DAO Object Variable Tags

Tag	Object Type	Tag	Object Type
cnx	Connection	prm	Parameter
cnxs	Connections	prms	Parameters
cnt	Container	prp	Property
cnts	Containers	prps	Properties
db	Database	qry (or qdf)	QueryDef
dbs	Databases	qrys (or qdfs)	QueryDefs
dbe	DBEngine	rst	Recordset
doc	Document	rsts	Recordsets
docs	Documents	rel	Relation
err	Error	rels	Relations
errs	Errors	tbl (or tdf)	TableDef
fld	Field	tbls (or tdfs)	TableDefs
flds	Fields	usr	User
grp	Group	usrs	Users
grps	Groups	wrk	Workspace
idx	Index	wrks	Workspaces
idxs	Indexes		

General Access Database Window Object Tags

Tag	Object Type	Tag	Object Type
cls	Class Module	rpt	Report
tbl	Table	mcr	Macro
qry	Query	bas (or mdl)	M
frm	Form		

Specific Access Database Window Object Tags*

Tag	Suffix	Object Type	Tag	Suffix	Object Type
tlkp	Lookup	Table (lookup)	qtot	Totals	Query (totals)
qsel	(none)	Query (select)	quni	Union	Query (union)
qapp	Append	Query (append)	qupd	Update	Query (update)
qxtb	XTab	Query (crosstab)	fdlg	Dlg	Form (dialog)
qddl	DDL	Query (DDL)	fmnu	Mnu	Form (menu)
qdel	Delete	Query (delete)	fmsg	Msg	Form (message)
qflt	Filter	Query (filter)	fsfr	SubForm	Form (subform)
qlkp	Lookup	Query (lookup)	rsrp	SubReport	Form (subreport)
qmak	MakeTable	Query (make table)	mmnu	Mnu	Macro (menu)
qspt	PassThru	Query (SQL pass-through)			

*Use either the general tag from the previous table plus the suffix from the table or the specific tag from this table with no suffix.

Access® 97 Developer's Handbook™

Third Edition

Paul Litwin
Ken Getz
Mike Gilbert

SYBEX®

San Francisco • Paris • Düsseldorf • Soest

Associate Publisher: Amy Romanoff
Acquisitions Manager: Kristine Plachy
Acquisitions & Developmental Editor: Melanie Spiller
Editor: Dusty Bernard
Project Editor: Kim Wimpsett
Technical Editor: David Shank
Book Design Director: Catalin Dulfu
Book Designer: Catalin Dulfu, Patrick Dintino
Graphic Illustrator: Patrick Dintino
Desktop Publisher: Maureen Forys
Production Coordinator: Amy Eoff
Indexer: Ted Laux
Cover Designer: Design Site
Cover Photograph: Furnished by FPG International

SYBEX is a registered trademark of SYBEX Inc.

Developer's Handbook is a trademark of SYBEX Inc.

TRADEMARKS: SYBEX has attempted throughout this book to distinguish proprietary trademarks from descriptive terms by following the capitalization style used by the manufacturer.

The authors and publisher have made their best efforts to prepare this book, and the content is based upon final release software whenever possible. Portions of the manuscript may be based upon pre-release versions supplied by software manufacturer(s). The authors and the publisher make no representation or warranties of any kind with regard to the completeness or accuracy of the contents herein and accept no liability of any kind including but not limited to performance, merchantability, fitness for any particular purpose, or any losses or damages of any kind caused or alleged to be caused directly or indirectly from this book.

Appendix A copyright ©1995–1997 by Gregory Reddick. All rights reserved. Used by permission.

Library of Congress Card Number: 96-70747
ISBN: 0-7821-1941-7

Manufactured in the United States of America

10 9

Software License Agreement:
Terms and Conditions

The media accompanying this book contains software ("the Software") to be used in connection with the book. SYBEX hereby grants to you a license to use the Software, subject to the terms that follow. Your purchase, acceptance, or use of the Software will constitute your acceptance of such terms.

The Software compilation is the property of SYBEX unless otherwise indicated and is protected by copyright to SYBEX or other copyright owner(s) as indicated in the media files (the "Owner(s)"). You are hereby granted a single-user license to use the Software for your personal, noncommercial use only. You may not reproduce, sell, distribute, publish, circulate, or commercially exploit the Software, or any portion thereof, without the written consent of SYBEX and the specific copyright owner(s) of any component software included on this media.

Software Support

Components of the supplemental software and any offers associated with them may be supported by the specific Owner(s) of that material but they are not supported by SYBEX. Information regarding any available support may be obtained from the Owner(s) using the information provided in the appropriate read.me files or listed elsewhere on the media.

Should the manufacturer(s) or other Owner(s) cease to offer support or decline to honor any offer, SYBEX bears no responsibility. This notice concerning support for the Software is provided for your information only. SYBEX is not the agent or principal of the Owner(s), and SYBEX is in no way responsible for providing any support for the Software, nor is it liable or responsible for any support provided, or not provided, by the Owner(s).

Warranty

SYBEX warrants the enclosed media to be free of physical defects for a period of ninety (90) days after purchase. The Software is not available from SYBEX in any other form or media than that enclosed herein. If you discover a defect in the media during this warranty period, you may obtain a replacement of identical format at no charge by sending the defective media, postage prepaid, with proof of purchase to:

SYBEX Inc.
Customer Service Department
1151 Marina Village Parkway
Alameda, CA 94501
(510) 523-8233
Fax: (510) 523-2373
e-mail: info@sybex.com

After the 90-day period, you can obtain replacement media of identical format by sending us the defective disk, proof of purchase, and a check or money order for $10, payable to SYBEX.

Disclaimer

SYBEX makes no warranty or representation, either expressed or implied, with respect to this media or its contents, its quality, performance, merchantability, or fitness for a particular purpose. In no event will SYBEX, its distributors, or dealers be liable to you or any other party for direct, indirect, special, incidental, consequential, or other damages arising out of the use of or inability to use the media or its contents even if advised of the possibility of such damage.

The exclusion of implied warranties is not permitted by some states. Therefore, the above exclusion may not apply to you. This warranty provides you with specific legal rights; there may be other rights that you may have that vary from state to state. The pricing of the book with the Software by SYBEX reflects the allocation of risk and limitations on liability contained in this agreement of Terms and Conditions.

Shareware Distribution

This Software media may contain various programs that are distributed as shareware. Copyright laws apply to both shareware and ordinary commercial software, and the copyright Owner(s) retains all rights. If you try a shareware program and continue using it, you are expected to register it. Individual programs differ on details of trial periods, registration, and payment. Please observe the requirements stated in appropriate files.

Copy Protection

None of the files on the disk is copy-protected. However, in all cases, reselling or redistributing these files without authorization is expressly forbidden except as specifically provided for by the Owner(s) therein.

ACKNOWLEDGMENTS

This book wouldn't have been possible without the concerted effort of many individuals in addition to the authors. First of all, we'd like to thank David Shank, our technical editor for the book. Because of his tireless attention to detail, this book is that much better. David is a programmer/writer who works on developer documentation at Microsoft. In fact, David contributed to the *Access Language Reference* and sample applications that shipped with both Access 95 and Access 97. Before working at Microsoft, David developed Visual Basic and Access applications for Applied Information Technologies, Inc.

Very special thanks go out to Greg Reddick, one of the coauthors of the first two editions of this book. Greg's contributions to those editions are still very much a part of the current edition. In addition, we continue to use his RVBA naming standard, which appears in Appendix A. Thanks, Greg, for all your hard work and friendship!

Special thanks also go out to Mike Gunderloy and Michael Kaplan. Mike was the technical editor for the second edition of the book and a contributor to several chapters in the first and second editions. His support continues to be invaluable. Michael wrote several sections in the second edition and helped edit several chapters of the current edition. He also supplied lots of early information to use for this edition.

Thanks go to Chris Bell, John Viescas, Michael Hernandez, and Richard Dickinson. Chris helped in deciphering form filter properties and events for the second edition of this book. John provided useful suggestions for examples and helped devise a technique we adopted for carrying forward values to a new row. Michael, a database design wizard, provided much of the inspiration for the database design chapter. Richard, a Microsoft Product Support Specialist, contributed immeasurably to our understanding of the new Internet and Office programmability features.

Thanks also go out to the several individuals who helped write chapters for the first edition of this book: Scott Alexander, Brian Randell, and Dan Haught.

We appreciate the work of the following people who provided ideas or technical editing support for of one or more editions of the book: Joe Celko, Desmond Chek, Mary Chipman, Michael Corning, Jim Ferguson, Pamela Hazelrigg, Sue Hoegemeier, Stan Leszynski, Joe Maki, Joe Morris, Jim Newman, and Erik Ruthruff.

Thanks to all the current and former members of the Access and Jet teams at Microsoft. In particular, the following individuals gave us early access to information, answered technical questions, or reviewed chapters: Kim Abercrombie, Steve Alboucq, Raj Batra, MariEsther Burnham, Neil Charney, Kevin Collins, Scott Fallon, Dan Frumin, Jim Hance, Roger Harui, Scott Horn, Debbie Johnson, Larry Jordan, Martis King, David Lazar, Jim Lucey, Michael Mee, Andrew Miller, Tad Orman, Chris Payne, Tony Poll, David Risher, Mike Risse, Joe Robison, Monte Slichter, Sterling Smith, George Snelling, and James Sturms.

Thanks also to all the individuals and companies who contributed content to the companion CD.

Of course, without the hard work and support of the staff at SYBEX, this book would be nothing more than a dream. We are especially appreciative of the efforts of our project editors Kim Wimpsett, Lee Ann Pickrell, and Kris Vanberg-Wolff, and our acquisitions manager Kristine Plachy. Of course, our superhuman development editor, Melanie Spiller, deserves special thanks for always keeping everything running smoothly and inspiring us when we didn't feel very inspired. An extra special thanks goes to Dusty Bernard, our tireless editor, who, after reading this book for the third time with an unerring eye for detail, must now know more about Access than any other editor on Earth.

Finally, we'd like to thank our friends, significant others, and family members who put up with us during yet another long and trying book-writing season.

CONTENTS AT A GLANCE

TABLE OF CONTENTS

PART III   **Presenting Data**   **293**

Chapter 7: Controlling Controls   **295**

APPENDIXES On the CD

FOREWORD

The nice part about writing forewords is you can be overtly enthusiastic and not be accused of self-promotion. After all, it's not my book. On that note, my advice to you, the prospective purchaser, is to buy this book. Now. And if you've already bought this book, let me be the first to say you did a good thing. Now, you are probably wondering why I am so excited about *Access 97 Developer's Handbook*, and there are a couple reasons....

First, this book is about Microsoft Access, the desktop database that is used by millions of users around the world every day. That's a lot of people using Microsoft Access, which is a good thing; it means you have a lot of company out there. Microsoft created this large user base by designing Microsoft Access to be a single database tool that all types of users could use—from database novices doing their first query to database developers building optimized inner-join double back flips. And we succeeded: Microsoft Access is the standard against which other tools are measured for ease of use and database development. There is nothing quite as much fun as finding reviews of some other product and reading "Product X lacks the ease of use of Microsoft Access" or "unlike Microsoft Access, which provides many programmability features, product X...." But then you probably knew that Microsoft Access defined the desktop database category—that's why you bought the product and why you are now contemplating the purchase of this book.

Second, this book is about Microsoft Access 97, a product entering the market at a time of mass upheaval and change in the PC marketplace. Of course, the PC marketplace is massively upheaved weekly, so it seems, but the point is that Microsoft Access 97 surfs the sources of these upheavals and puts you, the developer, in the driver's seat. Are you a net head that's wired to the gills? Check out the new Internet functionality that lets you save database objects to HTML or put your database on the Web. A developer building client-server solutions? New ODBCDirect functionality lets you get straight to server-based data sources like Microsoft SQL Server. A mobile worker? Microsoft Access now supports partial data replication for faster updating of information over slow connections. A developer of solutions? New Visual Basic for Applications 5.0 (now being licensed to other software vendors, so you'll see it in many places) makes code writing easier.

Or perhaps you know a first-time database user who doesn't know what any of those other sentences meant. For that user there's an Office Assistant to help explain how things work. When you look at how Microsoft Access 97 turns these technologies into benefits and makes them easy to learn and use, you'll see why the Access team is so excited about this product.

Finally, this book was written by three of the most widely quoted, published, and acknowledged Microsoft Access experts on the planet. Paul Litwin, Ken Getz, and Mike Gilbert are members of the Microsoft Access "insider community" that helps us define Microsoft Access by providing feedback and comments on our long-term direction. (The first comments weren't too polite, but they got better over time.) Each has spent years in the database world, and they have come to understand everything from the fundamentals of database design to the subtleties of the Microsoft Windows API. With this knowledge, they've written a great book on a great product that is going to help you make your work even easier—like training wheels for your surfboard.

Now that you've made up your mind to acquire this book, you can dive right in to get the most out of using Microsoft Access 97!

Michael Risse
Microsoft Access Group Product Manager

ABOUT THE AUTHORS

Paul Litwin

Paul Litwin is a senior consultant with MCW Technologies, focusing on application development employing Access, Visual Basic, Microsoft Office, SQL Server, Internet Information Server, and related technologies. Paul is also the editor of *Smart Access*, a monthly newsletter from Pinnacle Publishing for Access developers, and has written articles and reviews for various publications, including *Smart Access, Visual Basic Programmer's Journal, Visual Basic Developer,* and *PC World.* He wrote the *Jet Engine White Paper* for Microsoft, as well as several other books on developing applications using Microsoft Access. Paul trains Access and VB developers for the Application Developers Training Company and is a regular speaker at conferences, including Tech*Ed, Windows Solutions, Windows Solutions Tokyo, DevDays, Access Teach, and VB Teach. In what little spare time he has, Paul enjoys spending time with his family, running, and coaching his ten-year-old son's soccer and baseball teams. You can reach Paul on the Internet at plitwin@mcwtech.com or on CompuServe at 76447,417.

Ken Getz

Ken Getz is a senior consultant with MCW Technologies, focusing on the Microsoft suite of products. He has received Microsoft's MVP award (for providing technical support on CompuServe) for the years 1993 through 1996 and has written several books on developing applications using Microsoft Access. Ken is also a contributing editor to *Smart Access* and a frequent contributor to other developer publications as well. Currently, Ken spends a great deal of time traveling around the country for Application Developer's Training Company, presenting training classes for Access and Visual Basic developers. He also speaks at many conferences and shows throughout the world, including Tech*Ed, Advisor Publication's DevCon, Windows Solutions, and Access and VB Teach. When taking a break from the computer, he turns the chair around and handles the other keyboard: the grand piano that fills the other half of his office. You can reach Ken on CompuServe at 76137,3650 or on the Internet at keng@mcwtech.com.

Mike Gilbert

Mike Gilbert is a senior consultant with MCW Technologies, specializing in application development using Microsoft Access, Visual Basic, SQL Server, and Microsoft Office. He has worked with Microsoft on numerous ventures, including the Workgroup Templates, Office Developer's Kit, and DevCast. He writes for several periodicals and is a contributing editor to *Smart Access* and *Access/Visual Basic Advisor.* He is a trainer with Application Developer's Training Company and a regular speaker at conferences such as Tech*Ed, Advisor Publication's DevCon, and VB Teach. He spends what spare time he has enjoying life in Richmond, Virginia, with his wife Karen and their two cats, Chicago and Cairo. You can reach Mike on CompuServe at 73427,1053 or on the Internet at mikeg2@mcwtech.com.

INTRODUCTION

When it was released in late 1992, Microsoft Access took the database world by storm because of its aggressive $99 price. But when the dust settled after the first million were sold, many users and developers were pleasantly surprised to find a *real database* hidden beneath that ridiculously cheap price tag. Access 1.0 and the soon-to-follow modest upgrade, version 1.1, were certainly far from perfect, but users found an instantly usable product that broke down the walls of database accessibility. At the same time, almost overnight, a large and healthy developer community (that included the authors of this book) was born and began to develop professional applications that ran businesses of all sizes throughout the world.

Since its introduction, Microsoft has released three major updates: version 2.0, which hit the streets in May of 1994; Access for Windows 95 (aka Access 95 or Access 7.0), which appeared in November of 1995; and Access 97 (aka Access 8.0), which appeared in January of 1997. These updates fixed most of the limitations and annoyances of version 1.x and made numerous improvements in the areas of usability, programmability, and extendability.

Access 97 is a wonderfully powerful development platform, but like any powerful product, it takes considerable time to master. Fortunately for you, the three of us spent many months and countless hours tearing apart Access 97, exposing its undocumented secrets, and making it do things that few have imagined were possible—all for your benefit.

About the Book

This book is not a substitute for the Microsoft documentation, nor is it meant as a comprehensive reference manual. Instead, we strove to address the major issues we feel will face most developers. When we had to choose whether to cover a given topic or feature—one has to stop somewhere—we tended to favor the undocumented or poorly documented over the well documented.

In addition to the text, this book includes the usual assortment of figures, examples, and tables. It also includes lots of notes, tips, and warnings to call special attention to certain features or "gotchas."

About This Edition

This edition of the book is a significant rewrite of the best-selling *Microsoft Access 95 Developer's Handbook.* Many chapters have changed in some way, but some chapters have changed more than others. You'll notice the most changes in the areas of Access that have changed the most. Thus, for example, we didn't change too much in the database design and SQL chapters, but we made major revisions to our coverage of OLE/ActiveX, replication, Office programmability, client-server development, and many other topics. We've added several new chapters ("Using VBA Class Modules," "Shared Office Programmability," "Web-Enabling Your Applications," and "Using Source Code Control") and have condensed or combined others.

One thing you can be sure of: this is *not* an Access 2 or Access 95 book with an Access 97 cover. It is very much an Access 97 book—from cover to cover.

Is This Book for You?

This book is for any Access developer or anyone who would like to become one. It doesn't matter whether you develop Access applications full time, as only one component of your job, or in your spare time during the evenings and weekends. What matters is that you take the product seriously and want your applications to be the very best.

If you only care to get your toes wet with Access and are happy to throw together quick-and-dirty applications that are automated with nothing more than a few macros, you probably don't need this book. However, if you're ready to dive into the thick of Access and get down to the business of developing industrial-strength applications that utilize Access to its fullest, you've picked the right book.

If you already own a copy of one of the prior editions of this book, you may be wondering if you should buy this book, too. Yes—if you're planning to develop applications with Access 97 and you liked the prior editions, we're sure you'll get a lot out of this edition as well. So much in Access has changed for the developer, and we cover it all—okay, not all, but almost all.

What You Need to Know

For you to benefit most from an advanced book such as this, we've had to dispense with the fundamentals and make several assumptions about you. We assume you already have a basic level of familiarity with the product. At a minimum, you should be comfortable creating tables and simple queries, forms, and reports and have at least a rudimentary understanding of macros and Access Basic or Visual Basic for Applications. If you aren't up to speed, you may wish to put down this book for the moment and spend some time with Access and the manuals (including the *Building Applications* guide), the help system, or an introductory text such as *Mastering Access 97* by Alan Simpson and Elizabeth Olson (SYBEX, 1997).

Conventions Used in This Book

It goes without saying that the professional developer must consistently follow *some* standard. We followed several standard conventions in this book to make it easier for you to follow along.

We have used version 4.0 of the Reddick VBA (RVBA) naming conventions for the naming of Access objects, which have been accepted by many Access and VBA developers as the naming standard to follow. Greg Reddick, a noted Access and Visual Basic developer and trainer, developed the standard, which bears his name. Even if you don't subscribe to the RVBA standard, however, you'll likely appreciate the fact that it has been consistently used throughout the book. These conventions, which were first published in *Smart Access,* are included in their entirety in Appendix A and excerpted in the inside front cover of this book. (In a few places, you'll find we have used tags that differ from those in Appendix A. This happened because Greg finalized version 4.0 of the RVBA standard only weeks before the book went to press.)

In addition to following the RVBA standard, we have prefaced all functions, subroutines, and user-defined types that you may wish to use in your own code with the "adh" prefix (which stands for *Access Developer's Handbook*), aliased all Windows API declarations using an "adh_api" prefix, and prefixed all global constants with "adhc". These conventions should avoid naming conflicts with any existing code in your applications. If, however, you import multiple modules from various chapters' sample databases into a single database, you may find naming conflicts as a result of our using consistent naming throughout the chapters. In that case you'll need to comment out any conflicting API declarations or user-defined types.

Chapter Walk-Through

This book consists of seven parts and two appendixes. In every chapter you'll find lots of examples, with all but the most trivial included in sample databases you can find on the CD that accompanies this book.

Part I: Overview of Access

Part I begins with Chapter 1, which includes a brief history of Access and an overview of what's new in Access 97. In Chapter 2 you'll find a discussion of Access' event model and the sequence of events in Access. Chapter 3 (new for this edition) discusses the creation of Access class modules—an exciting new addition to Access 97.

Part II: Manipulating Data

When you design your database, you need to follow the principles of relational database design theory, which are detailed in Chapter 4. Here you'll also find a discussion of primary and foreign keys, relationships, the normal forms, and integrity constraints.

You can use Chapter 5 as the Access SQL reference that Microsoft never provided. This chapter provides the syntax of every Access SQL statement and clause, with numerous examples, and a discussion of how Access SQL differs from the ANSI SQL standards.

In Chapter 6 you'll find a discussion of Data Access Objects (DAO), the programmatic interface to the Jet engine. Here you'll learn how to programmatically create TableDefs, QueryDefs, Relationships, and other objects; how to set and retrieve object properties; how to manipulate recordsets; and—using the Containers and Documents collections—how to build your own replacement database container.

Part III: Presenting Data

Chapter 7 presents a comprehensive discussion of controls and their properties and methods, along with numerous examples. In this chapter you learn about list-filling functions, creating paired multi-select list boxes, using the Tag property, using the new tab control, and creating forms and controls programmatically.

After you've mastered controls, you'll be ready to think about the forms themselves, which is the topic of Chapter 8. In this chapter you'll find a thorough discussion of advanced ways of using forms in your applications. You'll also find numerous examples and reusable generic routines—some quite extensive, such as the example that shows you how to make any form resolution independent.

In Chapter 9 you'll learn how to master sorting and grouping, as well as the myriad of report properties and events. Again, you'll find lots of examples you can use in your applications.

Chapter 10 explains how to programmatically retrieve information about your printer, change print destinations, and perform many other printing wonders by using the prtDevMode, prtDevNames, and prtMip report properties.

Part III concludes with Chapter 11. In this chapter (new for this edition) you'll learn about three of the shared Office 97 programmable objects. These technologies are all completely new in Office 97. In this chapter, you'll learn how to programmatically control command bars, the new object model exposed by the shared Office toolbars and menu bars. You'll also learn how to programmatically manipulate the shared FileSearch object and the Office Assistant.

Part IV: Multiuser Issues

In the chapters contained in Part IV, you'll learn how to *think* multiuser. Chapter 12 covers the use of Access in a shared file-server environment. You'll find discussions of page-locking options, development strategies, transaction processing, linked table management, forcing record locking, determining who has a database open, and multiuser error handling.

Chapter 13 focuses on replication. In this chapter you'll learn about various replication options and strategies, synchronization and conflict management, using Replication Manager, and how to programmatically manipulate replication, synchronization, and conflict resolution. You'll also learn about Internet synchronization and partial replication (both features new with Access 97).

Chapter 14 discusses the *right* way to secure your Access databases. In this chapter you'll find a complete discussion of the Jet security model, the Access Security Wizard, accounts, permissions, and ownership. You'll also learn how to manipulate security programmatically.

Chapter 15 provides an introduction to Access client-server development. This chapter begins by detailing the difference between client-server and file-server development and discusses when to use one versus the other. It provides a comparison of the various data access methods, including the use of normal Access queries, SQL pass-through queries, and ODBCDirect. The chapter also discusses various client-server design strategies, potential problems, application optimization, and the Microsoft Upsizing Wizard.

Part V: Building Applications

In Chapter 16 you'll find a discussion of application debugging strategies and how to handle and recover gracefully from application errors. This chapter includes a generic set of routines for logging errors.

In Chapter 17 you'll learn how to optimize the various Access components, including queries, forms, reports, and VBA code. After you read this chapter, you should be able to make any sluggish application run more quickly.

Part VI: Interoperability

Part VI concentrates on interacting with the outside world from Access. Chapter 18 explains how to use the Windows API and other Dynamic Link Libraries (DLLs) to do things that are otherwise impossible using Access itself. This chapter includes a discussion of the Windows Registry and how to manipulate it using the Windows API, as well as a discussion of 16-bit to 32-bit DLL conversion issues.

In Chapter 19 you'll discover how you can use the undocumented tricks of the Wizards. In order to accomplish some of their tricks, the Wizards use tools that VBA doesn't directly supply. This chapter exposes a number of the functions exported by MSACCESS.EXE for use by the Wizards (and by your applications, as well, once you've learned the tricks).

In Chapter 20 you'll learn how to manipulate other applications using Automation (formerly OLE automation). This chapter includes examples that demonstrate how to use Automation to control Microsoft Outlook, Word, and Excel. The chapter also covers how to use ActiveX controls.

Chapter 21 presents the flip side of Chapter 20. Here you'll learn how to manipulate Access from Visual Basic, Excel, and other Automation controllers. The chapter includes an example Access reporting system that is controlled from Excel.

Part VII: Finishing Touches

Chapter 22 shows you, with examples, how to build and install Access Wizards, builders, libraries, and other add-ins you can use to enhance your Access applications. The chapter also discusses the practical side of VBA references and examines the new programmatic features of Access modules.

Chapter 23, which is new for this edition, explores Access 97's Internet and intranet capabilities. Here you'll find a discussion of hyperlinks and browsing the

Web from your Access applications. You'll also learn how to publish your Access databases so users can access your data using a standard Web browser.

Finally, Chapter 24, also new for this edition, discusses integrating Access 97 with a source code control system like Microsoft's Visual SourceSafe. In this chapter you'll learn how to use Access with Visual SourceSafe's version control and team development capabilities.

Appendixes

This book contains two appendixes on the CD. Each appendix exists in its own Adobe Acrobat (PDF) file. If Adobe Acrobat Reader is installed on your computer, you can open the appendix files by double-clicking on them. If Adobe Acrobat Reader is not installed on your computer, you can install it by double-clicking on the ACROREAD.EXE file in the Appendix folder on the CD. When the installation is complete, open the appendix files by double-clicking them.

Appendix A provides a description of the RVBA naming conventions used throughout this book. You'll find this useful both when reading this book and if you wish to use the same naming conventions in your own development work.

Appendix B discusses database startup properties and the GetOption and SetOption statements. This information is crucial for anyone attempting to distribute applications, but it just didn't fit in with any of the other chapters' material. Check out this appendix when it comes time to put the finishing touches on your application.

About the CD

The CD that comes with this book (attached to the inside back cover) is a valuable companion to the book. It includes all the chapter databases discussed in the book, as well as several extra goodies that should make your Access development work more efficient. (For late-breaking information about the CD, including additional files and utilities, see README.TXT in the root directory of the CD.)

What's on the CD?

On the CD we've included the chapter databases and two appendixes. We've also included three chapters from the second edition of this book that we had to remove from the text of the book in this edition to make room for new material. Because you may not have the *Microsoft Access 95 Developer's Handbook,* we decided to include these chapters on the CD. They are QUERIES95.DOC, a discussion of the creation of Access queries using Access' QBE interface; UI95.DOC, a discussion of user interface design issues; and DDE95.DOC, a discussion of dynamic data exchange. The first two topics (queries and user interface design) are still very much relevant in Access 97, but we felt these topics were of less importance than the other 24 chapters we included in the text of the book. DDE, on the other hand, has pretty much been supplanted by Automation. However, you may have the occasional need to make use of this older interapplication technology. These three chapters are included in their original format with their Access 95 sample databases. If you wish to use the samples with Access 97, you'll have to first convert them to Access 97 format.

We've also included white papers, freeware and shareware utilities, and demo versions of several commercial products on the CD. Most of these files have some restrictions on their use; please read the provided supporting documentation and respect the rights of the vendors who were kind enough to provide these files. For shareware programs, please register these programs with the vendor if you find them useful.

The CD files are described here:

- **Appendixes A–B:** (\Appendix) We've included in this folder the text of the two appendixes to this book. Each appendix exists in its own Adobe Acrobat (PDF) file. If Adobe Acrobat Reader is installed on your computer, you can open the appendix files by double-clicking on them. If Adobe Acrobat Reader is not installed on your computer, you can install it by double-clicking on the ACROREAD.EXE file in the appendix folder on the CD. When the installation is complete, open the appendix files by double-clicking them.

- **Old Chapter Text:** (\OldChap) We've included in this folder the text of the three chapters that we displaced in this edition of the book. The text of each chapter is included in a Microsoft Word 6.0 format (DOC) file that you should be able to read with most word processors or with the Windows 95/NT WordPad program. We've also included the sample databases for these chapters in this folder.

- **Chapter Databases:** (\Chapter) Here's where you'll find the chapter databases containing all the examples from the text. Each chapter database includes the tables, queries, forms, reports, macros, and modules discussed in the book so you can try out the examples yourself. These databases also include lots of reusable code and other objects you can copy and paste into your own applications. We've also included several Access add-ins and a few other supporting files in the Chapter folder.

- **FMS Power Pack 8.0 for Access 97:** (\Other\Fms) From FMS, Inc. FMS has provided the free Power Pack add-in for Access 97. This add-in provides six useful FMS utilities: Complexity Meter, Module Compiler, Jet Control Panel, Reference Manager, DAO Dumper, and Text Effects. To install the add-ins, run the FMSPWR80.EXE program.

- **Transcender Certification Test Demo Sampler:** (\Other\Transcnd) From Transcender Corporation. This is a demo sampler version of Transcender's preparation program for 13 of Microsoft's Certified Professional certification exams. Use the setup program (SETUP.EXE) to install the demo. See README.TXT for more details. Information is also provided on ordering the full Transcender products.

- **Process Custom Control:** (\Other\Wright\Process) From Wright Futures. You can use this shareware ActiveX custom control to manage external processes from within Access. Run the provided setup program (SETUP.EXE) to install this control. For information on using the control, see WPROC.HLP.

- **Registry custom control:** (\Other\Wright\Registry) Also from Wright Futures. This book discusses several different methods for reading and writing to the Registry. Less Wright has made it even easier, however, with this shareware custom control. Run the provided setup program (SETUP.EXE) to install this control. For information on using the control, see WREG.HLP.

- **Replication White Paper:** (\Other\Msft\Repwp) From Microsoft. This is a useful white paper from Microsoft that discusses Jet replication. It includes a few details that are not discussed in Chapter 13. Copy REPLWHTE.DOC to your hard disk and open it with Word for Windows or Windows 95/NT WordPad.

- **Jet Locking White Paper and DLL:** (\Other\Msft\Jetlock) From Microsoft. This folder includes a white paper, a dynamic link library, a utility program, a sample Access 97 database, and a sample Visual Basic application. You'll find this white paper and supporting files very useful for understanding how Jet locks records, for viewing locking information, and for determining which users have a database open. To use it, copy the MSLDBUSR.DLL file to your Windows\System folder and the remaining files to a new folder on your hard disk. Open JETLOCK.DOC with Word for Windows or WordPad for more details. An example of calling MSLDBUSR.DLL is included in Chapter 12.

- **Unsecured Wizard code:** (\Other\Msft\Wizards) From Microsoft. The Wizards that ship with Access 97 are secured, so you cannot open them. This is unfortunate because the Wizard code provides lots of examples of undocumented calls and techniques advanced developers can learn from. Fortunately,

Microsoft has graciously provided these unsecured copies of the Access 97 Wizards. To use them, back up the secured copies of the Wizards and copy the unsecured Wizards to your Access folder. From then on, you're on your own; Microsoft provides no support for the unsecured Wizards. It's best if you use these Wizards only on test machines because the unsecured version of the Wizards will be slower. See WIZREAD.TXT for more details.

- **Win32 API text file:** (\Other\Msft\Win32api) From Microsoft. This is a free text file that contains all the declarations for the Win32 API. To use it, copy this text file to a new folder on your hard disk and open it with any text editor.

- **WinZip 6.2:** (\Other\Winzip) From Nico Mak Computing, Inc. This is a shareware evaluation version of WinZip 6.2. WinZip is a Windows 95/NT utility for zipping and unzipping files. It includes its own zipping and unzipping routines, but it also can be configured to call PKZip, LHA, and other archiving programs. Run the provided setup program (WINZIP95.EXE) to install WinZip. See the online help for more information on using WinZip and registering the product.

- **SPEED Ferret Help File:** (\Other\Ferret) From Black Moshannon Systems. This is a help file that describes SPEED Ferret, a global search-and-replace add-in for Access 97. (Access 2 and Access 95 versions are also available.) This utility will propagate object name changes throughout your database.

- **What's New in Windows 95 Help and WinHelp Inspector:** (\Other\Bluesky\ WhatsNew) From Blue Sky Software. Blue Sky has provided a help file explaining what's new in the Windows 95/NT help system. Also includes WinHelp Inspector, which allows you to investigate the contents of existing Windows 95 help files. To install this help file, run SETUP.EXE.

- **Blue Sky HelpInfo Compilation:** (\Other\Bluesky\HelpInfo) From Blue Sky Software. Includes several white papers on Windows Help, RoboHelp, and the emerging HTML-based help standards. To install the white papers, copy the files to a folder on your hard disk.

Using the Files from the CD

The CD that accompanies this book is organized into several folders (subdirectories) that contain the chapter databases and other files. See the README.TXT file in the root folder of the CD for any late-breaking details on the CD files.

Installing the Chapter Samples

The sample chapter databases are located in the \Chapter folder. To install and use the files, follow these instructions:

- Most chapters contain only one database, named CHxx.MDB. To use this database, simply copy the file to a new folder on your hard disk and open the database with Access 97.

- For some chapters we've included multiple database files, all of which begin with the name CHxx. In this case, copy all these files to a new folder on your hard disk and open the database with Access 97. See the description of these files in the text of the chapter for more details.

- A few chapters have other non-database supporting files. These include Access add-ins (xxx.MDA) and Dynamic Link Libraries (xxx.DLL). See the descriptions of these files in the text of the chapters for more details.

Installing the Appendixes

To read an appendix file, double-click APPx.PDF from the \Appendix folder of the CD. If Adobe Acrobat Reader is installed on your computer, you can open the appendix files by double-clicking on them. If Adobe Acrobat Reader is not installed on your computer, you can install it by double-clicking on the ACROREAD.EXE file in the appendix folder on the CD. When the installation is complete, open the appendix files by double-clicking them.

Installing the Other Files

All other (non-chapter) files are located in subfolders of the \Other folder. See the section "What's On the CD?" earlier in this introduction for a description of the files and installation details.

> **WARNING** Most of the files cannot be run directly off the CD. Copy them to a folder on your hard disk before using them, or—when it's provided—run the setup program, which will copy and prepare the files for you. Also, please note that if you use File Manager, Windows Explorer, or the DOS COPY command to copy the files to your hard disk, the files will be marked as read-only. You will need to change the file attributes of the file before you can use the files. If you use the DOS XCOPY32 command, the files will not be marked as read-only.

How to Use This Book

While you may find it easiest to read the chapters in the order in which they appear in the book, it's not essential. One of our goals as we wrote the book was to make it possible for you to pick up and read any individual chapter without having to read through several other chapters first. Thus, the book is *not* a linear progression that starts with Chapter 1 and ends with Chapter 24. Instead, we have logically grouped together similar chapters, but otherwise (with a few exceptions) the chapters do not particularly build upon each other. To make it easy for you to jump from one chapter to another, we have included cross-references throughout the book.

While we've done a lot of the work for you, you'll get the most benefit from this book by putting the material to real use. Take the examples and generic routines found in the book and expand on them. Add and subtract from them as you incorporate them into your applications. Experiment and enjoy!

PART I

Overview of
Access

CHAPTER
ONE

What's New in Access 97

- Learning the history of Access changes

- Understanding what's new in Access 97

- Understanding what's new in Jet 3.5

Chances are, if you're reading this book, you've already decided that Microsoft Access 97 (we'll refer to it as *Access 97*) is a worthy platform for your development endeavors. Chances are, you're right. Microsoft has created a serious, full-featured, and powerful development environment for creating database applications on single-user and networked personal computers.

A Brief Access History

Access 1.0 really opened the eyes of many database developers. It was one of the first relational database products available for the Windows 3 platform, and it was certainly the first to fill the needs of many developers, both corporate and independent. Besides its ease of use in getting started, Access 1.0 made it very easy to create simple applications. It did have some limitations when developers got past a certain point in their applications, and it had a severe limitation in that databases couldn't be larger than 128 megabytes. Access 1.1 fixed that limitation, expanding the maximum database size to 1 gigabyte, and fixed some other limitations as well. Still, many professional features were lacking. Programmers used to Visual Basic's nearly complete flexibility were stymied by Access' inability to change control and form properties at run time, for example. On the other hand, there was no simpler way to get data in and out of forms than Access, so developers worked around Access 1.1's limitations.

Access 2.0 offered great gains for developers. Although it also provided numerous improvements for end users, the greatest leap from 1.1 came in the improvements for the developer community. For the professional programmer, Access 2.0 added features in almost every area of the product, including:

- A vastly extended object and event model
- Run-time access to most form and report properties
- Event procedures
- Cascading updates and deletes for referential integrity
- Engine-level enforcement of rules
- New query types—union, data definition, and pass-through queries—and support for subqueries

- Rushmore query optimization

- Data access objects (DAO), a consistent object model for the manipulation of Jet engine data

- OLE automation client support

- Programmable security

- Support for 16-bit OLE custom controls

Access 95 was a major undertaking. Both Access and Jet were ported from 16-bit Windows to 32-bit Windows. The Access Basic language and integrated development environment (IDE) were replaced with Visual Basic for Applications (VBA) and its enhanced IDE. Numerous other improvements were added; the most significant changes are listed here:

- Support for multi-instance forms

- Addition of the KeyPreview property for forms

- Support for multiselect list boxes and improved combo box performance

- New lightweight image control

- Ability to detect and alter the type of a control with the ControlType property

- Addition of a built-in query-by-form feature, Filter by Form

- Support for form class modules with public functions (methods) and Let, Get, and Set property procedures

- The ability, with the NoData event of reports, to choose not to print a report if there are no records

- Addition of the RepeatSection property, which lets you repeat a group header at the top of continuation pages

- Replacement of counter fields with the more flexible AutoNumber datatype

- Addition of new With...End With and For Each...Next VBA constructs

- Addition of the line continuation character

- Support for named parameters, optional parameters, and parameter arrays

- Support for new Date, Boolean, and Byte datatypes

- Improvements to the editor and debugger, including Watch variables and color-coded syntax

- Support for replication

- Several concurrency and performance improvements to the Jet 3.0 Engine

- OLE automation server support

- Addition of startup properties that let you disable access to the database window and change the application's title bar and icon

Access 97–the Best Access Ever

Things only get better with Access 97. This release is minor in comparison to Access 95. Still, there are lots of new features and improvements to existing features. Several areas received extra attention: Internet/intranet features, the VBA integrated development environment, shared Microsoft Office programmability features, and data access objects. Stability and performance have also been improved significantly. In the next few sections we detail the most important new features for Access developers.

Access 97 Internet and Intranet Features

It probably comes as no surprise that Microsoft has focused on making Access more Internet/intranet friendly. A host of features has been added, including these:

- Tables have a Hyperlink datatype.

- Label, command button, and picture controls have new hyperlink-related properties. This means you can click one of these controls and jump to a URL, all within the confines of your Access form.

- The Publish to the Web Wizard makes it easy to publish static or dynamic data on the Internet or your corporate intranet.

- You can export tables and queries to HTML.

- You can import or link to tables or lists located in an HTML file.

- You can insert the WebBrowser control into any Access form.

- From VBA code, you can make use of the HyperlinkPart function, as well as the HyperLink property and Follow and FollowHyperlink methods.

These features are discussed in detail in Chapter 23 and in other chapters throughout the book.

Access 97 Forms and Reports

The improvements to forms and reports in Access 97 are not very extensive. The most significant changes are

- Access 97 forms load and execute faster than in Access 95.

- You can create special lightweight forms that load even faster because they don't have any code behind them.

- The native tab control makes it easy to create a tabbed dialog.

- There's no need to use macros to create menus anymore. Use Tools ➤ Toolbars ➤ Customize to create and customize both menus and toolbars.

- Menus and toolbars are completely programmable using the CommandBars collection and CommandBar object.

- The Chart Wizard has been improved.

These changes are discussed in detail in Chapters 7, 8, 9, and 11.

Access 97 Queries

Queries have been tuned a bit for this release. Changes include the following:

- The RecordSet property allows you to specify that a query should return a snapshot.

- The FailOnError query property controls whether errors terminate bulk update queries against ODBC data sources.

- Using the MaxRecords query property, you can specify the maximum number of records that will be returned by queries against ODBC data sources.

These changes are discussed in Chapters 5 and 15.

Access 97 Modules

Microsoft has significantly improved the usability of the Access VBA integrated development environment. There have also been a few changes to modules. Thanks to these changes, coding in Access has never been easier:

- Class modules are now a reality in Access. These new modules allow you to create your own objects, complete with Initialize and Terminate events.

- The new Modules collection means you can now programmatically search through your code and replace, add, and delete lines of code.

- You can use a menu command or toolbar button to directly run (or step through) the current procedure without having to use the Debug window.

- When typing VBA code, you can have Access display a list of functions, methods, and properties to choose from to complete the current word.

- Using shortcut keys or menu commands, you can display a list of constants or properties and methods of the currently selected object. If you use the Auto List Members feature, Access will display these lists automatically as you type.

- Another shortcut key/menu command lets you display a list of parameters for any built-in or user-defined procedure. If you use the Auto Quick Info feature, Access will display this list automatically as you type.

- The VBA project name is now exposed, so you can reference your application from code.

- You can now tell Access to always place the Debug window on top.

- Support for drag-and-drop means you can pick up a snippet of code and move it to a new location with the mouse.

- The new Locals pane in the Debug window plus the Auto Data Tips feature (see the next item) may mean that you never have to create a Watch variable again.

- Move the mouse over a variable, constant, or expression while your code is suspended, and Access will automatically display its current value.

- Use the Step Out command to run the remainder of the current procedure and resume Single Step mode back in the calling procedure.

- Use the Compile and Save All Modules command to ensure that all the code in the database is in a compiled state.

- Use the Edit ➤ Bookmarks command to set and jump to bookmarks in your code.

- The Copy to Clipboard, Go Back, Go Forward, Help, Search, and View Definition buttons in the Object Browser make this tool much more usable.

Class modules are the subject of Chapter 3. Many of the other changes are discussed throughout the book.

Access 97 Database Engine: Jet 3.5 and DAO 3.5

Access 97 provides several significant changes to the Jet engine and its access language, DAO. The changes include the following:

- You can create partial replicas that contain only a subset of the rows from a table.

- You can replicate your databases over the Internet or across your intranet.

- Access supports a new client-server connection mode called ODBCDirect. This lets you establish a direct connection to a server database. Several new objects, properties, methods, and options have been added to DAO to support ODBCDirect.

- Several changes to the Jet Engine should improve the performance of database operations.

- The SetOption method of the DBEngine object temporarily overrides Jet Engine registry settings.

These changes are discussed in more detail in many of the chapters in this book, including Chapters 6, 12, 13, 14, and 15.

Other Access 97 Improvements

Additional changes have been made to the product that don't fit neatly into any of the above categories, including the following:

- You can now save your database in a special MDE format that removes all the VBA source code. The code will continue to run, but it cannot be viewed or edited, and the size of your database will be reduced. And because the source code won't be loaded into memory, performance should improve a bit too.

- You can search for files using the Office FileSearch object.

- Office and Access have an agent called the Office Assistant that offers users a helping hand. Plus, you can manipulate the Assistant object programmatically.

- You can now use the Compact and Repair utilities directly on the currently open database.

- The handling of dates with two-digit years has changed to be ready for the approaching millennium. Entries between 00 and 29 are now assumed to refer to 21st century dates.

- The References collection makes it easy to manage project references programmatically.

Many of these miscellaneous changes are discussed throughout the book.

Summary

Access is the best-selling desktop database program on the market today. It has the right mix of features for both users and developers. The changes Microsoft has made to the product for this release make this version the best Access ever.

CHAPTER

TWO

The Access Event Model

- ■ Working with objects and events

- ■ Reacting to form and control events

- ■ Handling data events

- ■ Determining the sequence of events

As with many applications that shield you from the details of working with Windows, one of the largest hurdles facing beginning Access developers is finding out how to make something happen. To create an application in Access, you must create and manipulate objects in response to events. An *object* in Access is one of the things you can see in the database window (also known as the database container or database explorer), plus the things these objects contain. Thus tables, queries, and forms are all objects, but so are fields, indexes, and controls. An *event* is a change in state that occurs when a user, a program, or the computer does something. For example, an event occurs when you move the mouse, click a button with the mouse, or press a key. An event also occurs when another application attempts to open a form using OLE automation or when the time-counting mechanism built in to your computer gets to the next increment in time.

The Access programming model uses an event-driven programming paradigm. In *event-driven programming,* the programming language operates in response to events that occur, usually in response to some user action. A relatively simple action by the user—moving the mouse over the form and clicking several controls, for example—causes Access to trigger many events, including the MouseMove, MouseDown, MouseUp, GotFocus, LostFocus, Enter, Exit, and Click events. At any of these events, you can step in and perform some action. The code that is activated when an event occurs is called an *event handler.*

> **NOTE**
>
> If you look in the property sheet listing the event properties for an object, you'll see names such as On Mouse Move and On Click. These names (with the spaces removed) are the names of the event properties. The events themselves, however, are named without the *On.* We'll refer to the MouseMove event (which corresponds to the OnMouseMove event property) or the Click event (which corresponds to the OnClick event property).

So Many Events, So Little Time

The more events Access generates when something happens, the finer the control you have, because you can take control at any point where an event is generated. On the other hand, it takes more work to react to lower-level events than to higher-level events. For example, when you type characters into a text box and press the Tab key, the KeyDown, KeyUp, KeyPress, Change, BeforeUpdate, AfterUpdate, Exit, and LostFocus events all occur. How do you know which event to react to, for any specific action you want to take? If you wanted to be able to open a popup form when the user pressed and released the Ctrl key twice, you would need to make use of the KeyDown and KeyUp events. If all you cared about was running a validation procedure when the user entered a new value into the text box, however, you'd be wasting your time working at this low keystroke-by-keystroke level. Instead, you'd likely want to use the BeforeUpdate event, which validates the entire value once the user is done entering it, instead of worrying about each key as it's typed.

For most of your Access programming, you'll deal with the higher-level events (BeforeUpdate, AfterUpdate), but it's nice to know that the lower-level events (KeyDown, KeyUp, KeyPress, Change, Exit, and LostFocus) are there when you need them.

Hooking In

Events happen continuously in Access, but they're not terribly interesting unless you can react to them. Access provides several ways for you to hook into events and react to them. You hook into an event in Access by placing a reference to an event handler in the property sheet of an object. In Table 2.1 you'll find the four kinds of event handlers, an example of calling each of them, and a description of when you should use them.

The last three event handlers in Table 2.1 use the Access VBA language. While macros are useful for quickly prototyping applications, we don't recommend their use in professional applications, because macros:

- Can't recover from errors

- Can't be used to call DLLs

- Can't easily be used for looping

- Can't be used to step through recordsets

- Can't be used in transaction processing

- Can't pass parameters

- Are difficult to debug

- Can be halted by users with Ctrl+Break (and this can never be turned off)

TABLE 2.1   Event Handlers

Event Handler	Example	When to Use It
Macro	mcrRunMe	In simple prototypes or single-user applications that don't need to be bulletproofed
Event procedure	[Event Procedure]	When you wish to have code encapsulated in the form or report or when you need parameters that are passed only to event procedures
Global module function	=GenericFunction	When you want to call generic code or when you want the ability to copy a control to another form or report and want its event handler reference to go with it. You can call only functions (not subroutines) directly from the property sheet
Form module function	=LocalModuleFunction	When you need to call the same event handler from multiple events or objects and you wish the code to be encapsulated within the form. Again, you can call only functions from here

The bottom line is that you should program using VBA code for all your Access application development, except when you only need to create a quick-and-dirty prototype or you wish to create a simple application that only you will use. (See Chapter 11 for more information on using macros in applications and for situations in which you don't have any choice about using them.)

Which type of VBA event handler you use depends on your coding style. Many developers use all three or use some combination of them. For example, you might create an event procedure that calls a function stored in a global module.

NOTE   Report events are not discussed in this chapter. You can find a detailed discussion of these in Chapter 9.

An Alternative to Event Handlers: Hyperlinks

Label, command button, and image controls have a new set of properties that allow you to establish *hyperlinks* to an Internet uniform resource locator (URL), a Microsoft Office document, or an Access object:

- HyperlinkAddress
- HyperlinkSubAddress

Using these new properties, you can create a control that, when clicked, jumps to your corporate home page or a bookmark in a Word document. In addition, you can use these properties to open an Access form or report without using an event handler.

For example, to create a hyperlink that opens the frmCustomer form in the current database, you would leave the HyperlinkAddress property blank and set the HyperlinkSubAddress to:

```
Form frmCustomer
```

Thus, you can use hyperlinks to create code-less switchboard-type forms. This is especially attractive because Access 97 supports something called *lightweight forms,* which are forms without any code. The advantage of using lightweight forms is that they load and display more quickly than forms containing modules.

You can view or change a form's "lightweight" status by manipulating the HasModule property of the form (or report). If you set an object's HasModule to No and it has existing code, that code will be deleted when you save the object, so be careful when manipulating this property.

If you attach both a hyperlink and a Click (or MouseUp) event procedure to a control, the processes are executed asynchronously, with the hyperlink jump occurring prior to the event procedure's execution.

Hyperlinks and other Internet/intranet features are discussed in more detail in Chapter 23.

Form Events

Three types of events can occur for a form:

- Form events
- Section events
- Control events

Form events are those events associated with the form itself. Some form events occur for all forms (for example, Open and Close); others (GotFocus, LostFocus) occur only if the form contains no controls; while still others come into play only in certain situations. (For example, the Timer event occurs only when the TimerInterval property is set to a nonzero value; the KeyDown, KeyUp, and KeyPress events occur only when the KeyPreview property is set to True.) Table 2.2 provides a description of each of the form events. (For more information on using Form, Section, and Control events, see Chapters 7 and 8.)

TABLE 2.2   Form Events

Event	Occurs	Can Be Canceled?
Current	When you move to a different record	No
BeforeInsert	When a new record is first dirtied	Yes
AfterInsert	After the new record is saved	No
BeforeUpdate	Just before edits to a record are saved	Yes
AfterUpdate	Just after edits to a record are saved	No
Delete	Just before each record is deleted. For multirecord deletes, occurs once per record	Yes
BeforeDelConfirm	After all records are deleted, but before the confirmation dialog	Yes
AfterDelConfirm	After the record is deleted or the deletion is canceled	No
Open	As the form is opened, but before data or controls are loaded	Yes

TABLE 2.2   Form Events (continued)

Event	Occurs	Can Be Canceled?
Load	After the form is loaded and the record source is opened	No
Resize	As the form is resized. Also occurs during form opening	No
Unload	When the form close is initiated, but before the form is actually closed	Yes
Close	When the form is closed, at the moment the form vanishes	No
Activate	When the form receives focus	No
Deactivate	When the form loses focus	No
GotFocus	After the form gets focus. Occurs only when the form contains no controls that can receive the focus	No
LostFocus	Before the form loses focus. Occurs only when the form contains no controls that can receive the focus	No
Click	When you click on the form's record selector or dead space* on a form	No
DblClick	When you double-click on the form's record selector or dead space* on a form	Yes**
MouseDown	When you click either mouse button on the form's record selector or dead space* on a form, but before the Click event fires	No
MouseMove	When you move the mouse over the form's record selector or dead space* on a form	No
MouseUp	When you release either mouse button on the form's record selector or dead space* on a form, but before the Click event fires	No

*Space that occurs when the form is sized larger than the height of its combined sections.

**Canceling this event cancels the second Click event.

***The Keystroke (and KeyPress, Change, and KeyUp events) can be canceled by setting KeyCode to 0.

†The Keystroke (and Change event) can be canceled by setting KeyAscii to 0.

††Although you can't cancel Error, you can suppress the display of Access' error message.

TABLE 2.2   Form Events (continued)

Event	Occurs	Can Be Canceled?
KeyDown	If KeyPreview is True, whenever you depress a key anywhere on the form (If KeyPreview is False, KeyDown occurs only when you depress a key while the record selector is selected.)	Yes***
KeyUp	If KeyPreview is True, whenever you release a key (If KeyPreview is False, KeyUp occurs only when you release a key while the record selector is selected.)	No
KeyPress	If KeyPreview is True, whenever you depress and release an ANSI key (If KeyPreview is False, KeyPress occurs only when you depress and release a key while the record selector is selected.)	Yes[†]
Error	Occurs when the form causes a run-time data error. This includes validation and datatype errors, as well as most locking errors	No[††]
Filter	When you choose to edit a filter, using either Records ➤ Filter ➤ Filter By Form or Records ➤ Filter ➤ Advanced Filter/Sort	Yes
ApplyFilter	When you apply a filter	Yes
Timer	When the timer interval has elapsed. You set the interval using the TimerInterval property	No

*Space that occurs when the form is sized larger than the height of its combined sections.

**Canceling this event cancels the second Click event.

***The Keystroke (and KeyPress, Change, and KeyUp events) can be canceled by setting KeyCode to 0.

[†]The Keystroke (and Change event) can be canceled by setting KeyAscii to 0.

[††]Although you can't cancel Error, you can suppress the display of Access' error message.

Each section on a form also has events, which are described in Table 2.3. It's unlikely that section events will play a major role in your applications, since these events are rather limited, essentially revolving around mouse movement and clicking on the background of sections.

Each type of Access control has a different set of events. Table 2.4 describes the events supported by each type of control. Table 2.5 describes when each control event occurs and whether it can be canceled.

TABLE 2.3   Section Events

Event	Occurs	Can Be Canceled?
Click	When you click on the background of a section	No
DblClick	When you double-click on the background of a section	Yes*
MouseDown	When you click either mouse button on the background of a section, but before the Click event fires	No
MouseMove	When you move the mouse over the background of a section	No
MouseUp	When you release either mouse button on the background of a section, but before the Click event fires	No

*Canceling this event cancels the second Click event

TABLE 2.4   Controls* and Events

Event	Label**, Image, or Box	Text Box	Option Group	Toggle Button, Option Button, or Check Box	Combo Box	List Box	Command Button	Object Frame	Sub-form
BeforeUpdate		√	√	√***	√	√		√†	
AfterUpdate		√	√	√	√	√		√†	
Updated								√	
Change		√			√				
NotInList					√				
Enter		√	√	√***	√	√	√	√	√

*The following controls do not have any events: line and page break.

**Listed events are for free-standing labels. Labels attached to other controls have no events.

***Only independent (when not a member of an option group) toggle button, option button, and check box controls have this event.

†Occurs only for bound object frames.

23

TABLE 2.4 Controls* and Events (continued)

Event	Label†, Image, or Box	Text Box	Option Group	Toggle Button, Option Button, or Check Box	Combo Box	List Box	Command Button	Object Frame	Sub-form
Exit		√	√	√***	√	√	√	√	√
GotFocus		√		√	√	√	√		
LostFocus		√		√	√	√	√		
Click	√	√	√	√***	√	√	√	√	
DblClick	√	√	√	√***	√	√	√	√	
MouseDown	√	√	√	√***	√	√	√	√	
MouseMove	√	√	√	√***	√	√	√	√	
MouseUp	√	√	√	√***	√	√	√	√	
KeyDown		√		√	√	√		√†	
KeyUp		√		√	√	√		√†	
KeyPress		√		√	√	√		√†	

*The following controls do not have any events: line and page break.

**Listed events are for free-standing labels. Labels attached to other controls have no events.

***Only independent (when not a member of an option group) toggle button, option button, and check box controls have this event.

†Occurs only for bound object frames.

TABLE 2.5 Control Events

Event	Occurs	Can Be Canceled?
BeforeUpdate	When you commit changes to a control by moving to another control or saving a record	Yes
AfterUpdate	After changes have been saved to a control	No

TABLE 2.5   Control Events (continued)

Event	Occurs	Can Be Canceled?
Updated	When you insert or update a source OLE object. May fire multiple times	No
Change	When data in control changes. May occur because a character was typed or a value was selected from the list	No
NotInList	When you enter a value in a combo box that is not in the list. Fires only when LimitToList is set to Yes	No*
Enter	When you have moved to a control that can receive the focus, but just prior to the control receiving the focus	No
Exit	When you have moved away from a control, but just prior to the control losing focus	Yes
GotFocus	After a control gets focus	No
LostFocus	Before a control loses focus	No
Click	When you click a control	No
DblClick	When you double-click a control	Yes**
MouseDown	When you depress either mouse button on a control, but before the Click event fires	No
MouseMove	When you move the mouse over a control	No
MouseUp	When you release either mouse button on a control, but before the Click event fires	No
KeyDown	When you depress a key while a control has focus	Yes***
KeyUp	When you release a key while a control has focus	No
KeyPress	When you depress and release an ANSI key while a control has focus	Yes†

*While you can't cancel NotInList, you can suppress the display of Access' error message.

**Canceling this event cancels the second Click event.

***The keystroke (and KeyPress, Change, and KeyUp events) can be canceled by setting KeyCode to 0.

†The keystroke (and Change event) can be canceled by setting KeyAscii to 0.

The Sequence of Events

Because there are so many events on Access forms, you may find it difficult to determine the event to use for a particular situation. In addition, you may need to know the exact sequence of events that occur for a particular scenario—for example, the opening of a form. In the sections that follow, we describe which events occur for various scenarios. While this is not meant to be comprehensive, we have tried to include the most commonly encountered situations.

Logging Events

One way to determine which events occur and in what order is to create a mechanism that will log events as they occur. In the CH02.MDB database you will find an event-logging facility made up of two forms: frmLog and frmEventTest. These forms allow you to test various scenarios and see the resulting event sequence (see Figure 2.1). To use this facility, load frmLog and adjust the level of event detail by checking and unchecking the ShowEvents check boxes. Then, load frmEventTest

FIGURE 2.1
Each and every event that occurs while frmEventTest is active gets logged to frmLog.

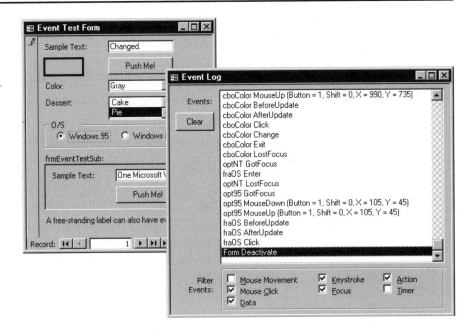

and try different actions on the form and its controls, noting the resulting events in frmLog. frmEventTest contains several types of controls, including a text box, label, subform, list box, combo box, option group, and others. You can add additional controls if you like.

How the Event-Logging Facility Works

Many of the components of the event-logging facility are based on topics discussed in later chapters. For this reason we'll just include a brief overview of how this facility works. If you want more information on the inner workings, just dig into the code—it's all there in the sample database.

Figure 2.2 shows frmEventTest in Design view. Notice that we've added event procedures for every event.

FIGURE 2.2

Event procedures are attached to every event on frmEventTest.

For example, frmEventTest contains this event procedure attached to the Click event of txtSample:

```
Private Sub txtSample_Click()
    adhLogEvent "txtSample Click", adhcEventMouseClick
End Sub
```

Each event procedure calls the adhLogEvent subroutine found in the basEvents module of the sample database. This procedure serves as the interface between the event-generating form (frmEventTest) and the event-logging form (frmLog). It has two parameters: strEvent, a brief description of the event; and intEvent-Type, the type of event. adhLogEvent calls the AddItem method of frmLog.

The AddItem method of frmLog verifies (by checking the status of the check boxes) that the event passed to it needs to be logged. If the event needs to be logged, AddItem places the event text in a module-level variable and requeries the list box. Finally, the item is added to the list box by a list-filling function attached to the lstLog list box.

General Form Actions

The following sections describe the sequence of events that occurs when you open and close a form or perform other general form actions.

Opening a Form

When you open a form, the following events occur:

```
Open → Load → Resize → Activate → Current →
1st Control (in tab order) Enter →
1st Control (in tab order) GotFocus
```

You can cancel the opening of the form from the Open event.

If the form contains a subform, the following events for the subform occur *prior* to the main form's Open event:

```
Open → Load → Resize → Current →
1st Control Enter → 1st Control GotFocus
```

During the Open event you don't normally have access to the values in the form's controls. If you need the control values, you should use the Load event instead. However, you can also force the Load event to occur within an event procedure attached to the Open event by using the following statement in the Open event procedure:

```
Me.SetFocus
```

Closing a Form

When you close a form, the following events occur:

```
Active Control Exit → Active Control LostFocus →
Unload → Deactivate → Close
```

This sequence assumes that any data on the form has already been saved. See the section "Data-Related Actions" later in this chapter for details on data-related events.

If the form contains a subform and one of the *main form's* controls has the focus, the following events occur instead:

```
Active Subform Control Exit →
Active Form Control Exit →
Active Form Control LostFocus →
Form Unload → Form Deactivate → Form Close →
Subform Unload → Subform Close
```

If the form contains a subform and one of the *subform's* controls has the focus, the following events occur (notice the addition of the main form's Exit event) instead:

```
Active Subform Control Exit →
Form Exit → Form Unload → Form Deactivate → Form Close →
Subform Unload → Subform Close
```

Form Resizing Actions

When you minimize a form, the following events occur:

```
Resize → Active Control LostFocus → Deactivate
```

When you restore a minimized form, the following events occur:

```
Activate → Last Active Control GotFocus → Resize
```

When you maximize a form or restore a maximized form, the following form event occurs:

```
Resize
```

When you resize a form, one or more Resize events will fire. The number will be affected by the speed and area of the resize. If the change in area is large or the resize occurs slowly, more resize events will occur than if the change in area is small or the resize occurs quickly.

Changing the Visibility of a Form

When you hide a form, the following events occur:

```
Active Control LostFocus → Deactivate
```

When you unhide a form, the following events occur:

```
Activate → Last Active Control GotFocus
```

Shifting Focus to Another Form

When you shift the focus from one form to another, by clicking the title bar of the second form, the following events occur:

```
Active Control on 1st Form LostFocus → 1st Form Deactivate →
2nd Form Activate → Active Control on 2nd Form GotFocus
```

Keyboard Actions

When you type a character into a control that accepts keystrokes (see Table 2.4), the following events occur:

```
KeyDown → KeyPress → Change → KeyUp
```

When you press a keystroke that causes the focus to move to another control (for example, Tab, BackTab, or Enter), some of the keyboard events will be received by one control and others will be received by the second control:

```
1st Control KeyDown → 1st Control Exit →
1st Control LostFocus → 2nd Control Enter → 2nd Control GotFocus →
2nd Control KeyPress → 2nd Control KeyUp
```

If the first control were updated prior to the navigation keystroke, the first control's BeforeUpdate and AfterUpdate events would also fire between the KeyDown and Exit events.

Using the KeyPreview Property

The form object doesn't normally receive keystrokes unless you have set the Key-Preview property of the form to Yes. When this is set, the form receives all keystrokes typed into controls on the form prior to the controls' receiving those same keystrokes.

Canceling Keystrokes

If you set the KeyCode parameter passed to your KeyDown event procedure to 0, Access cancels the remaining events, and the keystroke will never appear on the screen.

If you set the KeyAscii parameter passed to your KeyPress event procedure to 0, Access cancels the Change event, and the keystroke will never appear on the screen.

If KeyPreview has been set to Yes and you set KeyCode for the form to 0 in an event procedure attached to the form's KeyDown event, the control's KeyDown event will receive a KeyCode of 0, and all other keyboard events will be canceled. Similarly, if KeyPreview has been set to Yes and you set KeyAscii for the form to 0 in an event procedure attached to the form's KeyPress event, the control's KeyPress event will receive a KeyAscii of 0, and the control's Change event will be canceled.

Using the KeyCode and Shift Parameters

You can use the KeyDown and KeyUp events to trap all keystrokes, including special non-ANSI keys, such as the function keys and the Ctrl, Shift, and Alt keys. You can determine which keys were pressed by investigating the KeyCode and Shift parameters that Access passes to your KeyDown and KeyUp event procedures. Microsoft has defined KeyCode constants you can use when checking for various keys. There are constants for alphanumeric keys (for example, vbKeyA and vbKey1) and special keys (for example, vbKeyBack, vbKeySpace, vbNumPad0, and vbKeyF10). You can find these constants and others listed in the Access type library using the Object Browser (View ➤ Object Browser) or in the Help file by searching on constants, keycode.

If you wish to check whether the Shift, Alt, or Ctrl key has been pressed in combination with another key, use the Shift parameter, applying the appropriate bit mask (acShiftMask, acCtrlMask, or acAltMask) to the passed parameter. For example, the following code sets three Boolean variables to match the state of the three corresponding Shift keys:

```
fShift = (Shift AND acShiftMask) <> 0
fCtrl = (Shift AND acCtrlMask) <> 0
fAlt = (Shift AND acAltMask) <> 0
```

KeyDown and KeyUp versus KeyPress

Unless you need to trap special (non-ANSI) keystrokes, you'll find it easier to react to the KeyPress event in your applications. Access passes the KeyPress event procedure the ANSI code of the key that triggered the event via the KeyAscii parameter. This parameter is similar to the KeyDown and KeyUp event procedures' KeyCode parameter, except that the KeyPress event never gets triggered for non-ANSI keys. In addition, KeyPress gets distinct codes for lower- and uppercase alphabetic characters. (KeyDown and KeyUp always get the hardware code of the key itself, not of the character that key represents; you must check whether the keystroke is lower- or uppercase by checking the Shift parameter.) Because the KeyPress event receives only ANSI keys, you can use the Chr and Asc functions to convert back and forth between the KeyAscii parameter and the equivalent ANSI character. For example:

```
strKey = Chr(KeyAscii)
KeyAscii = Asc(strKey)
```

Repeating Keyboard Events

If you press and hold down a key, the KeyDown event occurs repeatedly until you release the key, at which point the KeyUp event occurs. If the key is an ANSI key, the KeyPress and Change events also repeat.

Mouse Actions

When you move the mouse cursor over a section, control, or other part of a form, the MouseMove event for that object is triggered. More MouseMove events are triggered the farther and more slowly the mouse is moved.

Mouse Click Actions

When you single-click the default (usually defined as the left) mouse button on a control, or the background of a section, or the record selector or dead space area of a form (the space that occurs when the form is sized larger than the height of its combined sections), the following events occur:

```
MouseDown → MouseUp → Click
```

Often you don't care about capturing the individual MouseDown and MouseUp events. In these cases you'll want to attach code to the Click event.

If one control has the focus and you click a second control, the following events occur:

```
1st Control Exit → 1st Control LostFocus →
2nd Control Enter → 2nd Control GotFocus →
2nd Control MouseDown → 2nd Control MouseUp →
2nd Control Click
```

If the first control were updated prior to the mouse click, the first control's Before-Update and AfterUpdate events would also fire before the Exit event.

Keystrokes That Cause Command Button Click Events

For command buttons, the Click event occurs (in addition to several keyboard events) in the following situations:

- If the command button has the focus and the spacebar is depressed and released

- If the Default property of the command button is set to Yes and the Enter key is depressed and released

- If the Cancel property of the command button is set to Yes and the Esc key is depressed and released

- If you've included an ampersand (&) character in the Caption property of the control to define a command button accelerator key and you depress and release the accelerator key along with the Alt key

Mouse Double-Click Actions

If you double-click the default mouse button on a control other than a command button, the following events occur:

```
MouseDown → MouseUp → Click → DblClick → MouseUp
```

If you double-click a command button, an additional Click event occurs after the second MouseUp event. This makes it virtually impossible for you to assign different actions to the Click and DblClick events of a button: both events occur when you double-click the button. There's no easy way to *not* have that first Click event's procedure execute, somehow knowing that there's a DblClick event to follow.

Data-Related Actions

When you change the data on forms, Access generates several additional events at various levels.

Access' Data Buffers

When you edit data on a bound form, Access maintains the following two buffers to support two levels of undo:

- Current record buffer
- Current control buffer

These buffers are depicted in Figure 2.3. When you move to a record, Access loads the values from the current record of the form's record source into the current record buffer. Then, as you move from field to field, Access loads the data from the current record buffer into the current control buffer.

When you change the value of a field and tab to another field, the control's Before-Update and AfterUpdate events occur. Between these two events, Access takes the value from the control buffer and uses it to replace the value in the record buffer. Similarly, when you save the current record—by explicitly saving the record, navigating to another record, or closing the form—Access replaces the data in the underlying record with the values in the current record buffer.

If, during the editing of data in a control, you press Esc or select Edit ➤ Undo, Access discards the contents of the current control buffer, refreshing it with the value from the current record buffer. If you press Esc a second time or select Edit ➤ Undo Record, Access discards the contents of the current record buffer, refreshing it with the values from the underlying record.

When using bound forms, you always edit the data in the control buffer; you never directly edit data in the underlying tables.

Changing Data in a Text Box

When you change the data in a text box control and tab to another control, Access triggers the following events (disregarding keyboard events):

```
1st Control Change (one for each typed character) →
1st Control BeforeUpdate → 1st Control AfterUpdate →
1st Control Exit → 1st Control Lost Focus →
2nd Control Enter → 2nd Control GotFocus
```

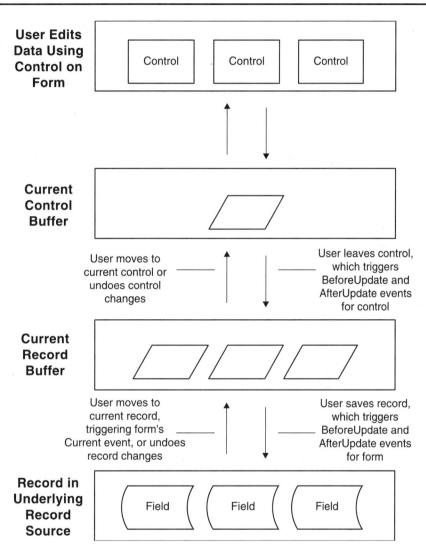

FIGURE 2.3

Access maintains a two-level undo buffer for bound forms.

Combo Box Actions

When you select a value from a combo box control that already has the focus, the following events occur (disregarding keyboard, MouseDown, and MouseUp events):

```
BeforeUpdate → AfterUpdate → Click → Change
```

The Click event occurs even when you select the value using the keyboard.

When you type an entry in a combo box and tab to another control, the following events occur:

```
1st Control Change (one for each typed character) →
1st Control BeforeUpdate → 1st Control AfterUpdate →
1st Control Click → 1st Control Exit → 1st Control Lost Focus →
2nd Control Enter → 2nd Control GotFocus
```

When the LimitToList property has been set to Yes and you enter a value that is not in the list, the following events occur:

```
Change (one for each typed character) → NotInList → Form Error
```

You may wish to create an event procedure for the NotInList event that adds a new row to the underlying list in this circumstance. You can prevent the form's Error event from occurring by setting the Response parameter of the NotInList event procedure. (See Chapter 7 for more information.)

List Box Actions

When you select a value from a list box control that already has the focus, the following events occur (disregarding keyboard, MouseDown, and MouseUp events):

```
BeforeUpdate → AfterUpdate → Click
```

The Click event occurs even when you select the value using the keyboard.

BeforeUpdate versus AfterUpdate for a Control

In many situations you can use BeforeUpdate and AfterUpdate interchangeably, attaching code to either event. Sometimes, however, it *does* matter which event you react to.

You should use a control's BeforeUpdate event when you need to:

- Validate the value entered into a control. You can cancel the committed changes by setting the Cancel parameter to True in the control's Before-Update event procedure.

- Compare the changed value with the previous value (which is available by using the OldValue property of the control).

You should use a control's AfterUpdate event when you need to:

- Change the value the user entered
- React to a change in value

The BeforeUpdate and AfterUpdate events are not triggered when you change the value of a control programmatically.

BeforeUpdate versus AfterUpdate for a Form

You should use a form's BeforeUpdate event when you need to:

- Validate the data entered for the current record. You can cancel the changes by setting the Cancel parameter to True in the form's BeforeUpdate event procedure.
- Make changes to the data in the current record before the record is saved. For example, you might want to save the current date and time in an event procedure attached to the BeforeUpdate event. (If you made these changes in an event procedure attached to the AfterUpdate event, you could get into an infinite loop because your changes would continue to dirty the record and cause it to trigger the AfterUpdate event repeatedly.)

You should use a form's AfterUpdate event when you need to react to the saving of the record.

Unlike the control's BeforeUpdate and AfterUpdate events, the form's BeforeUpdate and AfterUpdate events *are* triggered when you change the value of any of the form's controls programmatically.

OLE Control Actions

When you insert an object into an empty bound object frame, the following event occurs:

```
Updated
```

When you change the source object of a bound object frame by double-clicking the control, editing the source, and returning to the form, the following events occur:

```
OLE Control Click → OLE Control DblClick →
OLE Control Updated (may occur multiple times)
```

The Updated event may occur multiple times if the source document changes are extensive.

The following additional events occur when you commit the changes by moving to another control:

```
OLE Control BeforeUpdate → OLE Control AfterUpdate →
OLE Control Click → OLE Control Exit →
OLE Control LostFocus → Other Control Enter →
Other Control GotFocus → OLE Control Updated (three times)
```

Additional events that occur for OLE custom controls are discussed in Chapter 20.

Saving and Navigating between Records

When you save the current record by either pressing Shift+Enter or selecting Records ➤ Save Record, the following events occur:

```
Control BeforeUpdate → Control AfterUpdate →
Form BeforeUpdate → Form AfterUpdate
```

If the current record is dirty (contains unsaved changes) and you move to another record, the following events occur:

```
Control BeforeUpdate → Control AfterUpdate →
Form BeforeUpdate → Form AfterUpdate → Control Exit →
Control LostFocus → Form Current → Control Enter →
Control GotFocus
```

When you navigate to another record without changing data in the current record, the following events occur:

```
Control Exit → Control LostFocus → Form Current →
Control Enter → Control GotFocus
```

Inserting a Record

The following events occur when you move to the new record:

```
Control Exit → Control LostFocus → Form Current →
Control Enter → Control GotFocus
```

When you then dirty the new record, the following event occurs (disregarding keyboard, MouseDown, and MouseUp events) prior to other events that would occur when changing data in a control:

```
Form BeforeInsert
```

Finally, when you save the new record, the following events occur:

```
Control BeforeUpdate → Control AfterUpdate →
Form BeforeUpdate → Form AfterUpdate → Form AfterInsert
```

Deleting a Record

When you delete the current record, the following events occur before the deletion confirmation dialog appears:

```
Control Exit → Control LostFocus → Form Delete →
Form Current → Control Enter → Control GotFocus →
Form BeforeDelConfirm → Form Error
```

For multirecord deletions, the Delete event occurs once per deleted record.

If the deletion is canceled, the following events occur:

```
Control Exit → Control LostFocus → Form AfterDelConfirm
```

If you have set the Confirm Record Changes option in the Edit/Find tab of the Tools ➤ Options dialog to False (or have used the SetOption method of the Application object to set the equivalent using VBA code), the BeforeDelConfirm and AfterDelConfirm events are skipped. If you have set off warnings by using the SetWarnings method of the DoCmd object, BeforeDelConfirm and AfterDelConfirm events still occur, but the confirming dialog is skipped.

When the Delete event occurs, Access removes the record and stores it in a temporary buffer. You can cancel the Delete event (and restore the deleted record) by setting its Cancel parameter to True in an event procedure attached to this event. This will serve to cancel the delete operation and all subsequent deletion events.

You can also cancel the BeforeDelConfirm by setting its Cancel event to True. This also cancels the deletion, but the AfterDelConfirm will still occur. If you want to create your own custom deletion message, you should display it from an event procedure attached to the BeforeDelConfirm event. If you wish to continue the delete operation but suppress the built-in deletion message, set the Response parameter to the acDataErrContinue constant.

You can't cancel the deletion from the AfterDelConfirm event. The records have already been deleted (or the deletion has already been canceled). This is a good time, however, to react to the deletion. You can use the Status parameter that is passed to event procedures attached to this event to determine what happened. The value of Status can be

Constant	Meaning
acDeleteOk	The deletion occurred
acDeleteCancel	The deletion was canceled by your VBA code
acDeleteUserCancel	The deletion was canceled by the user

The Error Event

If you attach an event procedure to the form's Error event, your procedure will be called whenever a trappable error occurs while the form is running. You can use the DataErr parameter passed to your event procedure to determine which error has occurred and react accordingly. For example, you might use the MsgBox statement to provide a custom error message to the user. By setting the response parameter to the acDataErrContinue constant, you can tell Access to skip the display of the built-in error message. (See Chapters 8, 12, and 16 for more information on the Error event.)

The Indispensable Timer Event

The form's Timer event occurs only when you have set the TimerInterval property to a value greater than 0. This property—measured in milliseconds—determines how often the Timer interval fires.

The Timer event is useful for performing some action at regular intervals of time. For example, you could create a Timer event procedure that waited ten seconds and then closed the form. You could also use the Timer event to check on a regular basis to see whether some state was true and do something when this was the case. For example, you could create an automated import procedure that checked every ten minutes to see whether mainframe data had been downloaded to a certain file.

You can also use the Timer event to simulate user-defined events. The possibilities are endless. For example, you could create a user-defined "Locked" event by attaching code to the Timer event that checked once a second to see whether the current record had been locked by another user. Similarly, you could use the Timer event to simulate a "Dirty" event that occurred whenever a record was changed. (You can find examples of using the Timer event to simulate Dirty and Locked events in Chapters 8 and 12, respectively.)

You can stop Access from triggering a form's Timer event by setting the Timer-Interval property back to 0.

Actions That Can't Be Trapped

The following actions cannot be trapped in Access:

- Selecting a menu command
- Scrolling
- Discarding changes using the Edit ➤ Undo command
- Clicking the right or middle mouse button
- Dirtying a record
- Another user's locking the current record
- Dragging and dropping an object
- Doing anything with toolbars

As mentioned in the preceding section, you can simulate some of these events by making use of the Timer event.

Summary

In this chapter we introduced you to the Access event model. We discussed

- The Access event model
- Event handlers
- The different types of events that occur on forms
- The sequence of form events
- Access' data buffers
- Which actions in Access can't be trapped

CHAPTER

THREE

3

Using VBA Class Modules

- Exploring what class modules are and how they work

- Creating your own object classes

- Implementing custom properties and methods

- Establishing a hierarchy of object classes

- Creating and managing collections of objects

With the introduction of VBA in Visual Basic 4.0, Microsoft endowed Basic developers with a new tool: class modules. While other Basic dialects (Visual Basic and Access Basic) had already introduced object-oriented constructs, class modules gave Basic programmers the ability to create and manipulate their own classes of objects. Access (and other Office applications) did not include class modules until the release of Office 97, and programmers who had been using class modules in Visual Basic 4.0 can now migrate their skills in creating classes to the Microsoft Office environment.

If you're new to class modules, don't worry. If you have programmed in other object-oriented languages such as SmallTalk or C++, you are familiar with the benefits class modules provide. If you haven't, we hope to surprise you with the power they give you as a programmer. Because examples in this book will use class modules whenever possible, it makes sense at this point to explain what they are and how they work and to demonstrate some examples of how you can use them in your applications.

Because this chapter deals with creating your own objects, it assumes you are familiar with using objects provided by VBA or a host application. That is, you should be comfortable with concepts such as properties and methods and know how to declare and use object variables. (For more information about object variables, see Chapter 6.)

Why Use Class Modules?

If you've been developing applications using Basic for any length of time, you might be thinking, "Why use class modules, anyway? I've been getting along without them for some time." Like any new product feature, class modules have their benefits and costs. The primary cost is the learning curve required to understand them so you can use them effectively. Although many VBA programmers take working with built-in objects (for example, the Debug and Err objects) for granted, they find the idea of creating their own object types difficult to comprehend. We hope that after reading this chapter, you won't feel that way.

Once you've mastered the basics of class modules, the benefits become clear. Your code is more manageable, self-documenting, and easier to maintain, especially if you deal with complex sets of related data. The sections that follow examine some reasons for using class modules.

Classes Let You Create Your Own Objects

Class modules allow you to create and use your own object types in your application. Why would you want to do this? Imagine that you want to write an application that tracks information on employees in your company. Using traditional Basic, you might create separate variables to store each employee's name, manager, and salary, among other things. If you're really clever you might create an array of user-defined datatypes. It's also likely that you'd write procedures to handle tasks such as hiring or transferring an employee or giving an employee a raise. The problem with this approach is that there is nothing inherent in the program or the language that ties all these bits of information and processes together. We've shown this situation in Figure 3.1. All the data and processes are free-floating. It's up to you, the programmer, to ensure that each element is used correctly.

FIGURE 3.1

Managing data using traditional Basic constructs—every item stands alone.

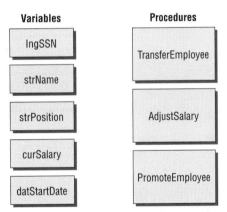

With nothing enforcing relationships between the items in Figure 3.1, chaos can result. For example, suppose two or more separate procedures modify the salary data using a particular set of rules. Changes to the rules necessitate changes to the program logic in several places.

Encapsulating these data and program components in an object makes the management task much easier. First of all, any references to data (properties) must be associated with a particular object, so you always know what "thing" it is you're operating on. Second, processes that operate on an object are defined as part of that object. In other words, the processes are defined as methods of the object. (For more information on properties and methods, see Chapter 6.) The consumers of the object—other procedures in your program—are insulated from the inner workings of each method and cannot modify properties directly unless you allow them to. This enforces a degree of control over data that the object represents. Finally, because each property and method is defined in one place (the object type's definition), any code modifications need be implemented only once. An object's consumers will benefit automatically from the change. This type of object-oriented development is represented in the diagram shown in Figure 3.2. All data and processes are defined as part of the object, and the application program interacts with them through a central point, a reference to an instance of the object.

FIGURE 3.2

Managing data using object-oriented techniques

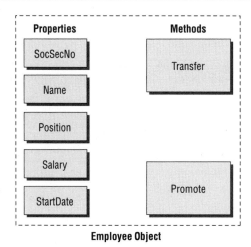

Employee Object

Classes Let You Abstract Complex Processes

If you find the idea of encapsulating data and processes within an object compelling, you'll be even more excited about the next benefit of using class modules: the ability to abstract complex processes. Suppose you are trying to create an application that manages internal purchases within an organization. Determining the amount to charge one department for goods or services received from another (called the *transfer price*) can be a complicated task. If you use traditional programming techniques, the logic for computing the transfer price might be an integral component of the application. Not only does embedding the logic in the application make the program code harder to maintain, it means that every programmer who works with the code must be able to understand the logic.

Is VBA Really Object-Oriented?

At this point many of you who have experience in other object-oriented languages are probably thinking, "What are they talking about? VBA isn't really object-oriented!" Although we concede that VBA does not exhibit some of the characteristics, such as polymorphism and inheritance (if you don't know what these are, don't worry), of a "true" object-oriented language, we believe that it just doesn't matter. VBA may not be as feature rich as C++ or SmallTalk, but for most people it's much easier to understand than those languages. More important, VBA offers a way for developers to think about applications in terms of a group of related objects, not masses of disparate data structures.

By using object-oriented techniques, on the other hand, you could create object classes for each good or service being transferred, making the transfer price computation logic part of each object class. This makes the application code easier to understand and write. The programmer using your class need only know that an object is being transferred and that the object knows how to compute the transfer price. The logic for computing that price is maintained separately, perhaps by another programmer more familiar with the intricacies of transfer pricing theory.

When you create an object you define an *interface* to that object. This isn't a user interface, but rather a list of the object's properties, methods, and collections. These items are all that consumers of the object (other programmers) need to know in order to use the object. It's then up to you to implement each feature in the object's source code using VBA class modules.

Classes Make Development Simpler

In the preceding example, imagine that another programmer was charged with the task of maintaining the transfer pricing logic encapsulated in the object being transferred. This brings up a continual challenge facing development managers: how to coordinate large, complex programming projects. Object-oriented techniques (which include using VBA class modules) can make the task of managing projects easier. Because objects are autonomous entities that encapsulate their own data and methods, you can develop and test them independently from the overall application. Programmers can create custom objects using VBA class modules and then test them using only a small amount of generic Basic code. After determining that the object behaves as desired, the programmer can use the object in an application simply by importing the appropriate class modules.

How Class Modules Work

We hope that by now we have convinced you that object-oriented techniques in general, and VBA class modules in particular, are worth learning about. In the following sections we explain how they work by discussing the difference between object classes and object instances.

Class Modules Are Like Cookie Cutters

VBA class modules define the properties and methods of an object, but you cannot use them, by themselves, to manipulate those properties. An object's definition is sometimes called an object *class*. You can think of VBA class modules, and thus object classes, as cookie cutters. A cookie cutter defines what a particular cookie will look like, but it is not itself a cookie. You can't have a cookie, however, without a cookie cutter.

In the case of VBA class modules, you define a set of properties, including their datatypes and whether they are read-only or read/write, as well as methods, including the datatype returned (if any) plus any parameters the methods might require. Figure 3.3 shows a simple example using the cookie analogy. You'll see in the next section how to add a class module to your Access database and how to use it to define properties and methods.

FIGURE 3.3

An imaginary cookie class, including three properties

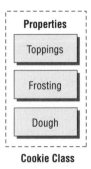

Cookie Class

Object Instances Are the Cookies

To actually make use of an object class, you must create a new *instance* of that class. Using the analogy, object instances are the individual cookies. Each has the set of properties and methods defined by the class, but you can also manipulate an instance individually as a real programming entity. When you create a new instance of a class, you can change its properties independently of any other instance of the same class. Figure 3.4 shows several instances of the cookie class with various property settings.

FIGURE 3.4

You can create multiple cookies from the same Cookie class.

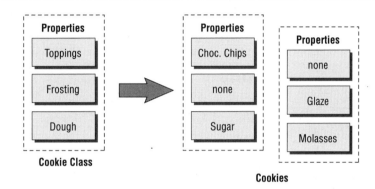

A Simple Example: A Text File Class

To demonstrate the basic techniques required to create and use class modules, we'll show you how to create a class that represents a text file. It will include properties that let you manipulate the file name and contents, as well as methods to read and write the contents from and to disk. Not only will this provide a relatively simple example for teaching class module concepts, it is a useful class you can add to your Access applications that must work with text files. (If you've ever attempted to maintain a log file for a running application, you'll appreciate the simplicity of this class.)

Creating an Object Class

As already mentioned, before you can start working with your own custom objects, you must create the object class from which they will be fabricated. You do this simply by adding a new class module to your database.

Inserting a New Class Module

To add a new class module to your database, select the Insert ➤ Class Module menu item. Access opens a new module window and adds the new class module to the database window. You edit class modules the same way you edit standard VBA code modules. The only difference is that class modules have two events, Initialize and Terminate, associated with the creation and destruction of a class instance. We'll explain these in more detail in the section "The Initialize and Terminate Events" a little later in this chapter.

Naming Your Class

All VBA class modules have a Name property that is integral to the definition of an object class: it determines the class name. Be sure to set the name of the class module to the name you want to use in your VBA programs that use the class. To name a class module, specify the class name when you first save the class module. Of course, you can alter the name at a later date; but you'll probably want to do that before you write any code that uses the class.

NOTE Although we are strong proponents of using sometimes obscure naming conventions with internal names and variables, you should choose a name for your class that is both easily understood and that identifies the "thing" the object class represents. Typically developers choose English words in the singular form. Capitalization is used to distinguish word breaks within an object class name. For example, these class names are appropriate: Application, Employee, and DrawingObject. For this example we've created a class named TextFile.

Creating a Property Using a Public Variable

Most objects have at least one property. Properties store values representing characteristics of the object. Although it's possible to create objects that implement methods for setting and returning values, we don't recommend this approach. Methods are normally used to implement actions an object can take.

The simplest approach to creating a property is to create a Public variable in the declarations section of the class module. (A second approach is described in the section "Using Property Statements" later in this chapter.) Consumers of your object will then be able to set and retrieve a value stored in that variable. (In other words, the property is read/write.) The variable's name determines the name of the property used by other parts of your program. For this reason, as with class names, choose a name with logical, symbolic meaning.

Although using Public variables to define properties is the simplest approach, this method does have one major drawback. Your class has no way of knowing when an outside process has changed the value of the property. This may be critical to your object for, say, restricting values to a given range or taking other actions in response to a change in value. (To meet these needs you must use Property procedures.) In addition, using Public variables to provide class properties keeps you from using one of Access 97's best features, the Object Browser, to view the properties and methods of the class. That is, properties defined as public variables may not show up in the Object Browser. (Public variables in classes contained within the current database do appear in the Object Browser, but if you're using automation to refer to classes from external projects, only properties created with Property procedures will appear. This, in itself, may be enough to keep you from using this simple technique.)

Creating a Method

Just as declaring a Public variable creates a property, declaring a Public procedure creates a method. You can create Public functions and subs, the only difference being that a Public function returns a value to the calling process and a sub does not. The TextFile class implements, among other things, a FileOpen method that carries out the task of opening the file specified by the Path property of the class. Listing 3.1 shows the VBA code that makes up the FileOpen method.

TIP

Although you might like to do so, you can't name this method *Open*. This name conflicts with a reserved word of the host application, Access. You may find that VBA reports a syntax error when declaring methods or properties. In these cases, make sure you haven't inadvertently used a reserved word, and change the method or property name if necessary.

Listing 3.1

```
Public Function FileOpen() As Boolean
    On Error GoTo HandleError

    ' If a file is already open, close it
    If Me.IsOpen Then
        Me.FileClose
    End If

    ' Get next available file handle
    mhFile = FreeFile

    ' Open file based on file open mode property
    Select Case Me.OpenMode
        Case tfOpenReadOnly
            Open Me.Path For Binary Access Read As mhFile
        Case tfOpenReadWrite
            Open Me.Path For Binary Access Read Write As mhFile
        Case tfOpenAppend
            Open Me.Path For Append Access Read Write As mhFile
        Case tfOpenReadOnlyExists
            Open Me.Path For Input Access Read As mhFile
    End Select

    ' Set IsOpen property variable and return value
    mfIsOpen = True
    FileOpen = True
ExitProc:
    Exit Function

HandleError:
    FileOpen = False
    Resume ExitProc
End Function
```

Although the code shown in Listing 3.1 is not earth shattering by any standard (it uses low-level file I/O functions that have been around for years), you should be able to see the benefits of encapsulating the code in a class. You no longer have to remember all the various forms of the Open statement. All you need to do is set the object's Path and OpenMode properties and call its FileOpen method. The code encapsulated in the class does the rest, including error handling.

One item of note in Listing 3.1 is the use of the reserved word Me (for example, Select Case Me.OpenMode). You use Me in class modules to refer to the current instance of that class. Just as you use Me in form modules to retrieve a reference to the current form, you use Me in a class module to retrieve a reference to the current object.

NOTE
Perhaps now you see why we refer to the module containing a form or report's code as its *class module*. In many senses, form or report class modules are equivalent to the class modules presented in this chapter. They both offer encapsulation, and both use the Me object to refer to the current instance. Stand-alone class modules offer the Initialize and Terminate events, which forms and reports don't, but that's one of the few differences between the modules attached to forms and reports and stand-alone class modules.

Table 3.1 lists all the properties and methods of the TextFile class. You may find it useful to follow the table through the class module and see how all the methods and properties have been declared.

TABLE 3.1   Methods and Properties of the Simple TextFile Class

Properties	Methods	Description
	Exists	Determines whether the file exists, based on a directory search. Returns True or False
	FileOpen	Opens the requested file, once you've supplied the Path (and optionally, the OpenMode) property. If you don't supply an OpenMode value, the code assumes you want read-only access
	FileClose	Closes the text file
	ReadNext	Reads the next line of text into the internal buffer. Use the Text property to retrieve the value
EOF		Contains True if you've reached the end of the text file (read-only)
Handle		Contains the operating system file handle for the opened file (read-only)

TABLE 3.1   Methods and Properties of the Simple TextFile Class (continued)

Properties	Methods	Description
IsOpen		Contains True if the file is currently open, False if not (read-only)
OpenMode		Contains the file open mode (0 for read-only, 1 for read/write, 2 for append, 3 for read-only for existing files) (read/write until the file is open, read-only after that)
Path		Contains the path of the text file (read/write until the file has been opened, read-only after that)
Text		Contains the text of the current line from the text file (read-only)

Using the Object Class

Now that you've defined a class and given it a few properties and methods, you can use it in other VBA procedures. The first step in using a class is to create a new instance of the class. This is analogous to cutting a new cookie in the earlier example.

Creating New Class Instances

To create a new class instance, declare an object variable based on the class. You'll use it to store a reference to a new class instance. Variables referencing custom classes adhere to the same rules as those referencing VBA or host application objects. You can declare them using the Dim, Private, Public, or Global reserved word. For example, the following code fragment declares a variable called objFile:

```
Dim objFile As TextFile
```

Note that the datatype in this example is the class name defined earlier. The next step is to create a new instance of the object and store a reference to it in the variable. To do this you use the Set statement in conjunction with the New keyword, as in:

```
Set objFile = New TextFile
```

Although the syntax might seem redundant, you must use the New keyword in the Set statement to create a new instance of the object. Otherwise VBA will generate run-time errors if you try to use any of the properties or methods of the class. Simply declaring a new object variable in this manner is not enough to create a new object instance.

If you want to create a new instance along with the variable declaration, you can make the New keyword part of the declarations itself, as in this example:

```
Dim objFile As New TextFile
```

Immediately after declaring an object variable in this manner, you can start using the object's properties and methods without first using Set.

You may be wondering why you would choose one technique over the other. The answer depends on when you wish the new instance of the object to be created. In the first example, VBA does not create a new instance of the TextFile object until it processes the Set statement. If this statement is never executed, the new instance is never created. Alternatively, in the second example, VBA creates a new instance of the TextFile object as soon as you use one of the object's properties or methods. Although the second approach is more convenient, requiring one line of code to create the new instance instead of two, it is not always clear which statement caused VBA to create the new instance. The first method is preferable because it provides greater control over when the new object is created.

> **NOTE**
>
> This method of object creation is called *instantiation. Instantiating* an object simply means creating a new instance of the object type. Whenever you use the New keyword, you're instantiating an object.

> **TIP**
>
> Remember to use the New keyword to create a new instance of a VBA class. If you don't, VBA generates an "Object variable or With block variable not set" error. If you receive this error on a statement involving an instance of your custom class, make sure you've created a new instance using New.

Using Properties and Methods

Once you have a variable storing a reference to a new class instance, you can use the properties and methods defined by the class module. Listing 3.2 shows some sample code that uses the TextFile class to open a file (AUTOEXEC.BAT, in this case) and print out each line using the properties (Path, EOF, Text) and methods (FileOpen, ReadNext, FileClose) of the class. This example is from basTestTextFile.

Listing 3.2

```
Function TestFile()
    Dim objFile As TextFile

    ' Create new instance of TextFile class
    Set objFile = New TextFile

    ' Set the Path property
    objFile.Path = "C:\AUTOEXEC.BAT"

    ' Try to open the file—if successful,
    ' read until the end of the file,
    ' printing each line
    If objFile.FileOpen() Then
        Do Until objFile.EOF
            objFile.ReadNext
            If Not objFile.EOF Then
                Debug.Print objFile.Text
            End If
        Loop
        objFile.FileClose
    End If

    ' Destroy class instance
    Set objFile = Nothing
End Function
```

Certainly, using this class is better than including the low-level I/O routines themselves in your code. In fact, if you've used DAO, the code should look familiar to you. It's similar to the way you manipulate database data using Recordset objects.

What's Going On?

In just a few lines of code we've accomplished a number of things. First, the code created a new instance of the object and stored a reference to it in the object variable objFile. It then used the reference to call the object's properties and methods. Programmers trained in other languages, such as C++ or Pascal, are used to calling this type of reference a *pointer*. (Think of a pointer as a variable that holds the memory address of another piece of data. In other words, it *points to* the other piece of data.) VBA doesn't expose the actual value of the pointer, but you don't really need it. All you need to know is that it points to some object you've defined and that you can use it to access that object's properties and methods.

It's important to remember that you can have more than one pointer pointing to the same object, and as long as an object has at least one pointer pointing to it, VBA keeps it in memory. For example, Listing 3.3 demonstrates how you could create two pointers to the same object by setting a second pointer variable equal to the first. You can tell whether two pointers refer to the same object by using the Is operator in a conditional statement.

Listing 3.3

```
Dim objFirst As TextFile
Dim objSecond As TextFile

' Create new instance of TextFile class
Set objFirst = New TextFile

' Create a second pointer to the new instance
Set objSecond = objFirst

' Compare the two pointers
If objFirst Is objSecond Then
    ' Both pointers refer to same object
End If
```

In a sense, VBA keeps the object alive until nothing points to it; that is, until it is no longer needed. When does this happen? It can occur when the last object variable pointing to the object goes out of scope. Also, you can explicitly break the connection between a pointer and the object it points to by setting the pointer variable to the intrinsic constant Nothing. That's what you saw in Listing 3.2. Although doing so was unnecessary (the pointer was local in scope, and Access automatically sets it to Nothing when it goes out of scope), it is good programming style to explicitly release objects you no longer need rather than rely on the rules of variable scoping to do it for you.

The Initialize and Terminate Events

Because VBA affords you the opportunity to run code when it creates and/or destroys an object instance, you should carefully consider exactly when those actions occur in your application. Unlike regular VBA modules, which have no events, class modules have Initialize and Terminate events that are triggered when an instance of the class is created and destroyed, respectively. You can use the Initialize event to do such things as setting default property values and creating references to other objects. Use the Terminate event to perform cleanup tasks. Remember that the Initialize event is triggered when VBA first creates a new instance of a class, and Terminate is triggered when the last pointer to the instance is released or destroyed.

Listing 3.4 shows the Initialize and Terminate event code for the TextFile class. During processing of the Initialize event, the code sets the default open mode property. In the Terminate event, the code checks to see whether a file is still open (in other words, whether the programmer has not explicitly called the FileClose method) and then closes it. If you want a clear example of when these events are triggered, try inserting a MsgBox statement in each and watching what happens as you use instances of the class.

Listing 3.4

```
Private Sub Class_Initialize()
    ' Set default file open mode property
    Me.OpenMode = tfOpenReadWrite
End Sub

Private Sub Class_Terminate()
    ' If a file is still open then close it
    ' before terminating
    If Me.IsOpen Then
        Me.FileClose
    End If
End Sub
```

Using Property Statements

You now know the basic techniques for creating and using class modules in VBA. If you've looked at the complete source code for the sample TextFile class, however, you will have noticed some things we have not yet discussed. The remainder of this chapter is devoted to more advanced class module techniques, beginning with the second way to implement custom properties: Property statements.

Class Modules and Multiple Instances of Forms and Reports

Access forms and reports, like VBA class modules, can have exposed custom properties and methods and allow for multiple instancing. In fact, the rules for defining properties and methods are the same for form and report class modules as they are for VBA class modules. Using Access forms and reports as classes, however, differs slightly.

First, VBA automatically adds the text "Form_" to the beginning of the form's name (and "Report_" to the beginning of a report name) to create the class name used to declare pointer variables. For example, to create a new instance of a form named frmTextFile, you would use code like this:

```
Dim objFile As Form_frmTextFile
Set objFile = New Form_frmTextFile
```

Second, unlike VBA class modules, form modules do not have Initialize and Terminate events. If you need to perform startup and shutdown tasks, use the Load and Close events, respectively.

Finally, creating a new instance of an Access form module creates a new instance of the form. Access adds it to the Forms collection, so beware of any existing code that manipulates this collection. In addition, although it initially loads hidden, the new form instance will show up in the Unhide dialog unless you set its Popup property to Yes.

What Are Property Statements and Why Use Them?

You've already seen how you can implement properties simply by declaring a Public variable in the declarations section of a class module. Consumers of your class can then reference that property using the *object.property* syntax. The major drawback to this approach is that your class has no way of knowing when the value of the property has changed. Property statements solve this problem. Property statements are VBA procedures that are executed when a property is set or retrieved. During the processing of a Property statement, you can take action regarding the property.

Property statements come in three varieties: Property Get, Property Let, and Property Set. You use Property Get statements to retrieve (or get) the values of class instance properties. You use Property Let and Property Set statements, on the other hand, to set the values of properties. The distinction between the two is that you use Property Let for scalar values (Integer, String, and so on), and you use Property Set for object datatypes. The following sections explain each of these in detail.

Retrieving Values with Property Get

The Property Get statement is probably the easiest of the three types of Property statements to understand. Its basic form consists of a declaration, which includes the property name and datatype, and a body, just like a normal function. It's up to you to return a property value by setting the statement name equal to the return value. For example, the following code is the Property Get statement for the Path property of the sample class:

```
Property Get Path() As String
    ' Return the path of the file from the
    ' Private class variable
    Path = mstrPath
End Property
```

The name of the Property statement, Path, defines the property name, and the return type (String, in this case) defines the property's datatype. When another procedure references the property using code like this:

```
Debug.Print objFile.Path
```

VBA calls the procedure, and the value of a Private class module variable (mstrPath) is returned. Of course, you can do anything within a Property procedure you can within any VBA procedure (such as performing a calculation or querying a database), so the way you arrive at the value to be returned is completely up to you.

TIP

Use the following technique when you want to control how a program sets and retrieves property values: declare a Private variable in the class module's declarations section to store the property value internally within the class. Then implement Property statements to set and/or retrieve its value.

In addition to following the simple example just presented, you can create Property Get statements that accept arguments. Property statement arguments are declared the same way as arguments of normal VBA procedures. For example, suppose your application requires you to compute weekly payroll dates. You might create a class with a PayDay property that accepts a week number and returns the associated payroll date. The declaration of that property might look like this:

```
Property Get PayDay(ByVal intWeek As Integer) As Date
    '
    ' Insert code here to compute the appropriate payroll date
    '
    PayDay = datSomeDate
End Property
```

Your program could then access the property by passing the arguments inside parentheses, after the property name:

```
datPayDay = objPayRoll.PayDay(12)
```

Setting Values with Property Let

The counterpart of Property Get is Property Let. You create Property Let statements to allow consumers of your object to change the value of a property. Listing 3.5 shows the Property Let statement for the Path property of the class.

Listing 3.5

```
Property Let Path(ByVal strPath As String)
    ' Set the path property of the file.
    ' If a file is already open, close it
    If Me.IsOpen Then
        Me.FileClose
    End If
    mstrPath = strPath
End Property
```

Notice that the Property Let procedure uses the same name (Path) as the corresponding Property Get. Property procedures (Let/Get, Set/Get) are the only pairs of VBA procedures that can have the same name within a single module. Notice also the argument to the procedure, strPath. VBA passes the value set by the object's consumer in this argument. For example, if another VBA procedure used a statement like this:

```
objFile.Path = "C:\AUTOEXEC.BAT"
```

VBA would pass the string "C:\AUTOEXEC.BAT" to the Property procedure in the strPath argument. In addition, the parameter passed to the Property Let procedure must have exactly the same datatype as the value returned from the Property Get or Set procedure.

> **NOTE**
>
> You need not have Property Get and Property Let procedures for each property you wish to implement. By defining only a Property Get procedure, you create, in effect, a read-only property—one that can be retrieved but not set. Likewise, defining only a Property Let procedure produces a write-only property. You'll see that the sample TextFile class makes heavy use of read-only properties. Although consumers of the class can't set the value of read-only properties, procedures inside the class can, by writing directly to the Private variables that store the property values.

Setting Values with Property Set

The Property Set statement is a variation of the Property Let statement designed to allow you to create object properties. *Object properties* are properties that are themselves pointers to objects, rather than scalar values. For example, suppose you want to create a property of one class that is itself a pointer to an instance of another class. You would need to define a Property Set statement to allow consumers of the first class to set the property value.

The code in Listing 3.6 defines a Property Set statement called SaveFile that might be part of a class representing text documents. The class stores a pointer to the TextFile object used for persistent storage of the document's contents.

Listing 3.6

```
' Private variable used to store a reference
' to the TextFile object associated with this class
Private mobjSaveFile As TextFile

Property Set SaveFile(objFile As TextFile)
    ' Make the private class variable point
    ' to the TextFile object passed to the procedure
    Set mobjSaveFile = objFile
End Property
```

VBA procedures could then set the pointer defined by the SaveFile property to point to another instance of the TextFile class. (Note the use of the Set reserved word.)

```
Set objDoc.SaveFile = New TextFile
```

Once the reference has been established, the procedure could then manipulate properties and call methods of the TextFile object pointed to by the document object's SaveFile property:

```
objDoc.SaveFile.Path = "C:\AUTOEXEC.BAT"
objDoc.SaveFile.FileOpen
```

At this point you might be wondering how to retrieve the value of an object property if you use Property Set to set it. As it turns out, you can use Property Get procedures for both scalar values and object pointers. You just need to declare the return value as an object datatype. For instance, if you wanted to write the corresponding Property Get statement for the SaveFile property, it might look like this:

```
Property Get SaveFile() As TextFile
    ' Return the pointer contained in the
    ' private class variable
    Set SaveFile = mobjSaveFile
End Property
```

Again, notice the use of the Set reserved word in all assignment statements involving object references.

A Simple Database Example

Although Access makes it trivial to create forms bound directly to data sources, as you start writing more advanced applications, you may need to use unbound forms more and more often. As described in Chapter 15, using unbound forms gives you better control in client-server and multiuser situations. You may find, in this type of situation, that using a class to represent your data can help make the task less formidable.

The sample class, Cats, tracks information about, well, cats. The sample form, frmCats (shown in Figure 3.5) demonstrates techniques you can use to load and save data from a table using a class to marshal the data between the table and the form. The Cat class module contains, for the most part, completely ordinary code, providing Property Let and Get statements to set and retrieve the value of each of the properties attributed to each Cat object (Name, Breed, Color, Birthdate, and so on). The class module also contains two routines that handle the transfer of data between the table and the class. The Load and Save methods, shown in Listing 3.7, do all the work and encapsulate data movement in the class module. You can call either method once you've set the ID property for the Cat object. The Load method loads the properties for a specific cat in tblCats. The Save method either saves the current Cat object to the correct row in tblCats or adds a new row and saves the data there (if the cat is new). (For more information on working with data programmatically, see Chapter 6.)

FIGURE 3.5

frmCats demonstrates using a class module to encapsulate simple data manipulation.

Listing 3.7

```
Public Function Save() As Boolean
    Dim rst As Recordset
    Dim db As Database

    On Error GoTo HandleErrors
    Set db = CurrentDb()
    Set rst = db.OpenRecordset( _
     "Select * from tblCats WHERE ID = " & Me.ID)
    With rst
        If .RecordCount = 0 Then
            .AddNew
            .Move 0, .LastModified
            ' Set the ID property for this new cat.
            Me.ID = !ID
        Else
            .Edit
```

```
        End If
        !Name = mstrName
        !Birthdate = mdatBirthdate
        !Sex = mstrSex
        !Breed = mstrBreed
        !Color = mstrColor
        !Neutered = mfNeutered
        .Update
    End With
    Save = True

ExitHere:
    If Not rst Is Nothing Then rst.Close
    Set rst = Nothing
    Set db = Nothing
    Exit Function

HandleErrors:
    Save = False
    Resume ExitHere
End Function

Public Function Load() As Boolean
    Dim rst As Recordset
    Dim db As Database

    On Error GoTo HandleErrors
    Set db = CurrentDb()
    Set rst = db.OpenRecordset( _
      "Select * from tblCats WHERE ID = " & Me.ID)
    With rst
        If .RecordCount > 0 Then
            mstrName = !Name
            mdatBirthdate = !Birthdate
            mstrSex = !Sex
            mstrBreed = !Breed
            mstrColor = !Color
            mfNeutered = !Neutered
            mlngID = !ID
        End If
    End With
    Load = True
```

```
ExitHere:
    If Not rst Is Nothing Then rst.Close
    Set rst = Nothing
    Set db = Nothing
    Exit Function

HandleErrors:
    Load = False
    Resume ExitHere
End Function
```

Although much of the code in the sample form's Class module deals with the particulars of the user interface (disabling and enabling controls at various points in the form's activity), two routines demonstrate a common technique: scattering the elements of an object to various controls on the form and gathering them back up from the form into the object. For examples of this technique, take a look at the ScatterFields and GatherFields procedures in frmCats.

Once you've created the class associated with your unbound form, as well as the routines to move the data between the member of the class and the form, writing the code to load and save the data is simple. For example, to retrieve a new row (a new cat, that is), you can use code like this, from cboCatID_AfterUpdate:

```
Set oCat = New Cat
' Set the new Cat's ID property, so you can
' use the Load method.
oCat.ID = Me!cboCatID
If oCat.Load() Then
    ' Display the loaded fields on the form,
    ' and then select the Name field.
    Call ScatterFields(oCat)
End If
```

The code necessary to save the changes on the form is also simple. The following procedure, called from several places within the form, saves data from the form back to the underlying table:

```
Private Sub SaveCat()
    Dim oCat As New Cat

    Call GatherFields(oCat)
    Call oCat.Save
End Sub
```

By emulating the techniques shown in this example, you can create unbound forms that load and save their data through an object class that mirrors the data in the underlying table. Be aware, however, that the code demonstrated here is missing a vital element: robust error handling. In an attempt to keep the code simple, this example includes very little error handling.

Advanced Class Module Techniques

Now that you've learned the basic principles behind creating and using VBA class modules, you're ready to explore some advanced techniques. The following sections cover these topics:

- Building class hierarchies
- Creating a Parent property for objects
- Implementing collections of objects

Object Hierarchies

It is almost always the case that when you model an application using object-oriented techniques, you discover relationships between object classes. Depicted graphically, the relationships between classes is sometimes called an application's *object model*. Usually, object relationships form a natural hierarchy. Consider the diagram shown in Figure 3.6, the object model for a fictitious accounting application.

You can see from this figure that a relationship exists between invoice and customer and between invoice and payment. It is generally a good idea to create a

FIGURE 3.6

Object model for a
fictitious accounting
application

sketch like the one in Figure 3.6 before beginning to program an application. It makes very clear which object classes exist and how they relate to one another.

Once you have an object model that represents your application, you can begin constructing class modules—one for each object in the diagram. To represent relationships between objects, declare pointers to child objects in the declarations section of parent class modules. For example, to model the relationship between invoice and customer (assuming classes named Invoice and Customer, respectively), you would declare a Customer variable in the declarations section of the Invoice class:

```
Public Customer As New Customer
```

Note that you can, in fact, declare object variables with the same name as the class they're based on, although naming conventions suggest that you not take advantage of this possibility.

When you create a new invoice, VBA creates a new instance of the Customer class automatically because you used the New keyword in the declaration, and the Invoice class includes a Customer object within it. You can use the Invoice object to set properties of the customer instance, as the following code fragment demonstrates:

```
Dim objInvoice As Invoice

Set objInvoice = New Invoice
With objInvoice.Customer
    .FirstName = "Jane"
    .LastName = "Smith"
End With
' and so on...
```

The ability to create object hierarchies using class-level pointer variables is a powerful feature of VBA. It lets you develop and test objects (such as the Customer object in this example) separately and then assemble them into a robust, object-oriented representation of your application.

NOTE The technique just described works great for one-to-one relationships, but what about one-to-many? For example, what if an invoice could have a number of customers associated with it? To model this situation, you need to use a collection. The sections "Collections of Objects" and "Creating Your Own Collections" later in this chapter cover this topic in detail.

Creating a Parent Property

In many object models, objects within the hierarchy implement a Parent property that contains a pointer to the instance of the object immediately above it in the hierarchy. This makes it convenient to traverse the hierarchy using VBA code: you can work your way down the tree using properties of class objects and work your way back up using the Parent property. For example, Excel Worksheet objects have a Parent property that points to the Workbook object in which the worksheets are contained.

You can implement a Parent property in your own classes by creating Property Set and Property Get procedures. For example, suppose you want to be able to reference the Document object from the TextFile object it contains. Listing 3.8 shows you how to do this.

Listing 3.8

```
' Private variable to store pointer to parent
Private mobjParent As Document

Property Set Parent(objParent As Document)
    ' If property hasn't been set yet, do so
    If mobjParent Is Nothing Then
        Set mobjParent = objParent
    End If
End Property

Property Get Parent() As Document
    ' Return the pointer stored in mobjParent
    Set Parent = mobjParent
End Property
```

In this case Parent is a *write-once property.* That is, after you set the value of the property, it cannot be set again. This prevents you from changing an object's parent after establishing the initial value. You set the value after creating a new object instance by using the Me object to refer to the parent class. Place the following code in the parent class:

```
Dim objFile As TextFile

Set objFile = New TextFile
Set objFile.Parent = Me
```

<table>
<tr><td>**NOTE**</td><td>In this example we've declared the Property procedures to accept and return a specific object type, Document. If you are creating a class that might be used by a number of other classes (and thus have different types of parents), you can use the generic Object datatype.</td></tr>
</table>

Collections of Objects

Often, when creating an object model for an application, you will find that the objects are related in a one-to-many relationship; that is, one instance of a class relates to many instances of another class. The set of related objects is typically called a *collection,* and that collection is contained by the parent object. Fortunately, VBA includes a Collection object you can use to create and manipulate your own custom collections. This section begins with a general discussion of collections and then shows you how to use VBA's Collection object to create your own.

Using Collections

You may already be familiar with collections from your experience using VBA or other Windows applications. For example, Microsoft Excel implements a Workbook object representing the data stored in an XLS file. This object, in turn, contains a collection of unique Worksheet objects. Each Worksheet object represents an individual worksheet tab within the workbook file.

If you're familiar with the way collections of objects work, you already know that you refer to objects in a collection using the collection name along with the name of one of the objects it contains. You can also use the relative position of the object in the collection by specifying a numeric index. For example, to examine the Visible property of a particular worksheet in the active workbook, you could use either of these statements:

```
Debug.Print ActiveWorkbook.Worksheets("Sheet1").Visible
Debug.Print ActiveWorkbook.Worksheets(1).Visible
```

<table>
<tr><td>**NOTE**</td><td>Collections are, in some respects, similar to arrays in that both contain a set of similar objects, and you can reference each using a numeric index. Collections are much more powerful when dealing with sets of objects and when implementing methods for adding, removing, and referencing objects.</td></tr>
</table>

Collection Properties and Methods

All collections implement a number of methods and properties designed to help you put other objects into the collection, take them out, and reference particular items. Unfortunately, not all products and components implement these properties and methods the same way. For example, to add a new worksheet to an Excel workbook, you call the Add method of the Worksheets collection. To add a new table to an Access database using Jet Data Access Objects, on the other hand, you first call the CreateTableDef method of a Database object. After setting properties of the new tabledef, you call the Append method of the database's TableDefs collection.

If this sounds confusing, don't worry. If you're interested only in creating your own collections of objects using VBA, you need to be concerned with only three methods and one property:

- Use the *Add method* to add objects to a collection. You pass a pointer to the object and an optional unique identifier as parameters.

- Use the *Remove method* to remove objects from a collection. You pass an object's unique identifier (or position in the collection) as a parameter.

- Use the *Item method* to reference a particular object in the collection and return a pointer to it. You pass an object's unique identifier (or position in the collection) as a parameter.

- Use the *Count property* to return the number of objects in the collection.

Manipulating Objects in a Collection

Once an object is in a collection, you can manipulate its properties and methods directly. To refer to an object in a collection, you refer to its place in the collection using either a unique identifier (or key) or its numeric position. You can also capture a pointer to the object in a variable, as in this example:

```
Dim wks As Worksheet
Set wks = ActiveWorkbook.WorkSheets(1)
```

Both of these techniques have been available in Microsoft Basic since the introduction of its object-oriented features. VBA added two new ways to work with objects and collections. The first, the With statement, is not limited to collections, but it can make working with complex object models much easier. The With statement lets you specify an object and then work with that object's properties or methods simply by starting each line with the dot separator character. Consider this example from Microsoft Excel:

```
With Workbooks("BOOK1.XLS").Worksheets("Sheet1"). _
  ChartObjects("Chart1").Chart
      .Rotation = 180
      .Elevation = 30
      .HasLegend = True
End With
```

This method of referring to the Chart object embedded on Sheet1 of BOOK1.XLS is certainly easier than repeating the collection syntax over and over.

Another VBA feature specific to collections is the For Each... loop. Like a regular For...Next loop, a For Each... loop uses a loop variable to iterate through a series of values. The values, however, are pointers to objects in a collection. To use a For Each... loop, you first declare a variable of the appropriate object type. You then use it in the For Each... statement, along with a reference to the collection you want to loop through. During iterations of the loop, the variable is reset to point to successive objects in the collection. For example, to display all the worksheets in an Excel workbook, you could use code like this:

```
Dim wks As Worksheet
For wksEach In ActiveWorkbook.Worksheets
    wks.Visible = True
Next
```

You can use both of these constructs with collections you create using VBA's Collection object.

Creating Your Own Collections

VBA allows you to create your own collections using a special Collection object. This VBA Collection object contains pointers to other objects. To use the Collection object, you must first create a new instance in your VBA code. For example:

```
Dim SomeObjects As New Collection
```

You can then add objects to the collection using the object's Add method. Assuming the variable objSomething contained a pointer to an object, you could use a statement like this:

```
SomeObjects.Add objSomething
```

When you add an object to a collection in this manner, however, the only way to refer back to it is by its position in the collection. Typically you don't want to rely on an object's position, because it might change as other objects are added or removed. Instead, you can specify an alphanumeric key as the second parameter to the Add method:

```
SomeObjects.Add objSomething, "Object1"
```

Having done this, you can refer to the object later on either by its position or by the unique key:

```
Set objSomething = SomeObjects(1)
' or
Set objSomething = SomeObjects("Object1")
```

Selecting unique key values for objects can be tricky. See the section "Setting Unique Object Keys" later in this chapter for more information.

NOTE Collections created using VBA's Collection object are one-based. There is no way to change this. The first object added is object 1, the second is 2, and so on. As objects are removed from the middle of the collection, higher numbers are adjusted downward to maintain continuity. You can also add objects to a collection at a specific point by specifying either the *before* or *after* parameter of the Add method (see online help for more information). It is for these reasons that you should not depend on an object's position in a collection.

You can represent one-to-many relationships in your object model by creating a collection as a property of an object class. For example, suppose the SomeObjects collection in the preceding example was declared as a Public variable of a class called Application. To add an object to the collection, you would use a statement like this (assuming objApp contained a pointer to an instance of Application):

```
objApp.SomeObjects.Add objSomething, "Object1"
```

Likewise, referring back to the object would require you to include a reference to the parent class:

```
Set objSomething = objApp.SomeObjects("Object1")
```

Although simple to implement, this approach does have its drawbacks. The section "Creating a Collection Class" later in this chapter explains what these drawbacks are and how to overcome them.

Collections and Pointer Lifetime

When you add an object to a collection, you create a new pointer to the object. The new pointer is stored as part of the collection. Consider the following code fragment:

```
Dim objSomething As SomeObject

Set objSomething = New SomeObject
SomeObjects.Add objSomething
' Does this terminate the object?
Set objSomething = Nothing
```

What happens to the new instance of SomeObject after you set the objSomething pointer to Nothing? The answer is: nothing. Even though the code explicitly destroyed the pointer contained in objSomething, an implicit pointer exists as part of the SomeObjects collection. Therefore, the new object instance is not terminated until it is removed from the collection.

Also, pay attention to where you declare your new Collection object variable. As a variable, it obeys VBA's rules concerning scope and lifetime. If you declare a Collection object variable in the body of a procedure, for instance, it will disappear when the procedure terminates, destroying all the objects it contains. Typically, you should declare collections as module or global variables.

Creating a Collection Class

VBA makes it simple to create your own collections using the Collection object. The Collection object does have one serious drawback, however. There is no way to limit the types of objects placed into a VBA collection. Traditionally, collections are made up of similar objects, but you can place pointers to any object type into a VBA collection. Unless you are extremely careful, this could lead to problems, especially in large development projects. For example, you can refer to an object's properties or methods using collection syntax, such as:

```
SomeObjects(1).Amount = 10
```

But what happens if the object represented by SomeObjects(1) doesn't have an Amount property? VBA generates a run-time error. To control the types of objects that are placed into a collection, you must create a collection class: a VBA class that defines a Private Collection object and implements methods to add, remove, retrieve, and count objects in the collection.

Because the Collection object is Private, you don't have to worry about external procedures cluttering it with invalid object pointers. Using your own class also gives you the ability to create custom replacements for the standard Add, Remove, and Item methods.

Normally, you create two classes to represent a collection of objects in this manner. One defines the object that will be contained in the collection, and the other defines the collection itself. Listing 3.9 shows the Line class module that defines a Line object, representing a line of text in the sample TextFile2 object class.

Listing 3.9

```
' Private variables for line of text
Private mstrText As String

' Private ID variable
Private mstrID As String

' Public variable for changed flag
Public Changed As Boolean

Property Get Text() As String
    ' Return value of private variable
    Text = mstrText
End Property

Property Let Text(ByVal strText As String)
    ' Change private variable and set changed flag
    mstrText = strText
    Me.Changed = True
End Property

Property Get Length() As Long
    ' Use Len function to return string length
    Length = Len(mstrText)
End Property

Property Get ID() As String
    ' Return value of private variable
    ID = mstrID
End Property
```

```
Private Sub Class_Initialize()
    ' Set the object's ID property to a random string
    mstrID = "Line" & CLng(Rnd * (2 ^ 31))
End Sub
```

Listing 3.10 shows the class module code for the Lines collection (the Lines class module from CH03.MDB). Note the Private New Collection object in the module's declaration section. Note also the Add, Remove, and Item methods, implemented as Public procedures, and the Count Property Get procedure.

NOTE This example also implements a Changed property that indicates whether any of the lines in the collection have been modified. This is another reason for using collection classes: you can create custom properties and methods of your collection, which is not possible with standard VBA Collection objects.

Listing 3.10

```
Option Explicit

' Private collection to store Lines
Private mcolLines As New Collection

Public Sub Add(ByVal strText As String, _
 Optional ByVal varBefore As Variant)

    ' Declare new Line object
    Dim objLine As New Line

    ' Set Text property to passed string
    objLine.Text = strText
    ' Add to private collection, using object's
    ' ID property as unique index
    mcolLines.Add objLine, objLine.ID, varBefore
End Sub

Public Sub Remove(ByVal varID As Variant)
    ' Call Remove method of private collection object
    mcolLines.Remove varID
End Sub
```

```
Property Get Item(ByVal varID As Variant) As Line
    ' Set return value of property to item within
    ' the private collection object specified by
    ' the passed index value (Note the return type!)
    Set Item = mcolLines(varID)
End Property

Property Get Count() As Long
    ' Return Count property of private collection
    Count = mcolLines.Count
End Property

Property Let Changed(ByVal fChanged As Boolean)
    Dim objLine As Line

    ' Set Changed property of each Line to fChanged
    For Each objLine In mcolLines
        objLine.Changed = fChanged
    Next
End Property

Property Get Changed() As Boolean
    Dim objLine As Line

    ' Loop through all Line objects in collection--
    ' if any Changed property is True then the
    ' Changed property of the collection is True
    For Each objLine In mcolLines
        If objLine.Changed Then
            Changed = True
            Exit For
        End If
    Next
End Property
```

Implementing the Remove method and the Count property in a custom collection class is straightforward. They are simple wrappers around the Collection object's method and property. The Add method is a bit more complex, however. Rather than being a simple wrapper, it's declared to accept a string parameter representing a line of text and, optionally, an index of an existing Line object before which to insert the new line. After creating a new instance of the Line class, the code sets the object's Text property to the string passed to the Add method. It then adds the object to the Private Collection object, using the new Line's ID property as the unique index. Finally, the Item method returns a particular object from the collection using an index passed to it.

The arguments to the Item and Add methods representing an object index are declared as Variants. This is necessary because the index could be either an object's unique alphanumeric identifier or its ordinal position in the collection.

Using a Collection Class

Using a collection class is similar to using any object class. You create a new instance of it and then manipulate its properties and methods. In the case of the Lines class, the TextFile class module creates a new instance, in effect producing a Lines collection within the TextFile object. The object even has the same name as the class:

```
Public Lines As Lines
```

You can then use the properties and methods of the class to add new instances of Line objects to the collection as you read each line of text from the file. Listing 3.11 shows a portion of the FileOpen method of the TextFile2 class (the more advanced text file class). After reading a line of text into the local variable strLine, the code adds a new object to the Lines collection.

Listing 3.11

```
Dim strLine As String

' ... other statements to open file

' Read all lines into the Lines collection
Set Lines = New Lines
If LOF(mhFile) > 0 Then
    Do Until EOF(mhFile)
        Line Input #mhFile, strLine
        Me.Lines.Add strLine
    Loop
End If
```

Once the collection of lines has been established, printing each one becomes trivial. You simply loop through each element in the collection, as demonstrated in Listing 3.12.

Listing 3.12

```
Dim cLines As Long

' Assume objFile is an open TextFile object

For cLines = 1 To objFile.Lines.Count
    Debug.Print objFile.Lines.Item(cLines).Text
Next cLines
```

WARNING Be careful when using the Remove method inside a loop. Because Access checks the value of the Count property only as it begins the loop but renumbers the items in the collection as you remove them, you will encounter a run-time error as the loop reaches its halfway point. To remedy this problem, loop backward from the initial Count value back to 1. The sample code in frmTestFile uses this technique to remove blank lines from a file.

Disadvantages of Collection Classes

Although collection classes give you an added level of safety and flexibility, there is a downside to using them: because VBA treats your class as a normal object, not a collection, you lose two very handy collection operators. (For a mediocre workaround, see the sidebar "Faking a Default Item Method.")

First, with true collections you normally don't need to specify the Item method when referring to objects within the collection. That's because Item is a collection's *default method*. For example, in Excel VBA, the following two statements are equivalent:

```
Debug.Print Workbooks.Item(1).Name
Debug.Print Workbooks(1).Name
```

When using a collection class, however, you must always specify the Item method. Perhaps someday the version of VBA in Office will support default methods for custom classes.

The For Each… loop is the second feature that will not work with collection classes. Because VBA treats your class as a single object, not a collection,

For Each... just will not work. If you wish to enumerate all the objects in your collection, you must use a standard For... Next loop with a numeric variable. Use the Count property to determine the number of objects in the collection and loop from 1 to this number.

Faking a Default Item Method

Although using collection classes does prevent you from using the VBA Collection object's default Item method, it is possible to create one of your own. To do this you need to create a private instance of your collection class and a procedure to return either a pointer to it or a particular instance.

Consider the following procedure:

```
Public Function Lines(Optional varID As Variant) As Object
    If IsMissing(varID) Then
        Set Lines = mobjLines
    Else
        Set Lines = mobjLines.Item(varID)
    End If
End Function
```

If placed in the TextFile class, you could write code like this to refer to an individual line:

```
Set objLine = objFile.Lines(1)
```

By passing a parameter to the function, the code accesses an object in the Private mobjLines collection. If you omit the parameter, however, you get back a pointer to the collection itself. This lets you access properties and methods of the collection, such as Count, Add, and Remove.

The disadvantage of this approach is that the code that returns a Line object from the Lines collection is part of the TextFile class, not the collection. Not only does this violate the whole idea behind object-oriented development, it means that any class that wants to use the Lines collection must contain this procedure.

Setting Unique Object Keys

We stated earlier that you should set a unique key for objects added to collections. It's worth noting, however, that this is not always intuitive or easy to do. First, an object's key cannot be numeric, making the generation of arbitrary, incrementing keys cumbersome. Second, once you set the key value, you cannot change it. Your only option is to destroy the object.

Ideally, you would use a property of the object being added. For example, the unique key for Excel Worksheet objects is the name of the worksheet. Unfortunately, you cannot mimic this feature in VBA, because the name of the object might change. If your object has a property that will not change, it's fine to use it. Otherwise, you can create a property of objects added to collections (for example, one called ID) to hold the unique key. Set the value of this property to an arbitrary (random) value during the Initialize event of the class. For example, this code fragment sets the value of a Private variable to a random, alphanumeric value:

```
Private Sub Class_Initialize()
    ' Set the object's ID property to a random string
    mstrID = "Line" & CLng(Rnd * (2 ^ 31))
End Sub
```

By setting this value in the Initialize event, you ensure that it will always have a value—the Initialize event is always triggered when an instance of the class is created. You can then use the value as the object's unique index in a collection. Consider the code shown in Listing 3.13. This code creates a new instance of the Line class and then adds it to a collection named mcolLines. The ID property of the new Line class is used as the unique key.

Listing 3.13

```
Public Sub Add(ByVal strText As String, _
 Optional ByVal varBefore As Variant)

    ' Declare new Line object
    Dim objLine As New Line

    ' Set Text property to passed string
    objLine.Text = strText

    ' Add to private collection, using object's
    ' ID property as unique index
    mcolLines.Add objLine, objLine.ID, varBefore
End Sub
```

Summary

In this chapter we've taken a look at VBA class modules, one of the most powerful features of VBA. By encapsulating complex functionality and code in class modules, you can develop applications that are easier to program and maintain. Of course, it all starts with thinking about the problem you're trying to solve in terms of object classes and the relationships between them. Once you've identified the components, it is relatively easy to model them using class modules. Simply create one class for each "thing" you want to model. In the case of one-to-many relationships between classes, you'll need an additional class to model a collection.

This chapter also explored class module coding techniques. It demonstrated how to create a class, its properties, and methods and how to create and use an instance of that class. You also saw how to create and use collection classes. Finally, the chapter presented a few useful class examples for reading and writing text files and for manipulating data.

When deciding how to take advantage of VBA class modules, you are limited only by your imagination. Just keep the following tips in mind:

- Create one class for each "thing" you want to model.

- Use Property procedures when you need to control how property values are set and retrieved.

- Use pointers to other classes to represent relationships between objects.

- Implement collection classes to protect and extend VBA's Collection object.

PART II

Manipulating Data

CHAPTER

FOUR

4

Database Design

- Database design and normalization theory

- Designing your databases: a practical, 20-step approach

- Normalizing a poorly designed database

Database design theory is a topic many people avoid learning; either they lack the time or they give up because of the dry, academic treatment the topic is usually given. Unfortunately, building a database without a solid understanding of relational database design theory is like building a house on a cracked foundation.

This chapter begins with an introduction to relational database design theory, including a discussion of keys, relationships, integrity rules, and normal forms. The chapter then presents a practical step-by-step approach to good database design and furnishes an example that demonstrates how to normalize an existing, poorly designed database.

The Relational Model

The relational database model was conceived in 1969 by E.F. Codd, then a researcher at IBM. The model is based on mathematical theory—or, more specifically, on the disciplines of set theory and predicate logic. The basic idea behind the relational model is that a database consists of a series of unordered tables (or relations) that can be manipulated using nonprocedural operations that return tables. This model was in vast contrast to the more traditional database theories of the time, which were more complicated and less flexible and were dependent on the physical methods used to store the data.

NOTE It is commonly thought that the word *relational* in the relational model comes from the fact that you *relate* tables to each other in a relational database. Although this is a convenient way to think of the term, it's not accurate. Instead, the word *relational* has its roots in the terminology Codd used to define the relational model. The table in Codd's writings was actually referred to as a relation (a related set of information). In fact, Codd (and other relational database theorists) use the terms *relations, attributes,* and *tuples* where most of us use the more common terms *tables, columns,* and *rows,* respectively (or the more physically oriented— and thus less preferable for discussions of database design theory—*files, fields,* and *records*).

The relational model can be applied to both databases and database management programs themselves. The *relational fidelity* of database programs can be compared using Codd's 12 rules (since Codd's seminal paper on the relational model, the number of rules has been expanded to more than 300) for determining how DBMS products conform to the relational model. When compared with other database management programs, Access fares quite well in terms of relational fidelity. Still, it has a way to go before it meets all 12 rules completely.

Fortunately, you don't have to wait until Access is fully relational before you can benefit from the relational model. The relational model can also be applied to the design of databases, which is the subject of the remainder of this chapter.

Relational Database Design

When designing a database, you have to make decisions regarding how best to take some system in the real world and model it in a database. This process consists of deciding which tables to create and which columns they will contain, as well as the relationships between the tables. While it would be nice if this process were totally intuitive and obvious or, even better, automated, this is simply not the case. A well-designed database takes time and effort to conceive, refine, and build.

The benefits of a database that has been designed according to the relational model are numerous, including the following:

- Data entry, updates, and deletions are efficient.

- Data retrieval, summarization, and reporting are efficient.

- Because the database follows a well-formulated model, it behaves predictably.

- Because much of the information is stored in the database rather than in the application, the database is somewhat self documenting.

- Changes to the database schema (the definition of the tables) are easy to make.

The goal of this chapter is to explain the basic principles behind relational database design and demonstrate how to apply these principles when designing a database using Access. This chapter is by no means comprehensive and is certainly not definitive. Many books have been written on database design theory; in fact, many careers have been devoted to its study. Instead, this chapter is meant as an informal introduction to database design theory for the Access developer.

NOTE   For a more detailed discussion of database design, we suggest *An Intro-duction to Database Systems, Volume I,* by C.J. Date (Addison-Wesley); *SQL and Relational Basics* by Fabian Pascal (M&T Books); or *Database Processing: Fundamentals, Design, and Implementation* by David M. Kroenke (Macmillan).

Tables, Uniqueness, and Keys

Tables in the relational model are used to represent "things" in the real world. Each table should represent only one type of thing. These things (or *entities*) can be real-world objects or events. For example, a real-world object might be a customer, an inventory item, or an invoice. Examples of events include patient visits, orders, and telephone calls.

Tables are made up of rows and columns. The relational model dictates that each row in a table be unique. If you allow duplicate rows in a table, there's no way to uniquely address a given row programmatically. This creates all sorts of ambiguities and problems.

You guarantee uniqueness for a table by designating a *primary key*—a column or set of columns that contains unique values for a table. Each table can have only one primary key, even though several columns or combinations of columns may contain unique values. All columns (or combinations of columns) in a table with unique values are referred to as *candidate keys,* from which the primary key must be chosen. All other candidate key columns are referred to as *alternate keys.* Keys can be simple or composite. A *simple key* is a key made up of one column, whereas a *composite key* is made up of two or more columns.

The decision as to which candidate key is the primary one rests in your hands; there's no absolute rule as to which candidate key is best. Fabian Pascal, in his book *SQL and Relational Basics,* notes that the decision should be based on the principles of minimality (choose the fewest columns necessary), stability (choose a key that seldom changes), and simplicity/familiarity (choose a key that is both simple and familiar to users). For example, let's say a company has a table of customers called tblCustomer that looks like the table shown in Figure 4.1.

FIGURE 4.1

The best choice for primary key for tblCustomer would be CustomerId.

CustomerId	LastName	FirstName	Address	City	State	ZipCode	Phone
1	Litwin	Elizabeth	1313 Mockingbird Lane	New York	NY	11358	2068886902
2	Wirkus	Mark	45-39 173rd St	Redmond	WA	98119	2069809099
3	Hinton	Mike	2345 16th NE	Kent	WA	98109	2067837890
4	Litwin	Geoff	1313 Mockingbird Lane	New York	NY	11358	2068886902

tblCustomer : Table

Record: 1 of 4

Candidate keys for tblCustomer might include CustomerId, (LastName + First-Name), Phone, (Address, City, State), and (Address + ZipCode). Following Pascal's guidelines, you would rule out the last three candidates because addresses and phone numbers can change fairly frequently. The choice between CustomerId and the name composite key is less obvious and would involve trade-offs. How likely is it that a customer's name will change (for example, because of marriage)? Will mis-spelling of names be common? How likely is it that two customers will have the same first and last names? How familiar will CustomerId be to users? There's no right answer, but most developers favor numeric primary keys because names do sometimes change and because searches and sorts of numeric columns are more effi-cient than searches and sorts of text columns in Access (and most other databases).

AutoNumber columns (referred to as counter columns prior to Access 95) make good primary keys, especially when you're having trouble coming up with good candidate keys and no existing arbitrary identification number is already in place. Don't use an Autonumber column if you'll sometimes need to renumber the values or if you must have an automatically incrementing number with no gaps in the sequence of values.

Determining Which Type of AutoNumber Column to Use

The AutoNumber datatype replaced the Counter datatype with the introduc-tion of Access 95. In addition, Microsoft has added two new field properties to the Auto-Number properties collection: FieldSize and NewValues.

You can set FieldSize to either Long Integer or Replication ID, with the default being Long Integer. Unless you're using the replication facilities of Access, you should leave this set to the default. (See Chapter 13 for more details on replication.)

You can set the NewValues property to Increment or Random. Access 1.x and 2.0 supported only Increment. Increment is a good choice when you want an AutoNumber column that increases by 1 for each new record and you want the number to approximate the number of records in the table. We use the term *approximate* here because an incrementing AutoNumber column will invariably contain gaps of records that were undone or deleted. You can't reuse the numbers that fall into these gaps.

A NewValues property setting of Random might be a better choice when you want to have data entered at multiple sites and then want to merge the separate databases at some later time (whether or not you are using Access replication). In this situation an incrementing AutoNumber column won't work, because each copy of the database would be assigning the same numbers. If you used a random AutoNumber column, however, there's only a slight chance that each copy of the database would use the same number.

Foreign Keys and Domains

Although primary keys are a function of individual tables, if you created databases that consisted only of independent and unrelated tables, you'd have little need for them. Primary keys become essential, however, when you start to create relationships that join multiple tables in a database. A *foreign key* is a column in one table that references the primary key of another table.

Continuing the example presented earlier, let's say you choose CustomerId as the primary key for tblCustomer. Now define a second table, tblOrder, that looks like the one shown in Figure 4.2.

CustomerId is considered a foreign key in tblOrder because you can use it to refer to a row in the tblCustomer table.

It is important that both foreign keys and the primary keys they reference share a common meaning and derive their values from the same domain. *Domains* are simply pools of values from which columns are drawn. For example, CustomerId

FIGURE 4.2

Customerid is a foreign key in tblOrder you can use to reference a customer stored in tblCustomer.

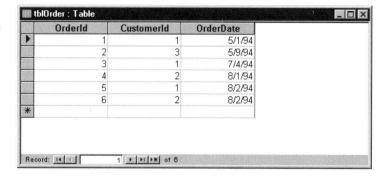

is of the domain of valid customer ID numbers, which might in this case be Long Integers ranging between 1 and 50,000. Similarly, a column named Sex might be based on a one-letter domain made up of the letters *M* and *F*. You can think of domains as user-defined column types, the definition of which implies certain rules the columns must follow and certain operations you can perform on those columns.

Access supports domains only partially. For example, Access will not let you create a relationship between two tables using columns that do not share the same datatype (for example, text, number, date/time, and so on). On the other hand, Access will not prevent you from joining the Integer column EmployeeAge from one table to the Integer column YearsWorked from a second table, even though these two columns are obviously from different domains.

Relationships

You define foreign keys in a database to model relationships in the real world. Relationships between real-world entities can be quite complex, involving numerous entities, all having multiple relationships with each other. For example, a family has multiple relationships among multiple people—all at the same time. In a relational database such as Access, however, you only consider relationships between two tables at a time. These pairs of tables can be related in one of three different ways: one-to-one, one-to-many, or many-to-many.

In Access, you specify relationships using the Tools ➤ Relationships command. In addition, you can create ad hoc relationships at any point, using queries.

One-to-One Relationships

Two tables are related in a *one-to-one* (1→1) relationship if, for each row in the first table, there is at most one row in the second table. True one-to-one relationships seldom occur in the real world. This type of relationship is often created to get around some limitation of the database management software rather than to model a real-world situation.

In Access, 1→1 relationships may be necessary in a database when you have to split a table into two or more tables because of security or performance concerns or because of the limit of 255 columns per table. For example, in a medical research database you might keep most patient information in tblPatient but put especially sensitive information (for example, patient name, social security number, and address) in tblPtConfidential (see Figure 4.3). Access to the information in tblPtConfidential could be more restricted than for tblPatient. Tables in a 1→1 relationship should always have the same primary key, which serves as the join column.

FIGURE 4.3

The tables tblPatient and tblConfidential have a one-to-one relationship. The primary key of both tables is PatientId.

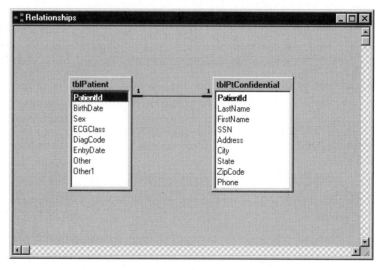

One-to-Many Relationships

Two tables are related in a *one-to-many* (1→M) relationship if, for each row in the first table, there can be zero, one, or many rows in the second table, but for each row in the second table, there is exactly one row in the first table. For example, each order for a pizza delivery business can have multiple items. Therefore, tblOrder is related to tblOrderDetail in a 1→M relationship (see Figure 4.4).

The 1→M relationship is also referred to as a *parent-child* or *master-detail* relationship. 1→M relationships are the most commonly modeled type of relationship. They are also used to link base tables to information stored in *lookup tables*. For example, tblPatient has a numeric field, DiagCode, that serves as a foreign key to the tblDiagCode table where the actual diagnoses are stored. In this case tblDiagCode is related to tblPatient in a 1→M relationship. (That is, one row in the lookup table can be used in zero or more rows in the patient table.)

FIGURE 4.4
There can be many detail lines for each order in the pizza delivery business, but each detail line applies to only one order. tblOrder and tblOrderDetail are therefore related in a one-to-many relationship.

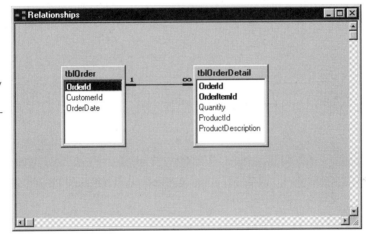

Many-to-Many Relationships

Two tables have a *many-to-many* (M→M) relationship when, for each row in the first table, there can be many rows in the second table, *and* for each row in the second table, there can be many rows in the first table. M→M relationships can't be directly modeled in relational database programs, including Access. These types of relationships must be broken into multiple 1→M relationships. For example, a patient may be covered by multiple insurance plans, and an insurance company covers multiple patients. Thus, the tblPatient table in a medical database would be related to the tblInsurer table using a M→M relationship. To model the relationship between these two tables, you would create a third table, a *linking table*, perhaps called tblPtInsurancePgm, that would contain a row for each insurance program under which a patient was covered (see Figure 4.5). Then the M→M relationship between tblPatient and tblInsurer could be broken into two 1→M relationships. (tblPatient would be related to tblPtInsurancePgm, and tblInsurer would be related to tblPtInsurancePgm, in 1→M relationships.)

FIGURE 4.5

A linking table, tblPt-InsurancePgm, is used to model the many-to-many relationship between tblPatient and tblInsurer.

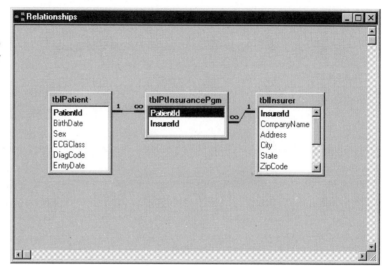

Normalizing a Set of Tables

As mentioned at the beginning of this chapter, when designing databases you are faced with a series of choices. How many tables will there be and what will they represent? Which columns will go in which tables? What will be the relationships between the tables? The answer to each of these questions lies in something called *normalization*, the process of simplifying the design of a database so it achieves the optimum structure.

Normalization theory gives us the concept of normal forms to assist in achieving the optimum structure. The *normal forms* are a linear progression of rules you apply to your database, with each higher normal form achieving a better, more efficient design. The normal forms are

- First Normal Form
- Second Normal Form

- Third Normal Form

- Boyce Codd Normal Form

- Fourth Normal Form

- Fifth Normal Form

In this chapter we discuss normalization through Third Normal Form.

Before First Normal Form: Relations

The normal forms are based on *relations,* special types of tables that have the following attributes:

- They describe one entity.

- They have no duplicate rows; hence there is always a primary key.

- The columns are unordered.

- The rows are unordered.

Access doesn't require you to define a primary key for each and every table, but it strongly recommends you do so. Needless to say, the relational model makes this an absolute requirement. In addition, tables in Access generally meet the third and fourth attributes listed above. That is, with a few exceptions, the manipulation of tables in Access doesn't depend on a specific ordering of columns or rows. (One notable exception is encountered when you specify the data source for a combo or list box.)

NOTE   For all practical purposes, the terms *table* and *relation* are interchangeable, and we use the term *table* in the remainder of this chapter. However, when we use this term, we actually mean a table that also meets the stricter definition of a relation.

First Normal Form

First Normal Form (1NF) says that all column values must be atomic. The word *atom* comes from the Latin *atomis*, meaning "indivisible" (or, literally, "not to cut"). 1NF dictates that for every row-by-column position, there exists only one value, not an array or list of values. The benefits from this rule should be fairly obvious. If lists of values are stored in a single column, there is no simple way to manipulate those values. Retrieval of data becomes much more laborious and less generalizable. For example, the table in Figure 4.6, tblOrder1, used to store order records for a hardware store, would violate 1NF.

FIGURE 4.6

tblOrder1 violates First Normal Form because the data stored in the Items column is not atomic.

You'd have a difficult time retrieving information from this table because too much information is stored in the Items column. Think how difficult it would be to create a report that summarized purchases by item.

1NF also prohibits the presence of *repeating groups* of information, even if they are stored in multiple columns. For example, you might improve upon the same table by replacing the single Items column with six columns: Quant1, Item1, Quant2, Item2, Quant3, Item3 (see Figure 4.7).

While this design has divided the information into several columns, it's still problematic. For example, how would you go about determining the quantity of hammers ordered by all customers during a particular month? Any query would have to search all three Item columns to determine whether a hammer was purchased and then sum over the three Quantity columns. Even worse, what if a customer ordered more than three items in a single order? You could always add more columns, but where would you stop—10 items, 20 items? Say you decided a customer

FIGURE 4.7

A better, but still flawed, version of the Orders table, tblOrder2. The repeating groups of information violate First Normal Form.

tblOrder2 : Table

OrderId	CustomerId	Quant1	Item1	Quant2	Item2	Quant3	Item3
1	4	5	hammer	3	screwdriver	6	monkey wrench
2	23	1	hammer				
3	15	2	deluxe garden hose	2	economy nozzle		
4	2	15	10' 2x4 untreated pine				
5	23	1	phillips screwdriver				
6	2	5	key				

Record: 1 of 6

would never order more than 25 items in any one order and designed the table accordingly. That means you would be using 50 columns to store the item and quantity information for each record, even for orders that involved only one or two items. Clearly, this is a waste of space. And someday, someone would want to order more than 25 items.

Tables in 1NF do not have the problems of tables containing repeating groups. The table in Figure 4.8, tblOrder3, is in 1NF, since each column contains one value and there are no repeating groups of columns. To attain 1NF, we have added a column, OrderItemId. The primary key of this table is a composite key made up of OrderId and OrderItemId.

FIGURE 4.8

The tblOrder3 table is in First Normal Form because all column values are atomic.

tblOrder3 : Table

OrderId	OrderItemId	CustomerId	Quantity	Item
1	1	4	5	hammer
1	2	4	3	screwdriver
1	3	4	6	monkey wrench
2	1	23	1	hammer
3	1	15	2	deluxe garden hose
3	2	15	2	ecomomy nozzle
4	1	2	15	10' 2x4 untreated pine board
5	1	23	1	screwdriver
6	1	2	5	key

Record: 1 of 9

You could now easily construct a query to calculate the number of hammers ordered. Figure 4.9 shows an example of such a query.

FIGURE 4.9

Because tblOrder3 is in First Normal Form, you can easily construct a totals query to determine the total number of hammers ordered by customers.

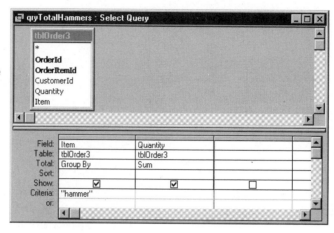

Second Normal Form

A table is said to be in Second Normal Form (2NF) if it is in 1NF and every non-key column is fully dependent on the (entire) primary key. Put another way, tables should store data relating to only one "thing" (or entity), and that entity should be fully described by its primary key.

The table shown in Figure 4.10, tblOrder4, is a slightly modified version of tblOrder3. Like tblOrder3, tblOrder4 is in First Normal Form because each column is atomic, and there are no repeating groups.

To determine whether tblOrder4 meets 2NF, you must first note its primary key. The primary key is a composite of OrderId and OrderItemId. Thus, in order to be 2NF, each non-key column (that is, every column other than OrderId and Order-ItemId) must be fully dependent on the primary key. In other words, does the value of OrderId and OrderItemId for a given record imply the value of every other column for that record? The answer is no. Given the value of OrderId, you know the customer and date of the order, *without* having to know the OrderItemId. Thus, these two columns are not dependent on the *entire* primary key, which is composed of both OrderId and OrderItemId. For this reason tblOrder4 is not 2NF.

FIGURE 4.10

The tblOrder4 table is in First Normal Form. Its primary key is a composite of OrderId and OrderItemId.

	OrderId	OrderItemId	CustomerId	OrderDate	Quantity	ProductId	ProductDescription
▶	1	1	4	5/1/97	5	32	hammer
	1	2	4	5/1/97	3	2	screwdriver
	1	3	4	5/1/97	6	40	monkey wrench
	2	1	23	5/9/97	1	32	hammer
	3	1	15	7/4/97	2	113	deluxe garden hose
	3	2	15	7/4/97	2	121	ecomomy nozzle
	4	1	2	8/1/97	15	1024	10' 2x4 untreated pine boards
	5	1	23	8/2/97	1	2	screwdriver
	6	1	2	8/2/97	5	52	key

tblOrder4 : Table — Record: 1 of 9

You can achieve Second Normal Form by breaking tblOrder4 into two tables. The process of breaking a non-normalized table into its normalized parts is called *decomposition*. Because tblOrder4 has a composite primary key, decomposition is simple: put everything that applies to each order in one table and everything that applies to each order item in a second table. The two decomposed tables, tblOrder and tblOrderDetail, are shown in Figure 4.11.

Two points are worth noting here:

- When normalizing, you don't throw away information. In fact, this form of decomposition is termed *non-loss* decomposition because no information is sacrificed to the normalization process.

- You decompose the tables in such a way as to allow them to be put back together using queries. Thus, it's important to make sure tblOrderDetail contains a foreign key to tblOrder. The foreign key in this case is OrderId, which appears in both tables.

Third Normal Form

A table is said to be in Third Normal Form (3NF) if it is in 2NF and if all non-key columns are mutually independent. One example of a dependency is a calculated column. For example, if a table contains the columns Quantity and PerItemCost, you could opt to calculate and store in that same table a TotalCost column (which would be equal to Quantity * PerItemCost), but this table wouldn't be in 3NF. It's better to leave this column out of the table and make the calculation in a query or

FIGURE 4.11

FIGURE 4.11

The tblOrder table (top) and tblOrderDetail table (bottom) satisfy Second Normal Form. OrderId is a foreign key in tblOrder-Detail that you can use to rejoin the tables.

tblOrder : Table

OrderId	CustomerId	OrderDate
1	1	5/1/97
2	3	5/9/97
3	1	7/4/97
4	2	8/1/97
5	1	8/2/97
6	2	8/2/97

Record: 1 of 6

tblOrderDetail : Table

OrderId	OrderItemId	Quantity	ProductId	ProductDescription
1	1	5	32	hammer
1	2	3	2	screwdriver
1	3	6	40	monkey wrench
2	1	1	32	hammer
3	1	2	113	deluxe garden hose
3	2	2	121	ecomomy nozzle
4	1	15	1024	10' 2x4 untreated pine boards
5	1	1	2	screwdriver
6	1	5	52	key

Record: 1 of 9

on a form or report instead. This saves room in the database and keeps you from having to update TotalCost every time Quantity or PerItemCost changes.

Dependencies that aren't the result of calculations can also exist in a table. The tblOrderDetail table in Figure 4.11, for example, is in 2NF because all its non-key columns (Quantity, ProductId, and ProductDescription) are fully dependent on the primary key. (That is, given the values of OrderID and OrderItemId, you know the values of Quantity, ProductId, and ProductDescription.) Unfortunately, tblOrderDetail also contains a dependency between two of its non-key columns, ProductId and ProductDescription.

Dependencies cause problems when you add, update, or delete records. For example, say you need to add 100 detail records, each of which involves the purchase of screwdrivers. This means you will have to input a ProductId code of 2 *and* a ProductDescription of "screwdriver" for each of these 100 records. Clearly, this is redundant. Similarly, if you decide to change the description of the item to "No. 2 Phillips-head screwdriver" at some later time, you will have to update all 100 records. As a further example, let's say you wish to delete all the 1997 screwdriver purchase records at the end of the year. Once all the records are deleted, you will no longer know what a ProductId of 2 is because you've deleted from the database both the history of purchases and the fact that ProductId 2 means "No. 2 Phillips-head screwdriver." You can remedy each of these anomalies by further normalizing the database to achieve Third Normal Form.

NOTE　　An *anomaly* is an error or inconsistency in the database. A poorly designed database runs the risk of introducing numerous anomalies. There are three types of anomalies: insert, delete, and update. These anomalies occur during the insertion, deletion, and updating of rows, respectively. For example, an insert anomaly would occur if the insertion of a new row caused a calculated total field stored in another table to report the wrong total. If the deletion of a row in the database deleted more information than you intended, this would be a delete anomaly. Finally, if updating a description column for a single part in an inventory database required you to make a change to thousands of rows, this would be classified as an update anomaly.

You can further decompose the tblOrderDetail table to achieve 3NF by breaking out the ProductId-ProductDescription dependency into a lookup table, as shown in Figure 4.12. This gives you a new detail table, tblOrderDetail1, and a lookup table, tblProduct. When decomposing tblOrderDetail, take care to put a copy of the linking column, in this case ProductId, in both tables. ProductId becomes the primary key of the new table, tblProduct, and becomes a foreign key column in tblOrderDetail1. This allows you to rejoin the two tables later using a query.

Higher Normal Forms

After Codd defined the original set of normal forms, it was discovered that Third Normal Form, as originally defined, had certain inadequacies. This led to several higher normal forms, including the Boyce/Codd, Fourth, and Fifth Normal Forms. This book does not discuss these higher normal forms because the discussion would require the introduction of additional terminology and concepts and, more important, because all that extra effort would give you little added value over 3NF.

FIGURE 4.12

The tblOrderDetail1 table (top) and tblProduct table (bottom) are in Third Normal Form. The ProductId column in tblOrderDetail is a foreign key referencing tblProduct.

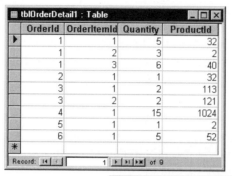

Instead we direct you to the books listed in the section "Relational Database Design" earlier in this chapter. Still, several points are worth noting here:

- Every higher normal form is a superset of all lower forms. Thus, if your design is in Third Normal Form, by definition it is also in 1NF and 2NF.

- If you've normalized your database to 3NF, you've likely also achieved Boyce/Codd Normal Form (and maybe even 4NF or 5NF).

- To quote C.J. Date, the principles of database design are "nothing more than *formalized common sense.*"

- Database design is more art than science.

This last item needs to be emphasized. While it's relatively easy to work through the examples in this chapter, the process gets more difficult when you are presented with a business problem (or another scenario) that needs to be computerized (or downsized). We outline one approach later in this chapter, but first we must introduce the subject of integrity rules.

Integrity Rules

The relational model defines several integrity rules that, while not part of the definition of the normal forms, are nonetheless a necessary part of any relational database. There are two types of integrity rules: general and database specific.

General Integrity Rules

The relational model specifies two general integrity rules: entity integrity and referential integrity. They are referred to as general rules because they apply to all databases.

The *entity integrity rule* is very simple. It says that primary keys cannot contain null (missing) data. The reason for this rule should be obvious. You can't uniquely identify or reference a row in a table if the primary key of that table can be null. It's important to note that this rule applies to both simple and composite keys. For composite keys, none of the individual columns can be null. Fortunately, Access automatically enforces the entity integrity rule for you; no component of a primary key in Access can be null.

The *referential integrity rule* says that the database must not contain any un-matched foreign key values. This implies that:

- A row may not be added to a table with a foreign key unless the referenced value exists in the referenced table
- If the value in a table that's referenced by a foreign key is changed (or the entire row is deleted), the rows in the table with the foreign key must not be "orphaned"

As defined by the relational model, three options are available when a referenced primary key value changes or a row is deleted:

- **Disallow:** The change is completely disallowed.
- **Cascade:** For updates, the change is cascaded to all dependent tables. For deletions, the rows in all dependent tables are deleted.
- **Nullify:** For deletions, the dependent foreign key values are set to null.

Access allows you to disallow or cascade referential integrity updates and deletions using the Tools ➤Relationships command (see Figure 4.13). There is no Nullify

FIGURE 4.13

Specifying a relationship
with referential integrity
between the tblCustomer
and tblOrder tables using
the Tools ➤ Relationships
command

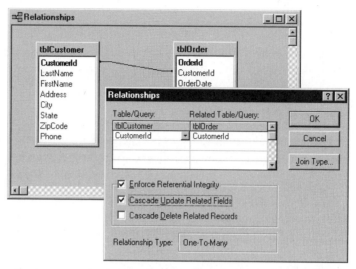

option. In the example shown above in Figure 4.13, any updates of CustomerId in
tblCustomer will be cascaded to tblOrder. Since the Cascade Delete check box hasn't
been checked, deletions of rows in tblCustomer will be disallowed if rows in
tblOrder would be orphaned.

Database-Specific Integrity Rules

All integrity constraints that do not fall under entity integrity or referential integrity are termed *database-specific rules*, or *business rules*. This type of rule is specific
to each database and comes from the rules of the business being modeled. Nonetheless, the enforcement of business rules is just as important as the enforcement
of the general integrity rules discussed in the previous section.

NOTE Starting with version 2.0, rules in Access are enforced at the engine level,
which means that forms, action queries, and table imports can no longer
ignore your rules as they could in version 1.x. Because of this change, however, column rules can no longer reference other columns or use domain,
aggregate, or user-defined functions. Access does, however, support the
specification of a table rule you can use to check columns against each
other. In addition, you can use form-based rules if you need to reference
domain, aggregate, or user-defined functions.

Without the specification and enforcement of business rules, bad data will get into the database. The old adage "garbage in, garbage out" applies aptly to the application (or lack of application) of business rules. For example, a pizza delivery business might have the following rules that would need to be modeled in the database:

- The order date must always be greater than or equal to the date the business started and less than or equal to the current date.

- The order time and delivery time can occur only during business hours.

- The delivery date and time must be greater than or equal to the order date and time.

- New orders cannot be created for discontinued menu items.

- Customer zip codes must be within a certain range (the delivery area).

- The quantity ordered can never be fewer than 1 or greater than 50.

- Non-null discounts can never be smaller than 1 percent or greater than 30 percent.

Access supports the specification of validation rules for each column in a table. For example, the first business rule from the preceding list has been specified in Figure 4.14.

FIGURE 4.14

A column validation rule has been created to limit all order dates to sometime between the first operating day of the business (5/3/93) and the current date.

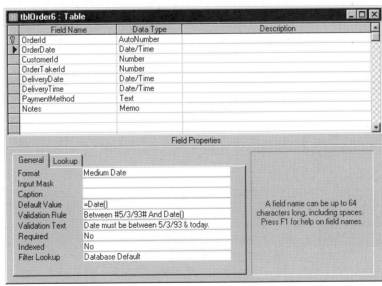

Access 2.0 added support for the specification of a global rule that applies to the entire table. This is useful for creating rules that cross-reference columns, as the example in Figure 4.15 demonstrates. Unfortunately, you can create only one global rule for each table, which can make for some awful validation error messages (for example, "You have violated one of the following rules: 1. Delivery Date >= Order Date. 2. Delivery Time > Order Time. . .").

FIGURE 4.15

A table validation rule has been created to require that deliveries be made on or after the date the pizza was ordered.

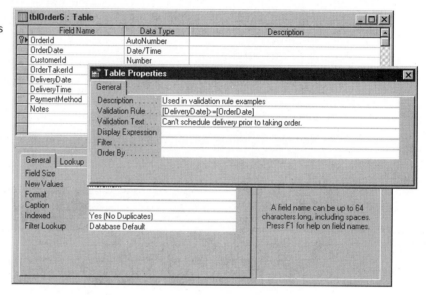

Although Access business rule support is better than most other desktop DBMS programs, it is still limited, so you will typically build additional business rule logic into applications, usually in the data entry forms. This logic should be layered on top of any table-based rules and can be built into the application using combo boxes, list boxes, and option groups that limit available choices; form-level and field-level validation rules; and event procedures.

TIP

Use application-based rules only when the table-based rules cannot do the job. The more you can build into rules at the table level, the better, because these rules will always be enforced and will require less maintenance.

A Practical Approach to Database Design

As mentioned earlier in the chapter, database design is more art than science. While it's true that a properly designed database should follow the normal forms and the relational model, you still have to come up with a design that reflects the business you are trying to model. Relational database design theory can usually tell you what *not* to do, but it won't tell you where to start or how to manage your business. This is where it helps to understand the business (or other scenario) you are trying to model. A well-designed database requires business insight, time, and experience. Above all, it shouldn't be rushed.

To assist you in the creation of databases, we've outlined the following 20-step approach to sound database design:

1. Take some time to learn the business (or other system) you are trying to model. This usually means meeting with the people who will be using the system and asking them lots of questions.

2. On paper, write out a basic mission statement for the system. For example, you might write something like, "This system will be used to take orders from customers and track orders for accounting and inventory purposes." In addition, list the requirements of the system. These requirements will guide you in creating the database schema (the definition of the tables) and business rules. Create a list that includes entries such as, "Must be able to track customer addresses for subsequent direct mail."

3. Start to rough out (on paper) the data entry forms. (If rules come to mind as you lay out the tables, add them to the list of requirements described in step 2.) The specific approach you take will be guided by the state of any existing system:

   - If this system was never before computerized, take the existing paper-based system and rough out the table design based on these forms. It's very likely that these forms will be non-normalized.

   - If the database will be converted from an existing computerized system, use its tables as a starting point. Remember, however, that the existing schema will probably be non-normalized. It's much easier to normalize the database *now* than later. Print out the existing schema, table by table, and the existing data entry forms to use in the design process.

- If you are starting from scratch (for example, for a brand-new business), rough out on paper the forms you envision using.

4. Based on the forms you created in step 3, rough out your tables on paper. If normalization doesn't come naturally (or from experience), you can start by creating one huge, non-normalized table for each form that you will later normalize. If you're comfortable with normalization theory, try to keep it in mind as you create your tables, remembering that each table should describe a single entity.

5. Look at your existing paper or computerized reports. (If you're starting from scratch, rough out the types of reports you'd like to see on paper.) For existing systems that aren't currently meeting user needs, it's likely that key reports are missing. Create them now on paper.

6. Take the roughed-out reports from step 5 and make sure the tables from step 4 include this data. If information is not being collected, add it to the existing tables or create new ones.

7. On paper, add several rows to each roughed-out table. Use real data if at all possible.

8. Start the normalization process. First, identify candidate keys for every table and, using the candidates, choose the primary key. Remember to choose a primary key that is minimal, stable, simple, and familiar. (See the section "Tables, Uniqueness, and Keys" earlier in this chapter.) Every table must have a primary key! Make sure the primary key will guard against all present *and* future duplicate entries.

9. Note foreign keys also, adding them if necessary to related tables. Draw relationships between the tables, noting whether they are 1→1 or 1→M . If they are M→M, create linking tables. (See the section "Relationships" earlier in this chapter.)

10. Determine whether the tables are in First Normal Form. Are all fields atomic? Are there any repeating groups? Decompose if necessary to meet 1NF.

11. Determine whether the tables are in Second Normal Form. Does each table describe a single entity? Are all non-key columns fully dependent on the primary key? Put another way, does the primary key imply all other columns in

each table? Decompose to meet 2NF. If the table has a composite primary key, you should, in general, decompose the table by breaking apart the key.

12. Determine whether the tables are in Third Normal Form. Are there any computed columns? Are there any mutually dependent non-key columns? Remove computed columns. Eliminate mutually dependent columns by breaking out lookup tables.

13. Using the normalized tables from step 12, refine the relationships between the tables.

14. Create the tables using Access. Create the relationships between the tables using the Tools ➤ Relationships command. Add sample data to the tables.

15. Create prototype queries, forms, and reports. While you are creating these objects, design deficiencies should become obvious. Refine the design as needed.

16. Bring the users back in. Have them evaluate your forms and reports. Are their needs met? If not, refine the design. Remember to renormalize if necessary (steps 8–12).

17. Go back to the Table Design screen and add business rules.

18. Create the final forms, reports, and queries. Develop the application. Refine the design as necessary.

19. Have the users test the system. Refine the design as needed.

20. Deliver the final system.

This list doesn't cover every facet of the design process, but you may find it useful as a framework from which you can start. (This approach is based on the writings of Access developer and database design wizard Michael Hernandez.)

Normalizing a Database with Existing Data

From time to time you may be faced with having to normalize a poorly designed database. You can usually accomplish this without loss of data by using a series of action queries. For example, you could normalize the version of the orders table (tblOrder4) shown earlier in Figure 4.10, taking it from 1NF to 3NF, using the following steps.

> **NOTE**
>
> Access 97 ships with a Wizard called the Table Analyzer. You start the Table Analyzer by choosing the Tools ➤ Analyze ➤ Table command. If you run the Table Analyzer against tblOrder4 in automatic mode ("Yes, let the wizard decide."), you can see how it fares: not so well. The Wizard only knows how to break out lookup tables (taking you from 2NF to 3NF). If you use the Wizard in manual mode ("No, I want to decide.") against tblOrder4, you'll find you can use it to break out the product information, but you can't decompose tblOrder4 further into order and order detail components. Perhaps the next version of this Wizard will be a bit smarter.

1. Make a copy of your table and work on the copy. For example, we have made a copy of tblOrder4 and named it tblOrder5. At this time it's also a good idea to make a backup copy of the database. Store it safely in case you make a mistake.

2. Break out the item-related columns that are dependent on both OrderId and Order-ItemId from tblOrder5 using a make-table query. This query, qmakOrderDetail5, will create tblOrderDetail5 and is shown in Design view in Figure 4.16. Don't delete any columns from tblOrder5 yet.

FIGURE 4.16

The qmakOrderDetail5 make-table query copies item-related data to a new table as part of the normalization process.

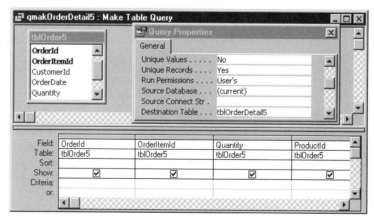

3. Move the product description information into a third table. Create this lookup table using a query based on tblOrderDetail5 with the UniqueValues property set to Yes. You use this type of query because you want only one record created for each instance of the ProductId code. This query, qmakProduct5, is shown in Design view in Figure 4.17. It creates the tblProduct5 lookup table. Don't delete any columns from tblOrderDetail5 yet.

FIGURE 4.17

The qmakProduct5 make-table query copies product-related data to a new lookup table as part of the normalization process.

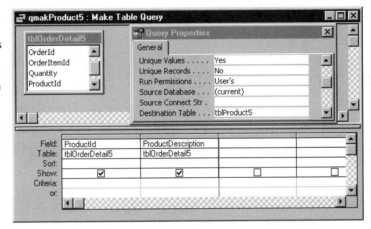

4. Open the tblOrder5 table in Datasheet view and make certain it contains the required information. It's important that things look okay before you delete any columns from the tables. Repeat this step for tblOrderDetail5 and tblProduct5.(You should still see duplicate rows in tblOrder5 and tblOrderDetail5, which you will fix in the next two steps.) At this point you may find it helpful to create a select query that rejoins the three tables to help you make certain all is well.

5. Create a third make-table query based on tblOrder5 to create the final orders table, tblOrder5a. This query, qmakOrder5a, is shown in Design view in Figure 4.18. In this query include only columns that will be in the final orders table (OrderId, CustomerId, and OrderDate). Because tblOrder5 contains duplicate rows, you must set the UniqueValues property of the query to Yes.

6. Create one more make-table query to create the final normalized version of the order details table, tblOrderDetail5a. This query, based on tblOrderDetail5, is shown in Design view in Figure 4.19. In this query include only columns that should remain in the final order details table (OrderId, OrderItemId, Quantity, and ProductId).

FIGURE 4.18
FIGURE 4.18

The qmakOrder5a make-table query creates the normalized version of the orders table.

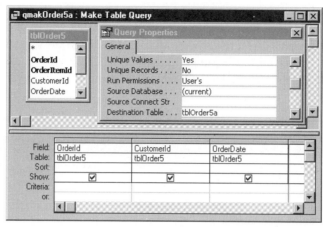

FIGURE 4.19

The qmakOrderDetail5a make-table query creates the normalized version of the order details table.

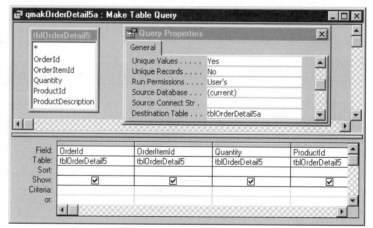

7. Open tblOrder5a, tblOrderDetail5, and tblProduct5, in turn, in Design view and define the primary key columns for each (OrderId, OrderId+Order-ItemId, and ProductId, respectively).

8. Create another select query that joins the three tables. If the datasheet looks okay, delete the original tables and rename the three new tables to their final names.

9. Create relationships between the tables using the Tools ➤ Relationships command. The screen in Figure 4.20 shows the relationships prior to renaming the tables.

FIGURE 4.20

Relationships for the normalized tables, which are now in Third Normal Form

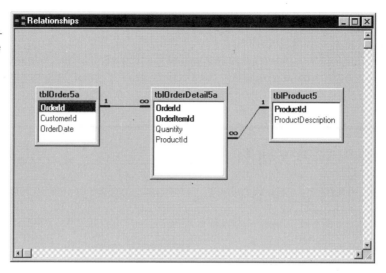

Breaking the Rules: When to Denormalize

Sometimes it's necessary to break the rules of normalization and create a database that is deliberately less normal than Third Normal Form. You'll usually do this for performance reasons or because the users of the database demand it. While this won't get you any points with database design purists, ultimately you have to deliver a solution that satisfies your users. If you do decide to break the rules and denormalize your database, however, it's important that you follow these guidelines:

- Break the rules deliberately; have a good reason for denormalizing.

- Be fully aware of the trade-offs this decision entails.

- Thoroughly document your decision.

- Create the necessary application adjustments to avoid anomalies.

This last point is worthy of elaboration. In most cases when you denormalize, you will be required to create additional application code to avoid insert, update, and deletion anomalies that a more normalized design would avoid. For example, if you decide to store a calculation in a table, you'll need to create extra event procedure code and attach it to the appropriate event properties of forms that are used to update the data on which the calculation is based.

If you're considering denormalizing for performance reasons, don't always assume the denormalized approach is the best. Instead, we suggest you first fully normalize the database (to Third Normal Form or higher) and then denormalize only if it becomes necessary for performance reasons.

When to Break the Rules

Here are two scenarios where you might choose to break the rules of normalization:

You decide to store an indexed computed column, Soundex, in tblCustomer to improve query performance, in violation of 3NF (because Soundex is dependent on LastName). The Soundex column contains the sound-alike code for the LastName column. It's an indexed column (with duplicates allowed), and it's calculated using a user-defined function. (If you're interested in such a function, see adhSoundex in the basSoundex module of CH04.MDB.) If you wish to perform searches on Soundex code with any but the smallest tables, you'll find a significant performance advantage in storing the Soundex column in the table and indexing this computed column. You'd likely use an event procedure attached to a form to perform the Soundex calculation and store the result in the Soundex column. To avoid update anomalies, you'll want to ensure that the user cannot update this column and that it is updated every time LastName changes.

To improve report performance, you decide to create a column named TotalOrderCost that contains a sum of the cost of each order item in tblOrder. This violates 2NF because TotalOrderCost is not dependent on the primary key of the table. TotalOrderCost is calculated on a form by summing the column TotalCost for each item. Since you often create reports that need to include the total order cost but not the cost of individual items, you break 2NF to avoid having to join these two tables every time this report needs to be generated. As in the preceding example, you have to be careful to avoid update anomalies. Whenever a record in tblOrderDetail is inserted, updated, or deleted, you will need to update tblOrder, or the information stored there will be erroneous.

If you're considering denormalizing because your users think they need it, investigate the reason. Often they will be concerned about simplifying data entry, which you can usually accomplish by basing forms on queries while keeping your base tables fully normalized.

Summary

This chapter has covered the basics of database design in the context of Access. Here are the main concepts we covered:

- The relational database model, created by E.F. Codd in 1969, is founded on set theory and predicate logic. A database designed according to the relational model will be efficient, predictable, self documenting, and easy to modify.

- Every table must have a primary key that uniquely identifies each row.

- Foreign keys are columns used to reference a primary key in another table.

- You can establish three kinds of relationships between tables in a relational database: one-to-one, one-to-many, or many-to-many. Many-to-many relationships require a linking table.

- Normalization is the process of simplifying the design of a database so it achieves the optimum structure.

- A well-designed database follows the Normal Forms: First Normal Form requires all column values to be atomic; Second Normal Form requires every non-key column to be fully dependent on the table's primary key; Third Normal Form requires all non-key columns to be mutually independent.

- The entity integrity rule forbids nulls in primary key columns.

- The referential integrity rule says the database must not contain any unmatched foreign key values.

- A well-designed database implements business rules (domain integrity) and requires business insight, time, and experience.

- You can normalize a poorly designed database using a series of action queries.

- Sometimes you may need to denormalize a database. Always have a good reason, and fully normalize to Third Normal Form before denormalizing.

CHAPTER

FIVE

5

Access SQL

- Understanding Access SQL

- Learning the differences between Access SQL and ANSI SQL

- Using subqueries and union queries

- Creating SQL pass-through queries

Structured Query Language (or SQL, pronounced both as "ess-cue-ell" and "see-quel"; we prefer the latter pronunciation) is by far the most popular non-procedural data access language today on computers of all sizes. Access includes support for this pervasive standard, but its implementation is incomplete and diverges from the standard in many places. Just pinning down Access' level of conformance is a chore; while Access SQL supports only a subset of SQL-89, at the same time it supports some elements of the newer SQL-92 standard. Thus, if you're already familiar with SQL, you may find Access' uneven support for the standard confusing. And if you're new to SQL and want to learn Access SQL in detail, you'll find a dearth of documentation on Microsoft's dialect of the standard query language. This chapter hopes to make up for this documentation deficiency.

A Brief History of SQL

Like many database standards, including the relational model itself and query by example, SQL was invented at an IBM research laboratory in the early 1970s. SQL was first described in a research paper presented at an Association for Computing Machinery (ACM) meeting in 1974. Created to implement E.F. Codd's relational model (originally described in an ACM paper in 1970), it began life as SEQUEL (for Structured English Query Language), briefly becoming SEQUEL/2 and then simply SQL.

Today there are hundreds of databases on platforms ranging from billion-dollar supercomputers down to thousand-dollar personal computers supporting SQL. This makes it the de facto data access language standard, but at the same time it's also an official standard. There are three American National Standards Institute (ANSI) SQL standards: SQL-86 (the most commonly implemented SQL today), SQL-89 (a minor revision), and the recently published SQL-92 (a major revision).

When most people speak of SQL, they are talking about the SQL-86 or SQL-89 standard, often extended by vendors to make it a more complete language. In the past few years vendors have begun to implement parts of the much more comprehensive SQL-92 standard. It will take years for many vendors (including Microsoft) to fully implement SQL-92.

Access SQL really shines in one crucial area: most of Access SQL directly maps to Access query by example (QBE)—in both directions. This means you can learn Access SQL by constructing queries using QBE and switching to SQL view to see the equivalent SQL. Conversely, the SQL-savvy developer can skip QBE entirely and directly enter queries using SQL view. In fact, such developers can use their SQL knowledge to learn Access QBE.

This chapter covers Access SQL in its entirety. It should prove useful to both the SQL-fluent developer coming to Access from other SQL implementations *and* the SQL-naive developer looking to make sense of this strange new language.

Where Can You Use Access SQL?

Unlike most other products that support SQL, Access has no SQL command line or similar facility into which you can directly enter SQL statements and press the ↵ key or click a button to view the results. The closest thing to this in Access is the VBA Debug window, but it doesn't allow you to directly enter SQL statements. Instead, you must enter SQL statements into the SQL view of the Access query facility and switch to Datasheet view to display the results.

Most of the time you'll find Access' way of doing things preferable to a SQL command-line interface because Access formats the data in a fully forward-and-backward-scrollable window. What's more, you can instantly switch between SQL view, where you enter the SQL statements; Query view, where you compose and view the equivalent query specification using QBE; and Datasheet view, where the results of the query are displayed.

If you find yourself still missing a SQL command-line type facility, you can always create your own using a simple form, such as the one shown in Figure 5.1. The main advantage of this type of SQL scratchpad facility is that you can view the SQL statement and its output simultaneously.

We created this scratchpad form using a text box, where the SQL statement is entered, and a list box control, where the results are displayed. A list-filling function (see Chapter 7) is used to fill the list box with the results of the query. We have included two additional text boxes to display the total number of returned records and any error messages encountered when running the query.

FIGURE 5.1

Simple SQL scratchpad form for testing SQL statements

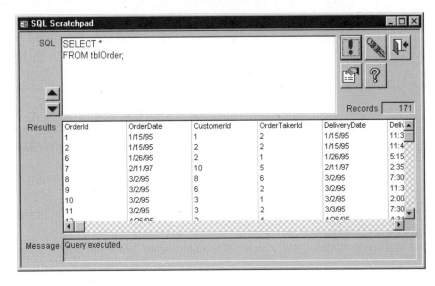

The form, frmSQLScratchpad, is included in the CH05.MDB database. Since we have implemented this form using event procedures, it will work without any changes if you import it into any other database. Many of the examples in this chapter are shown using this simple SQL scratchpad form.

> **NOTE**
>
> The SQL scratchpad form and all the tables and queries used in the examples in this chapter are included in the CH05.MDB database on the companion disk. In addition, we have created an add-in version of this form, SQLSCRAT.MDA, which you can also find on the CD included with this book. Once you install this add-in, you can call up the SQL Scratchpad form from any database using the Tools ➤ Add-ins command.

In addition to SQL view, there are several other places in Access where you can use SQL statements. You can use SQL as the record source for a form or report or the row source for a combo box, list box, or embedded graph control. You can also use SQL to create and modify query definitions that are manipulated with Access' data access objects (DAO) (see Chapter 6).

Learning Access SQL

Although SQL may seem at first daunting in complexity, when it comes right down to it, it's a fairly straightforward language to learn and use. Except for a few additions, Access SQL is pretty much a subset of ANSI SQL-89. The remainder of this chapter describes Access SQL in detail.

SQL Syntax Conventions

This chapter uses the following conventions for the specification of SQL syntax:

Items in all UPPERCASE indicate keywords you must enter literally. Items in *italicized* lowercase indicate placeholders for specific values you enter.

If the placeholder includes the word *list* or *clause,* this indicates a simplification of a more detailed syntax that is discussed elsewhere in the chapter. For example, "WHERE *where-clause"* is the syntax for a simplified WHERE clause.

Square brackets ([item]) in the syntax diagrams in this chapter denote optional items. For example, "CONSTRAINT [UNIQUE] *index"* indicates that CONSTRAINT is required, that the keyword UNIQUE is optional, and that you must enter the name of an index in place of *index.*

Curly braces combined with vertical bars ({OPTION1 | OPTION2}) denote a choice. In this case you can choose only OPTION1 *or* OPTION2.

An ellipsis (...) combined with the square brackets notation indicates a repeating sequence. For example, *"column1* [,*column2* [, ...]]" indicates that you may include one or more columns.

You customarily start each clause of a SQL statement on a new line, but this is done only for the sake of clarity; you may break the lines wherever you please. Another custom is to enter keywords in all caps, but this is not required. We follow these customs throughout this chapter. You should terminate SQL statements with a semicolon, although Access (but not many other SQL implementations) will still process SQL statements that lack semicolon terminators.

The SELECT Statement

The *SELECT statement* is the bread and butter of Access SQL, or any SQL, for that matter. If you learn the SELECT statement and all its clauses, you'll know most of what's to know about SQL. Select queries *select* rows of data and return them as a dynaset recordset.

The basic syntax of the SELECT statement is

SELECT *column-list*

FROM *table-list*

[WHERE *where-clause*]

[ORDER BY *order-by-clause*];

SELECT statements *must* include SELECT and FROM clauses. The WHERE and ORDER BY clauses are optional.

The SELECT Clause

You use the *SELECT clause* to specify which columns to include in the resulting recordset. The column names are analogous to fields dropped onto the QBE grid with the Show box checked. The syntax of the SELECT clause is

SELECT {* | *expression1* [AS *alias1*] [, *expression2* [AS *alias2*] [, ...]]]}

The expressions can be simple column names, computed columns, or SQL aggregate functions. Just as in QBE, you can use an asterisk (*) to indicate all fields from a table like this:

```
SELECT *
```

You indicate a single column—for example, LastName—like this:

```
SELECT LastName
```

You choose multiple columns—for example, Customer#, FirstName, and LastName—like this:

```
SELECT [Customer#], LastName, FirstName
```

In the preceding example, the Customer# column is enclosed in square brackets because its name contains a *nonalphanumeric* character. You need to use square brackets to delimit all column names that include these characters or spaces. (Don't confuse these *required* brackets with the square brackets used in the syntax diagrams to indicate optional parameters.) At your discretion you may also use brackets to enclose names that don't require brackets. For example, you could enter the preceding statement as:

```
SELECT [Customer#], [LastName], [FirstName]
```

You can change the name of output columns and create computed columns using SQL, just as you can in QBE. To create a computed column, enter an expression instead of a table-based column. To rename a column, add "AS *aliasname*" after the column or expression.

For example, to return Customer#, renamed as "ID", and the concatenation of first and last names, renamed as "Customer Name", you could enter the following:

```
SELECT [Customer#] AS ID, [FirstName] & " " & [LastName] AS
[Customer Name]
```

If you include multiple tables (or queries) in the SELECT statement (see the section "Joining Tables" later in this chapter), you will likely need to refer to a particular column that has the same name in more than one table included in the query. In this case you must use the fully qualified version of the column name using this syntax:

table-or-query.column

For example, you could select the column OrderId from table tblOrderDetails using the following:

```
SELECT tblOrderDetails.OrderId
```

NOTE Access QBE *always* generates SQL that uses fully qualified column names, even for single-table queries.

The FROM Clause

You use the *FROM clause* to specify the names of the tables or queries from which to select records. If you use more than one table, you must specify here how the tables are to be joined. See the section "Joining Tables" later in this chapter for more details on multitable queries. For now, here's the simplified single-table syntax:

FROM *table-or-query* [AS *alias*]

For example, you would enter the following SELECT statement to return all columns and all rows from table tblOrder. (This query was shown earlier in Figure 5.1.)

```
SELECT *
FROM tblOrder;
```

If you wished to return only the OrderId and OrderDate columns, you could enter the following SELECT statement:

```
SELECT OrderId, OrderDate
FROM tblOrder;
```

As with the SELECT clause, where you can alias (temporarily rename) columns, you can alias table names in the FROM clause. Include the alias, sometimes called a *correlation name,* immediately after the table name, along with the AS keyword. To expand on the last example, you could have renamed tblOrder as Orders Table using the following SELECT statement:

```
SELECT OrderId, OrderDate
FROM tblOrder AS [Orders Table];
```

Correlation names are often used for convenience—correlation names such as T1 and T2 (where T1 stands for *table 1*) are often used to reduce typing—but *sometimes* they are required. You must use them for the specification of self joins (see the section "Self Joins" later in this chapter) and certain correlated subqueries (see the section "Subqueries" later in this chapter).

The WHERE Clause

You use the optional *WHERE clause* to restrict or filter the rows returned by a query. The WHERE clause corresponds to the Criteria and Or lines of QBE. Columns referenced in the WHERE clause needn't be included in the SELECT clause column list. (You can accomplish the same end in QBE by unchecking the Show box under a column used to set criteria.) A WHERE clause in Access SQL may contain up to 40 columns or expressions linked by the logical operator AND or OR. You may also use parentheses to group logical conditions.

The syntax of the WHERE clause is

WHERE *expression1* [{And | Or} *expression2* [...]]

For example, you could restrict the rows returned by the SQL statement presented earlier to only those orders in which OrderTakerId = 2 with the following SELECT statement:

```
SELECT OrderId, OrderDate
FROM tblOrder
WHERE OrderTakerId = 2;
```

Figure 5.2 shows the result of this query.

WHERE clause expressions take the same format as expressions in QBE. You may reference columns, built-in and user-defined functions, constants, and operators in each expression. Here are several examples of valid WHERE clauses:

```
WHERE CustomerId = 4
```

FIGURE 5.2

Sample select query that displays OrderId and OrderDate for all orders taken by order taker

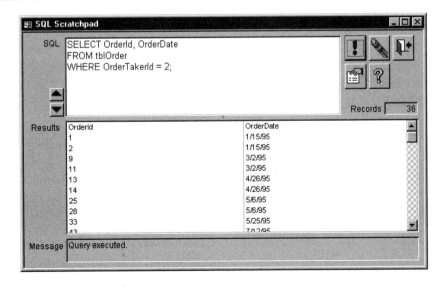

127

```
WHERE Sex = "Female" AND Age BETWEEN 21 AND 29
WHERE LastName IS NOT NULL OR (LastName IS NULL AND
  FirstName = "Joe")
WHERE OrderDate > DateAdd("yyyy", -1, Date())
```

Access SQL is less forgiving than Access QBE about the specification of criteria, so you need to keep the following rules in mind when entering expressions:

- Always enclose text strings in WHERE clauses in quotes; either single or double quotes are fine. For example:

```
WHERE LastName = "Jones"
```

- Enclose dates with the pound sign (#). For example:

```
WHERE OrderDate > #4/15/95#
```

- Always use the keyword LIKE with wildcard characters when you wish to use inexact pattern-matching criteria. For example:

```
WHERE FirstName LIKE "P*"
```

NOTE ANSI SQL uses double quotes the same way Access uses square brackets. In ANSI SQL you can use only single quotes for text strings.

The ORDER BY Clause

You use the optional *ORDER BY clause* to sort the rows returned by the query by one or more columns. You use the ASC or DESC keyword to specify ascending or descending order. Ascending is the default. The ORDER BY clause corresponds to the Sort line in QBE. As with QBE, precedence in sorting is left to right.

NOTE The sort order Access uses is specified at the time you create the database using the Tools ➤ Options ➤ General ➤ New Database Sort Order setting. By default, Access uses the "General" (U.S.) sort order, which you can change to some other sort order. Once a database is created, a change in sort order has no effect until you compact the database.

Just as with the WHERE clause, columns referenced in the ORDER BY clause needn't be included in the SELECT clause column list. You can sort text, numeric, and date/time columns, which will be sorted alphabetically, numerically, and chronologically, respectively, just as you'd expect. Don't include memo or OLE-object type fields in an ORDER BY clause; you cannot sort on these column types. The ORDER BY syntax is as follows:

ORDER BY *column1* [{ASC | DESC}] [,*column2* [{ASC | DESC}] [, ...]]

For example, if you wanted to list your customers alphabetically by last and then first name, you could use the following SQL statement:

```
SELECT *
FROM tblCustomer
ORDER BY LastName, FirstName;
```

You can also use expressions in an ORDER BY clause. For example, you could achieve the same result with:

```
SELECT *
FROM tblCustomer
ORDER BY LastName & ", " & FirstName;
```

If you have a choice (as in this example), it's best to sort on columns rather than expressions because sorting on expressions is slower.

Joining Tables

If you've properly normalized your database (see Chapter 4), you'll undoubtedly need to create queries that draw data from more than one table. When you access multiple tables in SQL, just as in Access QBE, you must *join* the tables on one or more columns to produce meaningful results. If you don't join the tables, you'll produce a Cartesian product query, which is usually undesired. (A *Cartesian product* is the arithmetic product of two or more input tables. For example, two 25-row tables joined this way result in a 625-row recordset.)

There are two ways to join tables in Access SQL (actually, three, if you include subselects, which are covered in the section "Subqueries" later in this chapter): in the FROM clause and in the WHERE clause. Joins in the WHERE clause have always been a part of SQL; joins in the FROM clause are a feature that was added to the ANSI standard in SQL-92.

Using the older SQL-89–compliant syntax, you join tables like this:

SELECT *column-list*

FROM *table1, table2*

WHERE *table1.column1 = table2.column2;*

Note that this syntax makes no provision for outer joins, although some vendors have suggested extensions to the standard.

In contrast, the SQL-92–compliant syntax looks like this:

SELECT *column-list*

FROM *table1* {INNER | LEFT [OUTER] | RIGHT [OUTER]} JOIN *table2*

ON *table1.column1 = table2.column2;*

The keyword OUTER is optional.

Say you wished to select OrderId, OrderDate, and CustomerName for all orders occurring on or after January 1, 1995. Using the older SQL-89–compliant join syntax, you would enter the SQL statement shown in Figure 5.3. Using the newer syntax, you would enter the equivalent statement shown in Figure 5.4.

Although it's useful to be familiar with the SQL-89–style join syntax (especially if you will be using other products that are SQL-89 compliant), we recommend using the SQL-92–compliant syntax for joining tables. It's more powerful, and it's consistent with the SQL generated by Access QBE. More important, recordsets produced using the SQL-89 syntax are not updatable.

Multiple Joins

As when using Access QBE, you can create SELECT statements that join more than two tables. A simplified syntax for specifying joins of multiple tables in the FROM clause is

FROM (... (*table1* JOIN *table2* ON *conditionA*) JOIN *table3* ON *conditionB*)
    JOIN ...)

You may find this nested-style syntax a little confusing. It implies a set order in which the joins are performed—for example, "first join table1 to table2 and then

FIGURE 5.3

SELECT statement that joins the tables tblOrder and tblCustomer using SQL-89–compliant join syntax. The results of this query will be read-only.

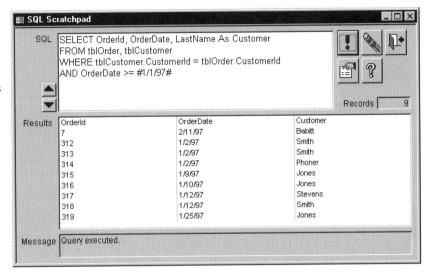

FIGURE 5.4

SELECT statement that joins the tables tblOrder and tblCustomer using SQL-92–compliant join syntax. The results of this query will be fully updatable.

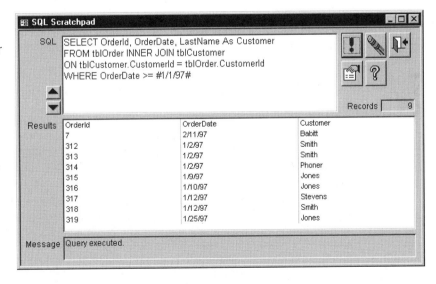

join that result to table3 and then...." But the order of joins doesn't really matter in Access. No matter how you specify the order in the FROM clause, the Jet query processor decides on the optimum ordering of joins for the sake of efficiency. This is the way it *should* be in the relational model.

NOTE To simplify the preceding syntax diagram, we've used the word *JOIN* to indicate *any* type of join. You would, of course, use one of the following instead: INNER JOIN, LEFT OUTER JOIN, or RIGHT OUTER JOIN.

So it would seem that this syntax is counter intuitive. Alas, this type of syntax *is* necessary for the specification of outer joins in the ANSI SQL standard because order *does* matter with outer joins. But there's yet another twist: even though ANSI SQL supports the use of parentheses to allow you to arbitrarily combine outer and inner joins in any order, Access does not. This arises from the fact that the Jet query processor ignores the placement of parentheses when processing queries. Because of this, Access SQL has very specific rules on how outer joins can be combined with inner joins or other outer joins.

The Jet engine enforces the following rules when combining joins in a single query:

- The nonpreserved table in an outer join *cannot* participate in an inner join.

- The nonpreserved table in an outer join *cannot* be the nonpreserved table of another outer join.

TIP In a left outer join, the unmatched rows in the table on the left side of the join are *preserved.* In a right outer join, the unmatched rows in the table on the right side of the join are preserved. As Access executes an outer join, it first looks at each row in the preserved table. If a row in the other (nonpreserved) table matches a row in the preserved table, Access creates a result row from the two. Otherwise Access creates a result row from the columns in the preserved table and fills the columns from the other (nonpreserved) table with nulls. An outer join will always have as many rows as or more rows than the equivalent inner join.

These rules can also be expressed using QBE: a table with an arrow pointing toward it *can't* also be connected to either a line with no arrow or another arrow pointing toward it.

So even though you must use the parentheses, for all practical purposes they are ignored as the Jet query engine processes your query. Instead, you must follow the preceding rules when combining outer joins. If you fail to, you will receive the "Query contains ambiguous outer joins" or "Join expression not supported" error message.

If you need to create a query that does not follow these rules, you can usually break it up into multiple stacked queries that Jet *can* handle. For example, say you wished to list all customers and the items they ordered but include customers who made no orders. To solve this problem, you might create a four-table, three-join query that looks like this:

```
SELECT LastName, OrderDate,
Quantity, MenuDescription
FROM ((tblOrder INNER JOIN tblOrderDetails
ON tblOrder.OrderId = tblOrderDetails.OrderId)
INNER JOIN tblMenu ON tblOrderDetails.MenuId = tblMenu.MenuId)
RIGHT JOIN tblCustomer ON tblOrder.CustomerId =
tblCustomer.CustomerId
ORDER BY LastName, OrderDate DESC;
```

Unfortunately, the preceding query will not work. If you attempt to execute it, you get the "Join expression not supported" error message. This is because the nonpreserved side of the outer join (in this case, a right outer join) is combined with several inner joins.

The solution to this dilemma is to create the query in two steps:

1. Create a query that joins the tables tblOrder, tblOrderDetails, and tblMenu using inner joins. Save the query, for example, as qryItems.

2. Create a second query that combines the result of qryItems with tblCustomer using an outer join.

The first query's SELECT statement (qryItems) would look like this:

```
SELECT CustomerId, OrderDate,
Quantity, MenuDescription
FROM (tblOrder INNER JOIN tblOrderDetails
```

```
ON tblOrder.OrderId = tblOrderDetails.OrderId)
INNER JOIN tblMenu
ON tblOrderDetails.MenuId = tblMenu.MenuId;
```

The second query would then look like this:

```
SELECT LastName, OrderDate,
Quantity, MenuDescription
FROM tblCustomer LEFT JOIN qryItems ON
tblCustomer.CustomerId = qryItems.CustomerId
ORDER BY LastName, OrderDate DESC;
```

You can use these two *stacked* queries, the datasheet for which is shown in Figure 5.5, to produce the correct answer.

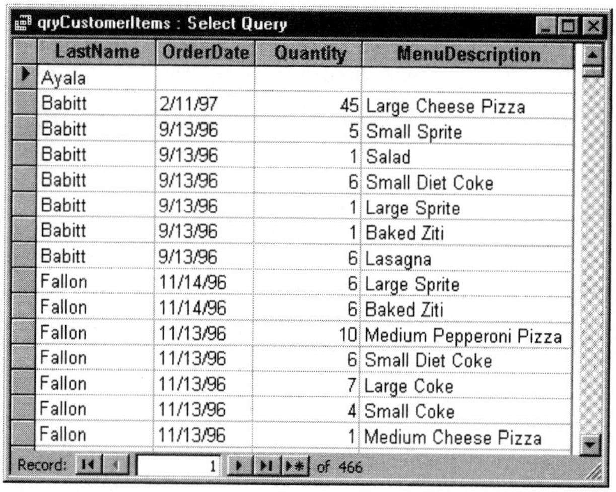

FIGURE 5.5

Customers and their orders, including rows where no orders were made. (Note the first row.) This query, because it requires combining outer and inner joins with inner joins on the non-preserved side of the outer join, must be created using two stacked queries.

LastName	OrderDate	Quantity	MenuDescription
Ayala			
Babitt	2/11/97	45	Large Cheese Pizza
Babitt	9/13/96	5	Small Sprite
Babitt	9/13/96	1	Salad
Babitt	9/13/96	6	Small Diet Coke
Babitt	9/13/96	1	Large Sprite
Babitt	9/13/96	1	Baked Ziti
Babitt	9/13/96	6	Lasagna
Fallon	11/14/96	6	Large Sprite
Fallon	11/14/96	6	Baked Ziti
Fallon	11/13/96	10	Medium Pepperoni Pizza
Fallon	11/13/96	6	Small Diet Coke
Fallon	11/13/96	7	Large Coke
Fallon	11/13/96	4	Small Coke
Fallon	11/13/96	1	Medium Cheese Pizza

Record: 1 of 466

Self Joins

Self joins are useful for answering certain types of queries when you have recursive relationships or when you wish to pull together and "flatten" multiple rows from a table. For example, if you stored the ID number of supervisors in an employees table, you could join the employees table to itself to display employees and their supervisors on a single row of a report. And in a database in which you stored multiple addresses of a customer in separate rows of an address table, you could also use a self join to pull together into a single record both home and work addresses.

The trick to creating self joins in QBE is to alias the second copy of a table so it is treated as though it were a separate table. You use this same trick to create self joins with SQL. For example, tblEmployee contains a column, SupervisorId, that is recursively related to EmployeeId (see Figure 5.6). Say you wished to view the names of all employees and their supervisors' names and include employees who lacked a supervisor. (This last requirement means you need to use an outer join to create the desired query.) The SELECT statement that accomplishes this is shown in Figure 5.7.

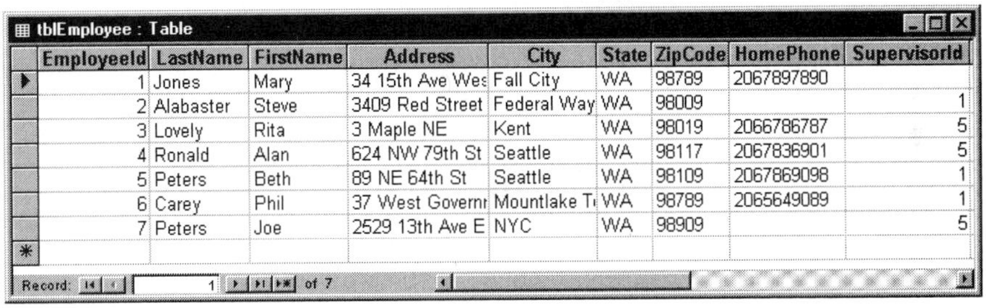

FIGURE 5.6

The tblEmployee table was designed with a recursive relationship between EmployeeId and Supervisorld. This design allows you to store information about both employees and their supervisors in a single table.

EmployeeId	LastName	FirstName	Address	City	State	ZipCode	HomePhone	SupervisorId
1	Jones	Mary	34 15th Ave Wes	Fall City	WA	98789	2067897890	
2	Alabaster	Steve	3409 Red Street	Federal Way	WA	98009		1
3	Lovely	Rita	3 Maple NE	Kent	WA	98019	2066786787	5
4	Ronald	Alan	624 NW 79th St	Seattle	WA	98117	2067836901	5
5	Peters	Beth	89 NE 64th St	Seattle	WA	98109	2067869098	1
6	Carey	Phil	37 West Govern	Mountlake T	WA	98789	2065649089	1
7	Peters	Joe	2529 13th Ave E	NYC	WA	98909		5

Record: 1 of 7

Non–Equi-Joins

All the joins discussed in this chapter so far have been *equi-joins*—joins based on one field being equal to another. You can also create *non–equi-joins* in Access using the operators >, >=, <, <=, <>, and Between. You'll likely use non–equi-joins far less frequently than the standard equi-join, but sometimes a non–equi-join is exactly what you need.

The CH05.MDB database includes a table called tblEvents that lists special sales events and the beginning and ending dates for each event (see Figure 5.8). Say you'd like to create a query that lists information on each order (from tblOrder) linked to the special events table and limited to Visa sales on or after July of 1996. Because the events from tblEvents are listed as a range of dates, you can't use an equi-join to link this table to tblOrder. You can, however, join the two tables using the BETWEEN operator like this:

```
ON (tblOrder.OrderDate BETWEEN tblEvents.BeginningDate AND
tblEvents.EndingDate)
```

FIGURE 5.7

This self-join query produces a list of all employees and their supervisors. By using an outer join, you can include the CEO, Mary Jones, even though she has no supervisor.

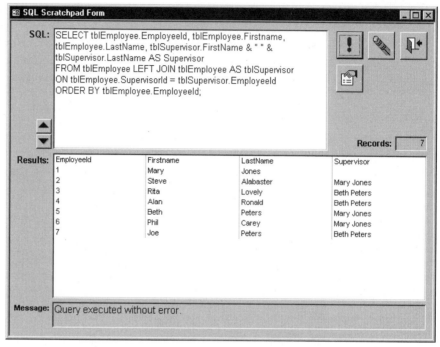

FIGURE 5.8

The tblEvents table tracks special events for a restaurant.

EventId	Event	BeginningDate	EndingDate	Comments
1	Presidents' DaySale 1996	2/1/96	2/3/96	a big flop
2	July 4th Two For One Sale 1996	7/1/96	7/4/96	50% increase in sales
3	Fall Clearance Sale 1996	10/5/96	10/5/96	better than last year
4	Say Goodbye to 1996 Sale	12/26/96	12/31/96	the turkey pizza didn't work
5	New Years Day Special 1997	1/1/97	1/1/97	good sales

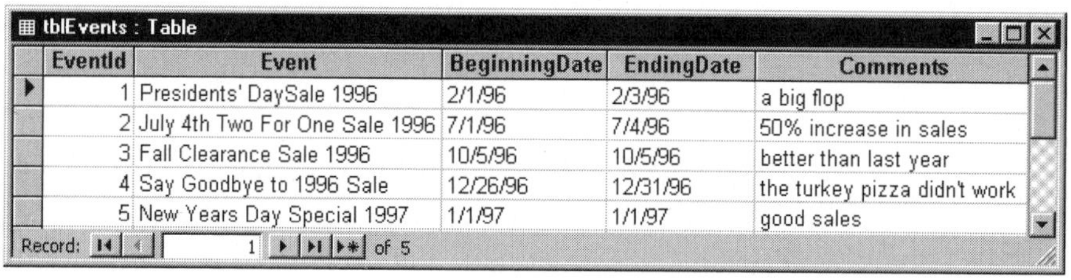

The complete query is shown in Figure 5.9. We used a left outer join to include all orders, not just those occurring during special events.

FIGURE 5.9

This query joins the tblOrder and tblEvents tables using the BETWEEN operator and a left outer join.

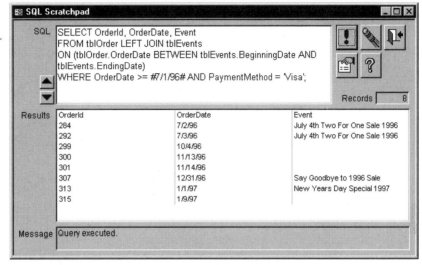

The ALL, DISTINCTROW, and DISTINCT Predicates

You can precede the SELECT clause column-name list with one of the mutually exclusive quantifier predicates: ALL, DISTINCTROW, or DISTINCT. (The DISTINCTROW predicate is unique to Access SQL.) These quantifiers control how duplicate values and duplicate records are handled. Here's the basic syntax of the SELECT clause predicates:

SELECT [{ ALL | DISTINCT | DISTINCTROW }] *column-list*

If you use no keyword, ALL is assumed. ALL returns all rows that meet the specified criteria. No special processing of the rows is performed to ensure uniqueness. This is equivalent in QBE to setting both the UniqueValues and UniqueRecords properties to No.

NOTE

When you created a query in prior versions of Access using QBE, Access by default set the UniqueRecords property to Yes, which is equivalent to using the DISTINCTROW predicate. In an effort to be more consistent with ANSI SQL, Access 97 QBE sets the UniqueRecords property by default to No, which is equivalent to using the ALL (or no) predicate.

If you use the keyword DISTINCT, Access eliminates any duplicate rows in the result set *based on the columns contained in the SELECT clause.* If more than one column is specified in the SELECT clause, Access discards duplicates based on the values of them all. When you use DISTINCT, the query's recordset is never updatable, and performance may be adversely affected. Thus, use DISTINCT only when necessary. Using the DISTINCT predicate in a SELECT statement is equivalent to setting the UniqueValues property to Yes in QBE.

If you use the keyword DISTINCTROW, Access eliminates any duplicate rows in the result set *based on all columns in the source tables.* DISTINCTROW has *no* effect when the query references only one table or returns at least one column from all included tables. In these cases, which include the vast majority of queries, using DISTINCTROW is equivalent to using ALL (or no predicate) and doesn't affect the performance of the query. The DISTINCTROW predicate corresponds to the UniqueRecords property in QBE. The DISTINCTROW predicate is unique to Access SQL.

It's worth noting that for most types of queries for which DISTINCTROW is applicable—queries with multiple tables *and* where at least one table is included in the FROM clause without a corresponding column in the SELECT clause (that is, a table is included without any output columns)—it produces the same result as the DISTINCT predicate, with one significant difference: the query's recordset is updatable.

For example, you might use the following query to list the descriptions of all menu items that have been ordered at least once since January of 1996:

```
SELECT ALL MenuDescription
FROM (tblMenu INNER JOIN tblOrderDetails ON tblMenu.MenuId =
tblOrderDetails.MenuId)
INNER JOIN tblOrder ON tblOrderDetails.OrderId =
tblOrder.OrderId
WHERE tblOrder.OrderDate > #1/1/96#
ORDER BY MenuDescription;
```

With the ALL predicate, this query returns 260 rows—one row for each Order Detail item since 1/1/96. Replacing ALL with DISTINCT returns 17 rows in a read-only recordset—one row for each distinct menu item ordered at least once since 1/1/96. Replacing DISTINCT with DISTINCTROW returns the same 17 rows, but this time the query is updatable. The datasheets returned by the three queries, each using a different predicate, are contrasted in Figure 5.10.

The TOP Predicate

You use the TOP predicate to return the top *n* rows or top *n* percent of rows from a recordset. This is useful when you wish to return only a select proportion of records meeting the query criteria. The TOP predicate is unique to Access SQL and is equivalent to using the TopValues property in QBE.

Unless you don't care which proportion of records you get, you should only use the TOP predicate with an ORDER BY clause. Otherwise you get a more or less random assortment of records. If you use an ORDER BY clause with the ASC keyword (or no keyword), TOP returns the bottom-most records. If you use an ORDER BY clause with the DESC keyword, TOP returns the top-most records.

TIP

The TOP predicate treats nulls as the smallest numeric value, earliest date, or first alphabetical text string. Thus, when you know in advance that the Top column may contain nulls, you may wish to explicitly exclude nulls in the WHERE clause.

There are two forms of TOP: alone and with PERCENT. You can combine either form of TOP with the ALL, DISTINCT, or DISTINCTROW predicate. The syntax is as follows:

SELECT [{ ALL | DISTINCT | DISTINCTROW }] [TOP *n* [PERCENT]] *column-list*

For example, to return the top seven most costly items ever ordered, where cost equals Quantity*Price*(1–Discount), you could use the SELECT statement shown in Figure 5.11.

Access processes the TOP predicate after all criteria, joins, sorts, grouping, and other predicates have been applied. Ties are treated like any other row, except

FIGURE 5.10

Three queries of menu items sold within the last year. The first query (top) uses the ALL predicate, which returns 260 rows, including duplicates. The second query (middle) uses DISTINCT and returns 17 rows, but the recordset is read-only. The third query (bottom) uses DISTINCTROW and also returns 17 rows, but the recordset is updatable. (Note the new-row asterisk at the bottom of the datasheet.)

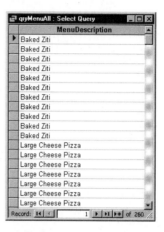

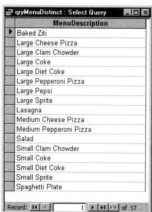

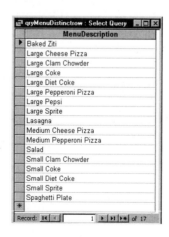

FIGURE 5.11

This query returns the top seven largest item sales by using the TOP predicate and a descending ORDER BY clause. Note that more than seven rows are returned because of a tie for seventh place.

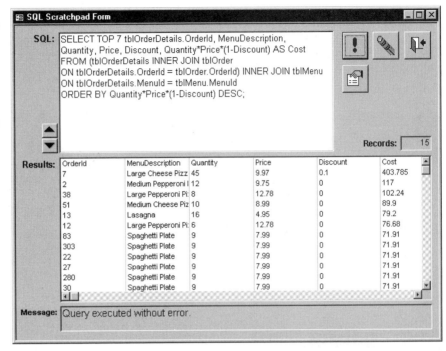

when multiple rows qualify as the last selected row—for example, the seventh row for a Top 7 specification (see Figure 5.11). When there is a tie on the last selected row, Access returns *all* rows with equivalent values. With no ORDER BY clause, Access uses all the columns from the SELECT clause to decide on ties. Otherwise Access uses only the columns contained in the ORDER BY clause to determine both the ordering of rows and the resolution of ties, even if some or all of the ORDER BY columns don't appear in the SELECT clause.

The WITH OWNERACCESS OPTION Declaration

You use the WITH OWNERACCESS OPTION declaration to allow users of a query you have created to inherit *your* security rights while running the query. This gives the users of a query you've created the ability to run the query, even if they don't have the necessary security permissions to one or more of the underlying tables. When you omit this declaration, the user without proper security clearance to the source tables does not inherit your security and thus cannot run the query. Using the declaration is equivalent to setting the RunPermissions property in QBE to "Owner's". Omitting the declaration is equivalent to setting it to "User's". The syntax for using the WITH OWNERACCESS OPTION declaration is as follows:

SELECT *column-list*

FROM *table-list*

[WHERE *where-clause*]

[ORDER BY *order-by-clause*]

[WITH OWNERACCESS OPTION];

The WITH OWNERACCESS OPTION declaration works only with saved queries; if you use it in a SQL statement that has not been saved as a query (for example, by directly entering a SQL statement in a form's RecordSource property), it has no effect.

Aggregating Data

Aggregate queries are useful for summarizing data, calculating statistics, spotting bad data, and looking for trends. These types of queries produce read-only recordsets.

You can construct three types of aggregate queries using Access SQL:

- Simple aggregate queries based on a SELECT statement *without* a GROUP BY clause

- GROUP BY queries using a SELECT statement *with* a GROUP BY clause

- Crosstab queries that use the TRANSFORM statement

All these queries have one thing in common: they use at least one aggregate function in the SELECT clause. The valid aggregate functions are detailed in Table 5.1.

TABLE 5.1   The SQL Aggregate Functions and Their Usage

Aggregate Function	Purpose
Avg([column[1]])	Mean or average of non-null values for the column
Count([column])	Count of the number of non-null values for a column
Count(*)	Count of the total number of rows in the result set, including rows with null values
Sum([column])	Sum of the non-null values for the column
Min([column])	Smallest non-null value for the column
Max([column])	Largest non-null value for the column
First([column])	Value of the column in the first row of the result set, which can be null[2]
Last([column])	Value of the column in the last row of the result set, which can be null[3]
StDev([column])	Sample standard deviation for the column. Null values are not included. This is a measure of the dispersion of values[4]
StDevP([column])	Population standard deviation for the column. Null values are not included. This is a measure of the dispersion of values[4]
Var([column])	Sample variance for the column. Null values are not included. The square of the sample standard deviation[4]
VarP([column])	Population standard deviation for the column. Null values are not included. The square of the population standard deviation[4]

[1]Although [column] is used throughout the table, you can also use expressions instead of columns in each of the aggregate functions.

[2]This may be null and is not the same as Min unless the query also sorts by the same column in ascending order and there are no null values.

[3]This is not the same as Max unless the query also sorts by the same column in ascending order and there are no null values.

[4]The sample standard deviation and variance use a denominator of $(n-1)$, whereas the population aggregate functions use a denominator of (n), where $n =$ the number of records in the result set. For most statistical analyses, the sample aggregate functions are preferable.

You can create expressions made up of a combination of aggregate functions combined mathematically. Aggregate functions can also reference expressions. For example, these aggregate expressions are all valid:

Aggregate Expression	Use
Sum(Abs(Discontinued))	Calculates the sum of the absolute value of the yes/no column Discontinued, which counts the number of Yes values
Sum(Abs(Discontinued+1))	Calculates the sum of the absolute value of the yes/no column Discontinued plus 1, which counts the number of No values (since Access stores Yes as –1 and No as 0)
Avg(DeliveryDate)–Avg(OrderDate)	Calculates the difference in the average delivery and order dates
Avg(Price*Quantity*(1–Discount))	Calculates the average cost of items

Aggregate Queries without a GROUP BY Clause

You can use an aggregate SELECT statement without a GROUP BY clause to calculate summary statistics on all rows meeting the WHERE clause criteria. This is useful for calculating grand totals for an entire table or a subset of a table. To create this type of aggregate SELECT, you must include aggregate functions and nothing *but* aggregate functions in the SELECT clause of a SELECT statement. (If you try to mix aggregate and nonaggregate expressions without a GROUP BY clause, you will get an error message.)

For example, say you wished to count the total number of orders in the tblOrder table and the earliest and latest times an order was taken. You could construct an aggregate query like the one shown in Figure 5.12.

FIGURE 5.12

This simple aggregate query calculates the total number of orders and the earliest and latest delivery times.

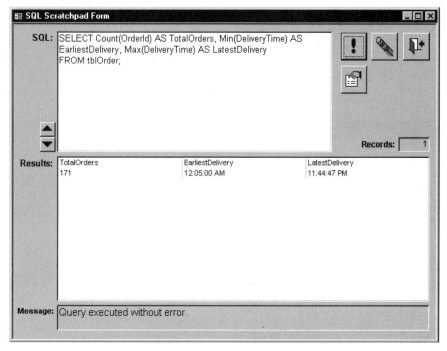

Using a GROUP BY Clause

You use a *GROUP BY clause* to define groups of rows for which you wish to calculate some aggregate function. Here's how the GROUP BY clause (and HAVING clause) fit into the overall SELECT statement syntax:

SELECT *column-list*

FROM *table-list*

[WHERE *where-clause*]

[GROUP BY *group-by-clause*]

[HAVING *having-clause*]

[ORDER BY *order-by-clause*];

The syntax of the GROUP BY clause is

GROUP BY *group-by-expression1* [*,group-by-expression2* [, …]]

Expressions in the GROUP BY clause can reference table columns, calculated fields, or constants. Calculations cannot include references to aggregate functions. The GROUP BY fields define the groups in the recordset. When you use a GROUP BY clause, all fields in the SELECT clause must be either arguments to an aggregate function or present in the GROUP BY clause. In other words, each column included in the resulting recordset must either define a group or compute some summary statistic for one of the groups. For example, the SQL statement in Figure 5.13 computes the number of orders by customer.

FIGURE 5.13
This GROUP BY SELECT statement counts the number of orders each customer made.

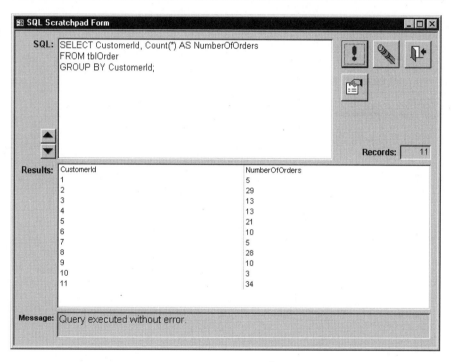

When you use multiple GROUP BY fields, the groups are defined from left to right, just as in an ORDER BY clause. The GROUP BY clause automatically orders values in ascending order without need of an ORDER BY clause (see Figure 5.13). If, however, you wish the groups to be sorted in descending order, you can reference the same fields in an ORDER BY clause with the keyword DESC.

For example, say you wished to count the number of orders by menu item and date, with menu items sorted alphabetically and dates sorted in descending order so as to show the most recent orders first. This GROUP BY SELECT statement is shown in Figure 5.14.

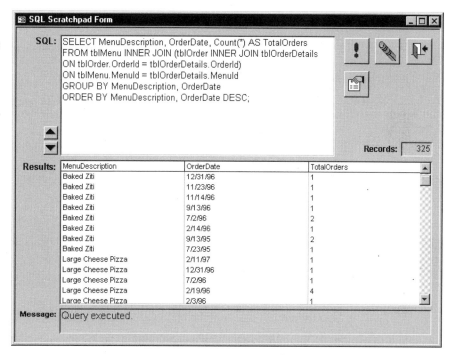

You may also find it useful to sort by one of the aggregate columns. For example, if you calculated total sales grouped by employee, you could sort by total sales in descending order rather than by employee. This would allow you to list the top-performing employees first.

You can specify up to ten GROUP BY fields, but be careful about adding unnecessary fields to the GROUP BY clause, because each additional field requires additional processing.

Using the HAVING Clause

Aggregate select queries may contain a WHERE clause, a *HAVING clause,* or both. Any criteria contained in a WHERE clause are applied *before* the grouping of rows. Thus, you can use WHERE clause criteria to exclude rows you don't want grouped. In contrast, any criteria contained in a HAVING clause is applied *after* grouping. This allows you to filter records based on the summary statistics calculated for each group. The syntax for the HAVING clause is similar to that for the WHERE clause:

HAVING *expression1* [{AND I OR} *expression2* […]]

For example, say you wished to calculate the average quantity ordered for each menu item but exclude any individual order from the calculation if a quantity of 5 or fewer were ordered. Since this requires the rows with a quantity of 5 or fewer to be excluded prior to grouping, you would use a WHERE clause. The SELECT statement would be constructed as follows:

```
SELECT MenuDescription, Avg(Quantity)
AS AvgOrdered
FROM tblMenu INNER JOIN tblOrderDetails ON tblMenu.MenuId =
tblOrderDetails.MenuId
WHERE Quantity > 5
GROUP BY MenuDescription;
```

On the other hand, you might want to calculate the same query but eliminate a menu item from the recordset if, *on average,* fewer than 6 of the item were sold for each order. This type of query requires the criteria to be applied *after* the average quantity has been calculated for each group, so you would use a HAVING clause instead. The SQL statement and result of this query are shown in Figure 5.15.

TIP

You can easily remember when WHERE and HAVING criteria are applied by looking at their placement in the SELECT statement. The WHERE clause comes before the GROUP BY clause, which corresponds with the fact that WHERE criteria are applied *before* grouping. The HAVING criteria come after the GROUP BY clause, which corresponds with the fact that HAVING criteria are applied *after* grouping.

FIGURE 5.15

The criteria for this group need to be applied after the grouping of data, so you use a HAVING clause.

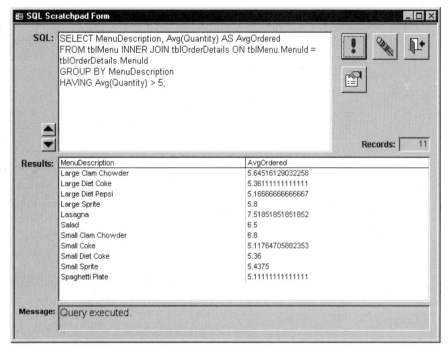

```
SQL: SELECT MenuDescription, Avg(Quantity) AS AvgOrdered
     FROM tblMenu INNER JOIN tblOrderDetails ON tblMenu.MenuId =
     tblOrderDetails.MenuId
     GROUP BY MenuDescription
     HAVING Avg(Quantity) > 5;
```

Records: 11

Results:

MenuDescription	AvgOrdered
Large Clam Chowder	5.64516129032258
Large Diet Coke	5.36111111111111
Large Diet Pepsi	5.16666666666667
Large Sprite	5.8
Lasagna	7.51851851851852
Salad	6.5
Small Clam Chowder	6.8
Small Coke	5.11764705882353
Small Diet Coke	5.36
Small Sprite	5.4375
Spaghetti Plate	5.11111111111111

Message: Query executed.

Creating Crosstab Queries with the TRANSFORM Statement

Microsoft added the *TRANSFORM statement* to Access SQL to support the creation of crosstab queries. The basic syntax of the TRANSFORM statement is shown here:

TRANSFORM *aggregate-function*

select-statement

PIVOT *column-headings-field* [IN (*value1*, [*value2*, [, ...]])];

The *aggregate-function* must be one of the SQL aggregate functions discussed earlier in this chapter. This aggregate function is used for the values of each cell of the crosstab table. The *select-statement* is a slightly modified GROUP BY SELECT statement. The *column-headings-field* is the field that is pivoted to become the column headings. The values in the optional IN clause specify fixed column headings.

Transforming a Group By Query into a Crosstab Query

The TRANSFORM statement is tricky to construct, especially because it is nonstandard SQL. An easy way to create a TRANSFORM statement is to start with an existing GROUP BY SELECT statement and transform it into a TRANSFORM statement.

Before you can hope to do this, however, you must have a suitable SELECT statement. It must have at least two GROUP BY fields and no HAVING clause. The TRANSFORM statement doesn't support the use of HAVING clauses. (You can work around this limitation by basing a crosstab query on the results of a totals query that has already applied the needed HAVING clause.) In addition, you'll want to make sure the column headings field won't have more than 254 values. (While this is the theoretical limit, in practice you'll find that crosstab queries are probably inappropriate where the column headings field contains more than 20 or so values.) As long as your SELECT statement meets these criteria, you can convert it into a TRANSFORM statement.

An example should help make this clearer. Say you wished to look at the total dinner sales for each dinner menu item by employee. You might start by constructing a GROUP BY query that joined the tables tblMenu, tblEmployee, tblOrder, and tblOrderDetails. The GROUP BY columns would be tblEmployee.LastName and tblMenu.MenuDescription. The query would look like this:

```
SELECT LastName AS Employee,
MenuDescription, Sum(Quantity*Price*(1-Discount))
AS Sales
FROM tblMenu INNER JOIN (tblEmployee INNER JOIN
(tblOrder INNER JOIN tblOrderDetails ON tblOrder.OrderId =
tblOrderDetails.OrderId) ON tblEmployee.EmployeeId =
tblOrder.OrderTakerId) ON tblMenu.MenuId =
tblOrderDetails.MenuId
WHERE Unit = "Dinner"
GROUP BY LastName, MenuDescription;
```

The datasheet for this query is shown in Figure 5.16.

Continuing with this example, say you wanted the result of this query displayed as a crosstab table instead. You could convert the SELECT statement into a TRANSFORM statement using the following steps:

1. Take the existing GROUP BY SELECT statement and plug it into the skeleton of a TRANSFORM statement. That is, insert a line with the word *TRANSFORM*

before the SELECT statement and a line with the word *PIVOT* after it. This would give you the following:

```
TRANSFORM
SELECT LastName AS Employee,
MenuDescription, Sum(Quantity*Price*(1-Discount))
AS Sales
FROM tblMenu INNER JOIN (tblEmployee INNER JOIN
(tblOrder INNER JOIN tblOrderDetails ON tblOrder.OrderId =
tblOrderDetails.OrderId) ON tblEmployee.EmployeeId =
tblOrder.OrderTakerId) ON tblMenu.MenuId =
tblOrderDetails.MenuId
WHERE Unit = "Dinner"
GROUP BY LastName, MenuDescription;
PIVOT;
```

2. Move the aggregate function that will define the value of each crosstab cell from the SELECT clause into the TRANSFORM clause. In this example you would move the expression that calculates sales. Thus, the SQL becomes

```
TRANSFORM Sum(Quantity*Price*(1-Discount)) AS Sales
SELECT LastName AS Employee, MenuDescription
FROM tblMenu INNER JOIN (tblEmployee INNER JOIN
(tblOrder INNER JOIN tblOrderDetails ON tblOrder.OrderId =
tblOrderDetails.OrderId) ON tblEmployee.EmployeeId =
```

FIGURE 5.16

This GROUP BY query computes the total sales of each menu item by employee.

Employee	MenuDescription	Sales
Alabaster	Baked Ziti	70.5
Alabaster	Lasagna	391.05
Alabaster	Spaghetti Plate	631.21
Carey	Baked Ziti	51.7
Carey	Lasagna	49.5
Carey	Spaghetti Plate	95.88
Jones	Baked Ziti	89.3
Jones	Lasagna	94.05
Jones	Spaghetti Plate	63.92
Lovely	Baked Ziti	4.7
Lovely	Lasagna	29.7
Lovely	Spaghetti Plate	535.33
Peters	Baked Ziti	18.8
Peters	Lasagna	138.6
Peters	Spaghetti Plate	209.338
Ronald	Baked Ziti	65.8
Ronald	Lasagna	297
Ronald	Spaghetti Plate	287.64

qtotEmployeeDinnerSales : Select Query

Record: 1 of 18

```
tblOrder.OrderTakerId) ON tblMenu.MenuId =
tblOrderDetails.MenuId
WHERE Unit = "Dinner"
GROUP BY LastName, MenuDescription;
PIVOT;
```

3. Move the field from the GROUP BY clause that will become the column headings to the PIVOT clause. Also, delete the reference to this field from the SELECT clause. Thus, you have

```
TRANSFORM Sum(Quantity*Price*(1-Discount)) AS Sales
SELECT LastName AS Employee
FROM tblMenu INNER JOIN (tblEmployee INNER JOIN
(tblOrder INNER JOIN tblOrderDetails ON tblOrder.OrderId =
tblOrderDetails.OrderId) ON tblEmployee.EmployeeId =
tblOrder.OrderTakerId) ON tblMenu.MenuId =
tblOrderDetails.MenuId
WHERE Unit = "Dinner"
GROUP BY LastName
PIVOT MenuDescription;
```

That's it! The crosstab datasheet produced by the preceding TRANSFORM statement is shown in Figure 5.17

FIGURE 5.17

This crosstab query is equivalent to the totals query shown in Figure 5.16. Note that the crosstab statement produces a more compact, readable summarization of the data.

qxtbEmployeeDinnerSales : Crosstab Query

Employee	Baked Ziti	Lasagna	Spaghetti Plate
Alabaster	70.5	391.05	631.21
Carey	51.7	49.5	95.88
Jones	89.3	94.05	63.92
Lovely	4.7	29.7	535.33
Peters	18.8	138.6	209.338
Ronald	65.8	297	287.64

Record: 1 of 6

NOTE

The datasheets shown in Figures 5.16 and 5.17 lack any field formatting. We could have used the field property sheet in Design view to format the cell values as currency. Alternately, we could have used the Format function to format the calculations directly in the Select clause. Unfortunately, you can't alter field properties from SQL view.

To recap the conversion process in more general terms, here are the steps for converting a SELECT statement into a TRANSFORM statement:

1. Ensure that the SELECT statement contains at least two GROUP BY fields, no HAVING clause, and a field suitable to become the column headings. Enclose the existing SELECT statement in a Transform "shell" like this:

```
TRANSFORM
select-statement
PIVOT;
```

2. Move the aggregate function that will be used for the Crosstab cell values from the SELECT clause into the TRANSFORM clause. The SQL should now look like this:

```
TRANSFORM aggregate-function
select-statement
PIVOT;
```

3. Move one of the GROUP BY fields—the one that is to become the column headings—to the PIVOT clause. Delete the reference to this same field from the SELECT clause. The resulting TRANSFORM statement should now produce a crosstab query:

```
TRANSFORM aggregate-function
select-statement
PIVOT column-heading-field;
```

Multiple Row Headings

TRANSFORM statements can include multiple row headings. You create the additional row headings by adding another GROUP BY field to the embedded SELECT statement. For example, you might wish to break down sales additionally by PaymentMethod. The SQL statement that creates this additional row heading and its output are shown in Figure 5.18. Note that the only difference between the earlier SQL statement and this one is the addition of PaymentMethod to the SELECT and GROUP BY clauses of the embedded SELECT statement.

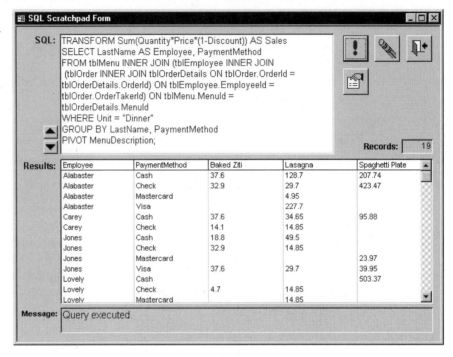

FIGURE 5.18

This TRANSFORM state-
ment produces a
crosstab table that con-
tains two row headings,
Employee and Payment-
Method.

Creating a Totals Column

You can create an additional column to calculate row totals in a crosstab query
by adding an additional aggregate field to the SELECT clause of the TRANSFORM
statement. Don't include the additional aggregate function anywhere else in the
TRANSFORM statement. Any aggregate functions you add to the TRANSFORM
statement's SELECT clause will be added to the crosstab between the row headings
field(s) and the column headings field. For example, the TRANSFORM statement
shown in Figure 5.19 was created by adding a Sum aggregate function to the
SELECT clause.

This additional aggregate function isn't limited to totaling the row values; you can
use any valid SQL aggregate function here. For example, you could calculate the
average sales per order. You could also include multiple aggregate functions in the
SELECT clause; each would be displayed between the row headings and column
headings fields.

FIGURE 5.19

By adding an aggregate function to the SELECT clause, you can create a column that totals the values for each row.

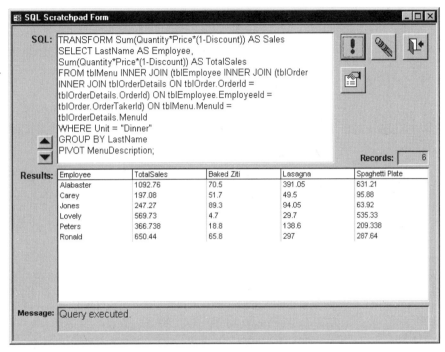

Using the IN Clause to Create Fixed Columns

You can create fixed column headings by using the *IN clause.* This is equivalent to using the ColumnHeadings property in QBE. Place the optional IN clause immediately after the PIVOT clause in the TRANSFORM statement. The syntax is

PIVOT *column-headings-field* [IN (*value1*, [*value2*, [, ...]])]

You can use the IN clause to order the values other than alphabetically (this is especially useful for alphanumeric date strings), exclude columns you don't wish to appear in the crosstab result, or include columns that may not exist in the recordset. For example, to create a crosstab table that excluded sales of "Spaghetti Plate" but included columns for "Baked Ziti", "Lasagna", and "Dinner Salad", even if there weren't any sales of these items, you would use the following PIVOT and IN clauses:

```
PIVOT MenuDescription IN ("Baked Ziti", "Lasagna","Dinner Salad")
```

Union Queries

Union queries are supported in Access only using SQL; there is no equivalent QBE method for creating a union query. UNION is not a SQL statement or even a clause. Instead it is an operator you can use to vertically splice together two or more compatible queries. The basic syntax is

select-statement1

UNION [ALL]

select-statement2

[UNION [ALL]

select-statement3]

[...]

Union queries produce *read-only* recordsets.

Access matches columns from each SELECT statement by their position in the SELECT statement, *not* by their names. For example, say you wished to create a query that combined the names and addresses of both employees and customers for a mailing you wished to do. You might create a union query like that shown in Figure 5.20.

WARNING
Although the Design view button is disabled when you create a SQL-specific (union, data definition, or SQL pass-through) query, you can always change the type of the query to a select or action query using the Query menu. Be careful, however, because when you change the query type of a SQL-specific query, your existing SQL statement is erased without so much as a confirming dialog.

FIGURE 5.20

This union query combines the names and addresses from the tblEmployee and tblCustomer tables.

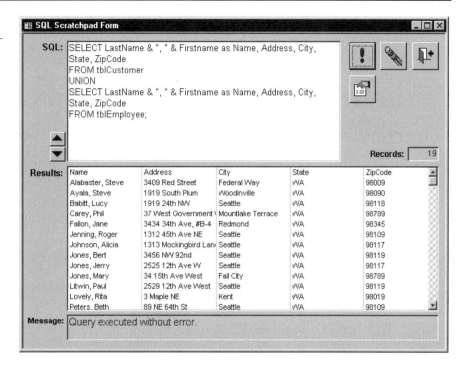

Using the TABLE Option

You can use a shortcut syntax when you wish to include all the columns from a table or another query. This syntax employs the TABLE option and allows you to replace any of the SELECT statements with:

TABLE *table-or-query*

which is equivalent to the following SELECT statement:

SELECT * FROM *table-or-query*

For example, the following two union queries are equivalent:

```
SELECT * FROM tblOrder
UNION
SELECT * FROM tblBackOrder;
```

and

```
TABLE tblOrder
UNION
TABLE tblBackOrder;
```

The ALL Option

By default, Access eliminates duplicate records for union queries. You can force Access to include duplicates, however, by using the *ALL option* after the UNION operator. Using the ALL option speeds up the execution of union queries even if they don't have any duplicate records because Access can skip the extra comparison step, which can be significant with large recordsets.

Sorting the Results

You can use an ORDER BY clause in the *last* SELECT statement of a union query to order the resulting recordset. If some of the column names differ, you need to reference the name assigned to the column by the *first* SELECT statement. For example:

```
SELECT LastName FROM tblNames
UNION ALL
SELECT EmployeeName FROM tblContacts
ORDER BY LastName;
```

While each SELECT statement in a union query *can* have an ORDER BY clause, all but the last one are ignored.

Compatible Queries

You can string together as many select queries as you like in a union query; you're limited only by the fact that as for all queries, the entire compiled query definition must fit into memory. The queries need to be compatible, however, which means they must have the same number of columns. Typically, the column names and datatypes of the unioned queries would be the same, but this isn't required. If they aren't the same, Access uses the following rules to combine them:

- For columns with *different names,* Access uses the column name from the first query.

- For columns with *different datatypes,* Access converts the columns to a single datatype that is compatible with all the columns' datatypes. For example, Access uses the Long Integer type when you combine an integer column with a long integer column. Similarly, text combined with a number produces a text column, date data combined with a yes/no column produces a text type, and so on.

- Access does not allow you to use memo- or OLE-type fields in a union query.

For example, the query shown in Figure 5.21 is valid syntactically, although it makes little sense.

FIGURE 5.21

This nonsensical but syntactically correct union query combines LastName from tbl-Customer with Order-Date and CustomerId from tblOrder. The datatype of the output column is text.

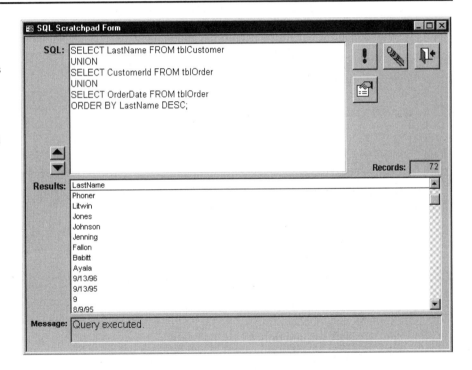

Subqueries

Subqueries are a useful part of SQL that allow you to embed SELECT statements within other SELECT statements (or action SQL statements, which are covered later in this chapter in the section "Updating Data with SQL"). Typically you use subqueries (which are also known as subselects) in the WHERE clause of a SQL statement to filter the query based on the values in another query (the subquery). There are three forms of syntax for subqueries:

- *expression* [NOT] IN (*select-statement*)
- *comparison* [{ANY | SOME | ALL}] (*select-statement*)
- [NOT] EXISTS (*select-statement*)

You may nest subqueries several levels deep; the actual limits on subquery nesting are undocumented. We discuss the use of each of the three types of subqueries in the next sections.

> **TIP**
>
> Most of the time you can use either a subquery or a join to create equivalent queries. You'll find a subquery is often easier to conceptualize than the same query that employs joins. On the other hand, a query containing a subquery usually executes more slowly than an equivalent query that uses joins.

> **NOTE**
>
> You can also use subqueries in Access QBE. Their use in QBE is analogous to their use in Access SQL. In QBE you can use subqueries in the Criteria or Field cell of a query.

Checking Values against a Lookup Table

Often you'd like to be able to check the value of a column against some list of values in another table or query. For these situations you use the IN form of a subquery. For example, say you wish to view the number, name, and price of all menu items that have ever been sold in quantities of ten or more. You could do this with the subquery shown in Figure 5.22. (Alternatively, this query could have been expressed using a join instead of a subquery. The equivalent join query is shown in Figure 5.23.)

This form of subquery can return only a single column. If it returns more than one column, Access complains with an error message.

FIGURE 5.22

This select query employs a subquery to find all menu items that have sold in quantities of ten or more.

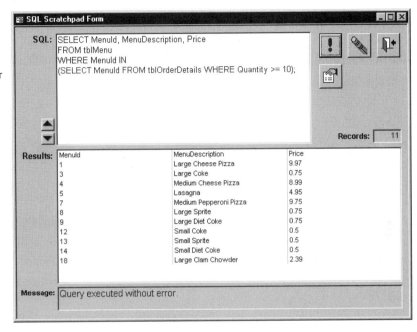

FIGURE 5.23

This select query uses a join to find all menu items that have sold in quantities of ten or more. This query produces the same result as the query in Figure 5.22.

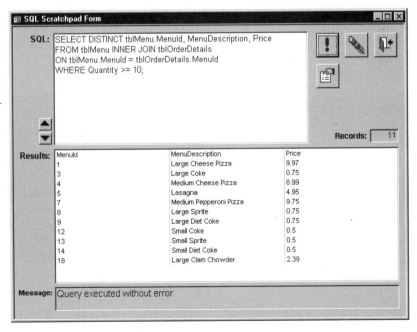

Using the NOT operator, you can also use this form of a subquery to look for values that are *not* contained in the list.

Comparing Values against Other Values

Subqueries also come in handy when you wish to compare a value against rows in another query. You can do this using the second form of the subquery syntax. This form of subquery is also limited to returning a single column. For example, you could use the subquery in Figure 5.24 to list all menu items that are more expensive than "Baked Ziti" (which sells for $4.70).

FIGURE 5.24

This query lists all menu items for which the price is higher than the price of baked ziti ($4.70).

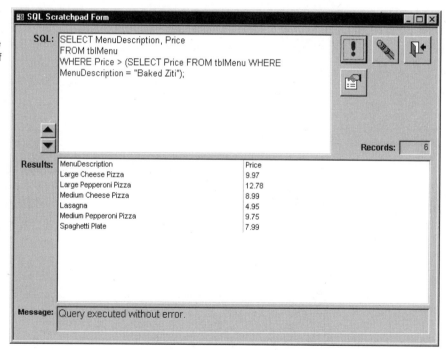

Note that the subquery in the query in Figure 5.24 returns one value, so you don't need to use a special predicate. If it had returned more than one row, it would have produced an error. When the output of a subquery is multiple rows, you must use one of the following predicates:

Predicate	Meaning
None	Makes a comparison with a single value
ANY or SOME	Is true if the comparison is true for any row returned by the subquery—in other words, if the comparison is true against the first row or the second row or the third row, and so on
ALL	Is true if the comparison is true for all rows returned by the subquery—in other words, if the comparison is true against the first row and the second row and the third row, and so on

If you don't use the ALL, SOME, or ANY predicate, you must guarantee that at most one value is returned. You can accomplish this by placing criteria on the subquery that select a row by its primary key value. Alternately, you could use a SQL aggregate function or a Top 1 predicate in the subquery. For example, the following three comparisons might all be used to ensure that Age is less than the age of the oldest student (assuming, of course, you knew in advance that student number 35 was the oldest):

```
WHERE Age < (SELECT Age FROM tblStudent WHERE StudentId = 35)
WHERE Age < (SELECT MAX(Age) FROM tblStudent)
WHERE Age < (SELECT Top 1 Age FROM tblStudent ORDER BY Age DESC)
```

You can use the ANY or SOME predicate (the two are equivalent) to make a comparison against any of the rows returned or use the ALL predicate to make a comparison against all the rows returned by the subquery. For example, the following comparison would select rows in which Age was less than the age of *any* of the students—in other words, where age was *less than the oldest student*:

```
WHERE Age < ANY (SELECT Age FROM tblStudent)
```

On the other hand, you could use the following comparison to select rows in which Age was less than the age of *all* of the students—in other words, where Age was *less than the youngest student*:

```
WHERE Age < ALL (SELECT Age FROM tblStudent)
```

NOTE The ANY, SOME, and ALL predicates will include rows with null values. This differs from the equivalent statements using the Min and Max aggregate functions, which exclude nulls.

Checking for Existence

The last form of a subquery comparison uses the EXISTS predicate to compare values against the existence of one or more rows in the subquery. If the subquery returns any rows, the comparison is True; if it returns no rows, the comparison is False. You can also use NOT EXISTS to get the opposite effect. Since you're checking only for the existence of rows, this form of subquery has no restriction on the number of columns or rows returned.

So far, all the subqueries presented in this chapter have been independent of the *outer* query (the query that contains the subquery). You can also create subqueries that are linked to the outer query. This type of subquery is termed a *correlated subquery* because it references the other query using its correlation name (discussed in the section "The FROM Clause" earlier in this chapter). The correlation name can be the same as the table name, or it can be a table's alias.

Each of the three types of subqueries can be correlated, but subqueries that use the EXISTS predicate are almost always correlated. (Otherwise they wouldn't be very useful.)

For example, you might want to find menu items that have never been ordered. You could accomplish this using the NOT EXISTS subquery shown in Figure 5.25. Running this query shows you that large anchovy pizzas have never been ordered.

The subquery in Figure 5.25 is termed a correlated subquery because it references the data in the outer query—the data in tblMenu—in the WHERE clause of the subquery.

Using Subqueries in the SELECT Clause

Typically you use subqueries in the WHERE clause of a query, but you may also find occasion to use a subquery that returns a single value in the SELECT clause. For example, say you wished to create a query similar to the one in Figure 5.25, but instead of listing only menu items that have never been ordered, you'd prefer to list all menu items with an additional field that indicates whether they've ever been ordered. You could accomplish this with the query shown in Figure 5.26. This

FIGURE 5.25

Using a NOT EXISTS correlated subquery, you can determine that no one has ever ordered a large anchovy pizza.

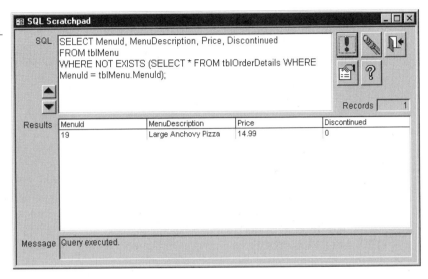

FIGURE 5.26

This query lists each menu item and whether or not it has ever been ordered. It accomplishes this using a correlated subquery in the SELECT clause of a query.

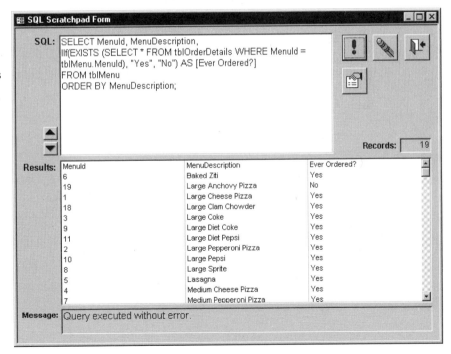

query moves the subquery into the SELECT clause, gives it an alias, "Ever Ordered?", and formats it using the IIf function.

You might also use a subquery in a SELECT clause to list a calculated constant that was used in selecting the rows. For example, you might want to list all menu items with prices higher than the average price, along with the average price as an output column. You could accomplish this with the following subquery:

```
SELECT MenuId, MenuDescription, Price,
(SELECT Avg(Price) FROM tblMenu)
AS AveragePrice
FROM tblMenu
WHERE Price > (SELECT Avg(Price) FROM tblMenu);
```

Example: Using a Subquery to Find Duplicates

Say you have a table called tblImport that contains duplicate orders that prevent you from designating OrderId as the primary key for the table. You can eliminate the duplicates using the following correlated subquery:

```
SELECT *
FROM tblImport
WHERE OrderId In (SELECT OrderId FROM tblImport
GROUP BY OrderId HAVING Count(*)>1) ORDER BY OrderId;
```

This subquery produces a dynaset with all the columns from tblImport but only the duplicate records. You can use this dynaset to visually scan through each of the duplicate rows and prune out the true duplicates. This is how the Find Duplicates Query Wizard works.

Subqueries have many more uses than the ones this chapter has presented. As mentioned previously, you can solve most queries as either subqueries or joined queries. Choose the method that makes the most sense for you.

Parameterized SQL

Just as in Access QBE, you can specify *parameters* to be resolved at run time using SQL. To do this, you use the PARAMETERS declaration. The syntax for its usage is

PARAMETERS *parameter1 datatype1* [*,parameter2 datatype2* [, …]];

sql-statement;

For example, if you want to list the date and employee number of all items for a particular order but have the user select the order when the query was run, you could construct a SELECT statement with a PARAMETERS declaration like this:

```
PARAMETERS [Enter Customer Number] Long;
SELECT OrderDate, OrderTakerId
FROM tblOrder
WHERE CustomerId=[Enter Customer Number]
ORDER BY OrderDate;
```

NOTE The SQL Scratchpad form (frmSQLScratchpad) does not work with parameter queries. If you want to try out this example in the sample database, you'll need to use the SQL view of a query instead.

You must choose the datatype for a parameter from the list of SQL datatypes in Table 5.2.

TABLE 5.2 SQL Datatypes and Their Counterparts in Table Design View

SQL Datatype and Synonyms	Table Design Field Type
BIT, BOOLEAN, LOGICAL, LOGICAL1, YESNO	Yes/No
BYTE, INTEGER1	Number, FieldSize = Byte
COUNTER, AUTOINCREMENT	Autonumber, FieldSize = Long Integer
CURRENCY, MONEY	Currency
DATETIME, DATE, TIME	Date/Time
SHORT, INTEGER2, SMALLINT	Number, FieldSize = Integer

TABLE 5.2   SQL Datatypes and Their Counterparts in Table Design View (continued)

SQL Datatype and Synonyms	Table Design Field Type
LONG, INT, INTEGER, INTEGER4	Number, FieldSize = Long
SINGLE, FLOAT4, IEEESINGLE, REAL	Number, FieldSize = Single
DOUBLE, FLOAT, FLOAT8, IEEEDOUBLE, NUMBER, NUMERIC	Number, FieldSize = Double
TEXT, ALPHANUMERIC, CHAR, CHARACTER, STRING, VARCHAR	Text
LONGTEXT, LONGCHAR, MEMO, NOTE	Memo
LONGBINARY, GENERAL, OLEOBJECT	OLE Object
GUID	Autonumber, FieldSize = Replication ID

Using External Data Sources

There are three ways to refer to data sources physically located outside an Access database in a SQL statement:

- Use linked tables.
- Use the IN clause.
- Use direct references to the external tables.

Using Linked Tables

By far the easiest and most efficient way to reference external tables is to use linked tables. (Prior to Access 95, these were known as attached tables.) Once a table is linked to an Access database, you refer to it in SQL statements exactly the same as you would if it were a native Access table. Chapter 12 discusses linked tables in more detail.

Although it is less efficient, you can also refer to nonlinked tables from a query using either the IN clause or the direct reference technique. These techniques are discussed in the next two sections.

Using the IN Clause

For nonlinked tables, you can use either the IN clause or the direct reference technique. To refer to one or more nonlinked tables located in the same Access database, the same ODBC database, or the same subdirectory for a given type of non-native ISAM database, it's easiest to use the IN clause. The syntax you use depends on the type of table you are querying. Be aware that this is one place where Access is not very forgiving; if you misplace a semicolon, a quote, or even, in some cases, a space, the SQL statement will fail.

Access Databases

For Access databases, you use the following syntax:

FROM *tablelist* IN *"path-and-database"*

The following SQL statement selects fields from the tblOrder and tblCustomer tables located in another Access database:

```
SELECT OrderId, OrderDate, LastName AS Customer
FROM tblOrder INNER JOIN tblCustomer
ON tblOrder.CustomerId = tblCustomer.CustomerId
IN "c:\bksybex3\paul\ch04\ch04.mdb";
```

External ISAM Databases

For external ISAM databases you use either the following syntax:

FROM *tablelist* IN *"path"* *"product;"*

or this syntax:

FROM *tablelist* IN *""* [*product*; DATABASE=*path*;]

You can find an up-to-date list of product names by searching online help under "Connect property."

NOTE   Unlike prior syntax statements in this chapter, the brackets in the preceding statement represent literal bracket characters.

When specifying the path for Excel files, you need to include the name of the spreadsheet and its extension. For Btrieve files, you need to include the name of the data definition file (DDF) and its extension. For all other products, include only the path to the subdirectory containing the table.

The following SQL statement selects fields from the FoxPro 3.0 Order and Customer tables (files) using the first version of the syntax:

```
SELECT OrderId, OrderDate, LastName AS Customer
FROM Order INNER JOIN Customer
ON Order.CustomerId = Customer.CustomerId
IN "d:\bksybex3\paul\ch05" "FoxPro 3.0;";
```

The next SQL statement uses the alternate syntax to return the same data:

```
SELECT OrderId, OrderDate, LastName AS Customer
FROM Order INNER JOIN Customer
ON Order.CustomerId = Customer.CustomerId
IN "" [FoxPro 3.0;DATABASE=d:\bksybex3\paul\ch05;];
```

Take care not to mix the two forms of the syntax. You must use one or the other; a hybrid will not work.

ODBC Databases

For ODBC data sources, you must use yet another syntax:

FROM *tablelist* IN "" [ODBC; *connect-string*;]

NOTE The brackets in the preceding statement represent literal bracket characters.

The exact connect string is dependent on the ODBC driver you use. Microsoft SQL Server uses a connect string like this:

DSN=*data-source*;UID=*user-id*;PWD=*password*;DATABASE=*database*

The *data-source* (DSN) is the name of the data source you have prespecified using the ODBC driver manager program. A DSN can refer to either a single database or multiple databases; if it refers to a single database, you don't need to use the DATABASE parameter. The UID and PWD parameters are optional. In a secured environment, however, you probably *won't* want to embed the password in the connect string. If you leave out these or any other parameters, you will be prompted for the missing parameters at run time.

The following SELECT statement selects data from two SQL Server tables that are part of the SQLPizza data source. This SELECT statement is analogous to those presented earlier in this chapter that used Access and FoxPro data sources.

```
SELECT OrderId, OrderDate, LastName AS Customer
FROM tblOrder INNER JOIN tblCustomer
ON tblOrder.CustomerId = tblCustomer.CustomerId
IN ""[ODBC;DSN=SQLPizza;UID=Bob;];
```

Anyone who executes this SQL statement will be prompted for Bob's password.

TIP

It is more efficient to use linked tables than the IN clause or direct external table references, although for ISAM data sources the difference in speed may not be noticeable. This is not true for ODBC data sources, however, where the IN clause or direct external table references are very inefficient. You should normally use linked tables for ODBC data sources because Jet can then manage the connections more efficiently.

Using Direct Table References

Sometimes you need to refer to multiple external data sources that are located either in different subdirectories/databases or in heterogeneous data sources. For example, you might want to join a table that's stored in dBASE format with a Para-dox table. In these cases the IN clause technique will not work, but Access provides another way to refer to these tables: the direct reference method. (This is our terminology, not Micro-soft's.) The syntax for each different data source type is detailed in the following table:

Data Source Type	Direct Reference Syntax
Access	[*path-and-database*].*tablename*
External ISAM	[*product*;DATABASE=*path*;].*tablename*
ODBC	[ODBC; *connect-string*;].*tablename*

The brackets in the preceding statements represent literal bracket characters.

For example, the query shown in Figure 5.27 joins two native Access tables, tblEmployee and tblOrderDetails, to an external FoxPro table, tblCustomer; a non-native Access table, tblOrder; and a SQL Server table, tblMenu; all in a single SELECT statement. Of course, this is an extreme example of what you *could* do, and a very inefficient example at that. In general, it's best to design your database and queries so that you minimize the number of heterogeneous joins (joins across tables from different data sources). This is of special importance when one of the data sources comes from a client-server database. Since this will almost always force Access to perform the join locally, it should be avoided. Also, it's worth repeating that you could improve efficiency by using linked tables. (See Chapters 15 and 17 for more information on creating efficient queries.)

FIGURE 5.27

This SELECT statement performs a heterogeneous join of two native Access tables, tbl-Employee and tblOrder-Details; a FoxPro table, tblCustomer; a non-native Access table, tblOrder; and a SQL Server table, tblMenu.

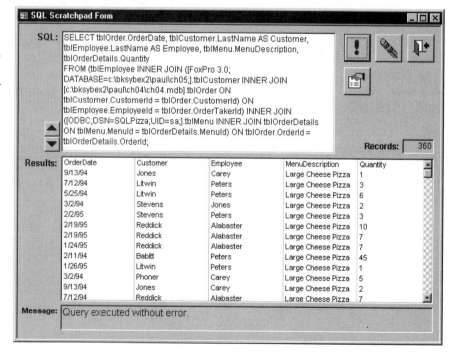

172

Updating Data with SQL

In addition to querying data, you can use SQL to make changes to data. You can use Access SQL to update records, delete records, or copy records to another table. Access SQL has four commands for updating data, all of which have analogous counterparts in Access QBE:

SQL Statement	QBE Query
UPDATE	Update
DELETE	Delete
INSERT INTO	Append
SELECT INTO	Make-table

All but the last one, SELECT INTO, are part of the ANSI SQL standard. (The ANSI standard uses SELECT INTO in a very different way to move a single row of data into a list of variables. The two usages are not equivalent.)

Once you have learned the SELECT statement and all its predicates, declarations, and clauses, you'll find learning the action SQL statements relatively easy. This is because each of these statements is similar syntactically to SELECT. Thus, even though each one includes WHERE clauses, for example, we will not repeat the discussion of WHERE clauses here. We will note, however, where there are differences between clauses in action SQL statements and the SELECT statement.

The UPDATE Statement

You use the *UPDATE statement* to change values in one or more columns in a table. The syntax is

UPDATE *table-or-query*

SET *column1 = expression1* [*,column2 = expression2*] [, ...]

[WHERE *criteria*];

You can update the values in either a table or a query, but if you use a query it must be updatable. The expressions in the SET clause can be a constant or the result of a calculation. For example, to increase the price of all non-pizza menu items by 10 percent, you could use the following update query:

```
UPDATE tblMenu
SET tblMenu.Price = [Price]*1.1
WHERE MenuDescription Not Like "*Pizza*";
```

The ANSI standard supports the use of subqueries in the SET clause, while Access SQL does not. Fortunately, Access SQL supports the use of joins in the UPDATE clause (this is nonstandard SQL), which gives you almost equivalent functionality. The syntax used for joins in the UPDATE clause is the same as the join syntax used for SELECT statements in the FROM clause. For example, to change the phone numbers in the tblCustomer table to new phone numbers stored in another table, tblCustomerMods—which you might have imported from another copy of the database on another machine—you could use the following UPDATE statement:

```
UPDATE tblCustomerMods INNER JOIN tblCustomer ON
tblCustomerMods.CustomerId = tblCustomer.CustomerId
SET tblCustomer.Phone = tblCustomerMods.Phone
WHERE tblCustomer.Phone<>tblCustomerMods.Phone;
```

This UPDATE statement uses a WHERE clause to limit the updates only to records that need to be modified—those in which the phone numbers are different.

The DELETE Statement

You use the *DELETE statement* to delete rows from tables. Its syntax is

DELETE [*table.**]

FROM *from-clause*

[WHERE *criteria*];

The use of *table.** is optional for delete queries that refer to only a single table.

NOTE Access also allows you to refer to a single column in the DELETE clause—for example, "DELETE tblOrder.OrderDate". In fact, Access QBE often generates DELETE statements in this misleading style, but don't let this confuse you; the entire record is deleted, not just the values in the column.

For single-table queries, the syntax can be simplified:

DELETE

FROM *table*

[WHERE *criteria*];

For example, to delete all discontinued items from tblMenu, you could use the following DELETE statement:

```
DELETE
FROM tblMenu
WHERE Discontinued = True;
```

You can create DELETE statements that reference multiple tables, but you must follow these rules:

- You can use the data in one table to decide which rows to delete from another related table. You can accomplish this by using a join in the FROM clause or by using a subquery in the WHERE clause. Tables can be related in either a one-to-one or a one-to-many relationship. (Note that you may be prevented from deleting rows from a table if referential integrity is turned on without cascaded updates.)

- You can delete rows from multiple tables in a single delete query if the tables are related in a one-to-one relationship.

- You can delete rows from multiple tables related in a one-to-many relationship with a series of DELETE queries.

For example, to delete all customers from tblCustomer who have not placed an order during the past year, you would create and execute the following DELETE statement, which uses a subquery to find the proper rows:

```
DELETE
FROM tblCustomer
WHERE tblCustomer.CustomerId NOT IN
(SELECT CustomerId FROM tblOrder WHERE OrderDate >
DateAdd('yyyy',-1,Date()));
```

Access SQL departs from the ANSI standard through its support for named tables in the DELETE clause and joins in the FROM clause.

If you wish to delete the value in one or more columns but not the entire record, use the UPDATE statement instead of DELETE and set the values to Null. For example, you could use the following UPDATE statement to set the LastName and FirstName columns in tblCustomer to Null for a particular customer:

```
UPDATE tblCustomer
SET LastName = NULL, FirstName = NULL
WHERE CustomerId = 4;
```

TIP

You can use a single DELETE statement to delete the records in two tables related in a one-to-many relationship if you've defined a relationship between the two tables and have turned on the cascading deletes option. In this case, if you delete a row from the "one" side of a relationship, Access automatically deletes the related rows in the "many-sided" table.

The INSERT INTO Statement

You use the *INSERT INTO statement* to copy rows from one table (or query) into another table. You can also use it to add a single row of data to a table using a list of values. The syntax of the first form of the INSERT INTO statement is

INSERT INTO *target-table*

select-statement;

TIP

The *target-table* reference can refer to an external table using the IN predicate or a direct reference. (See the discussion in the section "Using External Data Sources" earlier in this chapter.)

In its simplest form, you can use this form of the INSERT INTO statement to copy the contents of one table to another. For example, to copy all the rows from tblCustomerNew to tblCustomer, you could use the following INSERT INTO statement:

```
INSERT INTO tblCustomer
SELECT * FROM tblCustomerNew;
```

You can use any valid SELECT statement that produces recordsets, including SELECT statements with GROUP BY clauses, joins, UNION operators, and sub-queries. This embedded SELECT statement can include references to one or more queries. For example, to append records from the SELECT GROUP BY statement presented earlier in the chapter in the section "Creating Crosstab Queries with the TRANSFORM Statement" to a table named tblEmployeeDinnerSales, you could use the following INSERT INTO statement:

```
INSERT INTO tblEmployeeDinnerSales
SELECT LastName, MenuDescription,
Sum(Quantity*Price*(1-Discount)) AS Sales
FROM tblMenu INNER JOIN (tblEmployee INNER JOIN
(tblOrder INNER JOIN tblOrderDetails ON tblOrder.OrderId =
tblOrderDetails.OrderId) ON tblEmployee.EmployeeId =
tblOrder.OrderTakerId) ON
tblMenu.MenuId = tblOrderDetails.MenuId
WHERE Unit="Dinner"
GROUP BY LastName, MenuDescription;
```

You use the second form of the INSERT INTO statement to add a single row to a table and populate it with values. Its syntax is

INSERT INTO *target-table* [(*column1* [,*column2* [, …]])]

VALUES (*value1* [,*value2* [, …]]);

If you omit the column references in the INSERT INTO clause, you must include a value for each column in the target table in the exact order in which the columns appear in the table definition. If you include the column references, you may omit columns (other than the primary key and other required columns) or change the order in which they appear in the table definition. For example, you could add a new row to tblMenu using the following INSERT INTO statement:

```
INSERT INTO tblMenu (MenuId, Price, MenuDescription)
VALUES (50, 29.99, "Family Platter");
```

The SELECT INTO Statement

You use the *SELECT INTO statement*, unique to Access SQL, to create a new table from the rows in another table or query. Its syntax is

SELECT *column1* [,*column2* [, …]] INTO *new-table*

FROM *table-list*

[WHERE *where-clause*]

[ORDER BY *order-by clause*];

For example, you could use the following SELECT INTO statement to copy all purchases made by CustomerId = 9 (Bert Jones) from tblOrder to a new table called tblJonesOrders:

```
SELECT OrderId, OrderDate, CustomerId, OrderTakerId,
DeliveryDate, DeliveryTime, PaymentMethod, Notes
INTO tblJonesOrders
FROM tblOrder
WHERE CustomerId=9;
```

Like the INSERT INTO statement, the SELECT INTO statement can include any valid SELECT statement that produces recordsets, including SELECT statements with GROUP BY clauses, joins, UNION operators, and subqueries.

NOTE Tables created by SELECT INTO statements will not contain primary keys, indexes, or any column or table properties other than the defaults assigned to any new table.

Data Definition with SQL

You can use two methods to programmatically create and manipulate table schemas in Access: data access objects (DAO) and Data Definition Language (DDL) queries. In this section we discuss the use of DDL queries. Chapter 6 covers using DAO to create and modify schemas.

It's important to note that DDL queries offer only a subset of the schema definition capabilities that either the Access user interface or DAO provides. For example, you can't define validation rules, define default values for fields, create foreign key relationships with cascading updates or deletes, or create a non-unique index for a table using a DDL query. But DDL queries still have their place: they help bridge the gap between the SQL standard and Access SQL. Furthermore, it's likely that the support for DDL queries will only get better in future versions of Access.

In the meantime, there's at least one good reason for using DDL rather than either of the alternatives: it's based on a standard language that has widespread support—SQL. If you already have a fair amount of experience with SQL, using DDL queries will likely seem more natural than the other language-based alternative, DAO. Still, be aware that Access DDL support is incomplete and you may be required to go elsewhere in Access to complete the job.

As with union queries, you must enter DDL queries using SQL view; there's no QBE counterpart. You can also execute a DDL query by defining and executing a querydef created using VBA.

Access SQL supports four DDL statements:

DDL Statement	Purpose
CREATE TABLE	Creates a new table schema
ALTER TABLE	Modifies an existing table schema
CREATE INDEX	Creates a new index
DROP	Deletes a table schema or an index

In addition, you can use the CONSTRAINT clause in either a CREATE TABLE or ALTER TABLE statement to create constraints. (In Access' simplified support of CONSTRAINT, this means the creation of indexes.) The next few sections discuss each of these statements, as well as the CONSTRAINT clause.

The CREATE TABLE Statement

You use the *CREATE TABLE statement* to create a new table. Its syntax is

CREATE TABLE *table*

(*column1 type1* [(*size1*)] [CONSTRAINT *column-constraint1*]

[,*column2 type2* [(*size2*)] [CONSTRAINT *column-constraint2*]

[, ...]]

[CONSTRAINT *table-constraint1* [,*table-constraint2* [, ...]]]);

You specify the datatype of a column using one of the Jet engine SQL datatype identifiers or its synonyms. They were summarized earlier in Table 5.2.

WARNING The Jet engine SQL datatypes and their synonyms, which are derived from ANSI SQL datatypes, differ from the Access datatypes in several subtle ways. Use care when selecting the correct datatype keyword. Most notably, using the SQL datatype INTEGER produces a number column with Size = *Long* because INTEGER in ANSI SQL is a 4-byte integer value (which in Access is a Long Integer).

You can use the optional *size* parameter to specify the length of a text column. If *size* is left blank, text columns are assigned a size of 255. Note that this differs from the default column size of 50 assigned when new tables are created with the user interface. Other datatypes do not use this option.

You can create two types of constraints using a CREATE TABLE statement: single-column indexes and multicolumn (or table) indexes. You specify both of these indexes using the CONSTRAINT clause, which is discussed in the next section.

For example, to create a table tblNewMenu to mimic the schema of the tblMenu table found in the CH05.MDB sample database, you would use the following CREATE TABLE statement:

```
CREATE TABLE tblNewMenu
(MenuId LONG, MenuDescription TEXT (50), Unit TEXT (50),
Price CURRENCY, Discontinued BIT);
```

The CONSTRAINT Clause

In the SQL-92 standard, constraints are used to restrict the values that can be added to a table. You can use constraints in SQL-92 to create primary and foreign keys, constrain columns to be UNIQUE or NOT NULL, and to create validation rules (the CHECK constraint). Access SQL supports each of these uses except for the NOT NULL and CHECK constraints. Since the only constraints Access currently supports are ones requiring the definition of indexes, you might find it convenient to think of the Access CONSTRAINT clause as being used to create indexes. (Be aware, however, that support for the NOT NULL and CHECK constraints may be added at a later date.)

You use the CONSTRAINT clause in CREATE TABLE and ALTER TABLE statements. The CONSTRAINT syntax takes two forms. You use the first form for single-column constraints:

CONSTRAINT *name* {PRIMARY KEY | UNIQUE |

REFERENCES *foreign-table* [(*foreign-column*)]}

The multiple-column version of the CONSTRAINT clause is

CONSTRAINT *name* {PRIMARY KEY (*column1* [,*column2* [, …]]) |

UNIQUE | REFERENCES *foreign-table* [(*foreign-column1*

[,*foreign-column2* [, …]])]}

For example, you could use the following CREATE TABLE statement to create the tblNewMenu table and a unique index on the column MenuDescription:

```
CREATE TABLE tblNewMenu
(MenuId LONG, MenuDescription TEXT CONSTRAINT MenuDescription
UNIQUE, Unit TEXT, Price CURRENCY, Discontinued BIT);
```

TIP

Anytime you create an index in Access, even a single-column index, you must assign it a name. Since the Access UI assigns primary key indexes the name PrimaryKey and single-column indexes the same name as the column and there's no good reason to do otherwise, we recommend using these same naming conventions in DDL queries. Less clear is what to name foreign key indexes; we have chosen here to use the naming convention "*referenced-tablename*FK". For example, a foreign key to tblCustomer would be tblCustomerFK. (The Access UI gives less descriptive names of the form *Reference, Reference1*, and so forth.)

As a second example, say you wished to create two tables, tblNewOrders and tblNewItems, and relate them in a one-to-many relationship. You need tblNewOrders to have the following columns: OrderId (the primary key), OrderDate, and CustomerId. Table tblNewItems should contain OrderId, ItemId, and ItemDescription. For tblNewItems, OrderId and ItemId will make up the primary key and OrderId will be a foreign key reference to the same-named column in tblNewOrders. You could use the following two CREATE TABLE statements, executed one after the other (you can't place multiple SQL statements in a DDL query), to create the two tables:

```
CREATE TABLE tblNewOrders
(OrderId LONG CONSTRAINT PrimaryKey PRIMARY KEY,
OrderDate DATETIME, CustomerId LONG );


CREATE TABLE tblNewItems
(OrderId LONG CONSTRAINT tblNewOrdersFK REFERENCES
tblNewOrders, ItemId LONG, ItemDescription TEXT (30),
CONSTRAINT PrimaryKey PRIMARY KEY (OrderId, ItemId) );
```

TIP For foreign key references you can omit the name of the foreign key column if it is the primary key in the referenced table.

Both forms of CONSTRAINT lack any way to create non-unique indexes within a CREATE TABLE or ALTER TABLE statement. This *is* consistent with the SQL-92 standard. Fortunately, you can use the CREATE INDEX statement, described in the next section, to create this type of index. Another shortcoming of Access' CONSTRAINT clause is that there's no support for the specification of foreign key relationships with either cascading deletes or updates. (ANSI SQL supports this feature.)

The CREATE INDEX Statement

In addition to the CONSTRAINT clause of the CREATE TABLE and ALTER TABLE commands, you can use the *CREATE INDEX statement* to create an index on an existing table. (CREATE INDEX is not a part of the ANSI standard, but many vendors include it.) The syntax of the CREATE INDEX statement is

CREATE [UNIQUE] INDEX *index*

ON *table* (*column1* [,*column2* [, ...]])

[WITH {PRIMARY | DISALLOW NULL | IGNORE NULL}];

If you include the UNIQUE keyword, the index disallows duplicate values. You must give a name to each index, even if it's a single-column index. See the preceding section for suggested index-naming conventions.

You can create a primary key index by using the PRIMARY option in the WITH clause. All primary key indexes are automatically unique indexes, so you needn't (but you can if you insist) use the UNIQUE keyword when you use the PRIMARY option.

You use the IGNORE NULL option to prevent Jet from creating index entries for null values. If the indexed column will contain nulls and there may be many nulls, you can improve the performance of searches on non-null values by using this option. This is equivalent to using the IgnoreNulls property of the index in Table Design view.

You can use the DISALLOW NULL option to have the Jet engine prevent the user from entering null values in the column. This is similar to setting the Required property of a column in Table Design view to Yes. Choosing this option has the same effect, but this "hidden" feature is maintained by the index, not the column, and has no analogous property in the UI. If you use this option, you won't be able to turn it off through the user interface—the Required property of the underlying column will act independently—unless you delete the index.

You can create a multicolumn index by including more than one column name in the ON clause.

You can create only one index at a time with the CREATE INDEX statement. Also, there's no facility for creating descending-ordered indexes using the CREATE INDEX statement; you must use the UI or DAO to alter the sort order of any indexes created using DDL queries.

You could use the following CREATE INDEX statement to add a unique index that ignored nulls to the column Price in tblNewMenu:

```
CREATE UNIQUE INDEX Price
ON tblNewMenu (Price)
WITH IGNORE NULL;
```

The ALTER TABLE Statement

You can use the *ALTER TABLE statement* to alter the schema of an existing table. With it you can add a new column or constraint or delete a column or constraint. (You can't modify the definition of either.) You can operate on only one field or index with a single ALTER TABLE statement. The ALTER TABLE statement has four forms.

You use the first form to *add a column* to a table:

ALTER TABLE *table* ADD [COLUMN] *column datatype* [(*size*)]

[CONSTRAINT *single-column-constraint*];

The keyword COLUMN is optional. As in the CREATE TABLE statement, you specify the datatype of the new column by using one of the Jet engine SQL datatype identifiers or its synonyms (see Table 5.2 earlier in this chapter). You can use the optional SIZE parameter to specify the length of a text column. If *size* is left blank, text columns are assigned a size of 255. You can also specify an optional index for the column using the CONSTRAINT clause. (See the section "The CONSTRAINT Clause" earlier in this chapter.)

For example, you could use the following ALTER TABLE statement to add the integer column Quantity to the tblNewItems table:

```
ALTER TABLE tblNewItems ADD Quantity SHORT;
```

You can use the second form of ALTER TABLE to *add constraints* to a table:

ALTER TABLE *table* ADD CONSTRAINT *constraint*;

For example, you could use the following ALTER TABLE statement to add an index to the new column:

```
ALTER TABLE tblNewItems ADD CONSTRAINT Quantity UNIQUE (Quantity);
```

As with the CREATE TABLE statement, you are limited to creating indexes that are unique or serve as primary or foreign keys.

You use the third form of ALTER TABLE to *remove a column* from a table:

ALTER TABLE *table* DROP [COLUMN] *column*;

Again, the keyword COLUMN is optional. For example, you could use the following ALTER TABLE statement to remove the ItemDescription column from tblNewItems:

```
ALTER TABLE tblNewItems DROP COLUMN ItemDescription;
```

NOTE   You can't remove an indexed column from a table without first removing its index.

You use the final form of ALTER TABLE to *remove an index* from a table:

ALTER TABLE *table* DROP CONSTRAINT *index*;

You refer to an index by its name. For example, to remove the primary key from tblNewOrders, you would use the following ALTER TABLE statement:

```
ALTER TABLE tblNewOrders DROP CONSTRAINT PrimaryKey;
```

> **NOTE**
> You can't delete an index that is involved in a relationship without first deleting all the relationships in which it participates.

The DROP Statement

You can use the *DROP statement* to remove tables or indexes. It has two forms.

You use the first to *remove a table* from a database:

DROP TABLE *table*;

For example, you could use the following DROP statement to remove the tbl-NewItems table from the current database:

```
DROP TABLE tblNewItems;
```

You use the second form of DROP to *remove an index* from a table:

DROP INDEX *index* ON *table*;

For example, to delete the index named Price from tblNewMenu, you could use the following DROP statement:

```
DROP INDEX Price ON tblNewMenu;
```

> **NOTE**
> To drop an index from a table, you can use either the ALTER TABLE statement or the DROP statement. You must use caution when using DROP because there is no confirming dialog when it is executed.

Creating SQL Pass-Through Queries

You can use SQL pass-through queries to send uninterpreted SQL statements to a server database. Pass-through queries can be used only with ODBC data sources. Access performs no syntax checking, interpretation, or translation of the SQL in a pass-through query. It's entirely up to you to compose your query using the proper syntax of the server's dialect of SQL.

You create a SQL pass-through query by creating a new blank query and then choosing Query ➤ SQL Specific ➤ Pass-Through. It's important that you choose this command rather than just switch to SQL view because if you don't, Access will think you are creating a normal (non–pass-through) query.

> **TIP**
>
> You can convert a non–pass-through query entered into SQL view by choosing Query ➤ SQL Specific ➤ Pass-Through from within SQL view.

When you create a pass-through query, Access adds several new properties to the query's property sheet. These new properties are summarized in Table 5.3 and shown in Figure 5.28.

FIGURE 5.28

This pass-through query creates a table on the SQLPizza data source.

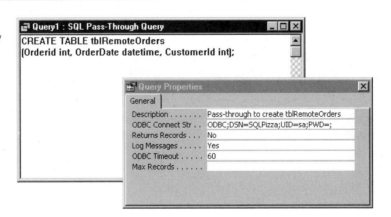

TABLE 5.3   Query Properties Unique to SQL Pass-Through Queries

Property	Description	Default Value
ODBCConnectStr*	The ODBC connection string to be used when executing the pass-through query	ODBC;
ReturnsRecords	Specifies whether or not the query returns any records	Yes
LogMessages	Specifies whether Access logs warning and informational messages from the server to a local table. Messages are logged to a table the name of which is derived from the user name (for example, Mary-00, Mary-01, Mary-02, and so on). This does not include error messages	No

*The DAO name for this property is "Connect".

TIP

To create a pass-through query programmatically, set the Connect property of the querydef to a valid connect string.

SQL pass-through queries are useful for:

- Using server-specific SQL that's not supported by ODBC
- Running SQL DDL (Data Definition Language) commands to create and modify the schema of server databases
- Executing stored procedures on the server
- Joining more than one database on the server (If run as a normal query, Jet would have to join the databases locally.)
- Forcing a query to be fully executed on the server

SQL pass-through queries have the following disadvantages:

- Any records returned in an SPT query are read-only.
- Jet will not check the syntax of SPT queries.
- You can't use Access' built-in or user-defined functions (although the server may have similar functions).

Most client-server applications will incorporate a combination of normal queries using linked tables and SQL pass-through queries. (See Chapter 15 for more information on creating client-server applications.)

When creating queries that go against ODBC data sources (both pass-through and non–pass-through queries), you may wish to take advantage of the new (for Access 97) MaxRecords property. Use this property to set a maximum limit for the number of records returned from a query. For ODBC data sources, this property is more efficient than using the TopValues property.

There are two types of pass-through queries: those that return records and those that don't. Pass-through select queries and some stored procedures return records. DDL queries and server action queries, as well as many stored procedures, do not return records.

FIGURE 5.29

The qsptRemoteOrders pass-through query executes a simple SELECT statement on the tbl-RemoteOrders table, returning a snapshot recordset to Access.

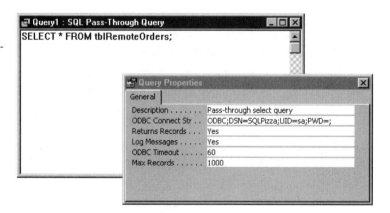

For example, a pass-through query that creates a three-column table, tblRemote-Orders, on a Microsoft SQL Server database is shown in Figure 5.28. Because this is a DDL query, its ReturnsRecords property is set to No. On the other hand, the pass-through query shown in Figure 5.29 returns a snapshot of records, so we have set its ReturnsRecords property to Yes.

The pass-through query shown in Figure 5.30 executes a SQL Server system stored procedure, sp_primarykey, to mark the OrderId column in tblRemoteOrders as the primary key.

FIGURE 5.30

This pass-through query executes a stored procedure, sp_primarykey, to mark the OrderId column in the tblRemoteOrders table as the primary key.

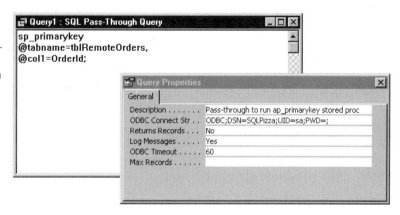

Differences between Access SQL and SQL-92

Access SQL is a hybrid SQL. It differs considerably from each of the SQL standards and doesn't *completely* support *any* of the ANSI SQL standards. It lacks large chunks of the standards, particularly in the areas of security and cursors. Sometimes it supports the same functionality found in one of the standards, but with a different syntax. For example, the syntax of the UPDATE statement is nonstandard but essentially equivalent to the functionality of the SQL-92 UPDATE statement. In other cases, similar functionality is provided elsewhere in Access. For example, you handle security in Access using either the UI or DAO. Finally, Access SQL has some useful extensions that are not present in any of the standards. A few of the extensions are dynaset updatability, support for crosstab queries, and the SELECT INTO statement.

The ANSI SQL standards are so varied that it's difficult to pin down all the differences between Access and the various flavors of SQL. Many of these differences have been noted throughout the chapter. Nonetheless, we have attempted to summarize the major differences between Access SQL and SQL-92 in Table 5.4. (Note that this table is not comprehensive; it covers only the major differences.)

TABLE 5.4   Major Differences between Access SQL and ANSI SQL-92

Feature	Supported by SQL-92	Supported by Access SQL	Comments
Security (GRANT, REVOKE, and so on)	Yes	No	Access' security system serves the same purpose
Transaction support (COMMIT, ROLLBACK, and so on)	Yes	No	Access offers a similar facility in DAO
Views (CREATE VIEW statement)	Yes	No	A saved query is equivalent to a view except that it is also updatable
Temporary tables (in the SQL-92 sense)	Yes	No	All tables are persistent
Joins in FROM clause	Yes	Yes	Access doesn't support all the variations on the syntax
Joins in UPDATE and DELETE statements	No	Yes	Unique to Access SQL
Support for FULL OUTER JOIN and UNION JOIN	Yes	No	A union join is different from the UNION operator
Full support for mixing heterogeneous joins	Yes	No	Access has limited support for mixing heterogeneous joins
Support for subqueries in the SET clause of UPDATE statements	Yes	No	Access offers support for joins instead
Support for multiple tables in DELETE statements	No	Yes	Unique to Access SQL
SELECT DISTINCTROW	No	Yes	Unique to Access SQL
SELECT TOP N	No	Yes	Unique to Access SQL
Cursors (DECLARE CURSOR, FETCH, and so on)	Yes	No	DAO supports the equivalent use of table cursors
Domain support (CREATE DOMAIN, ALTER DOMAIN, and so on)	Yes	No	Access doesn't support domains

TABLE 5.4   Major Differences between Access SQL and ANSI SQL-92 (continued)

Feature	Supported by SQL-92	Supported by Access SQL	Comments
Complete support for constraints	Yes	No	Access supports only a subset of constraint functionality
Assertions (CREATE ASSERTION, DROP ASSERTION, and so on)	Yes	No	Access doesn't support system-wide rules
Row value constructors	Yes	No	Access doesn't support this feature
Case expressions	Yes	No	Similar functionality is found using the IIf function
Full referential integrity support in CREATE TABLE statement	Yes	No	Access only partially supports this feature in SQL. Cascade support is also provided using the Access UI
Standardized system tables and error codes	Yes	No	Access uses its own system for naming system tables and error codes
Standard datatypes	Yes	Yes	Access supports most but not all the SQL datatypes
Standard string operators	Yes	No	Access provides several alternative string-manipulation functions
Standard wildcard characters	Yes	No	Access uses ? and * instead of the SQL _ and %
Support for VBA functions	No	Yes	You can use most VBA functions in Access SQL
Additional aggregate functions	No	Yes	StDev, Var, StDevP, and VarP are unique to Access SQL
TRANSFORM statement	No	Yes	For creating crosstab queries
Parameters	No	Yes	For defining parameters to be determined at run time
SELECT INTO statement	No	Yes	Unique to Access SQL

Summary

In this chapter we have covered all the components of Access SQL, including

- The SELECT statement and all its clauses, predicates, and variations

- The various types of joins: inner, outer, self, and non–equi-joins

- The ALL, DISTINCT, and DISTINCTROW predicates

- The TOP predicate

- The WITH OWNERACCESS OPTION declaration

- Aggregate queries, including GROUP BY and TRANSFORM (crosstab) queries

- Union queries

- Subqueries and all their variations

- Parameterized SQL

- Using external data sources

- Action SQL: UPDATE, DELETE, INSERT INTO, and SELECT INTO

- Data Definition Language (DDL) SQL: CREATE TABLE, CONSTRAINT, CREATE INDEX, ALTER TABLE, and DROP

- SQL pass-through queries

- The differences between ANSI SQL and Access SQL

CHAPTER

SIX

6

Using Data Access Objects

- Handling Access objects programmatically

- Creating, deleting, and modifying database objects from VBA

- Working with recordsets

- Creating a simple database window replacement

No matter which program you're using as an interface to your data, at times you'll need programmatic access to your database's structure and to its data. You might want to retrieve the schema of a table, create a new index, or walk through the data returned by a query, one row at a time. Perhaps you need to manipulate your application's security or find a particular row on a form. You can accomplish any of these tasks thanks to Access' use of data access objects (DAO), a shared component of Microsoft Office that is not only part of Access but is also exposed through Automation. In this chapter we'll cover the basics of DAO and present some useful examples along the way.

In previous versions of Access, DAO was a programmatic interface exclusively to the Jet database engine. Starting with Access 97, however, DAO is treated as a programmatic interface to data in general. DAO supports two separate data sources in this version (Access 97 includes DAO 3.5): Jet and ODBCDirect. ODBCDirect is a thin wrapper on the ODBC API, and you'll find out more about programming this layer in Chapter 15. This chapter, however, focuses on using DAO with Jet.

Although Microsoft introduced the Jet engine in Access 1.0, it's since been substantially upgraded. As of this writing, any application that supports Automation can use the Jet engine to work with database objects. Due to this shared use of the technology, the Jet engine must be application independent. The services it supplies must work with any application that needs those services. Therefore, you'll see throughout this chapter references to *engine-defined properties* and *application-defined properties*. Those things the engine must support need to be generic enough that all the applications that call the engine requesting data services can use it.

Dueling Object Hierarchies

Although it can be confusing, before investigating DAO you must realize that Access supports its own object hierarchy, in addition to that supplied by DAO. That is, Access provides a mechanism whereby you can gather information about any open form, report, or module, write to the Debug object, or retrieve information from the Screen object, for example. This application hierarchy is completely separate from the Jet engine hierarchy (see Figure 6.1). In addition, DAO 3.5 supports many objects, properties, and methods that work only with ODBCDirect objects. This chapter completely ignores those objects, deferring to the coverage in Chapter 15.

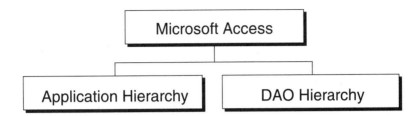

FIGURE 6.1

The two object hierarchies in Access

NOTE

Saying that Access supports two object hierarchies is so completely Access-centric as is to be rude. Actually, Access supports an infinite number of object hierarchies. It handles DAO the same way it handles the object model for Word, Excel, the Office Assistant, or any other OLE component. It's just that it's hard to use Access without encountering the DAO object model, and beginning developers tend to see Access as a single product. It's not; DAO is just another of the many components available to Windows developers. Of course, it's the most crucial component for Access developers.

The application hierarchy consists of the UI objects that Access itself maintains. These objects consist of all the open forms, reports, and modules; the controls, sections, and class modules associated with those objects; and the Application, DoCmd, Screen, Err, and Debug objects. These objects will play only a peripheral part in this chapter because the focus is the Jet engine hierarchy—the objects the database engine supports. These objects are outlined in Figure 6.2.

NOTE

If you're converting from Access 2, you may be confused by the change in the DoCmd statement. It used to be a statement, and now it's an object? Why this transformation? To enable automation, DoCmd must be an object. That way, you can perform macro actions from outside Access. In the same vein, the Application object has more properties and methods in each succeeding version of Access.

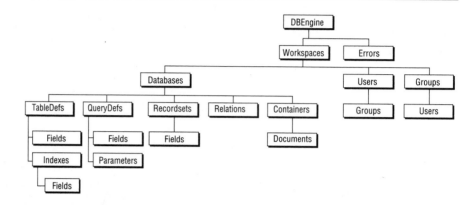

FIGURE 6.2

The Jet engine DAO hierarchy

Nuts and Bolts: Syntax Explained

To use DAO, you'll need to be able to refer to objects and use the correct syntax when building expressions. The next few sections discuss issues surrounding the various methods of using and referring to objects.

Properties and Methods

Objects have both properties and methods. *Properties* are attributes of objects that can normally be retrieved and (sometimes) set. For example, most objects expose a Name property, which returns the name of the object. You could use the following statement to retrieve the name of a TableDef object referred to by the variable tdf:

```
strName = tdf.Name
```

You can think of properties as the adjectives that describe objects.

Methods are actions that can be applied to objects. For example, Recordset objects provide the MoveNext method, which moves the current record pointer to the next record. You could use the following statement to move to the next record of the recordset referred to by the variable rst:

```
rst.MoveNext
```

You can think of methods as the verbs that act upon objects.

Using Object Variables

Through the course of this book, we make many assumptions about your knowledge of Access and VBA. We use standard variable types without explanation, assuming you'll understand statements like the following:

```
Dim intX as Integer
```

On the other hand, *object variables,* the basis of all your program code surrounding DAO, require a little explanation.

When you create a normal variable, you're asking Access to reserve enough space to hold the information for which you've specified a datatype. If you don't specify a datatype, Access assumes the most space the variable might need and uses a Variant-type variable. When you create an object variable (a variable that will refer to either a user-interface object or a data access object), Access creates only a "pointer." That is, the variable it creates only *refers* to a real object; it's not a real object itself.

For example, when you write code like this:

```
Dim db As Database
Dim rst As Recordset
Dim frm As Form
Dim ctl As Control
```

none of those variables actually hold any data, nor do they refer to any real objects at this point. To make an object variable actually refer to a real object, you must use the Set keyword. In every case you use Set to "point" the variable either at a real object (which must already exist) or at an instance of the object created with the New keyword. (See the section "Displaying Multiple Instances of Forms" in Chapter 8 for more information.) For example, using the variables in the previous example, you might see code like this:

```
Set db = CurrentDb()
Set rst = db.OpenRecordset("tblCustomers")
Set frm = Forms!frmCustomers
Set ctl = frm.Controls!txtCompanyName
```

In each case you've made the object variable refer to an actual object. Without this step, the object variables are just placeholders, waiting to actually refer to something.

If in the course of your code you point a data access object variable (such as a tabledef or recordset) at an actual object, Access will destroy the reference when the variable goes out of scope. If you have qualms about Access releasing the memory your object references use, you can explicitly delete the linkage by setting the variable equal to the predefined value Nothing:

```
Set rst = Nothing
```

In addition, if you created or opened an object as part of your assignment and want to be completely overt about your intentions, you should also use the Close method of the object to close it:

```
Set db = CurrentDb()
Set rst = db.OpenRecordset("tblCustomers")
  .
  .
  .
rst.Close
Set rst = Nothing
```

Although these steps aren't required, and we, too, tend to count on Access for these housekeeping details, you may want to consider these options. As you'll see in the section "CurrentDb versus DBEngine(0)(0)" later in this chapter, however, you should close only objects you've created as part of your code. CurrentDb, for example, returns a reference to the current user database. Although you can write

```
Set db = CurrentDb()
  .
  .
  .
db.Close
```

in your code, there's no reason to do so. Because you didn't open CurrentDb in your code, you can't close it. On the other hand, if being symmetrical is important to you, go ahead and use it. Db.Close will fail silently, without triggering an error.

DBEngine and the Workspaces Collection

The DBEngine object is the top-level object in any DAO reference. To refer to any object in the Jet hierarchy, you'll always start by referring to the DBEngine object. As you can see in Figure 6.2, the DBEngine object contains two collections: the collection of open workspaces and the Errors collection.

If you're using DAO from outside Access, you have no choice: the DBEngine object is the only way to get to any object. From within Access, you can and should use the CurrentDb function to obtain a reference to the current database. (See the section "CurrentDb versus DBEngine(0)(0)" later in this chapter for more information.) To reference objects that aren't part of the current database, however, you'll need to start with a reference to DBEngine even within Access.

NOTE We could list, in this chapter, all the properties and methods of each object. However, this information is neatly encapsulated in Access' online help. For each object type, search through online help and choose the object summary page for a complete list of the properties and methods each object exposes.

A workspace object represents a user's session. It contains all the open databases and provides for transaction processing and a secure workgroup. The Workspaces collection (of the DBEngine object) is the collection of all active workspaces. Unless you need to open an additional workspace, you'll rarely have any interaction with any workspace besides the default workspace Access opens for you.

As you can see in Figure 6.2, each workspace object contains three collections: Databases, Users, and Groups. The Databases collection contains all the opened databases, and the Users and Groups collections contain information about (you guessed it) all the users and groups in the current workgroup. (If you're working with ODBCDirect, a workspace object also contains a Connections collection. See Chapter 15 for more information.)

Referring to Objects

You refer to data access objects by following the hierarchy presented in the preceding section. Start with the DBEngine object and work your way down. The general format for referring to objects is

DBEngine.*ParentCollectionItem.ChildCollection!ChildObject*

where it may take several iterations through parent collections before you get to the child collection you're interested in.

Access provides a special way to refer to the current user database: the CurrentDb function. (See the next section, "CurrentDb versus DBEngine(0)(0)," for more information.) From code, we'll almost always refer to the user's database with the CurrentDb function, because this is the preferred method. In addition, you can use the CurrentDb function when retrieving properties, like this (the parentheses following CurrentDb are optional, and seldom used, in this syntax):

```
Debug.Print CurrentDb.TableDefs(0).Name
```

To refer to any member of any collection, you can use one of four syntactical constructs. Table 6.1 lists the four available methods. (In each example you're attempting to refer to the database named Sales that you'd previously opened as the only database in the default workspace (the one with the ordinal position 0).

TABLE 6.1   Methods for Referring to Objects

Syntax	Details	Example
collection("name")		DBEngine.Workspaces(0).Databases("Sales")
collection(*var*)	Where *var* is a string or variant variable	strDatabase="Sales"DBEngine.Workspaces(0).Databases(strDatabase)
collection(*ordinal position*)	Where *ordinal position* is the object's position within its collection	DBEngine.Workspaces(0).Databases(0)
collection!*name*collection![*name*]	Brackets are necessary if *name* contains a nonstandard character, such as a space	DBEngine.Workspaces(0).Databases!Sales

WARNING   Access and DAO number all built-in collections with ordinal values beginning with 0. Almost all other components in the Microsoft "world" number their collections starting with 1, and user-defined collections within Access are also numbered starting with 1. This is a point about which you'll want to be very careful.

All objects except DBEngine have an associated collection that contains all the objects of the given type. For example, the TableDefs collection contains a TableDef object for each table saved in the database. Collections make it easy to "visit" all the objects of a specific type, looping through all the items in the collection. Because you can refer to all the items in a collection either by name or by position, you have the best of both worlds. If you know the specific object's name, you can find it by name, as in the following code fragment:

```
Debug.Print CurrentDb.TableDefs("tblCompanies").RecordCount
```

If you want to refer to an object by number, you can do that, too:

```
Debug.Print CurrentDb.TableDefs(0).Name
```

By the way, in Access 2, a subtle problem made it impossible to chain together references below the current database in the DAO hierarchy until you had already referred to the current database itself at least once. Therefore, all Access 2 code had to declare a database variable, set it equal to a database, and then create references from there:

```
Dim db As Database
Dim tdf As Tabledef
Set db = DBEngine.Workspaces(0).Databases(0)
Set tdf = db.TableDefs(0)
Debug.Print tdf.RecordCount
```

This problem was fixed in Access 95, and you can now create references in one long string, if you wish. Either of the following statements will work:

```
Debug.Print DBEngine.Workspaces(0).Databases(0). _
  Tabledefs(0).RecordCount
```

or

```
Debug.Print CurrentDb.TableDefs(0).RecordCount
```

> **TIP**
>
> The "strung-out" reference using CurrentDb is useful only for retrieving properties; you cannot use it reliably to retrieve object references. In some situations it will work, but you're best off creating a variable that refers to the database and then using that variable for retrieving other references, just as you did in Access 2. You can use DBEngine.Workspaces(0).Databases(0) or CurrentDb to retrieve references directly, in one statement, but it's simpler to subscribe to the old technique: get an object variable that refers to the current database, and work from there.

CurrentDb versus DBEngine(0)(0)

To retrieve a reference to the current user's database, the DAO solution is to start with the DBEngine object, work your way through the Workspaces collection (Access creates Workspaces(0) for you when you log in to Access) and through the Databases collection (Access opens the user database as Databases(0)), all the way to:

```
DBEngine.Workspaces(0).Databases(0)
```

which you can shorten to:

```
DBEngine(0)(0)
```

if you count on default collections. (See the section "Using Default Collections" later in this chapter.)

Why, then, does Access *also* provide the CurrentDb function, which returns a reference to the current user's database? And why, when Microsoft stated quite clearly in Access 2 that CurrentDb was to be faded out and that the DAO reference was the preferred method for referencing the user's database, have they turned around and stated that CurrentDb is again the preferred method?

It all boils down to this: Jet and Access are two separate products. Jet provides the database services that Access requires, but Access provides its own layer on top of Jet, which you're using if you're designing applications inside Access. Access provides CurrentDb as a reference to the current database, and Jet provides DBEngine.Workspaces(0).Databases(0) (which can be condensed to DBEngine(0)(0)).

Certainly, the DBEngine(0)(0) syntax is required if you're working outside of Access. That is, if you're using OLE automation to control DAO, this is the only way to get a reference to the user's database in Access. On the other hand, Access provides the CurrentDb function, which will always refer to the current database from within Access.

Access presents some rather subtle problems having to do with the currency of the reference to the user's database. CurrentDb and DBEngine(0)(0) are not the same object internally, although they do both refer to the same database. Every time you retrieve a reference using CurrentDb, you're asking Access to create a new internal object that refers to the current database. On the other hand, Jet maintains only a single reference to the current database, DBEngine(0)(0). This explains why you can't create references using CurrentDb in a single long string: as VBA executes the line of code, Access creates a new database reference and gives you an object reference in that database. It's as though you've executed an explicit OpenDatabase on the current database. As soon as the line of code has finished executing, Access closes the database reference it just opened. For certain types of objects (recordsets, in particular), Access attempts to keep the reference to the recordset viable. For other types of objects, however, Access does not maintain the open reference, and further attempts at using the object will fail.

For example, attempting to run this procedure:

```
Sub ThisDoesntWork()
    Dim doc As Document
    Set doc = CurrentDb.Containers!Tables.Documents(0)
    Debug.Print doc.Name
End Sub
```

will fail with an error when the code attempts to print doc.Name. The database object that was used to reference that particular document is long gone, and *doc* becomes an invalid reference. Note, however, that if you were to replace CurrentDb with DBEngine(0)(0), this procedure would work fine. If you change the code to use a database variable instead of a single long reference, it will also work fine:

```
Sub ThisDoesWork()
    Dim db As Database
    Dim doc As Document

    Set db = CurrentDb()
    Set doc = db.Containers!Tables.Documents(0)
    Debug.Print doc.Name
End Sub
```

How do you choose between CurrentDb and DBEngine(0)(0) in your applications? If you're working with Access using Automation, your answer is simple: you use DBEngine(0)(0) to refer to the current database. If you're working in Access, however, you can use either CurrentDb or DBEngine(0)(0) to refer to the current database. Certainly, using CurrentDb is simpler, and it is easier to understand as you peruse code. On the other hand, it's slower. (Experimentation has shown that retrieving a reference using CurrentDb can be an order of magnitude slower than using DBEngine(0)(0). See Chapter 17 for details on testing this out.) There's one big difference between the two that may make your decision for you: the database referred to by CurrentDb is always up to date with the user interface. You must call the Refresh method before you use any collection retrieved using a reference through DBEngine(0)(0). The Refresh method is quite expensive (slow, that is) and will immediately obviate any speed gains you made by choosing

DBEngine(0)(0) over CurrentDb. Almost every example in this book that refers to the current database uses CurrentDb.

> **TIP** Although Microsoft has made no such promises, it's quite possible that a future version of Access will support multiple databases open on the Access desktop. If so, at that point there will be another difference between CurrentDb and DBEngine(0)(0): CurrentDb will always refer to the database containing the code that is currently executing, but DBEngine(0)(0) might refer to another database, the one that was added to the Databases collection first—that is, the one that was opened first. Therefore, using CurrentDb adds a tiny amount of "forward-thinking" to your code, although we can only speculate at this point as to whether it will ever make a difference.

Bang (!) versus Dot (.)

The bang (!) and dot (.) identifier operators help describe the relationships among collections, objects, and properties in an expression. They indicate that one part of an expression belongs to another.

In general, you follow the bang with the name of something you created: a form, report, or control. The bang also indicates that the item to follow is an element of a collection. You'll usually follow the dot with a property, collection, or method name.

You can also think of the uses of these operators this way: a bang separates an object from the collection it's in (a field in a table, a form in the Forms collection, a control on a form), while a dot separates an object from a property, method, or collection of that object.

Ordinal Positions

As you've seen, you can refer to an object using the ordinal position within its collection. Jet assigns and maintains these ordinal positions, and they always start with position number 0. For the Workspaces and Databases objects, ordinal position 0 always refers to the current workspace and the current database (the one that's open in the user interface). For example, when you start Microsoft Access, it opens a Jet engine session, creates a workspace, and assigns it to the first ordinal position in the Workspaces collection. When you open a database through the user interface (using the File ➤ Open Database menu item), Access assigns the database to the first ordinal position in the Databases collection.

For objects other than workspaces and databases, an object's ordinal position is dependent on the order in which it was added to its collection. The first table you create will have a lower ordinal position than tables you create later. As you create and delete objects, an object's ordinal position changes within its collection. Additionally, Access creates objects (such as the system tables) that may preclude your objects from starting at ordinal position 0. For this reason it is not a good idea to refer to a specific object using its ordinal position. You should use the ordinal position of objects only as loop indexes, for iterating through all the objects in a collection.

NOTE   Using an object's ordinal position has become less important since Access 2, with the addition of the For Each...Next construct. There are times, however, when you must loop through the entries in a collection. If your action changes the number of elements in the collection, using For Each...Next will, in general, fail. In cases when you're closing objects or deleting them from their collection, use a For...Next loop, using the objects' ordinal position to refer to them.

Using Default Collections

You can see from previous examples that a simple object reference can result in a long line of code. Fortunately, DAO provides default collections for most object types: if you don't specify a collection, Access assumes you're referring to the default collection for the parent object. You can use the default collection behavior of objects to make your code more compact (but somewhat less readable). Table 6.2 lists the default collection within each object type.

Using default collections, you can shorten this expression:

```
DBEngine.Workspaces(0).Databases(0).TableDefs(0)
```

to

```
DBEngine(0)(0)(0)
```

This expression means, "Refer to the first tabledef within the first database within the first workspace" because the default collection for DBEngine is the Workspaces

TABLE 6.2   Default Collections for DAO Objects

Object	Default Collection
Container	Documents
Database	TableDefs
DBEngine	Workspaces
Group	Users
Index	Fields
QueryDef	Parameters
Recordset	Fields
Relation	Fields
TableDef	Fields
User	Groups
Workspace	Databases

collection, the default collection for a workspace object is the Databases collection, and the default collection for a database object is the TableDefs collection.

You can use similar contractions to simplify your code. Be aware, though, that using default collections to reduce your code also makes it less readable: whoever is reading the code will have to understand the meaning of the expression without any visual clues.

Enumerating Objects in Collections

Because you can access any object in any collection by its position in the collection, you can use a loop to look at or modify any object in the collection. Use the Count property of a collection to determine the size of the collection. Remember that the ordinal position of objects within a DAO collection starts at 0; if a collection contains three elements, they'll be numbered 0 through 2.

For example, you could use code like this to print out the names of all the tables in your database:

```
Dim db As Database
Dim intI As Integer
Dim tdf As Tabledef

Set db = CurrentDb()
For intI = 0 To db.TableDefs.Count - 1
    Set tdf = db.TableDefs(intI)
    Debug.Print tdf.Name
Next intI
```

The simplest way to loop through any collection, however, is to use the For Each...Next syntax. This syntax requires you to create a variable that can refer to the object type in the collection you're looping through and then use code like this to do the work:

```
Dim db As Database
Dim tdf As TableDef

Set db = CurrentDb()
For Each tdf In db.TableDefs
    Debug.Print tdf.Name
Next tdf
```

In this case, For Each...Next does the "Set" operation for you.

Working with Properties

If you have worked with forms, reports, and controls, you are already familiar with referencing properties. (See Chapters 7 through 9 for more information on user interface objects.) However, the interaction between the Jet engine and Microsoft Access introduces new subtleties when you are working with properties.

Properties for data access objects behave somewhat differently from Microsoft Access properties. As you saw earlier in this chapter, every object has a collection of properties. For Access objects (forms and reports, for example), every property in the Properties collection that will ever exist for the object exists when you create the object. This is not necessarily the case for data access objects. Properties may not exist in the collection until you set them to a value, depending on the specific object. Therefore, it's important that you understand the differences among the different types of properties used in DAO.

Types of Properties

DAO properties can be either built in or user defined.

Built-in properties always exist for an object. They define the basic characteristics of an object and are available to any application that uses the Jet engine. For example, for Field objects, *Name* and *Type* are built-in properties. They define the basic characteristics of a field.

User-defined properties are added to the Properties collection of an object. These properties may be added either by Microsoft Access as a client of the Jet engine or by you as an application developer. If Microsoft Access added the property to the object, it's treated as a special case of a user-defined property. The properties Access adds are properties it needs in order to do its job. The Jet engine can't provide them, because they're specific to Access.

User-defined properties do not exist until they are added to the object's Properties collection. While this may seem obvious, it does cause some unexpected behavior. For example, a field's description is not a built-in property. Even though you can enter a field's description while defining the table, the Jet engine doesn't know about it until you've actually typed it into the property list for the field. If you try to retrieve the Description property of an object that has not yet had this property set, you will get a trappable run-time error.

Referring to Data Access Object Properties

As in referencing any other property, you can use the standard

object.property

syntax for referring to a built-in property of an object. On the other hand, to refer to a user-defined property (whether the "user" is you, your application, or Access as a client of the Jet engine), you must refer to the property through the Properties collection of the object (and this syntax always works, even for built-in properties):

object.Properties("property")

or

object.Properties!property

For example, to retrieve the Description property for the tblClients table, you could use code like the following. (Note that this code will fail with a run-time error if the Description property hasn't already been set.)

```
Dim db As Database
Dim tdf As TableDef
Dim strDescription As String

Set db = CurrentDb()
Set tdf = db.TableDefs!tblCustomers
strDescription = tdf.Properties!Description
```

(For more information on adding user-defined properties, see the section "Creating Your Own Properties" later in this chapter.)

Enumerating the Properties

Listing 6.1 shows code you could use to print out all the properties of any table:

Listing 6.1

```
Function ListProperties(strTable As String)
    Dim db As Database
    Dim tdf As TableDef
    Dim prp As Property

    Set db = CurrentDb()
    ' You could use the following expression:
    ' Set tdf = db.TableDefs(strTable)
    ' but the TableDefs collection is the default collection
    ' for a database object, so its use is unnecessary
    ' in the expression.
    Set tdf = db(strTable)

    For Each prp In tdf.Properties
        Debug.Print prp.Name, prp.Value
    Next prp
End Function
```

You'll find ListProperties in basTestProperties (in CH06.MDB). The output from the preceding code might look something like the output shown in Figure 6.3.

FIGURE 6.3

Sample property listing for tblCustomers

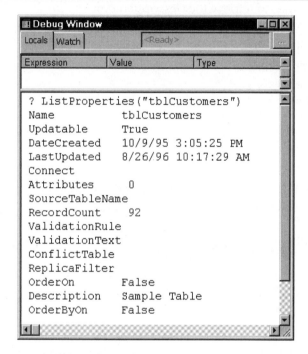

Setting and Retrieving Properties

To make it simpler to set and get properties of objects, we've provided the adhGetProp and adhSetProp functions in basHandleProps (in CH06.MDB). The adhSetProp function takes as its parameters an object reference, a property name, and a value. It attempts to set the property, and if it fails, it attempts to create the property and then set its value. Of course, this feature can work only for objects that allow you to create user-defined properties (Database, Field, Index, QueryDef, or TableDef). For example:

```
Set db = CurrentDb()
varRetval = adhSetProp(db.TableDefs("tblCustomers"), _
  "Description", "This is the customer table")
If Not IsError(varRetval) Then
```

```
    MsgBox "Description set successfully!"
End If
```

will set the Description property. If that property hadn't existed before the function call, adhSetProp would have created it and then set it. (See basHandleProps for the details.)

The adhGetProp function is simpler: it just attempts to retrieve the requested property, and it returns the value if the property exists or an error value otherwise. For example:

```
Set db = CurrentDb()
varRetval = adhGetProp( _
 db.TableDefs("tblCustomers").Fields("CustomerID"), _
 "Description")
If Not IsError(varRetval) Then
    MsgBox "The Description property was: " & varRetval
End If
```

will return either the Description property for the CustomerID field in tblCustomers or an error value if that property doesn't exist.

Data Definition Using DAO

The previous sections have been using data access objects to refer to existing objects and properties. A large portion of DAO's power, though, lies in its ability to programmatically create and manipulate objects. Using the CreateD… and Append methods, you can create and modify virtually any data access object.

Creating Objects

To create a new object, follow these three steps:

1. Use one of the Create… methods to create the object (CreateTable, CreateIndex, and so on).

2. Define the new object's characteristics by setting its properties. Some properties (such as its name) are essential to its existence and must be specified when you create the object. Others may be specified later. (In most cases this step can be

rolled up into the previous one. All the Create... methods accept optional parameters letting you specify essential properties of the new object.)

3. Append the object to its collection to make it a permanent part of your database.

In cases where the new object contains other objects (a table contains fields, for instance), you must create the main object, then create the subordinate objects, append them to the appropriate collection, and then append the main object to its collection. You can use this same technique when creating a new table, index, or relation programmatically. Each operation is unique in one way or another, so consult the online help for more information on the CreateTable, CreateField, CreateIndex, CreateProperty, and CreateRelation methods. The following sections demonstrate how to create these complex objects.

Creating a New Table

The following example creates a new table called tblOrders and adds two fields to it. You'll find the complete function in basCreateTable in CH06.MDB.

```
Function CreateOrdersTable()
    Dim db As Database
    Dim tdfOrders As TableDef
    Dim fld1 As Field
    Dim fld2 As Field

    Set db = CurrentDb()
    Set tdfOrders = db.CreateTableDef()
    tdfOrders.Name = "tblOrders"

    Set fld1 = tdfOrders.CreateField("OrderID", dbLong)
    Set fld2 = tdfOrders.CreateField("CustomerName", _
     dbText, 30)
```

At this point the new table and its two fields exist only in memory. To make the new objects a permanent part of the database, you must use the Append method. If you do not append a new object to a collection, it will not be saved as an object in the database.

WARNING Creating objects and giving them properties is not enough. You must take the step of appending them to the correct collection, or Access will never know of their existence. If your program exits before you've used the Append method to add them to a collection, they will be discarded.

The next lines save the new objects to the database:

```
With tdfOrders.Fields
    .Append fld1
    .Append fld2
End With

With db.TableDefs
    .Append tdfOrders
    .Refresh
End With
```

Finally, you can refresh the TableDefs collection to ensure that the new objects are included in it. In a multiuser environment, the new table may not be immediately available to other users unless you refresh the collection. The following line refreshes the TableDefs collection:

```
db.TableDefs.Refresh
```

Even using the Refresh method, Access won't update the database window itself until it must. It will only show the new table you've created once you move to a different collection and then back to the list of tables. To solve this problem, Access 97 adds the RefreshDatabaseWindow method of the Application object. Adding this line of code will refresh the database window's display:

```
Application.RefreshDatabaseWindow
```

NOTE   This simple example does not include error handling and will therefore fail if you attempt to run it more than once. If you want to try it again, first delete the table the example created from the database window.

TIP   The With…End With syntax can make it simpler to modify multiple properties or use multiple methods of an object. The previous example used the syntax only for the purpose of introducing it, but it can both simplify your code and make its intent clearer. You'll want to use it whenever possible.

You can also use the

Dim objectVar As New *Object*

syntax to create the objects. When you do this, Access creates the reference and then instantiates the object automatically. Rather than having to call CreateTable explicitly, Access creates the tabledef for you when you write

```
Dim tdf As New TableDef
```

This syntax creates, at the same time, both the object variable and the object to which it points. Once you've created an object this way (by running the procedure that includes the declaration), you still need to assign the values of the properties of the object, and you need to append it to the appropriate collection.

For example, you could rewrite the preceding function as shown here:

```
Function CreateOrdersTable2()
    Dim db As Database

    Dim tdfOrders As New TableDef
    Dim fld1 As New Field
    Dim fld2 As New Field

    Set db = CurrentDb()
    ' The tabledef's already created, so
    ' just assign the properties.
    tdfOrders.Name = "tblOrders"

    ' The fields are already created, so just
    ' assign the properties.
    With fld1
        .Type = dbLong
        .Name = "OrderID"
    End With

    With fld2
        .Type = dbText
        .Size = 30
        .Name = "CustomerName"
    End With

    With tdfOrders.Fields
        .Append fld1
        .Append fld2
    End With
```

```
    With db.TableDefs
        .Append tdfOrders
        .Refresh
    End With
    Application.RefreshDatabaseWindow
End Function
```

We can't recommend a real preference for either method, except that calling the Create… methods directly makes your code more *explicit:* on viewing the code, it's easier to see exactly what it's doing. In addition, using the Create… method allows you greater control over when the object comes into being: when you use the New keyword, Jet creates the object the first time you attempt to set or retrieve a property of the object.

The Create… Methods

For each data access object that you can create programmatically, there's an associated *Create* method. Table 6.3 summarizes the methods and their syntax.

TABLE 6.3   Object Creation Methods

Object	Method	Arguments	Datatype	Description
Table	CreateTableDef	Name	String	Name of the new table
		Attributes	Integer	Settings for attached, system, and hidden tables
		Source	String	An attached table's base table type information
		Connect	String	An attached table's base table path and file name
Field	CreateField	Name	String	Name of the new field
		Type	Integer	Datatype of the new field
		Size	Integer	Size of the field if it is a text field
Index	CreateIndex	Name	String	Name of the new index
Query	CreateQueryDef	Name	String	Name of the new query
		SQLText	String	Valid SQL string that defines the new query

TABLE 6.3   Object Creation Methods (continued)

Object	Method	Arguments	Datatype	Description
Relation	CreateRelation	Name	String	Name of the new relation
		Table	String	Name of the relation's primary table
		ForeignTable	String	Name of the relation's foreign table
		Attributes	Integer	Settings for relationship type, enforced referential integrity, and cascaded updates and deletes
Workspace	CreateWorkspace	Name	String	Name of the new workspace
		User	String	Name of an existing user. This user will become the owner of the new workspace object. For code that references the new workspace object, *User* will, in effect, be the user executing the code
		Password	String	Password for the new workspace object. Can contain any characters except ASCII null (Chr$(0))
		Type	Long	Value indicating the data source (dbUseJet for Jet, or dbUseODBC for ODBCDirect)
Database	CreateDatabase	DatabaseName	String	Name of the file that contains the database
		Locale	String	Collating order of the database
		Options	Integer	Options for the new database. You can specify whether or not the database is to be encrypted and which version (2.0 or 3.0) of the file format to use when saving the database

TABLE 6.3   Object Creation Methods (continued)

Object	Method	Arguments	Datatype	Description
Group	CreateGroup	Name	String	Name of the new group
		PID	String	Personal identifier for the new group
User	CreateUser	Name	String	Name of the new user
		PID	String	Personal identifier for the new user
		Password	String	Password for the new User object (up to 14 characters)

Creating an Index

As part of your applications, you may need to create an index programmatically. Follow these steps to create a new index:

1. Use the CreateIndex method of a TableDef object to create the index object, and set its Name property (either in the function call itself or by assigning a value to the Name property sometime before you append the index to the Indexes collection).

2. Assign values to the new index's properties, as appropriate. All the properties are read/write for an index object that hasn't yet been appended to the Indexes collection but are read-only once that has occurred. The ones you'll most likely be interested in are the Name, Primary, Unique, and Required properties.

3. Use the CreateField method to create a field object for each field that makes up part of the index, and append each to the index's Fields collection. This collection of fields indicates to the index the fields for which it must maintain values in order to keep itself current.

4. Use the Append method of the original TableDef object to append the index object to its Indexes collection.

NOTE   Because all the properties of an index object are read-only once the object has been appended to its collection, if you need to modify a property of an index once it's been created, you must delete the object and then create a new one.

In Access, using DAO, you can name your indexes any way you wish. If you have code you're using, however, that counts on your primary key being named PrimaryKey (and almost anyplace you're using the Seek method in your code, you will), you must ensure that your primary keys are named with the standard value, PrimaryKey. Otherwise, existing code might break.

The adhCreatePrimaryKey function in Listing 6.2 creates the primary key for any specified table. You pass to this function the name of the table, the name of the primary key, and a variant that may contain an array of field names or just a single field name to use as part of the primary key. Along the way, adhCreatePrimaryKey calls the FindPrimaryKey function, which returns the name of the primary key if it exists or Null if it doesn't. If a primary key already exists, adhCreatePrimaryKey deletes the primary key so it can create a new one. We've also included a test procedure, TestCreatePK, to test the functionality. You'll find all these examples in the module basPK in CH06.MDB.

Listing 6.2

```
Function adhCreatePrimaryKey(strTableName As String, _
 strKeyName As String, ParamArray varFields() As Variant) _
As Boolean
    Dim db As Database
    Dim idx As Index
    Dim tdf As TableDef
    Dim fld As Field
    Dim varPK As Variant
    Dim varIdx As Variant
    Dim idxs As Indexes

    On Error GoTo CreatePrimaryKey_Err

    Set db = CurrentDb()
    Set tdf = db.TableDefs(strTableName)
    Set idxs = tdf.Indexes

    ' Find out if the table currently has a primary key.
    ' If so, delete it now.
    varPK = FindPrimaryKey(tdf)
    If Not IsNull(varPK) Then
```

```
            idxs.Delete varPK
        End If
        ' Create the new index object.
        Set idx = tdf.CreateIndex(strKeyName)

        ' Set up the new index as the primary key.
        ' This will also set:
        '    IgnoreNulls property to False,
        '    Required property to True,
        '    Unique property to True.
        idx.Primary = True

        ' Now create the fields that make up the index,
        ' and append each to the collection of fields.
        For Each varIdx In varFields
            AddField idx, varIdx
        Next varIdx

        ' Now append the index to the TableDef's
        ' index collection
        idxs.Append idx
        adhCreatePrimaryKey = True

CreatePrimaryKey_Exit:
    Exit Function

CreatePrimaryKey_Err:
    MsgBox "Error: " & Err.Description & " (" & Err.Number & ")"
    adhCreatePrimaryKey = False
    Resume CreatePrimaryKey_Exit
End Function

Private Function FindPrimaryKey(tdf As TableDef) As Variant

    ' Given a particular tabledef, find the primary
    ' key name, if it exists.

    ' Return the name of the primary key's index, if
    ' it exists, or Null if there wasn't a primary key.

    Dim idx As Index

    For Each idx In tdf.Indexes
        If idx.Primary Then
```

```
            FindPrimaryKey = idx.Name
            Exit Function
        End If
    Next idx
    FindPrimaryKey = Null
End Function

Private Function AddField(idx As Index, varIdx As Variant) As _
  Boolean
    ' Given an index object, and a field name, add
    ' the field to the index.
    ' Return True on success, False otherwise.

    Dim fld As Field

    On Error GoTo AddIndex_Err
    If Len(varIdx & "") > 0 Then
        Set fld = idx.CreateField(varIdx)
        idx.Fields.Append fld
    End If
    AddField = True

AddIndex_Exit:
    Exit Function

AddIndex_Err:
    AddField = False
    Resume AddIndex_Exit
End Function

Sub TestCreatePK()
    Debug.Print adhCreatePrimaryKey("tblCustomerItems", _
      "PrimaryKey", "CustomerID", "ItemID")
End Sub
```

Creating Relationships

To create a relationship, use the CreateRelation method of a database object. Follow these steps to create a new relation:

1. Open the database that will be the basis for your relation.

2. Verify that the referenced table (the primary table in the relation) has a primary key in place.

3. Use the CreateRelation method of the database to create the relation object. Either set the relation's properties when you create it or set them one by one after the fact. These properties include the Table, ForeignTable, and Attributes properties.

4. Create a field object for each primary key field from the primary table involved in the relationship. For each field object, supply the ForeignName property, which corresponds to the name of the matching key field in the secondary table. Append each new field object to the relationship's Fields collection.

5. Use the Append method to append the new relation object to the database's Relations collection.

The following table lists all the possible values for the Attributes property of a relation object:

Constant	Description
dbRelationUnique	Relationship is one-to-one
dbRelationDontEnforce	Relationship isn't enforced (no referential integrity)
dbRelationInherited	Relationship exists in the database that contains the two attached tables
dbRelationLeft	Relationship is a left outer join
dbRelationRight	Relationship is a right outer join
dbRelationUpdateCascade	Updates will cascade
dbRelationDeleteCascade	Deletions will cascade

Set the property to be the sum of any of these constants. (Most programmers use the Or operator to combine these sorts of flags, just to make it clear they're working with flag values, not doing some sort of arithmetic.) If you set no value for the Attributes property, Access attempts to create a one-to-many inner-joined relationship with referential integrity enabled.

Listing 6.3 demonstrates, in the simplest case, the steps involved in creating a relationship. This function (from basRelations in CH06.MDB) creates a left outer join between tblCustomers and tblCustomerItems and enables cascading updates. Just to make sure the function succeeds, if it finds that the relation already exists, it deletes that relation and re-creates it.

Listing 6.3

```
Const adhcErrObjectExists = 3012

Function CreateRelationship() As Boolean

    ' Create a relationship between tblCustomers and
    ' tblCustomerItems.
    ' The relation will be a left outer join,
    ' with cascading deletes enabled.

    Dim db As Database
    Dim rel As Relation
    Dim fld As Field

    On Error GoTo CreateRelationship_Err

    Set db = CurrentDb()

    ' Create the new relation object.
    Set rel = db.CreateRelation()

    ' Set the relation's properties.
    With rel
        .Name = "Relation1"
        .Table = "tblCustomers"
        .ForeignTable = "tblCustomerItems"

        ' Create a left outer join containing
        ' tblCustomers and tblItems, with cascading
        ' updates enabled.
        .Attributes = dbRelationLeft Or _
         dbRelationDeleteCascade
    End With
    ' Or you could set all the properties when you create
    ' the object:
    ' Set rel = db.CreateRelation("Relation1", _
    '   "tblCustomers", "tblCustomerItems", _
    '   dbRelationLeft Or dbRelationDeleteCascade)
```

```
        ' Set the relation's field collection.
        Set fld = rel.CreateField("CustomerID")
        ' What field does this map to in the OTHER table?
        fld.ForeignName = "CustomerID"
        rel.Fields.Append fld
        ' You could append more fields, if you needed to.

        ' Append the relation to the database's
        ' relations collection.
        db.Relations.Append rel
        CreateRelationship = True

CreateRelationship_Exit:
    Exit Function

CreateRelationship_Err:
    Select Case Err.Number
        Case adhcErrObjectExists
            ' If the relationship already exists,
            ' just delete it, and then try to
            ' append it again.
            db.Relations.Delete rel.Name
            Resume
        Case Else
            MsgBox "Error: " & Err.Description & _
            " (" & Err.Number & ")"
            CreateRelationship = False
            Resume CreateRelationship_Exit
    End Select
End Function
```

Creating Your Own Properties

Access' support for DAO makes it possible for you to create your own properties and append them to the Properties collection for an object. For example, you might like to add a LastUpdated property to a table to keep track of the last time a user touched the table. Just as for adding an object of any other type, you take three steps:

1. Use the CreateProperty method to create the new property.

2. Define the new property's characteristics by setting its properties. (You may have done this in step 1.)

3. Append the object to the Properties collection to make it a permanent part of your database.

The code in Listing 6.4 creates the LastChanged and LastUser properties and appends them to the tblCustomers table. (You can find the function in basTestProperties in CH06.MDB.) The following paragraphs examine the function in detail.

The function's caller has passed in the name of the table on which to operate, so the first step is to set up a reference to the correct TableDef object:

```
Dim db As Database
Dim tdf As TableDef
Dim prpLastChanged As Property
Dim prpLastUser As Property
Dim prp As Property

Set db = CurrentDb()
Set tdf = db.TableDefs(strName)
```

Then you need to create the new property objects. When you call CreateProperty, you may supply the property's name, type, and initial value. You may also set those properties later, before you append the property to the table's Properties collection. In this case it's simpler just to do it all in the call to CreateProperty. You set the LastChanged property to contain the current time and the LastUser property to contain the current user ("Admin", unless you've logged in as someone else). (This step corresponds to steps 1 and 2 in the previous list of steps necessary to create new properties.)

```
Set prpLastChanged = tdf.CreateProperty("LastChanged", _
  dbDate, Now)
Set prpLastUser = tdf.CreateProperty("LastUser", _
  dbText, CurrentUser())
```

Use the Append method to add the properties to the table so they become persistent. Because the Append method triggers a run-time error if you've already appended the properties, you can avoid the problem by turning off error checking while appending:

```
On Error Resume Next
With tdf.Properties
    .Append prpLastChanged
    .Append prpLastUser
End With
```

```
On Error GoTo 0
```

To list the properties, you can loop through the Properties collection:

```
Dim prp As Property
For Each prp In tdf.Properties
    Debug.Print prp.Name, prp.Value
Next prp
```

To modify the LastChanged property, use one of the two possible syntax variations:

```
tdf.Properties!LastChanged = Now
```

or

```
tdf.Properties("LastChanged") = Now
```

Listing 6.4

```
Function TestAddProps(strName As String)
    Dim db As Database
    Dim tdf As TableDef
    Dim prpLastChanged As Property
    Dim prpLastUser As Property
    Dim prp As Property

    Set db = CurrentDb()
    Set tdf = db.TableDefs(strName)

    ' Create the two new properties.
    Set prpLastChanged = tdf.CreateProperty("LastChanged", _
     dbDate, Now)
    Set prpLastUser = tdf.CreateProperty("LastUser", _
     dbText, CurrentUser())

    ' This code will fail if the properties have already
    ' been added, so just let the errors occur,
    ' and keep on going.
    On Error Resume Next
    With tdf.Properties
        .Append prpLastChanged
        .Append prpLastUser
    End With
    On Error GoTo 0
```

```
      ' Now list out all the properties.
      For Each prp In tdf.Properties
            Debug.Print prp.Name, prp.Value
      Next prp

      ' Reset the LastChanged property, just to show how:
      tdf.Properties!LastChanged = Now
      ' or:
      ' tdf.Properties("LastChanged") = Now
End Sub
```

Modifying Objects

You can modify an existing object using DAO methods and properties without having to open the object in Design view. There are, however, other restrictions to keep in mind when setting properties of data access objects. Some properties can be set only when the object is created and cannot be changed after the object has been appended to its collection. The Attributes property of TableDef objects is an example of this restriction: you cannot change the Attributes property of an existing TableDef object but must set this value when you first create the object. If you must alter the Attributes property for a given tabledef, you need to create a new one, copy in all the information from the existing one, and set the Attributes property before you use the Append method to add the tabledef to your database. Also, you need to be aware that some properties do not exist for a data access object until they have been set to a value. (See the section "Types of Properties" earlier in this chapter for a reminder about this limitation.)

Connecting and Reconnecting Attached Tables

The Connect property of TableDef objects gives you control over attached tables. Using this property in conjunction with the SourceTableName property and the RefreshLink method, you can alter the location of the table feeding data to Access.

The Connect Property

Every TableDef object has a Connect property—a string that identifies the type of attached table and its location in the system's file structure. It does not specify the particular table (or file name, in the case of many of the external datatypes). The SourceTableName property contains the actual file name. (For local native Access tables, the Connect property is a zero-length string [""].) For a complete listing of values for the Connect property, see Access' online help.

In general, the Connect string names the database that contains the table to which you want to connect. Notice that for native Access tables, the database is the actual MDB file. For many other datatypes, use the directory that contains the table as the database. This makes sense because other DBMS programs, such as Paradox and FoxPro, use the DOS directory structure as the database; there is no single central file as with Access.

Creating an Attached Access Table

The function in Listing 6.5 creates an attached table in the current database, pulling in data from a different MDB file. To use it, you might try this:

```
fSuccess = CreateAttached("AttachedTable", _
"C:\AppPath\MDBFile.MDB", "tblContacts")
```

To create a new attached table, you must follow the same steps that have been covered already: create the object, set its properties, and then append it to the parent collection. CreateAttached first creates the new TableDef object:

```
Dim db As Database
Dim tdf As TableDef
Dim strConnect As String
Dim fRetval As Boolean

On Error GoTo CreateAttachedError

Set db = CurrentDb()
Set tdf = db.CreateTableDef(strTable)
```

Then the function must set the appropriate properties. For an attached table, you need to set the Connect and SourceTableName properties. Because you're attaching a native Access table, the Connect string doesn't specify a data source; it just describes the path to the MDB file.

```
With tdf
 .Connect = ";DATABASE=" & strPath
 .SourceTableName = strBaseTable
End With
```

Finally, the code must append the new TableDef object to the TableDefs collection:

```
db.TableDefs.Append tdf
```

In addition, the function adds some error handling. For example, you might already have created a TableDef object with a particular name, or you might try to attach data from an .MDB file that doesn't exist. In either case the error handler pops up a message box and causes the function to return a False value (instead of the True value it returns if it succeeds in creating the new TableDef object). You'll find CreateAttached in the module basAttach in CH06.MDB.

Listing 6.5

```
Function CreateAttached(strTable As String, strPath As String, _
  strBaseTable As String) As Boolean

    Dim db As Database
    Dim tdf As TableDef
    Dim strConnect As String
    Dim fRetval As Boolean

    On Error GoTo CreateAttachedError

    Set db = CurrentDb()
    Set tdf = db.CreateTableDef(strTable)

    With tdf
        ' Set up the tabledef's properties.
        ' Set the path to the MDB file.
        .Connect = ";DATABASE=" & strPath
        ' Set the source table name.
        .SourceTableName = strBaseTable
    End With

    ' Append the new tabledef to the Tabledefs collection.
    db.TableDefs.Append tdf
    fRetval = True
```

```
CreateAttachedExit:
    CreateAttached = fRetval
    Exit Function

CreateAttachedError:
    MsgBox "Error: " & Err.Description & " (" & Err.Number & ")"
    fRetval = False
    Resume CreateAttachedExit
End Function
```

Modifying an Existing Attached Table

As users work with your application, sooner or later its attached tables will need to be moved to a new location in the system's file structure. Your application will trigger a run-time error when it later tries to access the moved table. To take care of this problem, you can write a function that checks attached tables and then reconnects them if necessary. The function CheckAttachedTable, in Listing 6.6, tests an attached table and makes sure it's still where Access thinks it is. ReattachTable, also in Listing 6.6, reattaches the table if necessary. Its code is very similar to that in CreateAttached (in Listing 6.5). You'll find both functions in basAttach in CH06.MDB. (For a more complete discussion on handling the problems that can come up in applications that use attached tables, see Chapter 12. That chapter discusses a generalized solution for reattaching tables.)

After setting up the requisite database and tabledef object variables, the code in ReattachTable checks the Connect property for the particular tabledef. If it's a zero-length string, the table is a native table, and there's nothing to be done. Otherwise it builds up the new connection string and assigns it to the Connect property of the TableDef object:

```
If Len(tdf.Connect) > 0 Then
    tdf.Connect = ";DATABASE=" & strNewPath
    '
    '
End If
```

The code's next step is to attempt to refresh the link between the local Access database and the foreign data. The function uses the tabledef's RefreshLink method to do this. If the link isn't valid, this RefreshLink fails and the error-handling code posts a message and returns a False value from the function. If it succeeds, the function returns a True value, indicating its success.

```
On Error Resume Next
tdf.RefreshLink
ReAttachTable = (Err = 0)
```

Armed with a function to reattach tables if necessary, you can attack the problem of checking to make sure your tables are correctly attached, reattaching them if necessary. CheckAttachedTable does this work for you.

The majority of the code in CheckAttachedTable can be summarized in a few steps:

1. Turn on inline error handling (On Error Resume Next).

2. Attempt to retrieve the Name property of the first field in the requested table.

3. If the attempt fails, call ReattachTable to attempt to reattach it. If that fails, post a failure message and return False.

4. If the recordset creation succeeded, just close the recordset and return a True value from the function.

Listing 6.6

```
Function CheckAttachedTable(strTable As String, _
  strNewPath As String) As Boolean

    ' Checks the named table and attempts to reattach it if
    ' it's not attached properly.
    '
    Dim db As Database
    Dim strName As String

    ' Assume success
    CheckAttachedTable = True

    On Error Resume Next
    ' Attempt to retrieve the name of the first field. This
    ' will fail if the attachment isn't valid.
    Set db = CurrentDb()
    strName = db.TableDefs(strTable).Fields(0).Name

    If Err.Number <> 0 Then
        If Not ReattachTable(strTable, strNewPath) Then
            MsgBox "Could not reattach table '" & strTable & "'"
            CheckAttachedTable = False
```

```
            End If
        End If
        On Error GoTo 0
    End Function

    Private Function ReattachTable(strTable As String, _
      strNewPath As String) As Boolean

        Dim db As Database
        Dim tdf As TableDef

        ' Assume success.
        ReattachTable = True

        Set db = CurrentDb()
        Set tdf = db.TableDefs(strTable)

        ' If Connect is blank, it's not an attached table
        If Len(tdf.Connect) > 0 Then
            tdf.Connect = ";DATABASE=" & strNewPath

            ' The RefreshLink might fail if the new path
            ' isn't OK. So trap errors inline.
            On Error Resume Next
            tdf.RefreshLink
            ReattachTable = (Err = 0)
            On Error GoTo 0
        End If
    End Function
```

Knowing Your Limitations

Access cannot allow you to change the data source type of an existing attached table; nor can you change the name of the base table. For example, you cannot change an attached Paradox table into an attached dBASE III table, and you cannot change an attachment based on MYCUST.DBF into one based on MYCUST2.DBF. You can change only the path of an existing attached table.

If you need to change the type or base table name of an existing attached table, you must first delete the attached table and then re-create it. Note that deleting an attached table does not delete the underlying table, only the Access link to that table.

Determining the Type of an Attached Table

When you examine an attached table, you may want to know its type. The function in Listing 6.7 (from basAttach in CH06.MDB) returns the type of an attached table as a string representing the portion of the Connect string that indicates the attachment type.

The logic behind the function is simple. It takes four steps to determine the attachment type, attempting to be as "smart" about it as possible. It first compares the Attributes property of the table in question against the intrinsic constant, db-AttachedODBC. If this comparison returns a nonzero value, you're assured that the table is an ODBC table, and the function returns "ODBC".

The rest of the tests count on the tabledef's Connect property. If the string is zero-length, the table must be native (nonattached). If the first character is a semicolon, the table must be an attached Access table. Otherwise the function returns the portion of the Connect property that falls before the first semicolon in the string.

Listing 6.7

```
Function adhGetTableType(strTableName As String) As String

    ' Return the type of table, given the name:
    '    "Unknown" (table doesn't exist?)
    '    "ODBC"
    '    "Access Native"
    '    "Access Attached"
    '    or the specific attachment type

    Dim db As Database
    Dim strTableType As String
    Dim strConnect As String
    Dim tdf As TableDef
    Dim strConnectType As String
    Dim intPos As Integer

    On Error GoTo adhGetTableType_Err
    Set db = CurrentDb()
    Set tdf = db.TableDefs(strTableName)

    If (tdf.Attributes And dbAttachedODBC <> 0) Then
```

```
                strTableType = "ODBC"
        Else
            strConnect = tdf.Connect
            If Len(strConnect) = 0 Then
                strTableType = "Access Native"
            ElseIf Left$(strConnect, 1) = ";" Then
                strTableType = "Access Attached"
            Else
                intPos = InStr(strConnect, ";")
                If intPos > 0 Then
                    strTableType = Left$(strConnect, intPos - 1)
                Else
                    strTableType = "Unknown"
                End If
            End If
        End If
    End If

adhGetTableType_Exit:
    adhGetTableType = strTableType

adhGetTableType_Err:
    adhGetTableType = "UNKNOWN"
    Resume adhGetTableType_Exit
End Function
```

Working with Recordsets

In almost any Access application, sooner or later you'll need to manipulate data from VBA. DAO provides a rich set of data access objects to allow you to view, edit, add, and delete fields, rows, and tables. In its attempt to be as flexible as possible, Jet provides three separate means of working with data: tables, dynasets, and snapshots. Each has its own uses and capabilities. The following sections discuss these issues.

Meet the Recordsets

Although Jet provides three types of recordset objects, the one you use in any given situation depends on the source of the data being referenced and the methods you need to use to access the data. Table 6.4 lists each recordset type, along with its benefits and drawbacks.

TABLE 6.4   Recordset Types and Their Benefits/Drawbacks

Recordset Type	Description	Benefits	Drawbacks
Table	Set of records in a table in a database	Can use indexes for quick searches. Data can be edited	Works only works for local Access tables, not attached tables
Dynaset	Set of pointers (bookmarks) referring to data in tables or queries in a database	Can include data from multiple tables, either local or attached. Can be based on a SQL string. Data can be edited in most cases	Some dynasets may not be editable. Cannot perform indexed searches using the faster Seek method
Snapshot	Copy of a set of records as it exists at the time the snapshot is created	Can optionally be set to scroll forward only, allowing faster operations	Data cannot be edited. All records in a record-set's data source are read before control is returned to the program. Doesn't reflect changes to data made in a multiuser environment. A snapshot is a picture of the data at the time the snapshot is created, and no updates will be reflected in its set of rows. Cannot perform indexed searches using the faster Seek method

Creating a Recordset

You use an expression such as one of the following to create a recordset:

Dim rst As Recordset

Set rst = db.OpenRecordset(*Source, Type , Options, LockEdits*)

or

Set rst = *object*.OpenRecordset(*Type, Options, LockEdits*)

(The Type, Options, and LockEdits parameters are optional.)

In the first example you're creating a new recordset based on something in the database referred to by the database variable db. The *Source* parameter indicates where the data will come from and must be one of the following:

- Name of an existing table
- Name of an existing query that returns rows
- A SQL statement that returns rows

For table-type recordsets, the source can only be the name of an existing table.

In the second example, *object* can be any previously opened database object that returns rows, such as a table, a query, or even another recordset variable. Because you've already specified the source of the data, you needn't specify it again when creating a recordset based on an existing object.

In both cases the *Type* parameter specifies the type of the recordset. It should be one of the following built-in constant values:

- dbOpenTable, to open a table recordset
- dbOpenDynaset, to open a dynaset recordset
- dbOpenSnapshot, to open a snapshot recordset
- dbOpenForwardOnly, to open a forward-only type recordset (cannot be cloned and supports only the MoveNext method)

If you don't specify a type, Access automatically chooses the type it will open for the given *Source*. For example, if you create a recordset based on a table in the current database and don't specify *Type*, Access automatically opens a table-type recordset. Likewise, if *Source* is an attached table, a query, or a SQL string and you've not specified the *Type* parameter, Access automatically opens a dynaset recordset. In addition, you cannot specify dbOpenTable unless the *Source* parameter is the name of a local table. If you do, Access triggers trappable error 3011, "Couldn't find object...," for SQL expressions or 3219, "Invalid operation," for attached tables.

The *Options* parameter controls the multiuser access and update behavior of the recordset. It can be one of the values listed in Table 6.5.

TABLE 6.5   Options for Recordsets

Constant	Description
dbAppendOnly	You can only append new records (Applies only to dynaset-type recordsets.)
dbSQLPassThrough	Causes the SQL to be passed through directly to the back-end server for processing (Applies only to snapshot-type recordsets.)
dbSeeChanges	Jet triggers a run-time error if another user changes data you're currently editing (Applies only to dynaset-type recordsets.)
dbDenyWrite	Other users can't modify or add records. This effectively write-locks the recordset's underlying data source(s). Note that when you lock a dynaset recordset, you are locking all the underlying tables
dbDenyRead	Other users can't view records. By setting this option you are completely locking other users out of viewing the table (Applies only to table-type recordsets.)
dbForwardOnly	The recordset is a forward-scrolling snapshot. Use this type of recordset when you are making only one pass through the records. Since a forward-only snapshot does not copy data into a scrollable buffer, it can run much more quickly. Supplied for backward compatibility—see the dbOpenForwardOnly option. (Applies only to snapshot-type recordsets and cannot be used in conjunction with the dbOpenForwardOnly option.)
dbReadOnly	You can only view records; other users can modify them. This is a useful safeguard that can keep your code from inadvertently modifying data
dbInconsistent	Inconsistent updates are allowed (Applies only to dynaset-type recordsets, and only one of dbConsistent and dbInconsistent is allowed.)
dbConsistent	Only consistent updates are allowed (Applies only to dynaset-type recordsets, and only one of dbConsistent and dbInconsistent is allowed.)

The *LockEdits* parameter controls the concurrency of multiple users' access to the new recordset. Choose one or more of the following values:

- **dbReadOnly:** You can only view records; other users can modify them. Use this flag in either the Options parameter or the LockEdits parameter, but not both.

- **dbPessimistic:** Use pessimistic locking. A page is locked as soon as you use the Edit method and stays locked as long as you're editing any data in the page. This is the default for Jet.

- **dbOptimistic:** Use optimistic locking. A page is locked only when you use the Update method and is therefore only locked long enough to write the data to the table.

See online help for more information on interactions between the various settings.

Consistent versus Inconsistent Updates

When you create a recordset object based on more than one table, Access by default allows you to make changes only to the "many" side of a join. This is known as a *consistent update*. At times you may want to update both sides of join. To do this, set the dbInconsistent option. This allows you to update fields in both sides of the join. Note that this may violate the relationships between tables that your application needs. It is up to you to provide the necessary code to ensure that any "implied" referential integrity is maintained.

If you've turned on referential integrity for a relationship and enabled cascading updates, the dbInconsistent and dbConsistent options will cause identical behavior. In this case the referential integrity takes control, and the cascading updates will update the "many" side of the relationship when you update the "one" side.

Creating Recordset Objects

The following examples show a number of ways you can create recordset objects. This list isn't exhaustive, but it does show some representative cases.

- **To create a recordset based on a table or a saved query:**

```
Dim db As Database
Dim rstCustomers As Recordset
Dim rstSales As Recordset

Set db = CurrentDb()

' This will create a table-type Recordset.
Set rstCustomers = db.OpenRecordset("tblCustomers", _
```

```
                dbOpenTable)

                ' This will create a dynaset-type Recordset.
                Set rstSales = db.OpenRecordset("qryCustSales", dbOpenDynaset)
```

- To create a dynaset-type recordset based on a SQL string:

```
        Dim db As Database
        Dim rstCustomers As Recordset
        Dim strSQL As String

        strSQL = "SELECT [Contact Name] As Name From Customers " & _
        "ORDER BY [Contact Name]"
        Set db = CurrentDb()
        Set rstCustomers = db.OpenRecordset(strSQL, dbOpenDynaset)
```

- To create a table-type recordset that locks other users out of the source's records:

```
        Dim db As Database
        Dim rstCustomers As Recordset

        Set db = CurrentDb()
        Set rstCustomers = db.OpenRecordset( _
        "tblCustomers", dbOpenTable, dbDenyRead)
```

- To create a snapshot-type recordset based on a table:

```
        Dim db As Database
        Dim rstCustomers As Recordset

        Set db = CurrentDb()
        Set rstCustomers = db.OpenRecordset("tblCustomers", _
        dbOpenSnapshot)
```

Moving through a Recordset

Once you've created a recordset, Access provides a variety of methods for navigating through the rows: MoveFirst, MoveLast, MovePrevious, and MoveNext. Each of these works in the manner you would expect, based on the name. In addition, Access provides the Move method, which can move a specified number of rows forward or backward, either from the current row or from a stored bookmark. If the object is a table-type recordset, the movement follows the order of the active index, which you can set using the Index property of the recordset. If you have not specified the index for table-type recordsets, the row order is undefined. Recordsets also support the AbsolutePosition and PercentPosition properties, which allow you to read and write the current position within the recordset, based on the data in the current set of rows. (Neither forward-scrolling nor table-type recordsets support the AbsolutePosition property, but the other types do. Forward-scrolling recordsets also don't support the PercentPosition property, although table-type recordsets allow you to use this property.)

Using the Move Method

Although the actions of the other Move... methods are obvious, based on their names, the Move method is a bit more ambiguous. The Move method of a record-set accepts one or two parameters:

rst.Move *rows*[,*start*]

The *rows* parameter indicates the number of rows to move (greater than 0 for forward, less than 0 for negative), and the optional *start* parameter can contain a saved bookmark. If you supply the value for the bookmark, Access starts there and moves the appropriate number of rows from that spot. If you don't specify the start location, Access assumes you want to start moving from the current row. See the section "Adding New Rows to a Recordset" later in this chapter for an example of using the Move method.

> **NOTE** When working with a forward-only recordset, the *rows* parameter must be a positive integer, and you can't specify a bookmark. You can only move forward a specific number of rows from the current location.

Using the AbsolutePosition and PercentPosition Properties

You can set the value of either the AbsolutePosition property or the Percent-Position property to move to a specific row in the recordset. If you wanted to move to the row approximately 50 percent of the way through your rows, you could use code like this:

```
rst.PercentPosition = 50
```

To move to the 35th row in the rows currently in the recordset, given the current filtering and sorting, you could try this:

```
rst.AbsolutePosition = 35
```

You can also use these two properties to tell where you are in the recordset.

TIP Table-type recordsets do not support the AbsolutePosition property. That's just one more reason not to use table-type recordsets for anything but lookups. In addition, forward-scrolling recordsets do not support either the AbsolutePosition or the PercentPosition property.

WARNING The AbsolutePosition property is *not* a record number and should not be thought of as such. It simply returns the current row's position within the current set of rows, and it will change as you modify the filter or the sort order of the rows. To be able to find a row, no matter how you've modified the sorting or filtering, you'll need to use a bookmark (see the section "Using Bookmarks" later in this chapter) or store the primary key for later retrieval.

Finding the Number of Rows in a Recordset

In spite of any implication made by its name, the RecordCount property of recordsets may not return the actual number of rows in a given recordset. It actually returns the number of rows *accessed so far* in the recordset if the recordset is not a table-type recordset. This common misconception leads to a lot of confusion. To find the actual number of rows in a recordset, you must first use the MoveLast method (and then move somewhere else, if you like) before checking the value of the RecordCount property. If you don't move to the last row, the RecordCount property returns either 0 (if there are no rows) or 1 (if one or more rows exist) when you first create the recordset.

Table-type recordsets maintain their RecordCount property, so you needn't move to the last row. When you work with linked TableDef objects (not record-sets based on them), Jet always returns −1 for the RecordCount property.

In a single-user environment, the RecordCount property always correctly returns the number of rows in the recordset, once you've let Access calculate how many there are by moving to the last row. If you delete a row, either interactively or programmatically, the RecordCount property stays in sync. In a multiuser environment things are a bit more complex. If you're sharing data with another user and you both have a recordset open that's based on the same data, deletions made on the other machine won't immediately show up on your machine. Access won't update the RecordCount value until the code actually accesses the deleted row, at which point Access decrements the RecordCount. Therefore, in a multiuser environment, if you must know exactly how many rows are currently in the recordset, you should take the following steps:

1. Use the Requery method on the recordset object.

2. Use the MoveLast method to move to the end of the recordset.

3. Check the RecordCount property for the current value.

You could use the GetRecordCount function in Listing 6.8 as a simple example. (You'll find GetRecordCount in basRecordset in CH06.MDB.) It uses the Restart-able property of the recordset to make sure it can requery the recordset and just returns −1 if it can't. In that case the caller would know that the GetRecordCount function wasn't able to requery the recordset and that it needs to find a less generic means of solving the problem. Once GetRecordCount knows it can requery the recordset, it follows the steps outlined above, preserving and reset-ting the position in the recordset using the recordset's Bookmark property. (See the section "Using Bookmarks" later in this chapter for more information.) This function is actually useful only for dynaset-type recordsets because table-type recordsets can't be requeried and snapshot-type recordsets don't need to be requeried. Because a snapshot-type recordset won't reflect any changes made by other users, its RecordCount property won't change once it's created.

Listing 6.8

```
Function GetRecordCount(rst As Recordset) As Long

    ' Return the current record count for a Recordset.
    ' If the Recordset isn't Restartable (and table-type
    ' Recordsets aren't) then just return -1, indicating
    ' that the caller needs to reopen the Recordset in order
    ' to pick up any foreign changes.

    Dim varBM As Variant

    With rst
        If .Restartable Then
            .Requery
            If .Bookmarkable Then
                varBM = .Bookmark
            End If
            .MoveLast
            GetRecordCount = .RecordCount
            If .Bookmarkable Then
                .Bookmark = varBM
            End If
        Else
            GetRecordCount = -1
        End If
    End With
End Function
```

Testing for Boundaries

Every recordset supports two properties, BOF and EOF, that indicate whether
the current row is currently at the end of the recordset (EOF) or at the beginning of the
recordset (BOF):

- If you use MovePrevious while the first row is current, BOF becomes True
  and there is no current row.

- If you use MovePrevious again, BOF stays True but a run-time error occurs.

- If you use MoveNext while the last row is current, EOF becomes True and there is no current row.

- If you use MoveNext again, EOF stays True but a run-time error occurs.

Testing for an Empty Recordset

Often when you create a recordset you want to know immediately whether that recordset actually contains any rows. It's quite possible to create a recordset that doesn't return any rows, and you might need to take different steps based on whether the result contained any rows.

You can test for an empty recordset in a number of ways, but the two methods that follow ought to serve your needs. The following expression:

```
Set rst = db.OpenRecordset("qryCust")
If Not rst.BOF And Not rst.EOF Then
    ' You'll only be in here if there are some rows.
End If
```

checks to see whether both the BOF and the EOF properties for the recordset are True. If so, there must *not* be any rows, because that's the only way the current position could be at both the beginning and the end of the recordset. In addition, you often will want to loop through the rows of your recordset. In that case you needn't check; just write the loop so that it won't even start if there are no rows:

```
Set rst = db.OpenRecordset("qryCust")
Do Until rst.EOF
    ' Process rows in here
Loop
```

You can also check the RecordCount property of a recordset: if it's 0, you know there aren't any records in the recordset. For example, you might use code like this:

```
Set rst = db.OpenRecordset("qryCust")
If rst.RecordCount > 0 Then
    ' You'll only be in here if there are some rows.
End If
```

You may find this technique easier to use.

Looping through All the Rows

Although you're likely to have less reason than you'd think to loop through all the rows of a recordset (that's what action queries are for), the syntax is quite simple. The code in Listing 6.9 walks through a recordset backwards, from the end to the beginning, and if there are any records to be had, it prints out one of the fields in the underlying data. (Look for ListNames in basRecordset.)

Listing 6.9

```
Function ListNames()
    Dim db as Database
    Dim rst As Recordset

    Set db = CurrentDb()
    Set rst = db.OpenRecordset("tblCustomers")
    ' Check first to see if there are any rows.
    With rst
        If .RecordCount > 0 Then
            ' Move to the end.
            .MoveLast
            ' Loop back towards the beginning.
            Do Until .BOF
                Debug.Print ![ContactName]
                .MovePrevious
            Loop
        End If
        .Close
    End With
End Function
```

Using Arrays to Hold Recordset Data

You can use the GetRows method of any recordset to copy its data into a variant variable. Access will create a two-dimensional array with enough space to hold the data:

```
varData = rst.GetRows(intRowsToGrab)
```

You don't have to dimension or size the array; Access will do that for you. Because arrays give you random access to any row or column within the array, you may find it more convenient to work with arrays than with the recordset itself. For example, if you want the fastest access to data that you don't need to write to, you might want to use a forward-only recordset. But using this type of snapshot limits your movement in the data. If you create a forward-only recordset and copy its data to an array, you've got the best of both worlds: fast access *and* random access.

If you ask for more rows than exist, Access returns as many as there are. Use the UBound function to find out how many rows were actually returned:

```
intRows = UBound(varData, 2) + 1
```

The ", 2" tells UBound to find the number of rows (the second dimension of the array); then you must add 1 to the result, because the array is zero-based.

TIP

Be careful when creating your recordset before calling the GetRows method. Because Access will copy all the columns, including memos and long binary fields, you may want to exclude large fields from the recordset before you create the array; they can consume large amounts of memory and can be slow to load.

The following code (from basRecordset in CH06.MDB) fills an array with data and then prints it out backwards:

```
Function TryGetRows()
    ' Use an array to process data in a recordset.

    Dim db As Database
    Dim rst As Recordset
    Dim varData As Variant
    Dim intCount As Integer
    Dim intI As Integer

    Set db = CurrentDb()
    Set rst = db.OpenRecordset("tblCustomers", _
     dbOpenSnapshot, dbForwardOnly)
    ' Pick some arbitrary large number of rows to retrieve.
    varData = rst.GetRows(1000)

    ' How many rows did it actually send back?
    intCount = UBound(varData, 2) + 1
    ' Loop through all the rows, printing out the
```

```
    ' data from the second column.
    For intI = intCount - 1 To 0 Step -1
        Debug.Print varData(1, intI)
    Next intI
End Function
```

Creating a Recordset Based on a Querydef

If you need to create a recordset based on any select query (about which you might know nothing at all until your program is running), you must be prepared to supply the recordset with all the parameters the querydef requires. Without DAO, doing so requires knowing in advance what the parameters are and supplying their values in your code. Using DAO, you can loop through all the parameters of your querydef and evaluate the necessary parameters. QueryDef objects provide a useful Parameters collection, each element of which represents a single query parameter.

A problem occurs because Access cannot fill in the parameters' values for you when you're creating a recordset based on a querydef, even if the parameter values are available to Access. It's up to you to supply those values for the querydef before you attempt to create the recordset.

TIP Your query won't be able to run at all unless all the necessary parameters are available. If your query uses form objects as parameters, for example, you need to make sure the appropriate form is open and running, with appropriate values filled in, before you attempt to run a query based on those parameters.

The following code works with any QueryDef object that represents a select query:

```
Dim db As Database
Dim qdf As QueryDef
Dim prm As Parameter
Dim rst As Recordset

Set db = CurrentDb()
```

```
Set qdf = db.QueryDefs("qrySomeQuery")
For Each prm In qdf.Parameters
    prm.Value = Eval(prm.Name)
Next prm
Set rst = qdf.OpenRecordset(dbOpenDynaset)
```

The code loops through all the parameters of the object (and there may be none, in which case the loop won't ever execute), pointing a parameter variable at each of the parameters for the querydef, one at a time. For each parameter, the code evaluates the Name property using the Eval function and assigns the return value to the Value property of the parameter. This retrieves the value of each parameter, without your having to know in advance where the parameter is getting its value.

For example, if your query has a single parameter, on the City field:

```
Forms!frmInfo!CityField
```

the QueryDef container contains a single parameter object, for which the Name property is Forms!frmInfo!CityField. Through the use of the Eval function, the code in the previous example retrieves the value stored in that field and assigns it to the *Value* property of the specific parameter object. This satisfies the needs of the QueryDef object, and you'll be able to create the recordset you need, based on that querydef. The Incremental Search example in Chapter 7 uses this mechanism to allow the underlying code to create a recordset on almost any select query, whether or not it requires parameter values.

Finding Specific Records

You handle the task of finding specific data in a recordset in different ways, depending on the type of the recordset. Table-type recordsets can use an indexed search to find data, but dynaset- and snapshot-type recordsets often cannot.

Finding Data in Table-Type Recordsets

If you've created a table-type recordset object, you can use the fast Seek method to locate specific rows. (Attempting to use the Seek method with any recordset other than a table-type recordset results in run-time error 3219, "Invalid Operation.") You must take two specific steps to use the Seek method to find data:

1. Set the recordset's Index property. This tells Access which index you'd like it to search through. If you want to use the primary key for searching, you must know

the name of the primary key. (It's usually PrimaryKey, unless your application has changed it.)

2. Use the Seek method to find the value you want, given a search operator and one or more values to search for. The search operator must be <, <=, =, >=, or >, indicating how you want Access to search. If the operator is =, >=, or >, Access searches from the beginning of the recordset. Otherwise it starts at the end and works its way backward. To indicate to Access what it needs to search for, you supply one or more values, corresponding to the keys in the index you selected. If you based your index on one value, you need to supply only one value here. If your index includes multiple columns, you must supply all the values unless your search operator is something other than =.

For example, if your database contained an index named OrderIndex consisting of three columns—OrderNumber, OrderItem, and OrderDate—and you wanted to find the first item for order number 3, order item 17, for any date, the following fragment could get you to the correct row:

```
rst.Index = "OrderIndex"
rst.Seek ">=", 3, 17
```

The values you send to the Seek method must match the datatypes of the values in the index. In this case the values were numeric. Had they been strings or dates, you would have needed to use matching datatypes in the call to the Seek method.

Once you've used the Seek method to find a row, you must, *without fail,* use the recordset's NoMatch property to check that you actually found a row. The following code expands on the previous fragment, handling the success or failure of the seek:

```
rst.Index = "OrderIndex"
rst.Seek ">=", 3, 17
If rst.NoMatch Then
    MsgBox "Unable to find a match!"
Else
    MsgBox "The item name is: " & rst![ItemName]
End If
```

> **TIP**
>
> The Seek method always starts at the beginning (or end) of the recordset when it searches. Therefore, using Seek inside a loop, searching for subsequent rows that match the criteria, is generally fruitless. Unless you modify the value once you find it so that further searches no longer find a match on that row, your loop will continually find the same row.

Finding Data in Dynaset and Snapshot-Type Recordsets

Unlike table-type recordsets, dynaset- and snapshot-type recordsets cannot use the Seek method for finding data. Because these recordsets might well be based on ordered subsets of the original data, Access can't always use an index to speed up the search. Therefore, a search involving dynasets or snapshots might be a linear search, visiting every row in the recordset until it finds a match. Access will use an index if it can.

On a bright note, however, Access provides much greater flexibility in dynaset/ snapshot searches. The four different methods (FindFirst, FindNext, FindPrevious, and FindLast) allow you to optimize the search so it has to look through the smallest number of rows to find the data it needs. Because you can use FindNext with these searches, you won't need to start back at the beginning of the recordset to find subsequent matches. In addition, you can use loops to walk your way through the records because you can restart the search without going back to the first row.

You use the same syntax for each of these methods:

Recordset.{FindFirst | FindPrevious | FindNext | FindLast} *criteria*

where *Recordset* is an open dynaset- or snapshot-type recordset variable and *criteria* is a WHERE clause formatted as though in a SQL expression, without the word *WHERE*. For example, the following fragment searches for a last name of "Smith".

```
rst.FindFirst "[LastName] = 'Smith'"
```

Just as with the Seek method, you must follow every call to a Find method with a check of the recordset's NoMatch property. If that property is True, there is no current row, and the search fails. Often, when performing some operation that requires looping through all the rows that match some criteria, you can use code like this:

```
strCriteria = "[LastName] = 'Smith'"
With rst
```

```
        .FindFirst strCriteria
        Do While Not .NoMatch
            ' Since you know you found a match,
            ' do something with the current row.
            Debug.Print ![FirstName]
            .FindNext strCriteria
        Loop
End With
```

Of course, many such loops can be replaced with action queries, which are almost always a better solution to the given programming problem.

Using Variables in Strings

In building criteria for Find methods and in several other places in VBA (when calling domain functions and when creating SQL strings, for example), you often need to embed variable values into a string. Because Jet has no way of finding the value of VBA variables, you need to supply their values before you ask it to do any work for you. This can cause trouble because Access requires delimiters (quotes for strings, # for dates) around those values, but they aren't part of the variables themselves. This causes many Access developers, expert and neophyte alike, a great deal of anguish.

Numeric values require no delimiters at all, and you can simply represent a string variable using an expression like this:

```
"[NumericField] = " & intNumber
```

Date variables need to be delimited with # in an expression. The general solution for the date problem would be

```
"[DateField] = #" & varDate & "#"
```

That's not so bad!

The difficulty arises when you attempt to embed a variable containing a string value inside a string. For example, imagine you have a variable named strName that contains the name you'd like to match in your call to the FindFirst method (for the sake of simplicity here, "Smith"). You need to build a string that represents the required WHERE clause:

```
[LastName] = "Smith"
```

As a first attempt, you might try this:

```
strCriteria = "[LastName] = strName"
```

When you attempt to run the search, Access complains with a run-time error. The problem is that the expression in strCriteria was this:

```
[LastName] = strName
```

Most likely, no one in your table has that particular last name.

As a second attempt, you might try a new approach:

```
strCriteria = "[LastName] = " & strName
```

When you attempt to run the search this time, Access again complains with a run-time error. In this case it was using the value

```
[LastName] = Smith
```

which won't work because Access expects string values to be enclosed in quotes.

It should be clear by now that you need to get the quotes into that string. Access provides no fewer than three solutions to this problem.

All the solutions need to arrive at a value for strCriteria that looks like this:

```
[LastName] = "Smith"
```

or like this:

```
[LastName] = 'Smith'
```

Following are several solutions to this particular problem. These exercises are actually easier to envision if you do the work in reverse order.

The first solution is based on the fact that Access treats two quote characters side by side inside a string as representing one quote character. Remembering that every string expression must be enclosed in a pair of quotes, the first step in the first solution involves enclosing the final expression in those quotes. When enclosed in quotes, each internal quote needs to be replaced with two. The expression then becomes

```
"[LastName] = ""Smith"""
```

With the name separated out, the expression becomes

```
"[LastName] = """ & "Smith" & """"
```

Finally, with the constant replaced with the variable, the expression becomes

```
"[LastName] = """ & strName & """"
```

This last expression is the one you'd use with the FindFirst method.

You could also replace each quote with its ANSI representation, Chr$(34). If you go to the Immediate window and ask Access to print out the value

```
? Chr$(34)
```

it responds by printing a double-quote symbol. Therefore, again working backward:

```
[LastName] = "Smith"
```

becomes

```
"[LastName] = " & Chr$(34) & "Smith" & Chr$(34)
```

which becomes

```
"[LastName] = " & Chr$(34) & strName & Chr$(34)
```

If you create a string variable (perhaps named strQuote) and assign to it the value Chr$(34), you can use this expression:

```
"[LastName] = " & strQuote & strName & strQuote
```

You can also create a constant and assign to it a value that will resolve to be the string that is just a quotation mark. You can't use the Chr$ function when creating a constant, so this is the only way to create a constant value that does what you need:

```
Const QUOTE = """"
```

This might be the most straightforward solution to the problem.

The third solution involves replacing each internal quote with an apostrophe. That is, following the same backward steps:

```
[LastName] = "Smith"
```

becomes

```
[LastName] = 'Smith'
```

which becomes

```
"[LastName] = 'Smith'"
```

which becomes

```
"[LastName] = '" & "Smith" & "'"
```

which becomes (finally)

```
"[LastName] = '" & strName & "'"
```

The main problem with this solution (which many developers use) is that the value stored in strName cannot contain an apostrophe. If it did, you'd end up with an apostrophe embedded within a string that's enclosed in apostrophes. That's not allowed in Access' syntax. Therefore, you can use this method only when strName contains a value that could never contain an apostrophe. (Of course, the previous two solutions will fail if the string in question contains a double quote ("). But that's far less likely to happen than to have a string contain an apostrophe.)

To summarize, when building a string expression in Access that needs to contain a variable that represents a string, you must ensure that the final expression includes the quotes that enclose that string variable. The three suggested solutions are

```
Const QUOTE = """"
strCriteria = "[LastName] = """ & strName & """"
strCriteria = "[LastName] = " & QUOTE & strName & QUOTE
strCriteria = "[LastName] = '" & strName & "'"
```

In each case the important issue is that you place the *value* of the variable into the string being sent off to FindFirst rather than the *name* of the variable. The Jet engine (which ultimately receives the request to find a row) has no clue as to what to do with an Access variable. It's up to your code to supply the value before requesting help from the Jet engine.

A General Solution for Strings

If you want to completely generalize this problem, what about the case in which you have both apostrophes and quotes inside the text you're trying to embed in a string? This can't work:

```
strName = Forms!txtStoreName
strCriteria = "StoreName = " & QUOTE & strName & QUOTE
```

if the text box on the form happens to contain the string

Joe's "Pizza" Store

because the string itself contains a quote. This won't work, either:

```
strCriteria = "StoreName = '" & strName & "'"
```

because the string contains an apostrophe, too.

Because you'll be able to use neither quotes nor apostrophes as delimiters, what's the solution? In this case, and if you wish to be as general as possible in your solution, the answer is always to modify the delimited value by doubling any occurrences of whatever delimiter you choose. To do this you'll need a function that accepts a string value and the delimiter character as parameters and returns the string with any occurrences of the delimiter inside it "doubled up." You'll find that function, adhHandleQuotes, in basHandleQuotes in CH06.MDB. It can solve the previous problem:

```
strCriteria = "StoreName = " & _
 QUOTE & adhHandleQuotes(strName, QUOTE) & QUOTE
```
or
```
strCriteria = "StoreName = '" & _
 adhHandleQuotes(strName, "'") & "'"
```

The adhHandleQuotes function looks for all the delimiter characters inside strName, doubles them, and returns the string. Because Access allows doubled quotes inside a quoted string, all will be well, no matter what the delimiter and the string. If you're interested in seeing how adhHandleQuotes works, look in basHandleQuotes; the code uses brute-force string manipulations. If you want to use this technique in your own applications, just import the basHandleQuotes module and call adhHandleQuotes yourself.

Using Bookmarks

One of the primary functions needed in any database product is the ability to move quickly to a specified row. Access provides a number of ways to move about in recordsets, as seen in the section "Moving through a Recordset" earlier in this chapter. In addition to the methods presented there, Jet provides the Bookmark property, which allows you to quickly preserve and restore the current location within a recordset.

What Is a Bookmark?

Every active recordset maintains a single current row. To retrieve a reference to that row, you can store the bookmark for that row. The bookmark itself is a 4-byte long integer, the exact value of which is of no particular importance to you. Access uses the value, but under no circumstances can you use the value in any sort of calculation. You can perform two basic operations with bookmarks:

- Retrieve the value of the bookmark, in order to store it for later retrieval
- Set the value of the bookmark to a previously stored value, effectively setting the current row to be the row where you were when you originally saved the bookmark

You can retrieve and store as many bookmarks for a given recordset as you wish to maintain. Manipulating bookmarks in Access is the fastest way to maneuver through rows. For example, if you need to move from the current row and then move back to it, you can use one of two methods:

- **Store the primary key value:** Move from the row, and use the Seek or Find-First method to move back to the original row, using the saved primary key value to find the row.
- **Store the bookmark:** Move from the row, and then use the bookmark to move back to the original row.

The second method, using the bookmark, is much faster than the first. (For proof of this, see Chapter 17.) The code to do this might look something like the following example:

```
Dim varBM as Variant

varBM = rst.Bookmark
' Move to the first row.
rst.MoveFirst
'
' Now do whatever you moved from the current row to do.
'
' Then move back to the original row.
rst.Bookmark = varBM
```

Bookmarks and Record Numbers

If you're moving to Access from an Xbase environment, you might be tempted to think of bookmarks as a replacement for record numbers. In reality, that's not the case. Because Access is set based, row numbers really have no validity here. Access neither stores nor maintains a record number in its data, and you can't count on a bookmark to act as a permanent locator for any given row. Once you close a recordset, the bookmark value is no longer valid. In addition, you cannot use bookmarks as locators across different recordsets, even though the recordsets might be based on the same data and might contain the same rows in the same order. On the other hand, as stated in the preceding section, bookmarks provide an excellent means of moving about in an open recordset.

To Bookmark or Not to Bookmark

Not all recordsets in Access support the Bookmark property. Some data sources make it impossible for Access to maintain bookmarks, so it is your responsibility as a developer to check the Bookmarkable property of a recordset before attempting to use bookmarks with that recordset. Any recordset based on native Access data always supports bookmarks, but external data may not. If the recordset does not support bookmarks, attempting to use the Bookmark property results in trappable error 3159, "Not a valid bookmark."

Also be aware that there is no valid bookmark when you've positioned the current row to be the "new" row in a recordset. That is, the following code will trigger run-time error 3021, "No Current Record":

```
rst.MoveLast
' Move to the "new" row.
rst.MoveNext
varBM = rst.Bookmark
```

TIP In 16-bit versions of Access, one of the few ways to know you were currently working with the "new" row on a form was to count on the fact that retrieving a bookmark for the new row would fail. Access forms now provide the NewRecord property, making this technique unnecessary.

The Clone Method

For bookmarkable recordsets, you can use the Bookmark property to set and retrieve a marker for the current row. If you need to refer to the same recordset in two different ways, with two different current rows, you can use the Clone method to create a clone of a recordset. (To retrieve a clone of a form's recordset, use the form's RecordsetClone property instead of the Clone method. See the next section for more information.) With a clone of the original recordset, you can effectively maintain two separate "current" rows. This way you can compare the values in two of the rows in the recordset, for example.

You might be tempted to ask, "Why use the Clone method instead of just creating a new recordset based on the same source?" The answer is clear: creating a recordset clone is faster, in most cases, than creating a new recordset object. When the source of the data is a querydef, the difference can be enormous. Rather than reexecuting the entire query to produce the new recordset, the Clone method just points a separate object variable at the original set of rows. This effectively gives you two current rows and two bookmarks, based on the same data. You can also assign the bookmark from one recordset to its clone because they really are the same recordset.

Be aware of these two issues:

- A recordset created with the Clone method is documented as not having a current row. (Experimentation has shown that the clone does, in fact, inherit the original recordset's current position. Because this is explicitly documented as not being so, however, don't count on it!) To set a specific row as the current row, use any of the Find or Move methods (FindFirst, MoveFirst, and so on) or set the recordset's Bookmark property with a value retrieved from the original recordset. Remember that bookmark assignments work only when applied to identical recordsets (as are the original and its clone).

- Using the Close method on either the original recordset or its clone doesn't affect the other recordset.

As an example of using the Clone method, imagine the following situation: you'd like to create a function to compare certain columns in the current row to see whether they have the same value as the same columns in the previous row. You could use the Clone method to handle this problem, as you'll see in Listing 6.10. In this case you just check the value in the Country field. This example also uses the form's RecordsetClone property to retrieve the underlying recordset, which is covered in the next section. The sample form, frmLookup in CH06.MDB, uses this function in the Current event of the form to display or hide a label if the current Country field has the same value as the field in the previous row. Figure 6.4 shows this form in action.

FIGURE 6.4

frmLookup displays or hides a label, based on the comparison of the current and previous values in the Country field.

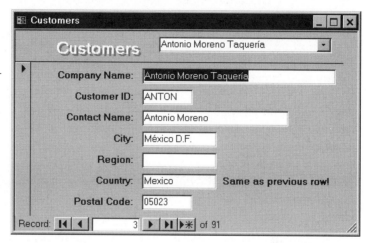

Listing 6.10

```
Function CheckPreviousRow(frm As Form, strFieldName As String) _
    As Boolean

    Dim rst As Recordset
    Dim rstClone As Recordset

    ' Set rst to refer to the form's Recordset,
    ' and set its bookmark to match the form's.
    Set rst = frm.RecordSetClone
    rst.Bookmark = frm.Bookmark

    ' Now create the Recordset clone, and make it
    ' refer to the same row as rst, which is on the same
    ' row as the form.
    Set rstClone = rst.Clone()
    rstClone.Bookmark = rst.Bookmark

    ' Move the clone Recordset to the previous row.
```

```
                ' If this puts us at the BOF, then the result has to be
                ' False, and leave the function.
                rstClone.MovePrevious
                If rstClone.BOF Then
                    CheckPreviousRow = False
                Else
                    ' If you're not at BOF, then retrieve
                    ' the necessary info.
                    CheckPreviousRow = _
                     (rst(strFieldName) = rstClone(strFieldName))
                End If

                rstClone.Close
            End Function
```

The RecordsetClone Property

You use the RecordsetClone property to retrieve a reference to a form's recordset. Any bound form maintains its own recordset, the set of rows onto which the form provides a window. You'll often need to manipulate that set of rows without showing your work on the visible form. To do this you create a recordset based on the form's recordset and do your manipulations there. For example, the code in List-ing 6.11, called from the AfterUpdate event of a combo box, searches for a specific company name on a form and sets the form to show the correct row once it finds a match. To see this form in action, try out frmLookup in CH06.MDB. Figure 6.5 shows this form in use.

FIGURE 6.5

Choosing a name from the combo box forces the code in Listing 6.11 to locate the correct row.

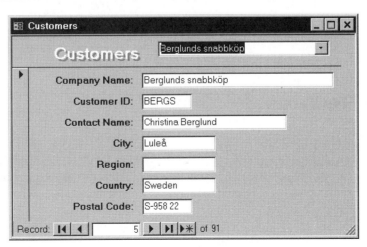

Listing 6.11

```
Const adhcQuote = """"
Sub cboCompany_AfterUpdate()
    Dim rst As Recordset

    Set rst = Me.RecordSetClone
    rst.FindFirst "[Company Name] = " & adhcQuote & _
     adhHandleQuotes(Me!cboCompany, adhcQuote) & adhcQuote
    If rst.NoMatch Then
        MsgBox "No match was found. Something is REALLY wrong!"
    Else
        Me.Bookmark = rst.Bookmark
    End If
    rst.Close
End Sub
```

> **NOTE**
>
> Assigning a recordset variable using the RecordsetClone property is the only time you set a recordset object without using the standard syntax, starting with a database object. Because you're retrieving a special kind of recordset, Access treats this case a bit differently. The results are almost the same, though: you end up with a recordset object variable referring to the set of rows filling the form. The recordset you're pointing to, however, doesn't support all the same properties as a real recordset. You can't set a form recordset's Filter or Sort property, for example. (For more information on using a form's RecordsetClone property, see Chapter 8. For more information on a recordset's Filter and Sort properties, see the next few sections.) Because you're not creating a new recordset, but obtaining a reference to an existing one, the current row is undefined once you return the reference.

Sorting Recordsets

When using recordsets as part of your applications, you'll often need to present the rows in a specific order. Again, Access treats table-type recordsets differently from dynaset- and snapshot-type recordsets. For all objects, however, remember that if you want a particular sort order, you must specify it yourself.

Sorting Table-Type Recordsets

For table-type recordsets, you can specify the ordering by setting the Index property. (Access does not allow you to set the Index property of any other type of recordset. Attempting to do so will only get you run-time error 3219, "Invalid Operation.") As soon as you set that property, the rows appear in their new ordering. After applying an index, Access appears to set the first row as the current row. This behavior is not documented, however, and you would be wise to explicitly set the current row after setting the Index property.

Listing 6.12 shows a function that lists the fields in the index, in index order, for each index in a specified table. ListIndexFields does its work by looping through the TableDef object's collection of indexes. For each index in the collection, it gathers up the index name and the field names and uses them to set the index and to print out the value of each field for each row in the recordset. To test ListIndexFields you might want to create a table with just a few rows and create an index for a few of the columns. Then, in the Immediate window, enter

? ListIndexFields("*YourTableName*")

replacing *YourTableName* with the name of your table. This should show all the indexes in your table, with the first indexed field in indexed order. (Look for ListIndexFields in basRecordset in CH06.MDB.)

Listing 6.12

```
Function ListIndexFields(strTable As String)
    Dim rst As Recordset
    Dim db As Database
    Dim tdf As TableDef
    Dim idx As Index
    Dim fld As Field

    Dim strField As String

    Set db = CurrentDb()
    Set tdf = db.TableDefs(strTable)
    Set rst = db.OpenRecordset(strTable, dbOpenTable)

    ' List values for each index in the collection.
    For Each idx In tdf.Indexes
        ' Set the index to use in the recordset
```

```
            rst.Index = idx.Name
            ' The index object contains a collection of fields,
            ' one for each field the index contains.
            Debug.Print
            Debug.Print "Index: " & rst.Index
            Debug.Print "============================="
            ' Move through the whole recordset, in index order,
            ' printing out the index fields, separated with tabs.
            rst.MoveFirst
            Do While Not rst.EOF
                For Each fld In idx.Fields
                    strField = strField & vbTab & rst(fld.Name)
                Next fld
                If Len(strField) > 0 Then
                    strField = Mid(strField, 2)
                End If
                Debug.Print strField
                strField = ""
                rst.MoveNext
            Loop
        Next idx
        rst.Close
End Function
```

Sorting Dynaset- and Snapshot-Type Recordsets

Just as with table-type recordsets, unless you specify a sorting order for dynaset- and snapshot-type recordsets, the rows will show up in an indeterminate order. The natural order for these derived recordsets is a bit more complex because it might depend on more than one table. In any case, if you need a specific ordering, you must set up that ordering yourself.

To create sorted dynaset- or snapshot-type recordsets, you have two choices, outlined in the next two sections.

Using a SQL ORDER BY Clause

You can create a recordset object using a SQL statement including an ORDER BY clause. To do so, specify the SQL expression as the row source for the OpenRecordset method. For example, this fragment:

```
Set db = CurrentDb()
```

```
Set rstSorted = db.OpenRecordset( _
 "SELECT * FROM tblCustomers ORDER BY [ContactName];")
```

creates a recordset based on tblCustomers, including all the columns, sorted by the LastName column. You can base a recordset on a SQL string only when creating recordsets based on a database object (as opposed to other uses of OpenRecordset, which can be based on tables, queries, or other recordsets). Attempting to do so will get you a run-time error. Creating a recordset using a SQL expression creates a dynaset-type recordset (unless you request a snapshot-type recordset).

Using the Sort Property

You can set the Sort property of any non–table-based recordset to change its sort order. The Sort property must be a string, in the same style as the ORDER BY clause of a SQL expression. You must specify the column on which to sort and, optionally, the ordering. The next time you create a recordset based on this recordset, the new sort order will take effect. (This is different from the way table-type recordset sorting works; there, the sorting takes effect immediately.) The following fragments show how to set the Sort property:

```
rst.Sort = "[LastName]"          ' Defaults to ascending
rst.Sort = "[LastName] Asc"      ' Ascending sort
rst.Sort = "[LastName] Desc"     ' Descending sort
```

Here are some items to remember when using the Sort property:

- The new sort order doesn't take effect until you create a new recordset, based on the old one.

- The Sort property doesn't apply to table-type recordsets. Use the Index property for them.

- It might be faster to open a new recordset based on a SQL expression than to use the Sort property.

The following code shows two methods for creating a sorted dynaset-type recordset:

```
Dim db As Database
Dim rst As Recordset
Dim rstSorted1 As Recordset
Dim rstSorted2 As Recordset
```

```
Set db = CurrentDb()
' Create a sorted Recordset using SQL.
Set rstSorted1 = db.OpenRecordset( _
 "SELECT * FROM tblCustomers ORDER BY [ContactName];")
' Create a sorted Recordset based on an existing Recordset.
Set rst = db.OpenRecordset("tblCustomers", dbOpenDynaset)
rst.Sort = "[LastName]"
Set rstSorted2 = rst.OpenRecordset()
'
' Do whatever you need to do here with the sorted recordsets
'
rst.Close
rstSorted1.Close
rstSorted2.Close
```

Filtering Non-Table Recordsets

Just as with sorting a recordset, you have two choices if you want to create a filtered subset of rows. These choices are outlined in the next two sections. You'll need to decide which method to use based on the circumstances of your application.

Using a SQL WHERE Clause

You can create a recordset by using a SQL statement including a WHERE clause. To do so, specify the SQL expression as the row source for the OpenRecordset method. For example, this fragment:

```
Set db = CurrentDb()
Set rstSorted = db.OpenRecordset( _
 "SELECT * FROM tblCustomers WHERE [ZipCode] = '90210'")
```

creates a recordset based on all the columns in tblCustomers, including only the rows where the ZipCode field is "90210". You can use this method only when creating recordsets based on a database object (as opposed to other uses of Open-Recordset, which can be based on tables, queries, or other recordsets). Attempting to do otherwise will get you a run-time error.

Using the Filter Property

You can also set the Filter property of any dynaset- or snapshot-type recordset to change the set of rows it contains. The Filter property must be a string, in the same style as the WHERE clause of a SQL expression. The next time you create a recordset based on this recordset, the new filtering will take effect. For example, you generally use the Filter property like this:

```
' rst is an existing recordset.
rst.Filter = "[Age] > 35"
Set rstFiltered = rst.OpenRecordset()
' Now rstFiltered contains all the rows from rst that
' have an [Age] field greater than 35.
```

Here are some items to remember when using the Filter property:

- The new filtering doesn't take effect until you create a new recordset based on the old one.

- The Filter property doesn't apply to table-type recordsets.

- It might be faster to open a new recordset based on a SQL expression than to use the Filter property.

- The new filtering will never retrieve additional rows from the original source tables. It will filter only rows that are in the base recordset you are filtering.

The following code shows two methods for creating a filtered dynaset-type recordset:

```
Dim db As Database
Dim rst As Recordset
Dim rstSQL as Recordset
Dim rstFiltered As Recordset

Set db = CurrentDb()
Set rstSQL = db.OpenRecordset( _
  "SELECT * FROM tblCustomers WHERE [ZipCode] = '90210';")
Set rst = db.OpenRecordset("tblCustomers", dbOpenDynaset)
rst.Filter = "[ZipCode] = '90210'"
Set rstFiltered = rst.OpenRecordset()
```

Editing Data in a Recordset Object

Of course, almost any database application needs to be able to add, update, and delete data. Access provides methods for accomplishing each of these tasks. The next few sections discuss the various data-manipulation methods that Access supports.

When Is a Recordset Modifiable?

You can modify data, of course, only if you have permission to do so. When you open a recordset, you may be able to retrieve the data for viewing only. If so, your attempts to modify the data will result in a run-time trappable error. You can always edit table-type recordsets unless someone else has placed a lock on that table (opened it exclusively or created a recordset based on it with an option that precludes others from changing its data). You can edit dynaset-type recordsets unless locks have been placed by other users, just as with table-type recordsets. In addition, join rules may prevent editing of certain fields. Snapshot-type recordsets are never modifiable, because they're read-only by definition.

Changing Data in a Recordset

To programmatically change the data in any recordset (assuming the recordset is updatable), take the following steps:

1. Move to the desired row.

2. Use the Edit method to put the current row in edit mode.

3. Make changes.

4. Use the Update method to save the edits.

Don't skip any of these steps, or your data won't be saved. The most important step, however, is the final one. If you make changes to the row but forget to use the Update method to commit those changes, Access treats the row as though you'd never made any changes at all. (If you want to explicitly discard a change, you can do so with the recordset's CancelUpdate method.)

The following code finds the first row in the recordset in which the LastName field contains "Smith" and changes it to "Smythe":

```
With rst
    .FindFirst "[LastName] = 'Smith'"
    If .NoMatch Then
        MsgBox "No Match was Found!"
    Else
        .Edit
            ![LastName] = "Smythe"
        .Update
    End If
End With
```

Adding New Rows to a Recordset

To programmatically add new rows to a recordset (assuming neither updatability nor security keeps you from doing so), follow these steps:

1. Use the AddNew method to add a new row. All fields will be set to their default values.

2. Fill in fields as needed.

3. Use the Update method to save the new row.

As in the preceding section, if you neglect to call the Update method before you leave the current row, Access discards any changes you've made and does not add the new row.

When you use the AddNew method, the current row remains the row that was current before you added the new row. If you want the new row to be the current row, employ the Move method, using as its parameter the bookmark returned from the LastModified property of the recordset.

The following example adds a new row to the recordset and fills in a few of the fields. Once it's done, it makes the new row the current row:

```
With rst
    .AddNew
        ![LastName] = "Smith"
        ![FirstName] = "Tommy"
```

```
    .Update

    .Move 0, .LastModified
End With
```

Dynaset-type recordsets treat new rows a bit differently than do table-type recordsets. For a dynaset-type recordset object, Access always places the new row at the end of the recordset. For table-type recordsets, if you've set the Index property, Access places the row at its correct spot in the index. For dynaset-type recordsets, Access adds the new row to the end of the underlying table. If you're working with a table-type recordset, though, new rows added to the table won't be seen by users who've based a recordset on that table until they refresh their rows.

In previous versions of Access (and the Jet database engine), adding new rows could result in page-lock collisions. With pessimistic locking, the final page of a table might have been locked, and your attempts to add a row would have failed. Starting with Access 95 (and Jet 3.0), these sorts of collisions should be a thing of the past. (See Chapter 12 for more information on inserting new rows and page locking.)

Deleting Data from a Recordset

To delete a row from a recordset, follow these steps:

1. Move to the desired row.

2. Use the Delete method to delete it.

> **TIP**
>
> You don't need to use the Update methods when deleting a row, unlike the other methods of modifying rows. Once you delete it, it's gone—unless, of course, you wrapped the entire thing in a transaction. In that case you can roll back the transaction to retrieve the deleted row.

> **TIP**
>
> After you delete a record, it is still the current record. The previous row is still the previous row, and the next row is still the next row. Use Move-Next to move to the next row, if that's where you'd like to be.

The code in Listing 6.13 deletes all the rows from a table, although it is not necessarily the best way to solve the problem. In reality, you'd use a delete query to do the work. To try this function out, check in basRecordset in CH06.MDB.

Listing 6.13

```
Function ZapTable(strTable As String)
    Dim db As Database
    Dim rst As Recordset

    Set db = CurrentDb()
    Set rst = db.OpenRecordset(strTable)
    With rst
        If rst.RecordCount > 0 Then
            .MoveFirst
            Do
                .Delete
                ' Without this MoveNext, Access would
                ' continually try to delete the same row,
                ' the first one.
                .MoveNext
            Loop Until .EOF
        End If
        .Close
    End With
End Function
```

Using Containers to Handle Saved Documents

A *container* object contains information about saved database objects. Its main purpose is to provide the Jet engine with some mechanism for knowing about all the Access UI objects. Because Jet provides security for Access, it must maintain information about ownership and permissions, and it does so in these containers. Some of the containers are provided by the Jet engine and some by the application. Table 6.6 lists the useful containers, the parent for each container, and what each contains.

Each container object contains a collection of Document objects, each of which is a saved object in the database. The Document objects contain information about

TABLE 6.6   Containers and Their Parents

Container	Parent	Contains Information about
Databases	Jet database engine	Containing database, database properties
Tables	Jet database engine	Saved tables and queries
Relationships	Jet database engine	Saved relationships
SysRel	Jet database engine	Saved relationship layout information
Forms	Microsoft Access	Saved forms
Reports	Microsoft Access	Saved reports
Scripts	Microsoft Access	Saved macros
Modules	Microsoft Access	Saved modules

the saved objects, but not about the data they contain. For example, the Tables container includes a Document object for each table and query in the database. Each document stores information about the permissions, creation date, and owner of the stored object. But documents in the Tables container don't store the actual data. The same goes for documents in the Forms container: each document object contains information about the form object but provides no information about the structure or content of the form itself. The Containers collection, and each container's collection of Documents, makes it possible to retrieve information about the documents in the database; this is how you can find out what exactly is *in* the database, when it was last modified, and so on.

TIP

Access 97 finally provides a method of working with code in modules, using the Modules collection. Seemingly unable to learn from past mistakes, the design team has again created a collection (that is, the collection of all *open* modules) with the same name as a container (the collection of all the *saved* modules). We thought that the confusion over the equivalently named Forms collection and Forms container would have taught the folks at Microsoft a lesson, but it appears not. For more information on working with the Modules collection, and programmatically creating and analyzing VBA code, see Chapter 22.

Each container object is a collection that contains non-engine objects. The Jet engine can get very limited information about them, such as their creator and creation time, through DAO. This allows the engine to know, in a limited sense, about the objects that are application specific. The main significance of containers is that they

- Give you information about the live Access objects; that is, they give you a mechanism you can use to walk through collections of non-DAO objects

- Provide the only method for retrieving information about your saved macros, modules, reports, and forms

- Let you treat non-engine objects as though they were data access objects instead of application-provided objects; that is, they let you use the set of DAO rules and tools with non-DAO objects

Because security is provided at the engine level, Jet has to know about non-DAO objects so it can handle their security. (For more information on this topic, see Chapter 14.)

To refer to a particular container, use the syntax

Containers("*name*")

or

Containers!*name*

where *name* is one of the items in the first column from Table 6.6.

NOTE The Forms, Reports, and Modules *containers* are very different from the Forms, Reports and Modules *collections*. Using the containers, you can work with any forms or reports in the database but can only retrieve information such as the owner, permissions, and date of creation. Using the collections, you can refer only to currently opened forms and reports, but you can retrieve information about the controls on the form, their layout, and so on.

To examine the various containers and their contents, run the function List-Containers in basContainers in CH06.MDB. This function can display, in the

Debug window, a list of containers and the documents within them and, if you like, all the properties and their values for each document. To make the function a bit more useful, you can pass it parameters that limit the output. (See the header comments for more information.) Listing 6.14 shows the function, and Figure 6.6 shows sample output.

FIGURE 6.6

ListContainers can display lists of all the containers and their properties.

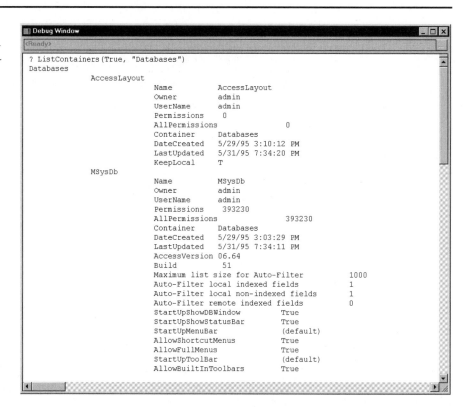

Listing 6.14

```
Function ListContainers(Optional fListProps As Variant, _
    Optional varContainer As Variant)

    ' List contents of containers, all or selected.
    ' Get lists of properties, too, if requested.

    ' In:
```

```
'    fListProps: (optional, default is False)
'        If True, list properties for all objects
'    varContainer: (optional, default is "ALL")
'        Leave blank for "ALL", or one of
'           "Databases", "Forms", "Modules", "Relationships"
'           "Reports", "Scripts", "SysRel", "Tables"

Dim db As Database
Dim con As Container
Dim doc As Document
Dim prp As Property

If IsMissing(fListProps) Then fListProps = False
If IsMissing(varContainer) Then varContainer = "ALL"

Set db = CurrentDb()
For Each con In db.Containers
    If varContainer = "ALL" Or (varContainer = con.Name) Then
        Debug.Print con.Name
        For Each doc In con.Documents
            Debug.Print , doc.Name
            If fListProps Then
                For Each prp In doc.Properties
                    Debug.Print , , prp.Name, prp.Value
                Next prp
            End If
        Next doc
    End If
Next con
End Function
```

Database Properties

Access allows you to set database properties with the File ➤ Database Properties menu. Those properties are stored as properties of the SummaryInfo document in the Databases container. If you set up user-defined properties for your database (choose the Custom tab on the File ➤ Database Properties dialog box to set these properties), they're stored as properties of the UserDefined document within the Databases container.

You may need to supply an interface for setting and retrieving your database's summary information from within your application. To get you started, we've supplied a simple form, frmSummaryInfo in CH06.MDB, that does the work for you and looks very similar to the built-in dialog box (see Figure 6.7).

FIGURE 6.7
frmSummaryInfo allows you to set and retrieve database summary info from your applications.

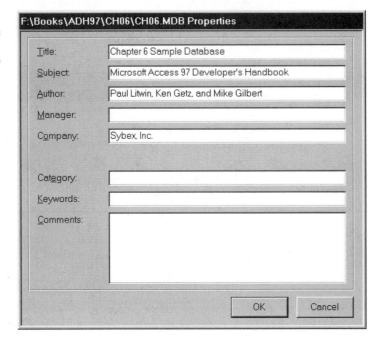

To use this form within your own applications, import it (frmSummaryInfo) and the module containing the property-handling functions, basHandleProps, from CH06.MDB. You may find it interesting to study the code in frmSummaryInfo's module. It makes several calls to the adhGetProp and adhSetProp functions, handling the various database summary information properties.

A Case Study: Using DAO

As an example of using DAO as part of an application, we've provided a simple replacement for the database window (see Figure 6.8) that you can import into any application. You can use it directly as is, or you can modify it to add new functionality. You might want to remove some of the objects for your own applications. For example, you might like to provide users with a list of only certain tables and queries. Perhaps you don't want to show your users a list of macros

FIGURE 6.8

The sample database container is simpler than the one you'll find in Access, but it provides many of the same features.

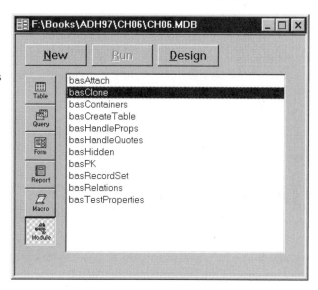

or modules. Given frmDBC as a starting place, you can make as many changes as you wish to fit your own needs. The point of the sample is to demonstrate the use of DAO when working with table and query objects and the Access-specific code to handle the other database objects: forms, reports, macros, and modules. In the interest of simplicity, we've modeled this form on the Access 2 database container. If your users are familiar with that interface, they'll be happy with this look. If not, you can certainly use one of the many custom controls available for Access to display this information in a different format. (For a different approach to this problem, see Chapter 19.)

Designing frmDBC

The design considerations for frmDBC were to

- Provide a list of all the tables, queries, forms, reports, macros, and modules in the current database

- Keep the interface as simple as possible

- Allow resizing of the list to match the size of the form

- Allow for customization

Although the interface is simple, the list box does resize to fit the form, no matter what size you choose for the form itself. Every time the form fires off its Resize event, the code figures out the current form size and resizes the list box inside the form accordingly.

The following sections discuss the form itself and how it does its work.

Choosing an Object Type and an Action

The buttons on the left side of frmDBC are part of an option group (grpObjects). When you click one of the buttons, the code attached to the option group's After-Update event refills the list box (lstObjects) that displays the list of objects. The particular list that lstObjects displays depends, of course, on the value of grpObjects.

> **TIP**
>
> To make the code as simple as possible, we've used the intrinsic constants acTable, acQuery, acForm, acReport, acMacro, and acModule wherever possible. These constants provide the values for the buttons in the option group and make up the choices available in all the Select Case statements within the code. Whenever possible, use the Access-defined constants in your code.

Once you've chosen an object type (and forced the list box to refill itself) and selected an object from the list, you can select one of the action buttons at the top of the form (New, Open, or Design). Depending on the circumstances, one or more of those buttons might have a different caption and might be disabled.

Displaying the Object List

To make the form work as simply as possible, frmDBC fills the list box (lstObjects) by providing a semicolon-delimited list of names as the RowSource property for the list box. This requires that the list box's RowSourceType property be set to "Value List", and the form's Open event procedure handles that chore. We could have used a list-filling callback function (see Chapter 7 for more information on list-filling callback functions) to fill the list box (and we did, in previous editions of this book) but decided on this simpler method instead. Because the RowSource property is limited to 2048 characters, the number of objects you can display in this sample form will be artificially constrained. The longer your object names, the fewer you'll be able to display in the list box. (Remember that every entry in the list will have an extra character, its trailing semicolon.) If you can accept that limitation, you may find this example a good starting place.

Filling the Object List

The GetObjectList function is the heart of this entire form. Given the object type to enumerate, it creates a semicolon-delimited list of object names and returns that string. Listing 6.15 shows the entire function, and the following sections go through the code, one bit at time.

Listing 6.15

```
Private Function GetObjectList( _
 ByVal intType As Integer) As String

    ' Returns a string with a semicolon-delimited list
    ' of object names.

    ' Parameters:
    '    intType -- one of acTable, acQuery, acForm,
    '               acReport, acMacro or acModule

    Dim db As Database

    Dim intI As Integer
    Dim fSystemObj As Boolean
    Dim ctr As Container
    Dim strName As String
    Dim fShowHidden As Boolean
    Dim fIsHidden As Boolean
    Dim strOutput As String
```

```
Dim fShowSystem As Boolean

On Error GoTo GetObjectListError
DoCmd.Hourglass True

Set db = CurrentDb()

' Are you supposed to show hidden/system objects?
fShowHidden = Application.GetOption("Show Hidden Objects")
fShowSystem = Application.GetOption("Show System Objects")

Select Case intType
    Case acTable
        Dim tdf As TableDef

        db.TableDefs.Refresh
        For Each tdf In db.TableDefs
            ' Check and see if this is a system object.
            fSystemObj = isSystemObject(acTable, _
             tdf.Name, tdf.Attributes)
            #If adhcTrackingHidden Then
                fIsHidden = IsHidden(acTable, tdf.Name)
            #Else
                ' If not tracking hidden objects,
                ' just assume it's not hidden!
                fIsHidden = False
            #End If
            ' Unless this is a system object and you're
            ' not showing system objects, or this table has its
            ' hidden bit set, add it to the list.
            If (fSystemObj Imp fShowSystem) And _
             ((tdf.Attributes And dbHiddenObject) = 0) _
             And (fIsHidden Imp fShowHidden) Then
                strOutput = strOutput & ";" & tdf.Name
            End If
        Next tdf
    Case acQuery
        Dim qdf As QueryDef

        db.QueryDefs.Refresh
        For Each qdf In db.QueryDefs
            ' Check and see if this is a system object.
```

```
                    fSystemObj = isSystemObject(acQuery, qdf.Name)
                    #If adhcTrackingHidden Then
                        fIsHidden = IsHidden(acQuery, qdf.Name)
                    #Else
                        ' If not tracking hidden objects,
                        ' just assume it's not hidden!
                        fIsHidden = False
                    #End If
                    ' Unless this is a system object and you're
                    ' not showing system objects, add it to
                    ' the list.
                    If (fSystemObj Imp fShowSystem) Then
                        If fIsHidden Imp fShowHidden Then
                            strOutput = strOutput & ";" & qdf.Name
                        End If
                    End If
                Next qdf
        Case acForm
            Set ctr = db.Containers("Forms")
        Case acReport
            Set ctr = db.Containers("Reports")
        Case acMacro
            Set ctr = db.Containers("Scripts")
        Case acModule
            Set ctr = db.Containers("Modules")
    End Select
    Select Case intType
        Case acForm, acReport, acMacro, acModule
            Dim doc As Document

            ctr.Documents.Refresh
            For Each doc In ctr.Documents
                #If adhcTrackingHidden Then
                    fIsHidden = IsHidden(intType, doc.Name)
                #Else
                    ' If not tracking hidden objects,
                    ' just assume it's not hidden!
                    fIsHidden = False
                #End If
                strName = doc.Name
                fSystemObj = isSystemObject(intType, strName)
                ' Unless this is a system object and you're
```

```
                        ' not showing system objects...
                        If (fSystemObj Imp fShowSystem) Then
                            ' If the object isn't deleted and its
                            ' hidden characteristics match those
                            ' you're looking for...
                            If Not isDeleted(strName) And _
                             (fIsHidden Imp fShowHidden) Then
                                ' If this isn't a form, just add it to
                                ' the list. If it is, one more check:
                                ' is this the CURRENT form? If so, and
                                ' if the flag isn't set to include
                                ' the current form, then skip it.
                                Select Case intType
                                    Case acForm
                                        If Not (conSkipThisForm And _
                                         (strName = Me.Name)) Then
                                            strOutput = strOutput & _
                                             ";" & strName
                                        End If
                                    Case Else
                                        strOutput = strOutput & _
                                         ";" & strName
                                End Select
                            End If
                        End If
                    Next doc
            End Select
        strOutput = Mid(strOutput, 2)

GetObjectListExit:
    DoCmd.Hourglass False
    GetObjectList = strOutput
    Exit Function

GetObjectListError:
    HandleErrors Err, "GetObjectList"
    Resume GetObjectListExit
End Function
```

The main body of GetObjectList, once it's initialized local variables and set up the environment by turning on the hourglass cursor, consists of a Select Case statement with one case for each of the possible object types. For tables and queries, the code uses DAO methods to compile the list. For forms, reports, macros, and modules, the code uses Access' version of DAO—its containers—to iterate through the different objects. (For a completely different solution to this same problem, see Chapter 19, which uses an undocumented function to retrieve lists of objects.)

Gathering Options

To emulate the built-in database window, frmDBC must know whether you've elected to display hidden and/or system objects. To gather this information, the GetObjectList function uses the Application.GetOption method. Based on the return values, the function sets the fShowHidden and fShowSystem variables; the function uses these variables to determine whether to include hidden and system objects in the output string. For more information on using Application.GetOption, see Appendix B.

Creating a List of Tables

The first step in compiling the list of tables is to refresh the TableDefs collection. This ensures that the collection is completely current and that it contains the entire list. Then, the code loops through each of the tabledefs, assigning the variable tdf to refer to each, in turn:

```
Dim tdf As TableDef
For Each tdf In db.TableDefs
'
'
Next tdf
```

Deciding Whether to Add a Table

For each particular tabledef, you may or may not want to add it to the output string. If you have not requested that the function include system tables and the current table is a system table, you'll want to skip it. In any case, the code always skips tables that have their hidden attribute set.

```
fSystemObj = isSystemObject(acTable, tdf.Name, tdf.Attributes)
' Unless this is a system object and you're not showing system
' objects, or this table has its hidden bit set,
' add it to the list.
If (fSystemObj Imp fShowSystem) And _
```

```
((tdf.Attributes And dbHiddenObject) = 0) _
And (fIsHidden Imp fShowHidden) Then
    strOutput = strOutput & ";" & tdf.Name
End If
```

Checking for System Objects

The first step in the preceding code was to determine whether or not the current table is a system object. To determine this you can call the function isSystemObject:

```
Private Function isSystemObject(intType As Integer, _
 ByVal strName As String, _
 Optional ByVal varAttribs As Variant)

    ' Determine whether or not the object named 'strName' is
    ' an Access system object.

    If IsMissing(varAttribs) Then
        varAttribs = 0
    End If

    If (Left$(strName, 4) = "USys") Or _
      (Left$(strName, 4) = "~sq_") Then
        isSystemObject = True
    Else
        isSystemObject = ((intType = acTable) And _
          ((varAttribs And dbSystemObject) <> 0))
    End If
End Function
```

In three instances the current object could be treated as a system object:

- If the name of the object is Usys followed by any text. This naming convention allows the user to create objects that Access will display, in the database container, only when the Show System Objects option is set to Yes.

- If the object is a query, built by Access for its own internal use with a name starting with "~sq_".

- If the object is a table and its Attribute field has its dbSystemObject bit set.

Checking for Inclusion

You'll want to include the table in your list unless one of the following situations exists:

- Its attribute includes the bit that indicates the table is to be hidden.
- You've asked to not include system tables, and this table is a system table.

Using Bitwise Operators to Check Attributes

Checking to see whether a particular attribute has been set for an object requires you to use the bitwise And operator. The And operator returns a non-zero value if the value you're checking and the appropriate intrinsic constant (dbSystemObject, in this case) have at least one bit set in the same position. Therefore, to check whether a particular object is a system table, you can use the following expression:

```
isSystemObject = ((intType = acTable) And _
  ((lngAttribs And dbSystemObject) <> 0))
```

This expression returns a True value if both parts of the expression are True; that is, if the type is acTable and the bitwise comparison of the object's attribute and dbSystemObject isn't 0.

To check whether the table's attribute includes the hidden bit, you need to check the return value from Anding it with dbHiddenObject. If

```
tdf.Attributes AND dbHiddenObject
```

returns a nonzero value, the matching bit is set in both values.

You also need to check whether to include a table, based on the fShowSystem setting and whether this particular table is a system table. Based on these two conditions, you have four possible outcomes, as shown in Table 6.7.

As you can see in Table 6.7, you'll want to include the current table in the output string unless the current table is a system table and you've elected not to include system tables. You could build a complex logical expression to indicate this information

TABLE 6.7   Decision Table for System Table Inclusion

System Table?	Include System Tables?	Include This Table?
Yes	Yes	Yes
Yes	No	No
No	Yes	Yes
No	No	Yes

to Access, but Access makes this a bit simpler by providing a single logical operator that works exactly as you need.

The IMP (implication) operator takes two values and returns a True value *unless* the first operand is True and the second is False. This exactly matches the truth table shown in Table 6.7. Given that the variable fSystemObj indicates whether or not the current table is a system object and the variable fShowSystem indicates whether or not you want to include system objects, you can use the expression

```
fSystemObj IMP fShowSystem
```

to know whether to exclude the table based on whether or not it's a system table. Therefore, to check both criteria for inclusion, you can use the following expression (which also checks for hidden objects in the same manner):

```
If (fSystemObj Imp fShowSystem) And _
  ((tdf.Attributes And dbHiddenObject) = 0) _
  And (fIsHidden Imp fShowHidden) Then
```

This expression returns a True value if all subexpressions return a True value.

Adding the Table

Once you've decided that a particular table is to be added to the list of tables, you'll want to place the Name property of the current tabledef in the output string:

```
strOutput = strOutput & ";" & tdf.Name
```

When the loop is done, the output string, strOutput, will contain one item for each acceptable table in the database.

Creating a List of Queries

To create a list of queries, the steps are almost completely parallel to the steps necessary to create a list of tables. The following sections discuss the few differences.

Using Different Datatypes

To manipulate queries rather than tables, you need to use querydef variables instead of tabledef variables. Therefore, the initialization code, when you are building the query list, looks like this:

```
Dim qdf As QueryDef
db.QueryDefs.Refresh
For Each qdf In db.QueryDefs
   '
   '
Next qdf
```

Aside from the changes from tabledef to querydef references, the code is identical to the code that handles tables.

Checking for System Objects

Because queries can't be system objects in the normal sense, the only way isSystemObject will return True is if the query has a name that starts with *Usys*. Therefore, in the call to isSystemObject, there's no point in passing in the object's attribute, because you aren't really interested in checking the attribute to see whether the query is a system object. The function call is

```
fSystemObj = isSystemObject(acQuery, qry.Name)
```

The third parameter (the object's attributes value) is optional because isSystemObject looks at the attribute only if the object happens to be a table.

Gathering Lists of Access Objects

Although the lists of objects in your Access database, aside from tables and queries, aren't handled by the Jet engine and aren't technically part of data access objects, we discuss them here just to complete the description of the replacement database container. From the users' point of view, there's no difference between Jet objects and Access objects, but from the developer's point of view, they're really separate entities.

Finding a Container

If you've asked GetObjectList to retrieve a list of the available forms, reports, macros, or modules, you won't be enumerating through a Jet collection. Instead, you'll be looping through one of four different Access containers. Because one container can be treated like any other, your first step is to create a variable of type Container to refer to the correct Access container. Following is the code from GetObjectList that performs this task:

```
Case acForm
    Set ctr = db.Containers("Forms")
Case acReport
    Set ctr = db.Containers("Reports")
Case acMacro
    Set ctr = db.Containers("Scripts")
Case acModule
    Set ctr = db.Containers("Modules")
```

Looping through the Containers

Once you've pointed the variable ctr at a particular container, the code to loop through all the elements of the container should look very familiar. Once you've determined that the current object matches the caller's interest in system objects, you have two new problems to handle:

- If this object is a form, should you list the current form?

- Is this object deleted? Access doesn't immediately remove deleted objects from the containers, and you won't want to display these objects in the list.

Set the constant conSkipThisForm, in the module's declarations area, to indicate whether you want to exclude the current form from the list. The following code fragment adds the current object name to the output string, depending on whether the item is deleted or hidden, and if it's the current form:

```
If Not isDeleted(strName) And _
 (fIsHidden Imp fShowHidden) Then
     ' If this isn't a form, just add it to
     ' the list. If it is, one more check:
     ' is this the current form? If so, and if
     ' the flag isn't set to include the current
     ' form, then skip it.
```

```
Select Case intType
    Case acForm
        If Not (conSkipThisForm And _
        (strName = Me.Name)) Then
            strOutput = strOutput & ";" & strName
        End If
    Case Else
        strOutput = strOutput & ";" & strName
End Select
End If
```

The isDeleted function takes a very low-tech approach to checking for deleted objects:

```
Private Function isDeleted (ByVal strName As String) As Boolean
    isDeleted = (Left(strName, 7) = "~TMPCLP")
End Function
```

The function looks for object names that start with ~TMPCLP, which is how Access renames deleted objects.

Finishing It Up

Finally, once you've created a string containing all the object names for the selected type, GetObjectList returns the string to the calling procedure. The calling function, ListObjects, uses that string to fill the list box's RowSource property.

Using frmDBC in Your Own Applications

To use frmDBC in your own applications, just import it. Because all the code it requires to run is encapsulated in its module, you need nothing else. However, you might want to consider making various alterations to it. For example, you might want to add some columns or remove some of the toggle buttons that appear along the left side of the form. In any case, we left the sample form simple so you can modify it for your own needs. Probably the only serious complication you'll run across is the resizing of the list box. You'll need to decide for yourself how resizing the form will affect the resizing of individual columns.

TIP

Although Jet does not expose a method for finding out whether any specific object is hidden (that is, you've set its Hidden property to True from the object's properties dialog), you can retrieve the information from a system table. This information is undocumented, and retrieving it for any specific object is slow, as well, because it requires a table access for each object. FrmDBC includes code to follow the setting of the Show Hidden Objects global option, but it's commented out and not included in the discussion here. If you want more information, look into basHidden in CH06.MDB. If you want to use this feature, you'll also need to distribute basHidden with frmDBC. See the comments in frmDBC for information on checking for hidden objects (using the adhcTrackHidden constant).

NOTE

We've actually included two versions of the sample database container. The second version, in frmDBCTab, uses the Access built-in tab control to choose the object type. Because this form uses techniques we won't discuss until Chapter 7, it seemed best to use and discuss the simpler version here. If you're interested, try out frmDBCTab—all the code is basically the same.

Summary

This chapter has presented a broad introduction to programming Jet's object model using DAO. Although we've made attempts to bring our own personal perspectives into this chapter, a full understanding of this material requires far more depth than we can cover here. Because of the similarities between the object models in Access, Visual Basic, and the rest of Microsoft Office, you would be well served to spend as much time as possible "digging in" to this material, because this is clearly the way future Microsoft products will be going.

This chapter has covered these major topics:

- Access' support for DAO with Jet
- Objects that Jet provides
- Referring to objects

- Iterating through collections

- Using properties

- Jet data definition using DAO

- Working with Jet's recordsets

- Using Access' application-supplied containers

There's much, much more to know. As a start, Chapter 14, focusing on Access Security, covers (among other things) programmatic control over security features using DAO. Chapter 15, which discusses client-server application development, will cover the other data access hierarchy, ODBCDirect.

PART III

Presenting Data

CHAPTER
SEVEN

7

Controlling Controls

- Using form and report controls

- Understanding control events and properties

- Using the Tag property in a standardized way

- Combining controls to work together

- Creating forms and controls programmatically

In this chapter you'll learn about some of the different Access controls, and you'll find some hints on deciding which control is best for a given datatype or situation, along with examples of many of the control types. In addition, you'll find a number of reusable solutions to common challenges you'll confront when designing your user interfaces.

Controls and Their Uses

Controls are the workhorses of Access applications. You can use them for inputting and outputting data, as well as for displaying static information. In addition, you can use controls as global variables, to calculate intermediate values, or to add aesthetic interest to your forms. Forms and reports share the same controls. (You can put a button on a report, for example, but it doesn't really make much sense to do so.) The focus of this chapter is on controls for forms.

You can think of controls in Access as being windows, just as all the other elements of a Windows application are windows. As with any window, a control can receive information from the user only when it has input focus. To allow a user to be able to enter text into a text box or to check an item in a check box, that control must first have been selected, either by the user or under your program's control.

Some controls have *values*, supplied by you at design time, by the data from which the control is being fed, or by the user at run time. The value of the control is the value you see displayed in that control. For a text box, the value is obviously the text displayed inside the box. For a list box, the value of the control is the chosen item (or Null, if no item is chosen).

Controls also have *properties* that your application can set and change. This chapter touches on the useful, pertinent, and difficult properties throughout its discussion of the various controls. If you're upgrading to Access 97 from Access 2, you'll find many new properties, and some new control types, as well.

> **TIP**
>
> Access 97 is far pickier about the datatypes you assign to properties than was any previous version of Access. For example, the ControlSource property of a text box previously accepted a string expression or a null value (indicating an empty ControlSource). No longer. You must now assign the correct datatype—String, in this particular case—to all properties. This change will be most evident when you attempt to convert existing applications to Access 97. Code that worked fine in earlier versions may fail to run correctly now, if you had been using Null to set property values that now require explicit types. VBA cannot catch most of these errors at compile time, so if you were in the habit of assigning null values to properties that should have been strings, you'll need to test existing converted code carefully. In addition, code that tested these property values to see if they were Null won't work any more—you'll need to check for an empty string, instead.

Code-Behind-Forms and Class Modules

In Access, every form and report can carry its own module with it. In Access 2 and Access 95, all forms and reports maintained a module; in Access 97, forms and reports are "born" without a module. You can cause Access 97 to create a module by adding any VBA code to the object, and you can remove the module by setting the object's HasModule property to False. The code in this module is sometimes referred to as *Code-Behind-Forms,* or *CBF,* and it's in this module that you'll usually attach code to any event property for any control. The module itself is called the form or report's Class module. Chapter 8 discusses this feature in greater depth, but be aware that when this chapter refers to attaching code to a given control or to a property of a control, it is talking about creating event procedure functions and subroutines that are stored with the form itself. You can gain access to the Class Module by clicking the Build (…) button next to the specific event on the property sheet and choosing Code Builder from the Choose Builder dialog box. Note that you can also reverse the order. If you choose [Event Procedure] from the row's drop-down list, you can then click the Build button, and Access will take you directly to the Class Module. You can also choose the Code button on the toolbar to access this code. The property sheet (with a builder button) is shown here:

Figure 7.1 shows the dialog box.

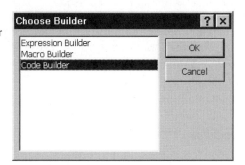

TIP	In response to suggestions from many Access users, Microsoft has added a feature in Access 97 allowing you to bypass the dialog you normally see when you click the Build (...) button, which asks whether you'd like to create an event procedure, create a macro, or use the Expression Builder. If you normally want to react to events using VBA code, choose the Tools ➤ Options menu, select the Forms/Reports tab, and make sure the Always Use Event Procedures check box is set. This way, you can bypass a mouse click every time you create an event procedure.

Some Standard Control Properties

Before we launch into a discussion of all the different controls and their various properties and events, this seems like a good time to discuss some of the standard properties and events that most controls share. Later in the chapter we'll discuss individual controls with their unique properties and events.

Using the Tag Property to Create Your Own Properties

Access provides the general-purpose Tag property, which allows you to specify and store up to 2048 characters of information attached to any control. Access never uses what's stored in this property, so it makes a perfect place to store information about a control that is pertinent to your application. You might find it tempting to place arbitrary values in this unused slot, but it's a good idea to avoid this urge. If you adopt a standard method of storing values in the Tag property, you can actually create your own user-defined properties for controls. In previous editions of this book, we proposed a standard that has gained acceptance within the Access development community for formatting this information.

We suggest using the following format for enabling the Tag property to contain user-defined information.

Name1=Value1; Name2=Value2; Name3=Value3;

This format guarantees that various pieces of your application won't overwrite information stored in the Tag property of a given control. If all access to the Tag property goes through a set of functions that set and get the specific values by their names, you have a very ordered and safe way to store and retrieve values. Using this method allows you to store multiple bits of information about a control and retrieve those bits when necessary.

To implement this functionality, we've provided a set of functions you can include in any of your applications. (To use the functions, import the module basParse from CH07.MDB.) We'll use the functions in basParse throughout this book, not only to work with the Tag property, but anyplace we need to store more than one item in a single string. The set of functions includes adhCtlTagPutItem, which puts a tag name and its value into the Tag property for a specific control, and adhCtlTagGetItem, which retrieves a specific tag value from the Tag property of a specific control. These two functions, described below, should provide the flexibility you need to use the Tag property to its fullest advantage. Figure 7.2 shows the adhCtlTagPutItem and adhCtlTagGetItem functions setting and retrieving the tag value, TimeModified.

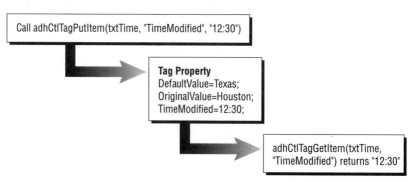

FIGURE 7.2
Use the adhCtlTagPutItem
and adhCtlTagGetItem
functions to place and retrieve values from the Tag
property of a control.

In addition, to make this interface as simple as possible, we've made the rules describing the structure of the Tag property string a bit stringent. In particular, the syntax for the Tag property is as follows:

TagName1=TagValue1; TagName2=TagValue2;...; TagNameN=TagValueN;

To use adhCtlTagGetItem and adhCtlTagPutItem, follow these rules:

- Separate each item name and value pair with an equal sign (=).

- Follow each pair with a semicolon (;), although you can change this particular separator by modifying the adhcSeparator constant in the code.

- Do not include the separator character (;) within the tag value itself.

If you use the provided functions to place values into the Tag property, these rules won't be a concern, since the code will follow them. The only problem occurs when you place values into the Tag property at design time. In that case, be careful to follow the rules exactly, since the provided functions may not work otherwise. The functions are declared as follows:

```
Function adhCtlTagGetItem(ctl As Control, _
 ByVal varItemName As Variant) As Variant
Function adhCtlTagPutItem(ctl As Control, _
 ByVal varItemName As Variant, _
 ByVal varItemValue As Variant) As Integer
```

The following list describes the parameters for each of the functions:

Argument	Description
ctl	Control containing the Tag property you want to manipulate
varItemName	String expression resulting in the name you want associated with the piece of data stored in the tag property
varItemValue	Variant expression resulting in the value you want to have stored in the Tag property of the specified control

TIP

To include the functionality described here in your own applications, include the basParse module from CH07.MDB.

NOTE

Access never records any property changes your running application makes while a form is in Form view. Just as with any other property, changes made to the Tag property with adhCtlTagPutItem will not appear in the property sheet. If you want to make persistent changes to any property, you need to make them when your form is in Design view.

TIP

The basParse module includes a second set of useful functions that work with any string, not just a control's Tag property. You'll find these functions to be more general-purpose, and we'll use them when necessary throughout the book. Take a look at the public functions in basParse for more information, if you wish.

The ControlType Property

In the 16-bit versions of Microsoft Access, you needed to use ugly and arcane syntax to find out the control type for a given control:

If TypeOf *control* Is *controlType* Then

   ' Do something

End If

Now, you can query the ControlType property of a control directly and get an integer that indicates the control type. Table 7.1 lists the different control types, along with their ControlType values and the Access constants that represent them.

TABLE 7.1   ControlType Property Values

Control	Integer	Constant
Label	100	acLabel
Rectangle	101	acRectangle
Line	102	acLine
Image	103	acImage
Command button	104	acCommandButton
Option button	105	acOptionButton
Check box	106	acCheckBox
Option group	107	acOptionGroup
Bound object frame	108	acBoundObjectFrame
Text box	109	acTextBox
List box	110	acListBox
Combo box	111	acComboBox
Subform/subreport	112	acSubform
Unbound object frame	114	acObjectFrame

TABLE 7.1 ControlType Property Values (continued)

Control	Integer	Constant
Page break	118	acPageBreak
Custom control	119	acCustomControl
Toggle button	122	acToggleButton
Tab control	123	acTabCtl
Page	124	acPage

In addition, the ControlType property is read/write in Design view. (You can't change a control's type while a form is running in Form view.) This makes it possible to write tools that directly manipulate the control's type (and this is just how the Format ➤ Change To menu item works).

The ControlTipText and ShortCutMenuBar Properties

Access 97 allows you to create *control tips* (those little boxes describing controls you see when you leave your mouse over a control for a short period of time) and *context-sensitive menus* (the menus you get when you right-click an object) for any control. The ControlTipText property can contain up to 255 characters of text, and you can modify this property at run time if you need to. Although you won't, in general, supply control tips for controls other than command buttons, they can be handy in other circumstances, as well. For example, frmFillTest, shown in Figure 7.3, allows you to fill a list with different items. (You'll see how frmFillTest fills its lists in the section "Changing the RowSource Property" later in this chapter.) Depending on which items you're displaying, you may want a different control tip for the list box. The fragment of the code that does the work, from the SetListBox-Contents procedure in the form's module, sets the ControlTipText property of the selected list box when you choose one of the command buttons:

```
Set ctl = Me!lstShowList
Select Case intFlag
    Case adhcShowProducts
        strField = "Products"
```

```
        strTable = "tblProducts"
        ctl.ControlTipText = "Choose a product"
    Case adhcShowLocations
        strField = "Locations"
        strTable = "tblLocations"
        ctl.ControlTipText = "Choose a location"
    Case Else
        Exit Function
End Select
```

FIGURE 7.3

Attach tool tips to controls with the ControlTipText property.

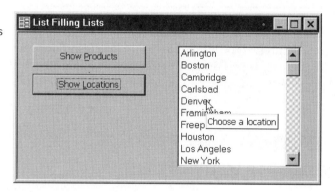

To supply a context-sensitive menu for a control, create a shortcut command bar and choose that command bar name for the ShortCutMenuBar property of the control. The sample form, frmFillTest, uses this technique on the list box, as shown in Figure 7.4. The two macros inside mcrChooseList end up calling the public SetListBoxContents function in the form's module, passing different parameters indicating which list to display.

Creating Shortcut Menus in Access 97

Because Access 97 uses command bar objects, supplied by Office 97, to create its menus, the techniques you'll use to create shortcut menus are new in this version. In addition, due to vagaries in the user interface Access supplies for creating menus and toolbars, it's not obvious what's going on as you create your shortcut menus.

If you want to convert existing shortcut menus (created with macros in previous versions of Access), first select your menu macro (not a macro containing the

FIGURE 7.4

Attach a context-sensitive menu to a control using the ShortCutMenuBar property.

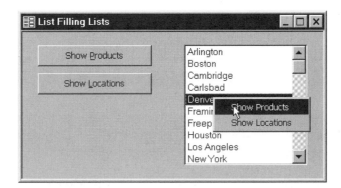

AddMenu actions, but one that contains the menu items themselves), and then select the Tools ➤ Macro ➤ Create Shortcut Menu from Macro menu item. This will create a new popup menu (stored as a command bar) for you.

Take the following steps to create a shortcut menu from scratch. (We'll use the example shown in Figure 7.4.)

1. Select the View ➤ Toolbars ➤ Customize menu item to start the process.

2. Click the New button on the Customize dialog to create the new, empty menu.

3. Supply a value for the name of the new menu. You'll now see a small, empty menu bar, awaiting your commands.

4. Select the Commands tab on the Customize dialog so you can set the new menu's commands.

5. Click and drag the Custom command from the right-hand column. (You'll do this once for each menu item you want to create.)

6. Once you see "Custom" on the new menu, right-click to set the properties of the item. Fill in at least the Name property (which sets the caption for the menu item). You can also set the image for the item here.

7. Click the Properties item at the bottom of the menu, and you'll see yet another dialog. This one allows you to enter properties of the menu control.

8. Select a value for the OnAction property. This tells Access what you want to do when someone selects the menu item. You can choose an existing macro

name from the drop-down list. You can also choose a public function in a standard module using the "=*FunctionName*()" syntax.

9. When you're done working with the properties of your menu control, close the dialog by clicking outside it.

10. Up to this point, everything you've done applies to normal menus, as well as to shortcut menus. To convert this menu into a shortcut menu, select the Properties button on the Customize dialog. Once you're on the Toolbar Properties dialog, change the Type property to "Popup". (You'll see an alert at this point—it's explained in the following paragraph.)

Access has no way, in its Toolbar customization user interface, to display shortcut menus. To work around this, all your shortcut menus appear under the Custom item on the ShortCut Menus toolbar. To edit your shortcut menu once you've set its Type property to Popup, follow these steps:

1. Select the View ➤ Toolbars ➤ Customize menu item to start the process.

2. Select the Shortcut Menus item at the very bottom of the list of available toolbars.

3. Click the Custom item at the far right of the Shortcut Menu "tree." Your shortcut menu should appear as one of the items on this list.

4. Edit your items just as you would any other menu.

Chapter 11 covers creating and manipulating the CommandBar object model programmatically. Most likely, you won't need that information to create and use your forms' shortcut menus. For more information on programmatic control over menus and toolbars, see Chapter 11.

Using the TabStop and TabIndex Properties

The TabIndex property allows you to control the order in which users will arrive at controls as they use the Tab or ↵ key to move from control to control on your form. The TabIndex property lets you assign an ordinal value (zero-based) to each control on your form, specifying how you want the user to move between controls. Access maintains the list, ensuring that no value is used twice and that no value is skipped. You can also use the View ➤ Tab Order menu item to edit the TabStop properties in a more visual environment.

The TabStop property (Yes/No) can remove a control from the form's tab list. Normally, if you press the Tab key to move from control to control on a form, the focus moves in tab order through the controls. If you set a control's TabStop property to No, Access skips that particular control. Controls that have their TabStop property set to No will still appear in the View ➤ Tab Order dialog box, however.

You can use the TabStop and TabIndex properties to gain complete control over the flow of your application's forms. You could, for example, change the tab order of fields based on a choice the user made. The example form, frmTabOrder (in CH07.MDB), changes the tab order from row-first to column-first, based on a choice the user made.

The code required to change the tab order at run time is simple. The following example was attached to the AfterUpdate event of the chkTabOrder control. All it needs to do is check the state of the check box and set the tab order accordingly.

```
Private Sub chkTabOrder_AfterUpdate()
    With Me
        If !chkTabOrder Then
            ' Use a column-wise ordering
            !txtFirstName.TabIndex = 1
            !txtLastName.TabIndex = 2
            !txtMiddleInitial.TabIndex = 3
            .
            .
            .
            !txtFax.TabIndex = 9
        Else
            ' Use the AutoOrder ordering.
            !txtFirstName.TabIndex = 1
            !txtAddress.TabIndex = 2
            !txtHomePhone.TabIndex = 3
            .
            .
            .
            !txtFax.TabIndex = 9
        End If
    End With
End Sub
```

Using the DisplayWhen Property

On forms, you can influence when Access will display a control with the Display-When property. (Report controls don't include the DisplayWhen property but must use the Visible setting instead.) If you want the control to appear only when you print the form, set the DisplayWhen property to Print Only (1). To make the control appear at all times, select Always (0), and to make it display only on screen and not at print time, choose Screen Only (2). You set the DisplayWhen property to Screen Only for all the controls you want displayed only when you're looking at the form on screen.

TIP Access 97 has added the IsVisible property for report controls, available only at print time. Using this property, you can find out whether a control has been hidden because you've turned on the HideDuplicates property and, for the current row, the value is the same as that in the previous row. See Chapter 9 for more information.

Using Labels

Labels are the simplest of all nongraphic Access controls. A label presents *static* text on a form or report. That is, the text doesn't change as you move from record to record. Labels can never receive input focus and thus can never be used to input data. The form's tab order skips over them. Labels, then, are best for displaying information on forms you never want your users to be able to change, such as data-gathering instructions or your company's name. Generally, you also use labels to display the field names for bound controls. Unless told otherwise, Access creates a label control to accompany any bound control you create, including the field name and a colon.

TIP

If you want to change the way Access creates labels for your bound fields, edit the default text box properties (and those of other controls you use). If you select the text box button in the toolbox, the property sheet heading should be "Default Textbox." Modify the AutoLabel and AddColon properties to match your preferences. In addition, you can set the LabelX and LabelY properties to control the offset of the label from the text box to which it's attached.

NOTE

You cannot create a label without text. That sounds obvious, but it's very disconcerting when you accidentally try to do it. If you size a label just right but then click some other control before entering a caption value, Access just removes the label as though you had never created it. You can delete the text once you've created it, however, but a label without text isn't very useful.

You can change the color, font name, font size, and text alignment for text in a label. You can also change the Color and SpecialEffect properties of the label itself. It's best to standardize the appearance of the field labels in your application, and you'll find that the control default properties can help you out. (See the section "Using Default Control Properties to Your Advantage" later in this chapter for more information.)

Once you've changed the font (name or size) for a particular label, you may find the text no longer fits inside the label. Double-clicking any of the control *handles* (the little black boxes that surround the control frame) causes Access to resize the control for best fit—that is, Access resizes the control so it's just big enough for your text. This can be useful if you're trying out different font sizes. It's equivalent to choosing the Format ➤ Size ➤ To Fit menu item. You can emulate this in your code using the SizeToFit method in Design view, as well.

The Parent Property

Although you won't find it on the property sheet, labels expose a Parent property, which returns to you the control that is the parent for the label. Other control types return the logical value for their Parent property: items in option groups return the option group as their parent, and all other controls return the form as their parent. (For more information on option groups, see the section "Using Option Groups—Controls inside Controls" later in this chapter.)

For example, imagine you have a label named lblTest that's attached to an option button, optTest, which resides inside the option group grpTest on frmTestParent. The Debug window session shown in Figure 7.5 demonstrates the relationships between controls and their parents. (You can try this out yourself by opening frmTestParent and the Debug window at the same time.)

FIGURE 7.5

The Parent property allows you to walk up the hierarchy of controls on a form.

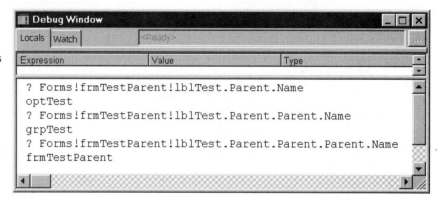

```
? Forms!frmTestParent!lblTest.Parent.Name
optTest
? Forms!frmTestParent!lblTest.Parent.Parent.Name
grpTest
? Forms!frmTestParent!lblTest.Parent.Parent.Parent.Name
frmTestParent
```

TIP

Just as you can use the Parent property of a label to find the control to which it's attached, you can now use the Controls collection of any control to find the label attached to it. See the section "Using Controls' Controls Collection" later in the chapter for more information.

Using Text Boxes

Although labels may be the simplest of all Access controls, text boxes are the most common. You can use text boxes to display data, as well as to capture it. They can contain single or multiple lines. They can display scroll bars if you wish. Text boxes can contain any amount of textual information, up to approximately 32,000 characters (although in reality this will probably be less, depending on your particular circumstances).

You can think of a text box as a mini-notepad, allowing you to enter free-form text. If you think your data entry will require more than one line or if you are using a text box to display information from a memo field, your best bet is to enable scroll bars. (Set the ScrollBars property to Vertical rather than None. Unfortunately, there is no way to have scroll bars appear only if you need them. They're either on or off.)

TIP

As is the Windows standard, the ↵ key causes Access not to insert a carriage return/line feed in your text box but rather to move to the next control. To move to a new line, you must press Shift+↵. To make the ↵ key insert a carriage return/line feed, set the EnterKeyBehavior property of the text box to New Line in Field. This makes the text box work more like what you might expect but less like the rest of Windows.

NOTE

Access text boxes can support only a single font and a single text attribute (bold, italic, or underline). Unless you care to embed an object (either the RTF text ActiveX control, available with Visual Basic and the Office Developer Edition, or a Word for Windows document), you will need to forego multiple fonts and formatting within text boxes.

Carrying Values Forward into New Records

In some instances your application may require the ability to carry forward existing field values into the new row when your user adds a new row using a form. Access does not provide this ability on its own, but it's not difficult to implement it in Basic. This functionality requires modifying the DefaultValue property of your controls, storing away field values. Then, when you add a new row, those default values will be placed into the controls for you.

This is a perfect situation in which you can make good use of the Tag property, as described in the section "Using the Tag Property to Create Your Own Properties" earlier in this chapter. For each control, you can use the Tag property to store the original DefaultValue property, so if you decide to stop carrying values forward for a specific text box, you can reset the original default value.

In addition, the example form, frmCarryTest, shown in Figure 7.6, allows you to interactively decide which fields will be carried. The form includes toggle buttons next to the fields you're likely to want to carry into a new row. Each of these toggle buttons includes, in its Tag property, a string indicating which bound control it's to be associated with.

The sample form, frm-
CarryTest, allows you to
selectively carry values
forward into a new row.

How Does It Work?

Each of the toggle buttons on the sample form includes, in its Tag property, a
string that associates the button with a bound control on the form. For example,
the toggle button next to the City field contains this string in its Tag property:

```
Ctl=txtCity;
```

The code called when you click the toggle button will use the Ctl keyword to find
out which control it needs to modify.

Each of the toggle buttons calls, from its AfterUpdate event, a common procedure:

```
=HandleCarry([Form],[Screen].[ActiveControl])
```

This common function, HandleCarry (in basCarry), handles all the details. Listing 7.1 shows the entire procedure.

TIP

You might be tempted to count on the ActiveForm, ActiveControl, and
PreviousControl properties of the screen object, which allow you to write
generic functions to be called from forms. For the most part you're better
off passing the Form property (from the property sheet) or the Me object
(from CBF) down to functions called in global modules. The main problem
is that often in the Access environment there is actually no current form or
control. Attempting to access one of these properties at those times
causes a run-time error. This makes it particularly difficult to debug code
that contains these objects. There is, however, no simple replacement for
Screen.ActiveControl, which is what we've used in this example.

Listing 7.1

```
Function HandleCarry(frm As Form, ctlToggle As Control)
    Dim ctlCarry As Control
    Dim varCtlName As Variant
    Dim varOldDV As Variant

    Const adhcQuote = """"""

    ' This constant must match the Tag value you
    ' used when creating the toggle buttons on the form.
    Const adhcCtlID = "Ctl"
    Const adhcDV = "DefaultValue"

    varCtlName = adhctlTagGetItem(ctlToggle, adhcCtlID)
    If Not IsNull(varCtlName) Then
        ' Get a reference to the control containing
        ' the data.
        Set ctlCarry = frm(varCtlName)
        If ctlToggle.Value Then
            ' The button is depressed, so set up associated
            ' control to carry forward.
            ' First, store away the current DefaultValue
            ' property, so it's there when you "untoggle".
            ' This'll put a string like:
            '    DefaultValue=Old Default Value
            ' in the control's Tag property.
            Call adhctlTagPutItem(ctlCarry, adhcDV, _
            ctlCarry.DefaultValue)

            ' Set the control's DefaultValue to be what
            ' you got from the Tag property,
            ' surrounded with quotes.
            ctlCarry.DefaultValue = adhcQuote & _
            ctlCarry.Value & adhcQuote
        Else
            ' The button is cleared, so reset the default
            ' value to its previous value.
            varOldDV = adhctlTagGetItem(ctlCarry, adhcDV)

            ' Make sure the old value gets set to a string,
            ' so tack on an empty string just to make sure.
```

```
            ctlCarry.DefaultValue = varOldDV & ""
        End If
    End If
End Function
```

To use this function, you pass to it a reference to the current form (in the example, by sending the form's Form property in the function call) and a reference to the current control (using Screen.ActiveControl in the sample form). The function first attempts to retrieve, from the current control, the name of the bound control with which it's associated:

```
varCtlName = adhCtlTagGetItem(ctlToggle, adhcCtlID)
```

If varCtlName isn't Null, the code sets a variable to refer to the bound control and then decides what to do based on the value of the toggle button. If the toggle button is depressed, the code stores the current DefaultValue property for the bound control in its Tag property and then sets its DefaultValue property to match its current value:

```
Call adhctlTagPutItem(ctlCarry, adhcDV, _
 ctlCarry.DefaultValue)
ctlCarry.DefaultValue = adhcQuote & _
 ctlCarry.Value & adhcQuote
```

If the button is raised, the code resets the bound control's DefaultValue property to the value retrieved from the control's Tag property:

```
varOldDV = adhctlTagGetItem(ctlCarry, adhcDV)
ctlCarry.DefaultValue = varOldDV & ""
```

NOTE   The DefaultValue property must be a string, and it must be enclosed in quotes. That explains why the code must wrap ctlCarry.Value in quotes (using the adhcQuote constant) before assigning it to ctlCarry.DefaultValue.

Carrying Values in Your Own Forms

To use this technique in your own applications, follow these steps:

1. Create your bound form, or use an existing bound form.

2. Add toggle buttons next to controls bound to fields that you might like to carry forward as you add new rows to the form.

3. For each toggle button, set the Tag property to indicate which bound control it is to be associated with, as discussed above.

4. Select all the toggle buttons, and call the HandleCarry function from the AfterUpdate event, as discussed above.

That's all there is to it. When you run your form and select one of the toggle buttons, HandleCarry will set the DefaultValue for the selected control to be the current value of the control. When you go to the new row, Access will supply the default value for you.

The ControlSource Property and Calculated Controls

Access developers often use text boxes to display calculated values. Figure 7.7 shows the sample form, frmControlSource, with a DueDate field, drawing its data from a table, and two text boxes displaying the number of days overdue for this payment. To create a calculated control, you have two choices:

- Use an expression.

- Use a user-defined function.

The second and third text boxes on the sample form use one of the preceding methods for calculating the number of days late.

In either case, you must precede the value in the property sheet with an equal sign (=), which indicates to Access that it must include what follows.

FIGURE 7.7

Using calculated controls on a form. Note that both methods (using an expression and using a function) return the same value.

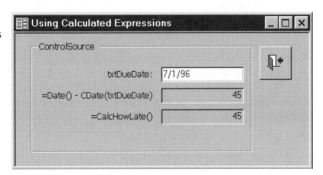

To create an expression that will be evaluated when the control gets recalculated—for example, to calculate the past due amount—use the expression

```
=Date() - CDate([txtDueDate])
```

This simple expression calculates the number of days since the due date and displays it. Figure 7.7 shows this example in action.

Your other option is to create a function that places a value in the text box.

> **NOTE**
>
> In general, if you want a specific event to place a value into a control on a form, it is not enough to specify a function call in the property sheet. Your function must explicitly place its value into the control. In most properties, Access completely disregards the return value from the function. Combined with the fact that Access can call only functions (which must return values), not subroutines (which do not return values), from the property sheet, it's easy to get confused. On top of that, Access is inconsistent as to how it treats function calls from the property sheet. The DefaultValue and ControlSource properties, for example, pass the return value from a function call on to the text box. All event properties disregard the return value.

Using the same example as above, you could create a function:

```
Function CalcHowLate()
    CalcHowLate = Date() - CDate(Me!txtDueDate)
End Function
```

To use a function to supply the ControlSource value, precede its name with an equal (=) sign. That is, use =CalcHowLate() in this example. Figure 7.7 shows this form in action.

> **NOTE**
>
> The expression in the previous example uses the CDate function to convert the value in the text box into a date. Because all control values are stored internally as variants but this calculation requires a date value, the CDate function ensures that Access understands what it is the expression needs to do.

Using Two-State Controls (the Yes/No Crowd)

All the controls described in the following sections (toggle button, option button, and check box) can represent data that has two states when used outside an option group on a form. (When grouped in an option group, they can represent more information.) Therefore, they all represent reasonable ways to present the user with yes/no data for acceptance. Each represents its two states differently, and you can use these differences to your advantage.

If you also need to represent a third state in which you don't yet know the value for the control, Access provides the TripleState property for toggle buttons, option buttons, and check boxes, as long as they're not embedded in an option group.

The Toggle Button

In an option group, the toggle button has two states: up and down. Its "up" state represents the False/No condition (unselected), and its "down" state represents the True/Yes condition (selected). It can display either text or a picture (but, unfortunately, not both). Access creates a dithered version of the picture on the button for its depressed state, relieving you from having to supply two separate bitmaps, one for the "up" state and one for the "down" state. Outside an option group, you can set the TripleState property to allow the button to also show a null value.

> **TIP**
>
> If you require a button that includes both text and a picture, you can create a bitmap in Paint that includes both and use that bitmap as the image for your button. From the user's perspective, it will look right, even though it's just a bitmap. You can even include a hot key: in your bitmap, underline the character you'd like to have activate the button, and include, in the button's Caption property, a string with that specific character preceded by an ampersand (&) ("&A", for example, to make Alt+A trigger your button).

Using toggle buttons to represent yes/no information to the user can make your forms more visually appealing than using simple check boxes, but they make sense in only a limited number of situations. If your user is inputting information that answers a simple yes/no question, toggle buttons aren't as clear as check boxes. On the other hand, if you are gathering other two-state information (alive or deceased, U.S. citizen or not), toggle buttons often are quite useful. Here's the real test: if you're tempted to use a toggle button alone on a form with a text description, use a check box instead. If you need a group of check boxes or if you can use a picture instead of text, consider using toggle buttons.

The Option Button

Option buttons do represent two states, but common usage suggests you use them most often in option groups to allow selection of a single item from the group. In that situation the two states can be thought of as "selected" and "not selected." For that reason, programmers often refer to option buttons as *radio buttons*, harkening back to the automobile radios of yesteryear with mechanical buttons that you could depress only one at a time to select a station and pressing one "unpressed" the rest.

When representing yes/no data, the option button displays a filled circle when it's in the True/Yes state. When representing the False/No state, it displays just an empty ring.

Although you can use option buttons alone on a form and can use the TripleState property in that situation, avoid using single option buttons on forms. You should limit their usage to the radio button image in option groups. If you need a single option button, use a check box instead.

The Check Box

The check box is the standard two-state control. When in the Yes (True) state, the control displays a check mark inside a box. When in the No (False) state, it displays just an empty box. Check boxes commonly stand alone or are used in groups to select multiple options. You can use check boxes in option groups, but common usage suggests you avoid this situation. Using check boxes in an option group allows you to choose only a single value, and this spoils the imagery of check boxes—allowing multiple choices. If you want to make a group of check boxes *look* like an option group, you can enclose them within a rectangle. Figure 7.8 shows all the combinations of subcontrols.

FIGURE 7.8

All the two-state controls (in rectangles, not option groups, so they can be null)

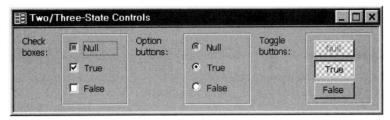

Using Option Groups—
Controls inside Controls

The option group allows you to group multiple controls (toggle buttons, option buttons, or check boxes) for the purpose of choosing a single value. Each subcontrol has its own value (set in its OptionValue property), and when it's chosen it assigns that value to the option group. Usually an option group consists of multiples of a single type of control. Figure 7.9 shows the sample form frmOptionGroups with three different option groups, one for each type of subcontrol. In addition, this figure includes an option group composed of various subcontrols. Although there's no reason not to create an option group combining different subcontrols, it's a good idea to avoid doing so since it's confusing and serves no real purpose.

TIP

Don't be shy about using the Control Wizards to help you build option groups. The Option Group Control Wizard can save you some steps, and you'll find it a useful tool. Don't believe anyone who tells you that real programmers don't use Wizards! Real programmers do anything that will save them time, and the Control Wizards are one such tool.

There's nothing keeping you from assigning the same OptionValue property to multiple subcontrols. As a matter of fact, if you copy a control within an option group, Access assigns the new control the same option value as the original control. This can be confusing because choosing one subcontrol will simultaneously select all subcontrols with the same OptionValue property. On the other hand, there's nothing keeping you from skipping option values. They need not be contiguous. The only limitation is that they must be Integer or Long Integer values (whole numbers).

FIGURE 7.9

Four option group examples. We don't recommend creating option groups composed of different subcontrols.

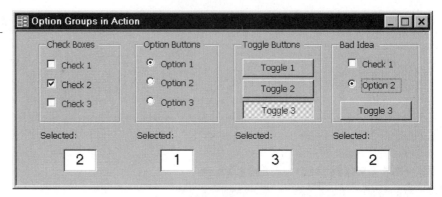

> **TIP**
>
> In the interest of preserving screen real-estate and simplifying your input forms, consider using a combo box if you find your option group includes more than five items. Option groups take up a great deal of space on the screen, and with more than five subcontrols in the group, it becomes difficult to choose the correct item.

The value of an option group can be only a single whole number, no matter how much you'd like an option group to return a string or any other datatype. This means the option value of each internal subcontrol is also limited to being a whole number. If you must use text values, for example, you can create an array of strings in your application and use the value returned from the option group as an index into your array. (See the section "Returning 'Real' Information from Option Groups" later in this chapter for information on returning string values.)

Access treats the option group, once it's populated with subcontrols, as a single control; when you select the container and move it, all the internal controls move, too. When you delete the container, Access deletes all the internal controls. Unless you're aware that this will happen, it can cause havoc in your development. Make sure you really intend to delete all the internal controls before you delete an option group!

TIP Because option groups can return only a single value, you are limited to making only one choice from the group of subcontrols inside it. This design indicates you would be better off using only toggle buttons or option buttons in an option group, because each of those is suited for making a single choice. If you need an option group that contains check boxes, allowing you to choose several items, consider creating a "faux" option group. To do this, enclose your check boxes within a rectangle (rather than within an option group). This way they'll look as though they are part of an option group but will allow multiple selections. Note, though, that you will have to examine each check box separately to find which ones you have selected. If you have controls inside an option group, you don't need to examine each separately, because all you care about is the single control you've selected, and Access assigns that value to the option group.

TIP Another alternative to the option group control is to use a tab control. The tab control, discussed later in this chapter, can contain almost any other control type (option groups can contain only the three types of controls shown in Figure 7.9), and it grants you some of the benefits of an option group without its limitation of one selected control. See the section "Using the Tab Control as a Container" later in this chapter for more information.

Moving Controls to a New Neighborhood

You'll find that moving a currently existing control into an option group does not work. Although the subcontrol will appear to be inside the option group, the two will not function together. (This same problem occurs with pages of a tab control, and you can use the same solutions.) To add items to an option group, use either of the following two methods:

- **Create a new control:** Select the option group and then choose your subcontrol from the toolbar and place it in the option group. Note that when you move the cursor to drop a subcontrol, the option group becomes highlighted as you pass the cursor over it. This visual prompt indicates that the option group is ready to receive a subcontrol.

- **Cut-and-paste an existing control:** Once you've used the Edit ➤ Cut menu item to cut the control, select the option group. With the option group selected, choose Edit ➤ Paste. Access places the control inside the option group as a real, active subcontrol.

> **NOTE**
>
> Controls in an option group lose their properties that deal with the underlying data, such as the ControlSource, TripleState, and ValidationRule properties, since they are no longer independent representations of data from the underlying record source. On the other hand, they gain the OptionValue property, since you must assign each a unique value. This is the value the control will return to the option group once you've made a choice. Therefore, you'll note that the property sheet for an independent control is a bit different from the property sheet for an identical control in an option group.

Assigning and Retrieving Values

Because the option group's value is the value of the chosen subcontrol, you can assign a value to the option group by making an assignment to the option group name. For example, the following code assigns the value 3 to the option group grpTestGroup:

```
Me!grpTestGroup = 3
```

Access would select the subcontrol in grpTestGroup that had the OptionValue of 3.

Likewise, you can retrieve the value of the option group just by referencing its name. The expression

```
varNewValue = Me!grpTestGroup
```

assigns the value chosen in grpTestGroup to the variant variable varNewValue.

To be completely clear, the reason the previous assignment works is that you're actually assigning the Value property of grpTestGroup to varNewValue. Because the Value property of a control is its default property, Access knows that's what you meant when you specified no property at all.

NOTE
The option group's value is Null when there are no items chosen. Therefore, just as with any other form control, consider retrieving its value into a variant-type variable that can handle the possible null return value.

Returning "Real" Information from Option Groups

Although option groups can return only integral values, you can work around this problem if you want an option group to gather and show information from a text field that has only a limited number of possible values. It may be that you're sharing data with other applications or that you just aren't able to change the field format to meet Access' requirements. In that case you'll need a few tricks to use option groups to represent textual information.

TIP
If at all possible, try to reorganize your tables in such a way that limited-option fields can be stored as whole numbers. Not only does this make it simple to use an option group to show the data, it cuts down on memory usage. Imagine you have 1000 records, with one of the following in the Delivery field: "Overnight", "2nd Day Air", or "Ground". Not only is this field prone to data entry problems, it's using a lot more disk/memory space than necessary. If you were to create a small table with those three values and an integer attached to each, you could just store the integers in your main table. Data entry would be simpler, you'd be using less memory, and everyone involved would be happier.

To bind the option group to text values rather than integer values, create an extra text box on your form. Normally you would make this text box invisible (set its Visible property to No), but for this example it will stay visible. Figure 7.10 shows the finished form, frmDelivery. For the purposes of this example, the option group's name is grpDelivery and the text box's name is txtDelivery. The text box is bound to the field containing the text, and the option group is unbound; the text box is the control that will send and receive data to and from the underlying table, and the option group will be used just to collect and display that data.

FIGURE 7.10

Binding an option group to a text value. Note the bound text box, which normally would be invisible.

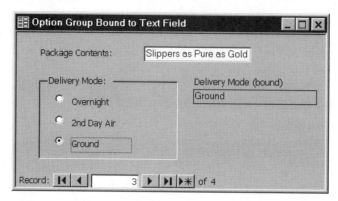

Once you have the bound text box on the form, you need to solve two problems:

- As you move from record to record, how do you get the right option in the option group to be chosen?

- As you make a choice in the option group, how do you get its value written out to the underlying data, if it's not bound?

To answer the first question you need to attach code to the form's Current event. Access fires off this event each time it makes a record current and allows you to set the value of the option group for each record. For this simple case you can use the Switch function, which returns the value corresponding to the first True statement it finds in its parameters:

```
Me!grpDelivery = Switch(Me!txtDelivery = "Overnight", 1, _
  Me!txtDelivery = "2nd Day Air", 2, _
  Me!txtDelivery = "Ground", 3, True, Null)
```

Using the Switch Function

You can use Switch to take the place of nested If...Then...Else...End If statements. Its general syntax is

retval = Switch(*expr1*, *var1* [,*expr2*, *var2*([,*exprN*, *varN*]])

where *expr1* through *exprN* are expressions that return either True (–1) or False (0) and *var1* through *varN* are the values to be returned if the corresponding expression is True. Switch returns the value corresponding to the first expression it finds in its list that returns True.

For example, the Switch function call in the previous example:

```
Me!grpDelivery = Switch(Me!txtDelivery = "Overnight", 1, _
 Me!txtDelivery = "2nd Day Air", 2, _
 Me!txtDelivery = "Ground", 3, True, Null)
```

could have been written as

```
If Me!txtDelivery = "Overnight" Then
    Me!grpDelivery = 1
ElseIf Me!txtDelivery = "2nd Day Air" Then
    Me!grpDelivery = 2
ElseIf Me!txtDelivery = "Ground" Then
    Me!grpDelivery = 3
Else
    Me!grpDelivery = Null
End If
```

Be aware of a few issues that arise when you use Switch:

- In previous versions of Access, you were limited to seven pairs of expressions. In Access 97, the list is basically unlimited. Common sense would indicate that you should limit your list to a reasonable, understandable number of entries.

- Switch returns Null if either none of the expressions return a True value or if the value associated with the first True expression is Null.

- Although only one of the expressions may be True, Access will evaluate every one of them. This can lead to undesirable side effects. For example, if you try this:

  ```
  varValue = Switch(x = 0 Or y = 0, 0, x >= y, x/y, x < y, y/x)
  ```

  you will inevitably end up with an Overflow error since, if either x or y is 0, you end up dividing by 0 even though it appears that you've checked for that in the first expression.

To answer the second question, you need to attach code to the AfterUpdate event of the option group. This code will place the correct value into the bound txtDelivery text box, which will, in turn, send it to the underlying data source. For this example, you should use code like this:

```
Me!txtDelivery = Choose(Me!grpDelivery, "Overnight", _
 "2nd Day Air", "Ground")
```

Using the Choose Function

Like the Switch function, the Choose function is yet another replacement for nested If...Then...Else...End If statements. It takes an integer as its first parameter and then a list of parameters from which to choose. Access returns the value corresponding, in position, to the index you passed as the first parameter. Its general syntax is

Choose(intIndex, *expr1* [,*expr2*]...)

Be aware of the following issues that arise when you use Choose:

- In previous versions of Access, you were limited to 13 possible values in the expression list. Access 97 allows a seemingly unlimited number of elements. Of course, if the list becomes too long, your execution speed and code maintainability will suffer.

- The index value can only be a value between 1 and the number of expressions you've provided, inclusive. If you pass a floating-point value, Access converts it to an integer following the same rules it does for the Fix function.

- Although Choose returns only one of the values, it evaluates them all. Beware of possible side effects. If you call a function in one or more expressions, each of those functions will be called. For example, if each of your expressions called the InputBox function, each and every one of the expressions would get evaluated, causing the InputBox dialog box to pop up multiple times as Access evaluated the list of expressions.

Using Controls' Controls Collection

In previous versions of Access, it was impossible to tell, given a reference to an option group, which controls were inside it. It was impossible to tell, programmatically, which label control on a form was attached to which text box. These problems, and others, have been resolved in Access 97, with the addition of the Controls collection of most control types.

For example, the Controls collection of an option group contains references to all the controls placed inside the option group. This seems so obvious that you have to wonder why it wasn't in the product from the very beginning. The following fragment (from the EnableAll procedure in the class module of frmControlsProperty) enables/disables all the option buttons in the option group:

```
Private Sub EnableAll(ctlMain As Control, fEnable As Boolean)
    ' Given a control, enable/disable all the
    ' option button controls it contains.

    Dim ctl As Control

    For Each ctl In ctlMain.Controls
        If ctl.ControlType = acOptionButton Then
            ctl.Enabled = fEnable
        End If
    Next ctl
End Sub
```

In previous versions of the product, this process would have required looping through all the controls on the form, checking the Parent property of each control, and for those option buttons in the right option group, setting the Enabled property. That might take a lot more time and effort.

Another useful artifact of the Controls collection is that you can now find out the label control attached to another control. For example, perhaps you want to set the foreground color of the label attached to a check box if that check box is selected. In previous versions of Access, you'd have to use some artificial naming convention, storing the attached control's name in the Tag property, or use some other work-around to find out which label was attached to the check box. Now, you can use the Controls collection—the label control will be the only control in the collection, for most control types. The following code fragment, from frmControlsProperty, sets the foreground color of the label attached to a check box to either black or red, depending on whether you've checked or unchecked the control.

```
Private Sub ColorLabel(ctl As Control)
    ' Depending on the value of ctl,
    ' set the label to black or red.
    Const conBlack = 0&
    Const conRed = 255&
    ctl.Controls(0).ForeColor = IIf(ctl, conRed, conBlack)
End Sub
```

It couldn't be much simpler than that!

In addition to the uses shown here, the Controls collection of various objects can aid you in many situations. For example, if you want to work with all the controls in the Header section of a form, you can enumerate all the controls in that one section. In previous versions of Access you had to work through all the controls on the form and, for each control, check its Section property. That is, instead of writing code like this:

```
Dim ctl As Control
For Each ctl in Me.Controls
    If ctl.Section = acHeader Then
        ' Use this control
    End If
Next ctl
```

you can now write the same fragment this way:

```
Dim ctl As Control
For Each ctl In Me.Sections(acHeader).Controls
    ' Use this control
Next ctl
```

The same technique applies to working with controls inside a page of a tab control. Use the Controls collection of the Page object to manipulate each of the controls on the page.

Using List and Combo Boxes

List boxes and combo boxes share many similar properties and uses. Combo boxes combine a text box and a list box in one control. Both list and combo boxes present a list of values, allowing you to choose a single item. They can present multiple columns of data, and you can use them as full data structures, with hidden columns that can contain data.

Differences between List and Combo Boxes

Although list and combo boxes share many of the same properties, events, and uses, several of their specific details are unique to their particular control type. Table 7.2 lists those idiosyncrasies.

TABLE 7.2   Differences between List and Combo Boxes

Item	List Box	Combo Box
Item choices	Allows you to choose only from the items already in the list	Allows you either to choose from the values in the list or to add new ones. This actually depends on the LimitToList property and also on which column is bound to the underlying field (For more information, see the section "The LimitToList Problem" later in this chapter.)
Screen real estate	Takes up as much space as you assign it. Works best when as many items as possible are immediately visible	Takes up the space of a single text box when it doesn't have the input focus and as many lines as you specify (in the ListRows property) when it has the focus
Keyboard handling	Matches only the first character of items in its list against letters you press. Pressing an M matches the first item that starts with M. Pressing it again finds the next, and so on. Pressing a different letter finds the first item that starts with that letter	Performs an incremental search as you type. That is, if you press M, it scrolls to find the first item that begins with M. If you then press i, it finds the first item that begins with Mi and scrolls to that item. Pressing Backspace returns the selection to the previous item you chose. In addition, if you've set the AutoExpand property to Yes, as you type, Access automatically finds and displays the first underlying data element that matches the number of characters you've typed so far. This auto-fill feature, similar to that found in several popular financial packages, is extremely useful, especially when combined with the LimitToList property. On the other hand, it does slow down data entry
Selected Items	List boxes can be configured to allow multiple selections. Once you set the MultiSelect property appropriately, you can choose one or more contiguous or noncontiguous items	Combo boxes can never select more than a single item

Important Properties of List and Combo Boxes

Access' Control Wizards can perform most of the work of creating list and combo boxes on your forms. At times, though, you might want to create the combo or list box from scratch if you find you don't get the flexibility you need when using the Wizard. List and combo boxes provide great flexibility in how they allow you, as a programmer, to display information to the user while controlling the input. Unfortunately, with this degree of flexibility, the plethora of options can be daunting. Many of the properties are interrelated and collectively affect how the control operates. The following sections detail some of the properties you need to understand to get the full benefit of these controls.

The Name Property

The Name property specifies the internal reference name for the control. The actual value of this property has no real significance, except as a convenience for the programmer.

> **TIP**
>
> Many beginning Access programmers confuse the Name property with the ControlSource property. The control name specifies only the name by which you, the programmer, will refer to the control. It has nothing to do with the underlying data, while the control source is actually linked with the data.

The ControlSource Property

The ControlSource property links the control with the underlying data. Specifying a field name tells Access where to retrieve the value of the control and where to place the value returned from the control once you select an item. The control returns the value from the column set in the BoundColumn property. With other controls, you can enter an expression preceded by an equal (=) sign for the ControlSource property. With list and combo boxes, this option succeeds only in making the control read-only.

The RowSourceType Property

The RowSourceType property specifies where to retrieve the rows of data the control displays. The options are

- **Table/Query:** The data comes from a table or query or from a SQL expression. In any case, the RowSource property specifies the table/query name or the SQL expression that will retrieve the dataset.

- **Value List:** The data comes from a list you specify explicitly in the RowSource property.

- **Field List:** The data will consist of a list of fields from the table or query specified in the RowSource property.

- **(User-Defined):** If you specify a function name with no equal sign and no trailing parentheses, Access calls it to fill the list or combo box. (See the section "Filling a List or Combo Box Programmatically" later in this chapter for more information.)

The RowSource Property

The RowSource property specifies which data to retrieve for presentation in the list or combo box. Its syntax depends on the RowSourceType property. Figure 7.11 (frmLists from CH07.MDB) demonstrates some of the methods of filling a list box via the property sheet. The following sections detail the information you need to supply for the RowSource property, based on your choice in the RowSourceType property.

Table/Query   Enter the name of a table, query, or SQL expression that will retrieve the data you wish to display. Here are some examples:

- **tblNames:** Retrieves as many columns from the table named tblNames as the ColumnCount property specifies.

- **SELECT Name, Address, Age FROM tblNames ORDER BY Age:** Retrieves a maximum of three columns from tblNames, ordered by age. If the number in the ColumnCount property is less than the requested number of columns in the RowSource, the ColumnCount property controls the number of columns Access displays.

FIGURE 7.11

One form showing some of the various methods of filling a list or combo box via the property sheet

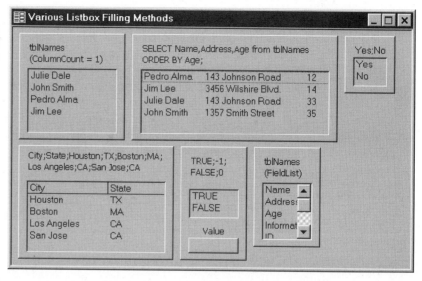

If you use a table name as the RowSource, you must be aware of changes to the table. For example, making a database replicable will add new columns to the front of every table and will therefore break such combo boxes. (See Chapter 13 for more information on replication.)

Value List   Enter a list of values, separated by semicolons, one row at a time (up to 2048 characters). If the ColumnHeads property is Yes, the first row of data will go into the column headings in the control. If you set the ColumnCount property incorrectly, the data will not go into the columns and rows as you had planned. Here are some examples:

- **Yes;No:** Displays just the two values Yes and No. Note that the display is also tied to the ColumnCount property. If the ColumnCount is 1, Yes and No each appears in its own row. If the ColumnCount is 2 or higher, Yes and No both appear on the first row of the control.

- **City;State;Houston;TX;Boston;MA;Los Angeles;CA;San Jose;CA:** Displays a two-column list with four rows of data, assuming these properties:

  ColumnCount = 2

  ColumnHeads = Yes

- **True;–1;False;0:** Displays just the two values True and False and stores a yes/no value back to the underlying field, given these properties:

    ColumnCount = 2

    ColumnWidths = ;0

    BoundColumn = 2

    ControlSource = a Yes/No field from the underlying data source

Figure 7.11 shows these examples, and more, in action.

Field List   Enter the name of a table or query from the form's record source. The fields will be listed in their physical order in the table or in the order in which they were placed into the query. There is no way to alphabetize the list.

The ColumnCount Property

The ColumnCount property controls the number of columns of data Access will store in the control's data area. The actual number of displayed columns can be no more than the number specified in this property, but it might be less, depending on the contents of the ColumnWidths property. Even if you render some of the data invisible (by using a ColumnWidth setting of 0), it's still loaded into the control, and you can retrieve it by using the Column property.

Set the ColumnCount property with a number or a numeric value. Access rounds nonintegral values to the nearest whole number.

The ColumnWidths Property

The ColumnWidths property sets the widths of the columns in the control and should be filled with a semicolon-delimited list of numbers, one per column. The default width is approximately 1 inch or 3 centimeters, depending on the unit of measurement. Leaving a value out of the list accepts the default width. A setting of 0 hides a column. If the physical area dedicated to the control is not wide enough to display all the columns, Access truncates the right-most column, and the control displays horizontal scroll bars. Note that a single-column control will never have horizontal scroll bars, no matter how wide that single column is.

For each of the examples, the control contains four columns and is 5 inches wide. All measurements are in inches:

- **2;2;2;2:** Each column is 2 inches wide. Since this is 3 inches wider than the control, Access provides horizontal scroll bars.

- **2:** The first column is 2 inches wide, and the rest assume the default width (1 inch).

- **2;0;3;0:** The first and third columns are displayed. The second and fourth are hidden.

- **(Blank):** All four columns are evenly spaced over the width of the control, since the control is wider than the sum of the default widths. If it were narrower than the total widths, the first three columns would each be 1 inch wide (the default width) and the last column would use the rest of the space (2 inches).

Figure 7.12 shows these example list boxes, from frmListWidths.

FIGURE 7.12
Various ColumnWidths settings

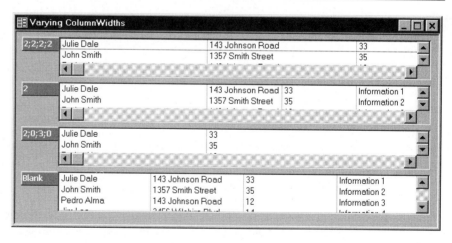

The ColumnHeads Property

The ColumnHeads property indicates whether Access should display a single row of column headings at the top of the control. (For combo boxes, Access displays this heading row only when you've asked it to expose the drop-down list.) When the RowSourceType property is ValueList, the first row of data goes into the header. If the RowSourceType is FieldList, the first field in the list goes into the header row. You should therefore not use the FieldList row source type when displaying column headers. If you do, Access displays field names in the header row.

The BoundColumn Property

The BoundColumn property indicates which of the columns in the control will actually be returned when you've made a selection from the list. This means the control returns the value from this column when you assign its value to a variable, for example.

Normal Operation   You must set the BoundColumn property as an integer between 0 and the number stored in the ColumnCount property. To retrieve the value from the control, use an expression like this:

```
varMyVariable = Me!cboTestCombo
```

The variable varMyVariable receives the value from the chosen row in cboTest-Combo, from the column specified in its BoundColumn property.

To set the value of the control, use an expression like this:

```
Me!cboTestCombo = varMyVariable
```

This code selects the first row in cboTestCombo in which the value in the column specified in the BoundColumn property matches the value stored in varMyVariable. If Access can't find a match, the control value will be Null.

The Special Case   If you set the BoundColumn property to 0, Access returns the selected row number in the control; the value of the control will be the row number of the selected row. Although this isn't very useful for bound controls—the chosen row number won't mean much when stored in a database—it can be very useful if you need to select a particular row in the control.

Suppose, for example, you want to make sure you've selected the first row of an unbound list box for each record, before the user even gets a chance to make a choice. Normally, to specify the row of the control you want selected, you would just assign a value to the control.

Unfortunately, in some cases (for example, when the RowSource of the control is a SQL query), you don't know the value of the bound field in the first row. To get around this problem, you can set the BoundColumn property to 0. Once you've done this, you can just assign the control the value 0, which will select the first row. (The row values are zero based.) To retrieve values from a control with the Bound-Column set to 0, use the Column property, discussed in the next section. For an example of setting the BoundColumn property to 0, see the section "Making Multiple Selections in a List Box" later in this chapter.

There are alternatives, of course. The ItemData method of a list or combo box returns the data from the bound column in any row you want. For example, rather than set the BoundColumn property to 0 in order to initialize a list box to the first row, you can set the default value to this expression instead:

```
=cboExample.ItemData(0)
```

The Column Property

The Column property of list and combo boxes is not available at design time but figures prominently at run time. It allows you access to data in any of the columns of any row of the control. The general syntax looks like this:

value = FormReference!ListOrCombo.Column(*column*[,*row*])

In a fit of nonstandardization, Access uses zero-based numbers for the column and row numbers: when you set the BoundColumn property to 1, you use Column(0) to retrieve the value stored there.

For example, to retrieve the data stored in the second column of the chosen row of cboTestCombo, use

```
varTestVariable = Me!cboTestCombo.Column(1)
```

To retrieve the value in the third column of the fourth row of cboTestCombo, use

```
varTestVariable = Me!cboTestCombo(2, 3)
```

Present a Name, Store an ID

Given these facts:

- A list/combo box can contain more than one column (ColumnCount > 0).

- The first visible column is the one Access displays in the text box portion of the combo box.

- Any column in the list/combo box can be bound to the underlying data (BoundColumn).

- You can set the width of any column to 0, rendering it invisible (Column Widths).

- List/combo boxes have their own separate source of data (RowSource).

it's easy to create a list or combo box that displays user-friendly information (such as a name) but stores information the user doesn't normally care to see (such as a counter value). Figure 7.13 (frmTextToID) shows such a combo box in action. In this example you're filling in a shipping form and want to choose the delivery method from a combo box. The delivery method is stored as an integer, but you can't expect users to remember the integer associated with each carrier. Therefore, you can use a query (qryDeliveryMethod) to feed the data for the combo's RowSource property. The second column in the combo has been made invisible (ColumnWidths set to ";0"), and the combo box will store the chosen value in its second column, the ID, to the underlying data (BoundColumn = 2, ControlSource = *DeliveryMethod*). You should be able to apply this same method to any situation in which you want to present the user with one piece of information but store a different, related piece of information.

FIGURE 7.13
Display text, but store an
ID to the underlying data.

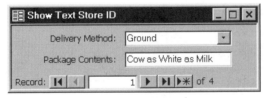

TIP

When your combo is bound to a numeric field (as it is in the previous example), you need to set the TextAlign property yourself. Because Access thinks you're really displaying a numeric value, it aligns the text to the right (which is how it treats numeric values). Set the TextAlign property manually to display the text the way you want it aligned.

Present a Calculated Value, List Individual Fields

Combo boxes can display only a single value in their text box portions, and it's always the value from the first visible column of the selected row in the control's drop-down list. What if you want to display a number of pieces of information in the text box portion but present discrete fields to the user in the drop-down list? Figure 7.14 shows such a scenario: the control displays a concatenated company, contact, and title in the text box portion but individual fields in the drop-down list.

How can you make this happen? It's simple, once you know the trick. It counts on the fact that Access displays in the text box the data from the first visible column in the control's drop-down list. In addition, the combo box can't physically display any column with a width set to less than $\frac{1}{100}$ inch. Therefore, you fill the combo with a query that performs the calculation you need and put that value in the first column of the combo. Figure 7.15 shows the query filling the example combo box. The first column creates a calculated field. The second becomes a hidden column containing the primary key, and the other columns make up the list portion of the control.

FIGURE 7.14

You can display a calculated field in the combo but display separate fields in the list.

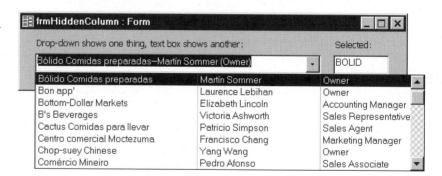

FIGURE 7.15

Count on Access' treatment of combo box columns to hide or display data.

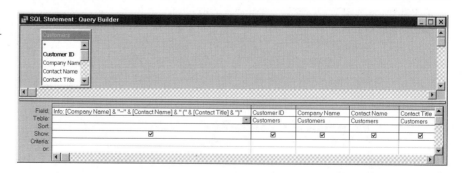

In the ColumnWidths property, set the width of the first column to 0.001 or so. (Depending on your screen resolution, Access may alter the value after you've entered it. The widths of the other columns are up to you.) Be sure to set the ColumnCount property to accurately match the number of columns you want to pull in from your query, and Access will do the rest. In this example, the Column-Widths property is set to 0.001";0";2";1.5";1", the ColumnCount property is set to 5, and the BoundColumn property is set to 2.

Multi-Select List Boxes

In 16-bit versions of Access, one of the most frequent complaints about list boxes was that you could select only a single item. Access 95 added a MultiSelect property for list boxes, allowing you to choose from three options, shown in the following table:

Setting	Description	Value
None	Single selection only (default)	0
Extended	Shift + click or Shift + arrow key extends the selection from the previously selected item to the current item. Ctrl + click selects or deselects an item	1
Simple	The user selects or deselects multiple items by choosing them with the mouse or pressing the spacebar	2

By choosing Extended or Simple, you can choose one or more items from the list box.

NOTE The MultiSelect property is read-only at run time. You won't be able to switch selection types while your form is in use; you can do so only at design time.

How can you tell which items are selected? There are two methods, and they're both read/write. That is, you can both retrieve the selected list and set it. Figure 7.16 shows a list box with its MultiSelect property set to Extended. As you select each item, code attached to the list box's AfterUpdate event updates the text box to its right.

FIGURE 7.16

The multi-select list box on frmMultiSelect allows you to use Shift+click and Ctrl+click to select multiple items.

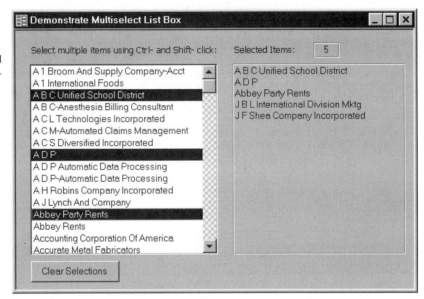

The Selected Property

The Selected property of a list box returns an array of Boolean values, one for each row of data in the list box. If there are 100 items in the list box, the Selected property will return an array of 100 True or False values. Each value in the array indicates whether the corresponding item in the list is selected. You can check to see whether the first item is selected:

```
If Me!lstCompanies.Selected(0) Then
    MsgBox "You've selected the first item!"
End If
```

or you can set the first four items as selected (as long as you've set the MultiSelect property to something other than None):

```
With Me!lstCompanies
```

```
    For intI = 0 To 3
        .Selected(intI) = True
    Next intI
End With
```

You cannot use the Selected array with a single-select list box during the list box's AfterUpdate event, because it hasn't yet been updated at that point. After that event it's current, but it will always have only one item that's True; the rest will always be False (because you can select only one item in the list box). This limits the Selected array's usefulness for single-select list boxes.

The ItemsSelected Property

If you want to do something with every selected item in a multi-select list box, you could use the Selected property to return an array of items and walk the array looking for rows in which the Selected array holds a True value. That is, you could use code such as this to list out the selected items:

```
Dim intI As Integer
With Me!lstCompanies
    For intI = 0 To .ListCount - 1
        If .Selected(intI) Then
            Debug.Print .ItemData(intI)
        End If
    Next intI
End With
```

This requires Access to loop through every single row of the Selected array, which is a lot of effort. To make this simpler, Access supplies the ItemsSelected property, which returns a collection of selected row numbers. To do something with each selected item, just walk this collection, working with each item in the collection, as in this fragment from frmMultiSelect (Figure 7.16):

```
' Show the list of selected companies.
With Me!lstCompanies
    For Each varItem In .ItemsSelected
        strList = strList & .Column(0, varItem) & vbCrLf
    Next varItem
    Me!txtSelected = strList
End If
```

This example also uses the ability of the Column property of a list box to return data from any column of any row. In this case you want the data from the first column (column number 0) in the row specified by varItem.

Like any other collection, the ItemsSelected collection provides a Count property that tells you how many items are currently selected. In frmMultiSelect, the text box showing the number of selected items has this expression as its ControlSource:

```
=lstCompanies.ItemsSelected.Count
```

The LimitToList Problem

The LimitToList property indicates to Access whether it should allow you to enter new values into a combo box. Setting this property to No allows you to disregard the current list of values and enter a new one, and setting it to Yes forces you to choose a value from the current list. If you set your combo box's Bound-Column property to any column aside from the first visible column, Access will (and must) set the LimitToList property to Yes.

You may not, at first thought, agree with this design decision. Imagine, though, for a moment, what's really going on here. Access displays and lets you enter values for the first visible column in the combo box. Therefore, if the control's BoundColumn property is set to 1, Access can take whatever it is you type and store it in the underlying data, even if it's not currently in the list. On the other hand, if the BoundColumn property is greater than 1 and you enter a value that's not already part of the list, Access needs to be able to store a value it doesn't have. Therefore, Access has no choice but to disallow new entries into combo boxes where the first column isn't displaying the bound field. Figure 7.17 shows, in pictorial form, why Access must make this limitation.

Combo boxes don't always do exactly what you might expect in terms of string matching. For example, if the LimitToList property is set to Yes, you might think that typing enough characters to find a match at all would be sufficient for Access to accept the selected value. That is not the case. You must type enough characters to indicate a *unique* match before Access will accept your value and let you leave the field. This can be frustrating for users who will type some characters, see the match in the combo box, and attempt to accept that value by pressing ↵. Unless the characters they've typed so far constitute a unique match, they'll need to keep typing. Combining the LimitToList property with the AutoExpand property, though, will make many users happy. If you set both LimitToList and AutoExpand to Yes, your users can leave the combo box as soon as Access has found any matching

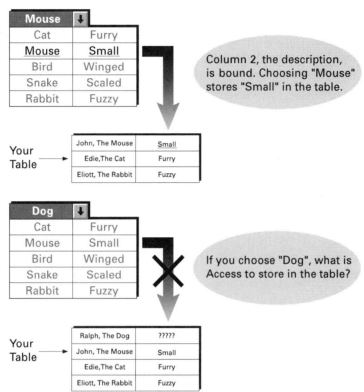

FIGURE 7.17
LimitToList must be set to Yes if you've bound your combo box to a column other than the first column.

Column 2, the description, is bound. Choosing "Mouse" stores "Small" in the table.

If you choose "Dog", what is Access to store in the table?

value in the list. This will, however, add some serious processing overhead. Although combo box performance in Access 97 has been greatly improved, if you find the performance still doesn't meet your needs, turn off the AutoExpand property.

In addition, null values are always a problem. If the LimitToList property is Yes and you type a value into a combo box and then delete it by backspacing over all the characters, the value now will not match any value in your list (unless you happen to have an empty value in the list). Prior to Access 95, you were not able to leave the combo box. Now, LimitToList accepts null values, so you can just delete the value and exit. Another easy way out is to press the Esc key, which undoes your change and lets you leave the control.

Taming the NotInList Event

When a user attempts to enter an item into a combo box (whose LimitToList property is set to Yes) that doesn't match one of the existing items in the list, Access triggers the NotInList event. If you have code in the form's module reacting to that event, you can take one of three actions, depending on how you fill in the Response argument that Access passes to the subroutine:

- If you place the value acDataErrDisplay in Response, Access displays its standard error message.

- If you place acDataErrContinue in Response, Access doesn't display its error message, giving you the chance to display your own. If you use this option, make sure you really do display your own error message. Otherwise, users will be confused.

- If you place acDataErrAdded in Response, you must add the item to the underlying record source, and then Access requeries the combo box for you, effectively adding it to the list.

Because the third option is the most interesting, it is the focus of the following discussion.

Access passes your procedure two parameters: NewData contains the current text in the combo box, and Response allows you to send back the results of your subroutine.

The following simple case, from frmNotInList in CH07.MDB, just asks the user whether to add the new item to the list:

```
Private Sub cboNotInList_NotInList(NewData As String, _
  Response As Integer)
    Dim strMsg As String
    Dim rst As Recordset
    Dim db As Database

    strMsg = "'" & NewData & "' is not in the list. "
    strMsg = strMsg & "Would you like to add it?"
    If vbNo = MsgBox(strMsg, vbYesNo + vbQuestion, _
      "New Company") Then
        Response = acDataErrDisplay
    Else
        Set db = CurrentDb()
```

```
      Set rst = db.OpenRecordset("tblCompanies")
      rst.AddNew
          rst!Company = NewData
      rst.Update
      Response = acDataErrAdded
      rst.Close
   End If
End Sub
```

The code first pops up a message box asking you whether to add the new value. If you consent, the procedure runs code to add the new value. By passing back acDataErrAdded in the Response parameter, you're telling Access it should requery the combo and then try again to verify that the item exists in the list. If the item still isn't in the list for some reason (the sample code doesn't deal with errors, and it ought to), you'll still see the default error message from Access.

In general, your situations won't be this simple. Most likely, you'll need to gather some information from the user before adding a new row to the table. In that case you'll probably want to pop up a form (using the acDialog WindowMode option), gather the information, add it to the table, and then send the acDataErrAdded back to Access to indicate that you've added the new row.

Auto-Drop Combo Boxes

In many situations you may want to have a combo box drop down automatically when you enter it. Although this was possible in earlier versions of Access, it was difficult to implement reliably. Starting with Access 95, Access provides the Drop-Down method for combo boxes, which forces a combo box to open.

The simplest solution is to add code to your combo box's GotFocus event:

```
Sub cboOpenSesame_GotFocus()
    Me!cboOpenSesame.DropDown
End Sub
```

That way, anytime you enter this combo box, it'll drop its list.

The BeforeUpdate and AfterUpdate Events

As with the other controls, Access fires off the BeforeUpdate event just before it attempts to update the underlying record set, and the AfterUpdate event occurs just after. You can attach code to either of these events to trap the selection event in either a list or combo box.

Even more interesting is the ability to trap *movement* in a list box. Access triggers both the BeforeUpdate and AfterUpdate events every time you move the selection bar in a list box. Access must do this because, were you to leave the list box with a Tab or Shift+Tab key at any point, the currently selected item would become the value of the control. This doesn't occur in a combo box, though, since Access won't write any value to the recordset until you've made a selection by clicking, pressing ↵, or leaving the combo. Since you can attach code to the Before/AfterUpdate events in a list box, you can make changes to other controls on your form based on the current value in the list box. Thus, you have the choice of using a "push" method for filling unbound controls on your form (that is, you *push* values into them) in addition to the simpler "pull" method, where the controls use expressions to pull in their values from other sources.

Using Combo and List Boxes to Fill In Other Controls

Access provides several methods by which you can choose a value and have the corresponding data from other fields filled in for you on a form. The method you choose depends on whether the controls to be filled in are bound and how many controls you want filled in.

Data Filled In for Free: Using AutoLookup

AutoLookup is a very misunderstood and underutilized feature. It comes into play anytime you have a one-to-many join, your form's RecordsetType property is set to Dynaset (or you're working with a raw query datasheet instead of a form), and you make a change to the joining field on the "many" side of the one-to-many relationship. If the field you change on the "many" side is the linking value between the two tables, Access knows only one set of data will match that value and fills in all the new data, based on the changed value. AutoLookup is really of value only when you're looking up some information for part of a larger form, such as information in an address on a shipping form, since the lookup must take place in a one-to-many relationship.

To see AutoLookup in action, open frmAutoLookupDemo. This form, shown in Figure 7.18, draws its data from qryAutoLookup: this query gets its data from the Customers and Orders tables. The important issue is that the combo box on frmAutoLookupDemo is bound to the Customer ID field from the Orders table. It's crucial in this situation that you take the linking field from the *"many"* side of the relationship. When you make a choice in the combo box, Access automatically looks up the values in the "one" side of the relationship, and those values are the ones you see in the etched read-only text boxes on the form.

FIGURE 7.18

AutoLookup makes it easy to look up values, but only in a one-to-many relationship.

Pulling versus Pushing Data into Controls

Imagine you want to provide a combo box from which you can choose a value. Once a value has been chosen, you want to fill in various other controls on the form with data found in the row that corresponds to the value the user just chose. The methods for doing this differ, depending on whether those other fields are bound. If the other controls are bound, you must "push" data into them; otherwise, they can "pull" the new data in themselves. You might think of the pull method as being *passive,* since the data just flows in, and the push method as being *active,* since you must provide code to copy the data from the list or combo box. For examples of each type of mechanism, you can investigate frmPullTest and frmPushTest in CH07.MDB. Figure 7.19 shows frmPullTest in action, and Figure 7.20 shows frmPushTest.

FIGURE 7.19

frmPullTest uses the Column property in each of its text boxes to retrieve the values from the current row.

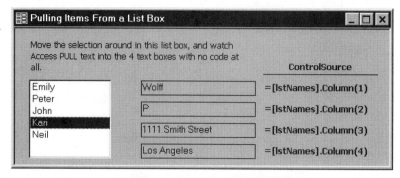

FIGURE 7.20

frmPushTest uses a small function to copy values from 1stNames to each of the text boxes.

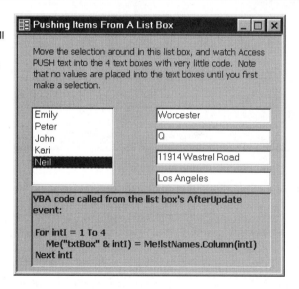

Pulling Data into Unbound Controls

If the controls to be filled in are unbound, their ControlSource property is otherwise empty, and you can use an expression to pull in data from the combo box where the user just made a choice. All references in this example work equally well for list boxes and combo boxes.

To pull in data from the combo box, follow these steps:

1. **Fill the combo:** Create a query (or use an existing table) that contains the data you want to present, plus any other fields you want filled in automatically

once the user makes a choice. Later steps will be simpler if you make sure the value to be displayed in the combo is the first field in the table or query, but that isn't imperative.

2. **Prepare the combo:** Set the ColumnWidths property so that the correct column is visible and the other columns are invisible. If the first column is the one you want displayed and you have five columns total, your Column-Widths setting would be

    ;0;0;0;0

    This tells Access to use the default width for the first column and 0 width (hidden) for the next four columns.

3. **Prepare the other controls:** Set the ControlSource property for each of the controls into which you want data pulled. In each case, set the ControlSource property to

    =*YourCombo*.Column(*n*)

    where *YourCombo* is the ControlName of the combo and *n* is the column number (starting at 0) you want pulled into the control.

Once you've set up the form, Access takes care of the rest. Anytime the combo box changes, the other controls on the form will recalculate and pull the value they need from the combo box. If you're pulling information from a list box, the information will be updated each time you move the selection bar in the list box. This is a convenient way for users to browse items as they move through the list box using the arrow keys. It takes absolutely no programming to accomplish a great deal!

NOTE   Although the method described above is very simple, it exacts a heavy price in performance. Because Access recalculates all dependencies on the form anytime you change a value on the form, you may find that pulling in data from a combo or list box is quite slow if the control contains a large number of rows. If you implement the "pull" method demonstrated here and your form slows down, you'll want to switch to the "push" method described in the next section.

TIP

Because the controls must have a calculated ControlSource for the method described above to work (and are therefore read-only), you might find it useful to also set the Locked property to Yes and the Enabled property to No. This way the control will appear normal, but your user won't be able to make changes.

Pushing Data into Bound Controls

If you need to fill in controls that are bound, their ControlSource property is not empty, and you can't use the "pull" method described in the previous section. In this case you'll need to push data into the controls once you've made a choice from the combo or list box. This is also simple, but it requires a bit of code.

The steps you follow to implement this method are the same as they were for the "pull" method. In this case, though, you need to leave the ControlSource property of the text boxes alone. The assumption is that you're using this method because those controls are bound to data fields. To apply the "push" method, you attach code to the AfterUpdate event of the combo or list box, which will fill the appropriate controls. In the example form, frmPushText, the code just loops through all the columns and sends out data to each of the four conveniently named text boxes:

```
Dim intI As Integer
For intI = 1 To 4
    Me("txtBox" & intI) = Me!lstNames.Column(intI)
Next intI
```

Filling a List or Combo Box Programmatically

Access provides you with many ways to get data into a list box without programming at all. You can supply a table or query name, a list of items, or a SQL string.

There is still at least one case in which you'll need to write code to fill a list box: if you need to fill the list box with values from an array, you must write code to do it. We suggest two such methods, but creative programmers can probably come up with others. You can either manipulate the RowSource property directly, providing a semicolon-delimited list of values, or write a callback function to provide Access with the needed values.

Changing the RowSource Property

Imagine a situation in which you have two buttons on your form. Choosing one of those buttons fills a list box with values from one specific field, and choosing the other fills the list box with values from a different field. Figure 7.21 shows a form like this in action (frmFillTest in CH07.MDB).

The following method creates a semicolon-delimited list of items for the list box (which must have its RowSourceType property set to ValueList) based on the recordset the user chose.

```
Set rst = db.OpenRecordset( _
 "SELECT [" & strField & "] FROM " & strTable & _
 " ORDER BY [" & strField & "]", dbOpenDynaset)
Do Until rst.EOF
    strFill = strFill & rst(strField) & ";"
    rst.MoveNext
Loop
ctl.RowSource = strFill
rst.Close
```

This code creates the Recordset object and walks through that object, building up a string in the format

Item1; Item2; Item3; Item4;…ItemN;

and then places that string in the list box's RowSource property. Since the Row-Source property can contain only 2048 characters, however, you're limited to small recordsets when you use this method.

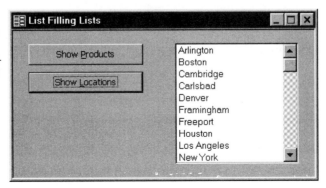

FIGURE 7.21

Click the Show Locations button to see a list of locations or the Show Products button to see a list of products.

Listing 7.2 shows the entire function. Interestingly, we performed some simple timing tests. Compared to the more obvious method, which is to set the RowSourceType to Table/Query and the RowSource to a SQL string describing the list, this method performed favorably for small lists. For larger lists, you'll have to try both and convince yourself.

Listing 7.2

```
Public Function SetListBoxContents(intFlag As Integer)
    Dim db As Database
    Dim rst As Recordset
    Dim strField As String
    Dim strTable As String
    Dim strFill As String
    Dim lst As ListBox

    Set lst = Me!lstShowList

    Select Case intFlag
        Case adhcShowProducts
            strField = "Products"
            strTable = "tblProducts"
            lst.ControlTipText = "Choose a product"
        Case adhcShowLocations
            strField = "Locations"
            strTable = "tblLocations"
            lst.ControlTipText = "Choose a location"
        Case Else
            Exit Function
    End Select
    db = CurrentDb()
    Set rst = db.OpenRecordset("SELECT [" & _
     strField & "] FROM " & strTable & " ORDER BY [" & _
     strField & "]", dbOpenDynaset)
    Do Until rst.EOF
        strFill = strFill & rst(strField) & ";"
        rst.MoveNext
    Loop
    lst.RowSource = strFill
    rst.Close
End Function
```

Using a Callback Function to Fill the List Box

To fill a list or combo box with an array of values or display information from an internal Access data structure, your best alternative is to use a list-filling function. Access allows you to supply a function that tells it all about the list or combo box you want displayed. You tell Access the number of columns, the number of rows, the formatting for individual elements, and the actual data elements. This is the only case in which Access directly calls a user-created function and uses the information it receives back from that function. This is, in effect, what makes your function a *callback* function—you are supplying information Access needs to do its job.

All this flexibility comes at a price, however. For Access to be able to communicate with your function, it needs to have a very specific interface, and it must respond in expected ways when Access requests information from it. Access calls your function at various times as it's filling the list box and indicates to your function exactly which piece of information it requires at that moment by providing an action code as one of the parameters. Metaphorically, every time Access calls this function, it's asking a question. It's up to your function to supply the answer. The question might be, "How many columns are there?" or "What value do you want displayed in row 1, column 2?" In any case, Access supplies all the information you need to retrieve or calculate the necessary answer. The return value from the function returns the question's answer to Access.

To attach your function to the list/combo box on a form, type its name (*without* a leading equal sign and *without* trailing parentheses) in the RowSourceType on the property sheet. This break in the normal syntax for the property sheet tells Access you're specifying a callback function. This is the property sheet set up to use a callback function:

```
Control Source . . . . . .
Row Source Type . . . .   FillTableOrQueryList
Row Source . . . . . . . .
```

Setting Up Your Callback Function

Any function that will be used as a list-filling callback function must accept exactly five parameters, the first declared As Control and the rest using simple datatypes. The following table lists the various parameters (the names used for them by convention; feel free to choose your own) and their descriptions:

Parameter	Description
ctl	Control-type variable that refers to the list box or combo box being filled
varID	Unique value that identifies the control being filled; you may find it more useful to check ctl.Name if you need to differentiate between controls using this code
lngRow	Row being filled in (zero-based)
lngCol	Column being filled in (zero-based)
intCode	The "question" Access is asking your function; its value indicates what action your function should take

A typical function declaration looks like this:

```
Function FillList(ctl as Control, varID as Variant, _
  lngRow as Long, lngCol as Long, intCode as Integer) _
As Variant
```

Your function reacts to each of the values in intCode, returning the information Access requests. Table 7.3 lists the possible values for intCode, their constant names as defined by Access, and the information Access is requesting when it sends you each of the constants.

When Access requests values for the list (acLBGetValue), it supplies a row and a column number in the lngRow and lngCol parameters, implying that you need to have random access to your data. Filling a list box from a recordset, then, is a tricky issue, because you don't really have random access to all Recordset objects in Access. (You can use the AbsolutePosition property to set the position directly for all but table-type recordsets.) You can emulate random access, however, using the Move method for Recordset objects. We present both methods of solving this problem. The first solution here suggests copying data from your recordset into an array, so you actually *can* access specific rows at will, but this method becomes quite slow when your datasets are large. The second solution uses the Move method to get to the exact record you need, based on the most recent record you were on and the new row number you need to get to. This method starts up more

TABLE 7.3 The acLB… Constants and Their Uses in Filling a List or Combo Box Programmatically

intCode	Constant	Meaning	Return Value
0	acLBInitialize	Initialize	Nonzero if your function can successfully fill the list; 0 or Null otherwise
1	acLBOpen	Open	Nonzero ID value if the function can successfully fill the list; 0 or Null otherwise. Many functions use the return value from the Timer function to get a unique value
2	Not used		Not used, although Access does call the function with this value. Its use is not documented
3	acLBGetRowCount	Number of rows	Number of rows in the list (can be 0); −1 if unknown. If you specify −1, Access calls the function to retrieve values (acLBGetValue) until you return a null value
4	acLGGetColumnCount	Number of columns	Number of columns in the list (can't be 0); should match the value in the property sheet. You can, of course, just pass back ctlField.ColumnCount or skip this option altogether
5	acLBGetColumnWidth	Column width	Width of the column specified in the varCol parameter (can be 0), measured in twips ($\frac{1}{1440}$ inch). Specify −1 to use the property sheet values, or just skip this option
6	acLBGetValue	Value	Value to be displayed at row varRow and column varCol
7	acLBGetFormat	Format string	Format string to be used in displaying the value at row varRow and column varCol. Specify −1 to use the default format, or skip this option
8	acLBClose	Not used	Not used, so no return value. Access does call your function with this value, though. Its use is not documented
9	acLBEnd	End	Returns nothing. Used when you close the form or requery the control. Use this portion of your function to release memory or clean up as necessary

quickly since it's not copying data into an array, but it's slower in execution since it must refer to actual data on disk to display its contents.

In general, your callback function will probably look something like the example code in Listing 7.3. It needn't be terribly complex, and once you've written a few of these functions, you should be able to cut-and-paste a new one in seconds.

Listing 7.3

```
Function FillList(ctl As Control, varId As Variant, _
 lngRow As Long, lngCol As Long, intCode As Integer) _
As Variant

    Dim varRetval as Variant
    Dim intRows as Integer
    Dim intCols as Integer
    Static aData() as Variant

    Select Case intCode
        Case acLBInitialize
            ' Initialization code
            ' Figure out how many rows and columns there are
            ' to be, and ReDim the array to hold them.
            ReDim aData(intRows, intCols)
            ' Code to fill the array would go here.
            varRetval = True

        Case acLBOpen
            ' Return a Unique ID code. The built-in Timer
            ' function works well.
            varRetval = Timer

        Case acLBGetRowCount
            ' Return number of rows
            varRetval = intRows

        Case acLBGetColumnCount
            ' Return number of columns
            varRetval = intCols

        Case acLBGetColumnWidth
            ' Return the column widths. If you return -1
            ' from this call, Access will use the default
            ' width for the specific column. That way,
```

```
            ' you can use the property sheet to supply the
            ' column widths.
            Select Case lngCol
                Case 0
                    ' Handle the first column
                    varRetval = 1440
                Case 1
                    ' Handle the second column
                    ' and so on.
                    varRetval = -1
            End Select

        Case acLBGetValue
            ' Return actual data.
            ' This example returns an element of the
            ' array filled in case acLBInitialize
            varRetval = aData(lngRow, lngCol)

        Case acLBGetFormat
            ' Return the formatting info for a given row
            ' and column.
            Select Case lngCol
                Case 0
                    ' Handle each column, setting the format.
                    varRetval = "ddd"
            End Select

        Case acLBEnd
                ' Clean up
                Erase aData
        End Select
        FillList = varRetval
End Function
```

Using a Callback Function

Displaying a list of table and/or query names is a prime candidate for using a callback function. Since you can get such a list only by enumerating Access objects, the callback function provides the most reasonable way to get the values into a list box. This example makes heavy use of data access objects to do its work. (See Chapter 6 for more information on the object collections.) Figure 7.22 shows the example form (frmListTables from CH07.MDB) in use. Open the form's module to follow the description of the code.

FIGURE 7.22

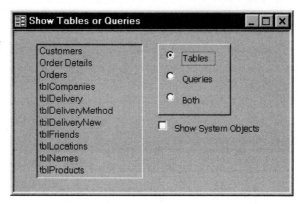

Choose Tables, Queries, or Both to display a list of the selected items.

In the acLBInitialize case, your goal is to set up the array to be used for later retrieval in the acLBGetValue case. In this example you need to find out how many tables and queries there are and store that value away. If there are no tables or queries (an unlikely event, since every database has at least the system tables), return a False value, telling Access your function is unable to initialize the list box:

```
Set db = CurrentDb()
' Figure out the greatest number of entries
' there might be.
db.TableDefs.Refresh
db.QueryDefs.Refresh
intItems = db.TableDefs.Count + db.QueryDefs.Count
If intItems = 0 Then
    varRetval = False
Else
.
.
.
```

Once you've found there are some tables or queries to display, your next step in the initialization case is to build up the array you will send to Access in the acLBGetValue case. Based on choices you've made on the form, the function will pull in different items for the list. For example, to get a list of queries, the code looks like this:

```
If ShowQueries() Then
    For Each qdf In db.QueryDefs
        If Not IsTemp(qdf) Then
            sastrNames(sintItems) = qdf.Name
```

```
                    sintItems = sintItems + 1
            End If
        Next qdf
End If
```

The variable sintItems will indicate the number of elements in the list box once you've finished all the looping, and this is the value you pass back to Access in the acLBGetRowCount case.

The rest of the code closely follows the skeleton example. It uses the default column widths and doesn't even bother dealing with the acLBGetFormat case, because it's just using the default formats. When asked to supply a value (in the acLBGetValue case), it just returns the value for the given row from the array it built in the acLBInitialize case. Finally, when Access shuts down the list box, the acLBEnd case uses the Erase command to release the memory the array uses.

To include this form in your own application, follow these steps:

1. Import the form frmListTables from CH07.MDB into your application.

2. Modify the AfterUpdate event of the list box lstTables to *do* something with the user's choice. Perhaps you'll want to place it into a global variable for later use.

Emulating a Permanently Open Combo Box

Access does not supply a drop-down list box control, and there will be times when you must have the list portion of a combo-like control permanently open. You can emulate this arrangement, however, with the pairing of a list box and a text box. The issue, of course, is performing the incremental search as you type into the text box, finding the matching elements of the list box as you type. Because Access provides the Change event for the text box, you can attach code to this event property that finds the first entry in the list box that matches the text you currently have in the text box. This functionality looks and feels just like the search capability in Windows Help and should fit well into many applications. Figure 7.23 shows a sample form, frmTestIncSrch from CH07.MDB, in action.

The drawbacks to this pairing, however, are somewhat serious. Because Access must do a lookup in the underlying data source for every change the user makes in the text box, response time can be slow in certain cases. On the other hand, if you can bind the list box to a table (and can guarantee the use of an index for lookups), the speed is quite reasonable even for large lists.

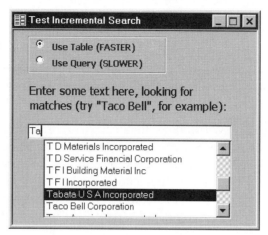

FIGURE 7.23

Typing into the text box
will find the first matching
value in the list box.

The sequence of steps necessary to accomplish this hybrid control is quite simple. Every time Access fires off the Change event for the text box, it calls the adhIncSrch function. This function tries to find the first entry in the list box's underlying recordset that matches the text currently in the text box. If the list box is bound to a table, the function uses the PrimaryKey index (or optionally, any index you specify) with the Seek method to find the first match. This method is quite fast. If the list box is bound to a query (and it must be bound to either a table or a query for this code to work at all), it uses the FindFirst method of the recordset to find the first match. This method can be much slower, depending on Access' ability to use an index for its search.

The function grlIncSrch uses some interesting techniques. (Look in basIncSearch for a complete listing.) First of all, rather than opening and closing a Recordset object for every lookup, it maintains a global Recordset variable. The first time you try to perform a lookup, the attempt to access the recordset will fail, triggering an error condition. The error handler calls SetUpRst, which first attempts to open a table-type recordset based on the data source. If it succeeds, and if it manages to set the Index property of the recordset, it's home free.

If SetUpRst can't open a table-type recordset, it'll open a dynaset-type recordset instead. In either case, the global variable mrst ends up pointing to the Recordset object, and the recordset will remain open until you close the form. (The code attached to the form's Close event closes the recordset.) Once everything is opened up, the function resumes back at the top, where it can now successfully do its work. The following code fragment shows the error-handling code in adhIncSrch:

```
Set mdb = CurrentDb()
' Set up the recordset.
If IsMissing(varIndex) Then
    varIndex = "PrimaryKey"
End If
If SetUpRst(ctlListBox.RowSource, varIndex) = 0 Then
    Resume LookItUp
Else
    Resume adhDoIncSearchExit
End If
```

Rather than just opening the Recordset object directly, adhIncSrch calls the SetUpRst function to do its work. As mentioned above, SetUpRst first attempts to open a table-type recordset and assign the Index property of the recordset. If both those steps succeed, it's done its work. If that fails, it now knows it will not be able to open a table-type recordset, and it attempts to open a querydef matching the row source it's been passed. To be as flexible as possible, SetUpRst attempts to resolve any parameters involved with the querydef. By walking through the Parameters collection, it can supply all the values for the query, as long as the values are available.

You should notice that the assignment

```
varValue = ctlTextBox.Text
```

uses the Text property rather than the Value property, which is the default property for text boxes. Since the value in the text box has not yet been committed at the point at which the function needs to access its contents, the Value property has not yet been updated. The Text property is always current while the control is active, but the Value property is not.

Doing the work is really quite simple. If the list box is bound to a table, the function uses the Seek method to find the first value greater than or equal to the value in the text box. If the list box is bound to a query, the function builds a string expression to be used as the criteria for the FindFirst method and uses it to search for the first match. In either case, if the NoMatch property is Yes after the search, there's not much the function can do (especially since the search really can't fail unless something is seriously wrong with the data), and it just displays a message box and quits:

```
If mintType = adhcObjTable Then
    mrst.Seek ">=", varValue
```

```
Else
    ' See Chapter 6 for more information on quotes within
    ' quoted strings.
    mrst.FindFirst strField & " >= " & _
     adhcQuote & adhHandleQuotes(varValue, adhcQuote) & _
     adhcQuote
End If
If Not mrst.NoMatch Then
    ctlListBox = mrst(strField)
Else
    ' This shouldn't happen, right?
End If
```

You might also notice that we've included code to fill in the text box with the currently selected value from the list box if you either click it in the list box or leave the text box at any point. This seems like reasonable and helpful behavior, similar to the way the AutoExpand property for combo boxes works.

In summary, the issues surrounding the use of this code are as follows:

- The list box's ControlSource must be either a table or a query.

- If the ControlSource is a table, the field you display must be the primary key, and the primary key must be named PrimaryKey, or you must pass in the name of the index as the final optional parameter.

- Using a query as the ControlSource is far more flexible, but it might be slower than using a table. This issue is far less important on small datasets.

- Because the code uses a global variable to refer to the list box's underlying recordset, you cannot use this code for more than one pair of controls at a time.

To include this functionality in your own application, follow these steps:

1. Import the basIncSrch and basHandleQuotes modules from CH07.MDB.

2. Create the text box and the list box.

3. From your text box's Change event, call the adhIncSearch procedure, replacing the control and field names with your own:

   ```
   Call adhIncSearch([txtIncSrch], [lstIncSrch], "Company")
   ```

4. From your text box's Exit event, call the adhUpdateSearch procedure:

   ```
   Call adhUpdateSearch([txtIncSrch], [lstIncSrch])
   ```

5. From your list box's AfterUpdate event, call the adhUpdateSearch procedure:

```
Call adhUpdateSearch([txtIncSrch], [lstIncSrch])
```

Making Multiple Selections in a List Box

Access list boxes allow multiple selections, as you saw in the section "Multi-Select List Boxes" earlier in this chapter. The only problem with using multiple-select list boxes is that it's difficult for users to see which items they've selected if the list is too long to fit on the screen. In addition, there's really no way, using a single list box, to change the ordering of the choices. (Wouldn't it be wonderful if Access list boxes supported the same functionality as Visual Basic's list boxes!)

Fortunately, you can code around these problems by showing the user two list boxes, one representing available items and the other representing selected items. By moving items from one list to the other, your users can select a group of items on which to work. Figure 7.24 shows a sample multi-pick list box (frmMultiPik from CH07.MDB) in action. Both list boxes on frmMultiPik allow multiple selections, so you can select as many items as you wish in either list box and move them all to the other list box. In addition, the buttons to the right of the Selected list box allow users to reorder their chosen items.

FIGURE 7.24

By clicking the buttons (or double-clicking the list boxes), the user can select a group of items.

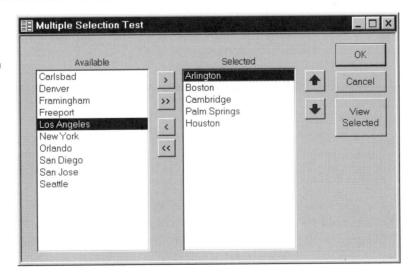

NOTE

Because of the way Access handles multi-select list boxes, it's not possible to alter the position of items in the list box if the MultiSelect property is set to Extended. Therefore, the right-hand list box has its MultiSelect property set to Simple. If you don't intend to allow users to alter the ordering of items in the list, or if you must use Extended multi-select (in which case you cannot alter positions), modify the MultiSelect property yourself.

VBA provides several ways to accomplish this goal, and we've chosen a method that allows you some flexibility. By using the code presented here, you'll be able to base your multiple-pick hybrid control on a recordset (either a table or a query) or on two arrays of values, one representing the available list and one representing the selected list. You might want to open frmMultiPik in CH07.MDB and experiment a bit while reading the following sections.

Our implementation of multiple-pick lists uses an array and two collections; the array holds the actual data and the selection status of the items. The two collections keep pointers to the rows in the master array that are available and those that are selected. The array (aFullArray in the code) is based on this structure:

```
Type typDataRow
    varData As Variant
    fSelected As Integer
End Type
```

The two collections (colAvailable and colSelected) do no more than store the index numbers of the available and selected items. When the code needs to fill in the Available or Selected list, it uses list-filling callback functions. (See the section "Using a Callback Function to Fill the List Box" earlier in this chapter.) In each case the callback function walks through each element of the available or selected collection and fills the appropriate list box with the data from the master array. Given that varRow represents an index in the Selected list box, the item displayed in the list box will be

```
aFullArray(colSelected.Item(varRow + 1)).varData
```

Like many other examples in this chapter, multiple-pick lists can be easily incorporated into your own applications. Rather than dissecting the full code for multiple-pick lists here, we refer you to basMultiPik in CH07.MDB. There are some points worth discussing here, though.

Filling the Two List Boxes

Unlike most other examples in this book, the two list boxes in this example have their BoundColumn property set to 0. As mentioned in the section "The Special Case" earlier in this chapter, setting the BoundColumn property to 0 effectively binds the list box to the selected row number, starting with 0. If the list box had a ControlSource (which these don't), you'd end up storing the chosen row number in the underlying data. In this case, setting the BoundColumn property to 0 makes it easier to programmatically specify the particular row to select.

In addition, these list boxes contain two columns. The first, visible, column contains the data from the master array. The second, hidden, column contains the master array index from which this particular piece of data came. Therefore, it takes two passes through the callback function to fill both columns. In one call to the function, when varCol is 0, Access retrieves the value for the first column. Access retrieves the value for the second column in a second call to the list-filling function:

```
Case acLBGetValue
    ' Get the data for each of the two columns.
    varValue = colSelected.Item(varRow + 1)
    If varCol = 0 Then
        varRetval = aFullArray(varValue).varData
    Else
        varRetval = varValue
    End If
```

One Callback or Two?

It's true that Access does pass your callback function a unique identifier for each control that calls into that function, and it also passes a handle to the control being filled. Given that information, it would seem that you could write a single function to fill the two list boxes used in this example. Actually, it turns out that combining these two functions, adhFillSelected and adhFillAvailable, into one function is more work than it's worth. The problem is, we found, that the two list boxes get filled in bits and pieces, overlapping in time. Although they could physically be combined, the resulting code would be so convoluted and difficult to maintain that it made more sense to separate them.

Retrieving the Selected List

This hybrid control, the pairing of two different list boxes, wouldn't do you much good if you couldn't easily find out which items the user had selected. Therefore, the module basMultiPik includes a function your application can call to retrieve an array containing the list of selected items. The sample form (frmMultiPik) displays the list in a message box when you click the View Selected button. To retrieve the list for your own use, call the function adhGetSelectedItems, passing in a reference to the active form and a dynamic array the function can fill in with the selected items. For example, in the sample form, the Click event of the View Selected button executes this code:

```
Private Sub cmdChosen_Click()

    Dim aSelected() As Variant
    Dim varItem As Variant
    Dim strShowIt As String

    ' Get an array filled with the selected items.
    Call adhGetSelectedItems(Me, aSelected())

    For Each varItem In aSelected
        strShowIt = strShowIt & varItem & vbCrLf
    Next varItem
    MsgBox strShowIt, Title:="Multiple Pick Test"
End Sub
```

Issues to Consider

The implementation of multiple-pick lists presented here is not completely generic. You should be aware of several issues before you attempt to use this hybrid control in your own applications:

- The code is non-reentrant—you can't have multiple forms with multiple pick lists on them at the same time. You can have multiple pick lists in your application, but when you move from one to the other, you'll need to reset the code, calling adhRegisterControlNames and adhFillMultiPikField or adhFill-MultiPikArray (depending on the data source).

- The data must come from either a table or query or from an array. To use a recordset variable to fill the list, you need to create arrays and fill them with the appropriate data before you call adhFillMultiPikArray.

- Think twice before using this method with large lists (more than 1000 data elements or so). It can take a long time to fill the collections when you have many elements.

- Multiple-pick lists make sense only when the data elements you present to the user are unique. You may need to concatenate multiple fields in a query, creating a list of unique values. Once you have that unique list, you can present it to the user.

To include multiple-pick lists in your own applications, follow these steps:

1. Import the module basMultiPik from CH07.MDB.

2. Create your form, including two list boxes and four data movement buttons. If you want to include the buttons to move selected data up and down, you can add those buttons, as well. You may find it easiest to just copy the eight controls from frmMultiPik in CH07.MDB by first importing frmMultiPik, then copying the appropriate controls, and then deleting frmMultiPik from your database.

3. If you want, set the AutoRepeat properties of all the command buttons to Yes.

4. Set the properties of the two list boxes, as shown here:

Column Count	2
Column Heads	No
Column Widths	;0"
Bound Column	0

You must set the ColumnCount to 2 and the BoundColumn to 0. The other two settings (ColumnHeads and ColumnWidths) presented in the preceding illustration are suggestions only.

5. Add procedure calls to various events, as shown in Table 7.4. The table uses the control names from the examples, but you're welcome to use any names you wish.

In addition, in the Form_Open event, you'll need to either call adhFillMulti-PikArray, passing to it the current form and the two arrays you want displayed:

```
call adhFillMultiPikArray(Me, varAvailable, varSelected)
```

or adhFillMultiPikField, passing to it the form reference, the name of the field to display, and the table from which to retrieve it:

```
Call adhFillMultiPikField(Me, "Locations", "tblLocations")
```

6. In the Declarations section in your copy of basMultiPik, change the values of the constants adhcSelectedList through adhcDeleteAllButton if your control names are different than ours. Again, if you copied the controls from the sample form, there's no need to change the names.

7. If you're filling your list boxes from arrays, you'll need to fill those arrays from your form's Open event, before you call adhFillMultiPikArray. The example form doesn't use this functionality, but if you want to try it out, change the constant USE_ARRAYS in frmMultiPik's module:

```
#Const USE_ARRAYS = False
```

to True. This causes the sample form to read its data from the arrays instead of from a table.

TABLE 7.4   Procedures Calls for MultiPik

Event Procedure	Procedure Call
lstAvailable_DblClick	Call adhMultiPikAddOne(Me)
lstSelected_DblClick	Call adhMultiPikDeleteOne(Me)
cmdAddOne_Click	Call adhMultiPikAddOne(Me)
cmdAddAll_Click	Call adhMultiPikAddAll(Me)
cmdDeleteOne_Click	Call adhMultiPikDeleteOne(Me)
cmdDeleteAll_Click	Call adhMultiPikDeleteAll(Me)
cmdUp_Click	Call adhBumpUp(Me)
cmdDown_Click	Call adhBumpDown(Me)
Form_Open	Call adhRegisterCtlNames(adhcSelectedList, adhcAvailableList, adhcAddOneButton, adhcAddAllButton, adhcDeleteOneButton, adhcDeleteAllButton)

Other Areas of Interest

If you're interested in studying user-defined collections, MultiPik's source code is a good place to start. It uses all the methods of collections (Add, Remove, Item) and exercises all the mechanisms for working with multi-select list boxes, as well. You'll find the routines that move selected items up and down the list (adhBumpUp and adhBumpDown) of particular interest, since these use many advanced features of collections.

The code that copies data from your table into aFullArray is interesting, as well. It uses the GetRows method of a recordset to return all the rows you care about in one single statement. Rather than looping through the rows of data one by one, this method returns all the rows you request into a variant array. In the sample case, because you need the data in an array of user-defined types, the code still has to walk the entire set of data. But the loop now is all in memory instead of looping through rows on the disk, one by one. The following code fragment is from adh-FillMultiPikField, in basMultiPik:

```
' Get all the data.
rst.MoveFirst
varData = rst.GetRows(intcount)
rst.Close


' Now copy that data into the array of
' total items, avarItemsToFill.
' The array returned by GetRows is 0-based.
Set colSelected = New Collection
Set colAvailable = New Collection
For intLoop = LBound(aFullArray) To UBound(aFullArray)
    ' aFullArray is 1-based, but the array from GetRows
    ' is 0-based. Therefore, the "intLoop - 1" in the
    ' next line.
    aFullArray(intLoop).varData = varData(0, intLoop - 1)
    aFullArray(intLoop).fSelected = False
    Call AddItem(colAvailable, intLoop)
Next intLoop
```

Isn't There a Better Way?

This really seems like a lot of code to do something that ought to be easy. Isn't there a better way? Of course. You can implement this same sort of functionality very easily, with a lot less code. The form frmMultiPikTable implements this technique. It works by using a Yes/No column named Selected in your table, which keeps track of which rows are selected. The code reacts to clicks of the selection buttons by setting the Selected field in the underlying table to either True or False and then refilling the list boxes with the appropriate (selected or not) subset of the data. Experiment with frmMultiPikTable to get a feel for how this works.

You may find this simple technique satisfies your needs, but you may also find some drawbacks that make it unsuitable:

- Because the code writes directly to the table, you'd have to take extra steps to make this work in a multiuser environment. You could create a new table that works in parallel with the main table, in a one-to-one relationship that's kept locally. This table could keep track of the selected items.

- The code fills the lists directly from the table. If you wanted to control the order of the selected list, you'd need to add another field to keep track of the order in which they were selected. Again, there are multiuser concerns involved.

On the other hand, this technique is quite fast: all it does is write directly to the table, setting the Selected field and then requerying the two list boxes.

How and When to Use Subforms

To display data from more than one table in any but a one-to-one relationship (a single form based on a query will handle the simple one-to-one case), you need to investigate subforms. Although you can use subforms in the one-to-one case, they are not required. A subform is nothing more than a related form displayed within a form; it can be displayed in Datasheet or Form view, and it can, in turn, contain another subform. Access allows nesting subforms two deep so you can display data in a one-to-many-to-many relationship. In addition, subforms have a bit of an identity crisis: from their own point of view, they're forms. From the point of view of their parent form, they're controls, just like any other control.

Creating a Subform

You first need to create the form you wish to use as a subform. It needs no special handling and can be any form you happen to have created. Remember that you will need to modify any special form-level properties for the subform on the form itself (not as a subform on some other form). You can make those changes at any point, though. The DefaultView, ViewsAllowed, and ScrollBars properties are important to consider when designing your subforms. If you save the form that will become the subform without scroll bars and in a particular view, that's how Access will display it on the main form.

Drag-and-Drop That Form

The easiest way to create a subform is to select and drag an existing form from the database window to your main form. Access will understand that you intend to create a subform and do the work for you. In addition, if you have created any default relationships between the tables on which you've based the form and subform, Access will fill in the LinkChildFields and LinkMasterFields properties for you. Note that this subform is not a copy of the original form, just a reference to it. That is, if you make changes to the original form that is now a subform, closing and reopening the main form will update all the information stored in the main form, and the subform will reflect any changes you've made.

NOTE   If your main form has its DefaultView property set to Continuous Forms and you place a new subform control on that form, Access displays a dialog box warning you that it will change the form to single-form mode. Access cannot display subforms on continuous forms.

Choosing a Control from the Toolbox

You can create a subform by choosing the Subform control from the toolbox. Once you place your control on the form, you can specify the source object, which tells Access where to retrieve the form at display time. Access provides you with a list of possible objects, which, in this case, will be a list of the currently defined forms in your database. In addition, you can change the SourceObject property while your form is in use. That is, when you change the SourceObject property for the subform control, Access pulls in different forms as you make the change.

TIP   Once your form is neatly embedded in a subform control on the main form, you can edit the form easily: just double-click the control in Design view. Access will bring up the subform control's form for you to work on. When you're done, close the form, and when you run the main form in Form view, your changes should take effect.

Relating the Parent to the Child

The LinkChildFields and LinkMasterFields properties control how the main form and the subform relate and interact. Once you have properly set these properties, record pointer movement in the master form will trigger appropriate movement in the child form. This way, the records displaying in the child form should always match the record displaying in the master form.

Allowable Settings

The LinkChildFields property applies to the subform, and the LinkMasterFields property applies to the main form. In each case, you can enter one of the following:

- A field name from the underlying recordset (a table or query), identified in the RecordSource property

- A list of fields, separated by semicolons

The number of fields you enter must match exactly in both property settings. Although the field names can match, there is no reason why they must. As long as the datatypes match and the data is related, this connection should work.

Setting the Values Automatically

Under either of the following two conditions, Access fills in the LinkChildFields and LinkMasterFields properties automatically:

- Both forms are based on tables, and the Tools ➤ Relationships menu item has been used to create default relationships between the two tables.

- Both forms contain fields of the same name and datatype, and the field on the main form is the primary key of the underlying table.

Always check the validity of the supplied links, because Access might make some incorrect assumptions. Unless one of the preceding conditions is true, Access cannot make a determination of how to link the forms and therefore leaves the properties empty.

Retrieving Calculated Values from Subforms

You may find it useful to employ subforms to display detail records and report on the total of some value displayed there on the main form. This is one of Microsoft AnswerPoint's most popular questions: how do you retrieve values from subforms back to the main form?

The complete syntax is rather complex and not at all obvious:

Forms![*Your Form Name*]![*SubForm Name*].Form.Controls![*Your Control Name*]

The important issue here is that you must use the Form property of the subform control to find the form contained within it and the Controls collection of that form to refer to controls on the form. To explore this syntax, you might take a look at the properties available when you have selected your subform in Design view. You'll notice that none of the actual form properties are available at this point. Therefore, were you to use the syntax

Forms![*Your Form Name*]![*SubForm Name*]

you'd have access only to those properties that you see in the property sheet. For example, you could set the Visible property of the subform:

Forms![*Your Form Name*]![*SubForm Name*].Visible = True

Luckily, you don't have to worry about any of these details. The default property of a subform control is its Form property. The default collection for a Form object is its Controls collection. Therefore, if you just use something like this:

```
Debug.Print Me!fsubOrder!txtTotal
' equivalent to:
Debug.Print Me!fsubOrder.Form.Controls!txtTotal
```

Access will know to look at the fsubOrder subform on the current form and then, on that form, to find the txtTotal text box and retrieve its value.

> **TIP**
> When creating references to subforms and the forms and controls they contain, remember that the only place to be concerned with the name of the form filling the subform control is in the control's SourceObject property. None of your code will care about, and none of your references will include, the actual name of the form. What your code needs is the name of the subform *control*, which will usually be different than the name of the form contained in the subform control.

Going All the Way

Access allows you to nest subforms two deep. That is, you can place a form that itself contains a subform as a subform on a form. This ability can be quite useful if you want to represent a one-to-many-to-many relationship on a form. For example, your client, a law office, might need to display information about each lawyer, the lawyer's clients, and billing information for each client. By nesting subforms, you could create a form that allowed your client to page through each lawyer and, for each, view each client. For each client, a third form could display the billable events for that client. Figure 7.25 shows a very simple form, frmNested, with two nested subforms.

> **NOTE**
> Since most of the interesting things you can do with subforms involve their acting as real forms, we cover subforms in detail in Chapter 8.

Using Command Buttons

Command buttons are most often associated with actions. Their most common use is with a macro or Basic code attached to their Click event. They have several interesting and useful properties and events, as described in the following sections.

Macros to Buttons, Automagically

Knowing that many people are likely to create macros and then assign them to command buttons on forms, Access allows you to select a macro name in the database window and drag it onto a form. Doing this creates a command button for

FIGURE 7.25

The main form represents a customer, the first subform represents one of the customer's orders, and the second subform represents the order items for that particular order.

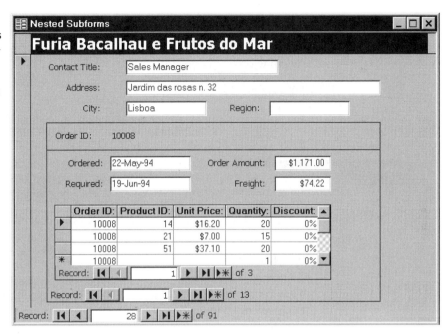

you, with the Caption property set to be the name of the macro. This feature is of limited value if you store more than one macro in a given macro group, but if you store one macro for each group, it's a nice feature. As a developer you're more likely to be writing modules than writing macros, so there's not much point dwelling on this feature.

Command Button Properties

Some of the properties associated with command buttons are different from those for all other controls, so it's worth a moment to go over the unique properties here.

The Picture Property

Unlike any other control, a command button can display either a bitmapped image or a text caption on its surface. (It would be nice if you could mix both on the button, but that option is not currently available. You can, however, use a graphics editor to create a bitmap image that includes text.) You can specify either a bitmap or an icon file to be placed on the surface of the button. Access displays your chosen picture centered and clipped on the button. In addition, Access attempts to display the *center* of your image in the center of the button; this way, if you shrink the button size so it's smaller than the picture, the center of the picture will still show. To simulate the button being depressed, Access shifts the bitmap to the right and down about 1 or 2 pixels. For this reason, very large bitmaps look rather strange when you click the button. You might consider sticking with icon-sized bitmaps for your buttons.

TIP

Access previously stored only the bitmap image, not a pathname reference to that image, in the button's properties. If you changed your mind about the image or just wanted to find out which file was currently being displayed in the button's picture, you were out of luck. Starting with Access 95, however, Access does store the full path to the image in the Picture property if you use your own image (as opposed to one retrieved from the Command Button Wizard). In addition, the PictureData property can return the bit-level image of the picture. You can also use the PictureData property to set the picture on a button. The simplest use for this is to copy a picture from one button to another by assigning a PictureData property from one to the other. See Chapter 19 for more information on using the PictureData property.

The Transparent Property

The command button's Transparent property turns off all display attributes but leaves the button active. This property allows you to overlay a button on another control that might not normally be able to receive focus or fire off events. For example, you could place a transparent command button on top of a line and assign an action to its Click event. To the user it would appear as though the line were reacting to the mouse click! You can also overlay transparent command buttons on bitmaps on forms, allowing various pieces of the bitmap to react to mouse clicks. Imagine a bitmap of the United States, with each state's name printed on the state. With a transparent button overlaid on the state's name, you could allow users to click the image of the state and have Access react to the click.

NOTE Do not confuse the Transparent property with the Visible property. When you set a control's Visible property to No, you completely disable that control. Not only is it invisible; Access removes it from the form's tab order, and it can never receive focus or trigger an event. When the Transparent property is Yes, Access turns off only the display attributes for the button. All the other attributes still apply. You can reach it by tabbing to it or clicking it. All its events are active.

The Default/Cancel Properties

Every form can have exactly one button that acts as the default button (its Click event gets triggered when you press ↵ on the form) and exactly one button that acts as the Cancel button (its Click event gets fired off when you press Esc on the form). A button with its Default property set to Yes acts as the form's default, and a button with its Cancel property set to Yes acts as the form's cancel button. Note that each form can have at most one of each of these, and setting a button's Default or Cancel property to Yes sets any other button's matching property to No.

You might think, as do many developers, that setting a button's Cancel property actually causes something to happen, perhaps closing of the form. This is simply not true. All that happens as a result of a button's Default or Cancel property being set to Yes is that that button receives focus and Access fires off its Click event when you press the correct key.

Give the assignment of Default and Cancel properties some serious thought. For situations in which something destructive might happen at the click of a button, make the Cancel button the default button. To do so, set both the Default and Cancel properties to Yes.

The Visible Property

Unlike the Transparent property, setting the Visible property to No for a button actually disables the button completely. This is the same behavior as with other controls, but it can be confusing for command buttons, which also support the Transparent property.

The DisplayWhen Property

If you are inclined to print single records from your form, you will find the DisplayWhen property indispensable. Since you probably will not wish to print the buttons on the form with the data, set the DisplayWhen property for the buttons to Screen Only. This way, when you print the form, the buttons won't print along with the data.

The Enabled Property

In modern, user-driven applications, it's important to make sure users can't make choices that shouldn't be available. It may have been reasonable at one point for a user to click a button only to be confronted with a dialog box that shouted, "This option is not currently available!" The correct way to handle this situation is for you to disable the button when the option isn't available so the user can't click it in the first place. Set the Enabled property to No when you want the button to be unavailable. Set it to Yes when you want the user to be able to click the button. You may be tempted to make unavailable buttons invisible, but many people find this distracting, since they tend to think, "I saw that option a minute ago; where did it go?"

The AutoRepeat Property

The AutoRepeat property determines whether Access will repeat the code attached to the Click event for a button while you hold down the button. Access fixes the initial repeat to be 0.5 second after the first repetition. Subsequent repeats occur each 0.25 second or at the duration of the macro, whichever is longer.

NOTE   The AutoRepeat property has no effect if the code attached to the button causes record movement on the form. Moving from row to row cancels any automatic repetitions.

One use for the AutoRepeat property is to simulate a spin-button control. In this sort of arrangement you create a text box and two little buttons, usually one with an up arrow and one with a down arrow. As you press the up arrow button, some value in the text box increases, and as you press the down arrow button, the value decreases. One issue to consider when doing this, though, is that Access performs the repeat without consideration for Windows' screen-painting needs. Therefore, your code will probably get far ahead of Windows' ability to repaint the text box. Anytime you cause screen activity using an auto-repeat button, you need to use DoEvents to allow Windows time to catch up.

Why bother creating your own spin buttons when there are ActiveX controls that perform this same function? First of all, most of the spin-button controls we've seen are unattractive. If you create your own, you control how they look. Also, ActiveX controls still exact a somewhat hefty overhead in terms of resources, speed, and application size. Because spin buttons are so easy to create using Access built-in controls, it seems like overkill to use an ActiveX control for this. In addition, because you're writing the code here, you can control the behavior. For example, the spin buttons we'll create here allow you to limit the range and, possibly, cycle back to the beginning or end once you reach an endpoint.

Example: Simulating Spin-Button Controls

Spin buttons provide one way to both control the values your users input and make it simpler for them to change numeric and date values. The basic concept should be familiar—it includes two buttons, one pointing up and the other pointing down, "attached" to a text box. Pressing the "up" button increments the value in the text box, and pressing the "down" button decrements the value. Although you could theoretically use this mechanism for text values, it's not often used that way. For the most part, spin buttons are restricted to date and integer entry.

In basSpin you'll find code that allows you to use spin-button controls in your own projects. We've provided two versions of the code—one for the simple case in which you just want to allow the spin buttons to cause the text box to go up or down in value, and one for the case in which you want to provide minimum and maximum values. This advanced version also allows for value wrapping at either end of the range or at both ends and also works with dates. Figure 7.26 shows the two spin buttons in action, along with text boxes displaying the function calls necessary to make them work. The sample form is frmSpinTest in CH07.MDB.

FIGURE 7.26

Examples of spin buttons. Note that the advanced example can spin through dates, as well as through numeric values.

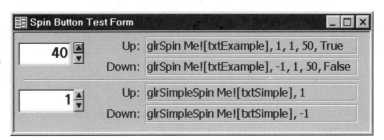

379

The simple case, in which the code doesn't limit the range your user can spin through, just pulls the current value from the attached text box, increments or decrements it, and then assigns it back to the text box. This code is in the function adhSimpleSpin in the module basSpin. (You'll find it useful to open this module as you read this discussion.) Of course, this action can cause an error, since the user could have entered a non-numeric value into the text box. The code disregards errors (using On Error Resume Next), so the buttons do nothing if they find an invalid value in the text box. If no error has occurred, the code uses DoEvents to allow Windows to repaint the screen as necessary to keep up with the changing values.

To use the adhSimpleSpin function, call it from the Click event of the buttons you want to use to control the text box. That is, use something like this:

adhSimpleSpin *txtYourTextBox*, *increment*

where *txtYourTextBox* is the text box containing the value your buttons are going to alter and *increment* is the amount to add to the value in the text box each time the button is pressed. (Generally, use +1 to go up and –1 to go down.) Figure 7.26 shows this function call in use.

The function adhSpin contains the more complex case, in which you can control the minimum and maximum values allowed in the text box. This function allows you to specify the control to manipulate, the increment (either positive or negative), the minimum and maximum values, and a True/False value indicating whether to allow wrapping. If you allow wrapping, the value will go from the maximum value back to the minimum value when moving up and from the minimum to the maximum when moving down. If you don't allow wrapping, no further movement will be allowed once the user reaches an endpoint (either the maximum or the minimum value). Since you call this function from the Click event of both spin buttons, there's nothing stopping you from putting in different parameters for the up button than for the down button. In some cases this makes sense. For example, if you want the user to be able to wrap back to the lowest value after reaching the highest value when moving up but not to be able to wrap after reaching the lowest value when moving down, you can do that.

To use the adhSpin function, attach a call to it from the Click event of your spin buttons:

adhSpin *txtYourTextBox*, *increment*, *min*, *max*, *allow wrap?*

where *txtYourTextBox* is the text box containing the value your buttons are going to alter and *increment* is the amount to add to the value in the text box each time the button is clicked. (Generally, use +1 to go up and –1 to go down.) The value *min* specifies the minimum value, and *max* specifies the maximum value. If you don't wish to specify a minimum or maximum value, don't specify a value for the appropriate parameter. In addition, if you specify both a minimum and a maximum value, you can enable wrapping by sending True as the final parameter. If you don't send both a minimum and a maximum value or if you send False for the final parameter, the function will not wrap as you move up or down with the spin buttons.

Once you have the correct procedure called from the Click event of the button, you must make sure the AutoRepeat property is set to Yes. This ensures that the action will repeat as you hold down the button. To decipher exactly what the adh-Spin function is doing, look at the code in basSpin. It's somewhat complex, due to the extra overhead of handling the wrapping and endpoints.

Command Button Events

Command buttons provide the same events as other controls, but you're likely to use just one of them, the Click event. You might be tempted to assign different actions to the Click and DblClick events. Don't bother. Access can't possibly differentiate between the two events and will always attempt to fire off the Click event before the DblClick event. This functionality can be useful to you at times, though. When you want the DblClick event to add to the Click event, it works to your advantage. In general, if you want to attach code to both events, make sure the code attached to the DblClick event extends the action done in the Click event. In actuality, you won't want to use the DblClick event for buttons very often.

The Tab Control

New in Access 97, the tab control is a built-in control that finally allows developers to create standard tabbed dialogs that match the Windows 95 "look." Figure 7.27 shows a simple example (frmTabSimple) using the tab control.

Developers have been asking for a built-in control like this one since the first version of Access hit the streets, and working around its absence has become an industry unto itself. Perhaps, in the past, you've used overlaid subforms or a multipage subform, controlled by a series of toggle buttons. Or perhaps you've used a technique demonstrated in the first edition of this book, *Microsoft Access 2 Developer's Handbook*, using graphical controls to "draw" a tab control on a form. Or perhaps you've used

FIGURE 7.27

The tab control makes it simple to create multi-page, standard tabbed dialogs.

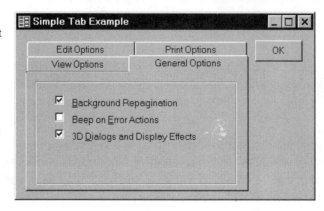

one of the several ActiveX controls available that provide this functionality. None of these techniques are necessary anymore. Although the built-in tab control is missing some useful functionality (you can't place the tabs anywhere except on the top edge of the control, and you can't change the color of individual tabs, for example), its simplicity and programmability far outweigh any perceived lacks.

What Works and What Doesn't

Because there are so many existing external tab-like solutions, it's important to provide a "level-set" here so you know what the tab control can do and what it can't. The following lists point out some of the features (and non-features) of the built-in tab control.

You can

- **Display multiple rows of tabs:** Set the MultiRow property to match your preference.

- **Place icons on the tabs:** Each page on the tab supports a Picture property, and you can display both a picture and text on the tab.

- **Hide the tabs altogether:** You can set the Style property to Tabs, Buttons, or None. Setting it to None provides a neat way to create multipage forms, just as Access has always been able to do, without most of the effort.

- **Place ActiveX controls on the pages:** No problem! Each page can contain its own set of controls, any of which can be ActiveX controls.

- **Float a control above the tab:** If you have a control you want to display at the same place on all pages, just place it on the form and then position it on top of the tab control. The sample form frmSimpleTab uses this technique to display the etched rectangle.

- **Hide/move pages at run time:** If you need to change the number of pages, or rearrange them, at run time, you can do it. Each Page object supports a Visible property that you can set to be True or False. Each Page object also supports a PageIndex property, which is read/write both when designing and when displaying the form, that allows you to set the order of the pages as they're displayed by the tab control.

You cannot

- **Nest tab controls:** Although you can float a tab control on top of another (so that the smaller control appears on every page of the larger control), you cannot place a tab control on a page of a tab control.

- **Provide transition effects:** Some ActiveX tab controls provide ways to show effects as you change from one page to another (page turning, slides, and so on). The Access tab control does not provide any such mechanisms.

- **Change orientation of the tabs:** With the Access tab control, you can have any text orientation you like, as long as it's horizontal, on the top of the control. The built-in Windows 95 control doesn't support placing the tabs along the sides or bottom, nor does it support rotating the text. Therefore, the Access tab control also doesn't support those features.

- **Drag-and-drop controls between pages:** Page controls work very much like option groups. To place a control on either control, you must either create it fresh or copy/cut/paste it from another location.

- **Create or delete pages at run time:** You can add to or delete from the Pages collection only in Design view. If you want to be able to control the number of pages at run time, you'll need to create as many pages as you think you might need at design time and then use the Visible property of the pages to display them when your form is opened. (The sample from, frmTabCustomers, uses this technique.)

TIP Although you can't place a tab control inside another tab control, you can work around this limitation by placing a tab control on a form and embedding this second form inside a page of your main tab control.

NOTE As mentioned above, the PageIndex property of a Page object determines its position within the tab control. This is the only place we know of in Access where you can set the position of an item within its collection without removing it first. In addition, it's the only place where an object's position within its collection is linked to the display of the object. There's no visible link between the position of a control within the Controls collection and its position on the screen, for example.

How the Tab Control Works

You can think of the tab control as a container for Page controls, each of which is a container for other controls. Only one Page object is visible at a time, and the tabs across the top allow you to switch from displaying one page to another.

The tab control provides a Pages collection that includes all the Page objects. You could, for example, write code like this to list out the Caption property for all the pages in a tab control:

```
Dim pge As Page
For Each pge In Me!tabItems.Pages
    Debug.Print pge.Caption
Next pge
```

Each Page object is also a member of the form's Controls collection. (For more information on forms and their Controls collection, see Chapter 8.)

Just as with any other collection (see Chapter 6 for more information on collections and referencing items in them), you can use several methods for referring to a Page object. For example, if the first page in a tab control were named "Page1", you could use any of the following methods to retrieve a reference to that page:

```
Dim pge As Page
Set pge = Me!tabItems.Pages(0)
' or
Set pge = Me!tabItems!Page1
```

```
' or
Set pge = Me!tabItems("Page1")
```

Each Page object provides a Controls collection, allowing you to programmatically visit every control within a specific page. For example, the following code fragment would change the ForeColor property of every control on a specific page to red:

```
Dim ctl As Control

' Disregard errors: Some controls don't support the
' ForeColor property.
On Error Resume Next
For Each ctl In Me!tabItems.Pages(0).Controls
    ctl.ForeColor = 255
Next ctl
```

In addition, Access makes all the Page objects, and all the controls on those pages, elements of the Controls collection of the form itself. Think of it this way: all the controls (the tab control itself, pages, and controls on each page) are elements of the form's Controls collection. Access just neatly "corrals" them into the Pages collection of the tab, and the Controls collection of each Page object, to make it easier for you to work with them.

TIP

When you first start working with tab controls, you may have a hard time selecting the entire control, as opposed to a specific page within the control. With the property sheet open, it's easy to tell which has been selected: just look at the title of the window. If you want to select a page, click the tab for that page. If you want to select the entire tab control, click the edge of the control—in other words, clicking on the right or bottom black border edge never fails.

An Advanced Example Using the Tab Control

As an example of the kinds of things you can do with a tab control, frmTab-Customers (see Figure 7.28) provides a tab for each different country in the Customers table. If you run the form, you'll see that it displays a single tab for each different country in the table, and once you select a tab, the form displays rows only for the selected country.

FIGURE 7.28

The sample form, frmTab-Customers, modifies the tab captions as it loads.

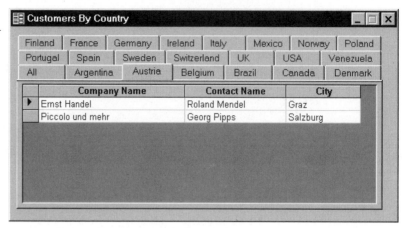

The mechanics of loading the tab labels is somewhat complex, mostly because you cannot add or delete pages at run time. This means that for an interface like this, you must create as many tabs as you'll ever need in Design view and then hide the extra tabs as you load the form. This means, of course, that this technique isn't as general purpose as it might be, but really, how many pages can a given tab control support, anyway? If your tab control has more than 30 pages or so, it's too complex. Even the example shown here is really pushing it.

Creating the Tab Control

Adding a page or two to a tab control isn't a problem, but adding 10 or 20 can become a chore. To simplify the task, you can use the PrepareTab procedure (in basTabSetup). This subroutine accepts two parameters: a reference to a tab control and the number of tabs you'd like that control to have. When the code runs, it either removes pages or adds them to get the page count to the value you request. The code, shown in Listing 7.4, does its work by sheer brute force.

Listing 7.4

```
Public Sub PrepareTab(ctl As TabControl, _
  ByVal intPages As Integer)
    Dim pge As Page
    Dim intI As Integer
    Dim pges As Pages
```

```
    On Error GoTo HandleErrors

    Set pges = ctl.Pages
    If intPages < 1 Then
        Exit Sub
    Else
        If intPages < pges.Count Then
            For intI = pges.Count - 1 To intPages Step -1
                pges.Remove intI
            Next intI
        Else
            For intI = 1 To intPages - pges.Count
                pges.Add
            Next intI
            ctl.MultiRow = True
        End If
    End If

ExitHere:
    Exit Sub

HandleErrors:
    Select Case Err.Number
        Case Else
            MsgBox "Error: " & Err.Description & _
            " (" & Err.Number & ")"
    End Select
    Resume ExitHere
End Sub
```

In this example, if the number of pages in the Pages collection is greater than the number you've requested, the code walks backward through the collection, using the Remove method to delete pages until the number of pages is correct. If there are fewer than you require, the code uses the Add method to add as many pages as necessary.

To create the sample control on frmTabCustomers (with 30 pages), add a tab control to the form, set its name (tabCustomers in this example), and then call Prepare-Tab like this:

```
Call PrepareTab(Forms!frmTabCustomers!tabCustomers, 30)
```

Modifying Tabs at Run Time

Once you've created a control that contains enough pages, modifying it at run time is simple: you simply set the Caption and Visible properties of each page you want shown and set the Visible property for those you want hidden. In the example, code called from the form's Load event (see Chapters 2 and 8 for more information on calling code in reaction to events) takes these steps:

1. Creates a distinct list of country names from the Customers table.

2. Sets the caption for the first page (page number 0) to "All".

3. Loops through the rest of the pages, copying country names to each page's caption and setting the Visible property to True. Stops when there are no more pages or no more countries.

4. If there are still pages (that is, there were fewer countries than pages), loops through the rest of the pages, setting the Visible property to False.

5. Finally, because the number of tabs affects the height of the display area for the pages, sets the size of the display subform to match the size of the first page. If there are only two countries, the display area will be larger than if there are 30 countries.

See Listing 7.5 for the entire procedure.

TIP

If you're going to be working with page captions programmatically, you may find it useful to disable form updates until you're finished. That way, you can avoid the flashing that occurs as Access updates the display of the tab control. To do this, use the Painting property of the form: set the property to False when you start, and set it to True when you're done.

Listing 7.5

```
Private Sub Form_Load()
    Dim rst As Recordset
    Dim db As Database
    Dim intI As Integer
    Dim lst As SubForm
```

```
' Fill the existing tabs on a tab control with the
' values from the selected field
On Error GoTo HandleErrors

Me.Painting = False

Set db = CurrentDb()
Set rst = db.OpenRecordset( _
 "SELECT DISTINCT " & conFieldName & " FROM " & conTable)
Set lst = Me(conSubform)
lst.Form.Filter = ""

intI = 0
' Work with the Pages collection.
With Me(conTabs)
    With .Pages
        With .Item(0)
            .Caption = conShowAll
            .Visible = True
        End With
        ' Loop through all rest of the pages. Once you run
        ' out of pages, you have to stop! If you hit the
        ' end of the records, jump out and make all the
        ' rest of the pages invisible.
        For intI = 1 To .Count - 1
            If rst.EOF Then
                Exit For
            End If
            With .Item(intI)
                .Caption = rst(conFieldName)
                .Visible = True
            End With
            rst.MoveNext
        Next intI
        ' Loop through any unused tabs, making
        ' them invisible.
        Do While intI < .Count
            .Item(intI).Visible = False
            intI = intI + 1
        Loop
    End With
    ' Set the list box to fit into the page, no matter
```

```
                     ' how many rows of tabs are showing.
                     With .Pages(0)
                         lst.Top = .Top
                         lst.Height = .Height
                         lst.Left = .Left
                         lst.Width = .Width
                     End With
                 End With
                 Me(conSubform).Form.FilterOn = True

ExitHere:
        If Not rst Is Nothing Then rst.Close
        Me.Painting = True
        Exit Sub

HandleErrors:
        Select Case Err.Number
            Case Else
                MsgBox "Error: " & Err.Description & _
                    " (" & Err.Number & ")"
        End Select
        Resume ExitHere
End Sub
```

Reacting to Page Changes

If you need to do something every time a different page is displayed on the tab, you can write code that reacts to the control's Change event. In the example, the control must apply a different filter to the subform every time a different country is selected. (See Chapter 8 for more information on using the Filter and FilterOn properties.)

To make this possible, use the Value property of the tab control. This property contains the PageIndex property of the selected page. The sample code uses this property to retrieve the caption for the selected page:

```
With Me(conTabs)
    strValue = .Pages(.Value).Caption
End With
```

Once the code knows the caption of the selected page, it builds a SQL WHERE clause and filters the subform accordingly. The following code, called from the tab control's Change event, does the work:

```
Private Sub tabGroups_Change()
```

```
    Dim strWhere As String
    Dim strValue As String

    On Error GoTo HandleErrors

    With Me(conTabs)
        strValue = .Pages(.Value).Caption
        If strValue = conShowAll Then
            strWhere = ""
        Else
            strWhere = _
                conFieldName & " = '" & strValue & "' "
        End If
    End With

    With Me(conSubform).Form
        .Filter = strWhere
    End With

ExitHere:
    Exit Sub

HandleErrors:
    Select Case Err.Number
        Case Else
            MsgBox "Error: " & Err.Description & _
                " (" & Err.Number & ")"
    End Select
    Resume ExitHere
End Sub
```

Using This Technique in Your Own Applications

It's simple to use this sample technique in your own applications. To do so, follow these steps:

1. Create the subform that will display the data. Include the fields you want displayed and set the DefaultView property to Datasheet.

2. Import frmTabCustomers into your own application and rename it appropriately.

3. If you will need substantially more or fewer than the 30 pages currently displayed on the form, use the PrepareTab procedure, as discussed in the earlier section "Creating the Tab Control," to set the number of pages.

4. Modify the SourceObject property of the subform control on frmTabCustomers so that it will load your new subform.

5. Modify the first two constants in the class module for frmTabCustomers. The first constant should be the name of the table filling your subform, and the second should be the name of the field you want to group on (Country, in this example).

That's all it takes. Remember, this technique won't be effective with more than 20–30 items, but it works well with dynamic sets of data up to that size.

Using the Tab Control as a Container

Although it may not be an obvious use, you can also turn off a tab control's labels (set the Style property to None) and use the control as a container for other controls. (If you also want to hide the border, set the BackStyle property to "Transparent".) Why would you want to do that?

Replacing Multipage Forms

The tab control makes a great replacement for Access' multipage forms. Rather than fighting with the 22-inch limit and working with forms that won't fit on your screen, you can place a tab control on your form and let its multiple pages handle the job a single multipage form used to handle. If you want to allow users to change from page to page, you can either react to the PgUp and PgDn keys or supply navigation buttons. In either case, set the Value property of the tab control to display a new page. Chapter 8 includes an example of using a tab control this way.

Augmenting Rectangles and Option Groups

The tab control is the only control (aside from the option group) that can contain other controls. You can surround a group of controls with a rectangle control, but that doesn't "connect" them in any way. When you move a tab control or an option group, all the contained controls move with it. You can cut-and-paste the entire group of controls to a different form by selecting just the container. You can also iterate the Controls collection of the container to take some action on each of the contained controls. (Try doing that for a group of controls surrounded by a rectangle!)

You can create a tab control with a single page, set the Style property to None (and the BackStyle to Transparent, if you don't want the border displayed), and then place controls inside it. You can place any control except another tab control inside a page, unlike an option group. You can also place a number of check boxes on a page and allow multiple selections, which doesn't work with an option group.

Using Default Control Properties to Your Advantage

Access stores default settings for each type of control with each form. To describe the settings for individual controls on the form, Access stores just the settings that *differ* from the default settings. Therefore, if a control has the same settings as the form defaults, Access won't need to store settings for that control. This affects only the stored image of the form; the comparison to the default values is only a save/load issue. All settings for all controls are available once Access loads the form (so there's no actual run-time memory savings).

You can change the default settings for a specific control in two ways. The first involves setting the properties before you actually create the control. The second lets you create the control, specify all its settings, and then tell Access to make those settings the default settings for that type of control.

Either way, when you specify the default settings, other controls of that type you create will inherit the default settings. Previously created controls won't be affected by changes to the default settings.

To set the default settings for a specific type of control before creating one, click that control in the toolbox. Notice that the title for the property sheet has changed to indicate that you're now setting properties for the *default* version of the control. Make whatever changes you want.

To set the default settings based on a specific control you've already created, create your control and set the properties you want. Once you're satisfied, choose the

Format ➤ Set Control Defaults menu option. This stores the settings used in the selected control in the form's default settings for that type of control.

Either way you do it, once you've set the default properties, any controls of that type that you create from then on, on the current form, will inherit those properties. When you save the form, Access will save only the properties for each control that differ from the default values. Judicious use of default properties can speed up your development time, as well as make forms smaller and therefore speed their load time.

Using the DefaultControl Method to Set Up Default Properties

What if you want to control properties for the default version of a control program-matically? In 16-bit versions of Access, you just couldn't. Now you can use the DefaultControl method of a form or report to retrieve a reference to the default control of any given type. Once you have that reference, you can set the properties of the default control, and any controls you create from then on will inherit those settings. This has two effects:

- You'll save steps, both in code and in the user interface. Controls you create will inherit the settings you want from the default controls.

- You'll save time and space. Because Access stores only control properties that differ from the default properties for that control type, if you've set the defaults for the control type and use those for most of your controls, you won't have to save most properties for most controls.

The DefaultControl method makes it possible to work settings that weren't available by any means in earlier versions of the product.

The syntax for calling DefaultControl looks like this:

Set *control* = *object*.DefaultControl(*controlType*)

where *control* is an object variable of type Control, *object* is a form or report reference, and *controlType* is one of the ac... constants that refer to controls (see Table 7.1 for a complete listing).

The control reference returned from a call to the DefaultControl method doesn't refer to a real control on the form or report, but rather to the internal representation of the default for that control type. Setting properties of this control won't make any changes to existing controls, or to the form or report on screen. On the other hand, once you've set the default properties for various control types, subsequent controls you create will use these new settings. Of course, the DefaultControl method works only when the form or report is in Design view.

For example, the following code fragment sets the default font name and size for all text boxes you create after calling this code:

```
With Me.DefaultControl(acTextBox)
    .FontName = "Tahoma"
    .FontSize = 10
End With
```

Creating Controls Programmatically

Access provides functions to create forms and reports, and the controls on these objects, programmatically. This is, of course, how the Access Form and Report Wizards work. They gather information from you about how you want the form or report to look, and then they go through their code and create the requested form or report. Chapter 22 covers in detail how you can create your own Wizards, but there are other uses for those functions. Specifically, if you want to create a form or report with many similar controls that can be easily described programmatically, you may be able to use one or more of these functions.

Functions That Create Forms and Controls

CreateForm and CreateReport create a form or report and return that object as the return value of the function:

CreateForm([*database* [,*formtemplate*]])

CreateReport([*database* [,*reporttemplate*]])

The form or report these functions create is "lightweight." (That is, it doesn't contain a module—its HasModule property is set to False—until you add some code.) The following table describes the parameters for these two functions:

Argument	Description
database	String expression representing the database in which to look for the template form. To look in the current database, omit this argument
template	String expression representing the form or report template to use in creating the new form or report. Use the word *Normal* to use the standard template. To use the template specified in the Tools ➤ Options menu, omit this argument

The following fragment will create a new form, with the caption "My New Form":

```
Dim frm As Form
Set frm = CreateForm("", "")
frm.Caption = "My New Form"
```

Use CreateControl and CreateReportControl to create new controls on forms and reports, respectively. The following fragment details the parameters you use when calling CreateControl and CreateReportControl:

```
CreateControl(formname As String, controltype As Integer _
 [, sectionnumber As Integer [, parent As String _
 [, fieldname As String [, left As Integer [, top As Integer _
 [, width As Integer [, height As Integer]]]]]]] )
CreateReportControl(reportname As String, _
 controltype As Integer[, section as Integer _
 [, parent As String[, columnname As String _
 [, left As Integer[, top As Integer _
 [, width As Integer[, height As Integer]]]]]]])
```

Table 7.5 lists the parameters for the two functions, along with the possible values for those parameters.

TABLE 7.5   Parameters for CreateControl and CreateReportControl

Argument	Description
formname, reportname	String expression identifying the name of the open form or report on which you want to create the control. If you've just created a form using CreateForm and have assigned the return value of that function to a variable (frmNewForm, for example), you can reference that form's FormName property here (frmNewForm.FormName)
controltype	Constant identifying the type of control you want to create:

Constant	Control Type
acLabel	Label
acRectangle	Rectangle
acLine	Line
acImage	Image
acCommandButton	Command button
acOptionButton	Option button
acCheckBox	Check box
acOptionGroup	Option group
acBoundObjectFrame	Bound object frame
acTextBox	Text box
acListBox	List box
acComboBox	Combo box
acSubform	Subform/subreport
acObjectFrame	Unbound object frame
acPage	Page
acPageBreak	Page break
acCustomControl	Custom Control

TABLE 7.5   Parameters for CreateControl and CreateReportControl (continued)

Argument	Description
	acToggleButton Toggle button
	acTabCtl Tab control
section	Constant identifying the section that will contain the new control:

Constant	Section
acDetail	(Default) Detail section
acHeader	Form or report header section
acFooter	Form or report footer section
acPageHeader	Form or report page header section
acPageFooter	Form or report page footer section
acGroupLevel1Header	Group-level 1 header section (reports only)
acGroupLevel1Footer	Group-level 1 footer section (reports only)
acGroupLevel2Header	Group level 2 header section (reports only)
acGroupLevel2Footer	Group level 2 footer section (reports only)

If a report has additional group level sections, the header/footer pairs are numbered consecutively beginning with 9

Argument	Description
parent	String expression identifying the name of the parent control. If you don't wish to specify the parent control, use ""
bound FieldName	String expression identifying the name of the field to which the new control should be bound. If you specify the boundFieldName, not only does it fill in the ControlSource property, it inherits the table properties, such as the Format and ValidationRule properties
left	Top, Integer expressions indicating the coordinates for the upper-left corner of the control, in twips
width	Height, Integer expressions indicating the width and height of the control, in twips

An Example Using CreateForm and CreateControl

As part of a project, you need to create a form with 42 similar command buttons, numbered 1 through 42, in 6 rows of 7 buttons each. You could do this by hand, spending a while getting all the controls just right. You could also do this with the CreateForm and CreateControl functions. Listing 7.6 contains the entire function you can use to create the form, as shown in Figure 7.29.

CreateCalendar creates the form by calling the CreateForm function. Since it specifies a zero-length string for both the database and the template, it will use the template specified in the Tools ➤ Options settings:

```
Set frm = CreateForm("", "")
frm.Caption = "Calendar"
```

All measurements specified for CreateControl must be in twips ($^1/_{1440}$ of an inch), so you need to convert all your values into twips before calling the function. These controls are to be 0.25 inch in height and 0.30 inch in width, with a 0.03-inch gap between them:

```
intHeight = .25 * adhcTwipsPerInch
intWidth = .30 * adhcTwipsPerInch
intGap = .03 * adhcTwipsPerInch
```

FIGURE 7.29

The Calendar form in Design view, after the CreateCalendar function has created all the buttons

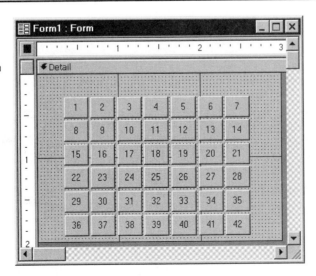

CreateCalendar loops through six rows of seven command buttons, creating each control with a call to CreateControl. It uses the width and height values to figure where to place the buttons and then sets the Width, Height, and Caption properties of the button it has just created. Note that this call to CreateControl uses the FormName property of the newly created form to reference the form, creates a control of type acCommandButton in the Detail section, and specifies no parent or bound field name.

Listing 7.6

```
Sub CreateCalendar()

    Const adhcTwipsPerInch=1440

    Dim frm As Form
    Dim ctl As Control

    Dim intI As Integer
    Dim intJ As Integer

    Dim intHeight As Integer
    Dim intWidth As Integer
    Dim intGap As Integer

    Dim intCols As Integer
    Dim intRows As Integer

    intCols = 7
    intRows = 6

    Set frm = CreateForm("", "")
    frm.Caption = "Calendar"

    ' Measurement properties are specified in TWIPS.
    ' So we need to convert all values from
    ' inches to twips, by multiplying by 1440.
    intHeight = 0.25 * adhcTwipsPerInch
    intWidth = 0.3 * adhcTwipsPerInch
    intGap = 0.03 * adhcTwipsPerInch
    With frm.DefaultControl(acCommandButton)
        .Width = intWidth
        .Height = intHeight
    End With
```

```
For intI = 1 To intRows
    For intJ = 1 To intCols
        With CreateControl(frm.Name, acCommandButton, _
        acDetail, "", "", intJ * (intWidth + intGap), _
        intI * (intHeight + intGap))
            .Caption = 7 * (intI - 1) + intJ
        End With
    Next intJ
    Next intI
End Function
```

TIP To create a control within a page of a tab control, specify the name of the page on which you want the control to appear as the Parent parameter. Coordinates you specify for the new control will be in relation to the upper-left corner of the page object, not the main form.

What Are These Controls, Anyway?

Those readers moving to Access from Visual Basic may be surprised to find out that the controls you see on forms, in Access, are not actual windows. (That is, they don't have window handles and don't respond to Windows messages.) The Access controls are just "paint on the screen," at least until each becomes the active control. Access uses this technique to conserve resources: because you may have 200, 300, or more controls on a single form, it's important that you not run out of window handles, graphics resources, and so on. (Yes, it's still possible to run out of resources under Windows 95. It's difficult, but possible. No one has managed to do this with Windows NT, as far as we know.)

But Visual Basic programmers are used to being able to manipulate controls as windows. You want to be able to use the SendMessage API function to control your controls. The fact is, this just isn't possible, in general, in Access. There are two important reasons why this won't work:

- The control becomes active at different times, depending on whether you enter it with the mouse or from the keyboard. Because you can't count on either the Enter or GotFocus event to magically transform a painted control into a real window, it's nearly impossible to find an event that will, in general, serve your purposes.

- The controls are subclassed versions of the Windows standard controls. They just don't react to many of the normal Windows messages, if any. Even if you manage to find a control when it's active, it will most likely ignore any message you send to it with SendMessage.

Using SendMessage to Limit Input Characters

You can't count on using SendMessage to manipulate any Access controls. On the other hand, it just so happens that by mistake, chance, or fate, Access text boxes do respond to at least one message: EM_SETLIMITTEXT. You can use the SendMessage Windows API function to limit the number of characters users can type into a text box. This can be useful if your text box is bound to a memo field and you want to allow users to enter, for example, no more than 1000 characters.

The sample form, frmLimitChars in CH07.MDB, allows you to specify the character limit and then calls the SendMessage API function to tell the text box the maximum number of characters it should accept. Figure 7.30 shows the form in use. Listing 7.7 shows all the code the form uses to limit the characters in the text box.

FIGURE 7.30

frmLimitChars shows how you can limit the number of characters typed into a text box.

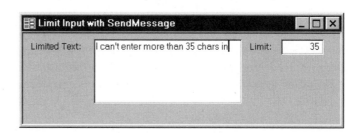

The one limitation on this technique is that you can't count on the control being a real window in either the Enter or GotFocus event, as mentioned above. The only time you're guaranteed that this control is a real window is in its Change event, so that's where we have hooked the code. (You can probably count on the Before-Update event, as well, but we've not tried that.) This means, of course, that the code calls the SendMessage API every time you type a character. Since this API call incurs so little overhead, compared to the speed at which you can type, the extra work just didn't seem to matter in this case.

The code first gets the window handle for the current window, using the Get-Focus API call:

```
' Get the window handle for the current window.
hWnd = GetFocus()
```

It then plays some tricks to make sure that, if you've set the maximum number of characters to less than the number of characters already in there, it will readjust the allowable number of characters to be the actual number of characters. (Otherwise, the text box wouldn't even let you delete one character at a time. If you have too many characters in a text box, Windows allows you to delete only the entire entry.) Each time you type a character, the code calls SendMessage again, so as you delete characters, the code continually resets the maximum size as necessary:

```
lngNewMax = Len(Me!Text0.Text & "")
lngLimit = Me!txtLimit.Value
If lngNewMax < lngLimit Then
    lngNewMax = lngLimit
End If
```

Finally, the code calls the SendMessage API function, which sends a message to the window identified by the supplied window handle:

```
SendMessage hWnd, adhcEM_SETLIMITTEXT, lngNewMax, 0
```

Experimentation has shown that although there are many EM_* messages that normal text boxes understand, Access text boxes respond to very few, if any, of these messages. You may find it interesting to dig through a Windows API reference, trying out various EM_* messages, as we've done here. Be warned: most won't work or will possibly crash Access. The technique we've shown here works not by design, but by chance. Therefore, although it's a useful technique, it may not work in future versions of Access.

Listing 7.7

```
Private Declare Function SendMessage Lib "user32" _
  Alias "SendMessageA" (ByVal hWnd As Long, _
  ByVal wMsg As Long, ByVal wParam As Long, _
  lParam As Any) As Long
Private Declare Function GetFocus Lib "user32" () As Long
```

```
Const adhcEM_SETLIMITTEXT = &HC5&

Private Sub Text0_Change()
    ' You actually CAN use SendMessage with
    ' Access controls, but you must remember that
    ' the changes you make are only active
    ' as long as this control has the focus.
    ' Therefore, if you want to limit the text in a text
    ' box, you MUST do it each time you enter the
    ' control. To be safe, the only place you can really
    ' do this is in reaction to the Change, BeforeUpdate
    ' or AfterUpdate event.

    Dim hWnd As Long
    Dim lngResult As Long
    Dim lngNewMax As Long
    Dim lngLimit As Long

    ' Get the window handle for the current window.
    hWnd = GetFocus()

    ' Hey, what if there's ALREADY too much text in
    ' there?  Limiting the text would make it
    ' impossible to type in there at all. You want
    ' to set the limit to be the max of the amount
    ' you want and the amount that's in there!
    lngNewMax = Len(Me!Text0.Text & "")
    lngLimit = Me!txtLimit.Value
    If lngNewMax < lngLimit Then
        lngNewMax = lngLimit
    End If

    ' Send the message to the current text box
    ' to limit itself to lngNewMax characters.
    SendMessage hWnd, adhcEM_SETLIMITTEXT, lngNewMax, 0
End Sub
```

Summary

This chapter has introduced each of the control types (except ActiveX controls, which are covered in Chapter 20). We've attempted to cover the nonintuitive properties and events and have suggested solutions to some common Access problems. In general, we covered the following topics:

- Working with Access controls and their properties, events, and methods which make up the bulk of your user interface

- Using VBA and the Tag property to emulate the creation of user-defined control properties

- Using VBA in combination with controls to emulate several hybrid controls that are not intrinsic to Access

- Using a control's default properties to ease the development burden

- Creating controls and forms programmatically, leading to a more uniform layout

- Working with the tab control and its pages

- For the adventurous, using the SendMessage API call to control Access controls, but only in a severely limited fashion

CHAPTER

EIGHT

8

Topics in Form Design and Usage

- Understanding the appearance and operation of forms

- Retrieving information about forms

- Resizing forms to match screen resolution

- Building form-based encapsulated tools

If your applications are like many of the Access applications in use, a large majority of their functionality is centered around forms. Most likely, from the user's perspective, your application *is* just a set of forms. In this chapter you'll find insights into using and creating forms in ways you might not otherwise have considered, focusing on the features added since Access 2. This chapter doesn't attempt to show you how to create or design forms, but rather how to use the forms you've created in original and interesting ways.

NOTE	Although you won't find a complete discussion of using the Windows API (Application Programming Interface) until Chapter 18, some of the examples in this chapter rely heavily on API calls. If you find yourself buried too deeply in the details, you may want to skip ahead to Chapter 18 and peruse the information there concurrently with this chapter.

Introduction to Class Modules

Access allows you to store program code and a form (or report) in one neat package. Each form and report can carry its own module with it (although new forms and reports are "born" without a module—you have to add code before Access creates the module for you), and, unless you specify otherwise, every procedure and variable in that module is private. This means that, as in Visual Basic, choosing an event from the property list takes you directly to a subroutine that is tied to that particular event. The event procedures are subroutines named

Private Sub *controlName_eventName*(*parameters*)

and their scope is, by default, private to the form. In several cases Access passes parameters to these procedures that provide information about the circumstances of the particular event. For example, mouse events receive information about the mouse location and clicked buttons, and key events receive information about the particular key that was pressed. This encapsulation makes it very easy to create forms that perform a single purpose, which you can reuse in various applications.

NOTE

Controls can contain spaces in their Name properties, but event procedures, being subroutines, cannot have spaces in their names. To solve this problem, Access must do some work on the names of controls that include illegal procedure name characters before it can name the event procedure. If you need to programmatically retrieve the event procedure name that corresponds to a control, check the EventProcPrefix property of any control on a form or report. This property, which doesn't appear on the property sheet, returns the modified name Access uses in its event procedures. If you're writing an application that creates event procedures, this property is essential.

To get to a form's module, you have several choices:

- From the database container window, once you see the list of forms, you can click the Code button on the toolbar. (This opens the form in Design view as well.)

- In Form Design view, click the same toolbar button.

- From the form's property sheet, for any event property, you can click the ... button, which takes you to the particular event procedure for this control.

- In Form Design view, right-click any control and choose the Build Event menu item.

A common misconception about controls and their attached event procedures causes new Access programmers a great deal of trouble. Most beginners assume that copying a control from one form to another also copies the control's event procedures to the new form. But this is not so, unfortunately. Copying a control copies only the control and its properties. You must manually copy its event procedures from one form's module to the other's.

Many of the forms demonstrated in this chapter rely heavily on form class modules to maintain their reusability. By keeping all their code in their own class module, these forms become encapsulated entities that you can import directly into your own applications. In 16-bit versions of Access, searching through source code using Access' Find/Replace options skipped over code in form or report (class) modules. Happily, Access' Find dialog box now includes an option to search through all the modules in the database, including form/report modules. Finding procedures hidden away in form (or report) class modules is no longer an onerous chore.

In addition, you may find that in our attempt to modularize the examples in this chapter, some procedures occur in multiple forms' class modules. If you import more than one of the forms from this chapter into your own applications, you might want to take a few minutes and peruse the imported forms' class modules. You will probably find some general-purpose procedures duplicated. We've attempted to point these out to you along the way. Moving those routines to standard modules can save you some memory overhead.

Windows Handles, Classes, Access Forms, and MDI

To make the best use of the different types of forms in Access, you must first have a basic understanding of Windows handles, classes, and parent-child relationships. These concepts will play a large part in your understanding the different form types in Access.

The Windows Handle (or hWnd)

In Windows, almost every object you see on the screen is an object with properties and events, just as in Access. Every button, scroll bar, dialog box, and status bar is a window. To keep all these windows straight, Windows assigns to each a unique window handle—a unique Long Integer—through which it can refer to the specific window. This window handle is generally referred to as the window's *hWnd* (handle to a *window*). Access makes this value available to you, for every form, in that form's hWnd property. (Like many other properties, the hWnd property is available only at run time and therefore can't be found in the form's property sheet.)

Windows Classes

In addition, every window is a member of a window *class*. Window classes share events and code, so windows of the same class can react the same way to outside stimuli. For example, all scroll bars are either part of the class SCROLLBAR or part of a class derived from the SCROLLBAR class. (Actually, not all scroll bars are necessarily based on this class, since a programmer can create a scroll bar from scratch. It's just a combination of bitmaps and code. But almost no one does it that way, because Windows provides this standard class with little effort on your part.) Every window type in Access has its own class name. You'll find some of these classes listed in Table 8.1, along with the parent for each window type (which will be important in the next section's coverage of the Multiple Document Interface used in Access). Figure 8.1 shows a simple class hierarchy diagram for these Access window classes.

TABLE 8.1   Sample Access Window Classes and Their Parents

Class Name	Description	Parent
OMain	Main Access window	
MDICLIENT	Access desktop	Main Access window
ODb	Database container	MDIClient window
OForm	Normal form frame	MDIClient window
OFormPopup	Popup form frame	Main Access window
OFormSub	Access form (the area that contains other controls)	Any normal or popup form window

FIGURE 8.1

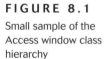

Small sample of the Access window class hierarchy

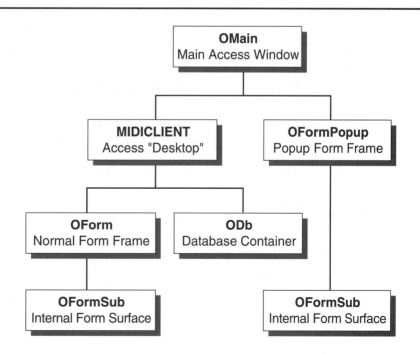

Multiple Document Interface (MDI)

The Multiple Document Interface (MDI) presents a standard way of writing applications for Windows in which one main window can contain many subordinate, or child, windows. Access is such an application, as is Excel, among many others. In MDI applications, the child windows minimize within the bounds of the parent window and show an icon (or tray, in Windows 95) when minimized. You can't size or drag child windows beyond the borders of their parent. The hierarchical organization of every MDI application is basically the same: you have a main window containing a special window—the MDI client—and within that window you have multiple child windows. In Access the MDI client window's class is MDICLIENT and the main Access window's class is OMain. As you'll note in Table 8.1, the MDI client's parent is the main Access window, for which the window class is OMain. It is actually the window that's situated within the Access main window; it contains all the other Access windows, including the design surfaces and running applications. This window normally extends from the bottom of the docked toolbars to the top of the status bar and from the left to the right of the main Access window.

Controlled Closing

You can disable or remove the standard Close button and provide your own Close button in an attempt to control the way users close your forms, but there is still at least one more way to close the form: users can use the Ctrl+F4 key (for normal forms) or the Alt+F4 key (for popup forms) to bypass your own form-closing mechanism. If you want complete control over your forms, you need to plug this one last hole.

To close this final loophole allowing users to close your forms behind your back, you must restrict the use of the Alt+F4 and Ctrl+F4 keys. Fortunately, you can accomplish this without having to check whether the user pressed either Alt+F4 or Ctrl+F4 to close your form. For this method to work, your form must include some method of allowing the user to close it, usually using a command button. It involves these four simple steps:

1. In your form's class module, in the declarations area, define a Boolean variable (fOKToClose, for this example).

2. In your form's Open or Load event, set the value of fOKToClose to False. Disable the Close button (set the CloseButton property to False).

3. In the code attached to the Click event of the button used to close your form, set fOKToClose to True.

4. In your form's Unload event, check the value of fOKToClose. If it's False, set the Cancel parameter to True, halting the form's closing.

That's all there is to it. Unless your user clicks your button, there's no way this form is going to close. Listing 8.1 shows the minimal code your form might contain to implement this method. You can investigate frmCloseTest in CH08.MDB to see it in action.

Listing 8.1

```
' Variable to control when the form can be closed.
Dim fOKToClose As Boolean

Private Sub cmdClose_Click()
    ' If you click the Close button, set the variable
    ' so the Unload event will let you out.
    fOKToClose = True

    ' Now that you've cleared the way, close the form.
    DoCmd.Close
End Sub

Private Sub Form_Load()

    ' Set the trap, so no one can close the form without
    ' clicking the Close button.
    fOKToClose = False
End Sub

Private Sub Form_Unload(Cancel As Integer)
    Cancel = Not fOKToClose
End Sub
```

If you really care to control when and how your users can close your form, you'll want to incorporate a combination of the suggestions discussed here. Of course, you'll want to remove the control box (set the ControlBox property to False) or disable the Close button and the Close item on the system menu (set the CloseButton property to False) so users won't attempt, in vain, to close the form using these items. In any case you'll probably want to set the Cancel variable to True in the Unload event so users can't close the form with an unanticipated keystroke.

NOTE

In previous versions of Access you could use the Windows API to modify the contents of, or enable and disable elements of, a form's system menu. Because all Access menus have been replaced with shared Office command bars, you can no longer work with menus programmatically in the same way you could before. Chapter 11 discusses some techniques you can use to replace existing code that uses the Windows API to work with standard menus. The system menu, however, is off limits.

Removing a Form's Caption Bar

As part of an application you may need to remove a form's caption bar. Although Access allows you to remove the entire border, this may not be what you need for a particular look. Removing the control menu and the Minimize/Maximize buttons and setting the form's caption to a single space will almost work, but it still leaves the thick bar above the form. Figure 8.2 shows a sample form (frmNoCaptionBar from CH08.MDB) with its caption bar removed.

FIGURE 8.2

Removing a form's caption bar leaves it with a sizable border, but you can't move the form by any means.

Removing the form's caption bar relies on changes to the form's window style. When any application creates a new window, it sets up some information about the style of that window. The Windows API provides functions to retrieve and set the style information, and you can change many of the window styles even after the window has been created. The presence or absence of the caption bar is one of those modifiable styles, and the code in Listing 8.2 (the adhRemoveCaptionBar function) works by changing the form's window style when called from the form's Open event.

TIP Even though you've removed the caption bar from the form, astute users will know they can access the items on the form's control menu, using the Alt+— (minus) keystroke. If you want to ensure that users can't move your form by any means, make sure you've set the ControlBox property to No.

Changing the Window Style

To change the window's style, follow these steps:

1. Retrieve the current window style (a Long Integer).

2. Turn off the particular bit in the value that controls whether the window has a caption bar.

3. Set the style for the window with the newly altered style value.

To retrieve and set the style value, you can call the Windows API functions GetWindowLong (aliased as adh_apiGetWindowLong) and SetWindowLong (aliased as adh_apiSetWindowLong), both declared in basFormGlobal. In each case you tell Windows which particular value you're getting or setting by passing the constant adhcGWL_STYLE.

To tell Windows to turn off the caption bar, you need to change the value returned from the call to GetWindowLong. Windows treats the 32-bit value as a set of 32 binary flags, each controlling one attribute of the window, where each can have a value of 0 (False) or 1 (True). For example, the window style value contains a bit controlling the display of the caption bar, the Minimize and Maximize buttons, and the control menu. The only one of these Access doesn't give you control over is the display of the caption bar.

To change one of the settings, you use either the And or the Or bitwise operator. The And operator takes any two values and returns 1 in any of the positions that was nonzero in both values and 0 in any of the positions where either or both were 0. The Or operator sets any position to 1 if either of the corresponding positions is 1, and 0 otherwise. Therefore, to force a specific bit to be on, you use the Or operator with a number that has all zeros except in the particular bit you care about, where you have a 1. (This works because any value Ored with 0 isn't changed, but any value Ored with 1 is set to 1.) To force a bit to be off, you use the And operator with 1's in all the bits except the one you care about, where you have a 0. (This works because any value Anded with 1 isn't changed, but any value Anded with 0 is set to 0.) To control whether you're turning bits on or off, you can use the Not logical operator, which flips all the bits of a value from 0 to 1 or from 1 to 0.

Therefore, given that the constant adhcWS_CAPTION contains the correct bit settings to turn on the display of the caption bar, you could Or it with the value returned from GetWindowLong to force the display on. To turn it off, you And it with NOT adhcWS_CAPTION. This leaves all the bits alone except the one controlling the caption bar display, which is set to 0. When you make this change and call SetWindowLong, Windows redisplays the window without the caption bar.

The following three lines of code execute the steps necessary to retrieve and set the window style value:

```
lngOldStyle = adh_apiGetWindowLong(hwnd, adhcGWL_STYLE)
lngNewStyle = lngOldStyle And Not adhcWS_CAPTION
lngOldStyle = adh_apiSetWindowLong(hwnd, adhcGWL_STYLE, _
 lngNewStyle)
```

Resizing the Window

Unless you do a little more work, the form will look rather odd at this point. Because you haven't told Windows to redraw the form, Access becomes confused: the caption will still show, but Access won't know it's there. You now must resize the form without the caption bar.

This section of code requires three Windows API functions:

- GetWindowRect (aliased here as adh_apiGetWindowRect) fills a user-defined datatype—a variable of type adhTypeRECT—with the current coordinates of the form.

- GetSystemMetrics (aliased here as adh_apiGetSystemMetrics) tells you the height of the caption bar that was just removed. When you pass in the adhcSM_CYCAPTION constant, Windows returns to you the height of the caption bar.

- MoveWindow (aliased here as adh_apiMoveWindow) moves the window. (Actually, it won't be moved; you'll just call MoveWindow in order to resize it. Other Windows API functions are available to resize windows, but this one is the easiest to call, given the coordinate information you'll know at this point.)

This code requires some brute-force calculations: figuring out the height of the old caption and subtracting that from the current height of the window. Subtracting the height of the caption bar from the current height of the form should leave you with a form that's the correct height. See Listing 8.2 for the details.

Listing 8.2

```
Function adhRemoveCaptionBar(frm As Form)
    ' Remove a form's caption bar
    adhRemoveWindowCaptionBar frm.hwnd
End Function

Sub adhRemoveWindowCaptionBar(ByVal hwnd As Long)

    ' Remove a window's caption bar, given its hWnd.

    Dim lngOldStyle As Long
    Dim lngNewStyle As Long
    Dim rct As adhTypeRect
    Dim intDX As Integer, intDY As Integer

    ' Get the current window style of the form.
    lngOldStyle = adh_apiGetWindowLong(hwnd, adhcGWL_STYLE)

    ' Turn off the bit that enables the caption.
    lngNewStyle = lngOldStyle And Not adhcWS_CAPTION

    ' Set the new window style.
    lngOldStyle = adh_apiSetWindowLong(hwnd, _
     adhcGWL_STYLE, lngNewStyle)

    ' The caption's been removed, but now resize
    ' the whole window to match the size of the interior.

    ' Get the current size, including the caption.
    adh_apiGetWindowRect hwnd, rct

    ' Calculate the new width and height.
    intDX = rct.X2 - rct.X1
    intDY = rct.Y2 - rct.Y1 - _
     adh_apiGetSystemMetrics(adhcSM_CYCAPTION)
```

```
' Move the window to the same left and top,
' but with new width and height.
' This will make the new form appear
' a little lower than the original.
Call adh_apiMoveWindow(hwnd, rct.X1, _
    rct.Y1, intDX, intDY, True)
End Sub
```

Using adhRemoveCaptionBar in Your Own Applications

To use adhRemoveCaptionBar in your own applications, follow these steps:

1. Import the modules basCaption and basFormGlobal from CH08.MDB into your own database.

2. Call adhRemoveCaptionBar from your form's Open event. You'll need either to place a call to it directly from the property sheet:

   ```
   =adhRemoveCaptionBar(Form)
   ```

   or to call it from the code you have currently attached to your Open event:

   ```
   Call adhRemoveCaptionBar(Me)
   ```

You can also call adhRemoveWindowCaptionBar, passing the function the window handle for any open window. As a matter of fact, the following fragment will remove Access' caption bar!

```
Call adhRemoveWindowCaptionBar(Application.hwndAccessApp)
```

Although attempting to remove the main window's caption bar did not work correctly in Access 95, in Access 97 it works perfectly. We haven't tried it with other Office 97 applications, but once you have a window's handle, you should be able to use this technique to change its window style and redraw the window.

Retrieving and Saving Information about Forms

You may find in your applications that you need more information about your forms than Access can give you. You may just want to be able to tell whether a specific form is open. You might, for example, need to save and restore your forms' locations from one session to the next. If your users can resize and move forms, this ability is especially important. (See the section "Screen Resolution and Distributing Forms" later in this chapter for more information on scaling forms as they're resized.) You may want to know what the current row is or whether the user has moved to the new row. You'll find the solutions to these problems in the sections that follow.

Which Form Is This?

If you write Visual Basic code attached to controls or sections on a form, you'll often need to pass to that code an object that refers to the current form. Many beginning developers count on the Screen.ActiveForm object to get this information. However, you should avoid this method if at all possible because Screen.ActiveForm often returns a reference to a different form from the one you'd intended.

Access provides a simple solution to this problem. From anywhere on the form's design surface, you can retrieve and pass to Visual Basic code any of the form's properties. One of these properties is the form's Form property, which is a reference to the form itself. You can pass this property as a parameter to any function you call from the property sheet so the function can identify the form with which it should be concerned. For example, if your form calls a function named FormOn-Current from its Current event, you could place this expression:

```
=FormOnCurrent(Form)
```

in the property sheet to pass a reference to the current form to the function. The function declaration would be something like this:

```
Function FormOnCurrent(frm as Form)
```

On the other hand, if your code exists in the form's class module, you can use the object reference returned in the Me property to refer to the current form. That is, in the external function declared above, you could retrieve the form's caption with this expression:

```
strCaption = frm.Caption
```

but in a form's class module, you could use this expression:

```
strCaption = Me.Caption
```

If you need to create global procedures that can be called from multiple forms, you can still call these from a form's class module. Just pass the Me object to those functions as a parameter from the form's event procedure. For example, to call the previously mentioned FormOnCurrent function from a form's module, use this:

```
Call FormOnCurrent(Me)
```

At the New Record?

It is sometimes vitally important for your application to be able to sense whether your user has moved to the "new" record (the extra record at the end of editable recordsets). Access provides a simple way for you to know whether or not users have positioned themselves on the new record: the NewRecord property. This property returns True if the form is displaying the new row and False otherwise. The sample form frmCategories, in CH08.MDB, includes a single line of code that will make a label visible if you're on the new row. Figure 8.3 shows this form, with the new row current. To set the visibility of the label, the form calls the following line from its Current event:

```
Me!lblNew.Visible = Me.NewRecord
```

That is, if the NewRecord property returns a True value, it sets the label to be visible and sets it to be invisible otherwise.

FIGURE 8.3

Use the NewRecord property to sense whether or not you're on the new row.

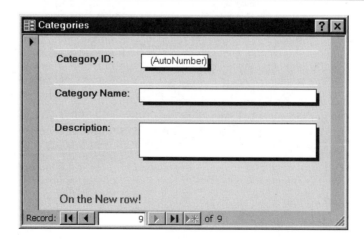

What's the Current Row, and How Many Rows Are There, Anyway?

For some applications, you'll want to turn off Access' navigation buttons for your forms. When you do, however, you lose the display of the current row and the total number of rows. Access makes it easy to find out what row you're on, however, by supplying the CurrentRecord property. Every bound form provides this property, allowing you to display the current row number.

The sample form frmNavigate, shown in Figure 8.4, re-creates the current row and total rows display that Access normally provides. (The section "Creating Self-Disabling Navigation Buttons" later in this chapter discusses how to create the navigation controls on the form.) Handling the current row is simple: in the form's Current event, the following statement updates the txtCurrRec text box:

```
frm!txtCurrRec = frm.CurrentRecord
```

FIGURE 8.4

Use form properties to determine the current row and the total number of rows.

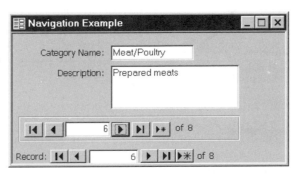

As for determining the total number of rows, you have to work a bit harder; this information isn't available from the form itself, but rather from the recordset that's filling the form. The recordset's RecordCount property ostensibly returns the number of rows that have, as of yet, been loaded. Common knowledge says you must use the MoveLast method to move to the end of the recordset before you can know the number of rows in the recordset. Experience shows that this isn't really necessary for some types of recordsets: if you just wait long enough, Access will actually update the RecordCount value, loading rows in the background until they've all been visited.

> **TIP**
>
> This technique does not appear to work with a form based on a table linked from SQL Server. This behavior is consistent with the Access 2 behavior of not doing background fetches on ODBC recordsets. If you find that the form doesn't update the record count automatically, you will need to perform an explicit MoveLast to fetch the record count.

The sample form counts on this behavior, although it would be simple to change. This is the code that does the work, pulled from code called by the form's Current event:

```
Set rst = frm.RecordsetClone
' Sooner or later, Access will figure out
' how many rows there really are!
frm!txtTotalRecs = rst.RecordCount + _
  IIf(frm.NewRecord, 1, 0)
End If
```

The code displays the current value in the recordset's RecordCount property, assuming that sooner or later it will be correct. For small recordsets, it's correct as soon as you move to a row other than the first row. For large recordsets, it may take a few seconds or longer to know the total number of rows. Every time you move from row to row and trigger the Current event, the sample form calls this code, which updates the display on the form itself.

If this updating display for large recordsets bothers you, there are a few alternatives:

- In the form's Open event, force the recordset to move to the last row (rst.MoveLast) and then back to the beginning (rst.MoveFirst) so it knows immediately how many rows there are. This can be slow, though, for large recordsets.

- In the form's Timer event, call code that uses a static variable to hold the Record-Count from the last time you called the routine. If the current value equals the previous value, you know the value has "settled," and you can change the Visible property of txtTotalRecs from False to True. You'll also want to disable the timer at that point (by setting the form's TimerInterval property to 0).

No matter how you solve this problem, you'll still want to update the text box during the form's Current event so it always reflects the actual number of rows.

TIP

If you use Access' built-in navigation buttons, the total number of rows increases by 1 when you're on the new row. That is, if there are eight rows in the table, when you're on the new row, Access displays "Record: 9 of 9." To emulate that, the example code adds 1 to the RecordCount property if it detects that you're on the new row.

Has the Form's Data Been Changed?

Access always knows if the data on the current form has been changed: if you have the form's RecordSelectors property set to True, you'll see the little pencil icon in the record selector when the data is "dirty." Access also makes this information available to you through the form's Dirty property.

Basically, it's simple: the Dirty property returns True when the little pencil would be visible on the record selector (regardless of whether you're actually displaying the record selector). You can use this property to provide your own indicator when the data has been changed or to cause your code to take action, depending on whether or not the data has been changed.

NOTE

Access doesn't trigger the form's Before/AfterUpdate events unless the data has been changed, so there's no point in checking the value of this property in those events. You wouldn't be there at all if the data weren't dirty.

The sample form, frmCategories from CH08.MDB, makes a label visible if you change the data on the form (see Figure 8.5). Every 250 milliseconds ($1/4$ second), Access calls the Timer event procedure, which checks the state of the Dirty property of the form and makes lblDirty visible if the form is dirty:

```
Private Sub Form_Timer()
    ' Turn the label on or off, depending on the state of
    ' the Dirty flag and the current visibility
    ' of the label.

    Dim fDirty As Boolean
    fDirty = Me.Dirty
    With Me!lblDirty
```

```
            If Not (fDirty Eqv .Visible) Then .Visible = fDirty
        End With
    End Sub
```

FIGURE 8.5

You can display a mes-
sage on your forms indi-
cating that the current
row has been changed.

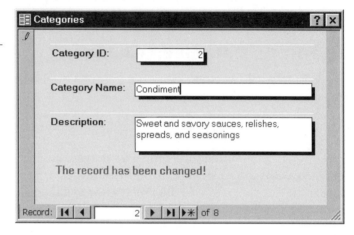

In addition, the Dirty property is read/write. You can set the Dirty property to
False, and if it's currently True, you'll force Access to save the current row, triggering the BeforeUpdate and AfterUpdate events. To test this, load frmCategories,
dirty the form (change a field on it), and then, from the Debug window, type

```
Forms!frmCategories.Dirty = False
```

This writes the data to disk and forces the "dirty" label to become invisible again.

TIP

When writing the code for this example, we were tempted to just set the
Visible property of lblDirty to be the same as the Dirty property of
the form—that is, if the form was dirty, make the label visible, and vice
versa. The problem is that if you set the Visible property of a control every
250 milliseconds, you're tying up a major portion of your application's
processing power in this tiny feature. To avoid that problem, the sample
code sets the Visible property only if it's not currently equivalent to the
form's Dirty flag. If the form is dirty and the label isn't visible, the code
makes the label visible. If the form isn't dirty but the label is visible (which
can happen if you change the data and then undo your change), the code
makes the label invisible. With this technique you avoid spending any
more processing power on this feature than necessary.

What Access really needs is an OnDirty event property for forms so you wouldn't have to perform hacks like the ones we've done here. Because there is no such event, you have to resort to adding code to your form's Timer event, watching for changes in the Dirty property or attaching code to check it in the AfterUpdate event of each control on the form. We're not sure why there still isn't a Dirty event (the Dirty property has been around since Access 2 so they've had time to hear the complaints and add it in), but it's not there.

Is a Specific Form Loaded?

Although Access doesn't provide a built-in mechanism to check whether a specific form is open, there's a simple way to detect whether a specific form (or any other object) is loaded into memory. The trick is to use the SysCmd function, which returns information about any object. If you call SysCmd, passing to it the constant acSysCmdGetObjectState—along with the name of your object and a constant indicating the object type (acForm, acReport, and so on)—it returns a value indicating the current state of that object. As long as the return value is nonzero, you know the object is open. Both basCalendar and basCalc call this function to check the state of their popup forms. If you pass the isOpen function just an object name, it assumes you want to know about a form. If you pass it both an object name and an object type, it will look for open objects of the specified type.

Here is the code:

```
Function isOpen(strName As String, _
  Optional intObjectType as Integer = acForm)
    ' Returns True if strName is open, False otherwise.
    ' Assume the caller wants to know about a form.
    isOpen = (SysCmd(acSysCmdGetObjectState, _
      intObjectType, strName) <> 0)
End Function
```

Which Rows Are Selected?

Access developers have always wanted a way to detect which rows the user has selected on a datasheet, and the 32-bit versions of Access finally include tools to make that possible. Using the SelLeft, SelTop, SelWidth, and SelHeight properties, you can tell exactly which cells the user has selected.

Take a look at frmSelTest in CH08.MDB. This form, shown in Figure 8.6, allows you to select a region of the datasheet by placing numbers into the text boxes on the right side of the form header, and every 500 milliseconds it updates the text boxes on the left part of the header with the current selected coordinates.

FIGURE 8.6

Use the SelTop, SelLeft, SelWidth, and SelHeight properties to work with the selected area in a datasheet.

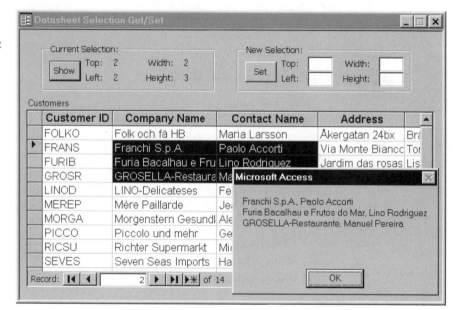

> **NOTE**   Access doesn't provide an event when the selection changes, so you'll need to use the Timer event to update those text boxes every now and then. Don't use this technique in an application; to keep the display relatively current, you would need to update the values far too often. That process ties up the computer too much for very little gain. If you run the form, you'll see that this repetitive code causes a great deal of flashing in Access' status bar as well.

Setting the Selection

Setting the selection is simple. If all the necessary values have been supplied, just set the various properties of the form:

```
Private Sub cmdSet_Click()
    If Not IsNull(Me!txtNewSelLeft + Me!txtNewSelTop _
    + Me!txtNewSelWidth + Me!txtNewSelHeight) Then
        With Me!subCustomers.Form
            .SelLeft = Me!txtNewSelLeft
            .SelTop = Me!txtNewSelTop
            .SelWidth = Me!txtNewSelWidth
            .SelHeight = Me!txtNewSelHeight
        End With
    End If
End Sub
```

This example sets the SelLeft, SelTop, SelWidth, and SelHeight properties of the form embedded in the control named subCustomers.

Retrieving the Selected Values

The sample form, frmSelTest, can also display a message box full of the selected values, as shown in Figure 8.6. The code to do this work, shown in Listing 8.3, walks through the rows and columns of the form's underlying recordset, matching the rows and columns selected on the form.

> **NOTE**
> Because the code in Listing 8.3 walks through the rows and columns of the form's recordset by number, it will work only if the layout of fields on the form matches the layout of fields in the underlying record source. If your form doesn't display all the columns the record source supplies, the listing of output fields may not be correct (depending on which columns are missing and which ones you select).

One small hitch: when you click the Show button, you move the selection from the subform datasheet to the button itself. When you do that, Access "loses" the selection in the datasheet. The code stores away the current values in the text boxes on the main form and immediately resets the selection for you once you click the Show button.

Listing 8.3

```
Private Sub cmdShow_Click()
    ' Demonstrate what you might do with the
    ' Sel... Properties.
    Dim strOut As String
    Dim rst As Recordset
    Dim lngCol As Long
    Dim lngRow As Long
    Dim lngSelLeft As Long
    Dim lngSelTop As Long
    Dim lngSelWidth As Long
    Dim lngSelHeight As Long
    Dim lngLastCol As Long
    Dim lngLastRow As Long

    lngSelLeft = Me!txtSelLeft
    lngSelTop = Me!txtSelTop
    lngSelWidth = Me!txtSelWidth
    lngSelHeight = Me!txtSelHeight

    ' If only part of the cell is selected,
    ' its height and width will be 0. Force them
    ' to 1 in that case.
    If lngSelWidth = 0 Then lngSelWidth = 1
    If lngSelHeight = 0 Then lngSelHeight = 1

    ' Track where to stop.
    lngLastCol = lngSelWidth + lngSelLeft
    lngLastRow = lngSelTop + lngSelHeight

    With Me!subCustomers.Form
        ' Set the subform's selection again, since you've
        ' just left there.
        .SelLeft = lngSelLeft
        .SelTop = lngSelTop
        .SelWidth = lngSelWidth
        .SelHeight = lngSelHeight
        Set rst = .RecordsetClone
    End With

    With rst
        ' Only do this if there are some rows!
```

```
        If .RecordCount > 0 Then
            lngRow = lngSelTop
            .MoveFirst
            .Move lngRow - 1
            Do While lngRow < lngLastRow
                lngCol = lngSelLeft
                Do While lngCol < lngLastCol
                    strOut = strOut & rst(lngCol - 1)
                    If lngLastCol - lngCol > 1 Then
                        strOut = strOut & ", "
                    End If
                    lngCol = lngCol + 1
                Loop
                lngRow = lngRow + 1
                strOut = strOut & vbCrLf
                .MoveNext
            Loop
            MsgBox strOut
        End If
    End With
End Sub
```

Saving and Restoring Form Locations

Many Windows applications save information about the size and location of their internal forms (or windows) from one invocation to the next. That way, when the user starts the program, the application is laid out just as it was when it was last used. Although you can explicitly save an Access form's location, you may not want (or be able) to save a form in order to preserve its size and location.

Storing Information in the System Registry

Most 32-bit applications that save their state do so in the System Registry. VBA provides four procedures that make it possible to read and write values to a specific location in the Registry:

Procedure	Description
SaveSetting	Saves a single item and value to the Registry
GetSetting	Gets the value of a single item in a subkey

GetAllSettings   Gets a list of settings and their respective values from a key in the Registry

DeleteSetting   Deletes a section or setting from the Registry

These procedures are extremely limited. They can work only with subkeys under this particular subkey:

```
HKEY_CURRENT_USER\Software\VB and VBA Programs
```

as shown in Figure 8.7. (If you want to dig in, Chapters 18 and 19 cover different ways to work with the Registry: Chapter 18 does its work from scratch, using the Windows API, and Chapter 19 uses functions exposed in the Access executable program that allow the Wizards to do their work.) The example shown in the section "Putting It All Together" a little later in this chapter will use the SaveSetting and GetSetting procedures to save and restore the window locations.

FIGURE 8.7

Use SaveSetting to write form locations to the System Registry.

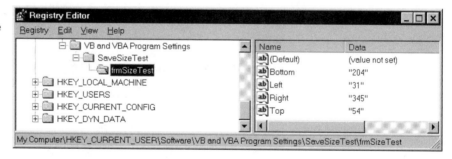

> **NOTE**
>
> In Access 95, SaveSetting created new subkeys for each different value you sent. In Access 97, SaveSetting writes the various values as subkeys of the main key, as shown in Figure 8.7. This is a more efficient use of the Registry and will result in fewer keys clogging Windows' search for values.

Nuts and Bolts: What Gets Stored Where

Because you can call the VBA Registry functions from Access and since you can call a function when a form loads and when it closes, you can read the information when your form opens and write it back out when the form closes. Each item will be stored in an individual subkey, as shown in Figure 8.7. The goal, then, of the necessary functions is to read the data from the Registry every time you load the form and to move the form to the correct size and location at that point. Then, when closing the form, you call a function to write the coordinates back out to the Registry. (Note that although we've used convenient names for the subkeys, the names are meaningful only to this application. You can use any subkey names you wish, as long as you look for the same subkey names when you save and restore the values.) You can find the necessary functions in the basSaveSize module in CH08.MDB.

NOTE In previous versions of Windows, the Registry was too difficult to work with to be of use for individual end-user applications, so most applications wrote their state information to text files, usually in the standard INI format. Because the Registry has now been deemed the correct place to store such information, you might want to get in the habit of using the Registry for saving information about your application. In addition, using RegEdit, you can save and load Registry subtrees, which gives you a way to move configuration information from one computer to another, as simply as you could use INI files in previous versions of Windows.

Using SaveSetting and GetSetting

SaveSetting allows you either to write to an existing subkey or to create a new one and write data there. The general syntax is this:

SaveSetting(*appname, section, key, setting*)

Use its parameters as described in the following table:

Parameter	Description	Example
appname	Name of the project or application	SaveSizeTest
section	Name of the item within the project	frmSaveSize
key	Name of the key for which you'd like to set the value	Bottom
setting	Value for the specified key	409

GetSetting works just about the same way. Here is its syntax:

GetSetting(*appname, section, key*[, *default*])

Use its parameters as described in the following table:

Parameter	Description	Example
appname	Name of the project or application	SaveSizeTest
section	Name of the item within the project	frmSaveSize
key	Name of the key whose value you'd like to retrieve	Bottom
default	Value to use if the key isn't found. If you don't specify a value, Access will use an empty string ("")	0

The Helpful Nz Function

The GetSetting function provides a useful way of ensuring that you get back a reasonable value when you try to query the Registry: it allows you to pass a final parameter that contains what it will return if it fails in its search.

Similarly, when you're programming, at times it would be useful to have a function that would return one value if a parameter was null and a different value if it was not. In Access 2, almost every programmer wrote a routine like this sooner or later, in order to convert null values to 0:

```
Function NullToZero(varValue As Variant) As Variant
    If IsNull(varValue) Then
        NullToZero = 0
    Else
        NullToZero = varValue
    End If
End Function
```

Access includes such a function, Nz, but it does much more.

Certainly, you can use Nz just as you would the NullToZero function above:

```
varConverted = Nz(varValue)
```

In this case Nz will return varValue's value if it isn't null and 0 if it is. But Nz also allows you to pass a second parameter, indicating what you'd like to return in the case where the first parameter is null. This makes it easy to supply a default value for possibly null parameters.

Consider this case (part of the sidebar "Sending Multiple Values in Open-Args" later in this chapter): you need to call the adhGetItem function to retrieve a portion of a string, but it's possible your search will fail and return a null value. In that case you'd like to supply a default value. In this example, you're searching for a string formatted like this:

```
Date=5/16/94
```

that starts with the word *Date* within the OpenArgs property of the current form. If it's there, adhGetItem returns "5/16/94". If not, it returns Null. In that case you'd like to override that value and return today's date instead. Nz allows you to do all that in one function call:

```
mvarDate = Nz(adhGetItem(Me.OpenArgs, "Date"), Date)
```

If you find yourself writing code that returns one value if a parameter is null and another if it's not, check out the very useful Nz function instead, and do it all in one line of code.

Putting It All Together

Once you know how to read and write information in the Registry, you still need to know how to retrieve and set the form's size and location. These steps require yet three more Windows API function calls:

```
Declare Function adh_apiGetWindowRect Lib "user32" _
  Alias "GetWindowRect" (ByVal hwnd As Long, _
  lpRect As adhTypeRect) As Long

Declare Function adh_apiMoveWindow Lib "user32" _
  Alias "MoveWindow" (ByVal hwnd As Long, _
  ByVal X As Long, ByVal Y As Long, ByVal nWidth As Long, _
```

```
            ByVal nHeight As Long, ByVal bRepaint As Long) As Long

Declare Function adh_apiGetParent Lib "user32" _
    Alias "GetParent" (ByVal hwnd As Long) As Long
```

Retrieving Window Coordinates

The GetWindowRect subroutine fills in a user-defined type with a window's current coordinates relative to the edge of the screen. MoveWindow moves and sizes a window relative to the window's parent (which in this case is most likely the Access main window). Therefore, when you retrieve a form's coordinates, you must make them relative to its parent's coordinates. To get information about the form's parent, you need the GetParent function. All three of these functions require a window handle, but this isn't a problem, because every form in Access provides its own handle through its hWnd property.

> **NOTE**
>
> Although Access provides the MoveSize macro action, it's not appropriate in all circumstances. Because it works only with the current form, it requires you to select a form before running the action. For the purposes of the example, this requires setting the focus to the form before changing its position. Even with the screen display turned off, the action on screen is quite distracting. In addition, using MoveSize requires you to specify coordinates in twips, not pixels. This requires some extra calculations to convert the retrieved screen location values from twips into pixels. In this example we've decided, for these reasons, to use the MoveWindow API subroutine instead of the Access MoveSize macro action.

Given the GetWindowRect function, you'll find it easy to retrieve a form's coordinates. This function by itself might be useful to you elsewhere because, although forms provide read-only WindowWidth and WindowHeight properties, they don't provide a Top or Left property. You can use the GetFormSize subroutine (Listing 8.4) in your own applications, filling in a typeRect variable with the coordinates of a form relative to its parent. The parent, by the way, will be either the Access MDI client window (for normal forms) or the Access main window (for modal forms).

Listing 8.4

```
' Store rectangle coordinates.
Type adhTypeRect
    X1 As Long
```

```
        Y1 As Long
        X2 As Long
        Y2 As Long
End Type

Private Sub GetFormSize(frm As Form, rct As adhTypeRect)

    ' Fill in rct with the coordinates of the window.

    Dim hWndParent As Long
    Dim rctParent As adhTypeRect

    ' Find the position of the window in question, in
    ' relation to its parent window (the Access desktop,
    ' the MDIClient window).
    hWndParent = adh_apiGetParent(frm.hwnd)

    ' Get the coordinates of the current window and
    ' its parent.
    adh_apiGetWindowRect frm.hwnd, rct

    ' Catch the case where the form is Popup (that is,
    ' its parent is NOT the Access main window). In that
    ' case, don't subtract off the coordinates of the
    ' Access MDIClient window.
    If hWndParent <> Application.hWndAccessApp Then
        adh_apiGetWindowRect hWndParent, rctParent

        ' Subtract off the left and top parent
        ' coordinates, since you need coordinates
        ' relative to the parent for the adh_apiMoveWindow
        ' function call.
        With rct
            .X1 = .X1 - rctParent.X1
            .Y1 = .Y1 - rctParent.Y1
            .X2 = .X2 - rctParent.X1
            .Y2 = .Y2 - rctParent.Y1
        End With
    End If
End Sub
```

This procedure, given a form object and a rectangle structure to fill in, first finds the parent of the form. It then finds the window coordinates of the two windows (the form and its parent) and calculates the coordinates of the child form as compared to the upper-left coordinates of the parent window. If the parent's hWnd does not equal the Access window handle, you know the current form is a popup form (a popup form's parent is the Windows desktop, not the Access main window), so there's no need to subtract the Access window's coordinates.

Moving Windows

When it comes time to place the form, with a specific size, at a specific location, use the MoveWindow API function. This function needs the window handle, the upper-left corner's coordinates, the width and height of the window, and information regarding whether or not to repaint the window immediately. The coordinates of the upper-left corner must be relative to the form's parent. Because you previously retrieved this information using the GetFormSize subroutine, this step should be simple.

The SetFormSize subroutine (Listing 8.5) takes a window handle and a rectangle structure filled with the new coordinates of that window, calculates the width and height based on the coordinates in the rectangle structure, and calls MoveWindow to move the form.

> **NOTE** Under Windows 95 (and Windows NT 4.0), there's a small (2-pixel) border inside the Access MDI client window. Access knows it's there, but the Windows API does not. Therefore, to make sure all the calculations aren't off by 2 pixels, the code includes two "fudge-factor" constants, adhcBorderWidthX and adhcBorderWidthY. These values take care of the small offset.

Listing 8.5

```
Private Sub SetFormSize(frm As Form, rct As adhTypeRect)

    Dim intWidth As Integer
    Dim intHeight As Integer
    Dim intSuccess As Integer

    With rct
        intWidth = (.X2 - .X1)
        intHeight = (.Y2 - .Y1)

        ' No sense even trying if either is less than 0.
        If (intWidth > 0) And (intHeight > 0) Then
```

```
              ' You would think the MoveSize action
              ' would work here, but that requires actually
              ' SELECTING the window first. That seemed like
              ' too much work, when this procedure will
              ' move/size ANY window.
              intSuccess = adh_apiMoveWindow(frm.hwnd, _
                .X1 - adhcBorderWidthX, .Y1 - adhcBorderWidthY, _
                intWidth, intHeight, True)
          End If
      End With
End Sub
```

The Final Steps

Once you know how to save and restore the information from the Registry and how to retrieve and set the window size, the only step left is to actually move the information to and from the Registry. When you open the form, you'll call the adh-GetCoords function, as shown in Listing 8.6. This function calls GetSetting for each of the four coordinates, using a default value of 0 for each coordinate. If the function didn't manage to retrieve nonzero values for the Right and Bottom coordinates, there's not much point in continuing.

Listing 8.6

```
Function adhGetCoords(strApp As String, frm As Form)

    ' This is the entry point for retrieving form info.
    ' Call this from the form's Open event.

    Dim rct As adhTypeRect
    Dim strName As String

    On Error GoTo adhGetCoordsErr

    ' Use the name of the application as the highest
    ' level, and the form's name as the next level.
    ' This way, you could have multiple forms in the same
    ' app use this code.
    strName = frm.Name
    With rct
        .Y1 = GetSetting(strApp, strName, adhcTop, 0)
        .X1 = GetSetting(strApp, strName, adhcLeft, 0)
        .Y2 = GetSetting(strApp, strName, adhcBottom, 0)
```

```
        .X2 = GetSetting(strApp, strName, adhcRight, 0)

        If .X2 > 0 And .Y2 > 0 Then
            Call SetFormSize(frm, rct)
        End If
    End With

adhGetCoordsExit:
    Exit Function

adhGetCoordsErr:
    MsgBox "Unable to retrieve all coordinates.", _
     vbInformation, "Get Coords"
    Resume adhGetCoordsExit
End Function
```

When you close your form, you'll need to call the adhSaveCoords function (Listing 8.7). This function is almost identical to adhGetCoords, except that it saves the settings rather than retrieving them.

Listing 8.7

```
Function adhSaveCoords(strApp As String, frm As Form)

    ' This is the entry point for saving form info.
    ' Call this from the form's Close event.
    Dim rct As adhTypeRect
    Dim strName As String

    On Error GoTo adhSaveCoordsErr

    ' Get the form's current size and position.
    GetFormSize frm, rct
    strName = frm.Name

    ' Use the name of the application as the highest
    ' level, and the form's name as the next level.
    ' This way, you could have multiple forms in the same
    ' app use this code.
    With rct
        SaveSetting strApp, strName, adhcTop, .Y1
        SaveSetting strApp, strName, adhcLeft, .X1
```

```
            SaveSetting strApp, strName, adhcBottom, .Y2
            SaveSetting strApp, strName, adhcRight, .X2
        End With

adhSaveCoordsExit:
    Exit Function

adhSaveCoordsErr:
    MsgBox "Unable to save all coordinates.", _
        vbInformation, "Save Coords"
    Resume adhSaveCoordsExit
End Function
```

Using adhGetCoords and adhSaveCoords in Your Own Applications

To use the adhGetCoords and adhSaveCoords functionality in your own applications, follow these steps:

1. Import the modules basSaveSize and basFormGlobal from CH08.MDB into your application.

2. Add a call to adhGetCoords to your form's Open event. Either add it to the code you already call or just call it directly. In either case, pass it an application name and a reference to the current form (the Form property, from the property sheet, or Me, from a form's class module).

3. Add a call to adhSaveCoords to your form's Close event. Either add it to the code you already call or just call it directly. In either case, pass it the application name and a reference to the current form.

When you open the form, the code attached to the Open event calls the adhGetCoords function and sizes and positions the form correctly. When you close the form, the Close event code stores away the current size and position information.

Retrieving and Using the Interior Coordinates of a Form

If you allow your users to resize your forms while your application is running, you may at some point need to know the dimensions of the interior portion of your form. (This information will be used extensively in the section "Screen Resolution and Distributing Forms" later in this chapter.) Aside from issues of screen resolution, though, you might want to move or resize controls on your form based on the form's size. The example in this section maintains a single button on a form, half the width and half the height of the form, and centered on the form, no matter how you resize it. Figure 8.8 shows three instances of the same form, sized differently. In each case the code attached to the form's Resize event has calculated the current dimensions of the form and has reset the size and position of the button accordingly.

What was a very difficult operation involving several API calls in Access 2 is now a trivial operation, due to the addition of the InsideWidth and InsideHeight properties of a form. These properties tell you the width and height of the inside area of a form window. (You can't use the Detail section's width to gather this information, because the Detail section's width may be different from the visible window width.) To size a control proportionally, all you need to do now is retrieve the InsideWidth and InsideHeight properties of the form, place the control accordingly, and set the height of the Detail section as well. Listing 8.8 shows the code attached to the Resize event of the sample form (frmCentered). Note that this example uses integer division ($\backslash$) rather than normal division ($/$) to center the control; this makes the form work more smoothly, because it has no need for the fractional parts of the measurements and can use integer math throughout.

FIGURE 8.8

The width and height of the form's border control the size and positioning of the button on the form.

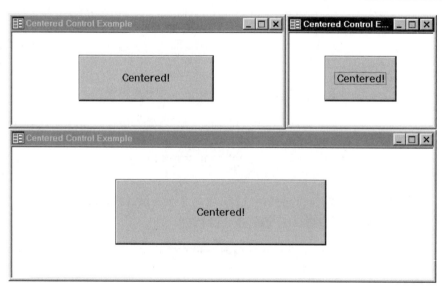

Listing 8.8

```
Private Sub Form_Resize()
    Dim intWidth As Integer
    Dim intHeight As Integer

    ' Get the current coordinates
    intWidth = Me.InsideWidth
    intHeight = Me.InsideHeight

    ' Set the detail section height
    Me.Section(0).Height = intHeight

    ' Set the coordinates of the button so that
    ' it's centered.
    With Me!cmdCentered
        .Width = intWidth \ 2
        .Height = intHeight \ 2
        .Left = (intWidth - .Width) \ 2
        .Top = (intHeight - .Height) \ 2
    End With
End Sub
```

Using Forms as Toolboxes

Although, thankfully, Access 97 has added a great deal of control over toolbars through the use of its CommandBars object model (see Chapter 11 for more information), these new objects still can't react to events unless you interact directly with them. In addition, they have only a single event to react to: the Click event. If you want to create toolbars that can react to changes on forms around them, you'll need to use forms that look and work like toolbars instead of the built-in toolbars. By setting the right combination of properties, you can make a form that you create look and act like a standard toolbox. (Although the terms *toolbar* and *toolbox* are often used interchangeably, we think of a toolbar as a group of buttons fixed to the application window, usually right below the menu bar, and a toolbox as a free-floating collection of buttons.) Generally, most application toolboxes have these characteristics in common:

- They float above all other forms in your application.

- They have a control menu and perhaps a Minimize button, but never a Maximize button.

- They have a nonsizable border.

- They consist of buttons with pictures indicating actions, perhaps with a status bar label.

Toolboxes usually provide generic buttons that work with any window your user might have loaded. For example, you might want to provide a record navigation toolbar that would allow your users to move from row to row in a form and would reflect the state of the form the user had most recently chosen. Toolboxes are also very useful when working with forms in Design view. Although Access provides a wide range of development tools, you might want to augment these with your own. The simple example you'll find here provides buttons to align groups of controls, as well as to center controls horizontally or vertically. Here is the sample toolbox, frmToolbox from CH08.MDB, in action:

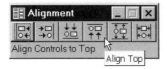

You should be able to take the example you see here and modify it for your own purposes.

Creating Your Toolbox

You'll want your toolbox to float above all the other windows in your Access application. To make this happen you need to set the form's Popup property to Yes. In addition, you need to set other properties to make the form act like a standard popup toolbox. Table 8.2 lists all the properties you'll need to set. Some of these property values are the Access default values, but make sure they're set correctly, in any case.

The Popup Property

As mentioned in the section "Retrieving Window Coordinates" earlier in this chapter, a form that has its Popup property set to Yes has a different parent than a normal window. Normal forms have the Access MDI client window as their parent (and can't be moved outside that window), but popup forms have the Access window itself as their parent. In addition, their Windows class is different, granting

TABLE 8.2   Toolbox Form Properties

Property	Value
Popup	Yes
BorderStyle	Dialog
ViewsAllowed	Form
ShortcutMenu	No
DefaultView	Single Form
ScrollBars	Neither
RecordSelectors	No
NavigationButtons	No
AutoResize	Yes
AutoCenter	No
MinMaxButtons	Min Enabled

them different properties. Therefore, you can move popup windows anywhere on the Windows desktop, and they stay "above" all the other, normal Access forms. Setting the Popup property to Yes, then, is crucial in order to allow your popup toolbox to function correctly; the code that locates the active form will rely on the fact that your toolbox has a different parent from the other forms.

The AutoResize Property

Although setting the AutoResize property to Yes isn't imperative, it certainly makes the design process simpler for you. Normally Access saves the dimensions and location of a form with the form when you save it. In Design view, though, Access always displays the horizontal and vertical scroll bars on a form. Because you're using your toolbox form without scroll bars, you'll want it just the right size to include the controls you've placed on it. Setting the AutoResize property to Yes causes Access to resize the form to the correct size to just contain the internal design surface when it loads the form. (If you want an exercise in design frustration, set this property to No and try to get your form sized correctly.)

Placing Objects on the Form

The sample toolbox form consists of command buttons and a label control. You'll want to choose buttons with pictures that are familiar to your users and actions that are clearly related to the pictures. For the example, we've chosen to use the alignment pictures Access itself uses for the Align Top/Left/Right/Bottom buttons and similar pictures for the Center Horizontal/Vertical buttons. In this case we've also added a simple status bar in the toolbox that updates to describe the current button as you move the mouse over the buttons or as you move from button to button with the keyboard. This provides a different text than the Control-TipText property might, so you can provide two different sets of text, one more verbose than the other, if you wish. There's no reason you can't include other control types in your own toolboxes, but this sample was meant to be simple.

Why Not Use Access' Status Bar?

The sample toolbox includes its own status bar. As you move the mouse over the various buttons, code attached to the MouseMove event of each button keeps the status bar updated. You may be wondering why we chose not to use the standard Access status bar. Yes, you can use the SysCmd function (with the acSyscmdSetStatus constant) to place text in the Access status bar. However, problems arise with that method:

- Access itself uses that status bar, and you have no control over the times at which that occurs. If you happen to run a query or any other action that requires Access to show a status meter, it will overwrite your status message without so much as a simple apology.

- Because you have no method for keeping track of exactly what is displayed in the status bar, you never can tell whether you actually need to update the text there. Therefore, all you can do is continually update the status bar. This can cause some unpleasant flashing as Access updates the screen. Using your own status bar on the form itself allows you to avoid this flashing.

- Many end users never notice what's displayed there. Because it's so far (in terms of distance) from the "action," the eye must travel too far to notice the text in the status bar at the bottom of the screen.

Updating the Status Label

Because you want the text updated every time the mouse enters each button and you also want it updated as each button gets the focus, you need code attached to both the MouseMove and Enter events. To keep from duplicating text in each place, we've used a common procedure, DisplayText, that takes as a parameter an Integer describing the button in question. These constants:

```
Const adhcClearText = -1
Const adhcAlignLeft = 0
Const adhcAlignRight = 1
Const adhcAlignTop = 2
Const adhcAlignBottom = 3
Const adhcCenterVert = 4
Const adhcCenterHoriz = 5
```

are used throughout the code to indicate which button is current. Then, from both the MouseMove and Enter events, the attached code calls DisplayText, passing the appropriate constant for each button.

The DisplayText procedure in the following listing can react to the parameter, placing the correct text into lblStatus:

```
Private Sub DisplayText(intWhich As Integer)
    Dim strText As String

    Select Case intWhich
        Case adhcAlignTop
            strText = "Align Controls to Top"
        Case adhcAlignBottom
            strText = "Align Controls to Bottom"
        Case adhcAlignLeft
            strText = "Align Controls to Left"
        Case adhcAlignRight
            strText = "Align Controls to Right"
        Case adhcCenterHoriz
            strText = "Center Controls Horizontally"
        Case adhcCenterVert
            strText = "Center Controls Vertically"
        Case Else
            strText = " "
    End Select

    If Me!lblStatus.Caption <> strText Then
        Me!lblStatus.Caption = strText
    End If
End Sub
```

Note that the code updates lblStatus only if the text to be placed there is different from the text that's already there. This reduces the flickering effect you'd see otherwise. Because Access fires off the MouseMove event every time the mouse moves even a tiny amount, this procedure would otherwise be updating the label for each move. This way it updates the label's caption only when there's new text to be placed there. You might find it interesting to try this function without checking the current text, comparing the way the status label looks in either case. You'll probably agree that the extra processing required to check the text first is worth the time it takes, based on the improvement in the screen display.

Beyond the Basics

Once you have your toolbox performing the basic functions (that is, appearing correctly and updating the status bar), you need to perform the following actions for each button:

- Determine the previous active window.

- Return to that window.

- Take the appropriate action.

Finding the Active Window

Once you've created your toolbox form and its buttons and status bar, you need to make it actually *do* something. If your intention is to have it take some action on the form at the point where the user was prior to clicking one of its buttons, it will need some way to figure out what the last active object was. To find this information you need to rely on the fact that Access uses the MDI model for its workspace. Open forms and reports are all children of the same MDI client window, while popup forms are children of the Access window itself. Luckily, the Windows API function GetWindow, when asked to retrieve information about children of a particular window, finds the top-most child window first. Because the active window is always the top-most window, you can get a handle to the window you want to find.

The module basWindowRelationships includes the functions you need in order to find the most recently active child of Access' MDI client window. To use them, you must have a list of the Windows class names for the objects you might need to find from your own toolboxes. Table 8.3 lists several objects and their class names.

TABLE 8.3   Sample Access Objects and Their Class Names

Object	Class Name	Comment
Database Container	ODb	There is only one Database container, so finding the first object with this class type is always sufficient
Form	OForm	All forms are of the same class
Report	OReport	All reports are of the same class
Macro Design Window	OScript	
Module Design Window	OModule	
Table	OTable	Whether the table is in Design or Datasheet view, the internal display is a window of the class OGrid
Query	OQry	

TIP

Table 8.3 lists just a few of the many window classes Access creates. If you want to explore on your own, you need a tool that can examine windows and give you information about them. One such tool is SPYXX.EXE, which ships with Microsoft's Visual C++ Compiler. That's the tool we used to gather the class name information you see here. You may also be able to find freeware tools that provide similar functionality.

To find the first occurrence of a particular child class, call adhGetAccessChild with the appropriate class name. For example,

```
hWnd = adhGetAccessChild("ODb")
```

returns to you the handle of the database container window. Calling the function as

```
hWnd = adhGetAccessChild("OForm")
```

returns the handle of the active standard form. It won't find popup forms because it only looks through the children of the MDI client window.

The more general-purpose function adhFindChildClass takes two parameters: the handle of a window through which to look for children and the class of the child you're interested in. You could find the database container's window handle by calling the function like this:

```
hWnd = adhFindChildClass(Application.hWndAccessApp, "ODb")
```

How the Functions Work

The adhGetAccessChild function starts by using code similar to the previous example to find the handle to the MDI Client window:

```
hwnd = adhFindChildClass(Application.hWndAccessApp, _
 adhcMDIClientClass)
```

Once it finds this handle it can call adhFindChildClass once more, requesting the necessary child of the MDIClient window:

```
If hwnd <> 0 Then
    ' Going into this function, hWnd is the handle
    ' for the main MDI client window. The return
    ' value is either the handle for the requested child
    ' or 0.
    hwnd = adhFindChildClass(hwnd, strClass)
End If
' It's possible that hWnd will be 0 at this point.
adhGetAccessChild = hwnd
```

adhFindChildClass uses the Windows API function GetWindow (aliased as adh_apiGetWindow), which can iterate through all the children of a window, looking for a specific class type. You can call it once with the adhcGW_CHILD flag, in which case it finds the window's first child. Calling it subsequently, with the handle of that child and the adhcGW_HWNDNEXT flag, finds siblings of that child. If adhFindChildClass looks through all the children and doesn't find one of the right type, it returns 0 (an invalid window handle), indicating failure. The loop boils down to these lines of code, iterating through all the children of the window for which the handle is hWnd:

```
hWndCurrent = adh_apiGetWindow(hwnd, adhcGW_CHILD)
fFound = False
Do While hWndCurrent <> 0
    intClassLen = adh_apiGetClassName(hWndCurrent, _
     strClassName, adhcMaxLen - 1)
    If Left(strClassName, intClassLen) = _
     strClassNameToMatch Then
        fFound = True
        Exit Do
```

```
            End If
            hWndTemp = adh_apiGetWindow(hWndCurrent, _
             adhcGW_HWNDNEXT)
            hWndCurrent = hWndTemp
Loop
```

Armed with adhFindChildClass and some program such as SPYXX.EXE from Microsoft, you should be able to find a handle to any child window for any application, should the need arise.

Making the Previous Form Current

Once you know the handle of the last-active form, you'll want to make it the current window again. That was the point of all this code. Unfortunately, Access provides no method for activating a window based on its handle. To do that you need one more Windows API function, SetFocus. Given a window handle, SetFocus makes the appropriate window active.

For the example toolbox you'll find in CH08.MDB, all the actions are appropriate only if the active form is in Design view. Therefore, the function you call that returns you to the previously active form must also check the mode of the form. It returns a True value if the form is opened in Design view (the CurrentView property is 0) and a False value otherwise. Listing 8.9 shows the GetToForm function, which the sample toolbox uses to return to the form that was active before you clicked a button on the toolbox. Each button's Click event code checks the return value of GetToForm before it takes any action. If the function returns a False value, each button does nothing at all.

Listing 8.9

```
' These are the class names used in Access.
Const adhcMDIClientClass = "MDICLIENT"
Const adhcAccessFormClass = "OForm"

Private Function GetToForm() As Boolean

    ' Move back to the first active form.
    Dim hwnd As Long
    Dim varTemp As Variant

    Const acDesignView = 0
```

```
        GetToForm = False

        ' Attempt to find the active form.
        hwnd = adhGetAccessChild(adhcAccessFormClass)
        ' If you found a form, then go to it.
        If hwnd <> 0 Then
            ' Set the focus to the selected form.
            varTemp = adh_apiSetFocus(hwnd)

            ' The form's hWnd had better match the active
            ' form's hWnd!
            Set mfrm = Screen.ActiveForm
            If mfrm.hwnd = hwnd Then
                If mfrm.CurrentView <> acDesignView Then
                    MsgBox "This command is available " & _
                        "only in design view!"
                Else
                    ' This is the only case in which
                    ' GetToForm is True.
                    GetToForm = True
                End If
            Else
                ' If the active form's hWnd doesn't match
                ' the one you just set the focus to, then
                ' something very strange is going on.
                MsgBox "An unknown error has occurred."
            End If
        End If
    End If
End Function
```

Taking Action

By checking the return value from GetToForm in each button's Click event code, you can be assured you won't perform an action that isn't reasonable for the form. If your toolbox is to perform actions that make sense in other contexts, you'll want to modify GetToForm to check that the object is opened in the appropriate context for your actions. In this case the four buttons that align groups of controls do nothing more than replicate menu items. A sample event code procedure might look like this:

```
Private Sub cmdAlignTop_Click()
    If GetToForm() Then
```

```
        On Error Resume Next
        DoCmd.RunCommand acCmdAlignTop
    End If
End Sub
```

NOTE

To spare current and future versions of Access from the horrible chore of managing and understanding multiple layers of old menu bars, Access 97 finally adds the RunCommand method. You no longer need to worry about exact menu locations as you did when using DoMenuItem—every possible menu action has a corresponding constant (beginning with "acCmd") you can use with the RunCommand method. The code in this book uses this new technique whenever possible. Declare a moratorium on old DoMenuItem code; use the new RunCommand method whenever possible.

The two buttons that center controls require more code because there are no built-in menu items to do that job. They both use the InSelection property, checking for inclusion in the selected group of controls. For any control in the selection, the code takes the appropriate action. (The mFrm variable is global to the form, filled in by the GetToForm function. This saves every event procedure needing to retrieve the form reference.) The following listing shows a function to center controls horizontally:

```
Private Sub cmdCenterHorizontal_Click()
    Dim intI As Integer
    Dim ctl As Control
    Dim intWidth As Integer

    If GetToForm() Then
        intWidth = mfrm.Width

        For Each ctl In mfrm.Controls
            With ctl
                If .InSelection Then
                    .Left = (intWidth - .Width) \ 2
                End If
            End With
        Next ctl
    End If
End Sub
```

> **TIP**
>
> The InSelection property is read/write. This means that if you want to write tools to be used when designing forms, you can now programmatically add items to the group of selected items on a form. Although this won't appeal to all developers, it's a welcome addition to the product.

Using frmToolbox in Your Own Applications

We've designed frmToolbox so you can just import it from CH08.MDB into your own application database (along with basFormGlobal and basWindowRelationships), open it in Form view, and use it while you're designing forms. You can use it, as is, as a development tool.

More likely, though, you'll want to take the concepts involved in frmToolbox and create your own toolboxes. If you're interested in using the underlying code but not the exact functionality, consider removing some of the code that's stored with the form. If you're going to use frmToolbox as part of your own application or library database, import it into your database. We've included the functions you'll need, along with the necessary declarations, in basWindowRelationships and basFormGlobal in CH08.MDB. To include those functions, just import those particular modules into your application.

Of course, if you don't need the status bar on your toolbox, you can just as easily create your standard toolbar (using the View ➤ Toolbars ➤ Customize menu). In that case, place your code into a standard module and set the OnAction function property of each toolbar button to call the appropriate function in your module. This requires a lot less code than handling everything yourself, as in this section's example. You give up some flexibility, however, by using the built-in mechanism.

Creating Self-Disabling Navigation Buttons

Access provides several methods for your users to move from one row of data on a form to another. You can use the standard form navigation buttons, but they provide absolutely no flexibility to you as a developer. You can also use the Button Wizard to create the navigation buttons on your form. In each case the solutions lack one feature that many clients request: they'd like buttons that don't do anything to be disabled. That is, if users are already at the last row in the recordset, the button that takes them to the last row ought to be disabled. If they're on the new row, the button that takes them there ought not be available. Few things are more frustrating to the end user than clicking a button and having nothing happen or, worse, clicking a button and finding out the action isn't available.

You can create your own buttons that replace the functionality Access provides and additionally give you the functionality described above. As an example, look at frmNavigate in CH08.MDB. This form includes buttons you can copy onto your own forms that handle form navigation for you. Figure 8.9 shows frmNavigate positioned at the last row in the underlying recordset. Note that the buttons that would move you to the next and last rows are currently disabled. (We've left the standard Access navigation buttons enabled for this sample form so you can compare the two sets. Of course, on a real form, you'd set the NavigationButtons property to No if you were going to use these new controls.)

FIGURE 8.9

Because the current row is the last row in the recordset, the Next and Last buttons are disabled.

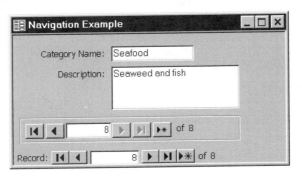

Forms and Their Data

Every bound form acts as a moving "window" for the form's underlying data. At any given time your form can display one or more rows from that dataset, and your Access Basic code can also manipulate that dataset. You can create a Recordset variable and assign to it the value of the form's RecordSetClone property. In this manner Access allows you to view and modify the same set of data that the user sees on the form. Because Access maintains separate record pointers for the form and for its underlying recordset, you can move around freely in the recordset, while the form's displayed record doesn't change at all.

In addition, when Access loads the data in a recordset, it creates a unique bookmark value for each row of data. You can read the Bookmark property of the form or of the underlying recordset. In either case, you're retrieving the bookmark associated with the current row. You can set the Bookmark property as well. This allows you to save and retrieve the form's bookmark independently of the form's recordset bookmark.

When you first retrieve a copy of the form's recordset (using the RecordSetClone property), your position in the recordset is officially undefined, and you'll need to position yourself on a particular row. You can use any of the Move... (MoveFirst, MoveLast, MoveNext, MovePrevious) methods to position the record pointer, or you can equate the recordset and the form's Bookmark properties. Doing so sets the current row in your recordset to be the same as the row currently shown on the form. Code to do this might look like the following:

```
Dim rst as RecordSet
Set rst = Me.RecordSetClone
rst.Bookmark = Me.Bookmark
```

Controlling Row Movement

Two issues are involved in controlling the row movement programmatically:

- Moving from row to row

- Disabling the correct buttons at the correct time

The issues involved in moving from row to row are simple. Each button calls, from its Click event, a distinct procedure in basNavigate. Each of these procedures calls into a common private procedure, NavMove, which performs the action. For example, the Last button calls this procedure:

```
Function adhNavLast(frm As Form)
    NavMove frm, acLast
End Function
```

(The constants acLast, acPrevious, acNewRec, acNext, and acLast are all defined by Access.) NavMove (Listing 8.10) uses the Move... methods of the form's recordset to move about, rather than using the GotoRecord method, because you can control the movement with more precision, trapping errors as necessary, if you move in the form's recordset first and then make the form display the new record once you've found it in the recordset.

Listing 8.10

```
Private Sub NavMove(frm As Form, intWhere As Integer)

    ' Move to the correct row in the form's recordset,
    ' depending on which button was pushed. This code
    ' doesn't really need to check for errors, since the
    ' buttons that would cause errors have been
    ' disabled already.
    '
Dim rst As Recordset
Dim fAtNew As Boolean

Const adhcErrNoCurrentRow = 3021

If frm.Dirty Then
    ' Put code here that you would have done in the
    ' form's AfterUpdate event. You can't use the
    ' AfterUpdate event if you've got these buttons
    ' in place, since they interfere pretty seriously.
End If

On Error GoTo NavMoveError
' This only works on the CURRENT form.
' You'll need to rethink this if you want
' the buttons on one form and the record
' movement on another.
If intWhere = acNewRec Then
    DoCmd.GoToRecord Record:=acNewRec
Else
    fAtNew = frm.NewRecord
    Set rst = frm.RecordsetClone
    rst.Bookmark = frm.Bookmark
    Select Case intWhere
        Case acFirst
            rst.MoveFirst
        Case acPrevious
            If fAtNew Then
                rst.MoveLast
            Else
                rst.MovePrevious
            End If
        Case acNext
            rst.MoveNext
```

```
              Case acLast
                  rst.MoveLast
          End Select
          frm.Bookmark = rst.Bookmark
      End If

NavMoveExit:
    Exit Sub

NavMoveError:
    If Err.Number = adhcErrNoCurrentRow And _
     frm.NewRecord Then
        Resume Next
    Else
        MsgBox Err.Description & " (" & Err.Number & ")"
        Resume NavMoveExit
    End If
    Resume NavMoveExit
End Sub
```

In theory, this code should be all you need to move around in your recordset. There are two problems, though. This code won't handle the disabling of unavailable buttons. It also causes an error condition (3021, "No Current Record") when you try to move past the last row or before the first row.

Disabling Buttons

To correctly enable and disable navigation buttons, you need to be able to retrieve the current row location. That is, if you're currently on the first row, you need to know that fact as soon as you get there so the appropriate buttons (Previous and First) can be disabled. If you're on the last row, you'll want the Next and Last buttons to be disabled. If you're on the new row, you'll want the New, Next, and Last buttons disabled.

Checking the Current Location

You can use the form's recordset and the Bookmark property to check the current row's location within its recordset. For example, you could take these steps to check whether the current displayed row in the form was the first row:

1. Retrieve a reference to the form's recordset using the RecordsetClone property.

2. Set the location in the recordset to be the same as that displayed on the form, using the Bookmark property.

3. In the recordset, move to the previous record, using the MovePrevious method. If the recordset's BOF property is now True, you must have been on the first row.

If you want to write a function that just checks to see whether you're on the first row, here's one way to do it:

```
Function AtFirstRow(frm As Form) As Boolean
    ' Return True if at first row, False otherwise.
    Dim rst as RecordSet
    Set rst = frm.RecordsetClone
    rst.Bookmark = frm.Bookmark
    rst.MovePrevious
    AtFirstRow = rst.BOF
End Function
```

You could apply the same logic to check whether you were at the last row. Armed with the knowledge assembled here, you should now be able to write a single function that checks all these states and disables the correct buttons.

There's one more issue, though. Some forms are not updatable at all. If they're based on nonupdatable queries or tables, if you've set the RecordsetType property for the form to Snapshot, or if you've set the AllowAdditions property for the form to No, you can't add a new row. In this case you also need to disable the New button.

The function you want should execute the following steps to determine which buttons are available as you move from row to row on the form:

1. Check the updatability of the form and its recordset, and set the New button's availability based on that information. Also, if you're on the new row, disable the button, since you can't go there if you're already there.

2. If you're on the new row already, enable the First and Previous buttons if there's any data in the recordset (disable them otherwise), and disable the Next and Last buttons.

3. If you're not on the new row, check for the beginning and end of recordset cases, as discussed above.

You'll find the procedure you need in Listing 8.11. adhEnableButtons takes a form reference as a parameter and enables and disables the navigation buttons on the form according to your location within the form's recordset. To use it, you must call it from the Current event of your form. Note that the code is dependent on the specific names for buttons (cmdFirst, cmdPrev, cmdNew, cmdNext, cmdLast). Make sure your buttons have the correct Name property before attempting to use this code.

Listing 8.11

```
Function adhEnableButtons(frm As Form)

    Dim rst As Recordset
    Dim fAtNew As Integer
    Dim fUpdatable As Integer

    frm!txtCurrRec = frm.CurrentRecord
    Set rst = frm.RecordsetClone
    ' Sooner or later, Access will figure out
    ' how many rows there really are!
    frm!txtTotalRecs = rst.RecordCount + _
     IIf(frm.NewRecord, 1, 0)

    ' Check to see whether or not you're on the new record.
    fAtNew = frm.NewRecord

    ' If the form isn't updatable, then you sure
    ' can't go to the new record!  If it is, then
    ' the button should be enabled unless you're already
    ' on the new record.
    fUpdatable = rst.Updatable And frm.AllowAdditions
    frm!cmdNew.Enabled = IIf(fUpdatable, Not fAtNew, False)

    If fAtNew Then
        frm!cmdNext.Enabled = False
        frm!cmdLast.Enabled = True
        frm!cmdFirst.Enabled = True And _
         (rst.RecordCount > 0)
        frm!cmdPrev.Enabled = True And (rst.RecordCount > 0)
    Else
        ' Sync the recordset's bookmark with
        ' the form's bookmark.
        rst.Bookmark = frm.Bookmark

        ' Move backwards to check for BOF.
        rst.MovePrevious
        frm!cmdFirst.Enabled = Not rst.BOF
        frm!cmdPrev.Enabled = Not rst.BOF
```

```
        ' Get back to where you started.
        rst.Bookmark = frm.Bookmark

        ' Move forward to check for EOF.
        rst.MoveNext
        frm!cmdNext.Enabled = Not (rst.EOF Or fAtNew)
        frm!cmdLast.Enabled = Not (rst.EOF Or fAtNew)
    End If
End Function
```

Doing Time on the New Row

While you're on the new row, you might enter data, finish the entry, and then want to move immediately to a *new* new row so you can add another record. The problem is that we've disabled cmdNew for as long as you're on the new row. To get around this problem, you can call code to reenable cmdNew as soon as the form becomes dirty. To make that happen, you'd follow these steps:

1. Set the form's KeyPreview property to Yes. This allows the form to react to keystrokes, no matter which control has the focus.

2. Call the adhHandleKeys procedure from the KeyPress event of the form. This procedure checks the enabled status of cmdNew and, if it's not enabled but the form is dirty, sets the button so that it's enabled.

Therefore, you'd need code like this in your KeyPress event:

```
Private Sub Form_KeyPress(KeyAscii As Integer)
    adhHandleKeys Me
End Sub
```

The adhHandleKeys subroutine looks like this:

```
Sub adhHandleKeys(frm As Form)
    ' Users want to be able to move to the new
    ' row from the new row, if they've already filled
    ' in their data. This procedure checks
    ' the Dirty flag for each key and enables the
    ' New button if the row is dirty.

    With frm!cmdNew
        If Not .Enabled And frm.Dirty Then
            .Enabled = True
        End If
    End With
End Sub
```

Specifying a Row Number

Just as with Access' own navigation buttons, these replacement controls allow you to type a row number into the text box, and once you leave that text box, the code will take you to the selected row. This code (adhMoveRow) does its work by moving to the first row in the recordset and then calling the Move method to move to the requested row:

```
rst.MoveFirst
If lngRow > 0 Then
    rst.Move lngRow - 1
End If
```

The Move method requires as its parameter a zero-based number, so the code must subtract 1 to perform the necessary conversion.

Listing 8.12 shows the entire function, which should be called from the After-Update event of the text box on your form.

Listing 8.12

```
Function adhMoveRow(frm As Form, ByVal lngRow As Long)

    ' Move to a specified row.
    On Error GoTo adhMoveRow_Err
    Dim rst As Recordset

    Set rst = frm.RecordsetClone

    ' Move to the first row, and then
    ' to the selected row.
    rst.MoveFirst
    If lngRow > 0 Then
        rst.Move lngRow - 1
    End If
    ' Sync up the form with its recordset
    frm.Bookmark = rst.Bookmark

adhMoveRow_Exit:
    Exit Function

adhMoveRow_Err:
    Select Case Err.Number
```

```
            Case adhcErrNoCurrentRow
                DoCmd.GoToRecord , , acNewRec
                Resume Next
            Case Else
                MsgBox Err.Description & " (" & Err.Number & ")"
                Resume adhMoveRow_Exit
        End Select
End Function
```

Creating Your Own Navigation Buttons

You can easily create your own navigation buttons. To do so, just follow these steps:

1. Import the module basNavigate from CH08.MDB.

2. Create five command buttons, or copy the five buttons from frmNavigate in CH08.MDB. They must be named cmdFirst, cmdPrev, cmdNew, cmdNext, and cmdLast. If you copy the whole set of controls from frmNavigate, you can skip steps 4 and 5.

3. Create the two text boxes (txtCurrRec and txtTotalRecs), or copy the controls from frmNavigate.

4. From each button's Click event, call the appropriate adhNav… function. For the cmdFirst button, for example, use

    ```
    =adhNavFirst(Form)
    ' or, from the form's module:
    ' Call adhNavFirst(Me)
    ```

    The functions to call are adhNavFirst, adhNavPrev, adhNavNew, adhNav-Next, and adhNavLast.

5. To be able to type a new row number into txtCurrRec, you must handle its AfterUpdate event. To do that, call adhMoveRow, passing to it the current form reference and the text box from which to retrieve the new row number:

    ```
    =adhMoveRow([Form],[txtCurrRec])
    ' or, from the form's module:
    Call adhMoveRow(Me, Me!txtCurrRec)
    ```

6. From your form's Current event, call the adhEnableButtons function. If this is the only item in the form's Current event, you can call it directly from the property sheet, using the expression

    ```
    =adhEnableButtons(Form)
    ```

If you already have code attached to your Current event, just call the function, passing it the form reference. That is, if you're calling it from the form's class module, you can use a statement like this:

```
Call adhEnableButtons(Me)
```

7. If you want to reenable cmdNew once you've entered data into the new row, also set the form's KeyPreview property to Yes, and have the KeyPress event call the adhHandleKeys function. From the property sheet, call

```
=adhHandleKeys(Form)
' or, from the form's module:
Call adhHandleKeys(Me)
```

8. If you've placed the function calls in the property sheet and your form has no other code in its module, set the HasModule property to No. This will allow your form to load a little more quickly.

Once you've set up the buttons and the event procedures, you should be able to open the form in Form view and use the navigation buttons to move about in your form's data.

NOTE
Even if you set these buttons' AutoRepeat property, they will not move you through rows as long as you keep them pressed. Because moving to a new row moves the focus away from the buttons, Access will not auto-repeat their actions.

Understanding the HasModule Property

When you load a form, Access must also load the module attached to that form. If there's no module, the form loads more quickly. (Sure, it's more complex than that, but at least you get the idea.) If you're working with forms that contain no code, you'll want to be sure to set their HasModule property to False, guaranteeing the fastest possible load time for the form.

In this case the form does call code from its events, so Access will still need to load the module, including all the navigation code, when you load a form that uses it. But there's a real benefit to placing code in standard modules if it's going to be called from multiple forms—only one form has to pay the price of loading the code. Once you've loaded one form that uses the navigation code, all other forms that have their HasModule property set to False will load more quickly: they don't have a module to load, and the code needed to perform the navigation has already been loaded.

NOTE	In Access 1, you had no choice but to place function calls in the property sheet in order to call Access Basic code in reaction to events. In Access 2, Microsoft introduced the concept of Code-Behind-Forms, so you could place code directly in a form's module. You have not been able to move controls from one form to another and carry attached code in any version of Access, so providing function names in the property sheet remains a viable solution for situations in which you must move controls from form to form, regardless of whether the form includes other procedures in its class module.

Other Tools

We've also included a popup toolbox record navigation tool in CH08.MDB, shown in Figure 8.10. You can use it as part of your own applications, and you might want to take the time to pick it apart because it uses some interesting design techniques. To use it, follow these steps:

1. Import the form frmRecNavPopup into your application from CH08.MDB.

2. Import the modules basFormGlobal and basWindowRelationships from CH08.MDB.

3. Import the module basRecNavToolbar. (This step is optional if you also skip step 4.)

4. For any form you want to use with frmRecNavPopup, modify the form's Current and Activate events to call the HandleRecNav function, passing a reference to the current form. (See the forms frmCategories and frmCustomers in CH08.MDB for examples.) Calling HandleRecNav ensures that the toolbar's display of the current position is correct even if you move from row to row on the form, not the toolbar. (This step is optional.)

To use the popup toolbox, open a form and then open the toolbox. Clicking the various buttons on the toolbox should navigate through the rows on the form. To fully appreciate the toolbox, though, you should also follow steps 3 and 4 above. If

FIGURE 8.10

Use frmRecNavPopup to control record navigation with any bound form.

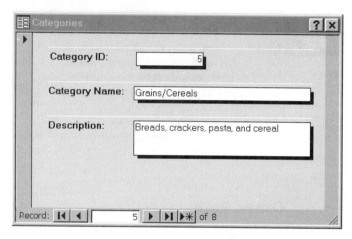

you add the function calls to your form's Current and Activate events, your forms can tell the popup toolbox what they're doing and where they are. This allows frm-RecNavPopup to track row changes when the user uses methods other than the toolbox to change rows, and it makes it possible for the toolbox to know exactly which form is the current form. If you're writing applications and want to use frm-RecNavPopup, we strongly suggest you set up your forms to call HandleRecNav.

Why Create Your Own Toolbox?

You could create a new toolbar using the tools that Access provides to control record navigation. However, if you create a toolbox from scratch (such as frmRec-NavPopup), you can include the features described here:

- You can maintain the current row number for the selected form.

- You can modify the toolbar caption to reflect the current form.

- By creating your own toolbox, you gain complete control over the actions your toolbox takes. Using Access' toolbars, your code can only react to clicks of the buttons. There's no way to react to mouse movement over the buttons on built-in toolbars, for example.

On the other hand, your own toolbox cannot dock itself the way Access' toolbars can. In addition, creating your own toolbox requires a great deal of handwritten code. Using Access' toolbars requires none.

Screen Resolution and Distributing Forms

When you set up Windows to run on your computer, you must choose a screen driver for use with your hardware. Your choice of screen driver allows your monitor to display a specific screen resolution, usually 640x480 (standard VGA), 800x600 (Super VGA), 1024x768 (XGA, Super VGA, or 8514/a), or 1280x1024. These numbers refer to the number of picture elements (*pixels*) in the horizontal and vertical directions.

If you create forms that look fine on your screen running at 1024x768, those same forms may be too large to be displayed by a user who's working at 640x480 (still the most popular screen resolution because it's the resolution most portable computers support). Similarly, if you create forms at 640x480, someone working at 1280x1024 will see them as very small forms. (A full-screen form created at 640x480 takes up about a quarter of the screen at 1280x1024—although this is not necessarily something your users will want to change. Many people who use large displays and high-resolution adapters appreciate the fact that they can see not only a full-screen form, but a great many other Access objects at the same time.)

One unattractive solution to this problem is to create multiple versions of your forms, one for each screen resolution you wish to support. This, of course, requires maintaining each of those forms individually. The following sections deal directly with the resolution issue. We present code you can use to scale your forms as they load, allowing them to look reasonable at almost any screen resolution. In addition, we include code you can attach to the Resize event of a form, allowing users to resize a form and all its controls at run time.

The sample form, frmScaleTest, demonstrates the technique of resizing a form to fit your screen resolution at load time. It also allows you to resize all the controls on the form as you resize the form. To try this out, load the form and select the Enable Automatic Resizing? check box.

Understanding Screen Resolutions

Before you can understand the solution to the screen resolution issue, you must understand the problem. Figure 8.11 shows a scale image of the four standard Windows screen resolutions, superimposed. As you can see, a form that appears full screen at 640x480 will take up only a small portion of a 1280x1024 screen, and a full-screen form at 1024x768 will be too large for a screen at 800x600.

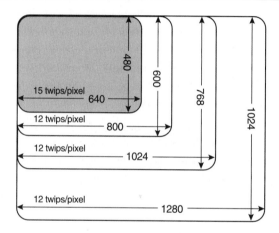

The difference in the number of pixels is only one of two issues you need to consider in scaling forms. You must also think about the size of the pixels—the number of pixels per logical inch of screen space. Each screen driver individually controls how large each pixel is in relation to what Windows thinks an "inch" is. Windows provides API calls to gather all this information, which we'll need later in this section. For now, the information of concern is the number of twips per pixel. (A *twip* is equivalent to $^1/_{1440}$ inch.) Practical experience shows that screens at 640x480 use 15 twips per pixel, and all other VGA screen resolutions use 12 twips per pixel. This means that at low-resolution VGA, 100 pixels take up 1500 twips (a little more than one logical inch), while at higher resolutions, 100 pixels take up 1200 twips (a little less than one logical inch). Therefore, to correctly scale your forms for different resolutions, you need to take both ratios into account. You need to compare, for both the screen on which the form was prepared and the screen on which it will be displayed, the pixels used and the twips-per-pixel value. The ratios of these values control how you scale the form.

The module basFormScale includes the code necessary to scale your forms at load time and to allow resizing by users at run time. This code makes extensive use of Windows API calls to retrieve information about the current display and the sizes of forms. (For more information about the Windows API and calling DLLs, see Chapter 18.)

Scaling Forms as They Load

To solve the problem of displaying forms so that they take up the same proportion of the screen real estate on different screen resolutions, it would seem that all you need do is calculate the ratio of the original screen dimensions to the current screen dimensions and scale the form accordingly. Unfortunately, the calculation is further complicated by the twips-per-pixel issue. Because different screen resolutions use a different number of twips for each pixel, you must also take this into account when calculating the new size for the form. The x-axis sizing ratio, when moving from 640x480 to 1024x768, is not just 1024/640. You must multiply that value by the ratio of the twips-per-pixel values. (Think of it this way: as far as Windows is concerned, pixels are "bigger" at 640x480. At higher resolutions, a pixel takes up fewer twips.) Figure 8.12 shows a single form, 400x120 pixels, created in 640x480 resolution, as it would display on a screen in 1024x768 resolution. The first example shows it unscaled, and the second example shows it scaled.

FIGURE 8.12

Scaling a form causes it to appear approximately the same on screens with different resolutions.

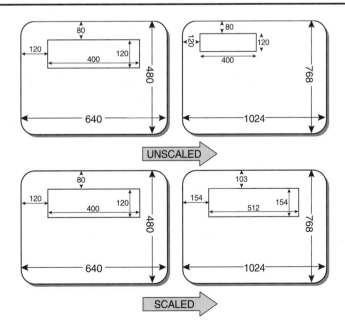

467

Necessary Information

To correctly scale your form, the code needs to know the screen resolution at which you created your form (so it can calculate the ratios between the screen widths and heights). It also needs to know the logical dots-per-inch values for the vertical and horizontal dimensions of the screen where you created the form. You may know, offhand, the screen resolution you use on your development machine, but you're unlikely to know the logical dots-per-inch values. Therefore, we've provided the frmScreenInfo form, shown in Figure 8.13. This form has one purpose in life: it provides information about your current screen settings so you can correctly call the adhScaleForm function described below.

The code in this form's class module calculates the current size of the screen, taking into account the area chewed up by taskbars docked to the edges of your screen. It also calculates the logical dots-per-inch values and formats the function call as you'll need for your form. Once you've run this form, cut the value in the text box to the clipboard and paste it into your form's Open event.

FIGURE 8.13

Use frmScreenInfo to calculate necessary screen coordinate information.

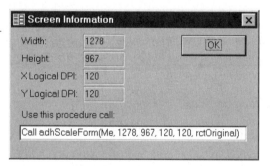

TIP

The information form, frmScreenInfo, takes taskbars into account when it calculates the screen resolution. If your users don't display their taskbars, you might want to set all taskbars on your system to be hidden when not in use. (Usually, this is the AutoHide property for the application.) That way, at worst, your form will scale too small (if you don't show taskbars but users do).

Retrieving Display Information

To scale your forms, you must first retrieve information about the current display driver so the code can compare the values to the information you supplied about your original screen settings. To do this, you need to use a Windows *device context,* a data structure that provides a link between the Windows API and the device driver. Actually, for this example, you can use an *information context,* which is a lower-powered device context, unable to write information back to the driver. Any calls to the Windows API dealing with the display driver must pass an information context or a device context handle as the first parameter. To get the information context handle, use the following code:

```
lngIC = adh_apiCreateIC("DISPLAY", vbNullString, _
 vbNullString, vbNullString)
```

Once you have the information context handle, lngIC, you can obtain the information you need about the current display driver. First of all, you must retrieve the pixel resolutions of the current display driver. You can use the Windows API function GetSystemMetrics to obtain this information:

```
intScreenX = adh_apiGetSystemMetrics(adhcSM_CXFULLSCREEN)
intScreenY = adh_apiGetSystemMetrics(adhcSM_CYFULLSCREEN)
```

Next, calculate the ratio of the current screen resolution to the resolution that was active when the form was created. The original values will have been passed in to this function in the parameters intX and intY:

```
sglFactorX = intScreenX / intX
sglFactorY = intScreenY / intY
```

However, as mentioned before, this isn't accurate enough. You need to take into account the differences in the number of twips per pixel between different display adapters. To do this, scale the scaling factors by the ratio of the twips-per-pixel value for the original display, as compared to the value for the current display:

```
sglFactorX = sglFactorX * (intDPIX / _
 adh_apiGetDeviceCaps(lngIC, adhcLOGPIXELSX))
sglFactorY = sglFactorY * (intDPIY / _
 adh_apiGetDeviceCaps(lngIC, adhcLOGPIXELSY))
```

Armed with the values for sglFactorX and sglFactorY, you have the information you need to correctly scale the form as you open it in the new display resolution. You should be able to just multiply the form's width, height, and position of the upper-left corner by that scaling factor and end up with the form in a relative position on the screen with the new width and height. Figure 8.12 earlier in this chapter demonstrates this calculation.

Scaling the Form's Contents

Scaling the form is only part of the problem, however. Just changing the size of the container won't help much if you can't see all the controls inside it. Therefore, you need a way to change the size of all the controls inside the form as well. The function adhScaleForm, called from your form's Open event, calls the adhResize-Form function to resize all the controls. You can also call this subroutine directly from your form's Resize event, allowing you to dynamically resize all the controls on the form every time the user resizes the form. This can be a striking feature, allowing the user to make a form take up less screen real estate but still be available for use. Figure 8.14 shows a form both full size and scaled down to a smaller size.

To accomplish this visual feat, you can attach a call to adhResizeForm to your form's Resize event. The adhResizeForm function loops through all the controls on the form, scaling them by the ratio between the previous size of the form and the current size of the form. Note that in this situation you don't care about any screen resolution issues; you're just comparing the current size of the form to the previous size of the form to find the sizing ratio.

FIGURE 8.14

Two copies of the same form, one at full size and another scaled to a smaller size.

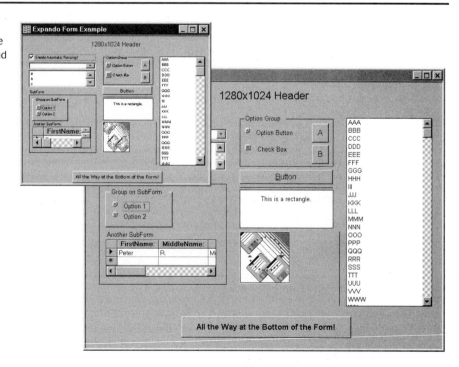

If you switch a form from Design view to Form view and the form will shrink at run time (it was designed at a higher screen resolution than the current resolution), Access will not repaint the screen correctly. You can force a screen repaint in the form's Resize event by uncommenting the lines of code in the sample that use the Application.Echo method. This creates its own problems, however, by causing unnecessary screen repaints. Unless you need to switch back and forth between Design and Form views, we recommend leaving those lines of code commented out.

The function first checks to make sure the user has not sized the form to its minimum size or minimized it, with no space inside the form. In those cases Access acts as though there were no active form, so the code cannot go any farther. The code calls the GetClientRect API function to find the form's height and just exits if the height is 0 or if it's iconized:

```
adh_apiGetClientRect frm.hwnd, rctNew
intHeight = (rctNew.Y2 - rctNew.Y1)
If intHeight = 0 Or adh_apiIsIconic(frm.hwnd) Then
    Exit Function
End If
```

Once the function has found the dimensions for the current form, it calculates the current width. Then it can calculate and store the scaling factors, based on the previous sizes stored in rctOriginal:

```
' Now get the actual window height and width.
adh_apiGetWindowRect frm.hwnd, rctNew

' Get the current width and height.
intHeight = (rctNew.Y2 - rctNew.Y1)
intWidth = (rctNew.X2 - rctNew.X1)
sglFactorX = intWidth / (rctOriginal.X2 - rctOriginal.X1)
sglFactorY = intHeight / (rctOriginal.Y2 - rctOriginal.Y1)
```

Finally, it stores away the current form sizes so it will have them available on the next pass-through here:

```
With rctOriginal
    .X1 = rctNew.X1
    .X2 = rctNew.X2
```

```
      .Y1 = rctNew.Y1
      .Y2 = rctNew.Y2
End With
```

Once all these preliminary steps have been taken, if there's resizing to be done, the function now calls the workhorse function, SetFormSize.

Scaling the Controls

In theory, SetFormSize does nothing more than just loop through all the controls on the form, scaling their locations and sizes by the scaling factors calculated in the calling function. In practice, there are a number of details that aren't, at first, obvious. These are some of the issues:

- The order of events is important. If your form is growing, you must expand the section heights before you allow the controls to expand. Otherwise the expanding controls will push out the boundaries of the sections and make the scaling invalid. The opposite holds true if your form is shrinking. In that case you cannot shrink the section heights until after you've sized all the controls. Otherwise you risk artificially compressing the control locations.

- You must deal carefully with controls that contain other controls. A group can contain toggle buttons, option buttons, and check boxes. A subform can contain any control and possibly yet another subform (nested, at most, two levels deep). To maintain the correct scaling, you need to walk through all the controls on the form, build an array containing information about all the container controls, scale all the controls on the form, and then scale the containers. In addition, if you run across a subform, you must recursively call the function again, scaling all the controls on that subform. If that subform contains a subform, you must call the function once more to handle that final subform. Once the function has handled all the controls on the form, it loops through the array of containers and scales them correctly.

- Some controls don't need their height or font scaled. For example, you can't really change the height of a check box. Several controls don't even expose a FontName property. The SetFormSize subroutine calls the ChangeHeight and ChangeFont functions to find out whether it should bother trying to change the particular property at all.

- You want to *move* forms only when they're first loaded. After that, moving forms should be up to the user. Therefore, the code that positions the form itself should be called only if the subroutine was called from adhScaleForm.

Steps to Successful Scaling

Due to limitations of the technology, the methodology presented here is far from perfect. Each time Access fires off the Resize event, the function calculates the current control or font size based on the previous size. This iterative calculation inevitably leads to round-off errors. Once your user compresses the form down beyond readability, attempts to expand it will often result in an unreadable mess. One alternative method would have been to store away the original size of each control on the form. Then, at each resize attempt, you could have compared the current size of the form to the original size, scaling each control accordingly. This method might have been more accurate but would have slowed down the process; in the trade-off of speed against accuracy, speed won again.

In any case, there are some rules you must follow to make it possible for this code to work:

- Use TrueType fonts for each control you will scale. This code will scale only the fonts in labels, buttons, and text, combo, and list boxes. Unfortunately, the default font used in all controls is not scalable. You must either modify your form defaults or select all the controls and change the font once you're finished designing. On the other hand, beware of using fonts that won't be available on your users' machines. All copies of Windows 95 and NT ship with Arial and Times Roman fonts; choosing one of these for your buttons, labels, and list, combo, and text boxes guarantees a certain level of success. Of course, all the Office 97 applications use the Tahoma font, and you may wish to use this font in order to "blend in" with the rest of Office.

- Do not design forms at 1280x1024 and expect them to look good at 640x480. By the time forms get scaled that far down, they're very hard to read. Using 800x600 or 1024x768 for development should provide forms that look reasonable at all resolutions.

- The current implementation of this code cannot resize subforms shown as datasheets. Although it may be possible to make this work, at this point you should be aware that the contents of datasheets will not scale, although their physical size will.

- Do not attempt to mix the AutoCenter property with a call to adhScaleForm called from the Open event. The AutoCenter property will attempt to center the form before it's resized and will cause Access to place the form somewhere you don't expect it to be.

- Make labels and text boxes a bit wider than you think you actually need. Windows doesn't always provide the exact font size the code requests, so you're better off erring on the generous side when you size your controls.

Scaling Your Own Forms

To include this functionality in your own applications, follow these steps:

1. Include the modules basFormScale and basFormGlobal from CH08.MDB in your database.

2. Ensure that all the fonts on your form are scalable. (Use TrueType fonts if possible, since they're all scalable.)

3. In the form module for each form you'd like to scale, declare a data structure to hold the size information for the form:

```
' The actual name doesn't matter, of course.
Dim rctOriginal As adhTypeRect
```

4. To scale the form to fit the current resolution when it loads, attach a call to adhScaleForm to your form's Open event. Pass to the function a reference to your form, the x- and y-resolutions of the screen for which it was designed, the logical dots-per-inch values for the horizontal and vertical dimensions of your screen, and the structure you created in step 3. (Use frmScreenInfo to generate this line of code.)

```
Call adhScaleForm(Me, 1280, 1024, 120, 120, rctOriginal)
```

5. To allow dynamic resizing of the form's controls, attach a call to adhResizeForm to your form's Resize event. The first parameter to adhResizeForm is a reference to your form, the second parameter tells the subroutine whether or not to actually do the resize, and the third is the structure holding the size of the form. If the second parameter's value is True, the subroutine changes all the controls. If it's False, it just resets the storage of the form's current size:

```
Call adhResizeForm(Me, True, rctOriginal)
```

Because your form always calls the function from the Resize event, regardless of whether you're actually resizing all the controls, the function always knows the form's previous size. This way, if you decide to allow resizing in the middle of a session, it will still work correctly. The example form bases this decision on a check box on the form itself.

Changing the Mouse Pointer

Access' Screen object supports a useful property that allows you a tiny bit of extra control over the current mouse cursor: the MousePointer property. You can set the mouse pointer using syntax like this:

Screen.MousePointer = *intPointer*

where *intPointer* can be one of the following values:

0: (Default) Shape determined by Access

1: Normal Select (Arrow)

3: Text select (I-Beam)

7: Diagonal Resize (Size NWSE)

9: Horizontal Resize (Size WE)

11: Busy (Hourglass)

The MousePointer property changes the cursor for the entire screen. (That is, Access provides no method for changing the cursor for specific objects.) None of the other integer values work; only the values in the table will work.

You can also retrieve the current setting of the mouse pointer:

```
intCurrentPointer = Screen.MousePointer
```

This way you can retrieve the current mouse pointer, store away its value, set it to a new value, and return it to its original state when you're done with it. As you can imagine, using

```
DoCmd.HourGlass True
```

sets the value of Screen.MousePointer to 11, as it should.

Filtering Data

As part of many applications, you'll be called upon to allow your users to choose a subset of rows and perhaps supply their own ordering from a table or query. Access provides two visual ways to filter data: Filter by (or Excluding) Selection and Filter by Form (often called "Query By Form", or QBF). The next few sections discuss these features and the form methods and properties that are associated with them. These include the Filter and FilterOn properties and the Filter and ApplyFilter events. Along the way, you'll also need to investigate the FilterLookup property for controls, because this property allows you to fine-tune the performance of your QBF forms.

The Filter Property

Forms and reports maintain a Filter property, which contains the current, or last applied, filter for the form. The Filter property takes the form of a SQL WHERE clause, such as

```
[LastName] = "Smith" And [City] Like "S*"
```

A filter can be either active or inactive, depending on the state of the FilterOn Property. (See the section "The FilterOn Property" a little later in this chapter for more information.) Filter By (or Excluding) Selection, Filter by Form, Advanced Filter/Sort (that's the mechanism that was available in Access 2), the ApplyFilter method, or direct manipulation via code or macro will update the Filter property. The results of these actions might be different, but they all do their work by modifying the Filter property.

Forms begin life with a null Filter property. Any of the actions listed above will insert a string into the Filter property, and the resulting filter can be either active or inactive, depending on the state of the FilterOn property. Subsequent uses of the actions mentioned above will either replace or add on to the existing Filter property, depending on the specific action and whether or not the filter was active when you took the action.

Filter by Selection

Filter by Selection allows you to create a filter by pointing to the values by which you'd like to filter. For example, selecting the value "Peter" in the FirstName field and then clicking the Filter By Selection toolbar button places

```
[FirstName] = "Peter"
```

in the form's Filter property. Selecting just the *P* in the Firstname field places

```
[FirstName] Like "P*"
```

in the Filter property, and selecting the *t* places

```
[FirstName] Like "*t*"
```

in the property.

If there was an existing value in the Filter property before you used Filter by Selection, Access' behavior depends on the setting of the FilterOn property. If the filter was active (the FilterOn property was set to True), using Filter by Selection will be cumulative: Access will place an And operator between the existing Filter property and the new expression generated by your activity in the Filter by Selection mode. Subsequent uses of Filter by Selection will continue to add to your criteria, using the And operator. If the filter was not active when you started your Filter by Selection session, Access replaces the Filter property value with the new criteria rather than adding on to it. When you close your form, Access will save the current Filter property along with the form.

WARNING   Access does not check the validity of your criteria. Because of the additive property of filters when you use Filter by Selection, you may end up with completely useless criteria. There's nothing Access can really do about this, so it's just a matter of being aware that it's possible to paint yourself into a corner using Filter by Selection.

Filter by Form

When you start a Filter by Form session, all the existing filter criteria are parsed into the current form's controls. When you leave Filter by Form mode, Access re-creates the filter from the criteria specified in each control. If the form's Filter property references fields that don't exist as controls on the form, then when you leave Filter by Form mode, Access drops the errant criteria from the Filter expression.

In any case, Filter by Form results always replace the current Filter property. Every time you use Filter by Form, Access parses the existing filter, allows you to change it, and then creates a new filter based on your selections in Filter by Form. (See the section "Fine-Tuning Filter by Form" later in the chapter for a few more details on Filter by Form.) When you close the form, Access saves the current Filter property with the form.

Advanced Filter/Sort

The Advanced Filter/Sort mechanism, left over from Access 2, allows you to create any type of filtering/sorting criteria you wish. In all cases, when you change the Filter property using Advanced Filter/Sort, Access completely replaces the value, regardless of whether it was active.

The ApplyFilter Method

Access allows you to apply a filter to a form, using the ApplyFilter method of the DoCmd object. You can specify a WHERE clause, a query, or both from which to extract the filter criteria. If you specify either a WHERE clause or a query name, Access places the appropriate criteria in the form's Filter property. That is (assuming the WHERE clause on qrySimple is "ID = 5"), the following two statements will have the same effect: the Filter property of frmSimple will contain the expression "ID = 5".

```
DoCmd.ApplyFilter FilterName:="qrySimple"
' or:
DoCmd.ApplyFilter WhereCondition:="ID = 5"
```

If you use both arguments, Access applies the WHERE clause to the results of the query you specify. In other words, it combines the two WHERE clauses, using the And operator.

Whether you supply one or both parameters to ApplyFilter, Access replaces the existing Filter property for the form with the new criteria specified by your parameters.

What Happens When You Change the Filter Property?

Any of the above actions (Filter by Selection, Filter by Form, Advanced Filter/Sort, or using the ApplyFilter action) will

1. Change the form's Filter property

2. Filter the form accordingly

3. Set the form's FilterOn property to True

4. Requery the underlying recordset

5. Set the "(Filtered)" description next to the form's navigation buttons

6. Put "FLTR" in the Access status bar

Changing the Filter Property Programmatically

When you change the Filter property programmatically (using VBA or macros), the result depends on whether or not the filter was active previously. If filtering is active when you change the Filter property programmatically, the new filter takes effect immediately. If filtering is inactive when you change the Filter property, it remains inactive, but the Filter property accepts the new value. The next time you work with the Filter property (either by setting the FilterOn property to True or by entering Filter by Form mode), Access will use your new filter. If you set the Filter property programmatically, Access will not automatically save the new Filter property when you close the form.

Removing the Filter

Access provides several methods you can use to remove the current filter from a form. If you use the ShowAllRecords method of the DoCmd object or click the Remove Filter toolbar button, Access leaves the current filter intact but sets the FilterOn property to False for you. If you change the form's record source or set the Filter property to an empty string, you'll actually remove the Filter property's value. The first methods leave the Filter property intact but make it inactive. Using the second set of methods actually removes the Filter property value altogether.

Saving the Filter Property

If you change the Filter property because of Access user interface operations (Filter by Form, Filter by Selection, or Advanced Filter/Sort), Access saves the new Filter property when you close the form, regardless of whether you specifically ask for the form to be saved. When you open a form with a Filter property set, Access will not automatically make the filter active; you'll need to set the FilterOn property to True for the filter to take effect. If you change the Filter property programmatically at any time while a form is open, Access will not save the Filter property when you close the form.

The FilterOn Property

When you open a form that has a non-empty Filter property, Access doesn't filter the data automatically. To cause Access to make the filtering active, set the FilterOn property of the form to True. This read/write property allows you to both set the filtering to be active or not and to find out whether filtering is active (Remember, changing the filter via the UI might set this property without your knowing about it.) For example, you could use code like this:

```
' Make a label on the form visible if filtering is active
Me!lblWarning.Visible = Me.FilterOn
' or
' Force filtering to be inactive.
Me.FilterOn = False
```

When you set the FilterOn property to True, Access applies the existing filter; it works the same as clicking the Apply Filter toolbar button. (As a matter of fact, if you set the FilterOn property for a form to True, Access will also select the Apply Filter toolbar button for you.) Setting the FilterOn property to False, if it's currently True, is the same as deselecting the Apply Filter toolbar button.

If you set the FilterOn property to True for a form with no Filter property, Access does not complain. The FilterOn property will be True; there just won't be any active filter. If you then subsequently set the Filter property, that filter will take effect immediately (because the FilterOn property is already set to True).

The Filter Event

Access triggers a form's Filter event whenever you select Filter by Form or Advanced Filter/Sort but before it actually goes into the filtering UI mode. Access passes two parameters to your event procedure: Cancel, which you can set to True to cause Access to cancel the filter activity that triggered the Filter event; and Filter-Type, which will be either 0 (acFilterByForm) for Filter by Form or 1 (acFilter-Advanced) for Advanced Filter/Sort.

You can use the Filter event to control what happens before a filtering session gets started. You could

- Make certain controls on the form invisible or disabled. If you do disable or hide controls, you'll want to reset them in the ApplyFilter event procedure. (See the next section for more details.)

- Clear out a previous Filter property so the filter starts "clean" every time. (Of course, changing the Filter property programmatically will prohibit its being saved with the form when you next close the form.)

- Cancel the event completely (set the Cancel parameter to True) or replace the standard Access interfaces with your own.

The sample form, frmQBFExample, uses the first technique to hide the button on the form that starts the Filter by Form session. The button, cmdQBF, uses RunCommand to switch into Filter by Form mode. When you're in Filter by Form mode, Access disables all buttons but doesn't change their appearance. To make the current mode clearer, the example hides the button, as well. It also disables the Address field, just to show that it's possible. This is the code attached to the form's OnFilter event property; it reacts only to requests to start a Filter by Form session:

```
Private Sub Form_Filter(Cancel As Integer, _
  FilterType As Integer)
    ' Disabling controls, and moving to the previous control,
    ' could trigger run-time errors. Just disregard them.
    On Error Resume Next
    If FilterType = acFilterByForm Then
        Me![Customer ID].SetFocus
        Me!cmdQBF.Visible = False
        Me!Address.Enabled = False
    End If
End Sub
```

The ApplyFilter Event

Once you've created your filter and wish to apply it to your form, Access triggers the ApplyFilter event. Access calls this event procedure for all user-initiated filtering (Filter by Form, Filter by Selection, Filter Excluding Selection, Advanced Filter/Sort) and most program-initiated filtering.

Access calls the ApplyFilter event procedure at different points, depending on the filtering action you've taken. The event is always triggered before Access modifies the Filter property, and it is a cancelable event. Using this event, you could

- Trap attempts to remove a filter, or set a new one, and request confirmation

- Modify the filter expression manually, before Access applies it (Of course, modifying the filter in code prohibits Access from saving the new filter with the form when you close the form.)

- Reset the display of the form, putting things back the way they were before you modified them in the Filter event

- Change or update the display of the form before Access applies the filter

Again, Access allows you to cancel the ApplyFilter event by setting the Cancel parameter it sends to your event procedure to True. In addition, Access sends you the ApplyType parameter, which can be 0 (acShowAllRecords) to remove the filter, 1 (acApplyFilter) to apply a new filter, or 2 (acCloseFilterWindow) if you attempted to close the filter window without specifying a new filter.

The example form, frmQBFExample, uses this event to reset the form to its previous state and to confirm changes. The event procedure, shown below, first makes the command button visible again and enables the Address field. Then, if you are attempting to set a new filter and that filter isn't empty, the form displays the filter string to be applied and requests confirmation. If you're trying to show all records or the filter you're applying is empty, the form requests confirmation to show all the rows:

```
Private Sub Form_ApplyFilter(Cancel As Integer, _
  ApplyType As Integer)
    Dim strMsg As String
    Dim strFilter As String
    ' Put things back the way they were before the
```

```
                ' Filter event changed them.
                Me!cmdQBF.Visible = True
                Me!Address.Enabled = True
                strFilter = Me.Filter
                If ApplyType = acApplyFilter And Len(strFilter) > 0 Then
                    strMsg = "You've asked to filter the form " & _
                     "given the condition:"
                    strMsg = strMsg & vbCrLf & vbCrLf & strFilter
                    strMsg = strMsg & vbCrLf & vbCrLf & "Continue?"
                    If MsgBox(strMsg, vbYesNo Or vbQuestion, _
                     "Apply Filter") = vbNo Then
                        Cancel = True
                    End If
                ElseIf ApplyType = acShowAllRecords Or _
                 Len(strFilter) = 0 Then
                    strMsg = "You've asked to show all records."
                    strMsg = strMsg & vbCrLf & vbCrLf & "Continue?"
                    If MsgBox(strMsg, vbYesNo Or vbQuestion, _
                     "Apply Filter") = vbNo Then
                        Cancel = True
                    End If
                End If
            End If
        End Sub
```

TIP

Because the ApplyFilter event can be canceled, you must place error handling around calls to the ShowAllRecords and ApplyFilter actions when called from VBA. If you don't handle the error, Access will trigger a run-time error if you cancel the filter, and your code will halt. This is similar to the way the Print action has always worked in Access: if you didn't handle errors and the user clicked the Cancel button while printing, your code would halt with a run-time error.

Fine-Tuning Filter by Form

When you enter Filter-by-Form mode, Access attempts to convert every text box on your form into a drop-down list, showing each unique item already in that field.

In general, this is very useful, but with large datasets it can be inordinately slow. You can control whether Access fills those lists with values in two ways:

- Find the text box in the Tools ➤ Option ➤ Edit/Find dialog that's labeled, "Don't display lists where more than this number of records read:". You can set that value to any number between 0 and 32766. Once you set the value, Access will read rows to fill your lists only until it reaches that number of rows. Once it has run out of rows, it knows not to display the list of values, but instead supplies only Is Null and Is Not Null as choices in the drop-down list. In other words, you're telling Access: "If you can't get all the unique values by reading fewer than this many rows, then just stop trying."

- You can also set the FilterLookup property for each control on your form. This property has three possible values: Never, if you never want Access to supply a list of values; Default, if you want to use the maximum number of rows described in the previous bullet point; or Always, if you always want Access to create the list, even if Access will have to read more rows than specified in the Options dialog.

The only remaining issue, then, is how many rows Access actually reads. The answer to this question is related to whether the field in question is indexed. If it is indexed, Access needs to read only unique values, so there's a much better chance you'll find all the unique values within the specified number of rows to be read. If the field is not indexed, Access has to look at every single row in order to create a unique list of values. Because Access will stop reading when it has reached the number of rows you specified in the Options dialog, you'll need to plan ahead before specifying that value. If you want Access to always pull up a list of unique values, set the option value to be at least as large as the number of rows in any nonindexed field in the underlying table. If, however, Access manages to build the full list of unique values before reaching the maximum number of rows to be read, it always displays just unique values, regardless of whether the field was indexed.

Ordering Your Rows

Just as with the Filter property, you can specify an OrderBy property for a form, report, query, or table and then make that order active by setting the OrderByOn property to True. This functionality corresponds to the quick-sort toolbar buttons: if you open frmQBFExample, choose the City field, and then click the Sort Ascending or Sort Descending toolbar button, you're actually setting the form's OrderBy property. To see this, check it out in the Debug window.

```
? Forms!frmQBFExample.OrderBy
```

will show you the current OrderBy value.

Just as it does the Filter property, Access saves the OrderBy property of the form when you close the form. If you want to make the sort order active, set the OrderByOn property to True.

If you want to sort on multiple fields, set the property to be the names of the fields, separated with commas:

```
Forms!frmQBFExample.OrderBy = "Country,City"
```

To make one or more of the fields sort in descending order, append DESC to the field name (just as you would in a SQL string, which is, of course, where this all comes from—you're just building the SQL ORDER BY clause):

```
Forms!frmQBFExample.OrderBy = "Country,City DESC"
```

When you open a form, Access does apply the OrderBy setting automatically (as opposed to the Filter property, which you must apply manually). Regardless of whether the OrderBy setting is active, it's stored with the form, and you can activate and deactivate it with the form's OrderByOn property.

Creating Popup Forms

If you write many applications, you will begin to notice a class of tools that is needed over and over—for example, popup calendars to select dates or popup calculators to calculate values. Once you create these items, you'd like to be able to use them in multiple applications.

The technique for providing a popup tool that returns a value is really simple in Access:

- Open the form using OpenForm, using the acDialog flag for the Window-Mode parameter. This forces all VBA code that follows the OpenForm action to pause, waiting for the form to be either closed or hidden.

- Pass parameters, as necessary, to the form in the OpenArgs parameter. (See the sidebar "Sending Multiple Values in OpenArgs" for information on passing multiple items in the single OpenArgs string.)

- In the form's Open event procedure, retrieve items from the OpenArgs property, as necessary. Using the code in basParse, and specifically adhGetItem, your form can retrieve specific items from a delimited list. (Again, see the sidebar for more information on using adhGetItem.)

- On the form itself, provide OK and Cancel buttons (or their equivalents). The OK button should make the form invisible, and the Cancel button should actually close the form.

- Once back in your original procedure, you know that the form has been either closed or hidden. To check which, use a function such as IsLoaded, as in the section "Is a Specific Form Loaded?" earlier in this chapter, to check whether the form is still open. If it is, you know the user clicked OK and wants to use the data from the form. If the form is not loaded, you know the user clicked Cancel and you should disregard anything the user did with the form open.

- If the form is still loaded, retrieve the value(s) as necessary from the form (which is currently invisible), and then close the form.

Sending Multiple Values in OpenArgs

When working with popup forms, you'll often find it useful to be able to send multiple values to the newly opened form in the OpenForm OpenArgs parameter. You're allowed to pass only a single string value, however, so how are you going to send multiple values? You'll use the delimited text technique we discussed in Chapter 7, of course! The basParse module includes just the two functions you need: adhSetItem and adhGetItem. In Chapter 7 you used this technique to place multiple values into the Tag property. In this case you'll just want to build up a string containing multiple values, pass it to the popup form in the OpenArgs parameter, and have the popup form retrieve the various items from its OpenArgs property.

For example, imagine you need to pass two values to a form as it opens: the initial date to be displayed and the background color to use. You'll need to build up a string that looks something like this:

```
Date=5/16/56;Color=255;
```

You can either do that by hand or use adhPutItem to do it:

```
Dim varItems As Variant
varItems = adhPutItem(varItems, "Date", "5/16/56")
varItems = adhPutItem(varItems, "Color", 255)
```

Once you've done that, you can send varItems to your popup form in the OpenArgs parameter:

```
DoCmd.OpenForm "YourForm", WindowMode:=acDialog, _
 OpenArgs:=varItems
```

On the receiving end, from the popup form, you can have code in the Open event that retrieves items from the OpenArgs parameter:

```
Dim mvarDate As Variant
Dim mvarColor As Variant
Sub Form_Open()
    ' Get the date, or use today's date if it's Null.
    mvarDate = Nz(adhGetItem(Me.OpenArgs, "Date"), Date)
    ' Get the color, or use black (0) if it's Null.
    mvarColor = Nz(adhGetItem(Me.OpenArgs, "Color"), 0)
End Sub
```

TIP

You don't actually have to close the form once you're done with it: if you want to leave it open but hidden, then the next time you open the form, Access will just make it visible, and it will still show the state in which the user last left it. Unfortunately, Access will not send the OpenArgs property unless it actually opens the form, so this technique will work only if you are not sending any parameters to the form.

Using Popup Tools

We've provided two popup tools, a calendar and a calculator, that fit into your application in the manner described in the previous section. In both cases you make a single function call that returns to your application the value returned from the popup form. In the case of the calendar, the return value will be the chosen date (or Null, if none was chosen). For the calculator, the function will return the result of the user's calculations. The inner workings of these tools aren't the issue here, but rather their interface to your application. Once you've seen how these forms work, you should be able to use the techniques from the previous section to create your own popup tools.

> **NOTE**
>
> Using forms this way, as encapsulated tools, is really taking advantage of the fact that every form carries with it its own class module. You can accomplish these same sorts of tasks using class modules on their own, as long as you don't need any user interface. For more information on building objects using class modules, see Chapter 3.

How Do the Sample Forms Work?

Both the calendar and calculator popup forms use the same technique, Property Let/Get/Set procedures, to set and retrieve user-defined properties of forms. (See the section "Using Property Let/Set/Get Procedures" later in this chapter for more information. Chapter 3 also contains information on this technique.) In this simple case, adhDoCalc retrieves the Value property of the popup form to return the result of the calculation.

Here is the code for the adhDoCalc function:

```
Const adhcCalcForm = "frmCalc"
Function adhDoCalc()

    ' Load frmCalc in dialog mode, and return the
    ' calculated value at the end of the session.

    DoCmd.OpenForm FormName:=adhcCalcForm, _
     WindowMode:=acDialog
    If isOpen(adhcCalcForm) Then
```

```
            ' Retrieve the return value
            ' then close the form.
            adhDoCalc = Forms(adhcCalcForm).Value
            DoCmd.Close acForm, adhcCalcForm
        Else
            adhDoCalc = Null
        End If
End Function
```

The code used to pop up the calendar is very similar to that used for the calculator. Again, in this case you'll check the Value property of the Calendar form (supplied by a Property Get procedure in the Calendar form) to see what date the user chose:

```
Const adhcCalendarForm = "frmCalendar"
Function adhDoCalendar(Optional varPassedDate As Variant) _
 As Variant
    '
    ' If the passed-in date is missing (as it will
    ' be if someone just opens the Calendar form
    ' raw), start on the current day.
    ' Otherwise, start with the date that is passed in.
    '
    Dim varStartDate As Variant

    ' If the user passed a value at all, attempt to
    ' use it as the start date.
    varStartDate = IIf(IsMissing(varPassedDate), _
     Date, varPassedDate)
    ' OK, so the user passed a value that wasn't a date.
    ' Just use today's date in that case, too.
    If Not IsDate(varStartDate) Then varStartDate = Date
    ' Open the form, and stand back!
    DoCmd.OpenForm FormName:=adhcCalendarForm, _
     WindowMode:=acDialog, OpenArgs:=varStartDate

    ' You won't get here until the form is
    ' closed or hidden.
    '
    ' If the form is still loaded, then get the
    ' final chosen date from the form. If it isn't,
    ' return Null.
    If isOpen(adhcCalendarForm) Then
        adhDoCalendar = Forms(adhcCalendarForm).Value
```

```
        DoCmd.Close acForm, adhcCalendarForm
    Else
        adhDoCalendar = Null
    End If
End Function
```

> **NOTE**
>
> To choose a date from the calendar form, either double-click or press Enter on the selected date. You could modify the form to include an OK button that does the same thing as selecting a date, but we felt it looks better without the extra button.

In this case you can pass to the function the date you want to have displayed on the calendar when it first appears. You can also pass a null value to have it use the current date or just leave the parameter out. (It's optional, so you don't have to supply a value at all.)

> **TIP**
>
> If you include more than one module from this book in your own application, you may find duplicated private functions or subroutines. Because we can't guarantee which combinations of modules and forms you'll want to include in your own applications, we've placed these small helper functions in the particular modules where they're needed. You may want to remove the Private keyword from one such instance, move it to a global module, and delete the other local instances; there's no need to carry around multiple copies of the same function.

Using the Sample Forms

You can easily include the popup calendar, the calculator, or both in your own applications. Follow these steps to include one or both:

1. From CH08.MDB, import the module basCalc or basCalendar.

2. Include the form frmCalc or frmCalendar.

3. When you want to pop up the calendar, call it with code like this:

```
varDate = adhDoCalendar(varStartDate)
```

where varStartDate is either null or a specific date/time value. The function returns the date the user selected by either double-clicking or pressing ↵ (see Figure 8.15).

4. When you want to pop up the calculator, call it with code like this:

```
varValue = adhDoCalc()
```

The function returns the result of the user's calculations (see Figure 8.16).

FIGURE 8.15

Calendar (frmCalendar, called from frmTestPopup (also in CH08.MDB)

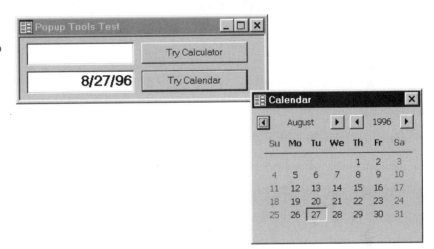

FIGURE 8.16

Popup calculator (frmCalc) in action

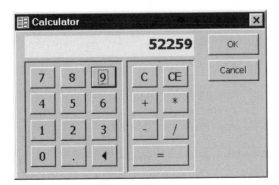

> **TIP**
>
> You might want to add the code discussed in the section "Saving and Restoring Form Locations" earlier in this chapter, which will preserve the location of the popup forms from one session to another. That way, once you place the Calendar form, for example, where you want it, that's where it will pop up the next time you invoke it. (See the earlier section for more information on adding that technique to your popup forms.)

Creating User-Defined Properties

In Access, you can create properties and methods of forms that "feel" just like built-in properties and methods from outside the form. These properties and methods correspond directly to the user-defined properties and methods of class modules, as described in Chapter 3. The next few sections explain how you can create your own form properties and methods. You'll use the Calendar form, presented earlier in this chapter, as an example.

Using a Public Form Variable

If the property you'd like to expose equates directly with a public module-level variable in the form's module, then there's no problem: just refer to the variable as though it were a property of the form. For example:

```
' In the module's declarations area
Public Value As Variant

' somewhere in your code
Forms!YourForm.Value = 5
```

will set the form's Value property to 5.

Using Property Let/Set/Get Procedures

If, on the other hand, you want to provide a property that requires some code to set or retrieve, you'll need to use VBA's Property Let/Set/Get procedures. Property Get procedures retrieve the value of a form property. Property Set procedures set the value of an object property of a form, and Property Let procedures allow you to set the value of a simple (nonobject) form property. These names, of course, correspond to the VBA Set and (seldom-used) Let keywords. (For example, for a form, you might want to create a ParentForm property that refers to the form that was active when you loaded the current form. That way you'd know which form to make current when you closed the current form again.) These procedures allow you to do any necessary work to set or retrieve information about the form. For example, in the calendar, this code allows you to set the FirstDay property:

```
Property Let FirstDay(intNewStartDay As Integer)
    ' Set the first day of the week.
    ' Fix up errant values.
    If intNewStartDay < 0 Or intNewStartDay > 7 Then
        intNewStartDay = 1
    End If
    mintFirstDay = intNewStartDay
    RedisplayCalendar
End Property
```

You don't actually call Property Let procedures. Instead, you set the value of the property as though it were a built-in property. Given the code in the previous example, setting the form's FirstDay property looks like this:

```
Forms!frmCalendar.FirstDay = 2
```

If you want to try this, load frmCalendar in Form view. In the Debug window, type the previous line (setting the FirstDay property to 2). The Calendar form will immediately redisplay itself with Monday as the first day of the week.

You can supply either the Property Let or Get procedure or both, but if you do supply both, the input datatype to the Let routine must match the output type for the Get routine. For example, the Calendar form supplies Let and Get procedures for the form's Value property:

```
Property Get Value() As Date
    ' Return the current value of this form,
    ' the selected date.
    Value = DateSerial(Me!Year, Me!Month, Me!Day)
End Property

Property Let Value(datNewDate As Date)
    ' Set the value of the form: the
    ' selected date.
    mdatStartDate = datNewDate
```

```
      RedisplayCalendar
End Property
```

To test this out, with frmCalendar open, enter the following statement in the Debug window:

```
Forms!frmCalendar.Value = #5/16/56#
```

This moves the calendar so that it has the specific date selected. To use the Property Get procedure, use standard property retrieval syntax:

```
Debug.Print Forms!frmCalendar.Value
```

The following table lists all the properties exposed by frmCalendar:

Property	Description
Value	Gets or sets the selected date
FirstDay	Gets or sets the first day of the week (1=Sunday, 2=Monday, and so on)

Using Form Procedures as Methods

VBA allows Access to expose any public function or subroutine as a method of that form. Using the Public keyword, you can create methods any other object can use to manipulate the form. The Calendar form does just this, making it a completely reusable, embeddable "object."

If you use form procedures as methods, no object outside the form needs to know anything about the form except its exposed methods and properties. For example, the Calendar form exposes the methods shown in Table 8.4. When your code calls these methods (for example):

```
Forms!frmCalendar.PreviousMonth
```

the Calendar form knows what to do and reacts by moving to the previous month.

If you create reusable objects so that they expose as many properties and methods as you need, you should be able to pick them up and move them from application to application, with no rewriting at all.

TABLE 8.4   Methods Exposed by frmCalendar

Method	Description
NextDay	Moves selection to the next day
NextWeek	Moves selection to the next week
NextMonth	Moves selection to the next month
NextYear	Moves selection to the next year
PreviousDay	Moves selection to the previous day
PreviousWeek	Moves selection to the previous week
PreviousMonth	Moves selection to the previous month
PreviousYear	Moves selection to the previous year
Today	Moves selection to the current date

To create a method for a form, all you need to do is add the Public keyword in front of the subroutine or function definition. Since the procedure is public, you can call it from anywhere else. For example, the code for the form's NextMonth method looks like this:

```
Public Sub NextMonth()
    ' The subroutine ChangeDate and the two
    ' constants tell the calendar what to do.
    ChangeDate adhcMonthStr, adhcMoveForward
End Sub
```

To test this from the Debug window, open frmCalendar in Form view, and type

```
Forms!frmCalendar.NextMonth
```

This moves the calendar to the next month after the one it's currently displaying.

To test this functionality, check out frmCalendarTest in CH08.MDB, shown in Figure 8.17. Clicking any of the buttons calls one of the exposed methods for the subform. For example, clicking the Next Month button calls this code:

```
Private Sub cmdNextMonth_Click()
    Me!Calendar.Form.NextMonth
    ' Make sure the screen repaints so
```

```
                    ' the user sees the cursor move.
                    Me.Repaint
                End Sub
```

FIGURE 8.17

Because frmCalendar exposes methods and properties, you can embed it and use it as a single entity.

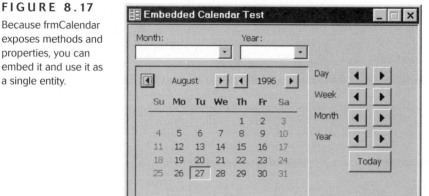

Form-Level Error Handling

Many errors can occur while your form is active. Some of these are standard run-time errors: perhaps a file is missing, a query your form expects to find isn't actually there, or the user does something you hadn't expected. Other errors are errors in the Access engine itself, and they can't be caught with normal error trapping. (For information on handling run-time errors, see Chapter 16.) You may find that you want to replace the standard Access behavior when these engine errors occur with behavior that is a little friendlier toward the user.

Access provides a form event to handle these errors. If you attach code to the Error event of a form, your procedure will be called whenever a trappable error occurs while the form is running. If you place your code in the form's class module (and you should, in this case), Access sends you two parameters. The syntax for the call is

Sub Form_Error (*DataErr* As Integer, *Response* As Integer)

The value *DataErr* will contain the error number for the error that just occurred, and *Response* allows you to specify how you want Access to handle the error. If your code handles the error to your satisfaction and you don't want Access to intervene or display its own message, place the value acDataErrContinue in *Response*. If you want Access to display its own error message, place acDataErrDisplay in *Response*.

The sample Form_Error subroutine shown in Listing 8.13 traps four errors that might pop up. In each case the procedure replaces the standard Access error message with its own. If an error occurs that it hadn't planned on, the subroutine just passes the responsibility back to Access. The form frmErrorSample in CH08.MDB includes this particular error handler. In this example, the following special conditions occur:

- The State field has a table-level validation rule. (Only "TX" will be allowed as the state.)

- The Age field is set up to accept numeric input only, between 0 and 255.

- The LastName field is set up as the key field.

The error-handling procedure reacts to any of the following events:

- The user enters a state other than "TX" in the State field.

- The user enters a non-numeric value in the Age field or a value out of range.

- The user creates or modifies a record such that the LastName field is empty.

- The user creates or modifies a record such that the LastName field (the primary key) is not unique.

In any of these cases the error-handling procedure takes over and displays the prepared message. If any other engine-level error occurs, Access' own error handling prevails.

TIP

Access behaves badly if your Form_Error event procedure contains a compile-time error. It won't compile this code for you when you run the form, only when it hits the error situation. At that time it complains of the compile error and then has Access handle the error. Make sure you compile your code before running your form.

Chances are you'll find a number of uses for form-level error handling. You could replace the error handling for these and other engine errors with your own, more personal, error handler. In Access 2, the Error event was not as powerful as it might have been in that it did not, in general, allow you to handle multiuser errors. Access now does handle these errors correctly. (For more information on trapping multiuser errors with the Form Error event, see Chapter 12.)

NOTE   The form error handler will not trap VBA run-time errors. If your code causes an error to occur or if the user is executing your code when an error occurs, your code should deal with those errors. The form-level error handler is meant to deal with errors that occur while the form has control and you're just waiting for the user to choose some action that will place your code into action again.

Listing 8.13

```
Private Sub Form_Error(DataErr As Integer, _
 Response As Integer)

    Const adhcErrDataValidation = 3317
    Const adhcErrDataType = 2113
    Const adhcErrDuplicateKey = 3022
    Const adhcErrNullKey = 3058

    Dim strMsg As String
    Select Case DataErr
    Case adhcErrDataValidation, adhcErrDataType
        strMsg = "The data you entered does not " & _
          "fit the requirements for this field."
        strMsg = strMsg & vbCrLf & "Please try again, " & _
          "or press Escape to undo your entry."
        MsgBox strMsg, vbExclamation
        Response = acDataErrContinue
    Case adhcErrDuplicateKey
        strMsg = "You've attempted to add a record " & _
          "that duplicates an existing key value."
        strMsg = strMsg & vbCrLf & "Please try again, " & _
          "or press Escape to undo your entry."
        MsgBox strMsg, vbExclamation
        Response = acDataErrContinue
    Case adhcErrNullKey
```

```
                strMsg = "You've attempted to add a new " & _
                  "record with an empty key value."
                strMsg = strMsg & vbCrLf & "Please supply " & _
                  "a key value, or press Escape to undo your entry."
                MsgBox strMsg, vbExclamation
                Response = acDataErrContinue
                ' You can even place them on the right field!
                Me!txtLastName.SetFocus
        Case Else
            ' It's an unexpected error. Let Access handle it.
            Response = acDataErrDisplay
    End Select
End Sub
```

Using Subforms in Your Applications

Subforms are most useful for displaying data from one-to-many relationships. In previous versions of Access they were often used as a means of grouping controls on forms. In Access 97, however, the tab control does a better job of grouping controls, for the most part. (See Chapter 7 for more information on using the tab control.) The next few sections deal with areas of subform use that may be giving you difficulty.

Nested Subforms versus Separate, Synchronized Subforms

As long as you're interested in displaying one-to-many relationships, you'll find it easy to drag-and-drop a form onto another form. If you've defined relationships for the tables involved, it becomes even easier, since Access fills in the LinkChild-Fields and LinkMasterFields properties for you.

This method has its good and bad sides. If you nest subforms, you're limited to having at most three levels of data: the main form plus two levels of nested sub-forms. On the other hand, forms involving nested subforms are simple to set up. Figure 8.18 shows an example from CH08.MDB, frmNestedMain, which draws on frmNestedOrders, which in turn includes frmNestedOrderDetail. The two inner forms are linked on OrderId, and the two outer forms are linked on CustomerID. This example requires absolutely no macros or VBA code.

FIGURE 8.18

Access makes it easy to create a form with two nested subforms, as long as you need only three levels and don't need to display any but the lowest-level forms in Form view.

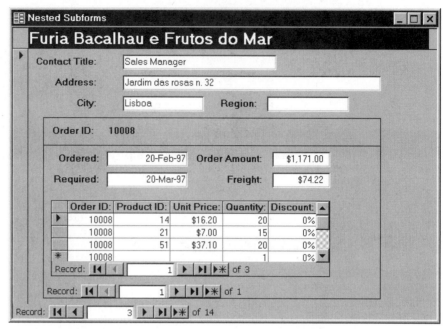

Although you'll find it easy to create examples like frmNested, you'll also run into some limitations if you want the form to look much different from the example. You can't, for example, make any form except the lowest-level form appear in Datasheet or Continuous Forms view, and you can't use more than two subforms. If you want any of the intermediate forms to appear in Datasheet or Continuous Forms view or if you need more than three levels of data displayed, you'll have to consider some other method.

The syntax for referring to objects on subforms, in its most complete form, used to be daunting. For example, to retrieve a value from txtName on the subform for which the ControlName property is frmSub1, which lives on frmMain, you could use the syntax

```
varName = Forms!frmMain!frmSub1.Form.Controls!txtName
```

The reference to frmSub1 takes you to the control that contains the subform. The ".Form" gets you to the actual form property of that control, from which you can access any control on the form through the Controls collection.

Referencing controls on nested subforms follows the same pattern. To reference a check box named chkAlive on frmSub2, which is a control on frmSub1, which is a control on frmMain, you'd use the syntax

```
fAlive = Forms!frmMain!frmSub1.Form.Controls!frmSub2. _
 Form.Controls!chkAlive
```

Fortunately, Access now makes this all a lot easier. The Controls collection is the default collection of a Form objects, so it is completely optional. In addition, in direct contrast to the syntax required by Access 2, the Form reference is no longer required. Finally, you can refer to objects on subforms with a simple syntax. For example, the previous reference to a control on a subsubform could be condensed to:

```
fAlive = Forms!frmMain!frmSub1!frmSub2!chkAlive
```

Yes, it's true: if you've struggled with subform references in Access 2, you can disregard all you've learned. The Form property is now the default property for the subform control, and the default collection for a form object is the Controls collection. Both references are therefore optional.

One more concern: the expression might be able to be abbreviated, depending on the current scope when you need to retrieve the value. For example, if you were trying to retrieve the value on frmSub2 as part of the ControlSource expression for a text box on frmSub1, you'd only need to refer to:

```
frmSub2!chkAlive
```

since you're already on the form contained in frmSub1.

TIP

The Access Expression Builder can help you create these complex references. Once in the Expression Builder, if you double-click the Forms item in the first list box, then double-click Loaded Forms, and then double-click the name of your main form, you should see the subform name. Double-click that subform name, and you see the name of the nested subform, if there is one. Once you've navigated to the form you want to reference, choose the appropriate control or property, and the Expression Builder builds up the necessary reference for you. The Expression Builder does include the Form property references, however, as though this were still Access 2.

Using Synchronized Subforms

Creating synchronized subforms in early versions of Access was a complicated process, due to some strange interactions between events on the different forms. In Access 2 the process became more straightforward, and it continues to work well. Figure 8.19 shows frmSyncMain with its included subforms, frmSyncOrders and frmNestedOrderDetail. Instead of nesting the two subforms, frmSynchMain synchronizes the two subforms. The mechanism is simple: in the "primary" subform's Current event, fill in a (normally) hidden text box. The code might look something like this:

```
Private Sub Form_Current()
    ' Disregard errors that would occur if you
    ' opened this subform as a normal form, without
    ' a parent property or without a text box
    ' named txtLink.
    On Error Resume Next

    ' Using the Parent property allows this form to
    ' be used as a subform on any form which happens
    ' to use a text box named txtLink to link it with
    ' other subforms.
    Me.Parent!txtLink = Me![Order ID]
End Sub
```

FIGURE 8.19

frmSyncMain with its included subforms

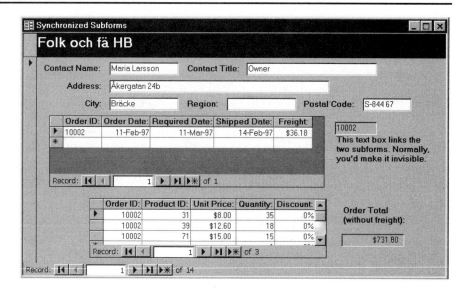

The error handler takes care of the case in which you might try to open the form on its own (without its being a subform of a form that contains a linking text box named txtLink).

The "secondary" subform's LinkMasterFields property is set to that same text box, with its LinkChildFields property set to the control name of the text box ([Order ID] in this example). Therefore, as the user moves from row to row in frm-SynchOrders, frmNestedOrderDetail will show only the orders with the same Order ID field as the chosen row in frmSynchOrders. This concept could be extended even further. If there were a one-to-many relationship starting from frm-NestedOrderDetail, its Current event could fill in a text box to which yet another form could be linked with its LinkMasterFields property.

Is It Loaded as a Subform?

You may have instances in which you'll want a form to work a certain way if loaded as a subform but a different way when loaded as a stand-alone form. For example, you may want to hide certain controls if the form is currently a subform.

There's no built-in function or property to get this information for you, but it's easy to write one yourself. The trick is that subforms always have a Parent property that refers to a real form, and stand-alone forms do not. Attempting to retrieve the Parent property of the form when it's not being used as a subform will always trigger a run-time error, and you can count on this error as you perform your test.

The following function, IsSubForm, from basFormGlobal, returns True if the form you inquire about is currently loaded as a subform and False if it's a stand-alone form. It does its work by attempting to retrieve the Name property of its parent. If that triggers a run-time error, you can be assured the form is not a subform.

```
Function IsSubForm(frm As Form) as Boolean
    ' Is the form referenced in the
    ' parameter currently loaded as a subform?
    ' Check its Parent property to find out.

    Dim strName As String
    On Error Resume Next
    strName = frm.Parent.Name
    IsSubForm = (Err = 0)
    On Error GoTo 0
End Function
```

To call the function, you could use code like this in your form's event procedures:

```
If IsSubform(Me) Then
    ' It's a subform.
Else
    ' You know it's not a subform.
End If
```

Controlling the Pesky Users

Much of your development time will be spent in limiting the actions users can take while your applications are running. That is, your application must be able to react to anything your users do, any key they press, any mouse button they click. The next few sections will discuss some ways you can take control over what actions the users can take while running your application.

Using the Cycle Property

In 16-bit versions of Access, as you moved past the last field on a bound form, Access automatically moved to the next row of data. Moving backward (Shift+Tab) past the first control moved you to the previous row. You could work around this through a bit of work, using hidden controls and a little bit of code, but it wasn't simple, and you had to do it on each and every form for which you wanted to restrict row movement.

You can now more easily restrict movement to the current row. The Cycle property of a form allows you to cause the cursor to wrap around the current form, or the current page of the form. The options for the Cycle property are listed in the following table:

Setting	Description	Value
All Records	Pressing Tab on the last control or Shift+Tab in the first control in the tab order moves to the next or previous row in the underlying data	0
Current Record	Wraps around to the first control on the form after pressing Tab on the last control, or to the last control after pressing Shift+Tab on the first control	1

Current Page	Wraps around to the first control on the page after pressing Tab on the last control, or to the last control after pressing Shift+Tab on the first control	2

Setting the Cycle property to 1 (Current Record) will handle the most common case: you'd like Access not to change the current row unless you tell it to. The sample form, frmCustomers in CH08.MDB, has its Cycle property set this way. Load it and give it a try. You'll see that you can't move to a new row using the Tab or Shift+Tab keys—you must use the navigation buttons or the PgUp or PgDn key. (If you wish to disable the PgUp and PgDn keys as well, see the next section, "Trapping Keys Globally: The KeyPreview Property.") (For multipage forms, you'll always want to set the Cycle property to 2 (Current Page). In this situation, having the user move from page to page inadvertently, using the Tab or Shift+Tab keys, can ruin the look of your form.)

Trapping Keys Globally: The KeyPreview Property

There are probably many situations in which you'd like to be able to trap keystrokes before Access sends them on to the controls on the form and perhaps react to them on a form-wide basis—for example, disabling the PgUp and PgDn keys. Without some global key-trapping mechanism, you'd have to attach code to the KeyDown event of each and every control on the form, watching for those particular keystrokes.

Access provides a mechanism to allow you to trap keystrokes before it sends them to controls on the form: the KeyPreview property of a form routes all keys you press while that form is active to the form's key-handling events before the active control's events get them. This way, you can react to, alter, or discard the keypresses at the form level.

Keep Users on a Single Row

For example, imagine you've set the form's Cycle property to 1 (Current Form) and you'd also like to make sure the user can't move from row to row by pressing the PgUp or PgDn key. In Access 2, this would have been inordinately difficult, requiring you to attach code to each control's KeyDown event. Now, you can set the form's KeyPreview property to Yes and attach code like this to the form's KeyDown event:

```
Private Sub Form_KeyDown(KeyCode As Integer, _
  Shift As Integer)
    If KeyCode = vbKeyPageDown Or KeyCode = vbKeyPageUp Then
```

```
            KeyCode = 0
        End If
End Sub
```

By setting the value of KeyCode to 0, you're telling Access to disregard the keystroke altogether. The sample form frmCustomers is set up this way. The only way to move from row to row on that form is to use the built-in navigation buttons.

Navigate Continuous Forms as Spreadsheets

Perhaps you'd like to make your continuous forms navigable as though they were spreadsheets. Out of the box, Access treats the → and ↓ keys the same way on a continuous form if an entire field is selected: it moves the highlight to the next field on the row, or to the first field on the next row if you're on the last field of the current row. However, you might want the ↓ key to move you to the current field in the next row, instead.

The KeyPreview property makes this possible. Once you've set the KeyPreview property to Yes, Access routes all keystrokes to the form's Key events first. Using a KeyDown event procedure such as the following causes Access to move to the previous row when you press the ↑ key or the next row if you press the ↓ key. In either case, the code sets the value of KeyCode to 0 once it's done so Access doesn't try to handle the keypress itself once this procedure has done its work.

```
Private Sub Form_KeyDown(KeyCode As Integer, Shift As Integer)
    ' Of course, pressing up or down could cause an
    ' error, when you get to the top or bottom of the
    ' set. Make sure to trap for errors, to avoid
    ' unsightly error alerts!
    On Error GoTo Form_KeyDown_Err
    Select Case KeyCode
        Case vbKeyDown
            DoCmd.GoToRecord Record:=acNext
            KeyCode = 0
        Case vbKeyUp
            DoCmd.GoToRecord Record:=acPrevious
            KeyCode = 0
        Case Else
            ' Do nothing at all!
    End Select

Form_KeyDown_Exit:
    Exit Sub

Form_KeyDown_Err:
```

```
Select Case Err.Number
    Case adhcErrInvalidRow
        KeyCode = 0
    Case Else
        MsgBox "Error: " & Err.Description & " (" & _
            Err.Number & ")"
End Select
Resume Form_KeyDown_Exit
End Sub
```

To see this procedure in action, take a look at frmCustomersTabular, shown in Figure 8.20. This form allows you to toggle the key handling on and off so you can see how it feels both ways.

TIP

Access includes intrinsic constants representing most of the keystrokes you'd ever want to use in your applications. (CH08.MDB uses these constants in several of its examples, including frmCustomersTabular, frmCalendar, and frmCalc.) To see the list yourself, open the Object Browser window (press F2 from the module editor), and then browse down the list of items until you find the objects starting with "ac". These objects are the enumerations for all the Access constants. The Object Browser will show, in its right-hand window (see Figure 8.21), a list of all the constants for each enumeration Access provides. You'll also find a list of all the constants provided by VBA, including the useful keycode names (under the KeyCodeConstants enumeration). Those are the key constants you'll use in your key-handling event procedures.

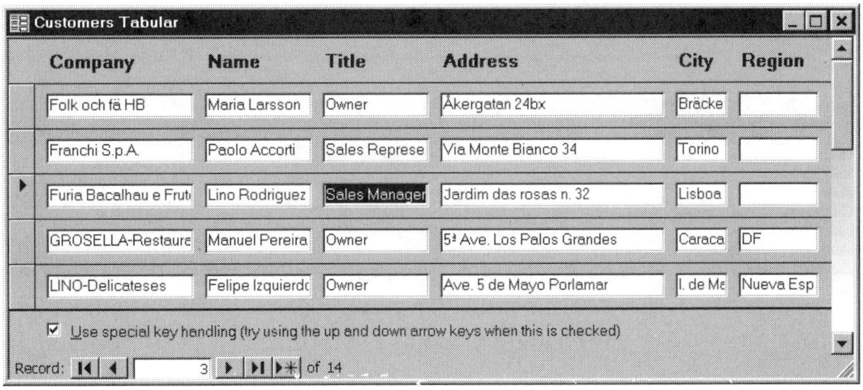

FIGURE 8.20

Use the form's Key-Preview property to handle keystrokes on a form-wide basis.

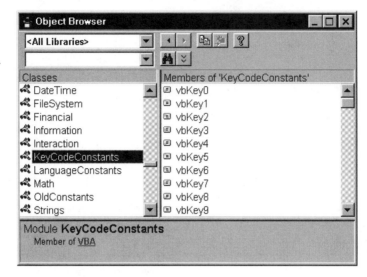

FIGURE 8.21

The Object Browser allows you to find a list of all the key constants.

Displaying Multiple Instances of Forms

In Access 2, if you wanted to display a form more than once in a given session, you needed to create as many physical copies of the actual form as you wanted to display. Now, you can open multiple instances of the same form (or report—the mechanism works the same for either) without making physical copies. There is no user interface for this functionality. If you want to display multiple instances, you'll need to write VBA code to make it happen.

NOTE   We could just as easily have placed this section of the chapter in Chapter 9, which discusses reports, but we feel you're more likely to need multiple instances of forms than reports, so we decided to place this material here.

Although you can create multiple instances of a master form, the original form is the only one for which you can permanently alter the properties. Access will not save any changes you make to the instances of the original form, although you are

•

allowed to make programmatic changes to the properties of any instance. You won't be able to switch the form instances into Design view, so any changes you wish to make to the instances will be through code, and they'll be temporary.

What Happens When You Create a New Instance?

When you create multiple instances of forms or reports, each new instance has its own set of properties, its own current row (if it's bound), and its own window. All instances of the same form or report share the same *name*, however, and this is a concept that takes some getting used to. Any place in VBA that requires you to supply a form or report name, therefore, will be generally useless when you are working with multiple instances. A side issue here is that because all the instances share the same name, you won't be able to use syntax like this:

```
Debug.Print Forms!frmCustomer.Caption
```

and expect to find any of the extra instances of frmCustomer. (On the other hand, Access does add an item to the Forms collection for each form instance you create, and you can always refer to these items by number. See Chapter 6 for information on the different ways you can refer to objects in collections.) Although Access does not create a named element of the Forms or Reports collection for each instance, it does add a reference in the collection, so this code will still work, even if several instances of forms are open:

```
For Each frm In Forms
    Debug.Print frm.Caption
Next frm
```

Because each form instance can (and should) have a unique caption, the previous example can actually be useful if you want a list of all the open forms, regardless of whether they're "real" forms or instances of real forms.

How Do You Create a New Instance?

Creating a new instance is simple: just declare a form variable and set it equal to a new form:

```
Dim frm As Form
Set frm = New Form_frmCustomers
```

The "Form_" syntax indicates to Access that you want a new member of the form class that's described by "Form_frmCustomers". The name of the form after the "Form_" must be a real, existing form, and by using the New keyword, you are asking Access to create a new instance for you. As soon as the variable referring to the new form goes out of scope, Access destroys the new form instance. What's more, you are asking Access to create the new form with its Visible property set to False; if you want to actually *see* the form, you'll need to set its Visible property to True.

It should be pretty clear, at this point, that if you write a procedure like this one:

```
Sub BadIdea()
    Dim frm As Form
    Set frm = New Form_frmCustomers
    frm.Visible = True
End Sub
```

you're never going to actually see that new form. Because Access will destroy the form when the reference to it goes out of scope, as soon as this procedure is complete, the form you created in it is history. What's the solution, then? You need to find some place to store that form reference until you're finished with it.

A simple solution is to make frm a static, or global, variable. That way it simply will never go out of scope. If you want to close it manually, you can always use code like this:

```
frm.SetFocus
DoCmd.Close
Set frm = Nothing
```

which sets focus to the form, closes it, and then releases the connection between the form variable and the object it was referring to. (Remember, you can't use the name of the object to close it, so you'll first have to make it the current form.)

A Better Solution

If you're going to be working with more than one extra instance of a form, you'll need a better way to manage the references to those new instances. One solution is to store the form references in a user-defined collection. (See Chapter 3 for more information on user-defined collections.)

For example, try out frmCustomers in CH08.MDB. Open the form itself, and then click the New Instance button a few times. Each time you click the button, you're running code that's creating a new form instance and placing a reference to it in a user-defined collection. If you want a list of all the extra instances, click the List Instances button on any of the forms, which will write a list of instance captions to the Debug window. Figure 8.22 shows what such a test might look like.

FIGURE 8.22

Use the New Instance button to create multiple instances of the main form.

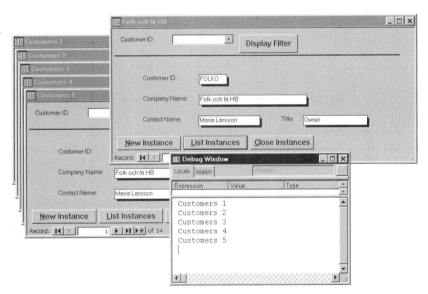

Every time you click the New Instance button, you're calling the NewCustomerForm procedure, which creates a new instance for frmCustomers and adds that new form reference to colForms, the collection of form instances:

```
Dim colForms As New Collection
```

```
Sub NewCustomerForm(frmOld As Form)
    Dim frm As Form

    Set frm = New Form_frmCustomers
    mintI = mintI + 1
    ' The Key value must be a string, so tack on an empty
    ' string to force the conversion. You'll
    ' use the hWnd later when you try to
    ' remove the window from the collection of windows.
    colForms.Add Item:=frm, Key:=frm.hwnd & ""
    frm.Caption = "Customers " & mintI
    ' These numbers are completely arbitrary.
    DoCmd.MoveSize (mintI + 1) * 80, (mintI + 1) * 350
    ' Preserve the original form's filter and whether or not
    ' that filter's active.
    frm.Filter = frmOld.Filter
    frm.FilterOn = frmOld.FilterOn
    frm.Visible = True
End Sub
```

NewCustomerForm increments a global variable, mintI, to keep track of which instance is the newest. That integer becomes part of the new instance's caption. When NewCustomerForm adds the new form reference to colForms, it stores the form reference itself, along with the hWnd (the window handle, guaranteed to be unique) as the key for the item. That way, later code can retrieve an item from the collection, given its window handle. (Remember, each form instance you create has the same name, so you can't refer to any instance individually by name.) The procedure also places the new form at a convenient location, sets its Filter and FilterOn properties to match the original form's, and then makes the new form visible.

Now that you've created these new form instances, you have a collection (colForms) that contains a reference to each of the forms. You can iterate through that collection (as you'll do when you attempt to close them all) or refer to a single form, given its hWnd.

Closing a Form Instance

If you close one of the form instances, you'll want to make sure the collection of form references is up to date. To make that happen, we've attached code to the form's Close event that removes the particular form from the collection:

```
Sub RemoveInstance(frm As Form)
    ' Each form calls this code when it closes itself.
    ' This is also hooked to the main
    ' form's Close event, so skip over the
    ' error that occurs when you try to close the
    ' main form (which doesn't have an entry in the
    ' collection!)
    On Error Resume Next
    colForms.Remove frm.hwnd & ""
End Sub
```

Each form calls

```
Call RemoveInstance(Me)
```

in its Close event. That way, the collection of instances always accurately reflects the current group of form instances.

NOTE The original form isn't in the collection of form instances—it never added itself, only the new instances. On the other hand, it has the call to RemoveInstance in its Close event, and its form reference is not in the collection. To avoid the error that would occur when trying to remove the form itself from the collection of instances, we just set up RemoveInstance so it doesn't complain about errors.

Closing All the Instances

If you want to close all the instances of the main form, you have a few choices. Here are two options:

- Remove each form reference from the collection. This forces each one to go out of scope and thus will close the instances.

- Set the focus to each instance in turn and then explicitly close each form.

We chose the second method, for a very specific reason. (The first method works fine in this simple example, and the code to do it appears in the CloseInstances procedure, although it's commented out.) If your forms were complex and perhaps had validation rules that had to be met, it's possible that the form wouldn't be allowed to close; imagine, for example, that you'd not fulfilled a validation rule. The second method, closing each form explicitly, guarantees that Access doesn't close the form before removing its form reference from the user-defined collection. It's just a cleaner way to close the forms, even though it does require physically setting the focus to each form in turn.

The code that's called from the Close Instances button, therefore, is quite simple (it's mostly comments):

```
Sub CloseInstances()
    Dim varItem As Variant
    ' The user may have closed some or all of the
    ' forms by hand. Skip any errors that
    ' occur because the collection count
    ' doesn't match reality.
    On Error GoTo CloseInstancesErr
    Application.Echo False
    For Each varItem In colForms
        ' Go to the form, and then close it.
        ' You can't close it given the name, because
        ' all the form instances have the same name.
        varItem.SetFocus
        DoCmd.Close
        ' You could also use
        '    colForms.Remove 1
        ' to remove the first element
        ' of the collection, over and over,
        ' but what happens if you can't close
        ' the form for some reason (Key violation,
        ' for example)? Explicitly closing
        ' the form is safer.

    Next varItem
    mintI = 0

CloseInstancesExit:
```

```
        Application.Echo True
        Exit Sub

CloseInstancesErr:
        Resume CloseInstancesExit
End Sub
```

All the example code for this simple test case is in basFormInstance. You'll need to modify it for any example in which you use it (because it requires the actual name of the form you're working with as part of its code), but the example ought to at least get you started.

> **NOTE**
>
> In this example, one form was different from all the rest: the original form. This needn't be the case. That is, you don't have to actually open the "seed" form in order to make instances of it. The form you refer to when you create the new instance can be closed, and as long as it's in the current database, Access can find it and create a new instance of it. If you follow this technique, then all open forms with the same name are equivalent—they're "clones" of the master.

Summary

Through the use of Windows API calls and VBA code, you can exact a great deal of control over the appearance and actions of your forms. In particular, you can control

- The border controls, individually or collectively

- The modality of the form

- When or whether your form gets closed

- The size and position of forms from one Access session to the next

- Form-level error handling

You've learned to create various Access tools, including

- Toolboxes

- Popup utilities
- Auto-sizing forms
- Self-disabling navigation buttons

You've seen some useful techniques, including

- Working with multiple instances of forms
- Controlling form filtering

And finally, along the way, you've encountered some useful tidbits, such as

- Reading and writing items in the System Registry
- Using the RecordsetClone property of bookmarks and forms
- Determining whether a specific form is loaded
- Detecting record position states
- Moving and sizing windows
- Enabling/disabling control menu items
- Resizing forms for various screen resolutions
- Using the Cycle and KeyPreview properties to control form behavior

Topics in Report Design

■ Using report and section events and properties

■ Controlling sorting and grouping programmatically

■ Altering the report layout programmatically

Designing reports ought to be a simple task. In theory, you never have to worry about data input, validation, movement from field to field, or capturing an endless number of different fields on the same form. On the other hand, designing a report that is both functional and aesthetically pleasing can be difficult. You may be attempting to simulate an existing report that exists on paper or in some other database system, or you may be designing your own reports. In this chapter we cover some of the basics involved in designing creative reports, focusing on the issues that elude or confuse many developers: report and section events and sorting and grouping. You won't find many Windows API calls in this chapter, since they won't normally help much when you're creating reports. Access gives you all the flexibility you need.

Learning to harness that flexibility is the challenge you face when you create reports. This chapter assumes you've already managed to create simple reports and now need to work with the various events and properties to add functionality. In addition, the chapter covers some common problem areas and suggests interesting solutions to those problems.

Report Properties New Since Access 2

Reports expose a number of properties you can manipulate at design time to get just the output you want. Access 95 added a few new properties, and this section focuses on those properties.

> **NOTE**   Access 97 added almost no functionality for reports. Perhaps the next version of Access will revamp the report writer, which hasn't changed much since Access 2.0.

Filtering and Sorting

The Filter, FilterOn, OrderBy, and OrderByOn properties for reports work very much the same way they work for forms. To see these properties in action, take a look at frmCustomers in CH09.MDB. This form allows you to filter your data any way you wish (using Filter by Selection, Filter by Form, or Advanced Filter/Sort) and, once you're ready, click the Preview Report button. That button's Click event executes this code:

```
Sub cmdPreview_Click()
    On Error GoTo HandleErr

    Dim strDocName As String

    strDocName = "rptPhoneBook"
    ' There are three possible scenarios:
    ' 1. No filter
    ' 2. Filter, but not applied
    ' 3. Filter, applied
    If Me.FilterOn And Len(Me.Filter & "") > 0 Then
        DoCmd.OpenReport ReportName:=strDocName, _
          View:=acPreview, WhereCondition:=Me.Filter
    Else
        DoCmd.OpenReport ReportName:=strDocName, View:=acPreview
    End If

ExitHere:
    Exit Sub

HandleErr:
    MsgBox Err.Description
    Resume ExitHere
End Sub
```

This code checks the form's Filter and FilterOn properties and, assuming all is correct, opens the report with either the form's current filter or no filter at all.

To see the OrderBy property at work, open rptOrderByProperty and frmOrderByProperty in CH09.MDB. When you make a choice on the sample form, code attached to the AfterUpdate event of the option group on the form sets the OrderBy property of the report:

```
Private Sub SortReport()
    On Error Resume Next
    Dim strOrderBy As String
    With Reports(adhcReportName)
        strOrderBy = Choose(Me!grpSort, _
          "[Company Name]", "Sales")
        If Me!chkDescending Then
            strOrderBy = strOrderBy & " DESC"
```

```
        End If
        .OrderBy = strOrderBy
        .OrderOn = True
    End With
End Sub
```

The OrderBy property becomes the highest-level sort, added on to the normal sorting applied in the Grouping/Sorting dialog box. You'll find you cannot override the sorting that's been done at design time, so you'll have the best luck using this property with reports that aren't currently sorted.

> **WARNING**
>
> Setting the OrderBy property for a report triggers that report's Close and Open events. If you have code attached to either of those events, be aware that changing the sort order for the report will run those event procedures as though you'd closed and then reopened the report.

To set the ordering based on multiple fields, separate their names with commas. To force one or more of the fields to sort descending, append DESC to the field name. The OrderBy expression works in addition to (that is, *after*) any sorting applied by the report's internal sorting. (See the section "Controlling Sorting and Grouping" later in this chapter for detailed information on controlling the report's internal sorting and grouping from your applications.)

Keeping Groups Together across Columns— the GrpKeepTogether Property

In the 16-bit versions of Access there really was no reasonable way to ensure that your sections didn't break across columns if you created a multicolumn report. Access 95 added the GrpKeepTogether property for reports, which allows you to specify that you want to group data for which you've specified either Whole Group or With First Detail kept together in a single column (Per Column) or on the whole page (Per Page).

To see this property in action, take a look at rptPhoneBook in CH09.MDB. This report prints in a phone book–type layout and is the subject of several examples in this chapter. The report's GrpKeepTogether property is set to Per Column so that groups aren't broken across columns. Try it out this way, and then change the setting to Per Page to see the difference it makes in the printout.

Is Anyone Home? Using the HasData Property

At times you need to know, after the report has opened, whether the report is showing any rows. Knowing this can be useful in places where you still want to view the report (or subreport) even if there are no rows, but you want to keep "#Error?" from displaying on your reports in places where you were performing calculations based on rows in the report.

The HasData property of a report, available only at run time, returns one of three possible values:

Value	Description
−1	Bound report with records
0	Bound report with no records
1	Unbound report

The sample report, rptBankInfo, uses this property to avoid showing incorrect summary data if rptBankInfoSub2 doesn't contain any rows. The subreport contains a list of all the computers in use at the company, and it includes a total value in its footer. The main report extracts that value and displays it in the text box, txtSummary. If there are no rows in rptBankInfoSub2, however, you don't want an error message in txtSummary. To avoid this problem, txtSummary's ControlSource is

```
=[Company] & " uses " & _
 IIf([rptBankInfoSub2].[Report].[HasData]=-1, _
 [rptBankInfoSub2].[Report]![txtSum], 0) & " computers."
```

In other words, if the company's list of computers includes some items, the control will indicate that. If not, it just indicates that the company uses 0 computers. Figure 9.4, shown later in this chapter, shows this report in use.

Controlling Sorting and Grouping

After layout of the controls on the report, the highest-level control you have over the results from a report is the sorting/groupings. It's impossible to completely separate these two issues, because grouping is so dependent on the sort order. Figure 9.1 shows a typical report layout, with groups set up based on the [Company Name] and [Contact Name] fields. If you've created any reports up to this point, you're probably well aware of the possibilities involved with using group headers and footers. What you might not have noticed is that group headers and footers, as well as every other section on the report, supply event hooks; you can use the "break" in the processing as a signal to your program code, which might need to react to the new group that is about to be printed or has just been printed. (We discuss report and section events throughout this chapter.)

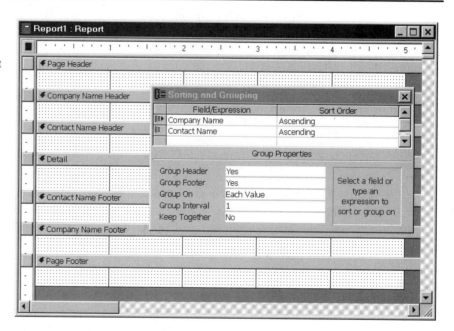

FIGURE 9.1

The sample report is grouped on the [Company Name] and [Contact Name] fields.

You also may be unaware that you can control the sorting and grouping properties of reports programmatically. You can create new reports or modify existing ones, creating new sections as necessary, and you can modify the sort information as well. The next few sections suggest methods for controlling the sorting and grouping characteristics of your reports from your VBA code.

The Section Property

Forms, reports, and all controls expose the Section property. For controls, the Section property is an indication of which section of the parent form or report it appears on, and this isn't the issue here (although the value returned from a control's Section property corresponds with the numbers used in specifying a form or report's section). For forms and reports, the Section property provides an array of all the sections contained in the given object, referred to by number, as shown in Table 9.1. To refer to any specific section, you treat it as an element from an array of sections, as in the following:

```
Reports!rptExample.Section(1).Visible = False
' or, because Access defines the constant acHeader to be 1:
Reports!rptExample.Section(acHeader).Visible = False
```

which makes the Report Header section invisible for rptExample.

TABLE 9.1   Section Numbers and Their Descriptions

Setting	Description	VBA Constant
0	Detail section	acDetail
1	Form or Report Header section	acHeader
2	Form or Report Footer section	acFooter
3	Form or Report Page Header section	acPageHeader
4	Form or Report Page Footer section	acPageFooter
5	Group-level 1 Header section (reports only)	
6	Group-level 1 Footer section (reports only)	
7	Group-level 2 Header section (reports only)	
8	Group-level 2 Footer section (reports only)	

Here are two more items to remember about sections:

- Aside from the sections listed in Table 9.1, group-level section headers and footers are numbered consecutively, starting with 9.

- Forms never contain more than five sections (numbered 0 through 4).

There's not much you can do with the Section property on its own; anytime you deal with the Section property, you'll be interested in the properties of that particular section. Unlike other property arrays in Access (the Column property, for example), the Section property does not ever return a value on its own—it just returns a reference to the section in question.

Referring to Sections by Name

Access allows you to refer to form and report sections by name, as well as by number. For example, if you create a new report, the Name property of its Detail section will be "Detail", and you can use that name in expressions:

```
Debug.Print Reports!rptSample.Detail.Height
```

That is, Access exposes a property of the report that matches the name of the section, through which you can access any property of that section. The name you type in your expression must match the name of the section, exactly as Access sees it in the property sheet for that section. Names of sections depend on the order in which they were created and are unique. To use the name in this context, you'll need to look in the property sheet to find the name of the section and then use that name (or change the name to one of your choosing) to refer to the section.

At the time of this writing the default names for the Page Header and Page Footer sections were PageHeader and PageFooter, respectively. Reports already expose PageHeader and PageFooter properties, so these names will conflict with the built-in property names. You won't be able to check the Page Header section's height using an expression like this:

```
Debug.Print rpt.PageHeader.Height
```

You'll need to either rename the section (change its Name property in the property sheet) or use the standard syntax:

```
Debug.Print rpt.Section (acPageHeader).Height
```

Setting Physical Characteristics Using the Section Property

In addition to setting the visibility of a specific section, you often need to set the height of a section. For example, perhaps you need to create a Footer section on a form, if one doesn't already exist, and then set its height. The code fragment in Listing 9.1 (which doesn't appear in the sample database) makes sure the Report Footer section is visible. To do this, it checks to see whether the report is already showing a footer section and, if not, creates one, setting the height of both the header and footer to 0. (Setting the height to 0 makes the section as small as possible, given the existing controls on the section. If there are no controls, the section shrinks to nothing.) Code later in the function might set the particular height for the footer. Note that if you create a report or page footer, you also create a header. This code sets the height of the header to 0 and sets its Visible property to False, ensuring that it won't be visible in the running report. This code fragment calls the IsSection function, which is discussed in the following section.

Listing 9.1

```
' If there isn't already a report footer,
' turn on headers and footers, and then
' hide the header.
If Not IsSection(Me, acFooter) Then
    ' Report Design/View/Report Header/Footer
    DoCmd.RunCommand acCmdReportHdrFtr
    Me.Section(acHeader).Height = 0
    Me.Section(acFooter).Height = 0
End If

' Make SURE the footer is visible and the
' header's invisible.
Me.Section(acHeader).Visible = False
Me.Section(acFooter).Visible = True
```

TIP

If you want a section to be as short as possible (just tall enough to include the controls inside it, with no extra vertical space), set the height to 0. A section can never obscure controls it contains, and setting its height to 0 is the quick and easy way to make the section just big enough. Of course, you may want to set it to 0, then retrieve its height (which will be just tall enough for the controls in the section), and then set it a bit taller, so there's some extra "breathing space" around your controls.

Determining Whether a Particular Section Exists

Access provides no simple way of determining whether a given section has been created on a form or report. The following function (from basSections in CH09.MDB) demonstrates one method: it attempts to retrieve the height of the section in question. If this attempt doesn't trigger a run-time error, the section must have existed. Just pass to it a reference to the form or report you're interested in, along with a number or constant representing the section on which you need to check.

```
Function IsSection(obj As Object, intSection As Integer) _
  As Boolean
     ' Returns TRUE if there currently is a form/report
     ' footer section, FALSE otherwise.
     ' Call as:
     '     If IsSection(Reports!Report1, acFooter) Then...
     ' to see if Report1 includes a footer section.
     Dim varTemp as Variant

     On Error Resume Next
     varTemp = obj.Section(intSection).Height
     IsSection = (Err.Number = 0)
End Function
```

Determining How Many Sections Exist

Forms are guaranteed to have no more than 5 sections but may have fewer. Reports may have up to 25 sections (5 standard, plus up to 10 groups, each with both a header and a footer). Access provides no built-in way to determine how many sections an object contains, and you may need to know this information. The function in Listing 9.2 demonstrates one solution to this problem: loop through the report, retrieving section heights and counting all the sections for which you don't trigger a run-time error. Because no report can contain more than 25 sections, that's as far as you need to look. You're also guaranteed that every form or report contains at least one section, Section(0) (the Detail section). You use that fact, in the function shown in Listing 9.2, to verify that the requested form is, in fact, loaded at the time you call the function.

NOTE　It was tempting, when trying to optimize this function, to make assumptions about the existence of sections. Unfortunately, all the sections aside from the paired page header/footer and report header/footer are individually selectable. This means you really do need to check out every section from 0 through 24.

Listing 9.2

```
Function adhCountSections(rpt As Report) As Integer
    ' Count the number of sections in a report.

    Dim intCount As Integer
    Dim intI As Integer

    On Error Resume Next
    intCount = 0

    ' Loop through all the sections,
    ' counting up the ones that exist.
    For intI = 0 To adhcMaxSections - 1
        If isSection(rpt, intI) Then
            intCount = intCount + 1
        End If
    Next intI
    adhCountSections = intCount
End Function
```

Creating New Report Sections

Aside from the method included in Listing 9.1 (using RunCommand), Access doesn't provide a method for creating Page or Report Header or Footer sections. For creating group headers and footers, though, Access provides the CreateGroupLevel function. Because sections beyond the Detail section and the page and report headers and footers are all manifestations of groupings, this function allows you to create all sections except the standard five (Detail, Report Header, Report Footer, Page Header, and Page Footer). This function takes four parameters:

intLevel = CreateGroupLevel(*strReport*, *strExpr*, *fHeader*, *fFooter*)

The following list describes the parameters:

- *strReport* is a string expression containing the name of the report on which to create the group.

- *strExpr* is the expression to use as the group-level expression.

- *fHeader* and *fFooter* are Boolean values that indicate whether to create sections for the header and/or footer. Use True to create the section, False otherwise.

The function returns an index into the array of group levels on your report. (See the next section for more information.) Access supports no more than ten group levels: Access returns run-time error 2153, "You can't specify more than 10 group levels," if you attempt to create more groups than that.

Accessing Group Levels

Access treats group levels in the same manner as sections. It maintains an array of group levels, which you access like this:

```
intOrder = Reports!Report1.GroupLevel(0).SortOrder
```

Just as with the array of sections, you cannot access the GroupLevel array directly; rather, you must access one of its properties. The expression

```
varTemp = Reports!Report1.GroupLevel(0)
```

generates run-time error 438, "Object doesn't support this method or property," because you've attempted to retrieve information about the group level itself rather than one of its properties. Just as with sections, Access externalizes no information about the number of group levels.

Although you can't access any properties of GroupLevel or Section objects, you can declare an object variable to refer to one and use that object variable in further references (just as you can with any other object type). For example, you can use code like this:

```
Dim glv As GroupLevel
Set glv = Reports!Report1.GroupLevel(0)
Debug.Print "Sort Order: "; glv.SortOrder
Debug.Print "Group Header: "; glv.GroupHeader
Debug.Print "Group Footer: "; glv.GroupFooter
```

to list information about a specific group level. (The next few sections provide details about various GroupLevel properties.)

To enumerate the group levels in a report, you need a function similar to that found in Listing 9.2 that will count or traverse the array of GroupLevels. See Listing 9.3 for such a function. Note that this function is much simpler than the similar one in Listing 9.2, because groups must be consecutively numbered. Removing a section bumps all the sections that follow it up the list. The adhCountGroups function does its work by attempting to retrieve the SortOrder property for every group. As long as it can continue without generating a run-time error, it keeps looping through groups. As soon as it can no longer retrieve the property, the code halts and returns the number of groups it worked through. You can find the functions presented in both Listing 9.2 and Listing 9.3 in basSections in CH09.MDB.

Listing 9.3

```
Function adhCountGroups(rpt As Report) As Integer
    ' Count the number of groups in a report.

    Dim intI As Integer
    Dim intOrder As Integer

    On Error Resume Next
    For intI = 0 To adhcMaxGroups - 1
        intOrder = rpt.GroupLevel(intI).SortOrder
        If Err.Number <> 0 Then
            Exit For
        End If
    Next intI
    adhCountGroups = intI
End Function
```

GroupLevel Properties

Just as with sections, you can access only properties of group levels, not the group levels themselves. To that end, the GroupLevel array exposes these properties: GroupFooter, GroupHeader, GroupInterval, GroupOn, KeepTogether, SortOrder, and ControlSource. The following sections describe each of these properties and its use.

GroupHeader and GroupFooter Properties

The GroupHeader and GroupFooter properties tell you whether a specific group level shows a Header and/or Footer section. In either case the property returns True (–1) so you can't use it to create new Header/Footer sections. You must use the CreateGroup-Level function mentioned earlier in this chapter to create new sections.

This code fragment determines whether there is a group header for group 0:

```
If Reports!rptTest1.GroupLevel(0).GroupHeader Then
    ' Do something
End If
```

The GroupOn Property

The GroupOn property specifies how data is to be grouped in a report. The values for the property depend on the datatype of the field or expression on which the GroupLevel is grouped. None of the settings except 0 (Each Value) is meaningful unless you have a group header or group footer selected for the group.

Table 9.2 displays all the possible values for the GroupOn property.

TABLE 9.2   Possible Values for the GroupLevel's GroupOn Property

Setting	Value
Each Value	0
Prefix Characters	1
Year	2
Qtr	3
Month	4
Week	5
Day	6
Hour	7
Minute	8
Interval	9 (see the GroupInterval property)

The GroupInterval Property

The GroupInterval property defines an interval that is valid for the field or expression on which you're grouping. You can set the property only when the report is in Design view, and Access' interpretation of its value is dependent on the value of the GroupOn property. As with the GroupOn property, the Access documentation states that you must have created a group header or footer before setting the value of this property to anything other than its default value (1). Actually, you can change it if you wish, but unless you have a group header or footer created, it won't have any effect. If the GroupOn value is 0 (Each Value), the GroupInterval property is treated as though it were 1, no matter what its value.

Set the GroupInterval property to a value that makes sense for the field or expression on which you're grouping. If you're grouping on text, the GroupInterval property defines the number of characters on which to group. If you're grouping on dates and you set the GroupOn property to 5 (Grouping on Weeks), setting the GroupInterval property specifies how many weeks to group together.

The following example (not in the sample database) creates a group, grouping on the time stored in a date/time field and breaking into groups of five minutes:

```
Dim intLevel As Integer

intLevel = CreateGroupLevel("rptTest", "DateField", _
 Header:=True, Footer:=False)
With Reports!rptTest.GroupLevel(intLevel)
    .GroupOn = 8
    .GroupInterval = 5
End With
```

TIP Although you'll almost always set the GroupOn and GroupInterval properties when you're creating a report programmatically, you can also set these properties from the report's Open event. You cannot create a group level except in Design view, but you can set properties for existing group levels from the report's Open event (and no other event).

The KeepTogether Property

The KeepTogether property specifies whether the data in the group level is to be kept together when printed. You can set the property only when the report is in Design view or, as with the GroupOn/GroupInterval properties, from the report's Open event. As with the other properties mentioned above, the Access documentation states that you must have created a group header or footer before setting the value of this property to anything other than its default value (0). Actually, you can change it if you wish, but unless you have a group header or footer created, it won't have any effect. The possible values for the KeepTogether property are shown in Table 9.3.

Under some circumstances Access is forced to ignore this setting. For example, if you've specified Whole Group (1), Access attempts to print the Group Header, Detail, and Footer sections on the same page. If that combination will not fit on a

TABLE 9.3   Possible Values for the GroupLevel's KeepTogether Property

Setting	Value	Description
No	0	Makes no attempt to keep the header, detail, and footer on the same page
Whole Group	1	Attempts to print the header, detail, and footer all on same page
With First Detail	2	Attempts to print the header and the first detail row on the same page

single page, Access is forced to ignore the setting and print it as best it can. The same concept can hold true if you've chosen With First Detail (2). In that case Access attempts to place the group header and the first detail row on the same page. If the combination of the two is larger than a single page, all bets are off and Access prints as best it can.

As with all the rest of the GroupLevel properties, you set the KeepTogether property through the GroupLevel array. For example, the following code fragment asks Access to attempt to print all of GroupLevel 0 on the same page:

```
Reports!rptTest.GroupLevel(0).KeepTogether = 2
```

The ControlSource and SortOrder Properties

The ControlSource property specifies the field or expression on which the group is to be grouped and/or sorted. By default, the ControlSource property matches the value you used to create the group level and should be identical to the second parameter you passed to the CreateGroupLevel function. Although you cannot use CreateGroupLevel to alter the field on which a group is based, you can change the group's ControlSource property. Like all the rest of the group-level properties, you change the ControlSource and SortOrder properties only when the report is in Design view or in the report's Open event.

Use the SortOrder property to set the sorting order of rows in the Detail section of a group level. Table 9.4 shows the possible values for the SortOrder property. You use this property in combination with the ControlSource property to define the sorting characteristics of the group.

TABLE 9.4   Possible Values for the GroupLevel's SortOrder Property

Setting	Value	Description
Ascending	0	Sorts values in ascending order (0–9, A–Z) (default)
Descending	−1	Sorts values in descending order (9–0, Z–A)

Using the GroupLevel Properties

In your application you may need to change the GroupLevel properties of an existing report. For example, you might want to allow the user to choose, from two or more fields, the field that's displayed on your report and still group rows correctly on the chosen field. CH09.MDB contains such an example; to try it out, load frmSortOrder (which will automatically load) and rptPhoneBook. Figure 9.2 shows the form and report in action.

FIGURE 9.2

Changing the sort order requires changing the GroupLevel's Control-Source property.

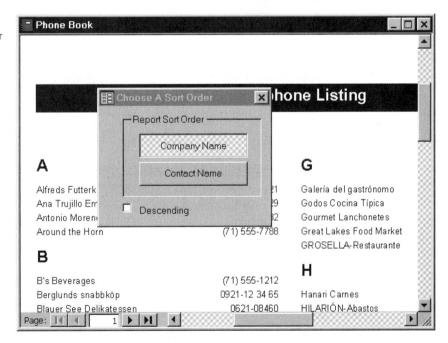

Depending on which of the option buttons you've selected, frmSortOrder sets up the report to group on either [Company Name] or [Contact Name], setting the header information appropriately. The code in Listing 9.4 does the work.

Listing 9.4

```
Const adhcDocName = "rptPhoneBook"

Private Sub chkDescending_AfterUpdate()
    Call ResetGroup
End Sub

Private Sub Form_Close()
    On Error Resume Next

    DoCmd.Close acReport, "rptPhoneBook", acSaveNo
End Sub

Private Sub Form_Open(Cancel As Integer)
    Dim intSortOrder As Integer
    Dim strControlSource As String

    On Error Resume Next
    DoCmd.OpenReport "rptPhoneBook", acPreview
    If Err <> 0 Then
        MsgBox "Unable to open 'rptPhoneBook'"
        Exit Sub
    End If

    ' Set the controls on the form to match the report
    ' itself, as it was last saved.
    With Reports!rptPhoneBook
        intSortOrder = .GroupLevel(0).SortOrder
        strControlSource = .GroupLevel(0).ControlSource
    End With
    Me!grpSort = IIf(strControlSource = "Company Name", 1, 2)
    Me!chkDescending = intSortOrder
End Sub

Private Sub ResetSort(adhcDocName As String, strField As String)
    With Reports(adhcDocName)
        !txtName.ControlSource = strField
```

```
        !txtLetter.ControlSource = _
         "=Left$([" & strField & "], 1)"
        .GroupLevel(0).ControlSource = strField
        .GroupLevel(1).ControlSource = strField
        .GroupLevel(0).SortOrder = Me!chkDescending
        .GroupLevel(1).SortOrder = Me!chkDescending
    End With
End Sub

Private Sub grpSort_AfterUpdate()
    Call ResetGroup
End Sub

Private Sub ResetGroup()
    On Error GoTo HandleErr

    Reports(adhcDocName).Painting = False

    DoCmd.OpenReport adhcDocName, acDesign
    Call ResetSort(adhcDocName, _
      IIf(Me!grpSort = 1, "Company Name", "Contact Name"))
    DoCmd.OpenReport adhcDocName, acPreview

    Reports(adhcDocName).Painting = True

ExitHere:
    Exit Sub

HandleErr:
    MsgBox Err.Description, vbExclamation, "ResetGroup"
    Resume ExitHere
End Sub
```

NOTE Because the example changes properties of the report in Design view, Access prompts you to save changes when you close the report unless you take steps to avoid this. Starting in Access 95, you can add the acSaveNo constant as the third parameter to the Close action. This causes Access to close the object and save no changes, without asking your permission. The example demonstrates this technique.

Events of Reports and Their Sections

As in all the other areas of Access, it's the events that drive the application when you're working with reports. As users interact with Access' user interface, it's up to your application to react to the events Access fires off. Reports themselves support only a few events besides the standard load/unload events (Open, Activate, Close, Deactivate, and Error)—that is, the Error, Page, and NoData events—but their sections react to events that occur as Access prints each record.

Report Events

Table 9.5 lists the events reports can react to. As indicated in the table, when you open a report, Access fires off the Open and then the Activate event. When you close the report, Access executes the Close and then the Deactivate event.

TABLE 9.5   Report Event Properties

Event	Event Property	Occurs When
Open	OnOpen	You open a report but before the report starts printing or becomes visible (before the Activate event)
Close	OnClose	You close the report (before the Deactivate event)
Error	OnError	A Jet error occurs while the report is printing
Activate	OnActivate	The report becomes the active window or starts printing (after the Open event)
Deactivate	OnDeactivate	You move to another Access window or close the report (after the Close event)
NoData	OnNoData	You attempt to open a report for printing or previewing, and its underlying record source provides no rows
Page	OnPage	The current page has been formatted but hasn't yet been printed

Activation versus Deactivation

When you switch from one report to another (in Preview view), the report you're switching away from executes its Deactivate event before the new report executes its Activate event. If you switch to any other Access window from a report, the report's Deactivate event still executes. If you switch to a different application or to a popup window within Access, the Deactivate event does not fire; that is, the Deactivate event fires off only when you switch to another window for which the parent is also the Access MDI Client window. (See Chapter 8 for more information on the MDI client window.)

Using the Open and Activate Events

When Access first opens the report, it runs the code attached to the report's Open event before it runs the query that supplies the data for the report. Given this fact, you can supply parameters to that query from the report's Open event. You might, for example, pop up a form that requests starting and ending dates or any other information your query might need. To see this in action, open rptPhoneBook-Param in CH09.MDB. (See Figure 9.3, although this figure is somewhat misleading—the form and the report would never actually be visible at the same time.)

In this example, rptPhoneBookParam's Open event executes the code found in Listing 9.5.

FIGURE 9.3

The report's Open event loads the parameter-gathering form, which, in turn, provides a parameter for the report's underlying query.

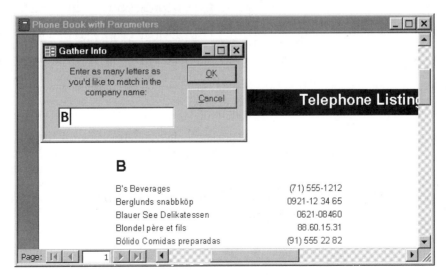

Listing 9.5

```
Private Sub Report_Open(Cancel As Integer)

    ' Set the global variable.
    strForm = "frmParam"

    DoCmd.OpenForm FormName:=strForm, WindowMode:=acDialog

    ' Set the Cancel flag if the form isn't still open.
    ' That would mean the user pressed the Cancel button.
    Cancel = Not IsOpen(strForm)
End Sub

Private Sub Report_Activate()
    DoCmd.Close acForm, strForm
End Sub
```

This code first opens frmParam modally so that code execution halts until you either hide or close the form. Just as described in Chapter 8, the OK button hides the form and the Cancel button closes the form altogether. On return from the OpenForm action, the code checks to see whether the form is still open, using the SysCmd function. If not, the report sets the Cancel parameter to True, to indicate that Access should abort the attempt to load the report.

Once Access has executed the Open event, it can go ahead and load the data that's going to populate the report. Because Access wouldn't be at this point at all for this report unless the parameter-providing form were still open (but hidden), you're assured that Access will be able to find the form it needs in order to supply the parameter for qryCustomerNameParam. The query uses the expression

```
Like Forms!frmParam!txtName & "*"
```

to filter its rows.

Finally, once the report executes its Activate event, the query no longer needs the form, and the code attached to the Activate event can close the form.

Avoiding Empty Reports—Using the NoData Event

There's nothing stopping you from choosing a filter for the report that returns no rows at all. In this case the report prints "#Error" in the Detail section. If you want to avoid this problem, you can add code to the NoData event of your report that reacts to this exact situation and cancels the report if there's no data to be printed. If you want to cancel the report if there aren't any rows, you can use code like this, from rptPhoneBookParam:

```
Private Sub Report_NoData(Cancel As Integer)
    MsgBox '"There aren't any rows to display!"
    ' Close the parameter form, as well.
    DoCmd.Close acForm, strForm
    ' Tell Access to just skip it.
    Cancel = True
End Sub
```

To test this code, try entering a value that is guaranteed to return no rows, such as "ZZ", when rptPhoneBookParam requests a value from you.

> **NOTE** Unsurprisingly, Access doesn't even bother with the NoData event for unbound reports. Finding out that an unbound report's recordset (which doesn't exist) doesn't contain any rows wouldn't be very useful information.

Using the Error Event

Access triggers a report's Error event when an error occurs in the Jet engine while the report is either formatting or printing. Although this eventuality is less likely with a report than it might be for a form, it can still occur. For example, if a table is opened exclusively by some user or a report is bound to a recordset that doesn't exist, Access triggers this error.

As with most other form and report events, you're better off using the report's class module to handle the Error event. In this case, Access provides two parameters to your event handler, allowing you some functionality you'd be missing if you called a macro or an external routine to handle this event. By using the class module, you can control how Access handles the error once you've investigated it.

Listing 9.6 shows a simple error-handling routine (from rptPhoneBookParam in the sample database). Although this example does little more than display a message box in response to the error that can occur when a user has removed the query or table to which a report has been bound, it should provide a starting place for your own error handlers.

> **NOTE** Because of the separation of VBA, the Access report engine, and Jet, you can't use the Err.Description property to return information on Jet errors. In this case you'll need to use the AccessError method of the Access Application object. This is just one of the many ways Access has changed due to the addition of the VBA shared component.

Listing 9.6

```
Private Sub Report_Error(DataErr As Integer, Response As Integer)
    Const adhcErrNoRecordSource = 2580

    Select Case DataErr
        Case adhcErrNoRecordSource
            MsgBox "This report is bound to a table or " & _
                "query that doesn't exist: '" & _
                Me.RecordSource & "'", vbExclamation
        Case Else
            MsgBox AccessError(DataErr)
    End Select
    DoCmd.Close acForm, strForm
    Response = acDataErrContinue
End Sub
```

The Page Event

You'll find there are some actions that you can't take at any time except when Access has finished formatting a page but before it actually prints the page. You can most easily draw a border around the page, for example, right before Access prints the page. The Page event gives you the flexibility you need to make any last-minute changes just before Access sends the formatted page to the printer.

The following code, from the Page event of rptBankInfo in CH09.MDB, draws a rectangle surrounding the entire printed page once Access has formatted the page (see Figure 9.4):

```
Private Sub Report_Page()
    Me.Line (0, 0)-(Me.ScaleWidth, Me.ScaleHeight), , B
End Sub
```

FIGURE 9.4

Use the Page event to draw on the report page once all the data for the page has been placed on the page.

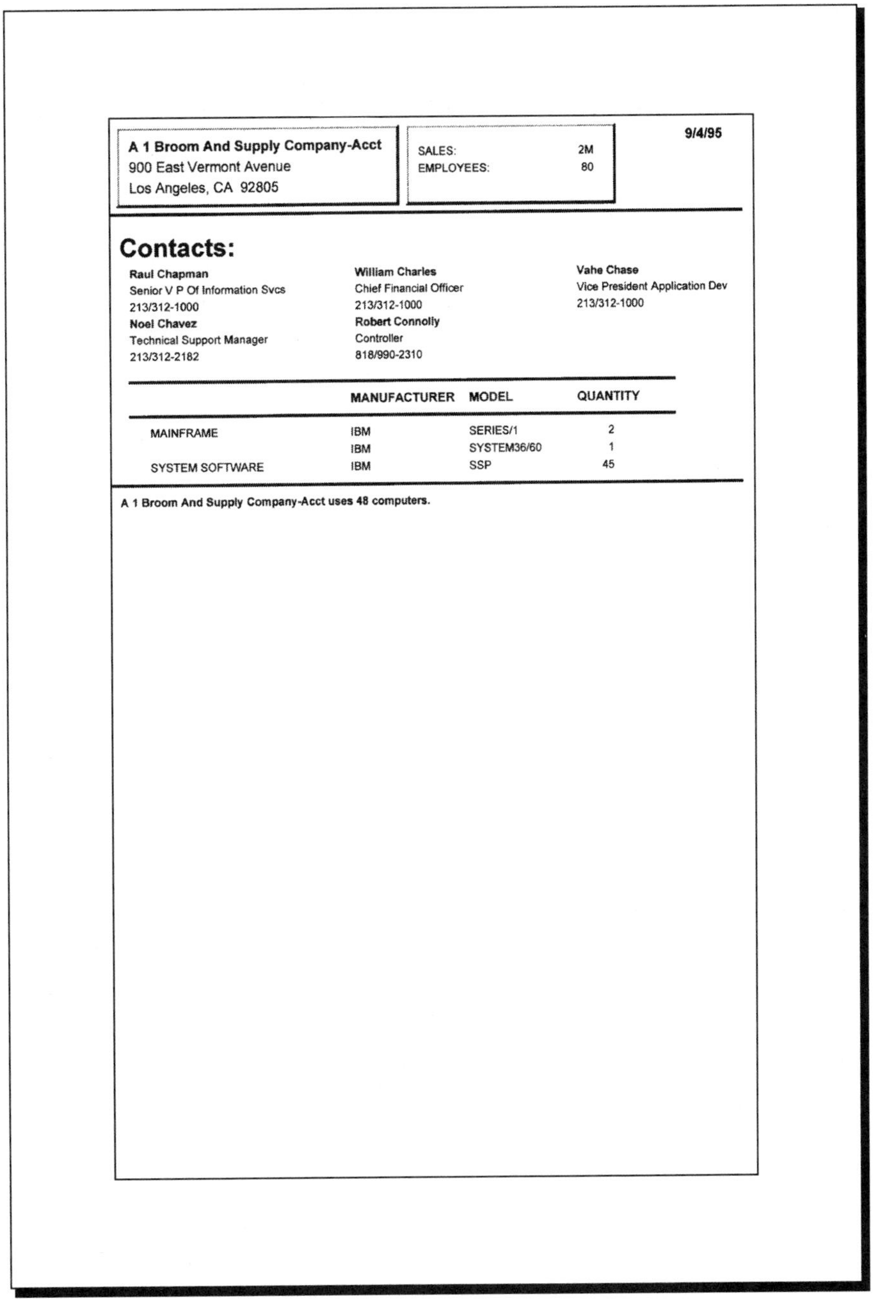

A 1 Broom And Supply Company-Acct		9/4/95
900 East Vermont Avenue	SALES: 2M	
Los Angeles, CA 92805	EMPLOYEES: 80	

Contacts:

Raul Chapman	William Charles	Vahe Chase
Senior V P Of Information Svcs	Chief Financial Officer	Vice President Application Dev
213/312-1000	213/312-1000	213/312-1000
Noel Chavez	Robert Connolly	
Technical Support Manager	Controller	
213/312-2182	818/990-2310	

	MANUFACTURER	MODEL	QUANTITY
MAINFRAME	IBM	SERIES/1	2
	IBM	SYSTEM36/60	1
SYSTEM SOFTWARE	IBM	SSP	45

A 1 Broom And Supply Company-Acct uses 48 computers.

NOTE You may find that printing a border around the printable region causes the border to extend past the printable region on your printer. In that case you may need to experiment with subtracting a few twips from Me.ScaleHeight until the entire border prints.

Section Events

Just as report events focus mainly on loading and unloading the report itself and on setting up the overall data that will populate the report, section events deal with the actual formatting and printing of that data. The following table lists the three events that apply to report sections:

Event	Event Property	Occurs When
Format	OnFormat	Access has selected the data to go in this section but before it formats or prints the data
Print	OnPrint	Access has formatted the data for printing (or previewing) but before it prints or shows the data
Retreat	OnRetreat	Access needs to move to a previous section while formatting the report

The Format Event

Access executes the code attached to a section's OnFormat event property once it has selected the data to be printed in the section but before it actually prints it. This allows you to alter the layout of the report or to perform calculations based on the data in the section at this particular time.

For a report's Detail section, Access calls your code just before it actually lays out the data to be printed. Your code has access to the data in the current row and can react to that data, perhaps making certain controls visible or invisible. (See the example in the section "Altering Your Report's Layout Programmatically" later in this chapter for more information on this technique.)

For group headers, the Format event occurs for each new group. Within the event procedure, your code has access to data in the group header and in the first row of data in the group. For group footers, the event occurs for each new group, and your code has access to data in the group footer and in the last row of data in the group. (For an example of using this information, see the section "The Sales Report" later in this chapter.)

For actions that don't affect the page layout or for calculations that absolutely must not occur until the section is printed, use the Print event. For example, if you're calculating a running total, place the calculation in the Print event because doing so avoids any ambiguities about when or whether the section actually printed.

If you've placed code for the Format event in the report's class module, Access passes you two parameters: FormatCount and Cancel. The FormatCount value corresponds to the section's FormatCount property. The Cancel parameter allows you to cancel the formatting of the current section and move on to the next by setting its value to True. This parameter corresponds to using

```
DoCmd.CancelEvent
```

from within your code.

The Print Event

Access executes the code attached to a section's OnPrint property once it has formatted the data to be printed in the section, but before it actually prints it. For a report's Detail section, Access calls your code just before it prints the data. Your code has access to the data in the current row. For group headers, the Print event occurs for each new group. Within the event procedure, your code has access to data in the group header and in the first row of data in the group. For group footers, the event occurs for each new group, and your code has access to data in the group footer and in the last row of data in the group.

For actions that require changing the report's layout, use the Format event. Once you've reached the Print event, it's too late to change the report's layout.

Just as it does for the Format event, Access passes two parameters to your code for the Print event if you place your code in the report's module. The PrintCount parameter corresponds to the section's PrintCount property. The Cancel parameter allows you to cancel the formatting of the current section and move on to the next by setting its value to True.

The Retreat Event

Sometimes Access needs to move back to a previous section while it's formatting your report. For example, if your group level's KeepTogether property is set to

With First Detail Row, Access formats the group header and then the first row and checks to make sure they'll both fit in the space available on the current page. Once it has formatted the two, it retreats from those two sections, executing the Retreat event for each. Then it again formats the sections and finally prints them.

If you've made any changes during the Format event, you may wish to undo them during the Retreat event. Because you really can't know during the Retreat event whether the current section will actually be printed on the current page, you should undo any layout changes made during the Format event.

Counting rows from the Format event makes a very simple example. If you include code attached to a section's Format event procedure that increments a counter for each row, include code in the Retreat event that decrements the counter. Otherwise the Format event may be fired multiple times for a given row, and the count will be incorrect. (Of course, there are several other ways to take care of this problem, including checking the FormatCount property. This example is intended only to explain why you might need to use the Retreat event.)

TIP

Access triggers the Retreat event in two very predictable places, among others. If you've created a group and set its KeepTogether property to With First Detail, Access triggers the Format event, then the Retreat event, and then the Format and Print events for the first row in the group as it attempts to fit the header and the first row on the same page. The same concept applies to groups in which you've set the KeepTogether property to All Rows, in which case Access formats each row, retreats from each row, and then formats the ones that will fit on the current page. Although there are many other circumstances in which Access will fire off the Retreat event, you can be assured that setting the group's KeepTogether property will force it.

Section Design-Time Properties

Report sections maintain a set of properties different from the properties of any other Access object. Table 9.6 lists those properties, and the following sections discuss some of them and give examples and hints for their use in designing your reports. Each of the properties in Table 9.6 applies to all report sections except the page header and footer.

TABLE 9.6   Report Section Properties

Property	Description	Settings
CanGrow	Determines whether the size of a section will increase vertically so Access can print all its data	True (−1); False (0)
CanShrink	Determines whether the size of a section will shrink vertically to avoid wasting space if there is no more data to print	True (−1); False (0)
NewRowOrCol	Specifies whether Access always starts printing a section in a multicolumn layout at the start of a new row (Horizontal layout) or column (Vertical Layout)	None (0); Before Section (1); After Section (2); Before & After (3)
ForceNewPage	Determines whether Access prints a section on the current page or at the top of a new page	None (0); Before Section (1); After Section (2); Before & After (3)
KeepTogether	Determines whether Access attempts to print an entire section on a single page	True (−1); False (0)
RepeatSection (Group Header sections only)	Specifies whether Access repeats a group header on the next page or column when a group spans more than one page or column	True (−1); False (0)

The CanGrow/CanShrink Properties

Setting either the CanGrow or CanShrink property causes other controls on the report to move vertically to adjust for changes in the sections' heights. Sections can grow or shrink only across their whole widths, so they must account for the maximum size needed within themselves. If you have a text box horizontally aligned with an object frame that cannot shrink, the section will not shrink, no matter how little text is in the text box. If you set a control's CanGrow property to Yes, Access sets the CanGrow property for the control's section to Yes, also. You can override this setting by changing the section's CanGrow property back to No if you need to.

Why CanShrink Doesn't and CanGrow Won't

Microsoft AnswerPoint suggests the following reasons why the CanGrow and CanShrink properties might not always do what you think they ought:

- Overlapping controls will not shrink, even when you've set the CanShrink property to Yes. If two controls touch at all, even by the smallest amount, they won't grow or shrink correctly.

- Controls shrink line by line (vertically). This means, for example, that if a group of controls is placed on the left side of a page and a large control (for example, an OLE picture) on the right side of the page, the controls on the left side will not shrink unless the picture is blank and hidden.

- Space between controls is not affected by the CanShrink or CanGrow property.

- Controls located in the page header or page footer will grow to, at most, the height of the section. Neither the Header nor the Footer section itself can grow or shrink.

The NewRowOrCol Property

The NewRowOrCol property applies only when your report uses multiple columns for its display. When you choose to use multiple columns in the Page Setup dialog (by selecting the Columns tab), you can select either a horizontal or a vertical layout for your items. Choosing Vertical prints items down the first column, then down the second, and so on. Choosing Horizontal prints across the first row, in the first column, the second column, and so on, and then goes on to the second row, printing in each column. You might use the Vertical layout for printing phone book listings and the Horizontal layout for printing mailing labels.

The NewRowOrCol property allows you to maintain fine control over how the Detail section of your report prints when it's using multiple columns. Table 9.7 describes each of the property's possible settings and how you can use it to control the layout of your report.

You'll want to experiment with the NewRowOrCol property if you're working with multicolumn reports. You can find an example of its use in the section "Companies, Contacts, and Hardware" later in this chapter.

TABLE 9.7 NewRowOrCol Property Settings

Setting	Value	Description
None	0	Row and column breaks occur naturally, based on the settings in the Page Setup dialog and on the layout of the current page so far (default)
Before Section	1	The current section is printed in a new row or column. The next section is printed in the same row or column
After Section	2	The current section is printed in the same row or column as the previous section. The next section is printed in a new row or column
Before & After	3	The current section is printed in a new row or column. The next section is also printed starting in a new row or column

The ForceNewPage Property

The ForceNewPage property allows you to control page breaks in relation to your report sections. Table 9.8 details the four options that are available for this property. Because you can control this option while the report is printing, you can, based on a piece of data in a particular row, decide to start the section printing on a new page. You can accomplish the same effect, although not quite as elegantly, by including a page break control on your report and setting its Visible property to Yes or No, depending on the data in the current row.

TABLE 9.8 ForceNewPage Property Settings

Setting	Value	Description
None	0	Access starts printing the current section on the current page (default)
Before Section	1	Access starts printing the current section at the top of a new page
After Section	2	Access starts printing the next section at the top of a new page
Before & After	3	Access starts printing the current section at the top of a new page and prints the next section starting on a new page, too

In addition, starting in Access 95, the ForceNewPage property is settable at run time, so you can insert page breaks easily from the Format or Print events of your sections. This ability should all but eliminate the need for setting the visibility of page break controls (a hokey hack, at best).

The KeepTogether Property

Setting the KeepTogether property to True asks Access to try to print a given section all on one page. If it can't fit on the current page, Access starts a new page and tries printing it there. Of course, if it can't fit on one page, Access must continue printing on the next page, no matter how the property is set.

The KeepTogether property for sections is much simpler than the KeepTogether property for groups. The Section property doesn't attempt to keep multiple sections together, as does the GroupLevel property. For sections, the KeepTogether property just attempts to have Access print the entire section on a single page, if possible.

The RepeatSection Property

Often, when you print a group on your report, Access has to start a new page or column in the middle of the group. In that case you may decide you'd like Access to reprint the group header for you on the new page or column. The Repeat-Section property for group headers controls whether Access repeats the group header at the top of the new page or column. The sample report, rptPhoneBook in CH09.MDB, uses this property to force Access to reprint the group header at the top of the column if a group has been broken across a column.

This property is available only for group headers, not the report header. For report headers you don't really need this functionality—you can just use a page header instead. If you're printing a subreport, however, and you'd like to emulate this behavior, you can fake it:

- In the subreport, create a group that's grouped on the string expression "=1". This creates a static grouping that won't change from row to row of data.

- Use this group header as the report header. (That is, don't show the Report Header section; use this group header instead, since it won't change throughout the report.) Because it's a group header, it will have a RepeatSection property, and Access will repeat it at the top of a new page.

Section Run-Time Properties

Some section events occur only while Access is formatting or printing the report (for example, the Format and Print events, discussed earlier in this chapter).

Table 9.9 lists the run-time properties, and the following sections present more information and suggestions for their effective use.

TABLE 9.9   Section Run-Time Properties

Property	Description	Settings
MoveLayout	Specifies whether Access should move to the next printing location on the page	True (−1): the section's Left and Top properties are advanced to the next print location; False (0): the Left and Top properties are unchanged
NextRecord	Specifies whether a section should advance to the next record	True: advance to the next record; False: stay on the same record
PrintSection	Specifies whether a section should be printed	True: the section is printed; False: the section isn't printed
FormatCount	Indicates the number of times the Format event has occurred for the current section	Read-only while the report is being formatted; not available in Design view
PrintCount	Indicates the number of times the Print event has occurred for the current section	Read-only while the report is printing; not available in Design view
HasContinued	Indicates whether the current section has been continued from the previous page	True or False: available in the section's Format event
WillContinue	Indicates whether the current section will continue on the next page	True or False: available in the section's Print event

The MoveLayout, NextRecord, and PrintSection Properties

The MoveLayout, NextRecord, and PrintSection properties, when combined, control exactly how Access moves from row to row in the underlying data and whether the current row will be printed. Table 9.10 presents all the possible combinations of the three properties and how they interact. By combining these three layout properties, you'll have a great deal of flexibility in how you lay out your reports. The examples in the sections "Printing Multiple Labels" and "Inserting Blank Lines" later in this chapter demonstrate the use of these properties.

TABLE 9.10   Section Run-Time Properties and Their Interactions

MoveLayout	NextRecord	PrintSection	Results
True	True	True	Moves to the next print location, moves to the next row, and then prints the row (default)
True	True	False	Moves to a new row and moves to the next print location, but it doesn't print the row (It leaves a blank space where the row would have printed.)
True	False	True	Moves to the next print location, stays on the same row, and prints the data
True	False	False	Moves to the next print location but doesn't skip a row and doesn't print any data. This effectively leaves a blank space on the paper without moving to a new row in the data
False	True	True	Doesn't move the print location but prints the next row right on top of the previous one. This allows you to overlay one row of data on another
False	True	False	Doesn't move the print location and doesn't print anything, but it skips a row in the data. This allows you to skip a row without leaving any blank space on the page
False	False	True	Not allowed
False	False	False	Not allowed

The FormatCount Property

Access increments a section's FormatCount property each time it executes the Format event for that section. Once it moves to the next section, it resets the FormatCount property to 0.

In some circumstances Access must format a section more than once. For example, as Access reaches the end of a page, it's possible that the current section won't fit. Access attempts to format the section and, if it doesn't fit, formats it again on the next page. It calls the Format event code twice, first with a FormatCount value of 1 and then with a FormatCount value of 2.

If you're performing some calculation or action from your Format event code, pay careful attention to the FormatCount value. For example, perhaps you want to increment counters only if the FormatCount value is 1. If you normally take an action in the Format event code, you must skip the action if the FormatCount value is greater than 1.

The PrintCount Property

Access increments a section's PrintCount property each time it executes the Print event for that section. Once it moves on the next section, it resets the PrintCount property to 0.

Access attempts to print a section more than once when a specific section spans more than one page. For example, if a section requires more than a single page for its output, Access calls the Print event code once for each page, incrementing the PrintCount property. If you're attempting to maintain running totals, adding in an amount each time a report section prints, you need to check the PrintCount property and add in the value only once. The following code might be used in a section's Print event code. (If you place the code in the report's class module, Access passes the PrintCount property to the code as a parameter. If not, you need to refer to the PrintCount property using the standard syntax.)

```
If PrintCount = 1 Then
    lngRunningTotal = lngRunningTotal + Me!OrderAmount
End If
```

The WillContinue/HasContinued Properties

The two report properties added in Access 95, HasContinued and WillContinue, are intended to allow code in your event procedures to react to the fact that a given section has continued from the previous page or will continue on the next page. These are both properties of sections, and they return either True or False. Each works a bit differently, and the following sections explain the details of using them. Unfortunately, they're both constructed in such a way that we were unable to find a use for either in any but the most trivial situations or by employing some difficult work-arounds. For the sake of completeness, however, the next few sections explain how they work.

The WillContinue Property

Access sets the WillContinue property during a section's Print event, and the property returns True if any portion of the current section will print on the next page. Therein lies the problem: Access' "trigger" is wound a bit too tightly. Access doesn't distinguish between white space and controls when setting this property, so it sets the WillContinue property to True for almost every page. All you care about is whether text has been printed on one page and continued on the next, not whether white space from the next row to be printed has touched the current page, but Access can't discern between these two situations.

Once Access has set the property to True for a given section, it remains True until the same section's next Print event (PrintCount > 1, on the next page). Therefore, you can use the value of the section's WillContinue property from the Format or Print event procedures of any section that will print before Access prints the rest of your section. (For Detail sections, this means you could check in the current page's Page Footer section or the next page's Page Header section, for example.) In our experimentation, the WillContinue property returned True for every single page of all our test reports except the last page, whether or not the rows actually carried over to the next page—even if the data occupied only a single row on the printed page! The only way we were able to avoid this situation was to print a report in which the Detail section's height was an integral factor of the printed page's height (1 inch, for example, on a 10-inch print area) and in which we didn't include any headers or footers. In that case, Access correctly did *not* set the WillContinue property for each page.

The HasContinued Property

Access sets a section's HasContinued property during the section's Format event, and it sets the property to True only if the FormatCount property is greater than 1 (which is, of course, exactly what it should do). As a matter of fact, our experiments found that Access always sets the HasContinued property correctly, even when it has incorrectly set the WillContinue property on the previous page.

The problem with the HasContinued property is that you can't check it from the location where it would be the most useful—when you're printing the page header. At that point Access hasn't yet set the FormatCount property for the section to a number greater than 1, so the HasContinued property will still be False if you examine the Detail section's properties from the page header. By the time you start printing the second portion of the Detail section (with its FormatCount property now set to 2), it's too late to do anything useful with the HasContinued property.

Of course, even though you can't set the visibility of a control based on the Has-Continued property, you can use the report's Print method to write text directly onto the report if you find the Detail section's HasContinued property is True. You may find this useful, but in our testing it appeared to be more work than it was worth.

Perhaps you can tell from the tone that we're a bit disappointed in the functionality these properties provide. They *sound* good, but they just don't provide the right results in the cases where they'd be most useful. We hope the properties will work correctly, or at least better, in future releases of the product.

Examples Using Report and Section Events and Properties

The following sections contain examples and solutions to some common problems. Each example refers to a specific report or form in CH09.MDB. In each case you might find it useful to open the specific report in Design view and follow along with the description you find here. Change properties and see what happens. Experimentation is the best way to find out how each of the report and section properties affects the printed output.

Printing Multiple Labels

Printing multiple labels based on a count stored with the label data makes a perfect example of the use of the MoveLayout, NextRecord, and PrintSection properties. In this example the user has stored, in the LabelCount column of a table, the number of copies of the row to be printed. Listing 9.7, which would be called from the Print event of the Detail section containing the label, shows the code necessary to print the correct number of labels. (See rptMultiLabel in CH09.MDB to test this example.) Given the data shown in Figure 9.5, the design surface shown in Figure 9.6 creates the labels shown in Figure 9.7.

FIGURE 9.5

Each row in the table contains a column indicating the number of labels to be printed.

Company Name	Contact Name	Address	City	Region	Postal Code	LabelCount
Ana Trujillo Emparedados y h	Ana Trujillo	Avda. de la Constitució	México D.F.		05021	0
Antonio Moreno Taquería	Antonio Moreno	Mataderos 2312	México D.F.		05023	1
Alfreds Futterkiste	Maria Anders	Obere Str. 57	Berlin		12209	7
Bon app'	Laurence Lebihan	12, rue des Bouchers	Marseille		13008	6
Bólido Comidas preparadas	Martín Sommer	C/ Araquil, 67	Madrid		28023	2
Blondel père et fils	Frédérique Citeaux	24, place Kléber	Strasbourg		67000	3
Blauer See Delikatessen	Hanna Moos	Forsterstr. 57	Mannheim		68306	5
B's Beverages	Victoria Ashworth	Fauntleroy Circus	London		EC2 5NT	3
Berglunds snabbköp	Christina Berglund	Berguvsvägen 8	Luleå		S-958 22	5
Bottom-Dollar Markets	Elizabeth Lincoln	23 Tsawassen Blvd.	Tsawassen	BC	T2F 8M4	5
Around the Horn	Thomas Hardy	120 Hanover Sq.	London		WA1 1DP	1
*						0

tblLabels : Table

Record: 1 of 11

FIGURE 9.6

The report design includes a visible control containing the LabelCount column. In your labels, this could be made invisible.

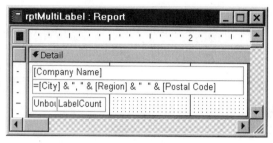

FIGURE 9.7

The labels will contain as many multiples as you requested in your table.

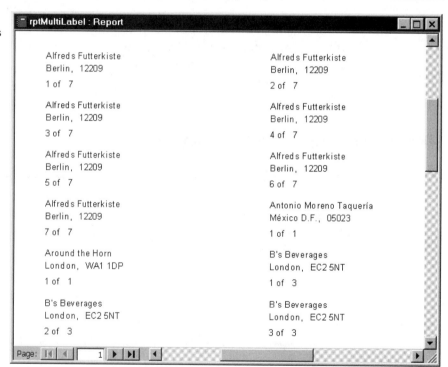

Listing 9.7

```
Sub Detail1_Print(Cancel As Integer, PrintCount As Integer)
    Me!txtLabel = PrintCount & " of "
    If Me!txtLabelCount = 0 Then
        Me.NextRecord = True
```

```
        Me.MoveLayout = False
        Me.PrintSection = False
    Else
        If PrintCount < Me!LabelCount Then
            Me.NextRecord = False
        End If
    End If
End Sub
```

To make this technique work, you must create a text box on your report for the field that contains the count. You can make it invisible, but it has to be on the report for the code to be able to get to it. (In this example the text box control is named LabelCount.) Unlike forms, reports must contain a control bound to any column they reference. Forms can reference any column in the underlying data without actually having to contain a control bound to that field.

This example does its work quite simply. If the user has requested no labels at all for the particular row, the code tells Access to move to the next record (NextRecord = True) but not to move to the next print position (MoveLayout = False) and not to print anything at all (PrintSection = False). Otherwise, if the PrintCount value is less than the number of labels to be printed (Me!LabelCount), don't move to the next record (NextRecord = False), but use the default value for the other properties. This causes Access to print the data from the current row and move to the next print location.

Although you might be tempted to attach this code to the Format event, it won't work correctly. Because Access must decide at format time how to lay out the labels on the page, the FormatCount value to which the Format event has access won't always be correct, especially when you've filled a page without completing the run of a particular row.

Printing Mailing Labels
Starting at a Specific Location

If you print mailing labels on full sheets of paper (as do most people with laser printers), you've probably needed, at one point or another, to start a printout at the first unused label on the page rather than on the first label. The technique to make this happen is very simple and uses the same properties used in the previous example: NextRecord and PrintSection. If you want to try out this technique, open rptSkipLabels in Preview view. This causes frmSelectLabel to pop up, requesting you to choose the first label on which to print. Once you've made a selection, the form disappears and the report prints, starting on the label you chose.

How Does It Work?

The basic idea is this: you call a function, adhGetLabelsToSkip (in basSelect-Label), that pops up a form requesting you to click the first label you want printed (see Figure 9.8). You send to this function information about the number of rows and columns for your labels, which label to choose by default, and whether you're printing across and then down or down and then across. Given that information, that form configures itself for your label situation and allows you to select the label on which you'd first like to print. When you click the form's OK button, the form hides itself, and the calling function in your report then knows how many labels to skip on the page. (For more information on creating popup forms that return values, see the section "Using Popup Tools" in Chapter 8.)

FIGURE 9.8

Choose a label from frm-SelectLabel on which to start printing.

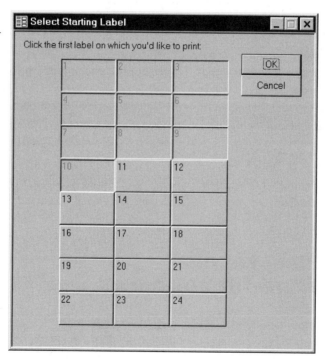

Your call to adhGetLabelsToSkip returns the first label you want printed, and it's up to your report to skip all labels before that one, but only on the first page. Figure 9.9 shows how rptSkipLabels will print after you've chosen to start on label 11, as in

FIGURE 9.9

Once you've selected a starting label, the report will skip labels up to that label number.

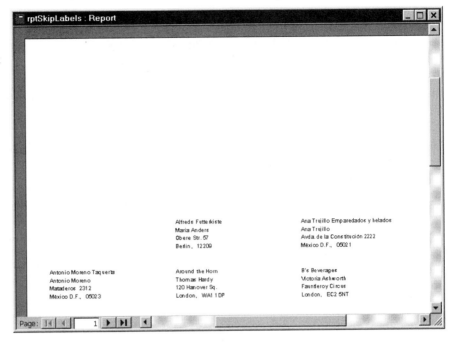

Figure 9.8. To do its work, rptSkipLabels calls the code shown here in reaction to the Report Header and Detail sections' Format events:

```
Dim intSkipped As Integer
Dim intToSkip As Integer

Private Sub Detail_Format(Cancel As Integer, _
 FormatCount As Integer)
   If intSkipped < intToSkip Then
      Me.NextRecord = False
      Me.PrintSection = False
      intSkipped = intSkipped + 1
   End If
End Sub

Private Sub ReportHeader_Format(Cancel As Integer, _
 FormatCount As Integer)
   intSkipped = 0
   intToSkip = adhGetLabelsToSkip(FormName:=frmSelectLabel, _
    Rows:=10, Cols:=3, Start:=1, PrintAcross:=True)
End Sub
```

Every time you print or preview the report, Access triggers the report header's Format event. There, you'll need to reset the count of skipped labels, intSkipped, back to 0 and then call adhGetLabelsToSkip. Pass adhGetLabelsToSkip information on the form to pop up; the number of rows and columns on your label sheets; which label to choose, by default; and whether you're printing across first (as opposed to down first). The function pops up the requested form, waits for a response, and returns the number of labels your printout should skip.

From the Format event of the Detail section, the code keeps track of how many labels it has skipped. Once it reaches the value in intSkipped, it actually starts printing labels. Up to that point, however, it sets the NextRecord and PrintSection properties to False, stalling until it reaches the right label.

As you can see from the previous two examples, you can use the MoveLayout, PrintSection, and NextRecord properties to create reports that would be difficult by any other means. Don't be put off by their apparent complexity; once you get the hang of it, you can make them do exactly what you need.

TIP To use this technique in your own applications, import frmSelectLabel and basSelectLabel from CH09.MDB. Copy all the event code from rptSkip-Labels (it's easier to do if you set the Tools ➤ Options ➤ Module ➤ Full Module View option) into your own report's module, and modify the call to adhGetLabelsToSkip to reflect your report's layout. Finally, make sure your report's property sheet has the Detail and Header sections' Format properties set to [Event Procedure]. When you open your report, it will pop up the form and request a starting label.

Handling Odd and Even Pages

Perhaps you print your reports double sided (either on a duplex printer or by using a printing utility such as ClickBook, from the ForeFront Group). In general, given that the first page of a document prints on the front of a piece of paper, odd-numbered pages appear on the right and even-numbered pages appear on the left when you bind the document. Quite often, in published documents, you'll want the page numbers to appear flush right on odd-numbered pages and flush left on even-numbered pages. Although Access doesn't provide a built-in method to accomplish this, it's easy to do. (See rptPhoneBook or rptPhoneBookParam for this example.)

To alternate left and right alignment for alternating pages, take these two steps:

1. Create your page footer control so that it spans the entire width of your report (see Figure 9.10). Enter the ControlSource value you'd like.

2. Attach the code in Listing 9.8 to the Format event of the Page Footer section. This handles setting the TextAlign property for the Footer section as each page gets printed. For every page, the code checks the page number MOD 2, which is 0 for even pages and 1 for odd pages. It sets the TextAlign property to acAlignRight for odd pages and acAlignLeft for even pages.

If you haven't used the MOD operator, this might appear confusing. Basically, the MOD operator returns the remainder you get when you divide the first operand by the second. That is, if you have

```
? 5 MOD 2
```

the result would be 1 because the remainder when you divide 5 by 2 is 1. The MOD operator is most useful for determining whether one number is a multiple of another since, if it is, the result will be 0. To tell whether a number is even, you can use the expression

```
If x MOD 2 = 0 Then ...
```

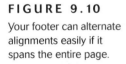

FIGURE 9.10

Your footer can alternate alignments easily if it spans the entire page.

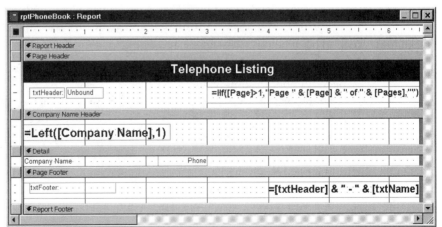

Listing 9.8

```
Private Function IsEven(intValue As Integer) As Boolean
    ' Is intValue even, or not?
    IsEven = (intValue Mod 2 = 0)
End Function

Private Sub PageFooter2_Format(Cancel As Integer, _
 FormatCount As Integer)

    ' Constants Access should supply, but doesn't.
    Const acAlignLeft = 1
    Const acAlignRight = 3

    Me!txtFooter.TextAlign = IIf(IsEven(Me.Page), _
     acAlignLeft, acAlignRight)
End Sub
```

Controlling the Starting Page Number

Every report supports a read/write property that indicates and/or sets the current page number. By inspecting the Page property of the current report, you can determine which page is currently active. You can also set the Page property, effectively resetting Access' understanding of the current page number. You could, if you had a reason to, set the Page property to 1 in the page header's Format event. Then, every time Access formatted a page header (once per page), it would reset the report's Page property to 1.

A more useful trick involving the Page property is the ability to set the starting page number to some value other than 1. This is especially useful if you need to chain reports or number chapters with a page number including the chapter number, with each chapter starting at page 1. The only tricky issue here is deciding when to reset the page number. If you want to print an entire report, starting at a particular page number, set the Page property in the report header's Format event. If you need to set the Page property based on data that could occur at the top of any given page, set the value in the page header's Format event.

For an example, see rptSales in CH09.MDB. This report sets the first page number to 6 in the report header's Format event. Numbers increase consecutively from there. The code to make this change is minimal, of course:

```
Sub ReportHeader0_Format(Cancel As Integer, _
 FormatCount As Integer)
    Me.Page = 6
End Sub
```

Because the report's Open event occurs before any of the formatting events, you could also use that hook to retrieve the starting page number, store it in a variable, and then assign the value of that variable to the Page property in the report header's Format event. (We discuss the other interesting features of this report, including the alternate gray bars, in the section "The Sales Report" later in this chapter.)

Numbering Items on a Report

Access makes it simple to number rows on a report. By changing two properties of a text box, you can create a row counter that will count rows either over the total report or just within a group. The report rptNumberRows in CH09.MDB demonstrates both types of row counters, as you can see in Figure 9.11.

To create a row counter on a report, set a text box's properties as follows:

Property	Setting
RunningSum	Over Group (1) or Over All (2)
ControlSource	=1

This technique takes advantage of the fact that setting the RunningSum property causes the current row's value to be the sum of all the previous rows' values plus the current row's value. Because the current row's value in this case is always 1, the running sum just increments by 1. You could, of course, place some other value in the ControlSource property to force it to increment by a different value.

You can examine rptNumberRows to see how it works, but the most important setting is that for the RunningSum property of the text boxes. If set to Over Group, it sums only over the current group. Every time Access starts a new group, its value

FIGURE 9.11

Use the RunningSum property to create a row counter in a report.

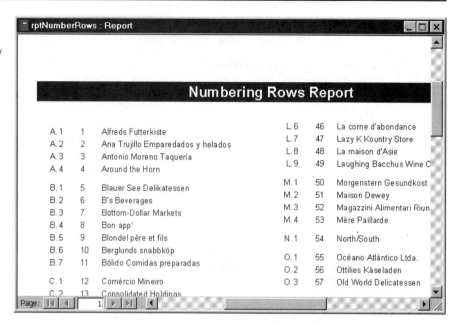

gets reset to 0. If set to Over All, the value gets reset only at the beginning of the report and continues to increment for the rest of the report.

Inserting Blank Lines

If your report consists of a long list of values, you may wish to insert a blank line at regular intervals. Figure 9.12 shows such a report, with a blank line inserted after each group of four rows.

This technique again involves the NextRecord and PrintSection properties. The code in Listing 9.9 does the work for you, and you can copy it into any of your own report's modules. (Look in rptBlankEveryNLines in CH09.MDB.) It does its work by counting up the lines that have been printed so far on each page; when the number is an even multiple of the group size plus 1 (that is, if you're breaking after every four lines, you'll be looking for line numbers that are a multiple of 5), the report skips to the next print location (MoveLayout = True) but does not move to the next record (NextRecord = False) and doesn't print anything (PrintSection = False). This inserts a blank row.

FIGURE 9.12

Insert a blank line to separate large groups into
readable chunks.

Listing 9.9 shows the HandleLine procedure.

Listing 9.9

```
Private Sub HandleLine()
    Dim fShowLine As Boolean

    Const adhcBreakCount = 4

    fShowLine = ((mintLineCount Mod (adhcBreakCount + 1)) <> 0)
    If Not fShowLine Then
        ' If you're not showing the current
        ' row, then don't move to the next record,
        ' and don't print the section.
        Me.NextRecord = False
        Me.PrintSection = False
        Me.MoveLayout = True
        mintLineCount = 0
    End If
```

```
        mintLineCount = mintLineCount + 1
End Sub
```

> **TIP**
>
> If you just want to insert a blank line between your groups and don't care about breaking them into specific-sized groups, you can set up a group footer that's blank (with its CanShrink property set to No). Then, when the group breaks, Access inserts a blank space between groups.

Some Simple Sample Reports

The following three reports show off some of the effects various properties can make on the printed output of an Access report. Each was designed to show off specific techniques:

- **Sales report:** Alternating gray bars, displaying report properties on the report, creating page totals

- **Telephone book:** Using multiple columns with full-page-width title, section titles, and footer page-range listing

- **Companies, contacts, and hardware:** Using multiple subreports and report properties to link separate reports

The Sales Report

The sales report (see Figure 9.13) lists companies in reverse order of sales and, within sets of equal sales, in alphabetical order by company name. For visibility, every other line is printed in gray, and each page contains a total sales amount for the companies printed on that page.

We'll take this in steps:

1. Create the basic report, with no gray and no totals.

2. Add the page total (using the Print event).

3. Add the alternate gray lines (using the Format event).

FIGURE 9.13

Company names in decreasing order of sales, with added alternate gray bars

COMPUTER SURVEY DATA

COMPANY NAMES IN DECREASING ORDER OF REVENUE
(Actual values have been altered to protect confidentiality)

COMPANY NAME	SALES (In Millions of $'s)
Bottom-Dollar Markets	4654
QUICK-Stop	675
Old World Delicatessen	454
Berglunds snabbköp	434
Galería del gastrónomo	356
GROSELLA-Restaurante	356
Hungry Coyote Import Store	356
Split Rail Beer & Ale	356
North/South	68
Morgenstern Gesundkost	57
Mère Paillarde	56
Océano Atlántico Ltda.	56
Suprêmes délices	56
Trail's Head Gourmet Provisioners	56
Bon app'	54
Que Delícia	54
Spécialités du monde	54
La maison d'Asie	46
B's Beverages	45
France restauration	45
La corne d'abondance	45
Laughing Bacchus Wine Cellars	45
Rancho grande	43
LINO-Delicateses	36
Maison Dewey	36
Magazzini Alimentari Riuniti	35
Blauer See Delikatessen	34
Cactus Comidas para llevar	34
FISSA Fabrica Inter. Salchichas S.A.	34
	8630

Report: rptSales (tblCustomers)

Page 6

Step 1: Creating the Basic Report–No Gray, No Totals

Figure 9.14 shows the design surface for the basic, no-frills sales report. The sorting and grouping have already been performed, using the setup shown in Figure 9.15. For this report, Access prints information from the Report Header section once, on the first page. It prints the information in the Page Header and Page Footer sections once on each page and prints the Detail section once for each row of data.

FIGURE 9.14

Plain sales report's design surface

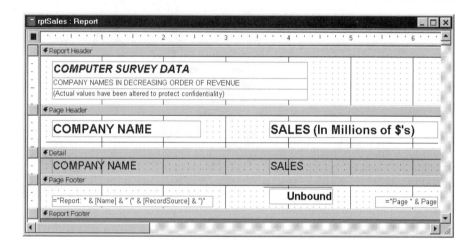

FIGURE 9.15

Sorting and Grouping dialog for the sales report

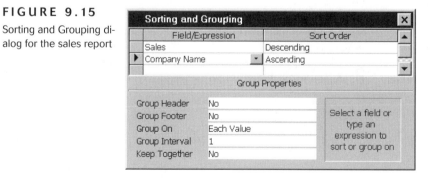

> **TIP**
>
> If you're using a calculated expression as the ControlSource property for a text box on a report, make sure its Name property does not match one of the fields in your expression. If the Name property is the same as one of the fields used to fill the control, Access can't know whether you want it to get the value from the field or from the control with that particular name. Confused, Access will place #Error into the text box when you run the report. This is a common occurrence when you create reports using the Report Wizards and then customize them. The Wizards use the field name as the Name property for each control, which can lead to just this sort of problem.

Using Report Properties

If you look carefully at the Page Footer section of the report, you'll notice that it's using some of the report's properties—Name, RecordSource, and Page—as values that are shown on the report. You can use any of the report's properties as built-in variables on the report printout. This same feature applies to forms, although it's not as useful in that context because form properties aren't nearly as interesting as report properties while the object's being viewed. (Forms don't support the Page property except when printing, for example.)

Step 2: Adding Page Totals

Unlike the Report and Group Header/Footer sections, page Header/Footer sections don't support aggregate functions, so you have to "fake out" Access in order to create page totals. Our solution (only one of many possible solutions) has two parts:

- As each page header is printed, reset the running total to 0 in preparation for accumulating the value for the current page.

- As each row is printed, accumulate the running total in a control in the page footer.

Each of these refers to a control in the page footer, necessary for accumulating the running total. In this sample report (rptSales), that text box is named txtPageTotal.

Because you surely do not want a value added into the running total unless that particular row has been slated to be printed on the current page, you should attach the code that updates the totals to the section's Print event. (If you insisted on using the Format event, you would need to add code to the matching Retreat event that would back out of the addition if the row were not to be printed.) In this simple example there's no chance that the Print and Format events will be fired off independently (since there's only one printed row per row in the data), but you need to think about the differences between the Print and Format events when deciding how to attach actions to events. Access fires off the Format event when it's formatting a section but isn't yet sure whether it will get printed. It fires off the Print event only when it's about to actually print the row.

Resetting the Total for Each Page

In the Page Header's Format event (which occurs only as each page starts its formatting process), call the following code:

```
Me!txtPageTotal = 0
```

This resets the text box in the page footer that will accumulate the total for each page.

Accumulating the Sales as You Go

In the Detail section's Print event, call the following code:

```
Me!txtPageTotal = Me!txtPageTotal + Nz(Me!txtSales)
```

(For more information on the Nz function, see the sidebar entitled "The Helpful Nz Function" in Chapter 8.)

This code adds the current row's sales value to the current page total. Remember that the Print event handler is the only event procedure that can access each and every row's data, once you're sure the data is to be printed on the current page. It's here that you need to place any code that must react to each row as it gets printed. When each page is finally pushed out of the printer, this total will be correct, since you've been maintaining it while Access has printed each row.

Step 3: Alternating White and Gray Bars

Although this sort of maneuver was tricky in previous versions of Access, starting in Access 95 you can easily create alternate gray and white bars. You can find the procedure AlternateGray (Listing 9.10) in CH09.MDB, in the report module for rptSales. Because Access now allows text boxes to be transparent, showing the background color through them, the exercise is trivial: for every alternate row, change the background color of the section. The controls are transparent, and the background color for the section will be the background color for the row.

The routine uses a module-global variable, fGray, to keep track of whether the current row should be printed. The procedure switches the variable between True and False:

```
fGray = Not fGray
```

If you want to ensure that the first row on each page is printed in white, set the value of fGray to False in the page header's Format event code.

Listing 9.10

```
Private Sub AlternateGray()

    Const adhcColorGray = &HC0C0C0
    Const adhcColorWhite = &HFFFFFF

    ' If the current section is to be printed in gray, then set
    ' the BackColor property for the section. This works only
    ' because the controls on the section are all set to
    ' be transparent.
    Me.Section(0).BackColor = IIf(fGray, adhcColorGray, _
    adhcColorWhite)

    ' Next time, do it the opposite of the way you did
    ' it this time.
    fGray = Not fGray
End Sub
```

TIP

To include this functionality in your own reports, copy the subroutine named AlternateGray from rptSales to your own report, declare the fGray integer variable in the declarations area in the report's class module, and add the necessary call to AlternateGray to the Format event of the Detail section. You might also set the value of fGray to False (or True) in the page header's Format event handler (to reset the first row on each page to a known color).

The Phone Book

Many people use Access to maintain their phone books and address lists. The report you'll see in this section creates a phone book–like listing of names and telephone numbers and adds a few twists. It incorporates large group separators, prints in two vertical columns, and puts a "names on this page" indicator at the bottom of the page. Figure 9.16 shows the layout of the first page of rptPhoneBook, in CH09.MDB.

Again, we'll take this in steps:

1. Create a basic list, sorted and grouped on Company Name, with a page number on each page.

FIGURE 9.16

Multicolumn, grouped by phone book

Telephone Listing

A

Alfreds Futterkiste	030-0074321
Ana Trujillo Emparedados y helados	(5) 555-4729
Antonio Moreno Taquería	(5) 555-3932
Around the Horn	(71) 555-7788

B

B's Beverages	(71) 555-1212
Berglunds snabbköp	0921-12 34 65
Blauer See Delikatessen	0621-08460
Blondel père et fils	88.60.15.31
Bólido Comidas preparadas	(91) 555 22 82
Bon app'	91.24.45.40
Bottom-Dollar Markets	(604) 555-4729

C

Cactus Comidas para llevar	(1) 135-5555
Centro comercial Moctezuma	(5) 555-3392
Chop-suey Chinese	0452-076545
Comércio Mineiro	(11) 555-7647
Consolidated Holdings	(71) 555-2282

D

Die Wandernde Kuh	0711-020361
Drachenblut Delikatessen	0241-039123
Du monde entier	40.67.88.88

E

Eastern Connection	(71) 555-0297
Ernst Handel	7675-3425

F

Familia Arquibaldo	(11) 555-9857
FISSA Fabrica Inter. Salchichas S.A.	(91) 555 94 44
Folies gourmandes	20.16.10.16
Folk och fä HB	0695-34 67 21
France restauration	40.32.21.21
Franchi S.p.A.	011-4988260
Frankenversand	089-0877310
Furia Bacalhau e Frutos do Mar	(1) 354-2534

G

Galería del gastrónomo	(93) 203 4560
Godos Cocina Típica	(95) 555 82 82
Gourmet Lanchonetes	(11) 555-9482
Great Lakes Food Market	(503) 555-7555
GROSELLA-Restaurante	(2) 283-2951

H

Hanari Carnes	(21) 555-0091
HILARIÓN-Abastos	(5) 555-1340
Hungry Coyote Import Store	(503) 555-6874
Hungry Owl All-Night Grocers	2967 542

I

Island Trading	(24) 555-8888

K

Königlich Essen	0555-09876

L

La corne d'abondance	30.59.84.10
La maison d'Asie	61.77.61.10
Laughing Bacchus Wine Cellars	(604) 555-3392
Lazy K Kountry Store	(509) 555-7969
Lehmanns Marktstand	069-0245984
Let's Stop N Shop	(415) 555-5938
LILA-Supermercado	(9) 331-6954
LINO-Delicateses	(8) 34-56-12
Lonesome Pine Restaurant	(503) 555-9573

M

Magazzini Alimentari Riuniti	035-640230
Maison Dewey	(02) 201 24 67
Mère Paillarde	(514) 555-8054
Morgenstern Gesundkost	0342-023176

N

North/South	(71) 555-7733

O

Océano Atlántico Ltda.	(1) 135-5333
Old World Delicatessen	(907) 555-7584

Alfreds Futterkiste - Old World Delicatessen

2. Print the list in two columns, with a full-span page header and page footer.

3. Add the "names on this page" indicator with alternating alignment, and hide the page number on the first page.

Step 1: Creating the Basic List

Because reports do their own sorting, based on the choices made in the Sorting and Grouping dialog box, this report is based on a table rather than on a query. (There would be no point in basing this report on a query: if the query sorted the data, the report would then just sort it again!) If you look at the report design (Figure 9.17), you'll notice that the list is grouped on [Company Name] (Prefix Characters:1), which means Access will start a new group every time the first letter of the last name changes. When that happens, it prints out the current value's group footer and the

FIGURE 9.17

Phone book's design surface

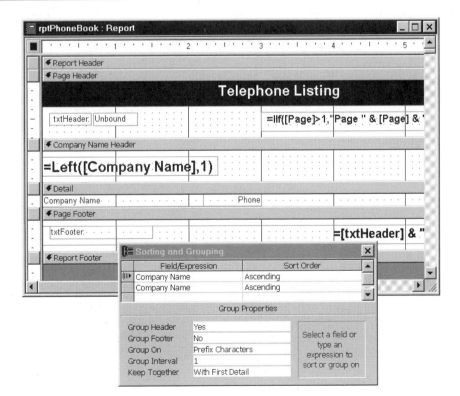

next value's group header. To get Access to sort the companies within the group, you must add [Company Name] to the Sorting and Grouping dialog again.

Each time Access starts a new group, it prints out the Company Name Header section, which consists of a large copy of the first letter of the company name at that moment. (Remember that the group header has access to the data from the first row of its section and the group footer has access to the last row of data in the section.)

Step 2: Printing the Multicolumn Report

Setting up reports to print in multiple columns requires digging around in a dialog box buried in the Page Setup dialog. Choose the Columns tab to find the options that control the number and type of columns you use in your report. Figure 9.18 shows the Page Setup dialog. Table 9.11 shows the items you'll be concerned with when creating a multicolumn report.

FIGURE 9.18

Choose the Columns tab in the Page Setup dialog to control the column settings for your report.

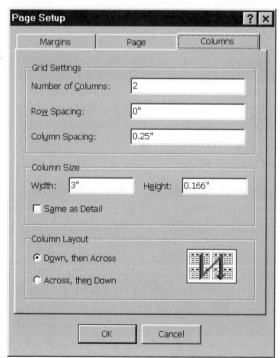

TABLE 9.11   Multicolumn Report Option Settings

Item	Description	Setting for the Phone Book
Items Across	Number of columns	2
Same as Detail	Determines whether each column is the same width as the Detail section in the report design	No (unchecked)
Width	Width of each column	3
Layout Items	Determines whether your columns will go across (Across, then Down) or up and down (Down, then Across)	Down, then Across

Making the changes outlined in the table should transform your report from a one-column list to a phone book–style layout.

One important point: if you want the header and footer to span the entire report (as you do in this case), you must set the report design surface width to the width of the entire report. Then, place controls in the Detail section (and its Header/ Footer sections) only as wide as your columns will be. Finally, make sure the Same as Detail option is unchecked, with the Width option set to the width each column will fill. This way the report's width determines the width of the Report Header and Footer sections, but the Width setting in the Page Setup dialog controls the width of each column.

You might also find it interesting to try setting the Item Layout property to print horizontally rather than vertically. In that case Access prints each row and then moves horizontally to the next print location. When all the columns are full across the page, it moves to the next row. You'll most likely want to try setting the NewRowOrColumn property for the group header to Before & After Section. This places each section header on a new row, by itself, with the data beginning on the following row. Figure 9.19 shows the horizontally arranged phone book.

FIGURE 9.19
Setting the Item Layout property to Horizontal changes the look of the phone book.

Telephone Listing			
A			
Alfreds Futterkiste	030-0074321	Ana Trujillo Emparedados y helados	(5) 555-4729
Antonio Moreno Taquería	(5) 555-3932	Around the Horn	(71) 555-7788
B			
B's Beverages	(71) 555-1212	Berglunds snabbköp	0921-12 34 65
Blauer See Delikatessen	0621-08460	Blondel père et fils	88.60.15.31
Bólido Comidas preparadas	(91) 555 22 82	Bon app'	91.24.45.40
Bottom-Dollar Markets	(604) 555-4729		
C			
Cactus Comidas para llevar	(1) 135-5555	Centro comercial Moctezuma	(5) 555-3392
Chop-suey Chinese	0452-076545	Comércio Mineiro	(11) 555-7647
Consolidated Holdings	(71) 555-2282		
D			
Die Wandernde Kuh	0711-020361	Drachenblut Delikatessen	0241-039123
Du monde entier	40.67.88.88		
E			
Eastern Connection	(71) 555-0297	Ernst Handel	7675-3425
F			
Familia Arquibaldo	(11) 555-9857	FISSA Fabrica Inter. Salchichas S.A.	(91) 555 94 44
Folies gourmandes	20.16.10.16	Folk och fä HB	0695-34 67 21
France restauration	40.32.21.21	Franchi S.p.A.	011-4988260
Frankenversand	089-0877310	Furia Bacalhau e Frutos do Mar	(1) 354-2534
G			
Galería del gastrónomo	(93) 203 4560	Godos Cocina Típica	(95) 555 82 82
Gourmet Lanchonetes	(11) 555-9482	Great Lakes Food Market	(503) 555-7555
GROSELLA-Restaurante	(2) 283-2951		
H			
Hanari Carnes	(21) 555-0091	HILARIÓN-Abastos	(5) 555-1340
Hungry Coyote Import Store	(503) 555-6874	Hungry Owl All-Night Grocers	2967 542
I			
Island Trading	(24) 555-8888		

Alfreds Futterkiste - Island Trading

Step 3: Indicating the Group Names and Hiding the First-Page Page Number

You have two final challenges in creating this report:

- Provide an indication of the group of names that are shown on the current page.

- Hide the page number on the first page. (Okay, Access will do this for you if you choose the Insert ➤ Page Number command, but it's worth understanding the details.)

Gathering Information, but Only in the Footer

To create a text box that displays the range of names on the current page, you need a bit more trickery. By the time Access formats the page footer, it has access to only the current row, which is the last row to be printed on the page. But you need to know the *first* name on the page, also. The trick here is to store away the first name when you can get it—when Access is formatting the page header. The easiest way to use it is to place it in a hidden text box in the report's page header during the page header's Format event. Then, as the control source for a text box on the page footer, you can retrieve the first name on the page from its storage place and concatenate it to the current (final) name. This works fine, except for one small problem: it can work only from the page footer. Because Access formats the page in a linear fashion (from the top section to the bottom), your names will be off by one page, one way or another, if you try this in any other sequence.

Therefore, in the Format event of the report's Page Header section, call the following code. In this example the text box named txtName contains the current row's Company Name field, and txtHeader is the text box in the page header that's used for storage:

```
Me!txtHeader = Me!txtName
```

Then, as the ControlSource for a control in the page footer, use this expression:

```
=[txtHeader] & " - " & [txtName]
```

This concatenates the stored first name and current final name in the control.

Printing the Page Range Anywhere

The Solutions database that ships with Access suggests an alternate method for gathering and printing the page range information, but it's quite complex and works only if you follow their rules exactly. On the other hand, it does allow you to print the information anywhere you like on the page.

The suggested solution requires that you use the Pages property somewhere on the report, which forces Access to make two passes through the report. Once you've done that you can calculate, during the first pass, the nameranges for each page and store them in a data structure in memory. Then, on the second pass, you can retrieve the values in the structure and use them on the report. If you absolutely must place the page range somewhere besides the page footer, this may be the best solution. See SOLUTIONS.MDB (shipped with Microsoft Access) for more information.

Hiding the Page Number

Hiding the page number on the first page requires a single step: set the Control-Source property of the text box such that it prints an empty string on the first page and the page number on all the rest:

```
=IIf([Page] > 1, "Page " & [Page] & " of " & [Pages],"Pages],"")
```

That is, all reports support the Page and Pages properties, and you can use them directly on your reports, as you can from your event procedures. (See the section "Controlling the Starting Page Number" earlier in this chapter.) In this case, if the current page number is larger than 1, display the current page number along with the total number of pages; otherwise, display nothing.

TIP Be aware that if you use the Pages property anywhere on your report, you're forcing Access to run your report twice—once to count the pages and once again to print it. Likewise, if you ask Access to calculate percentages of totals in the body of your report, it will have to make a first pass to calculate the totals and then another to print the report. If you're printing a long report, this extra overhead may be noticeable. If you can avoid using the Pages property for long reports, you may be able to run the reports more quickly.

Avoiding Widows

In 16-bit versions of Access, it was difficult to ensure that groups didn't break across columns, leaving "widows"—headers with no matching detail rows in the same column. Now, it's simple: use the report's GrpKeepTogether property (set to "Per Column") to have your groups' settings take effect over columns. (How you've set your groups' KeepTogether property will be affected either by page breaks—Per Page—or by column breaks, as well—Per Column.) It is confusing that this is a *report* property, not a group property, but because it applies to all groups, it therefore must be a global property.

Companies, Contacts, and Hardware

Sometimes you'll find that one complex report really requires several smaller, linked reports. The report in Figure 9.20 is one such report. It shows a single company site, the listed contacts for that site, and the computer hardware and software the company uses at that site. The data comes from three different tables:

- A list of companies' sites (with SiteID as the primary key)

- A list of names, with each row also containing a SiteID field—a foreign key from the site table

- A list of hardware and software items, one row per item, again with a SiteID field as a foreign key from the site table.

Figure 9.20 shows the required output, created with almost no code at all.

FIGURE 9.20

Subreports make this complex report possible.

Designing the Report

Looking at the report, you see three distinct sections: the site information, the contact information, and the hardware/software list. Because there isn't any way to create those three different sections within the confines of a single report, this situation is a perfect candidate for using subreports. You create this report in three steps, by creating three separate reports and then combining them:

1. Contact Information

2. Hardware/Software List

3. Site Information (the main report)

The main report will contain the site information, and its SiteID will link it with the two subreports. As the report prints, moving from SiteID to SiteID, Access will display only the contacts and hardware/software for the specific SiteID. You should be able to create each of the subreports independently, as long as you plan ahead and include the linking field, SiteID, somewhere on the report surface (and it can be invisible, of course). Although the final report is rather complex, each piece is simple.

The Multicolumn Contact List

After building the phone book list in the previous example, creating the multi-column contact list should be easy. The only differences in this case are that the items are to increment horizontally rather than vertically and that each item is in a vertical clump of data rather than a horizontal one. Figure 9.21 shows the design surface for this report (rptBankInfoSub1 in CH09.MDB).

FIGURE 9.21
Design surface for the
three-column contact list

Pertinent Properties

To get the report just right, set the properties for the Header section as follows:

Property	Value
NewRowOrCol	After Section
ForceNewPage	Before Section (necessary only when the report is not used as a subform)

Set the Sorting and Grouping dialog so that the report is sorted/grouped on Company, then Last, and then First, with the properties on the first grouping as shown here:

Property	Value
GroupHeader	Yes
GroupFooter	No
GroupOn	Each Value
GroupInterval	1

Finally, open the Page Setup dialog and set the properties there, as shown in the following table, so the report will print in three columns:

Property	Value
Number of Columns	3
Same As Detail	No (unchecked)
Column Layout	Across, then Down

As you set these properties, try variations and run the report. The best way to learn what each property does is to experiment with an existing report, changing properties and seeing how the output changes. Use Print Preview, of course, to save a few trees.

Hardware/Software List

The hardware/software report should seem simple compared with the other reports you've been creating. Figure 9.22 shows the design surface for this simple report (rptBankInfoSub2 in CH09.MDB).

FIGURE 9.22

Design surface for the simple list of hardware and software

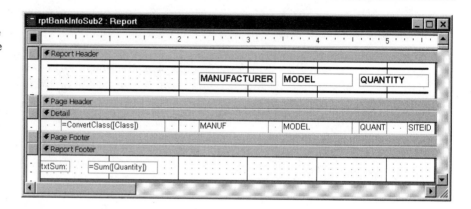

The only interesting feature of this report is its use of a simple function to convert the code representing the class type into an English word for that class. You can call any function to provide the contents of a report control: just assign the function you want placed in the control as the return value from the function. In the property sheet entry for the ControlSource property, enter

```
=ConvertClass([Class])
```

Access calls the ConvertClass function shown in Listing 9.11 and places the return value from the function in the text box. The function itself can reside in either the report's module or a stand-alone module.

Listing 9.11

```
Function ConvertClass(varClass As Variant)
    Select Case varClass
        Case "CPU"
            ConvertClass = "MAINFRAME"
        Case "OPR"
            ConvertClass = "SYSTEM SOFTWARE"
        Case "PRG"
```

```
            ConvertClass = "APPLICATION SOFTWARE"
        Case Else
            ConvertClass = "UNKNOWN"
    End Select
End Function
```

TIP

To avoid the display of consecutive items with the same class name, you can set the HideDuplicates property of the txtClass text box to Yes. In that case Access won't display the class name if it matches the one used in the previous row

TIP

Access 97 adds the IsVisible property for controls on reports, which you can check from a section's Print event. You can use this property to detect whether a particular control has been hidden because you've set the HideDuplicates property to True and, for the current row, the value displayed in your control is in fact a duplicate of the previous row. During the Print event of the section, each hidden control's IsVisible property will be False, indicating that the control has been hidden because it's a duplicate of the value from the previous row. (Don't confuse this property with your controls' Visible property, which you manage yourself, either at design or run time.)

The Main Report

The main report consists of little more than a few fields showing information about the particular site, and the two subreports you just created (rptBankInfo in CH09.MDB). Figure 9.23 shows the design surface for the main report.

The simplest way to create a report with subreports is to make the main report design surface and the database window visible at the same time. Then, drag the subreport from the database window directly onto the report. In this case, you'll want to remove the labels Access attaches to the subreports.

FIGURE 9.23

Design surface for the
main report

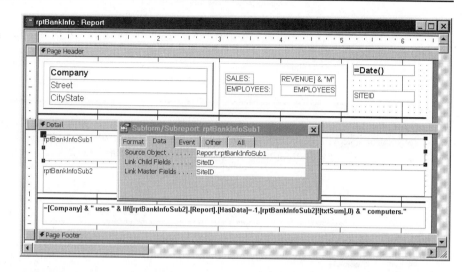

Linking It All Up

Once you've created the main report, the only job left is to link it all up. To do this you set some properties for the newly created subreports. From the main report's point of view (and that's where you are now—on the main report), these subreports are just controls, like any other report control. They have properties just like all other controls. In Figure 9.23 you can see the property sheet for the first subform, showing just the data properties for the subform.

To link the master and child reports, Access uses the LinkMasterFields and LinkChildFields properties in the subreport control. The LinkMasterFields property tells Access the name of the field(s) from the main report that must match the value(s) of the field(s) specified in the LinkChildFields property. In this case, as the report moves from SiteID to SiteID, you want to display just the rows in the two subreports for which the SiteID fields match the current siteID on the main report. It's important to remember that Access needs the actual name of the field, not the name of the control that displays that field, in the LinkChildFields property. Control names are acceptable in the LinkMasterFields property. (For more information on subforms and subreports and how Access links them with their parents, see the section "How and When to Use Subforms" in Chapter 7.)

Other Important Properties

Before leaving this report, you need to concern yourself with a few other properties, as described in the following sections.

The CanGrow Property

In this example there's no way to know ahead of time how much vertical space the two subreports will require. Access provides the CanGrow property so you can decide whether to allow the subreport control to grow as necessary. Sometimes you'll want a fixed-size subreport. Here, though, you set the CanGrow property to Yes so all the information will be visible.

CanShrink Property

Some of the sites might not list any contacts. In that case you'll want the contacts subreport to take up no space at all. To make that happen, you set the CanShrink property for the subreport control to Yes. (For details about when Access restricts the functionality of the CanShrink and CanGrow properties, see the section "Why CanShrink Doesn't and CanGrow Won't" earlier in this chapter.)

TIP

Just as with forms, reports load more quickly if they don't have a class module attached—that is, if they're "lightweight." When you first create a report, Access sets its HasModule property to No because it doesn't have a module attached. If you ever enter any code for the report, however, Access creates a module at that time and sets the HasModule property to Yes. If you later delete the code, Access doesn't delete the module for you. To ensure that your lightweight reports are as lightweight as possible, check the HasModule property yourself. If your report has no code attached, setting this property back to No will visibly improve the load time for the report.

Altering Your Report's Layout Programmatically

In some instances you may need to alter the complete layout of the Report Detail section on a row-by-row basis. Imagine, for example, you're printing a questionnaire and each question can be a yes/no, multiple-choice, write-in, or 1-through-10 type question. Your table containing the questions includes a column that indicates which question type to use on the report. RptQuestions in CH09.MDB is such a report; it makes different controls visible, depending on which question type is currently being printed. Figure 9.24 shows the printed report.

FIGURE 9.24

The printed survey shows different controls, depending on the question type.

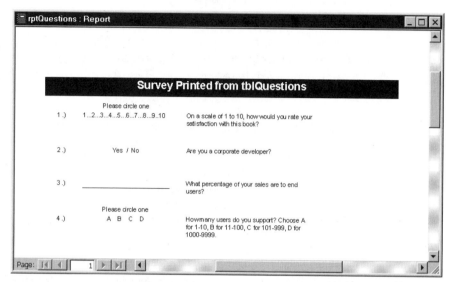

The concept here is simple. The report has several controls that always show up: dsptxtQuestion, dsptxtCount, and dsplblCount. (We're using the "dsp" prefix to indicate that these controls display for each row.) In addition, it contains five controls (four text boxes and a line) that Access displays or hides, depending on the question type. Figure 9.25 shows the design surface, with the controls spread out. Normally, all the user-response controls overlay one another. To make them easier to see, we've spread them out vertically.

FIGURE 9.25

Design surface for the questionnaire

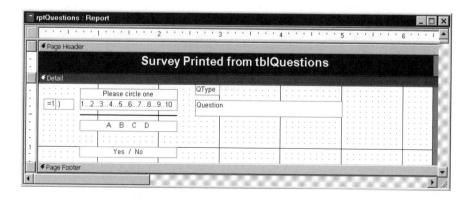

Listing 9.12 contains the code that controls which of the user-response controls are visible in each printed row. Because Access calls this code for each row in the Detail section, it must first hide all the user-response controls and then enable the ones that apply to this particular row. Once it has hidden all the nonessential controls, it shows the controls that are necessary for this particular question type.

Listing 9.12

```
Private Sub Detail0_Format(Cancel As Integer, _
 FormatCount As Integer)
    Const adhcTypeFillIn = 1
    Const adhcType1To10 = 2
    Const adhcTypeABCD = 3
    Const adhcTypeYesNo = 4

    Dim intI As Integer
    Dim ctl As Control

    ' Turn off all the controls in the Detail section,
    ' except the question and its label, which never go away.
    For Each ctl In Me.Detail0.Controls
        If Left(ctl.Name, 3) <> "dsp" Then
            If ctl.Visible Then
                ctl.Visible = False
            End If
        End If
    Next ctl

    Select Case Me!QType
        Case adhcType1To10
            Me!lbl1To10.Visible = True
            Me!lblCircleOne.Visible = True

        Case adhcTypeABCD
            Me!lblABCD.Visible = True
            Me!lblCircleOne.Visible = True

        Case adhcTypeYesNo
            Me!lblYesNo.Visible = True
```

```
        Case adhcTypeFillIn
            Me!linFillIn.Visible = True

        Case Else
            ' Do nothing, right now.
    End Select
End Sub
```

Of course, this isn't the only solution to this problem. If you knew the user-response controls could all be labels, you could just as easily change the Caption property of the labels, based on the question type. In this case, though, because one of the controls is a line, that method isn't workable.

If you expand on the "questionnaire" method, you can create very complex reports that, in Design view, take up just a very small amount of space. This can be particularly useful when you remember that your reports are limited to 22 inches of design space! Rather than iterate through your questions by hand, create a report to create the questionnaire for you.

Summary

In this chapter we've taken a look at reports from several angles. We covered these issues:

- New report properties
- Programmatically controlling sorting and grouping
- Report events and properties
- Section events and properties
- A series of tricky report issues
- A group of sample reports, using events and properties

We've worked through some problematic issues in report design, but we've barely scratched the surface. Once you get deeply into it, you'll find that report design can be even more complex, challenging, and rewarding than forms design. As long as you keep forward motion of the report engine in mind, you can learn to control the flow of events on your reports.

CHAPTER

TEN

Controlling Your Printer

- Retrieving information about your printer

- Creating a list of available output devices

- Changing print destinations programmatically

- Using the Windows printing mechanisms to control printed output

10

Although Access provides a standardized Print Setup dialog box, you'll find it difficult to programmatically control printing options using the standard means. You might be tempted to try using SendKeys to control the print settings, but you'll quickly run into obstacles when you try to control specific printer settings, such as paper size, for which each printer driver provides a list. Even worse, every printer's Options dialog box is different, making the control of that portion completely impossible with SendKeys.

Controlling Print Setup Information

Luckily, Windows provides a standardized mechanism for conversing with the printer driver to retrieve and set information. The Windows API defines two user-defined types, generally referred to as the DEVMODE and DEVNAMES structures by the Windows SDK documentation. Listing 10.1 shows the VBA–type declarations for appropriate user-defined types to contain the information stored in the DEVMODE and DEVNAMES structures, as well as the Access-defined prtMip information, described later in this section. You can find all these declarations in basPrtGlobal, in CH10.MDB.

Access makes all this information available to you so you can retrieve and change very specific printer settings. All reports and forms provide three properties: prtDevMode (associated printer-specific settings), prtDevNames (associated with the specific chosen printer), and prtMip (defined only in Access to support margin settings and page layout information). Later in this chapter we discuss methods for retrieving all the information, setting new values, and replacing the values in the properties. Listing 10.1 shows the user-defined data structures we use throughout this chapter when we refer to each of the different (prtDevMode, prtDevNames, and prtMip) properties.

> **NOTE**
>
> The Access Wizards use structures very similar to those shown in Listing 10.1. We could have used those exact structures throughout the book and not have bothered to create our own. Because you can't distribute the Wizard code with applications you create with the run-time version of Access, however, we wanted to enable you to write code you could distribute. If you use the declarations and examples from this chapter, there's no limitation on distribution.

Listing 10.1

```
Const adhcDeviceNameLen = 32
Const adhcFormNameLen = 32
' This is an arbitrary value. Based on experience,
' it ought to be large enough.
Const adhcExtraSize = 1024


' Structure for prtDevMode
Type adh_tagDevMode
    strDeviceName(1 To adhcDeviceNameLen) As Byte
    intSpecVersion As Integer
    intDriverVersion As Integer
    intSize As Integer
    intDriverExtra As Integer
    lngFields As Long
    intOrientation As Integer
    intPaperSize As Integer
    intPaperLength As Integer
    intPaperWidth As Integer
    intScale As Integer
    intCopies As Integer
    intDefaultSource As Integer
    intPrintQuality As Integer
    intColor As Integer
    intDuplex As Integer
    intYResolution As Integer
    intTTOption As Integer
    intCollate As Integer
    strFormName(1 To adhcFormNameLen) As Byte
    intLogPixels As Integer
    lngBitsPerPixel As Long
    lngPelsWidth As Long
    lngPelsHeight As Long
    lngDisplayFlags As Long
    lngDisplayFrequency As Long
    lngICMMethod As Long
    lngICMIntent As Long
    lngMediaType As Long
    lngDitherType As Long
    lngICCManufacturer As Long
    lngICCModel As Long
    bytDriverExtra(1 To adhcExtraSize) As Byte
```

```
        End Type

        ' Structure for prtDevNames
        Type adh_tagDevNames
            intDriverPos As Integer
            intDevicePos As Integer
            intOutputPos As Integer
            intDefault As Integer
        End Type

        ' Structure for prtMip
        Type adh_tagMarginInfo
            lngLeft As Long
            lngTop As Long
            lngRight As Long
            lngBottom As Long
            lngDataOnly As Long
            lngWidth As Long
            lngHeight As Long
            lngDefaultSize As Long
            lngItemsAcross As Long
            lngColumnSpacing As Long
            lngRowSpacing As Long
            lngItemLayout As Long
            lngFastPrinting As Long
            lngDataSheet As Long
        End Type
```

NOTE The main job of a visual development tool such as Access is to shield you from the details of the operating system. In a perfect world, it would be impossible to do anything from VBA that could cause you to halt Access or Windows or that could cause any sort of data loss. In general, that's true. Access usually buries most of the workings of Windows under a thick layer of protective wrapping. The properties we're discussing here, however, are extremely "raw." That is, there's almost no protective layer between you and the operating system when you're modifying Access' prtDevMode or prtDevNames property. If you set the values incorrectly or place an inappropriate value into one of the properties, you're likely to cause Access to crash. The routines we've provided here make the use of these properties as painless as possible, but be aware that there's not much of a net underneath you when you're working this close to the surface.

Introducing the prtDevMode Property

The prtDevMode property of a form or report contains information about the printing device you've selected for printing the object. It contains, among other things, the name of the device, information about the driver, the number of copies to print, the orientation of the printout, the paper tray to use when printing, and the print quality to use. All this information corresponds directly with Windows' DEVMODE structure, used by every single Windows program that ever intends to do any printing.

Although Access makes all this information available to you so you can retrieve and set print properties for reports and forms, it doesn't make it easy. The prtDevMode property is nothing more than a text string with all the information from the DEVMODE structure strung together. It's up to your code to pick apart the text string, make changes as necessary, and reassign the property. And unlike almost every other property in Access, the prtDevMode property is only read/write when the report or form is in Design view. You won't be able to make changes to the prtDevMode property while running the report—which makes sense, because you really can't be changing such things as the printer name or margins while printing the report. Table 10.1 lists each field in the DEVMODE structure, its datatype, and a short description. Some of the fields contain enumerated data, and the choices for those items are listed in Tables 10.2 through 10.6.

TABLE 10.1   prtDevMode Fields and Their Contents

Setting	Datatype	Description
Device Name*	32-byte string	Name of the device supported by the driver: "HP LaserJet 4", for example
Specification Version*	Integer	Version number of the DEVMODE structure in the Windows SDK
Driver Version*	Integer	Driver version number assigned by the driver developer
Size*	Integer	Size, in bytes, of the DEVMODE structure
Driver Extra*	Integer	Size, in bytes, of the optional driver-specific data, which can follow this structure
Fields	Long	Specifies a set of flags that indicate which of the members of the DEVMODE structure have been initialized. It can be 0 or more of the values in Table 10.2, added together

*Read-only for any specific printer.

TABLE 10.1 prtDevMode Fields and Their Contents (continued)

Setting	Datatype	Description
Orientation	Integer	Paper orientation. It can be either 1 (Portrait) or 2 (Landscape)
Paper Size	Integer	Size of the paper on which to print. The value can be chosen from Table 10.3. If you choose 256 (User-Defined Size), specify the length and width of the paper in the Paper Length and Paper Width members
Paper Length	Integer	Paper length in tenths of a millimeter. Overrides the setting in the Paper Size member
Paper Width	Integer	Paper width in tenths of a millimeter. Overrides the setting in the Paper Size member
Scale	Integer	Factor by which the printed output is to be scaled. The apparent page size is scaled from the physical page size by a factor of Scale/100. Has an effect only if your printer supports scaling
Copies	Integer	Number of copies printed if the printing device supports multiple-page copies
Default Source	Integer	Default bin from which paper is fed. See Table 10.4 for a list of possible values
Print Quality	Integer	Printer resolution. See Table 10.5 for a list of device-independent values. If you specify a positive value, it's treated as the x-resolution, in dots per inch (DPI), and is not device independent. In this case the Y-Resolution field must contain the y-resolution in DPI
Color	Integer	Specifies Color (1) or Monochrome (2) printing if the device supports color printing
Duplex	Integer	Specifies Simplex (1), Horizontal (2), or Vertical (3) print mode for printers that support duplex printing
Y-Resolution	Integer	Specifies the y-resolution for the printer, in dots per inch (DPI). If this value is specified, you must also specify the x-resolution in the Print Quality member. These values are device specific
True Type Option	Integer	Specifies how TrueType fonts should be printed (See Table 10.6 for a list of possible values.)

*Read-only for any specific printer.

TABLE 10.2 Initialized Field Flags for prtDevMode

Constant	Value
adhcDMOrientation	&H0000001
adhcDMPaperSize	&H0000002
adhcDMPaperLength	&H0000004
adhcDMPaperWidth	&H0000008
adhcDMScale	&H0000010
adhcDMCopies	&H0000100
adhcDMDefaultSource	&H0000200
adhcDMPrintQuality	&H0000400
adhcDMColor	&H0000800
adhcDMDuplex	&H0001000
adhcDMYResolution	&H0002000
adhcDMTTOption	&H0004000

TABLE 10.3 Available prtDevMode Paper Sizes

Value	Paper Size
1	Letter (8.5 × 11 in.)
2	Letter Small (8.5 × 11 in.)
3	Tabloid (11 × 17 in.)
4	Ledger (17 × 11 in.)
5	Legal (8.5 × 14 in.)
6	Statement (5.5 × 8.5 in.)
7	Executive (7.25 × 10.5 in.)
8	A3 (297 × 420 mm)
9	A4 (210 × 297 mm)

TABLE 10.3   Available prtDevMode Paper Sizes (continued)

Value	Paper Size
10	A4 Small (210 × 297 mm)
11	A5 (148 × 210 mm)
12	B4 (250 × 354)
13	B5 (182 × 257 mm)
14	Folio (8.5 × 13 in.)
15	Quarto (215 × 275 mm)
16	11 × 17 in.
18	Note (8.5 × 11 in.)
19	Envelope #9 (3.875 × 8.875 in.)
20	Envelope #10 (4.125 × 9.5 in.)
21	Envelope #11 (4.5 × 10.375 in.)
22	Envelope #12 (4.25 × 11 in.)
23	Envelope #14 (5 × 11.5 in.)
24	C size sheet
25	D size sheet
26	E size sheet
27	Envelope DL (110 × 220 mm)
28	Envelope C5 (162 × 229 mm)
29	Envelope C3 (324 × 458 mm)
30	Envelope C4 (229 × 324 mm)
31	Envelope C6 (114 × 162 mm)
32	Envelope C65 (114 × 229 mm)
33	Envelope B4 (250 × 353 mm)
34	Envelope B5 (176 × 250 mm)

TABLE 10.3   Available prtDevMode Paper Sizes (continued)

Value	Paper Size
35	Envelope B6 (176 × 125 mm)
36	Envelope (110 × 230 mm)
37	Envelope Monarch (3.875 × 7.5 in.)
38	6-3/4 Envelope (3.625 × 6.5 in.)
39	US Std Fanfold (14.875 × 11 in.)
40	German Std Fanfold (8.5 × 12 in.)
41	German Legal Fanfold (8.5 × 13 in.)
256	User-defined

TABLE 10.4   Available Paper Source Values for prtDevMode

Value	Paper Source
1	Upper or only one bin
2	Lower bin
3	Middle bin
4	Manual bin
5	Envelope bin
6	Envelope manual bin
7	Automatic bin
8	Tractor bin
9	Small-format bin
10	Large-format bin
11	Large-capacity bin
14	Cassette bin
256	Device-specific bins start here

TABLE 10.5 Available Print Quality Values for prtDevMode

Value	Print Quality
−4	High
−3	Medium
−2	Low
−1	Draft

TABLE 10.6 Available True Type Options for prtDevMode

Value	True Type Option
1	Print TrueType fonts as graphics. This is the default for dot-matrix printers
2	Download TrueType fonts as soft fonts. This is the default for Hewlett-Packard printers that use Printer Control Language (PCL)
3	Substitute device fonts for TrueType fonts. This is the default for PostScript printers

We'll show how to retrieve and modify the prtDevMode property in the next section. For now, here are some ideas to keep in mind as you peruse the tables that describe the DEVMODE information:

- Not all forms or reports will necessarily have a non-empty prtDevMode property. Any code you write should be able to handle this situation.

- Before providing your user with a list of choices (paper sizes, TrueType options, and so on), check the capabilities of the current device and limit your choices to options the device supports. Although Access does not provide this capability, you can use the Windows API to retrieve the information. We cover this functionality (calling the DeviceCapabilities API function) in the section "Retrieving Printer Capabilities" later in this chapter.

- Many printer drivers store additional information immediately following the DEVMODE structure. Therefore, when retrieving and setting the prtDevMode property, be aware that most often it will require more than the documented size. Plan on 512 bytes or more, and check the intDriverSize and intExtraSize fields when manipulating the values. (The code in our examples does all this for you.)

Retrieving the prtDevMode Information

Actually retrieving the prtDevMode information is, of course, trivial. Since prt-DevMode is a property of forms and reports, you can retrieve the information by simply copying it from the object into a string variable. Once it's there, though, you must somehow get it into a structure with the appropriate fields set up for you. The portion of the adh_tagDevMode structure shown here demonstrates how the raw property overlays the user-defined structure:

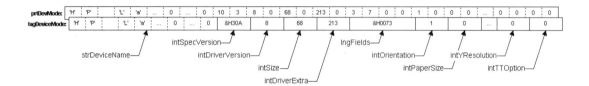

However, you also need a method for getting the string you've read directly from the object's property into the structure. The answer is VBA's LSet statement.

LSet allows you to copy bytes of data from one variable to another, even if they are of different datatypes. Normally, Access allows you to copy information between two variables of the same datatype. In this case you need to copy data from a string datatype to a variable of type adh_tagDevMode. The value returned by the prtDevMode property is laid out perfectly, so performing a byte-by-byte copy into the adh_tagDevMode structure fills in all the fields correctly. The previous graphic shows this "overlay" in progress. In the graphic, the top row represents the prtDevMode string, and the bottom row represents the variable of type adh_tagDevMode into which you've copied that data. The LSet command makes it easy to perform this operation, although there are a few issues you need to understand first, as described in the following sections.

Using LSet to Copy Unformatted Data

The LSet command has two variations. In the first variant, LSet allows you to left-align text within a string variable type, padding the extra room with spaces. In the second variant, LSet overlays the data stored in one user-defined type into a variable of a different user-defined type. This is the functionality you'll need. Note, however, the use of the term *user-defined*. Both variables must be of a user-defined type. Because your goal here is to move data from a string variable (the data retrieved directly from the object's prtDevMode property) into a user-defined variable, you must first take one intermediate step: place the data into a user-defined type that is nothing more than a fixed-length string:

```
' This is the number of bytes in the fixed portion of
' the DEVMODE structure. We've just broken the
' two sizes apart in case the fixed portion of
' the structure changes.
Const adhcDevModeSize = 148
Const adhcDevModeMaxSize = adhcDevModeSize + adhcExtraSize

' Temp structure for prtDevMode info.
Type adh_tagDevModeStr
    strDevMode As String * adhcDevModeMaxSize
End Type
```

Given a type declaration for such a datatype, you could retrieve the prtDevMode property and assign it to a variable of type adh_tagDevMode, as in the following code fragment:

```
Dim DM as adh_tagDevMode
Dim DMStr as adh_tagDevModeStr

DMStr.strDevMode = Reports!Report1.prtDevMode
LSet DM = DMStr
```

That code overlays the value retrieved from the prtDevMode property of Report1 into the adh_tagDevMode variable, DM. You should now be able to access any member of DM, just as you would with any other user-defined type. For example,

```
Debug.Print ANSIToUni(DM.strDeviceName)
```

should print the name of the printer assigned to print this particular report. (See the sidebar in this section for information on converting from ANSI to Unicode.)

ANSI versus Unicode

The 32-bit versions of Windows (Windows 95 and Windows NT) support two separate character sets: ANSI, in which each character takes 1 byte of storage and there are only 256 different possible characters; and Unicode, in which each character takes up 2 bytes of storage and there are 65,536 different possible characters. VBA, Access' programming language, supports Unicode only. In general, this works in your favor, allowing support for many languages, including those that use character sets different from the English ones.

There's one area of Access in which the Unicode support causes trouble: the prtDevMode and prtDevNames properties return the character strings in their values in ANSI format. This means that if you attempt to view the pieces of those properties directly, you'll just see garbled characters because Access is attempting to convert them to Unicode as it displays them.

This is why you'll find the ANSIToUni() and UniToANSI() functions in bas-Strings, in CH10.MDB. These functions handle each byte in the ANSI strings and convert back and forth between ANSI and Unicode, calling the built-in StrConv function. You shouldn't need these routines anywhere in Access aside from working with prtDevMode and prtDevNames, but it's important that you understand their purpose, should you ever want to write your own functions to handle these properties.

Using LSet to Replace the Data

Once you've made the necessary changes to the data in the adh_tagDevMode structure, you'll want to replace the value of the prtDevMode property. To do so, use the LSet command again:

```
Dim dm as adh_tagDevMode
Dim dmStr as adh_tagDevModeStr

dmStr.strDevMode = Reports!Report1.prtDevMode
LSet dm = dmStr
'
' Do work here, manipulating dm.
```

```
'
LSet dmStr = dm
Reports!Report1.prtDevMode = dmStr.strDevMode
```

A Simple Example Using prtDevMode

Anytime you want to manipulate the values in the prtDevMode property, follow these steps:

1. Declare variables of type adh_tagDevMode and adh_tagDevModeStr.

2. Copy the prtDevMode property from the report or form into the strDevMode member of the adh_tagDevModeStr variable.

3. Use LSet to copy the bytes into the adh_tagDevMode variable.

4. Make whatever changes you wish. You must inform Windows of the changes you've made, using the Or operator to set the appropriate bits in the lngFields member of the DEVMODE structure. (See the examples in the next few sections for more information.)

5. Use LSet to copy the bytes back into the adh_tagDevModeStr variable.

6. Replace the value of the prtDevMode property for the form or report from the adh_tagDevModeStr variable. Note the use in our examples of the MidB function, which treats the string as a series of single bytes (ANSI) instead of 2-byte Unicode values.

For example, Listing 10.2 demonstrates changing the number of copies of a given report to be printed. (Look in basSetCopies in CH10.MDB for SetCopies and SetCopies2, presented in the next section of this chapter.)

Listing 10.2

```
Function SetCopies(obj As Object, intCopies As Integer)

    ' This simple function would require
    ' error checking for real use. In addition,
    ' it requires that the report in question be
    ' already open in Design view (you can't set the
    ' prtDevMode property except in Design view).
    ' For example:
    ' retval = SetCopies(Reports!rptCompany, 3)
```

```
' 1. Declare variables of type adh_tagDevMode and
'       adh_tagDevModeStr.
Dim DM As adh_tagDevMode
Dim DMStr As adh_tagDevModeStr
Dim dr As adh_tagDeviceRec

' Some objects may have an empty prtDevMode property
' (if you've never touched their printer settings).
' In that case, use the default printer's
' DEVMODE structure instead.

If Len(obj.prtDevMode & "") = 0 Then
    If adhGetCurrentDevice(dr, ",") Then
        DMStr.strDevMode = adhGetDefaultDM(dr)
    End If
Else

    ' 2. Copy the prtDevMode property from the
    '       report or form into the
    '       adh_tagDevModeStr variable.
    DMStr.strDevMode = obj.prtDevMode
End If

' 3. Use LSet to copy the bytes into the
'       adh_tagDevMode variable.
LSet DM = DMStr

' 4. Make whatever changes you like, and set
'       the lngFields entry accordingly.
DM.intCopies = intCopies
DM.lngFields = DM.lngFields Or adhcDMCopies

' 5. Use LSet to copy the bytes back into the
'       adh_tagDevModeStr variable.
LSet DMStr = DM

' 6. Replace the value of the prtDevMode
'       property for the form or report from the
'       adh_tagDevModeStr variable.
obj.prtDevMode = MidB(DMStr.strDevMode, 1)
End Function
```

And a Bit Simpler

To make it a bit easier for you to retrieve and set values in the prtDevMode property, we've provided functions in basDevMode (in CH10.MDB): adhRetrieveDevMode and adhSetDevMode. Each takes two parameters:

- A reference to the form or report to use
- A variable of type adh_tagDevMode (adhRetrieveDevMode will fill this in from the object's prtDevMode property, and adhSetDevMode will place its value into the object's prtDevMode property.)

Each function returns either True or False, indicating the success of the operation.

Using these functions you could rewrite SetCopies as follows:

```
Function SetCopies2(obj As Object, intCopies As Integer)

    ' For example:
    ' retval = SetCopies2(Reports!rptCompany, 3)
    Dim DM As adh_tagDevMode

    ' Assume failure.
    SetCopies2 = False
    If adhRetrieveDevMode(obj, DM) Then
        DM.intCopies = intCopies
        DM.lngFields = DM.lngFields Or adhcDMCopies
        SetCopies2 = adhSetDevMode(obj, DM)
    End If
End Function
```

An Important Reminder

Remember, all the properties mentioned in this section (prtDevMode, prtDevNames, and prtMip) are available only in *Design view*. You must make sure your report or form is open in Design view before attempting to set any of these properties. (You can *retrieve* the properties, of course, no matter what the mode.)

Changing Paper Size

Contrary to the information presented above, many printers do not allow you to specify a user-defined page size. In addition, some printers use a page size of 0 to indicate a user-defined size, and some use 256. You need to retrieve information about the specific printer (see the section "Retrieving Printer Capabilities" later in this chapter for information on this) before trying to set a specific nonstandard page size.

If you find that you can change the size, you must change a number of fields in the prtDevMode string. You not only need to inform the printer that you're setting a user-defined size, you need to send the coordinates. The code listed here changes the paper size to 1000×1000 units (10 cm $\times$ 10 cm):

```
DM.intPaperSize = 256
DM.intPaperLength = 1000
DM.intPaperWidth = 1000
DM.lngFields = DM.lngFields Or adhcDMPaperSize Or _
  adhcDMPaperLength Or adhcDMPaperWidth
```

You must set the lngFields value so that the driver knows you've changed the paper size values.

Using the prtDevMode Property in Your Applications

If you want to use any of the procedures discussed in the preceding sections in your own applications, you should import basPrtGlobal, basDevMode, basPrt-Dest, and basStrings from CH10.MDB. Once you have those modules in your application, you should be able to call the functions you need in order to manipulate the prtDevMode property effectively.

Controlling Print Layout Information

Access makes the print layout information for a given report or form available to you through the object's prtMip property. This information includes margin settings, number of columns, spacing between columns, and the layout (horizontal or vertical) of those columns. Just as with the prtDevMode property, Access provides this information as a single string value, which you must pick apart yourself. Table 10.7 shows the elements of this property and their possible values. Listing 10.1, presented earlier in this chapter, shows an Access user-defined type you can use to extract and set information in the prtMip property.

TABLE 10.7 prtMip Fields and Their Contents

Setting	adh_tagMarginInfo Field	Description	Possible Values
Left	lngLeft	Left margin, in twips ($1/1440$ inch)	Limited logically by the paper dimensions
Top	lngTop	Top margin, in twips	Limited logically by the paper dimensions
Right	lngRight	Right margin, in twips	Limited logically by the paper dimensions
Bottom	lngBottom	Bottom margin, in twips	Limited logically by the paper dimensions
Data Only	lngDataOnly	Print only the data, without gridlines, borders, or graphics	True (−1) or False (0)
Item Size Width	lngWidth	Width, in twips, for each column	Limited logically by the paper dimensions
Item Size Height	lngHeight	Height, in twips, for each column	Limited logically by the paper dimensions
Default Size	lngDefaultSize	Specifies whether each column should be the same size as the Detail section or use the Width and Height settings	1, use the width of the Detail section; 0, use the Width and Height settings
Items Across	lngItemsAcross	Number of columns across for multicolumn reports or forms	Limited logically by the paper dimensions
Column Spacing	lngColumnSpacing	Space between detail columns, in twips	Limited logically by the paper dimensions
Row Spacing	lngRowSpacing	Space between detail rows, in twips	Limited logically by the paper dimensions
Item Layout	lngItemLayout	Specifies vertical or horizontal layout	1953 for Horizontal, 1954 for Vertical
Fast Printing	lngFastPrinting	Undocumented, and perhaps unused in this version?	
Print Headings	lngDataSheet	Print page headings for datasheets?	True, False

Just as with the prtDevMode property, the steps you use when modifying one or more prtMip options are as follows:

1. Declare variables of type adh_tagMarginInfo and adh_tagMarginInfoStr.

2. Copy the prtMip property from the report or form into the adh_tagMargin-InfoStr variable.

3. Use LSet to copy the bytes into the adh_tagMarginInfo variable.

4. Make whatever changes you like.

5. Use LSet to copy the bytes back into the adh_tagMarginInfoStr variable.

6. Replace the value of the prtMip property for the form or report from the adh_tagMarginInfoStr variable.

For example, Listing 10.3 demonstrates changing the number of columns and the column width for a given report. (Look in basSetColumns in CH10.MDB for Set-Columns and SetColumns2, presented in the next section.)

Listing 10.3

```
Sub SetColumns(rpt As Report, intCols As Integer, _
sglWidth As Single)
    ' Set the number of columns for a specified
    ' report. Pass in a reference to the report, the
    ' number of columns to print, and the width of
    ' each, in inches.
    ' For example,
    ' SetColumns Reports!rptPhoneBook, 3, 2.25

    ' To keep this example simple, all error checking
    ' has been removed.

    ' 1. Declare variables of type adh_tagMarginInfo
    '      and adh_tagMarginInfoStr.
    Dim MIP As adh_tagMarginInfo
    Dim mipTemp As adh_tagMarginInfoStr

    ' 2. Copy the prtMip property from the report or
    '      form into the adh_tagMarginInfoStr variable.
    mipTemp.strMIP = rpt.prtMip

    ' 3. Use LSet to copy the bytes into the
```

```
'      adh_tagMarginInfo variable.
LSet MIP = mipTemp

' 4. Make whatever changes you like.
MIP.lngItemsAcross = intCols
' Convert inches to twips.
MIP.lngWidth = adhcTwipsPerInch * sglWidth
' Tell the report not to use the detail section
' width.
MIP.lngDefaultSize = False

' 5. Use LSet to copy the bytes back into the
'      adh_tagMarginInfoStr variable.
LSet mipTemp = MIP

' 6. Replace the value of the prtMip property for
'      the form or report from the
'      adh_tagMarginInfoStr variable.
rpt.prtMip = mipTemp.strMIP
End Sub
```

Making It a Bit Simpler

To simplify your interactions with the prtMip property, we've supplied the adhRetrieveMIP and adhSetMIP functions, in basPrtMip (CH10.MDB). These two functions operate exactly like the adhRetrieveDevMode and adhSetDevMode functions described earlier in this chapter. You pass in an object reference and an appropriate structure to fill in—in this case, an adh_tagMarginInfo structure. Using the two functions adhRetrieveMIP and adhSetMIP, you could rewrite the SetColumns procedure like this:

```
Sub SetColumns2(rpt As Report, intCols As Integer, _
 sglWidth As Single)
    ' For example,
    ' SetColumns2 Reports!rptPhoneBook, 3, 2.25
    Dim MIP As adh_tagMarginInfo

    If adhRetrieveMIP(rpt, MIP) Then
        MIP.lngItemsAcross = intCols
        MIP.lngWidth = adhcTwipsPerInch * sglWidth
        MIP.lngDefaultSize = 0
        adhSetMip rpt, MIP
    End If
End Sub
```

Using these functions relieves you of dealing with LSet or the intermediate adh_tagMarginInfoStr structure.

Using prtMip in Your Own Applications

To retrieve or modify settings in an object's prtMip property, you need to import the basPrtMip and basPrtGlobal modules from CH10.MDB. Once you have that code in your application, you should be able to use the functions there to manipulate all the margin settings you need.

Introducing the prtDevNames Property

Both reports and forms support a property that contains information about the current output device associated with that form or report. That is, if you use the Print Setup menu option to select a specific printer for a form or report, that information is stored with the object. When you print the form or report, Access attempts to send the printout to the specified device, based on what it finds in the prtDevNames property of the object. To momentarily change the output device (to send the report to the fax instead of to the printer, for example), you need to retrieve the prtDevNames property, set it to the fax device, print the document, and then set it back.

The prtDevNames property stores three pieces of information about the specific output device in a manner that's convenient for programmers working in C or C++ (the standard Windows programming languages) but not as convenient for Access programmers. The property itself is just an exact copy of the DEVNAMES structure that's used as part of the Windows SDK. The DEVNAMES structure contains the device name, the driver, and the output port in a variable-length string, with each piece of information followed by a null character (CHR$(0)). In addition, the property starts out with a group of four integers. Each of the first three integers contains the offset of one of the three strings that follow, and the fourth contains a 0 or a 1, depending on whether the current device is the Windows default output device. Table 10.8 lists the members of the DEVNAMES structure, stored in the prtDevNames property. The order of the three strings in the structure is not important, as long as the offsets are consistent with that ordering. In the examples, you'll find the device name, then the driver name, and finally the output port. You'll discover that the three pieces of information the prtDevNames structures need are the same three pieces of information we'll gather from WIN.INI (or the System Registry) in the section "Controlling Your Destination" later in this chapter. Therefore, it should be simple to build up a new prtDevNames property based on the user's choice from the list of possible output devices. Here is an example prtDevNames string, using the Generic/Text Only driver:

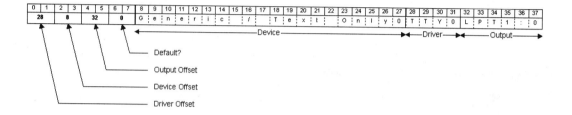

TABLE 10.8   prtDevNames Fields and Their Contents

Member	Description
Driver Offset	Offset from the beginning of the structure to a null-terminated string that specifies the file name (without the extension) of the device driver
Device Offset	Offset from the beginning of the structure to a null-terminated string that specifies the name of the device
Output Offset	Offset from the beginning of the structure to a null-terminated string that specifies the MS-DOS device name for the physical output port
Default	Specifies whether the strings in this structure identify the default Windows printer (1 if True, 0 if False)
Device Name	Specified device name. It cannot be longer than 32 characters (including the trailing null) and must match one of the items from WIN.INI in the [devices] section
Driver Name	Specified driver name. It cannot be longer than 9 characters (including the trailing null)
Output Name	Specified output port. It cannot be longer than 9 characters (including the trailing null)—for example, "LPT1:"

Using the prtDevNames Property

To use the prtDevNames property, you must be able to perform two basic manipulations: build up the string and break it apart. The module basDevNames in CH10.MDB contains two functions that perform these tasks. The function adhBuildDevNames takes as a parameter a structure of type adh_tagDeviceRec (containing the device name, the driver name, and the output location) and builds up an appropriate string. This function just takes the three strings, concatenates them with a null character inserted between them and at the end, and calculates the offsets for each.

To store away the offsets, you'll find it easiest to store them as integers in a user-defined type with four elements:

```
Type adh_tagDevNames
    intDriverPos As Integer
    intDevicePos As Integer
    intOutputPos As Integer
    intDefault As Integer
End Type
```

Once you've filled in all the values, you can use the LSet command to copy the structure, byte by byte, into a string-type variable. Once you have the four integers in the string variable, you can concatenate the list of three strings onto the end of the string variable. Just as before, you must create a simple user-defined type, consisting of just the string you want, into which you can LSet the values in the adh_tagDevNames structure. That is, given the user-defined type

```
Type adh_tagDevOffsets
    strDevInfo As String * 4
End Type
```

you can use the LSet command to copy the 8 bytes of information into that string. (Each character in a string is 2 bytes, so the structure has room for all 8 bytes.) The code might look like this:

```
Dim devNames As adh_tagDevNames
Dim devStr As adh_tagDevOffsets

.
. ' Fill the values in devNames here
.

LSet devStr = devNames
```

Listing 10.4 contains the adhBuildDevNames function, which creates the prt-
DevNames string, given the three pieces of information it needs.

Listing 10.4

```
Function adhBuildDevNames(dr As adh_tagDeviceRec) As Variant

    ' Given the printer's device name, driver name,
    ' and port, create an appropriate prtDevNames
    ' structure.

    Dim DN As adh_tagDevNames
    Dim devStr As adh_tagDevOffsets
    Dim varTemp As Variant

    ' Check for maximum length for the device name
    ' (leaving room for the null terminator)
    If Len(dr.strDeviceName) > adhcMaxDevice - 1 Then
        MsgBox "Invalid Device Name!", vbCritical, _
         "adhBuildDevNames()"
        Exit Function
    End If

    ' The first offset is always offset 8
    DN.intDriverPos = adhcDevNamesFixed
    DN.intDevicePos = DN.intDriverPos + _
     Len(dr.strDriverName) + 1
    DN.intOutputPos = DN.intDevicePos + _
     Len(dr.strDeviceName) + 1

    ' Because you're forcing a new printer setting, tell
    ' Windows that it's not the default printer.
    DN.intDefault = 0

    ' Both sides of the LSet need to be user-defined types,
    ' so use devStr (of type adh_tagDevOffsets) instead of
    ' just a plain ol' string.
    LSet devStr = DN

    ' Copy array to a variant, so it's easy to
    ' concatenate into output string.
    varTemp = devStr.strDevInfo
```

```
    ' The prtDevNames property is ANSI, so we've got
    ' to now convert these three strings BACK from
    ' Unicode to ANSI.
    adhBuildDevNames = varTemp & _
     UniToAnsi(dr.strDriverName) & ChrB$(0) & _
     UniToAnsi(dr.strDeviceName) & ChrB$(0) & _
     UniToAnsi(dr.strPort) & ChrB$(0)
End Function
```

Pulling apart the pieces of the prtDevNames property is easier. The function adh-ParseDevNames (in basDevNames in CH10.MDB) takes in a prtDevNames string and fills in the appropriate pieces of the adh_tagDeviceRec structure. In addition, the function returns True if the selected device is the default Windows output device and False otherwise. Once the function has used LSet to copy the four integer values into the adh_tagDevNames structure, it can use the offsets in the structure to pull apart the pieces. Note that the function uses the adhTrimNull function to get rid of everything past the first null character in the string that's past the beginning of the output port string. Listing 10.5 shows the entire adhParseDevNames function.

> **NOTE**
>
> Access is not neat about the value returned in the prtDevNames property. You will often find trailing "junk" after the information you're interested in. Since you can't count on its length, you must be careful to copy out only the parts that are of interest to you. When you're retrieving the property from a form or a report, be sure to throw away all but the first 58 characters of the string. (That gives you room for 8 bytes of offsets, 32 bytes for the device, and 9 bytes each for the port and the driver name.) Note the use of the ANSIToUni function, since the prtDevNames property stores its strings internally in ANSI format, just like the prtDev-Mode property.

Listing 10.5

```
Function adhParseDevNames(ByVal varDevNames As Variant, _
 dr As adh_tagDeviceRec) As Boolean

    Dim DN As adh_tagDevNames
    Dim temp As adh_tagDevOffsets

    ' To use LSet, both sides must be user-defined types.
```

```
' Therefore, copy the string into a temporary
    ' structure, so you can LSet it into dn.
    temp.strDevInfo = LeftB(varDevNames, adhcDevNamesFixed)
    LSet DN = temp

    dr.strDriverName = adhTrimNull(ANSIToUni( _
     MidB(varDevNames, DN.intDriverPos + 1)))
    dr.strDeviceName = adhTrimNull(ANSIToUni( _
     MidB(varDevNames, DN.intDevicePos + 1)))
    dr.strPort = adhTrimNull(ANSIToUni( _
     MidB(varDevNames, DN.intOutputPos + 1)))
    adhParseDevNames = CBool(DN.intDefault)
End Function
```

Controlling Your Destination

Windows allows you to print a document to any of the installed printer devices just by changing the current printer selection, using the Print Setup dialog. You can install a fax printer driver that will intercept your printing and send your document out the fax modem, for example, or just have multiple printer choices installed for various printing jobs.

Almost every Windows application uses the standard Print Setup dialog provided with Windows. This works fine in an interactive environment. Under program control, however, you must find some other way to specify a list of possible devices and provide a method for the user to choose a new output destination. Then, once you've changed the document's destination and told your application to send the document to that device, you need to set things back the way they were.

CH10.MDB contains a form demonstrating the use of the prtDevNames (and prtDevMode) property, allowing you to choose a form or report from your database and print it to any of the installed print devices. The form, zfrmPrintDest, displays a list of all the forms and reports and a list of the installed printer devices (see Figure 10.1 later in the chapter). Once you select an object and an output device, you can print either to the original device or to the chosen device. The code in zfrmPrintDest accomplishes this goal by changing the value of the prtDevNames property for the chosen object, and it changes it back once it's been printed.

WARNING It is imperative that you set the prtDevMode property at the same time you set the prtDevNames property if you are changing the output destination. Changing just the prtDevNames property will cause Access to crash unless you happen to be very lucky. In the examples that follow, you'll see that before you change the prtDevNames property, you should request the default DevMode structure from the printer driver, perhaps copy over the current user settings, and set the object's prtDevMode property before changing the prtDevNames property. Failure to follow these steps will, sooner or later, cause Access to crash.

The problem of providing your users with a means of selecting a specific output device and sending the current document to that device has two parts. First of all, you must be able to build a list of all the installed output devices. Then, once your user has chosen a device from the provided list, you must be able to use the prtDevNames property to control the destination of the particular document. Neither of these steps is terribly difficult, once you know the tricks.

Providing a List of Output Devices

Windows maintains a list of all the installed output devices in WIN.INI, under the "[devices]" heading. For example, the [devices] section in your WIN.INI might look like this:

```
[devices]
Microsoft Fax=WPSUNI,FAX:
Rendering Subsystem=WPSUNI,PUB:
HP LaserJet 4=HPPCL5MS,\\GATEWAY\HPLJ4
HP LaserJet III=HPPCL5MS,LPT1:
```

Each line represents one device, and the syntax of each line can be represented as

Device Name=Driver, Output

To provide your users with a list of devices, you need to read all the items from WIN.INI and create an array of these items in Access. Luckily, Windows provides

NOTE

Although Windows 95 and Windows NT store all the printer output information in the system registry, all the Microsoft Office 97 products still rely on WIN.INI for information about the current printer, since this is the method recommended in the 32-bit Windows SDK. Although the Win32 API provides methods for enumerating the list of installed printers, with more flexibility than the method we're using, this method is much simpler. In addition, under Windows NT, the information is actually stored in the system registry: Calls to GetProfileString retrieve the data they need from the registry, not from WIN.INI.

a mechanism for reading one (GetProfileString) or all (GetProfileSection) of the items within a section at once. In general, the syntax for GetProfileString is this:

GetProfileString(*strSection, strEntry, strDefault,*

strReturnBuffer, lngReturnBufferSize) As Long

where the following is true:

- *strSection* is the name of the section in WIN.INI from which to read. In this case the section will be "devices".

- *strEntry* is the item within the section to retrieve. Windows places the portion of the matching entry to the right of the equal sign in *strReturnBuffer.*

- *strDefault* is the value to return in *strReturnBuffer* if no match can be found. This value must never be null. You know that your search didn't find any matches if *strReturnBuffer* is the same as *strDefault* after the function call.

- *strReturnBuffer* is the string buffer into which Windows will place the text the function call finds. If *strEntry* is a single item, *strReturnBuffer* will contain either the portion of that specified entry to the right of the equal sign (if it's found) or the string in *strDefault* (if it's not).

- *lngReturnBufferSize* is the size, in characters, of *strReturnBuffer.* As with all Windows API calls, you must specify the width of the buffer before passing it to the Windows DLL. For example, to create a 1024-character buffer, you can use either

```
Dim strReturnBuffer as String * 1024
```

or

```
Dim strReturnBuffer as String
strReturnBuffer = Space$(1024)
```

The function returns the number of characters returned in *strReturnBuffer*.

On the other hand, to get a string containing all the different installed output devices, you would instead use the GetProfileSection function. To call this function, pass to it the section name, a buffer, and the size of that buffer. (We've provided the adhGetProfileSection function in basSetPrinter to handle all the details for you.)

```
Dim strMatch as String * 2048
lngCount = GetProfileSection("devices", strMatch, 2048)
```

You'd then need code to pull apart this string, breaking it at each null value and placing the values into an array. You can find the code to do this in the function adhGetDevices (in basSetPrinter in CH10.MDB). adhGetDevices fills the array passed to it with information about each of the devices found in WIN.INI, using the brute-force method of walking through the string returned from GetProfile-String, pulling off pieces until there are no more characters.

Your final goal, then, is to create an array of information about output devices. Each element of this array will contain a specific output device name, its driver name, and an output port. The user-defined type used as the basis for this array is declared in the module basPrtGlobal—the adh_tagDeviceRec:

```
Type adh_tagDeviceRec
    strDeviceName As String
    strDriverName As String
    strPort As String
End Type
```

On return from adhGetDevices, the application will have a global array of structures, each containing a specific combination of device, driver, and port.

Armed with this array, you now have all the information you need. Given an array that you want to present to the user as a list or combo box, your best solution in Access is to write a list-filling callback function. The function adhFillDeviceList calls the functions mentioned above to fill the array in its initialization case and then uses the values from that array when asked to provide data. Figure 10.1 shows the sample form in use with the list of devices visible. You should be able to easily use the code provided in basSetPrinter in your own applications once you've imported the module. Listing 10.6 shows the function that fills the list of devices.

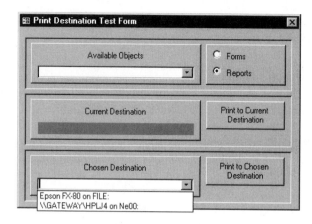

FIGURE 10.1

The sample form, zfrm-PrintDest, shows the list of all available output devices and their ports.

You can call this function directly from your own applications once you've imported basPrtGlobal and basSetPrinter. (For more information on filling list or combo boxes programmatically, see Chapter 7.)

Listing 10.6

```
Function adhFillDeviceList(ctlField As Control, _
 varID As Variant, varRow As Variant, varCol As Variant, _
 varCode As Variant) As Variant

    Static intCount As Integer
    Dim varRetval As Variant

    Select Case varCode
        Case acLBInitialize
            ' Initialize
            ' Go fill the array aDevList() with
            ' all the devices.
            intCount = adhGetDevices(aDevList())
            varRetval = (intCount > 0)
        Case acLBOpen
            ' Get ID
            varRetval = Timer
        Case acLBGetRowCount
            ' Number of rows
            varRetval = intCount
```

```
      Case acLBGetValue
          varRetval = aDevList(varRow).strDeviceName & _
          " on " & aDevList(varRow).strPort
      Case acLBEnd
          Erase aDevList
  End Select
  adhFillDeviceList = varRetval
End Function
```

Retrieving the Default DevMode Structure

Before you attempt to change the values stored in the prtDevNames property, you must also be able to retrieve a particular printing device's default DEVMODE structure. This really has nothing to do with Access, but rather with the fact that Access has exposed some rather low-level functionality. If you change the prtDevNames settings, you're in effect telling Access to use a different printing device. If you don't also change the prtDevMode property to match that new device, it's guaranteed that the two properties will collide. (Remember, the prtDevMode property also contains the name of the printing device.) In many cases this isn't catastrophic, and you'll never notice the difference. Switching between some pairs of printers, on the other hand, can be detrimental to the health of your application, any other applications that are currently running, and possibly even Windows.

Every printer maintains default values for each of the fields, and you can retrieve the default DEVMODE from the driver, using the OpenPrinter and DocumentProperties API functions. Once you have the default values, you can copy the user-modifiable values from your form or report's prtDevMode property into your copy of the default DEVMODE structure. Then you can use this new combined DEVMODE structure as the prtDevMode property for your object. The read-only fields (device name, DEVMODE size and extra size, and so on) must not be changed, however. Given an adh_tagDeviceRec structure containing information about the specific printer driver, the adhGetDefaultDM function, shown in Listing 10.7, retrieves the DEVMODE structure associated with that driver and returns it as a string.

Listing 10.7

```
Function adhGetDefaultDM(dr As adh_tagDeviceRec) As Variant
    Dim dmDefault() As Byte
    Dim hPrinter As Long
```

```
        Dim lngSize As Long
        Dim dmTemp As adh_tagDevModeStr
        Dim DMFull As adh_tagDevMode
        Dim varTemp As Variant
        Dim bytTemp As Byte

        Const adhcDMOutBuffer = 2

        If adh_apiOpenPrinter(dr.strDeviceName, _
         hPrinter, 0) Then
            ' This test shouldn't be necessary, but sanity
            ' checks never hurt!
            If hPrinter > 0 Then
                ' Call adh_apiDocumentProperties to get
                ' the size of the default devmode structure.
                lngSize = adh_apiDocumentProperties( _
                 0, hPrinter, dr.strDeviceName, _
                 bytTemp, bytTemp, 0)
                If lngSize > 0 Then
                    ReDim dmDefault(1 To lngSize)
                    If adh_apiDocumentProperties(0, hPrinter, _
                     dr.strDeviceName, dmDefault(1), _
                        dmDefault(1), adhcDMOutBuffer) > 0 Then
                            ' Copy the variant to the string
                            ' portion of a DevModeStr structure
                            ' so you can LSet it into a real DevMode
                            ' structure.  That way, you can pull
                            ' it apart and get the full size from
                            ' two of its member elements.
                            varTemp = dmDefault()
                            dmTemp.strDevMode = varTemp
                            LSet DMFull = dmTemp

                            adhGetDefaultDM = LeftB(varTemp, _
                             DMFull.intSize + DMFull.intDriverExtra)
                    End If
                End If
            End If
            Call adh_apiClosePrinter (hPrinter)
        End If
End Function
```

Copying Values from One DEVMODE to Another

Once you've retrieved the printer driver's default DEVMODE structure, you copy the settings for the current document that apply to the new printer into that DEVMODE structure. We've provided a function in basDevMode, adhCopyDMValues, that does the work for you. It looks at each bit in the lngFields member of the structure, and for each field that has been initialized by the new driver, it copies the data from the original prtDevMode property. Listing 10.8 shows the entire function.

Listing 10.8

```
Sub adhCopyDMValues(varOldDM As Variant, varNewDM As Variant)

    Dim dmOld As adh_tagDevMode
    Dim dmNew As adh_tagDevMode
    Dim dmTemp As adh_tagDevModeStr
    Dim intI As Integer

    ' Copy the string into a structure, using LSet.
    ' Because both sides of LSet must be user-defined types,
    ' copy the string into a temporary structure first.

    dmTemp.strDevMode = varOldDM
    LSet dmOld = dmTemp
    dmTemp.strDevMode = varNewDM
    LSet dmNew = dmTemp

    ' Copy all the old settings.
    ' Some of these may not apply to the newly chosen printer.
    ' Check the flags so only applicable ones get copied over.
    If dmNew.lngFields And adhcDMOrientation Then
        dmNew.intOrientation = dmOld.intOrientation
    End If
    If dmNew.lngFields And adhcDMPaperSize Then
        dmNew.intPaperSize = dmOld.intPaperSize
    End If
    If dmNew.lngFields And adhcDMPaperLength Then
        dmNew.intPaperLength = dmOld.intPaperLength
    End If
    If dmNew.lngFields And adhcDMPaperWidth Then
        dmNew.intPaperWidth = dmOld.intPaperWidth
    End If
```

```
       If dmNew.lngFields And adhcDMScale Then
           dmNew.intScale = dmOld.intScale
       End If
       If dmNew.lngFields And adhcDMCopies Then
           dmNew.intCopies = dmOld.intCopies
       End If
       If dmNew.lngFields And adhcDmDefaultSource Then
           dmNew.intDefaultSource = dmOld.intDefaultSource
       End If
       If dmNew.lngFields And adhcDMPrintQuality Then
           dmNew.intPrintQuality = dmOld.intPrintQuality
       End If
       If dmNew.lngFields And adhcDMColor Then
           dmNew.intColor = dmOld.intColor
       End If
       If dmNew.lngFields And adhcDMDuplex Then
           dmNew.intDuplex = dmOld.intDuplex
       End If
       If dmNew.lngFields And adhcDMYResolution Then
           dmNew.intYResolution = dmOld.intYResolution
       End If
       If dmNew.lngFields And adhcDMTTOption Then
           dmNew.intTTOption = dmOld.intTTOption
       End If
       If dmNew.lngFields And adhcDMCollate Then
           dmNew.intCollate = dmOld.intCollate
       End If

       ' Copy the value back into a string. Again,
       ' this must go through the temp structure because that's
       ' the only way LSet can work.
       LSet dmTemp = dmNew

       varNewDM = LeftB(dmTemp.strDevMode, _
         dmNew.intSize + dmNew.intDriverExtra)
    End Sub
```

Saving, Printing, and Restoring

Once you know how to put together and break apart the prtDevNames string and how to retrieve the default DEVMODE structure for the new driver, you're ready to control print destinations for forms and reports. The code to do this is embedded in the cmdChosen_Click procedure in the form module attached to zfrmPrintDest, and it breaks down into seven steps:

1. Get the old prtDevNames and prtDevMode properties.

2. Create the new prtDevNames string, based on the chosen output device.

3. Retrieve the default prtDevMode string for the newly selected printer.

4. Copy the current printer settings into the new prtDevMode string.

5. Set the new prtDevNames and prtDevMode strings for the form or report.

6. Print the form or report.

7. Replace the old prtDevNames string. (If you're not planning on saving your changes, this step is unnecessary.) Also, replace the original prtDevMode string.

Retrieving the Old Properties

To retrieve the old prtDevNames property, the sample application calls the adhRetrieveDevNames function, passing to it an object name and that object's type (acForm for forms or acReport for reports). The adhRetrieveDevNames function attempts to open the appropriate object, retrieves its prtDevNames property, and leaves the object open in Design view so later code can alter its properties. It also fills in the strOldDM variable so you can both replace the value of the prtDevMode property when you're done and copy values from it to the new DEVMODE structure you'll retrieve from the new output device:

```
varOldDevName = adhRetrieveDevNames(strName, _
  intType, varOldDM)
```

Creating the New prtDevNames String

Before you can print to a new destination, you must have chosen an item from the list of output devices. Because the combo box showing the list of devices, cboDestination, has its BoundColumn property set to 0, the value of the control is the index of the chosen item. That number corresponds to an element in the array that filled the combo. So given the value of the control, your code knows the specific device that was chosen. Passing the chosen item number to adhFillStructure returns an adh_tagDeviceRec structure filled in with the information from the array of installed output devices. Once you have the adh_tagDeviceRec structure filled in, you can call adhBuildDevNames to build the appropriate value to be used as a new prtDevNames string:

```
dr = adhFillStructure(ctl)
varNewDevName = adhBuildDevNames(dr)
```

Retrieving the Default DEVMODE Structure for the New Printer

As mentioned earlier, before you can change the output device you need to have the default DEVMODE structure for the new device to which you're switching. You can call the adhGetDefaultDM function to retrieve that information. You can then use the adhCopyDMValues procedure to copy the values from the current DEVMODE structure to the new one:

```
varDM = adhGetDefaultDM(dr)
adhCopyDMValues varOldDM, varDM
```

Setting the New Properties

To set the new prtDevNames string, your application must open the form or report in Design view and assign the newly created string to its prtDevNames property. (Remember that none of the prtDevMode, prtDevName, or prtMip properties are modifiable at run time.) To avoid problems when switching printer drivers, you must also assign the new printer's DEVMODE structure to the object's prtDevMode property at this point.

The simple matter of assigning the prtDevNames and prtDevMode properties is complicated in this application only because the object to be printed can be either a form or a report. The subroutine adhSetDevName (in basPrtDest) does the work for you in this case:

```
adhSetDevName strName, intType, varNewDevName, varDM
```

Listing 10.9 shows the adhSetDevName subroutine. Note the use of the MidB function to copy the data from the input values to the properties of the object. Unless you take steps to convince Access that these are just streams of bytes, as opposed to strings, Access will convert them to Unicode strings, which will make a mess of your prtDevNames and prtDevMode properties. Using MidB leaves the values intact as ANSI strings.

Listing 10.9

```
Sub adhSetDevName(strName As String, intType As Integer, _
  varDevNames As Variant, varDevMode As Variant)
```

```
        Dim obj As Object
        Select Case intType
            Case acForm
                DoCmd.OpenForm strName, acDesign
                Set obj = Forms(strName)
            Case acReport
                DoCmd.OpenReport strName, acDesign
                Set obj = Reports(strName)
        End Select
        ' Use the MidB() function to convert
        ' the variant into a string of bytes. Otherwise,
        ' Access assumes you're sending in a string
        ' and converts it from Unicode to ANSI, which ISN'T
        ' what you want here.
        obj.prtDevMode = MidB(varDevMode, 1)
        obj.prtDevNames = MidB(varDevNames, 1)
End Sub
```

Printing the Object (Finally!)

To print the object, you can use the PrintOut method. You'll probably want to switch to Normal view (instead of Design view) for printing. In addition, you may or may not want to close the object when you're done printing. (If you do close it without saving, you needn't worry about resetting the prtDevNames and prt-DevMode properties.) The DoPrint subroutine in zfrmPrintDest's CBF takes care of the printing and closing details for you. It opens the object in an appropriate view for printing, does the printing, and then either puts it back into Design view, so the caller can restore its state, or closes it. If you asked DoPrint to close the object, it calls the DoClose subroutine to do the work. (You'll find both procedures in zfrmPrintDest's CBF.) This procedure uses the third parameter of the Close macro action, indicating that Access shouldn't ask whether or not to save the object; this code just closes it without saving. It also resets some objects on the main example form, cleaning up after the print job.

Replacing the Old Properties

Finally, to reset the prtDevNames property to its original state, you can call the adhSetDevName subroutine again, this time passing the old prtDevNames value. This restores the original state of the form or report's prtDevNames and prtDev-Mode properties, allowing you to print to the originally chosen device:

```
adhSetDevName strName, intType, varOldDevName, varOldDM
```

All the rest of the code in the sample application deals with manipulating the form or report object you've selected to print and with the user interface of the application itself. You may find it useful to study the code in the application, but in any case you should be able to adopt it to your own needs quite easily.

Retrieving Printer Capabilities

To use the prtDevMode property to its fullest, you'll want to provide a means of allowing your users to make choices about their printed output. You might want to allow them to programmatically choose a particular page size, the number of copies, or the paper source. Access, though, does not provide a means of determining your printer's capabilities. Windows, of course, does provide just such a mechanism, although using this mechanism from within Access requires a bit of effort.

When Access (or any other Windows application) presents you with a Print dialog box, it has requested information from the printer driver to know which options to make available to you. Windows exposes this information directly from the printer driver, using the DeviceCapabilities API function. You can call this function from your own applications, retrieving information about which features the printer supports.

In the next few sections we first describe the DeviceCapabilities function as Windows implements it and then discuss how you can use it in your own applications. You have choices as to how to interact with the DeviceCapabilities API function. You can, of course, call it directly. Table 10.9 lists the various capabilities for which you can query DeviceCapabilities, along with the associated high-level function we've provided (see Table 10.10) to get the information for you.

You could also call the higher-level functions we've provided, which shield you from having to worry about many of the details involved in calling the API directly. We strongly recommend that you use the higher-level functions, because they make your use of this information much, much simpler. Table 10.10 lists all the high-level functions, the parameters to each, and the return values.

TABLE 10.9   Options Available When Calling DeviceCapabilities

Value	High-Level Function in basPrintCap	Meaning
adhcDCBinNames	adhGetBinNames	Copies an array containing a list of the names of the paper bins into the strOutput parameter. To find the number of entries in the array, call adh_apiDeviceCapabilitiesLng with the lngOutput parameter set to 0; the return value is the number of bin entries required. (Each bin name can be up to 24 [adhcBinNameSize] bytes long.) This allows you to make sure your output string is long enough to hold all the entries. Otherwise the return value is the number of bins copied
adhcDCBins	adhGetBins	Retrieves a list of available bins. The function copies the list to lngOutput as an array of integers. If you call adh_apiDeviceCapabilitiesLng with lngOutput set to 0, the function returns the number of supported bins, allowing you to allocate a buffer with the correct size. (See the description in Table 10.1, earlier in this chapter, of the Default Source member of the DEVMODE structure for information on these values.)
adhcDCCopies	adhGetCopies	Returns the maximum number of copies the device can produce
adhcDCDriver	adhGetDriverVersion	Returns the printer-driver version number
adhcDCDuplex	adhGetDuplex	Returns the level of duplex support. The function returns 1 if the printer is capable of duplex printing. Otherwise the return value is 0
adhcDCEnum–Resolutions	adhGetEnumResolutions	Returns a list of available resolutions. If lngOutput is 0, adh_apiDevice-CapabilitiesLng returns the number of available resolution configurations. Resolutions are represented by pairs of long integers representing the horizontal and vertical resolutions

TABLE 10.9 Options Available When Calling DeviceCapabilities (continued)

Value	High-Level Function in basPrintCap	Meaning
adhcDCExtra	adhGetExtraSize	Returns the number of bytes required for the device-specific portion of the DEVMODE structure for the printer driver
adhcDCFields	adhGetFields	Returns the lngFields member of the printer driver's DEVMODE data structure. The lngFields member indicates which members in the device-independent portion of the structure the printer driver supports
adhcDCFile–Dependencies	adhGetFileDependencies	Returns a list of files that also need to be loaded when a driver is installed. Call adh_apiDeviceCapabilitiesLng with lngOutput set to 0 to return the number of files. Call adhDeviceCapabilities to fill a string buffer with an array of file names. Each element in the array is exactly 64 (adhcFileDependencySize) characters long
adhcDCMaxExtent	adhGetMaxExtent	Returns a typePOINT variable containing the maximum paper size the intPaperLength and intPaperWidth members of the printer driver's DEVMODE structure can specify
adhcDCMinExtent	adhGetMinExtent	Returns a typePOINT variable containing the minimum paper size the intPaperLength and intPaperWidth members of the printer driver's DEVMODE structure can specify
adhcDCOrientation	adhGetOrientation	Retrieves the relationship between portrait and landscape orientations in terms of the number of degrees portrait orientation is to be rotated counter-clockwise to get landscape orientation. It can be one of the following values: 0 (no landscape orientation); 90 (portrait is rotated 90 degrees to produce landscapes—for example, PCL); 270 (portrait is rotated 270 degrees to produce landscape—for example, dot-matrix printers)

TABLE 10.9   Options Available When Calling DeviceCapabilities (continued)

Value	High-Level Function in basPrintCap	Meaning
adhcDCPaperNames	adhGetPaperNames	Retrieves a list of the paper names supported by the model. To find the number of entries in the array, call adh_apiDeviceCapabilitiesLng with the lngOutput parameter set to 0: the return value is the number of paper sizes required. (Each paper size name can be up to 64 [adhcPaperNameSize] bytes long.) This allows you to make sure your output string is long enough to hold all the entries. Otherwise, the return value is the number of paper names
adhcDCPapers	adhGetPapers	Retrieves a list of supported paper sizes. The function copies the list to lngOutput as an array of integers and returns the number of entries in the array. If you call adh_apiDeviceCapabilitiesLng with lngOutput set to 0, the function returns the number of supported paper sizes. This allows you to allocate a buffer with the correct size. (See the description in Table 10.1 of the Paper Size member of the DEVMODE data structure for information on these values.)
adhcDCPaperSize	adhGetPaperSize	Copies the dimensions of supported paper sizes in tenths of a millimeter to an array of typePOINT structures pointed to by lngOutput. This allows an application to obtain information about nonstandard paper sizes
adhDCSize	adhGetDMSize	Returns the Size member of the printer driver's DEVMODE data structure

TABLE 10.9 Options Available When Calling DeviceCapabilities (continued)

Value	High-Level Function in basPrintCap	Meaning
adhDCTrueType	adhGetTrueType	Retrieves the driver's capabilities with regard to printing TrueType fonts. The return value can be one or more of the following capability flags: adhcDCTTBitmap (1): device is capable of printing TrueType fonts as graphics; adhcDCTTDownload (2): device is capable of downloading TrueType fonts; adhcDCTTSubdev (4): device is capable of substituting device fonts for TrueType. In this case the strOutput parameter should be 0
adhcDCVersion	adhGetSpecVersion	Returns the specification version to which the printer driver conforms

TABLE 10.10 High-Level Functions for Retrieving Printer Driver Capabilities

Function Name	Parameters	Return Values
adhGetBinNames	dr As adh_tagDeviceRec, astrBinNames() As String	Fills in astrBinNames, returns the number of bins
adhGetBins	dr As adh_tagDeviceRec, aintList As Integer	Fills in aintList, returns the number of bins
adhGetCopies	dr As adh_tagDeviceRec	Returns the number of copies
adhGetDMSize	dr As adh_tagDeviceRec	Returns the size of the DEVMODE structure for the specified device
adhGetDriverVersion	dr As adh_tagDeviceRec	Returns the driver version number
adhGetDuplex	dr As adh_tagDeviceRec	Returns 1 if duplex allowed, otherwise 0
adhGetEnumResolutions	dr As adh_tagDeviceRec, aptlngList() As typePOINT	Fills in aptlngList, returns the number of resolutions
adhGetExtraSize	dr As adh_tagDeviceRec	Returns the "extra" size of the DEVMODE

TABLE 10.10 High-Level Functions for Retrieving Printer Driver Capabilities (continued)

Function Name	Parameters	Return Values
adhGetFields	dr As adh_tagDeviceRec	Returns the DEVMODE lngFields value
adhGetFileDependencies	dr As adh_tagDeviceRec, astrList() As String	Fills in astrList, returns the number of file dependencies
adhGetMaxExtent	dr As adh_tagDeviceRec, ptValue As typePOINT	Fills in ptValue with the max X and Y dimensions
adhGetMinExtent	dr As adh_tagDeviceRec, ptValue As typePOINT	Fills in ptValue with the min X and Y dimensions
adhGetOrientation	dr As adh_tagDeviceRec	Returns the orientation (see Table 10.9)
adhGetPaperNames	dr As adh_tagDeviceRec, astrNames() As String	Fills in astrNames, returns the number of paper names
adhGetPapers	dr As adh_tagDeviceRec, aintList() As Integer	Fills in aintList, returns the number of papers
adhGetPaperSize	dr As adh_tagDeviceRec, aptList()y As typePOINT	Fills in aptList, returns the number of paper sizes
adhGetDMSize	dr As adh_tagDeviceRec	Returns the size of the DEVMODE structure
adhGetTrueType	dr As adh_tagDeviceRec	Returns the TrueType flag (see Table 10.9)
adhGetSpecVersion	dr As adh_tagDeviceRec	Returns the driver spec version

The Printer Driver's DeviceCapabilities Function

To request information about the capabilities of the printer driver, you can call the DeviceCapabilities API function. In Listing 10.10 you'll find three Declare statements for the function, because you need to call DeviceCapabilities in different ways. If you pass 0 for the fourth parameter, the driver returns the number of items in the array you're requesting. If you pass it the address of a string buffer in the fourth parameter, it returns the actual data. To make it possible to call the function both ways, we've provided two ways of calling it. If you call adh_apiDeviceCapabilitiesLng, you pass a long integer in the fourth parameter. If you call adh_apiDeviceCapabilitiesStr, you pass the address of a string buffer in the fourth parameter. In addition, we've provided the declaration for adh_apiDeviceCapabilitiesAny, which allows you to pass anything you wish in that fourth parameter. You use this declaration when you need to pass a user-defined datatype to the API call, for example. This difference in calling conventions points out one more reason why you'd be better served in using the high-level functions discussed below.

Listing 10.10

```
Declare Function adh_apiDeviceCapabilitiesStr _
 Lib "winspool.drv" Alias "DeviceCapabilitiesA" _
 (ByVal strDeviceName As String, ByVal strPort As String, _
 ByVal lngIndex As Long, ByVal strOutput As String, _
 ByVal lngDevMode As Long) As Long
Declare Function adh_apiDeviceCapabilitiesLng _
 Lib "winspool.drv" Alias "DeviceCapabilitiesA" _
 (ByVal strDeviceName As String, ByVal strPort As String, _
 ByVal lngIndex As Long, ByVal lngOutput As Long, _
 ByVal lngDevMode As Long) As Long
Declare Function adh_apiDeviceCapabilitiesAny _
 Lib "winspool.drv" Alias "DeviceCapabilitiesA" _
 (ByVal strDeviceName As String, _
 ByVal strPort As String, ByVal lngIndex As Long, _
 lpOutput As Any, ByVal lngDevMode As Long) As Long
```

No matter which way you call DeviceCapabilities, it requires five parameters. Table 10.11 lists those parameters and gives information about each.

TABLE 10.11 Parameters for DeviceCapabilities

Parameter	Description
strDeviceName	The device name, as listed in WIN.INI ("HP LaserJet 4/4M")
strPort	The output port, as listed in WIN.INI ("LPT1")
lngIndex	An item chosen from the first column of Table 10.9, indicating the capability about which to inquire
strOutput, lngOutput, lpOutput	A string buffer or a user-defined type to be filled, or 0 to indicate that you're requesting the number of elements the function will return
lngDevMode	By definition, the address of a DEVMODE variable, 0 for your purposes

An Example of Calling adhDeviceCapabilities Directly

This example calls DeviceCapabilities directly. You will most likely find it easier to call the high-level functions (listed in the second column of Table 10.9) than to use this example's code directly. We started out using code like this but quickly realized that much of the code was the same among the different capabilities. Although you might never use this code, it does demonstrate how to use Device-Capabilities in case you need it for purposes we haven't considered.

Retrieving a List of Paper Names

The code in Listing 10.11 requests a list of the supported paper names from a specific printer driver. You pass to it a filled-in adh_tagDeviceRec variable, along with a dynamic array that it can fill with the list of names. It returns the total number of items it received from the driver. The function that called GetPaperNames would need to fill in the adh_tag-DeviceRec structure, create the dynamic array, and then call the function (see Listing 10.11).

GetPaperNames must first retrieve the number of items in the array Device-Capabilities will be returning so you can allocate enough space in the string buffer it will fill in. To do this, call adh_apiDeviceCapabilitiesLng, passing a 0 in the fourth parameter and the capability ID in the third parameter. If this call succeeds, it returns to you the number of elements in the array of names:

```
lngItemCount = adh_apiDeviceCapabilitiesLng( _
  dr.strDeviceName, dr.strPort, adhcDCPaperNames, 0, 0)
```

Once you know how many elements there will be, you can use ReDim to resize the output array to fit them all. Given a known size for each element you'll be retrieving from the driver (adhcPaperNameSize, in this case), you can use Access' String function to make sure the string buffer is large enough. Failure to execute this step will surely cause Access to crash, because it might very well overwrite code or data with the output values when you call DeviceCapabilities. Finally, you can call adhDevice-Capabilities to retrieve the necessary string buffer full of information from the driver:

```
' Reset the size of the array to fit all the items.
ReDim astrList(0 To lngCount - 1)

strItemName = String(adhcPaperNameSize * lngCount, 0)

lngTemp = adh_apiDeviceCapabilitiesStr(dr.strDeviceName, _
  dr.strPort, adhcDCPaperNames, strItemName, 0)
```

You're still missing the final step at this point, though. You need to pull apart the pieces of the array. (They're stored in one big, continuous stream in strItemName.) This is simple enough, of course, because you know the length of each piece. It's just a matter of pulling out each piece with the Mid function, trimming off trailing nulls (using the adhTrimNull function), and assigning the substring to the current row in astrList:

```
If lngTemp <> -1 Then
    For intI = 0 To lngCount - 1
        astrList(intI) = adhTrimNull( _
        Mid(strItemName, intI * _
        adhcPaperNameSize + 1, adhcPaperNameSize))
    Next intI
End If
```

As you'll see in the next section, we've done all this work for you. You should be able to retrieve any of the printer's capabilities easily with the high-level functions listed in the second column of Table 10.9.

Listing 10.11

```
Function GetPaperNames(dr As adh_tagDeviceRec, _
 astrList() As String) As Long

    ' Retrieve a list of strings from the driver, returning
    ' the number of strings in the output list.

    Dim lngCount As Long
    Dim strItemName As String
    Dim lngTemp As Long
    Dim intI As Integer

    On Error GoTo GetPaperNamesErr

    ' Find out how many items there are in the list.
    lngCount = adh_apiDeviceCapabilitiesLng( _
     dr.strDeviceName, dr.strPort, adhcDCPaperNames, 0, 0)
    If lngCount <> -1 Then
        ReDim astrList(0 To lngCount - 1)

        If lngCount > 0 Then
            ' This code places the entire string list in one
            ' string buffer and then parses it out later.
            strItemName = String( _
             adhcPaperNameSize * lngCount, 0)
            lngTemp = adh_apiDeviceCapabilitiesStr( _
```

```
            dr.strDeviceName, dr.strPort, _
            adhcDCPaperNames, strItemName, 0)
        If lngTemp <> -1 Then
            For intI = 0 To lngCount - 1
                astrList(intI) = adhTrimNull( _
                Mid(strItemName, intI * _
                adhcPaperNameSize + 1, _
                adhcPaperNameSize))
            Next intI
        End If
    End If
  End If

GetPaperNamesExit:
    ' Set the return value now.
    GetPaperNames = IIf(lngTemp = -1, 0, lngCount)
    Exit Function

GetPaperNamesErr:
    lngTemp = -1
    Resume GetPaperNamesExit
End Function
```

Saving Effort by Calling the High-Level Interfaces

To save you some time (and us, as well), we've provided a high-level interface to each of the printer capabilities. We've listed the name of each of these functions in Table 10.10. The second column of this table lists the parameters you need to pass to each function, and the third column lists the return values. You'll probably find it much simpler to call these functions directly, since they perform for you almost all the work shown in Listing 10.11. The code in Listing 10.12 is quite similar to the code you'd need to retrieve any of the printer's capabilities.

GetPaperNameList, in Listing 10.12 (from basPaperNameList in CH10.MDB), first fills in an adh_tagDeviceRec structure. This example pulls its information from the default printer listed in WIN.INI, using the adhGetCurrentDevice function (see basSetPrinter in CH10.MDB):

```
' Set up the device rec.
If adhGetCurrentDevice(dr, ",") Then
' ...
End If
```

Once GetPaperNameList has the device information, it can call adhGetPaper-Names directly. This fills in the dynamic array, astrNames, and returns the number of elements in the array:

```
' Get the list of paper sizes.
lngCount = adhGetPaperNames(dr, astrNames())
```

Finally, once you have the array of paper names, you can use it however you wish. This simple example just displays the list in the Immediate window:

```
' You might use astrNames() to fill a list box, for example.
For intI = 0 To lngCount - 1
    Debug.Print astrNames(intI)
Next intI
```

Listing 10.12

```
Function GetPaperNameList()
    Dim dr As adh_tagDeviceRec
    Dim astrNames() As String
    Dim lngCount As Integer
    Dim intI As Integer

    ' Set up the device rec.
    If adhGetCurrentDevice(dr, ",") Then
        lngCount = adhGetPaperNames(dr, astrNames())

        ' You might use astrNames to fill a list box,
        ' for example.
        For intI = 0 To lngCount - 1
            Debug.Print astrNames(intI)
        Next intI
    End If
End Function
```

A Major Example

To see an example of all this technology in action, check out frmDevCaps in CH10.MDB (see Figure 10.2). This form provides a list of installed printer devices, allows you to select a device, and then displays all the information it can retrieve from the printer driver about the selected device. The code you'll find in the form module deals mostly with displaying the information, but in it you'll find lots of calls to the functions listed in Table 10.10. Although it's doubtful you'll need all this information in any of your applications, you may well need one or more of the items from frmDevCaps when you present lists of formatting options to your users.

FIGURE 10.2

The form frmPrtCaps demonstrates all the values available by calling DeviceCapabilities.

Device Capabilities

Available Devices
\\GATEWAY\HPLJ4 on Ne00:

Driver Information

DEVMODE Size:	156 bytes
Extra Size:	112 bytes
Spec Version:	1025
Driver Version:	769
Minimum Size:	0 by 0
Maximum Size:	0 by 0
Maximum Copies:	32767
Landscape:	90 degrees
Duplex:	☐

Supported Paper Sizes

	Page Size Name	ID	Dimensions (in mm)
1.	Letter	1	215.9 by 279.4
2.	Letter Small	2	215.9 by 279.4
3.	Legal	5	215.9 by 355.6

Supported Bins

	Bin Name	ID
1.	Printer Folder Setting	15
2.	Auto Select	268
3.	Upper Paper tray	1

Supported Resolutions

1) 600 by 600 dots/inch
2) 300 by 300 dots/inch
3) 150 by 150 dots/inch
4) 75 by 75 dots/inch

True Type Font Support

☑ Print TrueType fonts as Graphics
☑ Download TrueType fonts
☐ Substitute Device Fonts for TrueType fonts

File Dependencies

DEVMODE Fields Initialized (incomplete list)

☑ dmOrientation	☐ dmPaperWidth	☑ dmDefaultSource	☐ dmDuplex	☐ dmCollate
☑ dmPaperSize	☐ dmScale	☐ dmPrintQuality	☐ dmYResolution	☑ dmFormName
☐ dmPaperLength	☑ dmCopies	☑ dmColor	☑ dmTTOption	☐ dmLogPixels

Summary

In this chapter we've taken a look at printing from several angles. We covered these issues:

- Using the prtDevMode property of objects to control printing details
- Using the prtMip property to control margins, columns, and so on
- Using the prtDevNames property to control the output device
- Retrieving printer capabilities using the DeviceCapability Windows API function

Although the information presented here is relevant to all of Windows, Access is alone in the manner in which it presents this information (unlike Word, Excel, or any of the other Microsoft products). Getting at and changing printer characteristics isn't easy with Access, but you have enough generic routines under your belt now to at least make it possible. You should be able to use the prtDevMode, prtDevNames, and prtMip properties in your own applications, given the sample routines in this chapter.

CHAPTER
ELEVEN

11

Shared Office Programmability

- Using the FileSearch object to find files

- Manipulating menus and toolbars using the CommandBars object model

- Animating applications using the Office Assistant

As Microsoft Office matures, more and more of the components of the individual applications are actually shared between multiple Office applications. Office Web, Office Art, and other major components are meant to be shared among all the Office applications. Office also provides a group of "internal" components, including the Office Assistant, command bars, and the FileSearch object, to each application. Each of these objects provides a rich programming model, making it possible for you to use them in your own applications. This chapter discusses each of these components in some depth, focusing on methods you can use to incorporate their functionality into solutions you write.

References Are Everything

To use any of the shared Office components programmatically, your application will need to include a reference to the Office 97 type library. Adding this type library reference to your project allows you to use early binding (declaring objects of variable types unknown to the host application), use the Object Browser to view the exposed Automation structure of the object, and use the online help files associated with the object.

To add the necessary reference to your project, follow these steps:

1. Open any module in Design view.

2. Choose the Tools ➤ References menu item.

3. From the list of installed type libraries, choose Microsoft Office 8.0 Object Library.

4. If this item doesn't appear on your list, choose the Browse button and search for MSO97.DLL (although this item should appear on your list if you've installed Office 97 correctly).

5. Choose the OK button, and you're ready to go.

The FileSearch Object Model

Access 95 provided the Microsoft Office File Open dialog, including its advanced search capabilities. Unfortunately, Access 95 didn't provide any way for you to use that functionality in your applications. Office 97 now provides a rich object model for its built-in FileSearch object. Your Access 97 applications (actually, applications written in any Office 97 component that supports VBA) can take advantage of the object model and provide full-featured searching for files across local, network, and remote drives.

You can use the dialog itself in its simple mode (see Figure 11.1) or its advanced mode (see Figure 11.2). The same is true for the FileSearch object. Using the simple mode, you can search with simple criteria; advanced mode allows you to specify a collection of PropertyTest objects that correspond to multiple search criteria. In addition, if you've enabled Microsoft's Fast Find feature (installed for you by default in your Startup group when you install Microsoft Office 97), the FileSearch object will use the indexes that program creates, providing extremely quick searches. The following sections and tables document how you can make use of this useful technology to find documents.

FIGURE 11.1

The simple Open dialog allows you to search on a few criteria.

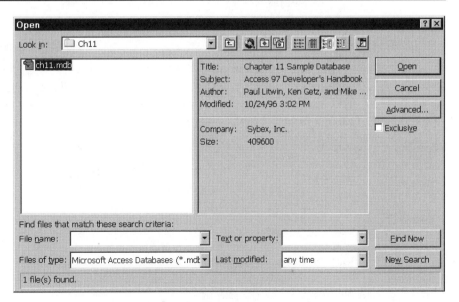

FIGURE 11.2

The Advanced Find dialog allows you to search for specific values in multiple properties, combined in complex Boolean searches.

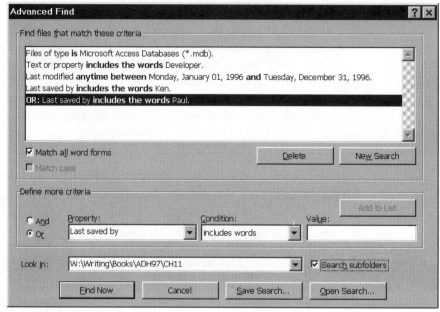

How Does It Work?

The Office programmability layer exposes only a single FileSearch object. That is, there's no collection of these objects, and the single object is pre-created for you. You needn't use the New keyword when working with the FileSearch object. You can use either of the two samples that follow to work with it:

```
Dim fs As FileSearch
Set fs = Application.FileSearch
With fs
...
End With

or

With Application.FileSearch
...
End With
```

> **NOTE**
>
> Because Automation always takes the current context into account, you needn't explicitly reference the Application object in code that handles the FileSearch object. We've gotten into the habit of using the explicit specification because it makes it clear, from reading the code, that FileSearch isn't a user-defined object.

In its simplest mode you'll use the FileSearch object like this:

1. Supply a criterion on which to search (a file name or a file type, perhaps), using the FileName or TextOrProperty property.

2. Use the Execute method of the FileSearch object to start the search.

3. The Execute method returns the number of matching files it found. You can check that value to see whether the search was successful.

4. Loop through the FilesFound collection, each element of which is a string containing the name of a found file, performing whatever action you need on each file.

For example, you might write a simple routine like the one shown in Listing 11.1, taken from basFileSearch in CH11.MDB. This procedure searches through the Windows directory for all files with .INI as the file extension. If it finds any matches, it displays the list in the Debug window.

Listing 11.1

```
Sub SimpleSearch()
    Dim varItem As Variant
    With Application.FileSearch
        .FileName = "*.ini"
        .LookIn = "C:\WINDOWS"
        .SearchSubFolders = False
        .Execute
        For Each varItem In .FoundFiles
            Debug.Print varItem
        Next varItem
    End With
End Sub
```

To perform more complex searches, you can replace the first step with a series of additions (using the Add method) to the PropertyTests collection. Once you've set up the PropertyTests collection, the rest of the steps are identical. (See "Using Advanced Search Techniques" later in this chapter for more information.)

To clear out your settings and start a new search, you can use the NewSearch method of the FileSearch object. This method only resets all the properties—it doesn't actually perform a search. You'll want to make sure your code uses this method anytime you start a new search. Otherwise you're likely to inherit settings from a previous search that don't apply in the current situation.

Creating Simple Searches

The following sections describe the properties you'll use when creating simple searches. The properties are cross-referenced with settings available in the File Open dialog, shown earlier in Figure 11.1.

Specifying What to Look For, and Where

Use the LookIn property to specify the drive and/or path in which to search. This property is a string expression and corresponds to the Look In drop-down list in Figure 11.1. Specify the FileName property to indicate the name (or file specification) of the files to search for. This can be a specific file name or a file specification (using the DOS wildcard symbols * and ?).

For example, the following code fragment searches for all text files in the root directory of the C drive:

```
With Application.FileSearch
    .LookIn = "C:\"
    .FileName = "*.txt"
    .SearchSubFolders = False
    .Execute
End With
```

Specifying How to Look for Files

You can use any of the following properties to help narrow down the search or to provide more information for the search engine when locating your files. By using these options you can place very fine control over the files you need to find.

- **TextOrProperty:** Use this string expression to specify text to search for in either the body or the properties of the document. There's no way to specify that the search should look only at one or the other. This option corresponds to the Text or Property combo box in Figure 11.1.

- **MatchAllWordForms:** Set this property to True to find matches on all word forms of the word entered in the TextOrProperty property. If you specify "talk" in the TextOrProperty property, setting this property to True will cause the search to find matches against "talk", "talks", "talking", and "talked". This option corresponds to the Match All Word Forms check box in Figure 11.2.

> **NOTE**
>
> The MatchAllWordForms property will have an effect only if you've installed and registered mswds_en.lex. (The name will be different for various localized versions.) If you used the Typical setup when installing Office 97, this option wasn't installed. You may need to rerun the Office 97 setup to install this feature.

- **MatchTextExactly:** If set to True, this property limits the search to an exact match on the text entered in the TextOrProperty property. This option corresponds to the Match Case check box in Figure 11.2.

- **SearchSubFolders:** If you set this property to True, the search will include not only the path specified in the LookIn property, but any folders contained within the specified folder. This option corresponds to the Search Subfolders check box in Figure 11.2.

- **FileType:** This property allows you to specify the file type to search for. You can specify one of the following values: msoFileTypeAllFiles, msoFileType-Binders, msoFileTypeDatabases, msoFileTypeExcelWorkbooks, msoFile-TypeOfficeFiles, msoFileTypePowerPointPresentations, msoFileTypeTemplates, msoFileTypeWordDocuments. This option corresponds to the Files of Type drop-down list in Figure 11.1. The default for this property is msoFileType-OfficeFiles, so unless you specify a file type or file specification in the FileName property, all you'll get is Microsoft Office files.

- **LastModified:** Set this property to any one of the following constants, indicating a range for the last modification date: msoLastModifiedAnyTime, msoLast-ModifiedLastMonth, msoLastModifiedLastWeek, msoLastModifiedThisMonth, msoLastModifiedThisWeek, msoLastModifiedToday, msoLastModifiedYesterday. This option corresponds to the Last Modified drop-down list in Figure 11.1.

Executing the Search

To run a search, use the Execute method of the FileSearch object. The Execute method accepts three parameters, all of which are optional:

```
With Application.FileSearch
    intFilesFound = .Execute(SortBy, _
    SortOrder, AlwaysAccurate)
End With
```

The method returns the number of matching files it located.

These are the optional parameters:

- **SortBy:** Indicates the attribute on which to sort the returned collection of file names. Use one of the following constants: msoSortbyFileName, msoSortbyFileType, msoSortbyLastModified, msoSortbySize.

- **SortOrder:** Indicates the sorting order. Use one of the following two constants: msoSortOrderAscending or msoSortOrderDescending.

- **AlwaysAccurate:** Ordinarily, the search uses only the saved indexes (if you're using the Fast Find program) to perform its search. If you want the search to also look on your disks so that the returned list is accurate (even if the saved indexes are not), set this parameter to True. The default, False, is faster, but it may not find files added or changed since the index file was last updated.

For example, the following fragment runs the specified search, returning values sorted by the last-modified date, in descending order, finding all matches regardless of whether they're in the Fast Find index:

```
With Application.FileSearch
    intFilesFound = .Execute _
    msoSortByLastModified, msoSortOrderDescending, True)
End With
```

Using All the Simple Features

To test out all the features mentioned in the preceding paragraphs, try out frmTestSimpleSearch in the sample database (see Figure 11.3). This form allows you to try out all the simple properties (and the parameters to the Execute method) on your own files, to see how they work. To make the form as simple as possible, the list box on the right is limited to 2048 characters. (It uses a semicolon-delimited list to supply a value for the RowSource property of the list box, and that's limited

FIGURE 11.3

Use all the simple search properties on this sample form.

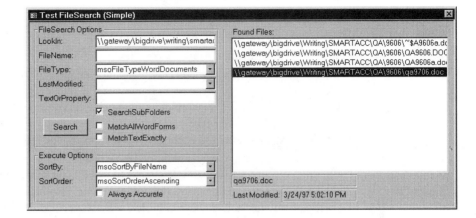

to just 2048 characters.) If you want to provide a real interface like this one, you'll need to modify the code to either write the file list to a table and fill the list box from there or use a list-filling callback function to supply the list's values.

Using Advanced Search Techniques

The FileSearch object also allows you to create a list of properties and values for those properties specifying the files to find. As shown earlier in Figure 11.2, you can create a collection of PropertyTest objects, each containing a property name, a condition, and a value or two to check for. The following sections explain how to use the PropertyTests collection to create very specific searches.

The PropertyTests Collection

The PropertyTests collection of the FileSearch object allows you to specify exactly the properties, and the values of those properties, you'd like to find as you search for files. When you run its Execute method, the FileSearch object will apply all the tests contained in its PropertyTests collection to each file that meets the location criteria (LookIn and SearchSubFolders properties). You can mix the simple FileSearch properties mentioned earlier in this chapter with the more complex PropertyTests items, although the behavior is undefined if you overlap conditions. (In our tests, it appears that specifying a FileName property takes priority over using the "File Name" PropertyTest item. This isn't documented, however, and you'd do best not to count on the behavior.)

Adding Items to the PropertyTests Collection

To add items to the PropertyTests collection, use the Add method of the collection. This method accepts up to five parameters, but only the first two (Name and Condition) are required. The allowed values for the properties are interrelated, and Tables 11.1 and 11.2 list the possible values for each. The general syntax for the Add method is

FileSearch.PropertyTests.Add(*Name, Condition, Value, SecondValue, Connector*)

The following list discusses each of the parameters and their values:

- **Name:** A string value corresponding to one of the built-in properties shown in Table 11.1, or a user-defined property name. Table 11.1 also indicates which values from Table 11.2 are available for a given property name.

- **Condition:** A numeric value from Table 11.2, indicating the condition applied to the property supplied in the Name parameter. Some conditions require no parameters, others a single value (supplied in the Value parameter), and others two parameters (supplied in the Value and SecondValue parameters). Table 11.2 indicates how many parameters each condition requires.

- **Value:** A variant, supplying the required value (if necessary) for the condition specified in the Condition parameter.

- **SecondValue:** A variant, supplying the second parameter (if necessary) for the selected condition.

- **Connector:** A numeric value, one of msoConnectorAnd and msoConnectorOr, indicating how the current member of the PropertyTests collection connects with other members that are modifying the same property Name. For example, in Figure 11.2, the two conditions applied to the "Last saved by" parameter would use the msoConnectorOr value for this parameter in the second "Last saved by" element of the collection.

TABLE 11.1   Built-In Office Document Properties and Their Associated Conditions

Property Name	Available Conditions, from Table 11.2
Application Name	Group 1
Author	Group 1
Category	Group 1

TABLE 11.1   Built-In Office Document Properties and Their Associated Conditions (continued)

Property Name	Available Conditions, from Table 11.2
Comments	Group 1
Company	Group 1
Contents	Group 2
Creation Date	Group 3
File Name	Group 4
Files of Type	Group 5
Format	Group 1
Hyperlink Base	Group 1
Keywords	Group 1
Last Modified	Group 3
Last printed	Group 3
Last saved by	Group 1
Manager	Group 1
Number of characters	Group 6
Number of characters + spaces	Group 6
Number of hidden slides	Group 6
Number of lines	Group 6
Number of multimedia clips	Group 6
Number of notes	Group 6
Number of pages	Group 6
Number of paragraphs	Group 6
Number of slides	Group 6
Number of words	Group 6
Revision	Group 1

TABLE 11.1   Built-In Office Document Properties and Their Associated Conditions (continued)

Property Name	Available Conditions, from Table 11.2
Size	Group 6
Subject	Group 1
Template	Group 1
Text or property	Group 1
Title	Group 1
Total Editing Time	Group 6
[User-defined Property]	Any constant, plus Group 7

TABLE 11.2   msoCondition Constants, Grouped by Functionality

Group 1

Condition Constant	UI Equivalent	Parameters Required*
msoConditionIncludes	includes words	1
msoConditionIncludesPhrase	includes phrase	1
msoConditionBeginsWith	begins with phrase	1
msoConditionEndsWith	ends with phrase	1
msoConditionIncludesNearEachOther	includes near each other	1
msoConditionIsExactly	is (exactly)	1
msoConditionIsNot	is not	1

Group 2

Condition Constant	UI Equivalent	Parameters Required*
msoConditionIncludes	includes words	1
msoConditionIncludesPhrase	includes phrase	1
msoConditionIncludesNearEachOther	includes near each other	1

TABLE 11.2 msoCondition Constants, Grouped by Functionality (continued)

Group 3

Condition Constant	UI Equivalent	Parameters Required*
msoConditionYesterday	yesterday	0
msoConditionToday	today	0
msoConditionLastWeek	last week	0
msoConditionThisWeek	this week	0
msoConditionLastMonth	last month	0
msoConditionThisMonth	this month	0
msoConditionAnytime	anytime	0
msoConditionAnytimeBetween	anytime between	2
msoConditionOn	on	1
msoConditionOnOrAfter	on or after	1
msoConditionOnOrBefore	on or before	1
msoConditionInTheNext	in the next	1

Group 4

Condition Constant	UI Equivalent	Parameters Required*
msoConditionIncludes	includes words	1
msoConditionBeginsWith	begins with	1
msoConditionEndsWith	ends with	1

Group 5

Condition Constant	UI Equivalent	Parameters Required*
msoConditionFileTypeDatabases		0
msoConditionFileTypeAllFiles		0
msoConditionFileTypeBinders		0

TABLE 11.2   msoCondition Constants, Grouped by Functionality (continued)

Group 5 (continued)		
Condition Constant	**UI Equivalent**	**Parameters Required***
msoConditionFileTypeExcelWorkbooks		0
msoConditionFileTypeOfficeFiles		0
msoConditionFileTypePowerPointPresentations		0
msoConditionFileTypeTemplates		0
msoConditionFileTypeWordDocuments		0

Group 6		
Condition Constant	**UI Equivalent**	**Parameters Required***
msoConditionEquals	equals	1
msoConditionDoesNotEqual	does not equal	1
msoConditionAnyNumberBetween	any number between…	2
msoConditionAtMost	at most	1
msoConditionAtLeast	at least	1
msoConditionMoreThan	more than	1
msoConditionLessThan	less than	1

Group 7		
Condition Constant	**UI Equivalent**	**Parameters Required***
msoConditionTomorrow	tomorrow	0
msoConditionNextWeek	next week	0
msoConditionNextMonth	next month	0
msoConditionIsYes	is yes	0
msoConditionIsNo	is no	0

*If 1, use the Value parameter. If 2, use both the Value and the SecondValue parameters.

Using the PropertyTests Collection

The example shown in Figures 11.1 and 11.2 provides a perfect test case for the PropertyTests collection. To produce the same search from code, you might run a procedure like the one shown in Listing 11.2, taken from basFileSearch. (You'll need to change the specified path to run the example in your own environment.)

Listing 11.2

```
Sub ComplexSearch()
    Dim varFile As Variant
    With Application.FileSearch
        .NewSearch
        .LookIn = "W:\WRITING\Books\ADH97\CH11"
        .SearchSubFolders = True
        .FileType = msoFileTypeDatabases
        .TextOrProperty = "Developer"
        With .PropertyTests
            .Add "Last Modified", msoConditionAnytimeBetween, _
                #1/1/96#, #12/31/96#
            .Add "Last Saved By", msoConditionIncludes, "Ken"
            .Add "Last Saved By", msoConditionIncludes, "Paul", _
                msoConnectorOr
        End With
        .Execute
        If .FoundFiles.Count > 0 Then
            For Each varFile In .FoundFiles
                Debug.Print varFile
            Next varFile
        End If
    End With
End Sub
```

Given all this flexibility, you should be able to find any file, local or remote, given any simple or complex set of criteria. Remember that using the Microsoft Fast Find indexing program will speed up your searches, but you don't need to use it to take advantage of the FileSearch object.

The CommandBar Object Model

Microsoft Office provides a shared mechanism for creating menus and toolbars in all its products. Access takes advantage of this technology, and all its menus and toolbars get their functionality from shared Office code. To provide a unified object model for toolbars and menu bars, the Office team has provided the new Command-Bar object hierarchy. A CommandBar object can appear in many guises, most obviously as a standard menu or as a toolbar.

Although the menu bar incarnation of a CommandBar resembles a standard Windows menu, it actually is a very different beast. Therefore, the bad news is that *any code you have that uses the Windows API to reference menus will fail in Office 97*. Even code that calls into menus created with macros will no longer work; those menus are created through the CommandBar code, as well. The good news is, of course, that Access programmers finally have complete control over their menus and toolbars. You can now create menus and toolbars programmatically, control their placement and docking characteristics, hide and show menu items whenever necessary, and much more.

The following sections discuss techniques you can use in applications to manipulate the new CommandBar object model, as well as ways in which you can replace existing code that uses the Windows API to manipulate existing menus. Along the way, you'll find techniques for solving typical programming problems involving menus, regardless of whether they were originally based on Windows API tricks.

In order to provide coverage of the CommandBar object model, we have made these assumptions:

- You've worked with Access 97's toolbars.

- You've created and modified toolbars and menus from the user interface.

- You already have an understanding of objects, properties, and methods. (For more information on these topics, see Chapters 3 and 6.)

- In any application where you want to programmatically control the CommandBar object model, you've set up a reference to the Microsoft Office 8.0 Object library.

TIP

When you load Access, all built-in CommandBar objects contain all the items they're ever going to contain (unless you modify them by adding or removing items, of course). Access simply hides and shows the various items as necessary. You need to be acutely aware of this fact as you work with the CommandBar object model, because you cannot take what you see at face value. Always inspect the Visible property of any built-in object you work with, and be aware that the count of visible menu items is almost always different from the Count property of the corresponding object. Examples throughout the following sections take this discrepancy into account.

NOTE

The CommandBar object model is just too large to be able to discuss fully in this limited space. The following sections provide suggestions on ways to use command bars and work through some sample code. In addition, this chapter will focus on menus, rather than trying to manage both menus and toolbars. The only differences, of course, are how they're displayed, so all the techniques shown here should work for both. Use this discussion to get started with this complex new technology, and then dig in through the Object Browser and the online help topics if you need to.

What's the Difference between Menus and Toolbars?

There's really not much difference between menus and toolbars. They're both stored the same way. The big difference is how they're displayed. A menu bar contains only text items, although the popup menus that "hang" off menu bars can contain text and graphics items. A toolbar, on the other hand, normally contains just graphics elements, with no text. The line can blur, of course, as you mix the text and graphics elements on a given command bar. The following sections focus mainly on the menu bar side of things because you're most likely to want to programmatically control the menus in your application. You can, of course, apply everything discussed here to either menus or toolbars—they "program" just the same. Although a given application can only have a single active menu bar, you can display any menu bar and as many toolbars as your screen can contain. You control whether an object displays as a menu bar or as a toolbar, where it appears, whether it's docked, and which items on the menu bar/toolbar are visible and enabled.

Where Are CommandBars Stored?

When you alter a built-in CommandBar object, Access stores that CommandBar information in the registry, on a per-user, per-machine basis. That way, changes to built-in CommandBars will affect all databases you (or any other user on your machine) open. If you create new menus or toolbars, however, Access stores the information with the current database. The menus and toolbars move around with the database in which they were created. On the other hand, some information about custom menus and toolbars is stored in the Registry, on a per-user, per-machine basis. Access stores information about the positions and visibility of the user-defined toolbars in the Registry, so people with different toolbar preferences can use the same database.

If you intend to distribute an application, make sure you test it on a "clean" machine (that is, a machine on which your menus and toolbars have never been used), emulating the end users' machines. That way you'll be able to see exactly what users will see when they attempt to use built-in and application-defined command bars. Remember that any specific settings about your application-defined command bars are stored in the Registry, and those Registry settings won't be distributed with your application. You'll need to programmatically set up the command bars the way you want them the first time a user runs your application.

What about Those API Calls?

No doubt about it: all code that uses the Windows API to manipulate menus will need to be rewritten for Office 97. The following sections provide some pointers and examples of using the CommandBar object model to replace your existing code. Rather than focus on individual API calls, however, we describe how to handle the most common scenarios that caused developers to work outside the tools Access provided natively and suggest methods for achieving the same results using the CommandBar object model instead of API calls.

> **NOTE**
>
> The SetMenuItem method of the DoCmd object will continue to work, of course. You won't need to change code that uses this method, although it will work only with menus you've created with macros. If you use the Tools➤ Macros ➤ Create Menu from Macro menu item to convert your macro-type menus to Command-Bars, SetMenuItem will no longer work. It never worked with built-in menus, and it won't work on menus you create as CommandBars, either.

> **WARNING**
>
> If you've used the Windows API to Manipulate a form's system menu (the menu hanging off the control box), you're out of luck—there's just no way to emulate that behavior in Access 97. Because those menus are now CommandBar objects, the API won't work. And because there's no exposed way to retrieve information about that menu from Access (unlike the rich CommandBar object model for menus and toolbars), there's just no reasonable way to work with these menus.

What Kinds of Objects Are There?

As you can see in Figure 11.4, there really are only two types of objects in the CommandBar object hierarchy: CommandBar objects and CommandBarControl objects. Each CommandBar object contains a collection of CommandBarControl objects. The interesting part is that the CommandBarControl object can be one of several types, as shown in Table 11.3.

FIGURE 11.4

The CommandBar object model is quite simple. Working with it is not.

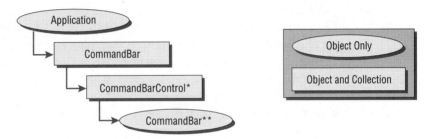

* Can be one of the CommandBarControlButton, CommandBarControlComboBox, CommandBarControlPopup subclasses. Each of the different classes adds its own set of properties and methods.

** Appears only if parent's Type is CommandBarControlPopup

TABLE 11.3   Base and Derived Classes for Command Bars

Object	Description
CommandBarControl	Base class for all the command bar controls. In addition to the three types listed below, you can create a simple edit box control, using the Add method of the CommandBarControls collection of a CommandBar
CommandBarButton	Derived type for command bar buttons. May look like a typical menu bar item or like a toolbar button
CommandBarComboBox	Derived type for various drop-down/combo box lists, like Access' list of controls when in Form Design view
CommandBarPopup	Derived type for a menu bar item that contains another menu bar. Use the CommandBar property of an item of this class to obtain a reference to the CommandBar object it contains

NOTE

Of course, things aren't this simple. Built-in CommandBar objects can contain control types other than the ones shown in Table 11.3. This table lists the control types *you* can create on command bars. As usual, what you can do programmatically is a version or so behind what the Microsoft programmers can do with the same objects. In a future version of Access you may be able to create drop-down grids and use all the other interesting command bar widgets that Access itself uses, but not now.

Office 97 supplies many properties and methods for the CommandBar family of objects, and Tables 11.4 through 11.9 introduce the most useful properties and methods of each of the objects. The sections that follow demonstrate the use of many of these methods and properties. The tables do not attempt to be definitive; we have included them here only to allow you to easily peruse the options available to you. (In these tables, if the Returns column includes an enumerated type, such as msoMenuAnimation, check the Object Browser for the complete list of values.)

TABLE 11.4   A Subset of the Methods and Properties of the CommandBars Collection

Name	Type	Returns	Read-Only?	Description
ActionControl	Property	CommandBar Control	Yes	In the code called from a control's OnAction property, returns a reference to the calling control. This allows your code to react differently depending on which button was selected
ActiveMenuBar	Property	CommandBar	Yes	Returns a reference to the active menu bar (There can be only a single active menu bar at any time.)
Add	Method	CommandBar		Adds a new, empty, initially hidden CommandBar to the CommandBars collection
Count	Property	Long	Yes	Returns the number of command bars in the collection
DisplayToolTips	Property	Boolean	No	Determines whether ToolTips are displayed for command bar controls. Its effect is Office-wide (If you change this property in Access, all other Office products will conform.)

TABLE 11.4   A Subset of the Methods and Properties of the CommandBars Collection (continued)

Name	Type	Returns	Read-Only?	Description
DisplayKeysIn-ToolTips	Property	Boolean	No	Determines whether shortcut keys are shown in ToolTips. Its effect is Office-wide
FindControl	Method	CommandBar-Control		Finds a specific control in the CommandBars collection. (See online help and the "Referring to Items Other Than CommandBars" section in this chapter for more information on the parameters the method uses.)
LargeButtons	Property	Boolean	No	Controls whether command bars are using large or small buttons. Its effect is Office-wide
MenuAnimation-Style	Property	msoMenu-Animation	No	Controls the current menu anima-tion style. Its effect is Office-wide
ReleaseFocus	Method			Releases the focus from the CommandBar objects in the UI. Even if a nested control has the focus, the focus is released completely (not just one level)

TABLE 11.5   A Subset of the Methods and Properties of a CommandBar Object

Name	Type	Returns	Read-Only?	Description
Built-In	Property	Boolean	Yes	Indicates whether the CommandBar object is built in
Controls	Property	CommandBar-Controls	Yes	Returns a reference to the collection of controls contained in this CommandBar
Delete	Method			Deletes the CommandBar from the UI. Fails for built-in CommandBar objects
Enabled	Property	Boolean	No	Indicates the enabled state of the CommandBar. For built-in CommandBars, setting the Enabled property to True simply allows Access to control the state

TABLE 11.5 A Subset of the Methods and Properties of a CommandBar Object (continued)

Name	Type	Returns	Read-Only?	Description
FindControl	Method	CommandBar-Control		Finds a specific control on this CommandBar only. To search all CommandBars, see the FindControl method of the CommandBars collection
Height	Property	Long	No	Returns the current height of the CommandBar (not counting the frame) in pixels. If you set the property, the height will be snapped to the closest valid value. Attempting to set this property will fail if the Command-Bar is not in a sizable state (docked or protected)
Left	Property	Long	No	Returns the X coordinate of the bar, in pixels. If floating, the value indicates screen coordinates. If not, the value is with respect to the docking area. If set, the value will be snapped to the nearest valid value and will fail if the bar isn't movable
Name	Property	String	No	Returns the name of the bar. For built-in bars, this is the English name of the CommandBar object, and it is read-only. Setting this property will fail if the name already exists in the CommandBars collection
NameLocal	Property	String	No	Returns the localized name for the CommandBar
Parent	Property	Object	Yes	Returns a reference to the parent of the CommandBar. If the CommandBar is a popup menu, its parent is the CommandBarPopup control to which it's attached
Position	Property	msoBarPosition	No	Indicates the current bar position. Setting this property to msoBarFloating returns the bar to its last floating position. You cannot set a bar's Position property to msoBarPopup; that value is available only to popup bars, and that setting is determined when you create the CommandBar object

TABLE 11.5 A Subset of the Methods and Properties of a CommandBar Object (continued)

Name	Type	Returns	Read-Only?	Description
Protection	Property	msoBarProtection	No	Indicates the bar's protection from various actions in the UI. You can combine the msoBarProtection values with the Or operator
Reset	Method			Resets a built-in CommandBar to its default state. Fails for user-defined CommandBars
ShowPopup	Method			Shows a popup menu at a specified location. Allows you to create your own popup menus anywhere on the screen
RowIndex	Property	Long	No	Indicates the logical row used by the bar when it docks. Set to a positive integer, or one of msoBarRowFirst (0) and msoBarRowLast (−1)
Top	Property	Long	No	Returns the Y coordinate of the bar, in pixels. If floating, the value indicates screen coordinates. If not, the value is with respect to the docking area. If set, the value will be snapped to the nearest valid value and setting the property will fail if the bar isn't movable
Type	Property	msoBarType	Yes	Indicates the command bar type (top-level toolbar, menu bar, or popup menu)
Visible	Property	Boolean	No	Indicates whether a CommandBar is currently visible. Cannot be set for popup menus, but it can be read. Use the Execute method of the parent control to make a popup menu visible. Setting this property to True will fail if the CommandBar isn't currently enabled
Width	Property	Long	No	Returns the width of the bar, in pixels. If floating, the value indicates screen coordinates. If not, the value is with respect to the docking area. If set, the value will be snapped to the nearest valid value and setting the property will fail if the bar isn't movable

TABLE 11.6   A Subset of the Methods and Properties of the CommandBarControls Collection

Name	Type	Returns	Read-Only?	Description
Add	Method	CommandBarControl		Adds a control to the collection and returns a reference to the newly added CommandBarControl object. See online help for complete details
Count	Property	Long	Yes	Returns the number of controls in the collection, not including gaps (toolbars) and separators (menus)

TABLE 11.7   A Subset of the Methods and Properties of a CommandBarControl Object

Name	Type	Returns	Read-Only?	Description
BeginGroup	Property	Boolean	No	Indicates that the control starts a group. On toolbars, the start of the new group appears as a gap. On menus, it appears as a divider line above the control
BuiltIn	Property	Boolean	Yes	Indicates whether the control is built in. Assigning a value to a control's OnAction property causes this value to be to False, and removing the property value causes this value to revert to its original setting (for built-in controls only)
Caption	Property	String	No	Returns the caption text. Use an ampersand (&) to include a keyboard mnemonic
Copy	Method	CommandBarControl		Copies the current control onto a specified CommandBar at a specified location

TABLE 11.7   A Subset of the Methods and Properties of a CommandBarControl Object (continued)

Name	Type	Returns	Read-Only?	Description
Delete	Method			Deletes a control (temporarily, if requested)
Enabled	Property	Boolean	No	Indicates whether the control is enabled. For a built-in control, Access maintains the enabled state. You can disable any built-in control, but you cannot enable a control that Access deems disabled. For non–built-in controls, this property is used without interpretation
Execute	Method			Executes the action associated with the control
Height	Property	Long	No	Returns the current height of the control, in pixels. If you set the property, the height will be snapped to the closest valid value. Set to 0 to use the default height
Id	Property	Long	Yes	Specifies the action associated with a built-in control
Left	Property	Long	Yes	Returns the current X coordinate of the control, in pixels, from the left edge of the screen
Move	Method	CommandBarControl		Moves a control to a specified CommandBar at a specified location

TABLE 11.7 A Subset of the Methods and Properties of a CommandBarControl Object (continued)

Name	Type	Returns	Read-Only?	Description
OnAction	Property	String	No	Indicates the action to take for a non–built-in control. Use the name of a macro, or a function in the form =*FunctionName*(), or just *FunctionName*. Due to limitations in the design, you can't call functions in form or report class modules. Instead, call functions in global modules
Reset	Method			Resets a control to its default state
SetFocus	Method			Moves the keyboard focus to the control. This will fail if the control isn't visible and enabled
Tag	Property	String	No	Can be used to store any user-defined data. Useful when searching for a control
ToolTipText	Property	String	No	Returns the text displayed in the control's ToolTip
Top	Property	Long	Yes	Returns the Y coordinate of the top of the control, in pixels, from the top of the screen
Type	Property	msoControlType	Yes	Returns the type of the control, as specified in the list of controls in msoControlType
Visible	Property	Boolean	No	Indicates the visibility of the control. Setting this property to True allows access to control the visibility
Width	Property	Long	No	Indicates the width of a control, in pixels. Not all controls can have their width changed

TABLE 11.8   Additional Properties for the CommandBarButton Object*

Name	Type	Returns	Read-Only?	Description
BuiltInFace	Property	Boolean	No	Indicates whether the button is displaying the built-in face. Setting this property to True forces the button to use the built-in face
CopyFace	Method			Copies the control's face to the clipboard
FaceId	Property	Long	No	Indicates the ID of the icon shown on the button. This value will be 0 if the button is showing a custom face
PasteFace	Method			Pastes the face on the clipboard onto the button
ShortcutText	Property	String	No	Indicates the shortcut key text ("Ctrl+O", for example) that displays in a menu. This doesn't cause the application to map the keystroke to an action, however. Your application must supply the necessary bindings to make this happen (perhaps using an AutoKeys macro). You can apply this property only to buttons that have an OnAction property value
State	Property	msoButtonState	No	Indicates the state of a button (up, down, or mixed). You can set this property only for buttons that have an OnAction property setting. If a button is on a menu and has no image, setting this property to msoButtonDown causes the item to have a check mark in front of it. Setting it to msoButtonUp removes the check
Style	Property	msoButtonStyle	No	Controls how the button displays its icon and/or caption. You can combine possibilities using the Or operator

*Not including those it inherits from also being a command bar control

TABLE 11.9   Additional Properties for the CommandBarComboBox Object*

Name	Type	Returns	Read-Only?	Description
AddItem	Method			Adds an item to the combo box. Fails for built-in controls
Clear	Method			Removes all items from the list. Fails for built-in controls
DropDownLines	Property	Long	No	Specifies the number of lines in the drop-down list. Set to 0 to have Access compute this for you. This property can be changed only for non–built-in controls
DropDownWidth	Property	Long	No	Specifies the width, in pixels, of the drop-down list. Set to 0 to use the width of the control. Set to –1 to use the longest item in the list. You can change this property only for non–built-in controls
List	Property	String	No	Returns an array (indexed starting with 1) allowing you to set or retrieve the text of any item in the list
ListCount	Property	Long	Yes	Returns the number of items in the list
ListHeaderCount	Property	Long	No	Indicates the number of items drawn above the separator line, commonly used as a most-frequently-used list (see frmCustomers in the sample database). Set to –1 (the default) to have no separator. Set to 0 to indicate an empty list. You can set this property only for non–built-in controls

TABLE 11.9   Additional Properties for the CommandBarComboBox Object* (continued)

Name	Type	Returns	Read-Only?	Description
ListIndex	Property	Long	No	Returns the index (starting with 1) of the selected item in the list. Returns 0 if nothing is selected
RemoveItem	Method			Removes the specified item from the list. Available only for non–built-in controls
Style	Property	msoComboStyle	No	Specifies the display style for the combo box
Text	Property	String	No	Returns the text displayed in the edit area of the control

*Not including those it inherits from also being a command bar control

CommandBars and CommandBarControls

Although the object model for CommandBars is simple, there are so many options and variations that the actual work becomes quite complex. Because there are so few object types and the objects all contain other objects, the recursion can get tricky. On the other hand, the basics of command bars can be boiled down to a few statements:

- Each CommandBar object contains a collection of CommandBarControl objects (its Controls collection).

- Each CommandBarControl object within the collection of controls can be a CommandBarComboBox, a CommandBarButton, or a CommandBarPopup.

- If the control is a CommandBarComboBox or CommandBarButton, it has its own set of properties and methods, but it cannot contain other controls.

- If the control is a CommandBarPopup, then it has a CommandBar property that refers to the CommandBar object it contains. The menus hanging off CommandBarPopup controls are called popup menus, and their Type property indicates that they're not menu bars.

Examples in the sections that follow demonstrate how to enumerate, modify, and create objects within these collections.

TIP

Because there is so little documentation on CommandBars and their subsidiary objects, you'll want to spend a lot of time in the Object Browser. Start with the top-level object you're interested in, and work your way down through the objects and their properties until you find the item you need. For example, to investigate the various control types you might find on a built-in menu bar, start with the CommandBarControl object on the left side of the Browser. On the right, find the Type property. In the bottom pane, you'll see "Property Type as MsoControlType." Click on "MsoControlType," and the Browser takes you to a list of the different control types. Make use of the Go Back and Go Forward buttons at the top of the Browser, as well, to move back to a previous location or forward to the next.

Working with the CommandBar Collections

CommandBar collections work just like collections of any other type of object. The only difficult issue is that a CommandBar object can contain a collection of CommandBarControl objects, each of which might contain a single CommandBar object itself, accessed through the CommandBar property of the control. The simple procedure in Listing 11.3, from basEnumerate, lists all the members of the CommandBars collection to the Debug window. You'll see right away that very few of the available CommandBar objects are actually visible. (Imagine the chaos that would ensue if all command bars were visible all the time!) Most likely, only the Menu Bar and Visual Basic CommandBar objects are visible when you run this code. Any CommandBar object with its Visible property set to True will be visible in Access.

Listing 11.3

```
Sub ListAllCBRs()
    Dim cbr As CommandBar
    For Each cbr In CommandBars
        Debug.Print cbr.Name, cbr.Visible
    Next cbr
End Sub
```

Perusing Controls on a CommandBar

Each CommandBar object contains a collection of controls, and you can enumerate the elements of this collection, as well. The example in Listing 11.4 prints a list of all the CommandBar objects, as well as the caption and type of each of the controls on each command bar.

To make the output from the procedure a bit more useful, it accepts an optional Boolean parameter. This parameter allows you to control whether the procedure displays all command bars or just the visible ones. If you want to see the list of visible command bars, either call it with no parameter or send it a True value (the default). If you want to see them all, pass a False value for the parameter.

Figure 11.5 shows the output from DumpCBRs (Listing 11.4, in basEnumerate). If you study the output you'll see that most of the items on the Visual Basic command bar are type 1 (msoControlButton), although the first item is type 14 (msoControlSplitButtonMRUPopup). You can create your own items of type 1, but you won't be able to create your own type 14s (at least, not in this version of Access). Also note that all the items on the CommandBar that is displayed as a menu are type 10 (msoControlPopup), as they should be. This is the type you'll find for all popup menus.

> **TIP**
>
> You can use any datatype for an optional parameter in Access 97. (In Access 95 you could use only a Variant type.) The IsMissing function, however, works only with Variants. If you want to pass a non-Variant optional parameter, don't count on using IsMissing to check for its existence. Instead, use the new ability to supply a default value directly in the procedure's format declaration. This is how the DumpCBRs procedure works.

Listing 11.4

```
Sub DumpCBRs(Optional VisibleOnly As Boolean = True)
    Dim cbr As CommandBar
    Dim cbc As CommandBarControl

    For Each cbr In CommandBars
        If VisibleOnly Imp cbr.Visible Then
            Debug.Print cbr.Name
            For Each cbc In cbr.Controls
                If VisibleOnly Imp cbc.Visible Then
                    Debug.Print , cbc.Caption, cbc.Type
                End If
            Next cbc
        End If
    Next cbr
End Sub
```

FIGURE 11.5

DumpCBRs provides a list of menu items and their types.

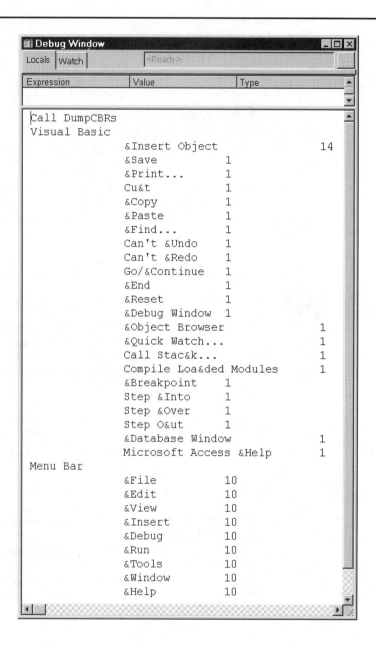

NOTE The Imp operator is an odd one—it's a seldom-used logical operator that returns a True value in all cases *except* when the first parameter is True and the second is False. In this case you want to display all command bars except when the VisibleOnly flag is True and the object's Visible property is set to False. You want to hide the object from the output only in that single case. You could get the same effect with a more complex logical expression, but the Imp operator is elegant and does exactly what you need in this example.

Looking at All Menu Items

The final example procedure in this section, DumpAllMenus (Listing 11.5, from basEnumerate), prints a list of all the items on the Access menus or on a specific popup menu. It displays each item's caption and its menu ID. DumpAllMenus calls the DumpMenu procedure to list items on a particular popup menu. That procedure calls itself recursively if it finds a control for which the type is Command-BarPopup on the current popup menu. (None of the Access menus are nested more than two levels deep, but you could nest your own menus more deeply than that and this procedure would still work correctly.)

You can call DumpAllMenus a number of ways. You can pass it no parameters, and it lists all the items on all the top-level popup menus and their nested menus. You can also pass the name of a top-level submenu ("File", "Edit", "Help", and so on), and DumpAllMenus will list all the items on that particular popup menu.

NOTE Because this procedure uses the particular popup menu name to obtain a reference to the menu, it will work only with the English-language version of Access. Access maintains English and localized versions for the names of all the built-in command bars themselves, but not for all the controls on those menus. If you look in the Object Browser you'll see that CommandBar objects expose both a Name and a NameLocal property, but these are the only objects that include both names. For the most part you cannot refer to CommandBar subobjects by name. Instead, you need to use the FindControl method, discussed in the section "Referring to Items Other Than CommandBars" a little later in this chapter.

Listing 11.5

```
Sub DumpAllMenus(Optional TopMenu As String = "Menu Bar")
    Dim cbr As CommandBar
    Dim cbp As CommandBarPopup

    Set cbr = CommandBars("Menu Bar")
    If TopMenu <> "Menu Bar" Then
        Set cbp = cbr.Controls(TopMenu)
        Call DumpMenu(cbp, 1)
    Else
        For Each cbp In cbr.Controls
            Debug.Print cbp.Caption
            Call DumpMenu(cbp, 1)
        Next cbp
    End If
End Sub

Sub DumpMenu(cbp As CommandBarPopup, intLevel As Integer)
    Dim cbc As CommandBarControl
    Dim intI As Integer

    For Each cbc In cbp.CommandBar.Controls
        ' Insert enough spaces to indent according to the
        ' level of recursion.
        For intI = 0 To intLevel
            Debug.Print "    ";
        Next intI
        Debug.Print cbc.Caption, cbc.Id
        If cbc.Type = msoControlPopup Then
            ' Call this routine recursively, to document
            ' the next-lower level.
            Call DumpMenu(cbc.Control, intLevel + 1)
        End If
    Next cbc
End Sub
```

> **NOTE**
> Because DumpAllMenus is only a diagnostic tool, it includes no error handling. In a real application this sort of routine would need to trap for the error that would occur if the caller supplied an invalid menu name.

In the basDumpIDs module in the sample database, you'll find a procedure (DumpIDs) that fills the contents of the tblControlID table in the
database with a list of all the built-in menu items and the Id property of
each. You'll need this information later if you want to programmatically
control any of the built-in menu items. Run this procedure once to fill the
table, and then use it to find the ID you need.

Referring to CommandBars and Their Items

Because there's no simple way for you to know which items exist in any given
CommandBar's collection of items, you'll need to take some special steps to obtain a
reference to a specific object within Access' hierarchy of CommandBars. The following
sections discuss the various techniques you can use to point at the object you need.

Referring to CommandBars

To make it easy for you to retrieve a reference to a specific top-level Command-
Bar object, you can refer to the object by its English name. Even though your application may be translated into a local language other than English, the English
references will work (just as they do for the GetOption and SetOption methods,
which require string parameters). That is, the following code will work in any
localized version of Access:

```
Dim cbr As CommandBar
Set cbr = CommandBars("Menu Bar")
```

Of course, the following code works just as well:

```
Dim cbr As CommandBar
Set cbr = CommandBars![Menu Bar]
```

and this code may even execute a tiny bit more quickly. On the other hand, it won't
do you any good, at any point when working with CommandBars and their
objects, to attempt to use syntax like this:

```
Set cbr = CommandBars(0)
```

unless you want to iterate through all the CommandBars. Although you can refer
to an element of the CommandBars collection by its ordinal position in the collection, you won't want to, for the most part. When you start Access (or any Office
application), the CommandBars collection contains all the built-in items, and the

application hides and shows them as necessary. Therefore, you can't figure out an item's index by looking at a menu or toolbar; all the hidden items take up an index "slot," as well. Instead, you'll most often refer to elements at the CommandBar level by name and at lower levels using the techniques shown in the next section.

Referring to Items Other Than CommandBars

Unfortunately, objects other than CommandBars don't expose both their local name and their English name (only their local name), so you'll need to take extra steps to find a particular object within a command bar. If you attempt to refer to items on a CommandBar by their English names, your code won't work in any other localized version of Access. If you don't care about this issue, you can build long strings of references, working your way through the collections. For example, to obtain a reference to the Tools ➤ Analyze ➤ Table menu item, you could use code like this:

```
Dim cbc As CommandBarControl
Set cbc = CommandBars("Menu Bar"). _
 Controls("Tools").CommandBar.Controls("Analyze"). _
 CommandBar.Controls("Table")
```

On the other hand, if you need to be able to find a specific control in any localized version of Access, you'll use the FindControl method. This method, of either the CommandBars collection or of a specific CommandBar object, makes it possible to find the exact CommandBarControl object you need.

The syntax for the FindControl method looks like this:

object.FindControl(*Type, Id, Tag, Visible, Recursive*)

For this method, all the arguments are optional, but you must at least supply one of Type, Id, and Tag. Table 11.10 describes each of the parameters.

Why is the FindControl method available to the entire CommandBars collection and to specific CommandBar objects as well? If you need to find a control and you don't know on which command bar the user has placed it, code like this will search all CommandBar objects until it finds a match:

```
CommandBars.FindControl Id:=123, Recursive:=True
```

If you want to search just a particular CommandBar object (the Menu Bar object, for example), you'll want to use code like this:

```
Dim cbrMenu as CommandBar
Dim cbcDebug as CommandBarControl
```

```
Set cbrMenu = CommandBars("Menu Bar")
' Find the Debug window menu item.
Set cbcDebug = cbrMenu.FindControl(Id:=560, Recursive:=True)
```

TABLE 11.10 Parameters for the FindControl Method*

Parameter	Description
Type	The type of control to be searched for. Must be one of the items from the msoControlType enumeration list from the Object Browser. Supply the constant value indicating which control type you're searching for
Id	The identifier of the control you're searching for. This is useful only if you're searching for a built-in control. Use the values from tblControlID. (Create this table by running DumpIDs in the sample database.)
Tag	The tag value of the control you're searching for. You're most likely to use this parameter if you're searching for a control your code created (and you set the Tag property when you created it)
Visible	Set to True to search only for visible controls. The default value is False
Recursive	Set to True to include the selected object and all its sub–command bars in the search. The default is False

*Applies both to the CommandBars collection or a specific CommandBar object

TIP

Although using the ID of a menu command is the only way to search for and find a specific built-in menu item, you'll want to refrain from using this technique. Because the menu Id property can and will change from version to version, you're leaving yourself open to maintainability problems if you use the ID directly. Unfortunately, you have no other choice if you want to find and modify an existing menu item. For menu items you create, you'll use the string you've set in the Tag property instead, so there will be no issues of upgradability. Of course, you can set the Tag property of a built-in menu item using the Access user interface (right-click on the item in Customize mode and choose the Properties item from the menu), but that doesn't help if you want to write an application to work on many users' machines.

Tips to Get You Started

If you've made it this far, you at least have a basic concept of what a CommandBar object is and how menu items "hang" off a CommandBar. The following sections contain a number of small tidbits, some with longer explanations, to help you further in your exploration of CommandBars. Using CommandBars is such a large topic, and so rich with possibilities, there's no way we can cover all the options here. These sections contain all the information you need to get started, and studying the examples is a great way to begin on your own CommandBar projects.

Referring to CommandBarControl Captions

You can use item names without the ampersand (&) (indicating the position of the hot key), and the names are not case sensitive. In addition, the trailing "…" included on some menu items is significant: if it's on the menu, you must include it in your object reference. (This tip really applies only if you're searching for the menu control by name. That's not a good idea if your intent is to write an application that will work in multiple localized languages.)

Everything's a Control

The objects on a given CommandBar are all controls. Whether you're displaying the command bar as a toolbar or a menu bar, most elements are command buttons. The difference between a toolbar and a menu is how the button is displayed.) Toolbars can also display controls besides command buttons (drop-down lists, for example); menus cannot.

Divide and Conquer

Divider lines in menus, and spaces in toolbars, aren't counted as controls. To indicate to the CommandBar that you want a divider line before a control, set the control's BeginGroup property to True. The divider/space has no effect on any item counts, nor does it affect indexes within collections.

For example, the example in Listing 11.6 (from basCommandBars) inserts a divider line before the third item ("Get External Data") on the command bar referred to by cbrPopup (the popup menu hanging off the first control on the main menu bar, the File menu).

Listing 11.6

```
Sub StartGroup
    Dim cbrMain as CommandBar
    Dim cbrPopup as CommandBar
    Set cbrMain = CommandBars("Menu Bar")
    Set cbrPopup = cbrMain.Controls(1).CommandBar
    cbrPopup.Controls(3).BeginGroup = True
End Sub
```

Roll Your Own? We Think Not

The controls used on command bars are specific to their implementation and aren't ActiveX controls, intrinsic Access controls, Office forms controls, or VBX controls. You cannot create your own control types, nor can you add to the list of controls that you can place on Access' command bars. You can add buttons and edit controls, drop-down lists, combo boxes, and popup menus. That's it.

IDs and Actions

A built-in CommandBar item's Id property indicates the action that control will take when it's selected, and it also indicates the image that appears on the built-in item by default. In addition, you can use the FaceId property to set just the image displayed on a control without affecting the action it takes. Finally, the OnAction property allows you to override the built-in action for any control that can take an action. The following list details the interactions between the three properties:

- You can use the Add method of a CommandBar's Controls collection, setting the Id parameter to match the ID of a built-in control to indicate that your control should match the appearance and action of the built-in control. This property is read-only once you've added the control to its collection.

- You can use the FaceId property of a control to set its appearance to match one of the built-in controls. See DumpIDs in basDumpIDs to create a complete list of controls' Id values.

- You can use the OnAction property of a control to specify an action that can override the action provided by the Id property for the control. See the next section for more information on using the OnAction property. If you want to take an action, you'll need to set the OnAction property to call a macro or a function that performs the action.

To make it easier for you to work with menu ID values, we've included the DumpIDs procedure, in basDumpIDs. This procedure writes all the Id property values to tblControlID, allowing you to find the exact ID value you need.

Using the OnAction Property

Use the OnAction property of CommandBarControl objects to execute an action when you select the item. The property can contain a string expression resolving to either the name of a macro (supply just the macro name, as a string) or a function call, in the form

=FunctionName()

(You can also just enter the function name without the leading "=" and the trailing "()".)

To cause a menu item to be checked, or to create a two-state button, the control must have its OnAction property set to call something. (To see two-state buttons in action, check out the View menu when the database window is selected; the Large Icons, Small Icons, List, and Details items all use a two-state button to indicate the current setting.)

Creating Your Own Menu Items

To create your own item on a menu (or toolbar), you use the Add method of a CommandBar object. Once you've created the new CommandBarControl object, you need to set its properties so it does what you need. You must at least set the Caption property so the control displays a caption. You should also set either the Id property so the control emulates one of the built-in controls or the OnAction property so the item does something when you select it. You can also set any or all of the other CommandBarControl properties, described in the Object Browser and online help.

For example, the code in Listing 11.7 (from basCustomItem) adds a menu item with the caption "Minimize Window" to the File menu, right before the "Save" item. The menu item will call the function MinimizeIt when it's selected. The code also sets the item's Tag property to match its caption so you'll be able to use the FindControl method later if you need to find the menu item again. To show that this works, the code also adds a Maximize Window menu item, using the FindControl method to find the previously added control and adding the new item right above it.

Listing 11.7

```
Sub AddMinimize()
    Dim cbr As CommandBar
    Dim cbc As CommandBarControl
    Dim cbcFile As CommandBarControl
    Dim cbcSave As CommandBarControl
    Dim cbcMinimize As CommandBarControl

    Set cbr = CommandBars("Menu Bar")

    ' Search for the top-level File menu.
    Set cbcFile = cbr.FindControl(Id:=30002, Recursive:=False)
```

```
' Search for the "Save" item on the File menu.
Set cbcSave = cbr.FindControl(Id:=3, Recursive:=True)

If Not cbcFile Is Nothing Then
    If cbcSave Is Nothing Then
        ' Add the item to the end of the menu.
        Set cbc = cbcFile.CommandBar.Controls.Add( _
        msoControlButton)
    Else
        ' Add the item before the Save item.
        Set cbc = cbcFile.CommandBar.Controls.Add( _
        msoControlButton, Before:=cbcSave.Index)
    End If
    With cbc
        .Caption = "Minimize Window"
        .OnAction = "MinimizeIt"
        ' Set the Tag property so you can
        ' get back to this item later using FindControl.
        .Tag = "Minimize Window"
    End With
End If
' Now, find the item you just added, and add a
' new item below it. Of course, you don't really have to
' search for the control here—you've already got it
' referred to in the cbc variable. Just trying to
' prove a point here.
Set cbcMinimize = cbr.FindControl( _
 Tag:="Minimize Window", Recursive:=True)
If Not cbcMinimize Is Nothing Then
    Set cbc = cbcFile.CommandBar.Controls.Add( _
    msoControlButton, Before:=cbcMinimize.Index)
    With cbc
        .Caption = "Maximize Window"
        .OnAction = "MaximizeIt"
        ' Set the Tag property so you can
        ' get back to this item later using FindControl.
        .Tag = "Maximize Window"
    End With
End If
End Sub

Function MinimizeIt()
    DoCmd.RunCommand acCmdDocMinimize
End Function
```

```
Function MaximizeIt()
    DoCmd.RunCommand acCmdDocMaximize
End Function

Sub ResetMenus()
    ' Use this procedure to reset your menus.
    CommandBars("Menu Bar").Reset
End Sub
```

> **TIP**
>
> When working with CommandBars, you'll often want to reset the main menu bar. To do so, include a subroutine like the ResetMenus procedure in Listing 11.7. That way, all you need to do is place your cursor in the routine and press F5 to run it; your menu bars will be reset to their "factory" state.

Working with Other CommandBarControl Objects

Although most of the controls you'll use on command bars will be command buttons, you may want to place an edit box or a combo box on a command bar. Each control has its own set of properties and methods, but the combo box control is interesting, and very useful.

The sample form, frmCustomers, creates a new command bar with a few normal command button controls (Print, Filter By Form, Filter By Selection, Apply Filter), and a combo box control as well. The combo box lists all the primary keys of all the rows displayed in the form's recordset and allows you to select a row to view. Listing 11.8 contains the code used to create the CommandBar and its controls. Note that the combo box calls, in its OnAction property, the FindRow function. Listing 11.9 contains the code for that function, found in the basCallback module.

> **TIP**
>
> Take some time to investigate the properties of the CommandBarCombo-Box control; it works more like the Visual Basic combo box than any Access control. In addition, it includes some new properties, such as the Style property, that control how it appears on the command bar.

Listing 11.8

```
Private Sub Form_Load()
    Dim cbr As CommandBar
    Dim cbo As CommandBarComboBox
    Dim ctl As CommandBarControl
    Dim rst As Recordset

    Set cbr = CommandBars.Add("Customers", _
     Position:=msoBarTop, Temporary:=True)
    With CommandBars("Form View").Controls
        .Item("Print...").Copy cbr
        .Item("Filter By Selection").Copy cbr
        .Item("Filter By Form").Copy cbr
        .Item("Apply Filter").Copy cbr
    End With
    With cbr
        Set cbo = .Controls.Add(msoControlComboBox, Before:=1)
        With cbo
            .Tag = "CustomerID"
            .Caption = "Select Customer &ID:"
            .Style = msoComboLabel
            .DropDownWidth = cbo.Width
            Set rst = Me.RecordsetClone
            Do While Not rst.EOF
                .AddItem rst!CustomerID
                rst.MoveNext
            Loop
            .OnAction = "FindRow"
        End With
        Me.Toolbar = "Customers"
    End With
End Sub
```

Listing 11.9

```
Public Function FindRow()
    Dim strID As String
    Dim rst As Recordset
    Dim varBM As Variant
    Dim cbc As CommandBarControl

    Set cbc = CommandBars.ActionControl
```

```
        strID = cbc.Text
        If Len(strID) > 0 Then
            With Screen.ActiveForm
                Set rst = .RecordsetClone
                rst.FindFirst "CustomerID = '" & strID & "'"
                If Not rst.NoMatch Then
                    .Bookmark = rst.Bookmark
                    Call AddToList(cbc, strID)
                    cbc.Text = ""
                End If
            End With
        End If
End Function
```

In addition, to make this example a bit more interesting, the FindRow function creates a collection of "most recently used" key values in the combo box. The Command-BarComboBox control allows you to create a dividing line in the list of items in the control. You can place items above the line or below it. In this case, once you've selected a key value, the code in AddToList (See Listing 11.10) adds the selected item to the top of the list. Like many solutions, this one assumes that if you wanted to find a particular row, you're likely to want to find that row again. By creating a "most recently used" list, you can quickly return to any of the rows you've already visited.

Listing 11.10

```
Private Function AddToList(cbc As CommandBarComboBox, _
 strID As String) As Boolean

    On Error Resume Next

    colFound.Add strID, Key:=strID
    ' Yes, this code should be smarter about errors.
    ' It's only example code!
    If Err.Number <> 0 Then
        AddToList = False
    Else
        ' Add the ID to the combo box on the command bar.
        ' Always add it at the top of the list.
        Call cbc.AddItem(strID, 1)
        cbc.ListIndex = cbc.ListIndex - 1

        ' The ListHeaderCount will be -1 the first time you
```

```
        ' come through here, indicating no divider line at all.
        ' If ListHeaderCount is 0, you have a divider line with
        ' nothing above it. This code either increments the value
        ' of the property or sets it to 1 in the first place.
        If cbc.ListHeaderCount > 0 Then
            cbc.ListHeaderCount = cbc.ListHeaderCount + 1
        Else
            cbc.ListHeaderCount = 1
        End If
        AddToList = True
    End If
End Function
```

Making Things Happen

To cause a CommandBarControl object to execute its action, you can use the object's Execute method. Of course, you can also use the DoCmd.RunCommand method to make a menu item do its thing, but that requires you to know the corresponding acCmd… constant. If your code is handed a CommandBarControl object, there's no simple way to map that control to its equivalent RunCommand constant. Therefore, the Execute method will come in handy if you've got a reference to the CommandBarControl and you want to "make it happen." You can also use this technique if you need to take an action that isn't normally available in the current context. The Execute method doesn't take the context into account, so you must take extra care when using it.

> **TIP**
>
> Be aware that you give up some readability and maintainability if you use this technique rather than the RunCommand method. That is, using the specific acCmd… constant in your code will make it explicitly clear what that code will do. Using the Execute method of a CommandBarControl object implicitly specifies the action, and you'll need to include a comment indicating what's actually going on. In addition, you're almost guaranteed that the built-in menu ID values will change from version to version.

For example, the code in Listing 11.11 displays the Debug window, but only if the menu item is currently available. This is one case in which it makes sense to use the Execute method; you have to get to the menu item to check its visibility anyway, so once there, you can just perform its Execute method. Listing 11.11, from basCommandBars, demonstrates this technique for finding a particular built-in menu item and executing its action. (Of course, you could also just use RunCommand to accomplish the same task. If you use that technique, however, you can't check the visibility of the menu item first.)

Listing 11.11

```
Sub ShowDebugWindow()
    Dim cbrMenu As CommandBar
    Dim cbcDebug As CommandBarControl

    Set cbrMenu = CommandBars("Menu Bar")
    ' Find the Debug Window menu item.
    Set cbcDebug = cbrMenu.FindControl( _
     Id:=560, Recursive:=True)
    If cbcDebug Is Nothing Then
        MsgBox "Unable to find the requested menu item!"
    Else
        With cbcDebug
            ' If the menu item is visible,
            ' execute its action (that is,
            ' display the Debug window).
            If .Visible Then
                .Execute
            End If
        End With
    End If
End Sub
```

Where Am I?

From within the code called by the string in the OnAction property, you can use the ActionControl property of the CommandBars collection to retrieve a reference to the control that called the code. This makes it possible to take different actions, depending on the menu or toolbar item that was just selected. If you've placed information in the control's Tag property, you can also use that in your code, once you've used the ActionControl property to find out just which control called the code. The example in the section "Checking/Unchecking a Menu Item" later in this chapter that shows how to group menu items will use this property in order to know which item was just selected.

Doing Things the CommandBar Way

Once you've got the hang of working with CommandBars, you'll want to start using some advanced techniques to really get them to do what you need. If you've used calls to the Windows API in Access 2 or Access 95, however, you'll need to replace those calls with code that will operate correctly with the new object model. The following sections provide details on making those replacements. Although there's no way to provide a one-to-one correspondence between specific API calls and VBA code, the discussion attempts to help in the conversion. The information presented here is not only useful for ex-API callers, however; these techniques are useful for anyone attempting to make CommandBars do their bidding.

References Rather Than Retrieving a Menu Handle

With the Windows API, almost every menu manipulation required you to provide a valid menu handle as one of the parameters to a function call. These menu handles are nowhere to be found in the CommandBar world; you'll never again make a call to the GetMenu or GetSubMenu API function.

Instead of retrieving menu handles, you'll need to retrieve and use references to CommandBar objects. To use an existing CommandBar object (for example, the menu hanging off the View ➤ Database Objects menu item), use code like this (in the English-language version of Access):

```
Dim cbr As CommandBar
Set cbr = CommandBars("Menu Bar").Controls("View"). _
 CommandBar.Controls("Database Objects").CommandBar
```

If you want to write code that will work in any localized version, you'll need to use the FindControl method of the CommandBar object:

```
Dim cbr As CommandBar
 ' Find the Database Objects popup menu.
Set cbr = CommandBars("Menu Bar").FindControl( _
 Id:=30107, Recursive:=True).CommandBar
```

This technique counts on your knowing the ID for each built-in menu item. Use the code in basDumpIDs to create tblControlID, a list of all the built-in ID values. Of course, as mentioned previously, you can use the Tag property to find a menu item you've created, as long as you set the Tag property when you create the item (or at least before you need to find the item).

Retrieving the Number of Items in a Menu

Your application may need to know the number of items on a menu. If your code previously called the GetMenuItemCount API function, you might try replacing it with simple code that retrieves the Count property of a given CommandBar. This won't work, however, because the Count property also includes all the items that aren't visible in the current context. You can use something like the function in Listing 11.12, from basCountItems, to replace calls to the GetMenuItemCount API function.

Listing 11.12

```
Function GetMenuItemCount(cbr As CommandBar, _
  Optional ByVal CountAll As Boolean = False) _
  As Integer

    ' Given a CommandBar reference, return the
    ' number of items it includes. Optionally, count
    ' all the items. The default is to just count visible
    ' items.

    Dim cbc As CommandBarControl
    Dim intCount As Integer
    Dim fCountAll As Boolean

    For Each cbc In cbr.Controls
        ' Increment the count if either
        ' you're counting all or this item
        ' actually is visible.
        If CountAll Or cbc.Visible Then
            intCount = intCount + 1
        End If
    Next cbc
    GetMenuItemCount = intCount
End Function
```

Disabling/Enabling a Menu Item

Disabling and enabling a menu item is as simple as changing the Enabled property of a control. Once you have a reference to the item you want to enable or disable, just set the value of its Enabled property, and you're all done. Using the Windows API, disabling and enabling a menu item required you to retrieve a menu handle and then call the EnableMenuItem API function.

To disable the Edit ➤ Undo Typing menu item programmatically, you might write code like the following. (Note that all the items that appear in the Undo slot share the same ID.)

```
Dim cbc As CommandBarControl
Set cbc = CommandBars("Menu Bar").FindControl( _
```

```
Id:=128, Recursive:=True)
cbc.Enabled = False
```

> **NOTE** Attempting to enable a menu item that Access wants disabled is a fruitless exercise. You're welcome to programmatically disable an enabled menu item, such as Edit ➤ Undo Typing, and Access will respect your changes. On the other hand, if you attempt to enable a menu item that Access thinks should be disabled, your change will be discarded without triggering an error. For example, attempting to enable the Edit ➤ Can't Undo menu item will have no effect as long as Access thinks it ought to be disabled. The same issues apply when you attempt to make a command bar visible; if Access doesn't want that item to be shown, nothing you can do will cause it to be displayed.

To try this out, open frmTestUndo, first click the Re-Enable Undo Command button (in case you tried the previous example, leaving you with the Undo item disabled). With the menus reset, click the Disable Undo Command button, modify some text, and then try to use the Edit ➤ Undo menu item. It will be disabled because the button (which calls the code shown above) disables it.

Checking/Unchecking a Menu Item

From a CommandBarControl's point of view, the "checked" state of a menu item is the same as the "selected" state for a two-state toolbar button. For example, in Form Design view, the Align Left, Center, and Align Right toolbar buttons could also be represented on a menu, with one of the three items being "checked." Using the Windows API, doing so required retrieving a menu handle for the parent menu and then using the CheckMenuItem API function.

You won't find a Checked property in the Object Browser or online help, because it doesn't exist. Instead, you'll use the State property of a CommandBarControl object to control the checked condition. To work with the checked state, your selected control must follow some rules. It must

- Either have no specific value set for its Id property or have a value set that doesn't insert a picture to the left of the menu item (You can also set the Style property so that the control doesn't display the associated image.)

- Not be a built-in control

- Call a macro or function from its OnAction property

So, when can you control the State property of a CommandBarControl? If you've created the item, set it up to call a macro or function when selected, and haven't set an image or explicitly hidden the image, you will be able to set its State property. If you attempt to set the State property for a built-in control, all you'll get for your efforts is a run-time error.

For example, the code in Listing 11.13 (from basCreateColors) creates a new menu containing five colors. Each item on the menu calls the HandleColors function when you select it, and that function places a check mark next to the selected item and clears the check for all other items. (Of course, in real life you'd want the Handle-Colors routine to also perform some action in response to the menu selection.)

Listing 11.13

```
Sub CreateColors()
    ' Create checked menus.
    Dim cbp As CommandBarPopup
    Dim varColors As Variant
    Dim intI As Integer

    ' Set up the array of colors.
    varColors = Array("Blue", "Green", "Pink", "Yellow", "White")

    ' Create the top-level menu.
    Set cbp = CommandBars("Menu Bar").Controls.Add( _
     msoControlPopup, Temporary:=True)
    cbp.Caption = "&Color"

    ' Loop through the array, adding one menu item for
    ' each element of the array.
    With cbp.CommandBar.Controls
        For intI = LBound(varColors) To UBound(varColors)
            With .Add(msoControlButton)
                .Caption = varColors(intI)
                .OnAction = "HandleColors"
            End With
        Next intI
    End With
End Sub


Public Function HandleColors()
    ' Function called from OnAction property.
    Dim strCaption As String
```

```
Dim cbc As CommandBarControl
Dim cbcItem As CommandBarControl
Debug.Print "Here"
' Get the selected control and store its caption.
Set cbc = CommandBars.ActionControl
strCaption = cbc.Caption

' Loop through all the controls in the CommandBar
' object that's the parent of the selected control.
For Each cbcItem In cbc.Parent.Controls
    With cbcItem
        ' Check the selected item, uncheck all the rest.
        If .Caption = cbc.Caption Then
            .State = msoButtonDown
        Else
            .State = msoButtonUp
        End If
    End With
Next cbcItem
End Function
```

Changing the Text of a Menu Item

Using the Windows API, you would have called the ModifyMenu and Draw-MenuBar functions in order to modify the text of a menu item (after you'd retrieved a handle to the parent menu). Using the CommandBar object model, you change the Caption property (and perhaps the ToolTipText, ShortCutText, and DescriptionText properties as well) of any control.

For example, to modify the text of the Edit ➤ Delete menu item, you could write code like this:

```
With CommandBars("Menu Bar"). _
 Controls("Edit").CommandBar.Controls("Delete")
    .Caption = "Remove"
    .ToolTipText = "Remove the selected item"
End With
```

Deleting a Menu Item

To delete a menu item, use the Delete method of a CommandBarControl—even a control on the main menu bar. (If the control is a CommandBarPopup control and has a menu hanging off it, the Delete method for the item will delete its child menu as well.) The Delete method replaces calls to the RemoveMenu API function.

Take note of these items:

- Think twice before deleting a menu item. It's much easier in the long run to set a control's Visible property to False instead. That way, if you need to show the item again, you don't need to re-create it. If your intent is to delete it from one place and insert it in another, consider the Move method instead.

- If you delete a built-in item by mistake, you can use the Reset method of a CommandBar object to set the menus back the way Access created them.

Displaying a Popup Menu

Access makes it easy to assign a shortcut menu to any control or form, but what if you want to pop up a menu at any location, at any time? The Windows API made this possible, although doing it in previous versions of Access was tricky; it required a lot of calculations, and creating a menu that didn't appear as part of the menu bar was quite a kludge.

Command bars make displaying a popup menu trivial. You can use the ShowPopup method of a popup CommandBar object—that is, a CommandBar object whose Style property has been set to 2 (msoBarTypePopup)—and specify the location if you like. If you don't specify the location, the menu will appear at the current mouse location.

The code in Listing 11.14, from basPopup, uses the ShowPopup method of a CommandBar object to display the popup menu either at the current location or at a specified location:

Listing 11.14

```
Function TrackPopupMenu(cbr As CommandBar, _
  Optional X As Variant, Optional Y As Variant)
' Display a popup menu at a specified location.
    If cbr.Type = msoBarTypePopup Then
      If IsMissing(X) And Not IsMissing(Y) Then
        cbr.ShowPopup , Y
      ElseIf IsMissing(Y) And Not IsMissing(X) Then
        cbr.ShowPopup X
      ElseIf IsMissing(X) And IsMissing(Y) Then
        cbr.ShowPopup
      Else
        cbr.ShowPopup X, Y
      End If
    End If
End Function
```

To pop up the Database Background menu at the current vertical position but at the left edge of the screen, you could call code like this:

```
TrackPopupMenu CommandBars("Database Background"), 0
```

Some Final Thoughts

The preceding sections have touched but a tiny portion of the functionality provided by the CommandBar object model. If you want to work with Office menus, take the time to dig through the online help topics and the lists of properties and methods in the Object Browser. You'll find much more flexibility in the new objects than was ever possible using the Windows API directly, and the code you'll write will be much cleaner. You will need to modify all your code that uses the Windows API to manipulate menus, but the final outcome will be simpler to read, maintain, and modify.

The Office Assistant

The Office Assistant is a third shared component provided by Microsoft Office. Its intent is to help users feel comfortable with all the Office applications and to provide suggestions that will help them make better use of the products. However you personally feel about the Assistant's usefulness, it's hard to discount the fact that the Assistant is just plain fun. The following sections explain what you can do with the Assistant in applications and how to take advantage of this technology to make your users more productive.

Using the Assistant: Advantages and Limitations

If you're like most developers we know, the first thing you'll want to do with the Assistant is turn it *off*! For developers, it's a cute little oddity that quickly wears thin. No matter what you want to do or need to know, if you've been developing applications with Access for a while, you can get the job done more quickly without the Assistant.

On the other hand, end users and beginners may find this addition to Office products a welcome helper. All Office 97 applications use the Assistant to provide help, tips, and guides as users work with the products. Because users can choose their own "character," with its own personality (see the section "Personality and Neighborhood" a little later in this chapter), many end users will find this seemingly simple yet quite complex technology a worthwhile addition to the product.

You can use the Assistant in your own applications to do the same sorts of things it does for the standard Office applications:

- Provide context-sensitive help

- Show specific animations, based on options the user has chosen, steps the user has taken, or any other whim of your imagination

- Use the Assistant's Balloon object to provide a powerful replacement for Access' MsgBox

The following sections examine the second and third of these options.

The Assistant Object Model

The Assistant object model is simple, and Figure 11.6 shows it in its entirety. Note that a Balloon object can contain a collection of up to five BalloonCheckBox objects (in the CheckBoxes collection) and up to five BalloonLabel objects (in the Labels collection), but you're not likely to use both of these object types at the same time.

FIGURE 11.6

The Assistant object model. Boxes with a shadow represent objects and collections; those without represent single objects.

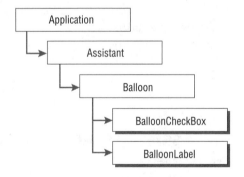

As you can see from Figure 11.6, the Assistant object can own a single Balloon object (that's the yellow area with buttons, labels, and icons that looks like a cartoon balloon). The balloon can contain up to five check boxes or up to five *labels* (the little blue "lights" on balloons that you can click). In addition, if you specify text for the Labels collection (the collection of BalloonLabel objects) you can display the text with blue lights, numbers, or bullets, depending on the BalloonType property.

NOTE The Assistant is available only to users who own a copy of Microsoft Office 97. If you're a Word or Excel developer, this isn't an issue, because anyone using your add-in or product will, of course, own the product. If you're an Access or VB developer, however, this complicates issues. Applications distributed with the run-time version of Access or as VB 4 (or later) executables don't have the legal rights to distribute the Office DLLs and character files that would be necessary to make the Assistant available to your application. Of course, if those users also have a copy of Office 97 installed, they can run applications that use the Assistant.

NOTE Attempting to use more than five labels or check boxes on a balloon will trigger a run-time error.

Working with the Assistant

What can you do with the Assistant? Even if you don't work with Balloon objects (discussed later in this chapter), you can make many choices about the activities and display of the Assistant. The following sections detail some of the properties and methods of the Assistant you'll be able to take advantage of in your own applications.

Personality and Neighborhood

The most important characteristic of the Assistant is its character. The specific animations and sounds associated with a given character are stored in files with the extension .ACT, normally in a folder inside the folder where you installed Office 97. You'll use the FileName property to retrieve and set the file name for the character you want displayed. Once you've selected a character, the Name property returns a user-friendly name for the character. (This is the name you see when you right-click the character and open the Choose Assistant dialog.)

Where Are Those Characters?

If you want to supply users with a list of installed characters, you can use a technique like that used in frmAnimations, shown in Figure 11.7. This form gathers a list of all the installed actors and provides that list to the user. The form also demonstrates

FIGURE 11.7

frmAnimations allows
you to select actors and
specific animations.

all available animations and some other visible option settings. The following sections discuss other features demonstrated by this form.

The code in frmAnimations retrieves the path for all the actor files from the Registry, using the GetActorPath function. If you're interested in learning how to retrieve arbitrary values from the Registry, you might take a peek at that function. Once the code knows where the files live (*.ACT), it uses the Dir function in the GatherList procedure to loop through all the files in the directory, setting the Assistant's FileName property to each file, in turn. While each actor is loaded, the code retrieves the Name property as well and then moves on to the next file. As the code works, it builds up a semicolon-delimited list of file names and actor names and stuffs that string into the RowSource property of the combo box on the form. Listing 11.15 shows the code from frmAnimations.

NOTE   Although this seems like a perfect situation in which to use the FileSearch object and its searching functionality, things aren't always what they seem. The FilesFound collection of the FileSearch object returns the full path of the files it finds. Dir, on the other hand, returns just the file name. In this case, because the code is attempting to set the FileName property of the Assistant and this property will not accept full path names (only file names), it makes more sense to use the Dir function than the FileSearch object.

Listing 11.15

```
Private Sub GatherList(strPath As String)
    ' Add all the actor file names and friendly names
    ' to the collection.
    Dim strFile As String
    Dim strName As String
    Dim strOut As String
    Dim strOldFile As String
    Dim fVisible As Boolean
    With Assistant
        ' The next line ought not be necessary, but
        ' test it on your own machine. You don't want
        ' to see the Assistant flashing through all the
        ' actors. Here, you don't see a thing.
        '.Visible = False
        strOldFile = .FileName

        strFile = Dir(strPath & "\*.act")
        Do While Len(strFile) > 0
            strOut = strOut & ";" & strFile
            .FileName = strFile
            strOut = strOut & ";" & .Name
            strFile = Dir
        Loop
        ' Put the file name back the way it was, and then
        ' force the Assistant to be visible.
        .FileName = strOldFile
        .Visible = True
        If Len(strOut) > 0 Then
            Me!lstActors.RowSource = Mid(strOut, 2)
        End If
    End With
End Sub
```

Along with the Name and FileName properties, you can set other properties that affect the location and display of the Assistant. Table 11.11 describes these properties.

Animations 'R' Us

The Assistant provides the Animation property, which allows you to control which animation the character displays at any time. You can choose only from the supplied animations, and not all characters respond to all the animations. For a list of possible values for the Animation property, see the Object Browser (msoAnimationType),

TABLE 11.11   Properties Controlling the Display of the Assistant

Property	Description
FileName	Specifies the file containing the animations and information for the actor. Actor files have .ACT as their extension. The ACP files are placeholders, containing no animations
Name	Contains the "user-friendly" name for the actor. Read-only
Top	Specifies the upper coordinate of the Assistant window, in pixels
Left	Specifies the left coordinate of the Assistant window, in pixels
Visible	Specifies the visibility of the Assistant window. Set to True or False to control whether the Assistant window is visible on screen

or check out tblAnimations in the sample database. The sample form, frmAnimations, allows you to try out all the settings with each actor.

NOTE   Some animation settings (msoAnimationGreeting, for example) contain more than one possible display. When you select a particular Animation property setting, there's no way for you to control exactly which of the possible animations you'll get; it's a random choice. You just have to give up a little control once in a while!

I'm Dancing as Fast as I Can!

No matter how hard you try, you cannot convince the Assistant to display a series of animations, strung together. Because the actor will "act" only during your computer's idle time to keep it from getting in the way of real work, there's no way for it to take over and perform animations serially. If you supply a list of actions, one after the other, you'll most likely see only the final animation in the list. You may be able to work around this by adding timing loops to your code, but don't. It's just not the point.

Try out the DanceTwerpDance procedure in basAssistant, shown in Listing 11.16. You'll see that although the code requests a series of animations, only one of them will be visible, most likely the final one.

Listing 11.16

```
Sub DanceTwerpDance()
    ' Note that the Assistant can handle animation only
```

```
    ' in "down time". In this case only the final animation
    ' will have any visible effect.
    With Assistant
        .Visible = True
        .Animation = msoAnimationGestureLeft
        .Animation = msoAnimationGestureRight
        .Animation = msoAnimationGestureUp
        .Animation = msoAnimationGestureDown
        .Animation = msoAnimationCharacterSuccessMajor
    End With
End Sub
```

Handling All the Options

Many of the Assistant's properties correspond one-to-one with options available in its Options dialog (right-click on the Assistant and choose Options). All the options shown in Table 11.12 contain Boolean values and are read/write.

TABLE 11.12   Assistant Properties Corresponding to the Options Dialog

Property	Corresponding Item
AssistWithAlerts	Display alerts
AssistWithHelp	Respond to F1 key
AssistWithWizards	Help with wizards
FeatureTips	Using features more effectively
GuessHelp	Guess help topics
HighPriorityTips	Only show high-priority tips
KeyboardShortcutTips	Keyboard shortcuts
MouseTips	Using the mouse more effectively
MoveWhenInTheWay	Move when in the way
SearchWhenProgramming	Search for both product and programming help when programming
Sounds	Make sounds
TipOfDay	Show the Tip of the Day at startup

Handling Balloon Errors

It's possible that you'll create a Balloon object and ask it to do something it can't or set its options in such a way that it can't be displayed. Anytime you use a Balloon object in a real application, you should check the Assistant's BalloonError property once it's been dismissed. That way your application can know if something went wrong while the balloon was in use. For a complete listing of BalloonError property values, check the Object Browser (msoBalloonErrorType) and online help.

For example, in Listing 11.17 (from basAssistant), the code attempts to create a modeless balloon with no buttons. Because Access won't allow you to create a modeless balloon that doesn't also supply a way to get rid of the balloon, you'll never see this balloon.

Listing 11.17

```
Sub NoButtonsNoBalloon()
    With Application.Assistant
        With .NewBalloon
            .Heading = "This will never show."
            .Text = "Imagine a balloon here."
            .Button = msoButtonSetNone
            .Mode = msoModeModal
            .Show
        End With
        If .BalloonError = msoBalloonErrorButtonlessModal Then
            MsgBox "You need a button to dismiss the balloon."
        End If
        .Visible = True
    End With
End Function
```

Assistant Methods

The Assistant object supplies three additional methods:

- **Help:** The Help method pops up a balloon filled with its guesses as to what you're trying to do, with jumps to the appropriate help topics.

- **Move:** The Move method allows you to move the Assistant window to any location on the screen. For example,

```
Assistant.Move 0, 0
```

moves the Assistant window to the upper-left corner. (Unlike other location values, these values must be supplied in *pixels*, not twips.)

- **ResetTips**: The ResetTips method resets the display of built-in tips back to the first item so users can see tips they've seen before.

Creating a New Balloon

A silent Assistant wouldn't do you much good, so Access allows you to create Balloon objects that display text from the Assistant. To create a balloon, you'll usually follow these steps:

1. Use the NewBalloon method of the Assistant object to create the new balloon. This balloon will be blank and invisible.

2. Set the Heading property to assign a heading.

3. Set the Text property to assign some text to the body of the balloon.

4. Specify text for controls (labels or check boxes) as needed.

5. Use the Show method to display the balloon.

6. If you're using a modeless balloon (see later sections for more information), use the Close method to dismiss the balloon.

The Assistant can display only a single balloon object at a time, and it has no mechanism for internally maintaining a collection of Balloon objects. You use the NewBalloon method of the Assistant to return a reference to a new Balloon object, and you can use this Balloon object to display text, labels, check boxes, and so on, to the user.

For example, Listing 11.18 (from basAssistant) creates and displays a very simple balloon. (The next section of this chapter offers more information about creating and using balloons and their text.)

Listing 11.18

```
Sub SimpleBalloon()
    Dim bln As Balloon
    Set bln = Assistant.NewBalloon
    With bln
        .Heading = "The Simplest Balloon!"
        .Text = "This is the simplest balloon you'll ever see!"
        .Show
    End With
End Sub
```

Working with Balloons

Balloon objects allow you to display text, request information, and interact in many ways with your applications' users. The following sections discuss the properties and methods of Balloon objects that allow you to create useful dialogs using the Balloon object.

What Can You Put on a Balloon?

A Balloon object can contain any or all of the following items:

- A heading (using the Heading property)

- A section of text (using the Text property)

- Up to five labels, buttons, or numbered items (using the predefined Labels collection)

- Up to five check boxes (using the predefined CheckBoxes collection)

- A group of command buttons (using the Button property)

- A graphic inserted into any text element

The example in Listing 11.18 showed how to create the Balloon object and assign its Heading and Text properties. Examples in the following sections show how to use the other Balloon object properties.

Inserting a Bitmap

You can insert a bitmap at any point in the text of a balloon. To do so, place a brace-delimited string indicating the image type ("bmp" for a bitmap) and the path to the bitmap directly into your text. For example, to place the Windows CIRCLES.BMP file into the header of your balloon, you could use code like this:

```
With Assistant.NewBalloon
    .Heading = "This is a picture " & _
    "{bmp C:\WINDOWS\CIRCLES.BMP} of circles."
    .Show
End With
```

You cannot, however, replace the numbers, bullets, or blue lights of the balloons with your own bitmaps.

To specify the graphic type, use one of the following text strings preceding the file name:

String	Meaning
bmp	Insert a Windows bitmap
wmf	Insert a Windows metafile
pict	Insert a Macintosh picture

Showing a Balloon

Once you've set up your Balloon object as you want it to appear, use the Show method to make it visible. See the example in Listing 11.18, which sets up the Heading and Text properties and then displays the balloon.

Getting Modal

You can display a Balloon object in one of three modalities: Modal, Modeless, or AutoDown. Table 11.13 lists the available settings and outlines the issues involved with each.

Using the Button Property to Handle Dismissals

Balloon objects require a dismissal method. If there's no way to make the balloon go away, Access won't even display it in the first place. If you display the Labels collection as bullet items, for example (see the next section for details), and don't otherwise provide some means for getting rid of the balloon, you'll never see the balloon.

Use the Button property of the Balloon object to indicate which combination of command buttons you'd like to see on the balloon. Table 11.14 lists the possible combinations. (See the msoButtonSetType enumeration in the Object Browser for complete details.)

Just as with the MsgBox function in VBA, the buttons don't actually do anything. When you select one of the buttons, the balloon either disappears or calls a function or macro, depending on the Mode property. If the balloon is opened with the msoModeModeless setting, clicking a button calls the function or macro specified in the CallBack property. If it's set to msoModeModal, clicking a button closes the balloon, and the return value of the Show method indicates which button you clicked.

TABLE 11.13 Available Settings for a Balloon's Mode Property

Modality	Constant	Description	Issues
Modal	msoModeModal	The balloon maintains the focus until you click on a label (if the BalloonType property is set to msoBalloonTypeBullets) or on a button, at which point it disappears (This is the default value of the Mode property.)	Use the return value of the Show method to find out exactly which label or button the user has selected.
Modeless	msoModeModeless	The balloon stays visible until you dismiss it with code	You must supply a Callback function or macro to react to clicks on the balloon. You can use the Close method only with a modeless balloon
AutoDown	msoModeAutoDown	The balloon disappears as soon as you click anywhere outside it	If your balloon includes buttons, the balloon will disappear once you click outside the balloon, regardless of whether you've clicked one of the buttons. This may be confusing to users of your applications

TABLE 11.14 Possible Button Combinations for Balloon Objects

msoButtonSetType Value	Buttons Displayed
msoButtonSetAbortRetryIgnore	Abort, Retry, and Ignore
msoButtonSetBackClose	Back and Close
msoButtonSetBackNextClose	Back, Next, and Close
msoButtonSetBackNextSnooze	Back, Next, and Snooze
msoButtonSetCancel	Cancel
msoButtonSetNextClose	Next and Close
msoButtonSetNone	No buttons at all
msoButtonSetOK	OK

TABLE 11.14   Possible Button Combinations for Balloon Objects (continued)

msoButtonSetType Value	Buttons Displayed
msoButtonSetOkCancel	Ok and Cancel
msoButtonSetRetryCancel	Retry and Cancel
msoButtonSetSearchClose	Search and Close
msoButtonSetTipsOptionsClose	Tips, Options, and Close
msoButtonSetYesAllNoCancel	Yes, Yes to All, No, and Cancel
msoButtonSetYesNo	Yes and No
msoButtonSetYesNoCancel	Yes, No, and Cancel

Table 11.15 lists the possible return values from the Show method. Note that if you've set the BalloonType property for the balloon to msoBalloonTypeButtons and you've supplied text for one or more of the Labels collection items (see the next section for more details), the Show method will return a number between 1 and 5, indicating which label was selected.

TABLE 11.15   Possible Return Values from the Show Method of a Balloon

msoBalloonButtonType Value	Button Selected
msoBalloonButtonAbort	Abort
msoBalloonButtonBack	Back
msoBalloonButtonCancel	Cancel
msoBalloonButtonClose	Close
msoBalloonButtonIgnore	Ignore
msoBalloonButtonNext	Next
msoBalloonButtonNo	No
msoBalloonButtonNull	No button was selected
msoBalloonButtonOK	OK

TABLE 11.15 Possible Return Values from the Show Method of a Balloon (continued)

msoBalloonButtonType Value	Button Selected
msoBalloonButtonOptions	Options
msoBalloonButtonRetry	Retry
msoBalloonButtonSearch	Search
msoBalloonButtonSnooze	Snooze
msoBalloonButtonTips	Tips
msoBalloonButtonYes	Yes
msoBalloonButtonYesToAll	Yes to All
Values: 1 through 5	If the BalloonType property is set to msoBalloonTypeButtons, indicates which label was selected

The procedure in Listing 11.19, from basAssistant, demonstrates the use of buttons and checking their value.

Listing 11.19

```
Sub TestShow()
    ' Demonstrate the Show method.
    Dim intRetval As Integer
    Dim strText As String
    Dim fVisible As Boolean
    ' Using multiple balloons doesn't look good unless the
    ' Assistant is visible to begin with.
    fVisible = Assistant.Visible
    Assistant.Visible = True

    With Assistant.NewBalloon
        .Heading = "Using Buttons and the Show method"
        .Text = "Select a button, and see what happens!"
        .Button = msoButtonSetBackNextClose
        .Mode = msoModeModal
        intRetval = .Show
        Select Case intRetval
            Case msoBalloonButtonBack
```

```
                strText = "You chose Back!"
          Case msoBalloonButtonNext
                strText = "You chose Next!"
          Case msoBalloonButtonClose
                strText = "You chose Close!"
      End Select
  End With
  ' Now create a new balloon, with the new text.
  ' Make this balloon go away as soon as you click
  ' anywhere outside the balloon.
  With Assistant.NewBalloon
      .Heading = "What Did You Choose?"
      .Text = strText
      .Mode = msoModeAutoDown
      .Show
  End With
  ' Put the Assistant away if he wasn't visible to
  ' begin with.
  Assistant.Visible = fVisible
End Sub
```

Using the Labels Collection

You can add up to five short paragraphs of text to a Balloon object, in the Labels collection. Depending on the value in the BalloonType property, the paragraphs will appear as numbered items, bulleted items, or as items in an option group. (You can select one, and only one, of the items in the collection.) Table 11.16 lists the possible values for the BalloonType property. (See msoBalloonType in the Object Browser.)

TABLE 11.16   Possible Values for the BalloonTypeProperty

BalloonType Value	Description
msoBalloonTypeBullets	Shows Labels collection as bullets
msoBalloonTypeButtons	Shows Labels collection as selectable options
msoBalloonTypeNumbers	Shows Labels collection as numbered items

The example shown in Listing 11.20 (from basAssistant) creates a simple set of labels from which the user can choose a value. Call the TestGetLevel procedure from the Debug window to test it out. Figure 11.8 shows the balloon in action.

FIGURE 11.8

Testing out the
Labels collection

Listing 11.20

```
Function GetLevel()
    ' Call a modal balloon and return the value of the
    ' selected label on the balloon.
    Dim bln As Balloon
    Set bln = Assistant.NewBalloon
    With bln
        .Heading = "User Information"
        .Text = "Select your skill level:"
        .Labels(1).Text = "Beginner."
        .Labels(2).Text = "Advanced."
        .Labels(3).Text = "Skip this information."
        .Mode = msoModeModal
        .BalloonType = msoBalloonTypeButtons
        .Button = msoButtonSetNone
        GetLevel = .Show
    End With
End Function

Sub TestGetLevel()
    Select Case GetLevel()
        Case 1
            Debug.Print "A beginner!"
```

```
        Case 2
            Debug.Print "An advanced user!"
        Case 3
            Debug.Print "Who knows?"
        Case Else
            Debug.Print "Invalid data!"
    End Select
End Sub
```

Controlling the Icon

You can control the icon displayed on your balloon. Set the Icon property to one of the constants listed in Table 11.17. (See the msoIconType enumeration in the Object Browser for more details.)

TABLE 11.17   Icon Constants for Assistant Balloons

msoIconType Value	Description
msoIconAlert	Displays an alert icon
msoIconNone	No icon at all
msoIconTip	Displays the tip icon (a light bulb)

The example shown in Listing 11.21 (from basAssistant) shows a balloon that uses an icon. Figure 11.9 shows the example as it's running.

Listing 11.21

```
Sub BadThing()
    ' This whole example is a bad idea.
    Dim fVisible As Boolean

    With Assistant
        fVisible = .Visible
        .Visible = True
        .Animation = msoAnimationCharacterSuccessMajor
        With .NewBalloon
            .Heading = "Terrible Disaster!"
            .Icon = msoIconTip
            .Text = "I need to format your hard drive."
```

```
                    .Button = msoButtonSetOkCancel
                    ' Because the Assistant is visible,
                    ' MsgBox will use it to do its work.
                    If .Show = msoBalloonButtonCancel Then
                        MsgBox "Sorry, it's too late for that!", _
                            vbExclamation, "Your Drive is Toast!"
                    End If
                End With
                .Visible = fVisible
            End With
        End Sub
```

FIGURE 11.9

The wrong animation, the wrong icon, and disasters don't mix.

Using the CheckBoxes Collection

Just as you can place up to five text paragraphs in the Labels collection, you can place up to five check boxes on a balloon, as well. (Normally, you'll use either labels or check boxes, but not both.)

To set a check box's caption, set its Text property. To determine whether it's been selected, look at its Checked property.

The example in Listing 11.22 demonstrates the simple use of the CheckBoxes collection, from basAssistant. It doesn't, however, allow you to find out which checks the user selected; that requires a modeless balloon and a callback function. Figure 11.10 shows this procedure running. See the next section for more information on providing callback functions and reacting to users' choices.

Listing 11.22

```
Sub ShowChecks()
    With Assistant.NewBalloon
        .Heading = "Your Menu"
        .Text = _
        "Choose the items you'd like included in your meal:"
        .Checkboxes(1).Text = "Appetizer"
        .Checkboxes(2).Text = "Salad"
        .Checkboxes(3).Text = "Soup"
        .Checkboxes(4).Text = "Main Course"
        .Checkboxes(5).Text = "Dessert"
        .Show
    End With
End Sub
```

FIGURE 11.10

Using check boxes on
a simple balloon

Supplying a Callback Function

If you create a modeless balloon, you'll need to supply a macro or function that
Access will call when you click any label or button. This function (and although you
can use a macro for this, you should not, because you won't get the information Access

passes to the function) will, at least, need to dismiss the balloon. In addition, it can determine which check boxes, if your balloon displays check boxes, the user's selected.

To supply the name of your callback function, set the Callback property value to be a string containing the name of the function or macro.

In the function, you can make decisions based on the check boxes on the balloon, and you can use the Close method to close the balloon. Access passes to your function three parameters:

- A reference to the balloon object
- An integer indicating which button, label, or check box was selected
- An integer representing the balloon's Private property

You can use these parameters to determine what action your callback function must take. Listing 11.23 demonstrates a simple example using check boxes and a callback function. To try it, run the GetStatistics procedure in basAssistant.

Listing 11.23

```
Sub GetStatistics()
    Dim bln as Balloon
    Set bln = Assistant.NewBalloon
    With bln
        .Heading = "Check your Statistics."
        .Checkboxes(1).Text = "Over 30."
        .Checkboxes(2).Text = "Smoker."
        .Checkboxes(3).Text = "Drinker."
        .Checkboxes(4).Text = _
         "Greater than 40 pounds overweight."
        .Text = "Which of the following " _
            & .Checkboxes.Count & " choices apply to you?"
        .Mode = msoModeModeless
        .Callback = "CountChecks"
        .Button = msoButtonSetOK
        .Show
    End With
End Sub

Function CountChecks(bln As Balloon, _
  intButton As Integer, intPrivate As Integer)
    ' Callback function from GetStatistics example.
```

```
        Dim intI As Integer
        Dim intCount As Integer
        Dim strText As String

        With bln
            For intI = 1 To 5
                If .Checkboxes(intI).Checked Then
                    intCount = intCount + 1
                End If
            Next intI
            .Animation = msoAnimationGestureDown
            Select Case intCount
                Case 0
                    strText = "No risk! Don't you have a life?"
                Case 1
                    strText = "Only one risk category. " & _
                        "You'll probably make it to 50."
                Case 2
                    strText = "Things are looking grim!"
                Case 3
                    strText = "Better think about life insurance."
                Case 4
                    strText = "Who's your next of kin?"
            End Select
            MsgBox strText, vbExclamation, "Health Survey"
        End With
        bln.Close
End Function
```

Using Multiple Balloons in a Session

The Assistant supports only a single Balloon object at any time. You can, however, use the Assistant.NewBalloon method repeatedly, creating all the balloon objects you need. Then, when you want to show one balloon or another, set its Visible property to True.

TIP

Because the Assistant supports only a single balloon at a time, if you use the Show method on one balloon, make sure you use the Close method on the one that was previously visible. If you don't, the Assistant gets confused.

If you're going to use multiple balloons in a given session, you'll often want to use modeless balloons. If you use modeless balloons, you'll want to use callback functions for those balloons, allowing you to take action based on the button clicked or the label selected.

Using a Callback with Multiple Balloons

If you intend to use a single callback function with multiple balloons, you've got to find some way to differentiate the balloons. You can set the value of your balloons' Private property. This property is simply a Long Integer that you can use for you own needs—Access never uses or modifies its value. When it calls your callback function, it passes the Private property for your balloon in the function's third parameter. You can then base decisions in the callback function on that value. The example shown in Listing 11.24, from basAssistant, takes advantage of this technique. It uses the value passed from the Private property in the third parameter in order to know which balloon is visible. Note that the example uses the callback function's second parameter to know which button was selected and takes appropriate action.

Listing 11.24

```
Dim bln1 As Balloon
Dim bln2 As Balloon

Sub MultipleBalloonsModeless()
    Dim fVisible As Boolean

    fVisible = Assistant.Visible
    Assistant.Visible = True
    Set bln1 = Assistant.NewBalloon
    Set bln2 = Assistant.NewBalloon
    With bln1
        .Heading = "This is balloon 1"
        .Private = 1
        .Mode = msoModeModeless
        .Callback = "MultipleBalloonCallback"
        .Button = msoButtonSetNextClose
    End With
    With bln2
        .Heading = "This is balloon 2"
        .Private = 2
        .Mode = msoModeModeless
        .Callback = "MultipleBalloonCallback"
```

```
            .Button = msoButtonSetBackClose
        End With
        bln1.Show
End Sub

Function MultipleBalloonCallback(bln As Balloon, _
 intButton As Integer, intPrivate As Integer)
    Select Case intButton
        ' No matter which balloon, the Close
        ' button closes both.
        Case msoBalloonButtonClose
            bln1.Close
            bln2.Close
        Case Else
            Select Case intPrivate
                Case 1
                    Select Case intButton
                        Case msoBalloonButtonNext
                            bln1.Close
                            bln2.Show
                        Case Else
                            ' No other buttons, right?
                    End Select
                Case 2
                    Select Case intButton
                        Case msoBalloonButtonBack
                            bln2.Close
                            bln1.Show
                        Case Else
                            ' No other buttons, right?
                    End Select
            End Select
    End Select
End Function
```

TIP

If you want the callback function to do anything with a balloon other than the current one, make sure the reference to the balloon is scoped so your function can "see" it. In most cases, you'll want to declare a variable that refers to the Balloon object at the module level so any procedure in the module can work with it. Of course, Access passes your callback function a reference to the current balloon, so that's not an issue.

Finishing Touches

Here are some additional thoughts on using balloons:

- **Plan carefully:** Plan your use of balloons carefully, before beginning to add them to your application. Because of the limitation on the number of checks and labels you can use, you'll need to design them very carefully.

- **One Assistant, many balloons:** If you want to use multiple balloons in a session, make sure the Assistant is visible first. Otherwise you'll see the Assistant appear and disappear for each balloon.

- **Respect the users' configurations:** If you use the Assistant, be sure to reset its visibility when you're done. Most of the examples in this portion of the chapter follow this suggestion.

- **No run-time distribution allowed**: Remember that run-time applications cannot use this functionality unless the intended user already has a copy of Office 97 installed. If you plan on shipping an application to a mixed group of end users (some using the retail version and others using only the run-time version), you'll need to provide forms or MsgBox calls to replace the balloons for run-time users.

Is There More?

This rounds out the introduction to the three shared Office components you can use in Access 97. Are there more? Of course! Almost all Office 97 components can be controlled via Automation, and they expose rich object models to allow you to control them. Office Art, Microsoft Graph, the Image Editor, and other features of Office all allow you to control them programmatically. Once you've set up the appropriate reference to the type library using the Tools ➤ References menu, you can program to your heart's content. Finding documentation, however, is another issue. Visit Microsoft's Web site (www.microsoft.com) to find what documentation there is. As time goes on, more and more of the shared components will become documented, and the Web site is the place to look for the new information.

Summary

In this chapter we've covered the three object models supplied by MSO97.DLL. We discussed finding Files with the FileSearch object, including:

- Using properties to provide a simple search

- Using the PropertyTests collection to provide complex searches

We examined the subject of programming command bars

- Perusing the CommandBars collection

- Creating new CommandBar objects

- Working with CommandBarControl objects

- Adding objects to command bars

- Using the OnAction property to take an action when an object is selected

We also took a look at controlling the Office Assistant, including:

- Using properties to control the Assistant

- Creating balloons

- Using Balloon properties to control a balloon's activities

- Using check boxes and labels on balloons

- Using Callback functions to react to actions on modeless balloons

Office 97 supplies a major increment in the number of Automation servers it provides, and the three covered here are just the tip of the iceberg. For more information, see Chapters 20 and 21, which deal directly with Access as an Automation controller and server.

PART IV

Multiuser Issues

CHAPTER

TWELVE

12

Developing Multiuser Applications

- Understanding page locking

- Contrasting optimistic and pessimistic locking

- Splitting a database to improve performance

- Handling multiuser errors with the Form Error event

- Determining who's logged on to a database

- Managing linked tables

Developing Access applications for multiuser systems requires extra planning and a shift from single-user application thinking, but it's not especially difficult to learn. In this chapter we explore the behavior of networked applications in Access. We don't cover network hardware or operating systems, but the good news is that you don't need to become a network administrator or a specialist in cabling and hubs to develop multiuser applications. Let your network administrator or hardware specialist worry about those aspects. (Of course, it can't hurt to communicate with this person and learn a bit about network hardware and operating systems over time.) We do, however, discuss how to *plan* and *think* multiuser and how to avoid the common pitfalls of multiuser development.

> **NOTE** There are three sample databases for Chapter 12 and one supporting .DLL file. CH12APP.MDB is the "application" database—it contains all the user interface objects and supporting code, including code that manages links to CH12DAT.MDB. CH12DAT.MDB is the "data" database—it contains only the tables. CH12AUTO.MDB contains the custom AutoNumber table discussed in the section "Using a Custom AutoNumber Routine." The frmViewUsers form in CH12APP.MDB calls the MSLDBUSR.DLL file, which can also be found on the companion CD in the \Other\Msft\Jetlock folder. Make sure you copy this file to your \Windows\System folder prior to using this form.

Setup on a Network

Before installing Access on a network, you need to decide whether Access will be installed only on the file server or on each workstation.

The first option, installing a single copy of Access on the file server, has several advantages:

- The network administrator has central control of the executables, minimizing maintenance chores.

- Hard-disk-space usage is kept to a minimum on workstations.

- Users with diskless workstations can run Access.

This scenario also has several significant disadvantages:

- Each time a workstation runs Access, the Access EXE, DLLs, and other files are sent over the network cable to each workstation. Because Access is much more than a single executable (it may call over 20 DLLs during execution, swapping portions of itself to and from memory), network traffic will be very high.

- Performance can vary from acceptable to abysmal.

A better alternative is to install a copy of Access on each workstation on the network. The major advantage of this scenario is performance. Access startup and execution will be significantly faster. Of course, this scenario does carry with it a disadvantage when compared with the file server–only scenario: you (or the network administrator) will have to maintain multiple copies of Access rather than just one. Still, we feel strongly that any added maintenance burden under this scenario is greatly overshadowed by the substantial increase in performance and reduction of network traffic.

TIP

Access provides an option for installing a special administrator version on the file server that you can then use to install individual copies of Access on each workstation. With this install technique, you need to use the disks or CD only once, and the installation process is much faster. (For more information on using the administrator setup options, see the NETWORK.TXT file on disk 1 of the Access disks or in the root directory of the Office Professional CD.)

Multiuser Settings

Several options and settings in Access affect how your applications behave in a multiuser environment, as described in the following sections.

Database Open Modes

You can affect the way a database is opened in Access in three ways:

- When you start Access, you can include a database name on the command line and either the /Excl or /Ro parameter to open that database in exclusive or read-only mode, respectively.

- You can check or uncheck the Exclusive check box or use the Open Read Only property when using the File ➤ Open Database dialog.

- You can change the default database open mode using the Tools ➤ Options command by changing the Default Open Mode setting on the Advanced tab of the Options dialog. The setting can be set to Exclusive for single-user access or Shared for multiuser access to the database.

TIP You can prevent a user from opening a database in exclusive mode by using the Tools ➤ Security ➤ User and Group Permissions command to uncheck the OpenExclusive permission of the database for that user. See Chapter 14 for more details.

The Refresh Interval

Using the Tools ➤ Options command, you can set the refresh interval. Access automatically checks the recordsets of open forms and datasheets to see whether changes have occurred at the frequency you have specified using this setting. The default refresh interval is 60 seconds, which may be too long for some applications. If you set the refresh interval to a very small value, however, you may create excessive network traffic. Finding the proper setting for your application may require some experimentation. In general, the smaller the network, the smaller you can set the refresh interval without adverse effect.

You can override the default refresh interval in your applications by using the Refresh method, the Requery method, or the Requery action. Record *refreshes*—either automatic refreshes by Access using the refresh interval or manual refreshes using the Refresh method—are faster than requeries. New records added by other users, however, appear only during a requery, and records deleted by other users vanish from your copy only after a requery. (All the values in the fields of deleted records, however, are replaced with the string "#DELETED" when the record is refreshed.)

Given the choice, you should use the Requery *method* rather than the almost equivalent Requery *action*. The method reruns the query that's already in memory, while the action reloads it from disk.

TIP Even if you set the refresh interval to a long value, Access automatically refreshes the current record whenever a user attempts to edit it. The benefit of a shorter refresh interval lies chiefly in providing quicker visual feedback that someone else has locked or changed a record while you are viewing it.

Locking Options

To provide concurrent access to records by multiple users, Access locks records. Unlike some other databases, however, Access doesn't lock individual records; instead it locks a 2K (2048 bytes) page of records. The advantage of page locking is that there's less overhead and thus generally better performance over true record locking. Unfortunately, this also means that Access usually locks more records than you would like. This is especially an issue when you employ pessimistic locking because this type of record locking allows users to keep records locked for long periods of time.

In a multiuser environment, you can open recordsets in one of three modes:

- **No Locks:** This is often called *optimistic locking* and is the default setting. With the No Locks setting, the page of records that contains the currently edited record is locked only during the instant when the record is saved, not during the editing process. This allows for concurrent editing of records with fewer locking conflicts.

- **Edited Record:** As soon as a user begins to edit a record, the page containing the currently edited record is locked until the changes are saved. This is known as *pessimistic locking.*

- **All Records:** This setting causes all the records in the entire recordset to be locked. You won't find this option very useful except when doing batch updates or performing administrative maintenance on tables.

You can adjust locking options for database objects that manipulate recordsets. Table 12.1 shows which locking options are available for each database object, as well as the point at which records are actually locked. The default RecordLocks setting for most of these objects is taken from the Default Record Locking option established using the Tools ➤ Options dialog.

TABLE 12.1 Available RecordLocks Settings for Various Access Objects

Access Object	No Locks	Edited Record	All Records	Default	When Records Are Locked
Table datasheets	Yes[1]	Yes[1]	Yes[1]	DRL	Datasheet editing
Select query datasheets	Yes	Yes	Yes	DRL	Datasheet editing
Crosstab query datasheets	Yes	Yes	Yes	DRL	Query execution
Union query datasheets	Yes	Yes	Yes	DRL	Query execution
Update and delete queries	No	Yes	Yes	DRL	Query execution
Make-table and append queries	No	Yes	Yes	DRL	Query execution[2]
Data definition queries	No	No	Yes	All Records[3]	Query execution
Forms	Yes	Yes	Yes	DRL	Form and datasheet modes
Reports	Yes	No	Yes	DRL	Report execution, preview, and printing
OpenRecordset	Yes	Yes	Yes	Edited Record[4]	Between Edit and Update methods

Yes = available option

No = option not available for this object

DRL = Default Record Locking option setting for the database

[1]There is no RecordLocks property for table datasheets. Datasheets use the Default Record Locking option setting for the database.

[2]For make-table and append queries, the target tables are locked.

[3]There is no RecordLocks property for data definition queries. Access locks the entire table.

[4]Changed using the LockEdits property of recordsets. Edited Record is the default unless you use the dbDenyWrite or dbDenyRead option of the OpenRecordset method, in which case the entire table is locked.

The Default Record Locking option is ignored when you use code to open recordsets using the OpenRecordset method. In this case Access employs pessimistic locking (Edited Record) unless you either set the option of the OpenRecordset method to dbDenyWrite or dbDenyRead or alter the LockEdits property. You use the dbDenyWrite option to lock all records for updates. You can go one step further and deny write *and* read access to table-type recordsets (only) by using the more restrictive dbDenyRead option. (These options apply only to native Access tables.)

NOTE
No record locking is performed for snapshot-type recordsets, because they are read-only.

If you haven't used either the dbDenyWrite or dbDenyRead constant when opening the recordset, you can use the LockEdits property of recordsets to specify the type of locking to be used. The default of True uses pessimistic (Edited Record) locking. You can force optimistic (No Locks) record locking by setting this property to False.

For example, the following piece of code opens a recordset against the tbl-Customer table using pessimistic locking:

```
Set rstPessimistic = db.OpenRecordset("tblCustomer")
' This recordset will employ pessimistic locking
With rstPessimistic
    ' This next line isn't really needed
    ' since LockEdits defaults to True
    .LockEdits = True

    .MoveFirst
    ' This next statement will produce Error 3260
    ' if another user has locked this page of records.
    .Edit
        ' ...
        ' This record will be locked
        ' for every statement between
        ' the Edit and Update methods
        ' ...
        !ZipCode = !ZipCode + 1
    .Update

    .Close
End With
```

Similarly, the next piece of code also opens a recordset against the tblCustomer table, this time using optimistic locking:

```
Set rstOptimistic = db.OpenRecordset("tblCustomer")
' This recordset will employ optimistic locking
With rstOptimistic
    .LockEdits = False

    .MoveFirst
    .Edit
        '  ...
        ' This record will not be locked
        ' until the Update method is executed.
        '  ...
        !ZipCode = !ZipCode - 1
' This next statement will produce Error 3197
' if another user has saved changes to this
' record since the Edit method was executed.
    .Update

    .Close
End With
```

Choosing a Locking Strategy

The *advantages* of *pessimistic* locking are

- It is simple for the developer.
- It prevents users from overwriting each other's work.
- It may be less confusing to the user than optimistic locking.

The *disadvantages* of *pessimistic* locking are

- It will usually lock multiple records. (How many depends on the size of the records.)

- Concurrency—the ability of multiple users to have simultaneous (concurrent) access to records—is worse than for optimistic locking because locks are held for longer time periods.

Because Access locks pages of records, optimistic locking is usually the better choice. The *advantages* of *optimistic* locking are

- It is simple to use.
- It provides better concurrency than pessimistic locking.
- It is less likely to lock other users out of editing multiple records.

The *disadvantages* of using *optimistic* locking are

- It may be confusing to the user when there's a write conflict.
- Users can overwrite each other's edits.

Unless you have a compelling reason to use pessimistic locking, we strongly recommend you consider optimistic locking. In most applications you don't want your users prevented from being able to edit records for potentially long periods of time.

In some applications you may need to use both strategies on different forms. For example, in an inventory application you must ensure that the QuantityOnHand column is pessimistically locked so that salespeople don't try to post a sale beyond QOH without invoking back-order processing. On the other hand, you might use optimistic locking on a vendor address form because it's unlikely that two change-of-address requests for the same vendor will be given to two different users for entry at the same time.

NOTE Microsoft has made several significant changes to improve multiuser performance in Jet 3.0 (Access 95) and Jet 3.5 (Access 97). Chief among these changes is that Jet no longer prevents users from adding new records when the last page of records in a table has been locked.

Default Optimistic Locking Behavior

As already mentioned, the main problem with optimistic locking is the potential for write conflicts. A *write conflict* occurs when:

1. A user begins to edit a record.
2. A second user saves changes to the record.
3. The first user then attempts to save his/her changes.

When a write conflict occurs in bound forms, Access displays the Write Conflict dialog, as shown in Figure 12.1 for the frmCustomerOptimistic1 sample form in the CH12APP.MDB database.

FIGURE 12.1

Under optimistic locking, users may encounter the Write Conflict dialog when attempting to save a record that has been changed by another user.

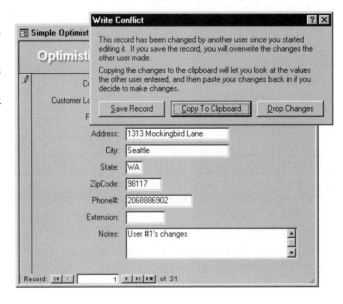

This dialog offers the user three options:

- **Save Record:** If the user selects this option, changes the user makes will over-write changes made by the other user. In most cases a user should not use this option; it blindly discards the other user's changes.

- **Copy to Clipboard:** This option copies the user's changes to the clipboard and refreshes the record with the other user's changes. This option is a good choice for the sophisticated user but requires too much understanding for the naive user. If you used this option in Access 2.0, you'll be happy to know that the bug that prevented formatted data from being pasted back to the form has been fixed.

- **Drop Changes:** If the user selects this option, that user's changes are dropped and the record is refreshed with the other user's changes.

FIGURE 12.2

This spurious error message can occur when you choose Save Record from the Write Conflict dialog.

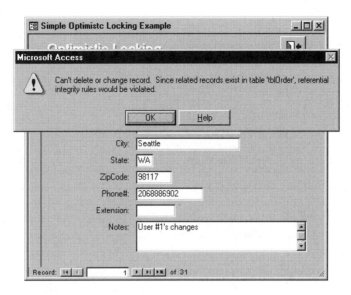

FIGURE 12.2

This spurious error message can occur when you choose Save Record from the Write Conflict dialog.

WARNING A bug in Access 97 (it was also in Access 2 and Access 95—some bugs are slow to be fixed) occurs when you have a one-to-many relationship defined for two tables *without* cascading updates turned on and you choose Save Record in the Write Conflict dialog for a record on the "one" side of the relationship. You will get a spurious referential integrity violation message even if you have not updated the primary key value (see Figure 12.2). (This message occurs because Access blindly copies values for all your fields over the values that have been saved by the other user, without bothering to check whether each field was actually changed. Because the fields include the primary key field, Jet thinks the primary key value has changed and displays the spurious error message.)

Optimistic Locking with Custom Error Handling

In Access 2.0, you were unable to trap and handle locking errors when using bound forms. Fortunately, you can now use the improved Form Error event to intercept write conflict errors and handle them using VBA code by creating an Error event procedure.

Access passes to your event procedure the DataErr and Response parameters. The two most common optimistic locking DataErr values are described in Table 12.2.

TABLE 12.2   Optimistic Locking Errors in Forms

Error Number	Access Error Message	Comment
7787	Write Conflict: This record has been changed by another user since you started editing it...	A second user saved changes while the first user was editing the record
7878	The data has been changed...	A second user saved changes while the first user was viewing the record

Error 7787 is the standard Write Conflict dialog error. It occurs when a user attempts to *save changes* to a record that has changed. Error 7878 occurs when a user *begins to edit* a record that has changed since that user began viewing it; this error is more likely to occur with long refresh intervals.

NOTE   The Error event (which was discussed in Chapter 8) is triggered anytime a data access error is generated, so any event procedure you create must also be prepared to deal with non-locking data access errors.

You can set the Response parameter to one of two built-in constants:

Response	When Used
acDataErrContinue	To tell Access to continue without displaying the error message; in the case of optimistic errors, this causes a refresh of the record, with the current user's edits discarded
acDataErrDisplay	To tell Access to display the normal error message; use this constant for errors you are not handling

You'll notice that there's no way to tell Jet to overwrite the record with "your" changes. Aside from choosing the built-in error message, your only option is to allow Jet to refresh the user's edits with those the other user has already saved to disk. The built-in Save Record functionality is provided by the Access UI and is, thus, not one of the options available programmatically. However, we have come up with a work-around that produces the same effect—without causing the bug mentioned in the preceding section.

The event procedure attached to the Error event of the frmCustomerOptimistic2 form in the CH12APP.MDB sample database demonstrates this work-around. Listing 12.1 includes this event procedure, as well as supporting code found in the Current event procedure of frmCustomerOptimistic2.

Listing 12.1

```
Dim mvarCustomerId As Variant

Const adhcErrWriteConflict = 7787
Const adhcErrDataChanged = 7878

Private Sub Form_Current()

    ' Store away primary key value.
    ' It may be needed later in the
    ' error handler for the form

    ' Value won't exist for a new record,
    ' so just ignore error that may occur
    On Error Resume Next
    mvarCustomerId = Me![Customer#]

End Sub

Private Sub Form_Error(DataErr As Integer, Response As Integer)

    ' Handle form-level errors

    On Error GoTo Form_ErrorErr

    Dim strMsg As String
    Dim intResp As Integer
    Dim rst As Recordset
    Dim fld As Field
    Dim db As Database
```

```
' Branch based on value of error
Select Case DataErr

Case adhcErrWriteConflict
    ' Write conflict error
    strMsg = "Another user has updated this record " & _
     "since you began editing it. " & vbCrLf & vbCrLf & _
     "Do you want to refresh your record with " & _
     "the other user's changes?" & vbCrLf & vbCrLf & _
     "Choose Yes to refresh your record, " & vbCrLf & _
     "or No to replace the record with your version."
    intResp = MsgBox(strMsg, _
     vbYesNo + vbDefaultButton1 + vbQuestion, _
     "Overwrite Conflict")

    ' Jet only allows the other user's changes to
    ' be saved, so we need to trick Jet into using our
    ' changes by writing our changes out to the underlying
    ' record, which Access will then copy over our changes.
    If intResp = vbNo Then

        Set db = CurrentDb

        ' Create recordset of one record that matches the
        ' PK value of the record when we began editing it.
        ' This value was stored away by the Current event
        ' procedure. This is necessary since we could've
        ' changed the PK value.
        Set rst = db.OpenRecordset("SELECT * FROM " & _
         "tblCustomer WHERE [Customer#] = " _
         & mvarCustomerId)

        ' Make sure PK value wasn't changed by other user.
        If rst.RecordCount = 0 Then
            strMsg = "Another user has changed the " & _
             "Customer# for this record. " & _
             "The record will need to be refreshed " & _
             "before continuing."
            MsgBox strMsg, vbOKOnly + vbInformation, _
             "Overwrite Conflict"
        Else
            ' Update values in underlying record with
```

```
                     ' any changed values from form.
                     ' Since Null comparisons will always return
                     ' False, temporarily convert Nulls to zero-
                     ' length strings for comparison.
                     DoCmd.Hourglass True
                     For Each fld In rst.Fields
                         rst.Edit
                             If Nz(fld) <> Nz(Me(fld.Name)) Then
                                 fld.Value = Me(fld.Name).Value
                             End If
                         rst.Update
                     Next fld
                 End If
             End If

             ' This will cause record refresh
             Response = acDataErrContinue

         Case adhcErrDataChanged
             ' This error occurs if Access detects that
             ' another user has changed this record when we
             ' attempt to dirty the record. Fairly harmless since
             ' we haven't actually made any changes.
             strMsg = "Another user has updated this record " & _
               "since you began viewing it. " & vbCrLf & vbCrLf & _
               "The record will be refreshed with the other " & _
               "user's changes before continuing."
             MsgBox strMsg, vbOKOnly + vbInformation, _
               "Record Refresh"

             ' This will cause record refresh
             Response = acDataErrContinue
         Case Else
             ' Otherwise, let Access display standard error message
             Response = acDataErrDisplay
     End Select

     DoCmd.Hourglass False

 Form_ErrorEnd:
     Exit Sub
```

```
Form_ErrorErr:
    ' It's possible to hit our own error while handling a
    ' data error. For example, someone could pessimistically
    ' lock the record while we are trying to update it.
    ' Report the error to the user and exit.
    MsgBox "Error " & Err.Number & ": " & Err.Description, _
        vbOKOnly + vbCritical, "Error Handler Error"

End Sub
```

The frmCustomerOptimistic2 form displays a custom write conflict message when error 7787 has been detected (see Figure 12.3). If the user chooses Yes, Response is set to acDataErrContinue and the event procedure exits. If the user chooses No, however, the event procedure takes the values from the form's current record and writes them out to a newly created recordset based on the conflict record. Then, when the event procedure sets Response to acDataErrContinue and exits, Jet copies "our" values back over the current record, thus providing the equivalent of the Save Record option. However, by copying only the values of fields that differ from the values the other user has saved, the code avoids the referential integrity error message:

```
For Each fld In rst.Fields
    rst.Edit
        If Nz(fld) <> Nz(Me(fld.Name)) Then
            fld.Value = Me(fld.Name).Value
        End If
    rst.Update
Next fld
```

This work-around depends on storing the primary key field value for the current record in a module-level global variable, mvarCustomerId, using an event procedure attached to the Current event. This is necessary because you need to be able to open a recordset based on the current record, but you have no guarantee that the user hasn't changed the primary key value. Thus, this technique uses the value of the PK field that was stored away during the Current event. An alternative way to handle this would be to make the PK field read-only or to use the inherently read-only AutoNumber datatype for your PK.

If your form uses a compound primary key field or a query based on multiple tables, you will have to store away each primary key field value.

FIGURE 12.3

The frmCustomer-
Optimistic2 form dis-
plays a custom write
conflict message.

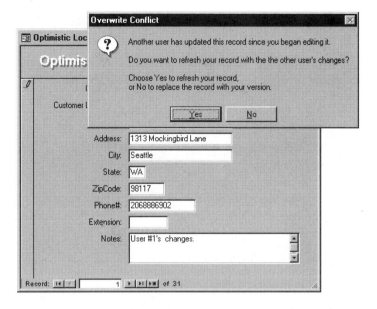

NOTE

In many applications, you may not wish to offer your users the ability to save their changes without first viewing the other user's changes. In these cases you may wish to use a much simpler optimistic locking error handler that simply informs the user that another user has saved changes to the record and then performs a record refresh. An example of this simpler event handler is also included in the sample database attached to the frmCustomerOptimistic3 form.

Default Pessimistic Locking Behavior

Forms that use pessimistic locking avoid write conflicts because only one user at a time is allowed to edit a record. The presence of the "slashed-O" icon in the record selector notifies other users that a record has been locked, as demonstrated by the frmCustomerPessimistic1 form from the sample database (see Figure 12.4).

FIGURE 12.4

Under pessimistic lock-
ing, the slashed-O icon in
the record selector noti-
fies users that the current
record is locked.

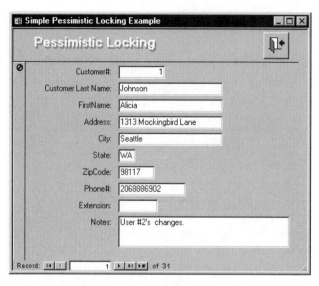

TIP

If you have set the RecordSelector property of a form to No, the slashed-
O icon does not appear when a record is pessimistically locked. Access
beeps at the user, but other than this audible signal, users won't have any
clue as to why they can't edit the values in the record. No trappable error
is generated, either, because this really isn't an error state. Thus, it's
important to leave the RecordSelector property set to Yes when using
pessimistic locking unless you create some custom mechanism for noti-
fying users of the lock, as described in the next section.

Pessimistic Locking with Custom
Lock Notification

While the default slashed-O lock icon works, it suffers from two shortcomings:

- It requires you to display the form's record selector.

- It doesn't tell you who locked the record.

Unfortunately, there's no event or error that occurs when the currently displayed
record has been locked. You can simulate such an event, however, by using the form's

Timer and Current events to check whether another user has locked the current record. We've included a form, frmCustomerPessimistic2, in the sample database that uses the Timer event to provide a custom lock notification message (see Figure 12.5). The code behind the frmCustomerPessimistic2 form is shown in Listing 12.2.

FIGURE 12.5

The frmCustomer-Pessimistic2 form uses VBA code attached to the Timer and Current events to report whether a record is locked and by whom.

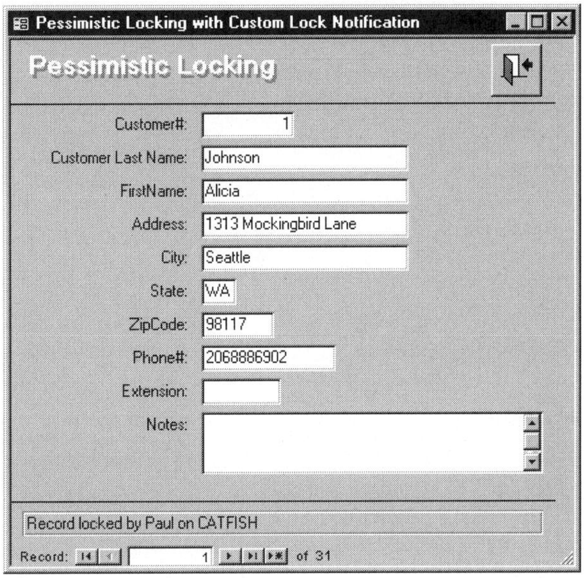

Listing 12.2

```
Const adhcRefreshInterval = 5

Private Sub Form_Current()
    Me!txtLockStatus = adhGetLockMsg(Me)
End Sub

Private Sub Form_Load()
    Me.TimerInterval = adhcRefreshInterval * 1000
End Sub

Private Sub Form_Timer()
    Me!txtLockStatus = adhGetLockMsg(Me)
End Sub
```

The Timer and the Current event procedures call the adhGetLockMsg function, which is located in the basLockingError module. adhGetLockMsg is shown in Listing 12.3.

Listing 12.3

```
Function adhGetLockMsg(frm As Form) As String

    On Error GoTo adhGetLockMsgErr

    Dim rst As Recordset
    Dim strUser As String
    Dim strMachine As String

    Set rst = frm.RecordsetClone
    rst.Bookmark = frm.Bookmark

    rst.Edit
        ' do nothing
    rst.Update

    adhGetLockMsg = "Record isn't locked by another user"

adhGetLockMsgDone:
    DoCmd.Hourglass False
    On Error GoTo 0
    Exit Function

adhGetLockMsgErr:
    Call adhGetLockInfo(Err.Number, Err.Description, _
     strUser, strMachine)
    If Len(strUser) = 0 And Len(strMachine) = 0 Then
        adhGetLockMsg = "Record isn't locked by another user"
    Else
        adhGetLockMsg = "Record locked by " & strUser & _
         " on " & strMachine
    End If
    Resume adhGetLockMsgDone

End Function
```

adhGetLockMsg works by cloning the form's recordset and synchronizing the current record pointer of the clone with the currently displayed record on the form.

Then, the function attempts to lock the record by using the Edit method of the recordset. If no error is generated, the record isn't locked, and adhGetLockMsg returns a message indicating that this is the case.

If an error is generated, code in the function's error handler passes the error number and message to the adhGetLockInfo subroutine, which checks whether the error is a standard locking error number and, if it is, parses the user and machine names from the error message. If the error is not a locking error, adhGetLockInfo returns empty user and machine names, which adhGetLockMsg interprets to mean that the record is not locked.

There's not much to the adhGetLockInfo subroutine, which is also located in the basLockingError module of CH12APP.MDB. It uses a brute-force algorithm to determine the user and machine names based on landmarks in the error message. The key part of this subroutine is shown here:

```
intUserStart = InStr(1, strErr, "by user") + _
 adhcLenByUser
intUserLen = InStr(intUserStart + 1, strErr, "'") - _
 intUserStart + 1
intMachineStart = InStr(1, strErr, "on machine") + _
 adhcLenOnMachine
intMachineLen = InStr(intMachineStart + 1, _
 strErr, "'") - intMachineStart + 1
strUser = Mid$(strErr, intUserStart + 1, intUserLen - 2)
strMachine = Mid$(strErr, intMachineStart + 1, _
 intMachineLen - 2)
```

The code attached to the Timer event of frmCustomerPessimistic2 uses the adhcRefreshInterval constant to determine how often to check whether the record is locked. We have set this constant to 5 seconds, but you may wish to lengthen it to reduce network traffic.

Forcing Access to Lock Individual Records

The main disadvantage of using pessimistic locking with bound forms is that Jet locks pages of records, not individual records. You can, however, force Access to lock individual records by creating record sizes that are larger than half a page—that is, larger than 1024 bytes. This works because Access won't store a new record on a partially filled page if it can't fit the entire record on that page. You can estimate the size of your records by using Table 12.3 and summing the size of each column.

TABLE 12.3   Number of Bytes (Not Counting Overhead) Used by Each Access Datatype

Field Datatype	Storage Size
Byte	1 byte
Integer	2 bytes
Long Integer	4 bytes
Single	4 bytes
Double	8 bytes
Currency	8 bytes
Counter	4 bytes
Yes/No	1 bit
Date/Time	8 bytes
Text	*variable*
Memo	14 bytes
OLE	14 bytes
Hyperlink	14 bytes
Replication ID	16 bytes

The contents of memo, OLE, and Hyperlink datatype columns are stored else-where in the MDB file, so you need to count the overhead only for their address pointers. Text columns require 1 byte for each actual stored character, with zero-length strings using 1 byte and null strings using 0 bytes. If your table is in a rep-licated database, you must also be sure to include the sizes of the system columns, which are visible only when you've used Tools ➤ Options ➤ View to make system objects visible.

You also have to account for overhead, which includes the following:

- Seven bytes per record for record overhead

- One byte variable-length column overhead for each text, memo, OLE, and hyperlink column

- One additional byte for every 256 bytes of the total space occupied by all text, memo, OLE, and hyperlink datatype columns

- One byte fixed-column overhead for each yes/no, byte, integer, long integer, counter, single, double, date/time, and replication ID column

NOTE These numbers were derived from a Microsoft Knowledge Base article (Q114215 INF: Estimating Microsoft Access Table Sizes), which states that these numbers can be used to calculate only an *estimated* record size.

An Example

The easiest way to pad a record to exceed 1024 bytes is to create one or more dummy text columns in the table with long default values. (Don't place these fields on your forms.) For example, if you estimated your record size to be at least 130 bytes (considering the minimal size of any text fields), you would calculate the needed dummy fields as follows:

- Bytes you will need to pad = (1025 – 130) = 895 bytes.

- Each whole dummy text field occupies = (255 + 2 bytes overhead) = 257 bytes.

Thus you would need three completely filled dummy fields (257 * 3 = 771) of 255 x's plus one partially filled dummy field of (895 – 771 – 1 overhead byte) = 123 x's.

Now, whenever a new record is created, Access will automatically create a record with the four x-filled dummy fields, which forces it to lock only a single record.

The sample database includes a simple table named tblForceRecordLocking (see Figure 12.6) and an accompanying form, frmForceRecordLocking, that uses this technique. Try it out with two machines on a network, and you will notice that Access locks individual records.

The Caveat

Now for the main caveat: this strategy wastes a lot of disk space and increases network traffic. Still, if you decide to use pessimistic locking and absolutely must have true record locking, you may wish to consider employing this technique.

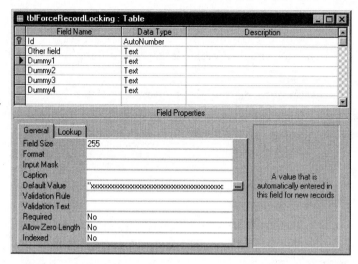

Alternative Locking Strategies

If you're not happy using either optimistic or pessimistic locking using bound forms and you don't wish to pad your record size to force the locking of records, you may wish to use one of the following alternative strategies:

- Use unbound forms to collect data, along with VBA code behind the unbound forms to handle the updating of records.

- Use forms bound to local transaction tables that are used to collect data offline. Then, create a system for downloading and posting transactions to the master data tables.

These strategies work best when you've split your database into data and application databases. (See the section "Splitting Databases" later in this chapter.) If you take either of these routes, be prepared for a lot of work; you'll have to handle everything Access bound forms normally handle for you (for example, reading records, navigating, writing records, and so on) and trap for and handle all the possible errors that might occur (both locking and other kinds of errors). It's not an easy task.

Recordset Error Handling

When using recordsets in a multiuser environment that are not bound to Access forms, you'll need to trap for any multiuser errors that can occur. The three most common errors are summarized in Table 12.4. Error 3197 is equivalent to the write conflict error code 7787 that occurs on bound forms.

TABLE 12.4 Common VBA Multiuser Error Codes

Error Code	Error Message	Comment
3186	Couldn't save; currently locked by user *username* on machine *machinename*	Usually occurs when you use the Update method with optimistic locking
3197	Data has changed; operation stopped	Usually occurs when you use the Edit or Update method with optimistic locking and another user changed the record while you were editing it. Following this message you get the Write Conflict dialog
3260	Couldn't update; currently locked by user *username* on machine *machinename*	Usually occurs when you attempt to use the Update method on a record that has been locked. This is most commonly encountered using pessimistic locking but may also occur with optimistic locking

When manipulating recordsets, you'll need to anticipate and handle each of the errors found in Table 12.4. To handle locked records, you will probably want to include some form of a retry loop that makes several attempts at gaining access to locked records. There's a good example of how to do this in the section "Using a Custom AutoNumber Routine" later in this chapter.

Transaction Processing

Transaction processing is a database term that refers to the process of grouping changes to your data into batches that are treated as single atomic units. Either the entire batch of *transactions* succeeds or they all fail. For example, when moving data from one account to another in a banking application, you wouldn't want to credit the new account without debiting the old account. Thus, you'd wrap this pair of updates in a transaction.

Transaction processing is useful in any application where one action *must* occur in concert with one or more other actions. Transaction processing is commonly required in banking and accounting applications, as well as in many others.

Access supports transaction processing with the BeginTrans, CommitTrans, and Rollback methods of the Workspace object. BeginTrans allows you to mark the start of a series of operations that should be considered as a single unit. CommitTrans takes everything since the most recent BeginTrans and writes it to disk. Rollback is the opposite of CommitTrans; it undoes all your changes back to the last Commit-Trans. In skeletal form, transaction processing usually looks something like this:

```
On Error GoTo Err_Handler

Dim wrkCurrent As WorkSpace
Dim fInTrans As Boolean

fInTrans = False
Set wrkCurrent = DBEngine.Workspaces(0)
' ...
wrkCurrent.BeginTrans
    fInTrans = True
    ' (Any series of data changes here)
wrkCurrent.CommitTrans
    fInTrans = False
' ...
Err_Handler:
    if fInTrans Then
        wrkCurrent.Rollback
    End If
    ' (further error processing)
```

Here are some issues you need to be aware of when using transaction processing:

- Not all recordsets support transaction processing. None of the non-native ISAM formats support transactions, but most ODBC data sources do. You can check the Transactions property of a Recordset object to see whether it supports transaction processing.

- Transactions affect *all* changes to data in the workspace. Everything you do after a BeginTrans method is committed or rolled back as a single unit. This even applies to changes across multiple databases open within a single workspace.

- You can nest transactions in Access databases up to five levels deep. Inner transactions must be committed or rolled back before the surrounding ones. You cannot nest transactions for ODBC tables. To maintain two independent transactions, you can use two separate workspaces.

- If you close a workspace without explicitly committing its transactions, all pending transactions are automatically rolled back.

- Access handles its own transaction processing on bound forms. You cannot use transaction processing in event procedures to group together changes made via bound forms.

Transaction Processing in a Multiuser Setting

Transaction processing has extra importance in multiuser applications. When more than one user is modifying the database, you can no longer depend on the results of one change being present when you start another unless you wrap the set of updates in a transaction. Thus, you may wish to use transactions in a multiuser setting.

NOTE When you use transactions, you increase the *integrity* of one user's set of changes at the expense of reduced *concurrency* of the entire shared application, because locks on multiple records are maintained for longer periods of time. Extensive use of transactions will likely cause an increase in the number of locking errors in your application.

When you use transaction processing in a multiuser setting, Access treats the entire transaction as a single disk write but otherwise respects your specified locking setting. Thus, if you're using pessimistic locking (LockEdits = True), Access locks a record when an Edit or AddNew method is encountered. If you're using optimistic locking (LockEdits = False) instead, Access doesn't lock the record until it encounters an Update method. Within the confines of a transaction, however, Access accumulates these locks without releasing them until the entire transaction has been either committed or rolled back.

If Access encounters a locked record within a transaction, the standard set of trappable errors occurs. When this happens you'll need to either obtain the necessary lock or roll back the transaction.

Implied Transactions

In addition to *explicit transactions* that you create using the BeginTrans, CommitTrans, and Rollback methods, Jet 3.5 (and its predecessor Jet 3.0) creates *implicit transactions* to improve the performance of recordset operations. In an exclusively used database, by default, Jet commits implicit transactions every 2 seconds; in a shared environment, Jet commits these transactions every 50 milliseconds. The default setting of 50 milliseconds should ensure no noticeable change in concurrency in a multiuser setting.

The exact effect implicit transactions have on concurrency depends on the values of several Registry settings. These settings are described in Table 12.5. To use non-default settings, you need to edit the Registry keys under the following node:

```
HKEY_LOCAL_MACHINE\SOFTWARE\Microsoft\Jet\3.5\Engines\Jet 3.5
```

T A B L E   1 2 . 5   Transaction Registry Settings

Key	Datatype	Effect	Default
UserCommitSync	String	Determines whether explicit transactions are executed synchronously (unnested transactions are performed one after the other)	Yes
ImplicitCommitSync	String	Determines whether Jet creates implicit transactions for recordset updates. A setting of No causes implied transactions to be used*	No
ExclusiveAsnycDelay	DWORD	Determines the maximum time (in milliseconds) before Jet commits an implicit transaction when the database is opened exclusively	2000
SharedAsyncDelay	DWORD	Determines maximum time (in milliseconds) before Jet commits an implicit transaction when the database is opened in shared mode	50

There may be some applications for which you wish to sacrifice concurrency for increased performance. In these cases you may want to increase the value of the SharedAsyncDelay key.

> **TIP**   You can override the Jet Registry settings by using the SetOption method of the DBEngine object. See Chapter 17 fror more information.

Multiuser Action Queries

Access 1.x provided no means of determining programmatically whether an action query failed. If any records failed to be updated because of locking conflicts or other errors, no trappable run-time error was triggered. With the introduction of Access 2.0, Microsoft improved the situation by adding an option (dbFailOn-Error) to the Execute method of querydefs. In Access 2, if an error was encountered, you could trap the error, but you still couldn't determine how many records were prevented from being updated, deleted, or appended.

In Access 97 (and Access 95) you can determine how many records were affected by the action query by checking the RecordsAffected property of the querydef after the query has executed. When executing a SQL statement rather than a stored query, you can use the RecordsAffected property of the DBEngine object to retrieve the same information. Unfortunately, you can't programmatically determine how many records were prevented from being updated because of locking conflict, key violation, or other reasons. (The Access UI provides this information when queries are executed interactively.)

Listing 12.4 shows an example of using the dbFailOnError option and the RecordsAffected property.

Listing 12.4

```
Function DeleteTempOrders()

    On Error GoTo DeleteTempOrdersErr

    Dim db As Database
    Dim wrk As Workspace
    Dim qdf As QueryDef
    Dim lngRecsEstimated As Long
    Dim lngRecsAffected As Long
    Dim intResp As Integer
    Dim strWhere As String
    Dim fInTrans As Boolean

    DeleteTempOrders = False
    fInTrans = False

    Set db = CurrentDb
    Set wrk = DBEngine.Workspaces(0)
```

```
        strWhere = "[Order#] BETWEEN 1 AND 100"

        lngRecsEstimated = DCount("*", "tblTempOrders", strWhere)
        Set qdf = db.CreateQueryDef("", _
         "DELETE * FROM tblTempOrders WHERE " & strWhere)

        intResp = MsgBox("About to delete " & lngRecsEstimated & _
         " records." & vbCrLf & _
         "Fail if any record can't be deleted?", _
         vbYesNo + vbInformation + vbDefaultButton1, _
         "Action Query Example")

    wrk.BeginTrans
        fInTrans = True
        If intResp = vbYes Then
            qdf.Execute (dbFailOnError)
        Else
            qdf.Execute
        End If
        lngRecsAffected = qdf.RecordsAffected
        If lngRecsAffected < lngRecsEstimated Then
            intResp = MsgBox("Only " & lngRecsAffected & _
             " out of " & lngRecsEstimated & _
             " records will be deleted." & vbCrLf & _
             "OK to continue?", _
             vbOKCancel + vbInformation, "Action Query Example")
            If intResp = vbCancel Then
                MsgBox "Transaction rolled back!", _
                 vbOKOnly + vbCritical, "Action Query Example"
                wrk.Rollback
                GoTo DeleteTempOrdersDone
            End If
        End If
    wrk.CommitTrans
    fInTrans = False

    DeleteTempOrders = True

DeleteTempOrdersDone:
    Exit Function

DeleteTempOrdersErr:
    If fInTrans Then
        wrk.Rollback
```

```
        MsgBox "Error occurred. Rolled back.", _
            vbOKOnly + vbCritical, "Action Query Example"
    Else
        MsgBox "Error#" & Err.Number & ": " & Err.Description, _
            vbOKOnly + vbCritical, "Action Query Example"
    End If
    Resume DeleteTempOrdersDone

End Function
```

In this example, which can be found in the basActionQueryExample module of CH12APP.MDB, DeleteTempOrders calculates the estimated number of records to be deleted by a delete query prior to its execution. Next, the function asks the user whether to use the dbFailOnError option.

If the user chooses Yes, the query is run using the dbFailOnError option. If a record is locked or if some other problem prevents one or more records from being deleted, the entire transaction is rolled back.

If the user chooses No, the query is run without the dbFailOnError option. If a record is locked or if some other problem prevents one or more records from being deleted, the query executes within a transaction, but the user is warned of the incomplete results and given the opportunity to roll back the transaction.

Microsoft has added two new properties to action queries for Access 97:

- FailOnError

- UseTransaction

You can use the FailOnError property instead of the dbFailOnError option of the Execute method; it has the equivalent effect. The advantage of using the new FailOnError property is that you can store this setting with the query definition. In addition, it allows you to cause an update query to fail if an error is received when executing queries outside of VBA code. The default value of this property is No (False).

By default, Access wraps each action query in a transaction. This behavior ensures that the entire query is executed in concert. Unfortunately, for very large queries this may cause Access to request a very large number of record locks from the operating system and can cause the query to fail due to the inability to receive those locks. (Even worse, this may cause the NetWare 3.x-based networks to crash.) The solution is to set the UseTransaction property of the query to No (False), which tells Access not to execute the action query as a single transaction.

Splitting Databases

No matter which locking scheme you employ, you are still left with the fact that, by default, Access puts all objects in a single database file. Performance can suffer considerably because every time an object (for example, a form) is used, it must be sent across the network to the user. In a production setting, where nothing but the data is updated, much of this network traffic is unnecessary.

You can eliminate this unnecessary traffic by splitting the database into an "application" database and a "data" database. Install the data database (with tables only) on the file server and a copy of the application database (containing all other objects) on each workstation. From each copy of the application database, use the File ➤ Get External Tables ➤ Link Tables command to link to the set of tables in the data database.

The *advantages* of this approach are

- Performance (especially user interface performance) is improved considerably.

- You can create temporary tables on each workstation and not worry about naming and locking conflicts for temporary objects.

- Splitting the database makes the updating of applications easier because the data and application are kept separate. Changes to the application can be made off site and easily merged back into the application database without disturbing the data.

The major *disadvantage* of this approach is that Access hard-codes the paths to linked tables. This means that if you move the data database, you have to fix up the table links.

Managing Linked Tables

Because Access hard-codes linked table paths, their use requires extra maintenance. If you move the data database with linked tables, you have three options for fixing the broken links:

- Delete and reestablish the link from scratch.

- Use the Access 97 Linked Table Manager Add-In to fix up the references and refresh the links.

- Create VBA code to manage links programmatically.

> **TIP**
>
> If you use universal naming convention (UNC) names when establishing your links (for example, \\ServerName\ShareName\Data.Mdb), you won't have to bother with fixing up links when you copy or move the application database from one computer to another within your LAN.

The sample database includes a module, basLinkedTables, that contains reusable code for managing linked tables. The entry point to the code is through the adhVerifyLinks function, which is shown in Listing 12.5.

Listing 12.5

```
Function adhVerifyLinks(strDataDatabase As String, _
  strSampleTable As String) As Integer

    On Error GoTo adhVerifyLinksErr

    Dim varReturn As Variant
    Dim strDBDir As String
    Dim strMsg As String
    Dim db As Database
    Dim varFileName As Variant
    Dim tdf As TableDef
    Dim intI As Integer
    Dim intNumTables As Integer
    Dim strProcName As String
    Dim strFilter As String
    Dim lngFlags As Long

    strProcName = "adhVerifyLinks"

    ' Verify Links using one sample table.
    varReturn = CheckLink(strSampleTable)

    If varReturn Then
        adhVerifyLinks = True
        GoTo adhVerifyLinksDone
    End If

    ' Get name of folder where application database is located
    strDBDir = GetDBDir()

    If (Dir$(strDBDir & strDataDatabase) <> "") Then
```

```
            ' Data database found in current directory.
            varFileName = strDBDir & strDataDatabase
        Else
            ' Let user find data database using common dialog
            strMsg = "The required file '" & strDataDatabase & _
             "' could not be found."
            strMsg = strMsg & " You can use the next dialog " & _
             "box to locate the file on your system."
            strMsg = strMsg & " If you cannot find this file " & _
             "or are unsure what to do choose CANCEL"
            strMsg = strMsg & " at the next screen and call " & _
             "the database administrator."
            MsgBox strMsg, vbOKOnly + vbCritical, strProcName

            ' Display Open File dialog using the adhCommonFileOpenSave
            ' function in the basCommonfile module
            strFilter = adhAddFilterItem( _
             strFilter, "Access (*.mdb)", "*.mdb")
            lngFlags = adhOFN_HIDEREADONLY Or _
             adhOFN_HIDEREADONLY Or adhOFN_NOCHANGEDIR

            varFileName = adhCommonFileOpenSave( _
                OpenFile:=True, _
                Filter:=strFilter, _
                Flags:=lngFlags, _
                DialogTitle:="Locate Data database file")

            If IsNull(varFileName) Then
                ' User pressed Cancel.
                strMsg = "You can't run database until you can " & _
                 "locate '" & strDataDatabase & "'."
                MsgBox strMsg, vbOKOnly + vbCritical, strProcName
                adhVerifyLinks = False
                GoTo adhVerifyLinksDone
            Else
                varFileName = adhTrimNull(varFileName)
            End If
        End If

        'Rebuild Links. Check for number of tables first.
        Set db = CurrentDb
        intNumTables = db.TableDefs.Count
        varReturn = SysCmd(acSysCmdInitMeter, "Relinking tables", _
         intNumTables)
```

```
        ' Loop through all tables.
        ' Reattach those with nonzero-length Connect strings.
        intI = 0
        For Each tdf In db.TableDefs
            ' If connect is blank, it's not a Linked table
            If Len(tdf.Connect) > 0 Then
                intI = intI + 1
                tdf.Connect = ";DATABASE=" & varFileName

                ' The RefreshLink might fail if the new path
                ' isn't OK. So trap errors inline.
                On Error Resume Next
                tdf.RefreshLink
                'If one link bad, return False
                If Err <> 0 Then
                    adhVerifyLinks = False
                    GoTo adhVerifyLinksDone
                End If
            End If

            varReturn = SysCmd(acSysCmdUpdateMeter, intI + 1)
        Next tdf

        adhVerifyLinks = True

adhVerifyLinksDone:
    On Error Resume Next
    varReturn = SysCmd(acSysCmdRemoveMeter)
    On Error GoTo 0
    Exit Function

adhVerifyLinksErr:
    Select Case Err
    Case Else
        MsgBox "Error#" & Err.Number & ": " & Err.Description, _
            vbOKOnly + vbCritical, strProcName
    End Select
    Resume adhVerifyLinksDone
End Function
```

The adhVerifyLinks function takes two parameters: strDataDatabase, the name of the data database containing the linked tables, and strSampleTable, the name of one of the linked tables. adhVerifyLinks starts by checking the validity of this sample linked table. It assumes that if this table's link checks out okay, then all the links are fine. (You can modify the code to check the integrity of all links instead.) The function verifies the links by calling the private function CheckLink, which is shown in Listing 12.6.

Listing 12.6

```
Private Function CheckLink(strTable As String) As Integer

    Dim varRet As Variant

    On Error Resume Next

    ' Check for failure. If can't determine the name of
    ' the first field in the table, the link must be bad.
    varRet = CurrentDb.TableDefs(strTable).Fields(0).Name
    If Err <> 0 Then
        CheckLink = False
    Else
        CheckLink = True
    End If

End Function
```

This simple function checks the validity of a link by attempting to retrieve the name of the table's first field. If this operation succeeds, the link is good; if it fails, it's assumed to be bad and the function returns False.

If CheckLink returns False, adhVerifyLinks attempts to find the data database in the same folder as the application database. If the database is found there, the function relinks all the tables using this database. If the data database isn't in the application folder, however, the function prompts the user with a common open file dialog.

adhVerifyLinks relinks the tables by modifying the Connect property of the tabledef and using the RefreshLink method. (See Chapter 6 for additional examples of linking and relinking linked tables.)

Integrating Linked Tables into Your Applications

When you split an existing single-database application into data and application databases, you may be required to alter some of your VBA code. You can't use table-type recordsets or the Seek method on linked tables. You can, however, use one of these alternative strategies instead:

- Create dynaset-type recordsets and use the slower FindFirst method.

- Use the OpenDatabase method to open the data database directly. You can then create table-type recordsets and use the Seek method just as though the tables were local.

Whichever method you choose, you'll almost certainly have to make changes to your application code.

> **TIP** Access 97 includes an add-in called the Database Splitter that makes it easy to split a single database into data and application databases.

Using a Custom AutoNumber Routine

Access 97 offers a great deal of flexibility in choosing AutoNumber fields (called Counter fields prior to Access 95). You can choose an AutoNumber field with Long Integer values that are made up of sequentially incremented or randomly chosen numbers, or you can use a 16-byte globally unique identifier (GUID) instead. (See Chapter 13 for more on GUIDs.) At times, however, you may prefer to use a custom routine for assigning some type of incremented value for one of the following reasons:

- You need to use an alphanumeric string.

- You need to use an increment greater than 1.

- You wish to recover values for discarded records.

- You need to create values that are computed using other fields in the record.

- You have the data stored in a non-native table that has no support for Auto-Number fields.

> **NOTE**
>
> It's important that you not place too much faith in surrogate primary keys, such as those that can be generated using AutoNumber (built-in or custom) ields. While these fields can certainly guarantee uniqueness of the record, you still have to ensure, through the use of additional indexes or event procedures, that a user can't create five customer records for the same customer.

Custom AutoNumber Setup

You can implement your own custom AutoNumber fields for an Access database by maintaining a separate table to hold the next AutoNumber value. You must lock this table when you retrieve a new AutoNumber value and trap for errors that may occur when multiple users attempt to retrieve a new value at the same time.

We have created a custom AutoNumber routine for the Menu# field of tblMenu in the CH12APP.MDB sample database. The routine is called from the frmMenu form; the table that holds the AutoNumber value is kept in the CH12AUTO.MDB database.

Implementing a Custom AutoNumber

We have split the activity of obtaining a new AutoNumber value into two parts. A low-level routine handles the AutoNumber increment or returns –1 if an AutoNumber value cannot be retrieved. A high-level routine handles the assignment of this Auto-Number to a new record and determines what to do about any errors. Both routines are contained in the module basAutoNumber in the CH12APP.MDB database.

adhGetNextAutoNumber is the low-level routine that interfaces directly with the AutoNumber database. It takes a single parameter—the name of the table that requires the new AutoNumber value. The next AutoNumber value is stored in a table (in the adhcAutoNumDb database) with _ID appended to the base table name. For example, the AutoNumber for tblMenu is stored in tblMenu_ID. This table has a simple structure: it consists of a single Long Integer field named NextAutoNumber. adhGetNextAutoNumber is shown in Listing 12.7.

Listing 12.7

```
' Public variable that is used to store
' the path and name to the AutoNumber database.
' This variable is set by adhInitAutoNum
```

```
Public gstrAutoNumDbName As String

' Database storing autonumber values
Public Const adhcAutoNumDb = "Ch12Auto.Mdb"

' Number of times to retry in case of locking conflicts
Public Const adhcMaxRetries = 5

'Error constants
Const adhcErrRI = 3000
Const adhcLockErrCantUpdate2 = 3260
Const adhcLockErrTableInUse = 3262

Function adhGetNextAutoNumber(ByVal strTableName As String) _
 As Long

    On Error GoTo adhGetNextAutoNumber_Err

    Dim wrkCurrent As Workspace
    Dim dbAutoNum As Database
    Dim rstAutoNum As Recordset
    Dim lngNextAutoNum As Long
    Dim lngWait As Long
    Dim lngX As Long
    Dim intLockCount As Integer
    DoCmd.Hourglass True

    intLockCount = 0

    ' Open a recordset on the appropriate table in the
    ' autonumbers database, denying all reads to others
    ' while it is open
    Set wrkCurrent = DBEngine.Workspaces(0)
    Set dbAutoNum = wrkCurrent.OpenDatabase(gstrAutoNumDbName, _
     False)
    Set rstAutoNum = dbAutoNum.OpenRecordset(strTableName _
     & "_ID", dbOpenTable, dbDenyRead)

    ' Increment and return the autonumber value
    rstAutoNum.MoveFirst
    rstAutoNum.Edit
        lngNextAutoNum = rstAutoNum![NextAutoNumber]
```

```
                rstAutoNum![NextAutoNumber] = lngNextAutoNum + 1
           rstAutoNum.Update

           adhGetNextAutoNumber = lngNextAutoNum

           rstAutoNum.Close
           dbAutoNum.Close

    adhGetNextAutoNumber_Exit:
        DoCmd.Hourglass False
        Exit Function

    adhGetNextAutoNumber_Err:
        ' Table locked by another user
        If Err = adhcErrRI Or Err = adhcLockErrCantUpdate2 Or _
         Err = adhcLockErrTableInUse Then
            intLockCount = intLockCount + 1
            ' Tried too many times, give up
            If intLockCount > adhcMaxRetries Then
                adhGetNextAutoNumber = -1
                Resume adhGetNextAutoNumber_Exit
            Else
                ' Calculate the wait time based on
                ' the number of retries and a random number
                lngWait = intLockCount ^ 2 * Int(Rnd * 20 + 5)
                ' Waste time, but let Windows
                ' multitask during this dead time
                For lngX = 1 To lngWait
                    DoEvents
                Next lngX
                Resume
            End If
        ' Unexpected error
        Else
            MsgBox "Error " & Err.Number & ": " & Err.Description, _
             vbOKOnly + vbCritical, "adhGetNextAutoNumber"
            adhGetNextAutoNumber = -1
            Resume adhGetNextAutoNumber_Exit
        End If

    End Function
```

When there is no contention for AutoNumber values, adhGetNextAutoNumber does its work by simply retrieving and incrementing the NextAutoNumber field. In a multiuser situation, however, it is possible for one user to request an AutoNumber value while another user already has the table locked. adhGetNextAutoNumber handles these types of errors using the following code:

```
intLockCount = intLockCount + 1
' Tried too many times, give up
If intLockCount > adhcMaxRetries Then
    adhGetNextAutoNumber = -1
    Resume adhGetNextAutoNumber_Exit
Else
    ' ...
End If
```

You'll need to set adhcMaxRetries to balance between potential failure and potential delays to the user. Depending on your network, you may find a value between 3 and 20 is appropriate. If the table is not free after a number of retries, it generally means that someone else has it locked for a reason unrelated to assigning Auto-Number values (for example, as a side effect of a GPF [General Protection Fault] encountered when assigning an AutoNumber).

The second part of the preceding If...Then...Else statement contains the code that forces the retry of the operation that encountered the lock:

```
Else
    ' Calculate the wait time based on
    ' the number of retries and a random number
    lngWait = intLockCount ^ 2 * Int(Rnd * 20 + 5)
    ' Waste time, but let Windows
    ' multitask during this dead time
    For lngX = 1 To lngWait
        DoEvents
    Next lngX
    Resume
End If
```

Rather than immediately retrying to obtain the lock, adhGetNextAutoNumber includes some time-wasting logic. It's useful to review this logic because it's likely you'll want to include similar code in all your routines that may experience locking conflicts. A Long Integer, lngWait, is calculated based on a formula that squares the number of retries and multiplies the result by a random number between 5 and 25. Then, a For...Next loop is executed for lngWait iterations to waste time. The inclusion of the DoEvents statement ensures that any other Windows tasks are given processor time during this "dead" time period. By including a random number and squaring the time for each retry, adhGetNextAutoNumber attempts to separate out any users who were requesting locks at the same time.

After the For...Next loop, the actual retry is accomplished with the Resume statement.

The function adhAssignID, also located in basAutoNumbers (and not shown here), handles the high-level AutoNumber assignment. It is called from the Before-Insert event of the form and is passed three parameters: the Form object, the name of the underlying table that holds the custom-AutoNumber field, and the name of the custom AutoNumber field. adhAssignID deletes any record that cannot be assigned an AutoNumber. Depending on your particular circumstances, you may need a more sophisticated high-level control routine. For example, you might want to save records that couldn't be assigned a value to a temporary local table rather than discard them entirely.

The basAutoNumber module also includes the adhInitAutoNum function, which determines the name and path of the AutoNumber database and sticks it in the gstrAutoNumDbName global variable. The sample database calls adhInitAutoNum during application startup, but you could alternately call this function from the Load event procedure of forms that employ adhAssignID.

You may wish to modify adhGetNextAutoNumber to return an AutoNumber in some custom format that uses an increment other than 1 or that uses an alphanumeric string.

Security

Although security is not really a multiuser-specific concern, it certainly becomes more necessary in a multiuser environment. As the number of workstations running your application increases, the more likely it is you'll want to prevent unauthorized users from gaining access to either the data *or* the application.

Using security also allows Access to accurately inform users as to who has locked a record. Even if you intercept Access' built-in locking-error messages, you still may want to parse out the user name and use it in any custom error messages. If you don't use security, every user will be named Admin. (See Chapter 14 for more details on security.)

Determining Which Users Have a Database Open

We've included on the CD that accompanies this book an unsupported DLL, MSLDBUSR.DLL (along with documentation), from Microsoft's Kevin Collins and Bob Delavan, that allows you to determine which users have a database open. This DLL works by reading information directly out of the .LDB file that Jet uses to maintain locking information.

To use the DLL you must include the following Declare statement in the declarations section of a module:

```
Private Declare Function LDBUser_GetUsers Lib "MSLDBUSR.DLL" _
(strUserBuffer() As String, ByVal strFilename As String, _
ByVal lngOptions As Long) As Integer
```

When you call the DLL, you pass it an array, the name of the database to check, and an options parameter; it returns the number of users and fills the passed array with the machine names of the users who have the database open. The lngOptions parameter can be any of the following:

Value	Purpose
&H1	Returns all users who ever had the database open during this session
&H2	Returns only currently active users
&H4	Returns users marked as corrupted only
&H8	Returns only the count of users

We've created a form, frmViewUsers, that calls MSLDBUSR and displays the machine names of active users in a list box control. frmViewUsers is shown in Figure 12.7.

For additional information on Jet locking issues and MSLDBUSR, including a discussion of an accompanying API call that returns various error conditions, see the white paper, JETLOCK.DOC, included on this book's CD along with the MSLDBUSR DLL.

FIGURE 12.7

This form calls MSLD-BUSR.DLL to determine the machine names of all users who have the specified database open.

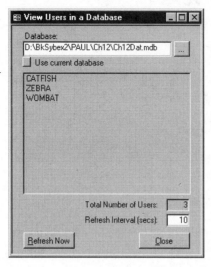

> **TIP**
>
> Access automatically creates an LDB file of the same name as the database whenever it finds that one does not exist. This file keeps track of record locks. If you experience a GPF or power failure or you reboot while a record is locked, the .LDB file will be left in a state that reports which records were locked at the time of the problem. Because this lock would now have no owner, the effect is a permanent lock of the record. The solution to this problem is to close the database (in a multiuser environment, all users must close it) and delete the LDB file. Access creates a new LDB file whenever none is found.

The Wire

When moving from single-user to multiuser applications, you need to start thinking about potential data bottlenecks. Remember that every time your application requests data, it is sent over the network (also know as *the wire*) to the workstation. Thus, you'll want to minimize sending large amounts of data over the wire, for the sake of both the user requesting the data and the network traffic.

One Record at a Time

One area that demands special attention is how *much* of a recordset you offer your users in a form. Although Access makes it easy to bind a form to an entire table or query, letting users navigate to their hearts' content, you'll quickly find this doesn't work well with even moderately large tables (more than 30,000–50,000 rows) on a network. You're better off presenting each user with a single record at a time and programmatically changing the record source of the form rather than using the FindFirst method to move to a specific record.

The frmOrderOneRec Sample Form

In CH12APP.MDB we've included a form, frmOrderOneRec, that demonstrates the technique of displaying only one record at a time to minimize network traffic. The form (see Figure 12.8) is bound to the tblOrder table. It also contains a subform bound to tblOrderDetails. frmOrderOneRec includes these features:

- It's bound to a SQL statement that initially returns no records:

```
SELECT DISTINCTROW * FROM tblOrder where [Order#] = 0;
```

- The user navigates to another order by entering an order number in a text box control, txtGotoOrder, located in the form header, and clicking the cmdGoto command button. This triggers an event procedure that builds a new SQL statement based on the value entered in the text box and changes the record source accordingly.

FIGURE 12.8

frmOrderOneRec form in edit mode

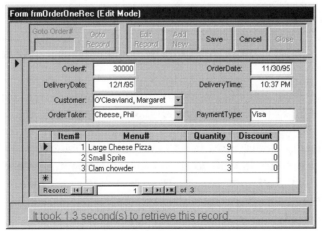

- The form switches among four modes (NoRecord, Browse, Edit, and AddNew); the current mode is indicated in the form's caption. Users switch among modes using buttons located in the form's header. When a record is made current, it's pulled up in Browse mode to minimize inadvertent changes to the data.

- When in Edit or AddNew mode, users are prevented from closing the form or navigating to a new record until they explicitly choose to save or cancel their changes.

You may wish to examine the code behind frmOrderOneRec and compare it with the code behind another form in the database, frmOrderAllRecs, which takes the default approach of offering the user all records at the same time.

NOTE There is some overhead associated with dynamically changing the form's record source. Thus, frmOrderOneRec will be slower in locating records than frmOrderAllRecs for recordsets with fewer than about 30,000–50,000 records. (The sample database contains far fewer records than this.) If you wish to add records to the sample database for the purpose of comparing these two techniques, you can use the frmCreateRandomRecords form that we've provided to automatically generate thousands of random order and order detail records for testing purposes.

Test, Test, Test!

You need to test your applications more thoroughly if they will be used on a network. The rule to remember here is, if something *can* go wrong, it will. This means you must set aside a significant amount of time for testing and debugging your multiuser applications.

One advantage of developing in the Windows environment is that you can develop, test, and debug multiuser applications on a single machine by starting two instances of Access and switching back and forth between the instances. While this should allow you to test for and fix many potential problems, you'll still need to test the application on the target network under a typical load of users to find all potential problems. In other words, there's no substitute for the real thing.

Summary

The important point to remember when writing multiuser applications is to anticipate problems. Multiuser applications need to handle—that is, recover from—the errors that occur when locks are placed on pages of records. In general, there is no set of perfect answers that applies to all multiuser applications. You'll have to develop the appropriate solution for your particular database and consider each of the following:

- Balance network security and maintenance against efficiency and speed when choosing whether to install Access on each workstation.

- Adjust your multiuser settings to achieve optimum performance for your particular application.

- Balance ease of use, data integrity, and ease of programming in developing your locking strategy.

- Be aware of the errors that can occur when multiple users share data.

- Use custom error-handling code when using bound forms with optimistic locking.

- Use custom lock notification code when using bound forms with pessimistic locking.

- Split your database into separate data and application databases for increased performance.

- Use VBA code to manage the linked tables in a split database architecture.

- Use transactions to ensure the integrity of your data when multiple operations must occur in concert.

- Use MSLDBUSR.DLL to see who has a database open.

- Minimize data going across the network wire.

- Be sure to adequately test your applications.

Mastering Replication

- ■ Understanding how replication works

- ■ Using Replication Manager

- ■ Creating a custom conflict resolution function

- ■ Synchronizing data over the Internet

- ■ Creating partial replicas

If you wanted to keep two or more copies of a database synchronized using Access 2, you faced many hurdles. In fact, this functionality required so much coding that few developers attempted it. With the support for replication and synchronization built right into Access 97 (as well as Access 95), replication is finally a reality for many developers. In this chapter we discuss Jet replication in detail, including how replication works and when to use it. In addition, we discuss how to replicate and synchronize databases and manage replication conflicts and errors—both through the built-in user interfaces and programmatically.

NOTE There are two sample databases for this chapter: CH13A.MDB and CH13B.MDB. CH13A.MDB contains a series of forms and generic code that can be used to manage replicated databases, this database is not replicated. CH13B.MDB is the pre-replicated design master for a sample replicated database that includes custom conflict and error resolution code. You'll need to replicate CH13B before you can start experimenting with the special replication code in that database.

Replication: What Is It and How Does It Work?

Replication is the act of making special copies of a regular Access database that are enabled in such a way that you can easily transfer changes made in one copy to each of the other copies. There are three basic steps to Jet replication:

1. Replication

2. Synchronization

3. Conflict and error resolution

Replication

When you replicate a normal Access database, Jet makes many changes to the schema of the database that enables it to exchange updates with other databases. These schema changes, which are discussed in more detail later in the chapter, include the addition of system tables, the modification of existing tables, and the creation of new properties of the database and many of its objects.

When you convert a nonreplicated database into a replicated database, you end up with the *design master* of a new *replica set*. A replica set of one, however, is not very useful since you wouldn't have anyone to exchange changes with, so you normally create a second member of the replica set by immediately replicating the design master. You can create additional members of a replica set by replicating any of its existing replicas.

Two replicas can exchange updates only if they are descendants of the same design master; that is, members of the same replica set.

The design master is a special member of a replica set. You can make schema changes only in the design master. You can, however, make changes to data in any replica of a replica set (unless you elect to make a replica read-only).

Synchronization

When you make updates to a replica that's a member of a replica set, Jet tracks the updates using the extra tables and fields it added to the database when you first replicated it. Jet does not, however, send changes to the other members of the replica set without your intervention. In fact, unlike networked databases in a multiuser file-server or client-server environment, replicas are not connected except when you temporarily connect them—two at a time—during a *synchronization exchange*.

When you synchronize two replicas, Jet sends updates from one replica to another. What makes replication so useful is that Jet has to send only the *updates*. This makes synchronization much more efficient than importing and exporting records between two nonreplicated databases. Normally, synchronization occurs in both directions, but you can elect to synchronize in only one direction if you wish. It's up to you to control when synchronization occurs and between which replicas.

Conflict and Error Resolution

It's possible that, in between synchronization exchanges, two users might modify the same row in two different replicas. When this occurs, Jet flags a conflict the next time the replicas are synchronized. Jet uses a simple algorithm to determine which record's changes are preserved that is based on which replica modified the record the greatest number of times. Access includes the Conflict Resolution Wizard, which you can use to alter this automated decision and swap the winning and losing records. In addition, you can write a custom conflict resolution function to use instead of Access' built-in Wizard.

The Many Faces of Replication

You can replicate and synchronize Jet databases through a variety of means, as shown in Table 13.1. Each method has its own set of advantages and disadvantages, as described in more detail in the next few sections. Your situation will usually dictate which method to choose. For example, if you're developing an application that will be run by sophisticated power users, you may wish to employ Briefcase replication or the Access menus. On the other hand, if you're developing an application for naive users, you'll need to use DAO or Replication Manager or some combination of the two.

TABLE 13.1   Various Mechanisms for Managing Jet Replication

Method	Advantages	Disadvantages	Comments
Windows Briefcase	Simple drag-and-drop action; can be performed by users	Requires user intervention; cannot be controlled programmatically; requires Windows Briefcase	Not as simple as it seems; can be confusing for some users. Can't create or populate partial replicas
Access menus	Simple; can be performed by users; includes basic conflict management facility	Requires user intervention and the understanding of basic replication terminology. Can't create or populate partial replicas	Requires retail copy of Access on each desktop
DAO methods and properties	Can be automated; insulates user from process. No need for Access; can be used with the Access run-time, Visual Basic, and Visual C++. Can create and populate partial replicas	Requires programming; no built-in conflict management mechanism	Probably the best solution for most developers
Replication Manager	Can be automated. Can be used with the Access run-time	Not all aspects of replication can be handled with Replication Manager. Not included with Visual Basic or Visual C++. Can't create or populate partial replicas	Only a partial solution; you will need to supplement with DAO or the Access menus

Briefcase Replication

The Windows Briefcase is an operating system utility that makes it easy for users to manage files on multiple PCs. Typically, you drag files to and from the Briefcase on your laptop. The Briefcase makes it easy to keep multiple copies of the same files synchronized. Normally, the Briefcase works at the file level, performing simple file date/time comparisons to ensure that the most recent copy of a file is never overwritten.

If you choose the replication option when you install Access, it registers a special Jet replication reconciler to be used instead of Briefcase's normal reconciler when an MDB file is dragged to and from the Briefcase. With the Jet replication reconciler installed and registered, the first time you drag an MDB file to the Briefcase, the MDB file is converted into a replication design master, and on your laptop, a replica of the database is made. Thereafter, when you choose the Update option within the Briefcase, the two replicas of the database are synchronized using the Jet replication reconciler.

To use the Windows Briefcase-based replication facilities, you must have

- Windows 95 or Windows NT 4.0 on the laptop with the Briefcase installed

- Access on the laptop with the replication option installed

There's no way to automate Briefcase replication or integrate it into an existing application, so its use for the professional developer is limited.

WARNING Once the special Jet replication reconciler has been registered, the Briefcase will attempt to replicate or synchronize all MDB files, even if the MDB file is an Access 2.0 database. There's no way to direct the Briefcase to perform file date/time comparisons only for certain MDB files.

Access Menu-Based Replication

The Access user interface includes a set of menus found under Tools ➤ Replication that expose most of the Jet replication functionality to the Access user. The Access replication menus are summarized in Table 13.2.

TABLE 13.2   Access Replication Menus

Menu	Description
Synchronize Now	Specifies another replica with which to synchronize; can also be used to transfer design master status to another replica
Create Replica	For nonreplicated databases, creates a design master and one replica; for replicated databases, creates an additional replica
Resolve Conflicts	If there are synchronization conflict or error records in the currently open replica, this command opens the Resolve Replication Conflicts dialog, which allows you to resolve conflict records (This command is automatically executed when you open a replica that contains synchronization conflicts or errors.)
Recover Design Master	If the currently open replica is not the design master, you can use this command to make this replica the design master for the replica set. You should use this command only if the design master has been damaged or destroyed

DAO Replication

While Briefcase replication and replication through the Access menus are useful, if you're a developer, you're probably most concerned about how to programmatically manipulate replication from DAO and VBA. The good news is that it's all there. Everything you can do from the Windows Briefcase or the Access menus is programmable through DAO—from Access, Visual Basic, and Visual C++. The only bad news is that the Access Conflict Manager Wizard is not accessible from DAO; it's available only through the Access UI. Fortunately, you can use your own conflict management routine to replace Access' Wizard.

The DAO replication properties and methods are summarized in Tables 13.3 and 13.4, respectively.

TABLE 13.3   DAO Replication Properties

Object	Property	Description	Read/Write Status
Database	DesignMasterID	Unique identifier assigned to the design master of a replica set	Read/write
	ReplicaID	Unique identifier for replica	Read-only
All document objects	KeepLocal	String property you set to the string "T" *before* the database is first replicated to make an object nonreplicated (local)	Read/write before the database has been replicated

TABLE 13.3 DAO Replication Properties (continued)

Object	Property	Description	Read/Write Status
	ReplicableBool*	Boolean property you set to True *after* the database is replicated to start replicating an object that was local; or to False to stop replicating an object	Read/write
Tabedefs**	KeepLocal	String property you set to the string "T" *before* the database is first replicated to make an object nonreplicated (local)	Read/write before the database has been replicated
	ReplicableBool*	Boolean property you set to True *after* the database is replicated to start replicating an object that was local; or to False to stop replicating an object	Read/write
	CollsGuid	The column in the table that serves as the globally unique identifier (GUID); usually s_GUID, but Jet will use a user-created field of type GUID if the table already contains one	Read-only
	ReplicaFilter	Determines the filter used to populate a partial replica with data. Can be a valid filter, True (all rows), or False (no rows—the default). Has no effect on full replicas	Read/write
Relations	PartialReplica	Determines whether Jet should include rows from the "many" side of this relationship when populating a partial replica. Can be True or False. Has no effect on full replicas	Read/write
MSysDB document of the Databases container	ReplicaId	GUID that identifies this replica	Read-only

*This property replaces the obsolete string Replicable property. Replicable is still available for backward compatibility but should not be used

**These properties are also available as properties of the table document object

TABLE 13.3   DAO Replication Properties (continued)

Object	Property	Description	Read/Write Status
	DefaultPartner	GUID that identifies the replica that's the default synchronization partner	Read-only
	RepVersion	Tracks whether VBA code at a replica needs to be recompiled	Read-only
	LastUpdater	GUID of the replica that last updated data in the replica set	Read-only
	ReorderTables	Undocumented	Read-only
	MostRecentSync-Partner	GUID of the replica that last made a synchronization exchange with this replica; used to maintain the Access synchronization dialogs	Read-only
	LastSynchViaInternet, LastInternetSynch-Mode	Whether or not the last synchronization was over the Internet, and if so, the type (send and receive, send only, and so forth); used to maintain the Access synchronization dialogs	Read-only
	LastTransXCoord, LastTransYCoord	Last horizontal and vertical coordinates of a replica in replication manager; used to maintain the replication manager map	Read-only
	ZoomCenterPoint, ZoomLevel	Zoom-level tracking information for replication manager; used to maintain the replication manager map	Read-only
UserDefined document of Databases container	ReplicationConflict-Function	Name of a custom function that's called when synchronization conflicts or errors are detected; called only when the database is opened; to reset to default conflict resolution, you must delete this property	Read/write

*This property replaces the obsolete string Replicable property. Replicable is still available for backward compatibility but should not be used

**These properties are also available as properties of the table document object

TABLE 13.4 DAO Replication Methods of the Database Object

Method	Description
MakeReplica	Makes a new replica from the current replica
Synchronize	Synchronizes the current database with another replica
PopulatePartial	Populates or repopulates a partial replica with records according to previously defined filters and relations

Replication Manager

If you've purchased a copy of the Microsoft Office Developer Edition (the replacement for the Access 95 ADT), you have an additional mechanism for managing replication and synchronization: Replication Manager and its companion program, Synchronizer (which was called Transporter in Access 95). Replication Manager is shown in Figure 13.1.

Using Replication Manager, you can

- Replicate a database
- Create additional replicas for a replica set
- Synchronize replicas
- Create a regular synchronization schedule for a replica set
- Review the synchronization history of a replica
- Manage various replica properties
- Set up a synchronization scheme for remote sites
- Set up Internet/intranet synchronization

Replication Manager makes it easy to plan your replication topology and manage the synchronization schedules for a replica set. This allows you to set up a regular synchronization schedule without programming. It also comes in handy if you need to review the synchronization history for a replica set.

You use Replication Manager to create replicas, design replication topologies, and set up synchronization schedules, but it is the accompanying Synchronizer program that actually carries out the scheduled synchronization exchanges, moving data between replicas at the times you have designated using Replication Manager.

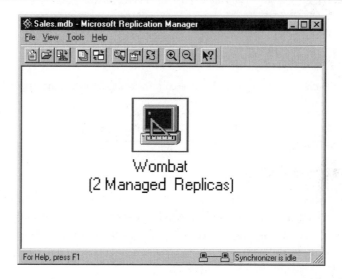

FIGURE 13.1

Replication Manager
is managing two Sales
replicas on a local
area network.

When you install Replication Manager, it defaults to loading Synchronizer when
you start Windows. If you don't plan on using Replication Manager and Synchronizer to perform synchronization, you'll want to remove the Synchronizer icon
from your startup group.

Synchronizers

When you use Replication Manager and Synchronizer to manage synchronization
of replicas on your LAN, you need to decide which PC will host the Synchronizer
program. This machine will need to load Synchronizer upon bootup and allow it
to remain running in the background. If your LAN server runs under Windows 95
or Windows NT, you can run Synchronizer directly on the server. If your server runs
under NetWare, Windows for Workgroups, or some other network operating system,
however, or you'd rather not increase the load on an already overburdened server,
you can elect to run the Synchronizer program from some other PC on the network.

You use a single synchronizer to manage the synchronization of all replicas on a
LAN. On a WAN, however, or in a distributed system of workgroups occasionally
connected by modem, you need to use multiple synchronizers, one for each workgroup (site). Each synchronizer manages the synchronization schedule of the local
workgroup's replicas and cooperatively manages (along with the other site's synchronizer) the synchronization between workgroups.

The Replication Manager Map

The Replication Manager user interface can be a bit confusing. For locally managed replicas, Replication Manager draws a single machine icon (labeled with the machine name) on the screen (the map) to represent a replica set. The total number of local replicas managed by the local synchronizer appears below the icon.

If replicas in the selected replica set are managed by multiple synchronizers, Replication Manager draws an icon for each synchronizer site (see Figure 13.2).

FIGURE 13.2

This replica set is managed by three synchronizers: one on the local PC (WOMBAT) and two remote PCs (CATFISH and MCWLA).

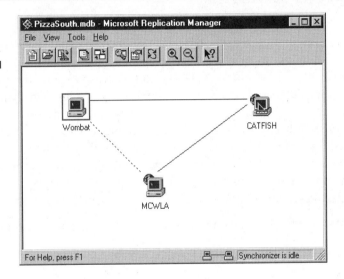

When to Use Replication

When you stop and think about it, replication is nothing more than a different way to share a database. Replication offers a major advantage over the more traditional file-server and client-server approaches: replicas don't have to be physically connected except during synchronization. Replication does have several drawbacks, however. For example, replication

- Adds overhead to a database
- Can't guarantee that a record is updated by only one user at a time

- Increases the likelihood that a record will be in different states for different users at the same time

Thus, you shouldn't use replication for situations in which the more classic file-sharing approaches are better suited. In many cases, it will be fairly obvious which file-sharing strategy is best suited for your particular application, but there are some situations where no one solution is obvious. The next few sections explore some of these situations.

Local Area Networks

When designing a system for a local area network (LAN), you may have difficulty deciding whether to share a single copy of a nonreplicated database (or at least a single copy of a "data" database in a classic split Access database system—see Chapter 12 for more details) across a workgroup or to distribute replicated copies of the database to each user and regularly synchronize changes between the replicated copies. In most cases the more traditional file-server approach makes more sense because of the need for the immediate dissemination of updates to all users. In a replicated system, there is a greater time lag between the dissemination of updates. This lag period may vary from an hour to several hours or days, depending on the number of users, the volume of updates, the frequency of conflicts, the synchronization topology, and the synchronization schedule.

On the other hand, using replication in this scenario might make sense if:

- Data is updated infrequently
- Updates do not usually affect other users
- The network is already overloaded
- The network is often down

In these cases it might make sense to use a replicated database instead of the traditional file-server approach.

Another alternative, especially when you have an overloaded network and can't afford to move to a client-server system, might be to create a hybrid system that uses replication *and* file-server sharing. Create multiple workgroups, each tied to a workgroup server machine. Users within a workgroup would use a split database system with the data database residing on the workgroup's file server. The data database would be replicated across workgroup servers, which would be synchronized on a regular schedule. This hybrid system would distribute the load over multiple servers.

Update latency—the time it takes for an update to be propagated to all replicas in the replica set—would be small within a workgroup but would be greater between machines in different workgroups.

Wide Area Networks

Wide area networks (WANs) are usually larger than LANs (have more nodes) and are spread out across greater distances. Perhaps most important, the speed of the connection between two nodes (computers) on a WAN is slower than on a LAN. These factors usually rule out the use of a file-server sharing model on a WAN in favor of a client-server system. With the introduction of replication, however, you may wish to consider using replication instead of a classic client-server system when using a WAN. Recall that synchronization exchanges transfer only the changed records, not whole tables, which makes replication well suited for WANs.

Replication may make sense on a WAN if:

- Data is updated infrequently

- Updates do not usually affect other users

- The network is already overloaded

- The network is often down

- The move to a client-server system is considered too expensive

On the other hand, replication is probably not a good candidate if:

- There are a great many updates, especially if multiple users will be updating the same records (creating a potentially large number of conflicts)

- There is a need for the immediate dissemination of updates to all users

- Data consistency is critical

In these situations you'd be better off using a more classic client-server, transaction-oriented approach or the replication services of a server database.

NOTE Microsoft has added Internet-based replication to Access 97. This makes it easier to use replication over WANs connected over the Internet or across corporate intranets.

Loosely Connected Networks

Mobile users on laptops connected to a network infrequently or connected over slow modem lines do not fit well into the classic file-server or client-server system, especially when two-way transfer of updates is needed. This type of system is often ideally suited for Jet replication.

Microsoft has added support for *partial replication* to Access 97. This makes replication more attractive for loosely connected networks because you can now partition tables so that each replica receives only a small subset of the rows present in the master database. See the section "Partial Replication" later in the chapter for more details.

Other Replication Uses

Replication may also be useful in the following situations:

- Warm backups
- Distribution of application updates

Even if you decide not to use replication to share data in a file-server environment, you may wish to consider using it for maintaining warm backups. By replicating a database and regularly (perhaps every 15 minutes or hourly) synchronizing it with another replica, you'll be ready in the event of a disaster that corrupts or destroys your main database. And if the backup replica is located on a different machine—perhaps even in another building—you're insulating yourself even further if the server itself goes down.

You may also wish to consider using replication to distribute application updates. This could significantly reduce the maintenance burden associated with updating an application that has been distributed to tens or hundreds of workstations. In this situation you'd synchronize with each workstation to distribute your update.

In both these scenarios, you'd have to weigh the potential benefits of using replication against the extra overhead replication adds to a database. (See the section "Changes Made to a Database When It Is Replicated" later in this chapter for more on replication overhead.)

Replication Topologies

When replicating a database, you must decide on a synchronization topology and schedule for the replica set. The *topology* defines which replicas exchange updates with which other replicas and the direction of these exchanges. The *schedule* defines when the exchanges occur and who initiates the exchanges. The topology and schedule you choose for your replica set affect the update latency.

LAN Topologies

Various topologies that might be used on a local area network (LAN) are depicted in Figure 13.3 and contrasted in Table 13.5.

FIGURE 13.3

Common replication topologies for a local area network

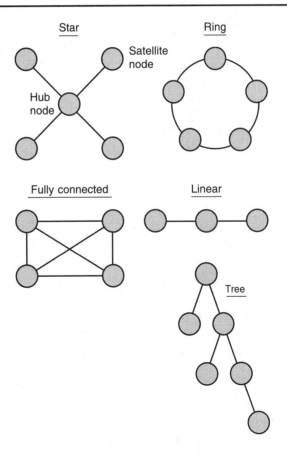

TABLE 13.5 Contrasting Various Replication Topologies

Topology	Latency	Load Distribution	Network Traffic	Reliability	Comments
Star	Moderate	Uneven	Low	Good as long as hub doesn't fail; bad if hub fails	Appropriate for many situations. Two rounds of synchronization exchanges may be necessary to fully propagate updates
Ring	Moderate	Even	Low	Good if direction can be reversed in the event of a node failure	Appropriate for many situations, especially when you need to evenly distribute the load
Fully connected	Low	Even	High	Good	Best latency but the most network traffic. Appropriate for applications with a small number of nodes where latency must be kept to a minimum
Linear	High	Even	Low	Bad; if any node fails, synchronization is disrupted	Simple to implement but worst update latency. May be appropriate for single-master model (data updates made only to the design master)
Tree	Variable	Uneven	Low	Depends on where the failure occurs	May be most efficient for applications where data updates occur only in selected nodes

Which synchronization topology you choose will depend on the importance of latency, network load, and synchronization reliability. If a very short latency is of utmost importance, network traffic is not a concern, and you don't have many nodes, then you may wish to use the fully connected topology. Otherwise, the star topology usually works best, with the ring topology another good choice. Replication Manager uses the star topology for locally managed replicas. The replica in the middle of a star topology is called the hub replica, and the other replicas are called satellite replicas.

WAN Topologies

All the topologies shown in Figure 13.3 are also possible on a wide area network (WAN) or a loosely connected network. More likely, however, you'll use a topology that interconnects several stars or rings, as depicted in Figure 13.4.

In a WAN or loosely connected network, each replica that exchanges updates with remote replicas is called a remote sync node. (This is our terminology, not

---

FIGURE 13.4

Common replication topologies for a wide area network

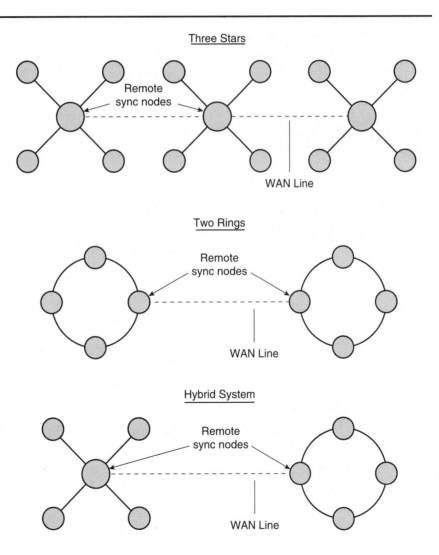

Three Stars

Remote sync nodes

WAN Line

Two Rings

Remote sync nodes

WAN Line

Hybrid System

Remote sync nodes

WAN Line

Microsoft's.) If you're using Replication Manager, the synchronizers will most likely be located on these machines. WANs and loosely connected networks actually have two sets of topologies: the topology that connects the remote sync nodes (this topology shows up in the Replication Manager map) and the topology used at each workgroup site. In a topology that consisted of several interconnected stars, the hubs of each star would also be remote sync nodes.

Design Master Location

We recommend placing the design master for a replica set on a non-hub computer when using the star topology. In addition, the design master should not be a remote sync node. This allows you to insulate the design master from the rest of the replicas and to better control when design changes are rolled out to the other members of the replica set.

When you will be making design changes over an extended time period, you should remove the design master from the normal synchronization schedule so that inconsistent design changes are not propagated to other members of the replica set.

Changes Made to a Database When It Is Replicated

When you replicate a database, Jet makes a number of changes to the database. These changes include

- Adding fields to each replicated table in the database

- Changing sequential AutoNumber fields to random AutoNumber fields

- Adding several system tables to the database

- Adding properties to database document objects

These changes, which can significantly increase the size of your database, are explored in the next few sections.

New Tables

Several new system tables are added to the database when it is replicated. These tables track the names and locations of replicas and replicated tables in the replica set, log synchronization exchanges, track deleted records, and log synchronization conflicts and errors. The replication system tables are summarized in Table 13.6.

TABLE 13.6   System Tables Added to a Replicated Database

Table	Present When	Purpose	Replicated?*
MSysErrors	Always	Tracks unresolved data synchronization errors for this replica set. This table is empty when all errors have been resolved	Yes
MSysExchangeLog	Always	Logs information on each synchronization exchange with this replica	No
MSysGenHistory	Always	Logs the history of every generation of updates in the replica set of which this replica is aware. Used to avoid sending unchanged records during synchronization exchanges	No
MSysOthersHistory	Always	Logs the generations received from other replicas in the replica set	No
MSysRepInfo	Always	Stores information about the replica set, including the GUID of the design master	Yes
MSysReplicas	Always	Stores the GUID of each replica in the replica set	No
MSysRepLock	Always	Used to log failed attempts to lock rows during a synchronization exchange	No
MSysSchChange	Always	Stores all schema changes made to the design master. Jet deletes records in this table periodically to minimize the size of this table	No
MSysSchedule	Always	Schedule information used by Replication Manager and the Synchronizer. Used only with these utilities	Yes

TABLE 13.6 System Tables Added to a Replicated Database (continued)

Table	Present When	Purpose	Replicated?*
MSysSideTables	After first conflict has occurred	Stores the name of the conflict table and GUID of the user table to which it applies. Contains one record for each table with outstanding conflicts	No
MSysTableGuids	Always	Stores the name of all replicated tables in the database and their GUIDs	No
MSysTombstone	Always	Stores the table and row GUIDs for all deleted rows in the replica	No
MSysTranspAddress	Always	Stores settings used by the Synchronizer	Yes
MSysTranspCoords	Replication Manager–managed replicas	Stores the x, y coordinates of the topology map used in Replication Manager	No

*Even though many of these tables are not replicated, the records in many of them are kept up to date across all replicas of a replica set.

All the replication system tables are read-only. Most of the fields in these tables are readable, although some of the fields are not because the data is stored in binary form as OLE objects. An example of one of the system tables, MSysRepInfo, is shown in Datasheet view in Figure 13.5.

In addition to the hidden system tables outlined in Table 13.6, Jet creates local (non-replicated) conflict tables whenever there are outstanding conflicts in a database table as a result of a synchronization exchange. Jet constructs the name of the conflict table by appending "_Conflict" to the end of the table that contains conflicts. For example, a conflict table for tblCustomer would be named tblCustomer_Conflict. The schema of the conflict table is the same as that of the original database table with which it is associated, except that the conflict table doesn't contain indexes (other than an index on the s_GUID field) or most field properties.

When a conflict occurs during synchronization because a row has been updated in both replicas, Jet creates a row in the conflict table (if this is the first conflict for a table, Jet first creates the conflict table) and stores the losing row in it. The algorithm used to determine the losing row is discussed in the section "Conflicts" later in this chapter.

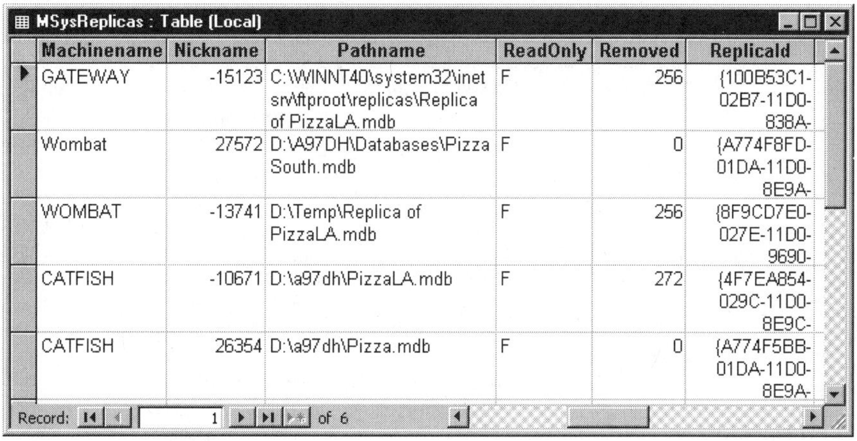

FIGURE 13.5

The MSysReplicas system table contains information on all replicas in the replica set.

Machinename	Nickname	Pathname	ReadOnly	Removed	ReplicaId
GATEWAY	-15123	C:\WINNT40\system32\inet srv\ftproot\replicas\Replica of PizzaLA.mdb	F	256	{100B53C1-02B7-11D0-838A-
Wombat	27572	D:\A97DH\Databases\Pizza South.mdb	F	0	{A774F8FD-01DA-11D0-8E9A-
WOMBAT	-13741	D:\Temp\Replica of PizzaLA.mdb	F	256	{8F9CD7E0-027E-11D0-9690-
CATFISH	-10671	D:\a97dh\PizzaLA.mdb	F	272	{4F7EA854-029C-11D0-8E9C-
CATFISH	26354	D:\a97dh\Pizza.mdb	F	0	{A774F5BB-01DA-11D0-8E9A-

Record: 1 of 6

Table Changes

Jet makes two types of changes to each replicated table when a database is replicated or a local table is made replicable.

- It adds new replication fields.
- It changes existing AutoNumber fields.

Additional Replication Fields

Jet adds several fields to each replicated table. The additional replication fields are summarized in Table 13.7. All the replication fields are read-only.

AutoNumber Fields

In addition to adding the fields from Table 13.7 to each database table, Jet alters the behavior of existing AutoNumber fields. If a table contains a Long Integer AutoNumber field with a NewValues property setting of Increment, Jet changes the property to Random. This significantly reduces the chance that two replicas assign the same AutoNumber value because each AutoNumber field will be based on a randomly selected number between –2 billion and and +2 billion. If for some reason this still produces too many duplicate values across a replica set, you may wish to use an AutoNumber field of type Replication ID instead. When you use an AutoNumber field with a Replication ID field size, Jet assigns numbers using a globally unique identifier.

TABLE 13.7 Replication Fields Added to Each Table

Field	Datatype	Purpose	Comments
s_Generation	Long Integer	Tracks changes (generations) to a row	Always present in replicated tables. If the s_Generation field value is 0, it represents an added row or a changed row that needs to be sent to other replicas during the next synchronization exchange. If it is a nonzero value, it represents the generation of the replica during which this change was made
s_GUID	AutoNumber— Replication ID	Added to most tables to uniquely identify the row across replicas, even if the primary key values change	This field will not be added to the table if the table contains an existing AutoNumber field with a field size of Replication ID. The CollsGuid property of the TableDef identifies which field is the GUID for the table— either s_GUID or a user-defined GUID field
s_Lineage	OLE Object	Tracks the history of changes to the record	
Gen_*Field*	Long Integer	One Gen field is added for each large object (memo or OLE object) user field in the table. This field tracks changes (generations) to the large object field independent of the other fields in the row	Its name takes the format Gen_*Field,* where *Field* is the name of the large object field. If this name is not unique, the rightmost characters are changed until a unique name is produced. The ColGeneration property of the large object field identifies the exact name of the accompanying Gen field

Globally Unique Identifiers (GUIDs)

While no system can ever guarantee that a number will *always* be unique, globally unique identifier (GUID) numbers have been designed with *global* uniqueness in mind. (These numbers are also sometimes referred to as universally unique identifiers, or UUIDs.) A Jet-generated GUID is a 16-byte string made up of several parts that, when concatenated, have an infinitesimal chance of ever generating duplicate values. And the *global* in GUID means that each GUID will be unique throughout the world, regardless of where or when it was generated. The datasheet for a replicated table with a GUID row identifier field (s_GUID) is shown in Figure 13.6.

GUIDs are used in several places in a replicated database to uniquely identify many parts of a replicated system, including:

- Rows in a replicated table

- Each table in a replicated database

- Each replica in a replica set

- Each synchronization exchange

- Each database generation

- Each schema change

- Each synchronizer

FIGURE 13.6

The normally hidden replication fields can be seen in the tblProduct table.

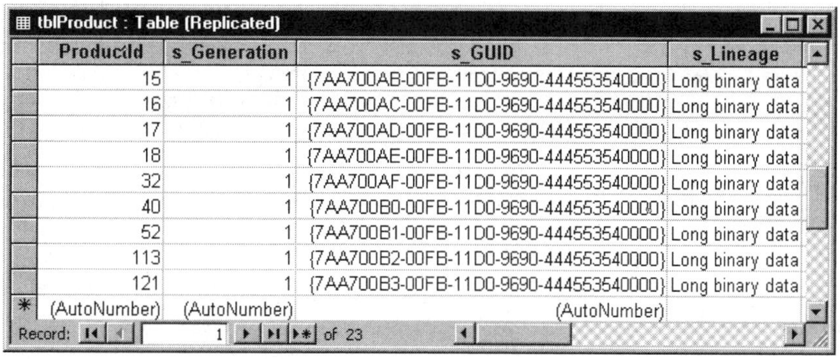

ProductId	s_Generation	s_GUID	s_Lineage
15	1	{7AA700AB-00FB-11D0-9690-444553540000}	Long binary data
16	1	{7AA700AC-00FB-11D0-9690-444553540000}	Long binary data
17	1	{7AA700AD-00FB-11D0-9690-444553540000}	Long binary data
18	1	{7AA700AE-00FB-11D0-9690-444553540000}	Long binary data
32	1	{7AA700AF-00FB-11D0-9690-444553540000}	Long binary data
40	1	{7AA700B0-00FB-11D0-9690-444553540000}	Long binary data
52	1	{7AA700B1-00FB-11D0-9690-444553540000}	Long binary data
113	1	{7AA700B2-00FB-11D0-9690-444553540000}	Long binary data
121	1	{7AA700B3-00FB-11D0-9690-444553540000}	Long binary data
(AutoNumber)	(AutoNumber)	(AutoNumber)	

tblProduct : Table (Replicated)

Record: 1 of 23

New Properties

Replicating a database adds properties to database objects. Earlier in the chapter, in Table 13.3, we described the DAO properties added to the database, TableDef objects, and document objects, including the MSysDB and UserDefined documents of the Databases container.

In addition, Jet adds the ColGeneration property to memo and OLE object fields. ColGeneration identifies the name of the field used to track generations for these large object fields.

Replicating a Database

The first step in employing Jet's replication services is to convert an existing non-replicated database into a replicated design master. You can do this using the Access menus, the Windows 95 Briefcase, Replication Manager, or DAO.

Regardless of which method you employ, you'll notice several Access UI changes in the look and behavior of the database that are a result of the underlying changes Jet makes to the database schema.

One of the first changes you will notice is to the title bar of the database window. Nonreplicated databases have title bars of the form *database_name*: *Database*. After replication, the title bar changes to *database_name*: Design Master, *database_name*: Replica, or *database_name*: Partial Replica.

In addition, when you save new database objects other than tables in a design master, the Save As dialog will include a new Make Replicable check box, as shown in Figure 13.7. To make a local object replicable in a design master, open the object's property dialog by using the View ➤ Properties menu command (or the equivalent right-click shortcut menu command) and check the Replicated check box. Similarly, to make a replicated object a local object, uncheck the Replicated check box in this dialog.

All saved objects in non–design master replicas will automatically be local. You can't change this. The only way you can make a local object replicable in a non–design master replica is to import that object into the design master, delete it from the replica, and then make it replicable in the design master by using the View ➤ Properties command.

FIGURE 13.7

Saving a form in a replicated database

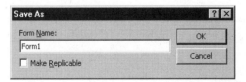

Replicating a Database Using the Access Menus

You use Tools ➤ Replication ➤ Create Replica to convert an existing nonreplicated database into a replicated design master. After executing this command, you are met with a warning dialog explaining that Access will close the database and then convert it into a replicated design master.

If you choose to proceed, you will see a second dialog asking whether you want Access to create a backup of your database before converting it. If you haven't already backed up the database, do so now, because there's no simple way to "un-replicate" a database. Access names the backup database name with the same root name and the extension .BAK. You won't have a chance to change this now, but you can always rename the backup later using Windows Explorer. After you dismiss this dialog, Access converts the database to the design master of the new replica set. After the database has been converted, Access displays a File Save As dialog, which asks for a name for the second replica of the replica set.

You can create additional replicas from any existing replica using the same command (Tools ➤ Replication ➤ Create Replica) you used to convert a database to a replicated design master.

Replicating a Database Using Replication Manager

You use the Tools ➤ Convert Database to Design Master command to convert a nonreplicated database into a replicated design master. Executing this command launches the Convert Database to Design Master Wizard. Like the Access menus, Replication Manager gives you the option of creating a backup with the .BAK extension when it converts the database.

Single Master Replica Sets

When converting a database to a design master, Replication Manager gives you the option of creating a replica set based on the *single master model* (see Figure 13.8). In this model, schema *and* data changes can be made only at the design master. If you choose the single master model (the second radio button option shown in Figure 13.8), all replicas other than the design master will be read-only (even if you specify otherwise when creating replicas using DAO). When you choose this option, Jet sets the SingleMaster field in the MSysRepInfo table to "T". Of course, you can get the equivalent effect in DAO by always creating read-only replicas, but there is no documented way to create a single master replica set from the Access UI or DAO.

> **WARNING** Take care before creating a single master replica set. There's no way to reverse this operation.

FIGURE 13.8

Using Replication Manager, you can create replica sets that allow data changes only in the design master. The default setting is to allow data changes in all replicas.

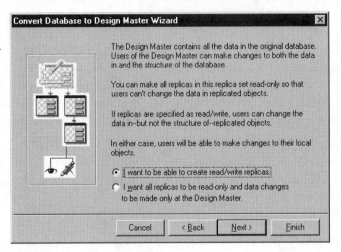

Managed Replicas

When converting a database to a design master or creating additional replicas with the File ➤ New Replica command, Replication Manager asks if you wish to have the replica *managed* by *this* synchronizer (see Figure 13.9). When a synchronizer manages a replica, it is able to schedule synchronizations that originate from the replica.

FIGURE 13.9

When creating a new replica, you need to decide whether you will manage the replica with this synchronizer.

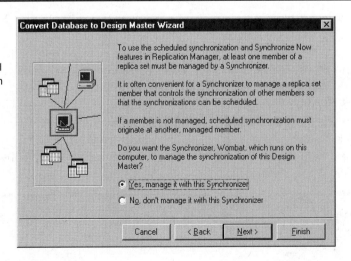

If you create an unmanaged replica, you will be unable to schedule synchronizations using the replica. To synchronize the replica you will have to either originate a synchronizer-based synchronization using another managed replica (or a different synchronizer that *is* managing this replica) or synchronize using Access or DAO.

The replica set shown in Figure 13.10 contains a single unmanaged replica and three managed replicas.

FIGURE 13.10

The left-most replica is unmanaged and thus synchronizations must originate from one of the other replicas.

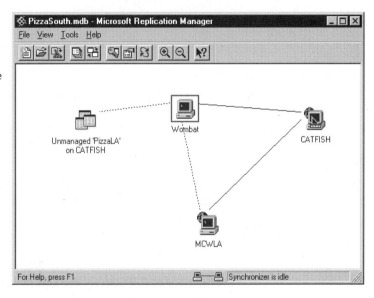

Replica Retention Period

Replication Manager exposes the ability to set the replica retention period. This value, which is stored in the MSysRepInfo table in the Retention field, controls how long Jet maintains schema changes and deleted records for replicas that have not been synchronized. This Integer value must be between 5 and 32,000 days and can be set only for the design master. You can alter the retention period value, which defaults to 1000 days for replica sets created by the Access UI or the Windows Briefcase and 60 days for replica sets created using Replication Manager or DAO, using the Replica property sheet in Replication Manager (see Figure 13.11). You can't change this value using the Access UI or DAO.

When you open a replica in Access or Replication Manager that is within five days of expiring, you are reminded of the impending replica expiration with a

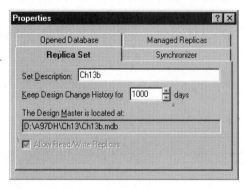

FIGURE 13.11

You can adjust the replica retention period for a replica set using the Replica properties sheet in Replication Manager.

warning message. If the retention period expires for a replica, Replication Manager and Access will refuse to synchronize changes between this replica and other replicas in the replica set.

Replicating a Database Using DAO

Using DAO, you convert a nonreplicated database into a replicated design master by setting the ReplicableBool property of the database to True. (You can also set the obsolete Replicable property to the string "T", but this property is present only for backward compatibility with Access 95–created replicas.)

Since the ReplicableBool property of the database will not exist until you set it for the first time, you'll need to add the property to the database's Properties collection in order to set it. For example, you could use the following code to make a new design master from the nonreplicated DatabaseToBeReplicated.MDB database:

```
Sub CreateNewReplicaSet()

    Dim db As Database
    Dim prp As Property

    Set db = DBEngine.Workspaces(0). _
      OpenDatabase("DatabaseToBeReplicated.MDB", _
      Options:=True)

    Set prp = db.CreateProperty("ReplicableBool", dbBoolean, True)
    db.Properties.Append prp

End Sub
```

Note that we have set the Options parameter of the OpenDatabase method to True. To convert a nonreplicated database to a replicated design master, you must have the database open exclusively. In addition, you *can't* convert the currently open database.

When you replicate a database using DAO, Access won't create a backup copy of the nonreplicated database. Thus, you should manually create a backup copy before replicating the database.

Creating Additional Replicas Using DAO

To create additional replicas, you use the MakeReplica method of the database object. The syntax of MakeReplica is

database.MakeReplica *pathname, description* [*, options*]

where *options* is one or both of the following constants:

Constant	Purpose
dbRepMakeReadOnly	Creates a read-only replica
dbRepMakePartial	Creates a partial replica

For example, you could use the following subroutine to create a new read/write replica based on the current database:

```
Sub CreateNewReplica()

    Dim db As Database

    Set db = CurrentDb()

    db.MakeReplica "Replica1.MDB", _
      "Replica of DatabaseToBeReplicated"

End Sub
```

The value of the description parameter is stored in the Description field of MSys-Replicas but otherwise is not used by Access or Replication Manager.

The basReplicationTools module in the CH13A.MDB database includes the adh-CreateReplicaSet and adhCreateReplica functions, which you can use to create new design masters and additional replicas, respectively.

Selectively Replicating Database Objects Using DAO

Prior to converting a database into a replicated design master, you can prevent objects from being replicated by setting their KeepLocal property to "T". By default, this property doesn't exist until you create it. If you wish to change your mind and replicate a local object before converting the database, set KeepLocal to "F". You can use the adh-GetKeepLocal and adhSetKeepLocal functions in basReplicationTools to get and set the KeepLocal property of objects, respectively. adhSetKeepLocal is shown in Listing 13.1.

Listing 13.1

```
Function adhSetKeepLocal(ByVal intObjType As Integer, _
 ByVal strObjectName As String, ByVal fKeepLocal As Boolean) _
 As Boolean

    ' Prevent an object from being replicated when
    ' the database is converted into a replicated design master.
    ' Can only be used on nonreplicated databases.
    ' First parameter should be one of the acObject constants.

    On Error GoTo adhSetKeepLocal_Err

    Dim db As Database
    Dim con As Container
    Dim doc As Document
    Dim varCon As Variant
    Dim varProp As Variant
    Dim strMsg As String

    Const adhcProcName = "adhSetKeepLocal"

    adhSetKeepLocal = False

    varCon = adhIntObjType2Container(intObjType)

    If Not IsNull(varCon) Then
        Set db = CurrentDb()
        Set con = db.Containers(varCon)
        Set doc = con.Documents(strObjectName)
```

```
        If fKeepLocal Then
            varProp = adhSetProp(doc, "KeepLocal", "T")
        Else
            varProp = adhSetProp(doc, "KeepLocal", "F")
        End If
    End If

    adhSetKeepLocal = True

adhSetKeepLocal_Exit:
    On Error GoTo 0
    Exit Function

adhSetKeepLocal_Err:
    Select Case Err
    Case Else
        strMsg = "Error#" & Err.Number & "-" & Err.Description
        MsgBox strMsg, vbCritical + vbOKOnly, "Procedure " & _
          adhcProcName
        Resume adhSetKeepLocal_Exit
    End Select

End Function
```

adhSetKeepLocal returns True if it succeeds. The intObjType parameter takes one of the acObject constants (acTable, acQuery, acForm, acReport, acMacro, or acModule). The strObjName parameter is the object name. You set the fKeepLocal parameter to True to keep an object local or False to make it replicable. This function uses the adhSetProp function from Chapter 6, as well as a private function, adhIntObjType2Container, which converts the acObject constants into the proper container name.

After you have replicated a database, the KeepLocal property becomes read-only. You can, however, use the ReplicableBool property of objects to make an object local or replicated. You can set this property to True or False in the design master, but you can't set this property to True for local objects in non–design master replicas. The adhGetReplicable and adhSetReplicable functions get and set the Replicable property of objects, respectively. adhSetReplicable is shown in Listing 13.2.

Listing 13.2

```
Function adhSetReplicable(ByVal intObjType As Integer, _
 ByVal strObjectName As String, ByVal fReplicable As Boolean) _
 As Boolean
```

```
' Makes an object replicated or local.
' Can only be used on a replicated design master.
' First parameter should be one of the acObjectType constants.

On Error GoTo adhSetReplicable_Err

Dim db As Database
Dim con As Container
Dim doc As Document
Dim varCon As Variant
Dim varProp As Variant
Dim strMsg As String

Const adhcProcName = "adhSetReplicable"

adhSetReplicable = False

varCon = adhIntObjType2Container(intObjType)

If Not IsNull(varCon) Then
    Set db = CurrentDb()
    Set con = db.Containers(varCon)
    Set doc = con.Documents(strObjectName)

    If fReplicable Then
        varProp = adhSetProp(doc, "ReplicableBool", _
            True)
    Else
        varProp = adhSetProp(doc, "ReplicableBool", _
            False)
    End If
End If

adhSetReplicable = True

adhSetReplicable_Exit:
    On Error GoTo 0
    Exit Function

adhSetReplicable_Err:
    Select Case Err
    Case Else
        strMsg = "Error#" & Err.Number & "—" & Err.Description
        MsgBox strMsg, vbCritical + vbOKOnly, "Procedure " & _
```

```
        adhcProcName
      Resume adhSetReplicable_Exit
  End Select

End Function
```

When you change the ReplicableBool property of an object from True to False, Jet makes the object local to the design master and deletes it from other replicas during the next synchronization.

Partial Replication

As mentioned earlier in this chapter, Microsoft has added support for partial replicas in Access 97. A *partial replica* is a replica that contains only a *subset* of data from one or more replicated tables. For example, if you're distributing your sales database to salespeople with laptops that contain limited hard disk space, it would be nice to be able to give each salesperson data pertaining only to that salesperson's sales territory.

You can create partial replicas only using DAO. There's no mechanism within the Access UI or Replication Manager for creating partial replicas.

> **TIP**
>
> Although it's not included in the box with Access, Microsoft has released a Partial Replica Wizard, which you can use to ease the creation of partial replicas. You can download a copy of this Wizard from microsoft.com.

Creating partial replicas is a bit more involved than creating regular (full) replicas using DAO, but it's not that difficult. The process involves three basic steps that you must follow in order:

1. Create an empty partial replica.
2. Define filters for the partial replica.
3. Populate the partial replica.

> **NOTE**
>
> You can't convert a partial replica into a full replica.

Creating an Empty Partial Replica

You use the MakeReplica method on a full replica with the dbRepMakePartial option to create an empty partial replica. For example, you could use the following sub-routine to create a new empty partial replica based on the currently opened full replica:

```
Sub CreatePartialReplica()

    Dim db As Database

    Set db = CurrentDb()

    db.MakeReplica "PartialRep.MDB", _
     Options:= dbRepMakePartial

End Sub
```

When you create an empty partial replica, the new partial replica contains all the replicated objects from the full replica, but the tables are empty.

You can't create a partial replica from an existing partial replica; you must use a full replica.

Defining Filters for a Partial Replica

You define the rows a partial replica will contain by setting the ReplicaFilter property of TableDef objects using the following syntax:

dbPartialReplica.TableDefs!*tabledef*.ReplicaFilter = *filter*

The filter should follow the same format as any standard Where clause (without the Where). The filter cannot reference subqueries, nor can it reference aggregate or user-defined functions. If you want all the rows from the full replica included in the partial replica's table, set the filter to True. If you don't want any rows, set the filter to False. Any tables for which you do not set the ReplicaFilter property will default to False; that is, no rows will be replicated to these tables.

TIP Synchronizations of partial replicas will be faster if your filters reference indexed fields.

For example, say you had a coffee importing business that operated in Poland and you wished to create a Northern Poland partial replica that contained orders from only the cities of Warsaw and Gdansk. You might use code like this:

```
dbNorthPoland.TableDefs!tblOrder.ReplicaFilter = _
 "City = 'Warsaw' Or City = 'Gdansk'"
```

When Jet populates the partial replica it includes all records from the "one" side of one-to-many relationships to maintain referential integrity. Thus, in the above example, Jet would copy rows into tblCustomer for customers located in Warsaw and Gdansk. Jet automatically includes rows that follow relationships from the many-to-one side. If Jet didn't do this automatically, the partial replica would contain unmatched foreign key values, which referential integrity forbids.

If you wish to include rows from the "many" side of a one-to-many relationship, you can set the ReplicaFilter property of the relationship to True. This causes Jet to automatically include all rows in the "many" table with matching rows in the "one" table. The syntax is as follows:

dbPartialReplica.Relations!*relation*.PartialReplica = True

For example, if the coffee import database contained a relationship called Order2Details that defined a one-to-many relationship between tblOrder and tblOrderDetail and you wished to include order detail rows in the partial replica that corresponded to tblOrder rows, you might use code like this:

```
dbNorthPoland.Relations!Order2Details. _
 PartialReplica = True
```

Often, however, you will not know the name of the relationship because Access names relationships for you automatically with nondescript names such as Relationship1. The basReplicationTools module of CH13A.MDB includes a function, adhSetRelFilter, that will set the PartialReplica filter of a Relation object based on the name of the two tables involved in the relationship. adhSetRelFilter is shown in Listing 13.3.

Listing 13.3

```
Function adhSetRelFilter(db As Database, strTable1 As String, _
 strTableM As String, Optional fFlag As Boolean = True) _
 As Variant

    ' Sets the PartialReplica property of
    ' any and all relations involving the
    ' primary table strTable1 and the related
```

```
' table strTableM.
' Returns the name of the last relation
' if successful; or Null if not.

On Error Resume Next

Dim rel As Relation

adhSetRelFilter = Null

For Each rel In db.Relations
    If rel.Table = strTable1 Then
        If rel.ForeignTable = strTableM Then
            rel.PartialReplica = fFlag
            adhSetRelFilter = rel.Name
        End If
    End If
Next rel

End Function
```

To set the PartialReplica property of a one-to-many relationship between tblOrder and tblOrderDetail in the current database, you could type the following into the Debug window:

```
?adhSetRelFilter(currentdb(),"tblOrder","tblOrderDetail")
```

> **NOTE** You must set the ReplicaFilter and PartialReplica properties of the Table-Def and Relation objects in the partial replica, not the full replica used to populate the partial replica.

Populating a Partial Replica

Once you've defined the filters for a partial replica, you use the PopulatePartial method to populate the partial replica with filtered rows from the full replica, using the following syntax:

dbPartialReplica.PopulatePartial *DbPathName*

where *DbPathName* is the name of the full replica that will be used to populate the partial replica.

The partial replica must be opened exclusively. In addition, the executing code can't be running from the partial replica.

For example, to populate the Northern Poland partial replica with rows from the FullPoland.MDB full replica, you could use the following (assuming the filters for the partial replica had already been defined):

```
Set dbNorthPoland = DBEngine(0).OpenDatabase(NorthPoland.MDB", True)
dbNorthPoland.PopulatePartial "FullPoland.MDB"
```

When you execute the PopulatePartial method, Jet performs the following steps in order:

1. Propagates any unpropagated changes to the full replica

2. Removes all existing records from the partial replica

3. Populates the partial replica with records based on the currently defined filters

You use the PopulatePartial method to both populate new replicas and repopulate existing replicas. When you execute this method on a replica with existing data, Jet clears out any orphaned records from the replica prior to the repopulation of records. A record can be orphaned when a user edits a record so that it no longer meets the currently defined filter.

> **NOTE** The PopulatePartial method is not equivalent to the Synchronize method and should be used only to repopulate data in an existing replica. Because Jet has to delete and recopy all records to the partial replica, the PopulatePartial method is much slower than the Synchronize method.

Preventing Replication

Only users with the Administer permission for a database can convert it to a replicated design master. However, any user who can open a replica has the necessary permissions to create additional replicas from an existing replica. This is unfortunate because each replica in a replica set takes some overhead to track. Of course, this may not be a problem if you do not give users the ability to create replicas in your application, but these users will still be able to create replicas if they can open the database outside the confines of your application using Access or Replication Manager.

Reversing Replication

Once replicated, a database can't be un-replicated—at least not directly. You can take the following steps, however, to create a nonreplicated version of a replicated design master. (You can't un-replicate a non–design master replica because you can't modify the design of its objects.)

1. Open the design master and document the existing relationships—either manually or by using the Database Documentor Add-In.

2. Delete all relationships in the design master.

3. Select a table in the database window and choose View ➤ Properties (or the equivalent shortcut menu). Uncheck the Replicated property and click the OK button. Repeat for all other replicated tables.

4. Create a new empty database and import all objects from the design master to the new database.

5. Open the new database created in step 4, which should now contain all the objects from the replicated database. Using the relationship documentation created in step 1, re-create all relationships in the new database.

> **NOTE**
>
> There's an unfortunate side effect of un-replicating a database using these steps. Any fields that were foreign keys in the replica will have their DefaultValue property set to "GenUniqueID()". Although this shouldn't cause any problems, Access will display "#Name?" in these fields when you are adding new rows to the tables. To remedy this situation, open the tables containing the foreign keys in design mode and delete the GenUniqueID function from the DefaultValue property of these fields. (Note, though, that the GenUniqueID function will reappear if you copy the table or import it into another database. If this is an issue, you'll need to duplicate the design of each of the problem tables and use append queries to copy the data to the new tables.)

Synchronizing Replicas

When you make a synchronization exchange between two replicas, Jet copies schema changes and data updates between the two replicas. The default exchange method is two-way, which means that updates move in both directions. If you are using DAO or Replication Manager to perform the synchronization exchange, you can also opt for a one-way data exchange between two replicas, but regardless of whether you choose two-way or one-way exchanges, Jet always propagates schema changes.

Synchronizing two databases is simple—Jet does all the work. It's up to you, however, to decide when to synchronize, with whom, how, and whether to use two-way or one-way synchronization. You're also responsible for making sure the two replicas are connected when you wish to synchronize them. In addition, you must be aware of how your replication topology affects the propagation of updates through your replica set. (See the section "Replication Topologies" earlier in this chapter.) Finally, you must manage any conflicts or errors that occur as a result of the synchronization exchange. This last item is discussed in the section "Managing Conflicts and Errors" later in this chapter.

Synchronizing Using the Access Menus

To synchronize two replicas using the Access menu commands, select Tools ➤ Replication ➤ Synchronize Now. Access responds with the Synchronize Database dialog, as shown in Figure 13.12. (This dialog will look different if you've used Replication Manager to distribute replicas to multiple synchronizers or if you've set up your system for Internet-based synchronizations.) Access fills the Synchronize With combo box with the list of all known replicas that it stores in the MSysReplicas system table. It also sets the default replica to the one you last synchronized with using Access. (This information is stored in the MostRecentSyncPartner property of the MSysDb document of the Databases container.)

When the synchronization is complete, Access displays a dialog informing you that some changes (schema changes) won't be visible until you close and reopen the database, and it offers to do this for you.

FIGURE 13.12

The Synchronize Database dialog

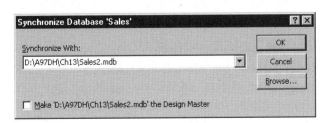

Synchronizing Using Replication Manager

In addition to using the capabilities previously discussed in the area of replica management, you can use Replication Manager (and its companion Synchronizer program) to create synchronization schedules, perform the synchronizations, and view the results of synchronization exchanges. Although you can do all of this using DAO, you may ask yourself, "Why bother?" Replication Manager is Microsoft's preferred method for managing and automating synchronization exchanges, and for good reason: it makes the synchronization management process very easy.

You can synchronize a replica set using the Tools ➤ Synchronize Now command. When you execute this command, Replication Manager displays a dialog similar to the one shown in Figure 13.13. At this time you can choose to synchronize the selected replica with one of the following:

- All local members of the replica set managed by this synchronizer

- All members of the replica set at all locations

- The replicas at a specified remote site

FIGURE 13.13

FIGURE 13.13
Replication Manager's
Synchronize Now
dialog box

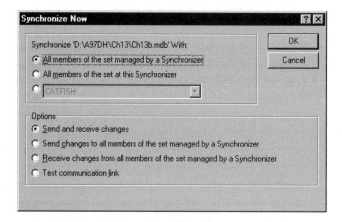

Scheduled Synchronizations

While the ability to synchronize replicas on demand is certainly useful, Replication Manager's scheduling abilities are its strong suit. You can set up a local synchronizationschedule for all replica sets managed by the local synchronizer by right-clicking the local machine icon on the Replication Manager map and choosing Edit Locally Managed Replica Schedule from the shortcut menu. When you do this, Replication Manager displays the dialog shown in Figure 13.14. You can schedule synchronizations on a weekly basis in 15-minute increments. This schedule applies to all local replicas managed by this synchronizer; there's no way to create individual schedules for different replica sets.

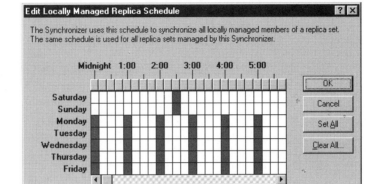

Direct versus Indirect Synchronization

Replication Manager and Synchronizer support both direct and indirect synchronization modes. When you initiate a synchronization exchange using Replication Manager/Synchronizer, your synchronizer performs the replication much as Access does. It opens both databases, determines which objects and records have changed, and proceeds to exchange data between the two replicas. This form of synchronization is called *direct synchronization* and works well when the replicas are located on two machines connected over a LAN.

Replication Manager and Synchronizer also support another form of synchronization called *indirect synchronization*. With indirect synchronization, your local synchronizer opens your local replica, establishes a link to a remote synchronizer, and exchanges packets of changes with the other synchronizer. This type of synchronization is safer and more efficient when using slower WAN and modem connections because the remote replica is not opened over the connection.

If you use the direct synchronization method over a WAN or modem connection, the exchange will likely be slower. More important, you risk corrupting your database because a communications glitch could occur during a write to one of the replicas. Thus, we strongly recommend you use the indirect synchronization method for WAN/modem connections.

Configuring Replication Manager for Indirect Synchronizations

When configuring Replication Manager, you must indicate you will be performing indirect synchronizations before you do so. You can use the Replication Manager Configuration Wizard (see Figure 13.15) to do this.

FIGURE 13.15

The second page of Replication Manager's Configuration Wizard asks if you want it to support indirect synchronization.

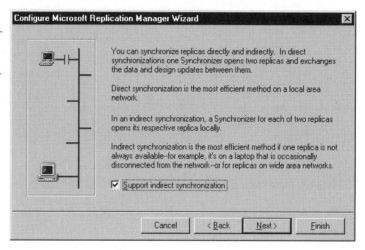

You will need to install and configure Replication Manager at each site that will be participating in indirect synchronizations.

Synchronizing Replicas Indirectly

When you set up Replication Manager to manage a replica set, it assumes you will be performing only direct synchronizations. By default, any replicas you create using Replication Manager or Access at this site will become managed or unmanaged local replicas supporting direct synchronization only. You'll need to follow these steps to create a remote replica at a site with which you wish to indirectly synchronize:

1. Run Replication Manager on your local computer and create (or open) a managed replica set.

2. Make a regular DOS/Windows copy of the replica (don't create an additional replica) and move that copy of the replica to the remote site.

3. Run Replication Manager at the remote site and select File ➤ Open Replica Set. Now, select File ➤ Start Managing 'xxx.mdb', where xxx is the name of the replica.

4. The two sites should now appear on the remote Replication Manager's map. Select the line connecting the two sites, right-click the mouse, and select Synchronize Now from the shortcut menu (see Figure 13.16).

5. If you have Replication Manager open at the local site, select Tools ➤ Refresh Synchronization Window so that the remote site's icon appears on the local Replication Manager map.

FIGURE 13.16

Right-clicking the line connecting the two sites brings up the indirect synchronization shortcut menu.

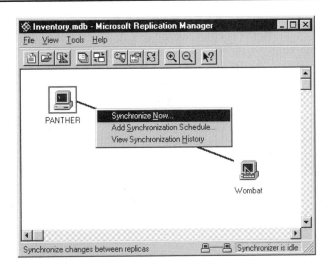

After creating a remote replica following these steps, you synchronize, schedule synchronizations, or view the synchronization history between the two sites by selecting the line connecting the two sites, right-clicking the mouse, and selecting the appropriate shortcut menu (see Figure 13.16).

To add the schedule for remote synchronization exchanges between two sites, right-click the line connecting the two sites and select Add Synchronization Schedule. (This menu changes to Edit Synchronization Schedule once you've established a schedule). The Edit Schedule dialog appears, as shown in Figure 13.17. The shading of each box indicates which synchronizer initiates the exchange; if the same

FIGURE 13.17

You can use this dialog to edit the synchronization schedule between the local and remote replicas.

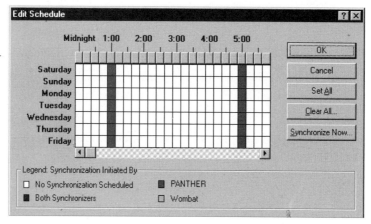

time point is selected by both sites, both sites will attempt to initiate the exchange at the same time.

Once you have scheduled remote exchanges, it's up to you to ensure that the connection will be made prior to the synchronization exchange. If it's not, the synchronizer will log the changes to a temporary database located in the drop-box folder for that synchronizer. (This was the location specified when you first configured Replication Manager; you can change it using the Tools ➤ Configure Microsoft Replication Manager command.) The local synchronizer then continues to check every 15 minutes to see whether it can connect to the remote site. When it eventually connects to the remote synchronizer, it transfers the updates that have accumulated in the drop-box to the target synchronizer.

This feature allows you to easily configure laptop copies of a database to be synchronized each time the laptop is connected to a network. Simply designate a dedicated drop-box folder for each laptop, which will receive all changes intended for that replica while the laptop is off the network. When the laptop returns, it will automatically be brought up to date.

NOTE Although similar in concept to indirect synchronization, Internet synchronization is handled differently. See the section "Internet/Intranet Synchronization" later in this chapter for details on synchronizing over the Internet or across a corporate intranet.

Reviewing Synchronization History

Replication Manager includes the ability to view the log of synchronization activity. If you right-click the local machine icon and select View Local Synchronization History, you'll be able to view the history of all local synchronization exchanges. Similarly, if you right-click a remote computer icon (or the line connecting your local computer and the remote site) and select View Synchronization History, you'll be able to view the history of exchanges between the local and remote replicas. A sample of a remote synchronization history log, which is sorted in descending order by the time the exchange was initiated, is shown in Figure 13.18.

FIGURE 13.18

The Synchronization History dialog lists each exchange in descending date/time order.

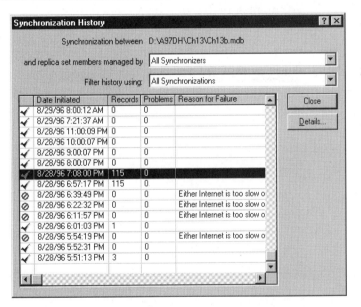

TIP

Regardless of whether you initially select to view the local or remote synchronization history, you can use the combo boxes that appear at the top of the dialog to filter the list so it includes the history of local exchanges, all exchanges, exchanges with a particular synchronizer, the last 25 exchanges, only successful exchanges, only exchanges with conflicts, and so on.

If you double-click a record (or click the Details button), a wealth of information regarding the selected exchange is revealed (see Figure 13.19), including:

- The direction of the exchange
- Whether the exchange was successful
- The number of data errors
- The number of conflicts
- The number and type of updates sent
- The number and type of updates received
- The number of design changes sent or received

FIGURE 13.19

The Synchronization Details dialog reveals a wealth of detail regarding a particular exchange.

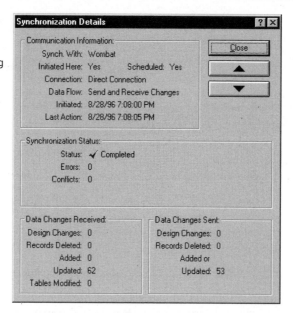

In an unfortunate omission, Replication Manager fails to list the names of the replicas involved in the exchange; it tells you only the name of the synchronizers involved.

TIP When you browse the local or remote synchronization history logs using Replication Manager, you are actually viewing the history of all synchronization exchanges, not just those initiated by Replication Manager or the Synchronizer program. Thus, even if you use the Access menus or DAO to synchronize replicas, you can still use Replication Manager to browse the exchange histories.

Synchronizing Using DAO

You can programmatically initiate synchronization exchanges using the Synchronize method of the database object. The syntax for this method is shown here:

database.Synchronize *DbPathName* [*,ExchangeType*]

where *DbPathName* is the path and name of the other replica you wish to exchange with and *ExchangeType* is either one of the first three constants from the following table or the fourth (dbRepSyncInternet) constant plus one of the first three constants:

Constant	Purpose
dbRepExportChanges	Only send changes to the other replica
dbRepImportChanges	Only receive changes from the other replica
dbRepImpExpChanges	Send and receive changes between both replicas (the default)
dbRepSyncInternet	Use Internet-based synchronization; when you use this constant, you must add it to one of the other constants

Just as when using Replication Manager, you're responsible for ensuring that any remote connections are made prior to initiating a synchronization exchange using DAO.

For example, to initiate a send-only exchange between the currently open database and "OtherReplica.Mdb", you could use the following:

```
CurrentDb.Synchronize "OtherReplica.Mdb", dbRepExportChanges
```

See the section "Internet/Intranet Synchronization" later in this chapter for details on Internet synchronization.

In basReplicationTools, we've created the adhDbSync function, which you can use to synchronize any two replicas programmatically. Listing 13.4 shows this function.

Listing 13.4

```
Function adhDbSync(ByVal strToDb As String, _
 Optional ByVal varFromDb As Variant, _
 Optional ByVal varExchType As Variant) As Variant

    ' Synchronizes two databases

    On Error GoTo adhDbSync_Err

    Dim dbFrom As Database
    Dim strMsg As String
    Const adhcProcName = "adhDbSync"

    If IsMissing(varFromDb) Then
        Set dbFrom = CurrentDb()
    Else
        Set dbFrom = DBEngine.Workspaces(0). _
         OpenDatabase(varFromDb)
    End If

    If IsMissing(varExchType) Then varExchType = _
     dbRepImpExpChanges

    dbFrom.Synchronize strToDb, varExchType

    adhDbSync = True

adhDbSync_Exit:
    On Error GoTo 0
    Exit Function

adhDbSync_Err:
    Select Case Err
    Case Else
        adhDbSync = CVErr(Err.Number)
    End Select

End Function
```

NOTE

If you execute synchronization code from a replica that has received design changes from a design master replica, you'll have to close and reopen the database for the changes to be incorporated into the schema of the open replica. Also, any conflict resolution code (either the built-in Access Conflict Resolution Wizard code or your custom code) will not automatically execute until you close and reopen the database. Unfortunately, there's no way to close and reopen the currently open database from code that is running from the open database.

Scheduling Synchronizations Using DAO

If you need to synchronize replicas on a regular basis and you've purchased the Microsoft Office Developer Edition, you may wish to use Replication Manager instead of DAO to schedule synchronizations. It's easier to use, requires no programming, and maintains an excellent history of the exchanges. Creating your own synchronization schedule using DAO, however, does have its own advantages:

- It allows you to deliver an Access-only solution; you don't have to install and use Replication Manager and Synchronizer.

- You're not limited to a day-of-week schedule. For example, you could create a schedule based on the day of the month.

- You can synchronize at times other than at 15-minute intervals beginning on the hour.

- You can create a hybrid synchronization system that is based on both a regular timed schedule and update load. (See the next section.)

If you decide to implement a synchronization system using DAO, you'll need to decide how the process will be driven. Most likely you'll employ a hidden form that's automatically loaded when the database is started with code attached to the form's Timer event. This form would likely follow a schedule that was stored in a table in the database. But where will this hidden form and table reside? Should it be part of the normal application database that runs on each desktop, or should it perhaps run only on selected desktops? One alternative might be to keep this form and table in a utility database that's kept separate from the rest of your application. This application could run off the file server or the database administrator's desktop.

Synchronization Based on Number of Updates

You may wish to implement a synchronization system that is based on update load rather than (or in addition to) a regular schedule. You can ascertain the update load by counting the number of records in each replicated table in the database where the s_Generation field equals 0. This number represents the number of records that have been updated or added since the last synchronization exchange. The sample form frmUpdateVolume in the CH13B sample database contains code that does just that. If you open this form and click its command button, the code in Listing 13.5 executes. After a brief delay, the number of updated records in the replicated tables in the database is displayed in a text box on the form (see Figure 13.20).

FIGURE 13.20

frmUpdateVolume counts the number of updated records since the last synchronization exchange.

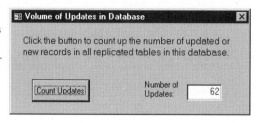

Listing 13.5

```
Private Sub cmdCount_Click()

    ' Count the number of updated/new
    ' records in any replicated tables
    ' in this database

    Dim lngCount As Long
    Dim ctlCount As TextBox
    Dim db As Database
    Dim tdf As TableDef

    DoCmd.Hourglass True

    Set ctlCount = Me!txtCount
    Set db = CurrentDb()
    lngCount = 0

    ' Iterate through all tabledefs
```

```
For Each tdf In db.TableDefs
    'Only check replicated tables
    If adhGetReplicable(acTable, tdf.Name) Then
        ' Count up number of records with
        ' s_Generation = 0
        lngCount = lngCount + _
        DCount("*", tdf.Name, "[s_Generation]=0")
    End If

Next tdf

ctlCount = lngCount
ctlCount.Enabled = True

DoCmd.Hourglass False

End Sub
```

Of course, this example doesn't do anything with the value, but once you've determined the number of updated or new records, you can easily decide whether it's time to synchronize. It's likely you'd call this code from a hidden form that is used to maintain a synchronization schedule for your application.

Synchronizing Partial Replicas

You can synchronize partial replicas using the Access UI, DAO, or Replication Manager. A partial replica, however, can be synchronized only with a full replica.

If you change replica filters (see the section "Defining Filters for a Partial Replica" earlier in this chapter) and try to synchronize the replica prior to executing the PopulatePartial method, you will get a trappable error (3570—"The filters defining a partial replica are out of sync with each other"). You may wish to trap for this error in your code and execute the PopulatePartial method when this occurs.

Internet/Intranet Synchronization

Access 97 includes support for synchronization over the Internet or an intranet. In order to use Internet/intranet synchronization your server must be running Windows 95 or Windows NT. In addition, you must:

1. Install a copy of Access or an Access run-time application on the server

2. Configure your server for Internet replication

3. Install a copy of Replication Manager on the server

4. Configure Replication Manager for Internet replication

5. Set up your replica set for Internet replication

Steps 2, 4, and 5 are discussed in the following sections.

Configuring Your Internet Server

Before you install Replication Manager on your Internet server machine, you need to prepare your Internet server. This involves three steps:

1. Configure the Internet server for anonymous connections.

2. Create a directory where the Synchronizer can run.

3. Create a directory where FTP file transfers are permitted. This directory will hold the message files that are exchanged during an Internet-based synchronization.

If you're using Microsoft's Internet Information Server (IIS), you should follow these (more specific) steps:

1. Using Windows Explorer, create a new subdirectory under your server's Scripts directory that will hold the Synchronizer executable file; you can name it anything you want, but we suggest calling it Sync. Also create a new subdirectory under the ftproot directory; again, you can name it anything you'd like, but we suggest calling it RepMsg.

2. Start the IIS Service Manager.

3. Right-click on the WWW service, and select Service Properties from the short-cut menu. Select the Directories tab and click the Add button. Enter the full path to the first subdirectory you created in step 1 (Sync) here. Enter an alias name of Sync; make sure the Read and Execute check boxes are checked; leave the other options at their default values. Click OK.

4. Right-click on the FTP service, and select Service Properties from the shortcut menu. Select the Directories tab and click the Add button. Enter the full path to the second subdirectory you created in step 1 (RepMsg) here. Enter an alias name of RepMsg; make sure the Read and Execute check boxes are checked; leave the other options at their default values. Click OK.

Configuring Replication Manager for Internet Synchronizations

After you've prepared your Internet server, you're ready to install Replication Manager on the server machine. Replication Manager is one component of the Microsoft Office Developer Edition. There's no need to install the other components of the ODE on this machine. During installation you are asked whether you want the Synchronizer included in your Startup group. Answer No. Your Internet server will start up an instance of the Synchronizer whenever needed, so this option is not necessary.

Start up Replication Manager. This also starts the Configuration Wizard. Follow these steps to configure Replication Manager/Synchronizer:

1. On the first page, click Next.

2. On the second page, uncheck the Support Indirect Synchronization check box. This is unnecessary for Internet synchronization.

3. On the third page, the Wizard asks, "Is this computer an Internet server?" Select Yes.

4. On the fourth page, the Wizard asks, "Do you want to use this Internet server to synchronize replicated databases?" Select Yes.

5. On the fifth page, you are asked to enter the Internet server name. Here you enter either the server's domain name if it's an Internet server (for example, "mydomain.com") or the server's machine name if it's a local intranet server (for example, "ralph").

6. On the sixth page, enter into the first text box the full path to the executable Synchronizer subdirectory you created when you prepared your server. If you're using IIS and you used our recommended name, you will enter something like "e:\inetpub\scripts\sync". Enter the alias name (without a preceding slash) in the second text box—for example, "Sync" (see Figure 13.21).

7. On the seventh page, enter into the text box the alias name of the FTP subdirectory you created when you prepared your server. This subdirectory will hold the synchronization message files. If you're using IIS and our recommended name, you would enter "RepMsg" (see Figure 13.22).

8. On the eighth page, you are asked to enter the path to the log file. The default name is fine.

9. On the ninth page, you are asked to name this synchronizer. To avoid confusion, you may wish to use a name that's either the machine name for intranet servers or the first part of the domain name—for example, "mydomain" for Internet servers.

10. On the tenth page, click Finish.

You should now be ready to create a new replica set and start synchronizing over the Internet or intranet.

FIGURE 13.21

On this page of the Replication Manager Configuration Wizard, you enter the name of the subdirectory (shared folder) and alias (share name) where the Synchronizer executable file will be stored.

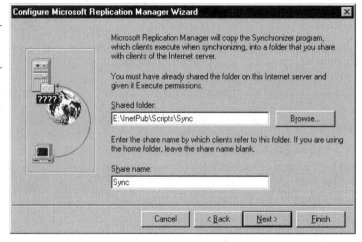

FIGURE 13.22

On this page you enter the name of the FTP subdirectory (FTP alias name) that will hold the synchronization message files.

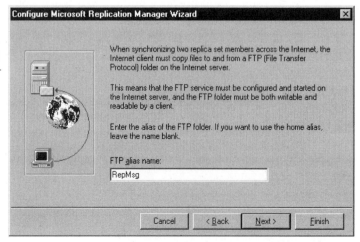

Setting Up a Replica Set for Internet Synchronization

Setting up a replica set for Internet synchronization is similar to setting up a replica set for indirect synchronization. Follow these steps:

1. Run Replication Manager on your server and create (or open) a managed replica set.

2. Make a regular DOS/Windows copy of the replica (don't create an additional replica) and move this "distribution" copy of the replica to a public FTP directory on the server.

3. When you want to add a new site that will synchronize using your server, log on to your server from the remote site using FTP and download a copy of the distribution replica.

4. Run Replication Manager at the remote site and select File ➤ Open Replica Set. Now, select File ➤ Start Managing '*xxx*.mdb', where *xxx* is the name of the replica.

5. The two sites should now appear on the remote Replication Manager's map; the server icon should have a globe behind its machine icon (see Figure 13.23). Select Tools ➤ Synchronize Now Across the Internet to synchronize this site with the Internet/intranet server machine.

6. If you have Replication Manager open at the server site, select Tools ➤ Refresh Synchronization Window now to make the remote site's icon appear on the server's Replication Manager map.

If you're not using Replication Manager at the remote site, you can skip steps 4 through 6 above.

Once you have all the pieces in place, you can synchronize over the Internet/intranet using any machine that has a copy of Access, Replication Manager, or Jet (with the replication DLLs). When you synchronize over the Internet/intranet, Jet performs a special type of indirect synchronization that is optimized for the TCP/IP, HTTP, and FTP protocols.

FIGURE 13.23

The icon on the left (Wombat) represents a regular Replication Manager site; the icon on the right (MCWLA) is an Internet server that has been enabled for Internet synchronization.

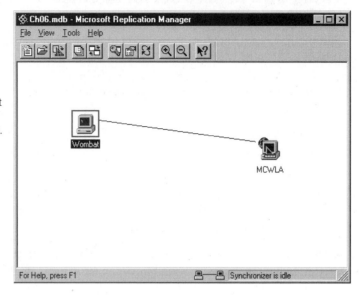

Synchronizing over the Internet Using Replication Manager

Select Tools ➤ Synchronize Now Across the Internet to synchronize a replica with an Internet/intranet server machine. During the synchronization exchange, Replication Manager performs several steps. It indicates its progress with several status messages as it establishes the connection to the server, sends data to the server, and receives data from the server (see Figure 13.24). Synchronization may take a while, especially if you have many changes or if you are using a slow dial-up line. If you are using a dial-up connection, you should establish the connection prior to synchronizing.

NOTE   You can't schedule synchronization exchanges over the Internet/intranet using Replication Manager. If you need to schedule this type of exchange, use DAO instead. See the section "Scheduling Synchronizations Using DAO" earlier in this chapter for details.

FIGURE 13.24

FIGURE 13.24

A status message displayed by Replication Manager during an Internet synchronization

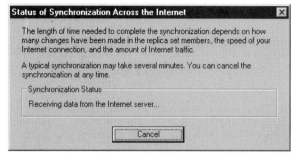

Synchronizing over the Internet Using Access

Before you can synchronize over the Internet using Access, you must make a DOS copy of a replica from the Internet/intranet server machine, as discussed earlier in the section "Setting Up a Replica Set for Internet Synchronization." Once you have done this, the replica should know where it came from, and synchronization should be straightforward.

Select Tools ➤ Replication ➤ Synchronize Now. Access displays the Synchronize Now dialog (see Figure 13.25). Select the second radio button to perform an Internet synchronization. Access displays another dialog, which asks you to select an Internet server (see Figure 13.26). Your server should appear in the list box; if it doesn't, you probably missed one of the steps in the "Setting Up the Replica Set for Internet Synchronization" section. Select the server and the type of exchange, and click the Synchronize button to begin the exchange.

FIGURE 13.25

The Synchronize Now dialog offers additional options when you synchronize a replica that came from an Internet server.

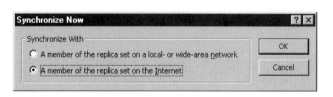

Unlike Replication Manager, Access does not display any messages during the exchange. This may lead you to prematurely believe that the session has hung, but be patient; the exchange will take several minutes when involving only a small amount of data. If you are using a dial-up connection, you should establish the connection prior to initiating the synchronization exchange.

FIGURE 13.26

When you select your server and click the Synchronize button, Access initiates a synchronization exchange over the Internet/intranet.

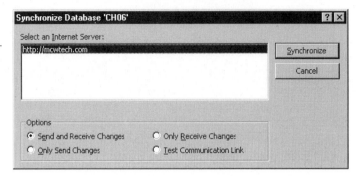

Synchronizing over the Internet Using DAO

To perform a synchronization exchange over the Internet, you use the Synchronize method of the database object along with the dbRepSyncInternet constant, using this basic syntax for an Internet server:

db.Synchronize *"domain/replica"*, dbRepSyncInternet + *exchange_type_constant*

where *domain* is the name of the Internet server's domain and *replica* is the name of the replica without any path. For some servers, you may also need to prefix the domain name with the name of the subdomain.

For example, to perform a two-way synchronization with a replica named Sales.Mdb over the Internet via a server named Remote.com, you'd use this:

```
db.Synchronize "remote.com/Sales.Mdb", _
  dbRepSyncInternet + dbRepImpExpChanges
```

To synchronize over an intranet, you should use this variation of the syntax:

db.Synchronize *"server_name/replica"*, dbRepSyncInternet + *exchange_type_constant*

where *server_name* is the name of the intranet server and *replica* is the name of the replica without any path.

For example, to perform a send-only synchronization with a replica named Invent.Mdb over a corporate intranet to a server named mis_dept, you'd use this:

```
db.Synchronize "mis_dept/Invent.Mdb", _
  dbRepSyncInternet + dbRepExportChanges
```

> **WARNING** You must add dbRepSyncInternet to one of the other constants. The synchronize method will not work if you include dbRepSyncInternet alone. In addition, make sure you use a forward slash to separate the domain or server name from the replica name.

Once again, if you are using a dial-up connection, you should establish the connection prior to using the Synchronize method.

Managing Conflicts and Errors

Three types of problems can occur as the result of a synchronization exchange (or an attempted synchronization exchange) between two replicas:

- Conflicts
- Data errors
- Design errors

Conflicts

Synchronization conflicts can arise when the same record has been modified in more than one replica since the last synchronization exchange. When this happens, Jet must declare one of the changes the winner in order to keep the replicas in agreement. In determining which update "wins" the exchange, Jet follows a fairly simple algorithm:

- If the row was updated more times in one replica than the other, its changes win.
- If rows were updated an equal number of times in the two replicas, Jet chooses the winner with the higher replica GUID.

When designing Jet replication, Microsoft realized that you may not want to resolve conflicts in this fashion, so Jet logs each losing row to a conflict resolution table. As mentioned in the section "Changes Made to a Database When It Is Replicated" earlier in this chapter, the conflict table name is constructed by appending "_Conflict" to the end of the name of the table that contains the conflicts.

Jet makes two other changes to the database when it creates a conflict table: it logs the name of the conflict table and its GUID to the MSysSideTables system table. In addition, it adds the ConflictTable property to the Properties collection of the original TableDef object, setting it equal to the name of the conflict table for that table.

Data Errors

A data error occurs whenever a record in one replica causes some type of error state in another replica. The different types of data errors are summarized in Table 13.8.

TABLE 13.8   Data Errors That Can Occur in a Replica Set

Error	Occurs When	How to Resolve
Duplicate keys	A record with the same primary key value or values is inserted in two or more replicas.	Delete one of the duplicate records or change the value of its primary key so it's no longer a duplicate
Validation rules	You change a table-level validation rule in one replica while at the same time, a user adds or updates records in another replica that fail to satisfy the new rule	Correct the new records so they meet the new rule
Referential integrity	A user inserts a new record in one table that references a primary key value in another table while at the same time, a second user deletes the referenced record in a second replica	Delete the record that references the deleted key (If you've enabled cascading deletes, this situation will correct itself during the next synchronization exchange.)
Locked records	A record that needs to be updated during a synchronization exchange is locked by another user	Release the lock (This is usually just a temporary problem that will correct itself during the next synchronization exchange.)

Data errors are stored in MSysErrors until they have been resolved. Unlike conflict records, data errors are replicated throughout the replica set, so MSysErrors will often contain multiple records for a given error. For example, information on both inserted records will be logged into MSysErrors for a duplicate key error. To resolve a data error, you must correct the offending situation and resynchronize. Sometimes you may have to synchronize more than once to completely resolve the data error. Jet deletes the row from MSysErrors when the data error has been resolved.

WARNING Because of the inherent complexities, only the database administrator or technically adept users should attempt data error resolution. At the very least, the database administrator should be contacted as soon as a data error occurs so it can be corrected quickly.

You can avoid many data errors by following these rules:

- Divide up the responsibility for adding new records by territory or some other criteria so it's unlikely that multiple users will be inserting the same records. If it's likely there will be some overlap, assign one user responsibility for okaying the new records.

- Make table validation rule changes and referential integrity rule changes only after you have synchronized all replicas in the replica set, and immediately synchronize the replicas after making the change. Also, you may wish to make these schema changes only during off hours.

Design Errors

Design errors can occur when a design change made at the design master replica conflicts with the design state of another replica.

TIP In Access 97, if you add a table at the design master replica and make it replicable, but a user has previously created a local table at another replica with the same name, a design error will no longer be generated. Instead, Jet will automatically rename the local table with the suffix "_Local" to make it unique.

During a synchronization exchange, Jet always applies design changes first, before data changes. Because of this, a design error will cause a synchronization exchange to fail.

> **WARNING** Because design errors prevent data from being exchanged, the database administrator must attend to them immediately.

Jet logs design errors into the MSysSchemaProb system table at the replica where the design change could not be applied. This means that the design master replica will never be notified of the design error since, unlike MSysErrors, MSysSchemaProb is not replicated. MSysSchemaProb is deleted once all design errors have been corrected. Like data errors, design errors require immediate attention by a database administrator, who should carefully review the records in MSysSchemaProb to determine how to fix the errors. This will require removing the blocking object at the non–design master replica.

Resolving Conflicts Using Access Menus

When a user opens a database in Access with conflicts or errors, Access displays a message and asks whether the user would like to resolve conflicts now. This message is displayed right after the execution of the database's AutoExec macro or the opening of the database's startup form. If the user answers Yes to this message box dialog, Access displays the Resolve Replication Conflicts dialog, as shown in Figure 13.27.

If the user highlights a conflict table and clicks the Resolve Conflicts button, Access launches the Conflict Resolution Wizard, which creates a custom conflict resolution form for the selected conflict table (see Figure 13.28). Using this form,

FIGURE 13.27

This Resolve Replication Conflicts dialog reports that there are 14 conflicts and one or more data errors.

FIGURE 13.28

The Conflict Resolution Wizard creates a custom conflict resolution form for each table with conflicts.

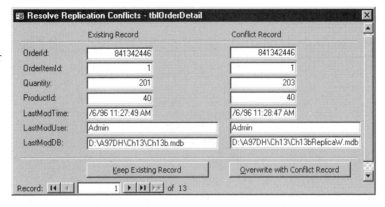

the user can review and possibly reverse the automated decision as to which version of the record was declared the winner. The conflict resolution form is deleted as soon as it is closed and re-created, if necessary, the next time the user clicks the Resolve Conflicts button for that table.

Once the user has either kept or overwritten each record in a conflict table, Access deletes the conflict resolution table, removes the entry from MSysSide-Tables, sets the ConflictTable property to Null, and displays a message box stating that all conflicts have been resolved.

Resolving Errors Using Access Menus

If data errors are present and you click the View Data Errors button, Access displays the Replication Data Errors form (see Figure 13.29). You can use this form to view the pertinent information regarding the data errors. Because this form (and its source of information, MSysErrors) does not log the primary key values for the offending records, you'll need to note the RecordId field (this is the value of the s_GUID field) for each record (as well as the table in which the error occurred and the nature of the error). You may wish to write down or copy this information to the Windows clipboard. (The ability to print a record from this form would be a nice enhancement.) With this information in hand, you'll next need to use the Tools ➤ Options command to turn on the display of system objects and then use a filter or the Find dialog to locate the offending records in the tables based on the s_GUID value. See Table 13.8 for some hints on how to resolve certain types of data errors.

FIGURE 13.29

The Replication Data Errors form reveals the offending data errors; in this case the error was caused by a duplicate key value.

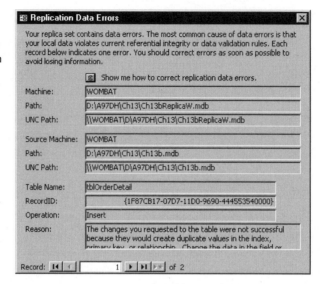

If you have an outstanding design error and you click the View Design Errors button, Access displays the Replication Design Errors form, which, unlike the more cryptic Replication Data Errors form, is fairly easy to interpret.

Resolving Conflicts and Errors Using DAO

If you are using the Access run-time system or a Visual Basic application, the Access Conflict Resolution Wizard will not be available. You will have to create your own facility for reviewing and resolving conflicts. Even if you are using Access, you may wish to resolve conflicts using a custom resolution algorithm rather than depend upon users to resolve conflicts.

Creating a Custom Conflict and Error Resolution Function

A custom conflict and error resolution function must take care of the resolution of conflicts, data errors, and design errors, so it's best to write a single high-level function that first determines the number of conflicts and errors in the database and then dispatches the appropriate procedure to deal with any problems that are present. For example, you might create a high-level function such as this:

```
Function adhResFun()

    ' Ignore errors in case MSys tables doesn't exist
    On Error Resume Next

    Dim lngConflictTables As Long
    Dim lngDataErrors As Long
    Dim lngDesignErrors As Long
    Dim fOK As Boolean
    Dim db As Database

    Set db = CurrentDb()

    lngConflictTables = _
     db.TableDefs("MSysSideTables").RecordCount
    lngDataErrors = db.TableDefs("MSysErrors").RecordCount
    lngDesignErrors = _
     db.TableDefs("MSysSchemaProb").RecordCount

    If lngDataErrors = 0 And lngDesignErrors = 0 Then
        If lngConflictTables > 0 Then
            ' Call conflict resolution function
        End If
    Else
        ' Call data error/design error processing function
    End If

End Function
```

Setting the ReplicationConflictFunction Property

If you're using Access or the run-time system, you can tell it to call your custom conflict and error resolution function (when there are conflicts or errors in the replica) at application startup by setting the ReplicationConflictFunction property of the UserDefined document of the Databases container to the name of your custom function. You must set this property to a string of the following format:

CustomFunction()

You must include the parentheses. To reset the conflict resolution facility to point to the default Access Wizard, you must remove this property from the UserDefined document's Properties collection; you can't set it to an empty or null string.

WARNING Besides having to create the ReplicationConflictFunction property before you can set its value, you must pass the CreateProperty method a True value for the usually optional fourth parameter, DDL. This Boolean parameter indicates that this property can't be changed or deleted unless the user has dbSecWriteDef permission. If you don't set this property to True, no error will occur, but your function will never be called.

The basReplicationTools module includes a function, adhSetConflictFunction, you can use to programmatically set this property. There are also related functions in basReplicationTools that you can use to get the name of the current conflict and error resolution function (adhGetConflictFunction) and reset the function back to the Access default (adhRemoveConflictFunction).

Resolving Errors

It's unlikely that users will be able to understand and fix data or design errors, so you may wish to simply alert users of the number and type of errors and ask them to call the database administrator when this type of error occurs. For example, you might call a simple function such as adhProcessErrors, which is shown in Listing 13.6.

Listing 13.6

```
Sub adhProcessErrors(lngDataErrors As Long, _
 lngDesignErrors As Long)

    Dim fOK As Boolean
    Dim strTitle As String
    Dim strMsg As String
    Dim strSol As String

    If lngDataErrors > 0 Or lngDesignErrors > 0 Then
        strTitle = "Database Synchronization Errors"
        strMsg = "* There are " & lngDataErrors & _
        " data errors." & vbCrLf & _
```

```
          "* There are " & lngDesignErrors & _
          " design errors."
          strSol = _
          "Contact your database administrator immediately!"
          MsgBox strTitle & "@" & strMsg & "@" & strSol, _
            vbCritical + vbOKOnly, "Serious Error"
      End If

  End Sub
```

adhProcessErrors, which you can find in basConflictMng in the CH13B.MDB database, uses the special formatting capabilities of MsgBox that were introduced in Access 95.

Resolving Conflicts

The basic idea behind a custom conflict resolution function is to iterate through each of the records in a conflict table, make a decision on how to resolve the conflict, resolve the conflict, and then delete the conflict record. The shell for a custom conflict resolution function might look like the function shown in Listing 13.7.

Listing 13.7

```
Function CustomConflictResolver()

    Dim db As Database
    Dim tdf As TableDef
    Dim rstResolve As Recordset
    Dim strTable As String
    Dim strConflict As String

    Set db = CurrentDb()

    ' Iterate through all TableDefs looking for tables
    ' with conflict tables
    For Each tdf In db.TableDefs
        strTable = tdf.Name
        strConflict = Nz(tdf.ConflictTable)

        If (strConflict <> "" And Not strTable Like "~TMPCLP*") _
        Then
            Set rstResolve = db.OpenRecordset(strConflict)
```

```
                    rstResolve.MoveFirst
                    Do While Not rstResolve.EOF
                        '  Resolve conflict
                        rstResolve.MoveNext
                    Loop

                    rstResolve.Close
                    db.TableDefs.Delete strConflict
                End If
            Next tdf

        MsgBox "Conflicts have been logged!", _
          vbInformation + vbOKOnly
    End Function
```

This function uses the ConflictTable parameter of the TableDef object to determine whether a conflict table exists for each tabledef in the database. It also compares the table name with "~TMPCLP*" to skip any deleted tables.

The difficult part of this process is deciding how to resolve the conflict. The Access Conflict Resolution Wizard leaves the onus on the user, which isn't a bad approach for a built-in UI tool, but it's arguable whether a professional application should leave conflict resolution up to the user.

In creating a custom conflict resolution routine, the simplest approach would be to simply delete the conflict tables and take for granted that the automated decision based on the number of times the record was updated is correct, or at least good enough. Other approaches might include

- Logging all conflict records to a table and then deleting them

- Determining the winning record based on who (the user's security level) made the change

- Making the last update always the winning update

- Offering some user control, such as the built-in Wizard

- A hybrid approach that would let users of a certain security level decide on the winning record, while the resolution for all other users would follow some other scheme

The sample database CH13B.MDB includes a form, frmConResFun, that uses the adhGetConflictFunction, adhSetConflictFunction, and adhRemoveConflictFunction functions to switch between the default Access Conflict Resolution Wizard and three different custom conflict and error resolution functions:

Conflict Function	Description	Constant
adhResSimple	Logs conflict record to a table; does not change default winner/loser	adhcCnflctResSimple
adhResTime	Switches winning and losing records if losing record was updated after the winning record	adhcCnflctResTime
adhResSecurity	Switches winning and losing records if the losing user's security level is higher than the winning user's security level	adhcCnflctResSecurity

If you wish to use any of these three conflict resolution functions in your own code, you'll need to add three fields to each table—LastModUser, LastModTime, and LastModDB—and add VBA code to each form so these fields are updated every time a record is saved.

Furthermore, if you wish to use the security-based function (adhResSecurity), you need to enable workgroup-based security and add the USystblConflictPriority table (see Figure 13.30) to your database.

FIGURE 13.30

The USystblConflict-Priority table

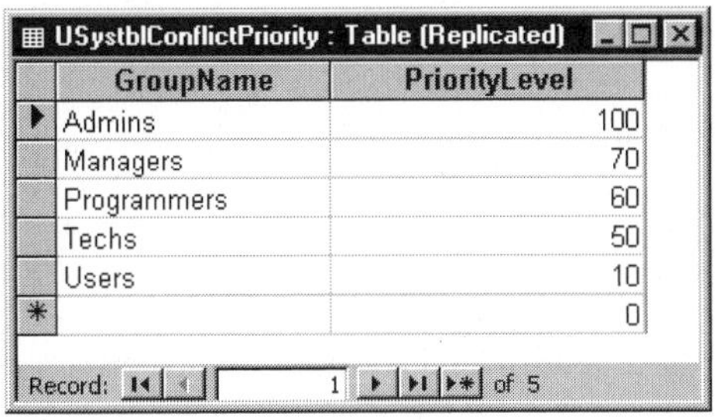

GroupName	PriorityLevel
Admins	100
Managers	70
Programmers	60
Techs	50
Users	10
	0

All of the three conflict functions are high-level functions that first check for conflicts, data errors, and design errors by calling the adhSyncInventory function. If conflicts are found, the functions call the adhResolveConflicts function with a parameter indicating the method of resolution to employ.

adhResolveConflicts (which you'll find in the basConflictMng module in the CH13B.MDB sample database) begins by checking to see whether the log table, the name of which is stored in the adhcCnflctLogTbl constant, exists. If not, it calls adhCreateConflictLogTbl, which creates it using a CreateTable DDL query. Next, it opens an append-only recordset based on the this table, where it will log its activity.

adhResolveConflicts then sets up a For Each loop to iterate through the Table-Defs in the database, just like the code for the CustomConflictResolver function from Listing 13.8, and uses an If…Then statement to disregard tables without any conflicts and any deleted tables.

The next part of the function determines the GUID field for the table and then adds the name of each of the primary key fields to a user-defined collection, strsPKFields.

Next, a recordset is created from a SQL statement that joins the conflict and user tables on the GUID field using a left outer join, and the function iterates through the records in this recordset.

If the intMethod parameter is set to adhcCnflctResSimple, Jet's automatic determination of the winning record is left unchanged. If intMethod is set to adhcCnflctResTime, however, the following piece of code is executed, comparing the update times of the winning and losing users and setting fChangeWinner to True when the losing record was updated at a later time:

```
If intMethod = adhcCnflctResTime Then
    ' Compare times of winning and
    ' losing users
    strMethod = "Last update check"
    If rstResolve("[" & _
     strTable & ".LastModTime]") < _
     rstResolve("[" & _
     strConflict & ".LastModTime]") Then
        fChangeWinner = True
    End If
```

This method of conflict resolution is dependent on one important factor: that the clocks of all replicas are synchronized. Note that if you have your replicas located in different time zones, you won't be able to use the Now function to record the last update time because it always returns the current time relative to the current time zone. Fortunately, the Windows API provides a function you can use to return a system time relative to Coordinated Universal Time (UTC) (also called Greenwich Mean Time (GMT)). We've created a function, adhUTCNow, which you'll find in basTimeZone in the CH13B.MDB sample database, that returns UTC time instead of the normal system time (see Listing 13.8).

Listing 13.8

```
Type SYSTEMTIME
        wYear As Integer
        wMonth As Integer
        wDayOfWeek As Integer
        wDay As Integer
        wHour As Integer
        wMinute As Integer
        wSecond As Integer
        wMilliseconds As Integer
End Type
Type TIME_ZONE_INFORMATION
        Bias As Long
        StandardName(32) As Integer
        StandardDate As SYSTEMTIME
        StandardBias As Long
        DaylightName(32) As Integer
        DaylightDate As SYSTEMTIME
        DaylightBias As Long
End Type

Declare Function adhGetTimeZoneInformation Lib "kernel32" _
 Alias "GetTimeZoneInformation" _
 (lpTimeZoneInformation As TIME_ZONE_INFORMATION) As Long

Public Function adhUTCNow() As Date

    ' Returns the current time relative to
    ' Coordinated Universal Time(UTC)

    Dim typTimeZone As TIME_ZONE_INFORMATION
    Dim lngRet As Long

    ' Make API call to determine number
```

```
' of minutes between this time zone and
' Coordinated Universal Time(UTC).
lngRet = adhGetTimeZoneInformation(typTimeZone)

' Return UTC Time
adhUTCNow = Now() + (typTimeZone.Bias / (60 * 24))
End Function
```

You'll need to use adhUTCNow instead of the Now function to record the time a record was updated. You'll find the following code attached to the BeforeUpdate event of all the data forms in CH13B.MDB:

```
Private Sub Form_BeforeUpdate(Cancel As Integer)
    Call adhSaveLastModInfo(Me)
End Sub
```

This code calls the adhSaveLastModInfo function, which makes the call to adhUTCNow. adhSaveLastModInfo is shown here:

```
Sub adhSaveLastModInfo(frm As Form)
    With frm
        !LastModTime = adhUTCNow()
        !LastModUser = CurrentUser()
        !LastModDB = CurrentDb().Name
    End With

End Sub
```

If the intMethod parameter is set to adhcCnflctResSecurity, the following piece of code is executed, comparing the security levels of the winning and losing users and setting fChangeWinner to True when the losing record has a higher security level:

```
ElseIf intMethod = adhcCnflctResSecurity Then
    ' Compare security level of winning and
    ' losing users and set fChangeWinner to True
    ' if losing user has higher priority
    strMethod = "Security check"
    If adhGetConflictPriority(rstResolve("[" & _
     strTable & ".LastModUser]")) < _
     adhGetConflictPriority(rstResolve( _
     "[" & strConflict & ".LastModUser]")) Then
        fChangeWinner = True
    End If
```

This code calls the adhGetConflictPriority function to check the security level of each user. adhGetConflictPriority determines the highest level of security by creating a recordset on USystblConflictPriority (see Figure 13.30 earlier in this chapter) sorted in descending order by PriorityLevel and then checking the first record (the record with the highest priority level) to see whether the user is a member of the group for that priority level. If so, the Do loop is exited, returning the PriorityLevel value of the record. If not, the next highest group is checked, and so on. Thus, by calling adhGet-ConflictPriority with both the winning and losing user names, the code is able to determine whether the losing user has a higher priority level than the winning user. If this is the case, fChangeWinner is set to True. Otherwise, if the losing user has the same or a lower priority level than the winning user, fChangeWinner is set to False.

Regardless of which method is used, adhResolveConlficts calls UpdateLogValues, passing it one set of parameters if fChangeWinner is False and a different set if it is True. (If fChangeWinner is True, it switches the names of the winning and losing tables and changes the "reason" text accordingly.) UpdateLogValues adds a new log record to rstLog for each conflict record, with the fields listed in Table 13.9 logged.

TABLE 13.9 The rstLog Fields

Field	Source	Description
LogTime	=Now()	Date/time
TableName	User record	User table name
RowGUID	User record	Usually the value of s_GUID
WinPKValues	Winning record	Primary key values of winning record
WinTime	Winning record	Date/time when winning record was last saved
WinUser	Winning record	User name when winning record was last saved
WinDB	Winning record	Name of replica where winning record was last saved
LosePKValues	Losing record	Primary key values of losing record
LoseTime	Losing record	Date/time when losing record was last saved
LoseUser	Losing record	User name when losing record was last saved
LoseDB	Losing record	Name of replica where losing record was last saved
ReasonText	N/A	Determined by glrResolveConflicts()

Finally, if fChangeWinner is True, the following code swaps the values in the winning and losing records:

```
If fChangeWinner Then
    rstResolve.Edit
        For Each fld In rstResolve.Fields
            ' SourceTable property gives you the
            ' field's underlying table
            If fld.SourceTable = strTable Then
                ' This will fail for read-only
                ' fields which we can ignore
                On Error Resume Next
                ' Copy conflict field value
                ' over data table field value.
                ' This works because recordset is
                ' updatable.
                fld.Value = rstResolve("[" & _
                  strConflict & "." & _
                  fld.SourceField & "]")
                ' Reset error handler
                On Error GoTo _
                  adhResolveConflicts_Err
            End If
        Next fld
    rstResolve.Update
End If
```

Other Issues to Consider

When developing database applications that will be replicated, you need to consider several other issues, as described in the next few sections.

Moving the Design Master

Normally, you won't need to change the design master status, but there may be times when you wish to designate another replica as the new design master. For example, say you are the database administrator for a replicated database and you will be going on vacation or transferring to another job. In cases like this you may wish to transfer design master status to your assistant, who normally uses a non–design master replica on the network.

Before you transfer design master status from one replica to another, compact the design master and synchronize all replicas with the current design master so they are at the same generation.

To transfer design master status from one replica to another using the Access menus, open the current design master and select Tools ➤ Replication ➤ Synchronize Now. In the Synchronize With combo box, choose the replica to which you wish to transfer design master status, and check the check box labeled "Make *'database'* the Design Master." (See Figure 13.12 earlier in this chapter.)

To transfer design master status using DAO code, follow these steps:

1. Exclusively open both the current design master and the replica you wish to make the new design master.

2. Set the current design master's DesignMasterID property to the ReplicaId property of the new design master.

3. Synchronize the two replicas.

You can use the adhDbTransferMaster function from basReplicationTools to transfer the design master status from one replica to another.

In some cases you may have to designate a new design master without the luxury of having the old design master around. This may be necessary, for example, if the design master becomes corrupted or was inadvertently deleted. In these cases you need to assign design master status to some other replica. You can do this by using Access' Tools ➤ Replication ➤ Recover Design Master command.

You can recover the design master using DAO code by opening the new design master database exclusively and setting its DesignMasterID property to its ReplicaId property. You can use the adhDbRecoverMaster function in basReplicationTools to do this.

After changing the design master, synchronize all replicas with the new design master.

Linked Tables

When you synchronize two replicas, Jet will exchange only the data in native Access tables, not in linked tables. You can, however, separately replicate and synchronize the database that contains the linked tables. If you're using a typical split database architecture (see Chapter 12), where users run an application from a local "application" database on their workstations linked to tables stored in a shared "data" database stored on the file server, you could choose to replicate the application database, the data database, or both.

> **NOTE** You cannot replicate data stored in external non-Access tables.

Design Considerations

If an application is to be used on a LAN only, you might keep a single nonreplicated data database on the file server with the application database replicated across the LAN, using a star topology with the file server as the hub node. As an alternative, you might wish to abandon the split database design and replicate the single database across the LAN using a star, ring, or fully connected topology.

If you wished to move a split application to a WAN or loosely connected network with, for example, multiple stars interconnected at their hub nodes, it may make sense to create two replica sets: one for the application databases that would be replicated to every desktop on the WAN, and a distinct replica set for the data databases that would remain on the file server hubs of each workgroup. Since application updates would be rare, you'd probably synchronize the application databases only when you needed to roll out a new version of the application. On the other hand, the data databases would be on a more regular synchronization schedule.

> **NOTE** When moving a replicated database with linked tables to another site, you'll have to update the Connect property of the tabledef and use the RefreshLink method at each site to fix up the linked tables so they point to the tables using a path that's valid for that site. (You can use either the Linked Table Manager Add-In or your own VBA linked table management code—see Chapter 12 for an example of such code—to fix up the links.) Jet doesn't consider making changes to the Connect property a design change, so you can make these changes at each replica.

Resolving Conflicts for "Data" Databases

Whenever you replicate a database that users will not normally open, you need to have in place some automated system for detecting and resolving conflicts and errors that might occur from synchronization exchanges between these replicas. This is necessary because the built-in Access Conflict Resolution Wizard or custom conflict resolution code will never be called, since the database won't normally be opened by a user. Thus, you'll have to create a VBA routine to automatically run after each synchronization exchange, logging and resolving conflicts and alerting the database administrator to any errors.

Security Issues

Jet doesn't support replicating the workgroup file (SYSTEM.MDW) in a secured workgroup environment. Thus, on a LAN you must either connect each replica to the workgroup file or copy the workgroup file to each workstation. For a WAN you'll need to copy the workgroup file to each remote synchronization replica.

> **NOTE** You can't replicate a database that has a database password. You must remove the password before proceeding. Similarly, you can't create a database password for a replicated database.

In a secured system that's normally centrally controlled by a single database administrator, this shortcoming shouldn't affect you. However, in situations where you would normally distribute security responsibilities among users, you will have to address the following issues:

- Because permission changes are considered design changes, they can be made only at the design master.

- Unless you restrict user access to the account management features, users will be able to make changes to user and group accounts (including the changing of passwords) from any replica.

> **NOTE**
> Security information is stored in two places. Account information is stored in the workgroup file (SYSTEM.MDW), and permission information is stored along with the objects in each user database. Thus, only permission information will be replicated in a replicated database.

Because you are restricted from making permission changes and these changes are kept in the user database, coordination of updates should not be a problem—they must be done at the design master and then propagated using the normal synchronization schedule. Changes to user accounts, however, present a problem: local account changes won't be replicated, since they are stored in the workgroup file. The best approach may be to limit these types of security changes to one database administrator who can see that the multiple workgroup files are kept in sync.

> **WARNING**
> It's important that any permission changes that are dependent on changes to accounts be made only *after* updated workgroup files have been copied to each workstation. Otherwise you run the risk of the replicated databases being out of sync with the workgroup files.

Compacting Replicas

When you make a number of schema changes at the design master, you should compact the database before synchronizing it with other replicas. This reduces the number of design changes that need to be transferred between replicas. In addition, it's a good idea to compact all replicas on a regular—perhaps daily or weekly—basis because replication will tend to bloat the databases.

> **TIP**
> When you compact replicated databases, you should compact each database *twice.* Jet performs the compact in two phases: first it performs the normal consolidation and recovery of deleted space, and *then* it goes through replicated objects and decides which ones to mark for deletion. However, because it has already finished reclaiming space from deleted objects, you need to compact a second time to finish the job. It won't hurt the replica to compact only once, but you will save additional space and make your replicas more efficient by compacting an extra time.

Summary

Replication is an exciting technology. In this chapter we've explored replication in detail and covered the following topics:

- How replication works
- All the tools you can use to manage replication: Windows 95 Briefcase, Access menus, Replication Manager, and DAO code
- When you should consider using replication
- Replication topologies
- The changes Jet makes to a replicated database
- Replicating a database
- Synchronizing replicas
- Resolving conflicts and errors
- Creating a custom conflict and error resolution function
- Moving the design master
- Replicating databases with linked tables
- Replicating secured databases
- Compacting replicas
- Partial replication
- Internet-based synchronization

CHAPTER
FOURTEEN

14

Securing Your Application

- Making your databases secure

- Programmatically creating user and group accounts

- Programmatically checking and setting object permissions

- Listing all users with blank passwords

- Preventing users from creating new objects

In this chapter we cover Jet security in detail, outlining how and why it works the way it does and how to avoid common "gotchas." We also show you how to manipulate security programmatically using Access' security objects.

> **NOTE** Security in Access is a function of the database engine, Jet, not the Access User Interface (UI). While the Access UI provides one means of managing security, Jet maintains security no matter what the client application—Access, Visual Basic, Excel, or other programs gaining access through the Access ODBC driver. Thus, in this chapter we use the term *Jet security* rather than *Access security*.

Security Basics

Jet 3.5 and Access 97 offer two overlapping security models:

- Workgroup-based security
- Database password security

Workgroup-Based Security

Since Access 1.0, the Jet engine has offered a sophisticated *workgroup-based* security model (it's also referred to as a user-based security model) rather than the more common database-based model most other desktop database management systems use. Under the simpler file-oriented model, security revolves around a database and is self-contained within the confines of that database. Each database has its own security system that is independent of others. In contrast, in Jet's workgroup-based security model, every database used by members of a workgroup shares the same security system.

Database Passwords

With the introduction of Jet 3.0 (Access 95), Microsoft added a much simpler alternative: database passwords. This system allows you to set a single password for a database that all users must know to open the database. While much simpler to implement and use, this system is very easily compromised because all users use the same password. In addition, it doesn't let you track individual users' activity in a shared database. However, you can use both workgroup-based security and database passwords at the same time.

You set a database password by selecting Tools ➤ Security ➤ Set Database Password. Once this option is set, whenever you open the database you will be met with the Password Required dialog, as shown in Figure 14.1. You must have the database open exclusively to set the database password.

FIGURE 14.1

Entering a password for a database

To open a database that's been password protected programmatically, you must use the connect parameter of the OpenDatabase method. For example, the following code opens the Test24 database with a password of "dirt":

```
Dim wrk As Workspace
Dim dbTest As Database

Set wrk = DBEngine.Workspaces(0)
Set dbTest = wrk. _
 OpenDatabase("d:\a97dh\ch14\test14.mdb", _
 False, False, ";PWD=dirt")
```

The connect parameter is case sensitive. In addition, you must set the exclusive and read-only parameters (the second and third parameters) if you use the connect parameter.

> **TIP**
>
> If you're using workgroup-based security, you may wish to prevent a user from creating or removing a database password. To do so, remove the user's Administer permission for the database object. You'll also need to remove this user from any groups that have this permission set. (See the section "Assigning Permissions" later in this chapter.)

The remainder of this chapter focuses on the more powerful workgroup-based security model.

NOTE You can't replicate a database for which you have set a database password; you must first remove the password.

Jet Workgroup-Based Security

Jet's workgroup-based security is based on *users and their permissions*, not passwords. Most desktop databases employ password-based security if they implement any security features at all. (Jet offers a limited password-based system, too—see the previous section.) In these systems users enter a password that identifies them to the system as valid users. Every user who shares a given security level shares that same password, so the system is incapable of identifying individual users. In contrast, Jet's security model requires each user to have both a user name and a password. The password merely verifies that users are who they claim to be. Once verified, the password leaves the picture. With Jet, users manage their own individual passwords, which they can change at will without affecting other users. Passwords can be more secure since they're not shared by lots of users.

In a password-based system, each object has passwords associated with it that define its security. For example, the Orders table in Paradox might have a read-only password and a read/write password, so a user named Joe who knew both passwords would have read/write access to the table. With Jet, however, an object doesn't have any associated passwords or permissions. Instead, a user (or a group of users) has an associated set of permissions on a per-object basis. Thus, in Access/Jet, the user Joe or the Managers group of which he is a member might have ReadData and UpdateData permissions for the Orders table.

Two Parts to Security

Jet security is made up of two parts:

- *User and group accounts and their passwords* are stored in the workgroup file. This file, usually kept centrally on a file server in a multiuser environment, is, by default, named SYSTEM.MDW.

- *Object permissions* are stored in each database.

For example, the security system for a small business, with three employees and four Access databases, might look like that shown in Figure 14.2. The workgroup for this company is defined by the company's workgroup file, BIZSYS.MDW, which contains the three user accounts and their passwords (Joe, Mary, and Sally) and the two group accounts (Managers and Programmers).

FIGURE 14.2

Security system for a small business. The workgroup file, BIZSYS.MDW, contains the three user and two group accounts. Object permissions are stored in each of the four databases.

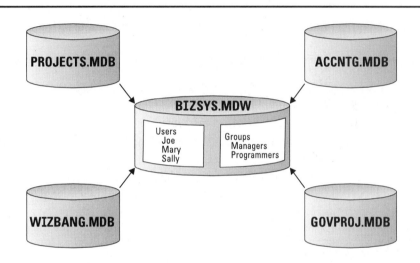

Each of the databases for this company—PROJECTS.MDB, ACCNTNG.MDB, WIZBANG.MDB, and GOVPROJ.MDB—would be tied to the BIZSYS.MDW workgroup file. Jet stores the access rights to each of the database objects in the individual databases. For example, the Managers group might have Administer rights on the table tblCustomers in ACCNTNG.MDB, while the Programmers group might have only ReadData and UpdateData rights for this table. The rights for this table and for all the other objects in ACCNTNG.MDB would be stored in this database, along with pointers to the account information stored in BIZSYS.MDW.

Enabling Security

Security in Jet is always on; it can't be turned off. The security system, however, remains invisible until you're ready to use it. This is possible because of the presence of several default user and group accounts.

Every workgroup file starts out with two predefined group accounts (Admins and Users) and one predefined user account (Admin). (Jet 3.x has dispensed with the Guest and Guests accounts, although these accounts will still be present if you're using a version 2.0 workgroup file. See the section "Migrating Secured Databases to Access 97" later in this chapter for more information on converting secured version 2 systems to Access 97.)

When a user starts an Access session, Jet always attempts to log on the user as *Admin* with a blank password. If this logon attempt fails, only then does Jet prompt the user for a user name and password using the Logon dialog. Thus, as long as you keep the Admin password blank (a zero-length string), security remains invisible.

Overriding Jet's Default Logon Attempt

Sometimes when you are developing an application, it would be nice if you could log on as a user, even when the Admin password is blank. You might want to do this, for example, to test out a user logging system. You can override Jet's attempt to log you on as Admin by using a startup option. For example, you can start Access as user Harpo with the password Marx using the following:

```
MSACCESS.EXE /User Harpo /Pwd Marx
```

Note, however, that this is useful only during testing. Your database will be anything but secure under this scenario.

Workgroups

Security in Jet revolves around *workgroups*. At the interface level, a workgroup is defined as a group of users who work together. At the Jet level, a workgroup is defined as all users sharing the same workgroup file.

The workgroup file is a special encrypted database, by default called SYSTEM.MDW, that Access and Jet use to store a number of pieces of information having to do with users, including:

- User account names, their personal identifiers (PIDs), and passwords
- Group account names and their PIDs

- Information regarding which users belong to which groups

- Various user preference settings, including custom toolbar settings

- A list of the last four opened databases (for each user)

In a multiuser environment you can choose to place the workgroup file either on the file server or on each workstation. Usually, you'll want to place it on the file server, which makes the maintenance of user and group accounts much easier. On the other hand, if your security settings are fairly static, you could reduce network traffic by placing a copy of the workgroup file on each workstation.

Creating a New Workgroup

Microsoft includes a utility program called the Workgroup Administrator (WRKGADM.EXE) you can use to create a new workgroup (workgroup file) or to change to another workgroup. (The Access install program copies this utility to the \windows\system folder and does not automatically add this program to the Start menu.) If you run this utility and choose to create a new workgroup, you are met with the Workgroup Owner Information dialog, as shown in Figure 14.3.

TIP

Because the workgroup file is such a vital part of security, we recommend regularly backing up this file and storing a copy of it safely off site. You should also consider storing a copy of the Name, Organization, and Workgroup ID fields in hard-copy form in a secure off-site location.

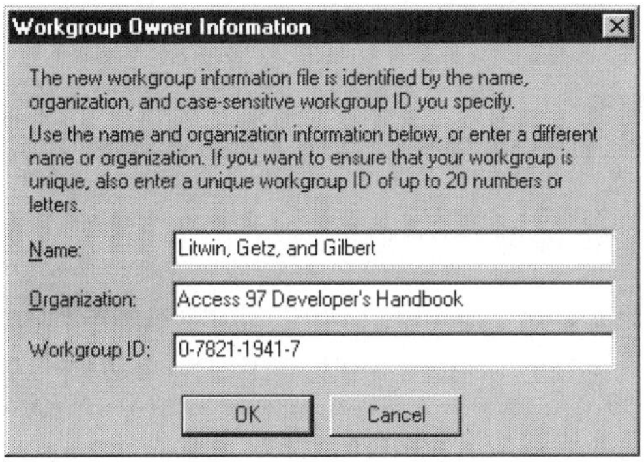

FIGURE 14.3

The information entered into the Workgroup Owner Information dialog is used to uniquely identify a workgroup.

855

By default, Jet takes your user and organization name from the Access installation parameters, which you can view using the Help ➤ About Microsoft Access command. This is the information Jet displays when the Workgroup Administrator program is started. You can change this information to anything you'd like at this time (but not at any other time).

The third field in the Workgroup Owner Information dialog, Workgroup ID, is the most critical one. You can enter from 0 to 20 numbers or *case-sensitive* letters into this field. Take extra care to keep this entry secret but backed up somewhere off site. If you leave this field blank, you'll be warned, but you won't be prevented from proceeding. Once you commit your entries to these fields by clicking the OK button, you will have one more chance to change your mind, and then you will never be able to view or change them again. Thus, it's important to write them down.

WARNING Access creates a default workgroup named SYSTEM.MDW when you install Access. To create this workgroup, it uses the name and company installation parameters and a blank Workgroup ID. *This makes the default workgroup file unsecure* because anyone who can get to the Help ➤ About Microsoft Access command with your copy of Access can break your security! When you need to secure a database, the first thing you should do is create a brand-new secured workgroup file.

Based on your entries in the Workgroup Owner Information dialog, Jet generates an encrypted binary ID called the Workgroup SID. Jet uses the Workgroup SID to uniquely identify the Admins group account in the workgroup. The significance of this built-in account is discussed in the section "Special Status: Built-In Accounts" later in this chapter.

You can also use the Workgroup Administrator program to join a different workgroup. This allows you to participate in multiple workgroups, although only one can be active at a time.

User and Group Accounts

Jet uses user and group accounts to dole out security permissions. Only users and groups can have permissions. Both types of accounts share the same name space, so you need to ensure that all names are unique for a workgroup. Thus, you can't have a user and a group with the same name.

Microsoft uses the convention whereby user names are singular and group names are plural (for example, the Admin user and the Admins group). We've adopted (and recommend that you adopt) this account-naming scheme.

In Access you use the Tools ➤ Security ➤ User and Group Accounts command to create and manage user and group accounts (see Figure 14.4).

Only members of the Admins group can add, delete, and change the membership for user and group accounts, but any user can view accounts (this is a change from Access 2) and change his or her account password.

FIGURE 14.4

The user Geoff is a member of the Users, Employees, and Programmers groups.

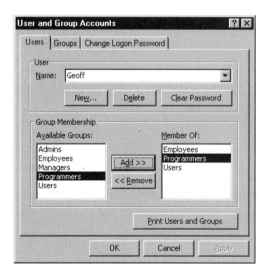

PIDs, SIDs, and Passwords

When you create a new user or group account in Jet, you must enter a nonblank, 4–20 character, case-sensitive *personal identifier* (*PID*). Jet combines the name of the account with the PID to create a *security identifier* (*SID*) for each user or group account. Once you've entered a PID, you can *never* view or change it.

After you create a new user account, you can add an optional 1–14-character, case-sensitive account password using the Change Logon Password tab of the User

TIP	We recommend that only a single database administrator create accounts and PIDs and that this individual keep a written off-site record. This will be useful if someone deletes an account that you need to re-create at a later date. This same person should keep a written off-site record of the user and organization names and the workgroup ID entered into the Workgroup Owner Information dialog, as well as a recent backup of the workgroup file.

and Group Accounts dialog. (Unlike PIDs, passwords are optional.) Jet uses passwords only at logon time to verify the identity of a user.

Only users can change their own passwords, but members of the Admins group can clear another user's password. (This is a restriction of the Access UI—using DAO, an Admins member can change another user's password without knowing the old password.) You *can't* view an existing password using either the UI or DAO.

Both passwords and PIDs are stored in the workgroup file in an encrypted format.

Jet uses the internally generated account SIDs to uniquely identify user and group accounts across workgroups. Except for some of the special built-in accounts that are discussed in the section "Special Status: Built-In Accounts" later in this chapter, Jet treats accounts in different workgroups with the same name but different PIDs (and thus different SIDs) as distinct.

Groups Are More Than Collections of Users

A group account is more than simply a collection of users. In many situations you can use a group account in place of a user account. The following table contrasts the two types of accounts:

Attribute	User Accounts	Group Accounts
Has associated permissions for objects	Yes	Yes
Has a personal ID (PID)	Yes	Yes
May own objects	Yes	Yes
May log on	Yes	No

Has password	Yes	No
May own a database	Yes	No

Although you cannot log on as a group, you can do almost anything else with a group account, including owning objects. A group account may not own a database.

Special Status: Built-In Accounts

As mentioned earlier in this chapter, the Jet security system includes several built-in accounts that make it possible for security to remain invisible until it's needed. These built-in accounts include the Admin *user* and the Admins and Users *groups*. It's important that you understand how these "special status" accounts work; otherwise your database won't be secure. The following table describes the three built-in accounts:

Account Type	Account	Same SID for All Workgroups?	Comments
User	Admin	Yes	Default user account
Group	Admins	No	Members have special privileges
Group	Users	Yes	All user accounts are members of Users

None of the special accounts can ever be deleted from a workgroup. Each of these accounts is described in more detail in the next few sections.

Admin User

All new workgroups initially contain the Admin user account with a blank password. As mentioned previously, unless a command-line option is used to override this behavior, Jet always attempts to log you on as the Admin user with a blank password. Only if this logon attempt fails does Jet prompt you for a user name and password.

You cannot delete the Admin user, but you can remove it from the Admins group as long as Admins has at least one other member. This is one of the steps for making a database secure that are discussed in the section "Properly Securing a Database with the Access Security Wizard" later in this chapter. *The Admin user will always have the same SID for all workgroups.*

The Admin user is somewhat misnamed; even though it is initially a member of the Admins group, it has no special administrative powers of its own. It might have been more accurate for Microsoft to have named the Admin user account User or DefaultUser.

As long as the Admin user is not the current user when you create objects, it will not have any permissions on newly created objects.

Admins Group

The Admins group is uniquely identified across workgroups. (This differs from all other built-in accounts, which are not unique from one workgroup to another.) In fact, the Admins group draws its SID from the workgroup SID created by the Workgroup Administrator program. Jet requires that there always be at least one member of the Admins group. This requirement makes it impossible to have a workgroup with no administrator.

Members of the Admins group have special, irrevocable administrative rights. Their membership in Admins, however, *is* revocable by another Admins member. As long as they are members of Admins, they can grant themselves permissions to all database objects in the databases in their workgroup. (Access, but not the Jet engine, enforces this. It is possible, using DAO, to revoke Administer permission from the Admins group for an object. The object's owner will retain Administer permissions for the object.) In addition, members of Admins always have the ability to manage user and group accounts in their workgroup.

By default, when you create a new object, the Admins group gets full permissions to the new object.

Users Group

The Users group is the default group for all Access users. All built-in user accounts—as well as new user accounts created using the Access UI—will be members of the Users group. Access won't allow you to remove users from the Users group. (This is an Access limitation, but it's not one that Jet enforces. Using DAO, you can remove user accounts from the Users group, but these users will no longer be able to log on to Access.)

Along with the Admin user account, it is the presence of the Users group account that allows Jet to keep security invisible until needed. This is possible because the Users group account has the same SID across all workgroups. Thus, if you wish to secure a workgroup, you must remove all object permissions from the Users group and refrain from using it to assign permissions. On the other hand, the easiest way to make a secure database unsecured is to assign full object permissions for each of its objects to the Users group.

By default, the Users group gets full permissions on newly created objects.

Assigning Permissions

Using the Access UI, you assign permissions to database objects with the Tools ➤ Security ➤ User and Group Permissions command (see Figure 14.5). Although you can change only one *type* of object at a time, you can select multiple objects (in contiguous or discontiguous groups) in the Permissions dialog.

FIGURE 14.5

The Programmers group account has ReadDesign and ModifyDesign permissions for the basSecurityUtilities module.

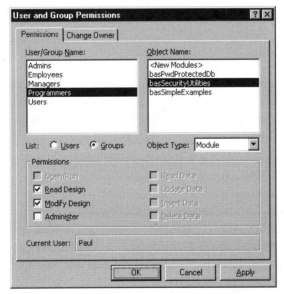

Which Objects Have Which Permissions?

Each database container object in Jet has a set of associated permissions you can set. Each type of object has a different set of settable permissions. For example, tables and queries don't have an Open/Run permission, but they have several permissions that control how data may be read or updated. On the other hand, forms, reports, and macros have no data permissions but do have an Open/Run permission. Table 14.1 lists each object and its permission set.

TABLE 14.1   Permission Sets for Each Type of Object

Object	Open/ Run	Read- Design	Modify- Design	Administer	Read- Data	Update- Data	Insert- Data	Delete- Data	Open- Exclusive
Table		√	√	√	√	√	√	√	
Query		√	√	√	√	√	√	√	
Form	√	√	√	√					
Report	√	√	√	√					
Macro	√	√	√	√					
Module		√	√	√					
Database	√			√					√

Only the database itself and database container objects have permissions. This is paralleled in DAO, where only containers and documents have permissions. Controls, columns, parameters, toolbars, and other Jet and Access objects do not have permissions—which means they are not individually securable.

With the release of Access 95, Microsoft added a new permission for the database object: Administer. Although its name implies otherwise, this permission does *not* control the ability to administer permissions for the database. The database's Administer permission, however, does control access to:

- Converting the database into a replicated design master (This doesn't include creating additional replicas; a user needs only the Open/Run permission to create additional replicas.)

- Creating and removing the database password (The user must also have the OpenExclusive permission.)

- Saving changes to the database startup properties (This affects only Access applications.)

Permissions are not completely independent of each other; some permissions imply other permissions. For example, you can't have UpdateData permissions if you don't also have ReadDesign and ReadData permissions. Thus, UpdateData permission also implies these other permissions. Table 14.2 shows the interdependencies of permissions for table and query objects.

TABLE 14.2 Relationship between Permissions for Table and Query Objects*

Permission	Read-Design	Modify-Design	Administer	Read-Data	Update-Data	Insert-Data	Delete-Data
ReadDesign	N/A						
ModifyDesign	√	N/A		√	√		√
Administer	√	√	N/A	√	√	√	√
ReadData	√			N/A			
UpdateData	√			√	N/A		
InsertData	√			√		N/A	
DeleteData	√			√			N/A

*If you have the permission in the first column, you also have the checked permissions to the right.

Permissions for New Objects

In addition to setting permissions on existing objects, you can set permissions on new objects. You do this by choosing <New *objectname*> in the User and Group Permissions dialog (see Figure 14.5). This setting does *not* control the ability to create new objects; it controls only the permissions the account will receive for new objects. Although you can remove all permissions for new objects, this will *not* prevent users from creating new objects. In addition, since they will become the owner of any objects *they* create, they can always grant themselves Administer rights to these objects.

By using DAO, however, you *can* prevent users from creating new objects. We include a function in the sample database, adhSetPermissionDocCreate, you can use for this purpose. (See the section "Programming Permissions" later in this chapter.)

Explicit versus Implicit Permissions

Users in the Jet security model have both implicit and explicit permissions. *Explicit permissions* are those permissions explicitly given to users and associated directly with a user account. *Implicit permissions* are those permissions users receive because of their membership in groups.

A user's set of permissions for an object will be based on the union of the user's explicit permissions and implicit permissions. A user's security level is always the *least restrictive* of the user's explicit permissions and the permissions of any and all groups to which the user belongs.

For example, say that user Alicia has no permissions for the table tblCustomer. Alicia also belongs to two groups: Managers and Programmers. The Managers group has Administer permissions (which implies all the other permissions for an object) for tblCustomer, and the Programmers group has only ReadDesign permissions for tblCustomer. Alicia will have Administer permissions for tblCustomer because this is the least restrictive (or highest) permission for tblCustomer.

> **WARNING** Don't make the mistake of removing a user's explicit permissions without bothering to check his or her implicit permissions.

Members of the Admins group (and those users having the Administer permission for a particular object) can directly view and set explicit permissions, but they can't directly view or set implicit permissions. Instead, you view implicit permissions by noting the group membership of a user and then looking at the permissions for each of these groups. To change implicit permissions, you must either modify the permissions for each of the groups to which a user belongs or add or remove the user from groups.

> **TIP** Jet 3.0 added a new property, AllPermissions, for the quick querying of a user's complete permission set. AllPermissions incorporates the union of a user's explicit and implicit permissions from DAO.

Who Can Change Permissions?

The following users can change object permissions:

- Members of the Admins group (for the workgroup in which the database was created) can always change permissions on any users. These rights can never be taken away using the Access UI (but they can be taken away using DAO).

- An object's owner—either the user who created the object or the user or group to which ownership of the object was transferred—can always modify the permissions for the object. This includes the ability of owners to give themselves Administer permissions for the object, even if someone else previously revoked these privileges. These rights can never be taken away.

- Any user with explicit or implicit Administer permissions to the object can administer permissions for that object. Another user with Administer rights can take away these rights.

- The database owner—the user who created the database—can always open a database and create new objects in it, even if the owner's rights to all the database's objects have been revoked. (The Access UI will allow members of the Admins group to *think* they have revoked the Open/Run permission from the database owner, but the owner will retain that right.) The only way to remove these rights is to import all of a database's objects into a new database and delete the original database.

What Happens to Permissions for Deleted Accounts?

When you delete a user or group account from a workgroup for an account that still has associated permissions, those permissions remain in the database. This can be a security concern; if someone can re-create the account and its PID, that person has a *backdoor pass* into your secured database. Thus, it's important that you remove all permissions (and transfer any objects the to-be-deleted account owns to a new owner) before deleting an account.

If someone re-creates an account with the same name but a *different* PID, Jet treats that account as a completely different account. It will not inherit any of the old account's permissions, because its SID is different from the SID of the old account.

> **TIP**
>
> The CurrentUser function returns only the name of a user and therefore cannot be counted on to distinguish between users with the same name but different SIDs (either in the same workgroup at different points in time or across workgroups). This might be an issue when you are using the value of CurrentUser to branch in your code or log activity to a file.

When you use the Change Owner tab of the User and Group Permissions dialog to list the owner of an object whose account has been deleted, Access lists the owner as "<Unknown>".

Ownership

In addition to the permissions that are granted to accounts, you need to be aware of ownership, because database owners and object owners have special privileges.

Who Owns a Database?

The user who creates a database is the database's owner. This user maintains special irrevocable rights to the database. As mentioned previously, this user will always be able to open the database. Only user accounts, not group accounts, can own databases.

Database ownership cannot be changed, but you can always create a new database using a different user account and import all the database's objects into another database. (This is how the Microsoft Security Wizard works.) If you then delete the original database and rename the new database to the name of the original, you have effectively transferred its ownership. The account used to transfer ownership must have ReadDesign and ReadData (where applicable) permissions to each of the database's objects.

You can use the Change Owner tab of the Tools ➤ Security ➤ User and Group Permissions command to view, but not change, the database owner.

Who Owns a Database's Objects?

Each database container object also has an owner. Initially, this is the user who created the object and may or may not be the same user account as the database owner. You can use the Change Owner tab of the Tools ➤ Security ➤ User and Group Permissions command to view and change object owners (see Figure 14.6).

The new owner for an object may be a group account. This is especially useful when you are managing OwnerAccess queries, which are discussed in the next section.

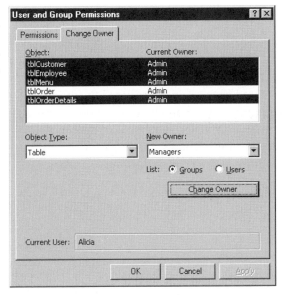

FIGURE 14.6

Using the Change Owner dialog, Alicia is about to change the ownership for four tables from Admin to the Managers group.

OwnerAccess Queries

Queries created in Access QBE have a property, RunPermissions, that governs whether Jet uses the query user's (the person running the query) permissions or the owner's permissions when checking the security permissions for each of the source tables in a query. In Access SQL, setting this property to "Owner's" translates to the "WITH OWNERACCESS OPTION" clause.

This property allows you to present data to users who lack access rights to the underlying tables. Using this feature, you can effectively apply column-level and row-level security to a table.

For example, using an OwnerAccess query, you could let members of the Programmers group view and update all the columns in the tblEmployee table except for the Salary field. To do this, you would perform the following steps:

1. Remove all permissions to tblEmployee for the Programmers group.

2. Using an account that has ReadData and UpdateData permissions to tblEmployee, create a query, qryEmployee, that includes all the columns from tblEmployee except Salary.

3. Set the RunPermissions property of qryEmployee to "Owner's" (or include the "WITH OWNERACCESS OPTION" clause in the SQL statement for the query).

One problem with OwnerAccess queries is that Jet allows only the query's owner to save changes to the query. Even other users with Administer rights to the query are prevented from saving changes to the query. This can present a problem if you are sharing the management of these queries among multiple users. In this case you may wish to transfer ownership of the query to a group account, but you'll have to temporarily change the RunPermissions property of the query back to "User's" before you can change the query's owner.

Encryption

As good as Jet security is, a very knowledgeable hacker equipped with a low-level disk editor might be able to directly open the MDB file and break into your database. The only way to guard against such a hacker is to encrypt the database. (Hacking your way into a database is far from a trivial task, but there are those who love such a challenge.)

Encrypting a database does not secure it. It is only one of a series of steps for properly securing a database. (These steps are discussed in the section "Properly Securing a Database with the Access Security Wizard" later in this chapter.)

Only the database owner or members of the Admins group can encrypt or decrypt a database. Jet uses an RSA- (Rivest, Shamir, and Adleman—the names of the inventors of the algorithm) based encryption algorithm with a key based on your workgroup ID to encrypt the database. Using Access, you can encrypt or decrypt a database using the Tools ➤ Security ➤ Encrypt/Decrypt Database command. The Access Security Wizard encrypts databases as its final step in securing a database.

Encryption has two negative side effects. First, it reduces database performance (according to Microsoft estimates) by approximately 10 to 15 percent. Second, it makes the database uncompressible by programs such as PKZip, LHA, Stacker, and DriveSpace. (You won't be prevented from compressing the database, but the compression step won't significantly reduce the size.)

Programming Security Using Data Access Objects

So far in this chapter we have focused on defining the Jet security model and showing you how to manipulate it using the Access UI. You can also use Jet data access objects (DAO) to manipulate security. In fact, DAO lets you manipulate Jet security in ways the Access UI does not currently support. (For an overview of DAO, see Chapter 6.)

In the sections that follow we introduce several reusable security functions, all of which can be found in the basSecurityUtilities module of the CH14.MDB database. Many of the functions are included in listings and described in detail; others are mentioned only briefly but are provided in basSecurityUtilities for your convenience. All the functions from basSecurityUtilities, however, are summarized in Table 14.3.

TABLE 14.3 Security Functions in basSecurityUtilities

Function	Purpose
adhAddGroupMember	Adds a user to a group
adhCheckPermission	Checks the particular bit or set of bits of a permission value for a document or container
adhCreateGroup	Creates a new group account
adhCreateUser	Creates a new user account
adhDeleteAccount	Deletes a user or group account from the workgroup
adhGetAccount	Checks for the existence of an account and returns the type (user or group) if found
adhGetObjectOwner	Gets the account name of an object's owner
adhIsGroupMember	Verifies whether a user is a member of a group
adhGetPermission	Gets the entire permission value for a document or container
adhListUsersWithBlankPwd	Prints all users with blank passwords to a text file
adhRemoveGroupMember	Removes a user from a group
adhSetDbCreate	Enables or disables an account from being able to create databases
adhSetDbPwd	Sets the database password

TABLE 14.3 Security Functions in basSecurityUtilities (continued)

Function	Purpose
adhSetOwner	Changes the owner of a document or container
adhSetPermission	Adds or subtracts a particular bit or set of bits, or replaces a permission value for a document or container
adhSetPermissionAdd	Adds a particular permission bit or set of bits for a document or container. Wrapper function that calls adhSetPermission
adhSetPermissionDocCreate	Enables or disables the ability of an account to create documents of a particular type. Wrapper function that calls adhSetPermission
adhSetPermissionReplace	Replaces a permission value for a document or container. Wrapper function that calls adhSetPermission
adhSetPermissionSubtract	Subtracts a particular permission bit or set of bits for a document or container. Wrapper function that calls adhSetPermission
adhSetPwd	Sets the password for a user account

NOTE

The functions presented here often work on a single object and a single user, which are passed to the function as parameters. This helps make these functions generic. Unfortunately, it also makes them inefficient to use if you need to work on many objects or many users. In these cases you'd be better off modifying these functions to work on more than one object at a time.

Programming security with DAO revolves around two object hierarchies that correspond to the division in Jet security discussed in the section "Two Parts to Security" earlier in this chapter:

Part of Security	Corresponding DAO Object Hierarchy
User and group accounts and their passwords	Users and Groups hierarchy
Object permissions	Containers and Documents hierarchy

The User and Groups Hierarchy

You manipulate user and group accounts—the elements of security that are stored in the workgroup file—using the object hierarchy shown in Figure 14.7.

FIGURE 14.7

Data access objects hierarchy for users and groups

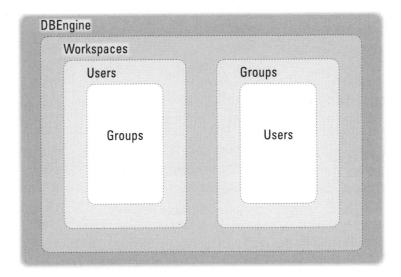

User and group objects are direct descendants of a workspace object; they are independent of any database objects. This is consistent with the physical location of the user and group account information—in the workgroup file.

The user and group object hierarchies overlap. Each user object contains a *Groups* collection that contains the names of all the groups to which a user belongs. Similarly, each group object contains a *Users* collection that contains the names of all users belonging to that group.

The Collections and Documents Hierarchy

You manipulate object permissions—the elements of security that are stored in databases—using the object hierarchy shown in Figure 14.8.

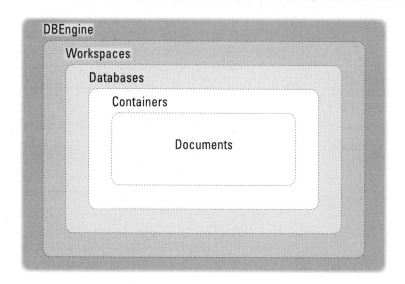

Unlike user and group objects, permissions are manipulated using container and document objects that *are* descendants of the database object. Again, this is consistent with the physical location of these security elements.

Managing Accounts

Using DAO, you can create, delete, and list user and group accounts. In addition, you can list the groups to which a user belongs and the users who are members of a group. Jet 3.5 lets any user view user and group account information, although only Admins members can update account information.

Users Collections and User Objects

There are two types of collections of users: collections of a workspace and collections of a group account. The Users collection for a workspace contains all the user accounts for that workspace. The Users collection for a group account contains all the members of the group.

The *Users collection* has a single property and three methods, described in Table 14.4.

The Users collection contains user objects. *User objects* have three properties and two methods, described in Table 14.5.

TABLE 14.4 Properties and Methods of the Users Collection

Type	Property/Method	Description
Property	Count	Number of user objects in the collection
Method	Append	Adds a new user to a collection
	Delete	Removes a user from a collection
	Refresh	Refreshes the collection

TABLE 14.5 Properties and Methods of User Objects

Type	Property/Method	Description
Property	Name	Name of the user. Read/write for new users not yet appended to the Users collection. Read-only otherwise
	Password	Case-sensitive password for the user account. Write-only for new users not yet appended to the Users collection. Not available otherwise
	PID	Case-sensitive personal identifier for the user account. Write-only for new users not yet appended to the Users collection. Not available otherwise
Method	CreateGroup	Creates a new group object. When appended to the user object's Groups collection, this method adds the user to that group
	NewPassword	Replaces an existing password with a new one

For example, you could use the following subroutine to enumerate the user accounts in the workgroup to the Debug window:

```
Sub ListUsers()

    Dim wrk As WorkSpace
    Dim usr As User

    Set wrk = DBEngine.Workspaces(0)

    Debug.Print "The Users collection has the following " & _
     wrk.Users.Count & " members:"
    For Each usr In wrk.Users
```

```
        Debug.Print usr.Name
    Next usr

End Sub
```

If you wished instead to list only user accounts that were members of the Managers group, you could use the following:

```
Sub ListManagers()

    Dim wrk. As WorkSpace
    Dim grpManagers As Group
    Dim usr As User

    Set wrk = DBEngine.Workspaces(0)
    Set grpManagers = wrk.Groups!Managers

    For Each usr In grpManagers.Users
        Debug.Print usr.Name
    Next usr

End Sub
```

To create a new user account, you use the CreateUser method of a workspace object.

Groups Collections and Group Objects

There are two types of collections of groups: collections of a workspace and collections of a user account. The Groups collection for a workspace contains all the group accounts for that workspace. The Groups collection for a user account contains all the groups to which that user belongs.

The *Groups collection* has a single property and three methods, described in Table 14.6.

TABLE 14.6 Properties and Methods of the Groups Collection

Type	Property/Method	Description
Property	Count	Number of group objects in the collection
Method	Append	Adds a new group to a collection
	Delete	Removes a group from a collection
	Refresh	Refreshes the collection

The Groups collection contains group objects. *Group objects* have two properties and a single method, described in Table 14.7.

TABLE 14.7 Properties and Methods of Group Objects

Type	Property/Method	Description
Property	Name	Name of the group. Read/write for new groups not yet appended to the Groups collection. Read-only otherwise
	PID	Case-sensitive personal identifier for the group account. Write-only for new groups not yet appended to the Groups collection. Not available otherwise
Method	CreateUser	Creates a new user object. When appended to the group object's Users collection, this method adds the user to the group

Groups don't have passwords; you can't log on as a member of a group.

You might use the following code to enumerate the names of all the groups in the Groups collection of the default workspace:

```
Sub ListGroups()

    Dim wrk As WorkSpace
    Dim grp As Group

    Set wrk = DBEngine.Workspaces(0)

    Debug.Print "The Groups collection has the following " & _
     wrk.Groups.Count & " members:"
    For Each grp In wrk.Groups
        Debug.Print grp.Name
    Next grp

End Sub
```

To create a new group account, you use the CreateGroup method of a workspace object.

Creating New Accounts

You can use the adhCreateUser function, located in the basSecurityUtilities module of CH14.MDB, to create a new user account. It takes as its parameters the name of the new user, the new user's PID, and the new user's password. It returns True if successful. This function, which requires the user running it to be a member of the Admins group, is shown in Listing 14.1.

Listing 14.1

```
Function adhCreateUser(ByVal strName As String, _
 ByVal strPID As String, ByVal strPW As String) As Boolean

    On Error GoTo adhCreateUserErr

    Dim wrk As Workspace
    Dim usrNew As User
    Dim strMsg As String

    Const adhcProcName = "adhCreateUser"

    adhCreateUser = False

    Set wrk = DBEngine.Workspaces(0)

    'Create new user account and append to Users collection
    Set usrNew = wrk.CreateUser(strName, strPID, strPW)
    wrk.Users.Append usrNew

    'Must also add user account to Users group
    usrNew.Groups.Append wrk.CreateGroup("Users")

    adhCreateUser = True

adhCreateUserDone:
    On Error GoTo 0
    Exit Function

adhCreateUserErr:
    Select Case Err
    Case adhcErrAccntAlreadyExists
        strMsg = "An account with the name '" & strName & _
        "' already exists."
    Case adhcErrBadPid
        strMsg = "You must enter a PID of between 4 " & _
        "and 20 characters."
```

```
        Case adhcErrNoPermission
            strMsg = "You don't have permission to perform " & _
            "this operation."
        Case Else
            strMsg = "Error " & Err.Number & ": " & Err.Description
        End Select
            MsgBox strMsg, vbCritical + vbOKOnly, "Procedure " & _
            adhcProcName
        Resume adhCreateUserDone

End Function
```

Creating a new user is much like creating any new object with DAO. adhCreateUser works by creating a new user object using the CreateUser method of the default workspace. The new user is created when the user's object is appended to the workspace's Users collection. To be consistent with the Access UI—and more important, to make it so the new account will be able to open databases in the workgroup—adhCreateUser finishes by appending the new account to the built-in Users group.

basSecurityUtilities also includes a similar function, adhCreateGroup, for creating new group accounts.

Checking for the Existence and Type of an Account

You can use adhGetAccount to check for the existence and type of account to which you pass the account name. It returns one of the following global constants that have been declared in the declarations section of basSecurityUtilities:

```
Global Const adhcAccntUser = 1
Global Const adhcAccntGroup = 2
Global Const adhcAccntNone = 0
```

adhGetAccount is shown in Listing 14.2.

Listing 14.2

```
Function adhGetAccount(ByVal strName As String) As Integer

    Dim wrk As Workspace
    Dim varAccntName As Variant

    Set wrk = DBEngine.Workspaces(0)
```

```
'Turn off error handling and check line by line
'to determine account membership
On Error Resume Next

varAccntName = wrk.Users(strName).Name
If Err = adhcErrNameNotInCollection Then
    'Reset error variable
    Err = 0
    varAccntName = wrk.Groups(strName).Name
    If Err = adhcErrNameNotInCollection Then
        adhGetAccount = adhcAccntNone
    Else
        adhGetAccount = adhcAccntGroup
    End If
Else
    adhGetAccount = adhcAccntUser
End If

End Function
```

adhGetAccount works by attempting to grab the name of a user account with the passed name. If error 3265 (adhcErrNameNotInCollection) occurs because the user account doesn't exist, adhGetAccount resumes and attempts to grab the name of a group account with the same name. If both attempts fail, the function returns 0. This function *doesn't* require the user running it to be a member of the Admins group.

Checking for Group Membership

You can check whether a user is a member of a group using adhIsGroupMember. This function takes as its input the name of the user and the group and returns True if the user is a member. adhIsGroupMember is shown in Listing 14.3.

Listing 14.3

```
Function adhIsGroupMember(ByVal strGroup As String, _
  Optional ByVal varUser As Variant) As Boolean

    On Error GoTo adhIsGroupMemberErr

    Dim wrk As Workspace
    Dim usr As User
    Dim grp As Group
    Dim strMsg As String
```

```
        Dim intErrHndlrFlag As Integer
        Dim varGroupName As Variant

        Const adhcFlagSetUser = 1
        Const adhcFlagSetGroup = 2
        Const adhcFlagCheckMember = 4
        Const adhcFlagElse = 0

        Const adhcProcName = "adhIsGroupMember"

        adhIsGroupMember = False

        'Initialize flag for determining
        'context for error handler
        intErrHndlrFlag = adhcFlagElse

        Set wrk = DBEngine.Workspaces(0)

        'Refresh users and groups collections
        wrk.Users.Refresh
        wrk.Groups.Refresh

        If IsMissing(varUser) Then varUser = CurrentUser()

        intErrHndlrFlag = adhcFlagSetUser
        Set usr = wrk.Users(varUser)

        intErrHndlrFlag = adhcFlagSetGroup
        Set grp = wrk.Groups(strGroup)

        intErrHndlrFlag = adhcFlagCheckMember
        varGroupName = usr.Groups(strGroup).Name

        If Not IsEmpty(varGroupName) Then
            adhIsGroupMember = True
        End If

adhIsGroupMemberDone:
    On Error GoTo 0
    Exit Function

adhIsGroupMemberErr:
```

```
      Select Case Err
      Case adhcErrNameNotInCollection
          Select Case intErrHndlrFlag
          Case adhcFlagSetUser
              strMsg = "The user account '" & varUser & _
                "' doesn't exist."
          Case adhcFlagSetGroup
              strMsg = "The group account '" & strGroup & _
                "' doesn't exist."
          Case adhcFlagCheckMember
              Resume Next
          Case Else
              strMsg = "Error " & Err.Number & ": " & _
                Err.Description
          End Select
      Case adhcErrNoPermission
          strMsg = "You don't have permission to perform " & _
            "this operation."
      Case Else
          strMsg = "Error " & Err.Number & ": " & Err.Description
      End Select
          MsgBox strMsg, vbCritical + vbOKOnly, "Procedure " & _
            adhcProcName
      Resume adhIsGroupMemberDone

End Function
```

This function checks for membership using the following statement:

```
varGroupName = usr.Groups(strGroup).Name
```

This statement attempts to set a variable to the Name property of the group object in the Groups collection of the user object. There's nothing special here about the Name property; any readable property of the group object would suffice. (With that said, however, you'll find that Name *is* the only readable property of a group or user object.) Because of the symmetry of the Users and Groups collections, adhIsGroupMember could have also checked for the name of the user object in the Users collection of the group object. The following alternate statement would yield the same result:

```
varUserName = grp.Users(strUser).Name
```

adhIsGroupMember *doesn't* require the user running it to be a member of the Admins group.

Adding a User to a Group

Members of the Admins group can use adhAddGroupMember to add a user to a group. This function takes as its input the name of the user to be added and the name of the group. It returns True if it succeeds. adhAddGroupMember is shown in Listing 14.4.

Listing 14.4

```
Function adhAddGroupMember(ByVal strUser As String, _
 ByVal strGroup As String) As Boolean

    On Error GoTo adhAddGroupMemberErr

    Dim wrk As Workspace
    Dim usr As User
    Dim grp As Group
    Dim strMsg As String
    Dim intErrHndlrFlag As Integer

    Const adhcFlagSetUser = 1
    Const adhcFlagSetGroup = 2
    Const adhcFlagElse = 0

    Const adhcProcName = "adhAddGroupMember"

    adhAddGroupMember = False

    'Initialize flag for determining
    'context for error handler
    intErrHndlrFlag = adhcFlagElse

    Set wrk = DBEngine.Workspaces(0)

    'Refresh users and groups collections
    wrk.Users.Refresh
    wrk.Groups.Refresh

    intErrHndlrFlag = adhcFlagSetUser
    Set usr = wrk.Users(strUser)

    intErrHndlrFlag = adhcFlagSetGroup
```

```
        Set grp = wrk.Groups(strGroup)

        intErrHndlrFlag = adhcFlagElse

        'Report error if user already a member of this group
        If adhIsGroupMember(strGroup, strUser) Then
            strMsg = "The user account '" & strUser & _
             "' is already a member of the group " & strGroup & "."
            MsgBox strMsg, vbCritical + vbOKOnly, "Procedure " & _
             adhcProcName
            GoTo adhAddGroupMemberDone
        End If

        'Append user to group
        grp.Users.Append grp.CreateUser(strUser)

        adhAddGroupMember = True

adhAddGroupMemberDone:
    On Error GoTo 0
    Exit Function

adhAddGroupMemberErr:
    Select Case Err
    Case adhcErrNameNotInCollection
        Select Case intErrHndlrFlag
        Case adhcFlagSetUser
            strMsg = "The user account '" & strUser & _
             "' doesn't exist."
        Case adhcFlagSetGroup
            strMsg = "The group account '" & strGroup & _
             "' doesn't exist."
        Case Else
            strMsg = "Error " & Err.Number & ": " & _
             Err.Description
        End Select
    Case adhcErrCantPerformOperation
        strMsg = "The user account '" & strUser & _
         "' is already a member of the group " & strGroup & "."
    Case adhcErrNoPermission
        strMsg = "You don't have permission to perform " & _
         "this operation."
    Case Else
```

```
        strMsg = "Error " & Err.Number & ": " & Err.Description
    End Select
        MsgBox strMsg, vbCritical + vbOKOnly, "Procedure " & _
          adhcProcName
    Resume adhAddGroupMemberDone

End Function
```

This function, as well as several others in the basSecurityUtilities module, uses a flag, intErrHndlrFlag, to declare a state before executing a statement that may cause an error. The functions use this flag to give the user better feedback when an error occurs. adhAddGroupMember, for example, uses this flag to replace a nonspecific missing account message for error 3265 (adhcErrNameNotInCollection) with a message that informs the user whether the nonexistent account is the passed user or group account.

adhAddGroupMember refreshes the workspace's collections before checking for membership in case anyone has altered the group membership recently. (Otherwise, any recent changes made in the Access UI or by another user in the workgroup would not be included.) It then checks for the existence of the user and group accounts and whether the user is already a member of the group (using adhIsGroupMember). If any of these checks turns up an error, adhAddGroupMember displays a dialog and exits. Otherwise, the CreateUser method is used to append the user to the group.

Changing Passwords

You can use adhSetPwd to change the password for either the current logged-in user or for another user's account. If you choose the latter, you must be a member of the Admins group. You pass adhSetPwd the name of the account, the old password, and the new password. This function can be found in Listing 14.5.

Listing 14.5

```
Function adhSetPwd(ByVal strUser As String, _
 ByVal strOldPwd As String, ByVal strNewPwd As String) _
 As Boolean

    On Error GoTo adhSetPwdErr

    Dim wrk As Workspace
    Dim usr As User
    Dim strMsg As String
```

```
        Const adhcProcName = "adhSetPwd"

        adhSetPwd = False

        Set wrk = DBEngine.Workspaces(0)

        'Point to user object
        Set usr = wrk.Users(strUser)

        'Only Admins members can change other users' passwords
        'For Admins members, old pwd is ignored
        usr.NewPassword strOldPwd, strNewPwd

        adhSetPwd = True

adhSetPwdDone:
    On Error GoTo 0
    Exit Function

adhSetPwdErr:
    Select Case Err
    Case adhcErrNameNotInCollection
        strMsg = "The user account '" & strUser & _
        "' doesn't exist."
    Case adhcErrNoPermission
        strMsg = "You don't have permission to perform " & _
        "this operation or you have entered the wrong " & _
        "old password."
    Case Else
        strMsg = "Error " & Err.Number & ": " & Err.Description
    End Select
        MsgBox strMsg, vbCritical + vbOKOnly, "Procedure " & _
        adhcProcName
    Resume adhSetPwdDone

End Function
```

adhSetPwd uses the NewPassword method of the user object. When you use this method, you are required to enter the correct old password if the account is the same as the value of CurrentUser; otherwise you don't have to enter the old password—the string is ignored. This behavior is consistent with the Access UI, where you can clear someone else's password. The difference is that with

DAO, you can both clear the password and set it to a new nonblank value in one step. (Of course, you have to be an Admins member to change the password of another user.)

The frmChangePwd form in CH14.MDB allows users to change passwords (see Figure 14.9). The event procedure attached to the Change Password command button calls adhSetPwd after ensuring that the password was verified properly. This procedure is shown in Listing 14.6.

FIGURE 14.9

frmChangePwd calls adhSetPwd to set a user's password

Listing 14.6

```
Private Sub cmdPwd_Click()

    Dim fOK As Boolean
    Dim ctlOldPwd As TextBox
    Dim ctlNewPwd As TextBox
    Dim ctlConfirmNewPwd As TextBox
    Dim strMsg As String

    Set ctlOldPwd = Me!txtOldPwd
    Set ctlNewPwd = Me!txtNewPwd
    Set ctlConfirmNewPwd = Me!txtConfirmNewPwd

' Perform a binary string comparison of the password
    ' and the confirmation password.
    If StrComp(Nz(ctlNewPwd), Nz(ctlConfirmNewPwd), _
    vbBinaryCompare) = 0 Then
        fOK = adhSetPwd(strUser:=cboUsers, _
        strOldPwd:=Nz(ctlOldPwd), _
        strNewPwd:=Nz(ctlNewPwd))
        If fOK Then
            strMsg = "Password changed!"
            ctlOldPwd = ""
```

```
            ctlNewPwd = ""
            ctlConfirmNewPwd = ""
        Else
            strMsg = "Password change failed!"
        End If
    Else
        strMsg = "New password entry does not match " & _
          "confirming password entry!"
    End If

    MsgBox strMsg, vbOKOnly + vbInformation, _
      "Change Password"

End Sub
```

The frmChangePwd form includes a combo box that allows Admins members to directly set the password for other users. The combo box is filled using a list-filling function. The list-filling function's initialization step, which fills an array with all users in the workgroup, is shown here:

```
sintUsrCnt = 0
swrk.Users.Refresh
ReDim sastrUsr(1 To swrk.Users.Count)
For Each usr In swrk.Users
    strName = usr.Name
    If strName <> "Engine" And strName <> "Creator" Then
        sintUsrCnt = sintUsrCnt + 1
        sastrUsr(sintUsrCnt) = strName
    End If
Next usr
ReDim Preserve sastrUsr(1 To sintUsrCnt)
```

Jet defines two built-in, but normally hidden, users—Creator and Engine—that have, or more likely just appear to have, blank passwords. (For those of you who are immediately thinking "security hole," there's no need to worry; even though these Jet-defined users appear in the Users collection, you cannot use them to log on to Access.) In any case, the adhcboUsersFill list-filling function skips over them. (See Chapter 7 for more details on list-filling functions.)

An event procedure attached to the form's Load event determines whether the current user is a member of Admins by calling adhIsGroupMember:

```
If Not adhIsGroupMember("Admins") Then
    With Me!cboUsers
```

```
        .Locked = True
        .Enabled = False
    End With
End If
```

This code ensures that the combo box is disabled if the user is not a member of Admins. Non-Admins members, however, can still use this form to change their own user password.

Listing All Users with Blank Passwords

A user account with blank passwords is the Achilles' heel of a supposedly secure workgroup. Using the Access UI, there's no way for a database administrator to quickly determine which users have left their passwords blank. Using DAO, however, you can accomplish this easily. We have written such a function, adhListUsers-WithBlankPwd, which is included in the basSecurityUtilities module. The essence of the function is shown here:

```
For Each usr In wrkDefault.Users
    strUser = usr.Name

    'Skip if special engine-level users
    If strUser <> "Creator" And strUser <> "Engine" Then
        'Initialize flag that tracks blank Pwd
        fNonBlankPwd = False

        'Attempt to log on to new workspace with blank Pwd
        Set wrkNew = DBEngine. _
         CreateWorkspace("NewWorkspace", strUser, "")

        'If an error occurred on last statement, then
        'error handler will set flag to True.
        'Otherwise, able to log on, so Pwd must've been blank.
        If Not fNonBlankPwd Then
            Print #1, strUser
            fAnyBlankPwds = True
        End If
    End If
Next usr
```

adhUsersWithBlankPW works by iterating through the Users collection in the default workspace and attempting to log on to each account using a blank password. If it is able to log on to an account, it prints the user name to a file.

Other Account Maintenance Functions

There are two other account maintenance functions in basSecurityUtilities. You can use adhDeleteAccount to delete a user or group account and adhRemove-GroupMember to remove a user from a group.

Programming Permissions

Permissions are properties of *documents* and their *containers*. Like other DAO collections, the Containers collection and Documents collection have a single property, Count, that indicates the number of objects in the collection. These two collections also have a single method, Refresh, you can use to make sure the collections are current.

Containers and Documents

Container and document objects (which were introduced in Chapter 6) have several properties. They are listed in Table 14.8.

TABLE 14.8 Properties of Containers and Their Documents

Object	Property	Description
Container	Inherit	Determines whether any changes are inherited by new objects. If you set permissions on a container and set Inherit to True, Jet uses these permissions when creating new documents for the container
	Name	Read-only. The name of the container. For example, the Tables container contains a database's tables and queries
	Owner	Read/write. The user or group account that owns the object. By default, all object containers are owned by the engine user (This can be changed, however, using DAO.)
	Permissions	Read/write. A Long Integer that stores explicit permission information for the container. When you use this property with the Inherit property, you can set permissions for new documents of a container
	AllPermissions	Read-only. A Long Integer that stores the union of explicit and implicit permission information for the container
	UserName	Read/write. When you read or write permissions for a container, the permissions are account specific. By default, this property points to the current user. You use UserName to view or set permissions for different user and group accounts

TABLE 14.8   Properties of Containers and Their Documents (continued)

Object	Property	Description
Document	Container	Read-only. The container to which the document belongs
	DateCreated	Read-only. The date the document was created
	LastUpdated	Read-only. The date the document's schema was last changed
	Name	Read-only. The name of the document
	Owner	Read/write. The user or group account that owns the object. By default, the owner is the document's creator
	Permissions	Read/write. A Long Integer that stores explicit permission information for the document
	AllPermissions	Read-only. A Long Integer that stores the union of explicit and implicit permission information for the document
	UserName	Read/write. When you read or write permissions for a document, the permissions are account specific. By default, this property points to the current user. You can use UserName to view or set permissions for different user and group accounts

Permission Constants

Microsoft predefines several database security constants you can use to simplify the reading and writing of permissions. These constants are outlined in Table 14.9. They also can be viewed with the Object Browser. The use of these constants is discussed in the next few sections.

TABLE 14.9   Jet and Access Security Constants

Constant	Meaning
dbSecNoAccess	No access to the object
dbSecFullAccess	Full access to the object
dbSecDelete	Can delete the object
dbSecReadSec	Can read the object's security-related information
dbSecWriteSec	Can alter access permissions

TABLE 14.9   Jet and Access Security Constants (continued)

Constant	Meaning
dbSecWriteOwner	Can change the Owner property setting
dbSecCreate	Can create new documents; valid only with a Container object
dbSecReadDef	Can read the table definition, including column and index information
dbSecWriteDef	Can modify or delete the table definition, including column and index information
dbSecRetrieveData	Can retrieve data from the Document object
dbSecInsertData	Can add records
dbSecReplaceData	Can modify records
dbSecDeleteData	Can delete records
dbSecDBAdmin	Gives user permission to make a database replicable, change the database password, and set startup properties
dbSecDBCreate	Can create new databases; valid only on the Databases container object in the workgroup file (SYSTEM.MDW)
dbSecDBExclusive	Can open the database exclusively
dbSecDBOpen	Can open the database
acSecMacExecute	Can run the macro
acSecMacReadDef	Can read the definition of the macro
acSecMacWriteDef	Can modify the definition of the macro
acSecFrmRptExecute	Can open the form or report
acSecFrmRptReadDef	Can read the definition of the form or report and its module
acSecFrmRptWriteDef	Can modify the definition of the form or report and its module
acSecModReadDef	Can read the definition of the global module
acSecModWriteDef	Can modify the definition of the global module

Reading Permissions

You can read the permissions of an object simply by checking the value of the Permissions or AllPermissions property of the object. Permissions returns explicit permissions only, whereas AllPermissions returns the union of explicit and implicit permissions. They both return the Long Integer corresponding to the user's permissions for the object. For example, you could query the permission of the tblOrder table and store the value into the variable lngPermission with the following assignment statement (assuming you have previously set the db object variable to point to a database):

```
lngPermission = _
    db.Containers!Tables.Documents!tblOrder.Permissions
```

Often, you'll want to check whether a user has some minimum permissions to an object. You can do this using bitwise arithmetic (also referred to as *bit twiddling*). This works because Jet stores each individual permission as a different bit of the 4-byte Long Integer value. You check a permission value for a specific set of bits—some permissions are actually the result of setting several bits—by using the And operator to mask off the bits in which you are interested and comparing the result of the operation to these same bits. Using the predefined permission constants makes this easy:

```
fOk = ((doc.Permissions And dbSecConstant) = dbSecConstant)
```

fOk will be set to True if the document object has that permission—as defined by dbSecConstant—set to True, and False if the document object does not.

For example, you could use the following function to determine whether the user Kizzie has read permission for tblCustomer:

```
Function CanKizzieRead() As Boolean

    ' Checks explicit permissions only

    Dim db As Database
    Dim doc As Document

    Set db = CurrentDb()
    Set doc = db.Containers!Tables.Documents!tblCustomer

    doc.UserName = "Kizzie"

    CanKizzieRead = _
      ((doc.Permissions And dbSecRetrieveData) _
```

```
              = dbSecRetrieveData)

End Function
```

If Kizzie has ReadData permission to tblCustomer, CanKizzieRead returns True; otherwise it returns False. The trick in this example is to use the bitwise And operator to mask off the complete permissions with only the permission you are interested in—in this case, dbSecRetrieveData (ReadData permission).

CanKizzieRead checks only for explicit permissions. We could have also checked Kizzie's implicit permissions by replacing the last part of the function with:

```
CanKizzieRead = _
 ((doc.AllPermissions And dbSecRetrieveData) _
 = dbSecRetrieveData)
```

There's another way to check a permission value against a constant that works *only* if one bit is set on in the constant:

```
fOk = (doc.Permissions And dbSecConstant) <> 0
```

This method, however, will *fail* with constants that have more than one bit set. Thus, because many of the security constants have multiple bits set, you shouldn't use it.

Writing Permissions

Writing permissions is similar to reading them. You have two choices when writing the permissions of an object:

- You can replace the existing permissions with a brand-new set of permissions.

- You can add or subtract a permission on top of the existing permissions.

To *replace* a set of permissions, you simply set the permissions to the new value. For example, you could change the permission for tblOrder to give the user ModifyDesign permission using the following code:

```
Set doc = db.Containers!Tables.Documents!tblOrder
doc.Permissions = dbSecWriteDef
```

To *add* a permission on top of the existing permission set, you use the bitwise Or operator. For example, you could use the following code to add ModifyDesign permission to the existing set of permissions for tblOrder:

```
Set doc = db.Containers!Tables.Documents!tblOrder
doc.Permissions = doc.Permissions Or dbSecWriteDef
```

Using this method of assigning permissions is often preferable because it guards against inadvertently removing other permissions the user may have. For example, if the user also had ReadData permission to tblOrder, that permission would be preserved using this technique. This would not be true in the previous example.

To *subtract* a permission from a user while preserving all other permissions, you use the bitwise And Not operator. For example, to take away the same permission from a user, replace the second line in the preceding example with the following:

```
doc.Permissions = doc.Permissions And Not dbSecWriteDef
```

Checking for a Specific Permission

You can use adhCheckPermission to check whether a user or group account has some permission bit (or multiple bits) set on. It takes these five parameters:

Parameter	Optional?	Purpose
lngPerm	No	Permission value of the object you wish to check
intObjType	No	One of the adhcObj constants (adhcObjDatabase, adhcObjForm, adhcObjModule, adhcObjReport, adhcObjScript, or adhcObjTable) defined in the declarations section of basSecurityUtilities to indicate the type of object to check
varObjName	Yes	Name of the document object to check; leave Null to check the document container
varAccount	Yes	Name of the user or group account to check; leave null to check permission for the current user
fAllPerm	Yes	For user accounts, set to True (the default) to check both explicit and implicit permissions; set to False to check only explicit permissions; for group accounts, this parameter has no effect

adhCheckPermission returns True if the account has the requested permission to the object. It's shown in Listing 14.7.

Listing 14.7

```
Function adhCheckPermission(ByVal lngPerm As Long, _
 ByVal intObjType As Integer, _
 Optional ByVal varObjName As Variant, _
 Optional ByVal varAccount As Variant, _
 Optional ByVal fAllPerm As Variant) As Boolean

    On Error GoTo adhCheckPermissionErr

    Dim wrk As Workspace
    Dim db As Database
    Dim cnt As Container
    Dim doc As Document
    Dim usr As User
    Dim strMsg As String
    Dim fPerm As Boolean
    Dim intErrHndlrFlag As Integer

    Const adhcFlagSetContainer = 5
    Const adhcFlagSetDocument = 6
    Const adhcFlagElse = 0

    Const adhcProcName = "adhCheckPermission"

    adhCheckPermission = False

    'Initialize flag for determining
    'context for error handler
    intErrHndlrFlag = adhcFlagElse

    'Optional parameters
    If IsMissing(varAccount) Then varAccount = CurrentUser()
    If IsMissing(fAllPerm) Then fAllPerm = True

    Set wrk = DBEngine.Workspaces(0)
    Set db = CurrentDb()

    'If setting permissions for database, you
    'actually need to use the MSysDB document
    If intObjType = adhcObjDatabase Then
        varObjName = "MSysDB"
    End If
```

```
        'Point to the right container
        intErrHndlrFlag = adhcFlagSetContainer
        Set cnt = db.Containers(intObjType)
        intErrHndlrFlag = adhcFlagElse

        'Refresh the container's docs
        cnt.Documents.Refresh

        intErrHndlrFlag = adhcFlagElse

        cnt.UserName = varAccount

        'Only point to a document if the name is non-blank
        If Len(varObjName) > 0 Then
            intErrHndlrFlag = adhcFlagSetDocument
            Set doc = cnt.Documents(varObjName)
            intErrHndlrFlag = adhcFlagElse
            doc.UserName = varAccount
        End If

        'Initialize permission flag
        fPerm = False

        If IsMissing(varObjName) Then
            If fAllPerm Then
                fPerm = ((cnt.AllPermissions And lngPerm) = lngPerm)
            Else
                fPerm = ((cnt.Permissions And lngPerm) = lngPerm)
            End If
        Else
            If fAllPerm Then
                fPerm = ((doc.AllPermissions And lngPerm) = lngPerm)
            Else
                fPerm = ((doc.Permissions And lngPerm) = lngPerm)
            End If
        End If

        adhCheckPermission = fPerm

adhCheckPermissionDone:
    On Error GoTo 0
    Exit Function
```

```
adhCheckPermissionErr:
    Select Case Err
    Case adhcErrNoPermission
        strMsg = "You don't have permission to perform " & _
        "this operation."
    Case adhcErrNameNotInCollection
        Select Case intErrHndlrFlag
        Case adhcFlagSetContainer
            strMsg = "Invalid object type constant."
        Case adhcFlagSetDocument
            strMsg = "The object '" & varObjName & _
            "' is not in the '" & intObjType & "' collection."
        Case Else
            strMsg = "Error " & Err.Number & ": " & _
            Err.Description
        End Select
    Case Else
        strMsg = "Error " & Err.Number & ": " & Err.Description
    End Select
        MsgBox strMsg, vbCritical + vbOKOnly, "Procedure " & _
        adhcProcName
    Resume adhCheckPermissionDone

End Function
```

adhCheckPermission, along with many other permission functions found in basSecurityUtilities, is flexible in that it allows you to query the permissions on a document object (for example, qryItems), a container (for example, Modules), or the database itself.

If you pass adhCheckPermission a non-null value for varObjName, it determines the permissions for that document.

If, instead, you pass the function a null varObjName parameter and one of the object constants for the parameter intObjType, it determines the permissions for the container itself. This is equivalent to determining the permissions for any newly created object.

If you pass the function a null varObjName parameter and the adhcObjDatabase constant for the intObjType parameter, adhCheckPermission determines the permissions for the database itself. adhCheckPermission accomplishes this by using a special document of the database container, MSysDB.

adhCheckPermission then sets the UserName property for the container object to the account name passed to it or, if a null account name was passed, to the current user.

If adhCheckPermission needs to check the permissions of a document, it sets the document object, doc, to point to the name of that object and also sets the User-Name property for the document.

Finally, adhCheckPermission uses the bitwise And operator to mask off the complete permissions with the value of the lngPerm parameter (the permission you wish to check). The following code accomplishes this for a document:

```
fPerm = ((doc.Permissions And lngPerm) = lngPerm)
```

Setting Permissions

You can add permissions to, subtract permissions from, or completely replace the permission value of an object for a user or group account using adhSetPermission. This function takes five parameters:

Parameter	Optional?	Purpose
lngPerm	No	Permission value of the object you wish to set
intObjType	No	One of the adhcObj constants (adhcObjDatabase, adhcObjForm, adhcObjModule, adhcObjReport, adhcObjScript, or adhcObjTable) defined in the declarations section of basSecurityUtilities to indicate the type of object to set
intAction	No	One of the adhcPermission constants (adhcPermissionAdd, adhcPermissionSubtract, or adhcPermissionReplace) defined in the declarations section of basSecurityUtilities to indicate the type of action to take
varObjName	Yes	Name of the document object to check; leave null to check the document container
varAccount	Yes	Name of the user or group account; leave null to set permission for the current user

adhSetPermission returns True if it succeeds in changing the permission. It's shown in Listing 14.8.

Listing 14.8

```
Function adhSetPermission(ByVal lngPerm As Long, _
 ByVal intObjType As Integer, _
 ByVal intAction As Integer, _
 Optional ByVal varObjName As Variant, _
 Optional ByVal varAccount As Variant) As Boolean

    On Error GoTo adhSetPermissionErr

    Dim db As Database
    Dim cnt As Container
    Dim doc As Document
    Dim strMsg As String
    Dim intErrHndlrFlag As Integer

    Const adhcFlagSetContainer = 5
    Const adhcFlagSetDocument = 6
    Const adhcFlagElse = 0

    Const adhcProcName = "adhSetPermission"

    adhSetPermission = False

    'Initialize flag for determining
    'context for error handler
    intErrHndlrFlag = adhcFlagElse

    'Optional parameters
    If IsMissing(varAccount) Then varAccount = CurrentUser()

    If intAction < adhcPermissionSubtract Or _
     intAction > adhcPermissionReplace Then
        strMsg = "Illegal intAction parameter."
        MsgBox strMsg, vbOKOnly + vbCritical, _
         "Procedure: " & adhcProcName
        GoTo adhSetPermissionDone
    End If

    Set db = CurrentDb()
```

```
'If setting permissions for database, you
'actually need to use the MSysDB document
If intObjType = adhcObjDatabase Then
    varObjName = "MSysDB"
End If


intErrHndlrFlag = adhcFlagSetContainer
Set cnt = db.Containers(intObjType)
intErrHndlrFlag = adhcFlagElse

'Refresh the container's docs
cnt.Documents.Refresh
'Set the container's inherit property so that
'any changes to it are inherited by new docs
cnt.Inherit = True
cnt.UserName = varAccount

'Only point to a document if the name is non-blank
If Not IsMissing(varObjName) Then
    intErrHndlrFlag = adhcFlagSetDocument
    Set doc = cnt.Documents(varObjName)
    intErrHndlrFlag = adhcFlagElse
    doc.UserName = varAccount
End If

'Overlay new permissions on top of the existing ones.
'Use Or to add permission; And Not to subtract permission.
If IsMissing(varObjName) Then
    If intAction = adhcPermissionAdd Then
        cnt.Permissions = cnt.Permissions Or lngPerm
    ElseIf intAction = adhcPermissionSubtract Then
        cnt.Permissions = cnt.Permissions And Not lngPerm
    Else
        cnt.Permissions = lngPerm
    End If
Else
    If intAction = adhcPermissionAdd Then
        doc.Permissions = doc.Permissions Or lngPerm
    ElseIf intAction = adhcPermissionSubtract Then
        doc.Permissions = doc.Permissions And Not lngPerm
    Else
        doc.Permissions = lngPerm
    End If
```

```
        End If

        adhSetPermission = True

adhSetPermissionDone:
    On Error GoTo 0
    Exit Function

adhSetPermissionErr:
    Select Case Err
    Case adhcErrNoPermission
        adhSetPermission = False
        Resume adhSetPermissionDone
    Case adhcErrNameNotInCollection
        Select Case intErrHndlrFlag
        Case adhcFlagSetContainer
            strMsg = "Invalid object type constant."
        Case adhcFlagSetDocument
            strMsg = "The object '" & varObjName & _
                "' is not in the '" & intObjType & "' collection."
        Case Else
            strMsg = "Error " & Err.Number & ": " & _
                Err.Description
        End Select
    Case adhcErrBadAccntName
        strMsg = "The account '" & varAccount & _
            "' doesn't exist."
    Case Else
        strMsg = "Error " & Err.Number & ": " & Err.Description
    End Select
        MsgBox strMsg, vbCritical + vbOKOnly, "Procedure " & _
            adhcProcName
    Resume adhSetPermissionDone

End Function
```

adhSetPermission works similarly to adhGetPermission. The major difference is that instead of getting the existing permission value, it adds, subtracts, or replaces the permission value for the object using the following code (for document objects):

```
If intAction = adhcPermissionAdd Then
    doc.Permissions = doc.Permissions Or lngPerm
ElseIf intAction = adhcPermissionSubtract Then
```

```
     doc.Permissions = doc.Permissions And Not lngPerm
Else
     doc.Permissions = lngPerm
End If
```

Because we've overloaded adhSetPermission with functionality, we've also provided several wrapper functions you can call instead, all of which do their work by calling adhSetPermission():

Function	Purpose
adhSetPermissionAdd	Adds a particular permission
adhSetPermissionSubtract	Subtracts a particular permission
adhSetPermissionReplace	Replaces a permission value with another
adhSetPermissionDocCreate	Enables or disables the ability of an account to create documents of a particular type

The last function, adhSetPermissionDocCreate, disables (or enables) the ability of a user to create a particular type of object by subtracting (or adding back) the dbSecCreate bit (&H1) of the permission property of the document's container. (If you use this function to remove the dbSecCreate permission of a user, you'll also want to make sure the user doesn't have implicit dbSecCreate permission by virtue of group membership.)

Disabling the Creation of New Databases

Jet includes a permission, dbSecDBCreate, that is not exposed by the Access UI. However, you can set this permission of the Databases container of the workgroup file (typically, SYSTEM.MDW) using DAO. The function adhSetDbCreate does just this. You pass it the name of the user or group account and a Boolean parameter that you set to False to disable database creation and True to reenable. Passing a False parameter will prevent the user or group account from being able to create new databases. (If you use this function to disable the dbSecDBCreate permission of a user, you'll want to make sure the user doesn't have implicit dbSecDBCreate permission.) adhSetDbCreate is shown in Listing 14.9.

Listing 14.9

```
Function adhSetDbCreate(ByVal strAccount As String, _
ByVal fEnable As Boolean) As Boolean

    On Error GoTo adhSetDbCreateErr

    Dim strSystemDB As String
    Dim dbSys As Database
    Dim cnt As Container
    Dim strMsg As String

    Const adhcProcName = "adhSetDbCreate"

    adhSetDbCreate = False

    strSystemDB = SysCmd(acSysCmdGetWorkgroupFile)

    Set dbSys = DBEngine.Workspaces(0).OpenDatabase(strSystemDB)
    Set cnt = dbSys.Containers!Databases
    cnt.UserName = strAccount

    'Turn on or off the permission to create new databases
    If fEnable Then
        cnt.Permissions = cnt.Permissions Or dbSecDBCreate
    Else
        cnt.Permissions = cnt.Permissions And Not dbSecDBCreate
    End If

    adhSetDbCreate = True

adhSetDbCreateDone:
    If Not dbSys Is Nothing Then dbSys.Close
    On Error GoTo 0
    Exit Function

adhSetDbCreateErr:
    Select Case Err
    Case adhcErrNoPermission
        adhSetDbCreate = False
        Resume adhSetDbCreateDone
    Case adhcErrNameNotInCollection
```

```
            strMsg = "The account '" & strAccount & _
            "' doesn't exist."
        Case Else
            strMsg = "Error " & Err.Number & ": " & Err.Description
        End Select
            MsgBox strMsg, vbCritical + vbOKOnly, "Procedure " & _
            adhcProcName
        Resume adhSetDbCreateDone

End Function
```

This function is analogous to adhSetPermission, except that it works on the Databases container of the *workgroup* file. To determine the name of the workgroup file, adhSetDbCreate uses the Access SysCmd function, passing it the acSysCmdGetWorkgroupFile constant.

Once the location of SystemDB has been determined, adhSetDbCreate creates a database object to point to it with the following Set statement:

```
Set dbSys = DBEngine.Workspaces(0).OpenDatabase(strSystemDB)
```

The permission is then set using this If…Then…Else statement:

```
If fEnable Then
    cnt.Permissions = cnt.Permissions Or dbSecDBCreate
Else
    cnt.Permissions = cnt.Permissions And Not dbSecDBCreate
End If
```

Changing Object Ownership

You can use the adhSetOwner function to change the name of the owner of an object. It takes as its parameters the object type, the name of the object, and the name of the new owner. It returns True if it succeeds.

adhSetOwner requires the current user to be either the owner of the object or a member of the Admins group.

You won't be able to change the owner of any OwnerAccess queries in the database. You must temporarily change the queries to non-OwnerAccess queries before using this function. (See the section "OwnerAccess Queries" earlier in this chapter for more details.) adhSetOwner is shown in Listing 14.10.

Listing 14.10

```
Function adhSetOwner(ByVal strNewOwner As String, _
 ByVal intObjType As Integer, Optional ByVal varObjName As _
 Variant) As Boolean

    On Error GoTo adhSetOwnerErr

    Dim db As Database
    Dim cnt As Container
    Dim doc As Document
    Dim strMsg As String
    Dim intErrHndlrFlag As Integer

    Const adhcFlagSetContainer = 5
    Const adhcFlagSetDocument = 6
    Const adhcFlagElse = 0

    Const adhcProcName = "adhSetOwner"

    adhSetOwner = False

    'Initialize flag for determining
    'context for error handler
    intErrHndlrFlag = adhcFlagElse

    Set db = CurrentDb()

    'Can't change owner of database
    If intObjType = adhcObjDatabase Then
        strMsg = "Can't change owner of database."
        MsgBox strMsg, vbOKOnly + vbCritical, _
          "Procedure: " & adhcProcName
        GoTo adhSetOwnerDone
    Else

    'Point to the right container
    intErrHndlrFlag = adhcFlagSetContainer
    Set cnt = db.Containers(intObjType)
    intErrHndlrFlag = adhcFlagElse

    'Refresh the container's docs
```

```
        cnt.Documents.Refresh

        'Set ownership on a document or a container
        If IsMissing(varObjName) Then
            cnt.Owner = strNewOwner
        Else
            intErrHndlrFlag = adhcFlagSetDocument
            Set doc = cnt.Documents(varObjName)
            intErrHndlrFlag = adhcFlagElse
            doc.Owner = strNewOwner
        End If

        adhSetOwner = True

    End If

adhSetOwnerDone:
    On Error GoTo 0
    Exit Function

adhSetOwnerErr:
    Select Case Err
    Case adhcErrNoPermission
        strMsg = "You don't have permission to perform " & _
            "this operation."
    Case adhcErrNameNotInCollection
        Select Case intErrHndlrFlag
        Case adhcFlagSetContainer
            strMsg = "Invalid object type constant."
        Case adhcFlagSetDocument
            strMsg = "The object '" & varObjName & _
                "' is not in the '" & intObjType & _
                "' collection."
        Case Else
            strMsg = "Error " & Err.Number & ": " & _
                Err.Description
        End Select
    Case adhcErrBadAccntName
        strMsg = "The account '" & strNewOwner & _
            "' doesn't exist."
    Case Else
        strMsg = "Error " & Err.Number & ": " & _
            Err.Description
```

```
      End Select
          MsgBox strMsg, vbCritical + vbOKOnly, _
            "Procedure " & adhcProcName
      Resume adhSetOwnerDone

End Function
```

adhSetOwner works by manipulating the Owner property of the object, as shown here for a document object:

```
doc.Owner = strNewOwner
```

basSecurityUtilities also includes a function, adhGetObjectOwner, you can use to get the name of an object's owner.

Properly Securing a Database with the Access Security Wizard

Securing a database properly takes great care. It's very easy to make a mistake and leave yourself open to possible security intrusions. Fortunately, Microsoft has created a Wizard that ships with Access to help secure databases properly. Using the Security Wizard, however, does not automatically guarantee a secure database; the Wizard is only one step in a series of steps you must follow to properly secure a database:

1. Use the Workgroup Administrator program (WRKGADM.EXE) to create a new workgroup with a non-null Workgroup ID.

2. Start Access and create a password for the Admin account.

3. Create a new user account that will be the administrator of the workgroup.

4. Add the new account to the Admins group.

5. Remove the Admin account from the Admins group.

6. Restart Access, logging on as the new administrator user, and create a password for this account.

7. Select Tools ➤ Security ➤ User-Level Security Wizard to run the Security Wizard.

8. Create the group accounts for your workgroup.

9. Create the user accounts for your workgroup, adding each user to the appropriate groups.

10. Set permissions on objects for the group accounts. If you wish to reduce permission maintenance, don't set any permissions for individual users.

11. (Optional) For the appropriate groups, set object permissions for the Database object and use the adhSetPermissionDocCreate and adhSetDbCreate functions to disable the ability to create objects and databases, respectively, as needed.

WARNING Don't skip any steps—except the optional step 11—or you run the risk of thinking you have a secured database when you do not.

Figure 14.10 shows the Access 97 Security Wizard's opening screen. You must be a member of the Admins group to run the Wizard. The Security Wizard works by performing a number of steps, including the following:

1. It creates a new copy of the database that is owned by the user running the Wizard (who must be a member of the Admins group and cannot be the Admin user).

2. It exports all objects to the new database.

3. It rebuilds attached tables and relationships in the new database.

4. It removes all permissions on selected types of objects in the new database for the Users group and the Admin user.

5. It encrypts the database.

NOTE With Access 97, the Security Wizard now removes the database's Open/Run permission for all user and group accounts except the Admins group and the user account of the user who ran the Wizard. This means that users who are not members of the Admins group will not be able to open the database after you've run the Wizard. You can, of course, add this permission to any user or group in the workgroup.

FIGURE 14.10

Opening screen of the
Access Security Wizard

FIGURE 14.10

Opening screen of the
Access Security Wizard

Securing Code

To secure VBA modules or forms or reports containing event procedures, you first need to follow the steps for securing your database.

You secure module-based code so that users can't see it by removing all permissions to it. Using DAO, set the permissions of the modules to dbSecNoAccess. Users will always be able to run your functions, but you will have to provide objects the user *can* read that hook into the secured functions.

You secure forms and reports with event procedures by removing all permissions but the Open/Run permission. Using DAO, you set the permissions to acSecFrmRptExecute. This also prevents users from modifying the form or report definitions.

If you will be installing your application at another site, make sure the owner of the objects you wish to secure and the owner of the database are secured users (not the Admin user or the Users group).

Grant permissions to the Users group for any objects to which you want users to have access.

Ship the database without the workgroup file with which you created it.

WARNING Many Access developers have taken to creating functions that create a new workspace using code that employs the CreateWorkspace method to log on as an Admins-level user. This requires embedding the password of an Admins group member user in the code. The modules containing this code are then supposedly secured by removing all permissions to all accounts but the Admins group. We don't recommend this practice because Access stores module code in the system tables, and it's likely that a determined hacker could decode the OLE object that is used to store this code enough to discover the embedded password. (Fortunately, the main reason for doing this—the need to query group membership—is no longer necessary since all users can now read this information in Access 97/Jet 3.5.)

Securing Data

It's likely you'll want to grant database users at least ReadData security on some tables or queries; there's not much sense in your users using a database without access to any of its data. Thus, you need to selectively grant permissions to users.

Follow the steps for securing any database. Set necessary permissions on tables. Then, set the necessary permissions on queries and use OwnerAccess queries where needed for column-level or row-level security.

Grant permissions to the Users group for any application objects to which you want all users to have access.

Securing the Database Structure

In some situations you may want to secure your database schema. For example, you might be in a service industry that provides valuable data with a proprietary database structure. In this case the database schema is at least as valuable as the data you provide.

In this scenario users will be able to see the names of the secured tables but will be unable to see the relationships between the tables or the columns in the tables. This works best if the unsecured users need only read-only access to the tables.

You can secure your database schema by following these steps:

1. Create a secure workgroup file.

2. If you are concerned about users being able to see the names of your tables, rename them to nonsense names that have no connection to their content.

3. Split the database into a pair of "data" and "application" databases. (See Chapter 12 for more details.)

4. Remove all relationships in the data database if you don't want users to be able to see relationships.

5. Secure both databases using the Security Wizard.

6. Log on as a secure user and open the data database. (*Don't* remove Open/ Run access to this database for unsecured users. If you do, unsecured users won't be able to read the data from linked tables.)

7. Grant yourself ReadData access for all tables in the data database. Make sure no unsecured user or group accounts have any access to these tables.

8. Using the same secure user account, open the application database and create OwnerAccess queries that use linked tables pointing to the data database.

9. Grant ReadData access to the Users group for the OwnerAccess queries.

10. Set the record source for all other objects in the database to the secured Owner- Access queries, not the underlying tables.

If you follow these steps, unsecured users will be unable to view either the contents of any of your tables or the OwnerAccess queries. They will, however, still be able to see the names of the tables and open the data database.

Unsecuring a Secured Database

You can reverse the process of securing a database by following these steps:

1. Log on as a member of the Admins group.

2. Grant full permissions, including Administer permission, to the built-in Users group for all objects in the database.

3. Clear the password for the Admin user.

4. Exit Access.

5. Restart Access and log on as Admin.

6. Create a new blank database and import all the secured database's objects using the File ➤ Get External Data ➤ Import command.

The trick to this technique is to give an unsecured group—Users—full permissions on all the objects and to then transfer ownership of the database and all its objects to an unsecured user—Admin.

Migrating Secured Databases to Access 97

You can move secured Access 2 databases to Access 97 by using one of the strategies listed in Table 14.10.

TABLE 14.10 Strategies for Moving Secured Access 2 Databases to Access 97

Strategy	Advantages	Disadvantages
Convert your secured database while joined to your existing Access 2 workgroup file; after conversion, continue to use the Access 2 workgroup file	Easy	You won't be able to take advantage of new security features, such as the ability of non-Admins members to view their group membership
Convert your secured database; create a new Access 97 workgroup file with the same WID; create the same accounts with the same SIDs as the Access 2 workgroup	Takes full advantage of new security features	Requires you to have a written record of all accounts and PIDs
Document existing security system (account names, group membership, object permissions); unsecure database by assigning all permissions of all objects to the Users group; convert the unsecured database; rebuild security system from the ground up using different PIDs	Takes full advantage of new security features; can be used when you don't have a written record of the workgroup WID or account SIDs	Requires the most work

If you're making the move from Access 95 to Access 97, you can continue to use your Access 95 workgroup file because security hasn't changed significantly between these versions.

Security and Linked Tables

When you secure linked tables in an application database of a classic split database architecture (see Chapter 12), you are securing only the links, not the data in the tables. To properly secure the data, you must secure the tables in the *data database*. Don't bother securing the links stored in the application database; this security will be overlaid on top of the security of the data tables and doesn't really add anything because users will always be able to directly open the tables in the data database.

To link to (or refresh links to) tables in the data database, users must have Open/Run (dbSecDBOpen) permission to the data database *and* the ability to create tables—dbSecCreate permission to the TableDefs container—in the application database.

Summary

In this chapter we have covered security in detail. You should now have a good understanding of the Access/Jet security model and how best to take advantage of it.

You have learned

- The basic structure of the Jet security model

- How to set database passwords

- How to use the more powerful workgroup-based security model

- That workgroup-based security in Access is made up of two components: user and group accounts stored in the workgroup file and object permissions stored in each database

- How to enable security

- How to use the Access security menus to manage security

- How to create a secure workgroup file

- How to manage user and group accounts

- How the special built-in user and group accounts work

- How to manage object permissions for users

- The difference between explicit and implicit permissions

- How object and database ownership works
- What OwnerAccess queries are and how to use them to get column-level and row-level security
- How encryption works and what it has to do with security
- The security object hierarchies
- How the security data access objects work
- What the permission constants are and how to use them to programmatically set permissions
- How to use DAO to manipulate accounts and permissions
- How to properly secure and unsecure databases
- How to migrate secured databases to Access 95

15

Developing Client-Server Applications

- Using Access as a database client

- Setting up and controlling ODBC and using ODBC data efficiently

- Managing connections to your server

- Controlling the flow of data

- Testing client-server applications

- Upsizing your Access application

The term *client-server* has come to represent many types of processing. In its most basic sense, a client-server application is one that divides the execution of tasks between two or more separate processes (running programs). A *server* is any process that offers services to other processes (the *clients*). These processes are typically located on different computers connected by some sort of network, but they need not be. Of interest to Access developers are *client-server database applications.* These are applications that shift the burden of data storage and manipulation to a dedicated application, usually running on a powerful server workstation on the network. (Often these are referred to simply as *client-server applications.*) Access' role in these applications is to provide the interface, or *front end*, to the server data. The Jet database engine is used only to communicate with the server, translating Access queries into those that can be executed by the server database engine.

In this chapter we discuss the use of Access as a front end to SQL-based database management servers. We focus on the use of ODBC, a Microsoft-sponsored standard for database connectivity, as the method of communication between Access and the database server. Because every server and every network are different, we can't give you complete advice on what to do in every client-server situation. However, we will show you the basic guidelines for understanding how Access functions as a client and demonstrate a method for testing with your own hardware and software.

The Difference between File-Server and Client-Server

Figure 15.1 shows schematically the five methods of retrieving data from a server we'll be discussing in this chapter:

- File-server

- Linked ODBC (Open Database Connectivity) tables

- Direct connection using Jet Data Access Objects (DAO)

- SQL pass-through (SPT) queries

- ODBCDirect, formerly called Remote Data Objects (RDO)

Linked ODBC, SQL pass-through, and ODBCDirect are variants of client-server computing.

FIGURE 15.1

Methods of data access. The client-server methods are distinguished by having a program that runs on the server.

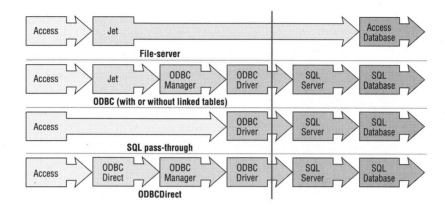

File-server Access is what you get when you simply move your database to a network server's hard drive. In this case no active components at all are running on the server. (The heavy black line in Figure 15.1 indicates the boundary between client and server components.) All data processing is done by the Jet database engine that runs on the client workstation. This is inherently inefficient due to the amount of data that must move across the network to satisfy queries. For example, suppose you need to retrieve all the customers in Alaska. In this case, assuming the State field of the customers table was indexed, the Jet engine would read the entire index for this field from the server. It would then retrieve the records it required.

Linking to server tables using *Open Database Connectivity* (*ODBC*) takes a more complex route to retrieve server data. In this case the Jet engine translates the original SQL for your query into a universal SQL dialect. This SQL, together with information on which server contains the data, is passed to the ODBC manager, a software component that runs on the client workstation. The ODBC manager locates the appropriate database server driver and hands it the SQL statement. The ODBC driver then translates the universal SQL to a SQL dialect understood by the particular database server and hands it to that server to process. Ideally, in this scenario the only network traffic is the SQL statement going out and the final result set coming back. The advantage of using linked tables is that you can still take advantage of Access features such as bound forms. You can even use DAO methods against the linked tables—Jet will take care of the translation to ODBC for you.

Connecting to data sources directly using *Jet DAO* is one more way you can programmatically manipulate server data. The key to this approach is the OpenDatabase method. Rather than specifying a local or network Jet database, you use

ODBC connection information to tell Jet to open a server database directly. You can then create recordsets and execute queries against the server database. The downside to this method, as we'll explain shortly, is that a fair amount of overhead is involved in the connection process, which you avoid when using linked tables.

SQL pass-through adds another wrinkle to this means of communication. Although the "plumbing" components are still present, none of them will perform any translation on a SQL pass-through query. Instead, you must write the exact SQL statement that the server will execute within Access itself. SQL pass-through is mainly of use when you need to use some advanced feature of your database server that ODBC SQL is incapable of understanding, although it can speed processing of regular queries because Jet and ODBC do not intercede to translate your SQL.

Finally, *ODBCDirect* provides another alternative to the standard ODBC connection. With ODBCDirect, instead of sending your query to Jet to be translated, you send it directly to the database server using an extension to the Jet DAO object model. ODBCDirect is integrated into the Jet DAO, so using it is a simple extension of using straight DAO. Rather than manipulating Jet data, however, ODBCDirect provides a very thin wrapper around native ODBC function calls and can produce additional execution speed because, like SQL pass-through, it sends queries directly to the server.

Using Client-Server versus File-Server

When you first look at using Access in a client-server system, you may think it's an easy task. After all, if you bought this book, you've probably developed in Access for a while. Migrating to client-server should just mean loading your data tables onto the server and changing the links, right?

Wrong. As you just saw, client-server systems are a completely different architecture from native Access. Migrating from one to the other often requires many changes in the design, implementation, and support of your application. Before you convert your application, you should understand the differences and the impact they will have on your application. Above all, if you're writing your first client-server application, be sure to leave plenty of time for testing in a nonproduction environment.

When you use Access in file-server mode, each instance of Jet manages its own cache of physical pages from the file, updates the pages on each client's machine, and sends the updated physical pages back over the network. Each copy of Jet performs the index updating, system table maintenance, and other database management functions required to process your application's work.

In marked contrast, when you use Access as a front-end application and the database resides on a database server, the database server provides all the data management functions for the application. Only the *database server* updates the physical file and sees the physical pages in the database. Each user's copy of Access sends requests to the database server and gets data, or pointers to the data, back from the server. It's this single point of control that makes client-server computing more robust than file-server computing, and that makes it a better choice for mission-critical applications.

Table 15.1 shows some of the key differences in processing between an Access-only multiuser application and a client-server application using Access and a database server.

TABLE 15.1 Key Differences between File-Server and Client-Server Applications

Process	Native Access (File-Server) Processing	Client-Server Access Processing
Updating data	Each user's machine retrieves the physical pages over the network, updates them, and writes them back to the shared drive. Because of this, a failure on any client machine has a good chance of corrupting the database and requiring shutdown and repair	The server database engine manages all updates of the physical database. Because of this, management problems with the network and individual machine failures are greatly reduced
Security	The Access security model covers all portions of a multiuser Access application	The Access security model is applied to the Access application portions of the application (forms, reports, modules, and macros). The security system of the database server controls accessing and updating the actual data. You still use Access security for forms, reports, modules, and queries, so both security systems must be kept current
Validation rules	Validation rules are part of native Access and the data engine	Validation rules and triggers must be defined at the server. They will not display the Access-defined error message when triggered. Your application will need to handle notifying the user appropriately

TABLE 15.1   Key Differences between File-Server and Client-Server Applications (continued)

Process	Native Access (File-Server) Processing	Client-Server Access Processing
Support for special datatypes	Supports Counter, OLE, and Memo datatypes	Server dependent
Referential integrity	Defined within Access	Referential integrity must be defined directly at the server if the server supports it. You cannot establish referential integrity rules across servers or between server data and Access stored data
Updatable queries/views	Access allows update of almost any type of join. Access allows update of both sides of a one-to-many join	Most servers prohibit updates to joined queries. Using ODBC will sometimes work around this by sending multiple updates. Using pass-through limits you to updates the server allows

By now you are probably wondering whether client-server is such a good idea after all. This is a good frame of mind from which to approach the native-Access versus client-server decision, because moving to a client-server implementation requires learning a new approach to application programming. It also requires giving up many of your familiar tools and losing some of the strong integration you find in Access. There are, however, several compelling reasons why you might choose to use a database server as a back end to Access applications:

- Reliability and data protection
- Transaction and data integrity
- Performance considerations
- Improved system management
- Unique server capabilities

NOTE   Each of the preceding reasons assumes you have a choice as to where to store the data. However, often you will consider using Access in a client-server environment simply because the data already resides on a database server and you wish to use Access to gain access to the data while continuing to keep the data on the server to support existing applications.

Reliability and Data Protection

Access runs a copy of the database engine on every client machine and has no synchronized transaction log or distributed transaction commit system. A failure of any single client machine or network component, therefore, has the potential to corrupt the entire database. Usually the database can be fixed, but repairing an Access database requires all users to log off the database. Repair of a large database can take several hours, and no user can use the database during the repair. On the other hand, because all updating and data management on a server occur at the *server*, failures on the network or client machines rarely affect the database. Also, most database servers have fast and robust recovery facilities. Database servers also typically run on operating systems such as Windows NT, UNIX, or MVS, which have their own fault recovery systems, making the database almost incorruptible. For example, you can literally pull the plug on a Windows NT server running Microsoft SQL Server with no data loss. Don't try that with your Access database!

Transaction Processing and Data Integrity

The transaction support built into Jet has access to the data only for its own current session. It cannot resolve problems left from a previous failed session or from another copy of Jet that failed somewhere else on the network. This transaction support also does not have full protection for the database if a failure occurs while Jet is committing a transaction. In addition, the current implementation of Jet can leave locks orphaned in the shared locking (LDB) file, requiring a shutdown and purge of the shared locking file before anyone can access or repair the data. As a result, failures that occur while a copy of Access is committing a transaction can result in data loss, data lockout, or database corruption. The windows are small, but they may be sufficient to cause you to seriously consider client-server if you are implementing systems that, for example, process real-funds transactions. In this case money will not be properly transferred or accounted for if the transaction partially commits. In contrast, most database servers are capable of maintaining a full audit trail, enabling the database administrator to reconstruct the state of the database at any time. Popular servers, such as Microsoft SQL Server, also offer hot backup facilities, letting you save a second copy of critical data in real time without needing to suspend database operations.

Performance Considerations

Performance is another important reason to consider client-server, but one that is often misrepresented. Unlike the reliability issues, there are many approaches to providing good performance from a native Access multiuser system. However, there are cases in which a server is the only way to achieve appropriate performance. Generally speaking, if you often need to find small amounts of data in a sea of records, client-server will provide a speed boost. On the other hand, if you're frequently analyzing records from the bulk of your database or running multiple reports with only slight variations between them, a client-server environment might prove slower than the equivalent file-server system.

It's important to remember that client-server is not a performance panacea. Simply moving your database tables to a server database will, in all likelihood, result in drastically *lower* performance. You must rethink your application in terms of client-server. We'll discuss this in more detail later in the chapter.

System Management

One often-overlooked area in client-server is overall system management and administration. Windows and the Access Workgroup Administrator program offer only very limited management services compared to a Windows NT Advanced Server or a UNIX server machine. Adding a robust, modern server database to the package further increases the management tools. Microsoft SQL Server, for example, is capable of monitoring its own operation and sending e-mail or even electronic pages to the database administrator in case of trouble.

Unique Server Capabilities

Sometimes you will need to use a server for your database simply because it offers some capabilities that Access doesn't. Here is a list of the most important features built into SQL Server that might make it the right choice for your applications:

- Data replication triggered by a specific transaction load.
- Central management of distributed servers.
- Scalability to high-performance machines. (SQL Server will make use of multiple processors; Access will not.)
- Support for very large databases (up to terabytes of data).
- Querying via electronic mail.
- Deadlock and livelock resolution, ensuring that two users cannot lock each other out of needed data.

- Dynamic backup, even while the database is in use.

- Automatic recovery—backups plus log files can be used to regenerate a database lost to hardware failure.

- Device mirroring—your data can be written to multiple drives at one time, for instantaneous backups.

- Integrated security resulting in a single logon for both the network and the database.

When you think about the amount of code you would have to write to get most of these capabilities in Access itself, you can see that a database server can save considerable development time and expense.

The Role of Access in Distributed Applications

Because Access is a full database management product, you have a great deal of flexibility in establishing the role of Access in your distributed application. The three main approaches we cover are

- Using Access as a true front-end process

- Using Access with both Jet tables and linked server tables

- Using Access as a store-and-forward application

NOTE You can also use ODBC to import data into an Access system and use the system as though there were no link to an outside data source. While we do not cover this approach in this chapter, it is often useful for data analysis and some decision-support systems, where up-to-the-second data is not necessary. It allows the use of outside data with the least impact on your Access development style. This approach is obviously dependent on having no more than a few hundred megabytes of data to deal with. If there is more data than that, the time it takes to move the data to your local computer and the storage space it requires become prohibitive.

Using Access as a True Front-End Process

You can implement a pure client-server application using Access as a front-end process, storing all data on the server and implementing all queries so that they run using the server's SQL engine. By doing this you centralize all the data administration functions on the server. All table maintenance and associated work are performed in a single environment. You can implement this approach by using SQL pass-through or ODBCDirect for all your queries, an approach we cover in the section "Using the Three Methods of Getting Data" later in this chapter. While it is possible to use ODBC and linked tables, you will find that Jet often generates rather inefficient SQL in response to your Access queries. We'll examine this in more depth in the section "Looking In on Jet and ODBC" later in this chapter.

The biggest advantage to this approach is performance. You will find that response time for a given query is less when using SQL pass-through or ODBCDirect than it is using Jet and ODBC. This is especially true for complex queries. The downside, however, is that creating a "true" client-server front end using Access is far less efficient in terms of developer productivity. You must have intimate knowledge of the server database you are communicating with. That is, you must express all queries in terms of the SQL that the server understands. You cannot use Jet SQL or the Access QBE grid.

Using Access with Both Jet Tables and Linked Server Tables

The most common approach to client-server with Access is to have a mix of local (Access-owned) and server-based data. The local data may be copies of relatively static data from the servers, or it may be data no one outside your workgroup needs to access. Common techniques that fall under this general approach are

- Downloading lookup tables to each client machine at login time

- Maintaining custom or auxiliary data in local databases

- Downloading bulk data to client machines for processing a series of reports or performing extended interactive analysis

Applications that use ODBC to link directly to server tables make for a smoother transition to client-server because Jet handles the task of translating your existing queries to those required by ODBC. Your application basically works the same way it does when using Access data. You may not be happy with the performance, however, because Jet often makes very inefficient decisions.

Using Access as a Store-and-Forward Application

An approach related to the preceding one is to use Access to perform store-and-forward processing to a server. In *store-and-forward processing*, Access is acting as a full database product for the user and then turning around and acting as a client to the database server to update the shared database. This approach is useful if your server is over a wide area network (WAN) rather than a high-speed local area network (LAN) but may also be useful in some cases even for local (non-WAN) processing.

One example of store-and-forward is an order entry application. In a pure client-server system, every detail item goes back to the server, perhaps multiple times, to validate and enter the item. In a store-and-forward approach, you use a set of local Access data tables to store the detail data as the order is entered and initial validation is made. After Access captures the entire order, it sends it to the server in a single transaction for final validation and loading into the shared database.

With Microsoft SQL Server 6.x and Access 97, you can also use database replication to your advantage in store-and-forward designs. You could, for example, set up multiple servers around your WAN and use replication between the servers to make sure every client has access to a local copy of the data. Alternatively, you could use Access' own replication to forward all the data to a single Access database located on the same LAN as the server and have it perform all the server updates.

The downside to the store-and-forward system is that you must maintain two different databases: your Access database and its server equivalent. Extra effort is required to build and maintain both databases, including the use of elements such as validation rules and referential integrity.

Understanding ODBC

Access uses the Open DataBase Connectivity (ODBC) standard to connect to servers. ODBC is a common language definition and a set of protocols that allow a client to interactively determine a server's capabilities and adapt the processing to work within the functions the server supports. You implement ODBC using components within Access, on each client machine running separately from

Access, and on the database server machine. To use ODBC to connect from Access to a back-end database, you need three things:

- A network that allows communications between the client machine and the machine that holds the back-end database
- The ODBC driver manager that comes with Access
- An ODBC driver that can work with your back-end database

Many sources exist for ODBC-compliant drivers. Many database and hardware vendors now provide them, and there are several third-party sources for drivers. If you have CompuServe access, you can find information on the latest ODBC drivers on the WINEXT forum.

ODBC processing consists of three major activities:

- Establishing connections
- Parsing queries
- Managing record sources

The key to getting reliable performance lies in understanding all three of these areas and how your specific ODBC driver and back-end server handle each.

Establishing Connections

ODBC processing revolves around *connections*. When a client needs access to data on a server, the ODBC software at the client end (in the case of Access, Jet and the underlying ODBC drivers) performs a number of steps to establish a connection. It

1. Finds the system and path information for the appropriate connection
2. Connects over the appropriate network(s) to the database server
3. Checks for a stored login for the database
4. Prompts the user (if required) for login and password information
5. Gathers information about the capabilities of the server
6. Gathers information about the capabilities of the ODBC driver
7. Gathers information about the table(s) that are being connected

To make a connection, an application must pass the ODBC manager an ODBC connect string. An *ODBC connect string* is a encoded stream that consists of the data source name and other required information. A sample connect string is shown here:

```
DSN=PerfTest;APP=Microsoft Access;UID=sa;PWD=;DATABASE=ADHTestDB;
```

You can see that each piece of information is designated by a code and separated from the next by a semicolon. Table 15.2 lists a few of the most common codes used in ODBC connect strings.

TABLE 15.2   Common ODBC Connect String Keys

Key	Description
DSN	Data source name
UID	User ID
PWD	User password
DATABASE	Database name (if the DSN does not specify a specific database, you can include it here)
APP	Application name (used by servers to identify the user of a connection)

One unique feature of ODBC is that every piece of connection information is optional. If the ODBC manager or database driver doesn't find what it needs in the connect string, it prompts the user for the missing information. When you link to an ODBC data source, Access stores the connect string in the linked table's Connect property. If you want to work with server data programmatically, you'll need to become comfortable constructing connect strings yourself.

Because of the cost of connecting to a data source, you generally want to make connections only once for each session. Once a connection has been established, you can execute multiple queries using it. This is what happens when you use linked tables, because Access caches connection information for linked tables locally. This in turn allows Jet to connect to the table when you reference it without all the overhead of a dynamic connection. When converting your Access application to a client-server application, you should examine all uses of the OpenDatabase function or method. When used against an ODBC data source, the OpenDatabase method triggers the steps listed above. If you need to open a database programmatically, consider opening a single connection and storing a pointer to it in a global Database variable.

Starting with the current release of ODBC (2.5), some drivers include a "fast connect" option. When you invoke this option (during the driver setup), the driver defers as much of the connection processing as possible until you actually request records from the data source. Using this option can speed the initial load of your application, at the cost of making the first access to each table slower.

Query Parsing

Jet handles a query for an ODBC connection in one of three ways. You can use any of the following:

- A regular Jet-optimized Access query
- A SQL pass-through (SPT) query
- A query passed using ODBCDirect

If you use an SPT or ODBCDirect query, Jet does no parsing of the query and passes the SQL string directly to the database server for processing. It is your responsibility to ensure that the string is a valid SQL statement. On the other hand, you can also use a regular Access query, whereupon Jet interprets and optimizes the query locally, determining the best execution path. During the optimization step, Jet partitions the query execution into a Jet-executed component and a server-executed component. It is at this point that Jet may make inappropriate choices concerning the best SQL to send to the server.

SQL pass-through and ODBCDirect querying generally work best for activities during which the server can do a large amount of processing or for which Access is incapable of expressing the query in native SQL. You might consider using one of these techniques in the following situations:

- To perform data definition language (DDL) operations or other administrative actions on the server. Often, there is no Jet equivalent for these queries.
- To execute SQL when the SQL syntax is not supported by Access.
- To execute very short SQL actions, such as single row retrievals or updates.
- To process SQL statements that join tables from two different databases on the same server.
- To process SQL updates when you need to check on the number of rows updated.
- To process large action queries within transactions.

Even in these cases it may be more efficient to use Jet-optimized Access queries, depending on your particular server and network load. Convert to pass-through queries only if you encounter a significant performance problem, such as a query that Jet fails to optimize properly. The normal SQL parsing for ODBC processing is similar to the Jet processing for native Access tables. The major difference is that once the Jet engine has isolated the commands that need to be processed at the server, it generates a SQL string in the common ODBC SQL dialect. This in turn is translated by your server-specific ODBC driver into your server's SQL dialect. When Jet executes the query, it executes all the portions of a query that are local and sends the translated SQL strings to the server for processing.

Managing Record Sources

When you convert to ODBC from native Access, you may find that complex forms open slowly compared to other forms. This is because there is more overhead associated with creating a connection to an ODBC data source than to a Jet table. Each record source on a form (the form itself, plus any subforms or list or combo boxes) may require its own connection. When you built your forms in native Access, you probably didn't worry about how many different sources of data the form used, because the data all came from local Jet tables. When you use ODBC you need to limit the number of different record sources on a form to ensure reasonable performance and usability.

As mentioned earlier in this chapter, ODBC uses connections to talk to the server. Depending on the server, a single physical connection may be opened or a separate physical connection may exist for each active recordset. If a recordset is updatable, Jet will maintain two connections (except when there are fewer than 100 records when only one connection is used). Whether they are physical links or logical links over a shared path, all connections use memory and processing resources. In addition, some servers impose a licensing limit on the number of open connections. Thus, to work efficiently under ODBC, you need to be careful about the number of active recordsets your application uses. Each row source on your form (whether for the form itself or a combo or list box) is a separate connection. Each bound subform will have one or more connections. A connection remains open in each of these situations:

- Until all associated data has been returned from the server

- While any transactions are outstanding

Jet may cache a connection, once made, to avoid the cost of reestablishing the connection the next time it requires the data. You can control this caching process by way of ODBC parameters in the Registry. (See the section "Configuring ODBC for Your System" later in this chapter.)

Configuring ODBC

Regardless of the approach you take to client-server development with Access, you'll need to know something about using ODBC. That's because all the techniques we've discussed thus far use ODBC, at a minimum, to identify a data source at which to direct queries. In this section we briefly discuss the ODBC Administrator applet you can use to configure ODBC data sources. If you've already mastered this tool, you can skip ahead to the section "Using the Sample Database."

ODBC Data Sources

Each distinct database you want to connect to is identified by an ODBC data source. You use the ODBC Administrator applet to manage data sources. Conceptually, a data source consists of three items:

- A name unique to the workstation on which the data source is defined

- The ODBC driver used

- Any other driver-specific information

ODBC supports both *user* and *system* data source names (DSNs). User DSN information is linked to a particular workstation user, while system DSNs are available to all users of a workstation. DSN information is stored in the registry in the Software\ODBC\ODBC.INI subkey of either the HKEY_CURRENT_USER hive (for user DSNs) or the HKEY_LOCAL_MACHINE hive (for system DSNs).

A new feature of ODBC version 3.0 is support for *file data sources*. File data sources store configuration information in a file rather than in the Registry. This makes it very easy, for example, to define a data source on one computer and transfer the definition to another. You just need to copy the definition file (which ODBC creates with a .DSN file extension) to the other computer. ODBC stores configuration files in the C:\Program Files\Common Files\Odbc\Data Sources directory.

NOTE

You can change the directory ODBC looks in to find file data sources. Modify the DefaultDSNDir entry of the HKEY_LOCAL_MACHINE\Software\ ODBC\ODBC.INI\ODBC File DSN Registry key.

Once you've established a data source, all an ODBC-compliant application such as Access needs to know in order to connect to it is the data source name. ODBC then allows the driver to prompt the user for any additional information.

Running ODBC Administrator

Although you can configure data sources by editing Registry settings, it is usually easier to use the ODBC Administrator applet. This software is installed as part of any application that supports ODBC and appears as a Control Panel icon labeled "32-bit ODBC." (You can also run the executable file, ODBCAD32.EXE, installed in the Windows directory, separately.) Figure 15.2 shows the Administrator's user interface. Using the tabs, you can view user, system, and file data sources, as well as information on ODBC drivers and system files.

FIGURE 15.2

ODBC Administrator applet showing user data source names

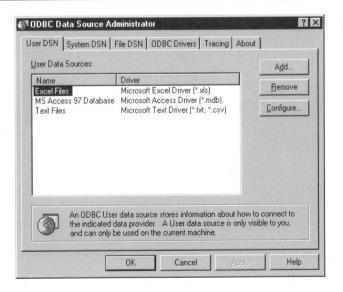

Setting Up a Data Source

To create a new user data source, click the Add button on the initial ODBC Administrator dialog. (To add a new system data source, click the Add button on the System DSN dialog.) You are prompted to select a driver from a list of those installed on your workstation (see Figure 15.3). As an example, we'll show you how to set up the Microsoft SQL Server data source our sample database uses. You start by selecting the SQL Server driver from the list and clicking the Finish button.

FIGURE 15.3

Choosing an ODBC driver for a new data source

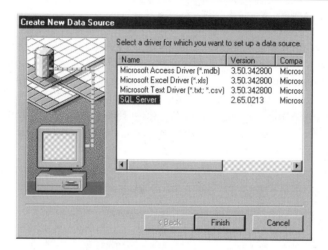

You should note that the list of ODBC drivers is built from registry entries in the HKEY_LOCAL_MACHINE\Software\ODBC\ODBCINST.INI subkey and should correspond to those installed on your workstation. If you do not see a particular driver listed, you should rerun that driver's setup program.

After selecting a driver, you see a dialog like the one shown in Figure 15.4. Don't be alarmed, however, if the one you see differs greatly, because the ODBC driver itself generates the dialog. It will therefore differ between drivers, given the varying pieces of information each needs.

At a minimum, however, you'll need to supply a name for the SQL Server data source. The name must be unique in respect to other DSNs defined on the same

FIGURE 15.4

Configuring the sample
SQL Server data source

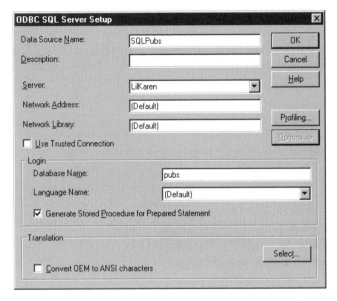

workstation. If you want to set up the data source for this chapter, fill out the remaining fields as shown in the dialog in Figure 15.4. (Substitute the name of your SQL Server in the Server field.)

Using the Sample Database

We've provided a sample database on the CD-ROM (CH15.MDB) that demonstrates various client-server development techniques. It is designed to be used with a Microsoft SQL Server database. Unlike the other sample databases for this book, the database for this chapter is not completely self contained. Because it contains attached Microsoft SQL Server tables, you can use it without modification only if you have installed Microsoft SQL Server (version 4.2 or above). The sample database also assumes you have installed the Pubs sample database that comes with SQL Server. In addition, to make sure the database works seamlessly, you'll need to create an ODBC data source named SQLPUBS that points to this database. If you have problems reading data from the attached tables even after defining a proper DSN, it's worth deleting the tables and reattaching them as a check.

Also, the sample database uses the default login of "sa" with no password throughout. If this is not a valid login on your SQL Server, you'll need to take two steps. First, drop and reattach the three tables in the sample. Second, open up frmTestbed in Design view and change the embedded login and password strings in the code to match your actual login.

Using the Three Methods of Getting Data

You can retrieve data in each of the three ways we've been considering—the native Jet query, SQL pass-through, and ODBCDirect—using VBA code. Let's look at the syntax for each of the three alternatives in turn, using the query shown in Design view in Figure 15.5. This query uses three of the tables from the Pubs database shipped with Microsoft SQL Server to retrieve information on authors and the books they have written.

FIGURE 15.5

The test query

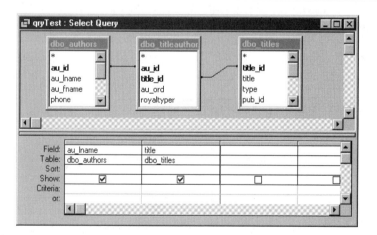

Native Jet Query

Finding the proper SQL for a native Jet query is simple: just construct the query on the QBE grid and switch to SQL view. Here's the Jet SQL for the sample query:

```
SELECT dbo_authors.au_lname, dbo_titles.title
FROM (dbo_authors INNER JOIN
```

```
dbo_titleauthor ON dbo_authors.au_id = dbo_titleauthor.au_id)
INNER JOIN  dbo_titles ON dbo_titleauthor.title_id =
dbo_titles.title_id;
```

frmTestbed in the sample database has CBF procedures to execute each of the query variations we're discussing here. For the native Jet query, we create a QueryDef object using the linked tables directly and then base a recordset on this querydef. Here's the relevant portion of the code:

```
Private Sub cmdExecuteAttached_Click()

    Dim wsCurrent As Workspace
    Dim dbCurrent As Database
    Dim qdfAttached As QueryDef
    Dim rstAttached As Recordset
    Dim intIterations As Integer
    Dim cIterations As Integer
    Dim lngStart As Long
    Dim lngTotal As Long
    Dim errAny As Error

    On Error GoTo cmdExecuteLinkedErr

    DoCmd.Hourglass True

    intIterations = CInt(Me!txtIterations)
    lngTotal = 0
    Set wsCurrent = DBEngine.Workspaces(0)
    Set dbCurrent = wsCurrent.Databases(0)

    ' This should set a global timeout for all queries run
    ' from this database. Unfortunately, a bug that persists
    ' from Access 2.0 ignores this property entirely. This
    ' is why we need to create a QueryDef object instead
    ' dbCurrent.QueryTimeout = 0

    Set qdfAttached = dbCurrent.CreateQueryDef _
      ("", Me!txtAttachedSQL)
    ' Tell Access to wait as long as the query takes
    qdfAttached.ODBCTimeout = 0
    For cIterations = 1 To intIterations
        lngStart = adh_apiGetTickCount()
```

```
        ' If query returns records create Recordset,
        ' otherwise execute it
        If Me!chkJetRec Then
            Set rstAttached = qdfAttached.OpenRecordset()
            rstAttached.MoveLast
            rstAttached.Close
        Else
            wsCurrent.BeginTrans
            qdfAttached.Execute
            wsCurrent.Rollback
        End If
        lngTotal = lngTotal + adh_apiGetTickCount() - lngStart
    Next cIterations
    Me!txtAttachedTicks = lngTotal / intIterations

cmdExecuteLinkedExit:
    DoCmd.Hourglass False
    Exit Sub
cmdExecuteLinkedErr:
    If Err.Number = DBEngine.Errors(0).Number And _
    DBEngine.Errors.Count > 1 Then
        For Each errAny In DBEngine.Errors
            MsgBox "Error " & errAny.Number & " raised by " _
                & errAny.Source & ": " & errAny.Description, _
                vbCritical, "cmdExecuteAttached()"
        Next errAny
    Else
        MsgBox "Error " & Err.Number & " raised by " _
            & Err.Source & ": " & Err.Description, _
            vbCritical, "cmdExecuteAttached()"
    End If
    Resume cmdExecuteLinkedExit
End Sub
```

(For more information on using Data Access Objects, such as the QueryDef and Recordset objects discussed here, see Chapter 6.)

The only major complication here is setting the query timeout. By default, Jet will wait only 60 seconds for a query to execute before deciding that the server is down and aborting all processing on that query. You can use the query's ODBCTimeout property (available through code, as shown here, or on any query's property sheet) to increase this time. If you set the timeout to 0, Jet will wait until either the server returns data or you give up and press Ctrl+Break to abort the query.

You should also note the error handling in this function. Because we're dealing with multiple components (Access, Jet, ODBC, and SQL Server), it's possible for a single operation to produce more than one error. If multiple errors occur in any Jet operation, Jet will populate the Errors collection of the DBEngine object with Error objects—one for each component to report an error. Jet will also put the last error into the Err object, which belongs to Access. However, if an error occurs in some nondata component (for example, VBA), Jet will not be notified, and consequently the Errors collection won't match the actual error. In this case you must retrieve the information from the Err object.

When it senses an error, the code checks to see whether there are multiple errors in the Errors collection and, if so, checks to see whether the first member of this collection matches the one stored in Err. If so, it dumps every member of the collection using a For Each loop. If not, it simply dumps the error information from the Err object.

SQL Pass-Through

To execute the same query using SQL pass-through, you must rewrite it in SQL the server can understand directly—which means you need to know the dialect of SQL used on your server. To translate this query to Microsoft SQL Server, you need to change the underlines in the table names back to dots and modify the join syntax, as shown here:

```
SELECT dbo.authors.au_lname, dbo.titles.title
FROM dbo.authors, dbo.titleauthor, dbo.titles
WHERE (dbo.titleauthor.au_id = dbo.authors.au_id)
AND (dbo.titleauthor.title_id = dbo.titles.title_id)
```

> **TIP**
>
> If you're unsure of the proper SQL but have a sniffer tool such as SQL Trace, which comes with Microsoft SQL Server (and is explained in detail in the section "Looking In on Jet and ODBC" later in this chapter), you can execute your query using the regular QBE grid and then inspect the trace of the conversation with the server to see how ODBC chose to translate it for you.

Executing a pass-through query in code also requires creating a QueryDef object. You create pass-through queries using the same technique as for normal queries, except that you set the querydef's Connect property to a valid ODBC connect string. In this case we're setting it to the return value of a function called Get-Connect. GetConnect constructs a connect string from values entered on the form.

```
Private Sub cmdPassthroughExecute_Click()

    Dim wsCurrent As Workspace
    Dim dbCurrent As Database
    Dim qdfPassthrough As QueryDef
    Dim rstPassthrough As Recordset
    Dim intIterations As Integer
    Dim cIterations As Integer
    Dim lngStart As Long
    Dim lngTotal As Long
    Dim errAny As Error

    On Error GoTo cmdExecutePassthroughErr

    DoCmd.Hourglass True

    intIterations = CInt(Me!txtIterations)
    lngTotal = 0
    Set wsCurrent = DBEngine.Workspaces(0)
    Set dbCurrent = wsCurrent.Databases(0)

    ' Create pass-through query
    Set qdfPassthrough = dbCurrent.CreateQueryDef("")
    qdfPassthrough.Connect = "ODBC;" & GetConnect()
    qdfPassthrough.SQL = Me!txtPassthroughSQL
    qdfPassthrough.ReturnsRecords = True

    ' Tell Access to wait as long as the query takes
    qdfPassthrough.ODBCTimeout = 0
    For cIterations = 1 To intIterations
        lngStart = adh_apiGetTickCount()

        ' If query returns records create Recordset,
        ' otherwise execute it
        If Me!chkPassRec Then
            Set rstPassthrough = qdfPassthrough.OpenRecordset()
            rstPassthrough.MoveLast
            rstPassthrough.Close
        Else
```

```
                qdfPassthrough.ReturnsRecords = False
                wsCurrent.BeginTrans
                qdfPassthrough.Execute
                wsCurrent.Rollback
            End If
            lngTotal = lngTotal + adh_apiGetTickCount() - lngStart
        Next cIterations
        Me!txtPassthroughTicks = lngTotal / intIterations

cmdExecutePassthroughExit:
    DoCmd.Hourglass False
    Exit Sub
cmdExecutePassthroughErr:
    If Err.Number = DBEngine.Errors(0).Number And _
     DBEngine.Errors.Count > 1 Then
        For Each errAny In DBEngine.Errors
            MsgBox "Error " & errAny.Number & " raised by " _
            & errAny.Source & ": " & errAny.Description, _
            vbCritical, "cmdExecutePassthrough()"
        Next errAny
    Else
        MsgBox "Error " & Err.Number & " raised by " _
        & Err.Source & ": " & Err.Description, _
        vbCritical, "cmdExecutePassthrough()"
    End If
    Resume cmdExecutePassthroughExit
End Sub
```

To create a pass-through query, you need to take the following steps in order. (Setting properties in the wrong order will result in a run-time error.)

1. Create the querydef.

2. Set the querydef's Connect property. If you're unsure of the syntax for the Connect property, check the Description property of a linked table from the same database.

3. Assign the proper server SQL to the query's SQL property.

4. Set the ReturnsRecords property to True if the query returns records. (You would set this to False for queries that don't return records, such as DDL queries.)

> **WARNING**
>
> If you want your pass-through query to execute with no user intervention, make sure you include every piece of information the server requires in your connect string. Otherwise the user may have to supply it by means of a driver-generated dialog. For example, if you omit the UID or PWD component when connecting to a SQL Server database, the ODBC driver will display a dialog each time the query is run.

Once you have created the proper querydef, a pass-through query behaves much like a native query in Jet—with one significant difference. Because Jet can't know how the server is retrieving these records, a pass-through query is always read-only. (If you need to update records in a pass-through query, you can write an update query and execute it by means of pass-through, as well.)

ODBCDirect

Because ODBCDirect queries also send their SQL directly to the server, they use the same SQL syntax as pass-through queries. The code needed to execute an ODBCDirect query, however, is quite different from SQL pass-through (though very similar to DAO):

```
Private Sub cmdRDOExecute_Click()

    Dim intIterations As Integer
    Dim cIterations As Integer
    Dim lngStart As Long
    Dim lngTotal As Long
    Dim wsDirect As Workspace
    Dim dbDirect As Database
    Dim cnDirect As Connection
    Dim rsDirect As Recordset
    Dim errAny As Error

    On Error GoTo cmdExecuteRDOErr

    DoCmd.Hourglass True

    intIterations = CInt(Me!txtIterations)
    lngTotal = 0
```

```
' Create an ODBCDirect workspace
Set wsDirect = DBEngine.CreateWorkspace _
 ("ODBCDirect", CurrentUser(), "", dbUseODBC)

' Open the database using an ODBC connect string
Set cnDirect = wsDirect.OpenConnection _
("ODBCDirectConnection",dbDriverComplete, False, "ODBC;" _
& GetConnect())

For cIterations = 1 To intIterations
    lngStart = adh_apiGetTickCount()

    ' If query returns records create Recordset,
    ' otherwise execute it
    If Me!chkODBCRec Then
        ' Open the recordset using server-specific SQL
        Set rsDirect = cnDirect.OpenRecordset( _
        Me!txtRDOSQL, dbOpenDynaset)
        rsDirect.MoveLast
        rsDirect.Close
        Set rsDirect = Nothing
    Else
        wsDirect.BeginTrans
        cnDirect.Execute Me!txtRDOSQL
        wsDirect.Rollback
    End If
    lngTotal = lngTotal + adh_apiGetTickCount() - lngStart
Next cIterations
Me!txtRDOTicks = lngTotal / intIterations

cnDirect.Close
wsDirect.Close

cmdExecuteRDOExit:
    DoCmd.Hourglass False
    Exit Sub
cmdExecuteRDOErr:
    If Err.Number = DBEngine.Errors(0).Number And _
    DBEngine.Errors.Count > 1 Then
        For Each errAny In DBEngine.Errors
            MsgBox "Error " & errAny.Number & " raised by " _
            & errAny.Source & ": " & errAny.Description, _
```

```
                    vbCritical, "cmdExecuteRDO()"
        Next errAny
    Else
        MsgBox "Error " & Err.Number & " raised by " _
         & Err.Source & ": " & Err.Description, _
          vbCritical, "cmdExecuteRDO()"
    End If
    Resume cmdExecuteRDOExit
End Sub
```

As you can see, ODBCDirect works much like DAO. The key is to create a new Workspace object using the dbUseODBC constant. This tells Jet that you want to use ODBCDirect for any database operations carried out in that workspace. Everything else should look familiar. Just remember to use server-specific SQL, not Jet SQL, when running queries.

Evaluating Query Alternatives

Choosing a query strategy blindly is unlikely to get you the best possible query performance. In any sizable application, you'll need to test at least Jet against pass-through for your important queries, and if you have ODBCDirect installed, you should test that as well. We've provided a simple test bed application in the sample database. It includes a form that lets you execute a query using each of the methods we've mentioned, as well as code to use the Windows API call GetTickCount to do precise timings.

On frmTestbed, you can type a SQL statement to be executed by any of the three methods of querying we've discussed. You can also choose the number of iterations of testing you wish to run. Always test a query multiple times when you're evaluating its performance because during a working session, data may end up cached on both the server and the client. You want your test to be extensive enough to get an average time, without the initial load of getting tables into memory.

Figure 15.6 shows some sample timings made on a copy of a test database with a 2000-row table on a lightly loaded network. The actual times in any situation will depend on many factors, including the type of query (Jet is very good at single-table select queries but tends to fall behind on complex joins or update queries, for example), the load on the network, the size of the server database, and the number of simultaneous users.

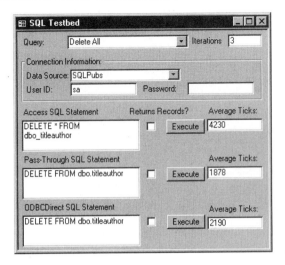

FIGURE 15.6

Sample query timings

Configuring ODBC for Your System

In the Windows Registry, Access provides a wide range of configuration options for controlling ODBC. All the settings in Table 15.3 are made in the \HKEY_LOCAL_MACHINE\SOFTWARE\Microsoft\Jet\3.5\Engines\ODBC Registry key. Table 15.3 contains descriptions of each configuration option and points out some potential settings for various conditions.

TABLE 15.3   Registry Settings for ODBC

Key Name	Value	Use
.TraceSQLMode (or SQLTraceMode)	0	Turns off tracing of Jet-to-server SQL statements (default)
	1	Traces all SQL statements sent from Jet to the ODBC interface. The output will be in a file named SQLOUT.TXT
.TraceODBCAPI	0	Disables tracing the ODBC API-level interface (default)
	1	Traces ODBC API calls into file ODBCAPI.TXT. You would use this only for debugging an ODBC driver or resolving a problem when working with a vendor. Normally, for working on your application's performance or debugging your SQL, use a SQL trace instead

TABLE 15.3 Registry Settings for ODBC (continued)

Key Name	Value	Use
.DisableAsync	0	Allows Access to continue processing while the server processes an ODBC request (default)
	1	Forces Access to wait for each ODBC request to complete before proceeding. You should set this only for debugging purposes or when dealing with a server that has problems with asynchronous queries, because it can have severe performance problems
.LoginTimeout	*s*	Aborts a login attempt if the server has not responded in *s* seconds (default: 20)
.QueryTimeout	*s*	Provides a default value for query-processing timeouts in seconds. Individual queries can override this with the ODBCTimeout property of the querydef. If you set this to 0, queries will not time out; instead, they will wait forever for data (default: 60)
.ConnectionTimeout	*s*	Sets the length of time in seconds during which Jet will maintain an inactive connection before releasing it. If your server is not licensed on a per-connection basis, setting this higher may improve response time. If you frequently run out of connections, lower this value (default: 600)
.AsyncRetryInterval	*m*	Sets the length of time, in milliseconds, Jet waits each time it checks on the progress of an async query (default: 500)
.AttachCaseSensitive	0	Does not use case when matching table names (default). If you use this setting, the first matching table that ODBC finds is attached
	1	Performs a case-sensitive search when opening tables
.SnapshotOnly	0	Allows processing that uses updatable recordsets (default)
	1	Forces the use of read-only Snapshot recordsets
.AttachableObjects	*string*	Includes the server's system objects in the selection list for attaching tables. *string* is a list of all the system objects to include in the selection list (default: TABLE, VIEW, SYSTEM TABLE, ALIAS, and SYNONYM)
.JetTryAuth	1	Try Jet Userid & Password before prompting the user for a different ID and password (default). You can use this setting if you keep IDs and passwords in sync between Access and the server
	0	Prompts the user for a different ID and password. Use this setting if your Access IDs are not kept in sync with the server

TABLE 15.3 Registry Settings for ODBC (continued)

Key Name	Value	Use
.PreparedInsert	0	Generates data-specific inserts that reflect only the supplied columns (default). You should normally use this setting
	1	Uses a predefined INSERT that uses all columns in the table. Using prepared INSERT statements can cause nulls to overwrite server defaults and can cause triggers to execute on columns that weren't inserted explicitly
.PreparedUpdate	0	Generates data-specific updates that reflect only the supplied columns (default). You should normally use this setting
	1	Uses a predefined UPDATE that updates all columns. Using prepared UPDATE statements can cause triggers to execute on unchanged columns
FastRequery	0	Uses a new SELECT statement each time a parameterized query is executed (default)
	1	Uses a prepared SELECT statement on the server when executing a parameterized query

Configuring Your Server for Access

You can provide additional information Access uses to manage your server connections in an optional table, MSysConf. You must add this table to each *server* database. It provides Access-specific information to assist in managing connections. Each time you connect to the database using Jet, Jet looks for this table and, if it exists, reads in the configuration information. The table should be defined as described in Table 15.4. Table 15.5 describes each of the settings for the MSysConf table.

TABLE 15.4 Structure of the MSysConf Table

Column Name	Data Type	Allows Nulls?
Config	2-byte integer	No
chValue	VARCHAR(255)	Yes
nValue	4-byte integer	Yes
Comments	VARCHAR(255)	Yes

TABLE 15.5   Settings in Your MSysConf Table

chConfig	nValue	Use
101	0	Does not store user IDs and passwords for attached tables. This value prompts the user for ID and password information each time the tables are attached
	1	Stores the user ID and password information with the connect string information for attached tables (default)
102	d	Sets the data retrieval delay time. Jet will delay d seconds between each retrieval of a block of rows from the server (default: 10; range: not documented [appears to be 1–32767])
103	n	Sets the number of rows to fetch from the server at each interval. You use these two settings (102 and 103) to control the rate at which data is brought from a server to Access during idle time (default: 100; range: not documented [appears to be 1–32767])

WARNING   If you include an MSysConf table on the server, it must have the proper format and data, or you won't be able to connect to that server at all.

Editing ODBC Data

You may on occasion link a server table only to discover that Access is treating it as a read-only data source. The Jet Engine requires a unique index for every non-Access table it will allow you to edit. When you link a table from an ODBC data source, Access chooses the clustered unique index as the primary key. If there is no clustered unique index, Access chooses the (alphabetically) first unique index as the primary key of the table. This has a couple of implications:

- A table with no unique index will always be read-only.

- If you have an index on the server that you wish to use as the primary key, you must make sure it is named something like AAA_PrimaryKey so that it will alphabetize before any other unique indexes, or you must make it a clustered unique index.

Should you have a table with no indexes, you can fix the problem in two ways. First, you can use whatever tools your server provides to create an index and then delete and relink the table. (Doing this forces Access to requery the server for the new structure of the table.) If someone other than yourself is maintaining your server database, this method may be the best way to go, because changing the table on the server will make it read-write for all users.

You can also correct the problem in Access by creating a pseudo-index. Access 97 automatically offers to do this for you when you link a table without a unique index on the server. You'll see the dialog box shown in Figure 15.7, and you can choose any combination of fields that you know is unique on the server.

FIGURE 15.7

Dialog box to select unique fields for a server view

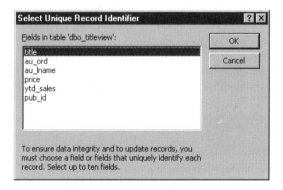

Alternatively, you can use a DDL (Data Definition Language) query in Access to create the pseudo-index. This has the general form

CREATE UNIQUE INDEX *index* ON *table* (*field* [ASC I DESC][, *field*
[ASC I DESC], …])

Using either the automatic method or the CREATE INDEX method causes Access to maintain a local index on the linked table, enabling it to update the data in the table.

Although any table with a unique index is updatable, you can make another optimization to speed updates on some servers. If your server supports a Timestamp datatype (a date/time field the server updates whenever any value in the record is changed), tables with a Timestamp field can be updated much more efficiently. Whenever Jet goes

WARNING A local index created in this manner is for your convenience only and may not reflect which fields in the server table actually determine uniqueness. Create these indexes with care! If you create a local index on fields that aren't unique, you could experience strange behavior when updating server tables.

to update a row using ODBC, it has to ensure that the record was not changed by another user while you were editing it. Normally it will check by retrieving all non-memo and non-OLE fields from the table and comparing them to the locally cached values, to make sure there were no changes to any field. If the table has a timestamp, it can just check to make sure the timestamp hasn't changed since you started editing the record.

Understanding Your Server

Part of the promise of ODBC is that you can develop applications that are server independent. It turns out, though, that while ODBC certainly makes it easier to move from server to server, it is still important to write your application with the target server in mind. Both the server and the connecting software will affect the processing of your SQL. The SQL language used in Access is far from any specific ANSI standard. (Chapter 5 outlines most of the differences.) Access has several features not supported by most servers and lacks features present in some servers.

ANSI SQL standards define datatypes differently from Access. You need to understand how ODBC maps datatypes, both from the server to Access and from Access tables to the server.

Some important areas to check for different servers are security, AutoNumber fields or their equivalent, joins, support for the use of multiple indexes within a single query, declarative referential integrity (DRI), and transaction processing support. The level of transaction support is a function of both the server and the ODBC driver. You need to match the features of your server with the features of Access that your application uses. If your application functionality is dependent on features your server does not support, you should look at a different server, rework your application, or consider not migrating the application. You will often end up splitting your application's logic between parts that can be performed on the server and parts that must be performed locally in the front end.

Consider the following server characteristics when picking a server and developing your Access applications:

- Does the server support SQL-92 Join syntax?
- What Join syntax is supported?
  - Inner joins only
  - Outer joins
  - Nested inner and outer joins (Note that this would require SPT or ODBCDirect queries.)
- Does the server support subqueries?
- Does the server support auto-incrementing or identity fields (counters)?
- Does the server support referential integrity?
- Does the server allow updates on any joined queries? If so, which updates and deletes are supported?
- Does the server support stored procedures or triggers?
- Does the server support cascading updates or deletes?
- Which built-in functions does the server support?
- Which date/time functions does the server support?

Designing an Efficient Client-Server Application

When implementing client-server systems, you need to address several design areas that you typically do not need to deal with in a stand-alone Access application. The next few sections cover each of these design areas in detail.

Establishing Rules for Transactions

You must clearly define and document all your data activity that is to be grouped together so that the transaction protection and recovery features of your server can work correctly.

Jet applies the following rules regarding transactions when processing against an ODBC data source:

- Forms must use optimistic locking.

- Recordsets must use optimistic locking.

- Only the outermost transaction is used if nested transactions are encountered.

- Only a single workspace is used for an ODBC connection. Multiple workspaces are consolidated.

- Action queries are processed in a single transaction.

- Recordsets created inside a VBA transaction are processed under that transaction.

Jet precludes the use of pessimistic locking because it has no way of knowing whether a particular record is locked. (This feature is not available through ODBC.) Therefore, bound forms are of limited usefulness in an update-intensive application where optimistic locking can lead to problems (records locked on save or data changing during edits). The same problems exist with records created using VBA, but with these you have much more control over how to handle the error.

You may, however, be able to successfully use bound forms directly against server tables or views in the following circumstances:

- When the form is based on a single table

- When the system is coded to handle update contention that will occur from optimistic locking

- When the data being updated does not need to be kept private while a set of changes is completed

- When the amount of data shown on the form at any one time is strictly limited

Forms that will usually meet these criteria include

- Inquiry-only forms (based on read-only recordsets)

- Master table maintenance forms

- Browse forms that accept a key value from the user and then change their record source to fetch only the record with that key

Processing that generally does *not* work well using bound forms in the client-server setup includes

- Updates or inserts of master/detail combinations, such as orders
- Updates in which multiple rows of a table must be changed at once

Using Local Tables

At times you will want to keep a local copy of some of your server database within the Access client application. When splitting the workload between Access and the server, always remember that Access is a complete database system. You can take advantage of this by caching data locally on each client machine as it is first used or even at login time, refreshing your local tables during your AutoExec macro or Startup Form Form_Open procedure. This way you can reduce both network traffic and the load on your server, allowing you to support many more concurrent users on the same server and network. This procedure is especially easy to implement if you are converting an existing application, because you already have the native Access processing coded.

Review all your data requirements and identify the data that matches the following conditions:

- Data is static or relatively static.
- Users do not need to see each other's changes immediately.
- Data is always used together as a set, with each set needing to be used together exclusively.

Also, review your processing requirements to look for the following situations:

- Data entry systems in which several detail records are entered to build a complete transaction. This may be an order, an invoice, a parts list, or one of several other cases matching the traditional header-detail data pairing.
- Reports showing several aspects of the same data.
- Reports that do a great deal of data consolidation.

When you have processing needs matching the above types, you can benefit by downloading the data onto the client machine for processing or, when going the other way, by capturing the user's activity locally and uploading data to the server only when the user's session or activity is complete.

If your application uses a number of lookup tables, set up your system to load these at startup time. You can then design your forms and reports to use the local data in pick lists, in combo boxes, or when displaying descriptive lookup text instead of codes.

If your users typically work on a particular set of data for an extended period and other users should not work on this same data concurrently, you have a prime candidate for downloading the data and processing it locally—for example, a problem management system or an order processing system.

Note that you'll have to choose carefully when to use the client copy of a table and when to use the server copy. A table of U.S. states used as the row source for a combo box, for example, should be the local copy because opening the combo will cause it to be requeried multiple times. On the other hand, when you're writing a query that joins that table with other server tables, you'll want to use the server copy, to avoid the heavy network traffic of doing a join between two different data sources.

Creating Efficient Queries

At the heart of any database application are queries. They are the way you interact with data. Creating efficient client-server queries requires that you follow two guidelines:

- Construct queries that can be executed entirely on the server.

- Move as little data as possible across the network.

Remember, your major benefits from a client-server application come when you move less data over the network cable than you would in a file-server application. These guidelines are discussed in the next two sections.

Execute on the Server

A database server's strength is its ability to process queries very quickly and efficiently. To take advantage of this, you must make sure that any queries you generate (including bound forms and update operations) are executed entirely by the server. When would this not be the case? If you're using pass-through queries or ODBCDirect, you needn't worry about this, because your queries are sent directly to the server with no intervention from Jet. If you're using linked tables, however, you can get into trouble.

Problems arise as Jet parses your query. Based on its knowledge of ODBC and the server you're using, Jet breaks down your query into the portions the server can execute directly and those it can't. It then executes one query for each server component, brings back the resulting data, and then processes the final result locally. This leads to longer execution time and increased network traffic.

Ideally, when Jet finishes parsing your query, it is left with a single SQL statement that it can then send to the server. Often, however, it will not be able to resolve your query to ODBC-compliant SQL. Specifically, Jet will need to perform local processing if you've used any of these features:

- Access or user-defined functions that take field values as inputs
- Access SQL that ODBC doesn't support (TRANSFORM/PIVOT is one example)
- Multiple-level GROUP BYs
- GROUP BYs including DISTINCT
- Joins over GROUP BYs
- Joins over DISTINCT clauses
- Certain combinations of outer and inner joins
- Queries stacked on unions
- Subqueries that include data from more than one source
- Joins between multiple data sources (ODBC or ISAM)
- Other complex queries

If you've used any of the elements listed above, you should rewrite those portions of the application to use simpler Jet queries, pass-through queries, or ODBCDirect.

For most developers, however, the final item in the list is of most concern. Often it is difficult to predetermine whether a particular query will result in local processing. To troubleshoot these situations, you need a way to see what SQL Jet is actually generating. (See the section called "Looking In on Jet and ODBC" later in this chapter for more information.)

Move Only What You Need

Network traffic is costly in terms of execution time, so you must reduce it as much as possible. If you've satisfied the first guideline above, you've met this one halfway. You've reduced the amount of data going *to* the server to a single SQL statement. The other half is to reduce the amount of data coming *back*.

It is important to avoid recordsets based on all fields and all rows of a table. If you really need this level of data, consider importing or downloading the data from the server instead of linking to it. You can always refresh the data from the server by dropping your local table and reimporting. For forms, always define a query for the record source, and always include a WHERE clause that is as restrictive as possible—one row is best but may not be enough to meet your needs. Avoid the use of the all-fields identifier (*) in your queries. Create form-specific queries that contain only the fields required for that form.

One way to limit the data returned when you're writing queries to serve as the record source for a form is to start with a blank record source. Force the user to make some type of selection that can be used in a WHERE clause to limit the rows returned. You can then include this in a SQL statement and dynamically change the RecordSource property at run time. (This strategy was also discussed for file-server applications in Chapter 12.) You can accomplish this by using an event procedure similar to this one:

```
Private Sub cboAuthors_AfterUpdate()
    Me.RecordSource = "SELECT * FROM dbo_authors WHERE " & _
      "au_id = '" & Me!cboAuthors & "'"
End Sub
```

In the sample database, frmAuthors demonstrates this same technique with the authors table from the SQL Server Pubs database. It also demonstrates another technique mentioned earlier: downloading lookup information to a local table. Author names and social security numbers are downloaded to a local table, and this information is used to populate a combo box on the form. After the user makes a selection, the remaining fields are retrieved. A Refresh button on the form lets the user download new values from the server table.

Another consideration concerns retrieving memo or OLE fields from the server. Because these tend to involve a substantial amount of data, they will vastly increase your network traffic. If you have an employees table with a picture of the employee, for example, you might start by bringing back only the text data and including a command button to retrieve the picture only if the user wants to see it.

For reports, consider defining the base data for the report as a local table and running an append query to load it from the server. Doing so avoids many of the pitfalls you will find when trying to interpret all the data access requirements of a report. It will also allow you to base multiple reports on the same set of data and yet query the server only once.

Building Your Forms

Building forms for client-server applications requires some special consider-ations beyond those covered in Chapter 8. You must pay special attention to how your searching and navigation processes work. You must also be closely aware of your data sources.

Choosing Bound and Unbound Fields

After you have identified all the data requirements and data sources for your forms, you need to create the forms and link all the fields to their data sources. Whenever possible, link bound fields to a field from the record source of the form rather than create a separate row source for each control. In a client-server environ-ment, each row source will result in a separate connection to the server.

If you do use controls bound to separate data sources (including subforms, list boxes, or combo boxes), make sure either that they are set to be hidden when the form opens or that the fields used to link to them or provide criteria for them are filled in during the form's Open event. Firing off the query for a subform with null criteria can create a major, unneeded workload for your network. This is especially important for subforms because they tend to be more complex than list boxes or combo boxes.

Choosing an Appropriate Design for Your Forms

Often an Access form allows a user both to navigate to a specific record and to then perform detailed work on the record. Several approaches to form design provide good performance for these situations. The goal of each approach is to present the user with a small subset of the fields to use to select the records they need and a sep-arate recordset for the detail. The form should be set up to fill the detail recordset only *after* the user selects the criteria.

Using an Unbound Main Form and a Subform for Detail

One of the simplest approaches you can use for forms mainly used to search or edit data is to create your edit form as though it will be used directly and then embed it as a subform on an unbound form. You can set the record source of the subform based on a query that references fields on the unbound main form rather than use the master and child linking fields. On the main form, create the controls users will use to establish the criteria for their final recordset. You should set the default value on each of the criteria fields to a value that will cause the subform to return no rows when the form is first opened. If you use a combo box, list box, or other pick-list mechanism to allow the user to find records, use a hidden field to hold the criteria and fill it in the AfterUpdate event procedure of the pick-list type control. Provide a command button, toolbar button, or menu selection for users to indicate that they are finished setting criteria. If the pick lists are based on fairly static data, such as order types, lists of valid codes, or processing status codes, this data should be downloaded to the client at startup. For more volatile data, you should accept the overhead of retrieving it from the server each time the form is opened to ensure that users receive the most current data.

Using a Dynamic Record Source

You can provide more flexibility by using a modified version of the form/sub-form model presented in the preceding section. Create the SQL for the detail form dynamically, based on the values filled in on the unbound main form. This eliminates the need for hidden fields for criteria and helps ensure that the most efficient SQL can be used for each alternative set of criteria. You must use dynamic SQL instead of a fixed query with parameters if you are using LIKE in your criteria and appending wildcard characters to the user's selections. If you use fixed criteria, you will end up with a full table scan because the optimizer cannot predict how to use the indexes. You should also use dynamic SQL instead of a fixed query if your table has multiple indexes but your server can use only a single index for each table in a query. By building the SQL based on the fields the user selects, you have the best chance of using the most restrictive index each time.

Using Unbound Controls in the Header or Footer

On a single form, you can use a variation on the approach just described. Place the unbound controls that are used for criteria entry in the header or footer, and at run time, either filter the form using the ApplyFilter action or reset the form's record source using the form's RecordSource property. (See the frmAuthors form in CH15.MDB for an example of this technique.) This approach has the advantage of using only a single bound form, but it offers fewer user interface design alternatives because the header and footer must always appear at a specific location.

Using FindFirst

One approach to record navigation and searching that works much better in client-server than in native Access is the FindFirst method. In Access this method always results in a scan, but with servers, Jet will often use a new query, and the server can process an efficient search. You can take advantage of this by placing your search criteria in the header or footer area of a form and using FindFirst to move the detail section to the desired data.

Building Reports

Reports often cause problems for client-server work in Access. Access has a powerful reporting module that offers many data-analysis tools. Most of these tools assume that the data with which they are working is local and that retrieving the data multiple times will not cause unacceptable overhead.

You may find that the easiest solution is to split your report processing into two parts. First, set up a query that extracts all the required data from your server. While building this query, do not worry about obtaining totals, grouping, or other reporting requirements. After you have isolated the data for the report, build the query or queries used by the report based on the server query. When you need to run multiple reports from a single data source, you should download the data into local Access tables and base the reports on these temporary tables.

Exceptions to this general approach are

- Generating a summary report from a very large database
- Generating a report using statistics (such as median) that are supported by your server directly but are not supported in Access

Effects of Grouping and Sorting

Access cannot send multiple-field GROUP BYs directly to servers. If you do not download the data into an Access table with indexes that support the GROUP BYs, the recordset is sorted on the client machine. The grouping and sorting in the report design will override the grouping and sorting in a query, so do not use grouping and sorting in the query when you are grouping and sorting data within the report.

Selecting Data Sources for Fields

Because reports represent a read-only snapshot of a database, you will find more cases in which downloaded data can be used than for forms. Applying all formatting on the report fields instead of the query fields also helps with query optimization.

Creating Header and Footer Fields and Expressions

You should try to base the summary fields in your headers and footers on fields from the Detail sections of your reports instead of on expressions against the tables.

Graphs

When including graphs in a report, you must pay close attention to the data source and the location of the OLE server. You usually use a separate record source for each chart on a report. Make sure the record source is restricted to exactly what should be graphed. Do not use the query to add formatting or titles or to provide anything other than the raw data for the graph. Provide all legends, titles, and formatting by means of Automation. Allowing the server to do what it does best—provide data from its tables—should keep your reports working smoothly.

Common Client-Server Migration Problems

It's likely you will encounter problems when moving existing file-server applications to a client-server environment. While much of this chapter has provided useful information for this process, the following sections offer additional troubleshooting assistance.

Nonupdatable Queries

One of the first problems you may run into is that queries (or views) that are updatable in Access will be read-only on your server. In these cases Jet processes the join operation locally and manages the retrievals and updates to the server's tables on the client side. This is not as efficient as handling the updates solely on the server, and it may also introduce increased contention problems, depending on how Access and your server define the transactions for these updates. You may want to consider redesigning your system to avoid doing updates on joined data. Typically, as long as your network is well designed, the server will be fast enough to allow the split in updating that Jet produces. The major problem comes with the increased network load that sometimes occurs with this type of system.

Converting Validation Rules

Validation rules are another area that requires special consideration during migration. Access-defined validation rules cannot be used by any current server. If your server supports triggers and stored procedures, you should be able to convert most Access rules to server-based triggers. If you do this, you will need to add in your own error handling to replace the validation text and error trapping you had in your native Access application. You will also need to test your specific server to determine the error processing related to stored procedures and triggers. Take extra care when converting table-level validation rules and validation rules that use Access functions. Most servers will not have the same set of predefined functions as Access, so you may need to have stored procedures written to replace them. In some cases you may need to do the validation locally in VBA before the data is sent to the server.

User-Defined Functions

Any queries that make use of user-defined functions or built-in Access functions also require special attention. Since the server will not support them, Jet returns them to your application to perform locally. This may not be too much of a problem if the functions are only on the final output, because they will be applied only as the data is sent from the server to the client. You will experience severe performance problems, however, if they are part of query criteria, ORDER BY, GROUP BY, or aggregate expressions. If you have any of these cases, look at converting the functions to stored procedures on the server. You could also split your query to allow all the server processing that doesn't involve the Access function to occur in one server query, returning a recordset that is then processed locally.

Counter, OLE, and Memo Fields

The presence of counter fields in your database requires the use of a stored procedure or special field datatype on many servers to provide a similar function. Most servers now support equivalents of OLE and memo fields, but if you use either of these, make sure you understand exactly *how* the server supports them.

Combo and List Boxes

Combo and list boxes that reference large numbers of server rows will be a problem. You'll get much better performance if you either cache the data locally or use appropriate criteria to restrict the list to a small number of entries.

Looking In on Jet and ODBC

To some extent, the interaction between Jet and ODBC is a black box. When you run queries against linked ODBC tables, you really have no control over how Jet retrieves or updates the data. This makes it difficult to troubleshoot problems involving Jet and ODBC and to make informed decisions regarding when to use features such as SQL pass-through or ODBCDirect. Fortunately, there may be a solution. Some database server vendors supply software that allows you to examine the actual SQL statements being sent to the server. While we can't cover every database server, in this section we'll look at using the SQL Trace tool that ships with Microsoft SQL Server 6.5.

> **NOTE** Prior to version 6.5, SQL tracing was possible through the use of a third-party program called SQLEye. Available on CompuServe and Microsoft's MDSN CD-ROM, this program works much the same way as SQL Trace.

Running SQL Trace

SQL Trace is one of the utilities you can install as part of the SQL Server package; it appears as an icon in your program group or Start menu. When you start SQL Trace for the first time, you are prompted to define a *filter*. Filters tell SQL Trace what to monitor—for example, which servers, processes, and activities. Click the Yes button to open the filter definition dialog shown in Figure 15.8.

You must give the filter a name that is unique among all other defined filters. You can optionally select individual logins, applications, or hosts to monitor. The default is to monitor everything. For convenience, you can set the application name to "Microsoft Access" to monitor only those SQL statements sent from Access.

Capture options refer to how SQL Trace should process the incoming statements. You can view them on the screen or save them to a file. If you choose to view them, check the Per Connection check box. This instructs SQL Trace to open a new window

Defining a SQL Trace filter to monitor statements sent to the server

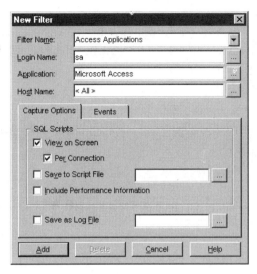

for each connection made to the server. Because Access will use multiple connections, it is easier to track them if each one has its own SQL Trace window.

The Events tab on the Define Filter dialog lets you select which server events you want to monitor. You can choose from connections, SQL statements, remote procedure calls (RPCs), attentions, and disconnections. For SQL and RPCs, you can also limit the individual statements you want SQL Trace to display.

Once you've defined at least one filter, you can begin monitoring activity. SQL Trace will update its display (if you chose to view information on the screen) with any active connections. You can define and use additional filters as you deem necessary.

Monitoring Jet and ODBC Interaction

As you execute queries (or anything involving the server you're monitoring, for that matter), SQL Trace displays the *actual statements* being sent to the server. If you're using linked ODBC tables, these statements will be the translated SQL coming from the SQL Server ODBC driver. In the case of pass-through queries or ODBCDirect, these will be statements you've defined yourself. If possible, run SQL Trace on a separate workstation from the one running Access and place the two monitors where you can see them both. This makes for the best viewing arrangement; you'll be able to see each connection as it is established, used, and terminated. (Sometimes this happens very quickly.)

When you begin using SQL Trace, you will find it enlightening just to watch the statements generated by Jet and the ODBC driver as you perform tasks such as linking to tables, running queries, and modifying data. Figure 15.9 shows the statements generated by opening the frmTitles form in the sample database immediately after opening the database itself.

FIGURE 15.9

Tracing commands sent to SQL Server using SQL Trace

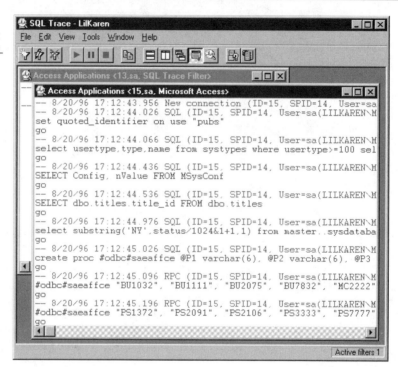

Each of the statements is described briefly here:

1. Access logs on to SQL Server and instructs the server to change to the pubs database.

2. The ODBC driver sets various configuration information.

3. Jet attempts to query the MsysConf table if it exists.

4. Jet queries the titles table for the primary key values.

5. Jet queries the sysdatabases table to determine whether the database is read-only.

6. The ODBC driver creates a stored procedure to retrieve additional field information based on a list of primary key values.

7. Jet calls this stored procedure twice to retrieve field values to place on the form.

What you don't see in Figure 15.9 is the data being returned to Access. You'll have to infer this from the SQL statements. For example, the statement requesting the primary key values might not make much of an impact with a 20-row table, but what if the table had a million records!

Troubleshooting Poor Performance

Using tools like SQL Trace, you can troubleshoot parts of your application that perform poorly after moving to client-server. For instance, suppose you use a delete query to remove rows from a table on the server. After migrating the data to SQL Server, you find that this query all of a sudden takes a very long time to execute. By using SQL Trace you'd notice that when you run a delete query against a linked ODBC table, Jet issues a DELETE statement for *each row in the table!* It does this to ensure that you delete only records that haven't changed since you created the result set. Armed with this knowledge, you could then replace the standard query with a SQL pass-through query that issued a single DELETE statement. As you become more familiar with how Jet and ODBC interact, you'll be able to spot instances where converting to SQL pass-through or ODBCDirect make sense.

The Upsizing Wizard

There is one special case in which you will find the mechanics of moving from Access to a server database to be considerably simplified: when you're moving from Access to Microsoft SQL Server. Microsoft has designed a separate product called the Access Upsizing Tools to make this transition easier. The original version was intended to convert an Access 2.0 database to use Microsoft SQL Server 4.21 tables. Microsoft updated this for Access 95, allowing you to move an Access 95 database to SQL Server 4.21, 6.0, or 6.5. Once again, Microsoft has updated the tool to work with Access 97 databases. Microsoft has made the tool available free of charge, and you can find it on their World Wide Web site at www.microsoft.com/accdev.

The Upsizing Wizard runs as an Access add-in. When you run it, it accomplishes the following tasks:

- Exports the structure of all tables to the SQL Server

- Creates indexes on the server

- Exports as many validation rules as possible to the server

- Creates stored procedures (for SQL 4.21) or Identity fields (for SQL 6.0) to replace counters

- Creates stored procedures (for SQL 4.21) or uses Declarative Referential Integrity (for SQL 6.0) to enforce your referential integrity on the server

- Renames tables and fields as necessary to conform with the SQL Server naming limits

- Exports your Access data to the server

- Links the SQL Server tables back to your Access application

- Creates queries as necessary to alias changed field and table names back to their original names

You can think of the Upsizing Wizard as the client-server equivalent of the Database Splitter that's included with Access 97. While it won't do anything to make the changes we've discussed above to make your application more efficient in a client-server environment, it will eliminate most of the tedious work, leaving you free to concentrate on the fine-tuning.

Resources

This chapter has merely scratched the surface of the issues involved in client-server development. *Access and SQL Server Developer's Handbook,* by John Viescas, Mike Gunderloy, and Mary Chipman (available from SYBEX) concentrates exclusively on client-server issues within the Microsoft product line. Several other sources of information may help further in this process. Books Online, the CD-ROM based documentation that comes with Office 97 Developer's Edition, includes a number of topics on ODBC and client-server applications.

Many Microsoft knowledge-base articles are also available from Microsoft on specific issues, problems, and work-arounds for both ODBC and client-server. Microsoft's *Jet Database Engine ODBC Connectivity* white paper also contains excellent information on using Access in a client-server environment. (You can access knowledge-base articles and the white paper on CompuServe, MSN, the MSDN, and TechNet CDs and through Microsoft's download services.) Your ODBC driver vendor and your database server vendor should be able to supply help in configuring the server and getting the ODBC links running properly.

Summary

In this chapter we have covered the basics of implementing a client-server system using Access. We introduced the major areas to consider when planning a client-server system or planning a migration to client-server. More specifically, we covered these issues:

- Understanding the mechanics of ODBC processing

- Choosing a query strategy for client-server applications

- Configuring Access for ODBC

- Mapping your transactions in client-server systems

- Taking advantage of Access' strengths in creating client-server applications

- Choosing the best form and control design for efficient processing

- Building efficient reports

- Identifying problem areas when migrating an application to client-server

- Using the Access Upsizing Tools

PART V

Building Applications

Error Handling and Debugging

- Dealing with compile-time errors

- Handling run-time errors

- Avoiding and resolving logic errors

- Techniques and strategies for debugging

In any programming environment, you have to deal with errors, and VBA is no different. These errors fall into three categories:

- Compile-time errors
- Run-time errors
- Logic errors

Compile-time errors occur when your code contains incorrect syntax. The compiler requires that these errors be fixed before the code will run. VBA flags the error either when you enter the improper syntax or when the code is compiled, depending on an option you set for the project.

Run-time errors occur when some condition makes your code invalid. For example, trying to open a table that doesn't exist will trigger a run-time error. If you don't trap run-time errors, VBA displays an error message and stops your code at that point. VBA provides a mechanism using the On Error statement that allows you to trap a run-time error and handle the problem.

Logic errors occur when your code doesn't do what you intended because of improper logic, a misunderstanding of how certain statements and functions work, or outright mistakes. For example, if you use a less-than operator (<) when you mean to have a less-than-or-equal-to operator (<=), you have a logic error. Logic errors are commonly known as *bugs*.

This chapter shows you how to reduce the number of each of these types of errors and how to deal with them when they do occur. All of the sample code shown in this chapter is available in CH16.MDB on the CD-ROM.

Dealing with Syntax Errors

VBA can report syntax errors at two points. If you select Tools ➤ Options and then look in the Module tab, you see a check box called Auto Syntax Check. This option controls when VBA will report syntax errors to you. If it is checked, VBA displays a message box as soon as you leave a line of code that has a syntax error in the module editor. If the option is unchecked, VBA merely changes the color to indicate that it doesn't understand the line. In either case, when VBA compiles the code, it reports the error.

Often you will write half a line of code and then discover you need to move up to the top of the module to declare the variable you are using. At this point VBA reports the line as having a syntax error if the Auto Syntax Check option is on. Since VBA shows lines with syntax errors in red, you already have immediate feedback that there is a problem, so you may prefer to turn off the option. You can always get complete details on the error by clicking the Compile Loaded Modules button on the toolbar.

There are also a number of syntax errors that VBA cannot immediately highlight. These errors occur in multi-line constructs, such as If...Then and Select...Case statements. Because a valid statement requires more than one line of code, VBA cannot check the syntax until the module is compiled. To check for these types of errors before running your application, click the Compile Loaded Modules button on the toolbar.

Dealing with Run-time Errors

When a run-time error occurs, you have several ways of dealing with it. If you do nothing, VBA responds by displaying an error message and stopping the execution of your code. While this behavior is fine in the development environment, it is rarely acceptable in production applications. For this reason you will usually want to include error-handling features in your code. Resolving errors that occur at run time requires three steps:

1. Invoking an error handler

2. Reacting to the error

3. Exiting the error handler

The following sections discuss these steps.

Invoking an Error Handler with the On Error Statement

You invoke an error handler with the On Error statement, which comes in several varieties, as described in the following sections. The On Error statement is actual VBA code that, when executed, tells VBA how to handle run-time errors that occur after the statement. Each procedure can have as many On Error statements as you wish. However, only the most recently executed On Error statement remains in force.

The On Error GoTo Label Statement

On Error Goto *Label* is the most powerful form of error handling because it gives you the most control over what to do in the event of a run-time error. You use the On Error Goto *Label* statement to cause VBA to jump to a specific location in your code if an error occurs. When an error occurs in code after an On Error GoTo *Label* statement, control passes to the assigned label. Listing 16.1 shows the most common format for an error handler.

Listing 16.1

```
Sub GenericSubWithHandler()
    ' Stub showing standard way to construct an error handler

    On Error GoTo GenericSubWithHandlerErr

    ' Some code that might generate a run-time error

GenericSubWithHandlerDone:
    Exit Sub
GenericSubWithHandlerErr:
    ' Error Handler
    Resume GenericSubWithHandlerDone
End Sub
```

When an error occurs, control immediately passes to the label specified in the On Error GoTo *Label* statement. The label must appear in the same procedure as the On Error GoTo *Label* statement. By convention, the error handler appears at the end of the procedure.

> **NOTE** Unlike previous versions of Access that used Access Basic as the programming language, VBA no longer requires that label names be unique across the entire module.

Use an Exit Sub or Exit Function statement to keep the normal flow of control from passing into the error handler. You can see this in the example, just after the GenericSubWithHandlerDone label.

Once an error has occurred and control has passed into the error handler, the code is treated as being in a special state. While the code is in this state, the following is true:

- The error handler defined by the On Error Goto *Label* statement is no longer in effect. This means any run-time error that occurs within the error handler is treated as though no error handler exists in this procedure.

- You can use a Resume statement (described in the section "The Resume Statement" later in this chapter) to return control back to the main procedure and resume normal error handling.

- You cannot execute an End Sub or End Function statement to "fall out" of an error handler. You must explicitly use an *Exit* Sub or *Exit* Function statement to exit the procedure. Commonly accepted software engineering practice says a procedure should have only one entry point and one exit point, so an even better idea is to use Resume *Label* to return control to the main code, where the procedure can be exited at a common point (as in our example).

The On Error Resume Next Statement

Creating an error handler with the On Error GoTo *Label* statement can require a considerable number of statements. Sometimes you want to ignore errors. Other times you know exactly which error to expect and want to handle it without having to write a full error handler. The On Error Resume Next statement informs VBA that you want control to resume at the statement immediately after the statement that generated the error, without any visible intervention from VBA. For example, if you are attempting to delete a file and don't care whether the file actually exists, you might have some code like that shown in Listing 16.2.

Listing 16.2

```
Sub Delfile(ByVal strFileName As String)
    ' Example showing an On Error Resume Next
    'Deletes a file if it exists

    On Error Resume Next

    Kill strFileName
End Sub
```

Normally, the Kill statement generates a run-time error if the file specified as its argument doesn't exist. However, the On Error Resume Next statement in this example causes the run-time error to be ignored, and control passes to the next line (in this case, the End Sub statement).

A slightly more complex example is shown in Listing 16.3.

Listing 16.3

```
Sub SetControlColors(frm As Form, ByVal lngColor As Long)
    ' Changes the color of all the controls on the
    ' form to the color specified by lngColor

    Dim ctl As Control

    On Error Resume Next

    For Each ctl In frm.Controls
        ctl.BackColor = lngColor
    Next
End Sub
```

This procedure loops through all the controls on a form specified by a form variable and changes the BackColor property of the controls to the value specified by the lngColor argument. Some controls, such as command buttons, do not have a BackColor property. When the code reaches these controls, a run-time error is normally generated. The On Error Resume Next statement lets the program ignore the error and continue. See the section "Inline Error Handling" later in this chapter for more on using On Error Resume Next.

The On Error GoTo 0 Statement

When you use an On Error GoTo *Label* or On Error Resume Next statement, it remains in effect until the procedure is exited, another error handler is declared, or the error handler is canceled. The On Error GoTo 0 statement cancels the error handler. VBA (or an error handler in a calling procedure, as described in the section "Hierarchy of Error Handlers" later in this chapter) again traps subsequent errors. This statement also resets the value of the Err object (see the section "Determining Which Error Has Occurred" later in this chapter), so if you need the values it contains, you must store away its properties.

Creating Intelligent Error Handlers

After trapping an error with the On Error GoTo *Label* statement, you will want to take some action. What you do depends on your application. If you are trying to open a table and the table doesn't exist, you might want to report an error to the user. On the other hand, you might decide instead to go ahead and create the table by executing a make-table query. To take action intelligently you must have some way to determine which specific error (of the literally thousands of possible errors) has occurred. This section explains how to do that using the VBA Err object.

Determining Which Error Has Occurred

VBA has a very convenient method of obtaining run-time error information: the Err object. The Err object has the properties listed in Table 16.1. These properties are set by VBA after a run-time error. By using the properties of the Err object, you can determine exactly which error has occurred.

TABLE 16.1   Err Object Properties

Property	Description
Description	Returns a descriptive string associated with an error
HelpContext	Returns a context ID for a topic in a Microsoft Windows Help file
HelpFile	Returns a fully qualified path to a Microsoft Windows Help file
LastDLLError	Returns a system error code produced by a call into a Dynamic Link Library (DLL). The GetLastError Windows API call gives the error code for the most recent Windows API call. When you are calling Windows API calls from VBA, though, you have a problem: VBA itself will make several Windows API calls between the time you make the call through VBA code and when you try to call GetLastError. When VBA does this, it wipes out the information that GetLastError returns. To get around this situation, VBA calls GetLastError for you after every API call
Number	Returns a numeric value specifying an error. Number is the Err object's default property
Source	Returns the name of the object or application that originally generated the error

NOTE   While the error number (Err.Number) associated with a particular error condition is fixed, the text (Err.Description) is not. Microsoft changes it from version to version to clarify error information and provide additional information. Also, if your program is ever run on an international version of Access, the error message will appear in the local language of the version of Access. For these reasons you should always use the Err.Number property in your error-handling code rather than the description strings from the Err.Description property.

Listing 16.4 shows an example of using the Err object in an error handler. The example tries to open a recordset based on a table that may or may not exist. If the table doesn't exist, VBA invokes the error handler, which examines the Err.Number property for the value 3011. Error number 3011 indicates that an invalid object name was supplied, in which case a custom error message is displayed. For all other errors the error handler displays a generic message using the Err.Number and Err.Description properties to provide the user with detailed error information.

Listing 16.4

```
Sub TypicalErrorHandlerSub()
    ' Example showing the construction of a procedure with an
    ' error handler.

    Dim rst As Recordset

    ' A constant for the error number
    Const adhcErrCannotFindObject = 3011

    On Error GoTo TypicalErrorHandlerSubErr

    ' Some code that might generate a run-time error
    Set rst = CurrentDb.OpenRecordset("tblTable", dbOpenTable)

    ' You would do some processing with rst here

TypicalErrorHandlerSubDone:
    On Error Resume Next
    rst.Close
    Exit Sub
TypicalErrorHandlerSubErr:
    Select Case err.Number
        Case adhcErrCannotFindObject    'Cannot find object
            MsgBox "tblTable doesn't exist. " _
            & "Call the database administrator.", _
            vbExclamation, "TypicalErrorHandlerSub"
        Case Else
            MsgBox "The application encountered unexpected " & _
            "error #" & err.Number & " with message string '" & _
            err.Description & "'", _
                vbExclamation, "TypicalErrorHandlerSub"
    End Select
    Resume TypicalErrorHandlerSubDone
End Sub
```

The Select Case statement uses the value in Err.Number to determine which error has occurred. You should use a Select Case statement even if you have only one case you want to handle, since this makes it easy for you to handle other errors later just by inserting another Case statement. Always use a Case Else to trap unexpected errors. You can use a MsgBox statement in the Case Else statement, or an error-reporting routine, as shown in the section "Creating an Error-Reporting Subroutine" later in this chapter.

It's important to realize that two or more statements in your main code can generate the same error (which would have occurred, for instance, if we had used OpenRecordset twice in the above example). If you want different things to happen in your error handler for each of those statements, you must set a flag in your main code and use If statements within the Case statement (or a nested Select Case statement) in your error handler. A more complicated method would define several different error handlers with On Error statements as you reached different parts of your code. Fortunately, most code doesn't require this complexity. If it does, it might be time to consider splitting the procedure into several smaller procedures.

Listing 16.5 shows an example of the use of flags.

Listing 16.5

```
Sub AddLineNumbers()
    Dim fState As Integer
    Dim strInput As String
    Dim lngLineNumber As Long

    ' State constants
    Const adhcFStateNone = 0
    Const adhcFStateOpeningFile1 = 1
    Const adhcFStateOpeningFile2 = 2

    ' Error constants
    Const adhcErrPermissionDenied = 70
    Const adhcErrPathFileError = 75

    On Error GoTo AddLineNumbersErr

    fState = adhcFStateOpeningFile1
    Open "c:\file1.txt" For Input As #1

    fState = adhcFStateOpeningFile2
    Open "c:\file2.txt" For Output As #2
```

```
        fState = adhcFStateNone

        lngLineNumber = 1
        Do Until EOF(1)
            Input #1, strInput
            Print #2, lngLineNumber, strInput
            lngLineNumber = lngLineNumber + 1
        Loop
        Close #2
AddLineNumbersCloseFile1:
        Close #1
AddLineNumbersDone:
        Exit Sub
AddLineNumbersErr:
        Select Case err.Number
            Case adhcErrPermissionDenied, adhcErrPathFileError
                ' Permission denied or Path/File access error
                Select Case fState
                    ' If error occurred trying to open file1...
                    Case adhcFStateOpeningFile1
                        MsgBox "Could not open 'c:\file1.txt'. " & _
                            "Something probably has the file locked.", _
                            vbExclamation, "AddLineNumbers"
                        Resume AddLineNumbersDone
                    ' If error occurred trying to open file2...
                    Case adhcFStateOpeningFile2
                        MsgBox "Could not open 'c:\file2.txt'. The " & _
                            "file may be write protected or locked.", _
                            vbExclamation, "AddLineNumbers"
                        ' Make sure to close file1!
                        Resume AddLineNumbersCloseFile1
                    Case Else
                        Stop     'Should never reach here.
                End Select
            Case Else
                MsgBox "Unexpected error #" & err.Number & ".", _
                    vbExclamation, "Add Line Numbers"
        End Select
        Resume AddLineNumbersDone
End Sub
```

This listing shows a procedure that opens an ASCII file named C:\FILE1.TXT. It reads each line, adds a line number to the beginning of the line, and writes a new file, C:\FILE2.TXT, with the changes. There are two Open statements in the procedure that can fail, and you want to show the user two different error messages, depending on which one failed. Also, if an error occurs while the second file is being opened, you need to close the first file before exiting the procedure. The variable fState holds a flag indicating which open statement is being processed. When an error occurs, this variable is checked to determine which error message to display. Using the constants adhcFStateOpeningFile1 and adhcFStateOpeningFile2 instead of just the numbers 1 and 2 makes the meaning of the current value of fState more explicit.

Another technique for handling the state information uses line numbers. Yes, VBA still allows line numbers, which were required in early versions of Basic, but you don't need them on every line. The Erl function tells you which line number was most recently executed. For example, the preceding code could be rewritten as shown in Listing 16.6.

Listing 16.6

```
Sub AddLineNumbers2()
    Dim strInput As String
    Dim lngLineNumber As Long

    ' Error constants
    Const adhcErrPermissionDenied = 70
    Const adhcErrPathFileError = 75

    On Error GoTo AddLineNumbers2Err

10  Open "c:\file1.txt" For Input As #1

20  Open "c:\file2.txt" For Output As #2

30  lngLineNumber = 1
    Do Until EOF(1)
        Input #1, strInput
        Print #2, lngLineNumber, strInput
        lngLineNumber = lngLineNumber + 1
    Loop
AddLineNumbers2CloseFile2:
    Close #2

AddLineNumbers2Done:
    Close #1

    Exit Sub
AddLineNumbers2Err:
```

```
        Select Case err.Number
            Case adhcErrPermissionDenied, adhcErrPathFileError
                ' Permission denied or Path/File access error
                Select Case Erl
                    ' Error occurred at line 10...
                    Case 10
                        MsgBox "Could not open 'c:\file1.txt'. " & _
                          "Something probably has the file locked.", _
                          vbExclamation, "AddLineNumbers"
                        Resume AddLineNumbers2Done
                    ' Error occurred at line 20...
                    Case 20
                        MsgBox "Could not open 'c:\file2.txt'. " & _
                          "The file may be write protected or " & _
                          "locked.", vbExclamation, _
                          "AddLineNumbers"
                        Resume AddLineNumbers2CloseFile2
                    Case Else
                        Stop      'Should never reach here.
                End Select
            Case Else
                MsgBox "Unexpected error #" & err.Number & ".", _
                  vbExclamation, "Add Line Numbers"
        End Select
        Resume AddLineNumbers2Done
End Sub
```

The Resume Statement

To return to the main part of the procedure from an error handler, you use the Resume statement. The Resume statement has three forms:

- Resume

- Resume Next

- Resume *Label*

They are described in the following sections.

Resume   Resume by itself returns control to the statement that caused the error. Use the Resume statement when the error handler fixes the problem that caused the error and you want to continue from the place where you encountered the problem. In the example shown in Listing 16.4, if the error handler ran a make-table query that created tblTable, you would use a Resume statement. Note, however, that if you didn't fix the problem that caused the error, an endless loop occurs when the original statement fails again. Use this form of Resume with extreme caution. In most cases you should provide a dialog where the user can choose to resume or exit the procedure.

Resume Next   Use the Resume Next statement inside an error handler when you either want to ignore the statement that caused the error or have taken other action that was unable to correct the error condition. Control returns to the statement following the one that caused the error, similar to the On Error Resume Next statement.

Resume Label   Use the Resume *Label* statement when you want to return to a line other than the one causing the error or the line that follows it. Resume *Label* is similar to a GoTo statement, except you can use it only from inside an error handler. The example in Listing 16.4 shows this use of the Resume statement to jump to the label TypicalErrorHandlerSubDone. This approach to exiting a procedure after a run-time error is preferred because there is only one exit point.

Raising Errors

At times you may want to generate an error yourself rather than wait for one to occur. Other times you may want to cause the error to happen *again* inside an error handler. You do this by raising an error, using the Err.Raise method. Raise can take as arguments all the properties of the Err object. Thus you can raise a user-defined error by using this code:

```
Err.Raise Number:=65535, Description:="A user defined error"
```

This code causes VBA to act as though an error with number 65535 occurred at this point in the code and defines the description as being the string "A user defined error". The normal handling of the error occurs, so if an On Error Goto statement is in effect, it then jumps to the error handler. The Err object's Number and String properties are set to the arguments of the Err.Raise method. If you don't specify an argument to the Raise method, VBA uses the default arguments for the error number.

Why might you actually *cause* an error to occur? Typically, errors are raised in situations where business and program logic rules have been violated. For example, suppose information being read from a text file and inserted into a table contains invalid data. Rather than include code in the body of a procedure to alert the user, you might instead raise a custom error and let your error handler cope with it. Centralizing *all* handling of errors, both run-time and business rule violations, in one part of your procedure makes code management a lot easier.

> **NOTE**
>
> In general, you can use any error number above 10,000 or so for your custom errors. Error numbers below this may be used by VBA, Access, or other components.

Inline Error Handling

If you have only one statement in a piece of code that can fail, you might not want to write a full error handler. The Err object used with the On Error Resume Next statement can catch errors in your main code. This is called an *inline error handler*. To use it, lay out your code so it looks like the code in Listing 16.7.

Listing 16.7

```
Sub OnErrorResumeNextExample()
    ' Example showing the use of On Error Resume Next

    Dim rst As Recordset
    Dim objError As New SavedError

    ' Error constants
    Const adhcErrNoError = 0
    Const adhcErrCantFindObject = 3011

    ' Suppress normal error messages
    On Error Resume Next

    ' Some code that might generate a run-time error
    Set rst = CurrentDb.OpenRecordset("tblTable", dbOpenTable)

    ' Save the error state
    objError.Save Err

    On Error GoTo 0

    ' Now do something with the saved error info
    Select Case objError.Number
        Case adhcErrNoError        ' No Error
            ' Do nothing
        Case adhcErrCantFindObject   'Can't find object
            MsgBox "tblTable doesn't exist. Call the " & _
```

```
            "database administrator.", vbExclamation
          GoTo SubNameDone
      Case Else
          ' Stop here with error message
          Call objError.Raise
    End Select

    ' Do some processing with rst
    rst.Close

SubNameDone:
End Sub
```

This code contains no error handler. Instead, an On Error Resume Next statement tells VBA to ignore any errors. However, anytime a statement can generate an error, the contents of the Err object are overwritten. If no error occurred, the Err.Number property is 0. Otherwise, the Err object will contain values for the error that occurred.

Because the contents of the Err object are constantly being overwritten, you may want to save the current error to use later. To do this we've created a custom VBA class called SavedError. It has the same properties as the VBA Err object, and two methods, Save and Raise. Note the declaration of objError as a New SavedError instance. After trying to create a recordset, we call the SavedError object's Save method, which accepts the Err object as an argument. The Save method, shown in Listing 16.8, copies the values from the Err object's properties to the SavedError object's. You can find the complete listing of the properties and methods of the class in the SavedError class module in CH16.MDB.

NOTE If you look in CH16.MDB, you'll also see that we've implemented a Saved-Errors (plural) collection class. By declaring a new instance of this class in the declarations section of a module, you can use its Add method to add new SavedError objects to the collection. This lets you collect a number of saved errors and examine their properties later in your code.

Listing 16.8

```
Public Sub Save(objVBAError As ErrObject)
    ' The Save method takes an ErrObject object
    ' and copies its properties to this object's
```

```
    ' properties
    With objVBAError
        mlngNumber = .Number
        mstrSource = .Source
        mstrDescription = .Description
        mstrHelpFile = .HelpFile
        mlngHelpContext = .HelpContext
        mstrLastDLLError = .LastDLLError
    End With
End Sub
```

Note that as soon as you have two different statements that can cause a run-time error, it is usually more efficient to write an error handler using the On Error GoTo *Label* syntax since the overhead of constructing the error handler is encountered only once. If you use the Err object with On Error Resume Next, always use a Select Case statement with a Case Else clause to trap unexpected errors. Otherwise, error numbers without Case statements are ignored and may produce unexpected results.

Hierarchy of Error Handlers

VBA uses a hierarchical approach to error handling when one procedure calls another. If the called procedure generates an error that isn't handled within the procedure, the calling procedure's error handler receives the error. VBA acts as though the procedure call itself generated the error. In effect, VBA looks backwards, up the call stack, until it finds an error handler. If it reaches the top without finding an error handler, it displays its own error message and halts the code.

> **WARNING**
>
> If you have any calls to user-defined functions or subs in your code, you need to be very aware of this feature of VBA's error handlers; it can cause control to unexpectedly jump into your calling procedure's error handler. For this reason we strongly recommend that you include an error handler in every procedure in your application. This may seem like a lot of work, and it definitely increases the size of your code, but the alternative is worse. You don't want an error in one procedure causing control to unexpectedly jump into another procedure's error handler. This can easily result in bugs in your code. The best way around this problem is to always handle run-time errors locally in *every* procedure. It's worth noting, however, that this does not mean you can't make use of generic error handling/reporting routines. (See the section "Creating an Error-Reporting Subroutine" later in this chapter.)

To demonstrate the hierarchy of error handlers, FunctionA calls SubB in Listing 16.9.

Listing 16.9

```
Function FunctionA()
    ' Sample function to show the hierarchy of
    ' error handlers.
    On Error GoTo FunctionAError

    Call SubB

    MsgBox "You might expect to get to here, but you don't."
FunctionADone:
    Exit Function
FunctionAError:
    Select Case Err.Number
    Case 1
        MsgBox "You got here from SubB", vbInformation
        Resume FunctionADone
    Case Else
        Error Err.Number
    End Select
    Resume FunctionADone
End Function

Sub SubB()
    ' Generates an error but doesn't handle it.

    ' Cause an error in this Sub.
    Err.Raise Number:=1
End Sub
```

VBA generates an error when it raises error number 1 in SubB. Since SubB doesn't contain an error handler, control immediately passes back to FunctionA. FunctionA does contain an error handler, so it processes the error. If FunctionA hadn't contained an error handler, control would have passed to the procedure (if any) that called FunctionA. If VBA gets to the top of the call stack without finding an error handler, it puts up an alert and stops executing the code.

VBA acts as though the Call statement itself generates the error. The Resume Next in FunctionA returns control to the statement following the Call statement; control doesn't return to SubB. If you use a Resume statement instead of a Resume

Next in FunctionA, the Resume statement returns control to the Call statement in FunctionA. This calls SubB again, which in this case puts you into an endless loop as the error repeats.

The OnError Property and the Error Event

When you are using a bound form or report, under the covers Access is using Jet for all data access. Anytime Access has to populate the fields on a bound form or fill a list box, it is making calls to Jet. Any of these calls might fail for reasons such as the database being opened exclusively by someone else or a table having been deleted. The On Error statements described earlier in the chapter are in effect only while your code is being executed. But what can you do about errors that happen while Access is manipulating a form or report? Access gives you a way to trap those errors through the use of the OnError property and its associated Error event procedure. This property allows you to specify a routine to be executed when an error occurs. When you run the Code Builder (by clicking the "…" button for the property and then selecting Code Builder) on this property, you see a procedure stub that looks like the following:

```
Sub Form_Error(DataErr As Integer, Response As Integer)

End Sub
```

DataErr is the value that would be returned by the Err.Number property had the error occurred in code. *Response* is a value you fill in before the procedure terminates. It tells Access whether or not it should report the error to the user. *DataErr* and *Response* are the variable names the Access Code Builder proposes, but you can rename them to any variable names. Listing 16.10 shows an example of a routine that handles the Error event.

Listing 16.10

```
Sub Form_Error(DataErr As Integer, Response As Integer)
    ' Reports errors for the form, attached to OnError property
    Const adhcErrNoError = 0
    Const adhcErrFieldNull = 3314
    Const adhcErrDuplicateKey = 3022
    Select Case DataErr
        Case adhcErrNoError       ' No error
        Case adhcErrFieldNull     ' Field '|' can't contain a
                                  ' null value.
            MsgBox "You have left a required field blank.", _
```

```
                vbInformation
            Case adhcErrDuplicateKey ' Duplicate value in index,
                                ' primary key, or relationship.
                                ' Changes were unsuccessful.
            MsgBox "This record contains the same primary key " _
            & "as another record. Try another value.", _
                vbInformation
            Case Else
            Stop      'Unknown Error
        End Select
        Response = acDataErrContinue
    End Sub
```

The Response argument can receive one of two values: acDataErrContinue or acDataErrDisplay. The value acDataErrDisplay causes Access to display the error message that would have appeared if you hadn't had an error handler attached to the form. acDataErrContinue causes this error message to be suppressed. By specifying acDataErrContinue you can substitute your own custom error message.

The function Error(DataErr) returns the Jet error string associated with the error. (For more information on the Form and Report Error events, see Chapter 8.)

NOTE Due to structural changes to error handling introduced with VBA, many error strings returned by the Error function aren't very helpful. In fact, for most error codes the Error function returns the string "Application or user-defined error". This is because VBA has no knowledge of a specific host's errors. It is up to the host (Access, in this case) to supply the descriptive information when an error occurs. To return error strings for Access errors, Access provides the AccessError method. It works the same way as Error but returns the real error description for a given error number.

Using the Jet Errors Collection

Anytime Jet is processing data, it can generate run-time errors. Since Jet may report multiple run-time errors from a single operation your code performs (especially when accessing ODBC data), it maintains a collection of those errors. Usually, you are concerned only with determining that an error has occurred and reporting that fact to the end user. In some cases, though, you may want to detail exactly the errors Jet generated. For this you use the Jet Errors collection.

The collection is a property of the DBEngine object. When you handle an error in an error handler in your code, or an Error event handler, you can then browse the Jet Errors collection to determine specifically which Jet errors occurred while processing a statement. The code in Listing 16.11 shows how you do this.

Listing 16.11

```
Sub JetErrorsCollection()
    Dim db As Database

    On Error GoTo JetErrorsCollectionErr

    CurrentDb.Execute "qappJetErrorsCollection", dbFailOnError
JetErrorsCollectionDone:
    Exit Sub
JetErrorsCollectionErr:
    Dim errCur As Error
    For Each errCur In DBEngine.Errors
        Debug.Print errCur.Description
    Next
    Resume JetErrorsCollectionDone
End Sub
```

In this code, when Jet generates a set of errors, each of the error descriptions is printed to the Debug window. The Err object will reflect the top-most of the objects in the Errors collection. The Errors collection is cleared before the next Jet Engine operation is executed.

Creating an Error-Reporting Subroutine

Because any robust application will have dozens, if not hundreds, of error handlers in its code, you may want to create a generic way of reporting them. We have created a generic routine you can use to report errors to the user. The error dialog created looks like the one shown in Figure 16.1. Typically this dialog is used in an error handler to report any unexpected run-time errors. Listing 16.12 shows adhHandleError, the generic error-handling routine that is called to invoke the error dialog.

Listing 16.12

```
Public Function adhHandleError() As Integer
    Static fInError As Boolean

    ' Make sure we're not currently in the
```

```
        ' error handler; otherwise we'll end up
        ' with an infinite loop
        If fInError Then
            MsgBox "Already in error handler!", vbCritical
            Stop
        Else
            fInError = True

            ' Make sure error form isn't open
            If SysCmd(acSysCmdGetObjectState, acForm, _
             adhcErrorForm) = acObjStateOpen Then
                DoCmd.Close acForm, adhcErrorForm
            End If

            ' Open the form in dialog mode—the form will
            ' use the LastError method of the global
            ' SavedErrors collection to get its information
            On Error Resume Next
            DoCmd.OpenForm FormName:=adhcErrorForm, _
             WindowMode:=acDialog

            ' Set return value and close the form
            If Err.Number = 0 Then
                adhHandleError = Forms(adhcErrorForm).Action
                DoCmd.Close acForm, adhcErrorForm
            End If

            ' Reset flag
            fInError = False
        End If
    End Function
```

FIGURE 16.1

Generic Error dialog

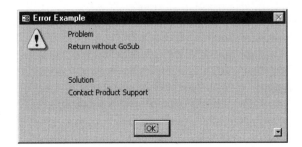

When you call adhHandleErr, it opens the error dialog, frmError. During the form's Open event it sets the value of the controls based on the last saved error that occurred. Listing 16.13 shows the code behind this event procedure. Since the form's Open event uses the SavedErrors collection's LastError property, it is important that when you encounter an error in a procedure, you add it to the collection using the collection's Add method.

Listing 16.13

```
Private Sub Form_Open(Cancel As Integer)
    Dim objLastError As SavedError

    ' Make sure there's an error for us to report on
    If gErrors.Count = 0 Then
        MsgBox "There are no errors to report on!", _
          vbInformation
        Cancel = True
    Else

        ' Set pointer to last error that occurred
        Set objLastError = gErrors.LastError

        With objLastError
            ' Call OverrideError to change property values to
            ' those in error table if one was specified
            Call OverrideError(.Number, .Display)

            ' Use DisplayError object properties to set up
            ' the main information on the form
            With .Display
                Me.Caption = .Title
                mlngButtonMap = .ButtonMap
                Call SetupIcon(.Icon)
                Call SetupButtons(.Buttons)
                Call SetupSolution(.Solution)
            End With
            ' Use SavedError object properties to set up
            ' the extended information on the form
            Me!txtErrorNumber = .Number
            Me!txtDescription = .Description
            Me!txtHelpFile = .HelpFile
            Me!txtHelpContext = .HelpContext
            Me!txtSource = .Source
```

```
                Me!txtDLLError = .LastDLLError

                ' Make sure we've got a valid message
                If .Display.Text = "" Then
                    Me!txtDisplayText = .Description
                Else
                    Me!txtDisplayText = .Display.Text
                End If
            End With

            ' Enable Log File button if specified
            ' in the SavedErrors collection's property
            Me!cmdLog.Enabled = (gErrors.LogFile <> "")
        End If
End Sub
Private Function OverrideError(lngNumber As Long, _
 objDisplay As DisplayError) As Boolean

    Dim db As Database
    Dim rst As Recordset
    Dim strSQL As String

    ' Build the query based on the error table
    ' and error number
    strSQL = "SELECT * FROM " & objDisplay.ErrorTable & _
     " WHERE Number = " & lngNumber

    ' Look for the error in the current database
    Set db = CurrentDb()
    Set rst = db.OpenRecordset(strSQL, _
     dbOpenDynaset, dbReadOnly Or dbForwardOnly)

    ' If found, override the error information
    With rst
        If Not .EOF Then
            objDisplay.Text = !Text
            objDisplay.Solution = !Solution
            objDisplay.Icon = !Icon
            objDisplay.Buttons = !Buttons
            objDisplay.ButtonMap = !ButtonMap
            OverrideError = True
        End If
        .Close
    End With
End Function
```

If you look at the definition of the SavedError class in CH16.MDB, you'll see it contains a public declaration of a new instance of another class called Display-Error. The DisplayError class implements properties such as Title, Icon, and Buttons, which are useful when building a dialog like frmError. The Open event uses these property values to configure the form.

One interesting property of the DisplayError class is ErrorTable. If this property is filled in with the name of a table, the error dialog will look in that table for error infor-mation, overriding the property values in the SavedError object. This lets you easily create custom error text for a few select errors. If an error isn't found in the table, the error dialog uses whatever property settings are contained in the SavedError object. Table 16.2 lists the fields the OverrideError procedure expects to find in the table. You can also look at our sample table, tblError, in CH16.MDB.

> **TIP**
>
> If you want to use our SavedError class in your own applications but don't want to create a generic error dialog, you can save a little overhead by deleting the DisplayError declaration from the class module.

TABLE 16.2 Column Names in Error Tables

Column	Description
Number	Number of the error message. This is the key value used to find the error in the table
Description	Description of the error
Solution	Solution for the error. If this is Null, no solution is displayed and the description box is expanded
Icon	Icon that should appear. Must be one of the following: vbInformation, vbExclamation, vbQuestion, or vbCritical
Buttons	Specifies which set of buttons appears in the dialog. Must be one of the following: vbOkOnly, vbOkCancel, vbYesNo, vbYesNoCancel, vbRetryCancel, or vbAbortRetryIgnore
ButtonMap	Maps the keys specified by varButtonSet to resume status value adhExitSub, adhResumeNext, or adhResume. Must be built by the adhKeyMap function

adhHandleError returns an integer value that will be one of three constants: adh-cExitSub, adhcResume, or adhcResumeNext. Based on this return value, your procedure can take appropriate action.

NOTE   The adhAssert function is described in the section "Using Assertions" later in this chapter.

You call the adhHandleError function using code similar to that found in Listing 16.14.

Listing 16.14

```
Public Sub ErrorExample()
    On Error GoTo ErrorExampleErr

    Call gProcStack.EnterProc("ErrorExample")

    ' Error constants
    Const adhcErrReturnWithoutGosub = 3
    Const adhcErrWeirdError = 42000
    Const adhcErrInvalidProcedureCall = 5
    Const adhcErrOverflow = 6

    ' One example
    err.Raise Number:=adhcErrReturnWithoutGosub
    ' Another example
    err.Raise Number:=adhcErrWeirdError
    ' A third example, overriding the description in the table
    err.Raise Number:=adhcErrInvalidProcedureCall, _
     Description:="Not what you'd expect"
    ' Another example, overriding everything
    err.Raise Number:=adhcErrOverflow

ErrorExampleDone:
    Call gProcStack.ExitProc("ErrorExample")
    Exit Sub
ErrorExampleErr:
    Dim objError As SavedError

' Add error to the errors collection
```

```
        Set objError = gErrors.Add(err)

' Add error log
    gErrors.LogFile = "C:\Error.log"

    ' Based on the error number you can change
    ' various property settings if you want
    Select Case objError.Number
        Case adhcErrOverflow
            With objError
                .Number = 27
                .Description = "Something didn't work!"
                With .Display
                    .Text = "It didn't work!"
                    .Solution = "Fix it!"
                    .Icon = vbCritical
                    .ErrorTable = "tblError"
                    .Title = "Something Happened"
                    .Buttons = vbOKCancel
                    .ButtonMap = adhButtonMap( _
                        adhcResumeNext, adhcExitSub, 0)
                End With
            End With
        Case Else
            With objError.Display
                .Title = "Error Example"
                .ErrorTable = "tblError"
                .ButtonMap = adhButtonMap( _
                    adhcResumeNext, 0, 0)
            End With
    End Select

    ' Now call adhHandleError and take action
    ' based on the value it returns
    Select Case adhHandleError()
        Case adhcResume
            Resume
        Case adhcResumeNext
            Resume Next
        Case adhcExitSub
            Resume ErrorExampleDone
        Case Else
            Call adhAssert(False)
```

```
        End Select
    Exit Sub
End Sub
```

This example uses Raise statements to force the invocation of certain errors. Normally you wouldn't include these types of statements in your code. You would, instead, just put in statements that might cause run-time errors.

In order to use the error form, the procedure adds each run-time error to the SavedErrors collection represented by the gErrors object variable. This makes the error information available to the form during its Open event. The procedure also sets the collection's LogFile property. This allows the user to save the error information to a file for later inspection. Finally, a Select Case statement block is used to change the properties of the error before calling adhHandleError. Based on the return value, the procedure executes the errant statement again, moves on to the next statement, or exits.

The user can obtain extended error information by clicking the small button in the lower right-hand corner of the error dialog (see Figure 16.1). Clicking this button expands the form to show information such as the VBA error number and help information, as shown in Figure 16.2. Drop-down lists at the bottom of the display list statistics such as free memory and disk space, along with the call stack. This information could be helpful when debugging your applications. If you're not around to view this information, the user can save it to a text file by clicking the command button at the bottom right of the form.

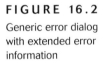

FIGURE 16.2

Generic error dialog with extended error information

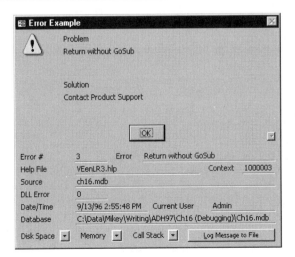

By using this error-reporting scheme, you can vastly reduce the complexity of your code at any given point because you can handle all generic errors within the errors table. In addition, you can override any of the information in the table to provide information that is specific to any particular error.

Implementing a Call Stack

When you are in the process of debugging a running procedure, you can select View ➤ Calls to see which function caused the error. Unfortunately, Access doesn't provide any method for retrieving this information from your code. When you get an unexpected error, it's useful to log what code is being executed at that point and how it got there. Since Access provides no way to get at the information it keeps internally (that is, the name of the currently executing procedure), you must maintain the information yourself if you need it.

We've implemented several VBA class modules to help with this process. The Procedure and ProcedureStack classes store information on each procedure in VBA's call stack by implementing a stack of their own. The only catch is that you have to write code in your subroutines and functions to add procedures to the stack; Access can't (and won't) do this for you. Listings 16.15 and 16.16 show the definitions of the Procedure and ProcedureStack classes, respectively.

Listing 16.15

```
' Procedure class
Private mstrName As String
Private mstrModule As String
Private mdatTimeEntered As Date
Private mobjNextProc As Procedure

' Name is the name of the procedure--
' note that it is a write-once property
Property Get Name() As String
    Name = mstrName
End Property
Property Let Name(strName As String)
    If mstrName = "" Then
        mstrName = strName
    End If
End Property

' Module is the name of the module this
```

```
' procedure is located in
Property Get Module() As String
    Module = mstrModule
End Property
Property Let Module(strModule As String)
    If mstrModule = "" Then
        mstrModule = strModule
    End If
End Property

' NextProc is used a pointer to the next
' procedure in the stack
Property Get NextProc() As Procedure
    Set NextProc = mobjNextProc
End Property
Property Set NextProc(objProc As Procedure)
    Set mobjNextProc = objProc
End Property

' TimeEntered is the date/time the class
' instance was created
Property Get TimeEntered() As Date
    TimeEntered = mdatTimeEntered
End Property

Private Sub Class_Initialize()
    ' Set date/time entered
    mdatTimeEntered = Now
End Sub
```

Listing 16.16

```
' ProcedureStack class
Private mobjTopProc As Procedure

Public Function Top() As Procedure
    ' This returns a reference to the top
    ' procedure so a caller can walk the stack
    Set Top = mobjTopProc
End Function

Private Function StackEmpty() As Boolean
    ' This makes sure the stack is not empty
    ' by checking to see if the top proc
```

```
        ' pointer is valid
      StackEmpty = (mobjTopProc Is Nothing)
End Function

Public Function EnterProc(Name As String, _
  Optional Module As String) As Procedure

    ' This pushes a new procedure onto the stack

    Dim objProc As New Procedure

    ' Set the procedure's name and module properties
    objProc.Name = Name
    objProc.Module = Module

    ' Make its NextProc property point to
    ' the one currently at the top of the stack
    Set objProc.NextProc = mobjTopProc

    ' Make the new procedure the one at the top
    Set mobjTopProc = objProc

    ' Return a reference to the new proc
    Set EnterProc = mobjTopProc
End Function

Public Function ExitProc(Name As String) As Boolean
      ' This pops a procedure off the stack--
      ' To enforce FILO behavior we check the
      ' name passed in against that of the top
      ' procedure

      ' Make sure the procedure stack is not empty
      If Not StackEmpty() Then

          ' If the name matches, pop the proc
          ' by making the next proc the top one--
          ' this destroys the pointer to the
          ' proc currently on top and it goes away
          If mobjTopProc.Name = Name Then
              Set mobjTopProc = mobjTopProc.NextProc
              ExitProc = True
          Else
              MsgBox "Error. Trying to pop wrong procedure. " & _
```

```
            "You passed '" & Name & "'. " & _
             "Current procedure is '" & _
             mobjTopProc.Name & "'.", vbCritical
            Stop
         End If
      End If
End Function
```

To implement a call stack using these procedures in your own applications, import the two class modules from CH16.MDB, declare a new instance of the ProcedureStack class in one of your global modules, and then place a call to the EnterProc method of the class at the entry point of every routine in your code. You must also put a call to the ExitProc method of the class at the exit point of every routine. Listing 16.17 shows an example of how to use these methods. It also shows how to print out the contents of the stack. (The code behind the call stack combo box in frmError uses this technique.)

Listing 16.17

```
Sub EnterAndExitExample()
' Call EnterProc to push proc onto the stack
    Call mProcStack.EnterProc("EnterAndExitExample")

    ' Call PrintCallStack which will print call stack
    ' to the Debug window so you can see that it works!
    Call PrintCallStack

    ' Make sure to call ExitProc!!
    Call mProcStack.ExitProc("EnterAndExitExample")
End Sub

Private Sub PrintCallStack()
    Dim objProc As Procedure

    ' Call EnterProc to push proc onto the stack
    Call mProcStack.EnterProc("PrintCallStack")

    ' Print it out by walking the stack
    Set objProc = mProcStack.Top
    Do Until objProc Is Nothing
        Debug.Print "Entered procedure '" & objProc.Name & _
        "' at " & objProc.TimeEntered
        Set objProc = objProc.NextProc
    Loop
```

```
        ' Make sure to call ExitProc!!
        Call mProcStack.ExitProc("PrintCallStack")
End Sub
```

Because you have to call the ExitProc method at the exit point, you will want to make sure you have only one exit point to your procedures. If you don't, you run the risk of trying to push the wrong procedure off the stack. If this happens you'll see a dialog like the one in Figure 16.3.

FIGURE 16.3

Error message indicating you tried to pop the wrong procedure

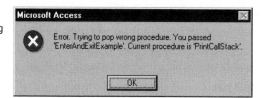

The payoff for using this call stack code comes when you are trying to determine the current state when an error has occurred. Anytime users get a run-time error, they can press the Log button in the extended info part of the dialog, which writes the current state to the log file. The log file is named in the SavedErrors collection's LogFile property. You can then have your user send you the log file, and then you can determine exactly what was going on when the error occurred.

Another advantage of having the EnterProc and Exit proc methods surrounding each entry and exit point of your code is that the Procedure class tracks the time it was initialized. Using this information, you can keep track of how much time is spent in the procedure. This is called *profiling.* You can use the profiling information to help determine which routines need optimization work.

Dealing with Logic Errors, AKA Bugs!

As stated at the beginning of this chapter, there are three kinds of errors: compile-time errors, run-time errors, and logic errors. VBA informs you of any compile-time errors when you use Debug ➤ Compile Loaded Modules or Debug ➤ Compile All Modules. Error handlers handle run-time errors. But what can you do about logic errors? If you were a perfect programmer, you'd never have any logic errors, because you'd never make mistakes; you'd always know exactly how Access works, and all your assumptions would always hold true. Professional programmers can't count on perfection, however. Logic errors, also known as bugs, are by far the most difficult type of error to find. In the remainder of this chapter we share some strategies for reducing the number of bugs in your code.

Avoiding Bugs

It's close to impossible to write a substantial application without any bugs, but certain strategies can help you avoid inserting unnecessary bugs. You should develop the necessary discipline to use these strategies whenever you write code, even if you think you're writing a function to use only in testing or for your own internal application. Good habits are hard to develop but are also hard to lose once you develop them. The next few sections describe how you can avoid letting bugs slip into your code by following these rules:

- Fix bugs as they appear.
- Use comments.
- Organize your code.
- Modularize your code.
- Use Option Explicit.
- Avoid Variants if at all possible.
- Use explicit conversion functions.
- Beware the simple Dim statement.
- Group your Dim statements.
- Use the tightest possible scoping.
- Watch out for "hidden" modules.
- Use consistent naming conventions.
- Use assertions.

Internalizing these suggestions will help you develop a good mind-set for avoiding bugs and for removing the ones that inevitably creep into your code.

As a single rule of thumb, the best bug-avoidance strategy is to take your time and to avoid the urge to make your code "cleverer" than necessary. At times you simply must use the newest, most complex features of any programming language, but in general, the simpler way is the better way. With this strategy in mind, there are some specific tactics that work well in Access coding to help avoid bugs.

Fixing Bugs As They Appear

It's critical that you fix bugs as they reveal themselves rather than wait until you have more features implemented; hurried cleanup at the end of a project will pressure you to apply bandages instead of real fixes. If your application is failing when the invoice amount is exactly $33.00, don't just patch the procedure like this:

```
If curInvoiceAmt=33 Then
    MyFunction = curTheCorrectValue
Else...
```

Instead, you must figure out *why* the call is failing and fix its cause instead of the apparent symptom. This requires steady and systematic testing, which is something programmers tend to avoid. Would you rather write 500 lines of code or try 50 test cases on existing code? Most of us would choose the former since writing code is fun and testing is boring. But if you keep in mind how little fun you'll have if your application doesn't work when it's shipped, you'll buckle down and do the boring testing work, too.

Using Comments

Old code is harder to debug than new code because it is less fresh in your mind. Depending on how busy you are, old code could be two weeks old, two days old, or two hours old! One way to help keep your code from aging rapidly is to insert comments. There's an art to sensible commenting: it depends on adding just enough to tell you what's going on without going overboard and cluttering up your code.

The comment should state the intention of the code rather than tell how the code is implemented. This is an important point. Novice programmers have a tendency to write comments that describe how the code is implemented, as in this example:

```
' Make sure the numbers in the combo box and the text box add up
' to less than the acceptable total
If cboStartTime + CInt(txtSlots) > MAX_SLOTS Then
    ' If not, put up an error message...
    MsgBox "Not enough time in day", vbCritical, _
    "Schedule Error"
```

```
    ' ...and exit the application
    GoTo cmdSchedule_Click_Exit
End If
' Find the last slot that needs to be modified
intSlotLast = cboStartTime + CInt(txtSlots) - 1

' Set an object to the current database
Set dbCurrent = CurrentDb()
' Open a querydef object with the Prospective schedule query
' loaded
Set qdfSchedule = _
 dbCurrent.OpenQueryDef("qryScheduleProspective")
' Get the first query parameter from the Installer combo box
qdfSchedule.Parameters(0) = cboInstaller
' Get the second query parameter from the Date combo box
qdfSchedule.Parameters(1) = cboDate
```

Reading through code like this is like trying to understand a telephone conversation with a bad echo on the line. By trimming down the number of comments to a more sensible level, you can highlight the overall structure of the code and note any particularly tricky spots for future programmers, including yourself. Remember, if you've named your variables using a consistent standard, their names will act as mini-comments in the code itself. Notice that the comments in this version of the same example describe the intention of the code, not how it is implemented:

```
' Check to see that we have enough hours left in the day
If cboStartTime + CInt(txtSlots) > MAX_SLOTS Then
    MsgBox "Not enough time in day", vbCritical, _
     "Schedule Error"
    GoTo cmdSchedule_Click_Exit
End If
intSlotLast = cboStartTime + CInt(txtSlots) - 1

' Get a list of open timeslots to check
Set dbCurrent = CurrentDb()
Set qdfSchedule = _
 dbCurrent.OpenQueryDef("qryScheduleProspective")
qdfSchedule.Parameters(0) = cboInstaller
qdfSchedule.Parameters(1) = cboDate
```

A comment that is not maintained is worse than no comment at all. Have you ever read a comment and then stared at the code below it and discovered it didn't seem to do what the comment said it did? Now you have to figure out whether it is the comment or the code that is wrong. If your code change requires a comment change, make sure you do it now, because you probably won't get around to doing it later.

To Strip or Not to Strip

One reason for keeping the number of comments to a reasonable level is that comments do take up space in memory while your database is loaded. Some programmers go so far as to encourage comment stripping, the practice of removing all comments from production code. If you choose to do this, make sure you only do it right before shipping and that you don't make changes to the stripped code. Otherwise you might end up with two different code bases. To facilitate removing comments from code, we've included an Access add-in that strips full-line comments from all modules in any given database. It won't work with comments that appear after a normal statement, but it can speed up the process of stripping comments from your code. For an explanation of how it works, see the section "Programmatic Control of Modules" in Chapter 22.

Organizing Your Code

In addition to commenting your code, you should do whatever you can to keep it organized. This means you should use indentation to organize the flow of code. It also means you should split large procedures into smaller ones.

Indent your code so that statements that "go together" are at the same indentation level and statements that are subordinate to others are indented one more tab stop. Although there is room for disagreement, most Access programmers lay out their code something like this:

```
' Initialize the array that governs visibility and
' set up records
For intI = 1 To intTotalTabs
    intShow(intI) = False
    rstLoggedData.AddNew
        rstLoggedData![State] = False
    rstLoggedDate.Update
Next intI
intShow(intTabNumber) = True
```

In VBA, many programmers use indentation both to match up traditional control structures (For...Next, If...Then...Else, Do...Loop, For Each) and to indicate levels of data access object activity (BeginTrans/CommitTrans, AddNew/Update, and so on).

Modularizing Your Code

Modularization is a fancy term for a simple idea: breaking up your code into a series of relatively small procedures rather than a few mammoth ones. There are several key benefits to writing code this way:

- You make it easier to understand each procedure. Code that is easier to understand is easier to maintain and to keep bug free.

- You can localize errors to a smaller section of the total code. If a variable is used only in one ten-line function, any error messages referring to that variable are most likely generated within that function.

- You can lessen the dangers of side effects caused by too-wide scoping of variables. If you use a variable at the top of a 500-line function and again at the bottom for a different loop, you may well forget to reinitialize it.

Using Option Explicit

In the Tools ➤ Options dialog, on the Module tab, you will find a check box labeled "Require Variable Declaration." Selecting this check box causes Access to insert the line "Option Explicit" at the top of any new module it creates. This statement forces you to declare all your variables before referring to them in your code. This will prevent some hard-to-find errors from cropping up in your code. Without Option Explicit, Access allows you to use any syntactically correct variable in your code, regardless of whether you declare it. This means that any variable you forget to declare will be initialized to a variant and given the value Empty at the point where you first use it. The hours you save in debugging time will make using this option well worth the effort.

Using Option Explicit is an easy way to avoid errors such as the one you'll find in the code in Listing 16.18. Errors like this are almost impossible to catch late in the development cycle, since they're buried in existing code. (Don't feel bad if you don't immediately see the error in the fragment; it's difficult to find.) That's why you'll want to use Option Explicit—to avoid just this sort of error.

Listing 16.18

```
Function UpdateLog(intSeverity As Integer, _
  strProcedure As String, strTracking As String) As Integer
    Dim dbCurrent As Database
    Dim rstUsageLog As Recordset
    Dim intFull As Integer
```

```
Dim qryArchive As QueryDef

Const adhcMinSeverity = 1
' Don't log activities that aren't severe enough to
' bother with
If intSeverity < adhcMinSeverity Then
    Exit Function
End If

DoCmd.SetWarnings False

' Append a new record to the usage log
Set dbCurrent = CurrentDb()
Set rstUsageLog = dbCurrent.OpenRecordset _
  ("zstblUsageLog", dbOpenDynaset)
rstUsageLog.AddNew
    rstUsageLog![Severity] = intSeverty
    If Err.Number Then
        rstUsageLog![ErrorCode] = Err.Number
        rstUsageLog![ErrorText] = Err.Description
    End If
    rstUsageLog![User] = CurrentUser()
    rstUsageLog![Date] = Now
'.
'. etc
'.
End Function
```

In case you missed it, the error occurred on this line of code:

```
rstUsageLog![Severity] = intSeverty
```

A small spelling error like this would cause only zeros to be stored in the Severity field and could cause you several hours of debugging time. Option Explicit lets you avoid these kinds of errors.

Avoid Variants If at All Possible

The Variant datatype is convenient, but it's not always the best choice. It's tempting to declare all your variables as variants so you don't have to worry about what's in them. The Access and VBA design teams did not put in explicit types to make your life difficult; they put them in because they're useful. If you think something will always be an Integer, dimension it as an Integer. If you get an error message later because you've attempted to assign an invalid value to that variable, the error message will point straight to the problem area of your code and give you a good idea of what went wrong. Variants are also slower than explicitly dimensioned variables for the same operations since they have the overhead of tracking which type of data they are holding at any given time. In addition, variants are larger than almost any other datatype and so take longer to move around in memory. These last two reasons alone should be enough to make you reconsider using variants whenever possible.

> **TIP**
>
> In some instances you have no choice about your datatypes. If you're assigning values to variables that might at some point need to contain a null value, you must use the Variant datatype. This is the only datatype that can contain a null value, and attempting to assign a null value to a nonvariant variable triggers a run-time error. The same goes for function return values. If a function might need to return a null value, the return value for that function must be a variant.

Use ByVal with Care

You need to be careful about passing information to routines that have parameters passed ByVal. While this is a good way to prevent subroutines from modifying variables passed to them (since ByVal creates a copy), you may lose information when calling the procedure. This is because information passed in is coerced to the datatype of the parameter. Therefore, if you pass a variable with the Single datatype to a parameter of type Integer, Access truncates the fractional component of the Single when it creates the Integer. You will have no warning of this, however, so make sure you know which datatype the procedures expect if you've used ByVal in the declaration.

Beware the Simple Dim Statement

Even the simple Dim statement can introduce subtle bugs into your code. Consider this statement:

```
Dim strFirst, strLast As String
```

The intent here is clearly to define two String variables on one line. If you've ever programmed in C or C++, you know that a similar declaration would do just that. However, this is not the way VBA works. The As clause applies only to the variable it immediately follows, not to all variables on the line. The result of the preceding declaration is that strLast is a String variable but strFirst is a Variant variable, with slightly different behavior.

For example, strFirst will be initialized to Empty and strLast to a zero-length string. You must explicitly define the datatype of every single variable in VBA. The simplest way to ensure this is to get into the habit of declaring only one variable for each statement.

Grouping Your Dim Statements

You can declare your variables anywhere in your procedures, as long you declare them before they are actually used, and Access will understand and accept the declarations. For the sake of easier debugging, though, you should get into the habit of declaring variables at the top of your procedures. This makes it easy to see exactly what a particular procedure is referring to and to find the declarations when you are in the midst of debugging.

Using the Tightest Possible Scoping

Always use the tightest possible scoping for your variables. Some beginning programmers discover global variables and promptly declare all their variables as global to avoid the issue of scoping altogether. This is a sloppy practice that will backfire the first time you have two procedures, both of which change the same global variable's value. If a variable is used solely in a single procedure, declare it there. If it is used only by procedures in a single module, declare it with module scope. Save global scope for only those few variables you truly need to refer to from widely scattered parts of your code.

If you need a variable to be available globally but want to restrict the scope of procedures that can change that value, you might consider "hiding" it from the rest of your application. To do so, create the variable as a private, module-level variable in a specific module. In that module, place any function that needs to modify the value of the variable. In addition, add one extra function that you'll use to retrieve the value from outside the module. If you want to be able to assign a new value to the variable from a different module, you can also include a procedure that will do that for you. In any case, no procedure in any other module will be able to modify the value of this variable. By hiding the variable in this manner, you can be assured that no other procedures in any other modules can modify your variable without going through your procedures. Listing 16.19 shows a simple case of this mechanism.

Listing 16.19

```
Private intCurrentValue As Integer
Sub SetCurrentValue(intNewValue As Integer)
    intCurrentValue = intNewValue
```

```
End Sub

Function GetCurrentValue()
    GetCurrentValue = intCurrentValue
End Function
```

Given the code in Listing 16.19, any procedure in any module can retrieve the value of intCurrentValue (by calling the GetCurrentValue function) and can set the value (by calling SetCurrentValue). If you made SetCurrentValue private, however, no procedure outside the current module could change the value of intCurrentValue. By protecting your *faux*-global variables in this manner, you can avoid errors that can easily occur in multiple-module applications, especially ones written by multiple programmers.

Using Consistent Naming Conventions

In addition to the conventions discussed here that help structure your code, consider adopting a consistent naming convention for objects and variables in your code. We (along with many other programmers) have standardized our naming conventions based on the RVBA naming conventions, which you'll find in Appendix A. A consistent naming standard can make it simple for you to find errors lurking in your programs, in addition to making them simpler for multiple programmers to maintain. By using the RVBA naming convention you gain two pieces of information about every variable: which datatype it is and what scope it has. This information can be very helpful during the debugging process.

Your Friend, the MsgBox Function

As an alternative to setting breakpoints, you can use the MsgBox function to indicate your program's state. With this strategy you decide what you would like to monitor and calls the MsgBox function to return particular information. You can enhance this technique by writing a wrapper for the MsgBox function so that these messages are posted only when you have a conditional compilation constant set to indicate that you want to see debugging messages. This flag controls whether the adhDebugMessageBox function should in fact interrupt execution of your code or whether it should just quietly return to the calling procedure. The adhDebugMessageBox function is shown in Listing 16.20. You'll find this function in the basError module in CH16.MDB. To use it in your own applications, import the module and call adhDebugMessageBox, as described in the following paragraphs.

Listing 16.20

```
#Const adhcFDebug = True

Function adhDebugMessageBox(ByVal varMessage As Variant, _
  strCaller As String) As Integer
     adhDebugMessageBox = True
#If adhcFDebug Then
     adhDebugMessageBox = (MsgBox(CStr(varMessage), _
      vbOKCancel Or vbQuestion, "Debug: " & strCaller) _
      = vbOK)
#End If
End Function
```

You can sprinkle as many calls to adhDebugMessageBox as you like into your code and make them all active or inactive at once by changing the value of the adhcFDebug constant. Typically, you can use these message boxes to return news on the state of the program's execution. For example, here's a possible code fragment from your application's AutoExec function (called from the AutoExec macro):

```
If Not adhDebugMessageBox("About to Start Logging", _
 "AutoExec") Then
    Stop
End If

varRet = StartLogging()

If Not adhDebugMessageBox("StartLogging returned " _
 & varRet, "AutoExec") Then
    Stop
End If
```

adhDebugMessageBox uses conditional compilation to include or exclude the body of the function. Conditional compilation tells the VBA compiler to include or exclude certain portions of code when it compiles the code. The #Const defines a conditional compilation constant. You can also define conditional compilation constants in the Advanced tab of the Options dialog. The #If and #End If define a block that is compiled only if the conditional compilation expression is true. Based on the value of the adhfDebug constant, the message box is either displayed or it's not. If the constant is not set, it just returns True, and your code can continue. However, if you are in debug mode instead, the function displays whatever you pass to it, as shown in Figure 16.4.

FIGURE 16.4

adhDebugMessageBox displays anything you send it.

If you click OK, the function returns a true value. If you click Cancel or press the Esc key, the function returns False, which in turn should halt your program execution back at the point where you called the adhDebugMessageBoxfunction. Using debugging message boxes is particularly useful when your code refers to the Screen object and its ActiveForm, ActiveReport, ActiveControl, and ActiveDatasheet properties because using the Debug window causes these objects to lose the focus and thus their context.

The Access Debugging Tools

Once you've recognized that you have a logic error, you will need to track it down. Access provides a set of tools for debugging your application. These include

- The Debug window
- Breakpoints and Single Step mode
- The call stack
- Watch expressions
- Quick watches
- Data Tips
- The Locals pane of the Debug window
- Debugging options in the Options dialog

This section briefly describes these features. The sections that follow show you how to use them to debug your VBA code.

The Debug Window

The Debug window, shown in Figure 16.5, gives you a place to investigate the effects of VBA code directly, without the intervention of macros, forms, or other methods of running the code. Think of the Debug window as a command line for VBA. You can use

FIGURE 16.5

Debug window showing how to call a sub named ErrorExample

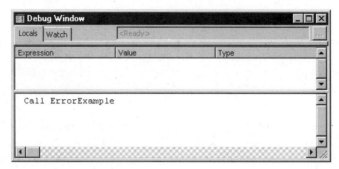

it to launch procedures and evaluate expressions. In fact, you can do almost as many things in the Debug window as you can in VBA procedure code. You open the Debug window by clicking the Debug Window button on the toolbar, selecting View ➤ Debug Window, or pressing Ctrl+G. Debug window contents are preserved as long as you are in a single session of Access, even if you close one database and open another.

NOTE You can choose whether Access treats the Debug window as a popup window (always on top) or as a normal MDI child window. The default is the latter. To make the Debug window a popup window, select the Debug Window on Top check box on the Module tab of the Tools ➤ Options dialog.

The Debug window displays the last 200 lines of output at all times. As more output is appended to the end, older lines disappear from the top of the list. With the capability to scroll back the Debug window, you can position the cursor on an evaluation line and press ↵, and Access will recalculate the expression and display its value. If you want to remove the lines in the Debug window above your current location, use Ctrl+Shift+Home to select them all and press Del. To remove lines below your current location, first select them with Ctrl+Shift+End.

Breakpoints

Breakpoints allow you to set locations in your code at which VBA will temporarily halt its execution of your code. Figure 16.6 shows code halted at a breakpoint. Note the highlighted line of code and the small arrow that appears in the left margin. These indicate the line of code *about to be executed.*

FIGURE 16.6

Code halted at
a breakpoint

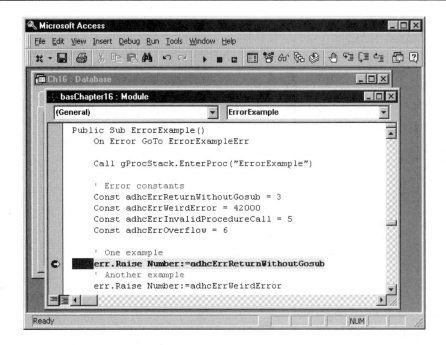

The Call Stack

Access has the ability to display the call stack when a function is paused at a breakpoint. The call stack lists each active function, with the current function at the top of
the list, the one that called it next on the list, and so on. If the function was originally
called from the Debug window, this is noted at the end of the list. If the function
is called from elsewhere in Access (for example, directly from a Click event or from
a RunCode macro action), there is no way to know from where it was called.
Figure 16.7 shows the call stack as it might appear at a breakpoint in your code.

FIGURE 16.7

VBA Calls dialog showing
the call stack

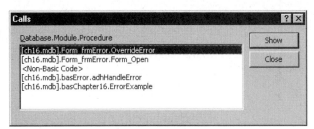

NOTE The entry <Non-Basic Code> indicates that another process, such as Access, VBA, or a DLL function, is involved in the call chain. In the example in Figure 16.7, the non-Basic code being run is the Access event handler.

To view the call stack, click the Call Stack button on the module toolbar, select the View ➤ Call Stack menu command, or press Ctrl+L. Once the Calls dialog opens, you can jump to any procedure in the call stack by selecting it from the list and clicking the Show button.

Watch Expressions

You use watches to track the values of expressions as code executes. VBA has implemented a full set of watch functionality. Watches come in three varieties, and you can view them interactively or add them to a list of persistent watch expressions. The three types of watches are

- Watch Expression
- Break When Expression Is True
- Break When Expression Has Changed

A watch expression is added to the top pane of the Debug window. Anytime you are debugging in break mode, all watch expressions are evaluated and shown. This is useful if you are single-stepping through code and want to watch the contents of a variable or an expression. It is also much more convenient than using the Debug window to print the contents of variables after each line of code executes.

The Break When Expression Is True and Break When Expression Has Changed functionalities allow you to specify a logical condition or expression. When that condition is true or changes, VBA immediately halts execution and puts you into break mode. These types of watches are useful for determining when and how a variable's value was changed. For example, say you know that somewhere in your code, a global variable named gintValue is getting set to 0. You can set a Break When Expression Is True watch with the expression "gintValue = 0". Then, as soon as gintValue becomes equal to 0, VBA puts you into break mode.

Quick Watches

The Quick Watch dialog, shown in Figure 16.8, is useful for quickly seeing the value of a variable. To use this dialog, position the cursor anywhere within a variable name and press Shift+F9. The Quick Watch dialog then shows you the present contents of a variable. You can also select an expression, and VBA will evaluate the expression. Clicking the Add button adds the expression as a regular Watch Expression.

FIGURE 16.8

Quick Watch dialog

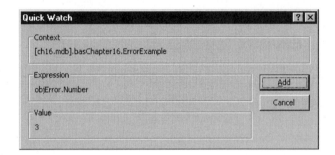

Data Tips

Data Tips are new to Access 97. They work like ToolTips in the Module window. To use Data Tips, move the mouse over any variable or property while your code is in break mode. Access displays a small ToolTip-type rectangle with the value of the expression. This is even quicker than using a quick watch.

The Locals Pane

Another feature new to Access 97 is the Locals pane of the Debug window. This pane (shown at the top of the Debug Window in Figure 16.9) lists all the variables currently in scope while your code is in break mode. You can expand and collapse objects to view their properties. In effect, this pane creates watch expressions for every variable in your code. Note that you use the tab at the top of the Debug window to switch between the Watch pane and the Locals pane.

Debugging Options in the Options Dialog

The Advanced tab of the Options dialog has two sections that let you fine-tune how Access handles errors and debugging. The first is a text box for conditional compilation constants. We mentioned conditional compilation in our discussion of

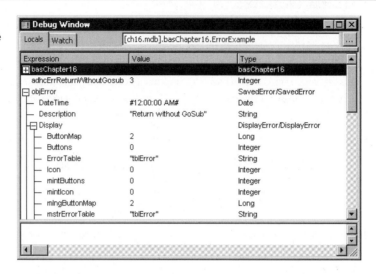

FIGURE 16.9

The Locals pane on the Debug window

the adhDebugMessageBox function. You can include the constants that control the behavior of conditional #If…#Then in your code (as we did in our earlier example) or enter them in the Options dialog. If you want to define more than one constant, just separate them with colons.

The other debugging option concerns error trapping and when Access enters break mode in response to run-time errors. You can choose among three options:

- **Break on All Errors:** Causes Access to enter break mode whenever a run-time error occurs, even if you've defined an error handler. Normally you want to use this option only while debugging an application, not after you distribute it.

- **Break in Class Module:** The default setting, this causes Access to enter break mode on all untrapped errors in global modules or class modules.

- **Break on Unhandled Errors:** Causes Access to enter break mode on all untrapped errors in global modules only. If an error occurs in a class module, Access enters break mode of the statement in a global module that called the class' property or method code.

Using the Debug Window

You can use the Debug window to test parts of an application interactively. From the Debug window you can launch procedures, view and change the values of variables, and evaluate expressions. You can also write VBA code to print information to the Debug window without your intervention.

Running Code from the Debug Window

You can easily run any function or subroutine that's in scope from the Debug window. To run a procedure, simply type its name (along with any parameter values) on a blank line in the Debug window and press ↵. Note that this also returns control to the Debug window. This technique works for both functions and subroutines. If, on the other hand, you want to run a function and have VBA return the result to the Debug window, you'll have to use the Print statement. For example, if you enter this expression:

```
Print MyFunction()
```

in the Debug window, VBA runs the function called MyFunction and prints out the return value.

VBA provides a shortcut for the Print method, as have most previous versions of Basic. In the Debug window, you can just use the ? symbol to replace the word *Print.* All our examples use this shortcut. Therefore, the preceding statement could be rewritten as:

```
? MyFunction()
```

Scoping rules apply as in normal code. That is, variables are available from the Debug window only if they're currently in scope. You can tell what the current scope is by looking at the text box at the top of the Debug window. It always reflects what it sees as the current scope.

Working with Expressions in the Debug Window

You can use the Debug window to evaluate expressions, be they simple variables or complex calculations. For example, you can view the current value of the variable intMyVar by typing

```
?intMyVar
```

in the Debug window and pressing ↵. Of course, the variable must already be dimensioned elsewhere in your code and must be in scope at the time. You cannot enter a Dim statement (or any of its cousins, including ReDim, Global, and Const) in the Debug window.

In addition to viewing expression results, you can use the Debug window to change variable values. To change the contents of intMyVar, you could use an expression like this:

```
intMyVar = 97
```

Any code that executes subsequent to your changing the variable value will see the new value.

Any statement you enter for direct execution in the Debug window must fit on a single line. You cannot, for example, enter a multiline If...Then...Else for evaluation in the Debug window, although you can execute a single-line If...Then statement. To get around this limitation, you can use the colon (:) character to separate multiple VBA statements on the same line.

For example, the following code will run a loop for you:

```
For intCount = 0 To 10:Debug.Print intCount:Next intCount
```

Printing Information to the Debug Window

You can use the Debug window as a way of tracking a running procedure by printing messages or expression values to it while your code is running. You use the Print method of the Debug object (the Debug window) to display any expression from within your running code. For example, running the function in Listing 16.21 (from the Fibo procedure in basChapter16 in CH16.MDB) produces the output shown in Figure 16.10. Note the Debug.Print statement inside the For...Next loop.

FIGURE 16.10

Output from running Fibo

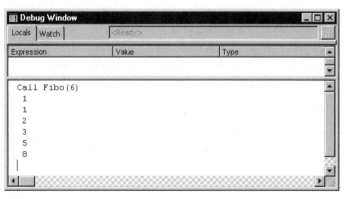

Listing 16.21

```
Function Fibo(intMembers As Integer)
    ' Print the requested number of elements of the
    ' standard Fibonacci series (s(n) = s(n-2) + s(n-1))
    ' to the Debug window.

    Dim intI As Integer
    Dim intCurrent As Integer
    Dim intPrevious As Integer
    Dim intTwoPrevious As Integer

    intPrevious = 1
    intTwoPrevious = 1

    Debug.Print intPrevious
    Debug.Print intTwoPrevious

    For intI = 3 To intMembers
        intCurrent = intPrevious + intTwoPrevious
        Debug.Print intCurrent
        intTwoPrevious = intPrevious
        intPrevious = intCurrent
    Next intI

End Function
```

Handling Remnant Debug.Print Statements

You can safely leave Debug.Print lines in your shipping code if you wish. As long as the user does not for some reason have the Debug window displayed, these lines will have no visible effect and only a slight performance penalty. However, if you are concerned about the performance hit of these lines, you can surround your debug code with conditional compilation statements. For example:

```
' In the declarations section:
#Const fDebug = True

' In some procedure:
#If fDebug Then
    Debug.Print "Some output"
#End If
```

Using Breakpoints

Using a breakpoint is the equivalent of putting a roadblock in your code. When you set a breakpoint, you tell VBA to stop executing your code at a particular line but to keep the system state in memory. This means that all the variables the function was dealing with are available for your inspection in the Debug window. You can also use the Step Into and Step Over functionality (using the menu items, the toolbar buttons, or the F8/Shift+F8 key) to move through your code statement by statement so you can watch it execute in slow motion. Access provides a toolbar, with appropriate breakpoint buttons, to aid in your debugging efforts. Figure 16.11 shows the Visual Basic toolbar, with each of the buttons labeled.

To set a breakpoint on a particular line of code, you can place your cursor anywhere on the line and do one of the following: click the Breakpoint button on the toolbar, choose Run ➤ Toggle Breakpoint, or press the F9 key. You can also create a breakpoint by clicking the mouse in the margin of the module window. Access highlights the chosen line in the Module window. (You can control the highlighting colors using the Module tab of the Options dialog.) When you're executing code and you hit a breakpoint, the focus switches to the Module window with the breakpoint showing, and a rectangle surrounds the statement where execution is halted. Additionally, if you have the module margin bar shown, Access displays a small arrow in the left margin indicating the current statement. Access suspends execution *before* it executes the particular statement. This way you can check or set the value of variables in your code before executing the chosen line of code.

FIGURE 16.11

The Visual Basic Toolbar

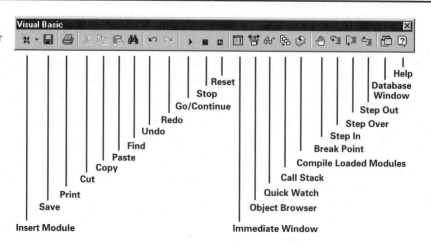

VBA does not save breakpoints with your code when you close a database. If you close a database and reopen it, any breakpoints you have set in your code vanish. (VBA does, however, preserve breakpoints when the Module window is closed, as long as you don't close the database.) If you need to preserve your breakpoints across sessions, you can use the Stop statement, which acts as a permanent breakpoint and is saved with your module. Just as with a breakpoint, Access pauses the execution of your code as soon as it encounters the Stop statement. Of course, you'll need to remove Stop statements from your code (or surround them with conditional compilation statements) before you distribute your application since they will stop the execution of your running code in any environment.

You can clear all breakpoints you have set with the Run ➤ Clear All Breakpoints item. This resets every breakpoint you have set, including those in global as well as in form and report modules.

Single Step Mode

When VBA halts your code at a breakpoint, you can choose how to continue. You can proceed at full speed once again by clicking the Go/Continue button on the toolbar, selecting the Run ➤ Go/Continue menu command, or pressing F5. You can also use *Single Step mode* to execute statements one at a time. To execute the next statement (the one highlighted with the rectangle), click the Step In button on the toolbar, select the Debug ➤ Step In menu command, or press F8. After executing the current line of code, VBA will bring you back to break mode at the next line.

Stepping In, Over, Out, and To

When VBA encounters one of your own procedures while in Single Step mode, it continues in one of three ways, depending on which Single Step command you use:

- Choosing Debug ➤ Step In, pressing the F8 key, or clicking the Step In toolbar button causes VBA to jump into your procedure, executing it one line at a time.

- Choosing Debug ➤ Step Over, pressing Shift+F8, or clicking the Step Over toolbar button also executes code one line at a time, but only within the context of the current procedure. Calls to other procedures are considered atomic by the Step Over action; it executes the entire procedure at once. This is especially useful if you are calling code you've previously debugged. Rather than take the time to walk through the other procedures, which you're confident are in working order, you can use the Step Over functionality to execute them at full speed while you're debugging.

- Choosing Debug ➤ Step Out, pressing Ctrl+Shift+F8, or clicking the Step Out toolbar button steps out of the current procedure. If it was called from another procedure, VBA returns to the line in that procedure following the call to the current one. This is useful if you have inadvertently stepped into a procedure you don't want to debug and want to return to the procedure from which you called it.

> **NOTE**
> You can never step into code in a DLL. You *can* step into code in an Access code library; however, you cannot set a breakpoint in a code library. To debug a library, you can either set a breakpoint in code in the current database and then single-step into the library code or open the library code using the Object Browser and set a breakpoint there. This does not work, however, with libraries that have had their source code removed with the Tools ➤ Database Utilities ➤ Make MDE File command.

Finally, you can also use the Run to Cursor functionality to continue to a given line. To do so, highlight any line after the currently executing one and select the Debug ➤ Run to Cursor command or press Ctrl+F8. Run to Cursor is also available from the right-click context menu. Run to Cursor causes VBA to continue execution until the line before the selected one is executed and then reenter break mode.

Other Single Step Options

While in Single Step mode you can move the current execution point to another location. Placing the insertion point on any statement in the halted procedure and choosing Debug ➤ Set Next Statement causes execution to begin at that statement when you continue the function. This command is also available from the right-click context menu. You can also change the current execution point by clicking and dragging the arrow in the module margin bar. You cannot skip to another procedure in this fashion, though. If you are wading through several open code windows, the Debug ➤ Show Next Statement item brings you back to the one where execution is paused.

Occasionally your code will become so hopelessly bug ridden that during the course of single-stepping through it, you want to throw up your hands and surrender. In this case you can choose the Run ➤ End command or click the End button on the toolbar to stop executing code. While this stops executing code and takes you out of break mode, it retains the contents of any module or global variables. To clear the contents of these variables, choose the Run ➤ Reset command, click the Reset toolbar button, or press Shift+F5 instead.

WARNING   While in break mode it is possible to launch other procedures. VBA maintains the current execution point for the first procedure while other procedures are executed. This can lead to unpredictable results, especially when you are running procedures that use the same data or variables. If you witness unpredictable behavior, make sure you don't have an outstanding break mode condition by selecting the Show Next Statement command, looking at the call stack, or selecting the Stop or Reset command.

Techniques and Strategies for Debugging

You can start developing a debugging strategy by understanding that bugs, despite the name, are not cute little things that scurry around in your code. Bugs are mistakes, pure and simple. And they're *your* mistakes; the program didn't put them there, and the end user didn't put them there. Removing these mistakes gives you an opportunity to become a better programmer.

Systematic Debugging

The first rule of debugging: You need a reproducible case to produce the error. If you cannot reproduce the error, you will have great difficulty tracking down the bug. You may get lucky and be in a situation where you can debug it when it happens, but if you can't reproduce it, your chances of fixing it are small. To reproduce the bug, you need as much information about the conditions that produced the bug as possible, but no more than that. If your users give you the hundred steps they performed that morning before the bug occurred, it makes your job difficult. Instead, if users limit the information to the essential three steps that actually cause the bug to occur, you can get somewhere. This isn't always that easy, though. Sometimes you can reproduce a bug only by following numerous steps or, for example, after the user has been using the application for four hours. As you can imagine, these types of bugs are much harder to find and fix.

The second rule of debugging: Debug data, not code. This means you should use the debugger and find out what the data is producing instead of staring at the code and speculating as to what it does. This seems a simple rule, but it is very effective at resolving bugs.

After you have found the bug but before you start fixing code, make sure you understand the nature of the problem. For example, a common error occurs when you declare variables to be of a specific simple datatype (Integer, Long, String, and so on) and, as part of your application, copy data from a table into these variables. In your own testing, everything works fine. At the client's site your client receives "Invalid Use of Null" messages.

There are two solutions to this problem, and each requires some understanding of the particular application. Clearly, you cannot place null values into Integer, Long, or String variables, so you might consider changing them all to variants. On the other hand, perhaps the solution is to disallow null entries into those particular fields in the table. Your decision on the solution needs to take into account the particular situation.

It seems obvious that you should change code only with a reason, but surprisingly, many programmers ignore this principle. "Experience" often masquerades as a reason when it is really a synonym for "wild guess." Don't just change your loop from

```
For intI = 0 To intCount - 1
```

to

```
For intI = 1 To intCount
```

until and unless you can point to your code and show exactly where and how the off-by-1 error is occurring. Take the time to thoroughly understand the bug before you try fixing it. Otherwise, you'll never know what you're fixing, and the bug will surely crop up somewhere else.

Finally, no matter how good you are and how sure you are of your work, make only one change to your code at a time, and then test it again. It's all too easy to fall into the trap of making multiple fixes without keeping records and then having to junk the current version and reload from a backup because you have no idea which things worked and which only made things worse. Take baby steps, and you'll get there faster. As an added measure, document changes to your code using comments in either individual procedures or the declarations section of a module. By logging changes with the date they were made, you can help track down problems introduced by various "fixes."

There are two more bits of debugging strategy you might want to consider. Many programmers find "confessional debugging" to be one of the most useful techniques around. Confessional debugging works something like this: you grab your printouts and go into the next cubicle, interrupt the programmer working there, and say, "Hey, sorry to bother you, but I've got this function that keeps crashing. See, I pass in the name of a form here and then declare a form variable and then—oh, wait, that's not the form itself, but the form's name. Never mind; thanks for your help." When you get good at it, you can indulge in this sort of debugging with non-programmers as the audience or even (in times of desperation) by talking things through with your dog or a sympathetic (but bored) loved one.

Of course, there are times when confessing your code isn't enough. If you have the luxury of working with peers, use them. There's a good chance that other programmers can see the bug that you can't.

If all else fails, take a break. It's easy to get stuck in a mental loop in which you try the same things over and over, even though they didn't work the first time. Take a walk. Have lunch. Take a shower. Your mind's background processing can solve many bugs while the foreground processes are thinking about something else altogether. Many programmers have told stories of waking up in the middle of the night, having just dreamed about a bug they weren't even aware existed until then, along with its solution. Having written down the information during the night, they've gone into work, found the previously unspotted bug, and fixed it on the spot.

Debugging Difficulties

As you debug, you'll come across some particular problems you'll need to watch out for. Most of them equate to the software version of the Heisenberg Uncertainty Principle: Halting code to investigate it can change the state of your program, either introducing spurious bugs or (perhaps worse) hiding actual bugs. Unfortunately, there often isn't much you can do about these problems other than to know they exist. Try using Debug.Print statements to find the program's state when you run into these sorts of bugs.

Resetting the Stopped State

If you set up a function to present the user with a particular environment and then stop it midstream, the application often won't be in the proper environment for you to proceed with your debugging. For example, you may have left screen echo off, warnings off, or the hourglass cursor on. You may also be shipping code with the toolbars turned off and yet want them handy when you're debugging things. The simplest solution to this problem is to have a utility function available, either in your production database or loaded in a library, to reset the environment to a more hospitable state. Listing 16.22 shows a function (from basError in CH16.MDB) you could possibly attach to a keystroke, using an AutoKeys macro that will reset most of your environment. Once you've assigned this function to a keystroke, it's just a simple matter of pressing one key combination whenever you stop the code and can't quite see what you're doing.

Listing 16.22

```
Function adhCleanUp()
    ' Return the application to normal programming mode.
    ' Reinstate screen updating,
    ' reset the cursor to its normal state,
    ' and reset warnings.

    On Error GoTo adhCleanUpErr

    Application.Echo True
    DoCmd.Hourglass False
    DoCmd.SetWarnings True
    Application.SetOption "Built-In Toolbars Available", True
```

```
adhCleanUpDone:
    On Error GoTo 0
    Exit Function

adhCleanUpErr:
    MsgBox "Error " & Err.Number & ": " & Err.Description, _
      vbCritical, "adhCleanUp"
    Resume adhCleanUpDone
End Function
```

Avoid Screen.ActiveForm and Screen.ActiveControl

Code that refers to Screen.ActiveForm or Screen.ActiveControl won't work properly when called from the Debug window. When the Debug window has the focus, there is no active form or active control. Any attempt to access Screen.ActiveForm or Screen.ActiveControl from your code while debugging will result in an error. In event procedures, you can work around this limitation by using the Me object instead of Screen.ActiveForm.

Problems with Focus Events

If you are debugging forms that have event procedures tied to their GotFocus or LostFocus event, those events will be triggered as you move away from the form to the Debug window and back. If you are trying to debug such events, or other low-level events such as KeyDown or MouseMove, you can't use any of the standard debugging tools. Instead, think about sprinkling adhDebugMessageBox calls into your code or even having the function dump status information continuously into a table or text file for later inspection.

Using Assertions

An *assertion* is a statement indicating that at a certain point the code should be in a certain state. If the code isn't in the expected state, an error message is reported.

The adhButtonMap function, shown in listing 16.23, displays several examples of assertions. This one function has six consecutive assertions.

Listing 16.23

```
Public Function adhButtonMap(ByVal bytButton1 As Byte, _
  ByVal bytButton2 As Byte, ByVal bytButton3 As Byte) As Long

    Call adhAssert(bytButton1 >= 0)
    Call adhAssert(bytButton1 <= adhcResumeMax)
    Call adhAssert(bytButton2 >= 0)
    Call adhAssert(bytButton2 <= adhcResumeMax)
    Call adhAssert(bytButton3 >= 0)
    Call adhAssert(bytButton3 <= adhcResumeMax)
    adhButtonMap = bytButton1 Or bytButton2 * 2 ^ 8 Or _
      bytButton3 * 2 ^ 16
End Function
```

These assertions state that the values being passed in fall within a certain range. You use assertions to validate the normal functionality of the program. Listing 16.24 shows the procedure adhAssert.

Listing 16.24

```
#Const adhcFDebug = True
Public Sub adhAssert(f As Boolean)
#If adhcFDebug Then
    If f = False Then
        Stop
    End If
#End If
End Sub
```

The code in adhAssert simply indicates that if the value passed is False, the code should be stopped at that point. The value passed in is usually the evaluation of a comparison expression.

Be sure to precede most assertions with a comment that describes why the assertion might fail: a value is out of range, the procedure name is not the same as the top of the stack, the code should never be reached, and so on. In some cases the comment might suggest how to fix the assertion. Liberal use of assertions in your code will help in finding many logic errors. The trade-off is that they add slightly to the size and reduce the speed of your code.

Summary

As you develop code, you will run into each of the three types of errors. By using the techniques described in this chapter, you can make your life much simpler by producing robust and easily maintainable code. Follow these suggestions:

- Use a generic error-reporting procedure.
- Plan your code in advance.
- Don't get too "clever."
- Structure and comment your code.
- Use indentation and naming conventions.
- Modularize your code.
- Use Option Explicit.
- Minimize your use of variants.
- Use the tightest scoping possible.
- Use assertions.

When bug avoidance fails, make sure you use a systematic and structured approach to bug removal:

- Reproduce the bug.
- Debug data, not code.
- Confirm your diagnosis before you try to fix it.
- Change code only with a reason.
- Make only one change at a time.

The temptation is always present to attempt a quick-and-dirty fix rather than plod along with the systematic approach. Don't let yourself fall prey to this temptation. It usually wastes much more time than it saves, muddying the waters before it forces you back to the approach outlined in this chapter.

By using these techniques you can create code that will stand up to the beating your users will give it. If your code does fail, you can quickly locate the problem and resolve it with minimum effort.

CHAPTER

SEVENTEEN

17

Application Optimization

- Making your applications run more quickly

- Understanding how the Jet engine optimizes queries

- Understanding and optimizing VBA's module loading

- Timing and comparing methods for solving a problem

As with any large Windows development environment, you can make choices when writing your own Access applications that will affect the performance of your application. How you create your queries, how you organize your tables, and how you write VBA code can all affect your application's speed. This chapter presents a number of issues you need to consider when optimizing your applications.

Tuning Your Application's Performance

The faster your application performs, the more usable it will be. No user (or developer) likes a slow application. Getting extra performance, however, sometimes requires you to make trade-offs and may affect other aspects of the application's usability, stability, and maintainability. Thus, it's important to keep these other issues in mind as you tune your applications for speed.

Some of the many aspects of performance tuning are outlined here:

- Hardware and memory

- Access configuration

- Database design

- Query design

- Forms design

- Reports design

- Single-user versus multiuser, file-server versus client-server application design

- VBA coding

To create applications that perform well, you will have to address many, if not all, of these areas. Depending on the design of your application, some issues will be less important than others. For example, an application that has only one or two simple reports may not need much attention paid to this component. On the other hand, the same application may need a lot of attention in the areas of query and form tuning.

> **NOTE** Although we've provided some limited multiuser and client-server performance tips in this chapter, look in Chapters 12 and 15 for additional performance suggestions specific to those areas.

Hardware and Windows Issues

Like most Windows-based programs, Access 97 runs more quickly on a faster machine. Microsoft recommends, at a minimum, a fast 486DX-based PC with at least 12MB of RAM on Windows 95 systems and 16MB of memory on Windows NT systems. This is really the *barest* of minimums, and you and your users will likely be dissatisfied with workstations of this nature. More realistically, the target machine should have

- At least a fast (66MHz or higher) 486-based processor

- 16MB or more of RAM (24MB when used on NT systems)

If you have to decide whether to get more RAM or a faster processor, we suggest you choose more RAM. For example, a 75MHz Pentium PC with 24MB of RAM will likely execute your applications more quickly than a 133MHz Pentium with 12MB of RAM.

For all installations you should also consider the following:

- Eliminate the loading of unused drivers and memory-resident utilities you rarely use.

- Remove screen savers, background pictures, and other unnecessary cycle-stealers.

- Eliminate disk-compression software, or at least consider placing your databases on uncompressed partitions. Access databases perform significantly more slowly on compressed partitions. Hard disk prices have fallen dramatically in the last few years; it may be time to buy an additional hard disk drive.

- Clean out your Recycle Bin regularly.

- Use a defrag utility regularly on your hard disks.

Understanding How the Jet Query Engine Works

One of the potentially biggest bottlenecks in your Access applications is query execution. Anytime your application creates a recordset, whether it be by executing a query, opening a form, printing a report, or opening a recordset in code, you are running a query.

The Jet query engine is responsible for the interpretation and execution of queries. Before you can optimize your queries, you need to understand how the Jet query engine works. Jet processes queries in four steps:

1. Definition
2. Compilation
3. Optimization
4. Execution

Query Definition

You can define queries using one of several mechanisms: QBE, SQL, or DAO. Whichever method you use to create the query definition, the query eventually gets converted to SQL, and it is passed to the Jet query optimizer, which then compiles and optimizes the query.

Query Compilation

Before Jet can optimize a query, it must parse the SQL statement that defines the query and bind the names referenced in the query to columns in the underlying tables. The Jet query engine compiles the SQL string into an internal query object definition format, replacing common parts of the query string with tokens. The internal format can be likened to an inverted tree: the query's result set sits at the top of the tree (the tree's root) and the base tables are at the bottom (the leaves).

Query definitions are parsed into distinct elements when compiled. These elements include the

- Base tables
- Output columns (the fields that will appear in the query's result set)

- Restrictions (in QBE, the criteria; in SQL, WHERE clause elements)

- Join columns (in QBE, the lines connecting two tables; in SQL, the fields in the JOIN clause)

- Sort columns (in QBE, sort fields; in SQL, the fields in the ORDER BY clause)

Each of these elements comes into play as the query optimizer considers different execution strategies, as described in the following sections.

Query Optimization

The query optimizer is the most complex component of Jet. It's responsible for choosing the optimum query execution strategy for the compiled query tree. The Jet query engine uses a cost-based algorithm, costing and comparing each potential execution strategy and choosing the one that's fastest. Jet calculates the cost for two major operations in the execution of queries: base table accesses and joins.

Base Table Access Plans

For each table in the query, the Jet query optimizer must choose a base table access plan. The three ways of accessing the rows in a table are

- **Table scan:** Scanning a table record by record without use of an index. This may be necessary if a restriction column is not indexed or if the restriction is not very selective (a large percentage of the base table rows are being requested). Each data page is read-only once for a table scan.

- **Index range:** Reading records in a table using an index over one of the single-table restrictions (query criteria). A data page may be read more than once for an index range.

- **Rushmore restriction:** A Rushmore restriction is used when there are restrictions on multiple indexed columns. By using multiple indexes, Jet is able to reduce considerably the number of data pages it needs to read. In many cases Jet can execute Rushmore queries without reading any data pages. (Of course, Jet still has to read index pages, but reading only index pages is almost always more efficient.)

Rushmore Query Optimizations

Jet 3.5 includes support for Rushmore query optimizations. In Jet 1.x, Jet could use only one index for a base table access. Using techniques borrowed from FoxPro, all versions of Jet since 2.0 have been able to use more than one index to restrict records. Rushmore-based query optimization is used on queries involving restrictions on multiple indexed columns of the following types:

- **Index Intersection:** The two indexes are intersected with And. Used on restrictions of the form

    WHERE Company = 'Ford' And CarType = 'Sedan'

- **Index Union:** The two indexes are unioned with Or. Used on restrictions of the form

    WHERE CarType = 'Wagon' Or Year = '1997'

- **Index Counts:** Queries that return record counts only (with or without restrictions). Used for queries of the form

    SELECT Count(*) FROM Autos

You can execute many queries much more quickly using the Rushmore query optimizer. Rushmore can't work, however, if you don't build multiple indexes for each table. It also doesn't come into play for those queries that don't contain index intersections, index unions, or index counts.

Join Strategies

For queries involving more than one table, the optimizer must consider the cost of joins, choosing from the following five types of joins:

- Nested iteration join
- Index join
- Lookup join
- Merge join
- Index-merge join

The Jet query optimizer uses statistics about the tables (discussed in the next section) to determine which join strategy to use. Each possible join combination is considered to determine which will yield the least costly query execution plan. The five join strategies are contrasted in Table 17.1.

TABLE 17.1   Jet Query Join Strategies

Join Strategy	Description	When Used
Nested iteration join	"Brute-force" iteration through the rows in both tables	Only as a last-ditch effort. May be used when there are few records or no indexes
Index join	Scans rows in the first table and looks up matching rows in the second table using an index	When the rows in the second table are small (or no data needs to be retrieved from this table) or when the rows in the first table are small or highly restrictive
Lookup join	Similar to the index join except that a projection and sort on the second table are done prior to the join	When rows in the second table are small but not indexed by the join column
Merge join	Sorts rows in the two tables by the join columns and combines the two tables by scanning down both tables simultaneously	When the two tables are large and the result set needs to be ordered on the join column
Index-merge join	Similar to a merge join, except that indexes are used to order the two tables	Instead of a merge join when each input is a table in native Jet database format. Each input must have an index over its join column, and at least one of the indexes must not allow nulls if there is more than one join column

Query Statistics

When evaluating various base table access plans and join strategies, the Jet query optimizer looks at the following statistics for each base table:

- Number of records in the base table.

- Number of data pages occupied by the base table. The more data pages that need to be read, the more costly the query.

- Location of the table. Is the table in a local ISAM format or is it from an ODBC database?

- Indexes on the table. When looking at indexes, the optimizer is concerned with

  - **Selectivity:** How "unique" is the index? Does the index allow for duplicates? A unique index is the most highly selective index because every value is distinct.

- **Number of index pages:** As with data pages, the more index pages, the more costly the query.

- **Whether nulls are allowed in the index:** Nulls in an index may rule out the usage of an index-merge join.

Putting It All Together

In determining the optimum query execution plan, the Jet query optimizer iterates through the various combinations of base table access plans and join strategies. Before choosing a join strategy, the optimizer selects a base table access plan. The optimizer then stores the estimated number of records returned and a cost indicating how expensive it would be to read the table using that plan. Next, the optimizer generates all combinations of pairs of tables and costs each join strategy. Finally, the optimizer adds tables to the joins and continues to calculate statistics until it finds the cheapest overall execution plan.

The query optimizer also considers the type of result set when costing various join strategies. When returning a dynaset, Jet often favors join strategies that are efficient at returning the first page of records quickly, even if the chosen execution strategy is slower at returning the complete result set. For dynasets, this tends to rule out joins that require sorting, such as lookup and merge joins.

For queries based on many tables, the time spent estimating the cost of all potential join combinations could easily exceed the time spent executing any given execution strategy. Because of this, the query optimizer reduces the potential number of joins it needs to consider by using the following rule: Consider joining only the results of a join to a base table. The query optimizer will never consider joining the results of one join to the results of another. This considerably reduces the potential number of joins Jet needs to look at.

After a query has been compiled and optimized by the Jet query optimizer, two additional steps are taken prior to the execution of the query.

For queries involving ODBC data sources, the remote post-processor determines how much of a query can be sent to the back end for processing by the database server application. The goal here is to send as much of the query as possible to the server, taking advantage of the server's abilities in executing queries involving server tables. This reduces the number of records that need to be sent across the network. The remote post processor identifies those parts of the query tree that can be satisfied by server queries and generates the server SQL strings for each remote query. (This partitioning of ODBC queries is discussed in more detail in Chapter 15.)

Finally, the post processor takes the compiled query tree and moves it to a new, cleaner, and smaller execution segment. This is the final step prior to query execution.

Query Execution

Once the optimizer has determined the optimum query execution plan, the query engine runs through the final query tree and executes each step to return the recordset.

You can, of course, direct Jet to create either a dynaset or a snapshot. When Jet runs a dynaset-based query, it creates a set of unique key values called a *keyset* in memory that points back to the rows in the underlying tables. This keyset-driven cursor model is very efficient because Jet needs to read only these key values and store them in memory (overflowing to disk if necessary). The values of the other columns in the dynaset aren't read until needed (such as when a user scrolls the datasheet to that screen of dynaset rows), minimizing the time needed to execute the query.

For snapshot-based queries, Jet must run the query to completion and extract all the query's columns into the snapshot. When the query contains many columns, it's likely that Jet won't be able to fit the entire snapshot into memory, requiring Jet to overflow the result set to disk, substantially slowing the query. Since Jet reads only the key values of dynasets into memory, the same dynaset-based query might fit entirely in memory, resulting in a significant performance boost. On the other hand, queries with a small number of columns and rows will likely execute more quickly as snapshots.

Forcing Jet to Recompile and Optimize a Query

Queries are compiled and optimized the first time you run a query. They are not recompiled until you resave and rerun the query. Make sure you run all queries at least once before delivering an application to users. This will eliminate subsequent compilations. Save the query in Design view and then run it without saving it again. You shouldn't save the query *after* running it or it may be saved in an uncompiled state.

Because Jet makes optimization decisions based on the size of source tables and the presence of indexes when you compiled the query, it's a good idea to force Jet to recompile a query after you've altered indexes or significantly changed the schema or number of rows in the tables. You can force recompilation by opening the query in design mode, saving it, and then reexecuting it.

Taking Advantage of Rushmore

There is no way to turn Rushmore on or off. Jet takes advantage of Rushmore optimizations anytime you have criteria that reference multiple indexed columns from the same table. If you have queries that *don't* include multiple restrictions or that contain restrictions on columns for which you haven't created indexes, Rushmore won't be used. Thus, it's important to create indexes on all columns that are used in query restrictions.

Rushmore works for both native and attached Access tables, as well as for attached FoxPro and dBASE tables. Queries involving ODBC, Btrieve, Paradox, or other ISAM tables do not benefit from Rushmore.

Keeping Statistics Accurate

The costing algorithms the query optimizer uses are dependent on the accuracy of the statistics provided by the underlying engine. Statistics for non-native tables will, in general, be less accurate than for native Access tables. For ODBC queries in which the whole query is sent to the server for processing, however, this is irrelevant since the server will be optimizing and executing the query.

For native Access tables, statistics may be inaccurate if many transactions are rolled back. Statistics can also be wrong if Jet (or the database application calling Jet) terminates abnormally without being able to update statistics to disk.

> **TIP**
>
> To force Jet to update the statistics in a Jet database, you should regularly compact the database. Compacting the database may also speed up queries because it writes all the data in a table to contiguous pages. This makes scanning sequential pages much faster than when the database is fragmented. Before compacting a database, it's a good idea to also run a disk defrag utility so that Jet can store the newly compacted database in contiguous space on disk.

Configuring the Jet Engine

The Jet 3.5 engine is an advanced desktop database engine that automatically optimizes many data access operations without user intervention. There are, however, several exposed Jet engine Registry settings you can adjust to help tune Jet for your unique situation. Make any changes to these settings with care because a change to one of the settings may have the exact opposite of your intended effect—that is, it may actually slow down the application. In addition, any change may have side effects that negatively impact concurrency or application robustness.

The Jet 3.5 Registry settings are summarized in Table 17.2. You can alter the Jet Registry settings in three ways:

- Use RegEdit to directly edit the default Registry settings.

- Create a user profile with Registry settings that override the default settings and start Access using the /profile command-line option.

- Use the SetOption method of the DBEngine object from your application to temporarily override the default or application Registry settings.

TABLE 17.2   Jet Engine Registry Settings

Key	Description	Default Value	Key Location	SetOption Constant
SystemDB	Path and file name of the security work-group file	*access_path*\ system.mdw	Engines folder*	N/A
CompactBy-PKey	If set to 1, Jet reorders records in primary key order during a compact operation; if set to 0, Jet places records in natural order (the order in which the records were originally entered)	1	Engines folder*	N/A
PageTimeout	Length of time in milliseconds a non–read-locked page is held in the cache before being refreshed	5000	Jet 3.5 folder**	dbPage-Timeout

TABLE 17.2 Jet Engine Registry Settings (continued)

Key	Description	Default Value	Key Location	SetOption Constant
UserCommit-Sync	If set to "Yes", the system waits for explicit record write operations to complete before continuing processing; if set to "No", Jet operates asynchronously when committing explicit transactions	Yes	Jet 3.5 folder**	dbUser-CommitSync
ImplicitCommit-Sync	If set to "Yes", the system waits for implicit record write operations to complete before continuing processing; if set to "No", Jet operates asynchronously when committing implicit transactions***	No	Jet 3.5 folder**	dbImplicit-CommitSync
SharedAsync-Delay	Time in milliseconds that Jet waits before committing implicit transactions*** in a shared environment	50	Jet 3.5 folder**	dbShared-AsyncDelay
ExclusiveAsync-Delay	Time in milliseconds that Jet waits before committing implicit transactions*** when the database is opened exclusively	2000	Jet 3.5 folder**	dbExclusive-AsyncDelay
FlushTransaction-Timeout	If nonzero, the number of milliseconds before starting asynchronous writes (if no pages have been added to the cache); a nonzero value disables the ExclusiveAsyncDelay and SharedAsync-Delay settings	500	Jet 3.5 folder**	dbFlush-Transaction-Timeout

TABLE 17.2 Jet Engine Registry Settings (continued)

Key	Description	Default Value	Key Location	SetOption Constant
MaxBufferSize	Size of Jet's cache in kilobytes; must be 512 or greater	((*total available RAM* − 12MB) / 4) + 512KB	Jet 3.5 folder**	dbMaxBufferSize
MaxLocks-PerFile	Maximum number of locks requested for a single transaction; if the number of locks exceeds MaxLocks-PerFile, the transaction is split and committed partially. This setting prevents problems that can occur with Novell NetWare 3.1 servers	9500	Jet 3.5 folder**	dbMaxLocksPerFile
LockDelay	Delay in milliseconds that Jet waits before retrying lock requests	100	Jet 3.5 folder**	dbLockDelay
LockRetry	Number of times to repeatedly attempt to lock a page	20	Jet 3.5 folder**	dbLockRetry
RecycleLVs	When set to 1, Jet will recycle long value (memo, OLE, and binary) pages	0 (disabled)	Jet 3.5 folder**	dbRecycleLVs
Threads	Number of background threads Jet uses	3	Jet 3.5 folder**	N/A

*The Engines folder is located at the \HKEY_LOCAL_MACHINES\Software\Microsoft\Jet\3.5\Engines key in the Registry.

**The Jet 3.5 folder is located at the \HKEY_LOCAL_MACHINES\Software\Microsoft\Jet\3.5\Engines\Jet 3.5 key in the Registry.

***See Chapter 12 for a discussion of implicit transactions.

Using SetOption is the most flexible of the four methods; it allows you to fine-tune performance on an application basis. In fact, you can change settings within the context of an application.

The syntax for using SetOption is very simple. For example, to improve performance for a batch of updates, you might lengthen the SharedAsyncDelay setting to 1 second using the following:

```
DBEngine.SetOption dbSharedAsyncDelay, 1000
```

See the "User Profiles" online help topic for more details on creating and using user profiles.

Not all Registry keys are settable using the SetOption method of DBEngine. Those keys that can be set have constants listed in Table 17.2. Any SetOption settings are in effect until you reset them with another SetOption method or DBEngine goes out of scope. In other words, these are temporary settings that affect only the current session; they are not written to the Registry. Also note that there is no corresponding GetOption statement or function.

In addition to the Registry settings in Table 17.2, there are several settings that apply only to ODBC access. See Chapter 15 or online help for more details.

Microsoft's Unsupported Jet Optimization Tools

Microsoft introduced two (officially) undocumented and unsupported Jet optimization tools in Access 95 that are available but still unsupported in Access 97:

- The ShowPlan option
- The ISAMStats method

Both these tools are part of Jet itself; you don't need any additional DLLs or other programs to make them work.

The ShowPlan Option

Jet 3.5 includes an undocumented Registry setting you can use to turn on the logging of query optimization plan information to a text file. To enable this option, you must create the following Registry key using the RegEdit program:

```
HKEY_LOCAL_MACHINE\SOFTWARE\Microsoft\Jet\3.5\Engines\Debug
```

Add the "JETSHOWPLAN" string value to this key and set it equal to "ON". (The "JETSHOWPLAN" string is case sensitive; be sure to enter it exactly as it appears here.) When you restart Access and open a database, Jet begins to log query optimization plan information to the file SHOWPLAN.OUT.

A sampling of a ShowPlan log is shown here:

```
--- qtotEmployeeDinnerSales ---

- Inputs to Query -
Table 'tblMenu'
Table 'tblEmployee'
    Using index 'PrimaryKey'
    Having Indexes:
    PrimaryKey 7 entries, 1 page, 7 values
      which has 1 column, fixed, unique, primary-key, no-nulls
    {98284CBC-D400-11CF-B58E-444553540000} 7 entries,
    1 page, 3 values
      which has 1 column, fixed
Table 'tblOrder'
    Using index 'PrimaryKey'
    Having Indexes:
    PrimaryKey 171 entries, 1 page, 171 values
      which has 1 column, fixed, unique, clustered and/or
      counter, primary-key, no-nulls
    OrderTakerId 171 entries, 1 page, 7 values
      which has 1 column, fixed
    CustomerId 171 entries, 1 page, 11 values
      which has 1 column, fixed
    {98284CBD-D400-11CF-B58E-444553540000} 171 entries,
    1 page, 7 values
      which has 1 column, fixed
    {98284CBB-D400-11CF-B58E-444553540000} 171 entries,
    1 page, 11 values
      which has 1 column, fixed
```

```
Table 'tblOrderDetails'
    Using index 'MenuId'
    Having Indexes:
    MenuId 465 entries, 3 pages, 18 values
      which has 1 column, fixed
    {98284CBF-D400-11CF-B58E-444553540000} 465 entries,
    3 pages, 171 values
      which has 1 column, fixed
    {98284CBE-D400-11CF-B58E-444553540000} 465 entries,
    3 pages, 18 values
      which has 1 column, fixed
- End inputs to Query -

01) Restrict rows of table tblMenu
      by scanning
      testing expression Unit="Dinner""
02) Inner Join result of '01)' to table 'tblOrderDetails'
      using index 'tblOrderDetails!MenuId'
      join expression "tblMenu.MenuId=tblOrderDetails.MenuId"
03) Inner Join result of '02)' to table 'tblOrder'
      using index 'tblOrder!PrimaryKey'
      join expression "tblOrderDetails.OrderId=tblOrder.OrderId"
04) Inner Join result of '03)' to table 'tblEmployee'
      using index 'tblEmployee!PrimaryKey'
      join expression "tblOrder.OrderTakerId=
      tblEmployee.EmployeeId"
05) Group result of '04)'
```

You'll likely find the earlier discussion of Jet query optimization helpful in interpreting the ShowPlan results. Examining the ShowPlan log for poorly performing queries may help you in determining how best to optimize these queries.

ShowPlan is completely undocumented and unsupported by Microsoft and should be treated like any other unsupported feature: with care. Here are some of the issues to consider when using it:

- If you close a database and open another database without exiting and restarting Access, the query plans for the new database will not be logged.

- The plans for some queries Access uses internally will appear in the log.

- The logging of plan information may adversely affect performance.

- The log file may get very large. You'll need to empty it out every so often.

- ShowPlan doesn't log the plan information for parameter queries or sub-queries and may incorrectly log the information for other queries.

To stop the logging of ShowPlan information, set the JETSHOWPLAN Registry key to "OFF".

The ISAMStats Method

Jet 3.5 includes an undocumented method of the DBEngine object, the ISAMStats method, that you can use to return a variety of pieces of information relating to disk reads and writes. The basic syntax of ISAMStats is as follows:

lngReturn = DBEngine.ISAMStats(*option*, [*reset*])

where *option* is a long integer representing one of the options from Table 17.3 and *reset* is an optional Boolean value that, when set to True, tells Jet to reset the counter for this particular option.

TABLE 17.3   ISAMStats Options

Value	Option
0	Disk reads
1	Disk writes
2	Reads from cache
3	Reads from read-ahead cache
4	Locks placed
5	Locks released

Each option of the ISAMStats method maintains a separate meter that counts the number of times that statistic occurred. The meter is reset back to zero whenever you use the reset option. To make use of ISAMStats, you need to call the method twice: once to get a baseline statistic and once to get a final statistic, after running some operation. You determine the actual value of the statistic by then subtracting the baseline statistic from the final statistic. For example, if you wanted to determine the number of disk reads Jet made while executing the qtotEmployeeDinnerSales query, you might use code like this:

```
Function GetReads()

    Dim lngStat1 As Long
    Dim lngStat2 As Long
    Dim db As Database
    Dim rst As Recordset

    Const adhcIsamReads = 0

    Set db = CurrentDb()

    lngStat1 = DBEngine.ISAMStats(adhcIsamReads)
    Set rst = db.OpenRecordset("qtotEmployeeDinnerSales", _
     dbOpenSnapshot)
    lngStat2 = DBEngine.ISAMStats(adhcIsamReads)

    GetReads = lngStat2 - lngStat1

End Function
```

NOTE
The previous example doesn't reset the ISAMStats "meter" but instead retrieves the current setting before and after running the query. You could, of course, reset the disk read meter by passing True as the second parameter before running the query. In that case you wouldn't need to subtract the "before" and "after" values in order to calculate the total disk reads.

ISAMStats is useful only when you use it to compare two possible ways of doing something. For example, if you wished to determine which of two different ways of creating a query was faster, you could use ISAMStats to determine the number of disk reads performed by each version of the query. Of course, you could always just time each query; using ISAMStats, however, may enable you to detect smaller differences that may not show up in timing comparisons. Why would you care about differences that wouldn't show up in timing tests? You may wish to perform tests using a small subset of data or using a fast development machine that you'd like to project to larger recordsets or slower target machines.

Speeding Up Queries and Recordsets

With Jet's sophisticated query optimizer, you don't have to be concerned about the order of columns and tables in queries. The Jet query optimizer decides on the most efficient query strategy and reorders the query's tables and columns to best optimize the query. You can, however, help the optimizer by following these guidelines:

- Create indexes on all columns used in ad hoc query joins (Jet already creates indexes for enforced relationships, so there's no need to create additional indexes for these types of joins), restrictions, and sorts.

- Use primary keys instead of unique indexes whenever possible. Primary key indexes disallow nulls, giving the Jet query optimizer additional join choices.

- Use unique indexes instead of non-unique indexes whenever possible. Jet can then better optimize queries because statistics on unique indexes are more accurate.

- Include as few columns as possible in the result set. The fewer columns returned, the faster the query, especially if you can completely eliminate columns from a table that is necessary only for restricting records.

- Refrain from using complex expressions, such as those involving the IIf function, in queries. If you are using nested queries (queries based on the results of other queries), try to move up any expressions to the highest (last) query.

- Use Count(*) instead of Count([*column*]). Jet has built-in optimizations that make Count(*) much faster than column-based counts.

- Use the Between operator in restriction clauses rather than open-ended >, >=, <, and <= restrictions. Using Between returns fewer rows. For example, use "Age Between 35 and 50" rather than "Age >= 35".

- When creating restrictions on join columns that are present in both tables in a one-to-many join, it is sometimes more efficient to place the restriction on the "one" side of the join. Other times it might be more efficient to place the restriction on the "many" side. You'll have to test which is more efficient for each query, because the ratio of the sizes of the tables and the number and type of restrictions determine which is more efficient.

- Normalize your tables, decomposing large tables into smaller normalized ones. Because this reduces the size of tables (and therefore the number of pages required to hold tables), it causes join strategies that involve table scans to execute more quickly.

- In some instances, it might also help to *denormalize* databases to reduce the number of joins needed to run frequently used queries. (See Chapter 4 for a discussion of denormalization and additional design details.)

- When you have the option of constructing a query using either a join or a subquery, it's worth trying both options. In some cases you will find the solution that employs the join to be faster; in other cases the subquery-based solution may be faster.

- Avoid using outer joins if possible because they require a complete scan of the entire preserved table (that is, the "left" table in a left outer join).

- For nontrivial queries, use saved queries instead of SQL because these queries will have already been optimized. (Access 97 creates hidden querydefs for SQL statements it finds in RecordSource and RowSource properties of forms and reports, but it won't create querydefs for SQL statements you have embedded in VBA code.)

- Manually recompile queries when the size of tables or the presence or type of indexes has changed. (See the section "Forcing Jet to Recompile and Optimize a Query" earlier in this chapter.)

- When possible, use action queries instead of looping through recordsets in VBA to update or delete batches of data.

- When you need to use a snapshot recordset and you don't need to move backward in the recordset, use a forward-scrolling snapshot.

- When you only wish to add new rows to a recordset, open the recordset using the dbAppendOnly option.

- When creating queries against client-server sources, consider using pass-through queries. (Pass-through queries, however, may not always be faster than regular queries.)

- When creating client-server applications, consider using ODBCDirect connections rather than standard Jet connections. (See Chapter 15 for more details on ODBCDirect and other client-server optimization strategies.)

- When running very large action queries, you may wish to set the UseTransaction property of the query to False, which tells Access not to execute the action query as a single transaction. (For moderately sized action queries, setting UseTransaction to False may actually slow down the query, so be careful using this property.)

When in doubt, experiment and benchmark various potential solutions. Don't assume one way to do it is faster just because it *should* be or because someone told you it was.

Speeding Up Forms

Most Access applications revolve around forms, so it goes without saying that any improvements to the performance of forms will realize large gains in the usability of your applications. The following sections detail several areas to consider when optimizing your forms.

Limiting a Form's Record Source with Large Recordsets

It's tempting to create forms in Access that are based on a huge recordset of tens or hundreds of thousands of records. However, you will quickly discover a severe performance penalty when opening such forms or attempting to navigate to a different record using the FindFirst method. The problems are exacerbated when you attempt to use these types of forms in a networked file-server or client-server environment, where forms will be retrieving remote data.

The solution is simple. Rather than giving users *all* the records and navigating around the form's dynaset, set up the form to serve up a single record (or some small subset of records) at a time. Then, instead of using the FindFirst method to move to a different record, change the form's RecordSource property. (Chapter 12 includes an example of this technique in the section "The Wire.")

Speeding Up Combo Boxes with Many Rows

Combo boxes are a great way to present a small or moderately sized list of items to a user, but you shouldn't use combo boxes to present more than a few thousand items. Consider alternative ways of presenting the same data.

For example, consider reworking the form so that the combo box contains fewer rows. You might use other controls on the form to refine the search and reduce the number of rows in the combo box's row source. For example, have the user enter an employee's territory into a territory control to reduce the number of entries in an EmployeeId combo box.

Although the AutoExpand functionality Access provides for combo boxes is very popular with users, it adds a large amount of overhead. Combo boxes will react to keystrokes more quickly if you turn off this property. (See Chapter 7 for more information.)

Other Form Speed-Up Tricks

Other things you can do to speed up your forms or reduce their memory usage include the following:

- Instead of opening and closing forms, load often-used forms hidden and make them visible and invisible. This uses up more memory and system resources, so you have to balance this technique against memory considerations.

- Consider using lightweight forms and hyperlinks for switchboard forms. (See Chapter 23 for more details.)

- Reduce the complexity of forms. Break complex forms into multiple pages or multiple forms or use the new native tab control.

- Don't use overlapping controls.

- Place controls containing memo and bound OLE objects on pages of a form other than the first or on ancillary forms that can be popped up using a command button. This allows users to browse quickly through records when they don't need to view these complex objects.

- If your form contains static pictures stored in unbound object frame controls, convert them to use lightweight image controls instead. To do this, right-click the control and select Change To ➤ Image.

> **TIP**
> You may find the Performance Analyzer Add-In (Tools ➤ Analyze ➤ Performance) helpful in locating and correcting performance bottlenecks in your application. Although its usefulness is limited, you may find it highlights problems you never thought of checking.

Speeding Up Reports

If you're creating complex reports, you may find they take longer to print than you'd expect. One reason for this is that Access creates a separate query for each section of the report. Many of the suggestions found in the section "Speeding Up Queries and Recordsets" earlier in this chapter also apply here because the speed of report output (or the lack thereof) is often more an issue of the underlying queries. In addition, you can try the following suggestions to improve report performance:

- Move query expressions onto the report.

- Avoid situations in which one query pulls the data from tables and a second query just filters the data. The more information you can pull together into one query, the better. One query uses less memory.

- Avoid including fields in the query that aren't used in the final output of the report.

- If you're using subreports, look at the queries on which they're based. Generally, you shouldn't use subreports when their record source is the same as the main report's record source. If the main and subform's record sources are the same, try rethinking your design so you can work without the subreport.

- Add subreports to replace multiple expressions that call domain functions such as DLookup or DSum. By using a subreport, you can often get the same functionality you get with the slower domain functions, without using any expressions. On the other hand, if you need to look up only a single value, using a domain function may be faster.

Optimizing VBA's Use of Modules and Compilation

Let's face it: when you first convert Access 2 applications to Access 97, they often run more slowly. Jet is much faster in its 32-bit incarnation, but the Access user interface just isn't as perky as it used to be. Although specific portions are faster (combo boxes, especially), the whole package may seem slower. Part of the slowdown can be attributed to the forms and reports engine, but a large portion may be due to the way Access and VBA interact. (On the other hand, Access 97 is much faster than Access 95 in almost all aspects. If you're converting from Access 95 to Access 97, you may be pleasantly surprised!) The following sections explain some of the issues involved in working with VBA, and the section "Speeding Up VBA: Testing Hypotheses" later in this chapter suggests some specific ways you can speed up VBA code.

Understanding How VBA and Compilation Work

Instead of being a tokenized, interpreted language, as was Access Basic, VBA is a compiled language. Although this advancement promises a great deal of power, it can be a drag if you aren't aware of the ramifications of using a compiled language. This discussion, through a series of questions and answers, explains the issues involved with compilation of your VBA code and what you can do to control it.

How Does VBA Load Code?

In Access 2, when you loaded an application, Access loaded all the global modules into memory at startup. Form and report modules were loaded as necessary, but the global modules were always available, having been loaded when the application loaded. This meant that although application load time might be longer, form and report loading could, at worst, cause the form or report module to be loaded. Of course, loading a large module takes time; the code must be loaded from disk and read into memory.

VBA loads code when it's needed, at execution time. In Access 95 and Access 97, only modules called during the application's startup sequence are loaded as the application loads. That is, only modules that are needed by the startup form (or the macro called at startup) are loaded with the application. Then, as your application calls various procedures, VBA loads the appropriate modules. (In Access 95, loading a module causes VBA to also load any modules containing code or variables used by the module. This "call-tree loading" contributed to Access 95's slow load speed for forms.) Certainly, for applications with large amounts of code, this "load on demand" feature allows faster load times. For Access 95, on the other hand, it will possibly contribute to slower form and report load times. As Access 95 loads each object, it might also need to load global modules called by procedures in the form or report module. This is not true for Access 97: now, VBA loads only the particular module it needs at any given moment to run your code.

VBA always loads an entire module if it needs any portion of the module. If it must use any procedure in a module, it loads the entire module. The same goes for a variable in a module: if your code attempts to set or retrieve the value of a Public variable in a module, VBA must load the entire module. This, too, can contribute to application slowdowns if you haven't planned accordingly.

> **TIP**
>
> If you'd like Access 97 to load modules the way Access 95 does (that is, all of them in the call tree, at once), you can still force this to happen. All you need do is refer to a single variable in each module, and you'll force VBA to load each module. If you want to preload all your modules, add a public variable to each and attempt to retrieve the value of each in your application's startup code. That way, you'll cause VBA to load each module you reference at that time. This may seem like a lot of work, but at least in Access 97 you have the choice of how to handle this; in Access 95, you had no choice at all.

Why Compile Code?

VBA must compile the code at some point before it can run the code. If the code hasn't been previously compiled, VBA must compile it on the fly, as needed. That is, as you open forms or reports with uncompiled code, VBA must compile the form/report module before Access can open the object, and compilation takes time. You can certainly see that this would cause your forms or reports to open more slowly.

What Gets Stored When Your Code Is Compiled?

When VBA compiles your code, it stores both the original text (it doesn't store it exactly as you type it but stores a tokenized version) and the compiled version. When Access prepares to run previously compiled code, it loads just the compiled version into memory and runs that compiled code. For uncompiled code, Access must load the original version into memory and then compile the code as needed.

When Should You Compile Loaded Modules?

When you choose the Debug ➤ Compile Loaded Modules menu item, you're instructing VBA to compile only the modules that are currently loaded, including any form and report modules. Using this menu item is equivalent to choosing the Compile Loaded Modules toolbar icon. Because this action compiles only the loaded modules, it's possible that even if you've compiled all the loaded modules, some saved modules will not yet have been compiled. These uncompiled modules could contain syntax errors that won't show up until you actually run the code. Use this menu item (or toolbar icon) to check for syntax errors in the code you're working on; it's the fastest way to do so.

When Should You Compile All Modules?

The Debug ➤ Compile All Modules menu item opens and compiles every module in your application, including the form and report modules. It performs a complete syntax check as well. This is the quickest way to completely compile your application, and you should perform this action before distributing any application. (More typically, you'll want to use the Debug ➤ Compile and Save All Modules menu item instead. That way, you know you've saved your compiled state.) If you continue to test your application using only Compile Loaded Modules, you may not be trying all the execution paths, which means that code you haven't worked on recently might contain a compile error.

You should consider the Compile All Modules action a waste of time, especially for large applications, until you're done writing code. When you're working on the application, you're guaranteed that some of the code will be in a decompiled state, and compiling all the modules in a large application can be quite time consuming. Use Compile Loaded Modules unless you're ready to distribute the application or when you want to check its performance. (Because running uncompiled code is always slower than running compiled code, you can't judge the actual performance until you've compiled all the modules.)

Unlike Access 95, Access 97 can store some modules in a compiled state and others in a decompiled state. When you choose to compile all (or compile and save), VBA just compiles the code that needs to be compiled, affording a substantial time savings.

How Does the Compile On Demand Option Fit In?

When the Compile On Demand option is checked (and that's the default for the option), VBA compiles only the code it must compile in order to run the current procedure. Although this does speed the development process somewhat (VBA isn't compiling code it doesn't need to compile for the current execution path), it's just delaying the inevitable. Sooner or later you must compile all your code. What's more, unless you understand the ramifications of this option, it can get you into trouble by leading you to believe your code is correct when, in fact, it's not.

To see the Compile On Demand option in action, follow these steps:

1. Use the Tools ➤ Options ➤ Module menu item to make sure the Compile On Demand option is turned on.

2. Create a new module, and enter the following code into it:

```
Function Test1()
    Test1 = Test2()
End Function
```

3. Create a second module, and enter the following code (which would normally cause a compilation error because the function Test4 doesn't exist):

```
Function Test2()
    Test2 = 1
End Function

Function Test3()
    Test3 = Test4()
End Function
```

4. In the Debug window, type the following, causing VBA to run Test1. Note that this doesn't trigger a compilation error, even though the code is not correct, because you've turned on Compile On Demand and you didn't demand that Test3 be compiled.

```
? Test1()
```

5. Go back to the Tools ➤ Options ➤ Module dialog and turn off the Compile On Demand option.

6. In the Debug window, repeat step 4. Note that there's still no error, because you're running code that's already compiled.

7. Modify Test1 so it looks like the code below, and then run it in the Debug window, as in step 4. Now you'll trigger a compile error because you've turned off Compile On Demand and caused the code to be recompiled.

```
Function Test1()
    Test1 = Test2()
    Debug.Print 1
End Function
```

What Does Compile and Save All Modules Do?

The Debug ➤ Compile and Save All Modules menu item (available only when you're editing a module) compiles all your modules and saves the compiled modules to disk. Access will now have saved both the original tokenized version and the compiled version. In addition, Access will track internally that all the modules are compiled and won't attempt to recompile anything before running your application. If you don't use this menu item, your modules' compiled state will be lost when you quit Access, and VBA will have to recompile before running the application. (If there have been no new changes to the code since it was last compiled, the Compile and Save All Modules menu item won't be available.)

What Causes Code to Be Decompiled?

Decompilation is the VBA programmer's curse. Compiling code can take time, and it's got to happen sometime between code changes and running the application. If you can save your code in a compiled state, you won't have to pay the compilation price at run time. To avoid decompilation of your code, you must know when it occurs and what causes it.

Access marks your VBA, module by module, as being decompiled anytime you save a change to an object that might affect VBA code: forms, reports, controls, or modules. If you modify a form (or a report) or its controls, modify code in a global or CBF module, or delete or rename any of these objects, you'll cause Access to tell VBA that the specific object needs recompilation. If you make a change but don't save it, you'll preserve the compiled state.

If you change an object or its code, in addition to the object that's been changed, VBA must recompile any module or object that refers to the changed object. That is, decompilation travels "upstream," not "downstream." If module A calls code in module B and you change something in module B that's used in module A, module A will need to be recompiled. If you change something in module A, however, module B will retain its compiled state (assuming that nothing in module B calls code in module A).

VBA stores the project name as part of its compilation status. Therefore, if you change the project name of a compiled application, Access sees it as being decompiled and forces VBA to recompile the entire application next time it's loaded. In Access 95, VBA used the database name as the project name, so if you renamed the database, your entire application became decompiled. In Access 97, you can use the Tools ➤ Options ➤ Advanced dialog box to change the project name, but the database name is no longer used—changing the database name no longer decompiles your application.

What Are the Effects of Compilation on Memory and Disk Usage?

Compiled applications require more disk space. As mentioned earlier in this chapter, when you compile all the modules, VBA stores both the decompiled and the compiled code in your database. On the other hand, compiled applications require less memory because VBA loads only the compiled code when it runs the application. If you attempt to compile code on the fly, VBA must load the decompiled code and then compile it as it runs.

Are Modules Ever Removed from Memory?

Modules are not removed from memory until you close the application. VBA loads modules into memory as it needs them, and once a module has been loaded, it's never removed from memory. That is, VBA supports dynamic loading of modules but doesn't support dynamic unloading. Don't forget that VBA will load a module if you reference either a procedure or a variable in that module.

During the development process, this dynamic loading of modules can cause memory usage to grow and free RAM to shrink. You may want to close and reopen the database occasionally to release the memory. Using the Debug ➤ Compile and Save All Modules menu item causes all the modules to be loaded into memory; make sure you close and reopen the database after compiling all the modules.

What You Can Do to Optimize the Use of Modules

Once you understand how VBA works with modules, you may want to take some extra steps to make your modules work as efficiently as possible. Although it may sound obvious, try to minimize the amount of extraneous code in each module. Because VBA always loads a full module to reference any procedure in that module, the less code it must load, the more quickly your forms and reports will open. Try to move unnecessary procedures from your modules, and group procedures, if possible, by their use. Don't forget that referring to a variable in a module will also cause VBA to load that module. The goal is to load as little code as possible at any given moment.

Unlike its behavior in Access 95, VBA in Access 97 will not decompile your entire application if a user adds a new form or report. Because of the "upstream" decompilation, you're guaranteed that no existing code relies on the new form or report, and your application will remain compiled. On the other hand, it's certainly possible for an end user to decompile specific modules by changing an existing form or report: if there's a change to an object that has code dependencies, VBA will have to decompile the code that depends on the object.

One More Consideration: No Circular References in Libraries

Because of a design limitation of VBA, Access projects do not support circular references. No matter how you try to obfuscate the path, no procedure can call a procedure in another module that ends up calling a procedure in the original module. Even if you call procedures in other modules along the way, the procedure call will fail if it eventually calls a procedure in the original module. This will most often occur if you write library databases (add-ins, Wizards, and so on). You will need to design your library database in such a way that you don't require circular references. One unfortunate solution is to place duplicate copies of procedures in multiple modules. (See Chapter 22 for more information on using library databases.)

What Else Can You Do?

There's no simple solution to maintaining the compiled state of your applications. You'll need to take special steps, and this will add extra overhead to your development process. The difference between running compiled code and decompiled code is quite obvious, even for moderate-sized applications, so it's worth taking the time to ensure that your applications are compiled when you need them to be.

Once you've tackled the major issues, you'll want to investigate ways to speed up the VBA code itself. The next portion of this chapter investigates some techniques you can use to improve the performance of the code. No such list could be exhaustive, and we've selected a series of ideas that we thought would make a difference in VBA code. The interesting part is that some things we *thought* would matter actually don't. In addition, some enhancements that made a small difference in Access 2 or Access 95 now make a very large difference in Access 97, and vice versa.

> **TIP**
>
> Although the conversion of a database to MDE format (using the Tools ➤ Database Utilities ➤ Make MDE File menu item) doesn't cause your code to run any more quickly, it does strip the source code itself from the database. That way, Access can load the file more quickly, and, because the database uses less memory (because there's no source code loaded), there's more memory available for your application to use. The more memory, the faster the application, so converting a large application to MDE format should afford one more way of speeding its execution. Of course, once you've converted your application to an MDE file, users can never cause the code to be decompiled, so you'll never again need to worry about the application's compiled state. (For more information on using MDE files, see Chapter 22.)

Speeding Up VBA: Testing Hypotheses

As in any programming language, in VBA there are often many ways to accomplish the same task. Because you're dealing not only with a language but also with the interface and the underlying data, all tied together in the programming environment, the choices are often even more complicated than with other, more standard languages. The following sections propose a series of selected optimizations, some more potent than others, and some that are based on incorrect assumptions (that is, they *don't* help at all and perhaps even hurt). Probably no single application will be able to use each of these, but you can add the ones that help to your "bag of tricks" as you program in Access. You'll also find a method for timing those optimizations so you can create your own test cases.

Creating a Stopwatch

Although you could use the VBA Timer function to calculate the time a specific process requires, it's not the wisest choice. Because it measures time in seconds since midnight in a single-precision floating-point value, it's not terribly accurate. Even though you'll most likely be timing intervals larger than a single second, you'll want a bit more accuracy than the Timer function can provide. The Windows API provides the timeGetTime function (aliased as adh_apiGetTime in the sample code), which returns the number of milliseconds that have passed since Windows was started.

Not that it matters for testing purposes, but Timer "rolls over" every 24 hours. timeGetTime keeps on ticking for up to 49 days before it resets the returned tick count to 0. Most likely, if you're timing something that runs for 49 days, you're not terribly interested in milliseconds, but that's what you get.

To test each of the proposed optimizations, you need some mechanism for starting and stopping the clock. The subroutine adhStartTimer stores the current return value from adh_apiGetTime into a global variable, lngStartTime. You must call this subroutine directly before any code you want to have timed. When you're done with the critical section of code, call the function adhEndTimer, which returns the difference between the current time and the time when you called adhStartTimer, or the elapsed time. Listing 17.1 shows the declarations and code for the timer functions.

Listing 17.1

```
Private Declare Function adh_apiGetTime Lib "winmm.dll" _
 Alias "timeGetTime" () As Long
Dim lngStartTime As Long

Sub adhStartTimer()
    lngStartTime = adh_apiGetTime()
End Sub

Function adhEndTimer()
    adhEndTimer = adh_apiGetTime() - lngStartTime
End Function
```

Most Windows programmers have used the GetTickCount function in previous versions of Windows to perform their high-resolution timing. Although that function returned its result in milliseconds, it was never more accurate than the clock timer in your PC, which measures time in increments of $1/18$ second. The timeGetTime function, introduced in Windows 3.0 as part of the multimedia extensions, uses a different hardware timer and can actually measure time with millisecond accuracy. Before Windows 95 and Windows NT, you couldn't have been sure your users had the correct multimedia DLLs on their system. With the new operating systems, you're assured that all users will have the necessary DLLs, and you can use timeGetTime without worry.

Getting Reasonable Results

You will find that running any given test only once doesn't provide reliable results. There are just too many external forces in play when you're running under Windows. To get a reasonable idea of the benefit of a given optimization test, you need to run the test code many times within the given test case and then run the test case many times, averaging the results. For simplicity, each of the tests in this chapter takes as its only parameter a Long value indicating the number of times you want to run the test. Each function loops the specified number of times with the clock running and provides the elapsed time as the return value of the function.

If you want to add your own tests to this test mechanism, you must follow those constraints when planning your tests. In addition, for each test case, you need two versions: a "slow" version (labeled Test1a in this example) and a "fast" version (labeled Test1b in this example). Once you've provided the two functions, you can call the function adhRunTests, which, in turn, calls both functions the specified number of times. adhRunTests averages the elapsed times the functions return and reports on the comparative speed of the two functions. Listing 17.2 shows the adhRunTests function. Notice that adhRunTests takes four parameters, as shown in Table 17.4. adhRunTests returns an Integer indicating the comparison between the first and second functions, measured as a percentage:

```
intAmount = Int((varResults1 - varResults2) / _
  varResults2 * 100)
```

TABLE 17.4   adhRunTests Parameters

Parameter	Description	Datatype
strFunc1	Name of the "slow" function to test	String expression
strFunc2	Name of the "fast" function to test	String expression
varReptFunc	Number of times to repeat the function call	Variant
varReptOp	Number of times to repeat the operation in the function	Variant

In addition, adhRunTests prints a string to the Debug window (so it's useful without an interface, for informal testing), like this:

```
Test1a vs. Test1b: 3.7        0.7              428%
```

This output shows the milliseconds elapsed while running each function, followed by the percentage improvement in the faster function.

For example, to call adhRunTests to test functions Test1a and Test1b, running each function 10 times to average the results and having each function loop internally 10,000 times, call adhRunTests like this:

```
strResult = adhRunTests("Test1a", "Test1b", 10, 10000)
```

Listing 17.2

```
Function adhRunTests(strFunc1 As String, strFunc2 As String, _
  varReptFunc As Variant, varReptOp As Variant) As Variant
    Dim varI As Variant
    Dim varResults1 As Variant
    Dim varResults2 As Variant
    Dim varDiff As Variant
    Dim intAmount As Integer
    Dim strResult As String
    Dim varTemp As Variant
    For varI = 0 To varReptFunc - 1
        Call SetStatus("Running " & strFunc1 & "() Pass " & varI)
        varResults1 = varResults1 + Eval(strFunc1 & _
        "(" & varReptOp & ")")
    Next varI

    For varI = 0 To varReptFunc - 1
        Call SetStatus("Running " & strFunc2 & "() Pass " & varI)
        varResults2 = varResults2 + Eval(strFunc2 _
        & "(" & varReptOp & ")")
    Next varI
    varResults1 = varResults1 / varReptFunc
    varResults2 = varResults2 / varReptFunc
    varDiff = varResults1 - varResults2
    If Abs(varDiff) < 0.005 Then varDiff = 0
    ' Better check for division by 0 and
    ' overflow, both of which can occur from
    ' a very small value in varResults1.
    On Error GoTo adhRunTestsError
    intAmount = Int((varResults1 - varResults2) / _
     varResults2 * 100)
    Debug.Print strFunc1 & " vs. " & strFunc2 & ":"; _
     varResults1, varResults2, intAmount & "%"
```

```
        adhRunTests = intAmount

adhRunTestsExit:
    ' Clear the status line.
    Call SetStatus
    Exit Function

adhRunTestsError:
    MsgBox Error, vbExclamation, "adhRunTests()"
    adhRunTests = 0
    Resume adhRunTestsExit
End Function
```

Using the Eval Function

adhRunTests uses the Eval function to execute each of the two tests. The Eval function takes as a parameter a string containing code you want Access to execute. If you intend to use Eval to execute functions, you should be aware of the various limitations involved in using this technique.

- Access performs no error checking on the string you send to Eval. If it works, great. If not, you get, at best, a "User Defined Error" message. At worst, you crash (and lose data). You would be wise to check the string you're about to send to Eval by using MsgBox or Debug.Print to display the string before its execution. This way you can verify that the string to be executed is, in fact, laid out exactly as you think it ought to be.

- Scoping rules are always an issue. Eval cannot interpret any local variables, nor can it handle private functions. You can remember the rules this way: any object you want to send to Eval must also work in macros. Just as VBA variables aren't available in macros, they aren't available once Eval gets hold of the string to be executed. adhRunTests uses local variables, but they become part of the string passed to Eval and are passed as values, not as variable names.

- The string you pass to Eval must represent a function that returns a value of some sort. That value will be the return value from the call to Eval. Neither subroutines nor expressions are allowed.

The effectiveness of each of the optimizations that follow depends on many factors, including the actual code in use at the time, the relative speed of your hard disk versus the processor in your computer, and other programs currently using Windows' memory and resources. Using Windows 95 or Windows NT and Access 97 makes the issues even more complex than they were when using Access 2. There might be a process running in the background that you're not aware of, and Access 97 and Jet both provide their own internal caching. The only sure way to provide accurate timings would be to remove all background processes and to reboot between each timing. That's not practical, so we'll mention again that the timing results presented here are for comparison purposes only. You'll need to decide for yourself in some of the marginal cases whether the optimization will really help. Therefore, a word of warning: take any suggestions of optimizations with a grain of salt. Try them out in your own applications before swearing by them. As they say in the auto industry, "These numbers are for comparison only. Your mileage may vary."

Eighteen Possible Optimizations

In this section we present 18 optimizations, in no particular order. Some will actually make a difference in your applications; others are interesting ideas we thought might make a difference (and used to, in Access 2 or Access 95) but no longer actually do in Access 97. We've left in the "losers," mostly to indicate that some perceived optimizations just don't help. To test each hypothesis, we've created two similar versions of a simple function. CH17.MDB includes the full source for both versions of each test so you can try them out yourself.

To simplify your experiments with the test cases we present here, you can use frmRunTests from CH17.MDB. Figure 17.1 shows this form in use. It includes a combo box from which you can choose the specific test case to run and spin buttons allowing you to specify how many loops to execute inside the routine, as well as how many times to call each routine. (See Chapter 7 for more information on creating your own spin buttons.) The View Slower and View Faster buttons pop up forms that pull the source code for the functions directly from the basTests module, so you can look at the code as you test. Finally, the clock button starts the test, running the slow version as many times as you've requested and then running the faster version the same number of times.

Clearly, this method of testing is far from perfect. The order in which you run the tests might make a difference, and Access, Jet, and the operating system caches all

FIGURE 17.1

frmRunTests allows you to choose a specific test and run it, resulting in a comparison between the slow and fast versions.

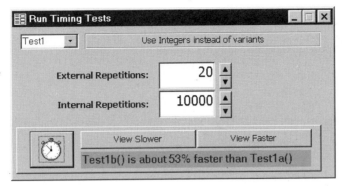

make a difference, too. In our informal testing (and that's all this can be—measurements of relative differences), none of these factors made much difference. Reversing the order of the tests made almost no difference. Remember, the goal of these tests is to determine which of two methods is faster, not to gather exact timings. In each case we ran the tests on a Pentium Pro 200 with 64MB of memory (which certainly removes the lack-of-hardware issue from the possible set of problems). The percentage differences we found depend totally on the specific tests we ran and the setup of our system, but we've tried to make them representative of the kinds of improvements you'd see, too.

> **NOTE** Some of the differences may disappear or reverse in low-memory situations as things are swapped back and forth from your Windows swap file.

The results of our performance tests are summarized in Table 17.5.

TABLE 17.5   Summary of the Results of the VBA Performance Tests

Test Number	Optimization	Approximate Effectiveness of Speedup
1	Integer variables instead of variants	50–60%
2	Integer division instead of real division	< 10%
3	Logical assignments instead of If...Then	30–35%

TABLE 17.5   Summary of the Results of the VBA Performance Tests (continued)

Test Number	Optimization	Approximate Effectiveness of Speedup
4	Len for testing for zero-length strings	30–40%
5	"Not var" to toggle True/False	60–70%
6	timeGetTime instead of Timer	Around 900% (no kidding!)
7	Use object variables	300–400%
8	Use implicit logical comparisons	10–20%
9	Refer to controls by number in loops	10–15%
10	IsCharAlphaNumeric instead of Asc	200%
11	Use DBEngine(0)(0) instead of CurrentDb	500–1000%
12	If...Then...Else instead of IIf	Depends on your code (100%, in the test case)
13	db.Execute instead of RunSQL	Around 100%
14	For Each...Next instead of For...Next	15–20%
15	Remove comments from code	No improvement
16	Use bookmarks rather than FindFirst to find rows	Around 900%
17	Drop default collection names in expressions	No difference
18	Refresh collections only when necessary	1500–2000% (depends on the number of objects)

Some of the comparisons are more dependent than others on the assumptions made. For example, Test2, which evaluates the difference between using Integer and real division, couldn't be constructed in too many different ways. It's doubtful you'd get results differing much from those in Table 17.5 by rewriting the code. On the other hand, Test12, which compares decisions made using IIf and the If...Then construct, will give widely differing results depending on the details of what you're doing in the "true" and "false" cases of the construct. Thus, it's important to be aware of the assumptions made for each test when interpreting the results.

In running these tests, we tried both the MDB file and a corresponding MDE file. In some of the tests, using an MDE file didn't change the comparative results but did make an improvement in the absolute results. That is, the ratio of slower to faster didn't change, but the time elapsed for each test, in total, was less.) These tests aren't particularly indicative of how real applications will benefit from conversion to MDE format, but certainly, the conversion could improve the speed of your compiled code.

We haven't listed the test code here. We describe the tests and the concepts involved, but you'll need to investigate CH17.MDB to see the exact details of the tests. In any case, you're very unlikely to use the specific code we've written in your own applications; it's the concepts that count. For each test case, the name of the procedure in basTests in CH17.MDB is Test$N$a (the presumed slow version) or Test$N$b (the supposedly faster version), where N is the test number. For example, the code corresponding to test case 5 is Test5a and Test5b.

Test 1: Use Integers Instead of Variants Whenever Possible?

Unless you specify otherwise, VBA creates all variables using its default type, Variant. To hold data of any simple type, variants must be at least as big and complex as any of the types they can contain. "Big and complex" equates with "slower," so avoid variants if at all possible. Of course, there will be many times when you can't avoid them, but if you're just ill-informed or being lazy, your code will suffer.

This optimization makes sense only within VBA. If you're working with data from tables in your code, you *must* use variants. Because variants are the only datatype that can hold null data, and it's usually possible for data from tables to be null, you'll avoid problems by using variants. In addition, you may find that attempting to use specific datatypes when working with Jet ends up *slowing* your code. Because Jet uses variants when it communicates with Access, when you place Jet data into specific datatypes, you're asking VBA to make a datatype conversion, and that takes time.

Test 2: Use Integer Division Whenever Possible?

Access provides two division operators, the / (floating-point division) and \ (Integer division) operators. To perform floating-point division, Access must convert the operands to floating-point values. This takes time. If you don't care about the fractional portion of the result, you can save some time by using the Integer division operator instead.

The results of this test were decidedly mixed. Using Integer division made almost no difference (and it did make a difference in Access 2). In some other examples—working with forms, for instance—this has made a difference. It may be that VBA is smart enough to use Integer math internally if it can tell that that's what will work most quickly.

Test 3: Use Logical Assignments When Possible?

Like many other languages, Access handles logical values as integers. In addition, Access performs right-to-left expression evaluation. The combination of these two features allows you to make logical assignments directly as part of an expression. For example, many people write code like this:

```
If x = 5 Then
    y = True
Else
    y = False
End If
```

This code is wordier than it needs to be. The intent is to set the variable y to True if x is equal to 5 and False otherwise. The expression (x = 5) has a truth value of its own—that is, it's either True or False. You can assign that value directly to y in a single statement:

```
y = (x = 5)
```

Although it may look confusing, VBA will interpret it correctly. Starting from the right, Access will calculate the value of the expression x = 5 (either True or False) and assign that value to the variable y. Other languages, including C and Pascal, use distinct assignment and equality operators, making this expression a little clearer. In C, for example, the statement would read

```
y = (x == 5)
```

with the "=" performing the assignment and the "==" checking the equality.

Anyplace you use an expression like the If…Then…End If statement above, you should be able to replace it with a single assignment statement.

If you find these logical assignments hard to read, you may choose to skip using them, because the improvement in performance is slight. If, however, logical assignments seem natural to use and read, then by all means use them.

Test 4: Use Len to Test for Zero-Length Strings?

There are several ways you can check to see whether the length of a particular string is 0. One method is to compare the string to "", and another is to compare the length of the string to 0. Comparing the results of the Len function to 0 is measurably faster.

Test 5: Use "Var = Not Var" to Toggle True/False?

In many circumstances you need to toggle the state of a variable between True and False. You might be tempted to write code like this:

```
If x = True Then
    x = False
Else
    x = True
End If
```

You might think that either of the following solutions would be an improvement over the original:

```
If x Then
    x = False
Else
    x = True
End If
  or
x = IIf(x, False, True)
```

Testing shows that neither is as good as the original expression (and the IIf solution is much slower). But the best solution is to use the following expression:

```
x = Not x
```

That way, if x is currently True, it will become False. If it's False, it will become True.

Test 6: Use timeGetTime Rather Than Timer?

As mentioned earlier in this chapter, the Windows API function timeGetTime (aliased as adh_apiGetTime in the examples) returns the number of milliseconds that have elapsed since you started the current Windows session. The VBA Timer function returns the number of seconds that have elapsed since midnight. If you're interested in measuring elapsed times, you're far better off using timeGetTime, for three reasons:

- timeGetTime is more accurate.

- timeGetTime runs longer without "rolling over."

- Calling timeGetTime is significantly faster.

Calling timeGetTime is no more complex than calling Timer, once you've included the proper API declaration for it. In the declarations section of any standard module in your application, you'll need to include the statement

```
Private Declare Function adh_apiGetTime Lib "winmm.dll" _
  Alias "timeGetTime" () As Long
```

With that declaration in place, you can call it from any module in your application, just as though it were an internal Access function.

Test 7: Cache Object References?

In writing code you often need to retrieve or set properties of the various forms, reports, and controls in your application. Generally, you refer to these objects with statements like this:

```
strCaption = Forms!frmTest!cmdButton1.Caption
```

For a single reference to an object, there's not much you can do to speed up the reference. If, on the other hand, you're going to be referring to many of the properties of that object or using that object in a loop of some sort, you can achieve a substantial speed increase by pointing an object variable at that object and using that variable to reference the object.

For example, if you were going to reference all of a specific control's properties, you would be well served to use code like this rather than refer to the control with the full syntax each time:

```
Dim ctl as Control
Set ctl = Forms!YourForm!YourControl
```

```
Debug.Print ctl.ControlName
Debug.Print ctl.Width
' etc...
```

In addition, using VBA's With...End With syntax affords the same improvements. Your code may end up being more readable if you use cached object references, but if you can use With...End With, it, too, can speed up your code.

Test 8: Don't Use Explicit Logical Comparisons?

When testing for the truth value of an expression in an IIf expression or an If...Then...Else statement, there is no point in actually comparing the condition to the value True. That is, these two expressions are completely equivalent:

```
If x = True Then
```

and

```
If x Then
```

Leaving out the explicit comparison will make only a small difference in the speed of your code. You'd have to use this construct many, many times before this optimization made any measurable difference in the speed of your code, but every little bit helps.

Test 9: Refer to Controls by Number If Possible?

Access gives you several choices when you're referring to controls on a form. For example, given a form with 16 command buttons, you could refer to the first button (cmdButton1) in your code several ways (assuming that cmdButton1 was the first control to be placed on the form):

```
Dim ctl as Control
Set ctl = Forms!frmTest1!cmdButton1
Set ctl = Forms!frmTest1("cmdButton1")
Set ctl = Forms!frmTest1(0)
```

If you intend to loop through all the controls on the form, you have fewer choices. You can either build up a string expression that contains the name of the control or refer to the controls by number. The latter method is measurably faster, but you should use it only where you are looping through controls.

Test 10: Use IsCharAlphaNumeric?

You may find yourself needing to find out whether a particular character is an alphanumeric character (that is, checking to see whether it falls in the range of characters from A–Z, a–z, or 0–9). One standard method for doing this in VBA is to compare the Asc(UCase(*character*)) to the ANSI values for the ranges. The Windows API provides a function specifically for this purpose, IsCharAlphaNumeric (aliased as adh_apiIsCharAlphaNumeric in the examples). In addition, you can use a similar API function, IsCharAlpha, to check a character to see whether it's between A and Z. An added bonus of using the Windows API functions is that they're internationalized. Many characters outside the normal A–Z range are considered legal text characters in other countries. The brute-force comparison method would fail on such characters. To top it all off, using the API method is significantly faster than performing the comparisons yourself.

To use IsCharAlphaNumeric, you need to include the following declaration in your application:

```
Private Declare Function adh_apiIsCharAlphaNumeric _
  Lib "User32" Alias "IsCharAlphaNumericA" (ByVal cChar As Byte)
```

Test 11: Use DBEngine(0)(0) If Speed Is the Only Concern?

If all you care about is raw speed, retrieving a reference to the current database with DBEngine(0)(0) is much faster than using CurrentDb. When you retrieve a reference with DBEngine(0)(0), like this:

```
Dim db As Database
Set db = DBEngine(0)(0)
```

Access returns a reference to an object that's already open. When you use CurrentDb, however, Access creates a new internal data structure, which obviously takes a bit longer—actually, a lot longer. In our sample tests, using DBEngine(0)(0) was 500 to 1000 percent faster.

However, don't forget the trade-offs. (See Chapter 6 for more information on CurrentDB versus DBEngine(0)(0).) When you retrieve a reference to CurrentDb, you're guaranteed that its collections are refreshed at that time. If you use DBEngine(0)(0), you can make no such assumption, and you should refresh any collections you need to use. On the other hand, refreshing the collection will usually make using DBEngine(0)(0) slower than using CurrentDB. You'll have to make up your own mind, given the facts here and in Chapter 6.

Test 12: Watch Out for Slow IIf Components?

Shorter code isn't necessarily faster. Although this fact is documented in both the Access online help and the manuals, it's easy to miss: in the IIf, Choose, and Select functions, VBA evaluates any and all expressions it finds, regardless of whether they actually need to be evaluated from a logical point of view. Given an expression like this:

```
varValue = IIf(fFlag, Function1(), Function2())
```

VBA will call both Function1 and Function2. Not only can this lead to undesired side effects, it can just plain slow down your program. In a case like this you're better off using the standard If...Then...End If construct, which will execute only the portions of the statement that fall within the appropriate clause. Given the statement

```
If fFlag Then
    varValue = Function1()
Else
    varValue = Function2()
End If
```

you can be assured that only Function1 *or* Function2 will end up being called. The same concepts apply for the Choose and Select functions. If you plan on calling functions from any of these functions, you may be better served by using an If...Then...End If or a Select Case statement.

Beyond any optimization considerations, IIf is very dangerous when dealing with numeric values and division. If this was your expression:

```
intNew = IIf(intY = 0, 0, intX/intY)
```

it would appear that you had appropriately covered your bases. Your code checks to make sure intY isn't 0 and returns an appropriate value if it is, rather than attempting to divide by 0. Unfortunately, if y is 0 this statement will still cause a run-time error. Because Access will evaluate both portions of the IIf expression, the division by 0 will occur and will trigger an error. In this case you need to either trap for the error or use the If...Then...Else statement.

Test 13: Use Execute instead of RunSQL?

When running an action query from your application, you have three choices: you can use the RunSQL macro action, you can use the Execute method of a database object to run SQL code, or you can create a QueryDef object and then use its Execute method. Using the Execute method of the database object or creating a temporary querydef and using its Execute method take about the same amount of time. On the other hand, using the Execute method of a database object requires one less line of code and seems like a simpler solution. Either solution is significantly faster than using DoCmd RunSQL.

The sample code shows two ways to accomplish the same goal: deleting all the rows from tblContacts. The slower method uses the RunSQL action to run the SQL string "DELETE * From tblContacts". The faster method uses the Execute method of the current database to execute the SQL string.

Using Temporary Querydefs

Access provides a useful mechanism for creating temporary QueryDef objects: just don't provide a name! If you use a zero-length string for the name parameter of the CreateQueryDef method, Access creates a temporary "in-memory" query. You no longer have to worry about the proliferation of querydefs and name collisions, and because Access doesn't write temporary querydefs to disk, they're a lot faster, too. Another plus: you don't have to delete temporary querydefs—they automatically disappear when the QueryDef object goes out of scope. For example, you can use code like this to create a temporary querydef:

```
Dim db As Database
Dim qdf As QueryDef
Set db = CurrentDb()
Set qdf = db.CreateQueryDef("", _
"SELECT * FROM tblCustomers WHERE Age > 30;")
```

Test 14: Use For Each...Next Rather Than For...Next?

VBA supplies the For Each...Next construct, which allows you to loop through all the members of a collection or array without having to know the number of elements in the collection. "Is it faster?" we wondered. The tests proved that it's marginally faster, but it just doesn't matter; it's such a useful addition to the language that we'd suggest using it even if it were slower than the old method.

Test 15: Remove Comments from Loops?

In Access 2, removing comments from your code did make a difference in the execution speed. VBA is a compiled language, and comments ought not make a difference. As our tests show, this is true: removing comments will not affect the speed of code, all other things being equal. Be aware that excess comments consume memory, however, if you're using the decompiled version of the code (editing, for example), so they can adversely affect performance due to memory usage. This shouldn't concern you unless you have a massive number of comments, however. Their use far outweighs their detriments.

In repeated trials, removing comments never seemed to help, and if anything, it caused slightly worse performance more times than not. We give this technique an unqualified "don't bother." Unless you can prove to yourself that removing comments in your particular application makes any difference, leave them in.

Test 16: Use Bookmarks Rather Than FindFirst to Locate Rows?

If you're working with recordsets as part of your application, you may need to find a specific row, move to a different row, and then move back to the first. You can accomplish this in a number of ways, and some are faster than others. The fastest way is to use the Seek method of a table-type recordset. However, it's not always possible to use table-type recordsets. In those cases you might try using FindFirst to find the row, move to wherever you need to go, and then use FindFirst again to get back to the original row. Although this will work, there's a better method: use a bookmark to store your location before you move away. Then, when you want to move back to the selected row, the bookmark can get you there almost instantaneously. (See Chapter 6 for more information on bookmarks and recordsets.)

The example procedures first use the FindFirst method of a recordset to find a row. Then they move to the first row and back to the original row. The first version uses FindFirst for both record moves. The second one stores away a bookmark instead and uses that bookmark to move back to the original record.

Your performance on this test will vary, of course, depending on the number of rows in the recordset, whether you can use an index for the search, and how many times you execute the search.

Test 17: Drop Default Collection References?

When working with DAO and its objects and collections, you always have the option of writing out complete object references or leaving out default collections in the references. (See Chapter 6 for more information on objects, references, and default collections.) Although leaving out the default collections in full references may help speed your code, it does make the code harder to read and its intent less obvious. The following examples compare using a full reference to the current database against using a shortened version:

```
Set db = DBEngine.Workspaces(0).Databases(0)
```

or

```
Set db = DBEngine(0)(0)
```

In our tests, using the shortened version provided little, if any, speed difference. Using different references might affect this acceleration, and you must always weigh the possible speed gains against readability losses.

Test 18: Refresh Collections Only When Necessary?

If you're using DAO and want to make sure the collections you're working with are completely up to date, you must first use the Refresh method of the collection. (See Chapter 6 for more information on refreshing collections.) On the other hand, refreshing collections is a very expensive operation in terms of time. The test case demonstrates just *how* expensive: in our sample case, with just two user-defined tables (and all the normal system tables), not refreshing the TableDefs collection before retrieving each tabledef's RecordCount property was more than 1300 percent faster than refreshing first. With more objects, this difference would be even more noticeable. This is one of the few optimizations presented in this chapter that can make a visible difference in your applications, even if you weren't using Refresh often. For large applications, the speed difference can be very noticeable. Of course, if you're working in a multiuser environment and need to peruse the entire list of objects, you don't have much choice; you may well miss newly added objects unless you refresh the collection first.

Summary

This chapter has presented a variety of suggestions for improving the performance of your Access applications. We covered the following topics:

- How the Jet engine optimizes and executes queries
- How to make use of the unsupported ISAMStats and ShowPlan options
- How to optimize Access
- How to optimize queries
- How to speed up forms
- How to improve the performance of reports
- How VBA compiles and loads code and how you can best take advantage of this
- Suggestions for optimizing your VBA code
- How to test your own optimization ideas

Although we attempted to cover the major areas of optimization, this chapter is not meant to be comprehensive, but it makes for a good start.

At every point in designing any application, you're faced with choices. These choices affect how well your application will work, and you need to be informed about the trade-offs in order to best make these choices. This chapter focused on the major areas in which you can improve the performance of your applications.

PART VI

Interoperability

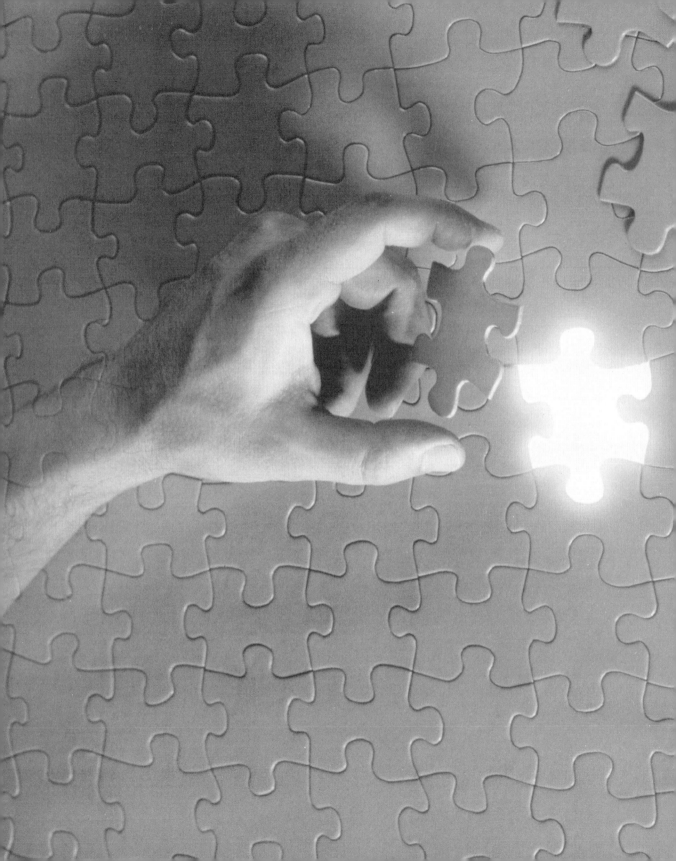

Accessing DLLs and the Windows API

- Explaining Dynamic Link Libraries

- Calling DLLs and the Windows API from VBA

- Declaring DLL procedures

- Discovering DLL details

- Converting 16-bit Windows API calls to 32-bit API calls

This chapter discusses one of the most powerful features of VBA: the ability to call Dynamic Link Libraries (DLLs) from VBA procedures. DLLs are primarily written in C or C++, but you can also create them using Pascal and Delphi. Calling a DLL provides a method of performing tasks that standard VBA functions and statements do not permit. For example, VBA has no intrinsic ability to retrieve the amount of system resources available, but you can do it easily with the Windows API.

Even if you are not proficient in C or C++, you can use DLLs someone else has written. The GLR32.DLL file on this book's companion disk, for example, allows you to perform tasks such as closing a program given its process identifier. Windows itself includes a number of DLLs with hundreds of useful functions. These functions are collectively called the *Windows API. API* is an acronym for "Application Programming Interface," and it is the set of functions Windows programs use to manipulate Windows.

Learning how to call the Windows API, and DLLs in general, allows you to vastly extend your ability to manipulate Windows. This chapter is divided into five main sections. The first section describes the basics of calling a DLL or Windows API call. The second section provides some examples of DLL calls. The third section, for more advanced users, shows how to construct a Declare statement to retrieve information from any arbitrary DLL. The fourth section takes a closer look at what goes on during DLL calls. The last section discusses how to convert 16-bit Windows API (from Windows 3.x) into 32-bit Windows API calls (Windows 95 and Windows NT).

Introducing Dynamic Link Libraries

In traditional DOS compiled languages, every application carries around every function it calls, and every application you create includes exactly the same shared code. For example, in standard C used from DOS, you call functions from the C run-time library to read a string from a file, get a character from the keyboard, or get the current time. These functions in the libraries are *statically linked* to the program, which means the code for the functions is included in the executable at the time the executable is created. The problem with this scheme is that if you have 200 programs that all write a string to the screen with the printf function, the code for this function is reproduced 200 times on your disk.

Windows uses a different approach: libraries are usually *dynamically linked* to the program. This means that if you have 200 Windows programs that all write a string to a window, only one copy of the ExtTextOut code resides on your hard disk. Each program includes only a very small amount of overhead to call this common code. These common routines reside in Dynamic Link Libraries, which normally have the extension .DLL and are stored in the Windows\System directory if more than one program uses them.

Programs that run under Windows call functions the operating system provides. These functions provide facilities to create a window, change its size, read and write Registry entries, manipulate a file, and so on. Windows stores most of these functions in three DLLs: USER32.DLL, GDI32.DLL, and KERNEL32.DLL.

To use a DLL you need to know the procedures in it and the arguments to each of those procedures. The Windows functions are well documented. To make a call to the Windows API, you just need to understand the documentation for the DLL call. For other DLLs you need to locate and understand the documentation for the DLL. Because traditionally DLLs have been designed to be called from C or C++, the documentation provided is usually stated in terms of calling functions from C or C++. For this reason you need to develop some skills in translating the terminology from the C perspective into the VBA perspective. This chapter provides most of the tools necessary and tells you where you can get the rest of the information you need.

NOTE The Windows API includes more than 1000 functions. Describing them all is beyond the scope of this book (whole books have been written on the subject), but they are documented in several places. The Access Developer's Toolkit for Office 97 Developer Edition contains a file named WIN32API.TXT. We have put a copy of this file on the CD-ROM that comes with this book. It has the Declare statements for most of the 32-bit Windows API calls, as well as the definition of most of the constants and structures used by the API calls. But to find out what the functions mean, you will need the Win32 documentation. You can find the complete documentation on the Microsoft Developer's Network (Level 1) CD-ROM or the Microsoft Solutions Development Kit CD-ROM. We highly recommend these tools as a source of information for developing Access applications.

Calling DLL Procedures from VBA

Calling procedures in DLLs is similar to calling procedures in standard VBA. The difference is that the body of the procedure resides in a DLL instead of inside a module. Before calling a function in a DLL, you need to tell VBA where to find it. There are really two kinds of DLLs, and you tell VBA how to call them in two ways:

- By specifying a type library
- By using a Declare statement

Using Type Libraries

The person who creates a DLL may do so in a special way, creating a file called a *type library,* which describes the procedures within the DLL. A type library usually has the extension .OLB or .TLB and is registered with the OLE component of Windows. The setup program that installs the DLL usually creates the proper entries with the Windows Registry to register the type library. If you select Tools ➤ References when an open module has the focus, the dialog shows all the registered type libraries that are available to Access. By placing a check next to the name of your type library, you tell Access that everything within the type library is available to VBA.

If you use a type library, there is no need to use Declare statements. The type library includes all the functionality of the Declare statement. In addition, type libraries avoid the difficulties of passing strings to DLLs. (See the section "Passing Strings to a DLL: The Real Story" later in this chapter.) The main drawback to all this is that the Windows API doesn't have a type library. You must use Declare statements to call the Windows API.

DAO in VBA is an example of a type library. The type library provides all the functionality of DAO to VBA; none of it is really intrinsic to VBA.

> **NOTE**   If you are calling a function specified with a type library, you can ignore the information in the rest of this chapter, which deals with calling DLLs through the use of Declare statements. You use functions specified with type libraries just as though they were an intrinsic part of VBA.

Using Declare Statements

A Declare statement is a definition you provide in the declarations section of a module that tells VBA where to find a function and how to call it. (You will find the details on the construction of a Declare statement in the section "How to Construct a Declare Statement" later in this chapter.) The important point here is that you need one to be able to call a DLL function that is not specified by a type library. Because there is no type library for the Windows API, you need to provide Declare statements for every Windows API call you make.

Because every Windows API function needs a Declare statement, someone has already constructed these statements for you. The Office 97 Developer Edition provides a file named WIN32API.TXT (you will also find it on the CD-ROM that comes with this book) that has all the Declare statements you need. You also need the definition of certain constants and user-defined type declarations. You can also find these definitions in WIN32API.TXT.

TIP

A tool named the API Text Viewer comes with Microsoft Office 97 Developer Edition (previously called the Access Developer's Toolkit). It also provides the Declare statements and other definitions you need. This tool simply searches the WIN32API.TXT and finds the proper entry. Unfortunately, the user interface on this tool makes it difficult to use; it is faster to use a text editor to find the Declare statement in the WIN32API.TXT file. Quite likely, shareware or freeware tools for providing Declare statements and other definitions will become available as the Win32 API increases in importance, so you may want to look for them on CompuServe or the Internet.

WARNING

Do not include all of WIN32API.TXT in a module. This large file has at least a thousand declarations within it. The amount of resources it consumes will substantially reduce the performance of your application. Because you will probably use at most several dozen of the declarations in your application, just copy the ones you use into your module.

This is an example of a Declare statement:

```
Public Declare Function WinHelp Lib "User32" Alias "WinHelpA" _
    (ByVal hwnd As Long, ByVal lpszHelp As String, _
    ByVal uCommand As Integer, dwData As Any) As Long
```

As mentioned earlier, you place Declare statements in the declarations section of a module. After you specify the Declare statement, you can use the procedure that has been declared just as though it were an intrinsic part of VBA, with a number of important exceptions. The following sections describe these exceptions.

> **WARNING**
>
> VBA provides a very safe environment in which to work. The environment is not as safe, however, when you are calling external DLL functions directly. Because you *will* eventually make a mistake attempting to call a Windows API and cause a General Protection (GP) fault, it is important to save your work before running any code that calls a DLL. The first time you attempt to call any given DLL function, or when you make a change to a Declare statement, you must be extra careful because that is when a GP fault will most likely occur. Keep recent backups of your database, just to cover the slight possibility that it becomes corrupt when Access crashes. DLLs are powerful, but they don't provide the protection from your mistakes that VBA normally gives you.

Passing Arguments to DLLs

You pass arguments to DLLs exactly the same way you pass arguments to any built-in function, with two exceptions, described in the sections "Returning Strings from a DLL" and "Using the Any Datatype" later in this chapter. For example, to find out information about the system on which Windows is running, you call the Windows API function GetSystemMetrics. You retrieve the Declare statement and some constants from WIN32API.TXT and place them in the declarations section of a module. The definitions look like this:

```
Declare Function GetSystemMetrics Lib "user32" _
  (ByVal nIndex As Long) As Long

' GetSystemMetrics() codes
Public Const SM_CXSCREEN = 0
Public Const SM_CYSCREEN = 1
Public Const SM_CXVSCROLL = 2
Public Const SM_CYHSCROLL = 3
Public Const SM_CYCAPTION = 4
' etc... There are 75 of them.
```

After putting the Declare statement and constant declarations in the declarations section of the module, you can call the GetSystemMetrics function just as though it were part of VBA. For example:

```
lngCyCaption = GetSystemMetrics(SM_CYCAPTION)
```

The form frmGetSystemMetrics is shown in Figure 18.1. It is based on the tblGet-SystemMetrics table, which contains one row for each constant used with the GetSystemMetrics function. It has fields for the constant, its value, and a description. The form calls GetSystemMetrics in a query used as its record source, passing the constant value for each row, and displays the results in the rightmost column.

FIGURE 18.1

The form frmGetSystem-Metrics shows each of the GetSystemMetrics constants, its value, its meaning, and the return value from calling the Windows API function GetSystemMetrics.

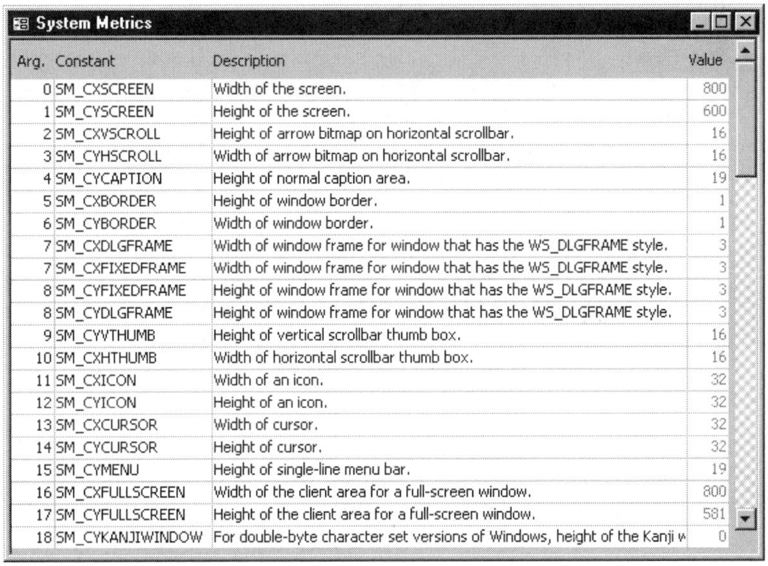

Arg.	Constant	Description	Value
0	SM_CXSCREEN	Width of the screen.	800
1	SM_CYSCREEN	Height of the screen.	600
2	SM_CXVSCROLL	Height of arrow bitmap on horizontal scrollbar.	16
3	SM_CYHSCROLL	Width of arrow bitmap on horizontal scrollbar.	16
4	SM_CYCAPTION	Height of normal caption area.	19
5	SM_CXBORDER	Height of window border.	1
6	SM_CYBORDER	Width of window border.	1
7	SM_CXDLGFRAME	Width of window frame for window that has the WS_DLGFRAME style.	3
7	SM_CXFIXEDFRAME	Width of window frame for window that has the WS_DLGFRAME style.	3
8	SM_CYFIXEDFRAME	Height of window frame for window that has the WS_DLGFRAME style.	3
8	SM_CYDLGFRAME	Height of window frame for window that has the WS_DLGFRAME style.	3
9	SM_CYVTHUMB	Height of vertical scrollbar thumb box.	16
10	SM_CXHTHUMB	Width of horizontal scrollbar thumb box.	16
11	SM_CXICON	Width of an icon.	32
12	SM_CYICON	Height of an icon.	32
13	SM_CXCURSOR	Width of cursor.	32
14	SM_CYCURSOR	Height of cursor.	32
15	SM_CYMENU	Height of single-line menu bar.	19
16	SM_CXFULLSCREEN	Width of the client area for a full-screen window.	800
17	SM_CYFULLSCREEN	Height of the client area for a full-screen window.	581
18	SM_CYKANJIWINDOW	For double-byte character set versions of Windows, height of the Kanji w	0

Returning Strings from a DLL

Windows has two ways of storing strings, known to C programmers as BSTR and LPSTR. The section "Passing Strings to a DLL: The Real Story" later in this chapter describes the details of how these are stored internally. All the Windows API calls except those dealing with OLE use LPSTRs, not BSTRs. DLLs cannot change the size of a LPSTR string once it has been created. This causes difficulties when you need the DLL to return a value in a string. In fact, DLL functions that deal with LPSTR strings don't actually return strings but instead modify them in memory.

Because a DLL that accepts an LPSTR cannot change the size of a string that is passed to it, the string needs to be big enough to accept the data to be returned before you pass it to the DLL. This means you need to fill the string with enough characters to create a buffer for the DLL to fill in. You normally accomplish this with the Space$ function. The DLL must not write past the end of the string, because that can result in a GP fault. DLL functions that modify strings normally require that you pass another argument that tells how much space has been allocated for the string.

The GetWindowText function is an example of a Windows function that manipulates a string in memory. You pass it a handle to a window, and it returns the text associated with the window into a buffer.

NOTE   A handle is a Long value that uniquely identifies an object to Windows. The first argument to GetWindowText is a handle to a window, also known as an *hwnd* or *hWnd*. Forms, reports, the Application object, and some ActiveX controls have an hwnd property that will return the handle to a window that can be passed into the GetWindowText function. You should always retrieve the hwnd property at the time you're calling such a function, because Windows will assign a new hwnd to a form each time you reopen it.

The following is a Declare statement for GetWindowText:

```
Declare Function GetWindowText _
 Lib "user32" Alias "GetWindowTextA" _
 (ByVal hwnd As Long, ByVal lpString As String, _
 ByVal cch As Long) As Long
```

When you call GetWindowText, control passes into the Windows USER32.DLL. The GetWindowText function inside the DLL looks up the handle in Windows' internal data structures and fills in the lpString parameter with the text that is associated with the window. You call GetWindowText like this:

```
Dim strReturnedString As String
Dim intRet As Integer

' Allocate enough space for the return value.
strReturnedString = Space$(255)

' Call the GetWindowsText function
intRet = GetWindowText(Me.hwnd, strReturnedString, _
```

```
Len(strReturnedString) - 1)

' Truncate the string down to the proper size
strReturnedString = Left$(strReturnedString, intRet)
```

The Space$ function in this example returns a string of 255 spaces followed by a null character. A null character has the ANSI value 0 and is used in LPSTRs to terminate a string. This allows you to use window captions up to 255 characters. In memory, strReturnedString looks like this:

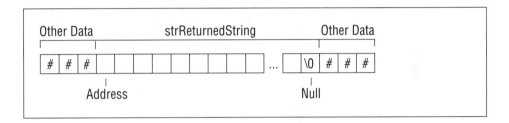

You can see from the illustration that the area in memory corresponding to strReturnedString is identified by an address marking the first byte in the string. You can also see why you don't want to let the DLL function modify too many bytes of memory. Overwriting memory that belongs to other variables or processes can lead to unpredictable results and GP faults.

The code then calls the GetWindowText function. The call has two effects:

- It changes the contents of strReturnedString to be the caption of the window indicated by the hwnd argument, followed by a null character.

- It returns the length of the string placed into strReturnedString, not counting the terminating null character.

After the call, strReturnedString looks like this in memory:

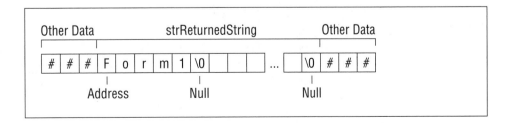

The length of the string hasn't changed, nor has any memory been deallocated—the string is still 255 characters long. Because the DLL cannot make the string shorter, before using strReturnedString you must truncate the string to just before the null character that GetWindowText placed at the end of the string it returned. Fortunately, the return value of the GetWindowText function tells us exactly how many characters should appear in the final string. You then use the Left$ function to truncate the string. If you pass an invalid value for the hwnd argument, Windows returns a value indicating that the API call failed.

If you call a DLL function that doesn't return a value telling you how many characters are in the returned string, you can search for the null character to determine how long the string should be. The Instr function combined with the Left$ function does the job:

```
strReturnedString = Left$(strReturnedString, _
  Instr(1, strReturnedString, vbNullChar) - 1)
```

Obviously, the GetTextString example shown above is useful, even though you can get the same information by just using the form's Caption property, because the window caption differs depending on which view the form is in. Furthermore, GetTextString works with *any* window in the entire operating system, not just windows that happen to be Access forms. We used the form's hwnd for this example because it was an easy hwnd to get. You can get the hwnd of other windows using other Windows API calls, such as FindWindowEx.

Using the vbNullString Constant

There are times when the documentation for a DLL function indicates that sometimes you need to pass a string and sometimes you need to pass a Null. A Null is a 4-byte zero placed directly on the stack. (For a full discussion of what this means, see the section "Understanding Passing by Value and by Reference" later in this chapter.) The main thing you need to know is that to pass a Null, you can use vbNullString.

For example, a Windows API function named SetVolumeLabel sets the label of a disk. The Declare statement for the function is

```
Declare Function SetVolumeLabel _
  Lib "kernel32" Alias "SetVolumeLabelA" _
  (ByVal lpRootPathName As String, _
  ByVal lpVolumeName As String) As Long
```

These are the two arguments to SetVolumeLabel:

Parameter	Meaning
lpRootPathName	Points to a null-terminated string specifying the root directory of a file system volume. This is the volume the function will label. If this parameter is Null, the root of the current directory is used
lpVolumeName	Points to a string specifying a name for the volume. If this parameter is Null, the function deletes the name of the specified volume

To set the volume label on the C drive to DRIVE_C, you execute the following code:

```
fRet = SetVolumeLabel("C:\", "DRIVE_C")
```

To delete the volume label using the method documented on the C drive, you need to pass a Null as the second argument. Normally VBA wouldn't allow this, because the arguments are declared as Strings, but vbNullString is a special value designed just for this purpose. To delete the volume label, execute the following code:

```
fRet = SetVolumeLabel("C:\", vbNullString)
```

NOTE Unfortunately, the current shipping version of Windows 95 contains a bug, and the code shown to delete a volume label does not work. (Windows 95 treats a Null as an invalid argument.) It does work as documented in Windows NT. This bug will probably be fixed in a future version of Windows 95. In the meantime, you can work around the bug by setting the label to an empty string ("").

Passing a User-Defined Type to a DLL

Sometimes you need to pass a user-defined type to a DLL. For example, many of the Windows functions expect a RECT structure, which is a user-defined type, as opposed to one that is supported implicitly by the C or VBA language. To do so, you need to define an equivalent type in VBA. You can find the declaration in WIN32API.TXT. The structure in VBA is

```
Type RECT
    left As Long
    top As Long
    right As Long
    bottom As Long
End Type
```

You must pass a structure by reference. The declaration of a function that takes a RECT as an argument is

```
Declare Function GetWindowRect Lib "user32" _
  (ByVal hwnd As Long, lpRect As RECT) As Long
```

The form frmGetWindowRect from CH18.MDB uses this function to retrieve the location of the form on the screen (from the upper left-hand corner and measured in pixels). Figure 18.2 shows this form.

FIGURE 18.2

Using the GetWindow-Rect Windows API call to determine the location of the window

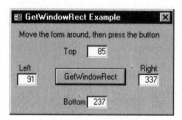

A call to GetWindowRect looks like this:

```
Dim rectForm As RECT

If GetWindowRect(Me.hwnd, rectForm) Then
    txtLeft.Value = rectForm.left
    txtTop.Value = rectForm.top
    txtRight.Value = rectForm.right
    txtBottom.Value = rectForm.bottom
End If
```

GetWindowRect returns True if it succeeds in filling in the rectForm structure passed in. It then uses the values from the structure to fill in text boxes on the form.

Passing an Array

You can pass individual elements of an array just as you would use any other variable. Sometimes, though, you'll want to pass an entire array to a DLL. You may do this—but only for numeric arrays, not for strings or user-defined ones, unless the DLL understands a special type called a SAFEARRAY. Documentation of the specific function will indicate when an array is expected. To pass an array, you pass its first element. This, in effect, tells the DLL function the memory address of the first element. Because arrays are always stored in contiguous blocks of memory, the DLL function can deduce the other elements given their size and count. For example, the call to the SetSysColors Windows API call is actually passed two different arrays:

```
Dim alngDisplayElements() As Long
Dim alngRGBValues() As Long
Dim lngCDisplayElements As Long

' Size the arrays for two elements
lngCDisplayElements = 2
ReDim alngDisplayElements(lngCDisplayElements - 1)
ReDim alngRGBValues(lngCDisplayElements - 1)

' Fill the arrays to set two system colors
alngDisplayElements(0) = COLOR_BTNHIGHLIGHT
alngRGBValues(0) = RGB(&HFF, 0, 0)
alngDisplayElements(1) = COLOR_BTNTEXT
alngRGBValues(1) = RGB(0, 0, &HFF)

Call SetSysColors(lngCDisplayElements, _
 alngDisplayElements(0), alngRGBValues(0))
```

This example is from code behind the form frmSetSysColors in CH18.MDB.

When passing an array to a DLL function, you must give the function some indication of the size of the array. You do this by passing another argument that gives the size of the array. Without this argument, the DLL cannot determine how large the array is and can go beyond the end of the array. If you pass in a size that is larger than the array that has been allocated, you are telling the DLL that more memory has been allocated than really has been. When the DLL tries to access the information past the end of the array, it will get either random bytes or a GP fault, depending on whether the memory it is trying to access actually exists. In other words, be very careful that you pass the correct size in that argument.

Note that while you cannot pass arrays of strings to DLL functions, you can pass what are called *double-null terminated* strings. These are strings in which individual fragments are separated by null characters and the entire string is terminated by two nulls. For example, to construct a double-null terminated string, you might write code like this:

```
Dim strDblNull As String

strDblNull = "First part" & vbNullChar & "Second part" & _
  vbNullChar & "Third part" & vbNullChar & vbNullChar
```

A few DLL functions require strings of this type. The functions parse data passed to them using the null characters.

Examples Using the Windows API

What follows are two sets of examples using the Windows API. The first deals with the clipboard, the second with the Windows Registry. These examples show Declare statements and calls. Due to space limitations, we've shown only a few lines of code. You can find the remainder in the sample database, CH18.MDB.

Using the Clipboard

Because, unlike Visual Basic, Access doesn't have a Clipboard object, this section demonstrates using Windows API calls to simulate the same functionality. The examples use the Windows API to produce two functions, adhClipboardSetText and adhClipboardGetText, that put text on the Windows clipboard and get the text from the Windows clipboard, respectively. The functions make use of 12 different Windows API calls and demonstrate most of the points mentioned in the chapter.

The adhClipboardSetText function performs the following tasks:

1. It uses the GlobalAlloc function to allocate some memory.

2. It moves the passed-in string into it.

3. It opens the clipboard.

4. It empties the current contents of the clipboard.

5. It writes the data onto the clipboard.

6. It closes the clipboard.

You can include these clipboard functions in your code by importing the module basClipboard from CH18.MDB.

The adhClipboardGetText function performs roughly the opposite:

1. It sees whether there is some text on the clipboard that can be read.

2. If so, it opens the clipboard.

3. It gets the current contents of the clipboard.

4. It copies the contents into a string.

5. It truncates the string to the right size.

6. It closes the clipboard.

If you look at the functions we've provided, you'll see several things common to working with the Windows API. First and foremost, a *lot* of functions need to be called. The Windows API tends to be very granular, with functions that perform small tasks. Only by combining these functions do you get rich functionality. Second, the clipboard functions use handles, just like other functions dealing with windows. You'll find the Windows API full of handles to just about everything. Individual functions are commonly structured to return a handle as a result or a zero if the function failed. For example, look at the call to the GlobalAlloc function, which allocates memory to a given program:

```
hMemory = adh_apiGlobalAlloc(GMEM_MOVABLE Or _
  GMEM_DDESHARE, lngSize)
If Not hMemory Then
    varRet = CVErr(adhCANNOTGLOBALALLOC)
    GoTo adhClipboardSetTextDone
End If
```

If GlobalAlloc is successful, it returns a handle to the allocated memory, which is then stored in hMemory. The procedure uses an If...Then test to see whether hMemory contains a valid (nonzero) handle. If it does not, the function returns an error code and exits the function.

The form frmClipboard in CH18.MDB, shown in Figure 18.3, demonstrates the two functions. First, you enter some text in the first text box and click the Copy button. This places the contents of the text box in the clipboard. You can then click the Paste button to paste it into the second text box. If you examine the code behind each button, you'll see that it simply calls our two clipboard functions.

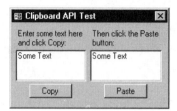

Registry Functionality

The System Registry is the cache for important data in Windows 95 and Windows NT. The Registry is organized as a hierarchical database of information. Data is indexed by a key and a value. The *key* indicates where within the database it can find the information. The *value* is the name given to a particular piece of information. You can store data of different datatypes in the Registry, including numbers, strings, and binary information.

You can look at the Registry under Windows 95 or Windows NT 4.0 by running REGEDIT.EXE (or REGEDT32.EXE on Windows NT 3.51). Figure 18.4 presents a picture of the Registry REGEDIT shows. The Registry is broken into a number of root entries, also known as *hives*:

HKEY_CLASSES_ROOT

HKEY_CURRENT_USER

HKEY_LOCAL_MACHINE

HKEY_USERS

HKEY_CURRENT_CONFIG

HKEY_DYN_DATA

Information about the current system is stored in the HKEY_LOCAL_MACHINE path. Information specific to the currently logged-in user is stored in the HKEY_CURRENT_USER path.

FIGURE 18.4

REGEDIT browsing
the Registry

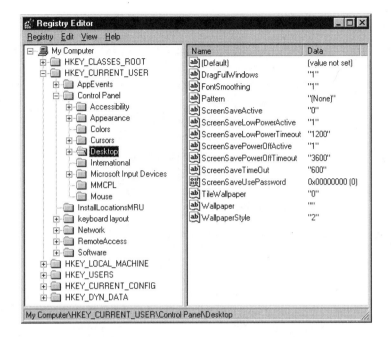

VBA provides some intrinsic functions that get and set some values within the Registry: GetSetting, SaveSetting, GetAllSettings, and DeleteSetting. While these functions are useful for setting and getting information about your program, they let you modify only a small part of the Registry database. Specifically, they let you modify only the HKEY_CURRENT_USER\Software\VB and VBA Program Settings branch of the database. It is often useful to be able to browse and modify other portions of the Registry.

Browsing the Registry

Figure 18.5 shows frmKeys from CH18.MDB. This form allows you to browse the HKEY_CURRENT_USER and HKEY_LOCAL_MACHINE branches of the Registry by selecting an option from the option group on the form. A list of keys is shown in the left-hand list box. When you double-click a key in the left-hand list box, the list is refreshed to show that key's subkeys. Single-clicking a key displays the values assigned to that key in the right-hand list box. Clicking a values name in the right-hand list box displays the contents of that value in the text box at the bottom of the form. Clicking the Reset button takes you back to the root key. This functionality demonstrates traversing the tree and getting values.

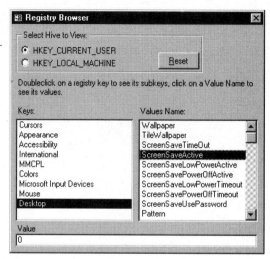

FIGURE 18.5

A Registry browser that
allows traversing the Registry tree

When you open the form, the form initializes the list boxes by calling the
cmdRoot_Click event. This function calls adhGetRegistryKeys from the basRegistry
module in the same database. adhGetRegistryKeys builds a semicolon-delimited
string, which sets the RowSource property of the list box. The function adhGet-
RegistryKeys is shown in Listing 18.1.

Listing 18.1

```
Public Function adhGetRegistryKeys(ByVal hKey As Long) As String
    ' Returns a semicolon-delimited list of all of
    ' the subkeys of this key

    Dim strRet As String
    Dim lngRet As Long
    Dim strClassName As String
    Dim cchClassName As Long
    Dim lngCSubKeys As Long
    Dim cchMaxSubKey As Long
    Dim cchMaxClass As Long
    Dim lngCValues As Long
    Dim cchMaxValueName As Long
    Dim cbMaxValueData As Long
    Dim cbSecurityDescriptor As Long
    Dim ftLastWrite As FILETIME
    Dim i As Long
```

```
Dim strKey As String
Dim cchKey As Long
Dim strClass As String
Dim cchClass As Long
Dim retCode As Long

strRet = ""
strClassName = Space$(256)
cchClassName = Len(strClassName)
Call adh_apiRegQueryInfoKey(hKey, strClassName, _
 cchClassName, 0&, lngCSubKeys, cchMaxSubKey, _
 cchMaxClass, lngCValues, cchMaxValueName, _
 cbMaxValueData, cbSecurityDescriptor, ftLastWrite)
For i = 0 To lngCSubKeys - 1
    strKey = Space$(cchMaxSubKey)
    cchKey = Len(strKey) + 1
    strClass = Space$(cchMaxClass)
    cchClass = Len(strClass) + 1
    cchKey, 0&, strClass, cchClass, ftLastWrite)
    retCode = adh_apiRegEnumKeyEx(hKey, i, strKey, _
    Select Case retCode And APPLICATION_ERROR_MASK
    Case ERROR_SEVERITY_SUCCESS
    Case Else
        Stop
        Exit For
    End Select
    strKey = Left$(strKey, cchKey)
    strRet = strRet & strKey & ";"
Next i

adhGetRegistryKeys = strRet
End Function
```

Each location in the path is a key. The Registry function operates by using handles to these keys. A handle to a key, or hKey, is a long integer that uniquely identifies a key. Various functions enumerate subkeys and values for keys.

The core functionality works like this:

1. The code retrieves a known handle to a key—in this case, HKEY_CURRENT_USER, stored in hKeyCurrent.

2. The code calls adhGetRegistryKeys with this handle to a key.

3. adhGetRegistryKeys calls RegQueryInfoKey to find out the number of subkeys under this Registry entry and the maximum length of the keys.

4. For each key, a call is made to RegEnumKeyEx. This gets the name of the key.

5. The code truncates the key down to the proper size, using the Left$ function.

6. The keys are concatenated together and placed in the RowSource property of the left-hand list box.

When you click an entry in the list box, the code shown in Listing 18.2 is called.

Listing 18.2

```
Private Sub lstKeys_Click()
    ' Fills the lstValues with a list of values based
    ' on the entry clicked on in lstKeys

    Dim hKeyNew As Long
    Dim lngRet As Long

    If hKeySelected Then
        Call adh_apiRegCloseKey(hKeySelected)
    End If
    lngRet = adh_apiRegOpenKeyEx(hKeyCurrent, lstKeys.Value, _
     0&, KEY_READ, hKeyNew)
    If lngRet = ERROR_SEVERITY_SUCCESS Then
        hKeySelected = hKeyNew
        lstValues.rowsource = adhGetRegistryValues(hKeySelected)
    End If
End Sub
```

> **NOTE** ERROR_SEVERITY_SUCCESS is a constant representing the value 0. It is returned by the Registry functions to indicate that the operation succeeded.

Whenever you select a key in a list box, the code opens the key and stores the hKey in hKeySelected. When you select another key, the code must close the first key, or Windows will continue to keep some memory allocated. The code then calls adhGetRegistryValues. adhGetRegistryValues is virtually same as adhGetRegistryKeys, except that it calls RegEnumValue to retrieve the names of the values. The difference is that one returns a list of subkeys and the other returns the list of values associated with a key.

When you double-click a key, the code traverses to that subkey. This code is shown in Listing 18.3. It opens the subkey with RegOpenKeyEx, closes the current key with RegCloseKey, and then gets the new values to fill the list box by calling adhGetRegistryKeys again. Finally, the code clears the right-hand list box and closes the currently selected key.

Listing 18.3

```
Private Sub lstKeys_DblClick(Cancel As Integer)
    ' Resets the list boxes to show the new key that
    ' was double-clicked

    Dim lngRet As Long
    Dim hKeyNew As Long

    lngRet = adh_apiRegOpenKeyEx(hKeyCurrent, lstKeys.Value, _
      0&, KEY_READ, hKeyNew)
    If lngRet = ERROR_SEVERITY_SUCCESS Then
        Call adh_apiRegCloseKey(hKeyCurrent)
        hKeyCurrent = hKeyNew
        lstKeys.RowSource = _
          Left(adhGetRegistryKeys(hKeyCurrent), 1024)
        If hKeySelected Then
            Call adh_apiRegCloseKey(hKeySelected)
        End If
        hKeySelected = 0
        lstValues.RowSource = ""
    End If
End Sub
```

Retrieving a value when the value name is selected is accomplished by calling GetRegistryValue, shown in Listing 18.4. It calls RegQueryValueEx twice. The first time it is called with the lpbData argument set to Null. This is to retrieve the datatype of the key into lngType. The second time it is called in different ways, depending on which type was retrieved. The return value of the function is set to the actual value retrieved.

Listing 18.4

```
Public Function adhGetRegistryValue(ByVal hKey As Long, ByVal _
  strValue As String) As Variant
    ' Returns a Registry value based on an hKey
    ' and a strValue
```

```
        Dim retCode As Long
        Dim lngType As Long
        Dim cbData As Long
        Dim strGetValue As String
        Dim lngValue As Long

        adhGetRegistryValue = "<Binary Data>"

        retCode = adh_apiRegQueryValueEx(hKey, strValue, 0&, _
         lngType, ByVal 0&, cbData)
        Select Case retCode And APPLICATION_ERROR_MASK
        Case ERROR_SEVERITY_SUCCESS
            Select Case lngType
            Case REG_NONE
                adhGetRegistryValue = CVErr(0)
            Case REG_SZ, REG_EXPAND_SZ
                strGetValue = Space$(cbData)
                retCode = adh_apiRegQueryValueEx(hKey, strValue, _
                 0&, lngType, ByVal strGetValue, cbData)
                adhGetRegistryValue = strGetValue
            Case REG_BINARY
            Case REG_DWORD, REG_DWORD_LITTLE_ENDIAN
                retCode = adh_apiRegQueryValueEx(hKey, strValue, _
                 0&, lngType, lngValue, cbData)
                adhGetRegistryValue = lngValue
            Case REG_DWORD_BIG_ENDIAN
            Case REG_LINK
            Case REG_MULTI_SZ
            Case REG_RESOURCE_LIST
            Case REG_FULL_RESOURCE_DESCRIPTOR
            Case REG_RESOURCE_REQUIREMENTS_LIST
            Case Else
                Stop
            End Select
        Case Else
            Call adhAssert(False)    'Should never happen
        End Select
    End Function
```

Another Registry Example

The previous example showed how to walk through the Registry, but what can
you use this technique for? It's very useful to be able to retrieve and set Registry
entries, given the path through the Registry to a value. For example, you may want

to retrieve the current value of HKEY_CURRENT_USER\Control Panel\Desktop\ScreenSaveActive. You do this by walking down through the various keys. We have provided a generic routine in the sample database, adhGetRegistryValueFromPath, that does the walking for you and returns the value of the key. You would call it with:

```
Dim strValue As String

strValue = adhGetRegistryValueFromPath _
  ("\HKEY_CURRENT_USER\Control Panel\Desktop\ScreenSaveActive")
```

> **NOTE**
>
> Chapter 19 provides another version of this code, which uses wrapper functions to call into MSACCESS.EXE. These functions perform similar functionality.

> **NOTE**
>
> Each Registry key has a default entry that has no value name. To retrieve the default entry for a key, follow the key name with a backslash when calling adhGetRegistryValueFromPath. For example, to retrieve the default value of the Desktop key mentioned previously in this chapter, you use \HKEY_CURRENT_USER\Control Panel\Desktop\.

The counterpart to adhGetRegistryValueFromPath is adhSetRegistryValueFromPath, which sets a value based on a path. It executes virtually the same code as adhGetRegistryValueFromPath, except that it looks at the result of the VarType function on the strValue key passed in and calls RegSetValueEx in the appropriate manner to write the value into the Registry. The only datatypes supported in this code are Strings and Longs. The other datatypes supported by the Registry (such as binary data) require a bit more code to support and are left as exercises for the reader.

How to Construct a Declare Statement

If you plan on using only Windows API functions, you won't need to construct Declare statements. Instead, you will get them from some source, such as

WIN32API.TXT. However, at some point you may call a DLL that doesn't have a Declare statement already prepared for it. In this case you need to construct a Declare statement from scratch. Also, the file WIN32API.TXT is not perfect. Some of the Declare statements don't allow you to call some of the Windows API calls with arguments of certain types. Also, we have found bugs in some of the Declare statements as we have worked with them. These may or may not be fixed in your copy of WIN32API.TXT, so understanding how to construct a Declare statement is a useful skill.

The Declare statement gives VBA six pieces of information about a procedure in an external library:

- The scope of the declaration

- The name of the procedure as you want to call it in your code

- The name and path of the containing DLL

- The name of the procedure as it exists in the DLL

- The number and datatypes of the arguments to the procedure

- If the procedure is a function, the datatype of the return value of the function

Given this information, VBA knows how to locate the function on the hard disk and how to arrange the arguments on the stack so they are acceptable to the DLL. The *stack* is a special segment of memory that programs use for storing temporary information. VBA pushes arguments onto the stack, the DLL function is called, and DLL manipulates the arguments. Then the return value is placed on the stack for VBA to return to your program.

The Declare statement defines the size of the arguments to a DLL function and what the arguments mean. It is *crucial* that the declaration be exactly what the DLL expects. Otherwise, you may be giving the DLL incorrect information, and that may cause the DLL to reference information in an invalid memory location. A GP fault results when a program tries to access memory it doesn't have the privilege to read or write. If you receive a GP fault, Access crashes without giving you a chance to save any changed objects. This is what most programmers call "a bad thing."

Defining the VBA Declare statement is similar to defining any other sub or function, except that there is no body to the procedure. The body of the procedure resides in the DLL. Once you have declared a DLL function, you can call it almost as though the code were part of VBA. Declare statements must appear at the module level in the declarations section. The Declare statement takes one of two forms, depending on whether the DLL function being called returns a value:

[Public | Private] Declare Sub subname Lib *"libname"*

  [Alias *"aliasname"*] [([*argumentlist*])]

or

[Public | Private] Declare Function *functionname* Lib *"libname"*

  [Alias *"aliasname"*] [([*argumentlist*])] [As type]

Here is an example of a Declare statement:

```
Private Declare Function FindWindow Lib "user32" _
 Alias "FindWindowA" _
 (ByVal lpClassName As String, _
 ByVal lpWindowName As String) As Long
```

If the function returns no value (that is, it is declared with the return type *void* in the C programming language), you use the Declare Sub format of the Declare statement. If the function returns a value (and almost all of them do), you use the Declare Function format.

Public versus Private

Just as any normal procedure declaration has a scope that determines what other procedures can call it, procedures defined by Declare statements also have a scope. You can call a DLL procedure from code only within the same form or module as the Declare statement if you prefix the Declare statement with the word *Private*. You can call a DLL function from any code if the Declare statement is prefixed with the word *Public*. Not using either Public or Private is the same as scoping the function with Public. A Declare statement in the declarations section of a form or class module must have Private scope. A Declare statement in a standard module can have either scope.

Specifying the Procedure Name

The function or sub name given in the Declare statement is the name that is used when you call it in your code. It must follow the same naming rules as for any VBA procedure name:

- It must begin with a letter.

- The other characters must be in the sets A–Z, a–z, 0–9, or an underscore character.

- It must be unique within the same scope.

- It must be no longer than 255 characters.

- It cannot be a VBA keyword.

If you don't supply an Alias clause, the name of the procedure must match the name of the function in the DLL. (See the section "Specifying the Alias" a little later in this chapter.)

Specifying the Lib

The Lib portion of the declaration tells VBA the DLL's name and also, potentially, its location on the disk. You must enclose the Lib name in quotes. It is not case sensitive. If the function you are declaring is in one of the main Windows DLLs, you can omit the .DLL extension. For example, you can use "User32", "GDI32", or "Kernel32". VBA appends the .DLL extension to these names. For other DLLs, you must include the DLL name.

If you do not include the path on the DLL name, Windows uses this order to search for the DLL:

1. The directory from which the application loaded (For Access, that's the directory from which Access is loaded, not the directory where your MDB is stored.)

2. The current directory

3. Windows NT only: the 32-bit Windows system directory (Windows\System32)

4. The Windows system directory (Windows\System)

5. The Windows directory (Windows)

6. The directories that are listed in the PATH environment variable

This order can cause some confusion. If you put a DLL in the Windows directory but there is an older version of the DLL in the Windows\System directory, the older version will get called. Furthermore, this order has changed from earlier versions of Windows.

Specifying the Alias

You may include an alias clause when you declare a procedure. The alias clause of the declaration is important because it allows you to change the name of the function from the way it was specified in the DLL to a different name in VBA. There are several reasons why you might use the alias:

- To change an invalid procedure name in the DLL to one that VBA allows

- To change the case of the DLL procedure call

- To set the procedure name to a DLL function that is only exposed by ordinal number

- To have a unique procedure name in an Access library

- To leave off the "A" required by ANSI versions of Windows API calls

These reasons are explained in more detail in the following sections.

Changing the Procedure Name in the DLL to One VBA Allows

The names that programming languages such as C allow for functions are different from those VBA allows. VBA function names must consist of alphanumeric or underscore characters and begin with a letter. C function names often begin with an underscore. The function name you specify in the Declare statement must be a valid VBA procedure name. If the name in the DLL doesn't match the VBA naming rules, you must use an alias. The name in the DLL might also be a reserved word in VBA, or it might be the name of an existing global variable or function, and in these cases, too, you must use an alias.

For example, VBA does not allow function names with a leading underscore. To use the Windows API function _lwrite, then, you might declare the function as

```
Declare Function lwrite Lib "Kernel32" Alias "_lwrite" _
 (ByVal hFile As Integer, ByVal lpBuffer As String, _
 ByVal intBytes As Integer) As Integer
```

This defines the function name lwrite as the _lwrite function in the Kernel32 Dynamic Link Library.

NOTE Although the _lwrite function still exists in Win32, it is provided only for backward compatibility with 16-bit Windows. You should use the WriteFile function in your code.

Changing the Case of the DLL Procedure Call

The name of the procedure given in the Declare statement is case sensitive. This means it must exactly match the case of the procedure name in the DLL. If you wish to have the procedure name in your code use a different capitalization than that given in the DLL, you must use an alias clause. This wasn't true in 16-bit Windows, so if you are converting Declare statements from old code, you need to be aware of this.

Setting the Procedure Name That Is Exposed by Ordinal Number

Every function in a DLL is assigned a number, called its *ordinal.* Every function in a DLL *may* expose its name but is not required to do so. The programmer writing a DLL chooses which procedures within the DLL can be called from code existing outside the DLL; these functions are *exposed.*

To call a function by ordinal, you must know the ordinal number for the function. You can find this information in the documentation for the DLL (if any) or in the DEF file for the DLL. Tools are also available that can examine a DLL. Whichever way you derive the ordinal, you specify #*ordinalnumber* for the alias name—that is, a pound sign followed by the decimal number of the ordinal. For example, the declaration for the _lwrite function presented earlier might be declared as

```
Declare Function lwrite Lib "Kernel32" Alias "#86" _
 (ByVal hFile As Integer, ByVal lpBuffer As String, _
 ByVal intBytes As Integer) As Integer
```

You may declare any function using its ordinal number, but if the name is exported, we recommend you use the name. This is especially important if you do not maintain the DLL. The DLL developer may assume that people will not call a function by ordinal if it is exported by name. Later versions of the DLL may not keep the same ordinal number for the functions in it but will most likely keep the same name.

Having a Unique Procedure Name in an Access Library

Each declared function at the same level of scope in VBA must have a unique name. Normally, this doesn't have huge implications, because you are not likely to give two different functions the same name or declare the same function twice in your own code. But if you are developing a library database that might be included on different systems and that library calls functions in a DLL (including Windows API calls), this issue becomes important.

Suppose your library calls the GetComputerName Windows API call. If you declare the function in the library with Public scope but without an alias, VBA uses the name GetComputerName. If users then decide to use GetComputerName in their own code and declare it as Public, the name in their code conflicts with the name in your library. For this reason, public declarations in a library should always use an alias. Thus, you might declare GetComputerName in a library as

```
Declare Function MYLB_GetComputerName _
 Lib "kernel32" Alias "GetComputerNameA" _
 (ByVal lpBuffer As String, nSize As Long) As Long
```

When you use the function in the library, you then use MYLB_GetComputerName as the function name. Doing this enables users to avoid conflicts if they also define GetComputerName.

Leaving Off the "A" Required by ANSI Windows API Calls

You can use the Alias clause to do any renaming of functions you wish. One common use is to rename ANSI Windows API calls that have a trailing "A" to the same name without the "A". The "A" is used in functions such as FindWindowA to indicate that the arguments being passed in are ANSI strings. (You can find a further discussion of ANSI and Unicode functions in the section "Unicode to ANSI and Back" later in this chapter.)

Specifying the Arguments

You pass arguments to a DLL on the stack. The DLL expects those arguments to be placed in a particular order and to have a certain size on the stack. When VBA places arguments on the stack, it looks to the Declare statement for direction. Arguments placed on the stack appear as a series of bytes. The DLL groups and decodes those bytes to use them in the parameters for the DLL call. If the VBA Declare statement and the DLL don't agree on what those bytes mean, incorrect data appears in the parameters for the DLL call. When the DLL tries to use the parameters, it gets the wrong information. Worse, if your program doesn't place enough data on the stack, the DLL will read data left over from previous use of the stack.

Correctly declaring arguments is the trickiest part of using a DLL from VBA. This subject is discussed in the following section.

Converting C Parameters into VBA Declarations

Most DLLs are written in C or C++. The documentation is usually in the form of a C header file (.h file) that provides the type and number of the arguments to the functions in the DLL. Based on the datatype required, you will need to convert it to an equivalent VBA datatype. Table 18.1 shows how to convert various C datatypes to VBA.

TABLE 18.1 Conversions between C Datatypes and Access Datatypes

C Datatype	Access Basic Datatype
ATOM	ByVal atom As Integer
BOOL	ByVal fValue As Integer
BYTE	ByVal bytValue As Byte
BYTE *	bytValue As Byte
CALLBACK	ByVal lngAddr As Long
char	ByVal bytValue As Byte
char _huge *	ByVal strValue As String
char FAR *	ByVal strValue As String
char NEAR *	ByVal strValue As String
DWORD	ByVal lngValue As Long
FARPROC	ByVal lngAddress As Long
HACCEL	ByVal hAccel As Long
HANDLE	ByVal h As Long
HBITMAP	ByVal hBitmap As Long
HBRUSH	ByVal hBrush As Long
HCURSOR	ByVal hCursor As Long
HDC	ByVal hDC As Long
HDRVR	ByVal hDrvr As Long

TABLE 18.1   Conversions between C Datatypes and Access Datatypes (continued)

C Datatype	Access Basic Datatype
HDWP	ByVal hDWP As Long
HFILE	ByVal hFile As Integer
HFONT	ByVal hFont As Long
HGDIOBJ	ByVal hGDIObj As Long
HGLOBAL	ByVal hGlobal As Long
HICON	ByVal hIcon As Long
HINSTANCE	ByVal hInstance As Long
HLOCAL	ByVal hLocal As Long
HMENU	ByVal hMenu As Long
HMETAFILE	ByVal hMetafile As Long
HMODULE	ByVal hModule As Long
HPALETTE	ByVal hPalette As Long
HPEN	ByVal hPen As Long
HRGN	ByVal hRgn As Long
HRSRC	ByVal hRsrc As Long
HTASK	ByVal hTask As Long
HWND	ByVal hWnd As Long
int	ByVal intValue As Integer
int FAR *	intValue As Integer
LONG	ByVal lngValue As Long
long	ByVal lngValue As Long
LPARAM	ByVal lngParam As Long
LPCSTR	ByVal strValue As String

TABLE 18.1   Conversions between C Datatypes and Access Datatypes (continued)

C Datatype	Access Basic Datatype
LPSTR	ByVal strValue As String
LPVOID	varValue As Any
LRESULT	ByVal lngResult As Long
UINT	ByVal intValue As Integer
UINT FAR *	intValue As Integer
void _huge *	bytValue() As Byte
void FAR *	bytValue() As Byte
WORD	ByVal intValue As Integer
WPARAM	ByVal intValue As Integer

More Advanced Details of Calling DLLs

At this point this chapter has discussed most of the details of calling a DLL. Really understanding what is going on, though, requires a fuller understanding of what happens during a DLL call.

Understanding Passing by Value and by Reference

You can pass an argument on the stack to a DLL in one of two ways: by value or by reference. *By value* means that a copy of the actual value of what is being passed is pushed onto the stack. *By reference* means that the address of what is being passed is pushed onto the stack. Unless you tell it otherwise, VBA passes all arguments by reference. On the other hand, most DLLs are written in C, and unless you tell the C compiler otherwise (by passing an address), C passes all arguments by value. The VBA declaration *must* be set up correctly to pass arguments the way the DLL expects them to be passed.

The semantic difference between passing by value and by reference is this:

- When you pass by value, a copy of the value is placed on the stack. Any changes to the value inside the DLL have an effect only on the copy and do not change the value for the calling code.

- When you pass by reference, the address of the original value is placed on the stack. If the DLL makes changes to the value, the calling code will be able to see those changes.

To understand the difference, look at the declaration in C of the function GetFileSize:

```
DWORD GetFileSize
    (
    HANDLE hFile,          // handle of file to get size of
    LPDWORD lpFileSizeHigh,  // address of high-order word
                           // for file size
    );
```

The GetFileSize function takes two arguments:

Parameter	Meaning
hFile	Specifies an open handle of the file whose size is being returned. The handle must have been created with either GENERIC_READ or GENERIC_WRITE access to the file
lpFileSizeHigh	Points to the variable where the high-order word of the file size is returned. This parameter can be Null if the application does not require the high-order word

The first, hFile, is a handle to a file by value. The second, lpFileSizeHigh, is a Long by reference. The function fills in the second argument. Suppose you call this function with the following code:

```
Function adhGetFileSize(ByVal strFile As String) As Long
Dim hFile As Long
    Dim lngHigh As Long
    Dim curSize As Currency

    hFile = CreateFile(strFile), _
    GENERIC_READ, FILE_SHARE_READ, ByVal 0&, OPEN_EXISTING, _
```

```
        0&, 0&)
    If Not Err.LastDllError Then
        curSize = GetFileSize(hFile, lngHigh)
        If lngHigh > 0 Then
            curSize = curSize + 2 ^ 32 * lngHigh
        End If
        adhGetFileSize = CLng(curSize)
        Call CloseHandle(hFile)
    Else
        adhGetFileSize = -1
    End If
End Function
```

At the point where GetFileSize is called, a diagram of the stack looks like this:

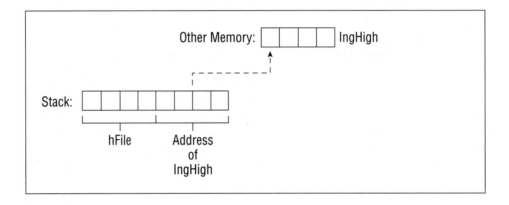

Notice that the value for hFile is directly on the stack (by value) and that a reference to lngHigh is placed on the stack (by reference). The important point to remember is that you must always declare the arguments the way the function expects to find them.

Passing Strings to a DLL: The Real Story

As mentioned earlier in this chapter, Windows has two ways of storing strings: LPSTR and BSTR. String parameters to DLL functions must specify which kind of string they accept. Internally, VBA uses BSTRs to store strings. If the function accepts an LPSTR as a parameter, the argument must be converted from a BSTR into an LPSTR before being passed in. The vast majority of DLLs that are passed strings expect to be passed LPSTRs, including all the Windows API calls (except OLE calls). This means you need some method of converting BSTRs to LPSTRs. To effect this, you should understand how BSTRs and LPSTRs are stored in memory.

An LPSTR is an address of a null-terminated string. A *null-terminated string* is a set of characters followed by a character with the ANSI value 0. An LPSTR is stored in memory like this:

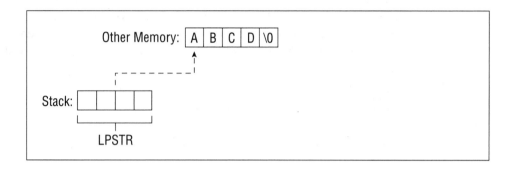

A BSTR is like an LPSTR except that the actual string data is preceded by a 4-byte value representing the size of the string. The address on the stack, however, still points to the first byte in the string. It is stored in memory like this:

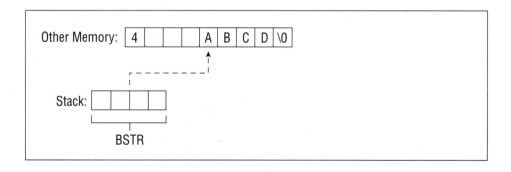

While these might seem like compatible datatypes, they're not. Unless a DLL function is specifically written to accept a BSTR (and most aren't), you must pass it an LPSTR. How do you tell VBA to pass an LPSTR rather than a BSTR? You declare the argument using the ByVal attribute. Don't worry about VBA placing a string *by value* (that is, all the bytes) on the stack; remember that when it comes to strings,

VBA always passes *by reference.* The type of reference (or pointer) it passes, however, differs, depending on whether or not you use ByVal in the declaration. To pass an LPSTR, declare string arguments using ByVal; to pass a BSTR, don't use ByVal.

Using vbNullString—A Closer Look

As shown in the section "Using the vbNullString Constant" earlier in this chapter, you can also pass a Null as the second argument to delete the volume label (at least in Windows NT). How can you pass a null pointer? You cannot pass an empty string, because that would pass a pointer to the empty string. (Remember that strings are passed by reference.) Passing an empty string would result in a stack like this:

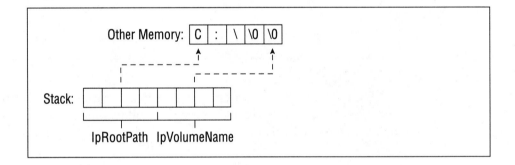

On the other hand, to pass a Null as the second argument, you want the stack to look like this:

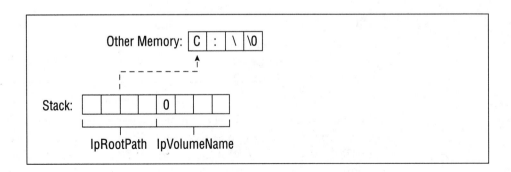

Notice that these two diagrams do not represent the same thing. The first stack passes a pointer to a null character, and the second stack passes a null pointer. How do you pass a null pointer? You pass the vbNullString constant as the second argument. VBA treats the vbNullString constant in a special way. It is a 4-byte-long zero, but no type checking is done on it when it is passed as a string argument. Because the second string argument is declared as being ByVal, passing vbNullString causes a 4-byte-long zero to be placed on the stack. To delete the volume label, you call SetVolumeLabel with:

```
Call SetVolumeLabel("C:\", vbNullString)
```

Unicode to ANSI and Back

The preceding discussion disregards one important subject about passing strings to DLL procedures: VBA stores strings internally as Unicode and converts those strings to ANSI at the time a DLL function call is made. *Unicode* is a character-encoding scheme that uses 2 bytes to represent each character, allowing representation of 65,536 different characters. The Unicode specification has assigned every character from every major language in the world to one of the Unicode values. ANSI uses only 1 byte per character and can represent only 256 different characters.

Internally, VBA represents every string in Unicode format. Whenever you make a function call, VBA intercepts the call if any argument is a string or a user-defined structure that contains a string. A temporary buffer is created, and then the strings are converted from Unicode, with the result placed in the temporary buffer. Then the pointers are fixed up to point to the converted strings. When the function returns, all strings are converted back from ANSI to Unicode before VBA returns control to you.

This conversion from ANSI to Unicode has several implications:

- You must never try to represent binary information within strings if you intend to pass these strings to DLL functions. If the information is not human readable as ANSI characters, you must pass an array of bytes. That's why VBA introduced the Byte datatype.

- You must call functions that expect ANSI strings. Any Win32 function that has strings as parameters comes in two versions. One ends in the letter "A" and accepts ANSI strings as arguments. The other ends in the letter "W" (for Wide) and accepts Unicode arguments. You must always call the function that ends in the letter "A". Typically, the Declare statement specifies an alias clause that defines the "A" version to be a generic name without either the

"A" or the "W". For example, GetWindowText is aliased to be the function GetWindowTextA within the DLL.

- VBA not only translates string arguments passed directly, it translates strings defined in user-defined types.

TIP If you receive the error message "DLL function not found" when trying to use a DLL function, check to see whether the function uses string arguments. If so, you must specify the ANSI version of the function using an Alias clause. This error often occurs when you forget to do so.

Using the Any Datatype

Certain API calls require different types of arguments, depending on how they are called. For example, the WinHelp function is defined in the C programming language like this:

```
BOOL WinHelp
    (
    HWND hwnd,          // handle of window requesting Help
    LPCTSTR lpszHelp,   // address of directory-path string
    UINT uCommand,      // type of Help
    DWORD dwData        // additional data
    );
```

The first two arguments are the hWnd of the parent window and the name of the Help file. The wCommand argument defines what you want Windows to do with the Help file. How the dwData argument is used is based on which constant is passed in for the wCommand argument. Two possible values for the wCommand argument are described in the following table.

wCommand	dwData	Meaning
HELP_ CONTEXT	Unsigned Long Integer containing the context number for the topic	Displays the topic identified by a context number that has been defined in the [MAP] section of the Help project file

| HELP_ PARTIALKEY | Long pointer to a string that contains a keyword for the requested topic | Displays the topic in the keyword list that matches the keyword passed in the dwData parameter, if there is one exact match. If there is more than one match, it displays the Search dialog box with the topics listed in the Go To box. If there is no match, it displays the Search dialog box |
| | | If you just want to bring up the Search dialog box without passing a keyword (the third result), use a long pointer to an empty string |

This presents a problem: HELP_CONTEXT wants a Long passed by value on the stack, whereas HELP_PARTIALKEY wants a string passed by reference; the way you call the function determines the datatype of the last argument. How can you declare the function so it allows both choices? The answer is the Any datatype. The Any datatype tells VBA that at the time you declare the function, you don't know what the datatype is or how big it is. It defers supplying this information until you call the procedure. This removes compile-time type checking, so all the responsibility for passing reasonable arguments is in your court: you must make sure you actually pass reasonable data to the DLL call. The declaration for this function would be

```
Public Declare Function WinHelp _
 Lib "User32" Alias "WinHelpA" _
 (ByVal hwnd As Long, _
 ByVal lpszHelp As String, _
 ByVal uCommand As Long, _
 dwData As Any) As Long
```

Notice that the datatype for the dwData argument is Any and that it is not declared using ByVal. At the time the function is called, you need to provide VBA with three pieces of information:

- The datatype of the argument

- Whether that datatype should be passed by value or by reference

- The contents of the argument

You can include ByVal or ByRef in both the Declare statement and the call. Whatever you use in the call overrides what is in the Declare statement.

You can call this function in two ways:

```
lngRet = WinHelp(Me.hwnd, Me.HelpFile, HELP_CONTEXT, ByVal 3&)
lngRet = WinHelp(Me.hwnd, Me.HelpFile, HELP_PARTIALKEY, _
 ByVal "FindThis")
```

The HELP_CONTEXT call to WinHelp passes a "ByVal 3&" in the dwData argument. This provides VBA with the following information:

- The information is to be passed by value.

- Four bytes are to be placed onto the stack.

- The contents of the 4 bytes should be the value 3.

The ByVal indicates that the argument is passed by value. The ampersand (&) is an indication that the constant is a Long, not an Integer. Without the ampersand, only 2 bytes would be placed on the stack, whereas the function wants 4.

The HELP_PARTIALKEY call to the function provides it with the following information:

- The information is to be passed by reference.

- The information is a string.

- The string should be converted from a BSTR to an LPSTR.

All strings are passed by reference, and the datatype of the argument is a string constant. The ByVal here performs the conversion between the BSTR and the LPSTR. Because a ByVal wasn't included in the Declare statement for this argument, the ByVal is required in the call statement.

Use the Any data type carefully because VBA is unable to do type checking at compile type. As an alternative, consider declaring the procedure multiple times using different names and specific datatypes. For example, the following code declares two versions of the WinHelp function—one that accepts a Long value and one that accepts a String value in the dwData argument:

```
Public Declare Function WinHelpContext _
 Lib "User32" Alias "WinHelpA _
 (ByVal hwnd As Long, _
```

```
ByVal lpszHelp As String, _
ByVal uCommand As Long, _
ByVal dwData As Long) As Long

Public Declare Function WinHelpPartialKey _
 Lib "User32" Alias "WinHelpA" _
 (ByVal hwnd As Long, _
 ByVal lpszHelp As String, _
 ByVal uCommand As Long, _
 ByVal dwData As String) As Long
```

Using Err.LastDLLError

When you call a Windows API call from Visual Basic, the possibility usually exists that the call will fail. The function indicates this failure by returning some special value, such as 0 or False. When you are using the Windows API from C, you can then call a function named GetLastError to find out why it failed. Unfortunately, calling GetLastError from VBA doesn't report accurate results. The reason is that VBA itself is also doing Windows API calls. By the time you get a chance to call GetLastError, VBA has already messed up the result GetLastError would have reported. To get around this problem, VBA implements the LastDLLError property of the Err object. This property is filled in with the error code of the last DLL call you made. You can use this property instead of calling GetLastError. For example:

```
fRet = SetVolumeLabel("C:\", vbNullString)
If Not fRet Then
    If Err.LastDllError = ERROR_INVALID_PARAMETER then
        MsgBox "Due to a Windows '95 bug, you can't delete " _
        & "the volume label. "
    End If
End If
```

Using Callback Functions

A small percentage of the Windows functions require a callback function. A *call-back* is a procedure *you* provide for *Windows* to call. Windows calls the callback multiple times, and with each call Windows passes arguments that reference an object in an internal data structure. For example, a call to the EnumWindows function requires a callback. The callback function is called once for each top-level window currently open and is passed a handle to it until they have all been enumerated. In the C declaration, the argument in which you indicate the address of the callback has the datatype FARPROC or CALLBACK.

Because VBA cannot intrinsically handle callback functions, there are two ways to handle external functions that require callbacks. One is to write a DLL that contains a function that can be used for the callback. The other is to use a special OLE control that already has the callback function written. The OLE callback procedure generates an event when Windows calls it.

The accompanying CD-ROM contains a special DLL (along with its source code) that implements a callback function. The CallBackDemo procedure in the sample database shows how to use the DLL with a function that requires a callback such as EnumWindows.

User-Defined Types and DWORD Packing

When VBA passes a user-defined type to a DLL, it refuses to allow any particular declaration within the structure to cross a DWORD (4-byte) boundary. Instead, it pads out bytes so that the next definition starts on a DWORD boundary. This means that if you compile your own DLL, you must either provide that padding yourself or use the Struct Member Alignment option the C compiler provides. For example, if you have a structure that looks like this:

```
Type TESTSTRUCT
    intTest As Integer
    bytTest As Byte
    lngTest As Long
End Type
```

the structure in memory is represented like this:

```
intTest
bytTest
One byte of padding to make the lngTest align to a DWORD boundary
lngTest
```

so the structure takes up 8 bytes in memory. If, instead, the structure is arranged like this:

```
Type TESTSTRUCT
    bytTest As Byte
    lngTest As Long
```

```
      intTest As Integer
End Type
```

it is padded out to look like this in memory:

```
bytTest
Three bytes of padding
lngTest
intTest
Two bytes of padding
```

and thus it takes up 12 bytes in memory.

If the DLL is compiled with the Struct Member Alignment option, the C compiler provides the appropriate padding to make the structure members line up with the way the structure is passed from VBA. On the other hand, you would be better off arranging the elements within the structure so they are DWORD aligned to begin with.

This implicit padding that VBA provides does not cause a problem with the Windows API, because the API structures have been DWORD aligned, but it can cause a problem if you use other DLLs. If the DLL is not compiled with the Struct Member Alignment option and has elements that cross DWORD boundaries, you cannot pass the bytes in the correct arrangement without doing a very tricky manipulation of the bytes within the structure.

Converting Windows API Calls from Access 2.0

If you are converting code from Access 2.0, you will need to revisit all your Windows API calls; many of them have changed. At a minimum, you'll need to update the Declare statements to refer to 32-bit DLLs and, possibly, adjust those requiring String arguments so that ANSI DLL functions are used. This is a significant amount of work.

Windows API calls come in five classes when ported to Win32:

- Calls that merely have to reference the Win32 libraries instead of the Win16 libraries

- Calls that must be modified to use the ANSI versions of Win32 API functions

- Calls that now have additional functionality under Win32

- Calls that have a new extended version (For example, GetWindowExt has a new extended version, GetWindowExtEx.)

- Calls that are not supported under Win32

Use the following steps as a guideline to make the conversion:

1. Start by finding each of your Declare statements in existing code.

2. Look in the Win32 documentation to determine in which one of the four classes of conversions the call falls.

3. Replace the Declare statement with the new Declare statement (unless the call is no longer supported in Win32).

4. Examine every function call to your Windows API calls. Make sure the arguments match the datatype of the parameters in the Declare statement. A great many of the arguments will need to be changed from Integers to Longs. Make sure these changes propagate throughout your code.

5. Save your database and make a backup copy.

6. Set a breakpoint on each of your API calls. Run your code. When you reach the breakpoint, verify that the arguments are both the correct value and the correct size. Then step through the call.

This is a lot of work, but it is absolutely necessary to get your code to work reliably under Win32.

Table 18.2 is not exhaustive, but it may help with some of the conversions.

TABLE 18.2   Some Windows 3.1 Calls That Need to Be Changed for Windows 95 or Windows NT

Win 16 Call	Replace with
GetWindowWord	GetWindowLong
SetWindowWord	SetWindowLong
GetClassWord	GetClassLong
SetClassWord	SetClassLong
GetPrivateProfileString	(VBA built-in function GetSetting or GetAllSettings)

T A B L E   1 8 . 2   Some Windows 3.1 Calls That Need to Be Changed for Windows 95 or Windows NT (continued)

Win 16 Call	Replace with
GetPrivateProfileInt	(VBA built-in function GetSetting)
WritePrivateProfileString	(VBA built-in statement SaveSetting)
MoveTo	MoveToEx
OffsetViewportOrg	OffsetViewportOrgEx
OffsetWindowOrg	OffsetWindowOrgEx
GetAspectRatioFilter	GetAspectRatioFilterEx
GetBitmapDimension	GetBitmapDimensionEx
GetBrushOrg	GetBrushOrgEx
GetCurrentPosition	GetCurrentPositionEx
GetTextExtent	GetTextExtentPoint
GetViewportExt	GetViewportExtEx
GetViewportOrg	GetViewportOrgEx
GetWindowExt	GetWindowExtEx
GetWindowOrg	GetWindowOrgEx
ScaleViewportExt	ScaleViewportExtEx
ScaleWindowExt	ScaleWindowExtEx
SetBitmapDimension	SetBitmapDimensionEx
SetMetaFileBits	SetMetaFileBitsEx
SetViewportExt	SetViewportExtEx
SetViewportOrg	SetViewportOrgEx
SetWindowExt	SetWindowExtEx
SetWindowOrg	SetWindowdOrgEx
AccessResource	(No longer exists in Win32)

TABLE 18.2 Some Windows 3.1 Calls That Need to Be Changed for Windows 95 or Windows NT (continued)

Win16 Call	Replace with
AllocDSToCSAlias	(No longer exists in Win32)
AllocResource	(No longer exists in Win32)
AllocSelector	(No longer exists in Win32)
Catch	(No longer exists in Win32)
ChangeSelector	(No longer exists in Win32)
FreeSelector	(No longer exists in Win32)
GetCodeHandle	(No longer exists in Win32)
GetCodeInfo	(No longer exists in Win32)
GetCurrentPDB	(No longer exists in Win32)
GetEnvironment	(No longer exists in Win32)
GetInstanceData	(No longer exists in Win32)
GetKBCodePage	(No longer exists in Win32)
GetModuleUsage	(No longer exists in Win32)
GlobalDOSAlloc	(No longer exists in Win32)
GlobalDOSFree	(No longer exists in Win32)
GlobalNotify	(No longer exists in Win32)
GlobalPageLock	(No longer exists in Win32)
LockData	(No longer exists in Win32)
NetBIOSCall	(No longer exists in Win32)
Throw	(No longer exists in Win32)
SetEnvironment	(No longer exists in Win32)
SetResourceHandler	(No longer exists in Win32)
SwitchStackBack	(No longer exists in Win32)

TABLE 18.2 Some Windows 3.1 Calls That Need to Be Changed for Windows 95 or Windows NT (continued)

Win 16 Call	Replace with
SwitchStackTo	(No longer exists in Win32)
UnlockData	(No longer exists in Win32)
ValidateCodeSegments	(No longer exists in Win32)
ValidateFreeSpaces	(No longer exists in Win32)
Yield	(No longer exists in Win32)
IsGdiObject	(No longer exists in Win32)
IsTask	(No longer exists in Win32)
DefineHandleTable	(No longer exists in Win32)
MakeProcInstance	(No longer exists in Win32)
FreeProcInstance	(No longer exists in Win32)
GetFreeSpace	(No longer exists in Win32)
GlobalCompact	(No longer exists in Win32)
GlobalFix	(No longer exists in Win32)
GlobalUnfix	(No longer exists in Win32)
GlobalUnwire	(No longer exists in Win32)
LocalCompact	(No longer exists in Win32)
LocalShrink	(No longer exists in Win32)
LockSegment	(No longer exists in Win32)
UnlockSegment	(No longer exists in Win32)
SetSwapAreaSize	(No longer exists in Win32)

Summary

This chapter has covered the following topics:

- Declaring a DLL procedure from VBA
- Specifying the arguments
- Understanding passing by value and passing by reference
- Converting C parameters into VBA declarations
- Using callback functions
- Returning strings from a DLL
- Understanding the Unicode-to-ANSI issue
- Using the vbNullString constant
- Using the Any datatype
- Passing a user-defined type to a DLL
- User-defined types and DWORD packing
- Passing an array
- Using type libraries
- Using the Windows API
- Converting Windows API calls from Access 2.0
- Examples using the Windows API

DLLs are one of the three ways by which you can reach outside the bounds of Access into other Windows programs, the other two being DDE and Auotmation. Automation is covered in Chapter 20. Due to space limitations, information on DDE has been moved to the CD-ROM (or you can refer to Chapter 20 of our *Microsoft Access 95 Developer's Handbook*). The DLL interface allows you to manipulate Windows directly through the Windows API, as well as to call your own DLLs. Combined with a C or C++ compiler and the appropriate knowledge, DLLs allow you to do virtually anything that is possible with Windows. However, even without the use of C or C++, the ability to call the Windows API vastly extends the power of Access.

Harnessing Wizard Magic

- File-handling functions

- Interfaces to Windows' common dialogs

- Font-handling functions

- Reading/writing values in the Registry

- DAO support

19

To make it possible for the Access Wizards to perform some of their wizardry, Access exposes some external functions as entry points into MSACCESS.EXE. The functions Access exports are meant to be called from VBA (because, of course, the Wizards are all written in VBA), and you can use them, too, in your own applications.

NOTE

> The functionality described in this chapter replaces that supplied in the library MSAU7032.DLL, which shipped as part of Access 95. Microsoft moved these functions into the base executable (rather than leaving them in an external DLL) to increase their loading speed. The functionality is the same, however: any Windows application can export public functions, just as a DLL does.

The list of public procedures includes a number of functions that break down into six basic categories:

- **File-handling functions:** Check for file existence; split file name components; retrieve a full path given a relative path

- **Interfaces to common dialogs:** Office File Open/Close and Color Choosers

- **Read and write Registry values:** Retrieve the number of subkeys and values for a given key; read and write keys and their values

- **Font-handling functions:** List available fonts and their sizes; retrieve the height and width of a given string in a specified font

- **Object-handling functions:** Retrieve a list of object names or a list of objects along with their types; sort an array of strings; sort an array of objects either by name or by type

- **Miscellaneous functions:** Check a file's national language; use Access' toolbar bitmaps; find the number of colors in a bitmap; retrieve programmatic information

This chapter discusses in detail many of the functions you can call that are exported by MSACCESS.EXE.

WARNING

Microsoft has documented none of the material in this chapter. That means that *any* of it can change for future versions of Access. Because the current Access Wizards use everything in this chapter at one point or another, though, we feel strongly that you're safe in using these procedures in Access 97. Most of these functions will continue to work in future versions of Access, but we (and Microsoft) can make no guarantees.

WARNING

The exposed functions in MSACCESS.EXE were written for a specific purpose: to allow the Wizards to do their work. They were not written for general-purpose use, and may not, at times, do what you'd expect them to do. We've documented them here because they may be useful to your applications. They work fine in the examples we've tried, but they may or may not work in the situations to which you apply them. If these functions do not work as you might expect, do not curse at us or at Microsoft for providing shoddy software—the functions do work correctly, in the environment for which they were written.

Using the Exported Procedures

To use the exported functions in MSACCESS.EXE, you need to have the Declare statements for the functions available to your application. In addition, many of the functions require specific user-defined datatypes. In the retail Access product, the function declarations and datatype definitions are scattered throughout various Wizards and library databases. Although you needn't do anything special to use these functions and datatypes as they're declared in the Access Wizards, you'll find yourself doing extra work if you intend to ship your application with the Access run-time version. If you use the run-time version, you can't distribute the Wizard databases with your application. Therefore, you'll need some method of reproducing those declarations and datatypes in your own applications.

To make things as simple as possible, we've created a single module including all the function declarations and datatype definitions you'll need. Import basDeclares (from CH19.MDB) into your application, and you'll be able to call any of the exported functions described in this chapter. We've aliased each of the functions and datatypes so they won't conflict with the corresponding declarations in the Wizards and libraries if they're loaded.

> **NOTE** The external procedure declarations in this chapter use numeric aliases. In Windows, when declaring the external procedure, you can refer to the item either by name or by ordinal number within the DLL or executable. Using the number is actually a tiny bit faster, and it protects you in case the author changes the name of the procedure in a future revision.

File-Handling Functions

MSACCESS.EXE provides three file-handling functions, each of which performs one of the following activities:

- Checks for the existence of a file
- Splits a full path reference into its component pieces
- Gets the full path associated with a file

The following sections deal individually with each of these functions.

Checking for the Existence of a File

You can check for the existence of a file by calling the adh_accFileExists function. To call it, use syntax like this:

```
intRetval = adh_accFileExists(strFileName)
```

This function returns 1 if the file exists or 0 otherwise.

For example, to check for the existence of C:\AUTOEXEC.BAT, you could use the following code:

```
If adh_accFileExists("C:\AUTOEXEC.BAT") = adhcFileExistsYes Then
    ' Do something
End If
```

Because of the way this function returns its success value (using 1 instead of the standard –1 that VBA normally uses), you won't be able to write code using the Not operator to check for the nonexistence of a file:

```
' Don't do this!
If Not adh_accFileExists("C:\AUTOEXEC.BAT") Then
    ' Don't to this, it won't work!
End If
```

If you must check for the nonexistence of a file, use code like this:

```
If adh_accFileExists("C:\AUTOEXEC.BAT") = _
 adhcFileExistsNo Then
    ' You know the file doesn't exist
End If
```

NOTE   This function does its work by attempting to open the specified file with read privileges and deny write access. If another process has already exclusively opened the file, you may find that this function returns incorrect results.

TIP   To use any of the functions from MSACCESS.EXE, import basDeclares (from CH19.MDB) into your own application. Many intricate dependencies exist between function declarations and user-defined data types, and it's just easier to import the entire module than to try to work out which pieces you need to copy.

Splitting a Full Path Reference into Components

As part of many applications, you'll need to take a full path reference, in the format

Drive:\Path\FileName.Ext

and retrieve any one of the single parts of the name (the drive, the path, the file name, or the extension) as a separate piece. The adhSplitPath subroutine (which calls the exported function adh_accSplitPath) will do the work for you, filling in each of the various pieces.

For example, running the code in Listing 19.1 produces the output shown in Figure 19.1.

FIGURE 19.1

The adhSplitPath procedure breaks a full pathname into its components

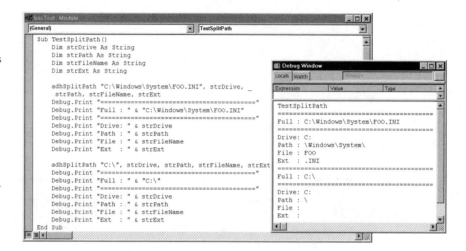

Listing 19.1

```
Sub TestSplitPath()
    Dim strDrive As String
    Dim strPath As String
    Dim strFileName As String
    Dim strExt As String

    adhSplitPath "C:\Windows\System\FOO.INI", strDrive, _
     strPath, strFileName, strExt
    Debug.Print "==========================================="
    Debug.Print "Full : " & "C:\Windows\System\FOO.INI"
    Debug.Print "==========================================="
    Debug.Print "Drive: " & strDrive
    Debug.Print "Path : " & strPath
    Debug.Print "File : " & strFileName
    Debug.Print "Ext  : " & strExt

    adhSplitPath "C:\", strDrive, strPath, strFileName, strExt
    Debug.Print "==========================================="
    Debug.Print "Full : " & "C:\"
```

```
        Debug.Print "========================================"
        Debug.Print "Drive: " & strDrive
        Debug.Print "Path : " & strPath
        Debug.Print "File : " & strFileName
        Debug.Print "Ext  : " & strExt
End Sub
```

Because the function in MSACCESS.EXE requires its parameter strings to be set up in a special fashion, you'll need to call this wrapper routine rather than the actual adh_accSplitPath function itself. The wrapper ends up calling adh_accSplitPath, but the calling conventions make it easier to call our wrapper instead.

Getting the Full Path for a File

You can use the adhFullPath function (which calls the adh_accFullPath routine in MSACCESS.EXE) to retrieve the full path for a file, based on a relative path. For example, if your current directory is the C:\Windows directory,

```
adhFullPath("..\OFFICE97\ACCESS\MSACCESS.EXE")
```

returns the value "C:\OFFICE97\ACCESS\MSACCESS.EXE", a fully qualified pathname for the file. If you pass an invalid path to adhFullPath, it returns a zero-length string.

> **NOTE** This function can be confusing in its intent. It looks at the current directory and the relative pathname you've sent it and creates a complete pathname for the file based on that information. It does nothing more; it does not check for the existence of the file (you can pass it anything you wish for the file name), nor does it check to see whether the actual directories exist. Its purpose is to turn relative paths into absolute paths.

Because the adh_accFullPath function requires a small wrapper function to make it easy to call, we've provided the adhFullPath function for you to call directly. To use it you must import the basDeclares module from CH19.MDB into your own application. The adhFullPath function ends up calling adh_accFullPath in MSACCESS.EXE, but it's simpler to call our wrapper function directly.

Using the Windows Common Dialogs

To standardize specific often-needed dialogs, Windows provides a series of common dialogs all applications can use. In addition, Office 97 provides its own version of the standard file-choosing dialog. Access provides no mechanism for you to get to any of the common dialogs for your own applications, but the code in MSACCESS.EXE provides a simple interface to the Office File Open/Save and Color Chooser dialogs. The following sections discuss how you can use these interfaces, along with the wrapper functions in basDeclares, making it simple for you to take advantage of these common dialogs in your own applications.

> **NOTE**
>
> Previous versions of the MSAU DLL included interfaces for the standard Windows Font and File Open/Save common dialogs. This version does not. If you need to use these common dialogs, you can either call the Windows API directly or use the Common Dialog OLE control that ships as part of the Office Developer's Edition and Visual Basic.

Using the Office File Open/File Save Common Dialog

You cannot have used Office 97 for long without noticing the standard File Open and File Save dialogs that all the Office applications use. This dialog, based on the common file dialog that Windows provides, makes it easy for you to allow users to select a file for opening or saving. The dialog also makes it possible for you to allow users to select a path, rather than both a path and file (and the standard Windows dialog doesn't supply this feature). The interface to these common dialogs requires you to send it some information, and Office will do its job, pop up the dialog, and return information to you. Whether you are opening or saving a file, you must create a variable of the adh_accOfficeGetFileNameInfo datatype. (We've defined this structure for you in basDeclares.) You fill out certain fields in the structure and then send it off to the adhOfficeGetFileName function. This function either requests a file to open or a name under which to save (depending on the value in one of its parameters) and returns the structure to you, all filled out with the information the user chose from the dialog.

> **NOTE**
>
> Neither the File Open nor the File Save dialog actually *does* anything with the file you select. These dialogs just return a file name to your application, where you can decide what you wish to do with that file. It's up to you to actually open or save the file.

The designers of MSACCESS.EXE set the structure of the user-defined type, adh_accOfficeGetFileNameInfo. If you were to call the common Windows dialog functions yourself, you'd use structures defined as part of the Windows SDK, which contain more fields and options. Because you're using MSACCESS.EXE to interface to the real library (COMDLG32.DLL), the available options are a bit limited. Table 19.1 lists all the fields in the structure, along with information on using those fields. Table 19.2 lists the possible values for the lngFlags field in this structure, and Table 19.3 lists the possible values for the lngView field.

TABLE 19.1 Fields in the adh_accOfficeGetFileNameInfo Structure

Field Name	Datatype	Description
hWndOwner	Long	Window handle for the parent of the dialog. Normally, supply Application.hWndAccessApp for this value
strAppName	String*255	Describes the application. Not currently used
strDialogTitle	String*255	Text that appears in a dialog caption
strOpenTitle	String*255	Text that appears on the Open button when choosing a file to open
strFile	String*4096	On input, contains the name of a file to have selected initially. On output, contains the file name or path of the selected item. If you've allowed multiple selections, contains the list of selected items delimited with a tab character
strInitialDir	String*255	Initial directory
strFilter	String*255	List of filter values, separated with "|". For example: "Text Files (*.txt)|Database Files (*.mdb)|All Files (*.*)"
lngFilterIndex	Long	Zero-based index into the array of filters, indicating which is to be selected when the dialog opens
lngView	Long	One of the values from Table 19.3, indicating which view of the directory is to be displayed when the dialog opens. This value is disregarded unless the lngFlags field includes the adhcGfniInitializeView constant

TABLE 19.2 Possible Values for the lngFlags Field in the adh_accOfficeGetFileNameInfo Structure

Constant Name	Value	Description
adhcGfniConfirmReplace	&H1	When choosing a file name in which to save, confirm with a dialog if the file already exists
adhcGfniNoChangeDir	&H2	Instead of changing the current directory to the selected directory, maintains the original directory after using the dialog
adhcGfniAllowReadOnly	&H4	Allows the (normally disabled) read-only option
adhcGfniAllowMultiSelect	&H8	Allows the user to select multiple items. Office returns multiple items in the strFile field delimited with a tab character (vbTab)
adhcGfniDirectoryOnly	&H20	Limits the user to selecting directories only. This flag overrides all others and turns the dialog into a directory picker
adhcGfniInitializeView	&H40	Allows the setting for the initial view to override the user's most recent choice. If this flag isn't set, the value in the lngView field is disregarded

TABLE 19.3 Possible Values for the lngView Field in the adh_accOfficeGetFileNameInfo Structure

Constant Name	Value	Description
adhcGfniViewDetails	0	Displays file details
adhcGfniViewPreview	1	Displays file preview, if available
adhcGfniViewProperties	2	Displays file properties, if available
adhcGfniViewList	3	Displays the file list (the standard view)

TIP

None of the values in the lngView field (chosen from Table 19.3) will have any effect unless the value in the lngFlags field includes the adhcGfniInitializeView flag. Make sure your code uses the Or operator to include this value if you want to specify the view.

To call the adhOfficeGetFileName function, you needn't supply values for all the fields in Table 19.1. Listing 19.2 shows a simple case of using the common dialogs to retrieve a file name to open. Figure 19.2 shows the dialog box this function pops up.

FIGURE 19.2

The code in Listing 19.2 causes this dialog to pop up.

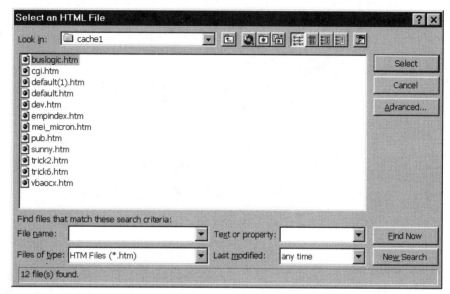

Listing 19.2

```
Sub TestGetFileName()
    Dim gfni As adh_accOfficeGetFileNameInfo
    With gfni
        .hwndOwner = Application.hWndAccessApp
        .strAppName = "Delete Extra HTML"
        .strDlgTitle = "Select an HTML File"
        .strOpenTitle = "Select"
        .strFile = ""
        .strInitialDir = "C:\Windows\" & _
        "Temporary Internet Files\Cache1"
        .strFilter = _
        "HTML (*.html;*.htm)|HTM Files (*.htm)|" & _
        "HTX Files (*.htx)|All Files (*.*)"
        .lngFilterIndex = 1
        .lngView = adhcGfniViewList
```

```
            .lngFlags = adhcGfniNoChangeDir Or adhcGfniInitializeView
        End With
        If adhOfficeGetFileName(gfni, True) = adhcAccErrSuccess Then
            MsgBox "You chose: " & Trim(gfni.strFile), _
             vbOKOnly, "Test Get File Name"
        End If
End Sub
```

There are a few items to note about this function:

- Because all the strings in the datatype are fixed-length strings, you need to use the Trim function to remove trailing spaces when you want to use the data that's in those strings.

- If you want to initialize the view (Details, Preview, List, or Properties) in the lngView field, you must also specify the adhcGfniInitializeView flag in the lng-Flags field. The example in Listing 19.2 does this.

- Most likely, you'll want to at least supply values for the fields used in Listing 19.2: strInitialDir, strDlgTitle, and strFilter. You can, of course, supply other values, but those will be the most useful ones. Note that you must end each entry in the strFilter field with a vertical bar and that each entry must consist of two parts: the text description of the filter item and, within parentheses, the file specification that will select that group. In addition, if you want to use two different filespecs within a group (as we did in Listing 19.2), separate them with a semicolon (;) in the second portion of the group.

- Calling the adhOfficeGetFileName function will return one of three values: adhcAccErrSuccess (0), indicating success; adhcAccErrGFNCantOpenDialog (–301), indicating there was some error in the parameters making it impossible to open the dialog; or adhcAccErrGFNUserCancelledDialog (–302), indicating that the user cancelled the dialog (with the Cancel button).

To choose a file name for saving, just set the second parameter to adhOfficeGet-FileName to False. That way, you've indicated to MSACCESS.EXE that you're trying to save a file rather than load it.

Trying Out All the Options

To make it easier for you to try out all the available options, we've supplied frmOfficeFileOpen, shown in Figure 19.3. This form allows you to choose the flags you want set, the text you'd like to use, and the initial view. Once you've made all your choices, you can click Test the Dialog to give it a try. The example places the selected file (or files) in the Results text box. Figure 19.3 shows the sample form set up to display the same dialog as the code in Listing 19.2.

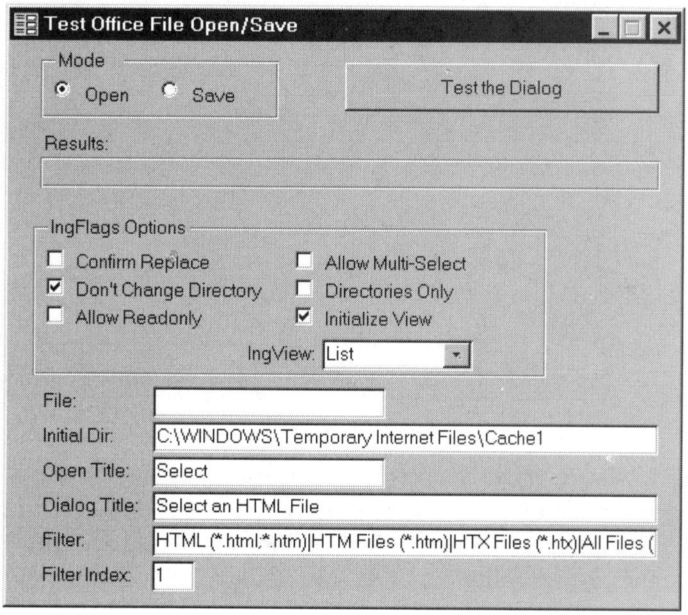

FIGURE 19.3

Use frmOfficeFileOpen to try out all the options for adhOfficeGetFileName.

Selecting Colors

If you need to allow your users to choose colors within your application, your easiest solution is to use the Windows common dialog Color Chooser. Figure 19.4 shows the Color dialog in action.

Just as with the file name–choosing dialog, MSACCESS.EXE makes it simple for you to use this dialog—you just call adhChooseColor. Because calling this function is far less complex, we've made the wrapper function's calling syntax a bit simpler: just pass to it a single long integer, indicating the initial color choice, and it will send the information to the common dialog for you. This wrapper function sets up the call to adh_accGetColor and returns the user's color choice to the calling procedure.

FIGURE 19.4

Windows color-choosing common dialog

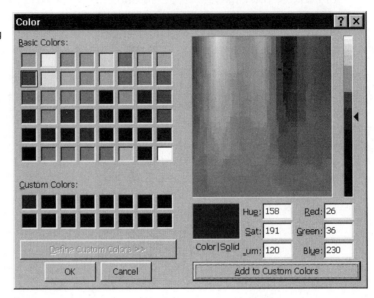

Unlike the File Open/Save dialog, there are no options you can change when dealing with the Color dialog when you call it through this simplified interface. Although the Windows API's version of the color selection dialog does afford some customization that this simple function does not, you get most of the functionality here with almost no effort.

To call adhChooseColor, pass in a color value. The function returns the value of the selected color:

```
lngNewColor = adhChooseColor(lngOldColor)
```

Reading and Writing Registry Values

Although you can use the Windows API to read and write Registry values (see Chapter 18 for more information), there just *has* to be a simpler way. The functions provided in MSACCESS.EXE make it a little simpler, although they still require a bit of effort on your part. The following sections highlight the six functions exported by MSACCESS.EXE that help you work with the System Registry.

> **TIP**
>
> If you simply intend to store your own application information in the Registry, you needn't fight with these functions. VBA supplies the GetSetting, SaveSetting, GetAllSettings, and DeleteSetting procedures, which allow you to get and set Registry values in a limited manner. See the section "Storing Information in the System Registry" in Chapter 8 for more information on using these functions.

To demonstrate many of the functions in this section, load and run frmStartup-Tips, shown in Figure 19.5. When you start Windows 95 or Windows NT 4.0 you have the option of displaying a splash screen that contains a "tip of the day." Figure 19.6 shows the startup screen after the change indicated in Figure 19.5 has been made. Windows maintains, in the Registry, a flag that indicates whether or not to show the tips, as well as the next tip to be displayed. Figure 19.7 shows the Registry key and values containing this information, which is stored separately for each user profile on the system. In addition, Windows stores all the tips themselves in a corresponding key, global for the entire machine. Figure 19.8 shows the tips as they appear in REGEDIT.EXE.

FIGURE 19.5

frmStartupTips allows you to edit existing startup tips or add new ones of your own.

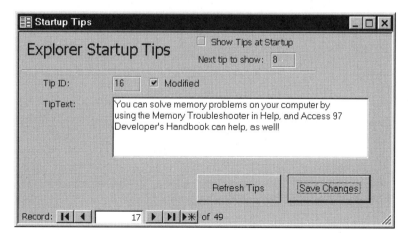

1147

FIGURE 19.6

You can control the tips in the Windows Explorer's startup screen by modifying the values in the Registry.

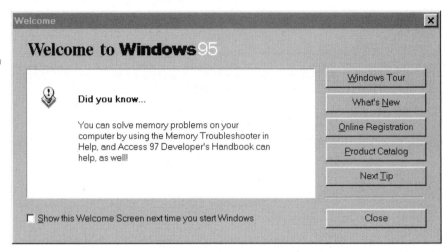

FIGURE 19.7

Windows stores state information about the tips for each individual user.

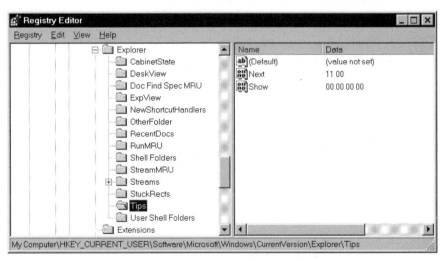

FIGURE 19.8

You can modify all the startup tips, and you can add your own as well.

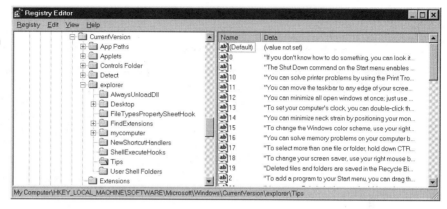

This example will work correctly only in Windows 95 or Windows NT 4.0. Although the functions provided in MSACCESS.EXE that work with the Registry will work equally well in any version of Windows NT or Windows 95, the startup tips this example manipulates just don't exist in Windows NT before version 4.0. If you need to discern which version of Windows you're running, take a look at the GetVersionEx Windows API function. This function can tell you which version (Windows NT or Windows 95) you're running.

You'll find the code for the Explorer tips example in basTips, in CH19.MDB. The fragments of code in the next four sections are extracted from that module as well.

Although these examples make heavy use of the Registry, this book does not intend to, nor can it, provide a reference or instructions on using the System Registry. Anytime you modify settings in the Registry, if you're not sure of what you're doing, you risk making your system unusable. Before you modify anything in the Registry, programmatically or manually, make sure you've backed up.

Retrieving Information about a Key

If you're interested in working your way through all the subkeys or values associated with a key in the Registry, you will need to know, before you start, how many of each exist. The adh_accRegGetKeyInfo function retrieves, for a given root key and path to a key, the number of subkeys and values associated with that key.

> **NOTE**
>
> The terminology surrounding the Registry can get confusing. From the Registry's point of view, a *key* is a node within the Registry, at any level within the hierarchy. A *subkey* of that key is any key located at the next lower level in the hierarchy. A *value* is a named quantity, displayed in the right pane of the Registry Editor, and can be text, numeric, or binary. The Registry includes a number of root keys as well, including HKEY_LOCAL_MACHINE and HKEY_CURRENT_USER.

In this example you want to retrieve tips from the specific key:

```
HKEY_LOCAL_MACHINE
    Software
        Microsoft
            Windows
                CurrentVersion
                    Explorer
                        Tips
```

as shown in Figure 19.8. The root key is HKEY_LOCAL_MACHINE, and the key to check on is

```
Software\Microsoft\Windows\CurrentVersion\Explorer\Tips
```

You need to know, in this case, how many values (startup tips) are associated with this key. To do this, call adh_accRegGetKeyInfo, passing to it the preopened value for the handle to the root key, HKEY_LOCAL_MACHINE (defined as the constant adhcHKEY_LOCAL_MACHINE), a string containing the path to the key in question, and two Long Integer variables the function will fill in with the number of subkeys and values:

```
lngRetval = adh_accRegGetKeyInfo(adhcHKEY_LOCAL_MACHINE, _
    adhcRegTips, lngSubKeys, lngValues)
```

MSACCESS.EXE will retrieve the information for you and pass it back in those final two variables. The syntax for calling adh_accRegGetKeyInfo is shown in Table 19.4.

TABLE 19.4 Syntax for Calling adh_accRegGetKeyInfo

Parameter	Type	Description	Comments
hkeyRoot	Long	Key to use as the root	Use one of the constants defined in basDeclares: adhcHKEY_LOCAL_MACHINE or adhcHKEY_CURRENT_USER, normally
strSubKey	String	Path to the key in question	Do not include the root key name or a leading backslash (\)
lngSubKeys	Long	Filled in by the function call with the number of subkeys underneath the specified key	Only subkeys located at the next lower level in the hierarchy are counted
lngValues	Long	Filled in by the function call with the number of values underneath the specified key	
Return Value	Long	Error code	adhcAccErrSuccess, adhcAccErrRegKeyNotFound, or adhcAccErrUnknown

For example, here's the code from adhFillTipTable that retrieves the number of tips to be had. (In this example adhcRegTips is a constant containing the path to the key.)

```
' Get the number of subkeys and values under the key.
' It's the number of values you really care about here.
lngRetval = adh_accRegGetKeyInfo(adhcHKEY_LOCAL_MACHINE, _
  adhcRegTips, lngSubKeys, lngValues)
For intI = 0 To lngValues - 1
    ' Retrieve the subkey information
Next intI
```

Retrieving a Value Name

To retrieve a value for a key, you must know the name of the value. (You can get around this restriction using the Windows API directly, but this chapter attempts to solve problems using MSACCESS.EXE with as few "raw" API calls as possible. For more information on using the API to get to the Registry, see Chapter 18.) For example, the tips are all named with numeric text between "0" and "48" (or possibly more, if you've added some tips). The code in adhFillTipTable loops through all the values associated with the key, retrieves their names, and then, given the names, retrieves the values themselves.

To retrieve the name of a value, use the adh_accRegGetValName function. As in the previous function, you supply it with a root key and a path to the key in question. You must also give it the index for the value for which you want to retrieve the name, a buffer in which to place the returned value, the size of that buffer, and a Long Integer into which the function can place the type of value (Text, Numeric, and so on) it retrieved. Table 19.5 shows the syntax for calling adh_accRegGetValName.

TABLE 19.5 Syntax for Calling adh_accRegGetValName

Parameter	Type	Description	Comments
hkeyRoot	Long	Key to use as the root	Use one of the constants defined in basDeclares: adhcHKEY_LOCAL_MACHINE or adhcHKEY_CURRENT_USER, normally
strSubKey	String	Path to the key in question	Do not include the root key name or a leading backslash (\)
lngValue	Long	Index of the value to retrieve	The index is zero-based
strValName	String	Buffer to contain the value name	Must be large enough to contain the string before you call the function (Use the Space function to "puff" it out, or use a fixed-length string.)
lngMaxLen	Long	Maximum characters in the output buffer	Initialize the output buffer with this much space before calling the function
lngType	Long	On return from the function, filled in with the datatype of the value	For a list of possible types, see the constants starting with adhcREG_ in basDeclares. In general, the only datatypes you'll care about are adhcREG_SZ (null-terminated string) and adhcREG_DWORD (Long Integer)
Return Value	Long	Error code	adhcAccErrSuccess, adhcAccErrRegKeyNotFound, or adhcAccErrRegValueNotFound

For example, once you've retrieved the number of values associated with the Tips key, you can walk through them all, retrieving their names, with the following code from adhFillTipTable:

```
For intI = 0 To lngValues - 1
    strValueName = Space(adhcMaxSize)
    ' Get the value name.
    lngRetval = _
     adh_accRegGetValName(adhcHKEY_LOCAL_MACHINE, _
     adhcRegTips, intI, strValueName, adhcMaxSize, lngType)
    If lngRetval = adhcAccErrSuccess Then
        strValueName = adhTrimNull(strValueName)
    End If
    ' Do more stuff...
Next intI
```

Retrieving a Value from the Registry

Given the name of a key's value, you can retrieve its actual value (yes, the terminology gets in the way here) using the adh_accRegGetVal function:

```
strValue = Space(adhcMaxSize)
lngRetval = adh_accRegGetVal(adhcHKEY_LOCAL_MACHINE, _
 adhcRegTips, strValueName, ByVal strValue, adhcMaxSize)
```

This function, as well as all the other MSACCESS.EXE Registry functions, requires you to tell it the root key and the path to the specific key. You also specify the name of the value to be retrieved, a buffer in which to place the value, and the size of that buffer. MSACCESS.EXE places the value into the buffer and returns a status code. Table 19.6 explains the syntax for calling adh_accRegGetVal.

TABLE 19.6   Syntax for Calling adh_accRegGetVal

Parameter	Type	Description	Comments
hkeyRoot	Long	Key to use as the root	Use one of the constants defined in basDeclares: adhcHKEY_LOCAL_MACHINE or adhcHKEY_CURRENT_USER, normally
strSubKey	String	Path to the key in question	Do not include the root key name or a leading backslash (\)

TABLE 19.6 Syntax for Calling adh_accRegGetVal (continued)

Parameter	Type	Description	Comments
strValName	String	Name of the value to retrieve	
lpData	Any	Buffer to contain the returned data	lpData can be of any datatype, but if you're returning text data, you *must* precede this parameter with the keyword ByVal when you call the function. This tells Access to convert the buffer into a null-terminated string that the function can fill with text data
lngMaxLen	Long	Maximum characters in the output buffer	Initializes the output buffer with this much space before calling the function if you're retrieving text, or places the length of the buffer if you're retrieving a Numeric type (You can use the Len function to find the length of the datatype.)
Return Value	Long	Error code	adhcAccErrSuccess, adhcAccErrRegKeyNotFound, adhcAccErrRegValueNotFound, or adhcAccErrBufferTooSmall

Writing a Value to the Registry

Once you've modified a startup tip, you'll need to write the new value back to the Registry. MSACCESS.EXE provides the adh_accRegWriteVal function to write data to a value associated with a given key. You tell it the (by now familiar) root key and path to the key, as well as the name of the value, the data, and the datatype.

This is the code fragment from adhSaveTipTable that loops through the recordset of tips and writes the modified ones back to the Registry:

```
Do While Not rst.EOF
    lngRetval = adh_accRegWriteVal(adhcHKEY_LOCAL_MACHINE, _
     adhcRegTips, rst!TipID, ByVal CStr(rst!TipText), _
     adhcREG_SZ)
    If lngRetval <> adhcAccErrSuccess Then
        Err.Description = "Unable to save tip " & rst!TipID
```

```
        Err.Raise lngRetval
    Else
        intCount = intCount + 1
    End If
    rst.MoveNext
Loop
```

Table 19.7 describes the syntax for calling adh_accRegWriteVal.

TABLE 19.7   Syntax for Calling adh_accRegWriteVal

Parameter	Type	Description	Comments
hkeyRoot	Long	Key to use as the root	Use one of the constants defined in basDeclares: adhcHKEY_LOCAL_MACHINE or adhcHKEY_CURRENT_USER, normally
strSubKey	String	Path to the key in question	Do not include the root key name or a leading backslash (\)
strValName	String	Name of the value to be written to	If the value does not exist, the function will create it
lpData	Any	Buffer containing the output data	LpData can be of any datatype, but if you're using text data, you *must* precede this parameter with the keyword ByVal when you call the function. This tells Access to convert the buffer into a null-terminated string that the function can fill with text data
lngType	Long	Datatype for the value in lpData. Must be either adhcREG_SZ (null-terminated string) or adhcREG_DWORD (Long Integer). Any other datatype will cause the function to return an error	This function's limitations, in terms of datatypes it will accept, make it difficult to use in many situations. It can write only String or Long Integer data to the Registry
Return Value	Long	Error code	adhcAccErrSuccess, adhcAccErrRegTypeNotSupported, adhcAccErrRegKeyNotFound, or adhcAccErrRegCantSetValue

As you can see in Table 19.7, adh_accRegWriteVal is limited in the types of data it can write to the Registry. If you need to write any values besides strings or Long Integers, you'll have to use the Windows API directly. Even in this example we've limited the functionality because of this: the values in the Registry that track the next tip to be shown and whether or not to show tips at all are stored as binary values. Although you can read the values with adh_accRegGetVal, you cannot write them out with adh_accRegWriteVal. (See Figure 19.7 for the exact Registry key and values. The adh-GetTipInfo procedure in basTips retrieves this information.) If you want to modify the example to allow you to save the values, you'll need to use the Windows API.

Retrieving the Name of a Registry Subkey

You may need at times to retrieve the name of a Registry subkey associated with a given key, given the subkey's index. For example, frmSoundList in CH19.MDB, shown in Figure 19.9, retrieves a list of all the default system events. Figure 19.10 shows those events as they appear in the Registry. (Look in basGetSoundList for more information.) To call adh_accRegGetKey, use the syntax shown in Table 19.8.

TABLE 19.8   Syntax for Calling adh_accRegGetKey

Parameter	Type	Description	Comments
hkeyRoot	Long	Key to use as the root	Use one of the constants defined in basDeclares: adhcHKEY_LOCAL_MACHINE or adhcHKEY_CURRENT_USER, normally
strSubKey	String	Path to the key in question	Do not include the root key name or a leading backslash (\)
lngSubKey	Long	Zero-based index of the subkey name to retrieve	
strName	String	Buffer to contain the subkey name	Must be large enough to contain the string before you call the function (Use the Space function to "puff" it out, or use a fixed-length string.)
lngMaxLen	Long	Maximum characters in the output buffer	Initializes the output buffer with this much space before calling the function if you're retrieving text, or places the length of the buffer if you're retrieving a numeric type (You can use the Len function to find the length of the datatype.)
Return Value	Long	Error code	adhcAccErrSuccess, adhcAccErrKeyNotFound, or adhcAccErrSubkeyNotFound

FIGURE 19.9

frmSoundList retrieves a list of all the default system events and plays the associated sounds.

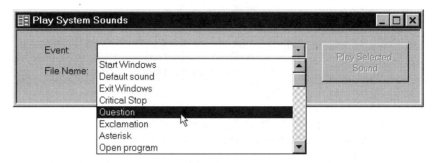

FIGURE 19.10

Default system events in the Registry

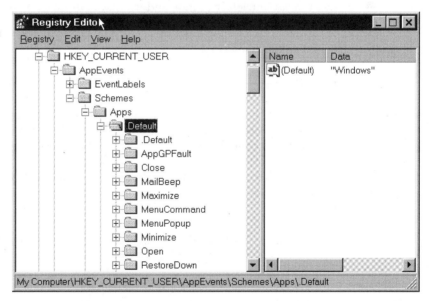

NOTE If your computer does not support sound, you will not be able to test frm-SoundList. If it can't find the requisite Registry keys, it will fail and display an alert. In order for the keys to exist, you must have the hardware installed, and you must have selected a sound scheme. Run the Control Panel applet, Sounds, to set up the sound scheme.

TIP The procedure that fills the combo box is actually a bit more complex than we've let on—it must do more than just retrieve the list of event names. Each event name has an associated "friendly" name, stored under a different key in the Registry. The example retrieves those friendly names and places them in the combo. You may find perusing the code useful as a learning tool.

The following code fragment shows the loop that retrieves all the default event subkeys. In this example adhcRegSoundList has been defined as

```
Const adhcRegSoundList = "AppEvents\Schemes\Apps\.Default"
```

and atypSounds is an array of data structures. In those data structures, one of the elements is strUnfriendlyName, and it's that item this loop is attempting to fill.

```
For intI = 0 To lngSubKeys - 1
    With atypSounds(intI)
      ' Initialize the buffer.
      .strUnfriendlyName = Space(adhcMaxSize)

      ' Given an index (intI), get the particular key.
      lngRetval = adh_accRegGetKey(adhcHKEY_CURRENT_USER, _
       adhcRegSoundList, intI, .strUnfriendlyName, _
       adhcMaxSize)
      If lngRetval <> adhcAccErrSuccess Then
          Err.Raise lngRetval
      End If
      ' Trim off extra junk at the end.
      .strUnfriendlyName = adhTrimNull(.strUnfriendlyName)

      ' Now go retrieve the friendly name. See
      ' basGetSoundList for the gory details.
    End With
Next intI
```

Creating a New Key

The final Registry-focused procedure in MSACCESS.EXE is also the simplest to use. It allows you to create a new key in the Registry. The adh_accRegWriteKey function is as user friendly as a function can be: it creates the key, and if the key is nested beneath other keys that need to be created, it creates those keys as well. In addition, if the key already exists, the function just leaves it alone.

For example, to create this scenario:

```
HKEY_CURRENT_USER
    Software
        MCW Technologies
            Marketing
                Application
```

you could call adh_accRegWriteKey with the following parameters:

```
lngRetval = adh_accRegWriteKey(adhcHKEY_CURRENT_USER, _
    "Software\MCW Technologies\Marketing\Application", "")
```

Windows will create the Application key, as well as any keys above it in the Registry that it must create in order to supply the path you've requested. Figure 19.11 shows the Registry after calling the code in the example. Table 19.9 shows the syntax for calling adh_accRegWriteKey.

FIGURE 19.11

Call adh_accRegWriteKey to create new Registry keys.

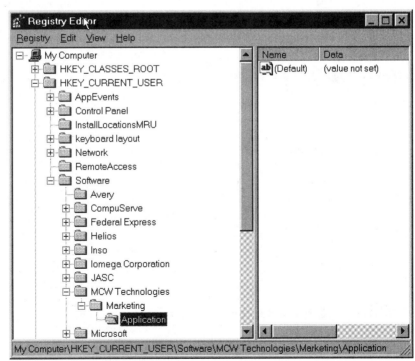

TABLE 19.9 Syntax for Calling adh_accRegWriteKey

Parameter	Type	Description	Comments
hkeyRoot	Long	Key to use as the root	Use one of the constants defined in basDeclares: adhcHKEY_LOCAL_MACHINE or adhcHKEY_CURRENT_USER, normally
strSubKey	String	Full path of the key you want to create	Do not include the root key name or a leading backslash (\). Windows will create any keys necessary to get to your new key if they don't already exist
strClass	String	Specifies the class (object type) of this key. Ignored if the key already exists. Normally unused	The Microsoft documentation (if you look up the RegCreateKeyEx API function) for this parameter is cloudy, to say the least. Until you can find more information about what this parameter is really for, perhaps it's best to leave it as an empty string
Return Value	Long	Error code	Either adhcAccErrSuccess or adhcAccErrRegCantCreateKey

Font-Handling Functions

If you need to supply users with a list of available fonts and their sizes, MSACCESS.EXE can help you out. Performing this task from Access without external help is difficult, if not impossible, because it requires a callback function, and that technique is not available from VBA in Office. MSACCESS.EXE provides functions to retrieve the count of installed fonts; a list of those fonts; and for each raster (bitmapped) font, a count of the available sizes and a list of those sizes. The next few sections cover the use of these functions. In addition, we've provided a sample form (frmListFonts in CH19.MDB) that ties together all these techniques. Because these topics will be much clearer with a real example to discuss, you might want to take a moment to exercise frmListFonts before digging into this material. Figure 19.12 shows the form in use.

Retrieving a List of Fonts

MSACCESS.EXE provides two functions you need in order to fill an array with a list of all the available fonts. The adh_accGetFontCount function returns the number of fonts, and adh_accGetFontList fills a passed array with the names of all those fonts. The code attached to frmListFonts' Open event calls both of these functions

FIGURE 19.12
frmListFonts allows you
to view any font in any
available point size.

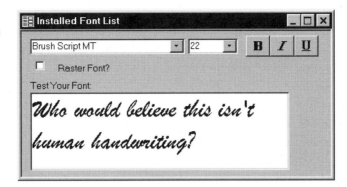

directly in order to fill the combo box on the form with a list of fonts. List-ing 19.3
shows the portion of the code that handles this process.

Listing 19.3

```
Dim hDC As Long
hdc = adh_apiCreateIC("DISPLAY", "", "", 0&)
If hdc <> 0 Then
    mlngCountFonts = adh_accGetFontCount(hdc)
    If mlngCountFonts > 0 Then
        ReDim mafiFonts(0 To mlngCountFonts - 1)
        mlngCountFonts = adh_accGetFontList(hdc, _
         mafiFonts())
        ' Get rid of the trailing null and spaces NOW.
        For intI = 0 To mlngCountFonts - 1
            mafiFonts(intI).strName = _
             adhTrimNull((mafiFonts(intI).strName))
        Next intI
    End If
End If
'
' the code continues...
'
Call adh_apiDeleteDC(hDC)
hDC = 0
```

As the first step when you work with fonts, you must retrieve information about
the current display device. To do so, call the Windows API function CreateIC (create
information context) or CreateDC (create device context). Either will do in this case
because you're retrieving information only about the display device. Were you

interested in modifying any of the device settings, you'd be forced to use CreateDC, which requires a bit more overhead than CreateIC. To get the handle you need, call CreateIC (aliased as adh_apiCreateIC in the example), sending to it the name of the device driver (DISPLAY, in this case), with all the other parameters set to empty strings or 0. This will retrieve a device handle referring to the current display device, as shown in the following code fragment:

```
Dim hDC As Long

hDC = adh_apiCreateIC("DISPLAY", "", "", 0&)
```

Once you have a device context, you can request the number of installed fonts from MSACCESS.EXE. To call adh_accGetFontCount, just send it the device context as a parameter, and it will return the number of fonts installed for that device:

```
If hDC <> 0 Then
    intFonts = adh_accGetFontCount(hDC)
```

Once you have the number of installed fonts, you can create an array to hold the list. That array will need to be made up of elements of the type adhFontInfo, as shown here:

```
Type adhFontInfo
    fRasterFont As Long
    strName As String * 32
End Type
```

where each element stores a True or False value, indicating whether or not the font is a raster font, as well as the name of the font. The code to resize the array looks like this:

```
ReDim mafiFonts(0 To intFonts - 1)
```

To fill in the list of font information, call adh_accGetFontList, passing to it the device context and the array. The function returns the actual number of fonts it filled in and actually fills in the entire array:

```
intFonts = adh_accGetFontList(hDC, mafiFonts())
```

As the final step in this process, you need to deal with the extra characters the function call left in the array. Because the adh_accGetFontList function treats the strings as though they were null terminated and Access doesn't deal well with null-terminated strings, the sample function here includes a pass through all the elements of the array, truncating them at the first null character each contains:

```
' Get rid of the trailing null and spaces now.
```

```
For intI = 0 To mlngCountFonts - 1
    mafiFonts(intI).strName = _
     adhTrimNull((mafiFonts(intI).strName))
Next intI
```

Last but not least, you must always release the device (or information) context handle when you're done with it. Windows maintains only a fixed number of these handles, so you must always conclude with code like this:

```
Call adh_apiDeleteDC(hDC)
hDC = 0
```

This code both releases the handle and resets its value back to 0 so subsequent code that checks the value of hDC knows it doesn't represent a device context anymore.

Retrieving a List of Sizes

For TrueType fonts, Windows generally presents you with a standardized list of font sizes:

```
8,9,10,11,12,14,16,18,20,22,24,26,28,36,48,72
```

The code attached to frmListFonts maintains an array, maintTTSizes, that contains those standard sizes. For raster fonts, however, it is the font itself that determines the available sizes. Therefore, for raster fonts, the code needs to retrieve the list of specific sizes for the font. The procedure in Listing 19.4, FillFontSizes, fills the global array malngRasterSizes with the available font sizes for the specified font.

Listing 19.4

```
Private Sub FillFontSizes(hdc As Long, _
 ByVal varFaceName As Variant)

    Dim strName As String

    If IsNull(varFaceName) Then
        Erase malngRasterSizes
        Exit Sub
    End If
    strName = CStr(varFaceName)
    mlngCountRasterSizes = adh_accGetSizeCount(hdc, strName)
    If mlngCountRasterSizes > 0 Then
        ReDim malngRasterSizes(0 To mlngCountRasterSizes - 1)
        mlngCountRasterSizes = adh_accGetSizeList(hdc, _
```

```
        strName, malngRasterSizes())
    End If
End Sub
```

To call FillFontSizes, you pass to it the device context you previously created and the name of the specific font. If the face name is null, of course, the procedure can't do its work and will need to empty out the array and just exit.

```
If IsNull(varFaceName) Then
    Erase malngRasterSizes
    Exit Sub
End If
```

Next, the procedure needs to determine how many sizes are available for the given font. To do this it can call the adh_accGetSizeCount function provided in MSACCESS.EXE. This function takes the device context and a font name and returns the number of available font sizes:

```
strName = CStr(varFaceName)
mlngCountRasterSizes = adh_accGetSizeCount(hdc, strName)
```

Once you have the number of fonts, all you need to do is redimension the global array to be large enough to contain the list of font sizes and then retrieve them. To fill the array with the list of available font sizes, you can call the adh_accGetSizeList function in MSACCESS.EXE:

```
If mlngCountRasterSizes > 0 Then
    ReDim malngRasterSizes(0 To mlngCountRasterSizes - 1)
    mlngCountRasterSizes = adh_accGetSizeList(hdc, _
      strName, malngRasterSizes())
End If
```

That's basically all there is to frmListFonts. When the user chooses a font from the list, the AfterUpdate event code requeries the list containing the available sizes for that font. In addition, it sets the properties of the text box that displays the same text to match the chosen values.

Finding the Screen Size for Text in a Given Font

At times you'll need to know the screen size for a piece of text, given a font name, its size, and its attributes. For example, you might want to set the size of a text box so that it just fits the text inside it, in which case you need to know how much space the text will take up. Or, imagine you'd like to set the width of a combo box so that it can display all the text of all its items. The MSACCESS.EXE exported function, adh_accTwipsFromFont, can do the job for you. Figure 19.13 shows a sample form (frmFontWidth) that calculates the width of the text for each value in a combo box's list and resizes the combo to match, based on the font being used in the control.

FIGURE 19.13

Calculate the maximum width of items in a combo box's list and resize accordingly.

To call adh_accTwipsFromFont, use the syntax shown in Table 19.10.

TABLE 19.10 Syntax for Calling adh_accTwipsFromFont

Parameter	Type	Description	Comments
strFontName	String	Name of the font	Must match one of the installed font names, or Windows will make a substitution
lngSize	Long	Size, in points (as shown in the font size drop-down list in Access)	The point size must be between 1 and 127
lngWeight	Long	Weight of the font, chosen from the following list: 100 (Thin), 200 (Extra Light), 300 (Light), 400 (Normal), 500 (Medium), 600 (Semi-bold), 700 (Bold), 800 (Extra Bold), 900 (Heavy)	
fItalic	Long	Logical value indicating whether or not the text is italicized	

TABLE 19.10 Syntax for Calling adh_accTwipsFromFont (continued)

Parameter	Type	Description	Comments
fUnderline	Long	Logical value indicating whether or not the text is underlined	
lngChars	Long	To use the average character width for the font in the calculations, specify the number of characters in this parameter	Fill in either strCaption or lngChars. If you fill in both, lngChars will take priority. This parameter interacts with the cchUseMaxWidth parameter: the function will use the maximum character width for the cchUseMaxWidth of the characters and use the average width for the rest, up to lngChars. Unless you fill in this parameter, the function disregards the value in cchUseMaxWidth
strCaption	String	Text for which you wish to calculate the width and height. Either supply the text here (the function will calculate the actual width, based on your character string) or supply a length in the lngChars parameter (the function will use the average character width)	
cchUseMaxWidth	Long	Number of characters for which you'd like to use the maximum character width for the font when making calculations	If you supply a value for lngChars, the function will use the average character width for the requested font when making its calculations. Supply a value in this parameter to specify for how many of those characters you'd like to use the maximum character width. This is useful if you want to display abbreviations, part numbers, and so on, that are short and must display all the characters, no matter what. The function will use the maximum character width for the first cchUseMaxChars characters and the average width for lngChars—cchUseMaxChars characters. This parameter is ignored if lngChars isn't greater than 0

TABLE 19.10 Syntax for Calling adh_accTwipsFromFont (continued)

Parameter	Type	Description	Comments
lngWidth	Long	Filled in by the function with the width, in twips, of the text	This value seems always to be a bit short, based on experimentation in Access. We found that multiplying it by 1.1 (or perhaps a value even closer to 1.0) makes the value match reality a little more closely. You may need to experiment to get this value exactly right
lngHeight	Long	Filled in by the function with the height, in twips, of the text	
Return Value	Long	True if the function succeeded, False otherwise	

The sample form, frmFontWidth, uses the code in Listing 19.5 to set the size for the combo box, based on the values in the CompanyName field of tblCustomers. It loops through each item in the combo's list, calling adh_accTwipsFromFont with the attributes of the control's font, and sets the width of the combo box to match the maximum width of the field. (For more information on the GetPixelsPerTwip function, used in this example to add in the width of the vertical scrollbar, see Chapter 8's discussion of resizing/rescaling forms at run time.)

Listing 19.5

```
Function GetMaxWidth(ctl As Control)
    Dim lngMax As Long
    Dim lngWidth As Long
    Dim intOK As Integer
    Dim strFont As String
    Dim intWeight As Integer
    Dim fItalic As Boolean
    Dim fUnderline As Boolean
    Dim lngHeight As Long
    Dim intSize As Integer
    Dim strText As String
    Dim intI As Integer
```

```
With ctl
    intSize = .FontSize
    strFont = .FontName
    intWeight = .FontWeight
    fItalic = .FontItalic
    fUnderline = .FontUnderline
End With
For intI = 0 To ctl.ListCount - 1
    strText = ctl.Column(0, intI)
    intOK = adh_accTwipsFromFont(strFont, intSize, _
     intWeight, fItalic, fUnderline, 0, strText, _
     False, lngWidth, lngHeight)
    If intOK Then
        If lngWidth > lngMax Then
            lngMax = lngWidth
        End If
    End If
Next intI
' Add in the width of the scrollbar, which we get in pixels.
' Convert it to twips for use in Access.
GetMaxWidth = lngMax * ahdcAdjustForScreen + _
 GetSystemMetrics(SM_CXVSCROLL) / GetPixelsPerTwip()
End Function
```

Object-Handling Functions

Many of the Access Wizards need to display lists of database objects. There are many factors to take into account when deciding which items you want to see on those lists: Are system objects visible? Are hidden objects visible? Exactly which types of queries do you want to see? Which kinds of tables (local, ISAM, ODBC) do you want to see?

You can make all these decisions using DAO (as shown in Chapter 6) to provide the list, but it's a lot of work and can be slow. To simplify this process, MSACCESS.EXE includes four functions to help you supply lists of objects. You can retrieve a list of names of objects and sort that list. You can retrieve a list of data structures that include names and object types, and you can sort that list. Each of the next sections details one of the four functions.

Retrieving a List of Object Names

If you need to provide a list of object names in your applications, you can certainly use DAO to create the list. (See Chapter 6 for more information.) On the other hand, MSACCESS.EXE makes it easy: you specify the object type and set some flags describing which subsets of that object you want, and the function fills in an array with a list of the items.

The sample form, frmDBCTab, in CH19.MDB (see Figure 19.14), is similar to frmDBCTab from CH06.MDB. Instead of using DAO to fill its lists, however, it uses MSACCESS.EXE, calling the adh_accGetObjNames function. Table 19.11 describes the syntax for calling adh_accGetObjNames.

FIGURE 19.14

frmDBC, using MS-ACCESS.EXE rather than DAO to fill itself

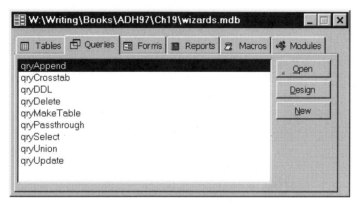

TABLE 19.11 Syntax for Calling adh_accGetObjNames

Parameter	Type	Description	Comments
varWrk	Variant	Reference to the workspace containing the database from which you want to retrieve object names	
varDB	Variant	Reference to the database from which you want to retrieve object names	
intObjType	Integer	One of the standard object types: acTable, acQuery, acForm, acReport, acMacro, acModule	

TABLE 19.11 Syntax for Calling adh_accGetObjNames (continued)

Parameter	Type	Description	Comments
lngFlags	Long	One or more values, combined with the Or operator, indicating which subset of objects you want to retrieve. For tables, use one or more of adhcBitTblLocal, adhcBitTblAttachedISAM, adhcBitTblAttachedODBC, and adhcBitTblAll. For queries, use the standard DAO Type constants (dbQSelect, dbQCrossTab, and so on), passed through the adhcvtQryTypeToBitfunction, or use adhcBitQryAll to get all queries. For any type of object, use adhcBitObjSystem and adhcBitObjHidden to control the display of Hidden and System objects	
astrObjects	String array	On return, filled in with the list of objects you requested	Before you call the function, you must dimension the array to hold as many elements as the maximum number of items to be returned. That is, if you're asking for a subset of the queries, make the array large enough to hold all the queries. On return, the intItemsFilled parameter will contain the number of items the function actually placed into the array, so you can dimension the array again at that point
intStart	Integer	Zero-based index, indicating where to start placing items into the array	Useful if you need to put more than one type of object into the array (if you want to list tables and queries at the same time, for instance)

TABLE 19.11 Syntax for Calling adh_accGetObjNames (continued)

Parameter	Type	Description	Comments
intItemsFilled	Integer	Filled in, on return, with the number of items the function placed into the array	If this value ends up being more than you'd prepared the array to hold, you're pretty much guaranteed to crash. Make sure you dimension astrObjects large enough to hold all possible items
Return Value	Long	adhcAccErrSuccess or adhcAccErrUnknown	

In frmDBCTab, look in the ListObjects list-filling function to find the interesting code. Listing 19.6, excerpted from the ListObjects procedure in frmDBCTab's class module, shows the initialization step of the function.

Listing 19.6

```
Dim db As Database
Static astrItems() As String
Static lngCount As Integer
Dim lngFlags As Long
Dim intSize As Integer

Select Case intCode
    Case acLBInitialize
        Set db = CurrentDb()

        ' Fill in astrItems() with the list of
        ' object names.
        lngCount = db.Containers(GetContainer( _
        Me!tabObjects)).Documents.Count
        If lngCount > 0 Then
            ' Set up the array.  It might be too
            ' many elements, but the code will resize
            ' the array at the end.
            ReDim astrItems(0 To lngCount - 1)

            ' Set up the flags, so you just open the
            ' items you want.  Assume you want all the
            ' tables (attached or otherwise), and then
```

```
' check on whether or not to show
' hidden/system objects.
Select Case Me!tabObjects
    Case acTable
        lngFlags = adhGetAppInfo(adhcBitTblAll)
    Case acQuery
        lngFlags = adhGetAppInfo(adhcBitQryAll)
    Case Else
        lngFlags = adhGetAppInfo(0)
End Select
' Now ask MSACCESS.EXE to fill in the array with
' the selected items.
Call adh_accGetObjNames(DBEngine(0), db, _
 (Me!tabObjects), lngFlags, astrItems(), _
 0, lngCount)
' If it returned any items, resize the array to
' just the right size.
If lngCount > 0 Then
    ReDim Preserve astrItems(0 To lngCount - 1)
    Call adh_accSortStringArray(astrItems())
End If
' code continues...
```

This code works in a series of steps that you'll also need to follow when using adh_accGetObjNames in your own applications:

1. **Dimension the array:** The array must be able to hold enough rows for all possible items. In this case, the code just retrieves the count of documents in the appropriate container. (The GetContainer function simply converts container numbers into the appropriate names.) Of course, when it gets the count of documents in the Tables container, it's going to get tabledefs and querydefs, but that's not a problem. Once the code has executed, you'll resize the array to just the right size.

```
Static astrItems() As String
' ...
lngCount = db.Containers(GetContainer( _
 Me!tabObjects)).Documents.Count
If lngCount > 0 Then
    ReDim astrItems(0 To lngCount - 1)
    ' code continues...
```

2. **Set the flags correctly:** In this example you want to see all items, honoring the system settings (Show System Objects/Show Hidden Objects). Therefore, call the adhGetAppInfo function, which combines its incoming parameter

with the appropriate flags (adhcBitObjHidden and adhcBitObjSystem) indicating whether or not to show system and hidden objects.

```
' From the list-filling function...
Select Case Me!tabObjects
    Case acTable
        lngFlags = adhGetAppInfo(adhcBitTblAll)
    Case acQuery
        lngFlags = adhGetAppInfo(adhcBitQryAll)
    Case Else
        lngFlags = adhGetAppInfo(0)
End Select
' the code continues...

Function adhGetAppInfo(lngFlags As Long) As Long
    ' Set the output based on whether or not
    ' you've selected to see hidden/system objects.
    If Application.GetOption("Show Hidden Objects") Then
        lngFlags = lngFlags Or adhcBitObjHidden
    Else
        lngFlags = lngFlags And Not adhcBitObjHidden
    End If
    If Application.GetOption("Show System Objects") Then
        lngFlags = lngFlags Or adhcBitObjSystem
    Else
        lngFlags = lngFlags And Not adhcBitObjSystem
    End If
    adhGetAppInfo = lngFlags
End Function
```

TIP

MSACCESS.EXE does not use the built-in DAO constants (dbQSelect, dbQCrosstab, and so on) to specify the query types you want to see. Internally, it uses a slightly different value to flag each query type. To convert from the normal query types to the flags MSACCESS.EXE expects to find, use the adhCvtQryTypeToBit function, in basDeclares. This function takes in DAO constants and returns the appropriate MSACCESS.EXE flag value.

3. **Call adh_accGetObjNames:** Now that everything is all set up, call the function. This fills lngCount with the number of items the function actually placed into the array.

```
Call adh_accGetObjNames(DBEngine(0), db, _
 (Me!tabObjects), lngFlags, astrItems(), _
 0, lngCount)
```

4. **Resize the array:** Once you've placed the data in the array, you must resize it so that it's just large enough to hold the items placed in it. If you're not going to sort it or you're going to add more elements, you can skip this step, but if you're sorting the array, this step is *crucial*. (See the next section for information on sorting the array.)

```
If lngCount > 0 Then
    ReDim Preserve astrItems(0 To lngCount - 1)
    Call adh_accSortStringArray(astrItems())
End If
```

Sorting a String Array

To support the adh_accGetObjNames function, MSACCESS.EXE includes adh_accSortStringArray. This function is useful in its own right: it can sort any array of strings you care to send it, not just object names.

Calling adh_accSortStringArray is simple: pass it an array filled with strings, and it will sort them in place. It returns adhcAccErrUnknown if anything goes wrong or adhcAccErrSuccess if it succeeds. You can use this function with any array of strings.

> **WARNING** If you pass an array to adh_accSortStringArray that has been dimensioned to contain more elements than it actually contains, the sort procedure will become confused and return your array with the empty elements sorted incorrectly. Make sure you redimension your array correctly before calling adh_accSortStringArray.

Retrieving a List of Objects and Their Types

At times you'll need to retrieve lists of multiple object types, stored in the same array, and be able to discern between them (as when the Wizards provide a list of tables and queries in the same control). MSACCESS.EXE includes a function, adh_accGetDbObjList, that fills an array with data structures:

```
Type adhDBObj
    intObjType As Integer
    strName As String
    lngFlags As Long
End Type
```

Because this structure contains both the object's name and its type, you can tell the different object types apart once they're in your array.

> **NOTE**
> Although this structure contains a lngFlags field, MSACCESS.EXE disregards this field and always places a value of 0 into it. You can't remove it from the structure, or the function call won't work, but you also shouldn't use the field.

The sample form, frmDBObjList, shown in Figure 19.15, allows you to experiment with all the options available for the lngFlags parameter to adh_accGetDBObjList. (The flags work just the same for adh_accGetObjNames, of course.) As you make choices, the form requeries the list box and shows the items in the array that has been filled by adh_accGetDBObjList.

FIGURE 19.15

Use frmDBObjList to test the functions that create lists of objects.

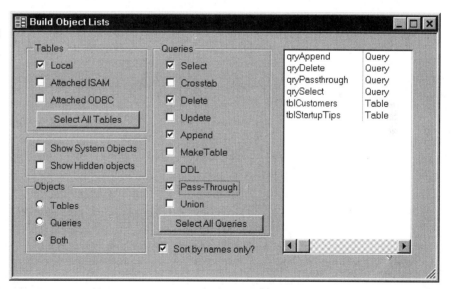

Table 19.12 shows the syntax you use to call adh_accGetDBObjList. You may find it interesting to dig in and see how frmDBObjList works, but in general, it follows the same set of steps outlined for working with adh_accGetObjNames.

TABLE 19.12 Syntax for Calling adh_accGetDBObjList

Parameter	Type	Description	Comments
varWrk	Variant	Reference to the workspace containing the database from which you want to retrieve object names	
varDB	Variant	Reference to the database from which you want to retrieve object names	
intObjType	Integer	One of the standard object types: acTable, acQuery, acForm, acReport, acMacro, acModule	
lngFlags	Long	One or more values, combined with the Or operator, indicating which subset of objects you want to retrieve. For tables, use one or more of adhcBitTblLocal, adhcBitTblAttachedISAM, adhcBitTblAttachedODBC, and adhcBitTblAll. For queries, use the standard DAO Type constants (dbQSelect, dbQCrossTab, and so on), passed through the adhcvtQry-TypeToBit function, or use adhcBitQryAll to get all queries. For any type of object, use adhcBitObj-System and adhcBitObj-Hidden to control the display of Hidden and System objects	

TABLE 19.12 Syntax for Calling adh_accGetDBObjList (continued)

Parameter	Type	Description	Comments
atypObjects	Array of glrDBObj data structures	On return, filled in with the list of objects you requested	You must dimension the array, before you call this function, to hold as many elements as the maximum number of items to be returned. That is, if you're asking for a subset of the queries, make the array large enough to hold all the queries. On return, the intItemsFilled parameter will contain the number of items the function actually placed into the array, so you can dimension the array again at that point
intStart	Integer	Zero-based index, indicating where to start placing items into the array	Useful if you need to put more than one type of object into the array (if you want to list tables and queries at the same time, for instance)
intItemsFilled	Integer	Filled in, on return, with the number of items the function placed into the array	If this value ends up being more than you'd prepared the array to hold, you're pretty much guaranteed to crash. Make sure you dimension atypObjects large enough to hold all possible items
Return Value	Long	adhcAccErrSuccess or adhcAccErrUnknown	

Sorting the Array of DBObj Structures

To sort the array of structures, MSACCESS.EXE provides the adh_accSortDBObjArray function. This function is simple to call: pass to it an array of adhDBObj structures all filled in and a Boolean flag, fNamesOnly, indicating whether you want to sort by object type and then names, or just by names. For example:

```
fSuccess = adh_accSortDBObjArray(atypNames(), True)
```

sorts atypNames in order of names only, disregarding the object types. If you pass False for the fNamesOnly parameter, the function sorts the array first by object type and then by name. Try out this feature on frmDBObjList (check and uncheck the Sort by Names Only? check box) to get a feel for the differences. The function returns either adhcAccErrSuccess or adhcAccErrUnknown, indicating the success or failure of the function.

> **WARNING**
> If you pass an array that is dimensioned to hold more elements than adh_acc-GetDBObjList actually placed into the array to adh_accSortDBObjArray, MSACCESS.EXE may crash. Make sure you redimension your array to the correct size after the call to adh_accGetDBObjList to avoid this crash.

Miscellaneous Functions

To round out your whirlwind tour of functions exported by MSACCESS.EXE, this final section includes a few functions that didn't fit any of the other categories. These functions include retrieving the current national language, using toolbar bitmaps in your own applications, and some miscellaneous programming tidbits, like these:

- Is a particular string a valid identifier?
- Does a specified global function already exist?
- Is an object's record source a table, a query, or a SQL string?

Retrieving National Language Info

You may have a need to find out the national language version of Access that's currently running, and that information isn't easy to recover using VBA alone. MSACCESS.EXE exports a simple function, adh_accGetLanguage, that can tell you which version of Access is currently running. It returns a number, indicating the current language. Table 19.13 lists some of the language code numbers defined by Windows—you can figure out which language is current using the values in this table, along with the constants provided in basDeclares.

TABLE 19.13 A Subset of Windows Language Codes

ID	Language	ID	Language
1046	Brazilian Portuguese	2058	Mexican Spanish
3084	Canadian French	1045	Polish
1034	Castilian Spanish	2070	Portuguese
1027	Catalan	1048	Romanian
1050	Croato-Serbian (Latin)	1049	Russian
1029	Czech	2074	Serbo-Croatian (Cyrillic)
1030	Danish	2052	Simplified Chinese
1043	Dutch	1051	Slovak
1035	Finnish	1053	Swedish
1036	French	4108	Swiss French
1031	German	2055	Swiss German
1032	Greek	2064	Swiss Italian
1037	Hebrew	1054	Thai
1038	Hungarian	1028	Traditional Chinese
1039	Icelandic	1055	Turkish
1040	Italian	2057	U.K. English
1041	Japanese	1033	U.S. English
1042	Korean	1056	Urdu

Although it's tricky to retrieve this information using API calls directly from Access, it is possible. This function makes it simple. To find out the language version, just call adh_accGetLanguage directly, perhaps like this:

```
Select Case adh_accGetLanguage()
    Case adhcUSEnglish
        ' You're running the US version
    Case adhcFrench
```

```
        ' You're running the French version
      ' and so on...
End Select
```

Retrieving Toolbar Bitmaps

As you've noticed if you've modified the button face of a toolbar button, Access provides a limited set of bitmaps from which to choose. More bitmaps are available for you to use on buttons, through the Button Wizard.

Office 97 stores this collection of bitmaps as a single "slab" in one of its DLLs. Storing the bitmaps this way saves on graphics resources, which are in short enough supply with major Windows applications running! In addition, Access provides its own set of button bitmaps.

To do its work, the Button Builder required some method of retrieving a single bitmap from the "slab," and MSACCESS.EXE provides the code necessary to retrieve that bitmap. To make it possible to use the same bitmaps on all screen resolutions, the function returns a device-independent bitmap. The function, adh_accGetTBDib, fills a buffer with the bytes of data. The function returns 0 if it fails for any reason and a nonzero value if it succeeds.

To add its own set of bitmaps to the ones Office supplies, the Access Wizards use a table (tblTBPictures in CH19.MDB) that includes offsets into the slab of images mentioned above, and actual bitmaps (stored in the table) for other images. You need this table, listing all the pictures and their ID values (which indicate to the function where to start pulling data, inside the bitmap), in order to call adh_accGetTBDib. You must include tblTbPictures in any application for which you'd like to supply this functionality.

> **WARNING**
>
> Because you're including this table in your application, you must be extremely careful to keep the table updated to match the current version of Access. The table we've supplied matches Access 97. Anytime the version of Access changes, you'll need to import bw_TblPictures from whichever library it's currently in. (In Access 97, it's in WZMAIN80.MDA.) Because Microsoft maintains complete control over both the table and the bitmap "slab," you have to make sure you have them synchronized. You could, of course, just link the table bw_TblPictures from WZMAIN80.MDA, rename the link to tblTBPictures, and use it externally. The problem with this solution is that you can't ship WZMAIN80.MDA with applications you distribute using the run-time application. If you import the table, you aren't fighting that restriction. We decided to import the table and not worry about the distribution problems.

Table 19.14 describes the three parameters for adh_accGetTBDib.

TABLE 19.14 Parameters for adh_accGetTBDib

Parameter	Datatype	Description
lngBMP	Long	Value from the TBBitmapID column in tblTBPictures, indicating which bitmap to retrieve
fLarge	Long	Flag: True to use large bitmaps, False to use small bitmaps
abytBuffer	Array of bytes	Buffer to hold the bitmap information

It's up to you to make sure strBuf is large enough to hold all the bitmap information before you call adh_accGetTBDib. We recommend you use the Space function to ensure that it's initialized to the correct size. For large bitmaps you'll need 488 characters. For small bitmaps you'll need 296 characters. You might use code like the following to set this up:

```
Const adhcLargeBitmapSize = 488
Const adhcSmallBitmapSize = 296

' Arbitrarily use small pictures, this time.
fUseLargePictures = False

strPictureData = Space(IIf(fUseLargePictures, _
 adhcLargeBitmapSize, adhcSmallBitmapSize))
```

To retrieve a specific bitmap from the array of bitmaps in the bitmap slab, you need to find the correct row in tblTBPictures, retrieve the TBBitmapID value from that row, and then call adh_accGetTBDib. Listing 19.7 shows code you could use to retrieve a bitmap and use the bitmap to replace the picture on a specific button.

Listing 19.7

```
Private Sub RetrieveDIB(ctl As Control, _
 lngPictureID As Long)
    Dim fUseLargePictures As Integer
    Dim abytBuffer() As Byte
    Dim varRetval As Variant
    Dim db As Database
    Dim rst As Recordset
```

```
Const adhcLargeBitmapSize = 488
Const adhcSmallBitmapSize = 296

    ' Arbitrarily use large pictures.
    fUseLargePictures = True

    Set db = CurrentDb()
    Set rst = db.OpenRecordset("Select PictureData, " & _
     "TBBitmapID from tblTBPictures where PictureID = " & _
     (lngPictureID), dbOpenSnapShot)

    ' If there is a row with the selected ID, then
    ' load that picture.
    If Not rst.EOF Then
        If Not IsNull(rst!TBBitmapID) Then
            ReDim abytBuffer(0 To IIf(fUseLargePictures, _
             adhcLargeBitmapSize, adhcSmallBitmapSize) - 1)
            If adh_accGetTbDIB(rst!TBBitmapID, _
             fUseLargePictures, abytBuffer()) Then
                ctl.PictureData = abytBuffer()
            End If
        Else
            ctl.PictureData = rst!PictureData
        End If
        rst.Close
    End If
End Sub
```

In the example code, you first need to find a particular row in tblTBPictures, given the primary key value for a row. The following code does that for you:

```
Set db = CurrentDb()
Set rst = db.OpenRecordset("Select PictureData, " & _
 "TBBitmapID from tblTBPictures where PictureID = " & _
 (lngPictureID), dbOpenSnapShot)
```

If you've found the row, you need to check the TBBitmapID column, because some of the rows don't pertain to data in the bitmap array but actually store their bitmap information in the PictureData column. For those rows you just copy the data directly out of the table instead of retrieving it from the bitmap slab:

```
If Not rst.EOF Then
    If Not IsNull(rst!TBBitmapID) Then
```

```
        ReDim abytBuffer(0 To IIf(fUseLargePictures, _
         adhcLargeBitmapSize, adhcSmallBitmapSize) - 1)
        If adh_accGetTbDIB(rst!TBBitmapID, _
         fUseLargePictures, abytBuffer()) Then
            ctl.PictureData = abytBuffer()
        End If
    Else
        ctl.PictureData = rst!PictureData
    End If
    rst.Close
End If
```

In either case, once the procedure has retrieved the data, it places it on the button's face by assigning it to the button's PictureData property.

Using adh_accGetTBDib

If you've used the Command Button Wizard, you know it supplies you with a list box full of pictures you can place on a button. The Wizard's main problem is that you can work with only a single button and its properties at a time. If you need to change the pictures for buttons you've already created, Access does provide a button picture builder, but going through the steps of using the builder for each button can be tedious. Figure 19.16 shows the Command Button Wizard in action.

We've created a small tool, frmButtonPix in CH19.MDB, that can take care of this task for you. Using the code shown in Listing 19.7, it can place any picture from tblTBPictures onto any button on any form you have loaded. This can be a very useful design-time tool, and it works fine at run time, too. Figure 19.17 shows frmButtonPix running.

> **NOTE**
>
> If you wish to use frmButtonPix to change the picture on a button permanently, you need to open the form containing that button in Design view, use frmButtonPix to change the button face, and then save the changed form. Changes made to forms at run time are not saved with the form.

Because there's no simple way for frmButtonPix to know that you've loaded or closed forms around it, we've supplied the Refill Lists button on the form. This button allows you to change which forms are currently loaded and then tell frmButtonPix about it.

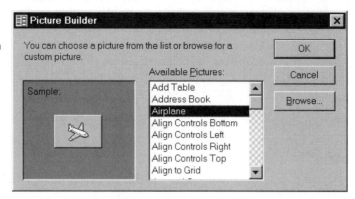

FIGURE 19.16

The Command Button Wizard supplies you with a choice of bitmaps for your buttons.

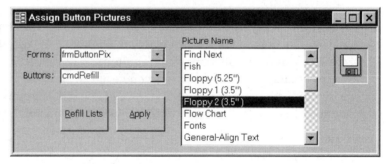

FIGURE 19.17

frmButtonPix can change the picture on any button on any form.

Once you've selected a form and a button on that form, you can click the Apply button (or double-click the picture image on the form), and the code will apply the chosen image to the chosen button:

```
Private Sub cmdApply_Click()
    On Error Resume Next
    Forms(Me!lstForms)(Me!lstButtons).PictureData = _
    Me!cmdSample.PictureData
End Sub
```

To use frmButtonPix in your own applications, import both the form and the table (tblTBPictures), along with the module basDeclares.

Programming Tidbits

In addition to the other functions exported by MSACCESS.EXE, you'll find a few useful tidbits the Wizard programmers needed that may also be useful in your own applications. The following sections introduce each of these little functions.

Is That String a Valid Identifier?

If you ever have any reason to parse expressions that users input, you'll need to be able to tell whether a given identifier is legal, as far as Access is concerned. A valid identifier:

- Can be up to 255 characters long

- Must begin with a letter

- Can include letters, numbers, or underscore characters (_)

- Can't include punctuation characters or spaces

- Can't be a Visual Basic keyword

Rather than check these rules yourself, you can call the adh_accIsValidIdentifer function, passing in the text to be tested. The function returns True if the identifier passes and False if it doesn't. For example, you might write code like this:

```
If adh_accIsValidIdentifier(strProposedId) Then
    ' You know the identifier is OK
End If
```

Does That Global Function Already Exist?

If you're programmatically creating code for users, you'll want to ensure that any global procedure you create doesn't already exist. To do so, call the adh_accGlobalProcExists function, passing it the name of your proposed procedure. If the procedure already exists, the function will return True; otherwise it'll return False. For example, the following fragment checks to see whether a specified procedure already exists:

```
If Not adh_accGlobalProcExists("adhTrimNull") Then
    ' Run code to insert the procedure
End If
```

What's That Record Source?

You may have a need to know whether a given object's RecordSource property contains the name of table or a query or an actual SQL string. Although you can accomplish this task by perusing the TableDefs collection, and then the QueryDefs collection, that's quite slow. The function adh_accTypeOfStrRS returns a value indicating the type of record source, without the need for any extra code. The function returns one of the values adhcAccRSTypeSQL (0), adhcAccRSTypeTable (1), or adhcAccRSTypeQuery (2).

To determine the type of record source, you might write code like this:

```
Select Case adh_accTypeOfStrRS(Forms!frmCustomers.RecordSource)
    Case adhcAccRSTypeSQL
        ' Form uses a SQL string
    Case adhcAccRSTypeTable
        ' Form's based on a table
    Case adhcAccRSTypeQuery
        ' Form's based on a query
End Select
```

Summary

This chapter has introduced some of the undocumented functions exported by MSACCESS.EXE and demonstrated how to use each function. As with any other undocumented feature, the exported functions in MSACCESS.EXE and their use could change with any future release. Everything in this chapter was current as of the writing of this book, and because the Access Wizards use all the features described here, chances are they won't change much.

Specifically, the sections in this chapter demonstrated these areas:

File-Handling Functions:

- Check for the existence of a file.
- Split a full path reference into component pieces.
- Retrieve the full path name for a file.

Common Dialogs:

- Use the Office File Open/File Save dialogs.
- Use the Color Chooser dialog.

Work with the Registry:

- Retrieve the number of subkeys and values for a given Registry key.
- Get a subkey name by its index.
- Get a key value.
- Get a value's name given its index.
- Create a Registry key.
- Write a key's value.

Work with Installed Fonts:

- Retrieve the count of available fonts.
- Retrieve the list of available fonts.
- Retrieve the count of available font sizes for a font.
- Retrieve the list of available font sizes for a font.

Work with DAO Objects:

- Retrieve a list of object names.
- Retrieve a list of objects and their types.
- Sort an array of strings.
- Sort an array of database objects, either by type or by name.

Miscellaneous:

- Retrieve the current running version of Access' national language.
- Retrieve a bitmap from the common button bitmaps.

In addition, we've provided sample forms that demonstrate a number of these techniques. You can easily import these forms directly from CH19.MDB into your own applications.

CHAPTER
TWENTY

20

Using Access as an Automation Client

- Understanding how Automation works

- Writing simple Automation code

- Creating integrated solutions using Microsoft Office 97

- Using Automation to manipulate ActiveX controls

- Creating event sinks to monitor other applications

The term *Automation* refers to a technology that allows two separate application components to communicate with each other. Communication can take the form of data exchanges or commands issued by one component for another to carry out. The driving force behind the creation and exploitation of this technology is the desire to be able to combine numerous independent software components into a single integrated solution. For several versions, Microsoft Access has supported the programming interfaces that make Automation possible. In this chapter we explain the basics of Automation and explore ways to use it to create integrated solutions using applications like those found in Microsoft Office. We also look at using Automation techniques with ActiveX controls, the bright star in the galaxy of reusable software components. After reading this chapter you should have an understanding of how the pieces of the Automation puzzle fit together and how you can use them to your advantage.

Automation Basics

Automation is a complex technology that is relatively simple to implement. Its greatest strength is that it lets you work with objects from other applications using the same techniques you use now with Access objects. Before beginning to write integrated solutions using Automation, you should be familiar with the basics. In this section we explain the terminology we'll be using, where Automation information is stored, and how to examine an Automation component's objects, properties, and methods.

Terminology

There have been some changes in Automation terminology since the last edition of this book. In addition, some of the terms used in this book have meanings that differ when taken outside the context of Automation. In both cases, it's important that you understand the specific meanings of these terms.

Changes in Terminology

The ActiveX wave took many developers by storm and left many confused. *ActiveX* is an umbrella term for a number of technologies designed to speed Internet-related development. It is also the new term for some existing technologies that used to be known as OLE (Object Linking and Embedding). The following list provides both the old and new terms for some of the technologies involved.

- OLE automation is now just Automation.
- OLE automation components are now Automation or ActiveX components.
- OLE custom controls or OLE controls are now ActiveX controls.
- OLE document objects are now ActiveX documents.

Terminology Used in This Chapter

Now let's clarify some common terms used in this chapter.

Automation requires a client (sometimes called a *controller*) and a server. The *server* is the application or component that provides services to the client. It may exhibit behaviors independently of the client, but for the most part it depends on the client's giving it commands to do things. The *client,* on the other hand, is the application that uses the services of an Automation server. In a narrow context, a client application is one that implements a development language allowing you to write code that controls a server. Access is an obvious example of an Automation client. Other Automation clients include Microsoft Excel, Word, PowerPoint, and Visual Basic. In fact, any application that supports VBA has Automation client capabilities. An Automation client need not be a development tool, but development tools such as Access are the ones of most interest here.

In addition to understanding clients and servers, you should be familiar with the difference between object classes and objects. *Object classes* are the types of objects that an Automation server makes available for you to control. Object classes have a defined set of properties, methods and, in some cases, events that dictate how instances of that object class look and act. When you write Automation code, you manipulate *objects*—particular instances of object classes. The same holds true for VBA class modules and the instances you create and manipulate. (For more information on class modules, see Chapter 3.) You can think of objects and object classes as being similar to variables and datatypes. VBA supports a fixed set of datatypes, but you can declare and use as many variables of a single type as you wish. In this chapter, when we discuss a server application's *object model,* we are talking about its set of object classes. When you write VBA code, you're using instances of those classes, which are called objects.

What's the Value of Automation?

Automation's biggest benefit is its capacity to let you use pre-built, robust, and debugged software components in your applications. Just think how your development project would be affected if you had to build your own spreadsheet module instead of using Microsoft Excel. Clearly, for simple tasks you may decide to "roll your own," but as the complexity of a component increases, the benefits of using off-the-shelf software increase as well. Automation takes component reuse one step further by allowing you to control objects using your own code, extending whatever built-in intelligence the objects may have. Finally, the architecture of Automation lets you do this unobtrusively. That is, you control objects using Automation the same way you control them in Access, using sets of properties, methods, and events. With a few extensions to your current understanding of Access and its objects, you can start controlling other applications' objects, such as those found in Microsoft Office (Excel, Word, PowerPoint, and Outlook) and ActiveX controls.

Object Classes

Before you can start controlling objects, you need to understand which objects are available to you. As you install applications and ActiveX controls, these components will make entries in the Registry that mark them to Windows as controllable. (Technically speaking, Automation servers are those applications that support the IDispatch programming interface.) Because each application may make more than one object class available to Automation clients, you need to know not only the application name, but the object type as well. This information is encapsulated in the program identifier, or ProgID, for the particular object class. ProgIDs are expressed as follows:

ApplicationName.ObjectClass

For example, Microsoft Excel exports a controllable Chart class that has an associated ProgID of "Excel.Chart". Furthermore, this convention lets you append a version number to the ProgID to restrict manipulation of the object to a particular version of the software. "Excel.Chart.5" refers to a Chart object that is manipulated by Excel version 5. Most applications register a pointer to the latest version installed on your computer, so leaving off the version number will force that version to be used.

WARNING As software versions are released at an ever-increasing pace, it occasionally becomes necessary to have multiple versions of a particular program installed on your computer. Furthermore, sometimes you will install an older version of a program on a computer that already has a newer version installed. When this happens with an Automation component, the older version sometimes overwrites the Registry information so that an unqualified ProgID (one with no version number appended) will point to the older version. Automation clients that use this ProgID and depend on features that exist only in the newer version will no longer work. When this happens you should reinstall the newer version. This should restore the Registry settings. As a precaution, however, you should always use qualified ProgIDs if you depend on certain features that aren't available in all versions.

While it is not always the case, most applications that feature a user interface (as opposed to "service only" servers, which operate transparently behind the scenes) register an Application class. Normally, this object represents the highest-level object in the application's object model, and from it you can derive most other object types. As we discuss the examples in this chapter, the use of ProgIDs should become clear.

Type Libraries: the Key to Classes

Most newer Automation components ship with a supplemental file called a type library. Type libraries are databases that list the objects, methods, properties, and events offered by a server application. Automation clients such as Access can use the information stored in a library to "learn" about another application. Type libraries offer a number of benefits:

- Access does not actually have to run the server application to interrogate its object model.

- The VBA editor and interpreter can use type libraries to perform syntax checking on your Automation code.

- You can obtain context-sensitive help for another application's keywords.

Most components' type libraries have a .TLB or .OLB (for object library) file extension, and you use them in your VBA project by adding them to the list of references in the References dialog. Most well-behaved components make the proper Registry entries to make this happen automatically. Occasionally, however, you must add it to the references list yourself. To do this, follow these steps:

1. Open any module.

2. Select Tools ➤ References. You should see a list of references similar to the ones shown in Figure 20.1.

3. Check the box next to the reference you want to add.

4. If the reference is not listed, click the Browse button and locate the type library or executable file of the component you want to use.

FIGURE 20.1

References dialog showing loaded and available references

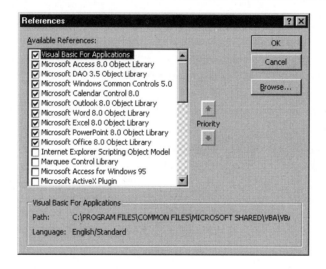

Once you've loaded a type library, you can use the objects, properties, and methods in your VBA code. VBA will be able to correctly verify syntax, as well as provide context-sensitive help for the server component's keywords. One important issue is that the complete path to the type library is stored with your VBA project. If you move the type library or install your application on another computer, you will need to reestablish the link to the type library.

Browsing Objects with Object Browser

Once you've added references to an Automation component's type library, you can use the VBA Object Browser to view a list of the component's classes, properties, and methods. To make Object Browser available, press the F2 key in Module view, click the Object Browser toolbar button, or select the View ➤ Object Browser menu command. Figure 20.2 shows Object Browser open to the Application class of Microsoft Excel's type library.

FIGURE 20.2

Object Browser showing details on Excel's Application object

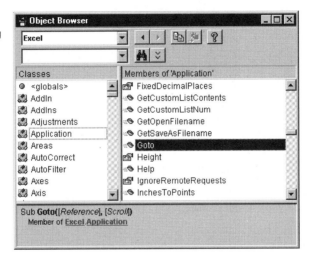

When Object Browser first opens, it displays a list of all the classes exposed by every referenced Automation component, including the current database. You can use the Project/Library drop-down list at the top left of the screen to select a single component, thus making the list of classes a bit more manageable. Object Browser changes the contents of the Classes and Members lists to reflect the change. The Classes list shows all the object classes available from the Automation component. Selecting any one of them causes Object Browser to display the methods and properties for that class in the right-hand list. Icons denote various elements of the type library, such as constants, classes, properties, and methods. Note that collections are also shown in the left-hand (object) list. When you select a collection, usually denoted as the plural form of the object class, Object Browser displays the methods and properties for the collection, not the object.

If you're not sure of the exact name of a property or method, you can use Object Browser's search engine. Enter a text string in the text box just below the list of libraries and click the Find button (the one with binoculars on it). After searching all the referenced type libraries, Object Browser opens the Search Results pane, as shown in Figure 20.3. You can collapse the pane by clicking the button with the up arrows.

FIGURE 20.3

Object Browser displaying search results

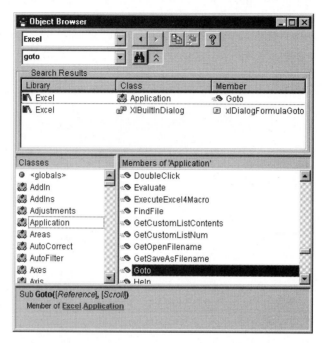

Figures 20.2 and 20.3 also show the Application object's Goto method highlighted in the right-hand list. Note the syntax example at the bottom of the dialog. Object Browser shows you the calling syntax of the property or method, including any arguments. You can highlight any portion of the syntax and use the Copy button to copy the highlighted portion to the clipboard for subsequent pasting into a module. If you don't highlight any of the syntax, the Copy button simply copies the method or property name to the clipboard. If the type library being viewed supports a Windows help file, pressing the Help button (the one with a question mark) opens that file to the proper page for the displayed property or method.

Object Browser can be especially helpful when you're using an Automation component for the first time. It gives you a class-by-class overview of the object model, allowing you to browse the individual classes and their properties and methods. As you become more familiar with a component, you'll be able to write Automation code from memory, but until then, Object Browser is a good place to start learning about what's available and how to use it.

Creating Objects

All Automation sessions begin with the client application creating an object. By *creating* an object, we mean establishing a conversation with the server application and telling it which of its objects you wish to control. The result of this creation process is a pointer to an instance of the server's object stored in an object variable. Using this object variable, you can control the server application's object using the same techniques you use to control Access objects—by manipulating their methods and properties.

Early Binding and Late Binding

There are two approaches to creating instances of Automation component objects: early binding and late binding. The approach you use is determined by the point at which you inform VBA of your intention to use a particular Automation component and object class. Each approach has its own pros and cons.

With *early binding,* you add a reference to a component's type library at design time and use the VBA New keyword to instantiate the object. For example, to create a new instance of Microsoft Excel's Application object, you set a reference to the Microsoft Excel 8.0 Object Library and use code like this:

```
Dim objXL As New Excel.Application
```

This technique is called early binding because VBA knows which object classes the component supports (along with all their properties and methods) before you execute your code.

> **NOTE**
> Notice that we prefaced the object class, Application, with the name of the server, Excel. You must qualify the object class with the server name whenever the object class is ambiguous. (Access also has an Application object.) If you're unsure of the server name to use, look at the list of libraries in Object Browser. Object Browser uses the name of each component, which is what you should use to qualify objects exported by that component.

Late binding, on the other hand, does not require a reference to a type library. Instead you use the VBA CreateObject or GetObject function with a ProgID passed as text to instantiate objects. This approach is known as late binding because VBA has no way of knowing what type of object will be created until run time.

Although not every Automation component supports it, you should use early binding whenever possible. Early binding offers several benefits:

- **Speed:** Because you tell VBA about a component in advance, it does not need to worry that a particular property or method might not be supported. With late binding, extra communication takes place to determine whether a statement is supported by the server. This decreases performance.

- **VBA editor support:** When you use early binding, VBA can perform syntax checking on your source code and provide such features as Auto List Members and Auto Quick Info.

- **Online help:** Early binding gives you context-sensitive help for components that have help files. Just highlight any member name and press F1.

Early binding has a drawback, however. Since you must use a reference to a type library, if the type library is ever moved or deleted (or you install your application on a computer lacking a copy of the Automation component), the reference will break. When this happens your code will not compile until you resolve the reference. Late binding solves this problem because it does not require a reference in the first place. If this issue concerns you, take a look at the section "Restoring References Using VBA" in Chapter 22. In general, you should use late binding only when an Automation component does not support early binding.

A Simple Early Binding Example

Controlling Automation components using early binding is extremely simple and very similar to the way you work with built-in Access components and custom classes constructed using VBA class modules. To demonstrate early binding, we've created a simple example that uses Microsoft Excel as an Automation server. If you already know everything there is to know about early binding, you can skip to the next section. Otherwise, start up Access and follow these steps:

1. Create a new database.

2. Add a new module to the database.

3. Open the References dialog by selecting the Tools ➤ References menu command.

4. Locate Microsoft Excel 8.0 Object Library in the list and mark the check box. Click OK to close the dialog.

5. Enter the VBA code shown in Listing 20.1 in the new module.

6. Highlight any line of code in the TestXL procedure and press F8 to step through the code.

Listing 20.1

```
Sub TestXL
    Dim objXL As New Excel.Application

    ' Reference a few properties (this will launch a
    ' new instance of Excel)
    MsgBox objXL.Name & " " & objXL.Version
    objXL.Visible= True
    objXL.Quit
    Set objXL = Nothing
End Sub
```

As you step through the code, you'll notice several things happen. First, you'll observe a slight delay and some disk activity as you execute the MsgBox statement. This is because a new instance of Excel is being launched. After the new instance loads, Access displays the message box.

At this point a new copy of Excel will be running, but you won't be able see it. That's because when Excel is launched in response to a request from an Automation client, it makes its main window invisible. This behavior is application specific. For more information on how the other Microsoft Office applications react, see the section "Differences in Application Behavior" later in this chapter.

To make Excel's main window visible, execute the next statement. Excel's Application object has a Visible property that controls this behavior. Changing the property to True displays Excel's main window.

Executing the next statement (objXL.Quit) terminates Excel. You'll notice another slight delay as Excel shuts down. The final statement, which sets the object variable to the intrinsic constant Nothing, is a housekeeping task that frees any memory VBA was using to manage the Automation session.

Delaying Instantiation

In the previous example you saw how a new instance of Excel was created when you executed a MsgBox statement. As with VBA class modules, if you declare an object variable using the New keyword, the object is instantiated the first time you reference one of its properties or methods. Sometimes, however, you will want to explicitly control when an object is instantiated. To do this, declare the object variable without using the New keyword. Then use a Set statement in your code in conjunction with New. For instance, you could modify the example as shown in Listing 20.2.

Listing 20.2

```
Sub TestXLDelayed()
    Dim objXL As Excel.Application

    ' Create new instance now
    Set objXL = New Excel.Application

    ' The rest is the same
    MsgBox objXL.Name & " " & objXL.Version
    objXL.Visible= True
    objXL.Quit
    Set objXL = Nothing
End Sub
```

In this case Excel will not be launched until VBA executes the Set statement. While this is actually one line sooner than in the previous example, it is explicit and easy to identify. If you don't use Set as we have done here, it may be hard to determine when an object becomes "live." If you try to use any of the object's properties or methods without first instantiating the object, VBA raises an "Object variable or With block variable not set" error.

Late Binding with CreateObject and GetObject

CreateObject and GetObject are VBA functions used to instantiate late-bound Automation component objects, and you can call them from your code just as you would any other function. Because they do nothing more than create an Automation object, you need to store the object pointer they return in an object variable. You can declare a variable using the generic Object datatype, or you can use a server-specific datatype if you have added a reference to the server's type library to your VBA project. For example:

```
' If you don't want to use the type library, do this:
Dim objExcel As Object
' If you are using the type library you can do this:
Dim objExcel As Excel.Application
```

Using CreateObject

CreateObject accepts a single argument, a string containing a component object's ProgID, as described in the section "Object Classes" earlier in this chapter. When you call CreateObject, VBA attempts to create an object of the type specified using the application specified. If it cannot create the object, perhaps because the application is not installed or does not support the object type, it fails with a run-time error.

If you want to try a simple example of late-bound Automation, create the procedure shown in Listing 20.3 and step through it.

Listing 20.3

```
Sub TestXLLateBound()
    Dim objXL As Object

    ' This creates a new instance
    Set objXL = CreateObject("Excel.Application")

    ' The rest is the same
    objXL.Visible = True
    objXL.Quit
    Set objXL = Nothing
End Sub
```

You'll notice that this is almost the same code as in the prior examples, except that we've used a generic Object variable to store the pointer to Excel's Application object. If you don't include a reference to a component's type library, you must use the Object datatype. We've also used CreateObject to instantiate the object variable rather than the New keyword. Note that the ProgID, "Excel.Application", is passed as text. We could have stored this in a variable that VBA could evaluate at run time. This is something that is not possible if you use early binding, because the ProgID must be part of the Dim statement.

Using GetObject

GetObject is similar to CreateObject, but instead of accepting a single argument, it allows for two optional arguments, a document name and/or a ProgID. The general form of a GetObject statement is

Set *objectvariable* = GetObject([*docname*], [*ProgID*])

Note that both arguments are optional, but you must supply *at least* one of them. GetObject is a more flexible function that you can use to create an object from an application's document (an Excel workbook file, for example) or from an existing instance of an application. The flexibility of GetObject is revealed by the combination of arguments used. Table 20.1 explains the results of these combinations.

TABLE 20.1   Various Uses of the GetObject Function

Combination	Example	Results
Document name only	Set objAny = GetObject ("C:\DATA\BOOK1.XLS")	The application associated with the document type is launched and used to open the specified document. If the application supports it, an existing instance will be used, and if the document is already open, the object pointer will refer to that instance
Object class only	Set objAny = GetObject (, "Excel.Application")	If the server application is running, an object pointer is created for the running instance; otherwise GetObject returns a run-time error
Object class and empty document name	Set objAny = GetObject ("", "Excel.Application")	Same behavior as CreateObject. Opens a new instance of the application
Both document name and object class	Set objAny = GetObject ("C:\DATA\BOOK1.XLS", "Excel.Application")	Redundant. Same behavior as passing only the document name, except that if the server does not support the document type, a run-time error occurs

As you can see, GetObject is more complex than CreateObject, although it does offer the benefit of using running instances of applications rather than launching new copies each time your Automation code runs. This is especially critical on low-memory computers.

Multiple-Use versus Single-Use Classes

In the preceding examples using the Application class, a new copy of Microsoft Excel is launched each time VBA requests a new instance of the class. This is because the Application class is, by default, a single-use class. Automation server classes fall into two broad categories: multiple-use and single-use. *Single-use classes* cause a new instance of the application to launch when a client application instantiates them. We've illustrated this in Figure 20.4. Each instance of the Application class created by client applications references an Application object created by a separate copy of Excel.

FIGURE 20.4

Single-use classes are each hosted by a different copy of the application.

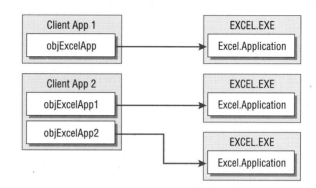

Multiple-use classes, on the other hand, allow Automation client applications to share the *same instance* of the class. An example of a multiple-use class is Microsoft Outlook's Application class. Only one instance of the class can exist at any given time. Figure 20.5 illustrates this type of class. Even though client applications might instantiate the class using the New keyword or CreateObject, all references point to the same instance in the server application. Applications that expose multiple-use classes are typically those that allow you to launch only one instance from the Windows shell.

FIGURE 20.5

Multiple-use classes are all hosted by a single copy of the application.

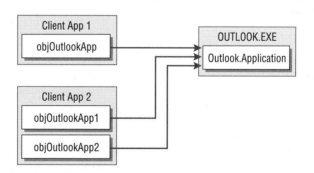

What's more, classes that are single-use by default can be used as a multiple-use class, as illustrated in Figure 20.6. For example, you can use Excel's Application class as though it were a multiple-use class even though it is single-use by default. To accomplish this you must first ensure that a copy of the application is already running. Then, instead of using the New keyword to instantiate an object, use a normal Set statement. Code in Listing 20.4 demonstrates this.

FIGURE 20.6

Using a single-use
class as though it
were multiple-use

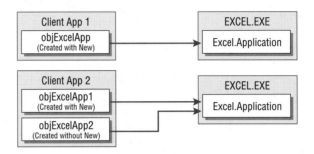

> **NOTE**
> While you can use most single-use classes in the multiple-use role, the converse is not true. Each time you request a new instance of a multiple-use class, you receive a new reference to a preexisting instance if one exists. Only the first request results in a copy of the application being launched.

Listing 20.4

```
Sub TestXLExisting()
    Dim objXL As Excel.Application

    ' Use an existing instance
    Set objXL = Excel.Application

    ' The rest is the same
    MsgBox objXL.Name & " " & objXL.Version
    objXL.Quit
    Set objXL = Nothing
End Sub
```

> **NOTE**
> The code shown in Listing 20.4 actually will work even if Excel is not running. This behavior seems to be peculiar to Excel and Access, however. If you tried to use this code with Word, and Word was not running, it would fail.

Table 20.2 lists the programs in Microsoft Office 97 and indicates whether they are single-use or multiple-use by default.

TABLE 20.2 Single-Use and Multi-Use Office 97 Applications

Application	Default Behavior	Multiple-Use?
Access	Single-use	Yes
Excel	Single-use	Yes
Outlook	Multiple-use	N/A
PowerPoint	Multiple-use	N/A
Word	Single-use	Yes

Controlling Other Applications

Now that you understand the basics of Automation, you're ready to start writing code to control Automation components, be they mega-applications, such as Microsoft Excel and Word, or smaller elements, such as ActiveX controls. The rest of this chapter explains how you can write code like this, using the other applications in Microsoft Office to illustrate.

Learning an Application's Object Model

The techniques involved in using another component's objects through Automation are the same as those for manipulating Access objects; the only difference is the set of objects themselves. Before beginning to write Automation client code, you must familiarize yourself with the server component's object model. Unfortunately, the availability and quality of documentation vary enormously, even among Microsoft products. As a general rule, those applications that have their own development language (such as VBA in Microsoft Excel, Word, and PowerPoint) have better documentation than those that don't (for example, Outlook). Resources are available that you can use to learn another application's object model. Some of them are listed here:

- The *Office Programmer's Guide* is included with Microsoft Office 97 Developer Edition and contains information on creating integrated solutions with Microsoft Office, including object model descriptions.

- The *Microsoft Solutions Development Kit* is a resource for those developing integrated solutions using Microsoft Office and BackOffice products. It is a CD-ROM product available from Microsoft.

As mentioned earlier, you can also use Object Browser to interrogate a component's object model. Even with online help, though, this tends to be a trial-and-error method that does not offer the supplementary information that other documentation sources do.

Differences in Application Behavior

When creating Automation objects, be aware that component applications exhibit unique behavior when used as Automation servers, specifically under two conditions:

- When the application first launches in response to an Automation client request
- When you destroy the object variable that references a server object

Differences in an application's behavior will dictate how you use it in your Automation client code. Table 20.3 lists differences in behavior of the Application object among the programs that make up Microsoft Office 97. As you use other Automation components, you may want to note how they behave in respect to the list provided.

TABLE 20.3   Differences in Behavior among Microsoft Office 97 Applications

Application	Differences in Behavior
Access	Launches as an icon with a Visible property of False. Changing the Visible property to True restores the main window; changing it to False minimizes the window. Additionally, destroying the object variable causes Access to terminate if it was launched via Automation. You can also use the Quit method
Excel	Launches as a hidden window with a Visible property of False. Changing the Visible property to True "un-hides" the window. Destroying the object variable does not cause Excel to terminate. Use the Quit method instead
PowerPoint	Launches as a hidden window with a Visible property of False. Changing the Visible property to True "un-hides" the window. Destroying the object variable does not cause PowerPoint to terminate. Use the Quit method instead
Outlook	Launches as a hidden window. The Application object does not have a Visible property. There is no way to make it visible using the object model. You must use the Windows API instead. Destroying the object variable does not cause Outlook to terminate. Use the Quit method instead
Word	Launches as a hidden window with a Visible property of False. Changing the Visible property to True "un-hides" the window. Destroying the object variable does not cause Word to terminate. Use the Quit method instead

Memory and Resource Issues

One very important piece of information to keep in mind when creating integrated solutions using Automation is how controlling multiple applications at the same time will affect the overall performance of a user's system. Large server applications such as Excel and Word consume a lot of memory. While it is now more difficult to produce the dreaded "Out of System Resources" error, thanks to better memory management in Windows 95 and NT, RAM is still an issue. Computers with fewer than 16 megabytes of RAM may perform poorly when many large applications are running, due to disk swapping. If low memory is a problem, you may want to consider closing each server after using it.

The other side of the coin is the time it takes to start and stop large applications. If you frequently use large applications as Automation servers, you may want to leave them open despite the effect this will have on memory consumption. In other words, you will likely have to experiment to get the right mix of performance and memory utilization.

Converting Access 2.0 Automation Code

If you wrote OLE automation code that used Access reserved words in Access 2.0, you may experience problems when converting your applications to Access 97. In Access 2.0 you could not use methods or properties of other applications that conflicted with Access reserved words. To get around this, Access Basic let you use brackets to indicate that the method or property belonged to an OLE automation object. Unfortunately, the workaround for Access 2.0 causes problems when used in Access 97. A particularly insidious problem exists in code that calls Microsoft Excel's Quit method. In Access 2.0 you had to write code that looked like this:

```
objExcelApp.[Quit]
```

This forced the Access Basic compiler to ignore whatever was between the brackets. In Access 97 you can use any method or property without brackets. The problem is that when you convert code like that shown above, it compiles and executes but does not actually do anything. Excel appears to ignore the Quit statement until the brackets are removed. If you notice that some of your legacy OLE automation code isn't working correctly, check for brackets around method and property names and remove any you find.

Creating Automation Solutions with Microsoft Office 97

Statistically speaking, if you are reading this book you already own a copy of Microsoft Office 97. Since most copies of Access are sold as part of Office, if you're developing Access applications, chances are your users own a copy of Office as well. This gives you an opportunity to leverage the vast functionality in those applications by creating integrated solutions based on Automation. To get you started, we'll spend a good portion of this chapter demonstrating several sample applications that use Office components. You'll be able to see examples of how each can be controlled from Access. We'll also point out some of the minor differences and idiosyncrasies that still exist in this supposedly integrated suite of products.

Specifically, we'll show you four applications:

- A mail-merge tool that inserts data from any form into a new Word document

- A time-reporting system that pulls schedule information from Outlook

- A tool that creates and runs a PowerPoint presentation based on Access data

- A data analysis system that uses Excel to summarize data from Access tables

Each of these examples will highlight a slightly different aspect of using Automation. First off, the Word application demonstrates the basics of controlling an Automation component and shows how to work with a document-oriented server. Our Outlook example explores the unique aspects of this all-in-one organizer, which relies on the Exchange messaging system. The PowerPoint example highlights the challenges involved in creating completely free-form documents (PowerPoint slides). Finally, the Excel example shows how to use existing documents as the target of Automation commands. As you read through the examples and test the sample code, keep in mind that the real message here is that Automation code is more *similar* to the code you're writing already than it is different.

Correcting Automation Typelib References

Before delving into the sample applications we've created for this chapter, we need to say a few words regarding references to type libraries that are part of the sample database. These references allow VBA to examine the properties and methods of a given server and are explained in detail in the section "Type Libraries: the Key to Objects" earlier in this chapter.

Type library references are hard coded. That is, the complete path to a type library is stored as part of a VBA project. Thus, moving or deleting a type library prevents VBA code that references it from compiling. Because the type libraries used in the samples are almost certainly stored in different locations on your computer than they are on ours, you will need to update the references before testing the samples. To do this, open any module in CH20.MDB and display the References dialog. For each reference marked as MISSING, click the Browse button and find the type library file on your computer.

If you cannot find the type library, perhaps because you don't have the particular product installed, uncheck its reference in the dialog and compile the VBA code. You will find several compile errors. To correct these errors, comment out the offending statements.

The Office Object Models

While we don't have nearly enough room in this chapter to fully explain the object models of Office 97 applications, we can describe some of their more significant aspects. This will provide a good basis for explaining the sample applications in the rest of the chapter. We've included diagrams that illustrate abridged versions of the object models. They include just a few of the applications' classes. Table 20.4 lists the classes that are exposed to Automation clients. All the other classes implemented by the applications are available through collections, methods, and properties of the exposed classes.

TABLE 20.4 Object Classes Exposed by Microsoft Office 97 Applications

Server Name	Class Name	Description
Access	Application	Pointer to an instance of Microsoft Access
Excel	Application	Pointer to an instance of Microsoft Excel
	Chart	Pointer to a new Chart object. Launches Excel and opens a new workbook if necessary
	Sheet	Pointer to a new Worksheet object. Launches Excel and opens a new workbook if necessary
Outlook	Application	Pointer to an instance of Microsoft Outlook
PowerPoint	Application	Pointer to an instance of Microsoft PowerPoint
Word	Application	Pointer to an instance of Microsoft Word
	Document	Pointer to a new Document object. Launches Word if necessary

Excel

Excel has what might be described as the "grand-daddy" of Office object models. It was the first application to integrate VBA (with version 5.0 in 1993), and with that came a very rich object model that allowed developers complete control over Excel worksheet-based applications. Figure 20.7 illustrates a small portion of the object model.

As you can see in Figure 20.7, Excel's object model follows its user interface design very closely. Its top-level class, Application, represents the main Excel application. Descending from that is a Workbooks collection representing all open workbooks (XLS files), and contained within each workbook is a collection of Worksheets.

Within each worksheet are collections of objects representing embedded charts, lines, pictures, and so on. What you won't see is any collection symbolizing data in individual cells. This is because implementing a Cells collection, for example, would require managing 16,777,216 objects (because an Excel worksheet is 256 columns wide by 65,536 rows deep)! Instead you use methods to return references to data. These references are stored using a generic Range object. A range can be a single cell, a block of cells, a discontinuous group of cells, or an entire row or column. You'll find numerous methods designed to return Range objects—for example, Cells, Range, Column, Row, Union, and Intersect. Once you have a valid Range

FIGURE 20.7

A very small portion of the Excel object model

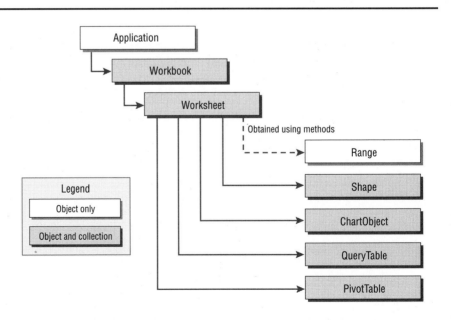

object, you can use some of its more than 160 properties and methods to manipulate data, change formats, and evaluate results.

Word

Word 97 is the first version of Microsoft's flagship word processor to have an exposed object model. While it has been an Automation component since version 2.0, prior versions have exposed only a single class, Word.Basic, representing Word's macro interpreter. You used this class to execute WordBasic commands against the current instance of Word. Without a rich object model, writing Automation code was cumbersome. WordBasic macros operate only on the currently selected text or object, so it took a great deal of code to ensure that the proper element was selected before you could execute a command that modified it.

Fortunately, this limitation became history with Word 97; Microsoft developers have created a full-featured, flexible object model for word processing documents. Figure 20.8 illustrates a small portion of Word's object model.

FIGURE 20.8

Highlights of Word 97's object model

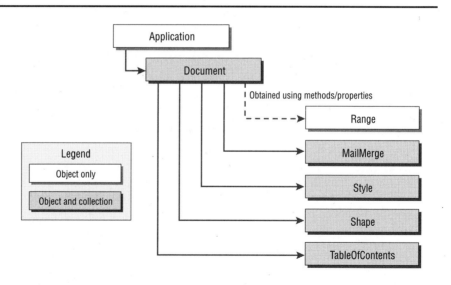

Word's object model shares a number of similarities with that of Excel. At its root is the Application object, which contains a collection of Document objects, one for each open document. Each Document object has several properties that allow you to manipulate text, including Sections, Paragraphs, Sentences, and Words. Each property returns a pointer to a Range object. Word Range objects are similar in concept to those in Excel in that they give you access to the contents and formatting of blocks of text.

PowerPoint

PowerPoint lived its last revision cycle in the shadow of other Automation components, such as Word and Excel. Microsoft introduced Automation support in PowerPoint 95, but it lacked a development language of its own and suffered from the short development cycle of Office 97. Not many developers took the time to learn how to use it. PowerPoint 97, which offers integrated VBA, complete with a macro recorder, will likely change that situation.

PowerPoint has a rich object model that, like Excel and Word, is aimed at managing the contents of documents. (In Excel, workbooks are the "documents.") PowerPoint's document paradigm, however, deals with presentations and slides. Figure 20.9 shows a portion of the PowerPoint object model, which should look familiar to you by now. It features the requisite Application object and Presentations and Slides collections.

Manipulating textual information in PowerPoint is a bit more convoluted than in Word or Excel because of the unstructured, free-form nature of PowerPoint

FIGURE 20.9

PowerPoint's object model deals with Presentation and Slide objects.

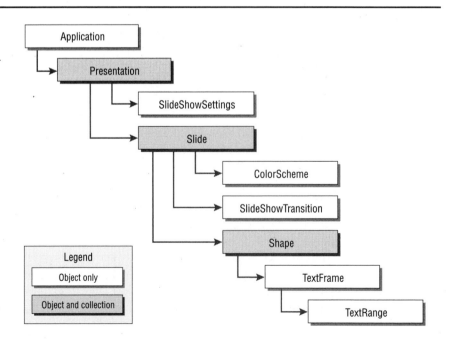

slides. Each Slide object has a collection of Shapes representing the various graphical components placed on the slide. For those shapes that can contain text there is a TextFrame object, which controls how contained text is displayed (margins, orientation, and so on). Finally, the TextFrame object contains a TextRange object with text and formatting properties and methods.

Outlook

If Excel's object model is the grand-daddy of the Office suite, then Outlook's object model might be described as the black sheep of the family. It is unlike any of the other Office products, primarily because it does not follow the same document-centric metaphor. The data it manipulates is far less structured and, like its predecessor Schedule Plus, the object model can be difficult to learn and use. Furthermore, Outlook is designed to be an integral part of your electronic messaging system and as such must cope with various service providers, addressing schemes, storage mechanisms, and electronic mail functions.

Figure 20.10 illustrates the Outlook object model, which may at first appear less complex than that of the other applications. It has an Application class at its root, but that's where similarities end.

First, Outlook requires that you create a reference to what it calls a Namespace class. This represents one of the messaging service provider layers that Outlook depends on for data storage (although "MAPI" is the only type of namespace Outlook currently supports). When you install Outlook on a computer with no other messaging component, the setup program also installs the MAPI-based Microsoft Exchange messaging system. (MAPI is an acronym for Messaging Application Programming Interface.)

FIGURE 20.10

Outlook's object model is quite different from other Office applications.

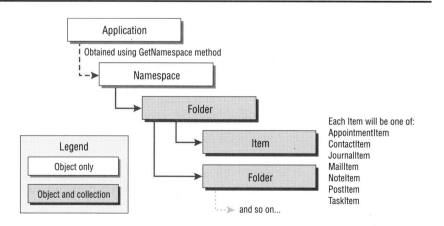

Each messaging system can implement persistent data storage using a hierarchical folder metaphor similar to disk subdirectories. Outlook's Namespace class contains a Folders collection representing the top-level folder of each installed storage system. Each of these, in turn, contains a Folders collection with members for each subfolder (Inbox, Outbox, and so on). Every folder object has a Folders collection, allowing for infinite nesting of data storage.

Data in folders is represented by an Items collection. Each element of this collection can be one of a variety of object classes that represent such things as mail messages, appointments, journal entries, contacts, and tasks. It is this uncertainty about what a folder contains that makes programming with Outlook challenging.

Office Objects

Finally, Microsoft Office implements a set of objects that individual programs share. These include the Office Binder, Office Assistant, command bars, a file search tool, Data Map, and Microsoft Graph. You'll find information about some of these objects elsewhere in this book. For the others, consult Object Browser or online help.

Example: Smart Mail Merge to Word

Our sample Microsoft Word application is an intelligent mail-merge tool you can use with any form in your database to copy data from the form to a Word document. The tool is intelligent in that it will try to match fields on your form with bookmark names in the document. Specifically, the tool must perform the following steps:

1. Launch Microsoft Word if it is not already running.

2. Load a copy of a preexisting Word template with one or more bookmarks defined.

3. Iterate through each control on the active form, trying to match control names with bookmark names.

4. Where a match is found, copy the data from the form to the Word document.

5. Give the user the option of printing the document after all data has been copied.

Since the code works with any form, you can add the code described below to any database and instantly give your users a simple export tool that integrates with their word processor.

Creating the Word Template

The sample application included in CH20.MDB relies on the existence of a Microsoft Word template file with predefined bookmarks that have names corresponding to fields on a form. We have included a sample template, THANKS.DOT, you can use to test the sample application. Copy this template to your Microsoft Office Templates directory before running the application. Figure 20.11 shows the template open in Microsoft Word. The vertical gray bars on the left side of the document are Word bookmarks.

FIGURE 20.11

Sample template showing the location of bookmarks

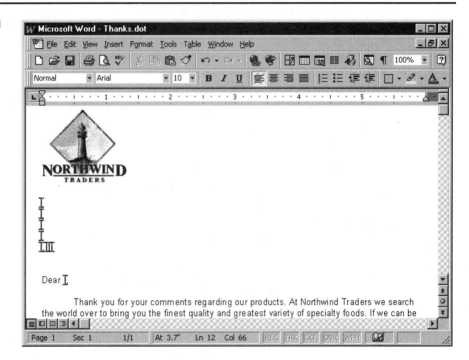

You define a bookmark by setting the insertion point at the spot in the document where you want to create the bookmark and then choosing the Insert ➤ Bookmark command. Figure 20.12 shows the dialog that appears. It lists any existing bookmarks, and you can click the Go To button to go to the point in the document marked by the bookmark. To create a new bookmark or redefine an existing one, enter the name of the bookmark in the text box and click the Add button.

You can see in Figure 20.12 that our sample template has a number of bookmarks already defined. These bookmarks are named after controls on a form we will

FIGURE 20.12

Word's Bookmark dialog, showing bookmarks defined in the sample template

use to drive the data-merge process. A function (we'll describe it shortly) will look for each bookmark that matches a control name on the active form and copy the contents of the control to the document at the appropriate spot.

If you want to use our function with your own document templates, you will need to define bookmarks that correspond to control names on your forms. If you have a control that must be used more than once, append a sequence number, starting with 1, after the control name (such as the txtContactName and txtContactName1 fields in the sample template). Our function will look for additional bookmarks when it processes the form.

Launching the Merge Process

CH20.MDB contains an AutoKeys macro that defines Ctrl+L as a shortcut key that launches our initialization process using a function named adhInitMerge, in basWord. AdhInitMerge opens a form, frmWord, that lets you select a Word template to use as the merge document. The procedure uses Screen.ActiveForm to capture the active form and then passes the name of this form to frmWord in its OpenArgs property. FrmWord will use the active form to get the data for the merge process.

> **NOTE**
> Due to a bug in VBA, if the reference to Word's type library is missing or broken, the AutoKeys macro will not run. Microsoft decided not to resolve this issue for Access 97. If you want to run the sample application, you should manually verify that the reference is valid.

Figure 20.13 shows frmWord, which features a list of Microsoft Word template files the user can choose from to use in the merge process. frmWord also offers users the option of printing the finished document. During the form's Load event, a new instance of Word's Application object is created, stored in a module-level variable (mobjWord), and used to locate the default Office Templates directory. The directory name is extracted from the path of Word's Normal template, the template all new documents are based on. The code that accomplishes this is shown here:

```
mstrTemplateDir = mobjWord.NormalTemplate.Path
```

FIGURE 20.13

frmWord showing a
list of Microsoft Word
templates

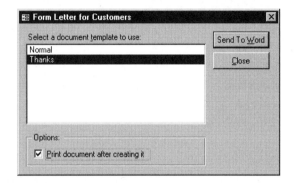

Copying Data to Word

After frmWord presents the list of templates to the user, the user can select one from the list and click the Send to Word button to copy the data on the active form to a new document created from the template. Listing 20.5 shows the adhCreate-FormLetter function (sans error handling), which performs the task of copying data from the active form to the Word document. It accepts three arguments: a pointer to a Word Application object (objWord), a pointer to a form from which to copy data (frmAny), and the path to a Word template file (strTemplate). Code in the Click event for frmWord's Send button calls adhCreateFormLetter.

Listing 20.5

```
Function adhCreateFormLetter(objWord As Word.Application, _
 frmAny As Form, ByVal strTemplate As String) As Long

    Dim objWordDoc As Word.Document
```

```
            Dim ctlAny As Control
            Dim intExtras As Integer
            Dim intCount As Integer

            ' Open a new document based on the selected template
            Set objWordDoc = objWord.Documents.Add(strTemplate)

            ' Loop through the controls on the form and attempt
            ' to goto Word bookmarks with the same name--
            ' Use adhValueFromControl to get the value from
            ' the control (this function copes with numeric and
            ' Boolean values, etc.)
            For Each ctlAny In frmAny.Controls
                ' Try to find a bookmark with the same name
                ' as the control
                If adhInsertAtBookmark(objWordDoc, ctlAny.Name, _
                 adhValueFromControl(ctlAny)) Then

                    ' For fields that may appear more than once,
                    ' look for bookmarks with the control name
                    ' and a sequential number (txtControl1,
                    ' txtControl2, etc.)
                    intExtras = 0
                    Do
                        intCount = intCount + 1
                        intExtras = intExtras + 1
                    Loop Until Not adhInsertAtBookmark(objWordDoc, _
                     ctlAny.Name & intExtras, _
                     adhValueFromControl(ctlAny))
                End If
            Next

            adhCreateFormLetter = intCount
    End Function

    Function adhInsertAtBookmark(objWordDoc As Word.Document, _
     strBookmark As String, strText As String) As Boolean

        With objWordDoc.Bookmarks
            If .Exists(strBookmark) Then
                .Item(strBookmark).Range.Text = strText
```

```
            adhInsertAtBookmark = True
        End If
    End With
End Function
```

The first thing adhCreateFormLetter does is create a new document based on the selected template by calling the Add method of Word's Documents collection. It then uses a For Each...Next loop to iterate through each control on the active form. Using the name of each control, the procedure attempts to insert the contents of the control at a point designated by a matching bookmark in the new document.

You'll notice that rather than just inserting the value of the control, we use a function, adhValueFromControl, to return a string to insert. We've done this so we can substitute meaningful strings for controls such as check boxes that hold numeric values.

Figure 20.14 shows a sample document created using our smart merge function. We used the frmCustomers form in CH20.MDB as the basis for this document.

FIGURE 20.14

A completed merge document created using the sample Customers form

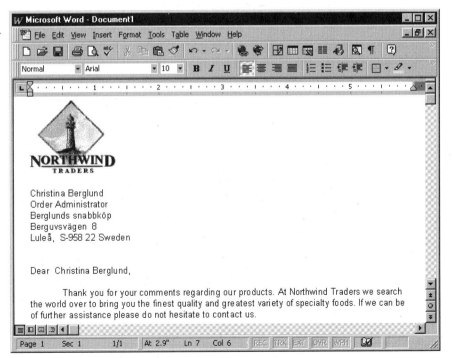

Example: Outlook Time Reporting

To demonstrate the basics of Automation, we've created a sample application that uses Access to control Microsoft Outlook. The application allows you to create journal entries and then load that schedule information back into an Access database. The application is a simple time-reporting system that tracks the length of time spent on various tasks using the Outlook journal.

To test this application you'll need a copy of Outlook installed on your computer. To get the maximum benefit, you'll also need to create some journal entries. You can do this by using the first component of this sample project or Outlook itself.

Outlook and Exchange

Even if you don't use Outlook to send and receive electronic mail, you're still using Exchange, Microsoft's messaging product, to some degree. This is because Outlook relies on Exchange, or more specifically MAPI (Messaging Application Programming Interface), for data storage. Exchange uses a hierarchical collection of folders for data storage. Every folder can have subfolders, *ad infinitum*. Individual folder items are just blobs of data. It's up to the applications that use them to make sense of the bits and bytes.

At a minimum, to use Outlook you'll need to create a set of *personal folders* on your hard drive. Exchange stores these in a PST (for *personal message store*) file. When you create your PST file, your set of personal folders will contain subfolders for electronic messaging (Inbox, Outbox, Sent Items, and Deleted Items). Outlook will create additional folders for its use (Calendar, Contacts, Journal, Notes, and Tasks). Part of creating Automation solutions with Outlook is navigating this folder hierarchy.

Finally, to access any of the folders managed by Outlook, you'll need to tell Outlook what messaging system, known as a *namespace,* to use. You do this by calling the GetNamespace method of Outlook's Application object. Currently only one namespace, MAPI, is supported, but this method allows for future extensibility.

Conversing with Outlook

Beginning an Automation session with Outlook involves creating a new instance of the Application class, specifying a namespace to use, and logging on to the messaging system. We've wrapped these steps inside a function in basOutlook called adh-GetOutlook, shown in Listing 20.6, that returns a pointer to the MAPI namespace after logging in.

Listing 20.6

```
Function adhGetOutlook() As Outlook.NameSpace
    Dim objOutlook As New Outlook.Application
    Dim objNamespace As Outlook.NameSpace
    Dim strProfile As String
    Dim strPassword As String

    Const adhcLogonForm = "frmChooseProfile"

    ' Open the logon form
    DoCmd.OpenForm FormName:=adhcLogonForm, _
     windowmode:=acDialog

    ' If the user didn't cancel, continue
    If SysCmd(acSysCmdGetObjectState, acForm, _
     adhcLogonForm) Then

        ' Get the profile and password to use
        strProfile = Nz(Forms(adhcLogonForm)!cboProfile)
        strPassword = Nz(Forms(adhcLogonForm)!txtPassword)
        DoCmd.Close acForm, adhcLogonForm

        ' Get a reference to the MAPI workspace
        Set objNamespace = objOutlook.GetNamespace("MAPI")

        ' Log on, creating a new MAPI session,
        ' using the profile and password
        Call objNamespace.Logon(strProfile, _
         strPassword, False, True)

        ' Return a reference to the namespace
        Set adhGetOutlook = objNamespace
    End If
End Function
```

We begin by opening a dialog, shown in Figure 20.15, that prompts the user for an Exchange profile and the password associated with it. Exchange profiles are used to define combinations of data storage and electronic messaging systems for use during an Exchange session. Once the user has made a selection, the adh-GetOutlook function calls GetNamespace, passing "MAPI" as the namespace type, and then calls the namespace's Logon method. Logon takes four arguments:

- The name of an Exchange profile

- The password associated with that profile

- A True/False value that determines whether a logon dialog is displayed

- A True/False value that determines whether a new Exchange session is created

FIGURE 20.15

Selecting an Exchange profile prior to working with Outlook

Creating New Journal Entries

adhGetOutlook is used by the two forms that make up the sample application to begin an Automation session. The frmOutlookWriteJournal form, shown in Figure 20.16, lets you create journal entries by selecting a date on the calendar ActiveX control, entering subject, start time, and end time information, and clicking the Log button.

FIGURE 20.16

The frmOutlookWrite-Journal form lets you create new journal entries.

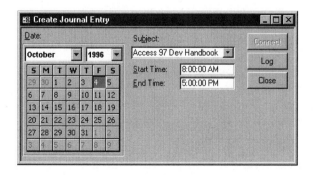

Before you click the Log button, however, you must click the Connect button to begin the Automation session. Code behind this button calls adhGetOutlook and stores the resultant Namespace object in a module-level variable. It does this so you can use the same namespace to create multiple journal entries without repeatedly starting and stopping Outlook. After you connect to Outlook, the button becomes disabled.

Code behind the Log button, shown in Listing 20.7, uses the Namespace object to create a new journal entry by first obtaining a reference to the Journal folder. It does this by calling the namespace's GetDefaultFolder method with the olFolderJournal constant. While you could use the Folders collection to navigate the hierarchy manually, using GetDefaultFolder is easier when you need to access any of the messaging or Outlook folders.

Listing 20.7

```
Private Sub cmdLog_Click()
    Dim objOLJournal As Outlook.MAPIFolder

    ' Make sure we have a valid reference
    If mobjOLNamespace Is Nothing Then
        Me!cmdConnect.Enabled = True
        Me!cmdConnect.SetFocus
        Me!cmdOK.Enabled = False
    Else
        ' Get a reference to the "Journal" folder
        Set objOLJournal = mobjOLNamespace. _
         GetDefaultFolder(olFolderJournal)

        ' Create a new journal item, set its
        ' properties, and save it
        With objOLJournal.Items.Add(olJournalItem)
            .Start = CVDate(Me!calMain.Value & " " & Me!txtStart)
            .End = CVDate(Me!calMain.Value & " " & Me!txtEnd)
            .Subject = Me!cboSubject
            .Type = "Task"
            .Save
        End With
    End If
End Sub
```

Once a reference to the Journal folder has been obtained, the procedure calls the Add method of the folder's Items collection. This creates a new journal entry. The procedure uses a With block to set various properties before calling the new object's Save method.

Loading Journal Information

Once you've created a few journal entries, you can use the frmOutlookReadJournal form shown in Figure 20.17 to load them into an Access table. The contents of this table, tblJournalEntries in the sample database, is displayed on the form as well as summarized on a report, rptTime. You can open the report by clicking the Report button.

FIGURE 20.17

The frmOutlookRead-Journal form loads and displays journal entries.

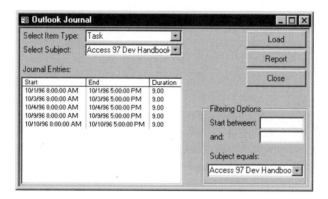

Reading journal entries from Outlook is quite similar to creating them. First, the applicaiton calls adhGetOutlook, then creates a reference to the Journal folder, and finally uses a For Each loop to iterate through each item in the folder. Listing 20.8 shows a portion of the code that accomplishes this. The rstJournal variable in the listing refers to a DAO recordset based on the tblJournalEntries table, and obj-FilteredItems is declared as an Outlook.Items variable.

Listing 20.8

```
' Get a reference to the "Journal" folder
Set objOLJournal = objOLNamespace. _
 GetDefaultFolder(olFolderJournal)

' Filter the items in the folder
Set objFilteredItems = _
```

```
    adhFilterItems(objOLJournal.Items)

' Process the items in the folder, adding them
' to the journal entries table
With rstJournal
    For Each outItem In objFilteredItems
        .AddNew
        !EntryID = outItem.EntryID
        !Type = outItem.Type
        !Subject = outItem.Subject
        !Start = outItem.Start
        !End = outItem.End
        .Update
    Next
End With
```

In addition to simply reading the items from the folder, we optionally apply a filter to them using the Items collection's Restrict method. Listing 20.9 shows the adhFilter-Items function that accomplishes this. It builds a filter string based on controls on the form. Applying the Restrict method does not change the existing Items collection but instead returns a new Items collection representing items that match the filter expression. It is this new collection that is returned as a result of calling adhFilterItems.

Listing 20.9

```
Private Function adhFilterItems(objItemsToFilter As _
 Outlook.Items) As Outlook.Items

    Dim strFilter As String
    Dim strQuote As String * 1

    ' Get a double quote for delimiters
    strQuote = Chr$(34)

    ' First check date range
    If IsDate(Me!txtFilterStart1) And _
     IsDate(Me!txtFilterStart2) Then

        strFilter = "[Start] >= " & strQuote & _
        Me!txtFilterStart1 & strQuote & " AND " & _
        "[Start] <= " & strQuote & _
        Me!txtFilterStart2 & strQuote
    End If
```

```
        ' Then check Subject
        If Not IsNull(Me!cboFilterSubject) Then
            If Len(strFilter) Then
                strFilter = strFilter & " AND "
            End If
            strFilter = "[Subject] = " & strQuote & _
             Me!cboFilterSubject & strQuote
        End If

        ' If we have a filter, apply it to the Items collection,
        ' otherwise just return the original collection
        If Len(strFilter) Then
            Set adhFilterItems = objItemsToFilter. _
             Restrict(strFilter)
        Else
            Set adhFilterItems = objItemsToFilter
        End If
End Function
```

The Restrict method (and its relative, the Find method) is useful when you have many items in a particular folder. Reading each item one at a time to locate specific ones can take a lot of time. Filter expressions used with the Restrict and Find methods must obey these rules:

- You can use any property name (for example, Subject), as long as it is enclosed in square brackets.

- You can use only property names and literal values.

- You can use only the =, >, <, >=, <=, and <> operators.

- You can combine individual expressions using the And, Or, and Not operators.

- Each individual expression must evaluate to True or False.

Example: Creating a PowerPoint Presentation

Our third sample Automation application uses Microsoft PowerPoint to create a slide presentation based on the data in tblJournalEntries. It demonstrates how to work with PowerPoint's somewhat cumbersome object model to create simple slide presentations, complete with transition effects and timings. While PowerPoint is a document-based application like Word and Excel, the documents (specifically, slides) are much less structured, containing various elements such as text, graphics, sound, and video clips. Creating complex presentations requires a bit of hard work, but once you've familiarized yourself with the basic structure of a PowerPoint slide, you should be able to accomplish this without much trouble.

Understanding PowerPoint Slides

On the surface, PowerPoint's object model is very similar to those of Word and Excel. At its root is the Application class, which contains a collection of Presentation objects. Each Presentation object, in turn, contains a collection of Slide objects. You add new slides to a presentation using the Add method of the Presentations collection. Add accepts two arguments: the position in the presentation where the new slide is to appear and a constant representing the slide layout. Layout options include blank, title and subtitle, title only, title and text, and so on. Layout options correspond to those shown in PowerPoint's Add Slide dialog.

From here the object model diverges greatly from its counterparts. The contents of a slide fall into the general category of Shapes. A shape could be a line, rectangle, text box, chart, picture, or one of a variety of other objects. You create new shapes by calling one of the methods listed in Table 20.5. Each method returns a pointer to a Shape object that you can manipulate using its properties and methods.

TABLE 20.5 Methods for Creating PowerPoint Shapes

Method	Shape Created
AddCallout	Callout with arrow
AddComment	Slide comment
AddConnector	Shape connector
AddCurve	Curved line
AddLabel	Text label
AddLine	Straight line
AddMediaObject	Media object (.AVI, .WAV, etc.)
AddOLEObject	Other embedded object

TABLE 20.5   Methods for Creating PowerPoint Shapes (continued)

Method	Shape Created
AddPicture	Graphical image based on a file
AddPlaceholder	Placeholder (a preset shape from the slide's original layout)
AddPolyline	Multi-segmented line
AddShape	Predefined shape (rectangle, circle, star, etc.)
AddTextbox	Text box
AddTextEffect	WordArt image
AddTitle	Title placeholder
BuildFreeForm	FreeForm drawing object

Depending on the style of slide you create, you may already have several shapes on the slide. For example, the ppLayoutText style (the traditional bullet point with title slide) has two Shape objects, one for the title and one for the bulleted text. In addition to the methods listed in Table 20.5, the Shapes collection has two useful properties, HasTitle and Title. HasTitle is a Boolean property that determines whether the slide has a shape designated as the title. If so, it will be the first Shape object in the Shapes collection, and you can use the Title property to return a pointer to it.

We've created a wrapper function for adding new slides to a presentation that handles the task of designating a layout style and setting title text, if applicable. The function, adhAddNewSlide, is shown in Listing 20.10 and included in the sample database's basPowerPoint module. You will notice that we've used optional arguments to provide sensible default values for various slide properties.

Listing 20.10

```
Function adhAddNewSlide(objPres As PowerPoint.Presentation, _
  Optional intStyle As Integer = ppLayoutText, _
  Optional strTitle As String = "", _
  Optional intIndex As Integer = 0) _
As PowerPoint.Slide

    Dim objSlide As PowerPoint.Slide
```

```
                ' Use the passed Presentation
            With objPres

                ' Find out where to put the slide
                If intIndex = 0 Or intIndex > .Slides.Count + 1 Then
                    intIndex = .Slides.Count + 1
                End If

                ' Create new slide
                Set objSlide = .Slides.Add(intIndex, intStyle)

                ' If the slide has a title, set it
                With objSlide.Shapes
                    If .HasTitle Then
                        .Title.TextFrame.TextRange.Text = strTitle
                    End If
                End With

                ' Return pointer to the slide
                Set adhAddNewSlide = objSlide
            End With
        End Function
```

After creating the new slide, adhAddNewSlide returns a pointer to it that the calling procedure can use to set slide properties. The code that sets the slide's title text requires a bit of explanation. For that we'll have to delve more deeply into the structure of PowerPoint Shape objects.

Working with PowerPoint Shapes

PowerPoint shapes are rather complex objects. A shape has properties that control its appearance, contained text, animation settings, and actions during a slide show. Of most interest to us are those that control the text contained in the shape. Other appearance properties, such as Fill, Rotation, and Shadow, should be fairly self-explanatory.

You cannot access contained text directly. Instead you must first reference a shape's TextFrame property, which returns a pointer to a TextFrame object. A TextFrame object is the rectangular region in which PowerPoint draws text. It has properties that control overall text margins, anchor points, and orientation. It also has a Ruler property that returns a pointer to a Ruler object. Using the Ruler object, you can set indentation levels and tab stops.

To actually manipulate text inside a shape, you use the TextFrame's TextRange property. TextRange returns a pointer to an object of the same name. TextRange objects are similar to Range objects in Word and Excel in that they contain actual data that you can manipulate. The default property of a TextRange object is Text, which returns the actual characters. You can also use properties such as Font and Paragraph-Format to control the text's appearance. The TextRange class also has a variety of methods for dissecting text, such as Paragraphs, Sentences, Words, and Characters, and others for editing text, such as Cut, Copy, Paste, InsertAfter, and InsertBefore.

We touch on only a few of these in our sample application. If you're serious about using PowerPoint as an Automation component, spend an afternoon using Object Browser and online help to explore its extremely rich object model.

Creating a Simple Presentation

Our sample application uses the data in tblJournalEntries, described earlier in this chapter, to create a slide presentation that details total time spent on various tasks. The process is initiated from the frmCreatePPT form shown in Figure 20.18. The form lets you specify text for a title slide, as well as options for a slide show you can run after the presentation has been created.

Code behind the OK button creates the new presentation. Listing 20.11 shows a portion of the code. (For a complete listing, refer to the form in CH20.MDB.) You'll notice that the procedure uses the adhAddNewSlide function mentioned earlier in this chapter.

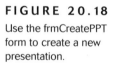

FIGURE 20.18

Use the frmCreatePPT form to create a new presentation.

Listing 20.11

```
Dim objPPApp As New PowerPoint.Application
Dim objPPPres As PowerPoint.Presentation
Dim objPPSlide As PowerPoint.Slide

' Create a new presentation
Set objPPPres = objPPApp.Presentations.Add

' If user wants a design template, apply it
If Me!chkTemplate Then
    objPPPres.ApplyTemplate mstrTemplatePath & _
    "\" & Me!lstTemplates & ".pot"
End If

' Add a new title slide
Set objPPSlide = adhAddNewSlide(objPPPres, _
 ppLayoutTitle, Nz(Me!txtTitle))
objPPSlide.Shapes(2).TextFrame.TextRange.Text = _
 Nz(Me!txtSubtitle)
Call adhSetSlideShowOptions(objPPSlide)
```

After creating a new presentation using the Add method of the Presentations collection, the procedure optionally applies a design template based on the user's selection. Design templates supply colors, fonts, and other aspects of a presentation. The procedure then adds a title slide using the ppLayoutTitle constant and the text from the form. At this point the new presentation contains a single slide. Figure 20.19 shows an example of what it might look like.

Additional slides are created inside a Do Until loop that iterates through data summarized from tblJournalEntries. A new slide is created for every month that appears in the summarized data. The code shown in Listing 20.12 enters details on tasks and times on the slide.

Listing 20.12

```
' Add a new slide
Set objPPSlide = adhAddNewSlide(objPPPres, , _
 rstPeriods!MonthYear)
Call adhSetSlideShowOptions(objPPSlide)

' Insert the main bullet point (Subject)
With objPPSlide.Shapes(2).TextFrame. _
```

```
TextRange.InsertAfter

    .IndentLevel = 1
    .Text = rstTime!Subject & vbCrLf

    ' Insert the sub head (Duration)
    With .InsertAfter
        .IndentLevel = 2
        .Text = Format(rstTime!Duration, _
        "0.00 hours") & vbCrLf
    End With
End With
```

FIGURE 20.19

Title slide from a newly created presentation

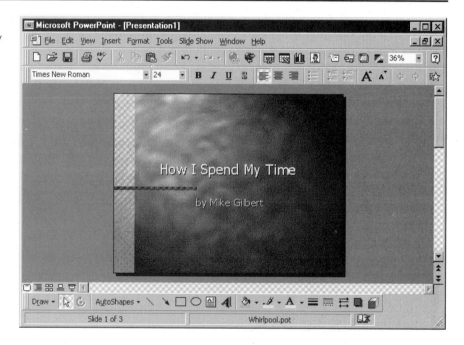

You can see how we use the TextFrame and TextRange properties of Shape(2). Shape(2) is the bulleted text frame on the slide. We make heavy use of the InsertAfter method. When called with a String argument, InsertAfter inserts the text after any existing text and returns a TextRange object that points to the newly inserted text.

When called with no arguments, it returns a pointer to an empty TextRange object at the end of the current text stream. Once we have this in a With block, we can set its IndentLevel and Text properties. Figure 20.20 illustrates what one of the slides created using this code looks like.

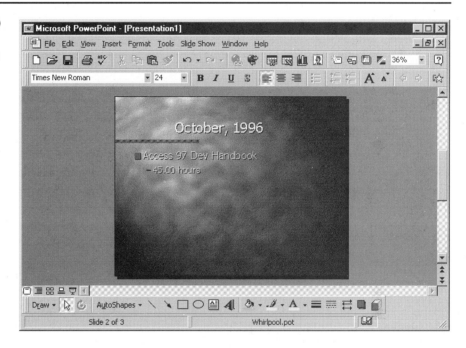

Apply Slide Show Effects

frmCreatePPT also contains controls for setting slide show options. Specifically, you can select a transition to use between slides, the amount of time before advancing to the next slide, and whether to start the slide show automatically after creating the presentation. The adhSetSlideShowOptions procedure shown in Listing 20.13 applies these choices.

Listing 20.13

```
Private Sub adhSetSlideShowOptions(objSlide _
 As PowerPoint.Slide)

    With objSlide.SlideShowTransition
```

```
        If Me!chkTransition Then
            .EntryEffect = CInt(Me!cboTransitions)
        End If
        If Me!chkAdvance Then
            .AdvanceOnTime = msoTrue
            .AdvanceTime = CSng(Me!txtSeconds)
        End If
    End With
End Sub
```

The procedure operates on the slide's SlideShowTransition object, setting the EntryEffect, AdvanceOnTime, and AdvanceTime properties. Calling the Run method of the presentation's SlideShowSettings object in the event procedure for the OK button actually starts the slide show. As you can imagine, there is a host of other properties and methods of these objects. Once again, use Object Browser to your advantage when exploring PowerPoint's object model.

Example: Populating an Excel Worksheet

Microsoft Excel is probably one of the most satisfying Automation servers you can work with. It has a rich, well-documented object model that lets you control just about every element of an Excel worksheet, right down to individual character formatting within a cell. In this section we show you how to update a simple worksheet and chart with data in an Access database. We've already discussed most of what you need to know about using Automation servers, so we'll keep this section brief.

Using an Existing File

One thing we haven't yet discussed is using an Automation server to manipulate an existing document. Manipulating existing documents is a technique that becomes critical when you need to retrieve data from a file that was edited by another process or even a (gasp!) human being. Because you don't have complete control over it, you must be careful when altering and saving it to make sure you don't inadvertently overwrite another person's changes. Using existing files is also a good compromise between completely manual and completely automated creation of documents. For example, the VBA code required to create a complex Excel chart can be quite long. It is often better to use an existing chart and modify only a few properties.

From a programming standpoint, you can approach this problem in one of two ways. You can either create an instance of Excel's Application object and use it to open an existing file or you can use the GetObject function, which will return a reference directly to the workbook. In this example we've used GetObject to demonstrate how to use it with existing documents. GetObject lets you specify a document name and path instead of a ProgID. As long as the file type is correctly registered, Windows will start the appropriate Automation component application (if it's not already running) and load the specified file.

Our Scenario

The scenario for our sample Excel application involves a fictitious airline. CH20.MDB contains a table of airport codes (tblAirports) and a table filled with randomly generated lost-luggage rates (tblLostCount) for each North American airport for the month of January 1997. In our example we've also created an Excel workbook called STATREQ.XLS that allows users to request data on any given airport. You might think of it as a query form a user can fill out and send to someone else for processing. The workbook contains two worksheets. The Query worksheet, shown in Figure 20.21, lets the user fill in an airport code (the standard, three-character code assigned by the International Air Transport Association) in a cell. Our Access application will query the database and, based on the current date, return information on month-to-date lost-luggage rates. The second worksheet in STATREQ.XLS, called Results, provides a table of data and a chart. In our example we show you how to perform the following steps using Automation to control Excel:

1. Open the workbook.

2. Retrieve the airport code from the Query worksheet.

3. Query the Access database.

4. Return the results to the worksheet.

5. Redefine the data range the chart uses to reflect new data.

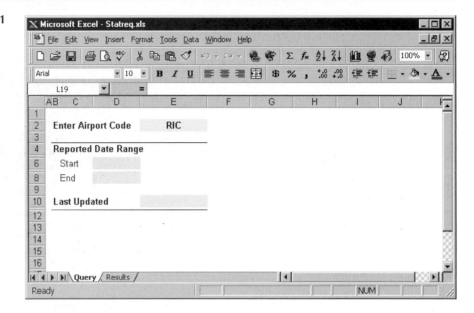

Creating an Object from an Existing Document

There is no user interface for our simple example function. Rather, we've created one procedure, called adhUpdateAirportStats, in basExcel, that handles all the processing. The module basExcel, in CH20.MDB on the companion disk, shows the entire subroutine. If you view the module in Design view, you can see from the variable declarations that we use quite a few Excel object variables in the procedure.

The first thing the procedure does is call GetObject, passing it the path to the STATREQ.XLS file. As long as Excel is installed correctly and the path is valid, GetObject should return a reference to an Excel workbook. This differs from the other examples we've discussed so far, which used the Application object of each Automation server. Keep this in mind as you create object references to documents. The object you create will be somewhere in the middle of the object hierarchy, not at the top, as is the case with Application objects.

Because we will want to manipulate Excel's Application object in addition to a Workbook object, we need a way to create a reference to it. Fortunately, rather than using another call to GetObject or CreateObject, we can use the Parent property of Excel objects to return a reference to the object immediately above the current object in the object hierarchy. Using the Parent property, we can create references to the Application object using the following code:

```
Set objXLApp = objXLBook.Parent
```

> **WARNING**
>
> With Excel 97, Microsoft has made a change to the way an XLS file is referenced using GetObject. Passing an XLS file now returns a Workbook object. In prior versions, GetObject returned a Worksheet object representing the first worksheet in the XLS file. This will undoubtedly break some existing applications. If you have existing VBA code that uses GetObject in this fashion, be sure to take note of this change in behavior.

Working with Excel Objects

Once we have a few object variables hanging around, pointing to some of the key objects in our Excel application, we can begin to manipulate the worksheets. Some aspects of controlling Excel objects are identical to Access VBA code. For example, to display the Excel main window and the STATREQ.XLS document window, we can set their Visible properties to True:

```
objXLApp.Visible = True
objXLBook.Windows(1).Visible = True
```

Other aspects, however, require that you write a bit more code. Excel, unlike Access, does not support the concept of default collections. For example, the following two lines of Access VBA code are identical because the Controls collection is the default collection for a Form object:

```
Forms("txtLastName").Enabled = True
Forms.Controls("txtLastName").Enabled = True
```

You must explicitly specify each collection when referring to objects in an Excel application. Therefore, the code that sets object references to the two worksheets in STATREQ.XLS, named Query and Results, looks like this:

```
Set objQuerySheet = objXLBook.Worksheets("Query")
Set objResultsSheet = objXLBook.Worksheets("Results")
```

Furthermore, Excel supports bang (!) syntax only for absolute range references on worksheets. You must use the syntax shown above, which utilizes the collection name and an object identifier (either a name or an index number) in parentheses, to refer to specific objects in a collection.

Updating the Worksheets and Chart

The bulk of the processing in adhUpdateAirportStats involves running a query against the tblLostCount table and poking the results into the Results worksheet in STATREQ.XLS. We do this by first querying the data and placing the results in a Variant array using the GetRows method of the Recordset object:

```
Set dbThis = CurrentDb
Set qdfLost = dbThis.QueryDefs("qryLostCount")

qdfLost.Parameters![pIATACode] = varIATACode
qdfLost.Parameters![pStart] = varStart
qdfLost.Parameters![pEnd] = varEnd

Set rstLost = qdfLost.OpenRecordset(dbOpenSnapshot)

varResults = rstLost.GetRows(31)
rstLost.Close
dbThis.Close
```

We then clear any existing data using the Clear method of a Range object corresponding to the data shown in Figure 20.22. This figure also shows the Chart object, which we will update once all the data has been copied.

FIGURE 20.22

Results worksheet showing a data table and chart

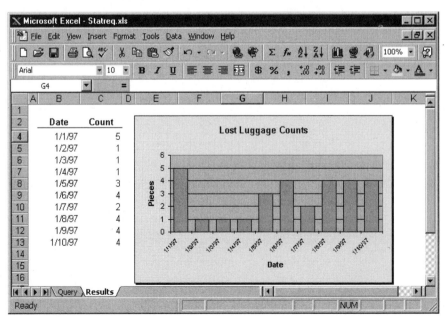

The code that clears the existing data is shown below. Notice that we use the worksheet's Range method with a named cell range.

```
objResultsSheet.Range("rngDataAll").Clear
```

We can now copy the results of our query into the Excel worksheet. The simplest and fastest way to do this is to construct a Range object that refers to the block of cells where the data belongs and set its FormulaArray property equal to the query results stored in our Variant array. The other alternative, iterating through each cell in the range, is extremely slow because Excel is running as an out-of-process server. (If you want to know more, see the sidebar "In-Process versus Out-of-Process Servers" later in the chapter.) The following code demonstrates how to use the FormulaArray property. Note that we need to use Excel's Transpose function because the array returned by GetRows is not oriented correctly.

```
Set objXLRange = objResultsSheet. _
  Range("B4:C" & 4 + UBound(varResults, 2))

objXLRange.FormulaArray = _
  objXLApp.Transpose(varResults)
```

The last task remaining once the data is on the worksheet is to redefine the source for the chart to reflect the current amount of data. We use Excel's Union method (a method of the Application object) to combine the data range computed in the prior step with cells B2 and C2, which contain the headings for the data and chart. We use this with the ChartWizard method of the Chart object on the Results worksheet to set the new data source equal to the existing data set:

```
objResultsSheet.ChartObjects(1). _
  Chart.ChartWizard Source:=objXLApp. _
  Union(objResultsSheet.Range("B2:C2"), _
  objXLRange)
```

To test adhUpdateAirportStats, you'll need to copy STATREQ.XLS to a directory on your hard disk and edit the adhcXLSPath constant accordingly. Then run adhUpdateAirportStats from the Access Debug window. AdhUpdateAirportStats should work regardless of whether Excel is currently running or STATREQ.XLS is currently loaded.

In-Process versus Out-of-Process Servers

Automation components can be grouped into two categories that describe how the operating system treats their program code. *In-process* servers are loaded into the same memory address space (or *process space*) as the client application. The Jet database engine is an example of an in-process server, as are ActiveX controls. When you reference the DBEngine object, for example, you're communicating with an instance of Jet loaded into Access' process space using Automation. You can also create your own in-process servers using Visual Basic, where they are called OLE DLLs.

Out-of-process servers, on the other hand, are loaded into their own address space. All the Microsoft Office applications, as well as normal Automation servers you create in Visual Basic, are out-of-process servers.

From a practical standpoint, the biggest difference between the two types of servers is the rate at which communication takes place between them and your client application. In-process servers are, as a rule, much faster than out-of-process. This is because Windows does not need to manage data and communications between two separate processes and address spaces.

While you can't control what type of server an Automation server is, you can modify your code when using out-of-process servers. Try to avoid repeated references to objects, properties, and methods. In our example we've taken advantage of the fact that you can insert several cells' worth of data into an Excel worksheet with a single statement. We avoided referencing individual cells one at a time.

Using ActiveX Controls

Access 2.0 was the first application to support ActiveX controls, then called OLE custom controls. ActiveX controls, or *OCXs*, as they are sometimes called because of their file extension, are the successors to VBX controls, the modular components that helped make Visual Basic such a success. ActiveX controls encapsulate a certain degree of functionality that you can integrate into your application simply by placing one on your Access form. Access 97 integrates ActiveX controls much better than Access 2.0, but in most respects controls are used in the same way.

In addition to their being self-contained chunks of functionality, you can control ActiveX controls the same way you control other applications using Automation. ActiveX controls implement their own objects, properties, methods, and events. In this section we show you how to control the calendar control that ships with Access 97.

ActiveX Control Registration and Licensing

Before you can use a ActiveX control, you must make sure it is properly registered. By this we mean that the correct entries are made in the Windows Registry to enable the control's functionality. If you purchase a development tool that includes ActiveX controls, such as Microsoft Visual Basic 4.0 or the Office 97 Developer Edition, the installation program usually installs and registers the controls for you. If you acquire controls separately or are installing controls on your users' computers to support your application, you will have to register the controls yourself.

To register controls, you can use either the ActiveX Controls dialog in Microsoft Access or the REGSVR32.EXE program that ships with Visual Basic. Figure 20.23 shows the Access 97 ActiveX Controls dialog. You display the dialog by selecting Tools ➤ ActiveX Controls. As you can see, the dialog lists the controls that are currently registered and features buttons for registering and unregistering controls. The unregistering feature is useful for deleting Registry entries for controls you no longer plan to use.

FIGURE 20.23

Access 97 ActiveX
Controls dialog

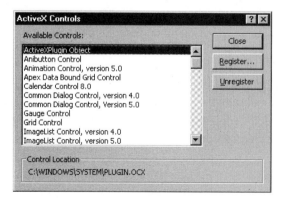

To register a new control, click the Register button and select the control from the file dialog that appears. To unregister a control, simply select it from the list and click the Unregister button.

If you are distributing your application to others whom you do not want messing with the ActiveX Controls dialog, you can register controls using a small program, REGSVR32.EXE. The syntax of REGSVR32.EXE is shown here:

REGSVR32.EXE [/u] *filename*.ocx

You run REGSVR32.EXE using the path to the ActiveX control you wish to register. The program uses information in the OCX file to create the proper Registry entries. You can use the /u switch to unregister a control.

If you're using the Setup Wizard that comes with the Office 97 Developer Edition, you can include any ActiveX controls your application uses as part of the installation file list. The installation program that installs your application will register the controls for you automatically.

If you plan to develop applications using ActiveX controls, you need to be aware of the new licensing scheme most control developers now use. Unlike Visual Basic VBXs, which used a simple text file located in the VBX directory, ActiveX controls use Registry settings to control whether you can use a particular control in Design view and/or at run time. These Registry settings are normally created when the controls are installed, usually by some type of installation program. Creating these entries yourself on a computer for which you did not purchase a copy of the ActiveX control is probably a violation of the vendor's license agreement.

Inserting ActiveX Controls

You place ActiveX controls on forms by selecting Insert ➤ ActiveX Control while in Form Design view. This action displays the Insert ActiveX Controls dialog, as shown in Figure 20.24.

The dialog's list box displays the controls that have been registered on your computer and are available to you. To insert the control, select the control name from the list and click the OK button. Access inserts the control on your form. You can then size it to meet your needs.

In addition to using the menu, you can create custom command bar buttons for each ActiveX control. To do this, open the Customize dialog by selecting the Customize command from the View ➤ Toolbars menu, select the Commands tab, and

FIGURE 20.24

Insert ActiveX Control dialog listing the available ActiveX controls

select ActiveX Controls from the list of categories. You should see a dialog like the one in Figure 20.25, listing the available controls instead of displaying buttons. To create a custom command bar button, just select an ActiveX control from the list and drag it onto a command bar. Access creates the button using the icon associated with the chosen control.

After creating a custom command bar button, adding the control to a form becomes simply a matter of clicking the button and then dragging a region on the form, just as for any of the built-in controls.

FIGURE 20.25

Creating a command bar button for an ActiveX control using the Customize dialog

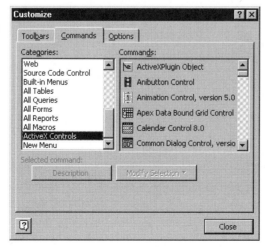

In addition to adding the control to your form, Access automatically adds a reference to the control's type library to your VBA project. You should see a reference for the control listed in the References dialog after inserting it on a form. This allows you to use the control's properties and methods in your VBA code. If you don't see a reference to the control, you'll need to add it yourself.

Modifying ActiveX Control Properties

ActiveX controls have properties, just like built-in controls. Because all ActiveX controls are hosted by a special object frame, when you select an ActiveX control in Design view, the Access property sheet displays properties associated with the object frame. If you want to modify those properties specific to the control, you have two choices. Your first choice is to select the Other (or All) tab from the control's property sheet. Here you will find most of the properties for the ActiveX control. For example, Figure 20.26 shows the property sheet for a copy of the calendar control that ships with Access 97.

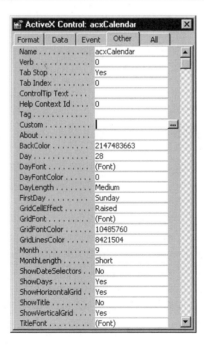

FIGURE 20.26

Custom properties for a calendar control

Your other option is to use the control's custom property dialog. Each ActiveX control implements a dialog that lets you modify its properties. Figure 20.27 shows the custom property dialog for the calendar control. You can display this dialog by clicking the Build button to the right of the Custom property on the Access property sheet (near the top of Figure 20.26) or by right-clicking the control and selecting *Control* Object ➤ Properties from the shortcut menu.

FIGURE 20.27

Custom property dialog for a calendar control

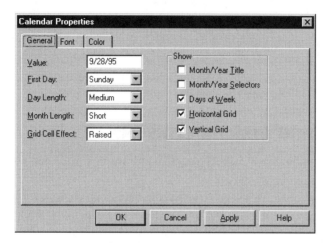

Using ActiveX Control Events

ActiveX controls differ from Access controls in that they do not expose their events through the property sheet. Access controls have properties such as OnClick, which you can use to call a macro, VBA function, or code contained in the form's module. ActiveX control events are available only from the form's module. When you add an ActiveX control to a form, VBA adds event procedure stubs to the form's module that correspond to those supported by the control. To view these event points, you must open the module, select the control from the Object list, and then select the event from the Procedure list. Figure 20.28 shows a module window open to the AfterUpdate event of a calendar control. Note, however, that some of the events in this list belong to the object frame, not to the control itself. These include the Enter, Exit, GotFocus, LostFocus, Click, DblClick, MouseDown, MouseMove, MouseUp, and Updated events.

FIGURE 20.28

FIGURE 20.28

Event procedure for
a calendar control's
AfterUpdate event

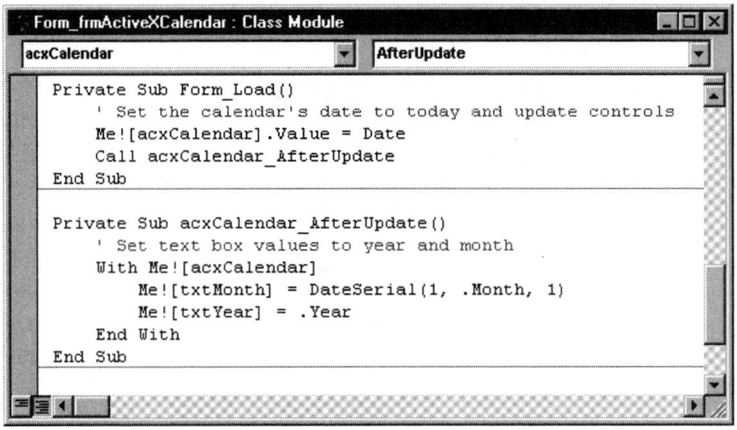

```
Form_frmActiveXCalendar : Class Module                         _ □ ×
acxCalendar                    ▼   AfterUpdate                 ▼
    Private Sub Form_Load()
        ' Set the calendar's date to today and update controls
        Me![acxCalendar].Value = Date
        Call acxCalendar_AfterUpdate
    End Sub

    Private Sub acxCalendar_AfterUpdate()
        ' Set text box values to year and month
        With Me![acxCalendar]
            Me![txtMonth] = DateSerial(1, .Month, 1)
            Me![txtYear] = .Year
        End With
    End Sub
```

Using Bound ActiveX Controls

A valuable feature of Access 97 is the support for bound ActiveX controls. For example, you can bind the calendar to a Date/Time field by setting the control's ControlSource property to the field name. There is no need to write any code; you simply choose the control source from the property sheet just as you would for an Access control. We've included a form, frmBoundCalendar, in CH20.MDB, which demonstrates this. This type of binding is called *simple binding* because the control is bound only to a single column. Some ActiveX controls also support *complex binding*—binding to an entire table, with the control managing individual fields. Some of the ActiveX controls that ship with Visual Basic support complex binding. Unfortunately, Access, unlike VB, does not support complex binding from the client side, so you won't be able to use these controls with Access.

Calendar Control Example

To demonstrate the use of ActiveX controls, we have created a simple example using the calendar control that ships with Access 97. Figure 20.29 shows our sample form, frmActiveXCalendar. It's a rather rudimentary form containing only the calendar control, two text boxes, and four command buttons. We can use it, however, to demonstrate manipulating ActiveX control events and properties.

You can use the buttons on the form to move from month to month and year to year. As the date changes, so do the month and year shown in the text boxes at the top of the form. You can use the mouse to click a day on the calendar, and that

FIGURE 20.29

A sample form using the calendar ActiveX control

changes the date as well. Double-clicking the calendar displays a message box containing the current date.

Listing 20.14 shows some of the code contained in frmActiveXCalendar's VBA module. You can view the complete listing by opening the form in Design view. It's not much code, a fact that testifies to the value of ActiveX controls.

Listing 20.14

```
Private Sub Form_Load()
    ' Set the calendar's date to today and update controls
    Me![acxCalendar].Value = Date
    Call acxCalendar_AfterUpdate
End Sub

Private Sub acxCalendar_AfterUpdate()
    ' Set text box values to year and month
    With Me![acxCalendar]
        Me![txtMonth] = DateSerial(1, .Month, 1)
        Me![txtYear] = .Year
    End With
End Sub

Sub cmdNextMonth_Click()
    ' Move to next month by calling the NextMonth method
    Me![acxCalendar].NextMonth
End Sub
```

As you can see from the code sample in Listing 20.14, using ActiveX controls is very much like using built-in Access controls. You set their properties the same way and call their methods the same way. You even respond to their events the same way—using the event procedures generated in the form's module (for example, acxCalendar_AfterUpdate). Access and VBA insulate you from the fact that the control is a separate software component.

ActiveX Control References

One issue that arises when you use ActiveX controls (or a type library from any Automation server) in your applications is that of type library references. When you insert an ActiveX control on a form, Access automatically creates a reference to that control's type library (normally stored in the OCX itself) in your VBA project. Access stores the full path to the control. This means that if you install your application in a different path on your user's computer, VBA will not be able to resolve the reference, and your ActiveX control–specific VBA code will not compile.

Access is somewhat intelligent about automatically resolving references for you. For instance, Access automatically reestablishes references if you create them for controls in the Windows\System directory or in the directory where Access itself is installed. If you plan to distribute ActiveX controls with your application, choose one of these locations as the destination for OCX and type library files. You can also reestablish references programmatically using VBA. For more information on how to do this, see Chapter 22.

Using ActiveX Controls from Other Products

As the number of ActiveX controls increases, you will have a wider selection to choose from when building your applications. Be aware, however, that not all ActiveX controls work well with Access. Many of the controls that ship with Microsoft Visual Basic, for example, have features not available through Access. For example, Access does not support the ability to embed one ActiveX control in another, so you won't be able to create the same visual effect with some controls that you can with Visual Basic. As this technology matures, it will be easier to share components among development tools. Until then, treat new ActiveX controls with a degree of caution.

ActiveX Controls—Reusable Components or Not?

One of the benefits of old OLE custom controls was that you could use them in any development tool that supported the custom control architecture. While this was not completely true (for instance, some custom controls that shipped with Visual Basic 4.0 could not be used with Access 95), the controls were reusable enough to make working with them worthwhile. With the advent of the "new and improved" ActiveX controls, one would think that this situation would, at worst, stay the same and perhaps even improve.

Things are not always as we would like them to be. As it turns out, many ActiveX controls are actually *less* reusable than their OLE control counterparts. The reason for this is easy to explain and understand, albeit disappointing.

The original OLE custom control specification defined a set of programming interfaces that controls, as well as the applications that hosted them, *had* to support. Many of these interfaces, however, were not necessary from the control's standpoint. Controls implemented the interfaces nonetheless and, as a result, carried around excess baggage in the form of unnecessary program code.

When Microsoft later developed the ActiveX control specification, one driving goal was the ability to make controls available over the Internet via Web browsers such as Microsoft Internet Explorer 3.0. Since download time is a critical issue for Web-based controls, they need to be as small as possible. Obviously, carrying around excess and unused code increases the time required to download the control to a user's computer. So rather than insist that controls implement every programming interface, Microsoft decided to let developers implement only those that were necessary for the control to function. It is up to the host application (a browser or development tool) to determine which ones the control supports.

The net result of this decision is that you will soon have a plethora of ActiveX controls installed on your computer, only a handful of which you'll be able to use with Access. Keep that in mind as you evaluate controls for use in your applications.

Tapping into Events Using WithEvents

You've just seen how ActiveX controls expose their events to Access and VBA so you can write code in response to them. Have you ever wondered how this works? When Access loads an ActiveX control, it queries the control's type library for the list of events and then registers event sinks with the control for each one. An *event sink* is simply a way for a control to call into VBA rather than VBA calling into the control, which is what happens when you access the control's properties or methods. Until now the only way Access developers could tap into these event sinks was through event procedures on forms. With the latest version of VBA, however, you can create your own event sinks using the new WithEvents feature.

What Is WithEvents?

WithEvents is a VBA keyword used in conjunction with an object variable declaration. It signals to VBA that in addition to exposing the object's properties and methods, you want VBA to notify you of any events that object exposes. WithEvents is most useful when using Automation components like those in Microsoft Office. After all, ActiveX controls already expose their events through the host form's VBA module. In theory, though, you can use WithEvents with any Automation component that exposes events.

How do you know if an Automation component exposes events? The easiest way to find out is by looking at the component's entries in Object Browser. When you select a class that exposes events, Object Browser lists them along with properties and methods, marking them with a lightning-bolt icon. Figure 20.30 shows Object Browser displaying information on Microsoft Word's Application class. Near the bottom of the Members list you can see the two events exposed by the class, DocumentChange and Quit.

> **NOTE** The only events that Access exposes in this manner are the ItemAdded and ItemRemoved events of the References collection.

FIGURE 20.30

Object Browser display-
ing events exposed by
Word's Application class

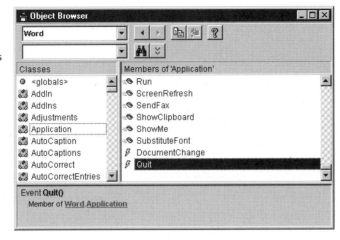

Using WithEvents

You use WithEvents in a variable declaration. There are a couple of catches, however. You can use it only in a class module (including form modules), and it must
appear in the declarations section. You can't declare a variable using WithEvents in
the body of a procedure. We've included a class module called clsWordEvents in the
sample database that contains the following declaration:

```
Private WithEvents mobjWordApp As Word.Application
```

Note that the WithEvents keyword is listed before the object variable name.
When you add a declaration using WithEvents to the declarations section of a class
module, VBA adds an entry to the Object drop-down list that corresponds to
the variable name. This is the same thing that happens when you add a control
(ActiveX or otherwise) to an Access form. Selecting that entry from the list displays
the object's events in the Procedure list. Figure 20.31 shows clsWordEvents open in
Design view with the DocumentChange event procedure selected. You can see that
we've responded to the event by opening a dialog that displays the name of the
current active document.

Before you can begin using the event functionality exposed by an Automation
component, you must do two things that are normally taken care of for you when
using ActiveX controls. You need to instantiate the Automation component class,
and you need to create an instance of the VBA class where the component class
variable is declared.

FIGURE 20.31

Editing mobjWordApp's
DocumentChange event
procedure

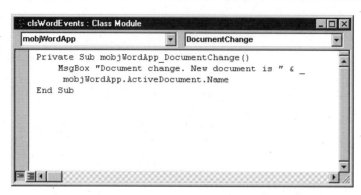

```
clsWordEvents : Class Module                              _ □ ✕

mobjWordApp              ▼   DocumentChange              ▼

    Private Sub mobjWordApp_DocumentChange()
        MsgBox "Document change. New document is " & _
            mobjWordApp.ActiveDocument.Name
    End Sub
```

We've satisfied the first requirement in the Initialize event of our class, using the following code:

```
Private Sub Class_Initialize()
    Set mobjWordApp = New Word.Application
    mobjWordApp.Visible = True
End Sub
```

NOTE   We could have used the New keyword in our declaration statement to instantiate mobjWordApp as soon as an instance of our VBA class was created.

To satisfy the second requirement, you need to create a new instance of the clsWordEvents class. We have included an example in basAutomation:

```
Global gobjWordEvents As clsWordEvents


Sub InitWordEvents()
    Set gobjWordEvents = New clsWordEvents
End Sub
```

That's all you need to create a custom event sink for Microsoft Word. Note that we've declared the object variable as Global. If we had declared it in the body of the InitWordEvents procedure, it would have been destroyed, along with our event sink, when the procedure terminated.

Figure 20.32 illustrates how event sinking with VBA works. Our object variable, gobjWordEvents, points to an instance of our VBA class, clsWordEvents. The class

FIGURE 20.32

How VBA event
sinking works

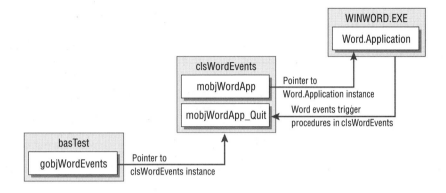

instance, in turn, contains another pointer (mobjWordApp) that references an
instance of Word's Application class. As the Application class generates events,
Word calls our VBA event procedures defined in clsWordEvents. The gobjWord-
Events variable is required only to give our event sink "life."

Using Event Sinking with Forms

We've included a second example of event sinking in the sample database. This
example uses a form, frmWithEventsWatchForm, instead of a VBA class module.
Opening the form creates a new instance of Word's Application class and logs each
event to a text box. Figure 20.33 shows an example of using the form to monitor the
active documents in Word.

The code behind the form is nearly identical to that explained in the previous
section except that we don't need a separate variable to store an instance of the
class. Since opening a form automatically creates a instance of the form's class
module, this step isn't required.

> **WARNING**
>
> Event procedures created using WithEvents are nothing more than
> functions that an Automation component calls when an event occurs.
> Just as with normal functions, the Automation component cannot con-
> tinue processing until an event procedure finishes. Beware of anything
> that could prevent or delay the completion of an event procedure (such
> as the MsgBox statement in our example).

FIGURE 20.33

FIGURE 20.33

Using a form to monitor
Word events

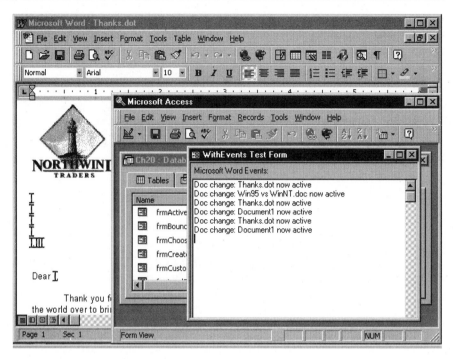

Summary

In this chapter we've explored the basic concepts behind Automation, including:

- The role of Automation clients and servers, the use of type libraries, and the creation of objects in another application

- The similarities between Automation code and the VBA code you write in Access

- How to manipulate other applications using objects, properties, and methods, just as you do Access objects

We used several sample applications that demonstrated how to use the other programs in the Microsoft Office suite in integrated solutions. We also showed how to manipulate ActiveX controls embedded on a form. In each example we stressed the similarities between Automation code and plain VBA code.

Automation can help you become more productive by giving you the tools to integrate other robust, feature-filled applications into a customized solution. In this chapter you've seen how you can use Access 97 to control other applications.

CHAPTER

TWENTY-ONE

21

Controlling Access as an Automation Server

- Deciding when to use Access as an Automation server

- Exploring the nuances of Access in the server role

- Creating a reporting system controlled from Microsoft Excel

- Learning to create Automation-friendly applications

Starting with Access 95, Microsoft added a capability long sought by developers looking for a way to integrate Access into solutions created with other tools. Access' capabilities as an Automation server are unchanged in Microsoft's latest release, Access 97. Having this capability at your disposal opens up a number of interesting possibilities. You can have one Access application that controls another. You can also create applications in Microsoft Visual Basic, or any of the Office applications that support VBA, that use the services of Access to do such things as print reports, create tables and queries, and display forms. In this chapter we'll examine the reasons to use Access as an Automation server and demonstrate an example of its capabilities by implementing a system that uses Access to preview and print reports. The sample code in this chapter is on the CD-ROM in text form so you can import it easily into any VBA project.

Looking at Access as an Automation Server

One paradox Access developers must face is that while it is possible to use Access as an Automation server, the need to do so is probably smaller than ever. As companies such as Microsoft move toward a component-based approach built on ActiveX technology, huge chunks of a program's functionality become available without the need to actually run the program. A case in point is the Jet database engine, the component responsible for manipulating data and objects in an MDB file. You can now use Jet objects and methods directly from any Automation client without going through Access. So, you ask, when does it make sense to use Access as an Automation server? Consider these situations:

- You need to do something that's possible only through Access, such as printing a report.

- You need to do something that requires launching a second copy of Access, such as compacting the current database.

- You need to create background processes that use information from an active Access session.

- You need to provide seamless integration between Access and another application.

Access 97 provides only one object that you can create using Automation: the Application object. Unlike other Office applications, such as Word and Excel, Access does not feature document objects (for example, Excel.Sheet). As you might expect, the class ID for Access' Application object is Access.Application. Using this ID with the New keyword or either CreateObject or GetObject gives you an object pointer to Access' top-level object, from which all other objects can be referenced.

Using the Access Type Library

When developing Automation applications, you will find it helpful for several reasons to include Access 97's type library, MSACC8.OLB, in the list of references for your project. First, it makes your code more readable by declaring object variables that map directly to the objects in Access. Second, VBA can use the type library to display context-sensitive help when you highlight an Access object name and press the F1 key. Third, if your development tool supports it, you can create an object reference using the New keyword rather than using CreateObject or GetObject. For example, the following code automatically creates a new reference to Access' Application object the first time the object is used:

```
' Create a new object of the proper class
Dim objAccess As New Access.Application

' Reference a property--Access will be started automatically
MsgBox objAccess.hWndAccessApp
```

Finally, if you use the New keyword with the syntax shown above, VBA can check your code for syntax using the list of objects, properties, and methods exported by Access. VBA would warn you, for example, if you misspelled the HwndAccessApp property or tried to use a property that did not exist.

Differences from Regular Access

Using Access as an Automation server is very much like developing applications the way you do now. The object model, methods, and properties are identical, regardless of whether you call them from a VBA module in an Access database or using Automation from an external application such as Excel or Visual Basic. Subtle differences do exist, however, in the way you use Access objects. First and foremost, all controllable objects descend from the Application object, to which you must create a pointer before using any other object, property, or method. When porting code from Access to another VBA-enabled application, make sure you qualify all "top-level" objects (those for which Access VBA can assume the context) with the object variable holding a pointer to the Access Application object. The following list identifies some of the common methods, descendant objects, and collections of the Access Application object that you must qualify when calling them from Automation code. For a complete list, use the Object Browser to interrogate the Application object for all its descendants.

AddAutoCorrect	Domain aggregate functions (for example, DMax)
BuildCriteria	
CodeContextObject	Echo
CodeDb	Eval
CreateControl	Forms
CreateForm	GetOption
CreateGroupLevel	hWndAccessApp
CreateReport	Nz
CreateReportControl	Quit
CurrentDb	RefreshDatabaseWindow
CurrentObjectName	RefreshTitleBar
CurrentObjectType	ReloadAddins
CurrentUser	ReplaceModule
DBEngine	Reports
DDE functions (for example, DDEInitiate)	Run
	SaveAsText
DefaultWorkspaceClone	Screen
DelAutoCorrect	SetOption
DeleteControl	ShortcutMenuBar
DeleteReportControl	SysCmd
DoCmd	Visible

For example, the following code snippet executes perfectly well in an Access module:

```
Dim frmAny As Form

Set frmAny = Screen.ActiveForm
frmAny.Visible = False
If frmAny.Caption = Forms(0).Caption Then
    DoCmd.Close acForm, frmAny.Name
End If
```

To mimic the functionality of these statements using Automation in Visual Basic, on the other hand, you would need to declare and initialize an object variable and prefix the Screen, Forms, and DoCmd objects with it, as shown in this code fragment:

```
Dim objAccess As New Access.Application
Dim frmAny As Form

Set frmAny = objAccess.Screen.ActiveForm
frmAny.Visible = False
If frmAny.Caption = objAccess.Forms(0).Caption Then
    objAccess.DoCmd.Close acForm, frmAny.Name
End If
```

You must also keep in mind that because Access is operating behind the scenes when used as an Automation server, you must not initiate actions that require user intervention. For example, any message box displayed as the result of running a query or macro or opening a form or report will cause your Automation client code to halt while it waits for a response from the user. If Access is not in a state in which it can accept input (if the main window is hidden, for instance), there will be no way for the code to continue executing. In the section "Hiding the Access Main Window" later in this chapter, we will explain how to manage the user interface to display Access forms and dialogs when necessary.

Access Automation Server Behavior

You saw in Chapter 20 various ways to create a pointer to an Automation server, including a direct reference using the New keyword as well as the CreateObject and GetObject functions. Access as an Automation server behaves differently depending on how it is called. It also implements its Visible property differently from other Microsoft Office applications. The following paragraphs explain this behavior, beginning with the simplest scenario, using CreateObject to obtain an object reference.

Access is by default a *single-use* Automation server. As with other single-use servers, using CreateObject will always create a new instance of Access, the result of the function call being a pointer to that instance. When a new instance of Access opens in response to an Automation client request, it cannot be terminated simply by selecting File ➤ Exit or clicking the Close button. Instead of closing in response to these actions, it closes the current database and minimizes the main window. Access knows it was started via Automation and will not shut down until a Quit request is made or the object variable storing the Application object reference is destroyed.

When you call GetObject, the counterpart to CreateObject, Access behaves differently, depending on which arguments you supply. GetObject accepts two optional arguments: a document name and an Automation Prog ID. If you pass an empty string as the first argument (the document name) and "Access.Application" as the second, a new instance of Access is created. Alternatively, you can cause Access to immediately open a database by passing a valid path and file name as the first argument. In this case the second argument is not really necessary, because Windows can infer which Automation server to use from the file extension. If you have given your database file an extension other than one of those registered by Access (.MDB, .MDA, and so on), you must supply both arguments. In addition, you can call GetObject, omitting the first argument altogether and passing only the class ID as the second argument. If a copy of Access is already running, GetObject will create a reference to the running instance; otherwise, a new instance will be created.

Finally, you can create a reference to Access using the New keyword in VBA applications. Using the New keyword always launches a new instance of Access. Additionally, whenever you create a new instance of Access via Automation, Access automatically shuts down when all pointers to it have been destroyed, *unless* the user has clicked on or otherwise interacted with the Access window.

Running Access Reports Using Automation

To demonstrate the general techniques required to use Access as an Automation server, we have written sample code that lets you browse and print reports stored in an Access database. We chose this example for a number of reasons. First, it allows us to demonstrate the very few additional techniques you need to master to use Access effectively as an Automation server. (After all, the rest of this book describes how to write an Access application *in Access*!) Second, printing reports is one thing Access does much better than most other development tools, including other databases, as well as applications such as Microsoft Word and Excel. Finally, printing Access reports from other applications, particularly those written in Visual Basic, is a capability a great number of developers who are disappointed with those applications' reporting capabilities have long sought.

The Sample Files

We have created a number of VBA procedures that control Access using Automation; you will find these in a text file called ACCSERVE.BAS on the CD-ROM. These procedures are generic, and you can use them in any VBA host application by including ACCSERVE.BAS in your VBA project. Table 21.1 lists the procedures and what each does.

TABLE 21.1   VBA Procedures for Using Access as an Automation Server

Procedure	Description
adhGetAccessObject	Creates a reference to an instance of Access and returns the pointer as a result. Accepts an optional True/False value indicating whether a new instance should always be created
adhOpenCurrentDatabase	Accepts a pointer to an Access instance and the path to an MDB file and instructs Access to open that database
adhListReports	Lists the reports contained in the current database. Accepts a pointer to an Access instance and a Variant variable by reference. When the procedure returns, the variable will contain an array of report names
adhPrintReport	Prints or previews an Access report. Accepts a pointer to an Access instance, the name of a report, and a True/False value. If the last argument is True, Access previews the report
adhQuitAccess	Quits an Automation session with Access by setting the object pointer to Nothing. Accepts a pointer to an Access instance and a True/False value indicating whether Access' Quit method should be called explicitly

TABLE 21.1   VBA Procedures for Using Access as an Automation Server (continued)

Procedure	Description
adhOpenPreventForm	Opens a special form in the current database (if it exists) that will prevent the database itself from being closed by the user
adhClosePreventForm	Closes the special prevention form
adhShowAccessWindow	Hides or displays the Access main window. Accepts a pointer to an Access instance and a True/False value

To demonstrate how to use the functions (and because we needed something to show), we've also included a Microsoft Excel application in CH21.XLS. Figure 21.1 shows the application's main menu.

The sample application was written in Microsoft Excel because many Access developers also have a copy of Excel. Having a copy of Excel will make it easy to test the sample code without writing an application of your own.

FIGURE 21.1

Main switchboard for a sample Automation applicaiton written in Excel

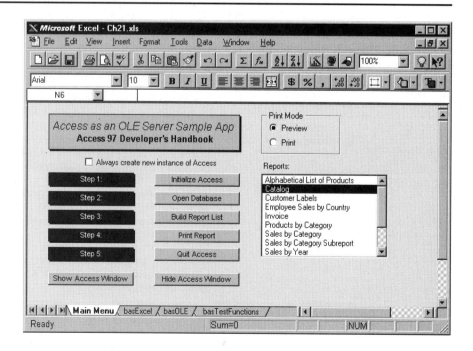

NOTE In this chapter we'll highlight the common VBA functions and downplay Excel-specific code.

Finally, we've created several procedures to test different aspects of Access as an Automation server. You'll find these procedures in the Excel workbook and in a text file called ACCTEST.BAS on the companion CD-ROM.

The Five-Part Process for Printing Reports Using Automation

CH21.XLS contains a worksheet called Main Menu, which holds the application's interface, and a module sheet called basAutomation, which contains our generic VBA code. The main menu worksheet features a list box and a number of buttons. Each of the buttons demonstrates one part of a five-part process for printing reports using Automation:

1. Initiating a connection to an instance of Access using Automation. A check box on the worksheet controls whether a new instance of Access is created or a running instance (if one exists) is used.

2. After a connection has been established, opening a database so a list of reports can be retrieved. Our sample code first determines whether a database is currently open and, if so, closes it.

3. Once a database has been opened, retrieving a list of reports and displaying it in the list box on the worksheet.

4. Printing or previewing the report, depending on the state of another check box on the worksheet.

5. Shutting down the instance of Access (if a new one was created) by destroying the object variable used to interact with it.

Each of these steps is explained in the paragraphs that follow, which also include the sample code. You'll notice several things about the way we constructed the sample application:

- We use a module-level Object variable to store the reference to Access' Application object. Using a module-level variable allows several different procedures to operate on the same instance of Access.

- We often compare the Object variable with the intrinsic constant Nothing to determine whether a valid Automation reference exists before using any of Access' properties or methods. Doing so prevents run-time errors if we inadvertently reinitialize the variable. (This is particularly critical with Excel VBA applications because Excel reinitializes all module- and global-level variables whenever you make *any* change to *any* module in the workbook.)

- After creating a new instance of Access, we hide the main Access window using a Win32 API function. This adds to the impression that the application is truly integrated and reduces the chance that the user will somehow mess things up by playing around with Access' user interface. You can choose to leave the Access window visible if you wish by commenting out the call to adhShowAccessWindow.

Initiating an Automation Session

The sample application uses a rather sophisticated procedure to initiate an Automation session with Access. The Initialize Access button on the Excel worksheet calls adhGetAccessObject (shown in Listing 21.1), which first attempts to create a reference to a running instance of Access using GetObject. If the call to GetObject fails because no copy of Access is running, the error-handling code calls CreateObject instead. Error 483 (represented by the constant adhcErrNoCreateObject) indicates that the object reference could not be created. You can override this behavior and always create a new instance of Access by checking a check box on the main menu worksheet. This passes a True value as the second parameter to adhGetAccessObject. An If...Then statement checks the value and triggers error 483, thus forcing a call to CreateObject.

Listing 21.1

```
Public Function adhGetAccessObject( _
 Optional ByVal varAlwaysNew As Variant) As Object
```

```
        ' Set up error handling to trap the case
        ' where no instance of Access is running
        On Error GoTo ErrorHandler

        Dim objAccess As Object
        Dim fAlwaysNew As Boolean

        ' If the user wants to create a new instance of
        ' Access, force an error to trigger a call
        ' to CreateObject instead of GetObject
        If Not IsMissing(varAlwaysNew) Then
            If VarType(varAlwaysNew) = vbBoolean Then
                fAlwaysNew = varAlwaysNew
            End If
        End If
        If fAlwaysNew Then
            Error adhcErrNoCreateObject
        Else
            Set objAccess = GetObject(, adhcClassID)
        End If

        ' Set return value of function to point to
        ' the instance of Access
        Set adhGetAccessObject = objAccess

ExitProc:
    Exit Function
ErrorHandler:
    Select Case Err
        Case adhcErrNoCreateObject
            ' Unable to create reference or the
            ' user wants to create a new instance
            Set objAccess = CreateObject(adhcClassID)

            Resume Next
        Case Else
            MsgBox Error(), vbExclamation, "Error " & Err
    End Select
    Resume ExitProc
End Function
```

The pointer to Access' Application object returned by adhGetAccessObject is stored in a module-level variable, mobjAccess.

Using Access as an Automation Server in a Secure Workgroup

The Automation specification assumes that calling CreateObject is all that's required to put an application in a state in which you can begin working with it. It was not designed to account for applications such as Access that, when operating in a secure workgroup, require a user ID and password just to start up. If you attempt to use the sample code we've provided in a secure workgroup, Access will wait for a user to enter the required logon information, and your Automation statement will time out and fail.

To use Access as an Automation server in a secure workgroup, you must first launch Access using the Shell statement, which can accept command-line parameters for the user name and password. Then, use GetObject to obtain a reference to the newly created Access instance. The adhTestSecureWorkgroup procedure shown below demonstrates this:

```
Sub adhTestSecureWorkgroup()
    Dim objAccess As Object
    Dim strUser As String
    Dim strPassword As String
    Dim strCommand As String

    ' Set user id and password
    strUser = "Admin"
    strPassword = ""

    ' Construct command line (alter this to reflect
    ' the path to Access on your system)
    strCommand = "C:\Program Files\Office97\Access\" & _
     "MSACCESS.EXE /User " & strUser & _
     "/Pwd " & strPassword & _
     "/NoStartup"

    ' Use the Shell function to launch Access with
    ' the user id and password
    If Shell(strCommand) Then
```

```
              ' Now get a reference to the running instance
              Set objAccess = adhGetAccessObject(False)

              ' Do stuff here

              ' Quit Access
              Call adhQuitAccess(objAccess, True)
       End If
End Sub
```

Note the use of the NoStartup command-line parameter as well. This suppresses Access' startup dialog.

Of course, this method is not perfect. If you have multiple instances of Access running, you can't be assured of getting a pointer to the most recently started one. However, short of changing the command line of Access in the Registry, it's your only alternative.

Opening a Database

Access provides two methods specifically designed to deal with opening and closing databases using Automation: OpenCurrentDatabase and CloseCurrentDatabase. While you can use CloseCurrentDatabase in Access applications, these two methods of the Application object are most useful in Automation code. Listing 21.2 shows adhOpenCurrentDatabase, a wrapper function that handles opening a database using Automation.

Listing 21.2

```
Public Function adhOpenCurrentDatabase(objAccess As Object, _
 ByVal strPath As String) As Boolean

   If Not objAccess Is Nothing Then

       ' Check to see if a database is already open
       If objAccess.DBEngine.Workspaces(0). _
       Databases.Count > 0 Then

           ' If so, close it
           Call adhClosePreventForm(objAccess)
```

```
                objAccess.CloseCurrentDatabase
        End If

        ' Open the selected database
        objAccess.OpenCurrentDatabase strPath

        ' Hide the database container--note that
        ' this next statement will fail if the
        ' database has a startup form
        objAccess.DoCmd.RunCommand acCmdHide

        ' Open the prevention form if it exists
        Call adhOpenPreventForm(objAccess)

        ' Set return value
        adhOpenCurrentDatabase = True
    End If
End Function
```

AdhOpenCurrentDatabase accepts a path to an MDB file and tries to load the selected database. It first checks to see whether a database is already open in the instance of Access pointed to by objAccess, by checking the number of databases open in the default workspace. If the count is greater than 0, the procedure calls CloseCurrentDatabase to close whichever database is open.

WARNING Be careful when calling CloseCurrentDatabase to close a database you didn't open through Automation. If you try to close a user database with open, changed objects, the user will have to dismiss a series of confirmation dialogs before Access can close the database. This may cause the CloseCurrentDatabase to time out and fail. Make sure your error handling is set up to cope with this possibility.

Opening the chosen database is a simple matter of calling OpenCurrentDatabase with the name of the database. OpenCurrentDatabase will accept any valid file name, including both full and partial path information. After opening the database, the procedure hides the Database window (an optional step) and then attempts to open a form called frmPrevent in the current database (by calling adhOpenPreventForm). This form helps prevent users from inadvertently closing a database while you are using it in your Automation code. (See the section

"Preventing Users from Closing the Database" later in this chapter for more information on how this form works.)

Getting a Report List

After opening a database, you can use the adhListReports procedure (see Listing 21.3) to populate a Variant variable with an array of report names from the current database. We use this in our Excel application to populate the list box on the Main Menu worksheet. AdhListReports uses a For Each...Next loop to enumerate all the Document objects in the database's Reports container.

Listing 21.3

```
Public Function adhListReports(objAccess As Object, _
 ByRef varList As Variant) As Boolean

    Dim db As Database
    Dim objRptDoc As Document
    Dim cDoc As Long

    ' Make sure object reference is still valid
    If Not objAccess Is Nothing Then

        ' Use a For Each...Next loop to iterate through
        ' all the document objects in the Reports
        ' container, adding them to the array
        Set db = objAccess.CurrentDb()
        If db.Containers("Reports"). _
         Documents.Count > 0 Then

            ReDim varList(1 To db. _
```

```
                    Containers("Reports").Documents.Count)

            For Each objRptDoc In db. _
             Containers("Reports").Documents
                cDoc = cDoc + 1
                varList(cDoc) = objRptDoc.Name
            Next

            ' Set return value
            adhListReports = True
        End If
    End If

End Function
```

There's really not much to say about adhListReports, because it uses the same technique to build a list of reports that you might use in an Access application. The only difference is the qualification of CurrentDb with the Object variable storing a reference to Access.

Previewing and Printing

Printing or previewing the report is where the fun starts in this sample application. Listing 21.4 shows the adhPrintReport procedure that manages this process. First, you must determine whether the report is currently open and, if so, close it before opening it a second time. AdhPrintReport uses objAccess to call the Syscmd function, which returns a value of acObjStateOpen if the report is open. You can see from this bit of code that including a reference to Access 97's type library makes coding easier by letting you use Access constants without your needing to redeclare them.

Listing 21.4

```
Private Declare Function adh_apiSetForegroundWindow _
 Lib "user32" Alias "SetForegroundWindow" ( _
 ByVal hwnd As Long) _
 As Long

Public Sub adhPrintReport(objAccess As Object, _
 ByVal strReport As String, ByVal fPreview As Boolean)

    Dim intMode As Integer
```

```
    If Not objAccess Is Nothing Then
        ' If report is already open, close it before
        ' trying to open it again
        If objAccess.SysCmd(acSysCmdGetObjectState, _
          acReport, strReport) = acObjStateOpen Then
            objAccess.DoCmd.Close acReport, strReport
        End If

        ' Set the open mode
        If fPreview Then
            intMode = acPreview
        Else
            intMode = acNormal
        End If

        ' Open the report in Access
        objAccess.DoCmd.OpenReport strReport, intMode

        ' Now if the report was opened in preview mode
        ' then we need to make sure the user can see it,
        ' right? So unhide the Access window and bring
        ' it to the front.
        If intMode = acPreview Then

            ' Show the Access window and switch to it
            objAccess.DoCmd.Maximize
            Call adhShowAccessWindow(objAccess, True)
            Call adh_apiSetForegroundWindow _
              (objAccess.hWndAccessApp)
        Else
            ' Hide the Access window
            Call adhShowAccessWindow(objAccess, False)
        End If
    End If
End Sub
```

Next, if a user decides to preview a report, we need to somehow put the Access main window in a position where the user can see it. We first maximize the report so it fills the Access window. (You'll notice that forms and reports opened via Automation are extremely small.) We then call a Win32 API function, SetForeground-Window, to bring the Access window to the front. SetForegroundWindow accepts a window handle as its sole argument and moves that window on top of all other open windows.

Quitting Access

The final step demonstrated in the sample application is quitting Access when you no longer need its services as an Automation server. AdhQuitAccess (see Listing 21.5) is a simple procedure that accomplishes this by setting the Object variable storing a reference to Access to the intrinsic constant Nothing. Not only does this free up resources used during the Automation session, it correctly terminates the connection to Access. By *correct* we mean that if we initiated the running instance, then that instance of Access will shut down. If, on the other hand, we did not initiate the instance (we used GetObject to use an existing copy of Access), Access will continue running. The latter case assumes that the user had already launched a copy of Access, and we should not automatically terminate it without warning. Occasionally, though, you will want to shut down Access, even if you didn't launch it using Automation. To accommodate this, adhQuitAccess accepts an optional flag that, if set to True, instructs the procedure to call Access' Quit method.

Listing 21.5

```
Public Sub adhQuitAccess(objAccess As Object, _
 Optional ByVal varForceQuit As Variant)

    If Not (objAccess Is Nothing) Then
        ' If a prevention form was opened, go
        ' ahead and close it from code
        Call adhClosePreventForm(objAccess)

        ' If the user wants to force a shutdown
        ' call Access' Quit method
        If Not IsMissing(varForceQuit) Then
            If VarType(varForceQuit) = vbBoolean Then
                If varForceQuit Then
                    objAccess.UserControl = False
                    objAccess.Quit
                End If
            End If
        End If

        ' Destroy the contents of the object variable--
        ' if we launched Access this will shut it down,
        ' if Access was already running it won't
        Set objAccess = Nothing
    End If
End Sub
```

The sample procedure also includes code to close a form called frmPrevent in the open database if it exists and is open. This form prevents users from inadvertently closing the active database while you are controlling it using Automation. (See the section "Preventing Users from Closing the Database" later in this chapter for more information on this technique.)

While the sample application is simple, it does demonstrate a number of key techniques required to use Access as an Automation server, including creating an object reference, calling Access methods and properties, and terminating an Automation session. Given your knowledge of Access, as well as the techniques described in the rest of this book, you should be able to extend the examples given here into fully functional Automation applications. The remainder of this chapter discusses additional topics related to using Access as an Automation server, including calling user-defined functions using Automation and creating databases that work equally well whether run from the Access user interface or from Automation.

Calling User-Defined Functions from an Automation Client

In addition to using the properties and methods of Access objects, you can call user-defined subroutines and functions via Automation. By using this capability you can leverage functions already written, eliminating the need to rewrite them in the client application. You use two different methods to call procedures in an Access database, depending on whether they are declared in a global module or a form's CBF module.

Global Functions

Public functions are executed using the Run method of Access' Application object. In Access, Run executes functions or subroutines declared in a database that is not referenced by the current database, using the References dialog. (You can call functions in libraries or databases that are referenced without using Run—see the examples in Chapter 22.) When controlling Access through Automation, you can use Run to call a procedure in the current database or any of the preloaded library databases, such as WZTOOL.MDA. Run accepts a variable number of arguments, up to 30, the first of which is the name of the function or subroutine you wish to execute. You use the remaining arguments of Run to pass any arguments the called procedure requires.

To demonstrate, CH21.MDB contains a function called adhListObjectsAutomation, which accepts a container name and an array (in the form of a Variant argument) as arguments and populates the array with the names of all documents in the chosen container. It also returns the number of documents as a result. You can call the function from an Automation client program by using Access' Run method. For example, the adhListReportsEx function in the basTestFunctions module of CH21.XLS (see Listing 21.6) uses this approach to print the names of reports from a database to the Debug window.

NOTE The adhListObjectsAutomation and adhListReportsEx functions are included only to demonstrate techniques for calling procedures and passing arguments to user-defined functions through Automation. The sample application does not call these functions. Because using adhListReportsEx requires that adhListObjectsAutomation be declared in the selected database, the generic approach using the Reports container described above is used instead.

Listing 21.6

```
Function adhListObjectsAutomation(strContainer As String, _
  varDocArray As Variant) As Integer

    Dim dbThis As Database
    Dim docAny As Document
    Dim intDoc As Integer

    ' Make sure argument is an array of variants
    If VarType(varDocArray) = vbVariant Or vbArray Then

        ' Clear existing values
        ReDim varDocArray(0) As Variant

        ' Get all document names in the container
        Set dbThis = CurrentDb
        For Each docAny In dbThis. _
          Containers(strContainer).Documents

            ' Increment the array and insert the name
            ReDim Preserve varDocArray(intDoc + 1)
            varDocArray(intDoc) = docAny.Name
```

```
            intDoc = intDoc + 1
        Next
    End If

    ' Set return value
    adhListObjectsAutomation = intDoc
End Function

Sub adhListReportsEx(ByVal strPath As String)

    Dim objAccess As Object
    Dim varRpt As Variant
    Dim intRpt As Integer
    Dim intCRpt As Integer
    Dim strProjectName As String
    Dim strProcToRun As String

    ' To pass an array to an Access function
    ' using Automation you must use a
    ' Variant variable and redimension it
    ' with one element (this forces VBA to
    ' treat the argument as an array)
    ReDim varRpt(1)

    ' Launch a copy of Access
    Set objAccess = adhGetAccessObject(True)

    ' Open a database
    If adhOpenCurrentDatabase(objAccess, strPath) Then

        ' Get the name of the VBA project; this will be
        ' used to construct the procedure call for
        ' the Run method
        strProjectName = objAccess.GetOption("Project Name")

        ' Create the procedure call from the project
        ' name and function name
        strProcToRun = strProjectName & ".adhListObjectsAutomation"

        ' NOTE: to run this next line you must
        ' have a function called adhListObjectsAutomation
        ' declared in the current database.
```

```
            ' You can copy the function from CH21.MDB
            intRpt = objAccess.Run(strProcToRun, "Reports", varRpt)

            ' intRpt will contain the number of
            ' reports in the loaded database—if
            ' there's at least one then print them
            ' to the Debug window
            If intRpt > 0 Then
                For intCRpt = 0 To intRpt - 1
                    Debug.Print varRpt(intCRpt)
                Next
            End If


            ' Close the database
            Call adhClosePreventForm(objAccess)
            Call adhQuitAccess(objAccess, True)
        End If
End Sub
```

By using the Run method you can pass literal values, as well as variables, as arguments to a procedure. If you pass a variable by reference, the called procedure can modify its value (as adhListObjectsAutomation does). When passing variables as arguments to called procedures via Automation, you must follow these guidelines:

- All passed variables must be declared as Variants in the calling procedure.

- Arguments can be declared as any scalar datatype in the called procedure.

- To pass an array, declare a Variant and redimension it with at least one element before passing it to the procedure.

The syntax of the Run method requires that you precede the name of the procedure with the name of the database's VBA project (AutomationServerMDB in CH21.MDB). You can find the name of a database's VBA project on the Advanced tab of the Options dialog. If you want to use the adhListObjectsAutomation function in your applications, you must copy the function either to a library database (and modify it to list the objects from the currently loaded user database) or to each individual database with which you want to use it. If you copy it to a library database, modify the statement that sets the value of strProjectName to reflect the VBA project in your library database. Otherwise this statement uses the GetOption method to return the project name of the loaded user database.

Form-Level Functions

Form-level functions, those declared in a form's module, are called differently from global functions. First of all, form-level functions must be explicitly declared as Public in order to be visible to calling programs. Once this is done, they become methods of the form and are called in the same way as any other methods using VBA. That is, you first obtain an object pointer to the form and then call one of its methods. The only difference with Automation is that you must qualify the Forms collection with a pointer to Access' Application object. Listing 21.7 shows a short procedure that calls a function named FClose, declared in the frmCloseMe form from CH21.MDB. FClose does nothing more than use the DoCmd.Close method to close the form, but it lets you express this as a built-in method of the form. Listing 21.8 shows the very small bit of code that makes up the FClose method, as well as an example of how you can call it from VBA code in Access. (We would have liked to call this function Close, but because that's a VBA reserved word, we had to choose something else.)

Listing 21.7

```
Sub TestFormMethod()
    Dim objAccess As Object
    Dim frm As Form

    ' Get a reference to Access
    Set objAccess = adhGetAccessObject(True)

    ' Open CH21.MDB--edit the line below
    ' to reflect the path to CH21.MDB on
    ' your computer
    If adhOpenCurrentDatabase(objAccess, _
     "C:\Data\Ch21.mdb") Then

        ' Open the form and set a pointer
        objAccess.DoCmd.OpenForm "frmCloseMe"
        Set frm = objAccess.Forms("frmCloseMe")

        ' Put some code in here that does something

        ' Close the form using its FClose method
        frm.FClose

        ' Quit Access
```

```
                    Call adhQuitAccess(objAccess, True)
            End If
    End Sub
```

Listing 21.8

```
Public Function FClose()
    ' This public function acts as a new method
    ' of this form object. You can call it from
    ' VBA code in Access (see the cmdClose_Click
    ' procedure) or using Automation
    DoCmd.Close acForm, Me.Name
End Function


Private Sub cmdClose_Click()
    ' Calls the new FClose method of this form
    Me.FClose
End Sub
```

If you've created a method that returns a value, you can capture that in a variable in the Automation client's code, just as you would for other methods that return values. Just make sure you include parentheses (as well as any arguments) after the method name.

Writing Automation-Friendly Applications

As you begin to use the Automation server features of Access, you may discover it makes sense to use the same database both as a user application in Access and as the subject of Automation control from another program. The suggestions in this section are aimed at helping you create an application that can serve both purposes well. By keeping in mind that your user may not always be at the helm, you can greatly leverage your time investment.

The UserControl Property

Access exports a property of its Application object that is very useful when creating databases that will be used by both end users and Automation clients. Called UserControl, this property returns True if Access was launched by an end user or

False if it was started by a request from an Automation client. UserControl also returns True if a user has interacted with Access after being started by Automation or even if the Access application window receives the input focus. You should use this property in your own application whenever you need to know whether a user or Automation client is in control. For example, you might use this in your error-handling code to suppress message boxes unless UserControl returns True. The section "Creating Your Own Error Stack" later in this chapter uses this technique.

Also check the UserControl property in your AutoExec function or the Open event of your startup form and suppress actions that don't make sense for a database being opened by another application. For instance, it is unlikely you'll want to waste time displaying a splash screen during an Automation session. In cases like this, the UserControl property allows you to selectively display forms and messages that make sense for a human user.

Hiding the Access Main Window

One problem with using Access as an Automation server is that the default behavior of Access' main window is to remain visible, regardless of the value of the Application object's Visible property. Unlike other applications, such as Microsoft Excel, Access minimizes, rather than hides, its main window when the Visible property is set to False. If the window is visible, there is always a chance a user will activate it and do something that would confuse your Automation code (close the active database, for instance). You saw in the section "The Five-Part Process for Printing Reports Using Automation," which described the sample application, that we hid the Access main window immediately after creating an object reference using the CreateObject function. This is the best way to prevent users from tampering with the application while your Automation code is running. Listing 21.9 shows the adhShowAccessWindow procedure, which displays or hides the Access main window based on the value of the fShow argument. It also lists the Windows API call ShowWindow, which is necessary to change the window's visibility.

Listing 21.9

```
Private Declare Function adh_apiShowWindow _
 Lib "user32" Alias "ShowWindow" ( _
 ByVal hwnd As Long, _
 ByVal nCmdShow As Long) _
 As Long
Private Const adhc_apiSW_HIDE = 0
Private Const adhc_apiSW_NORMAL = 1
```

```
Public Sub adhShowAccessWindow(objAccess As Object, _
 fShow As Boolean)
    ' Show the Access main window using ShowWindow
    ' with the SW_NORMAL constant
    If Not objAccess Is Nothing Then
        If fShow Then
            Call adh_apiShowWindow(objAccess.hWndAccessApp, _
              adhc_apiSW_NORMAL)
        Else
            Call adh_apiShowWindow(objAccess.hWndAccessApp, _
              adhc_apiSW_HIDE)
        End If
    End If
End Sub
```

Both procedures use the hWndAccessApp property of the Application object, which returns the window handle of Access' main window. ShowWindow accepts the window handle and changes the state of the window based on a constant passed as the second argument.

Preventing Users from Closing the Database

If you don't want to hide the Access window when using Access as an Automation server (perhaps because you're using an instance of Access launched by the user), another approach to prevent tampering is to keep the database open until your Automation code no longer needs it. You can accomplish this by opening a form that cannot be closed until code is run from your Automation client application. CH21.MDB contains a form called frmPrevent, which uses a module-level variable to determine whether or not the form can be closed. Listing 21.10 shows the contents of the form's module.

Listing 21.10

```
Option Compare Database
Option Explicit

' Private variable to control whether form
' (and thus database) can be closed--set by
' public Property Let statement
Private mfCanClose As Boolean
```

```
Property Get CanClose() As Boolean
    ' Property Get for the CanClose property--
    ' returns the value of the form variable
    CanClose = mfCanClose
End Property

Property Let CanClose(fCanClose As Boolean)
    ' Property Let for the CanClose property--
    ' sets the value of the form variable and
    ' sets the state of the form's check box
    mfCanClose = fCanClose
    Me![chkCanClose] = fCanClose
End Property

Private Sub chkCanClose_AfterUpdate()
    ' Checking the check box lets the user
    ' close the form
    mfCanClose = Me![chkCanClose]
End Sub

Private Sub Form_Unload(Cancel As Integer)
    ' This code prevents the form from closing
    ' if the CanClose property is False--to
    ' close the form the user must click the
    ' check box or Automation code must
    ' set the value of CanClose to True
    If Not Me.CanClose Then

        ' If the form cannot be closed, display
        ' a warning to the user if UserControl
        ' is True, otherwise just beep once
        If Application.UserControl Then
            MsgBox "Cannot close.", vbCritical
        Else
            Beep
        End If

        ' Cancel the close
        Cancel = True
    End If
End Sub
```

Code in the form's Unload event checks a user-defined property of the form called CanClose, which is initialized to False. If the property is still False during processing of the Unload event, the event procedure prevents the form from closing. Because Access will not unload the database if the form cannot be closed, preventing the form from closing prevents the database from being closed as well. Code in adhOpenCurrentDatabase in the sample application attempts to load frmPrevent by calling adhOpenPreventForm. Code in both adhOpenCurrentDatabase and adhQuitAccess calls adhClosePreventForm, which closes frmPrevent, thus allowing the database to be closed. AdhOpenPreventForm and adhClosePreventForm are shown in Listing 21.11.

> **NOTE**
>
> AdhOpenPreventForm checks the value of the UserControl property before attempting to open the form. If UserControl is True and the form does not exist in the loaded database, Access opens an error dialog. By temporarily setting UserControl to False, we suppress the Access error and handle it in our code instead.

Listing 21.11

```
Private Const adhcPreventForm = "frmPrevent"

Public Sub adhOpenPreventForm(objAccess As Object)
    On Error GoTo ErrorHandler

    Dim fUserControl As Boolean

    If Not objAccess Is Nothing Then
        ' Capture current state of UserControl
        fUserControl = objAccess.UserControl

        ' If the user was in control we need to temporarily
        ' take control away, otherwise Access will display
        ' an error dialog
        If fUserControl Then
            objAccess.UserControl = False
        End If

        ' Try to open the form
        objAccess.DoCmd.OpenForm formname:=adhcPreventForm, _
         windowmode:=acHidden
    End If

ExitProc:
```

```
' If the user had control and we took it away then
' we need to give it back
If (Not objAccess Is Nothing) And fUserControl Then
    objAccess.UserControl = True
End If


Exit Sub
ErrorHandler:
    Select Case Err
        Case adhcErrFormNoExists
            ' This error is generated if the form doesn't
            ' exist, so just ignore it
        Case Else
            MsgBox Error(), vbExclamation, "Error " & Err
    End Select
    Resume ExitProc
End Sub

Public Sub adhClosePreventForm(objAccess As Object)
    ' If the prevention form was opened, set its
    ' CanClose property to True, allowing it to
    ' be closed, then close it
    If Not objAccess Is Nothing Then
        If objAccess.SysCmd(acSysCmdGetObjectState, _
        acForm, adhcPreventForm) = acObjStateOpen Then

            objAccess.Forms(adhcPreventForm).CanClose = True
            objAccess.DoCmd.Close acForm, adhcPreventForm
        End If
    End If
End Sub
```

AdhClosePreventForm uses Access' SysCmd function to determine whether frm-Prevent is open in the loaded database. If so, the procedure sets the form's CanClose property to True and then closes the form. As explained in the previous paragraph, this will allow the database itself to close. If you want to use this technique in your applications, be sure to copy the frmPrevent form from CH21.MDB to your database files.

Being User-Input Aware

When designing your applications, keep in mind that any type of forced user input will interrupt the successful completion of actions initiated via Automation. A good example is the Employee Sales by Country report in NORTHWIND.MDB. It's based on a parameter query that requires users to enter a range of dates before it can print. Launching this report from Automation (especially if the Access main window were hidden) would cause your client code to time out and fail. If you need to use objects that require user input, you should at the very least display and activate the main Access window so users can take action while your Automation code is waiting. Ideally, however, you should not use objects that halt the processing of an object's method.

Creating Your Own Error Stack

If you want to call your own functions from an Automation client, one challenge you face is returning meaningful error information to your application. If a user-defined function called via Automation fails, your client application will receive an Automation error that may or may not be meaningful. One alternative is to maintain your own error stack in the server application, which the client can query to determine the status of any run-time errors. CH21.MDB contains code to do this in basErrorStack (see Listing 21.12). It works by opening a form containing an unbound list box and adding error information to the list. Because Access 97 forms can expose methods and properties, you can retrieve error information from your Automation client application.

> **NOTE** If you write Automation server applications using Visual Basic, you can use the Raise method of VBA's Err object to return error information to an Automation client. VBA documentation states that not all host applications support using the Raise method in this fashion. Unfortunately, Access falls into this category. Using the Raise method in your code will produce a run-time error in your Access application, but this error will not be returned to any Automation client application.

Listing 21.12

```
Option Compare Database
Option Explicit

Const adhcErrForm = "frmErrorStack"

Sub adhInitErrs()
    ' If the error form is open, call its ClearErrors
    ' method; otherwise just open the form (the
    ' error list starts out blank)
```

```
        If SysCmd(acSysCmdGetObjectState, acForm, _
         adhcErrForm) = acObjStateOpen Then

            Call Forms(adhcErrForm).ClearErrors
        Else
            DoCmd.OpenForm _
             formname:=adhcErrForm, _
             windowmode:=acHidden
        End If
End Sub

Sub adhPushError(ByVal lngError As Long, _
 ByVal strError As String, ByVal strProc As String)

    ' If the error form is open add the error
    ' information to the list
    If SysCmd(acSysCmdGetObjectState, acForm, _
     adhcErrForm) = acObjStateOpen Then

        Call Forms(adhcErrForm).AddError( _
          lngError, strError, strProc)
    End If
End Sub

Sub TestStack()
    ' Set up error handling
    On Error GoTo TestStack_Error

    ' Flush any existing errors
    Call adhInitErrs

    ' Fake an error
    Debug.Print 1 / 0

TestStack_Exit:
    Exit Sub
TestStack_Error:
    ' If Access was launched by the user, display
    ' a dialog box; otherwise push the error
    ' information onto our homemade stack
    If UserControl Then
        MsgBox Err.Description, vbExclamation, _
          "Error " & Err.Number
    Else
```

```
            Call adhPushError(Err.Number, _
              Err.Description, "TestStack")
        End If
        Resume TestStack_Exit
    End Sub
```

Listing 21.12 shows the contents of basErrorStack, which includes two procedures for managing the error information and one for testing purposes. The first procedure, adhInitErrs, opens the error stack form (frmErrorStack) and clears existing error information. Note that we open the form hidden so it is not obvious to users who may be working with Access. You should call adhInitErrs at the head of any procedure within which you want to trap errors.

After calling adhInitErrors, call adhPushError in your error-handling code to push error information onto the stack. AdhPushError requires three parameters—the error number, the error description, and the procedure name—and calls the AddError method of the error stack form (see Listing 21.13). TestStack demonstrates the use of the previous two procedures. You'll notice that it calls adhInitErrors immediately after establishing error handling with the On Error Goto statement. Farther down in the procedure's error handling code, it calls adhPushError with the error information only if UserControl returns False. If the UserControl property returns True, the procedure displays a message box. This illustrates how an application could be used both interactively by a user and as the server for an Automation client.

Listing 21.13 shows the code contained in frmErrorStack's VBA module that manages the list of errors on the form. It includes public methods to clear the error list (ClearErrors) and add items to it (AddError). It also includes Property Get statements to return error information. You call each of the properties, ErrNo, ErrDesc, and ErrProc, by passing an index into the collection of errors, with 0 being the most recent error. Note the similarities between this technique and the DAO Errors collection. To determine how many errors exist on the stack, you can query the ErrCount property.

Listing 21.13

```
Option Compare Database
Option Explicit

Property Get ErrNo(ByVal intErr As Integer) As Variant
    ' Property Get statement to return a particular
    ' error number--works by changing the BoundColumn
    ' property and returning the data for a given row
    If intErr > Me![lstErrors].ListCount Then
```

```
            ErrNo = -1
        Else
            Me![lstErrors].BoundColumn = 1
            ErrNo = Me![lstErrors].ItemData(intErr)
        End If
End Property

Property Get ErrDesc(ByVal intErr As Integer) As Variant
        ' Property Get statement to return a particular
        ' error description--works by changing the BoundColumn
        ' property and returning the data for a given row
        If intErr > Me![lstErrors].ListCount Then
            ErrDesc = "#Error#"
        Else
            Me![lstErrors].BoundColumn = 2
            ErrDesc = Me![lstErrors].ItemData(intErr)
        End If
End Property

Property Get ErrProc(ByVal intErr As Integer) As Variant
        ' Property Get statement to return a particular
        ' error procedure--works by changing the BoundColumn
        ' property and returning the data for a given row
        If intErr > Me![lstErrors].ListCount Then
            ErrProc = "#Error#"
        Else
            Me![lstErrors].BoundColumn = 3
            ErrProc = Me![lstErrors].ItemData(intErr)
        End If
End Property

Property Get ErrCount() As Long
        ' Property Get statement to return the number of
        ' errors--works by returning the ListCount of the
        ' list box
        ErrCount = Me![lstErrors].ListCount
End Property

Public Sub ClearErrors()
        ' Public method to clear the error list
        Me![lstErrors].RowSource = ""
End Sub

Public Sub AddError(ByVal lngErrNo As Long, _
 ByVal strErrDesc As String, ByVal strProc As String)
```

```
     ' Public method to add an error to the list--
     ' works by adding text to the RowSource property
     Me![lstErrors].RowSource = lngErrNo & ";" & _
       strErrDesc & ";" & strProc & ";" _
       & Me![lstErrors].RowSource
End Sub
```

To demonstrate how this error stack works, we've included a test procedure in the basTestFunctions module of CH21.XLS called adhTestErrorStack (see Listing 21.14). It calls the TestStack function in basErrorStack using the Application object's Run method. You can see from Listing 21.12 that we've intentionally forced a division-by-zero error in TestStack. After opening CH21.MDB, the procedure then calls the TestStack function, which contains the division-by-zero error. Because UserControl is False, this will place the error information on our custom stack rather than display an error message.

Listing 21.14

```
Sub adhTestErrorStack()
    Dim objAccess As Object
    Dim frmErrors As Object
    Dim intCErr As Integer

    ' Create Access Application object using
    ' CreateObject--this is necessary to create
    ' an instance where the UserControl
    ' property returns False
    Set objAccess = adhGetAccessObject(True)

    ' Open CH21.MDB--edit the line below
    ' to reflect the path to CH21.MDB on
    ' your computer
    If adhOpenCurrentDatabase(objAccess, _
      "C:\Data\Ch21.mdb") Then

        ' Run the TestStack routine in CH21.MDB--
        ' this will generate an error and put it on
        ' the stack
        objAccess.Run "TestStack"

        ' Get a pointer to the error stack form
        Set frmErrors = objAccess.Forms("frmErrorStack")

        ' Check the error count--if it's greater than
        ' zero, loop through each, displaying a message
```

```
        If frmErrors.ErrCount > 0 Then

            For intCErr = 0 To frmErrors.ErrCount - 1

                ' Create an error message in this app
                ' by calling the ErrDesc, ErrNo, and
                ' ErrProc properties of the error form
                MsgBox frmErrors.ErrDesc(intCErr), _
                 vbExclamation, "Error " & _
                 frmErrors.ErrNo(intCErr) _
                 & " in " & frmErrors.ErrProc(intCErr)
            Next

                ' Clear the error stack now that we're done
                frmErrors.ClearErrors
        End If

        ' Quit Access
        Call adhQuitAccess(objAccess, True)
    End If
End Sub
```

After calling the test procedure, adhTestErrorStack gets a reference to the error stack form and stores it in the frmErrors object variable. It then uses this variable to examine the ErrCount property of the form. If there's at least one error (which there will be in this test case), adhTestErrorStack loops through each one, using the ErrDesc, ErrNo, and ErrProc properties to extract the relevant information and display it in an Excel message box. Finally, the procedure calls the ClearErrors method to flush the error stack. Figure 21.2 shows what your screen might look like if you ran adhTestErrorStack on your own computer. Figure 21.3, on the other hand, shows frmErrorStack after being made visible with the Window ➤ Unhide command. To view this yourself, you'll have to pause execution before calling the ClearErrors method.

The downside to this approach is that you must manually query the stack's error count after each call to a user-defined function using Automation. This is because there will be no run-time error in your client application; from your application's perspective, everything will be fine. If you call a lot of user-defined functions with Automation, however, the additional information provided by our error stack may be well worth the effort.

FIGURE 21.2

Excel session showing error information returned from our custom stack

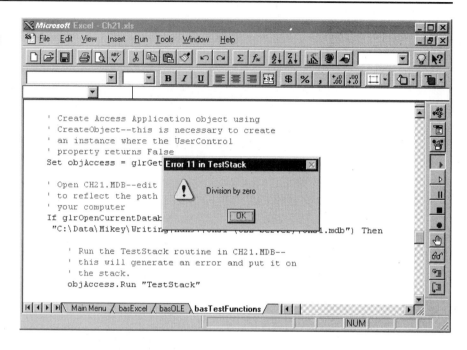

FIGURE 21.3

Error stack form in Access showing a single error

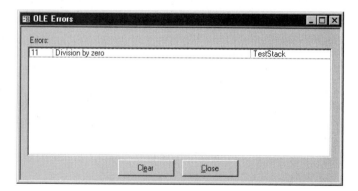

Switching Back to the Client Application

In the sample application the user can print or preview a report. If the user chooses to preview the report, the code opens it in Preview view, displays the Access window, and moves it to the foreground. At this point it relinquishes control to the user, who can print the report, close it, or take any number of other actions. For users uncomfortable with the idea of switching between multiple applications, you can provide a way for them to return to your Automation client application from Access.

VBA offers an AppActivate method that accepts a window title as an argument. It activates the first application with a top-level window with a caption matching that title. If it can't find an exact match, it looks for a window with a caption that begins with the string passed as an argument. This is helpful for MDI applications (such as those in Microsoft Office) that include the caption of a child window in the title bar when the child window is maximized. For example, this statement would activate a running instance of Microsoft Excel, no matter which worksheet has the input focus:

```
AppActivate "Microsoft Excel"
```

If you expose the Access user interface to your users, as we do in the sample application, you can give them a way to switch back to your application by calling App-Activate in response to some event. Figure 21.4 shows a report from CH21.MDB in Print Preview view. If you look carefully at the command bar, you'll see that we have added a custom button entitled "Return to Excel." This button calls adhReturn-ToApp, a function declared in basReturn. This function accepts a window title and passes it to AppActivate. We set the OnAction property of the command bar button to "=adhReturnToApp("Microsoft Excel")". Using this technique adds to the impression that Access is part of an integrated solution rather than an odd-ball component.

FIGURE 21.4

A custom toolbar button activates Microsoft Excel.

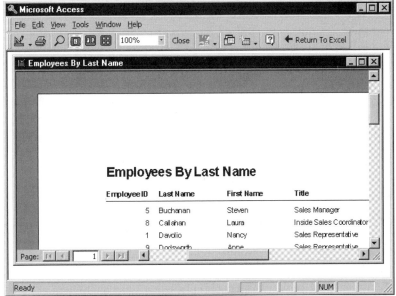

Summary

In this chapter we've introduced you to the few concepts you need to be familiar with in order to use Access as an Automation server. Because you can use all the same objects, properties, and methods you can when programming in Access alone, you should be able to write or port code that uses Access as an Automation server very quickly and easily. In summary:

- You create a reference to Access.Application using CreateObject, GetObject, or New.

- All Access properties and methods must be qualified with an object variable.

- You can use the Run method to call user-defined global functions.

- You can use UserControl and other properties to create Automation-friendly applications.

PART VII

Finishing Touches

CHAPTER

22

Building Add-Ins

- Understanding what Access add-ins are

- Creating library databases, including menu add-ins

- Developing property builders

- Designing and implementing custom Wizards

- Using the new Access 97 features for libraries

Access is a unique product in that it is aimed both at end users seeking an easy-to-use database and at developers looking for a powerful development platform. Somewhere in between is a group of users who demand more than a simple list manager but don't have the level of expertise required to call themselves developers. For this group of people Microsoft has provided extensions to Access generally known as *add-ins*. Add-ins are designed to simplify complex tasks by walking the user through various steps using easy-to-understand dialogs. You can create your own add-ins to assist your users or make working with Access easier for yourself. If you're really ambitious, you can create add-ins that can be sold commercially. In this chapter we explain how to create a variety of add-ins and give a number of examples to get you started. We also explain some exciting new Access 97 features: managing references using VBA, programmatic control of modules, and the ability to distribute your add-ins *without the source code* using the Make MDE function.

Libraries and Wizards and Builders, Oh My!

In this chapter we discuss several categories of add-ins:

- *Libraries* are add-ins that contain functions users can call from VBA code in their database. Access documentation often refers to any type of add-in as a library database. In this book we use this term for databases that contain nothing but VBA code called from procedures in other databases.

- *Builders* are add-ins that assist the user in setting a property of a database object, usually through some type of dialog. Access' property sheets feature Build buttons (the small buttons with an ellipsis [...] that appear next to property values) that launch a builder when clicked.

- *Wizards* are add-ins that create new objects in a user's database. You can build Wizards that create new tables, queries, forms, and reports. You can also build Wizards that create new form and report controls.

In the following sections we explain some of the common elements of Access add-ins. We follow this up with extensive discussions of each type of add-in, including how to create, install, and distribute them.

Unsecured Wizard Code

The Wizards that accompany Access 97 are shipped in a secured state using the new MDE format, so you cannot look at any of the source code they contain. The decision to secure the Wizards was made to keep the Wizard code in a compiled state for best performance and to protect a large investment by Microsoft in the Wizard technology, which is now almost as big a part of the base functionality as the program code itself. Microsoft has, however, made available unsecured versions of the Wizards with the proprietary code removed. They have also granted the right to distribute these libraries on the companion CD-ROM.

If you are serious about writing Wizards that look and act like those that come in the Access box, you might find a trip through the source code interesting. You won't find any comments, and the code is, at times, difficult to follow, but it offers numerous examples and tidbits of information that have proven invaluable to many Access developers.

Entry Points for Add-Ins

Access provides five ways for a user to launch an add-in. This chapter explains how to write add-ins to take advantage of these entry points, shown in Table 22.1.

TABLE 22.1   Entry Points for Access Add-Ins

Entry Point	Remarks
Menu add-in	To make menu add-ins available, select Tools ➤ Add-ins from Access' menus
Wizard	Table, Query, Form, and Report Wizards are available from the list of Wizards Access displays when a user creates a new object
Control Wizard	Users launch Control Wizards when they create a new control on a form or report. Users can disable Control Wizards by toggling the Control Wizard button in the toolbox
Builder	Builders help users set property values. Users initiate builders by clicking the Build button on an Access property sheet
Library functions	Users call library functions directly from their own VBA code

All add-ins, regardless of their purpose or entry point, are initiated by a function call. With the exception of library functions, Access calls all add-in functions directly in response to the events listed in Table 22.1, and the declaration of these functions is predetermined. The sections that follow detail the proper way to declare each type of function.

CurrentDB versus CodeDB

One important difference between writing DAO code in library databases versus normal databases is your use of the CurrentDB function. In a normal database, CurrentDB returns a pointer to the database in which the executing code is located. This is merely a coincidence, however, because CurrentDB is actually designed to return a reference to the database that is loaded in Access' user interface. Using CurrentDB in a library database can be problematic if you are trying to reference the library database, not the current user database.

To reference a library database, use the CodeDB function instead. CodeDB returns a pointer to the database that contains the executing code. When you are developing your library databases in Access' user interface, CodeDB works just like CurrentDB. When running in a library database, however, CodeDB will reference it, not the user database. You'll see an example of using CodeDB in the section "A Sample Form Wizard" later in this chapter.

Add-Ins and the Registry

Access 97 depends heavily on settings in the Windows Registry, and add-ins are no exception. Add-in information is stored in the Registry tree in several locations. Figure 22.1 shows the Registry open to the Access 97 branch (HKEY_LOCAL_MACHINE\Software\Microsoft\Office\8.0\Access). Normally, Access stores add-in information directly under the 8.0 key. If you're using Access user profiles, however, Access may also store add-in information on a user-by-user basis under the profile key for each user.

The following sections on libraries, builders, and Wizards explain how to create Registry entries for each type of add-in.

Creating Library Databases

FIGURE 22.1

Windows Registry settings showing keys for add-ins and Wizards

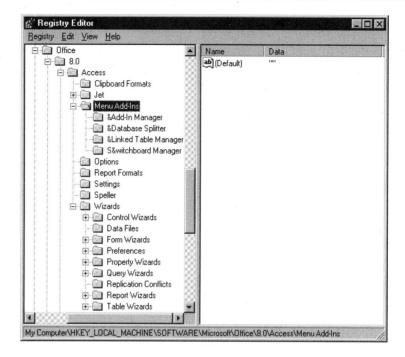

Creating Library Databases

Library databases are those that contain code modules with common functions shared by a number of applications. The benefit of creating a code library is that it relieves you from having to create and maintain a separate version of a function in each database where it is called. Creating library databases in Access 97 is relatively straightforward. The trick is making them available to other applications. (The concept of references, introduced in Chapter 20, comes into play here.) In this section we explain a number of issues related to creating library databases, including structuring library code modules, using library databases, and some of the reference issues involved.

Structuring Library Code Modules

What you put in an Access library database is really up to you. As you write more and more applications, you will find common functions on which you depend. These are all good candidates for library databases. How you structure your library databases, though, is important; it will dictate how well your applications perform and the amount of memory they require. Assuming that a "good" library database is one that loads quickly and consumes little memory, you can make decisions on how to structure library databases to meet these goals. To determine the best way to structure library databases, you need to understand how Access treats the VBA code they contain.

One improvement in Access 97 is *dynamic loading* of VBA code. In Access 2.0, all global modules (as opposed to form and report modules) were loaded into memory when a database was opened. This applied to library databases, as well as to user databases opened through the user interface. As a result, users paid a penalty of increased load time, especially of large applications, even if they never called a function in a global module. Access 97, on the other hand, does not load a VBA module until it is needed. Users still suffer slightly during the initial load process, but now this takes place incrementally rather than all at once. The important thing to understand about this process, from a developer's standpoint, is how Access determines when a module is needed.

Obviously, if your code calls a function in a particular VBA module, Access must load that module into memory. Access loads the entire module, even if you're going to call only a single function. The same holds true if you reference a global variable declared in a VBA module. Therefore, the first rule for creating library databases is to separate those functions that are called frequently from those that are called infrequently. By putting infrequently called procedures in separate modules, you will prevent Access from loading them until they are actually used. In fact, it is not too outrageous to suggest placing procedures that are called extremely infrequently in individual modules of their own. Alternatively, by centralizing frequently used functions in one module, you virtually ensure that the module will already be loaded into memory when you call a function it contains.

Using a Library Database

In Chapter 20 we introduced the concept of code references as a way for you to write VBA code that called methods and used properties implemented by Automation servers. We also explained the consequences of moving, deleting, or otherwise altering a reference once you had created it. Access library databases are subject to the same reference requirements as Automation server type libraries. That is, before you can call a function in a library database, you must establish a reference to it.

We've included a sample library database called CH22LIB.MDA that contains two small but useful functions, adhMin and adhMax, which compute the minimum and maximum values, respectively, within a list of numbers. The module basLib-Functions, in CH22LIB.MDA on the companion disk, shows the definition of these two procedures. Both use a ParamArray argument to accept a variable number of parameters. We can use CH22LIB.MDA to demonstrate the process of setting a library reference and calling a library function.

To demonstrate the referencing process, you'll need to create a new database. Then, follow these steps:

1. Create a new module in the database.

2. Select Tools ➤ References to display the References dialog.

3. Click the Browse button on the References dialog.

4. Select "Add-ins (*.mda)" from the list of file types on the Add Reference dialog that appears.

5. Locate the CH22LIB.MDA file and click OK. You should now see CH22LIB in the Available References list box on the References dialog.

6. Click OK to close the References dialog.

You can now call adhMin and adhMax from the new database. To test this, enter the subroutine shown here (or something similar) in the new module and run it from the Debug window:

```
Sub TestFunctions()
    MsgBox "Minimum: " & adhMin(3, 7, 8.9, -3, 10)
    MsgBox "Maximum: " & adhMax(3, 7, 8.9, -3, 10)
End Sub
```

As long as you maintain the reference to CH22LIB.MDA, the test procedure will continue to compile and work. If you break the link, by either moving or renaming the library database, Access complains that the reference to CH22LIB.MDA cannot be found. If this happens you must reestablish the reference either manually, using the References dialog, or through VBA code. For more information on the latter, see the section "Restoring References Using VBA" later in this chapter.

NOTE The entry that appears in the References dialog is the name of the database's VBA project. If you are converting a database from Access 95, the project name will be the same as the database name, including the file extension. New Access 97 databases use the database name without the file extension. You can change the project name to be whatever you want using the Advanced tab of the Options dialog.

TIP One quirk of Access references appears when you have a broken reference in a database with a startup form. If you call VBA functions in your code, Access will highlight one of these functions and report a missing reference. Obviously, the invalid reference is not for VBA but for something else. Don't be confused. Just open the References dialog and look for the missing reference.

Library Database Reference Issues

In Chapter 20 we discussed what happens when your VBA project loses a reference to an Automation server's type library. Access issues an error stating that the "Project or library cannot be found" and then opens the References dialog to display the offending reference. Access exhibits the same behavior when it cannot find a library database reference by another VBA project (see Figures 22.2 and 22.3). When this happens, you have the same two options. You can either use the Browse button to find the missing database or uncheck the box next to the reference to remove it from the project. If you opt for the latter, you must remove or comment out all references to procedures or variables declared in the missing library.

Lost references become an issue if you plan to distribute your library database to other users who might not install it in the same directory. Of course, you can insist that they install it to a particular directory, but most users don't take kindly to developers who insist on anything. Fortunately, there are several alternatives that will prevent references from becoming lost. First, if VBA is unable to locate a reference based on the *absolute path* that is saved with the project, it automatically tries to find the library using the same *relative path* as the database in which it is referenced. This means that Access will be able to find library databases if they are in the same directory as the database that uses them or in the same relative location. For example, if you create a database in C:\Test\Libs and reference it from a database in C:\Test\Apps, you can easily move them to C:\Prod\Libs and C:\Prod\Apps, respectively, with no problem.

FIGURE 22.2

You see this warning message when compiling a module after moving or renaming a library database.

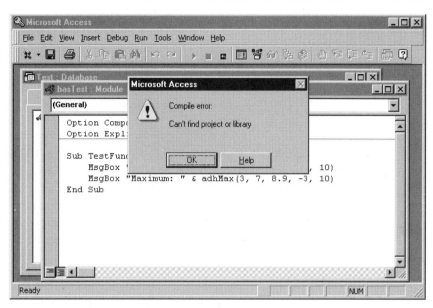

FIGURE 22.3

References dialog showing that the reference to CH22LIB.MDA is missing

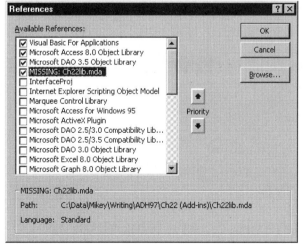

If a relative path search proves unsuccessful, Access searches for the library database in the following places:

- The directory where Access is installed

- The Windows and Windows\System directories

- Any directory included in the environmental PATH variable

Finally, you can create a Registry entry that specifies another secondary location. This is a good idea if you plan to distribute several library databases because it lets you choose one distinct location for installing all of them. To create these entries, add a Registry key called RefLibPaths under the HKEY_LOCAL_MACHINE\ Software\Microsoft\Office\8.0\Access key. For each library, create a new string value with the name of the library database and a value indicating the path to that database. Figure 22.4 shows an example of this Registry setting.

FIGURE 22.4

Registry key given an alternative location for library databases

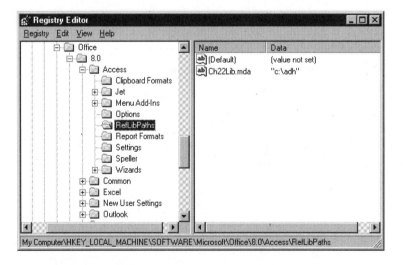

Circular References Are Not Allowed

Due to changes imposed by the integration of VBA into Access, you can no longer create circular references among libraries and databases. This was never an issue in

Access 2.0 because all public functions shared the same global name space. Procedures in any library could call procedures in any other. This is no longer the case. Any level of circularity is illegal. For example, Figure 22.5 shows two scenarios of references.

FIGURE 22.5

Stacked, but not circular, references are allowed.

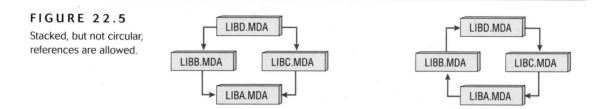

Given the first scenario in Figure 22.5, procedures in libraries LIBB.MDA and LIBC.MDA can call procedures in library LIBA.MDA. Procedures in library LIBD.MDA, in turn, can call procedures in libraries LIBB.MDA and LIBC.MDA. The second scenario is not allowed, however, because the referencing of LIBA.MDA to LIBB.MDA to LIBD.MDA to LIBC.MDA and back to LIBA.MDA results in a circular reference.

Editing Loaded Library Code

Once you've created a library database, you should install it as described in the previous sections and test it by calling library functions from a user database. If you find problems in your code, you can easily make modifications without unloading the library and restarting Access. To do this, you first set a reference to your library and then open the Object Browser dialog and select your library from the drop-down list of references at the top of the dialog (see Figure 22.6). You can then use the Object Browser to view both the modules in your library and the procedures they contain.

To view a procedure definition, select it from the list of procedures shown in the Members list box and click the View Definition button (it's the one to the left of the question mark) or double-click the procedure name. Access opens a module window and brings up the appropriate code. You can then make changes and continue to test your library.

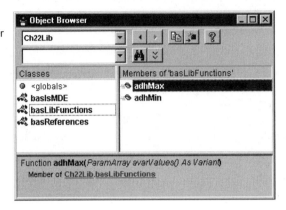

FIGURE 22.6

Using the Object Browser to view procedures in a loaded library database

> **NOTE**
>
> If you converted the library to an MDE file (see "Creating MDE Files" near the end of this chapter for more information), the View Definition button will be disabled and you will not be able to view or edit any code.

Using Application.Run to Run Procedures

You saw in Chapter 20 how you could use the Run method of Access' Application object to execute procedures in an Access database using Automation. You can use the same technique to call procedures in library databases. The advantage of this approach is that VBA does not require a reference until run time.

Run accepts the name of a procedure and up to 30 of the procedure's arguments. You can use it to execute both subroutines and functions. For example, you could modify the sample procedure listed above to use the Run method. The sample procedure shown below demonstrates this. (Note that the first argument to Run is the name of the procedure and that it is preceded by the VBA project name of the library.)

```
Sub TestFunctionsUsingRun()
    MsgBox "Minimum: " & Application.Run( _
    "Ch22Lib.adhMin", 3, 7, 8.9, -3, 10)
End Sub
```

Using the LoadOnStartup Key with Application.Run

If you want to use Application.Run, you must give Access a way of finding the database containing the procedure you're calling. You do this using the LoadOn-Startup Registry key. When you use the Run method and Access cannot find the specified procedure in any of the loaded or referenced libraries, it searches for it in any databases listed under this key. Figure 22.7 shows the key and two sample entries. You must add this key yourself (it is not created by default) under the HKEY_LOCAL_MACHINE\Software\Microsoft\Office\8.0\Access\Wizards key and add string values for each of the libraries in which you want Access to look.

LoadOnStartup uses a format similar to the Libraries section of Access 2.0's initialization file, MSACC20.INI. Each string value contained in the key is named after a library database, including the complete path if it is *not* located in the Access 97 directory. The value must be either "rw", for read/write, or "ro", for read-only. Unless you have code in the library that needs to update tables that are also in the library, you should specify "ro". Unlike Access 2.0 libraries, however, databases listed under the LoadOnStartup key are not loaded into memory when

---

FIGURE 22.7

LoadOnStartup Registry key showing additional libraries to search

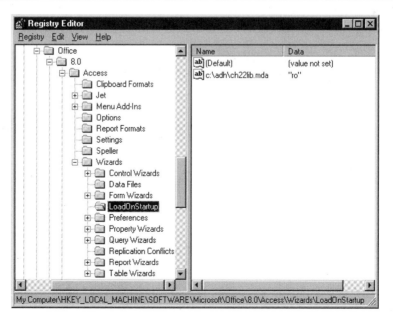

Access 97 starts, as the key name implies. Instead, Access loads only the module and procedure lists. The modules themselves are not loaded until a procedure is executed using Application.Run.

Always Compile Your Libraries

One final topic regarding library databases relates to VBA code compilation. Because a library database contains nothing but code, you don't have to worry about the database becoming decompiled once you have compiled it. Therefore, since compiled VBA code loads and executes more quickly than uncompiled code, be sure to compile and save all modules prior to distributing it to users. You can ensure the compiled state by creating an MDE file, as covered in the section "Creating MDE Files" later in this chapter.

Menu Add-Ins: the Simplest Add-Ins

Perhaps the simplest add-in you can create is a menu add-in. Menu add-ins are functions that are called by a menu command under Access' Tools ➤ Add-ins menu. You can call any function from a menu command by making a few entries in the Windows Registry. Figure 22.8 shows the Registry keys for the default add-ins, along with the Registry values for our sample comment stripping add-in. (See the section "Programmatic Control of Modules" later in this chapter for more information on this add-in.)

FIGURE 22.8

Registry entries for menu add-ins

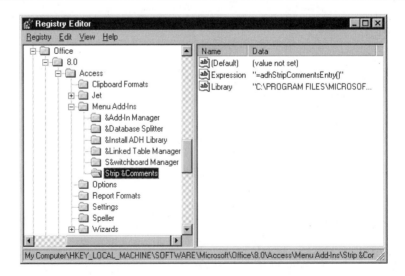

To create a menu add-in, you first add a new Registry key beneath the Menu Add-Ins key shown in Figure 22.8. Access will use the name of the key as the menu command on the Add-ins fly-out menu. You can see from Figure 22.8 that you can precede a character with an ampersand to make that character the access key for the menu command. After creating the key, you must create two String values, named Library and Expression.

Access uses the Library value to identify which database contains the add-in's main function. The Expression value contains the code fragment that Access must evaluate to invoke the add-in itself. In Figure 22.8, the value for Expression, "=adh-StripCommentsEntry()" is a function call, including the equal sign and parentheses. You can create your own menu add-ins very simply by calling a function in a library database.

Building Your Own Builders

Builders (sometimes called Property Wizards) are functions in library databases that assist you in setting properties of objects in an Access database. When you select a property in an Access property sheet and the Build button appears, that's your cue that a builder is available for that property. Access ships with a number of builders. In addition, you can write your own builders by following the few simple rules outlined in the following sections. We also describe two sample builders that are included with this book's sample files.

The Sample Builders

We've created two sample builders to demonstrate the basic requirements for creating your own builders. Both builders are implemented in CH22BLD.MDA.

You can use the System Color Builder to set Access color properties to Windows system colors by selecting them from a dialog that emulates Windows' Display Properties dialog. Because there are three properties that relate to color, we'll need to install this builder to work with each one of them.

You can use the Recordset to Form Builder to create VBA statements that transfer data from a Recordset variable to controls on a form and vice versa. This type of code is often used in client-server applications where querying is done using DAO or ODBCDirect and unbound forms are used to present the data.

> **NOTE**
>
> Access 97 is much better than version 2.0 about using system colors. The default background color for new forms, for example, is the system color for 3D objects (like command buttons). When a user makes changes to these colors through the Control Panel, Access automatically updates each form. This was not the case in Access 2.0. You will find the System Color Builder useful when updating forms created in version 2 to make them compatible with Access 97 forms.

Writing a Builder Function

You create builders by writing VBA functions that Access uses to set property values. Access requires that builder functions follow a strict set of rules. These rules can be summarized as follows:

- Builder functions must be declared with a specific set of three arguments.
- Builder functions must return the new property value as a string.
- Any forms opened through code in the builder function must be opened in dialog mode.

The following table lists the required builder function arguments:

Argument	Datatype	Description
strObject	String	Name of the table, query, form, report, or module object on which the builder function is operating
strControl	String	Name of the control to which the property applies
strCurVal	String	Current property value

Note that the argument names are arbitrary. Only their position in the declaration is important. When you initiate a builder, Access calls the builder function, passing it values in the three arguments. This is similar in concept to the callback functions for filling list boxes (see Chapter 7).

In the body of your builder function, you can use the information provided by the arguments to decide how your builder function should continue. Once you've computed the new value for the property, you must return it as a String result of the builder function.

How you compute the new value is where writing builder functions gets interesting. You can do just about anything you wish inside the builder function: open dialogs, call other procedures, or query databases. The only restriction Access places on you is that you must open forms as dialogs. This ensures that code execution in your builder function will halt until the dialog form is closed or hidden. Access requires, when a builder function terminates, that the screen be left in the same state it was in when the function was called. Leaving nonmodal forms hanging around would violate this rule.

The structure of builder functions will become clear as we explain the two sample builders we've included with this book—a builder that lets you set object color values to Windows system colors and a builder to create VBA statements (sometimes called a *code builder*). First, however, we must explain how Access knows a builder has been installed. For that we'll need to take yet another trip into the Windows Registry.

Builder Registry Entries

The Registry settings for Access include a host of keys and values that relate to builder functions. Access maintains individual builder keys beneath HKEY_LOCAL_MACHINE\Software\Microsoft\Office\8.0\Access\Wizards\ Property Wizards. Each Registry key is named after the property to which it applies. When Access starts up, it reads the list of keys from the Registry and makes the Build button available for properties that have builders defined. Access does not attempt to execute a builder function, however, until a user actually clicks the Build button. Although only a small number of properties are assigned builders when you install Access, you can create builders for every built-in Access property. See the next section, "Creating New Builder Entries," for information on how to add Registry keys to do this.

Access allows more than one builder for each property. Each individual builder is denoted by separate Registry keys beneath the key that corresponds to a property. Figure 22.9 displays the Registry tree expanded to show the settings for our System Color Builder. When Access finds two builders defined for the same property, it displays a dialog like the one shown in Figure 22.10 that allows the user to choose which builder to use.

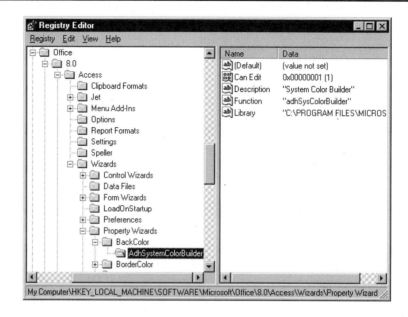

FIGURE 22.9

Registry Settings for
our sample System
Color Builder

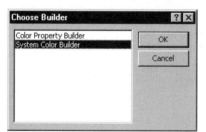

FIGURE 22.10

Access dialog for select-
ing which builder to use

> **NOTE**
>
> Some builders, like the default color builders, are implemented as part
> of Access itself, not as part of a separate library database. In these cases
> you'll see a dialog like the one in Figure 22.10 even though there is only
> one builder entry in the Registry.

The key name for each builder (adhSystemColorBuilder in this example) is arbitrary and serves only to identify the builder to Access. Each separate key needs to
be unique, however. When deciding on a name for your builders, be sure to keep
that in mind.

Each individual builder key must contain four values. You can see them in the right pane of the Registry Editor window in Figure 22.9. Each of these values is explained in Table 22.2.

TABLE 22.2 Registry Values for Property Builders

Value Name	Value Type	Remarks
Can Edit	DWORD	Set to 1 to allow a builder to operate on an existing value. It is hard to imagine an Access property with no existing value (even a null), but if you ever find one and don't want your builder to change it, make the Can Edit value 0
Description	String	Set to the description of your builder. Access will use this description in the builder dialog when more than one builder is defined for the same property
Function	String	Set to the name of your builder function with no arguments or parentheses. Remember that builder functions have a fixed set of arguments that Access will supply when the function is called
Library	String	Set to the path to the library database that contains the builder function. You can omit the path if your library database is located in the Access directory

Creating New Builder Entries

To add a new builder and have Access recognize it, you must create a new set of entries. In this section we show you how to make the entries to install the sample builders. Normally, though, you won't have to do this manually. The section "Distributing and Installing Add-Ins" later in this chapter discusses how to set up your library database so Access' Add-in Manager can automatically create the entries for you.

To install our sample builders, you'll need to create a set of Registry entries for each. We'll start with the System Color Builder. To install the System Color Builder, create an entry for the BackColor property, as shown in Figure 22.9. Then add an entry under the BackColor key (our example uses adhSystemColorBuilder) and add the values listed in Table 22.3. When you're finished your Registry should look like the one shown in Figure 22.9.

WARNING Before making any changes to the Registry, it's a good idea to make a backup. You can do this by creating a Startup disk or by using the Registry Editor to export the entire Registry database as a text file.

TABLE 22.3   Registry Values for the System Color Builder

Value Name	Value Type	Value
Description	String	System Color Builder
Can Edit	DWORD	1
Function	String	adhSysColorBuilder
Library	String	Set this to indicate the path to CH22BLD.MDA on your computer. For example: C:\ADH\CH22BLD.MDA

That's all it takes to install the System Color Builder to work with any BackColor property in Access. If you want to install the builder to use the other color properties, ForeColor and BorderColor, you will need to repeat the preceding steps to create new builder keys beneath each property key. If you find this too tedious, wait for the section "Using Add-In Manager" later in this chapter. We'll explain how you can use it to create these keys.

Installing the Recordset To Form Builder requires basically the same steps we just described. As with our System Color Builder, the Recordset To Form Builder operates on a property for which there is no Registry key. You can install builders for properties that are not set up by Access by adding a new Registry key under Property Wizards, setting its name to the name of the property you want to manipulate. The Recordset To Form Builder, however, is a special builder because it operates on VBA code, not an Access property. Therefore, to install it, you first need to create a key called "Module" beneath Property Wizards. You can then create a new key for our builder (for example, adhRTFBuilder) and add the values shown in Table 22.4.

TABLE 22.4   Registry Values for the Recordset to Form Builder

Value Name	Value Type	Value
Description	String	Recordset to Form Builder
Can Edit	DWORD	1
Function	String	adhRSToFormBuilder
Library	String	Set this to indicate the path to CH22BLD.MDA on your computer. For example: C:\ADH\CH22BLD.MDA

If you do not follow this Registry structure exactly, Access issues an "Invalid add-in entry for *addinname*" message when you first launch it, where *addinname* is the name of the Registry key with invalid entries. Access does not provide any information in addition to the Registry key causing the problem, however. (For instance, it would be helpful to know the property key where the errant add-in was located.) If you see this error and can't find the problem, you can use the Registry editor's search capability to look for a key with the name of the errant add-in.

Now that the builders are installed, we can look at how they work.

The System Color Builder

How many times have you consulted the Access Help file to find the values for Windows system colors? While VBA provides constants for these values, you still need to enter the literal numbers in Access property sheets. The System Color Builder (shown in Figure 22.11) is a simple tool that sets these values using a dialog. Listing 22.1 shows the tool's builder function, adhSysColorBuilder. (You can find this function in basBuilders in CH22BLD.MDA.)

FIGURE 22.11

Sample System
Color Builder

Listing 22.1

```
Function adhSysColorBuilder(strObjName As String, _
    strControl As String, strCurVal As String) As String

    On Error GoTo adhSysColorBuilder_Error
```

```
     ' Constant holds the name of builder form
     Const adhcFrmSysColBld = "frmSysColorBuilder"

     ' Open the builder form in dialog mode--this
     ' halts the code until the form is closed
     ' (by the Cancel button) or hidden (by the
     ' OK button)--note that we pass the current
     ' property value in the OpenArgs argument
     DoCmd.OpenForm FormName:=adhcFrmSysColBld, _
      WindowMode:=acDialog, _
      OpenArgs:=strCurVal

     ' Check to see if the form is still open--
     ' if so then the user clicked OK
     If SysCmd(acSysCmdGetObjectState, acForm, _
      adhcFrmSysColBld) = acObjStateOpen Then

         ' Set the return value to the value
         ' of the color combo box
         adhSysColorBuilder = CStr(Forms( _
          adhcFrmSysColBld)![cboColors])

         ' Close the builder form
         DoCmd.Close acForm, adhcFrmSysColBld
     Else
         adhSysColorBuilder = strCurVal
     End If

adhSysColorBuilder_Exit:
     Exit Function

adhSysColorBuilder_Error:
     MsgBox Err.description, vbExclamation, _
      "Error " & Err.Number
     Resume adhSysColorBuilder_Exit
End Function
```

adhSysColorBuilder simply opens the builder form, frmSysColorBuilder, in dialog mode and waits for the user to take some action. It passes the current property value (stored in the strCurVal argument) to the form in its OpenArgs property. Code in the form's Load event procedure sets the initial value of the system color combo box to this value. If the user clicks OK, VBA code in the form's module hides the form by setting its Visible property to False. Alternatively, if the user clicks the Cancel button, the form is closed. At this point adhSysColorBuilder continues executing and SysCmd is called to determine whether the form is still open (but hidden).

If SysCmd returns acObjStateOpen, the builder assumes the user clicked OK. In this case adhSysColorBuilder reads the value of the system color combo box and returns it to Access. It then closes the form. If, on the other hand, the user canceled the dialog, adhSysColorBuilder returns the original property value. Note that you must return something as the result of a builder function; otherwise the property will be set to an empty string.

adhSysColorBuilder is an example of a basic procedure that demonstrates the minimum requirements for an Access builder function. It accepts the current value of a property, changes it in the body of the procedure (in this case, using a dialog form), and returns the changed value as a result.

> **NOTE** The System Color Builder form, which actually manages the process of accepting user input, contains a good deal of rather uninteresting code. Most of the VBA code is contained in Click and DblClick event procedures and is used to set the value of the combo box in response to mouse clicks. We have chosen not to include the actual code here.

The Recordset To Form Builder

If you create applications only with bound forms you won't find the Recordset-ToForm Builder terribly useful. If, on the other hand, you use unbound forms to display data from DAO recordsets, you'll see the value of this builder right away. That's because you write lots of code that looks like this:

```
Forms!frmSomeForm!txtField1 = rstSomeRecordset!Field1
Forms!frmSomeForm!txtField2 = rstSomeRecordset!Field2
Forms!frmSomeForm!txtField3 = rstSomeRecordset!Field3
Forms!frmSomeForm!txtField4 = rstSomeRecordset!Field4
Forms!frmSomeForm!txtField5 = rstSomeRecordset!Field5
' ...
```

The code shown here populates controls on a form using field values from a recordset. The Recordset To Form Builder (shown in Figure 22.12) will write this code for you, given a *bound* form and the name of a recordset variable. To make the builder work you'll need a form bound to the same record source that the recordset variable is based on. After the code has been written, you can convert the form to an unbound one.

FIGURE 22.12

Our sample Recordset To Form Builder form

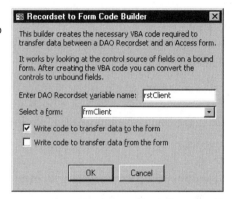

Listing 22.2 shows the function that invokes the builder form, adhRsToForm-Builder. Like adhSysColorBuilder, this function is very small, serving only to open the builder form, frmRsToFormBuilder, in dialog mode. Code in the form's VBA module (in the Public Result function) manages the construction of VBA statements.

NOTE To save space we've chosen not to include the listing for the Result function here. In brief, it opens a form in Design view, loops through all the bound controls, and builds a text string using the control's Name and ControlSource properties. If you want to explore how this is accomplished, open the frmRsToFormBuilder form in CH22BLD.MDA.

Listing 22.2

```
Function adhRsToFormBuilder(strObjName As String, _
 strControl As String, strCurVal As String) _
 As String

' Name of the builder form
```

```
Const adhcRTFForm = "frmRsToFormBuilder"

' Open form in dialog mode
DoCmd.OpenForm FormName:=adhcRTFForm, _
 windowmode:=acDialog

' If form is still open grab the value
' in the Result property
If SysCmd(acSysCmdGetObjectState, acForm, _
 adhcRTFForm) = acObjStateOpen Then

    adhRsToFormBuilder = Forms(adhcRTFForm).Result
    DoCmd.Close acForm, adhcRTFForm
End If
End Function
```

The important thing to point out is that adhRsToFormBuilder returns a string containing the VBA statements (along with comments). Like all code builders, the string is inserted into the active module *at the current insertion point.* Figure 22.13 shows a module with the insertion point positioned just below a statement opening a DAO recordset. You invoke a code builder by selecting Build from the right-click shortcut menu. Any code generated will be inserted at the point where the right mouse button was clicked.

FIGURE 22.13

Module code prior to invoking a code builder

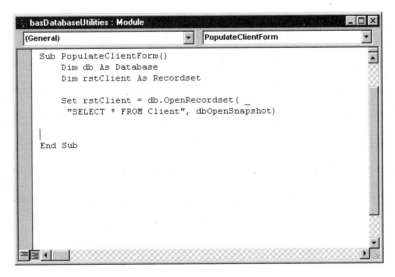

With code builders, Access always displays the Choose Builder dialog shown earlier in Figure 22.10. There appears to be no way to circumvent the Choose Builder dialog. (Even the new Always Use Event Procedures option has no effect.)

Figure 22.14 shows the results of VBA code to populate the form from a DAO recordset. Note that Access inserts a line break before inserting the code generated by the builder and that all indentation must be part of the generated text. Additionally, you need to make sure the controls referenced in the code are unbound—that is, they have no ControlSource setting.

FIGURE 22.14

Results of inserting builder-generated code

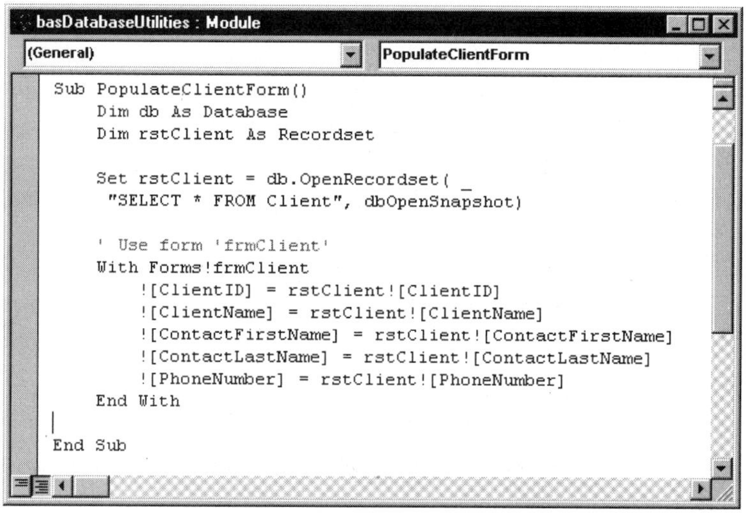

```
basDatabaseUtilities : Module                              _ □ ×
(General)                          ▼  PopulateClientForm          ▼

Sub PopulateClientForm()
    Dim db As Database
    Dim rstClient As Recordset

    Set rstClient = db.OpenRecordset( _
    "SELECT * FROM Client", dbOpenSnapshot)

    ' Use form 'frmClient'
    With Forms!frmClient
        ![ClientID] = rstClient![ClientID]
        ![ClientName] = rstClient![ClientName]
        ![ContactFirstName] = rstClient![ContactFirstName]
        ![ContactLastName] = rstClient![ContactLastName]
        ![PhoneNumber] = rstClient![PhoneNumber]
    End With

End Sub
```

> **NOTE**
>
> The Recordset To Form Builder dynamically generates a relatively small amount of VBA code. For code builders that create large blocks of code, it is often impractical to embed all of this code in the builder's module. In these cases you should use an Access table to store the generated code. Not only is this easier to manage, it makes updating the code easier as well, because you can edit data in a table using much less effort than when editing multiple lines of VBA source code. The section "Using an Access Table to Store Code" later in this chapter explains how to do this.

Developing Custom Wizards

One of the most interesting areas of Access development is the creation of custom Wizards. Wizards let you extend the product in a way that is both unique and tightly integrated. In a sense, your Wizards become part of the product itself. In this section we show you how to create new Wizards using a framework that manages the mechanics of wizardry and lets you focus on defining the functionality of your Wizards. We demonstrate this framework using a sample Form Wizard that lets you create simple dialog boxes.

Access Wizard Functions

Before digging into creating custom Wizards, we must explain the built-in functions Access provides for creating new objects. Objects you can create with Wizards generally fall into two categories: data access objects (DAO) and user-interface objects. You create data access objects—tables and queries—using data access objects and methods. Chapter 6 provides a detailed discussion of DAO and how to use it to create and modify tables and queries. If you want to create Wizards that build data access objects, you'll need to integrate code from Chapter 6 into the Wizard framework we describe in the following section.

User-interface objects—forms and reports—are handled by a completely different set of functions. Access provides six functions that create and delete forms, reports, and controls. Table 22.5 lists each of these. In this section we provide a brief overview of each function. The section "Finishing the Process" later in this chapter gives examples of how to use them.

TABLE 22.5   Access Wizard Functions

Function	Description
CreateForm	Creates a new form based on the current form template
CreateReport	Creates a new report based on the current report template
CreateControl	Creates a new control on a form
CreateReportControl	Creates a new control on a report
DeleteControl	Removes a control from a form
DeleteReportControl	Removes a control from a report

CreateForm and CreateReport both take two optional String arguments that let you select a form or report template to use as the basis for the new object. The first argument is the path to a database containing the desired template, and the second argument is the name of the template. If you leave both arguments blank, the default template will be used (the form or report specified in the Forms/Reports tab of the Options dialog). Using templates lets you create new objects that already have a number of properties, such as size and color, predefined. Both functions return a pointer to the newly created object.

CreateControl and CreateReportControl take a relatively large number of arguments and create a form or report control as a result. Like the previously mentioned functions, both also return a pointer to the new control object. Table 22.6 lists the arguments for each. Note that only the first two, FormName/ReportName and ControlType, are required.

TABLE 22.6 CreateControl/CreateReportControl Arguments

Argument	Type	Remarks
FormName/ReportName	String	Specifies the name of the form or report on which Access should create the new control
ControlType	Integer	Specifies the type of control to create. It should be one of the control type constants listed in online help (for example, acTextbox)
Section	Integer	Number of the section where Access should create the control. It defaults to 0 (the Detail section) but can be any section (including report group levels) on the form or report
Parent	String	Specifies the parent of the new control. Controls that have parents, such as attached labels, move with them
ColumnName	String	Specifies the name of the field to which the control should be bound. For unbound controls, this should be an empty string (the default)
Left, Top, Height, Width	Integer	Sets the location and size of the control in twips. There are 1440 twips per inch. If you omit any of these arguments, the default property for the control type is used

When you create a new control using either of these two functions, it is automatically endowed with the default properties for that control type. If you want to change any of these values, you can do so using the control object returned by the function. You will see, in the section "Finishing the Process" later in this chapter, that we do not use any of the optional arguments in our sample form Wizard. Instead we use the control object returned by the functions to set properties of the new control individually. We think using explicit property names makes code more readable.

DeleteControl and DeleteReportControl are subroutines that accept two mandatory String arguments, the first being the name of a form or report and the second being the name of a control. If successful, these procedures remove the specified control permanently. Finally, although it should be obvious, you can use these functions, as well as CreateControl and CreateReportControl, only in Design view.

One thing you should notice about these procedures is that they are not very object oriented. For instance, wouldn't it make more sense for CreateControl to be a method of form and report objects? Unfortunately, we are still bearing the burden of the original, undocumented (not to mention un–object oriented) Wizard functions from Access 1.0. As you read through the rest of this chapter, though, it should become clear how to use these procedures effectively in your own Wizards.

Defining a Wizard Framework

There are many ways to create Access Wizards or programs that use the Wizard functions. In this chapter we've chosen to develop a framework for writing Wizards that we think is both powerful and flexible. Our framework concentrates on the mechanics of a Wizard—eliciting user input and moving between pages on a dialog—freeing you to focus on writing code to make the Wizard do what you want.

Our Wizard framework is premised on the idea of using one main Wizard dialog to store information provided by the user and manage navigation using standard Next, Back, Cancel, and Finish buttons. Individual Wizard options are set by controls on one or more subforms that are dynamically loaded and unloaded in response to navigation commands. Each Wizard page corresponds to a different

Wizard state. An Access table manages each state, including which subform object to load, as well as which buttons to enable or disable.

A Sample Form Wizard

To demonstrate both our framework and the Access Wizard functions, we've created a simple Form Wizard in CH22WIZ.MDA for creating input dialogs like the one shown in Figure 22.15. You can use this Wizard to create forms that ask simple questions or accept typed input. This example demonstrates a variety of Wizard techniques. Not only will you see how to create forms and controls, you will see how our Wizard framework lets us respond to choices the user makes.

FIGURE 22.15

Dialog created using the sample Form Wizard

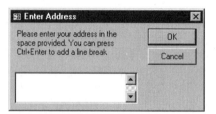

Our Wizard has three distinct states, each of which is represented by options on a separate subform. The first Wizard state requires the user to choose a dialog type—either a simple prompt or an input box. Depending on the user's selection, the Wizard can then proceed directly to the last state, where final choices are made before creating the form, or to an intermediate state, where details for the input box are specified.

We will control the program flow by making entries in the state table and by adding decision logic to the VBA modules for each Wizard page. Figures 22.16, 22.17, and 22.18 show the sample Wizard's three states, each of which is implemented as a separate form.

How to Use the State Table

Each Wizard state can be represented by a set of values that control such things as which subform to display and which buttons to enable. Also crucial is the state to which a Wizard should move if the user clicks either the Next or Back

FIGURE 22.16

The first Wizard state uses sbfWizDialog1 to set caption, message, and type information.

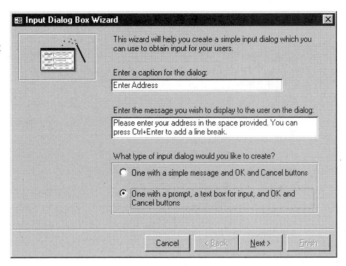

FIGURE 22.17

The second Wizard state uses sbfWizDialog 2 to set input box properties.

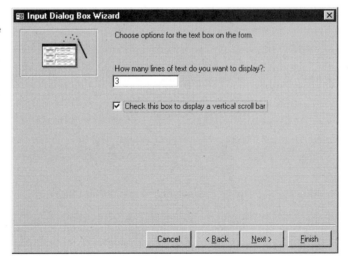

FIGURE 22.18

The third Wizard state uses sbfWizDialog3 to save and display the completed forms.

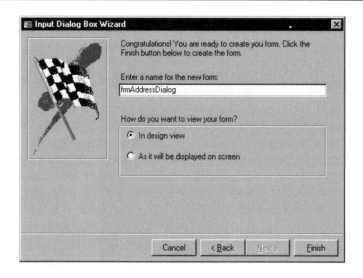

button. We've chosen to store this information in an Access table (called tblWiz-State in CH22WIZ.MDA) because this makes it very easy to add new Wizards and states, as well as to modify existing state information. Table 22.7 lists the fields in tblWizState.

TABLE 22.7 Field Definitions for tblWizState

Name	Type	Purpose
Wizard	Text	Wizard identifier
WizardState	Integer	State number
WizardForm	Text	Subform to load for this state
Comment	Text	Descriptive comments of the Wizard state
BackState	Integer	State reached by clicking the Back button
NextState	Integer	State reached by clicking the Next button
OptionalState	Text	State reached by clicking the optional button or the name of a function to call when the button is pressed
OptionalLabel	Text	Caption to display on the optional button

TABLE 22.7 Field Definitions for tblWizState (continued)

Name	Type	Purpose
ShowOptional	Yes/No	Indicates whether the optional button should be displayed
EnableBack	Yes/No	Indicates whether the Back button should be enabled
EnableNext	Yes/No	Indicates whether the Next button should be enabled
EnableFinish	Yes/No	Indicates whether the Finish button should be enabled
ConfirmCancel	Yes/No	Prompts the user to confirm canceling the Wizard

When adding your own Wizards to our framework, you'll need to create one record in the table that represents each Wizard state. To describe which values to enter, let's look at the records in the table for our sample Form Wizard. Table 22.8 lists the most important field values.

TABLE 22.8 State Table Values for Our Sample Form Wizard

WizardState	WizardForm	BackState	NextState	EnableBack	EnableNext	EnableFinish
1	sbfWizDialog1	−1	2	No	Yes	No
2	sbfWizDialog2	1	3	Yes	Yes	Yes
3	sbfWizDialog3	2	−1	Yes	No	Yes

Our Wizard uses three sequentially numbered states. The state numbers need not be sequential, but it is easier to follow the program logic if they are. The first state uses sbfWizDialog1 as the source object for the Wizard's subform control. From the first state the user can enter a caption for the dialog and a message to display on the form and can choose between a simple dialog or one with a text box for user input. You can see from the values in the state table that the only choice of movement is forward. An EnableBack setting of No disables the Wizard form's Back button, and a BackState value of −1 ensures that even if the button were enabled, no state information would be found in the table.

By default, if the user clicks the Next button, the Wizard moves to state 2 (determined by the NextState value). Later on, in the section titled "Creating Wizard Pages," we'll show how to adjust this logic using VBA code to skip state 2. In this state, which uses sbfWizDialog2 to elicit input on how the input box should appear, the user can move either backward or forward. (EnableBack and EnableNext are both Yes.) Finally, in state 3 the Next button is disabled, preventing the user from overrunning the Wizard. Also notice that the Finish button is enabled only in states 2 and 3. This forces the user to enter information on the first Wizard page before building the form.

You should be able to see a pattern in how the Wizard state values are specified. When you create your own Wizards, you will need to map their logic to records in the state table.

Looking at the Wizard Host Form

Our Wizard framework uses one form that acts as the host for the subforms that make up individual Wizard states. Figure 22.19 shows the sample host form, frm-WizardFrame, in Design view. The entire Detail section of the form is filled with a subform object. Our Wizard code will dynamically change the control's Source-Object property, depending on which state the Wizard is in.

Command buttons in the form's footer are used for Wizard navigation (Back, Next) and control (Cancel, Finish). You can use the button on the left, which has no caption, for an optional command. For example, it might make sense to include an

FIGURE 22.19

Sample Wizard host form in Design view

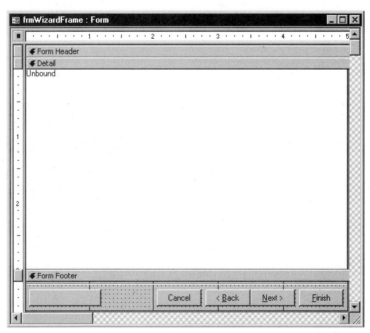

Advanced or Options button in a particular form state. Our Wizard functions will dynamically update this control based on settings in the state table.

Code behind the Host Form

If you open frmWizFrame in CH22WIZ.MDA on the companion disk in Design view, you can browse the contents of the host form's VBA module. We have chosen not to include it here to save space. If you examine it you will see that it is a very small amount of code. Generic code in the basWizards module handles most of the navigation tasks. The code that resides in the form itself is mainly responsible for initializing the Wizard and maintaining its current state. Several module-level variables are defined in the declarations section of the frmWizFrame's module. CurrentState is defined as a Public Integer, and we use it to store the Wizard's current state number. NextState is another Public Integer, which we use to store the state to which the Wizard moves when the user clicks the Back or Next button. We have declared these as Public so we can access them from other procedures. Similarly, StateTable is a Public Recordset variable, which we use as a pointer to records in tblWizState that apply to the current Wizard. We use a Private Boolean variable, mfCanceled, to denote whether a user has canceled the Wizard by clicking the Cancel button. We will use this variable later on when processing the form's Unload event. When creating your own Wizards using our host form as a template, you should not change or delete any of these variables. You should, however, change the value of the adhcWizID constant. This is the Wizard identifier specified by the Wizard field in tblWizState, and it should correspond to the value you use in that table to identify your Wizard.

Code in the form's Load event establishes the recordset used to retrieve state information. We use a SQL statement to query the tblWizState table based on the adhcWizID constant declared in the form. Once we have a pointer to the recordset, we can retrieve information about individual states and take some action, such as enabling or disabling buttons, and so on. If the SQL statement produces a valid recordset (that is, one containing records), we set the value of the form's Current-State property to 1 and call the global function adhWizGotoState, described in the section "Global Wizard Functions" later in this chapter.

Alternatively, code in the form's Unload event performs clean-up duties by closing the Recordset object. It is also responsible for issuing a message box dialog if the user tries to cancel the form and the current Wizard state calls for a confirmation. Code in the Click event for the cmdCancel button sets mfCanceled to True and calls DoCmd.Close to close the form. If the recordset's ConfirmCancel field is set to True when the user cancels the Wizard and the user does not answer Yes to the prompt, the procedure cancels the Unload event and resets the mfCanceled flag.

Code that responds to the Click events for the Back and Next buttons (cmdBack and cmdNext, respectively) calls a global function, adhWizGotoPage. Each passes a reference to the Wizard form using the Me object, as well as a Boolean value. Which state to go to is determined by the value in the state table's BackState and NextState fields.

Finally, there is no code attached to the Finish button's Click event. This is where you place code that is specific to your Wizard. As we look at the sample form Wizard, it will become clear how to use this button's event.

An Example Wizard Form

The module frmWizardFrame showed the VBA code contained in our template host form. When you create your own Wizard forms, you will need to add code to the existing module that is specific to your Wizard. Listing 22.3 shows the additional code contained in our sample form Wizard. It is composed of nothing more than several form-level variables we will use to store values the user selected. The reason there isn't much code is that all the work of eliciting and validating user input is handled by the subforms that make up individual Wizard pages.

Listing 22.3

```
' ****************************************************
' ** Add your own properties here                  **
' ****************************************************
' Change this constant to reflect your wizard id
' as set in the state table
Const adhcWizID = "SimpFormWiz"

' Public properties to store user selections
Public DialogType As Integer
Public DialogCaption As String
Public DialogMessage As String
Public LinesOfText As Integer
Public VerticalScrollbar As Boolean
Public OpenMode As Integer
Public NewFormName As Variant

Private Sub Form_Load()
    ' See frmWizardFrame for the rest of the code
```

```
      ' ***************************************
      ' ** Add your own startup code here **
      ' ***************************************
      ' This sets an initial value for LinesOfText
      Me.LinesOfText = 1
End Sub

Private Sub cmdFinish_Click()
    If Me.sbfWizard.Form.StateExit(True) Then

          ' ***************************************
          ' ** Add your own Finish code here **
          ' ***************************************
          If adhFormWizFinish(Me) Then
              DoCmd.Close acForm, Me.Name
          End If
      End If
End Sub
```

The most relevant code is in the declarations section of the form's module. Here we've declared a number of Public variables we will use to store selections the user makes. These variables, described in Table 22.9, map directly to the user input controls on our Wizard pages. As the user leaves each page, values in the controls are saved in the Public variables. When the user clicks the Finish button, our Wizard uses these values to create a new form.

TABLE 22.9   Sample Form Wizard Variables

Variable	Purpose
DialogType	Type of dialog to create—simple message (0) or text input (1)
DialogCaption	Caption for dialog box
DialogMessage	Text message to appear on the dialog
LinesOfText	For input dialogs, how many lines of text to allow
VerticalScrollbar	For input dialogs, whether the text box should have a vertical scroll bar
OpenMode	Whether the new form should be displayed in Design view (0) or Form view (1)
NewFormName	Name for the new form

You'll also notice that code in the form's Load event sets an initial value for the LinesOfText property (1). A validation rule on the text box for this property restricts user input to values between 1 and 10. You'll want to initialize any variables your own Wizard uses in the Load event, as well.

Global Wizard Functions

While each Wizard you create requires a separate copy of the host form, all Wizards share a set of common functions in a global VBA module (basWizards). These functions handle the mechanics of Wizard navigation and control. Listing 22.4 shows the first of these functions, adhWizGotoState. adhWizGotoState accepts two arguments: frmWiz, a pointer to a Wizard form; and fForward, a flag indicating whether the user is moving forward or backward in the Wizard process.

Listing 22.4

```
Function adhWizGotoState(frmWiz As Form, _
 ByVal fForward As Boolean) As Boolean

    Dim strBookmark As String
    Dim strCurrentForm As String
    Dim frmWizPage As Form

    ' Record the current position in the recordset
    ' in case we have to go back
    strBookmark = frmWiz.StateTable.Bookmark
    strCurrentForm = frmWiz!sbfWizard.SourceObject

    ' Call the StateExit method of the current
    ' subform to make sure it's okay to leave it
    If frmWiz!sbfWizard.Form. _
     StateExit(fForward) Then

        ' Find the record in the state table that
        ' corresponds to the given state
        frmWiz.StateTable.FindFirst _
         "WizardState = " & frmWiz.NextState

        ' Make sure there's a match
        If Not frmWiz.StateTable.NoMatch Then
```

```
            ' Turn off form painting
            frmWiz.Painting = False

            ' If so, then bring up the next subform
            ' based on the entry in the state table
            frmWiz!sbfWizard.SourceObject = _
             frmWiz.StateTable!WizardForm

            ' Now call the StateEnter method of the
            ' new subform to make sure it's okay
            ' to proceed
            If frmWiz!sbfWizard.Form. _
             StateEnter(fForward) Then

                ' If so, call adhSetWizardControls
                ' to set the state of the host
                ' form's navigation controls
                Call adhSetWizardControls(frmWiz)

                ' Set the host form's CurrentState
                ' property to the new state
                frmWiz.CurrentState = frmWiz.NextState
            Else

                ' Otherwise restore the current
                ' state by reloading the original
                ' subform and resetting the recordset
                ' to its original location
                frmWiz.StateTable.Bookmark = _
                 strBookmark
                frmWiz!sbfWizard.SourceObject = _
                 strCurrentForm
            End If

            ' Restore form painting
            frmWiz.Painting = True
        End If
    End If
End Function
```

adhWizGotoState is responsible for moving between Wizard states, a process comprising several steps. First, the procedure records data on the current Wizard state, including the position in the Wizard's recordset and the current subform SourceObject property. We may need to use this information later to return to the current state if an error occurs. After we've collected this information, the procedure executes the recordset's FindFirst method to jump to the row containing state settings for the given state. Once we have this information, we can update the Wizard's host form to reflect the new state by loading the appropriate subform.

Before doing that, however, we must make sure it is okay to do so. Why wouldn't it be okay? There are a number of situations in which you would not want a user to leave or enter a particular Wizard state until certain tasks had been completed or options selected. For example, suppose one Wizard state features a list of database objects from which the user must pick. Until the user actually makes a selection, we need a way to prevent the user from going forward. adhWizGotoState verifies that it is okay to leave the current state by calling a custom method of the currently loaded subform called StateExit (see the next section, "Creating Wizard Pages," for more information).

We pass the fForward flag to StateExit so the method knows the direction in which the user is moving. If StateExit returns False, the procedure terminates; otherwise it loads the subform acting as the desired state's Wizard page into the host form by setting the SourceObject property to the value of the recordset's WizardForm field. Immediately after the form is loaded, we call a complementary method of the new subform object, StateEnter. Similar to StateExit, StateEnter determines whether it is okay to enter the desired state. If this method returns True, adhWizGotoState calls adhSetWizardControls (which enables or disables the host forms' command buttons) and updates the host form's CurrentState property. If, on the other hand, the method returns False, the procedure restores the previous state's subform Source-Object setting and recordset position (by resetting its Bookmark property).

Creating Wizard Pages

Now that we've explained the code behind the host form and the global Wizard functions module, we can discuss the creation of individual Wizard pages using Access forms. Creating a new Wizard page involves making a copy of the sbfWizardPage form in CH22WIZ.MDA. SbfWizardPage contains sample image and label controls, and it is the correct size to fit in the Detail section of the host form. Its VBA module also includes function stubs for the StateEnter and StateExit methods. After making a copy of this form, you should edit the form and its VBA module to add controls and code particular to your Wizard page. You will need to include the following bits of code:

- Code in the Form_Load event that reads current values from the host form into local variables.

- A Public function called StateEnter that returns True if state entry is allowed and False if it is not.

- A Public function called StateExit that returns True if state exit is allowed and False if it is not. If state exit is allowed, this function should transfer data from any local variables to the host form's variables.

Because the module in sbfWizardPage is only a shell for your own Wizard code, it is easier to describe the requirements of our framework if we look at the module of one of the sample Wizard pages. Listing 22.5 shows the code in sbfWizDialog1, the first page of our sample Form Wizard. The code listing contains the minimum amount of code you will need to provide as part of your own Wizard pages.

Listing 22.5

```
Const adhcWizStateFirst = 1
Const adhcWizStateLast = 3
Const adhcWizDlgTypeMessage = 0
Const adhcWizDlgTypeInput = 1

Private Sub Form_Load()
    ' Enter initialization code here
    Me![txtMessage] = Me.Parent.DialogMessage
    Me![txtCaption] = Me.Parent.DialogCaption
    Me![grpType] = Me.Parent.DialogType
End Sub

Public Function StateEnter(fForward As Boolean) As Boolean
    ' Enter code to accept or prevent state entry here
    StateEnter = True
End Function

Public Function StateExit(fForward As Boolean) As Boolean
    ' Enter code to accept or prevent state exit here
    StateExit = True
```

```
' This makes sure the user entered some text for
' the dialog message
If fForward And Len(Me![txtMessage] & "") = 0 Then
    MsgBox "You must provide a message to display.", _
        vbExclamation
    Me![txtMessage].SetFocus
    StateExit = False
    Exit Function
End If

' This is logic to jump to the final state if the
' user selected the simple dialog option
If Me![grpType] = adhcWizDlgTypeMessage _
  And fForward Then
    Me.Parent.NextState = adhcWizStateLast
End If

' Enter termination code here
Me.Parent.DialogMessage = Me![txtMessage]
Me.Parent.DialogCaption = Me![txtCaption] & ""
Me.Parent.DialogType = Me![grpType]
End Function
```

When the user moves to this page in our sample Form Wizard, we need to update the controls on the form with the current dialog properties. We do this in the Form_Load event procedure by examining the value using the subform's Parent property. Parent returns a pointer to the form in which the subform is embedded. Note that Form_Load will be executed when we set the SourceObject property of the subform object to sbfDialog1.

After the subform loads, the adhWizGotoState procedure calls its StateEnter method. Note that we have declared both StateEnter and StateExit as Public functions, thus making them accessible to procedures outside the form's VBA module. In our example we don't need to perform any validation before allowing entry to this particular state, so StateEnter simply returns True.

Our StateExit function, on the other hand, is slightly more complex. Before moving to the next Wizard state, the user must enter a value for the dialog text. An If...Then statement examines the length of the text in txtMessage to determine whether it is greater than 0. If the user has not entered any text and is trying to move to the next state, the procedure issues a warning message, sets its return value to False, and terminates. This prevents adhWizGotoState from moving to a new state. If, on the other hand, all the conditions for leaving the current state are met (the user has entered a message), StateExit returns True. This allows adhWiz-GotoState to load the next Wizard page.

Finally, another If…Then statement examines the value in the dialog type control (grpType) that determines whether the new form will be a simple message dialog or will accept user input. If the user selects a simple dialog, it does make sense to display the second Wizard page—the one that lets the user set properties for the input box control. In this case the procedure sets the NextState property to the final Wizard state number. This has the effect of bypassing the logic in the state table and jumping to a different state. You can use similar logic in your own Wizards to alter the user's path through your dialogs.

Finishing the Process

After working with various Wizard pages to make selections, users can click the Finish button to have the Wizard transform their choices into a beautiful new object. Depending on the complexity of your Wizard, this may require large amounts of VBA code. The code attached to the Finish button on our sample Form Wizard, shown in Listing 22.6, is extremely simple, however.

Listing 22.6

```
Private Sub cmdFinish_Click()
    If Me.sbfWizard.Form.StateExit(True) Then


        ' ************************************
        ' ** Add your own Finish code here **
        ' ************************************
        If adhFormWizFinish(Me) Then
            DoCmd.Close acForm, Me.Name
        End If
    End If
End Sub
```

You should notice two things about this code. First, we are calling a separate function (adhFormWizFinish) to create the new form, and second, the function is located in a separate module in the database (basFormWizFinish). Since the form creation process could involve a large amount of VBA code, it would be nice if we could delay loading this into memory until the user actually clicks the Finish button. Placing adhFormWizFinish in a separate module prevents Access from loading the module until the procedure statement is executed. This technique provides better Wizard load time because Access does not need to load basFormWizFinish along with the Wizard form itself. Of course, if the user cancels the Wizard process, we never waste time loading this Finish code at all.

Creating Forms and Controls

As we just mentioned, we use a separate function, adhFormWizFinish, to create the dialog form defined by the user's selections in our Wizard. The module bas-FormWizFinish, in CH22WIZ.MDA on the companion disk, shows adhFormWiz-Finish, a procedure that uses Access' Wizard functions to create the dialog form and its controls. To save space we've included only the highlights in this section. adhFormWizFinish accepts a single argument, frmWiz, that points to the Wizard form. Because we have defined the variables that hold Wizard settings as Public, frmWiz is all that's required to reference them from this global procedure.

Logically, the first thing adhFormWizFinish does is create the form that will be used as our dialog box, using the CreateForm function and no arguments. Access creates a new form in the current database based on the default form template and returns a pointer to it in the frmNew variable. We can now use frmNew to set several form properties appropriate for a dialog box. For example, we remove the record selector, navigation buttons, and scroll bars and change the form's size to 3 inches wide by 1 inch tall. As the following code fragment shows, we also change its grid settings and caption. We set the latter to the Wizard form's DialogCaption property:

```
' Build the form
Set frmNew = CreateForm()
frmNew.Width = 3 * adhcTwipsPerInch
frmNew.Section(0).Height = 1 * adhcTwipsPerInch
frmNew.Caption = frmWiz.DialogCaption
frmNew.GridX = 16
frmNew.GridY = 16
frmNew.AutoCenter = True
frmNew.AutoResize = True
frmNew.RecordSelectors = False
frmNew.ScrollBars = 0
frmNew.NavigationButtons = False
frmNew.MinMaxButtons = 0
```

After creating the form, the procedure goes on to create a label control and, if the user chose an input dialog, a text box. The following code fragment shows our use of the CreateControl function, passing it the name of the form to create the control using our new form variable, frmNew, and the control type. The return value, a pointer to the newly created control, is stored in ctlNew:

```
Set ctlNew = CreateControl(frmNew.Name, acTextBox)
```

Although we could have passed additional arguments to indicate its control source, position, and size, we did not, opting instead to set these properties individually. Using specific property names makes the code easier to understand:

```
With ctlNew
    .Height = frmWiz.LinesOfText * _
      adhcLineHeight * adhcTwipsPerInch
    .Width = 1.875 * adhcTwipsPerInch
    .Top = 0.75 * adhcTwipsPerInch
    .Left = 0.0625 * adhcTwipsPerInch
End With
```

After the procedure creates the text box and adjusts the height of the form accordingly, it creates two command buttons—one labeled OK and the other Cancel. It places these on the right-hand side of the form. Once the command buttons have been created and their property values assigned, we must also insert some VBA code to make the controls work. We do this by calling a function, adhInsertCode, which we describe in the next section. If the user chose to create an input dialog, we call adhInsertCode to insert VBA code for the form's Load event to set an initial value of the control when the form is opened.

Finally, after the procedure creates the form and its controls and all the VBA code has been inserted, we can display and, optionally, save the form. The code that does this, shown below, first makes sure the new form is the active object by calling its SetFocus method. It then uses the Save method of the DoCmd object to save the active object (the new form) using the name provided by the Wizard form's NewFormName property. Finally, it calls the OpenForm method to display the new form in Form view if the user selected that option.

```
frmNew.SetFocus
If Not IsNull(frmWiz.NewFormName) Then
    DoCmd.Save , frmWiz.NewFormName
End If
DoCmd.Restore

If frmWiz.OpenMode <> 0 Then
    DoCmd.OpenForm frmNew.Name, acNormal
End If
```

Wizard code that you write is likely to be very different from the code in our sample Wizard because your code is specific to your Wizard's function. It should, however, have a similar structure—that is, a CreateForm statement followed by one or more CreateControl statements and finishing with an action that saves and/or displays the completed object.

Using an Access Table to Store Code

Our sample Wizard must insert code into the newly created form's VBA module to enable the two command buttons. Rather than embed large amounts of code in the Wizard module, we store it in an Access table. This lets us modify it easily, without having to edit the Wizard code. The code table, tblWizCode, contains three fields, CodeID, CodeText, and CodeDesc. CodeID is a text field that acts as the unique identifier for each code fragment in the table. CodeText is a memo field containing the actual VBA code. CodeDesc lets you specify a descriptive comment for the code fragment. Figure 22.20 shows tblWizCode open in Datasheet view. You can see that it contains VBA code fragments that we will use in our Form Wizard.

FIGURE 22.20

VBA code stored in tblWizCode

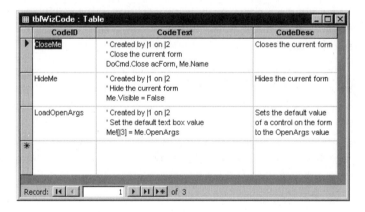

We've also created a function, adhInsertCode, shown in Listing 22.7, that inserts the code into a form's VBA module. adhInsertCode accepts five arguments and returns a Boolean value indicating success or failure. Table 22.10 lists each of these arguments and its purpose.

TABLE 22.10 Arguments to adhInsertCode

Argument	Type	Remarks
strCodeID	String	Should be a value in the CodeID field of tblWizCode; finds the block of text to insert into the form's VBA module
frmAny	Form	Specifies the form containing the module into which we will insert code
ctlAny	Control	Specifies the control to which the event code applies. Note that this can be Nothing, indicating that the code applies to the form itself, not a control
strEvent	String	Specifies the name of the event to which the code applies (for example, "Click")
avarTokens	Variant	This ParamArray argument lets you pass substitution strings to the procedure that the procedure, in turn, will insert into the code

Listing 22.7

```
Function adhInsertCode(ByVal strCodeID As String, _
 frmAny As Form, ctlAny As Control, ByVal strEvent _
 As String, ParamArray avarTokens() As Variant) _
 As Boolean

    Dim dbWiz As Database
    Dim rstCode As Recordset
    Dim varToken As Variant
    Dim intToken As Integer
    Dim strCode As String

    Const adhcTokenChar = "|"

    ' Query the code table to get the code for the
    ' selected CodeID
    Set dbWiz = CodeDb()
    Set rstCode = dbWiz.OpenRecordset("SELECT " & _
     "CodeText FROM tblWizCode WHERE CodeID = '" & _
     strCodeID & "'", dbOpenSnapshot)

    ' If we found a match go ahead and build the code
    If Not rstCode.EOF Then

        ' Build the declaration using the form
```

```
' or the control name--if we didn't
' supply a control reference then
' we must want to add code to the form's
' event procedures
If ctlAny Is Nothing Then
    strCode = "Sub Form"
Else
    strCode = "Sub " & ctlAny.Name
End If

' Add the '()' and a carriage return
strCode = strCode & "_" & strEvent & _
 "()" & vbCrLf

' Add the code from the table
strCode = strCode & rstCode![CodeText]

' For each token replacement call adhReplace
' to insert the replacement text
For Each varToken In avarTokens
    intToken = intToken + 1
    strCode = adhReplace(strCode, _
     adhcTokenChar & intToken, _
     varToken)
Next

' Add a carriage return and 'End Sub'
strCode = strCode & vbCrLf & "End Sub"

' Insert the code into the form's module
frmAny.Module.InsertText strCode

adhInsertCode = True
    End If

rstCode.Close
dbWiz.Close
End Function
```

The bulk of the code that makes up adhInsertCode handles the task of building a text string that will eventually be inserted into the form's module using the module's InsertText method. You will notice that adhInsertCode adds "Sub" and "End Sub" strings to the text it retrieves from tblWizCode. You should not, therefore, include an event procedure's declaration in tblWizCode.

adhInsertCode uses a For Each loop to iterate through any additional arguments passed to the procedure using the ParamArray argument, avarTokens. It calls adhReplace (not shown in this chapter) to replace all instances of a token (the pipe symbol, |, followed by a number) in the VBA code with an argument from the array.

> **NOTE**
>
> As it is written, adhInsertCode works only with event procedures that do not require arguments. If you wish to use it with those that do (for example, BeforeUpdate), you will need to modify adhInsertCode so that it appends the argument list to the procedure declaration instead of empty parentheses.

If you refer to the adhFormWizFinish procedure in CH22WIZ.MDA, you'll see how we use adhInsertCode in our sample Form Wizard. The statement that inserts code for the form's Load event is repeated here:

```
Call adhInsertCode("LoadOpenArgs", frmNew, _
 Nothing, "Load", CurrentUser, Now, strInputControl)
```

In this example the code fragment in tblWizCode is identified by the string "Load-OpenArgs". Once adhInsertCode has retrieved it from the table, it is inserted into the form's module. Passing the symbolic constant Nothing as the control argument forces adhInsertCode to create an event procedure for the form, as opposed to a specific control. Finally, three additional arguments are passed to the function. Tokens in the code stored in tblWizCode (you can see the tokens, |1, |2, and |3, in the code in Figure 22.20) will be replaced with these values.

Launching the Wizard

Like builders, Wizards are normally initiated by a function call from Access. While you can launch your Wizards any way you wish, if you want to integrate them into the list of standard Access Wizards, you must create a function with a specific declaration. There are two varieties of Access Wizard functions—one for tables and queries and one for forms and reports. Wizard functions for forms and reports must define at least one argument, regardless of whether you use it in your code. No arguments are required for Table and Query Wizards. Listing 22.8 shows the function used to initiate our sample Form Wizard, adhFrmWizEntry.

Listing 22.8

```
Function adhFrmWizEntry(strRecordSource _
 As String) As Variant

    ' Name of wizard form
    Const adhcFrmWizForm = "frmWizDialog"

    ' Open wizard form and let it do its stuff
    DoCmd.OpenForm FormName:=adhcFrmWizForm, _
     Windowmode:=acDialog

End Function
```

The argument to a Form or Report Wizard function such as ahdFormWizEntry must be a string, which Access will fill in with the name of a record source for the new object. This could be the name of either a table or a query. Access gets this value from the combo box on the initial Wizard dialog. Our sample Wizard creates an unbound form, so we ignore this argument. If you are creating a bound form, however, you would use this to examine the record source for field names and types. Access does not pass anything to Wizard functions that create new tables or queries.

You can define additional arguments to your Wizard functions if you plan on calling them from elsewhere in your application. For example, you might create a common Wizard function that handles both forms and reports, depending on the value of a second argument. (In fact, this is how the Access Wizards work.) If you do this, however, you need to tell Access about the additional argument; otherwise the normal Wizard functionality will be impaired. Informing Access of additional arguments requires making additional Registry entries, as explained in the next section.

WARNING You must adhere exactly to the rules for declaring Wizard functions. Any error in your Wizard function, including declaration, syntax, and compile errors, will result in Access issuing a "This feature is not installed" error when you attempt to invoke your Wizard. As you can see, this is far from being the most descriptive Access error message ever written. If you receive this error, you will need to shut down Access before attempting to edit your code. This is because, once an Access database has been loaded as a library, it cannot be opened in the user interface.

The only task that remains is to tell Access about our Wizard so our users have the option of selecting it from the standard list of Form Wizards. To do that we'll need to make some more (you guessed it) Registry entries.

Wizard Registry Entries

Access separates Wizard entries into groups based on the type of object the Wizard creates. Figure 22.21 shows the Registry keys for Control Wizards and Form Wizards. Not visible are the keys for Table Wizards, Query Wizards, and Report Wizards. Figure 22.21 also shows the Form Wizard subkeys that define the individual Wizards themselves. To add a new Wizard to Access' list of installed Wizards, you must add a new subkey beneath the appropriate Wizard type key. Access will use the name you give to the subkey in the list of Wizards displayed to the user, so choose something short but descriptive. For example, to install our sample Form Wizard, create a new subkey called Dialog Form Wizard beneath the Form Wizards key.

In addition to the subkey, you'll need to create several Registry values. Table 22.11 lists the required value names for Table, Query, Form, and Report Wizards, along with the values for our sample Wizard. To complete the installation of our Wizard, you'll need to add these values to the Dialog Form Wizard Registry key.

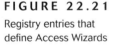

FIGURE 22.21

Registry entries that define Access Wizards

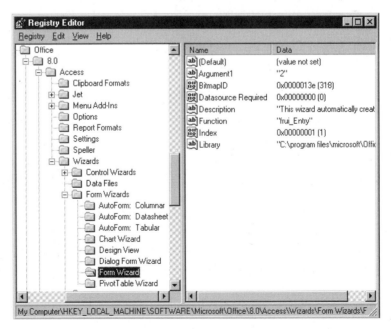

TABLE 22.11 Object Wizard Registry Key Values

Value Name	Value Type	Sample Value	Remarks
Bitmap	String	Path to ADHWIZ.BMP	Defines the path to a bitmap (BMP) file containing an image that Access displays in the new object dialog when the Wizard is selected
BitmapID	DWORD	N/A	Resource ID of the bitmap to use for this Wizard. Access Wizards use resource IDs to reference bitmaps included as part of the MSACCESS.EXE executable file
Datasource Required	DWORD	0	If set to 1, Access requires the user to select a data source for the object. A value of 0 means a data source is optional
Description	String	"Creates a simple dialog that displays a message or accepts input"	Lets you create a description of the Wizard that Access will display in the new object dialog
Function	String	adhFrmWizEntry	Defines the name of the Wizard function Access calls to initiate the Wizard
Index	DWORD	7	Defines the position of the Wizard in the list of Wizards. Must be between 0 (the first in the list) and 1 less than the number of installed Wizards. Must also be unique among other Wizards. If omitted, Access adds the Wizard at the end of the list
InternalID	DWORD	N/A	Marks the Wizard as one implemented by MSACCESS.EXE, not a library database, and indicates which internal Wizard function to use (You can't really use this setting; we've included it here for the sake of completeness.)
Library	String	Path to CH22WIZ.MDA	Defines the path to the library database containing the Wizard function. You can omit the path if the library is located in the Access directory

If you have declared additional arguments to your Wizard function, you also need to create values for each one in the Wizard's Registry key. You can see in Figure 22.21 the values for Access' built-in Form Wizard and an additional String value named Argument1. In addition to the required String argument, Access' Wizard function, frui_Entry, declares an Integer argument denoting which type of object is being created. Since, by default, Access will pass the Wizard function only one argument (the record source), this Registry value forces Access to pass a second one (in this case, with the value 2). If your Wizard function accepts more than one argument, you must define additional Registry values named Argument1, Argument2, and so on, one for each additional argument. After creating the additional Registry entries, assign them the values you want Access to pass to the additional arguments when Access invokes your Wizard function. These must be hard coded as strings and cannot be evaluated at run time.

Figure 22.22 shows the Registry updated to reflect settings for our sample Form Wizard. To test the Wizard, open any Access database and click the New Form button on the toolbar or select the Insert ➤ Form menu command. Figure 22.23 shows the New Form dialog with the sample Wizard selected. Note the Wizard's name, description, and bitmap. These are all defined using the Registry entries described earlier in this chapter.

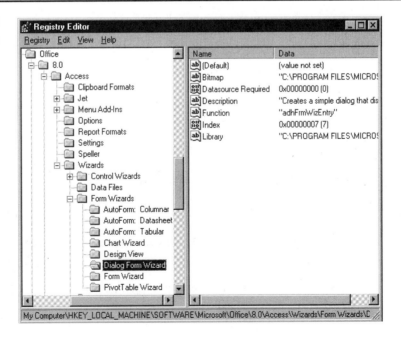

FIGURE 22.22

Registry entries for the sample Form Wizard

FIGURE 22.23

New Form dialog show-
ing details for the sample
Form Wizard

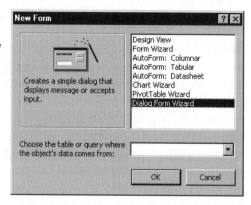

NOTE   If you want our custom bitmap to appear in the New Form dialog, you must copy ADHWIZ.BMP from the CD-ROM to your hard disk and set the Bitmap registry value appropriately.

Our Framework in Summary

We have presented a great deal of information in this chapter describing how to create Access Wizards. The discussion included both the Access Wizard functions and our framework for creating Wizard dialogs. Try not to confuse the two. You can use the Access Wizard functions (CreateForm, CreateControl, and so on) in any VBA procedure to create new objects. We have included a description of our framework because we believe it is a powerful yet easy-to-implement way of creating Wizards that look and act like those that come with Access.

If you choose to use our framework, there are a number of things you need to do. We have described them in detail in this chapter. To summarize the steps for creating new Wizards using our framework:

1. Create a copy of frmWizardFrame. This will act as the host form for your Wizard.

2. Change the adhcWizID constant to the unique ID for your Wizard.

3. Add Public variables to the host form's declarations section to hold user choices.

4. Add code to the Load event of the host form to initialize the Wizard.

5. Add code to the cmdFinish_Click procedure that calls your object-creation code.

6. For each Wizard page, create a copy of sbfWizardPage.

7. Add code to the subform's Load event to initialize that page.

8. Add validation code to the StateEnter procedure to restrict entry to that state.

9. Add validation code to the StateExit procedure to prevent users from leaving that state.

10. Add code to the StateExit procedure to save values from the subform to the host form's Public variables.

11. Set the SourceObject property for the subform object on your host form to the name of the first Wizard page.

12. Add a record to tblWizState that defines the subform and options for that state.

13. Create a function that accepts a pointer to the host form and uses the form's custom properties to create a new object.

14. Create a Wizard function that opens the host form in dialog mode.

15. Register your Wizard so Access can display it to users and call its Wizard function.

Control Wizards: A Hybrid

In addition to object Wizards, such as our sample Form Wizard, Access supports Control Wizards that are invoked when a user creates a new control on a form or report. Access' Combo Box Wizard is an example of a Control Wizard. Additionally, you can create ActiveX control Wizards that are called when a user adds a new custom control to a form or report. We briefly describe how to create a Control Wizard in this section. You will find, however, that the overall process differs little from regular Wizards and builders.

To use a Control Wizard, the user must have enabled this option by clicking the Control Wizards button on the form design command bar. We've created a simple Wizard that is invoked when a user creates a new text box. Figure 22.24 shows the Wizard's main form, frmTBWiz. Our Control Wizard is extremely simple. In fact, we've reused the second page of our Form Wizard.

FIGURE 22.24

Sample Text Box Wizard

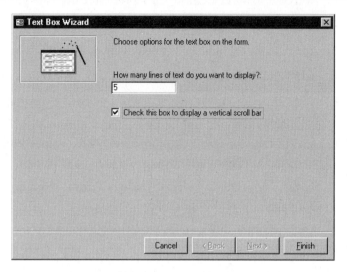

Control Wizard Functions

Like regular Wizards, Control Wizards must be invoked by a function. Access passes the name of the newly created control and its label (if it has one) as String arguments to the Wizard function. Listing 22.9 shows the function for the Text Box Wizard that we've included with this book.

Listing 22.9

```
Function adhTextBoxWizEntry(strControlName As _
    String, strLabelName As String) As Variant

    Dim ctlNew As Control
    Dim frmWiz As Form

    ' Constants for line height
    Const adhcTwipsPerInch = 1440
    Const adhcLineHeight = 0.1575
    ' Name of wizard form
    Const adhcTextBoxWizForm = "frmTBWiz"

    ' Check the active object and make sure it's
    ' a form (scroll bars don't make sense
    ' for reports)
```

```
If Application.CurrentObjectType = acForm Then

    ' Get a reference to the newly
    ' created control
    Set ctlNew = Forms(Application. _
     CurrentObjectName).Controls( _
     strControlName)

    ' Make sure it's a text box
    If ctlNew.ControlType <> acTextBox Then
        MsgBox "You can only use this wizard " _
         & "with text boxes.", vbExclamation
    Else
        ' Open wizard form and let it do its stuff
        DoCmd.OpenForm FormName:=adhcTextBoxWizForm, _
         Windowmode:=acDialog

        ' If form is still open, proceed
        If SysCmd(acSysCmdGetObjectState, acForm, _
         adhcTextBoxWizForm) = acObjStateOpen Then

            ' Get reference to wizard form
            Set frmWiz = Forms(adhcTextBoxWizForm)

            ' Set control properties
            ctlNew.Height = frmWiz.LinesOfText * _
             adhcLineHeight * adhcTwipsPerInch

            ' Text box scroll bars
            ctlNew.ScrollBars = ( _
             Abs(frmWiz.VerticalScrollbar) * 2)

            ' Close the wizard form
            DoCmd.Close acForm, adhcTextBoxWizForm
        End If
    End If
End If
End Function
```

There are several things to note about this function. First, before any substantial processing begins, the procedure checks the return value of Access' CurrentObject-Type method to ensure that the active object is a form. You can use this technique (as we have in this case) to take a different action if the active object is a report rather than a form. Next, this procedure sets a reference to the newly created control (stored in the ctlNew Control variable) using the control name Access passes to the function. You could use Screen.ActiveControl, but using the control's name is much safer and more intuitive. Once the reference is set, the procedure checks to make sure the control is, in fact, a text box and then opens the Wizard form.

Code attached to the cmdFinish button on the Wizard's host form simply hides the form and lets adhTextBoxWizEntry continue. adhTextBoxWizEntry then sets the Height and ScrollBars properties of the newly created control. Keep in mind that Access has already added the control to the form or report before it invokes your Wizard. The only thing your Wizard needs to do is set its properties.

Control Wizard Registry Entries

The Registry entries for Control Wizards are similar to those for builders. Figure 22.25 shows the entries for our sample Text Box Wizard. You can have more than one Wizard for each control, and these are grouped under the Control Wizards Registry key. There is a subkey for each control type (you can add ones that are not created by default), and each of these has subkeys for each Wizard that applies to the control. If you wanted to add a second text box builder, for example, you would create a new, unique subkey beneath the TextBox key shown in Figure 22.25.

FIGURE 22.25

Registry entries for
Control Wizards

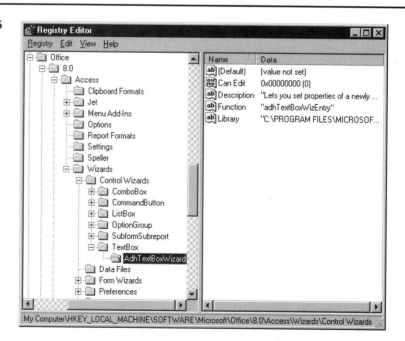

The Registry values themselves (in the right-hand pane in Figure 22.25) are the same for builders and were listed in Table 22.2 earlier in this chapter. The only significant difference is in the use of the Can Edit value. In the case of builders, you almost always want this value to be 1, indicating that the builder can be invoked for an existing property value. Control Wizards, on the other hand, are normally used to create new objects. In this case it may not make sense to invoke the builder on an existing control. For this reason the Can Edit value should be 0. You can have reentrant Control Wizards, of course, but you may have to write extra code to account for this.

ActiveX Control Wizards

We have one final word on Wizards. If you develop and distribute your own ActiveX controls, you can also install special Wizards to work with them. Access will recognize a Registry key for custom controls that follows the same rules as for normal Control Wizards, with a few exceptions.

First, before you install your Wizard you must create a new Registry key called OLE CONTROL WIZARDS (it must be uppercase) beneath the normal Access "Wizards" key. Then, instead of a control type, you must create a new subkey beneath the OLE CONTROL WIZARDS key using the class name of the custom control. For example, DBOutl.DataOutline is the class name for the data outline control.

From here the rules are the same as for regular Control Wizards. Create a new subkey beneath the control subkey with the values listed in Table 22.2.

Distributing and Installing Add-Ins

Once you've created a Wizard, you can easily distribute it to others by providing them with a copy of the library database. The only complication involves installing it on another person's computer and making the appropriate Registry entries. Fortunately, Access provides two mechanisms to ease this task: Add-in Manager and the USysRegInfo table. In this section we describe each of these and how to use them to distribute your own custom add-ins.

Using Add-In Manager

Using the Access Add-in Manager is usually the easiest way to install and uninstall Access Wizards, builders, and add-ins. Add-in Manager uses a special table in the Wizard database called USysRegInfo to create or delete the Registry entries required for the add-in to operate. You invoke Add-in Manager by selecting Tools ➤ Add-ins ➤ Add-in Manager from the Access menus. Figure 22.26 shows the Add-in Manager dialog.

FIGURE 22.26

Access' Add-in
Manager dialog

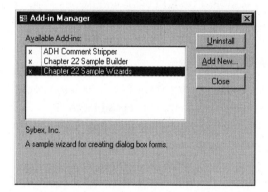

The list box displays all the add-ins Add-in Manager knows about. Access builds this list by looking at all the library databases in the Access directory and examining their database properties. Add-in Manager examines three properties for each library database in the Access directory: Title, Company, and Comments. Figure 22.27 shows the Summary tab of the Database Properties dialog for our sample Form Wizard database, CH22WIZ.MDA. You can see how values in these three properties are displayed in the Add-in Manager dialog in Figure 22.26.

NOTE You must have Open/Run permission on a library database in order for Add-in Manager to read its properties. If you do not have permission to open the database, Add-in Manager displays a warning dialog and omits the add-in from the list.

A check box next to the add-in description in the Add-in Manager dialog tells you whether the add-in is currently installed. Add-in Manager makes this determination by looking for values in the Registry that match those in the add-in's USysRegInfo table (which we describe in the next section). If the library database does not have a USysRegInfo table, Add-in Manager cannot determine its installed

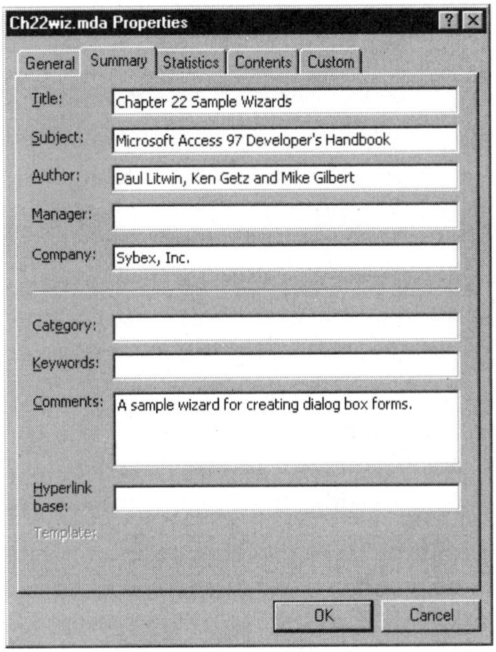

FIGURE 22.27

Document properties
used by Add-in Manager

FIGURE 22.27

Document properties
used by Add-in Manager

state. You can toggle the installed state of an existing add-in by double-clicking the add-in on the list or by selecting it and clicking the Uninstall button. For add-ins that are not currently installed, the caption of this button changes to "Install," and clicking it installs the selected add-in.

You can also install new add-ins that aren't in the list by clicking the Add New button. This opens a browse dialog with which you can locate the library database containing the add-in. After you have found the add-in, Add-in Manager automatically copies it to the Access directory and installs it. There is no way to prevent Add-in Manager from copying the file. You can have add-ins in other directories, but your users will not be able to use Add-in Manager to administer them.

Creating the USysRegInfo Table

Add-in Manager depends on the existence of a table called USysRegInfo in your library database that contains your add-in's required Registry entries. USysRegInfo is composed of four fields. Table 22.12 lists each of these fields and its datatype.

TABLE 22.12 Field Layout for the USysRegInfo Table

Field	Type	Remarks
Subkey	Text	Contains the name of the Registry subkey containing a specific Registry setting
Type	Number	Defines the type of entry to create: key (0), string (1), or DWORD (4)
ValName	Text	For Registry values, defines the name of the value
Value	Text	For Registry values, the actual value as text

The value in the Subkey field is the name of the Registry subkey you want Add-in Manager to create when it installs your add-in. Previous sections of this chapter described the keys that are necessary to install each of the various add-in types. You can have as many sets of entries in USysRegInfo as you wish. However, Registry entries that apply to a given add-in must all have the same value in the Subkey field.

When adding records to the USysRegInfo table for your own add-ins, the first record in each group should consist of the subkey name and the value 0 in the Type field. A Type of 0 instructs Add-in Manager to create the subkey. You must do this prior to adding values to it. Once you have created the subkey, you add values to it by adding more records to USysRegInfo.

The format of the Subkey value is important. All values in this field must begin with either "HKEY_LOCAL_MACHINE" or "HKEY_CURRENT_ACCESS_PROFILE". These strings have an identical effect when installing your add-in, except when you are using User Profiles. In this case the latter string instructs Add-in Manager to create Registry entries beneath the current profile instead of beneath Access' normal Registry structure. Normally you should use HKEY_CURRENT_ACCESS_ PROFILE unless you want to force Add-in Manager to create entries under HKEY_LOCAL_MACHINE\Software\Microsoft\Office\8.0\Access. The remainder of the Subkey value is the Registry key structure beginning with the Access Registry key, including any pre-existing keys.

Figure 22.28 shows the USysRegInfo table from our sample Form Wizard. Note the Subkey values that point to a new Registry key called Dialog Form Wizard. The first entry in the table creates the key (Type equals 0) and the rest add appropriate values for Library, Description, and so on. Note the string "|ACCDIR" in the Library entry's Value field. This is a token Add-in Manager will replace with the full path to the Access directory when it installs the add-in.

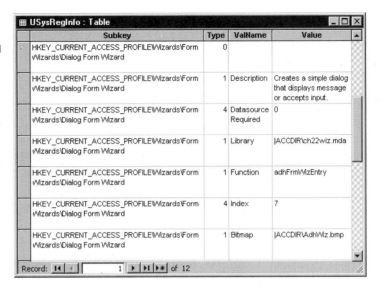

FIGURE 22.28

USysRegInfo values for the sample Form Wizard

Examine the USysRegInfo tables in the other sample add-ins to see how to create Registry entries for every type of Wizard, builder, and add-in.

Advanced Add-in Topics

Finally, there are a few advanced Access 97 features that relate to the development and distribution of add-ins. We discuss those in this section.

Restoring References Using VBA

In Access 95, references were, to say the least, troublesome. They were necessary due to the new architecture of VBA, yet developers had no programmatic control over them. The only way for an end user to use a library database was to add the reference manually. Fortunately, that's changed for the better in Access 97, although the current solution is not yet perfect. Access' Application object now contains a References collection populated with one Reference object for each reference in the current VBA project. You can use the collection and objects to view and even change VBA references. This gives you the capability to install and rebuild references using VBA code.

Table 22.13 lists the properties of a Reference object. You can use these to examine the characteristics of existing references using VBA code as follows. (You can find this code in the basListRefs module in CH22LIB.MDA.)

```
Dim ref As Reference

For Each ref In Application.References
    With ref
        Debug.Print .Name,
        Debug.Print .FullPath,
        Debug.Print IIf(.BuiltIn, "Required", ""),
        Debug.Print IIf(.Kind, "Project", "TypeLib: " _
          & .Guid),
        Debug.Print .Major & "." & .Minor,
        Debug.Print IIf(.IsBroken, "Missing!", "")
    End With
Next
```

TABLE 22.13 Properties of a Reference Object

Property	Description
BuiltIn	True if the reference is required for Access to operate. (For example, Access, DAO, and VBA are all required.) Required references cannot be removed
Collection	Pointer to the parent References collection
FullPath	Full path to the type library, executable, or Access database the reference is linked to
Guid	The GUID (Globally Unique Identifier) for the reference. Only type libraries and executable programs have GUIDs
IsBroken	True if the reference has been broken (shown as Missing in the References dialog)
Kind	Type of reference. Returns 0 for a type library or executable and 1 for a VBA project (that is, an Access database)
Major	Major version number. Always 0 for VBA projects
Minor	Minor version number. Always 0 for VBA projects
Name	Reference name. For VBA projects this is the project name unless the reference is broken. In this case it will be the full path to the database (that is, the same as the FullPath property)

All the properties listed in Table 22.13 are read-only. You make changes to references using methods of the References collection. In addition to a Remove method, which you can use to remove broken references, the collection has two methods for adding references. AddFromFile accepts the path to an Access database as its only argument and adds a reference to it to the current project. AddFromGuid accepts a type library's GUID (Globally Unique Identifier) plus major and minor version numbers. This method looks up the GUID in the Windows Registry and adds a reference to the type library associated with it.

We've provided code in CH22LIB.MDA that adds a reference to the sample library to a user database. The function that accomplishes this, adhAddReference, is shown in Listing 22.10.

Listing 22.10

```
Function adhAddReference() As Variant
    Dim ref As Reference
    Dim strDBName As String
    Dim fOK As Boolean

    ' VBA project name
    Const adhcProject = "Ch22Lib"

    On Error GoTo HandleError

    ' Get the name of this database
    strDBName = adhGetJustMDBName(CurrentDb.Name)

    ' Make sure reference isn't already added
    For Each ref In Application.References

        ' If reference name equals project name
        ' then we're okay!
        If ref.Name = adhcProject Then
            fOK = True
            Exit For

        ' If database name is contained in
        ' reference name then we've got a broken
        ' reference
        ElseIf adhGetJustMDBName(ref.Name) = strDBName Then

            ' Delete the bad reference
            References.Remove ref
```

```
            Exit For
        End If
    Next

    ' If we haven't fixed it then we have to add it
    If Not fOK Then
        References.AddFromFile CodeDb.Name
        MsgBox "Reference to " & CodeDb.Name & _
          " added.", vbInformation
    End If
ExitProc:
    Exit Function
HandleError:
    MsgBox Err.Description, vbExclamation, _
      "Error " & Err.Number
    Resume ExitProc
End Function
```

adhAddReference works by examining each of the references in the current project, comparing its name with the library's project name, Ch22Lib. If a match is found, the reference exists and is valid. If, on the other hand, the database name is found, the reference exists but is currently broken. (When a reference to a database is broken, the Name property returns the last known path to the database.) In this case the bad reference is removed.

After removing the missing reference (or failing to find any reference to the database at all), adhAddReference uses the AddFromFile method to create a new reference to the library.

So how does a user call this function if there is no reference to the library? Our sample library database contains a USysRegInfo table that establishes a Menu Add-in command to call the function. With this approach end users can install the library once using Add-in Manager and then select the menu command to add a reference to any database they want!

NOTE Programmatic control of references is a step forward, but its implementation is not yet perfect. Because the References collection is a descendant of the Application object, it allows you to manipulate only references in the currently loaded database. References, however, are unique to each VBA project (database). Perhaps a future version of Access will enhance the References collection to allow a finer degree of granularity.

Programmatic Control of Modules

Another new (and as yet imperfect) feature in Access 97 is programmatic control of VBA modules. In prior versions of Access, control of module code was extremely limited. While Access exposed a Module object, it had only one method, InsertText. Access 97 enhances this somewhat by including a few more properties and methods, but control is not as granular as, for example, Microsoft Word or PowerPoint, which let you control text down to individual letters. Programmatic control of module code is a capability long sought by library and add-in developers.

Table 22.14 lists the properties and methods of the enhanced Module object. Using these properties and methods, you can perform tasks such as enumerating the procedures in a module, searching for and replacing selected text strings, creating new event procedures, and inserting and deleting lines of code.

TABLE 22.14 Properties and Methods of a Module Object

Property or Method	Description
CountOfDeclarationLines property	Returns the number of lines in a module's declarations section as a long integer
CountOfLines property	Returns the number of lines of code in a module, including the declarations section
Lines property	Returns a string containing VBA code from the module, given a starting line number and line count
Name property	Name of the module
ProcBodyLine property	Returns the line of code containing the declaration of a procedure, given its name and type (sub or function, Property Let, Property Get, or Property Set)
ProcCountLines property	Returns the total number of lines that make up a procedure, given its name and type. This includes any comments or conditional compilation statements that immediately precede the declaration
ProcOfLine property	Returns the name of a procedure that contains a given line of code in the module. Returns the type of procedure in a passed variable
ProcStartLine property	Returns the line at which the body of a procedure begins, given a procedure name and type. The beginning of a procedure includes any comments or conditional compilation statements that appear immediately before the declaration

TABLE 22.14 Properties and Methods of a Module Object (continued)

Property or Method	Description
AddFromFile method	Adds the contents of a text file to a module. All text is inserted after the declarations section and before the first procedure if one exists
AddFromString method	Adds the contents of a text string to a module. All text is inserted after the declarations section and before the first procedure if one exists
CreateEventProc method	Creates an event procedure stub in a form or report module, given the event name and object name. Returns the line of code where the declaration begins
DeleteLines method	Deletes lines of code from a module, given a starting line and line count
Find method	Searches for text in a module. Returns True if text was found or False if it was not. Variables passed as arguments will be filled in to return the line and column where the specified text begins
InsertLines method	Inserts lines of text into a module, given a starting line
InsertText method	Inserts text at the end of a module, after all existing procedures
ReplaceLine method	Replaces a line of text in a module with a new text string

To demonstrate this functionality we've created a simple library that performs a frequently needed service: stripping comments from a module. Many developers strip comments from their applications before distributing them because it saves disk space and memory. The add-in is contained in NOCOMM.MDA on the CD-ROM, and you can use Add-in Manager to install it. It will create a new command on the Tools ➤ Add-ins menu.

While we can't include here all the code in the library, we can explain the highlights. The code works by iterating through all the modules in the current database, using the DAO Documents collection of the Forms, Reports, and Modules containers. With each document, it opens the module in Design view. For global and class modules, it uses the OpenModule method of the DoCmd object:

```
DoCmd.OpenModule docAny.Name
```

For form and report modules it's a bit trickier. First the form or report must be opened in Design view. Then the library must check to see whether the object has

a module (using the HasModule property), since lightweight forms and reports won't. Finally, if the object has a module, the library opens it using the OpenModule method. Note that the module name is the same as the object name with either "Form_" or "Report_" prepended to it. Here is the code that accomplishes all this:

```
DoCmd.OpenForm docAny.Name, acDesign
If Forms(docAny.Name).HasModule Then
    DoCmd.OpenModule "Form_" & docAny.Name
    cDeleted = cDeleted + _
     adhStripCommentsFromModule( _
     Application.Modules("Form_" & docAny.Name))
    DoCmd.Close acForm, docAny.Name, acSaveYes
Else
    DoCmd.Close acForm, docAny.Name, acSaveNo
End If
```

The code that actually deletes the comments is shown in Listing 22.11. It works by walking backward through each line of code in the module (determined using the CountOfLines property), looking for lines that begin with an apostrophe. If one is found it is deleted.

Listing 22.11

```
Private Function adhStripCommentsFromModule _
  (modAny As Module) As Long
    Dim lngLines As Long
    Dim cLine As Long
    Dim cDeleted As Long

    ' Walk backward from the total count of
    ' lines looking for those that start with
    ' apostrophes, deleting them
    For cLine = modAny.CountOfLines - 1 To 0 Step -1
        If InStr(Trim(modAny.Lines(cLine, 1)), "'") = 1 Then
            modAny.DeleteLines cLine, 1
            cDeleted = cDeleted + 1
        End If
    Next

    adhStripCommentsFromModule = cDeleted
End Function
```

Note that the adhStripCommentsFromModule function strips only full-line comments. It will not work with comments that appear on a line after a VBA statement. This is because doing so would require parsing the line to determine whether the apostrophe was a comment or part of a valid VBA statement.

Creating MDE Files

The final new feature of Access 97 that we discuss in this chapter is the ability to create MDE files. MDE files are Access databases containing modules that have been saved without the VBA source code. Instead, only the compiled VBA pseudocode is stored. This makes for a much smaller database than a normal MDB file, and one that is inherently much more secure. Since the source code is not included, there is no danger of an unscrupulous individual breaking in and stealing it.

NOTE This is actually how the Wizards in Access 95 were secured. At the time, Microsoft said they were secured using "an undocumented technique." Since the functionality was developed late in the development cycle, Microsoft chose not to make it available in Access 95 but instead to use it only to secure the Wizards.

Creating an MDE file is simple. Select Make MDE File from the Tools ➤ Database Utilities menu. At the prompt, you enter a new file name, to which Access appends the .MDE extension. When Access creates an MDE file, it compiles all the VBA source code and saves only the compiled state, discarding the source code itself. Access also compacts the database during the save process.

The database you use to create an MDE file must meet certain criteria:

- The code must be free of compile errors.

- If the database has been secured, you must have Read Design privileges for all objects.

- The database cannot be a replica or design master. (Once you create the MDE file, however, you can replicate it.)

- If the database references other Access databases, they must first be compiled into MDE files.

After conversion, some of the functionality of your database is altered due to the removal of VBA source code:

- You cannot view any module in the database.

- You cannot create any new forms, reports, or modules.

- You cannot use the Module methods described in the previous section to view or alter source code.

- You cannot change any references in the VBA project.

- You cannot change the VBA project name.

- You cannot export or import forms, reports, or modules; however, you can export and import tables, queries, and macros.

- The View Definition button in the Object Browser will be disabled if you examine modules and procedures in an MDE file.

Since creating an MDE file alters your database dramatically, be sure to keep a copy of the original MDB or MDA file. This copy will be necessary should you have to fix any errors in your VBA code.

> **WARNING** MDE files are version specific. That is, if you create an MDE file using Access 97, there is no guarantee that it will work with future major versions of Access. If you want to use your MDE with Access 98 (or whatever the next version is called), you'll need to retain the original version of the database, convert it to the new version of Access, and then use the new version to create another MDE. What about minor releases (for example, 8.0a, 8.1, and so on), if there are any? Microsoft has stated they will make every effort not to break MDE functionality with minor (sometimes called *point*) releases, but they're not making any promises. In any event, make sure you keep a copy of the original database just in case.

To programmatically determine whether a database has been converted to the MDE format, you can check a user-defined property of the database that Access adds during the conversion process. This property, called MDE, will return the letter "T " if the database is an MDE file. If the database is not an MDE file, the property will not exist. Listing 22.12 shows the adhIsMDE function, which accepts a database object pointer and returns True or False, depending on whether the database is an MDE.

Listing 22.12

```
Function adhIsMDE(dbAny As Database) As Boolean
    Dim varRet As Variant

    On Error Resume Next
    varRet = dbAny.Properties("MDE")
    adhIsMDE = (varRet = "T") And (Err.Number = 0)
End Function
```

WARNING Be careful when creating MDE files from libraries containing a USys-RegInfo table. If you create an MDE file, make sure you change the library name in the table to reflect the .MDE file extension. Otherwise Access will be unable to locate your add-in.

Summary

In this chapter we've explored the very powerful capabilities of Access Wizards. Creating custom Wizards allows you to invest your users with specialized tools that appear as built-in features of Access. Specifically, we covered the following topics:

- Where Wizard Registry entries are stored
- How to launch a function from the Add-ins menu
- How to create a builder to help users change property settings
- How to design a custom Wizard using our Wizard framework
- How to make it easy for your users to install your add-in using Add-in Manager
- How to change references using VBA code
- How to manipulate module code using VBA
- How to create an MDE file

The information contained in this chapter should help you create your own custom Wizards easily and quickly.

Web-Enabling Your Applications

- Understanding hyperlinks and HTML

- Using hyperlinks for intra-database navigation

- Creating a Web-search form

- Publishing Access data on the World Wide Web

- Updating data from the Web using an ASP page

Unless you've been living under a rock lately, you've probably run across a phenomenon called *the Internet*. This pervasive global network, along with its associated protocols and standards, has turned the computer industry on its ear. One of the biggest and most exciting facets of the Internet is the World Wide Web (*the Web*, for short). The Web is the hypertext and multimedia side of the Internet. Using a relatively simple piece of software called a browser, you can browse the Web for an almost unlimited amount of easily accessible information.

While publishing on the Web is a great idea if you want to publicly advertise your services or make some information available to millions of users, many businesses are also discovering that they can apply the protocols and standards of the Internet, and the elegant simplicity of the Web browser, to private TCP/IP-based networks called *intranets*.

Access 97 includes a host of new Internet/intranet features. In general, these new features fall into one of two areas:

- Browsing
- Publishing

The *browsing* (or Internet client) features allow you to insert hyperlinks into your tables, forms, and reports that allow users to jump to Internet or intranet documents, as well as Microsoft Office documents and local files.

The *publishing* (or Internet server) features allow you to make data in your Access databases available to other users over the Internet or your corporate intranet.

NOTE   The term *Internet* generally refers to the public global network based on TCP/IP (Transfer Control Protocol/Internet Protocol), HTTP (Hypertext Transfer Protocol), HTML (Hypertext Markup Language), FTP (File Transfer Protocol), URL (Uniform Resource Locator), and related protocols. The term *intranet* generally refers to private corporate networks that employ the same protocols. In this chapter, though, we often use the term *Internet* (or *Web*) to refer to both public Internet and private intranet networks.

What Are Hyperlinks?

To understand how Access stores and uses hyperlinks, you need to know a little about what they are and how they're formed. Hyperlinks allow you to navigate to other documents both on and off the Web using Universal Resource Locators (URLs). URLs support Web addresses (such as the ever-popular http://www.microsoft.com), as well as file locations on your hard disk. Normally you activate, or *follow,* a hyperlink by pointing to and clicking its text with your mouse. When a browser application follows a link, it locates the document at the given URL and processes it. Web browsers such as Microsoft Internet Explorer and Netscape Navigator use HTML (Hyper-Text Markup Language) to display formatted text and graphics. Office 97 applications have special provisions for navigating to documents created by other Office apps, launching the appropriate program and displaying the file.

A hyperlink actually consists of a number of components:

- **Address:** Specifies the path to an object, document, Web page, or other destination.

- **Display text:** Optional text that Access displays to the user at the hyperlink location. If you don't supply display text, Access displays the address instead.

- **Subaddress:** A particular location in a document specified by the address.

Table 23.1 lists some of the types of hyperlink addresses and subaddresses Access supports. This table is not meant to be comprehensive. In addition to the protocols noted there, hyperlinks can contain references to mailto:, gopher:, news:, nntp:, telnet:, and other addresses. Check the Access online help for the full details. Of course, a protocol won't work if it hasn't been properly installed on your machine. You can't send e-mail from Access, for example, if your installation doesn't already know how to send e-mail.

TABLE 23.1 Types of Hyperlink Addresses and Subaddresses

Hyperlink Type	Address	Subaddress
Access	Path to an Access database	Name of Access form or report
Excel	Path to an Excel workbook file	Sheet name and range
PowerPoint	Path to a PowerPoint presentation file	Slide number

TABLE 23.1   Types of Hyperlink Addresses and Subaddresses   (continued)

Hyperlink Type	Address	Subaddress
Word	Path to a Word document	Name of a bookmark in the document
World Wide Web	URL to a Web page	An anchor on the HTML page*
ftp file	URL to an ftp file	Not supported
Local file of registered type	Path to a file on a local machine or on a LAN	Not supported

*A bug in Internet Explorer 3.0 prevents the subaddress of a hyperlink from working properly with Web page anchors; Netscape Navigator 3.0, however, has no problem with them.

Access stores hyperlinks as plain text, with each component separated from the others by pound symbols (#). The general format is

DisplayText#*Address*#*Subaddress*

DisplayText is optional, but you must specify either an address *or* a subaddress. If you don't include a *DisplayText* component, Access displays the address (or the subaddress, if no address is specified). Table 23.2 lists some hyperlink examples, including the text Access displays to the user.

NOTE   A subaddress is *supposed* to work with Web pages, causing the hyperlink to jump to a named anchor on a Web page. Unfortunately, when used with Internet Explorer 3.0, the subaddress portion of a link to a Web page from Access doesn't work correctly. At this time the subaddress works only with Microsoft Office documents and Internet Explorer. Interestingly, the subaddress *does* work when used with Netscape Navigator 3.0 and may or may not work with other Web browsers.

TABLE 23.2 Hyperlink Examples

Hyperlink	Description	Access Displays
http://www.microsoft.com	Link to the default HTML document at http://www.microsoft.com	http://www.microsoft.com
Microsoft's Home Page# http://www.microsoft.com	Link to the default HTML document at http://www.microsoft.com	Microsoft's Home Page
Sales Figures#\\salesserver \data\sales.xls#B5	Link to cell B5 on the Last Quarter Sales Figures worksheet in the sales.xls workbook on the salesserver server	Sales Figures
Main Menu#file://c:\My Documents\MyApp.mdb #Form frmMain*	Link to the frmMain form in C:\My Documents\MyApp.mdb	Main Menu
##Form frmOrder	Link to the frmMain form in the current database	Form frmOrder

*The file:// protocol designator is optional.

Where to Find the Links

You'll find hyperlinks in Access in three places:

- Stored in tables in fields of the Hyperlink datatype
- Embedded in special properties of command button, label, and image controls of forms and printed reports
- In VBA code

Field-Based Hyperlinks

Microsoft has added a special Hyperlink datatype to Jet tables so you can store hyperlinks in a table just like normal text. The difference is that when Access displays the hyperlink—on a datasheet or in a bound control on a form—you can click it with your mouse to follow the link.

The CH23.MDB database contains a form, frmHyperlinks, that provides several examples of using hyperlinks on forms. If you click the Field Links tab of this form, you'll see an embedded subform bound to the tblHyperlink1 table (see Figure 23.1). If you click a Web-based hyperlink, Access launches your default browser, bringing up the Web page associated with the hyperlink, as shown in Figure 23.2 with Internet Explorer and in Figure 23.3 with Netscape Navigator.

FIGURE 23.1

Various types of hyperlinks are displayed on the Field Links tab of the frm-Hyperlinks form.

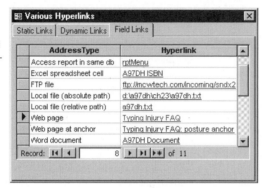

FIGURE 23.2

Result of clicking a Web hyperlink when using Internet Explorer as your default browser.

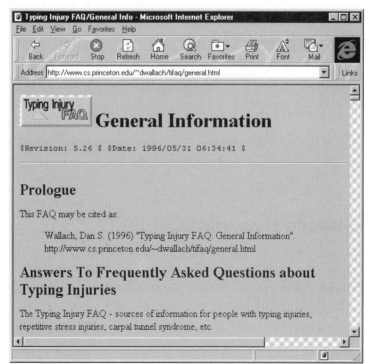

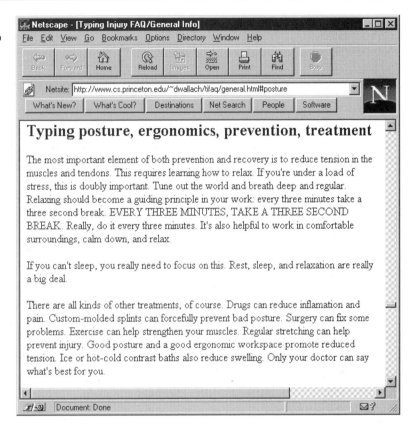

FIGURE 23.3

Result of clicking a Web hyperlink when using Netscape Navigator as your default browser.

You can enter a hyperlink into a table by typing it directly (using the syntax described earlier in this chapter) or by using the Edit Hyperlink dialog shown in Figure 23.4.

NOTE When inserting a hyperlink into a Null field, you actually use the Insert Hyperlink dialog; thereafter you use the Edit Hyperlink dialog to edit the hyperlink.

FIGURE 23.4

The Edit Hyperlink dialog lets you build hyperlinks interactively.

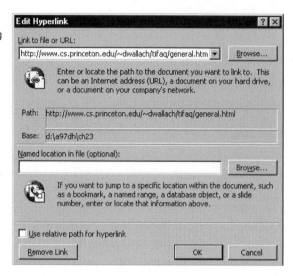

You use the "Link to file or URL" combo box on the Edit Hyperlink dialog to enter the address portion of a hyperlink. Here you can enter a URL directly; select one from your browser's history list using the drop-down list; or use the Browse button to choose a file on your hard drive, a network share, or an Internet FTP (File Transfer Protocol) site.

Use the "Named location in file (optional)" text box to enter the optional subaddress portion of the hyperlink. If you're establishing a link to an object in an Access database, you can use the Browse button to select an object from the database.

The Edit Hyperlink dialog also contains a check box you can check when you want to use relative paths for local or network-based files. This option works with the Hyperlink Base property of the database. You can specify a base address to be used for all relative addresses with the Hyperlink Base property of the database. You can edit this property using the Database Properties dialog (see Figure 23.5). You can also set this property using code similar to this:

```
Currentdb.Containers!Databases.Documents!SummaryInfo. _
  Properties![Hyperlink Base] = "d:\a97dh\ch23"
```

FIGURE 23.5

You can specify a Hyperlink Base address on the Summary tab of the Database Properties dialog.

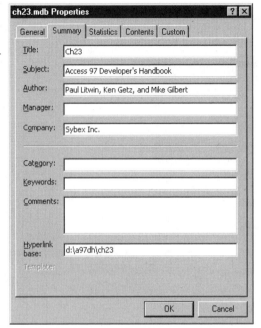

You can't enter the DisplayText portion of a hyperlink using the Edit Hyperlink dialog. You can, however, right-click the field and select Hyperlink ➤ Display Text from the shortcut menu to enter display text for the link (see Figure 23.6).

NOTE   Underneath the covers, Jet stores hyperlink data internally as a memo field with a special bit mask (dbHyperlinkField, value 32768) on the field's Attributes property. Hyperlinks are really a function of how Access interprets these special memo fields. In fact, if you access hyperlink fields from outside of Access—for example, from Visual Basic programs—you will get memo data with no special hyperlinking capabilities.

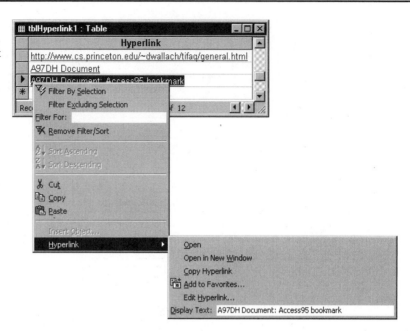

FIGURE 23.6

Using the shortcut menu, you can enter display text for a hyperlink.

Control-Based Hyperlinks

Access forms support hyperlinks in several places. First, you can use text box, combo box, and list box controls bound to fields with a Hyperlink datatype. You can also associate hyperlinks with the following types of unbound controls:

- Labels

- Command buttons

- Image controls

NOTE Access includes limited support for hyperlinks in list box controls. The hyperlinks appear correctly in list boxes and can be manipulated programmatically, but users can't follow the hyperlinks from the UI.

For example, the Static Links tab on frmHyperlinks contains the three types of unbound controls that can contain hyperlinks (see Figure 23.7).

You create control-based hyperlinks by entering each of the hyperlink parts into three different properties of the control:

Hyperlink Part	Control Property
Address	HyperlinkAddress
Subaddress	HyperlinkSubAddress
DisplayText	Caption

The image control doesn't have a Caption property; you must use the image itself for this purpose.

As with field-based links in tables, you can use the Edit Hyperlink dialog to help create the hyperlink. Click the Build button to the right of either the Hyperlink-Address or the HyperlinkSubAddress property on the control's property sheet to bring up this dialog.

You can create statically linked controls as demonstrated on the Static Links tab (see Figure 23.7) of frmHyperlinks. You can also set the HyperlinkAddress and HyperlinkSubAddress properties of label, command button, and image controls at run time to create dynamically linked controls. The Dynamic Links tab of frm-Hyperlinks (see Figure 23.8) demonstrates this feature. When you choose a hyperlink from the combo box list, code attached to the combo box control's AfterUpdate

FIGURE 23.7

You can associate command button, label, and image controls with hyperlinks.

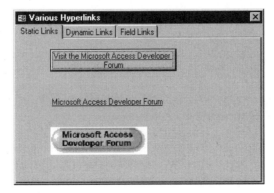

FIGURE 23.8

The command button's
hyperlink is created
dynamically by code
attached to the combo
box's AfterUpdate event.

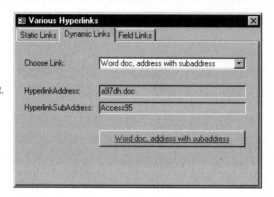

event sets the command button's HyperlinkAddress, HyperlinkSubAddress, and
Caption properties:

```
Private Sub cboLinks_AfterUpdate()

    Dim ctlLinks As ComboBox
    Set ctlLinks = Me!cboLinks

    If Not IsNull(ctlLinks) Then
        Me!txtAddress = ctlLinks.Column(1)
        Me!cmdGo.HyperlinkAddress = ctlLinks.Column(1)

        Me!txtSubAddress = ctlLinks.Column(2)
        Me!cmdGo.HyperlinkSubAddress = ctlLinks.Column(2)

        Me!cmdGo.Caption = ctlLinks
    End If

End Sub
```

The row source for the cboLinks control is tblHyperlink2. The code also sets the
value of the two text boxes for display purposes only.

Hyperlinks on Reports

Hyperlinks operate differently on reports than they do on forms. Hyperlinks are
operational only when the report is exported to an HTML document. You can do
this by using the File ➤ Save As/Export or the File ➤ Save As HTML command.

(These commands are discussed in more detail later in the chapter.) Hyperlinks are visible but do not function in Print Preview view.

In reports, you use unbound label or bound text box controls to store hyperlinks. When exported as HTML documents, the reports can be published on a Web server, or the files can be directly loaded using your Web browser. This latter option may be useful because it allows you to distribute HTML versions of your reports without having to have a copy of Access on each user's desktop.

For example, Figure 23.9 shows the rptMenu report as it looks in Internet Explorer. We've included a label in the report's header with the following HyperlinkAddress:

```
MailTo:plitwin@mcwtech.com
```

FIGURE 23.9

The HTML version of a simple Access report with a label containing a MailTo: hyperlink.

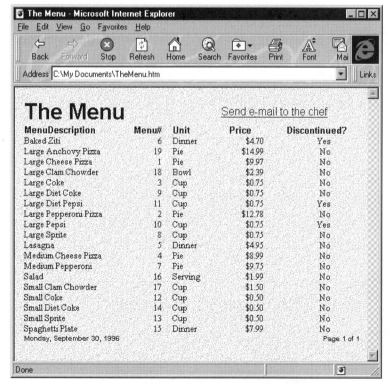

Using Hyperlinks for Intra-Database Navigation

While you might not need to link your workgroup's reporting system to the World Wide Web, you may wish to use hyperlinks to navigate within a database. Using just the subaddress portion of a hyperlink, you can jump from one database form or report to another.

By combining this technique with another new feature of Access 97, lightweight forms, you can create user interfaces without any code or macros. Lightweight forms are forms with no VBA class module associated with them. Since Access does not need to load VBA when opening the form, it opens the form more quickly than a form that has VBA code behind it. Hyperlinks don't need VBA and thus are great for use with lightweight forms.

frmLWSwitchboard, shown in Figure 23.10, is a switchboard form that lets you navigate among several forms and reports in the CH23.MDB database. This lightweight form was constructed using no VBA code or macros; thus it loads more quickly than the equivalent code-based switchboard form.

All Access forms start out as lightweight. Access adds a class module only if you try to insert VBA code. You can make a "heavyweight" form lightweight by setting its HasModule property to No in Design view. This, however, destroys any existing VBA code in the form's module.

While using hyperlinks for database navigation is nice, it does have several drawbacks. First, Access displays the text of the command button as it does other hyperlinks, using colored, underlined text. After you've followed a hyperlink, the text changes color.

You can control Access' formatting of hyperlinks by setting properties on the Hyperlinks/HTML tab of the Options dialog. Unfortunately, because this is a global

---

FIGURE 23.10

This lightweight switchboard form contains no code or macros but is fully functional.

setting, it will affect all hyperlinks. A better solution is to change the formatting properties of the *control* (ForeColor and FontUnderline) after you've inserted the hyperlink address; these settings will override the settings that Access made when you added the hyperlink to the control. Access also changes the mouse cursor to the hyperlink hand when you move it over the control. You can't change this, but it's a small price to pay for simple, no-code navigation.

Controlling Hyperlinks with VBA

As mentioned earlier in the chapter, you can set the HyperlinkAddress and HyperlinkSubAddress properties of a control using VBA code. In addition, you can manipulate hyperlinks as objects. Hyperlink-based controls (unbound label, command button, and image controls, *and* text box, combo box, and list box controls that have been bound to Hyperlink type fields) have an additional property, HyperLink, that doesn't appear on the controls' property sheet. You use this property to establish a reference to a Hyperlink object. The methods and properties of the Hyperlink object are summarized in Table 23.3.

TABLE 23.3 Properties and Methods of the Hyperlink Object

Type	Property/Method	Description
Property	Address	Address component of the hyperlink
	SubAddress	Subaddress component of the hyperlink
Method	AddToFavorites	Adds the hyperlink to the favorites list
	Follow	Jumps to the hyperlink using the default browser

The Address and SubAddress Properties

The following code prints the hyperlink information for a text box named txtLink to the Debug window using the Hyperlink object properties:

```
With Me!txtLink.Hyperlink
    Debug.Print .Address
    Debug.Print .SubAddress
End With
```

The AddToFavorites Method

As you can probably guess from its name, the AddToFavorites method adds the hyperlink to your browser's list of favorite sites. Its syntax is quite simple because it has no parameters:

Hyperlink.AddToFavorites

For example, to add the hyperlink stored in the txtLink text box control to your browser's favorites list, you might use the following code:

```
Me!txtLink.Hyperlink.AddToFavorites
```

The Follow and FollowHyperlink Methods

The Follow method links directly to a specified hyperlink. It takes several parameters, as shown here:

Hyperlink.Follow [*newwindow*], [*addhistory*], [*extrainfo*], [*method*], [*headerInfo*]

The parameters are described in Table 23.4.

TABLE 23.4 Parameters of the Follow Method

Parameter	Description	Default Value
newwindow	Boolean value that, when set to True, opens the document in a new window	False
addhistory	Boolean value that, when set to True, adds the hyperlink to the History folder	True
extrainfo	String or byte array that specifies additional information about the hyperlink. You can use this to specify a search parameter for an IDC or ASP file	Null
method	Integer that specifies the format of the *extrainfo* argument. Can be msoMethodGet, for a string argument that is appended to the address (it appears at the end of the address with a question mark separating the string from the rest of the address), or msoMethodPost, for a string or byte array that is posted to the page	Null if *extrainfo* is Null; msoMethodGet for non-null *extrainfo* values
headerinfo	String that specifies additional http header text that is passed to the browser	Zero-length string

The FollowHyperLink method of the Application object is very similar to the Follow method of the Hyperlink object. With the FollowHyperLink method, however, you don't need to establish a reference to a Hyperlink object. Instead you can use FollowHyperLink to jump to any arbitrary address. Its syntax is shown here:

[Application.]FollowHyperLink *address*, [*subaddress*], [*newwindow*], [*addhistory*], [*extrainfo*], [*method*], [*headerInfo*]

where *address* and *subaddress* are the address and subaddress parts of the hyperlink. The rest of the parameters are the same as for the Follow method.

A Simple Example

The frmHyperlinkObject form in the chapter database demonstrates the use of the various properties and methods of the Hyperlink object. The code behind the frmHyperlinkObject form is shown in Listing 23.1.

Listing 23.1

```
Private Sub cmdAddress_Click()
    MsgBox Me!txtLink.Hyperlink.Address, _
    vbInformation + vbOKOnly, Me.Caption
End Sub


Private Sub cmdFav_Click()
    Me!txtLink.Hyperlink.AddToFavorites
End Sub


Private Sub cmdFollow_Click()
    Me!txtLink.Hyperlink.Follow
End Sub


Private Sub cmdSub_Click()
    MsgBox Me!txtLink.Hyperlink.SubAddress, _
    vbInformation + vbOKOnly, Me.Caption
End Sub
```

For example, if you clicked the Display Address of Hyperlink command button of frmHyperlinkObject, Access would display the message box shown in Figure 23.11.

FIGURE 23.11

The hyperlink address of the text box is displayed when you click the Display Address of Hyperlink button of frmHyperlinkObject.

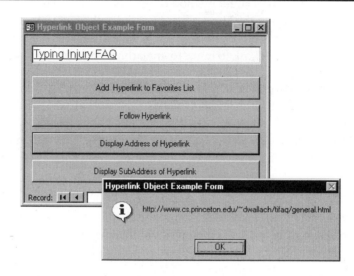

Creating a Web Search Form Using the ExtraInfo and Method Parameters

The frmWebSearch form in the sample database illustrates how you can use the extrainfo and method parameters of the FollowHyperlink method of the Application object to pass search parameters to a Web page. This form lets you enter a string to search for on the Web using one of three popular search engine sites: Alta Vista, Yahoo, or Excite (see Figure 23.12). If you enter a search string like that shown in Figure 23.12, the FollowHyperlink method will open your default browser and pass it the hyperlink address and extrainfo parameters, in this case displaying the results of the search, as shown in Figure 23.13.

FIGURE 23.12

When you click the Perform Search button on frmWebSearch, code behind the button uses the FollowHyperlink method to navigate to the selected Web search site and perform a search on the entered search string.

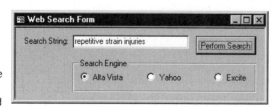

FIGURE 23.13

Result of the search specified in Figure 23.12.

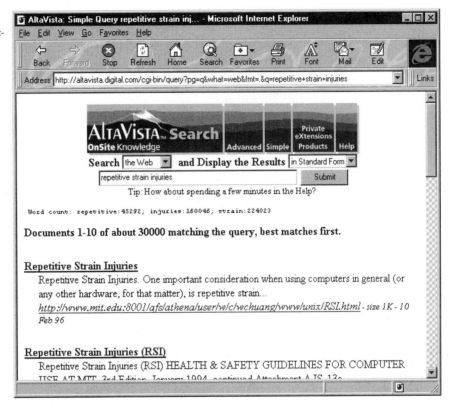

The code attached to the Click event of the cmdSearch button is shown in Listing 23.2. The subroutine begins by replacing spaces in the search string with a plus sign (+) using the adhReplaceAll function. The subroutine then uses the FollowHyperlink method of the Application object, passing it the address of the selected Web search engine. The extrainfo parameter is formatted in the correct syntax for the particular search engine. This varies from a simple *"p=searchstring"* for the Yahoo engine to more complex strings for the AltaVista and Excite sites. (We determined the correct strings by performing searches using our browser and observing the address passed to the search page.) In addition, the method parameter is set to "msoMethodGet".

Listing 23.2

```
Private Sub cmdSearch_Click()

    Dim varSearch As Variant

    Const adhcSiteAltaVista = 1
    Const adhcSiteYahoo = 2
    Const adhcSiteExcite = 3

    varSearch = adhReplaceAll(Me!txtSearch, " ", "+")

    Select Case Me!optSite
    Case adhcSiteAltaVista
        Application.FollowHyperlink _
          Address:="http://altavista.digital.com/cgi-bin/query", _
          ExtraInfo:="pg=q&what=Web&fmt=.&q=" & _
          varSearch, Method:=msoMethodGet, _
          AddHistory:=True
    Case adhcSiteYahoo
        Application.FollowHyperlink _
          Address:="http://search.yahoo.com/bin/search", _
          ExtraInfo:="p=" & varSearch, _
          Method:=msoMethodGet, _
          AddHistory:=True
    Case adhcSiteExcite
        Application.FollowHyperlink _
          Address:="http://excite.com/search.gw", _
          ExtraInfo:="search=" & varSearch & _
          "&collection=Web&searchButton.x=11&searchButton.y=8", _
          Method:=msoMethodGet, _
          AddHistory:=True
    End Select
End Sub
```

You can use the extrainfo and method parameters to pass information to CGI, IDC, or ASP pages.

The HyperlinkPart Function

The HyperlinkPart function accepts a complete hyperlink and returns a specified part of it, such as the display text or subaddress. Its syntax is shown here:

strReturn = HyperlinkPart(*hyperlink*, [*part*])

part, which defaults to acDisplayedValue, can be any of the following constants:

acAddress

acDisplayText

acDisplayedValue

acSubAddress

For example, the LinkToSite subroutine shown in Listing 23.3 (from basHyperlink) searches for a Web site in a table of favorite sites and then links to the Web site.

Listing 23.3

```
Sub LinkToSite(strSite As String)
    Dim db As Database
    Dim rst As Recordset

    Dim strAddress As String
    Dim strSubAddress As String

    ' Find record in database
    Set db = CurrentDb()
    Set rst = db.OpenRecordset( _
     "SELECT Hyperlink FROM tblWebJumps WHERE " & _
     "SiteName = '" & strSite & "'", dbOpenSnapshot)

    ' If record was found, link to site
    If Not rst.EOF Then
        strAddress = HyperlinkPart(rst!Hyperlink, acAddress)
        strSubAddress = HyperlinkPart(rst!Hyperlink, acSubAddress)
        Debug.Print "Site found...linking to " & _
         IIf(strSubAddress = "", "", strSubAddress & " at ") & _
         strAddress
        FollowHyperlink strAddress, strSubAddress
```

```
        Else
            Debug.Print "Site not found."
        End If

        rst.Close
    End Sub
```

LinkToSite attempts to locate the record in the tblWebJumps table with a Site-Name equal to the passed-in strSite parameter. If it finds a match, it uses the HyperlinkPart function to parse the address and subaddress portions of the address stored in the Hyperlink field and then uses the FollowHyperlink method to jump to that hyperlink. For example, if you entered the following in the Debug window using the CH23.MDB sample database, the http://www.fmsinc.com page would appear in your browser:

```
Call LinkToSite("FMS")
```

Using the Microsoft Web Browser Control

When you click a Web-based hyperlink or execute code that employs the Follow or FollowHyperlink method, Access starts up your default Web browser and passes it the necessary information to display the desired Web page. This works well in many situations, but sometimes it would be nice if you could browse Web pages in place on a form. You can accomplish this by using a Web ActiveX control such as Microsoft's Web browser control (WebBrowser). The Microsoft control is automatically installed when you install Internet Explorer 3 (or later) on your machine.

WebBrowser has a couple of idiosyncrasies:

- Unlike most other ActiveX controls, its properties (except for the TopLevel-Container and Busy properties) are not merged with the Access property sheet or exposed via a custom property sheet.

- Help for the control does not come with Internet Explorer.

Fortunately, a help file is available; in fact, it's included in the Valupack\Access\Web-help folder of the Office 97 installation CD. (If you can't locate your CD, you can also find a copy at http://www.microsoft.com/intdev/sdk/docs/iexplore/default.htm.) In addition, you can get at the control's event properties by opening the form's VBA module and selecting the control using the Object drop-down list.

The WebBrowser control's properties and methods are summarized in Table 23.5.

TABLE 23.5 Properties and Methods of the Microsoft Web Browser Control (the WebBrowser Object)

Type	Property/Method	Description
Property	Application	Object variable pointing to the application that contains the WebBrowser object
	Busy	Boolean value specifying whether the WebBrowser control is engaged in a navigation or downloading operation
	Container	Object variable pointing to the container of the WebBrowser control
	Document	Object variable pointing to the active document, if any
	Height	Returns or sets the height, in pixels, of the frame window that contains the control
	Left	Returns or sets the distance between the left edge of the control's container and the left edge of the control in the coordinate system of the container
	LocationName	Returns the name of the currently displayed resource—either the title of the Web page or, if the browser is displaying a folder or file, the UNC path
	LocationURL	Same as LocationName except that for Web pages, LocationURL returns the URL address of the page
	Parent	Object variable pointing to the form that contains the control
	Top	Returns or sets the distance between the top edge of the control's container and the top edge of the control in the coordinate system of the container
	TopLevelContainer	Boolean value indicating whether the browser object is a top-level container
	Type	String representing the type of the contained document object
	Width	Returns or sets the width, in pixels, of the frame window that contains the control

TABLE 23.5 Properties and Methods of the Microsoft Web Browser Control
(the WebBrowser Object) (continued)

Type	Property/Method	Description
Method	GoBack	Navigates backward one item in the history list
	GoForward	Navigates forward one item in the history list
	GoHome	Navigates to the home page as specified in the Internet Explorer Options dialog box
	GoSearch	Navigates to the search page as specified in the Internet Explorer Options dialog box
	Navigate	Jumps to a new URL; takes one required parameter, *URL*, and four optional parameters, *Flags, TargetFrameName, PostData,* and *Headers*; *Flags* can be one or more of: navOpenInNewWindow (1), navNoHistory (2), navNoReadFromCache (4), and navNoWriteToCache (8)
	Refresh	Reloads the currently displayed page
	Refresh2	Reloads the currently displayed page; takes one parameter, *Level,* which can be REFRESH_NORMAL (1), REFRESH_IFEXPIRED (2), or REFRESH_COMPLETELY (3)
	Stop	Stops any pending navigate or download operations

The CH23.MDB sample database contains an example of using the WebBrowser control in a form named frmWebBrowser (see Figure 23.14). This Access-based Web browser form, complete with search capabilities, was created with surprisingly little code. The code behind frmWebBrowser is shown in Listing 23.4.

Listing 23.4

```
Private Declare Function adh_apiGetSystemDirectory _
 Lib "kernel32" _
 Alias "GetSystemDirectoryA" (ByVal lpBuffer As String, _
 ByVal nSize As Long) As Long

Private Sub cmdBack_Click()
    On Error Resume Next
    Me!ocxWeb.GoBack
End Sub
```

FIGURE 23.14

You can use the Microsoft Web browser control to create a Web browser embedded in an Access form.

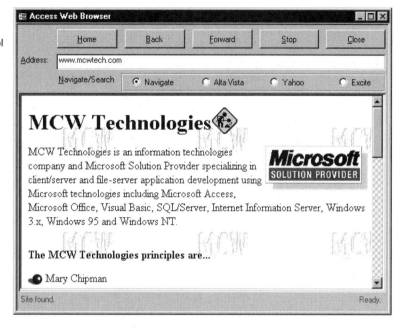

```
Private Sub cmdClose_Click()
    DoCmd.Close
End Sub

Private Sub cmdForward_Click()
    On Error Resume Next
    Me!ocxWeb.GoForward
End Sub

Private Sub cmdHome_Click()
    On Error Resume Next
    Me!ocxWeb.GoHome
End Sub

Private Sub cmdStop_Click()
    Me!ocxWeb.Stop
    Me!lblStatusNav.Caption = ""
    Me!lblStatusDL.Caption = "Download aborted."
End Sub
```

```
Private Sub Form_Load()

    Dim strSysDir As String
    Dim lngChars As Long

    Const adhDirLen = 260
    strSysDir = Space(adhDirLen)

    lngChars = adh_apiGetSystemDirectory(strSysDir, adhDirLen)
    If lngChars > 0 Then
        strSysDir = Left$(strSysDir, lngChars)
    Else
        strSysDir = ""
    End If

    Me!ocxWeb.Navigate strSysDir & "\BLANK.HTM"
End Sub

Private Sub ocxWeb_BeforeNavigate(ByVal URL As String, _
 ByVal Flags As Long, ByVal TargetFrameName As String, _
 PostData As Variant, ByVal Headers As String, _
 Cancel As Boolean)
    Me!lblStatusNav.Caption = "Navigating to " & URL & "..."
    Me!txtSearch = URL
End Sub

Private Sub ocxWeb_DownloadBegin()
    Me!lblStatusDL.Caption = "Downloading data..."
End Sub

Private Sub ocxWeb_DownloadComplete()
    Me!lblStatusDL.Caption = "Ready."
End Sub

Private Sub ocxWeb_NavigateComplete(ByVal URL As String)
    Me!lblStatusNav.Caption = "Site found."
End Sub

Private Sub optSite_AfterUpdate()
    Call txtSearch_AfterUpdate
End Sub
```

```
Private Sub txtSearch_AfterUpdate()

    Dim varSearch As Variant

    Const adhcSiteNavigate = 0
    Const adhcSiteAltaVista = 1
    Const adhcSiteYahoo = 2
    Const adhcSiteExcite = 3

    If Not IsNull(Me!txtSearch) Then
        varSearch = adhReplaceAll(Me!txtSearch, " ", "+")

        Select Case Me!optSite
        Case adhcSiteNavigate
            Me!ocxWeb.Navigate Me!txtSearch
        Case adhcSiteAltaVista
            Me!ocxWeb.Navigate _
              "http://altavista.digital.com/cgi-bin/query?" & _
              pg=q&what=web&fmt=.&q=" _
              & varSearch
        Case adhcSiteYahoo
            Me!ocxWeb.Navigate _
              "http://search.yahoo.com/bin/search?p=" _
              & varSearch
        Case adhcSiteExcite
            Me!ocxWeb.Navigate _
              "http://excite.com/search.gw?search=" _
              & varSearch & _
              "&collection=web&searchButton.x=11&searchButton.y=8"
        End Select
    End If
End Sub
```

The Microsoft Web browser control is not as programmable as some third-party controls. The Sax Webster control (Sax Software, http://www.saxsoft.com), for example, allows you to grab the HTML text for a page and cancel the loading of the page based on its content. On the other hand, the Microsoft control is free and very easy to program.

An HTML Primer

As mentioned at the beginning of this chapter, Access 97 supports database publishing, which allows you to make data in your Access databases available to other users over the World Wide Web.

Hypertext Markup Language (HTML) is the language of the Web. While it's not necessary to learn HTML to publish data to the Web, it certainly helps. In this section we present a brief overview of HTML. If you're already fluent in HTML, you may wish to skip to the next section.

HTML is made up of text and embedded tags that are enclosed in angle brackets. For example, the following HTML snippet tells the browser to create a title for an HTML page:

```
<TITLE>Access 97 Developer's Handbook Web Page</TITLE>
```

Most tags, including the <TITLE> tag used in this example, have corresponding closing tags. The closing tag tells the browser to stop applying the tag. In this case, </TITLE> tells the browser it has reached the end of the title. Some tags, such as the line break tag, <BR>, have no corresponding closing tag.

The basic layout of an HTML page is shown here:

```
<HTML>

<HEAD>
heading information
</HEAD>

<BODY>
body text goes here
</BODY>

</HTML>
```

Some of the more commonly used tags are summarized in Table 23.6.

TABLE 23.6 Basic HTML Tags

Tag	Closing Tag	Description
<HTML>	</HTML>	Denotes the start of an HTML document
<HEAD>	</HEAD>	Denotes the start of the heading section of the page. The title of the page goes in this section; other descriptive information that is not displayed on the page may also be placed here
<TITLE>	</TITLE>	Designates the title of the page; most browsers display the title in the title bar of the browser
<BODY>	</BODY>	Designates the body of the Web page; this is where all text other than the title goes. Use the optional BACKGROUND subtag to indicate a background image for the page. No other tags except for the </HTML> tag may appear after the </BODY> closing tag
<H#>	</H#>	Creates a header; # may be an integer between 1 and 6; the smaller the number, the larger the header
<P>	</P>	Starts a new paragraph; paragraphs are separated with a blank line
 	None	Starts a new line
<!--	-->	designates a comment; comments are not displayed on the page. Comments are sometimes used for Web extensions; Access uses comments to designate sections of templates
<B>	</B>	Makes the text bold
<I>	</I>	Makes the text italicized
<CENTER>	</CENTER>	Makes the text centered; you can also use the ALIGN subtag within a header tag to indicate the alignment for a header—for example,<H1 ALIGN=CENTER>Imports and Exports</H1>
<IMG>	*None*	Inserts an image—for example, <IMG SRC="car.gif" ALT="an image of a car">. The SRC subtag indicates the location of the image on the server; the ALT subtag indicates substitute text that displays on text-only browsers; use the ALIGN subtag to create an image with wrapped text
<HR>	*None*	Inserts a horizontal rule; the SIZE, WIDTH, and ALIGN subtags control the size and look of the line

TABLE 23.6   Basic HTML Tags (continued)

Tag	Closing Tag	Description
<A>	</A>	Creates a link to another URL. Use the HREF subtag to indicate either a URL address—for example, <A HREF="http://www.mcwtech.com"MCW Technologies</A>—or a link to a named anchor in the current HTML document—for example, <A HREF="#posture"Posture Section</A>. Use the NAME subtag to create an anchor to which you can jump—for example, <A NAME="posture"Posture Section</A>. The text between the HREF/NAME subtag and the closing tag is displayed on the page
<TABLE>	</TABLE>	Creates a table; within a table, use the <TR> and </TR> tags to denote rows, <TH> and </TH> to denote header cells, and <TD> and </TD> to denote regular (non-header) cells

For example, the HTML shown in Listing 23.5 and included on the companion CD would produce the Web page shown in Figure 23.15.

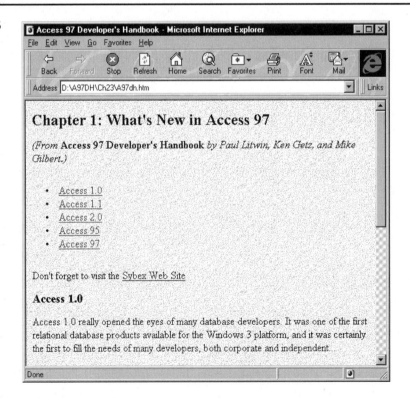

Chapter 1: What's New in Access 97

*(From **Access 97 Developer's Handbook** by Paul Litwin, Ken Getz, and Mike Gilbert.)*

- Access 1.0
- Access 1.1
- Access 2.0
- Access 95
- Access 97

Don't forget to visit the Sybex Web Site

Access 1.0

Access 1.0 really opened the eyes of many database developers. It was one of the first relational database products available for the Windows 3 platform, and it was certainly the first to fill the needs of many developers, both corporate and independent...

Listing 23.5

```
<HTML>

<HEAD>
<TITLE>Access 97 Developer's Handbook</TITLE>
</HEAD>

<BODY BACKGROUND="gray.jpg">

<H2>Chapter 1: What's New in Access 97</H2>
<p><I>(From </I><B>Access 97 Developer's Handbook</B> <I>
by Paul Litwin, Ken Getz, and Mike Gilbert.)</I></p>

<UL>
<LI><A HREF=#A10>Access 1.0</A>
<LI><A HREF=#A11>Access 1.1</A>
<LI><A HREF=#A2>Access 2.0</A>
<LI><A HREF=#A95>Access 95</A>
<LI><A HREF=#A97>Access 97</A>
</UL>
<BR>

<P>Don't forget to visit the
<A HREF="http://www.sybex.com">Sybex Web Site</A>
</P>

<H3><A NAME=A10>Access 1.0</A></H3>
Access 1.0 really opened the eyes of many database developers.
It was one of the first relational database products available
for the Windows 3 platform, and it was certainly the first to
fill the needs of many developers, both corporate and independent...

<H3><A NAME=A11>Access 1.1</A></H3>
Access 1.1 fixed that limitation, expanding the maximum
database size to 1 gigabyte, and fixed some other limitations as
well.
Still, many professional features were lacking...

<H3><A NAME=A2>Access 2.0</A></H3>
Access 2.0 offered great gains for developers. Although it also
provided numerous improvements for end users, the greatest leap
from 1.1 came in the improvements for the developer community...
```

```
<H3><A NAME=A95>Access 95</A></H3>
Access 95 was a major undertaking. Both Access and Jet were
ported from 16-bit Windows to 32-bit Windows. The Access Basic
language and integrated development environment...

<H3><A NAME=A97>Access 97</A></H3>
Things only get better with Access 97. This release is minor
in comparison to Access 95. Still there's lots of new features
and improvements to existing features. Several areas received
extra attention: Internet/intranet features, ...

</BODY>

</HTML>
```

HTML is processed locally and rendered on the user's desktop by the user's Web browser. Because of this you can view the HTML source for a page you are browsing by selecting the source command in your browser. For example, in Internet Explorer, you'd use View ➤ Source (the results of this command are shown in Figure 23.16); in Netscape Navigator, you'd use View ➤ Document Source.

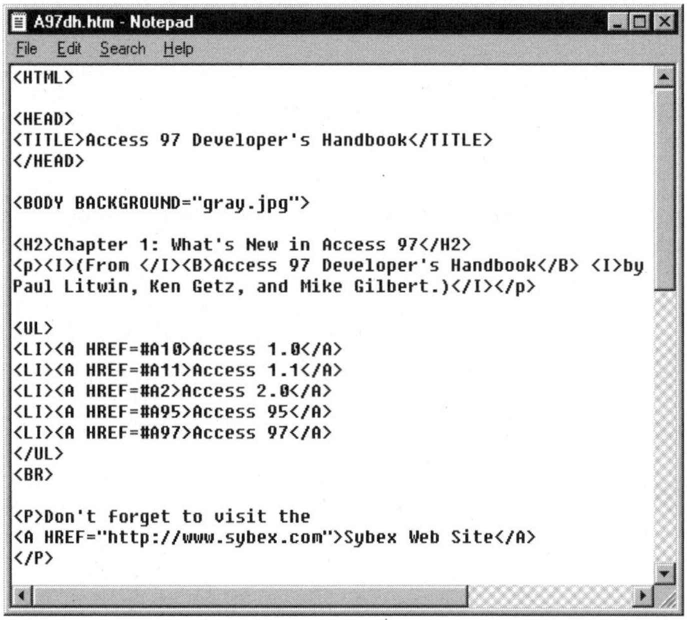

FIGURE 23.16

The source code for the Web page shown in Figure 23.15 displayed by selecting Internet Explorer's View ➤ Source command.

```
A97dh.htm - Notepad                            _□×
File  Edit  Search  Help
<HTML>

<HEAD>
<TITLE>Access 97 Developer's Handbook</TITLE>
</HEAD>

<BODY BACKGROUND="gray.jpg">

<H2>Chapter 1: What's New in Access 97</H2>
<p><I>(From </I><B>Access 97 Developer's Handbook</B> <I>by
Paul Litwin, Ken Getz, and Mike Gilbert.)</I></p>

<UL>
<LI><A HREF=#A10>Access 1.0</A>
<LI><A HREF=#A11>Access 1.1</A>
<LI><A HREF=#A2>Access 2.0</A>
<LI><A HREF=#A95>Access 95</A>
<LI><A HREF=#A97>Access 97</A>
</UL>
<BR>

<P>Don't forget to visit the
<A HREF="http://www.sybex.com">Sybex Web Site</A>
</P>
```

The Publish to the Web Wizard

Access 97 includes a Wizard for publishing your Access data on the World Wide Web. You invoke the Publish to the Web Wizard by selecting the File ➤ Save As HTML command. You can publish data in three formats:

- Static HTML

- Dynamic Internet Database Connector (IDC) pages

- Dynamic Active Server Pages (ASP)

You select the output format on page 4 of the Wizard (see Figure 23.17). If you select multiple objects to publish, you can select different output formats for each different object.

FIGURE 23.17

On the fourth page of the Publish to the Web Wizard, you select the output format.

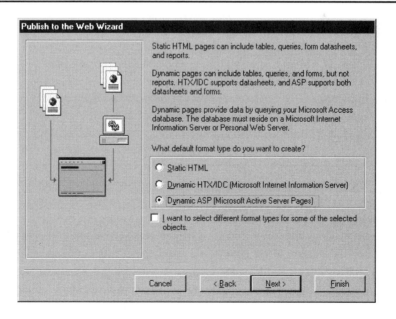

1405

You can publish table and query datasheets, as well as the record source for forms and reports, using the *static HTML* format. You can also elect to produce dynamic Web pages using one of two choices: *Internet Database Connector (IDC)* pages or *Active Server pages (ASP)*.

The three publishing formats are contrasted in Table 23.7. As you can see from this table, the dynamic formats work only with certain servers and browsers, while the static format works with all servers and any browser that supports tables (virtually all browsers). We discuss each of the output formats in more detail in the following sections.

TABLE 23.7   Publish to the Web Wizard Formats

Format	Wizard Output	Servers Supported	Browsers Supported	Comments
Static HTML	HTML files	All	All	Simple, standard; doesn't require an ODBC connection to a database
IDC pages	IDC and HTX files	Microsoft IIS 1.x/2.0 (running NT 3.1/4.0), Microsoft Peer Web Services (NT 4.0), or Microsoft Personal Web Server (Windows 95)	All	Requires IIS, Peer Web, or Personal Web server with an ODBC connection to your database; data is dynamic but read-only
Active Server Pages	ASP files	Microsoft IIS 3.0 (NT 4.0), Microsoft Peer Web Services (NT 4.0), or Microsoft Personal Web Server (Windows 95)	Internet Explorer 3.0 (For published forms you'll also need the ActiveX HTML Layout control, which you can download from microsoft.com.)	Requires IIS 3.0, Peer Web, or Personal Web server; data is dynamic and editable (forms only)

Publishing Static HTML

The static HTML format is a good choice anytime you wish to create a static table of data that will be updated infrequently. Access creates one or more pages with the data laid out in HTML tables. The user will not be able to query the database using this format or update the data. This format is much like the results of a printed report and represents a snapshot of the data at the time it was published.

For example, if you publish the tblMenu table from the CH23.MDB database, you'll produce an HTML page that looks like the page shown in Figure 23.18.

Of course, you can easily doctor up the pages the Wizard produces. For example, you might take the output shown in Figure 23.18 and alter the title, add a background image, and so forth. The Wizard is responsible for outputting the data; it's up to you to make it look the way you want. Fortunately, the Wizard supports templates you can use to apply a standard look to all your published pages. Templates are discussed in the section "Wizard Templates" later in this chapter.

As you can see from Table 23.7, the static HTML format doesn't require any special Internet server, nor does it require a special browser. This is a big advantage. On the other hand, you'll have to republish the data anytime you wish to update the page. You can, however, use a Wizard profile to ease the burden of repeatedly

FIGURE 23.18

Result of publishing the tblMenu table as a static HTML page

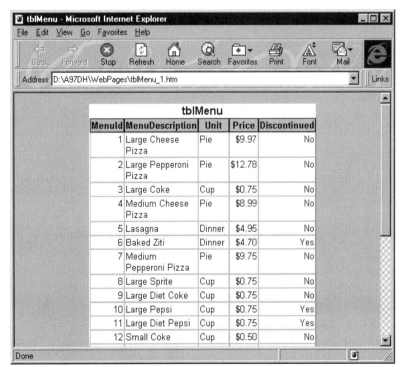

producing static HTML pages. Profiles are discussed in the section "Using and Manipulating Profiles" later in this chapter.

 TIP If you publish hyperlink fields using the static HTML format, Access creates hyperlinks for the field on the generated Web page. (This feature is not supported by the IDC and ASP formats.)

Publishing Internet Database Connector Pages

The Internet Database Connector (IDC) format is a good choice if you need to produce dynamic tables that always contain the latest information. When you choose the IDC (or ASP) format, you're asked to provide a data source name (DSN) and an optional user name and password (see Figure 23.19). Don't worry if you haven't created the data source yet; the Wizard won't actually look for the data source at this time, so you can create it later.

FIGURE 23.19

This page of the Wizard requests information on the data source the Internet server will use to query your Access database at run time.

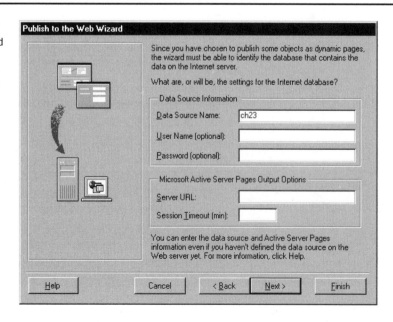

You create a data source using the ODBC Data Source Administrator program (also called the ODBC Driver Manager). You need to create the data source on the server machine that will be hosting your Web site. In addition, the data source must be a system data source, not a user data source. A system data source is a data source that's available to all users system-wide, not just the user who created it. You create system data sources using the System DSN tab of the ODBC Data Source Administrator program (see Figure 23.20).

FIGURE 23.20

You create and configure system data sources using the System DSN tab of the ODBC Data Source Administrator program.

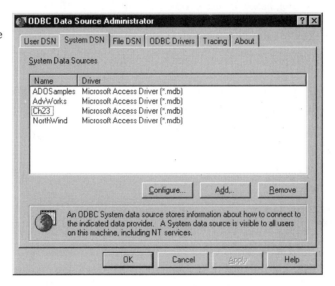

Obviously, if the data you are publishing is stored in an Access database, you'll need to create a system data source that uses the Microsoft Access ODBC driver (and this means you'll need to install the Access driver on your server if it's not already there). While you must create the system data source on the Internet server machine, the actual database doesn't have to be located on this particular server. See Chapter 15 for more information on ODBC and the ODBC Data Source Administrator program.

For IDC pages, the Wizard doesn't produce an HTML file. Instead, the Wizard creates two files your browser never sees:

- Internet Database Connector (IDC) file

- HTML extension (HTX) file

The IDC File

The Internet Database Connector (IDC) file is the main file used to produce an IDC page. It's a simple text file that follows this basic format:

Datasource: *system_DSN*

Template: *htx_file_name*

SQLStatement: *sql_statement*

[Password: *optional_password*]

[Username: *optional_username*]

The *system_DSN* is the name of the system data source.

htx_file_name is the name of the accompanying HTX file. The Wizard names this file with the same root as the IDC file.

sql_statement is the SQL query that returns the desired rows. If the SQL statement is continued on multiple lines, you need to begin continuation lines with a plus sign. For example:

```
SELECT MenuID, MenuDescription
+ FROM tblMenu
+ ORDER BY MenuDescription
```

The *username* and *password* parameters are required only when you wish to log in to a secured database. Unfortunately, there's no way to prompt the Web user for a user name and password and pass it to an IDC file. Thus, you have to hard-code the user name and password into the IDC file.

> **NOTE** There are additional optional IDC file parameters that we won't discuss here. See your server's documentation for more details on these additional parameters.

The IDC file generated by the Wizard for the tblMenu table in the sample database is shown here:

```
Datasource:ch23
Template:tblMenu.htx
```

```
SQLStatement:SELECT * FROM [tblMenu]
Password:
Username:
```

The HTX File

The HTML extension file (HTX) describes the layout of the records that will be generated by the IDC query. It's mostly made up of standard HTML, with some embedded placeholders for the data. The basic format of the .HTX file is

```
<HTML>
<HEAD>
<http_header_info>
<TITLE>title</TITLE>
</HEAD>
<BODY>
<TABLE><CAPTION><B>table_caption</B></CAPTION>

<THEAD>
<TR>
<TH>col_1_heading</TH>
<TH>col_2_heading</TH>
 .
 .
<TH>col_n_heading</TH>

</TR>
</THEAD>
<TBODY>
<%BeginDetail%>
  <TR VALIGN=TOP>
  <TD><%field_1%><BR></TD>
  <TD><%field_2%><BR></TD>
 .
 .
<TD><%field_n%><BR></TD>

  </TR>
<%EndDetail%>
</TBODY>
<TFOOT></TFOOT>
</TABLE>
</BODY>
</HTML>
```

We've left out all the font tags and other tags the Wizard uses to control the formatting of the table, but this is all standard HTML. The only thing that's not standard HTML is the section that falls between the <%BeginDetail%> and <%EndDetail%> tags. These tags tell the Internet Database Connector to place the data—one table row for each record returned by the IDC query—here, substituting each of the query's fields for each <%*field_n*%> tag. The field names must correspond to the names of the fields used in the SQL statement in the IDC file.

A portion of the HTX file produced by the Wizard for the tblMenu table displayed using Notepad is shown in Figure 23.21.

FIGURE 23.21

HTML template file for the IDC version of the Wizard-published tblMenu table.

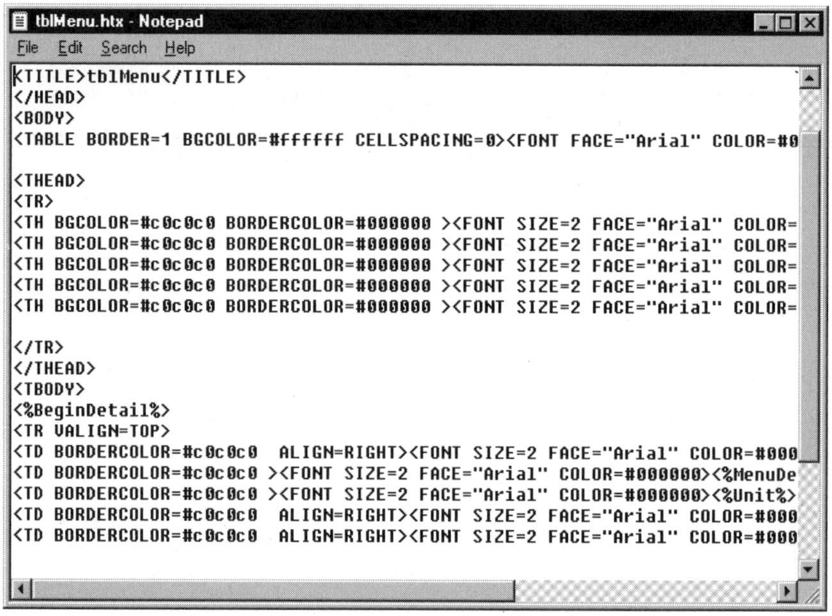

```
tblMenu.htx - Notepad
File  Edit  Search  Help
<TITLE>tblMenu</TITLE>
</HEAD>
<BODY>
<TABLE BORDER=1 BGCOLOR=#ffffff CELLSPACING=0><FONT FACE="Arial" COLOR=#0

<THEAD>
<TR>
<TH BGCOLOR=#c0c0c0 BORDERCOLOR=#000000 ><FONT SIZE=2 FACE="Arial" COLOR=
<TH BGCOLOR=#c0c0c0 BORDERCOLOR=#000000 ><FONT SIZE=2 FACE="Arial" COLOR=
<TH BGCOLOR=#c0c0c0 BORDERCOLOR=#000000 ><FONT SIZE=2 FACE="Arial" COLOR=
<TH BGCOLOR=#c0c0c0 BORDERCOLOR=#000000 ><FONT SIZE=2 FACE="Arial" COLOR=
<TH BGCOLOR=#c0c0c0 BORDERCOLOR=#000000 ><FONT SIZE=2 FACE="Arial" COLOR=

</TR>
</THEAD>
<TBODY>
<%BeginDetail%>
<TR VALIGN=TOP>
<TD BORDERCOLOR=#c0c0c0  ALIGN=RIGHT><FONT SIZE=2 FACE="Arial" COLOR=#000
<TD BORDERCOLOR=#c0c0c0 ><FONT SIZE=2 FACE="Arial" COLOR=#000000><%MenuDe
<TD BORDERCOLOR=#c0c0c0 ><FONT SIZE=2 FACE="Arial" COLOR=#000000><%Unit%>
<TD BORDERCOLOR=#c0c0c0  ALIGN=RIGHT><FONT SIZE=2 FACE="Arial" COLOR=#000
<TD BORDERCOLOR=#c0c0c0  ALIGN=RIGHT><FONT SIZE=2 FACE="Arial" COLOR=#000
```

Hyperlinking to an IDC Page

The Internet Database Connector produces the actual HTML file at the time the page is requested by submitting the SQL statement from the IDC file to Access and merging the results of the request with the HTX file. This produces a temporary HTML file that is then sent over the Internet/intranet to the client browser. Because the browser receives standard HTML, IDC files can be used with any browser.

The hyperlink to the IDC page must be in this format:

http://*web_site*/*idc_file*.idc?

For example, if you wished to link to the TBLMENU.IDC file located at pizza.com, you'd use the following hyperlink:

```
http://pizza.com/tblMenu.idc?
```

The question mark tells the server that the request can take parameters. In this case there are no parameters, but the question mark is still required. The IDC version of the tblMenu page is shown in Figure 23.22 as it would look in Netscape Navigator.

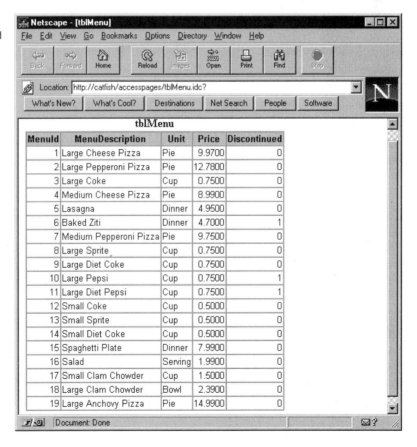

FIGURE 23.22

tblMenu table published using the IDC format

Parameter Queries

In addition to standard queries, the Publish to the Web Wizard supports parameter queries. When you ask it to publish a query with one or more parameters, the Wizard creates a third file, an HTML document with the .HTML extension, that prompts the user for the parameters.

For example, if you published the qryOrderDetailsParam query from the sample database using the GRAY.HTM HTML template, the Wizard would create these three files:

qryOrderDetailsParam_1.IDC

qryOrderDetailsParam_1.HTX

qryOrderDetailsParam_1.HTML

The HTML file uses standard HTML to create a text box for each parameter. The qryOrderDetailsParam_1.HTML is shown here:

```
<HTML>

<TITLE>qryOrderDetailsParam</TITLE>

<BODY background = gray.jpg>

<FORM METHOD="GET" ACTION="qryOrderDetailsParam_1.IDC">
Customer ID #? <INPUT TYPE="Text" NAME="Customer ID #?"><P>
<INPUT TYPE="Submit" VALUE="Run Query">
</FORM>


</BODY>

<BR><BR>

<IMG SRC = "msaccess.jpg">

</HTML>
```

The lines in the file between the <FORM> and </FORM> tags create the text box (Type="Text") and command button (Type="Submit") controls that appear on the form. Figure 23.23 shows this page as it looks in Internet Explorer. Figure 23.24 shows the result of the query when a customer ID number of 5 is entered.

FIGURE 23.23

Parameter page created by the Publish to the Web Wizard for the qryOrder-DetailsParam query

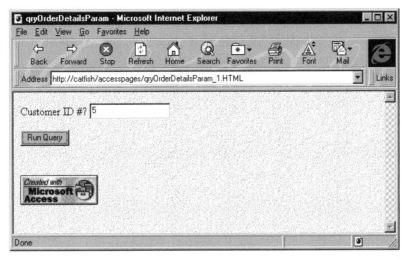

FIGURE 23.24

Results of the parameter query with Customer ID # = 5

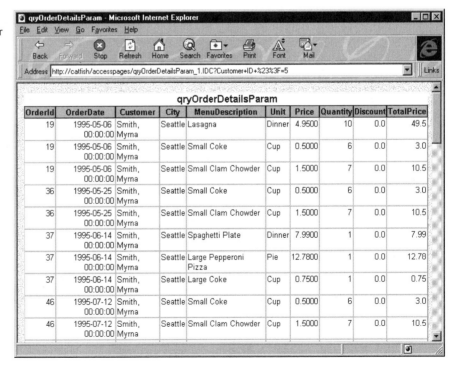

qryOrderDetailsParam

OrderId	OrderDate	Customer	City	MenuDescription	Unit	Price	Quantity	Discount	TotalPrice
19	1995-05-06 00:00:00	Smith, Myrna	Seattle	Lasagna	Dinner	4.9500	10	0.0	49.5
19	1995-05-06 00:00:00	Smith, Myrna	Seattle	Small Coke	Cup	0.5000	6	0.0	3.0
19	1995-05-06 00:00:00	Smith, Myrna	Seattle	Small Clam Chowder	Cup	1.5000	7	0.0	10.5
36	1995-05-25 00:00:00	Smith, Myrna	Seattle	Small Coke	Cup	0.5000	6	0.0	3.0
36	1995-05-25 00:00:00	Smith, Myrna	Seattle	Small Clam Chowder	Cup	1.5000	7	0.0	10.5
37	1995-06-14 00:00:00	Smith, Myrna	Seattle	Spaghetti Plate	Dinner	7.9900	1	0.0	7.99
37	1995-06-14 00:00:00	Smith, Myrna	Seattle	Large Pepperoni Pizza	Pie	12.7800	1	0.0	12.78
37	1995-06-14 00:00:00	Smith, Myrna	Seattle	Large Coke	Cup	0.7500	1	0.0	0.75
46	1995-07-12 00:00:00	Smith, Myrna	Seattle	Small Coke	Cup	0.5000	6	0.0	3.0
46	1995-07-12 00:00:00	Smith, Myrna	Seattle	Small Clam Chowder	Cup	1.5000	7	0.0	10.5

Customizing IDC Pages: An Example

The Publish to the Web Wizard makes it very easy to get data published on the Web, but you'll likely want to customize the pages the Wizard creates. For example, say you've published the qryOrderDetailsParam query from the last section but you'd like to improve the final product in these ways:

- Make the Customer ID # text box on the parameter page into a combo box that looks up customers from the customer table

- Format the OrderDate, Cost, Discount, and TotalCost columns of the query output so they look more standard

- Remove the repeating data elements of the query output—CustomerName and City—from the table and place them in the header of the page

You can improve the usability of the parameter page by changing the text box into a combo box that draws its values from the qryCustomerSorted query in the sample database. Because you will need to establish a connection to the CH23.MDB database to populate the combo box, you'll have to create a pair of IDC and HTX files to grab the combo box row source from the database. The result of this query will then be used to generate a dynamic parameter page that prompts the user for the parameter and passes the parameter along to a second pair of IDC and HTX files that generate the output of the parameter query. This is depicted schematically in Figure 23.25.

FIGURE 23.25

The pieces of the customized parameter IDC query

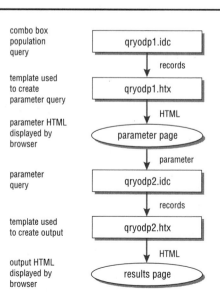

1416

The QRYODP1.IDC File

You specify the query that will populate the combo box using the QRYODP1.IDC file, which is shown here:

```
Datasource:ch23
Template:qryODP1.HTX
SQLStatement:
+ SELECT CustomerID, CustomerName
+ FROM qryCustomerSorted
```

The QRYODP1.HTX File

The query returns two columns, CustomerID and CustomerName, which are then merged with the QRYODP1.HTX file to create the HTML form. The HTX file is shown here:

```
<HTML>

<TITLE>Customer Query</TITLE>

<BODY background = gray.jpg>

<FORM METHOD="GET" ACTION="qryODP2.IDC">
Select customer:
<SELECT NAME="Customer ID #?" SIZE=1>
<%begindetail%>
     <OPTION VALUE=<%CustomerID%>><%CustomerName%>
<%enddetail%>
</SELECT>
<INPUT TYPE="Submit" VALUE="Run Query">
</FORM>

</BODY>

<BR><BR>

<IMG SRC = "msaccess.jpg">

</HTML>
```

This HTX file produces the combo box from the results of the QRYODP1.IDC query. The combo box is defined by the lines between the first pair of <SELECT> and </SELECT> tags, which contains a <%begindetail%>, <%enddetail%> pair.

Thus, for each row returned by the query, the IDC/HTX files create a new OPTION VALUE, generating the following HTML combo box code:

```
<SELECT NAME="Customer ID #?" SIZE=1>
    <OPTION VALUE=12>Ayala, Steve
    <OPTION VALUE=10>Babitt, Lucy
    <OPTION VALUE=7>Fallon, Jane
    <OPTION VALUE=6>Jenning, Roger
    <OPTION VALUE=1>Johnson, Alicia
    <OPTION VALUE=9>Jones, Bert
    <OPTION VALUE=4>Jones, Jerry
    <OPTION VALUE=11>Litwin, Paul
    <OPTION VALUE=8>Phoner, Phil
    <OPTION VALUE=2>Reddick, Greg
    <OPTION VALUE=5>Smith, Myrna
    <OPTION VALUE=3>Stevens, Ken
</SELECT>
```

The resulting parameter query prompt page is shown in Figure 23.26.

FIGURE 23.26

Parameter page produced by the QRYODP1.IDC and QRYODP1.HTX files

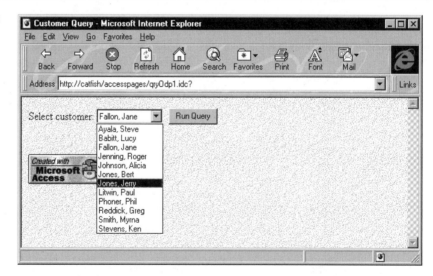

The QRYODP2.IDC File

When you select a customer and click the Run Query button, the second IDC query is executed. If you look back at the output from the query produced by the

Wizard (see Figure 23.24), you'll see that the Date, Price, TotalPrice, and Discount fields are formatted poorly. Unfortunately, there's no way to format the results using the HTX file. Perhaps a future version of the HTX file will support this need, but it's not there at this time.

Instead, you will have to do all the formatting using formatting functions in the SQL SELECT statement in the IDC file. Be aware that not all Access functions are supported here; only a small subset of functions is available through ODBC. In particular, we've found the following functions to work:

Format	Mid
Month	Instr
Day	Int
Year	Date
Left	Now
Right	

Other functions may work here as well; this list represents only the functions we were able to get to work in our limited testing.

The QRYODP2.IDC file looks like this:

```
Datasource:ch23
Template:qryODP2.htx
SQLStatement:
+ SELECT tblOrder.OrderId,
+ tblCustomer.FirstName & ' ' & tblCustomer.LastName AS Customer,
+ Format(OrderDate,'mm/dd/yy') AS OrderDate1,
+ tblCustomer.City, MenuDescription, Unit,
+ Format(Price,'$#,##0.00') AS Price1, Quantity,
+ Format(Discount,'0%%') AS Discount1,
+ Format([price]*[quantity]*(1-[discount]),'$#,##0.00')
+ AS TotalPrice
+ FROM tblMenu INNER JOIN
+ (tblEmployee INNER JOIN (tblCustomer INNER JOIN
+ (tblOrder INNER JOIN tblOrderDetails
+ ON tblOrder.OrderId = tblOrderDetails.OrderId)
+ ON tblCustomer.CustomerId = tblOrder.CustomerId)
+ ON tblEmployee.EmployeeId = tblOrder.OrderTakerId)
```

```
+ ON tblMenu.MenuId = tblOrderDetails.MenuId
+ WHERE (((tblCustomer.CustomerId)=%Customer ID #?%))
+ ORDER BY OrderDate;
```

When creating IDC SQL statements, keep in mind the following:

- You must use single quotes in expressions.

- You must enclose parameters in percent symbols (%).

- If you want to pass percent symbols (%) through to Access, you'll need to double them (as we did for the Discount field).

The QRYODP2.HTX File

The final .HTML extension file, QRYODP2.HTX, formats the output records. It's similar to the Wizard-produced HTX file, with a few improvements.

We improved the heading with the following HTML:

```
<CAPTION><B>Orders for <%City%> Customer: <%Customer%>
 (Customer# = <%idc.Customer ID #?%>)</B></CAPTION>
```

Because the value of Customer and City is constant for a particular customer, there's no need to print it in the table. Instead, we've moved the value of the fields to the header. In addition, we've included a reference to the value of the parameter that was passed to the IDC file. The format used to reference a parameter is

<%idc.*parameter_name*%>

We also included code to deal with the situation in which no records are returned by a query. This is handled by the following code, which we've placed after the table:

```
<%if CurrentRecord EQ 0%>
  <CENTER><I><B>Sorry, this customer has no orders.</B></I></CENTER>
<%endif%>
```

This works because the special CurrentRecord variable, which is incremented from 0 to $n-1$ (where n equals the total number of records), will equal to 0 after the detail section is printed when no records are returned by the query.

The final output page is shown in Figure 23.27.

FIGURE 23.27

Output of the parameter query produced by the QRYODP2.IDC and QRYODP2.HTX files

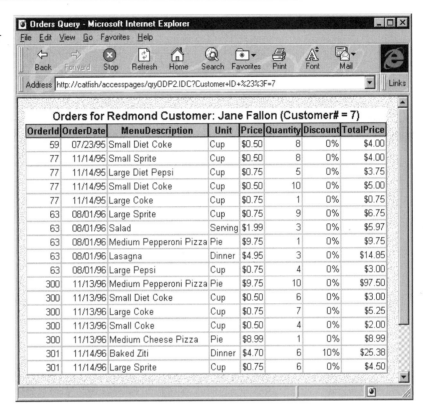

Orders for Redmond Customer: Jane Fallon (Customer# = 7)

OrderId	OrderDate	MenuDescription	Unit	Price	Quantity	Discount	TotalPrice
59	07/23/95	Small Diet Coke	Cup	$0.50	8	0%	$4.00
77	11/14/95	Small Sprite	Cup	$0.50	8	0%	$4.00
77	11/14/95	Large Diet Pepsi	Cup	$0.75	5	0%	$3.75
77	11/14/95	Small Diet Coke	Cup	$0.50	10	0%	$5.00
77	11/14/95	Large Coke	Cup	$0.75	1	0%	$0.75
63	08/01/96	Large Sprite	Cup	$0.75	9	0%	$6.75
63	08/01/96	Salad	Serving	$1.99	3	0%	$5.97
63	08/01/96	Medium Pepperoni Pizza	Pie	$9.75	1	0%	$9.75
63	08/01/96	Lasagna	Dinner	$4.95	3	0%	$14.85
63	08/01/96	Large Pepsi	Cup	$0.75	4	0%	$3.00
300	11/13/96	Medium Pepperoni Pizza	Pie	$9.75	10	0%	$97.50
300	11/13/96	Small Diet Coke	Cup	$0.50	6	0%	$3.00
300	11/13/96	Large Coke	Cup	$0.75	7	0%	$5.25
300	11/13/96	Small Coke	Cup	$0.50	4	0%	$2.00
300	11/13/96	Medium Cheese Pizza	Pie	$8.99	1	0%	$8.99
301	11/14/96	Baked Ziti	Dinner	$4.70	6	10%	$25.38
301	11/14/96	Large Sprite	Cup	$0.75	6	0%	$4.50

More on the Internet Database Connector

Although the Wizard doesn't create pages that update data, you can create your own IDC files that submit INSERT, UDPATE, or DELETE SQL statements to Access. The best place to look for additional information on IDC is the "Publishing Information and Applications" chapter of the *Installation and Administration Guide* that comes with Microsoft Internet Information Server. (This is an electronic document in HTML format that is copied to your server when you install IIS.)

Publishing Active Pages

Like the IDC format, the Active Server Pages produced by the Publish to the Web Wizard also support dynamic read-only querying of the data. In addition, the Wizard publishes Active forms that can be used for form-based record navigation and editing of the data from your browser.

Unlike the IDC format, the Active format requires only one file, the Active Server Page (ASP) file, where you specify both the query and output format.

TIP

When publishing ASP pages using the Publish to the Web Wizard, you can normally leave the Server URL text box (see Figure 23.19) blank. When publishing forms with embedded subforms, however, it's essential you enter the correct URL. If you don't, the server won't be able to link the subform ASP files.

The ASP File and VBScript

The ASP file is a combination of HTML and the VBScript language. VBScript is a special, limited version of VBA adapted for Web use. In VBScript, all variables are variants, and many of the advanced aspects of the language have been removed to make the language "lean and mean," but it's still the same basic language used in Access, VB, and Microsoft Office.

The Active pages also make use of a new type of database connection, the Active Data Object (ADO). This is an object layer on top of ODBC that is similar to ODBCDirect, which was described in Chapter 15. ADO is optimized for Internet/intranet data access.

A Simple Active Example

If you take a look at an ASP file, you'll notice that it looks quite a bit more complex than the equivalent IDC/HTX files. The ASP file, however, looks a lot less intimidating once you understand what the code is doing.

For example, if we published the qryEmployeeDirectory query from the sample database to ASP format, the Wizard would create a page that looked like the one in Figure 23.28.

Let's take a look at the QRYEMPLOYEEDIRECTORY_1.ASP file used to produce that page. To make it simpler, we'll break the file into several smaller parts.

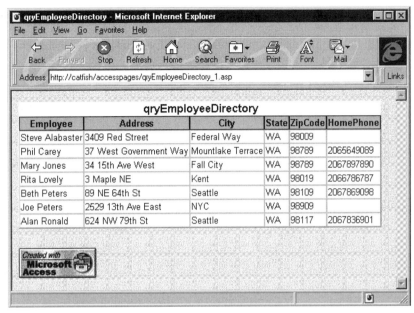

FIGURE 23.28

The qryEmployeeDirectory query was published using the ASP format.

Part 1: The HTML Header

The first part of the ASP file is just standard HTML that generates the header of the page. Here's the code:

```
<HTML>

<HEAD>
<TITLE>qryEmployeeDirectory</TITLE>
</HEAD>

<BODY background = tiles.jpg>
```

Part 2: Establishing the Connection

The second part of the Wizard-produced ASP file is made up of VBScript statements, which establish (and maintain) an ADO connection to the Access database. The IsObject function checks whether the connection has already been made. This can occur when a user moves to another page and then returns or when the user refreshes the page. By using this code the Wizard is able to reduce the number of connections that need to be dropped and reestablished:

```
<%
Param = Request.QueryString("Param")
Data = Request.QueryString("Data")
%>
<%
If IsObject(Session("ch23_conn")) Then
    Set conn = Session("ch23_conn")
Else
    Set conn = Server.CreateObject("ADODB.Connection")
    conn.open "ch23","ch23","","ch23","ch23","",""
    Set Session("ch23_conn") = conn
End If
%>
```

Notice that all the VBScript commands are enclosed by <% and %>. This tells the server that this code is not standard HTML and needs to be interpreted by the VBScript interpreter before the server passes the HTML to the client.

Part 3: Executing the Query

The third part of the ASP file runs the query that generates the data for the page:

```
<%
If IsObject(Session("qryEmployeeDirectory_rs")) _
 And Not (cstr(Param) <> "" And cstr(Data) <> "") Then
    Set rs = Session("qryEmployeeDirectory_rs")
    rs.Resync
Else
    sql = "SELECT [FirstName] & ' ' & _
     " [LastName] AS Employee," & _
     " tblEmployee.Address, tblEmployee.City, " & _
     " tblEmployee.State," & _
     " tblEmployee.ZipCode, tblEmployee.HomePhone  " & _
     " FROM tblEmployee  "
    If cstr(Param) <> "" And cstr(Data) <> "" Then
        sql = sql & " WHERE " & cstr(Param) & " = " & cstr(Data)
    End If
    sql = sql & " ORDER BY tblEmployee.LastName, " & _
         " tblEmployee.FirstName    "
    Set rs = Server.CreateObject("ADODB.Recordset")
```

```
    rs.Open sql, conn, 3, 3
    Set Session("qryEmployeeDirectory_rs") = rs
End If
%>
```

Once again, the code uses the IsObject function to check whether the recordset already exists.

The code after the Else statement should look familiar; it's fairly standard DAO-like code that you would use to create a recordset using Access VBA code. There are a few twists, however. The recordset object is created with this line of code:

```
Set rs = Server.CreateObject("ADODB.Recordset")
```

and the recordset is populated by the query with this line of code:

```
rs.Open sql, conn, 3, 3
```

Part 4: The Table Header

Next, the header for the table is created using the name of the published object—in this case, qryEmployeeDirectory—and the name of each of the fields in the query. This is all standard HTML:

```
<TABLE BORDER=1 BGCOLOR=#ffffff CELLSPACING=0>
<FONT FACE="Arial" COLOR=#000000><CAPTION>
<B>qryEmployeeDirectory</B></CAPTION>

<THEAD>
<TR>
<TH BGCOLOR=#c0c0c0 BORDERCOLOR=#000000 >
<FONT SIZE=2 FACE="Arial" COLOR=#000000>Employee</FONT></TH>
<TH BGCOLOR=#c0c0c0 BORDERCOLOR=#000000 >
<FONT SIZE=2 FACE="Arial" COLOR=#000000>Address</FONT></TH>
<TH BGCOLOR=#c0c0c0 BORDERCOLOR=#000000 >
<FONT SIZE=2 FACE="Arial" COLOR=#000000>City</FONT></TH>
<TH BGCOLOR=#c0c0c0 BORDERCOLOR=#000000 >
<FONT SIZE=2 FACE="Arial" COLOR=#000000>State</FONT></TH>
<TH BGCOLOR=#c0c0c0 BORDERCOLOR=#000000 >
<FONT SIZE=2 FACE="Arial" COLOR=#000000>ZipCode</FONT></TH>
<TH BGCOLOR=#c0c0c0 BORDERCOLOR=#000000 ><FONT SIZE=2 FACE="Arial"
COLOR=#000000>HomePhone</FONT></TH>

</TR>
</THEAD>
```

Part 5: The Table Data

The next stretch of code is a mixture of HTML and VBScript. The HTML generates the table; the VBScript populates the rows of the table with the records from the open recordset:

```
<TBODY>
<%
On Error Resume Next
rs.MoveFirst
do while Not rs.eof
 %>
<TR VALIGN=TOP>
<TD BORDERCOLOR=#c0c0c0 ><FONT SIZE=2 FACE="Arial"
COLOR=#000000><%=Server.HTMLEncode(rs.Fields("Employee").Value)%>
<BR></FONT></TD>
<TD BORDERCOLOR=#c0c0c0 ><FONT SIZE=2 FACE="Arial"
COLOR=#000000><%=Server.HTMLEncode(rs.Fields("Address").Value)%>
<BR></FONT></TD>
<TD BORDERCOLOR=#c0c0c0 ><FONT SIZE=2 FACE="Arial"
COLOR=#000000><%=Server.HTMLEncode(rs.Fields("City").Value)%><BR>
</FONT></TD>
<TD BORDERCOLOR=#c0c0c0 ><FONT SIZE=2 FACE="Arial"
COLOR=#000000><%=Server.HTMLEncode(rs.Fields("State").Value)%><BR>
</FONT></TD>
<TD BORDERCOLOR=#c0c0c0 ><FONT SIZE=2 FACE="Arial"
COLOR=#000000><%=Server.HTMLEncode(
rs.Fields("ZipCode").Value)%><BR>
</FONT></TD>
<TD BORDERCOLOR=#c0c0c0 ><FONT SIZE=2 FACE="Arial"
COLOR=#000000><%=Server.HTMLEncode(
rs.Fields("HomePhone").Value)%><BR>
</FONT></TD>

</TR>
<%
rs.MoveNext
loop%>
</TBODY>
<TFOOT></TFOOT>
</TABLE>
```

The rs.MoveFirt, rs.MoveNext, and Do…Loop commands all use standard VBA-like syntax. The field values are dropped into the table cells using code like this:

```
<%=Server.HTMLEncode(rs.Fields("Employee").Value)%>
```

Part 6: The HTML Footer

The rest of the page is standard HTML:

```
</BODY>

<BR><BR>

<IMG SRC = "msaccess.jpg">

</HTML>
```

That's all there is to it. Things get more complicated, however, when you publish Active forms, which are discussed in the next section.

An Active Form Example

The Active pages the Wizard produces don't offer much of an advantage over the IDC pages when publishing datasheets—both formats produce similar results. It's the publishing of forms where the ASP format shines. When you publish forms using the IDC format, the Wizard doesn't actually publish the form. Instead, it merely publishes the datasheet for the form's underlying recordset. When you publish forms using the Active format, however, the Wizard generates an Access form–like page that can be used to browse, update, insert, and delete records!

For example, say you'd like to publish the frmMenu form from the sample database. The Access version of this form is shown in Figure 23.29. If you publish the form using the ASP format and browse the form using Internet Explorer with the HTML ActiveX Layout control, you should see a Web page similar to the one in Figure 23.30.

The Wizard creates two ASP files for each published form. The main ASP file (*form_name*_1.ASP), which is the file to which you need to establish a hyperlink,

---

FIGURE 23.29

The frmMenu form is a standard Access form.

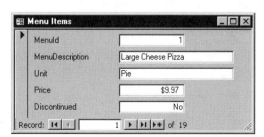

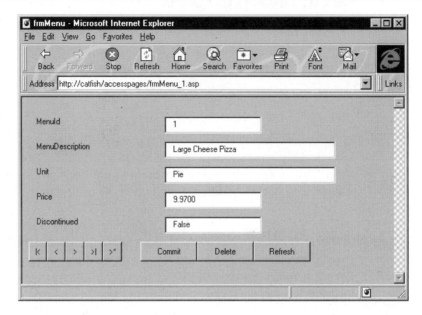

FIGURE 23.30

ASP version of the frmMenu form

queries the data and reacts to the navigation button events. The second file (*form_name*_1ALX.ASP), which is referenced by the main file, is responsible for creating the form layout using the ActiveX HTML Layout control.

The code in the main ASP file is similar to the ASP file generated for datasheets. It includes two additional sections: VBScript code responsible for the navigation buttons and VBScript code that references the HTML Layout control.

The Navigation Button Code

The navigation button code is found in the main ASP file. It's all VBScript:

```
<%
tempVar = Request.QueryString("nav_btn")
If cstr(tempVar)="nav_btn_MoveFirstRecord" Then
    rs.MoveFirst
End If
If cstr(tempVar)="nav_btn_MovePrevRecord" Then
    rs.MovePrevious
    If rs.bof Then
        rs.MoveNext
    End If
End If
```

```
If cstr(tempVar)="nav_btn_MoveNextRecord" Then
    rs.MoveNext
    If rs.eof Then
        rs.MovePrevious
    End If
End If
If cstr(tempVar)="nav_btn_MoveLastRecord" Then
    rs.MoveLast
End If
If cstr(tempVar)="nav_btn_MoveAddRecord" Then
    rs.AddNew
End If
If cstr(tempVar)="nav_btn_MoveCommitRecord" Then
    rs.Update
    rs.Requery
End If
If cstr(tempVar)="nav_btn_MoveCancelUpdate" Then
    rs.CancelUpdate
    rs.Resync
End If
If cstr(tempVar)="nav_btn_MoveDeleteRecord" Then
    On Error Resume Next
    rs.Delete
    On Error Goto 0
    rs.MoveNext
    If rs.eof Then
        rs.MovePrevious
        If rs.bof Then
            rs.AddNew
        End If
    End If
End If
%>
```

The ActiveX HTML Layout Control Code

The code at the end of the main ASP file references the layout ASP file using the OBJECT tag:

```
<OBJECT ID="frmMenu_1alx"
CLASSID="CLSID:812AE312-8B8E-11CF-93C8-00AA00C08FDF"
STYLE="TOP:0;LEFT:0;">
<PARAM NAME="ALXPATH" VALUE="frmMenu_1alx.asp">
</OBJECT>
```

The code in the layout ASP file is voluminous; it's responsible for precisely positioning all the elements of the form using the HTML Layout control. We won't go into the details, but here's a sample of the HTML Object tag used to position the Price field from the FRMMENU_1ALX.ASP file:

```
<OBJECT ID="Price"
CLASSID="CLSID:8BD21D10-EC42-11CE-9E0D-00AA006002F3"
STYLE="TOP:120;LEFT:204;WIDTH:144;HEIGHT:24;
TABINDEX:3;ZINDEX:10;">
<%If Not IsNull(rs.Fields("Price").Value) Then%>
<PARAM NAME="Value" VALUE="<%=Server.HTMLEncode(
rs.Fields("Price").Value)%>">
<%End If%>
<PARAM NAME="BackStyle" VALUE="1">
<PARAM NAME="BackColor" VALUE="16777215">
<PARAM NAME="ForeColor" VALUE="0">
<PARAM NAME="FontHeight" VALUE="160">
<PARAM NAME="Font" VALUE="MS Sans Serif">
<PARAM NAME="FontName" VALUE="MS Sans Serif">
<PARAM NAME="Size" VALUE="3744;624">
<PARAM NAME="SpecialEffect" VALUE="2">
<PARAM NAME="VariousPropertyBits" VALUE="2894088219">
</OBJECT>
```

What's Published for Active Forms?

Obviously, the Publish to the Web Wizard won't be able to publish every Access control on every Access form you've ever created; it does have some limitations:

- The Picture property for the form is not supported.

- All code behind the form or any of its controls is lost.

- Some controls are not supported.

Table 23.8 details the relationship between Access and ASP controls.

The Wizard automatically creates navigation buttons that work just like Access' built-in navigation buttons. In addition, it creates Commit, Delete, and Refresh buttons.

NOTE   When using ASP-produced forms to edit data, you'll be repositioned at the beginning of the recordset when you save or delete any records.

TABLE 23.8 Access Form Controls and Their Corresponding ActiveX Server Page Controls

Access Control	ASP Control	Comments
ActiveX control	ActiveX control	Any code behind the control is lost
Check box	Check box	
Combo box	Combo box	
Command button	Command button	If the Access command button includes a hyperlink, a hyperlink is created for the ASP button. Code behind the Access button isn't carried over to the ASP form
Image control	Not supported	
Label	Label	If the Access label includes a hyperlink, a hyperlink is created for the ASP label
Line	Not supported	You can simulate using a label control with no caption
List box	List box	
Option group	Option group	No frame is drawn
Object frame	Not supported	
Option button	Option button	
Page break	Not supported	
Rectangle	Not supported	You can simulate using a label control with no caption
Subform	Subform	Only datasheet subforms that are read-only objects
Tab control	Not supported	
Text box	Text box	If the Access text box contains a hyperlink field, the address will be displayed, but a hyperlink won't be created
Toggle button	Toggle button	

The Publish to the Web Wizard supports the use of embedded subforms, but the subform fields are read-only. A Wizard-generated main/subform form is shown in Figure 23.31. As mentioned earlier, if you use an embedded subform, you must enter the correct server URL in the Wizard (see Figure 23.19). If the subform does not display on your form, you likely left this field blank or got the URL wrong.

FIGURE 23.31

ASP page generated by the Wizard for the frmOrder main/subform form

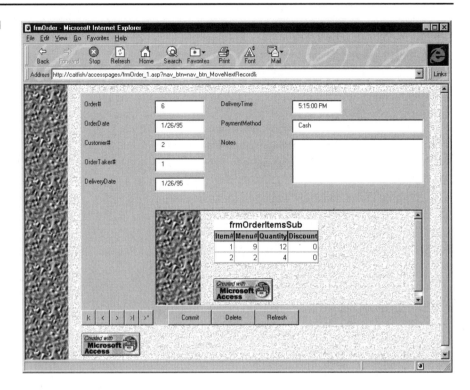

More on ASP and VBScript

We've only scratched the surface of information on Active Server Pages, VBScript, and ADO. If you wish to dig in further, use the Wizard to publish additional forms and datasheets and pull apart the code generated by the Wizard. Make some modifications to the code and see what happens. A good resource for further information is the documentation and samples that are copied to your server when you install IIS 3.0.

Wizard Templates

On the third page of the Publish to the Web Wizard, you are asked whether you wish to use a template for the published pages (see Figure 23.32). Microsoft has defined several tokens that you can embed in your template to control where Access places the elements of the generated page. These tokens are detailed in Table 23.9.

FIGURE 23.32

Template page of
the Wizard

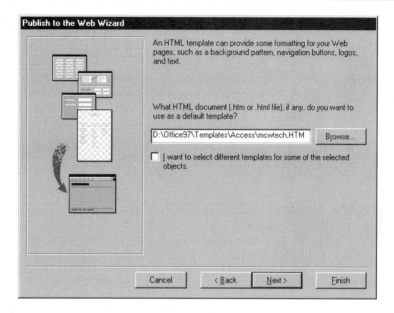

TABLE 23.9 Access Template Tokens

Token	Wizard Replaces Token with
<!--AccessTemplate_Title-->	Name of the exported object
<!--AccessTemplate_Body-->	The details rows
<!--AccessTemplate_FirstPage-->	A hyperlink to the first page of output; useful only for reports
<!--AccessTemplate_PreviousPage-->	A hyperlink to the prior page of output; useful only for reports
<!--AccessTemplate_NextPage-->	A hyperlink to the next page of output; useful only for reports
<!--AccessTemplate_LastPage-->	A hyperlink to the last page of output; useful only for reports
<!--AccessTemplate_PageNumber-->	Current page number; useful only for reports

The last five tokens in Table 23.9 make sense only when the Wizard generates multiple pages of output, which it does only when publishing reports. Thus, you may wish to have two versions of each template: one version for reports that includes these tokens and one version for all other pages that doesn't include these tokens.

> **TIP**
>
> If you refer to images in your template file, make sure you copy these graphics to the folder containing the published HTML, IDC, HTX, or ASP files.

A sample template that you might use with reports is shown here:

```
<HTML>

<HEAD>
<IMG SRC = "CONSTRUCTION.GIF" ALIGN=LEFT>
<TITLE><H1>MCW Technologies<H1></TITLE>
<H2><!--AccessTemplate_Title--></H2>
</HEAD>

<BODY background = gray.jpg>
<!--AccessTemplate_Body-->
</BODY>

<BR><BR>
<A HREF=<!--AccessTemplate_FirstPage-->>[|< First]  </A>
<A HREF=<!--AccessTemplate_PreviousPage-->>  [< Prior]  </A>
<A HREF=<!--AccessTemplate_NextPage-->>  [Next >]  </A>
<A HREF=<!--AccessTemplate_LastPage-->>  [Last >|]</A>

<P ALIGN=center>
Page <!--AccessTemplate_PageNumber-->.
</P>

</HTML>
```

A report generated with this template is shown in Figure 23.33.

> **TIP**
>
> You can set the default directory where the Wizard looks for templates using the Hyperlinks/HTML tab of the Tools ➤ Options dialog.

FIGURE 23.33

Last page of a report
generated using a Wizard
template

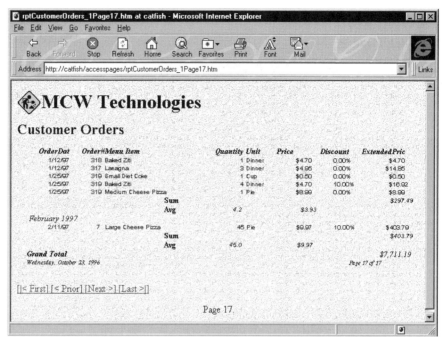

Using and Manipulating Profiles

On the last page of the Publish to the Web Wizard, you are given the opportunity
to save a publication profile based on the currently specified settings of the Wizard.
If you find yourself generating the same or similar pages repeatedly, you'll save
yourself a lot of time and trouble by creating publication profiles. You can load a
saved publication profile on the first page of the Wizard (see Figure 23.34).

Publication profiles are not saved as files; instead they are saved as properties of
the database and its objects. This has several implications:

- Each database can have a different set of publication profiles.

- There's no way to move publication profiles from one database to another.

- The Wizard doesn't support deleting or renaming publication profiles.

The publication profile properties and their formats are detailed in Table 23.10.

FIGURE 23.34

Using a publication profile will save you lots of time and trouble.

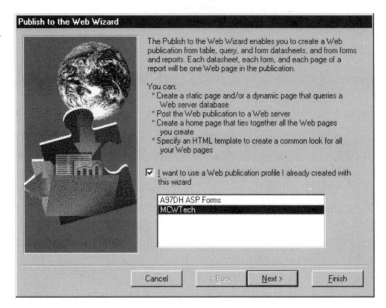

TABLE 23.10 Publication Profile Properties

Object	Property	Purpose	Example
Currentdb.Containers!Databases!MSysDb	pubwiz_SpecName	Name of profiles delimited with semicolons	A97DH ASP Forms; MCWTech
Currentdb.Containers!Databases!MSysDb	pubwiz_*profilename*	Database-level information for the profile as specified on the Wizard pages. Must follow this order: home page name; WebPost friendly name; data source name; user name; password; publishing directory; default template; default output format (1 for HTML, 2 for HTX/IDC, 3 for ASP); Active server URL; Active session timeout	MCWTechHome;;ch23;;; D:\A97DH\WebPages; D:\Office97\Templates\Access\mcwtech.HTM;1; http://catfish/accesspages;

TABLE 23.10 Publication Profile Properties (continued)

Object	Property	Purpose	Example
Document object	pubwiz_ *profilename*	Object-level information for the profile. Must follow this order: output file name; output format (1 for HTML, 2 for HTX/ IDC, 3 for ASP, −1 for default); template name ("<<Default>>" for default template)	tblMenu;−1;<<Default>>

You can delete a publication profile by directly deleting the property.

TIP

Even if you don't use publication profiles, you can save several publication parameters using the Hyperlinks/HTML tab of the Tools ➤ Options dialog.

The Web Publishing Wizard

The second to last page of the Publish to the Web Wizard offers to publish your Web pages to an Internet/intranet server using the Web Publishing Wizard if you installed this Wizard (also known as the WebPost Wizard) from the Office ValuPack.

If you choose the second option on this page, which is shown in Figure 23.35, the Web Publishing Wizard will start right after the Publish to the Web Wizard has finished generating the published files.

If you've previously used the Web Publishing Wizard, you can use the third option on this page to refer to an existing "friendly name." A friendly name is just an alias for a previously specified server.

FIGURE 23.35

You can use the Web Publishing Wizard to ease the process of moving your published files to your Internet/intranet server.

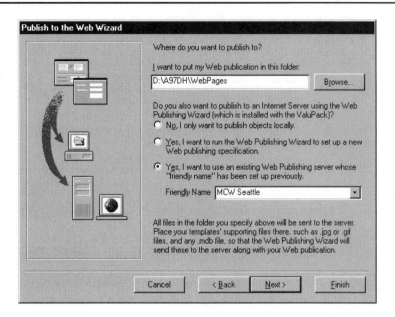

> **NOTE**
>
> The Web Publishing Wizard will copy every file from the local web publication folder to your server. (This folder is specified using the text box shown at the top of Figure 23.35.) Before running the Wizard, you'll want to make sure the local publication folder contains all the necessary files, including databases and images that will be needed on your server. In addition, make sure you delete any files from this folder that you do not wish the Wizard to copy to your server.

Publishing without the Wizard

There are two ways to publish an object in Access that don't require you to use the Publish to the Web Wizard (at least not directly). They are

- Using the File ➤ SaveAs/Export command.
- Using the OutputTo method of the DoCmd object (or the OutputTo macro action).

Using the SaveAs/Export Command

You can use the File ➤ SaveAs/Export command to publish a single database object without going through the many Wizard pages. Follow these steps:

1. Select the object in the database container.

2. Select File ➤ SaveAs/Export and choose to save the object "To an External File or Database" when the Save As dialog appears.

3. Select the appropriate output format—"HTML Documents (*.html;*.htm)", "Microsoft IIS 1-2 (*.htx;*.idc)", or "Microsoft Active Server (*.asp)"—using the Save as Type combo box.

4. Enter any optional parameters in the Output Options dialog.

Using the OutputTo Method

You can use the OutputTo method of the DoCmd object (or the OutputTo macro action) to programmatically generate Web pages in HTML, IDC, or ASP format. The syntax of the OutputTo method is shown here:

DoCmd.OutputTo *objecttype*, [*objectname*], [*outputformat*], [*outputfile*], [*autostart*], [*templatefile*]

The parameters are described in Table 23.11.

TABLE 23.11 Parameters of the OutputTo Method

Parameter	Description	Default Value
objecttype	One of the object type constants (acOuputForm, acOutputModule, acOuputQuery, acOutputReport, or acOutputTable)	None; required
objectname	Name of the object you wish to output	The active object
outputformat	One of the output format constants (acFormatASP, acFormatHTML, acFormatIIS, acFormatRTF, acFormatTXT, or acFormatXLS)	*None*; if left missing, Access prompts you for the value
outputfile	Name of the output file	*None*; if left missing, Access prompts you for the value

TABLE 23.11 Parameters of the OutputTo Method (continued)

Parameter	Description	Default Value
autostart	Boolean value when True; Access automatically starts the host application for that object after the output file is generated (This is ignored for the acFormatActiveServer and acFormatIIS formats.)	False
templatefile	Name of an optional template file	None

For example, you might use the following subroutine (which can be found in the basPublish module of the sample database) to publish tables using the OutputTo method, as shown in Listing 23.6.

Listing 23.6

```
Sub PublishTable(strTable As String, _
 strOutputFile As String, _
 varFormat As Variant, _
 Optional strTemplateFile As String = "")

    On Error GoTo PublishTableErr

    DoCmd.Hourglass True
    If strTemplateFile = "" Then
        DoCmd.OutputTo ObjectType:=acOutputTable, _
          ObjectName:=strTable, _
          OutputFormat:=varFormat, _
          OutputFile:=strOutputFile, _
          AutoStart:=False
    Else
        DoCmd.OutputTo ObjectType:=acOutputTable, _
          ObjectName:=strTable, _
          OutputFormat:=varFormat, _
          OutputFile:=strOutputFile, _
          AutoStart:=False, _
          TemplateFile:=strTemplateFile
    End If

    DoCmd.Hourglass False

    MsgBox "The " & strTable & _
      " table was successfully published to the " & _
```

```
          strOutputFile & " file.", _
          vbInformation + vbOKOnly, "PublishTable Sub"

PublishTableEnd:
    Exit Sub
PublishTableErr:
    DoCmd.Hourglass False
    MsgBox "Error " & Err.Number & ": " & Err.Description, _
     vbCritical + vbOKOnly, "PublishTable Error"
    Resume PublishTableEnd

End Sub
```

Getting Additional Information on Web Publishing

We've sampled only some of the functionality of standard HTML, the use of HTML forms, the Internet Database Connector, and Active Server capabilities. If you'd like to learn more about basic HTML or HTML forms, you may wish to perform a search using your favorite Web search tool for sites that have information on HTML and Web page authoring. There are plenty of excellent sites. Here are a few we've found useful:

- http://www.library.carleton.edu/Webtutorial/welcome.html

- http://gort.ucsd.edu/iassist/

- http://www.w3.org/pub/WWW/

- http://www.ncsa.uiuc.edu/General/Internet/WWW/HTMLPrimer.html

- http://www.microsoft.com/workshop/author/default.htm

As mentioned previously, the best place for information on the Internet Database Connector and Active Server is the documentation and samples that come with Microsoft Internet Information Server.

Of course, there are also good books from Sybex and others on Web publishing and some of the newer technologies, such as IDC and ASP. In addition, several magazines and newsletters cover these subjects. And don't forget to search the Web for information on these and other publishing topics; the Web is often your best bet for up-to-date information on emerging technologies.

Recognizing Access' Limits as an Internet Data Server

Access is a file-server database and thus is limited in the number of simultaneous users it can support. Every time a user launches a dynamic Web page (IDC or ASP) on your server, IIS will need to load the Jet Engine DLLs and open the shared database. This shouldn't be a problem within a limited corporate intranet environment with ten users—perhaps even more if you're using read-only pages—but going much beyond this will likely cause speed, contention, or corruption problems.

If you plan on having many users—especially if they will be concurrently updating records—or if you're unhappy with the response time of your Access-published pages, you may wish to consider upsizing to a client-server back end, such as Microsoft SQL Server or Oracle. You can edit the pages produced by the Access Publish to Web Wizard so they point at a client-server database system data source instead of your Access data source. See Chapter 15 for more details on client-server databases.

Back to the Stone Age?

Using the Internet to browse and update data stored in database tables may seem like going back to the Stone Age. In many ways, it is! Many of the tools, as well as the final product produced by these tools, are primitive when compared with the robust tools and applications you can pull together using only a desktop database such as Access. While you may find it amazing when your published Active Server pages work (we did at first), we all like to reach for slightly higher functionality. Web-based applications are slow and lack much of the functionality you've come to expect from standard (Web-less) database applications.

The point we are trying to make is that there's a lot your Internet/intranet-enabled applications just simply cannot do or can do only rather poorly. This means there still *is* a place for your regular old Access applications.

When it makes sense to publish on the Web, by all means publish, but it's probably a bad idea at this time to start converting all your applications to Web-only applications. That's not to say there won't be a time in the future when most or all of the UI of desktop applications will be run through a Web browser. That day may come—perhaps sooner than we'd like.

> **TIP**
>
> Using the Active Server format to publish Access forms allows you to make your Access data available for editing to Mac users. (As this book went to press, a beta version of the ActiveX HTML Layout control was available for the Mac; a UNIX version may also be available at some time in the future.)

Summary

The Internet is an exciting frontier. Access 97 has many enhancements that make it easy to create applications for the Internet or your corporate intranet. In this chapter we've explored Access' browser enhancements in detail, including:

- Understanding hyperlinks
- Creating hyperlink fields
- Creating hyperlink controls on forms
- Creating hyperlinks on reports
- Programmatically manipulating hyperlinks
- Creating lightweight forms
- Using hyperlinks for intra-database navigation
- Using ActiveX browser controls

We've also explored Access' publishing features, including:

- Hypertext markup language
- Publishing data using the Publish to the Web Wizard
- Publishing data as static HTML, dynamic Internet Database Connector pages, and dynamic Active Server pages
- Publishing parameter queries
- Creating ActiveX forms
- Creating and using Wizard templates and publication profiles
- Using the SaveAs/Export command to publish individual objects
- Programmatically publishing data using the OutputTo method
- Limits of Access as an Internet/intranet server and limits of Web-based applications

CHAPTER

TWENTY-FOUR

24

Using Source Code Control

- Understanding source code control

- Exploring source code control integration in Access 97

- Using Microsoft Visual SourceSafe with Access

- Controlling Visual SourceSafe with VBA

As the popularity of Microsoft Access grew over time among both commercial and corporate developers, it began to show a weakness when multiple developers used it to contribute to a single database development project. Not only was it difficult for two or more developers to work simultaneously on a single database (for instance, changes to modules required other developers to close and reopen the database), but it was impractical, if not impossible, to track changes to individual database objects. "Pure" language developers (those working in C, C++, Basic, and so on) created a solution to this problem long ago in the form of *source code control* applications. These applications use a network directory to store copies of a program's source files and regulate access to them. Until now Access has been incompatible with source code control programs because, instead of having separate source files that are combined to create a single executable program, Access applications are stored in a single, binary file format. Microsoft has finally remedied the situation, however, and built source code control compatibility into Access 97. In this chapter we look at how source code control is supported, as well as how to use it with Microsoft's control program, Visual SourceSafe.

What Is Source Code Control?

The driving principle behind source code control (abbreviated SCC in this chapter) is simple. Any programmer involved in a development project is allowed to use source files to compile, or *build*, a version of the application. Only one developer, however, is given the privilege to modify a source file at any given time. This eliminates the chance that two developers will overwrite each other's changes by working on the same source file at the same time. If the development tool has properly integrated source code control, the mechanics of making this work are transparent to the developer. The following sections explain the concepts encompassed in source code control, all of which apply generally to development tools that support SCC. Later sections cover how Access 97 supports and uses these concepts.

Source Code Control Provider

At the heart of source code control is the actual software that manages access to source files, called the SCC *provider*. Microsoft offers a provider called Visual SourceSafe you can use with its Visual Basic, Visual FoxPro, and Visual C++ languages, as well as with Access 97. Other, third-party software is also available. A provider can follow either the file-server or client-server deployment model, with provider software running on each developer's computer or on a centralized server. In each case a centralized database or directory structure stores source code files.

SCC provider software usually supports distinct user accounts, just as the database server or network software does. Each developer wishing to use any managed source code files must have an account with the provider. This ensures that only authorized users can access the valuable files and provides a convenient way to track changes to them.

Projects and Source Files

Before you can begin using source code control with your programming language you must set up a *project* on the server. Most providers let you do this as a separate step or by importing an existing development project. At a minimum, the SCC project defines the source code files to be managed. Depending on the provider, you may also be able to set other project options.

Most providers let you share source files among several projects. This is extremely useful for managing "utility" functions that are used in many different applications.

Check In and Check Out

When you want to work on a particular source file, you must "check it out" from the project on the server. After making sure no other developer already has the file checked out, the provider copies the latest version of the file to your computer so you can modify it. When you have made your changes and want others to be able to use them in their copies of the application, you check the file back in. In this sense source code control is like a library with the SCC provider acting as librarian.

Multiple Check Out and Merge

Some source code control providers offer the ability to have multiple developers check out the same source file. While this can potentially lead to problems, it is sometimes necessary, especially with source files for generic or "utility" functions. During the check in process, the SCC provider compares the version being checked in with the current version. If it detects conflicts it cannot resolve, you must manually merge the two files. Many provider programs automatically resolve some conflicts (for example, if the file being checked in is a complete superset of the current version), but you will have to cope with many conflicts yourself.

Get

If you don't want to modify a particular file but want only to include it in your copy of the application, you perform what's known as a *get*. This copies the most recent copy from the server to your computer, overwriting the existing version stored there. Developers typically perform gets periodically during the day to bring in changes to source code files made by other developers.

Diff and Restore

Most SCC providers support *versioning*. When a developer checks in a source file, rather than simply overwriting the copy on the server, the provider archives it, logging the date and time it was checked in and by whom. This allows you to compare versions, called performing a *diff* (for difference). The provider software usually displays the versions side by side with any changes highlighted. Should you wish, you can *restore* an older version of the source file, making it the current one.

Support for Source Code Control in Access 97

As mentioned earlier in this chapter, the main reason earlier versions of Access were incompatible with source code control programs was their single, binary file structure. Not only did this make check in and check out useless, but given the changing structure of the binary file contents, performing a diff on two functionally equivalent databases would always show changes. It took an act of Access Program Management to add specific support for SCC programs to the base product. In this section we explain how Microsoft chose to support source code control in Access 97.

Source Code Control Add-In

Before you can use Access' source code control features, you must purchase a copy of the Microsoft Office 97 Developer Edition (ODE) CD-ROM. This replacement to the Access Developer's Toolkit includes the add-in and DLLs that implement the link between Access and a source code control provider. Once you've installed the add-in from the ODE and a source code control provider, Access invokes the add-in at key points in the development process (when you open a database or create a new object, for example). The add-in then communicates with the SCC provider using a standard set of functions to perform acts such as check in, check out, and get.

The add-in uses a standard set of functions, so you can use any source code control provider that supports these. Microsoft Visual SourceSafe and PVCS are two products that were available as this book went to press.

The Process

In the section "Working with VSS from Access 97" later in this chapter, we explain the exact steps to manage a database project using a source code control provider. Here, however, we discuss the process in general.

After installing the appropriate software (a provider and the SCC add-in), you (as a single developer who has the most up-to-date copy of the MDB file) begin the process by creating a source code control project from an existing Access database. Creating a project from an existing database produces the appropriate source files on the source code control server and makes them available to other developers.

Once the project exists on the server, you want to allow other developers to begin using it. You start by creating a new Access database on each developer's work-station and, in effect, importing all the objects from the project on the server. These developers work on their own copies of the database. You create each database using the SCC add-in menu commands, however, not by creating a database and importing objects yourself. Other developers can then work with the objects in their own copies of the database, checking objects in and out as necessary.

Eventually you'll want to remove a database from source code control so you can distribute it to your users. To do this you simply compact the database. Access asks, each time you compact a database, whether you want to remove it from source code control. If you answer yes, Access breaks the link from the SCC project, and you will no longer be able to use SCC commands.

WARNING Once you've removed a database from source code control, there is no way to reestablish the link with the SCC project. The only solution is to create a new database based on the project.

Object Exchanges

An Access database stores two things that are normally separate in other development environments: data and application objects (queries, forms, reports, macros, and modules). Access 97 treats these separately when it comes to source code control. When Access exchanges application objects with an SCC provider, it exports each object as a separate text file. These files define the properties of each object and, where applicable, any VBA code the object contains, using a format similar to the one Microsoft Visual Basic has used for years. Everything else an Access database can contain (tables, relationships, command bars, custom properties, and import/export specifications) remains in a single, binary file that the SCC add-in treats as a separate component.

Figure 24.1 illustrates how Access treats objects under source code control. When you retrieve them from the SCC provider, Access reassembles them into a single MDB file. For details on the file structure, see the section "Object Text File Formats" later in this chapter.

FIGURE 24.1

How Access treats database objects under source code control

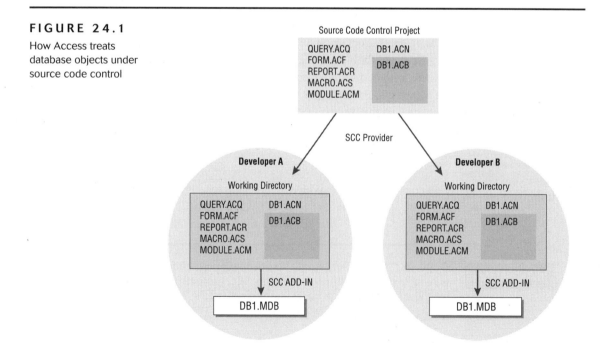

The binary file containing a database's tables, relationships, and other objects is, itself, an Access database that contains these objects and nothing more.

While the exchange of objects is accomplished with text files, it is important to remember that developers themselves still work with an Access database. The conversion to text files and back is completely transparent. Developers working with a database under source code control each maintain a separate MDB file on their own hard disk. When you check out or get objects from the SCC project, the SCC add-in copies them, as text, to your hard drive and then integrates them into your local MDB file. When you check them back into the project, the process is reversed. The add-in instructs Access to export the objects to your local hard drive and then copies them back to the project on the server.

Check In and Check Out Rules

To modify database objects and save them back to the project, you must check them out from the SCC project. You can check out application objects individually, just as with other language products such as Visual Basic and C++. If you want to modify any data objects (tables, and so on), however, you must check out the entire binary database component. While you have objects checked out, no other user can check them out. The exception to this rule is modules. Multiple developers can check out a single module and then merge their changes during the check in process.

When you have a database under source code control, Access prompts you to check out objects whenever you attempt to open them in Design view. This goes for all the traditional application objects, as well as such things as relationships and VBA project information. You can bypass these dialogs by using the SetWarnings action to turn them off.

Local Objects

In addition to objects that are part of an SCC project, you can maintain local objects in your copy of the Access database. This applies to everything except tables. (You can't create local tables, because all tables are stored as a single binary object.) Local objects exist only in your database and are useful for testing and experimentation. After creating a local object, you can add it to the SCC project.

Local Source File Storage

Because Access breaks up a database into separate source files while working with an SCC provider, it must have a place to store these files. In SCC nomenclature, this location is sometimes called the *working directory*. It is the place on a developer's hard drive where files are stored when they are checked out, as well as before they are checked back in to the project.

Access implements a working directory by creating a subdirectory beneath the directory where the local MDB file is stored. This subdirectory has the same name as the database and an extension of .SCC. For example, if the database was called CH24.MDB, the working directory would be called CH24.SCC. Within this directory the SCC add-in would place all the source files for the database as necessary during exchanges with the SCC provider.

> **NOTE**
>
> Access and the SCC add-in create this directory when you open the database and delete it when you close it. While it exists, any files it contains that are not checked out will be marked as read-only to prevent inadvertent changes. Unlike other development tools, however, these files are *not* used to build a compiled program directly. You should not, therefore, edit these files; if you do, your changes will be lost during the next get, check out, or check in action.

Source Code Control Options

Access lets you customize how it interacts with your source code control provider via the Options dialog shown in Figure 24.2. Open the dialog by selecting the source code control Options command from the Tools ➤ SCC menu. The options for each of the four questions shown in Figure 24.2 are Yes, No, and Ask. Select Ask if you want Access to prompt you. Select one of the other options if you want actions to happen automatically.

Changes to Objects under Source Code Control

Placing a database and its objects under source code control produces changes to those objects and the way you use them. First of all, Access adds a number of properties to the database and its objects. Table 24.1 lists the properties that are added

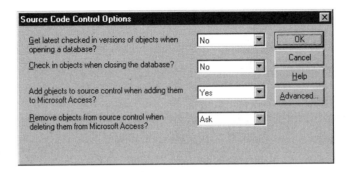

FIGURE 24.2

Options dialog that controls how Access works with your SCC provider

to the Database object. The one of most interest is SccStatus, which indicates the status of an object in regard to source code control.

TABLE 24.1   Properties Added to a Database under Source Code Control

Property	Description
SccStatus	Bit mask indicating the current status of an object. See code examples for bit mask values
SccDatabasePath	Local path of the database under source code control
SccPath	Path to the source code control project containing the database
SccAuxPath	Additional directory information used by a source code control provider
SccUserName	Source code control user name of the developer who created this copy of the database

WARNING   The information in this section is based on our own experimentation. The SCC properties are not documented or officially supported by Microsoft. As with any undocumented feature, these properties may change in future versions. Use this information at your own risk.

Additionally, the SccStatus property is added to each DAO Document object in the database under source code control. Local objects do not have an SccStatus property. The bit mask values are the same as those for a database.

You can use the SccStatus property to determine the status of any object in a database. For example, the adhSccStatus function shown in Listing 24.1 accepts an object variable and returns a status message. Note the error handling. This is required because the SccStatus property won't exist for objects that aren't under source code control.

Listing 24.1

```
Public Const adhcUnderSCC = &H1
Public Const adhcCheckedOutByMe = &H2
Public Const adhcCheckedOutByOther = &H4

Function adhSccStatus(objAny As Object) As String
    Dim lngStatus As Long
    Dim strTemp As String
    Dim fOk As Boolean

    On Error GoTo HandleError

    ' Make sure object is valid
    If TypeOf objAny Is Database Then
        fOk = True
    ElseIf TypeOf objAny Is Document Then
        fOk = True
    End If
    If Not fOk Then
        MsgBox "You can only use this function with " & _
          "Database and Document objects.", vbExclamation
        Exit Function
    End If

    ' Get status value--this will cause an error if the
    ' object isn't under source code control
    lngStatus = objAny.Properties("SccStatus")

    ' Build base string
    strTemp = "Object is under source code control and "

    ' Compare status against constants
    If (lngStatus And adhcCheckedOutByMe) Then
        strTemp = strTemp & "checked out by you."
    ElseIf (lngStatus And adhcCheckedOutByOther) Then
```

```
                strTemp = strTemp & "checked out by someone else."
        Else
                strTemp = strTemp & "not checked out."
        End If

        adhSccStatus = strTemp

ExitProc:
    Exit Function
HandleError:
    Select Case Err.Number
        Case 3270    ' Property not found
            adhSccStatus = _
              "Object is not under source code control."
        Case Else
            MsgBox Err.Description, vbExclamation, _
              "Error " & Err.Number
    End Select
    Resume ExitProc
End Function
```

Access also provides visual feedback for objects that are under source code control. Special icons in the database window designate these objects. You can see them in Figure 24.3. They include the lock, indicating an object in the SCC database; the check mark, indicating that you have the object checked out; and the small person, indicating that another user has the object checked out. Local objects won't have any icons at all.

FIGURE 24.3

Access uses icons to indicate the status of objects in a database under source code control.

In addition to the new properties, you should be aware that changes to an object may affect the source file in the server project. For example, renaming an object in your copy of the database renames it in the project as well. The next time another developer's copy of the database changes, that developer's local object will be renamed. Given the potential complications involved in renaming objects (hard-coded references in code being one), you should use care when renaming objects. You must check out the binary data object in order to rename tables, command bars, or relationships. Renaming an object will fail if another user has the object checked out.

Deleting an object also has an effect on the project. When you delete an object from your database, the SCC add-in asks whether you want to delete it from the project as well. If you choose to do this, other developers will not be able to check out or use the object.

Source Code Control Restrictions

While source code control offers many benefits, there are several restrictions regarding which Access features are allowed in databases under source code control. Specifically, there are three classes of databases that you cannot place under source code control: secured databases, replicated databases, and enabled databases. If you want to secure or replicate a database, develop it under source code control first, and then apply security or replication to the finalized database.

Another restriction concerns relationships involving queries. Any relationship involving a query is ignored when you place a database under source code control. This is necessary for Access to treat queries as separate objects and not part of the binary data object.

Finally, beware of changes made to a database programmatically using DAO. For example, it is possible to create a new table using VBA. Since Jet knows nothing about the presence of a source code control add-in, it will not create the property values necessary to add the database to an SCC project. The next time the binary data object is updated, your changes will be overwritten.

Using Microsoft Visual SourceSafe

If you don't currently have a source code control provider, you can purchase a copy of Microsoft's SCC product, Visual SourceSafe (VSS). VSS ships as a separate product and is also bundled with Visual C++ and Visual Basic, Enterprise Edition.

To demonstrate how to take advantage of source code control in Access, we'll show you examples that use VSS. If you use another provider, the concepts will remain the same, but the exact steps and dialogs will obviously be different.

Setting Up Source Code Control

Installing Visual SourceSafe is a two-step process. First, you install the server components on a networked computer. This creates a database that VSS will use to store project files. Then VSS copies setup files that developers can use to install the client software on their computers. You must install the client files on each computer where you want to use source code control.

> **TIP**
>
> You can install both the server and client files on a single computer. This allows you to use source code control features such as versioning and histories (see the section "Working with Histories and Differences" later in this chapter) even if you're the only developer working on a project.

Installing SourceSafe Server Files

To install the VSS server files, run SETUP.EXE from the VSS CD-ROM. You have the option of installing just the server files, just the client files, or, if you select the Custom installation option, both (see Figure 24.4). Be sure to install both sets of files if you intend to use the computer as both a VSS server and a client.

Figure 24.5 shows the Setup dialog associated with a custom installation. The first option, Create SourceSafe Database, is a critical option for a server installation. It creates the directory structure VSS uses to store project files. If you want other developers to be able to install VSS from the server, be sure to include the Network Client Setup option as well.

After installing the server files, you should share the install directory. This allows others to install the client software directly from the server. Furthermore, since VSS is a file-server–based applicaiton, you'll need to give developers access to the directory where the VSS database is stored.

Installing SourceSafe Client Files

Once the server files have been installed, you can install client files on each workstation that needs access to project files. The simplest way to do this is to run the

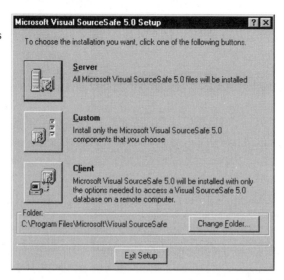

FIGURE 24.4

The VSS Setup dialog lets you specify the installation type.

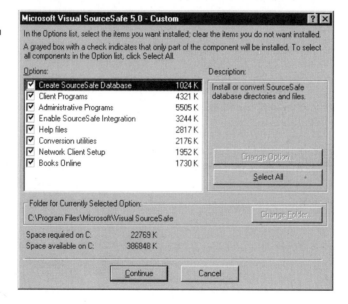

FIGURE 24.5

VSS custom installation options

NETSETUP.EXE file from the directory on the server where you installed VSS. To do this, connect to the VSS share and run NETSETUP.EXE. The setup program copies the VSS program files and automatically creates a reference to the VSS database.

Creating SourceSafe User Accounts

Visual SourceSafe includes an integrated security component to ensure that only authorized developers have access to project files. Before using VSS with Access, you should use the VSS Administrator application to add user accounts. When you install the server files, the setup program creates an icon for the Administrator program. Figure 24.6 shows the program's main window. It lists the existing user accounts and which ones, if any, are logged into VSS.

FIGURE 24.6

VSS Administrator program showing user accounts

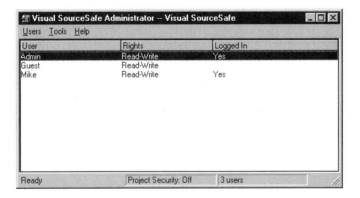

VSS creates two accounts for you: Admin and Guest. Admin is the administrator account you must use to create user accounts. When you launch VSS or the Administrator program, you are prompted to log in. Figure 24.7 shows the Login dialog. You'll also need to log in the first time you use a VSS function from Access.

TIP
You can have VSS use a user's network name and password as that user's login information. This eliminates the need for developers to manually log in to VSS. To enable this feature, use the Options dialog in the VSS Administrator application.

FIGURE 24.7

Visual SourceSafe
Login dialog

Admin is created with a blank password, so leave that field blank when you log on for the first time. We recommend, however, that you change the password as soon as possible. To change an account's password, select the account from the Administrator program's main window and select Users ➤ Change Password.

To create new accounts for your developers, select Users ➤ Add User. Figure 24.8 shows the Add User dialog, where you specify a name and password. You can also designate the account as read-only. Read-only accounts can perform gets on project files but cannot check them out.

FIGURE 24.8

Adding a new VSS
user using the Add
User dialog

NOTE   User-level authentication is the default security scheme VSS uses. This allows any user with a valid VSS account complete access to any and all projects and files. Using the VSS Administrator application, you can enable project-level security, which restricts access to projects and files on a user-by-user basis.

Running Visual SourceSafe

While you'll normally interact with VSS or other source code control providers through Access' user interface, you can run VSS interactively as a separate product.

Figure 24.9 shows the VSS Explorer window. It operates just like the Windows Explorer. The left-hand pane shows all the projects that VSS is currently managing. The right-hand pane shows the source files that make up the project.

VSS uses a hierarchical structure to manage projects. Every project can have subprojects, which, themselves, can have subprojects, and so on. All projects descend from a root project represented by the symbols $/ in the left-hand pane. You can create projects that are part of other projects and operate on them independently or as a component of their parent (called *recursively* by VSS documentation). For example, you can perform diffs on entire projects in VSS, including any subprojects.

When you select a project from the left-hand pane, VSS displays all the files that make it up in the right-hand pane. VSS displays the file name (note that those in Figure 24.9 are Access components), the date and time it was last modified, and check out information if applicable. If a file has been checked out, VSS shows you who checked it out and the directory on the workstation to which that user copied it.

Using VSS Explorer, you can create new projects, add and remove files from projects, view file histories, perform diffs and restores, and print a number of reports. We'll leave exploring all its functionality up to you and concentrate on the Access VSS interface in the remainder of this chapter.

FIGURE 24.9

Visual SourceSafe Explorer showing details on a project

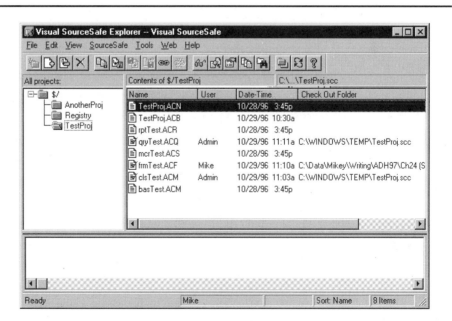

> **TIP**
>
> The Visual SourceSafe Explorer is most useful to project managers and lead developers. It shows who has what checked out, and you can use it to troubleshoot errors by performing diffs and restores.

Working with VSS from Access 97

This section explains the basics of using VSS from within Access 97. It is not meant to replace the Access or VSS documentation, so not every aspect of using VSS is covered. This section should, however, provide you with a fundamental understanding of how Access and VSS interact.

To use VSS from Access, you need to install both the VSS client files and the Access source code control option that comes on the Microsoft Office 97 Developer Edition CD-ROM. Once you've accomplished that, you'll be able to access the source code control commands on the Tools menu. If you install the SCC support files but do *not* install VSS or another SCC provider, you'll receive the error message shown in Figure 24.10. Click No to dispense with the dialog and prevent it from appearing again.

FIGURE 24.10

Error message you receive if you install SCC support but no SCC provider

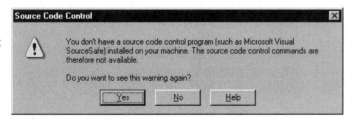

> **TIP**
>
> Some users inadvertently perform a complete install of the ODE without realizing that it includes the source code control integration features. If you see the warning dialog and want to remove the source code control add-in, you can rerun the setup program and choose the Add/Remove option.

Placing a Database under Source Code Control

The first step in using an Access database with source code control is to add it to a VSS project. To place a database under VSS source code control, open it in Access and select Tools ➤ SourceSafe ➤ Add Database To SourceSafe. Access warns you that it must first close the database before it can add it to SourceSafe. If you have any open, changed objects, you can click No and save them and then select the menu command again. Otherwise you will be prompted with a dialog for each object.

> **WARNING**
> Do not use the Add Files command in VSS Explorer to add a database to a project. VSS by itself cannot cope with an MDB file's binary structure. It will add the entire file to the project instead of exporting and adding individual object files.

Selecting a VSS Project

After you give Access permission to add the database to SourceSafe, it closes and reopens the database. You will then have to log in to VSS using the Login dialog shown earlier in Figure 24.7. Access then prompts you with a dialog like the one shown in Figure 24.11, listing all the VSS projects and subprojects. You can either enter the name of a new project in the text box or select an existing project from the tree view window. If you want to create a new project, you can either enter a complete path in the text box (for example, "$/Sales/Inventory") or select an existing project and enter just the name of the new subproject. In the latter case VSS creates a new subproject beneath the selected project. The Create button creates a new project immediately and displays it in the tree view window. If you don't click the Create button, VSS automatically creates the new project when you click OK.

> **WARNING**
> Make sure you leave the text box blank if you want to place the database into an existing project. Otherwise VSS will create a new subproject beneath the selected project and place your database there.

FIGURE 24.11

Use this dialog to select or create a VSS project for your database.

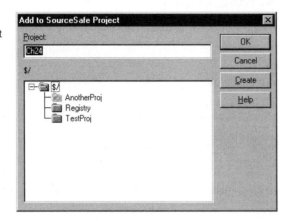

Add to SourceSafe Project

NOTE Access will not let you add a database to a VSS project that already contains a database under source code control.

Adding Objects to the Project

After choosing a VSS project name, you are presented with another dialog. This one, shown in Figure 24.12, gives you the opportunity to add database objects (including the binary data object) to the VSS project. You need not add any objects at this time. This dialog is accessible whenever you're working in a database under source code control. If you decide not to add any objects, Access will create only the ACN file (the one that defines the database name) in the VSS project.

You can select as many or as few objects as you like from the "Objects to be added" list. If you have a lot of objects in your database, you can view only those of a given type by selecting it from the Object Type combo box. Note the highlighted entry in Figure 24.12 ("Other: Data and Misc. Objects"). This is the entry for the binary data component.

After making your selections, click OK to add them to the VSS project. You'll see a VSS dialog that logs the status of each object as it is added to the project. Normally this dialog, shown in Figure 24.13, disappears automatically after all the objects have been added successfully. If any errors or warnings occur, it remains open so you can examine them.

FIGURE 24.12

Use this dialog to add objects to the VSS project.

FIGURE 24.13

The Visual SourceSafe dialog shows status and error messages during processing.

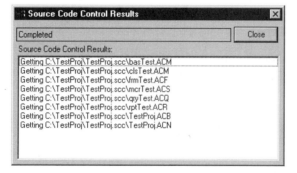

Creating a Database from a VSS Project

Once one developer has created a VSS project from an Access database, other developers can begin working with it. You cannot, however, simply copy the MDB file to other workstations, because it contains custom properties that apply to the original VSS user. If you attempt to open a database placed under source code control and you aren't the VSS user who created it, Access issues a warning message and disables all source code control functions.

To begin working with a database under source code control, you must use the SourceSafe menu to create a new database. Select Tools ➤ SourceSafe ➤ Create

Database from SourceSafe Project. You'll be prompted with the dialog shown in Figure 24.14 to specify a local working directory and to select a VSS project folder. Select the VSS project containing the database you created using the previously listed steps.

FIGURE 24.14

Creating a new database from a Visual SourceSafe project

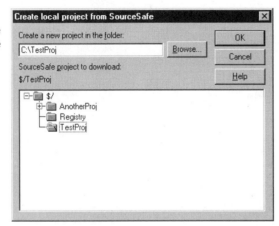

After making your selections, click the OK button. Access and Visual SourceSafe will create a new MDB file and copy all the objects from the VSS project on the server. You can then start working with database objects under source code control.

Working with Objects in a VSS Project

Adding objects to a VSS project is only the first step in using source code control features with Access. If you want to make changes to objects, you'll need to check them out, as described in the next section.

> **NOTE**
>
> If you decided not to add all the objects in the database when you added it to SourceSafe, or if you have created new local objects, you can add objects to a VSS project by selecting the Add Objects command from the SourceSafe menu.

Checking Out Objects

As mentioned earlier in this chapter, Access prompts you to check out objects whenever you attempt to open them in design mode. You can also check out objects interactively using a VSS-supplied dialog. To open this dialog, shown in Figure 24.15, select the Check Out command from the Tools ➤ SourceSafe menu.

> **TIP**
>
> Access also features a Source Code Control command bar with buttons for the most frequently used SCC commands. To display this command bar, use the View ➤ Toolbars menu command or the command bar right-click menu.

The dialog lets you select one or more objects to check out at the same time. Use the Object-Type drop-down list to view objects of a given type or all objects in the project. Mark those you wish to check out with a check mark in the Objects to be Checked Out list. Use the Comment text box to enter a comment regarding why you are checking out these objects. Comments are stored in the VSS database and can be read and/or printed by the project administrator.

Clicking the Advanced button opens the dialog shown in Figure 24.16. The options shown on the dialog control what happens during the check out process. Table 24.2 describes these options and what they are used for.

FIGURE 24.15

Visual SourceSafe dialog for checking out objects

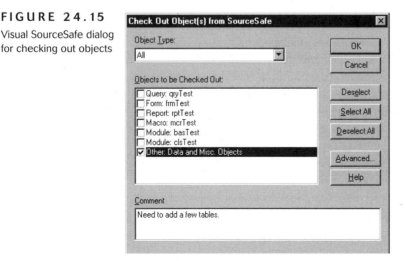

FIGURE 24.16

Visual SourceSafe
advanced check out
options

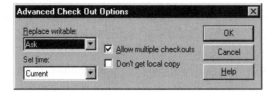

TABLE 24.2 Advanced Check Out Options

Option	Description
Replace Writable	Determines how VSS reacts when it finds a file in the working directory that is not read-only. It can prompt you (Ask), replace the file with the one being checked out (Replace), skip the file (Skip), or merge the two files (Merge)
Set Time	Determines what date and time information VSS sets on the checked out file. Your choices are Current, for the current date and time; Modification, for the last time the file was modified; and Check In, for the date and time the file was last checked in
Allow multiple check outs	If checked, VSS allows multiple check outs on the file
Don't get local copy	If checked, VSS marks the file as checked out but does not copy the latest version to your working directory

Undoing a Check Out

Occasionally you may want to reverse or "undo" a check out. For example, suppose that after checking out an object and making numerous changes, you discover you've approached a problem from a completely wrong direction—that you've reached a programming dead end. Rather than trying to remember all the changes you've made to the object and repealing each one individually, you can use VSS to undo the check out, thus reverting to the current VSS project version.

To do this, select the Undo Check Out command from either the Tools ➤ SourceSafe menu or the right-click menu for an object in the database window. SourceSafe warns you that undoing a check out will overwrite any changes to the object.

Checking In Objects

Once you have made changes to an object that you want to share with others, you must check the object back in to the VSS project. Select the Check In menu command to open the dialog shown in Figure 24.17. Like the Check Out dialog, you can view only those objects of a particular type or all objects. You can also supply a comment indicating what changes were made that will be saved along with the objects.

FIGURE 24.17

Visual SourceSafe dialog for checking objects back in to VSS

If you want to continue working on the objects, select the "Keep checked out" check box. This instructs VSS to check the objects in to the project on the server so other developers can retrieve them, along with your changes, but leaves the objects checked out to you so you can continue editing them.

Before checking in the objects, you can view the differences between them and those currently in the VSS project on the server by clicking the Differences button. For application objects, this displays the VSS Differences dialog. See the section "Working with Histories and Differences" later in this chapter for more information on using this dialog. For the binary data object, VSS informs you if there is a difference but does not display the information in the Differences dialog.

Retrieving Checked In Objects

If you are working with multiple developers on the same database project, you will occasionally want to merge changes made by other developers into your copy of the database. To do this, select an object in the database window and activate the Get Latest Version command from the SourceSafe or right-click menu. This replaces the current version of the object with the one stored in the VSS database.

> **WARNING**
>
> Be cautious about doing this with code-bearing objects such as forms, reports, and modules. Other developers may have checked in their changes with references to other procedures you may not have declared in your copy of the database. This will prevent your application from compiling.

Merging Changed Modules with Multiple Check Outs

Visual SourceSafe allows multiple users to check out any text file from a VSS project. This lets more than one person make changes to an object at the same time. While it is preferable to restrict check outs to a single developer, sometimes multiple check outs are necessary due to the size and complexity of a source file. Access supports multiple check outs for code modules only.

> **NOTE**
>
> To enable multiple check outs you must run the VSS Administrator application and select this option from the Options dialog.

When checking in source files that have been checked out by multiple developers, VSS must merge the file being checked in with the one in the VSS database. Merging involves integrating changes made to the local copy with the current version in the VSS project. VSS uses a rather sophisticated pattern-matching algorithm to process the merge and to spot conflicts. Therefore, VSS can often perform the merge automatically if there are no direct conflicts between files. For example, if only new procedures are added to a code module, VSS adds the new procedures to the VSS database copy of the file. Changes to the same line of code, or any other change that short-circuits the pattern-matching algorithm, will cause conflicts that VSS cannot resolve on its own.

When conflicts are detected, VSS displays its Visual Merge dialog, shown in Figure 24.18. This dialog contains three panes. The upper-left and -right panes show the current VSS project version of the file alongside the local version. The lower pane shows the results of the merge. It is up to you to sort out the differences and, where there are conflicts, to pick a "winner."

To make the process easier, VSS color-codes each conflict to indicate which lines have been added, changed, or removed. You can use the toolbar to move quickly from one conflict to the next. For each conflict, you have the option of discarding your changes and reverting to the VSS database version, discarding the version in the VSS database, or accepting both sets of changes where applicable. For example, if two new, different procedures exist in the two versions, you could decide to accept both. On the other hand, in the case of conflicts within a single line of code, you must pick one winner. To select a winner, simply click on it in the appropriate upper pane. You can also right-click on a conflict and select from menu commands that accept the change, discard it, or apply both.

FIGURE 24.18

The Visual Merge dialog lets you resolve conflicting changes to a file.

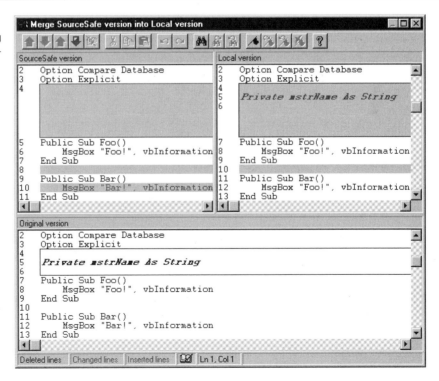

When you are done merging the two files, close the Merge dialog. VSS prompts you to confirm that the merge was successful. If you were able to resolve all the conflicts, click Yes to check in the file. If not, perhaps because you needed to check with another developer, Click No to keep the object checked out.

Working with Histories and Differences

As you begin to save numerous versions of an object, you may want to look back at previous incarnations. This is called viewing the *history* of an object. VSS makes this information available via the History dialog shown in Figure 24.19. You access this dialog by selecting the Show History command on the Tools ➤ SourceSafe menu.

FIGURE 24.19

Viewing the history of check ins made for a source file

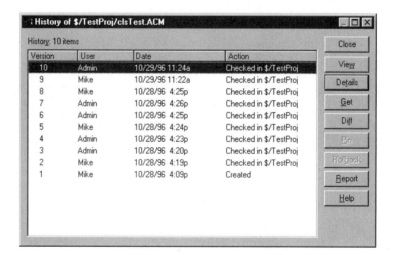

The dialog lists the version number, the user name of the developer who checked in that version, the date and time of the check in, and the action that initiated the new version. You can view a version's details, such as any comments or labels associated with it, by clicking the Details button. This opens a secondary dialog.

You can also take action from this dialog. For example, you can retrieve any version of the file into your copy of the database by clicking the Get button. You can also view the differences between your local copy and any other version by selecting that version and clicking the Diff button. If there are differences between the two versions, VSS displays the Differences dialog shown in Figure 24.20.

FIGURE 24.20

Viewing differences
between two versions
of a source file

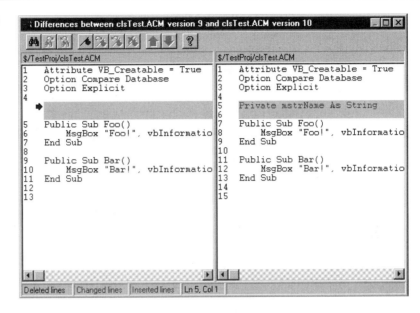

VSS uses the same highlighting as the Visual Merge dialog. You can use the toolbar to move from difference to difference, but you cannot make changes using this dialog. You'll have to manually note the differences and change them in your local copy.

In addition to viewing differences between your local copy of an object and a version in the history list, you can view the differences between any two versions in the VSS database. Just select the first version you want to examine, hold down the Ctrl key, and click on another version. Now click the Diff button.

> **TIP**
>
> You can also compare your local copy of an object with the version in the VSS database by selecting the Show Differences command from the Tools ➤ SourceSafe menu.

If you discover a critical error in your local version of an object and correcting it manually would be impractical, you can use the History dialog to restore a prior version. Simply select the version you want to restore (click the View button to examine it if you're unsure) and click the Rollback button. Restoring a version of an object deletes all subsequent versions permanently, so use care when doing this. VSS does not, however, merge the restored version into your local copy of the database. Your database will still contain the newer, yet flawed, version. We recommend, therefore, that after performing a rollback, you immediately get the latest version.

Sharing and Branching

If you've been developing applications for a while, you probably have modules of source code that you share between projects. This is an especially useful technique for utility functions that are not application dependent. VSS also supports sharing of source files among projects. When you share a source file using VSS, only one copy of the file actually exists in the VSS database; however, you can include it in as many projects as you like. Whenever you make changes to the file in one project and check it back in to the VSS database, all other projects that use the file are affected. The next time a get is performed in those projects, your changes will appear.

When using source code control integration in Access, you can select source files from any other project for inclusion in the current database. You do this using the Share With dialog shown in Figure 24.21. To access this dialog, select the Share Objects command from the Tools ➤ SourceSafe menu.

Use the Projects list to view source files in a particular project. You can select any project except the current one. If you select the current project, no files are displayed

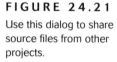

FIGURE 24.21

Use this dialog to share source files from other projects.

in the "Files to share" list. This list is a multiple-selection list box. You can choose one or more files to share from this list. After making your selections, click the Share button. This marks the files as shared in the VSS database, adds them to the current project, and copies the latest version of each to your local database. You can then work with them as you would any other source file.

The opposite of sharing is branching. *Branching* is performed on a shared file and breaks the link between projects using the file. It creates a new, native copy of the file in the project where the branch is created. From that point forward, changes in the new copy do not affect other projects that use the file.

You cannot perform branching directly through Access. You must run Visual SourceSafe itself. To do this, select Run SourceSafe from the Tools ➤ SourceSafe menu. From the VSS Explorer window, select the project where you want to create the branch and select the shared file. Select Branch from the SourceSafe menu or click the Branch Files toolbar button.

Controlling SourceSafe with VBA

Visual SourceSafe version 5.0 supports an Automation interface that allows you to execute SourceSafe procedures using any Automation client, including Microsoft Access. Using this interface plus a few undocumented Access methods, you could write your own VSS integration tool. In the next section we briefly explain the Automation interface and show you how to use it. This section is not meant to replace the VSS documentation or tools such as the Object Browser. We do not, therefore, include complete descriptions of every object class, property, and method. Instead we highlight a select few using simple examples. For a complete reference to the VSS Automation interface, consult the VSS Web page at http://www.microsoft.com/ssafe.

> **NOTE** It is not clear to the authors *why* you would want to reinvent the wheel by using the VSS Automation interface in this manner. Understanding how VSS and Access work together, however, may help you in using the products effectively. You might also choose to integrate the functionality into other VBA host products.

To demonstrate some of these techniques, we've developed a small application called the VSS Project Explorer (see Figure 24.22). To use this application, just open the frmVSSExplorer form in CH24.MDB. You are prompted to log in to a VSS database, and then the form displays a list of all the projects in that database. Double-click on a project name to view any subprojects. Use the Files tab to see a list of the files associated with a project.

FIGURE 24.22

Our VSS Project Explorer demonstrates the VSS Automation interface.

You can use the VSS Explorer to view source files in a separate window or print version and to check out information to the Debug window. Most of the source code included in this section is contained in the Explorer form's module.

Visual SourceSafe Object Model

Visual SourceSafe features a fairly simple and straightforward object module. In fact, it consists of only four object classes: VSSDatabase, VSSItem, VSSVersion, and VSSCheckout. All of these except VSSDatabase also have associated collections. Figure 24.23 illustrates the object model. Note that the VSSItem object below VSSDatabase represents the results of calling the database's VSSItem method. Once you have a pointer to this object, you can access collections of all the other objects it contains.

FIGURE 24.23

Visual SourceSafe Auto-
mation object model

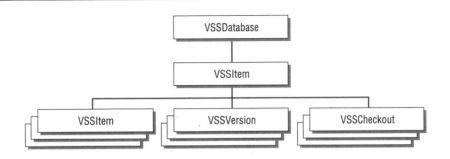

NOTE

Before attempting to write any Automation code, be sure to add a reference to the Visual SourceSafe 5.0 Object Library to your VBA project. If
the type library is not added to the reference list when you install VSS,
you can find it in the \win32 subdirectory of your VSS install directory.
The type library file name is SSAPI.DLL.

The VSSDatabase Class

SourceSafe's VSSDatabase class represents an entire VSS database, including all
the projects and subprojects defined therein. All Automation sessions begin by
declaring a new instance of this class and calling its Open method. Open accepts
three arguments: a path to a VSS INI file containing the database to use, a VSS user
name, and a password. The following code snippet illustrates this:

```
Dim vdb As New VSSDatabase

' Make sure the path to srcsafe.ini is accurate!
vdb.Open "C:\VSS\SRCSAFE.INI", "Admin", ""
```

Once you've opened the database, you can start manipulating items in the database. To obtain a pointer to an item (represented by the VSSItem class, explained in
the next section), use the VSSDatabase's VSSItem method. VSSItem accepts an item
specification (similar in concept to a file path and name) as an argument. Depending
on the specification, you can get a pointer to any project or item in the database. For
example, to get a pointer to the root project, you could use the code shown here:

```
Dim vit As VSSItem

' Get a reference to the root project
```

```
Set vit = vdb.VSSItem("$/")
```

Alternatively, the following code fragment obtains a reference to a file called basSccFunctions.acm in the Chapter24 project:

```
Dim vit As VSSItem
```

```
Set vit = vbd.VSSItem("$/Chapter24/basSccFunctions.acm")
```

The VSSItem Class

As you may have deduced by now, the VSSItem class can refer to either a project or a source file. Once you have a pointer to a VSSItem object, you can check its Type property to determine exactly what it is. Type returns 0 (VSSITEM_PROJECT) for a project and 1 (VSSITEM_FILE) for a file.

While we can't include all the details here, suffice it to say that the VSSItem class implements obvious properties such as Name, IsCheckedOut, IsDifferent, Local-Spec, Parent, and VersionNumber, among others. For methods, you can use Add, CheckIn, CheckOut, Get, and UndoCheckout.

The VSS Project Explorer uses some of these properties and methods to copy a version of a source file to a temporary directory where it can be viewed using the frmVSSFileViewer form (see Figure 24.24). Listing 24.2 contains the ViewFile procedure that accomplishes this.

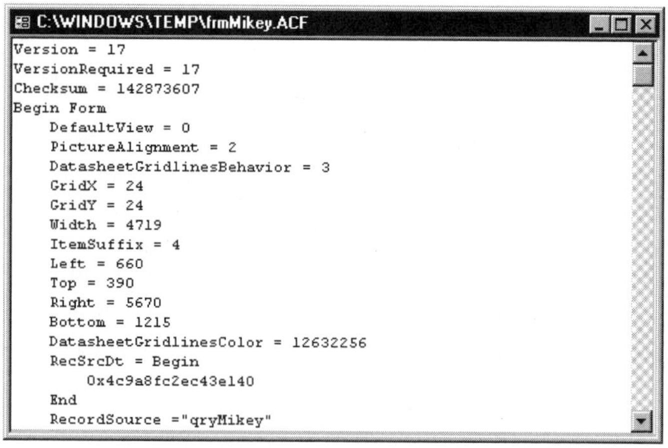

FIGURE 24.24

Viewing a source file from a VSS project

```
C:\WINDOWS\TEMP\frmMikey.ACF
Version = 17
VersionRequired = 17
Checksum = 142873607
Begin Form
    DefaultView = 0
    PictureAlignment = 2
    DatasheetGridlinesBehavior = 3
    GridX = 24
    GridY = 24
    Width = 4719
    ItemSuffix = 4
    Left = 660
    Top = 390
    Right = 5670
    Bottom = 1215
    DatasheetGridlinesColor = 12632256
    RecSrcDt = Begin
        0x4c9a8fc2ec43e140
    End
    RecordSource ="qryMikey"
```

Listing 24.2

```
Private Sub ViewFile(vitFile As VSSItem)
    Dim strTempFile As String
    Dim frmViewer As New Form_frmVSSFileViewer
    Dim frmAny As Form
    Dim cb As Long

    ' Make sure it's a file
    If vitFile.Type = VSSITEM_PROJECT Then
        MsgBox "Cannot view projects.", _
            vbExclamation, Me.Caption
    ' Make sure it's text
    ElseIf vitFile.Binary Then
        MsgBox "File is binary and cannot be viewed.", _
            vbExclamation, Me.Caption
    Else

        ' Create a temp file name
        strTempFile = Space(255)
        cb = adh_apiGetTempPath(255, strTempFile)
        If cb > 0 Then
            strTempFile = Left(strTempFile, cb)
            strTempFile = strTempFile & mvitCurrFile.Name

            ' See if we already have it open
            For Each frmAny In mcolViewers
                If frmAny.File = strTempFile Then
                    frmAny.SetFocus
                    Exit Sub
                End If
            Next

            ' Perform a "get" to grab the file
            vitFile.Get strTempFile

            ' Set the viewer form's File property (this
            ' reads the file's contents)
            frmViewer.File = strTempFile

            ' Make the form visible and add it to our
            ' collection to keep it around
            frmViewer.Visible = True
            mcolViewers.Add frmViewer
```

```
                        ' Getting the file makes it read-only.
                        ' Remove this attribute
                        SetAttr strTempFile, vbNormal

                        ' Delete the temp file
                        Kill strTempFile
                End If
        End If
End Sub
```

You'll notice that the procedure first verifies that the VSSItem being passed in is, in fact, a file and not a project by examining its Type property. It then checks the Binary property to ensure that it's a text file. After constructing a file name from the system temp directory and the VSSItem's Name property, the procedure calls the object's Get method. This instructs VSS to copy the file from the VSS database to the location specified by the method's argument. After this happens a new instance of frmVSSFileViewer is opened, and it reads the file into a text box. The ViewFile procedure can then delete the file by calling the Kill function (after removing the read-only attribute VSS placed on the file during the Get operation).

The VSSVersion Class

Since one of the reasons for using a source code control program is to maintain past versions of files, the VSS Automation interface implements a class that allows you programmatic access to these. The VSSVersion class has properties specific to a particular version of a source file, such as Comment, Date, Username, and VersionNumber. Additionally, the VSSVersion class implements a VSSItem property, which returns a pointer to a VSSItem object representing the actual source file. Using the VSSItem property, you can manipulate all the versions of a file, including the current one.

You access versions using properties of a VSSItem. Use the Versions (plural) property to iterate through all versions using a For Each loop, or the Version (singular) property to reference an individual version. (VSSItem objects do not have a true Versions collection.) For example, the following procedure iterates all the versions of a given file, printing information to the Debug window:

```
Private Sub PrintVersionInfo(vit As VSSItem)
    Dim ver As VSSVersion

    Debug.Print "Version info for " & vit.Name
    Debug.Print "===================================="
    For Each ver In vit.Versions
        With ver
```

```
        Debug.Print "Version " & .VersionNumber, _
            .UserName, .Date, .Action, .Comment
      End With
    Next
End Sub
```

To reference a particular version of a file, however, you would use code like the following, which prints the file name of the original version:

```
Debug.Print vit.Version(1).Name
```

The IVSSCheckout Class

Finally, the IVSSCheckout class implements properties pertaining to the status of an object when it is checked out. You can use the Checkouts collection of a VSSItem object to view this information. If an object is not checked out, there will be no members of this collection. Check outs will contain a single IVSSCheckout object under normal situations when a user has the object checked out. If you allow multiple developers to check out an object, the collection could potentially contain multiple IVSSCheckout objects.

The IVSSCheckout class implements properties such as UserName, Machine, LocalPath, Date, and Comments that inform you of who has the object checked out, where it is, and when that user checked it out. The following procedure lists information for a given VSSItem object:

```
Private Sub PrintCheckoutInfo(vit As VSSItem)
    Dim vck As IVSSCheckout
    Dim c As Integer

    Debug.Print "Check out info for " & vit.Name
    Debug.Print "===================================="
    For Each vck In vit.Checkouts
        c = c + 1
        With vck
            Debug.Print "Check out " & c, _
            .UserName, .Machine, .LocalSpec, .Date, _
            .Comment
        End With
    Next
End Sub
```

Access Source Code Control Methods

To support source code control integration, Access now implements two new methods: SaveAsText and LoadFromText. Normally these are called only by the

SCC integration add-in that comes with the ODE. You can, however, write VBA code that calls these methods.

The SaveAsText Method

SaveAsText does just that—it saves an Access object to a text file so it can be loaded into VSS or some other source code control application. SaveAsText takes three arguments: an object type (use the Access constants acQuery, acForm, and so on), an object name, and a file name. Access will create a text definition of the object at the specified location. As an example, the following code creates a text file called C:\QUERY1.ACQ containing the definition of a query, Query1:

```
Application.SaveAsText acQuery, "Query1", "C:\QUERY1.ACQ"
```

The LoadFromText Method

The counterpart to SaveAsText is LoadFromText. LoadFromText takes the same three arguments and uses the definition information in the text file to create or re-create an object in the current database. The code snippet shown here creates a new version of Query1 from the text file:

```
Application.LoadFromText acQuery, "Query1", "C:\QUERY1.ACQ"
```

While LoadFromText will create the object in the database, it does not mark it as being under source code control. To do that you must add the SccStatus property to the object's associated DAO Document object yourself.

Object Text File Formats

We could fill most of a chapter discussing just the text file formats Access uses for exchanging objects. Obviously we can't do that, but we do want say a few words about it. Because you can use the SaveAsText and LoadFromText methods apart from source code control, the text file format does open up some interesting possibilities.

File Usage and Naming

We've already mentioned that Access exports individual text files for each of the application objects in a database, plus one binary file for the data objects. Access names these files using the object or database name and a file extension that denotes the object type. You can see this in Figure 24.9, shown earlier in the chapter. Access uses the file extensions .ACQ, .ACF, .ACR, .ACS, and .ACM to denote queries, forms, reports, macros (scripts), and modules, respectively. The extension .ACB denotes the binary data object. Finally, Access creates a zero-byte file with the file extension .ACN to denote the name of the database. It's important that you do not delete this file from the project. If you do, other developers will not be able to create new databases based on the project.

Object Definitions

Access uses a format that is similar to that used by Visual Basic. It uses a nested, hierarchical structure to describe objects. Components of an object are represented by blocks of text that specify property values. Listing 24.3 shows the definition of a simple query that selects all the fields from a sample table with a criterion on the ID field.

Listing 24.3

```
Operation = 1
Option = 0
Where ="(((tblTest.ID)=5))"
Begin InputTables
    Name ="tblTest"
End
Begin OutputColumns
    Expression ="tblTest.*"
End
dbBoolean "ReturnsRecords" ="-1"
dbInteger "ODBCTimeout" ="60"
dbByte "RecordsetType" ="0"
dbBoolean "OrderByOn" ="0"
Begin
End
```

```
Begin
    State = 0
    Left = 40
    Top = 22
    Right = 778
    Bottom = 323
    Left = -1
    Top = -1
    Right = 731
    Bottom = 144
    Left = 0
    Top = 0
    ColumnsShown = 539
    Begin
        Left = 38
        Top = 6
        Right = 134
        Bottom = 83
        Top = 0
        Name ="tblTest"
    End
End
```

You can see evidence of properties in the listing. Some, such as ODBCTimeout and RecordsetType, are DAO properties. Others are used by Access to build the QBE display. Listing 24.4 shows a simple macro with two actions. The first action opens a form and the second displays an informational dialog.

Listing 24.4

```
Version = 131074
ColumnsShown = 0
Begin
    Action ="OpenForm"
    Argument ="frmTest"
    Argument ="0"
    Argument =""
    Argument =""
    Argument ="-1"
    Argument ="0"
End
Begin
    Action ="MsgBox"
    Argument ="The form has been opened!"
    Argument ="-1"
```

```
        Argument ="4"
        Argument ="Test Macro"
End
```

Again, notice the properties and their values. In the case of macros, each Begin…End block marks a single macro action. Begin and End statements denote complex properties and, in the case of forms and reports, are nested to indicate object containment.

While it will take you some time to fully explore and map the structure of these files, it does open the door for additional approaches to object creation.

> **TIP**
>
> To make viewing these files from the Windows Explorer easier, we've included a Registry file, SCCFILES.REG, that you can merge into your Windows Registry. This will create file associations for the Access source code control files so you can open them in Notepad simply by double-clicking on them in Explorer.

Summary

In this chapter we've explained the basic concepts behind source code control. We showed you how Access fits into the source code control universe by decomposing its databases into separate components. We explained how to use Access with one particular source code control provider, Microsoft Visual SourceSafe. Finally, we explored using SourceSafe's Automation interface to manage source code control projects using VBA. The chapter covered these key concepts:

- What source code control projects are

- How you work with source files in a controlled environment

- How Access supports source code control integration

- How to install and use Microsoft Visual SourceSafe

- How to manage a database project using source code control

- How to control VSS using Automation from VBA

With this knowledge in hand (and Access 97's source code control integration features), managing large development projects involving numerous programmers should be easier than ever.

INDEX

Note to the Reader: Throughout this index **boldface** page numbers indicate primary discussions of a topic. *Italic* page numbers indicate illustrations.

A

<A> HTML tag, 1402
absolute paths for libraries, 1306–1308
AbsolutePosition property, 241–242
abstraction, class modules for, **46–47**
acAlignLeft value, 561
acAlignRight value, 561
.ACB files, 1483
Access SQL
    aggregate data with, **142–144**
        with GROUP BY clause, **145–147**, *146–147*
        without GROUP BY clause, **144**, *145*
        with HAVING clause, **148**, *149*
        with TRANSFORM, **149–155**, *151–152*, *154–155*
    copying data in, **176–177**
    creating tables in, **177–178**
    data definition in, **178–185**
    deleting data in, **174–176**
    external data sources for, **168–172**, *172*
    learning, 123
    parameterized, **167–168**
    pass-through queries in, **186–189**, *186*, *188–189*
    SELECT statement in. *See* SELECT statement
    vs. SQL-92, **189–191**
    subqueries in, **159–166**, *161–162*, *165*
    syntax conventions in, **123**
    union queries in, **156–159**, *157*, *159*
    updating data in, **173–174**
    using, **121–122**, *122*
AccessError method, 542
acCmd constants, 451

accounts. *See* users and user accounts; workgroups and group accounts
ACCSERVE.BAS file, 1263
ACCTEST.BAS file, 1265
acDataErrAdded response, 344–345
acDataErrContinue constant, 39–40
    for forms, 497
    for NotInList, 344
    with OnError property, 987
    for optimistic locking, 732, 736
acDataErrDisplay response
    for forms, 497
    for NotInList, 344
    with OnError property, 987
    for optimistic locking, 732
acDeleteCancel constant, 40
acDeleteOk constant, 40
acDeleteUserCancel constant, 40
.ACF files, 1483
acForm constant, 278
acLBClose constant, 355
acLBEnd constant, 355, 359
acLBGetColumnCount constant, 355
acLBGetColumnWidth constant, 355
acLBGetFormat constant, 355
acLBGetRowCount constant, 355, 359
acLBGetValue constant, 355, 358–359, 365
acLBInitialize constant, 355, 358–359
acLBOpen constant, 355
.ACM files, 1483
acMacro constant, 278
acModule constant, 278
.ACN files, 1483
acObjStateOpen constant, 1272, 1321

B

C

E

F

G

H

I

N

0

P

S

T

U

V

Y

Z

What's on the CD?

This CD is a valuable companion to the book. It provides a wealth of information in a readily usable format to aid in your Access development efforts. We've included every significant example presented in the text, and not just the VBA code; we've also included all the tables (with sample data), queries, forms, reports—*everything* to get you up and running instantly. The CD also contains two appendices, the text of the three chapters that we displaced in this edition of the book, several free and shareware utility programs, several demos of commercial products, and several Access add-ins to make application development even easier.

Here's just a sampling of what you'll find on the CD:

- An Access add-in that serves as a scratchpad facility for entering SQL statements on the fly and viewing the output

- A set of six utilities from FMS that help you optimize your queries, document your objects, and perform several other useful tasks

- A set of routines for creating screen-resolution–independent forms, so you can develop your forms in one resolution and deliver them to your users using a *different* resolution

- Ready-to-use popup calendar and calculator forms you can call from your code

- An ActiveX custom control for reading and writing values in the Registry

- Several free utility programs for working with help files

- A shareware Windows program for zipping and unzipping files

- The unsecured Access 97 Wizards

- Demo version of Transcender certification test preparation tool

For more information about the CD, including installation instructions, see the section "About the CD" in the Introduction of this book and the README.TXT file in the root folder of the CD.

Please note that if you use File Manager, Windows Explorer, or the DOS Copy command to copy the files to your hard disk, the files will be marked as read-only. You will need to change the file attributes of the file before you can use the files. If you use the DOS XCOPY32 command, the files will not be marked as read-only.

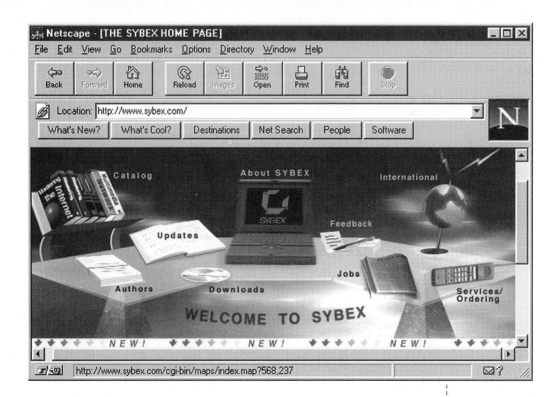